Lecture Notes in Computer Science 12894

Igor Farkaš · Paolo Masulli ·
Sebastian Otte · Stefan Wermter (Eds.)

Artificial Neural Networks and Machine Learning – ICANN 2021

30th International Conference on Artificial Neural Networks
Bratislava, Slovakia, September 14–17, 2021
Proceedings, Part IV

Editors
Igor Farkaš
Comenius University in Bratislava
Bratislava, Slovakia

Paolo Masulli
iMotions A/S
Copenhagen, Denmark

Sebastian Otte
University of Tübingen
Tübingen, Baden-Württemberg, Germany

Stefan Wermter
Universität Hamburg
Hamburg, Germany

ISSN 0302-9743 ISSN 1611-3349 (electronic)
Lecture Notes in Computer Science
ISBN 978-3-030-86379-1 ISBN 978-3-030-86380-7 (eBook)
https://doi.org/10.1007/978-3-030-86380-7

LNCS Sublibrary: SL1 – Theoretical Computer Science and General Issues

This Springer imprint is published by the registered company Springer Nature Switzerland AG
The registered company address is: Gewerbestrasse 11, 6330 Cham, Switzerland

Preface

Research on artificial neural networks has progressed over decades, in recent years being fueled especially by deep learning that has proven, albeit data-greedy, efficient in solving various, mostly supervised, tasks. Applications of artificial neural networks, especially related to artificial intelligence, affect our lives, providing new horizons. Examples range from autonomous car driving, virtual assistants, and decision support systems to healthcare data analytics, financial forecasting, and smart devices in our homes, just to name a few. These developments, however, also provide challenges, which were not imaginable previously, e.g., verification of raw data, explaining the contents of neural networks, and adversarial machine learning.

The International Conference on Artificial Neural Networks (ICANN) is the annual flagship conference of the European Neural Network Society (ENNS). Last year, due to the COVID-19 pandemic, we decided not to hold the conference but to prepare the ICANN proceedings in written form. This year, due to the still unresolved pandemic, the Organizing Committee, together with the Executive Committee of ENNS decided to organize ICANN 2021 online, since we felt the urge to allow research presentations and live discussions, following the now available alternatives of online conference organization. So for the first time, ENNS and the Organizing Committee prepared ICANN as an online event with all its challenges and sometimes unforeseeable events!

Following a long-standing successful collaboration, the proceedings of ICANN are published as volumes within the Lecture Notes in Computer Science Springer series. The response to this year's call for papers resulted, unexpectedly, in a record number of 557 article submissions (a 46% rise compared to previous year), of which almost all were full papers. The paper selection and review process that followed was decided during the online meeting of the Bratislava organizing team and the ENNS Executive Committee. The 40 Program Committee (PC) members agreed to check the submissions for the formal requirements and 64 papers were excluded from the subsequent reviews. The majority of the PC members have doctoral degrees (80%) and 75% of them are also professors. We also took advantage of filled-in online questionnaires providing the reviewers' areas of expertise. The reviewers were assigned one to four papers, and the papers with undecided scores also received reports from PC members which helped in making a final decision.

In total, 265 articles were accepted for the proceedings and the authors were requested to submit final versions. The acceptance rate was hence about 47% when calculated from all initial submissions. A list of PC members and reviewers who agreed to publish their names is included in the proceedings. With these procedures we tried to keep the quality of the proceedings high while still having a critical mass of contributions reflecting the progress of the field. Overall we hope that these proceedings will contribute to the dissemination of new results by the neural network community during these challenging times and we hope that we can have a physical ICANN in 2022.

Finally, we very much thank the Program Committee and the reviewers for their invaluable work.

September 2021

Igor Farkaš
Paolo Masulli
Sebastian Otte
Stefan Wermter

Organization

Organizing Committee

Cabessa Jérémie	Université Paris 2 Panthéon-Assas, France
Kerzel Matthias	University of Hamburg, Germany
Lintas Alessandra	University of Lausanne, Switzerland
Malinovská Kristína	Comenius University in Bratislava, Slovakia
Masulli Paolo	iMotions A/S, Copenhagen, Denmark
Otte Sebastian	University of Tübingen, Germany
Wedeman Roseli	Universidade do Estado do Rio de Janeiro, Brazil

Program Committee Chairs

Igor Farkaš	Comenius University in Bratislava, Slovakia
Paolo Masulli	iMotions A/S, Denmark
Sebastian Otte	University of Tübingen, Germany
Stefan Wermter	University of Hamburg, Germany

Program Committee

Andrejková Gabriela	Pavol Jozef Šafárik University in Košice, Slovakia
Atencia Miguel	Universidad de Malaga, Spain
Bodapati Jyostna Devi	Indian Institute of Technology, Madras, India
Bougie Nicolas	Sokendai/National Institute of Informatics, Japan
Boža Vladimír	Comenius University in Bratislava, Slovakia
Cabessa Jérémie	Université Paris 2 Panthéon-Assas, France
Di Nuovo Alessandro	Sheffield Hallam University, UK
Duch Włodzisław	Nicolaus Copernicus University, Poland
Eppe Manfred	Universität Hamburg, Germany
Fang Yuchun	Shanghai University, China
Garcke Jochen	Universität Bonn, Germany
Gregor Michal	University of Žilina, Slovakia
Guckert Michael	Technische Hochschule Mittelhessen, Germany
Guillén Alberto	University of Granada, Spain
Heinrich Stefan	University of Tokyo, Japan
Hinaut Xavier	Inria, France
Humaidan Dania	University of Tübingen, Germany
Jolivet Renaud	University of Geneva, Switzerland
Koprinkova-Hristova Petia	Bulgarian Academy of Sciences, Bulgaria
Lintas Alessandra	University of Lausanne, Switzerland
Lü Shuai	Jilin University, China
Micheli Alessio	Università di Pisa, Italy

Oravec Miloš	Slovak University of Technology in Bratislava, Slovakia
Otte Sebastian	University of Tübingen, Germany
Peltonen Jaakko	Tampere University, Finland
Piuri Vincenzo	University of Milan, Italy
Pons Rivero Antonio Javier	Universitat Politècnica de Catalunya, Barcelona, Spain
Schmidt Jochen	TH Rosenheim, Germany
Schockaert Cedric	Paul Wurth S.A., Luxembourg
Schwenker Friedhelm	University of Ulm, Germany
Takáč Martin	Comenius University in Bratislava, Slovakia
Tartaglione Enzo	Università degli Studi di Torino, Italy
Tetko Igor	Helmholtz Zentrum München, Germany
Triesch Jochen	Frankfurt Institute for Advanced Studies, Germany
Vavrečka Michal	Czech Technical University in Prague, Czech Republic
Verma Sagar	CentraleSupélec, Université Paris-Saclay, France
Vigário Ricardo	Nova School of Science and Technology, Portugal
Wedemann Roseli	Universidade do Estado do Rio de Janeiro, Brazil
Wennekers Thomas	Plymouth University, UK

Reviewers

Abawi Fares	University of Hamburg, Germany
Aganian Dustin	Technical University Ilmenau, Germany
Ahrens Kyra	University of Hamburg, Germany
Alexandre Frederic	Inria Bordeaux, France
Alexandre Luís	University of Beira Interior, Portugal
Ali Hazrat	Umeå University, Sweden
Alkhamaiseh Koloud	Western Michigan University, USA
Amaba Takafumi	Fukuoka University, Japan
Ambita Ara Abigail	University of the Philippines Diliman, Philippines
Ameur Hanen	University of Sfax, Tunisia
Amigo Galán Glauco A.	Baylor University, USA
An Shuqi	Chongqing University, China
Aouiti Chaouki	Université de Carthage, Tunisia
Arany Adam	Katholieke Universiteit Leuven, Belgium
Arnold Joshua	University of Queensland, Australia
Artelt André	Bielefeld University, Germany
Auge Daniel	Technical University of Munich, Germany
Bac Le Hoai	University of Science, Vietnam
Bacaicoa-Barber Daniel	University Carlos III of Madrid, Spain
Bai Xinyi	National University of Defense Technology, China
Banka Asif	Islamic University of Science & Technology, India
Basalla Marcus	University of Liechtenstein, Liechtenstein
Basterrech Sebastian	Technical University of Ostrava, Czech Republic
Bauckhage Christian	Fraunhofer IAIS, Germany
Bayer Markus	Technical University of Darmstadt, Germany

Bečková Iveta	Comenius University in Bratislava, Slovakia
Benalcázar Marco	Escuela Politécnica Nacional, Ecuador
Bennis Achraf	Institut de Recherche en Informatique de Toulouse, France
Berlemont Samuel	Orange Labs, Grenoble, France
Bermeitinger Bernhard	Universität St. Gallen, Switzerland
Bhoi Suman	National University of Singapore, Singapore
Biesner David	Fraunhofer IAIS, Germany
Bilbrey Jenna	Pacific Northwest National Lab, USA
Blasingame Zander	Clarkson University, USA
Bochkarev Vladimir	Kazan Federal University, Russia
Bohte Sander	Universiteit van Amsterdam, The Netherlands
Bouchachia Abdelhamid	Bournemouth University, UK
Bourguin Grégory	Université du Littoral Côte d'Opale, France
Breckon Toby	Durham University, UK
Buhl Fred	University of Florida, USA
Butz Martin V.	University of Tübingen, Germany
Caillon Paul	Université de Lorraine, Nancy, France
Camacho Hugo C. E.	Universidad Autónoma de Tamaulipas, Mexico
Camurri Antonio	Università di Genova, Italy
Cao Hexin	OneConnect Financial Technology, China
Cao Tianyang	Peking University, China
Cao Zhijie	Shanghai Jiao Tong University, China
Carneiro Hugo	Universität Hamburg, Germany
Chadha Gavneet Singh	South Westphalia University of Applied Sciences, Germany
Chakraborty Saikat	C. V. Raman Global University, India
Chang Hao-Yuan	University of California, Los Angeles, USA
Chang Haodong	University of Technology Sydney, Australia
Chen Cheng	Tsinghua University, China
Chen Haopeng	Shanghai Jiao Tong University, China
Chen Junliang	Shenzhen University, China
Chen Tianyu	Northwest Normal University, China
Chen Wenjie	Communication University of China, China
Cheng Zhanglin	Chinese Academy of Sciences, China
Chenu Alexandre	Sorbonne Université, France
Choi Heeyoul	Handong Global University, South Korea
Christa Sharon	RV Institute of Technology and Management, India
Cîtea Ingrid	Bitdefender Central, Romania
Colliri Tiago	Universidade de São Paulo, Brazil
Cong Cong	Chinese Academy of Sciences, China
Coroiu Adriana Mihaela	Babes-Bolyai University, Romania
Cortez Paulo	University of Minho, Portugal
Cuayáhuitl Heriberto	University of Lincoln, UK
Cui Xiaohui	Wuhan University, China
Cutsuridis Vassilis	University of Lincoln, UK

Cvejoski Kostadin	Fraunhofer IAIS, Germany
D'Souza Meenakshi	International Institute of Information Technology, Bangalore, India
Dai Feifei	Chinese Academy of Sciences, China
Dai Peilun	Boston University, USA
Dai Ruiqi	INSA Lyon, France
Dang Kai	Nankai University, China
Dang Xuan	Tsinghua University, China
Dash Tirtharaj	Birla Institute of Technology and Science, Pilani, India
Davalas Charalampos	Harokopio University of Athens, Greece
De Brouwer Edward	Katholieke Universiteit Leuven, Belgium
Deng Minghua	Peking University, China
Devamane Shridhar	KLE Institute of Technology, Hubballi, India
Di Caterina Gaetano	University of Strathclyde, UK
Di Sarli Daniele	Università di Pisa, Italy
Ding Juncheng	University of North Texas, USA
Ding Zhaoyun	National University of Defense Technology, China
Dold Dominik	Siemens, Munich, Germany
Dong Zihao	Jinan University, China
Du Songlin	Southeast University, China
Edwards Joshua	University of North Carolina Wilmington, USA
Eguchi Shu	Fukuoka University, Japan
Eisenbach Markus	Ilmenau University of Technology, Germany
Erlhagen Wolfram	University of Minho, Portugal
Fang Tiyu	University of Jinan, China
Feldager Cilie	Technical University of Denmark, Denmark
Ferianc Martin	University College London, UK
Ferreira Flora	University of Minho, Portugal
Fevens Thomas	Concordia University, Canada
Friedjungová Magda	Czech Technical University in Prague, Czech Republic
Fu Xianghua	Shenzhen University, China
Fuhl Wolfgang	Universität Tübingen, Germany
Gamage Vihanga	Technological University Dublin, Ireland
Ganguly Udayan	Indian Institute of Technology, Bombay, India
Gao Ruijun	Tianjin University, China
Gao Yapeng	University of Tübingen, Germany
Gao Yue	Beijing University of Posts and Telecommunications, China
Gao Zikai	National University of Defense Technology, China
Gault Richard	Queen's University Belfast, UK
Ge Liang	Chongqing University, China
Geissler Dominik	Relayr GmbH, Munich, Germany
Gepperth Alexander	ENSTA ParisTech, France
Gerum Christoph	University of Tübingen, Germany
Giancaterino Claudio G.	Catholic University of Milan, Italy
Giese Martin	University Clinic Tübingen, Germany

Gikunda Patrick	Dedan Kimathi University of Technology, Kenya
Goel Anmol	Guru Gobind Singh Indraprastha University, India
Göpfert Christina	Bielefeld University, Germany
Göpfert Jan Philip	Bielefeld University, Germany
Goyal Nidhi	Indraprastha Institute of Information Technology, India
Grangetto Marco	Università di Torino, Italy
Grüning Philipp	University of Lübeck, Germany
Gu Xiaoyan	Chinese Academy of Sciences, Beijing, China
Guo Hongcun	China Three Gorges University, China
Guo Ling	Northwest University, China
Guo Qing	Nanyang Technological University, Singapore
Guo Song	Xi'an University of Architecture and Technology, China
Gupta Sohan	Global Institute of Technology, Jaipur, India
Hakenes Simon	Ruhr-Universität Bochum, Germany
Han Fuchang	Central South University, China
Han Yi	University of Melbourne, Australia
Hansen Lars Kai	Technical University of Denmark, Denmark
Haque Ayaan	Saratoga High School, USA
Hassen Alan Kai	Leiden University, The Netherlands
Hauberg Søren	Technical University of Denmark, Denmark
He Tieke	Nanjing University, China
He Wei	Nanyang Technological University, Singapore
He Ziwen	Chinese Academy of Sciences, China
Heese Raoul	Fraunhofer ITWM, Germany
Herman Pawel	KTH Royal Institute of Technology, Sweden
Holas Juraj	Comenius University in Bratislava, Slovakia
Horio Yoshihiko	Tohoku University, Japan
Hou Hongxu	Inner Mongolia University, China
Hu Ming-Fei	China University of Petroleum, China
Hu Ting	Hasso Plattner Institute, Germany
Hu Wenxin	East China Normal University, China
Hu Yanqing	Sichuan University, China
Huang Chenglong	National University of Defense Technology, China
Huang Chengqiang	Huawei Technology, Ltd., China
Huang Jun	Chinese Academy of Sciences, Shanghai, China
Huang Ruoran	Chinese Academy of Sciences, China
Huang Wuliang	Chinese Academy of Sciences, Beijing, China
Huang Zhongzhan	Tsinghua University, China
Iannella Nicolangelo	University of Oslo, Norway
Ienco Dino	INRAE, France
Illium Steffen	Ludwig-Maximilians-Universität München, Germany
Iyer Naresh	GE Research, USA
Jalalvand Azarakhsh	Ghent University, Belgium
Japa Sai Sharath	Southern Illinois University, USA
Javaid Muhammad Usama	Eura Nova, Belgium

Jia Qiaomei	Northwest University, China
Jia Xiaoning	Inner Mongolia University, China
Jin Peiquan	University of Science and Technology of China, China
Jirak Doreen	Istituto Italiano di Tecnologia, Italy
Jodelet Quentin	Tokyo Institute of Technology, Japan
Kai Tang	Toshiba, China
Karam Ralph	Université Franche-Comté, France
Karlbauer Matthias	University of Tübingen, Germany
Kaufhold Marc-André	Technical University of Darmstadt, Germany
Kerzel Matthias	University of Hamburg, Germany
Keurulainen Antti	Bitville Oy, Finland
Kitamura Takuya	National Institute of Technology, Japan
Kocur Viktor	Comenius University in Bratislava, Slovakia
Koike Atsushi	National Institute of Technology, Japan
Kotropoulos Constantine	Aristotle University of Thessaloniki, Greece
Kovalenko Alexander	Czech Technical University, Czech Republic
Krzyzak Adam	Concordia University, Canada
Kurikawa Tomoki	Kansai Medical University, Japan
Kurpiewski Evan	University of North Carolina Wilmington, USA
Kurt Mehmet Necip	Columbia University, USA
Kushwaha Sumit	Kamla Nehru Institute of Technology, India
Lai Zhiping	Fudan University, China
Lang Jana	Hertie Institute for Clinical Brain Research, Germany
Le Hieu	Boston University, USA
Le Ngoc	Hanoi University of Science and Technology, Vietnam
Le Thanh	University of Science, Hochiminh City, Vietnam
Lee Jinho	Yonsei University, South Korea
Lefebvre Grégoire	Orange Labs, France
Lehmann Daniel	University of Greifswald, Germany
Lei Fang	University of Lincoln, UK
Léonardon Mathieu	IMT Atlantique, France
Lewandowski Arnaud	Université du Littoral Côte d'Opale, Calais, France
Li Caiyuan	Shanghai Jiao Tong University, China
Li Chuang	Xi'an Jiaotong University, China
Li Ming-Fan	Ping An Life Insurance of China, Ltd., China
Li Qing	The Hong Kong Polytechnic University, China
Li Tao	Peking University, China
Li Xinyi	Southwest University, China
Li Xiumei	Hangzhou Normal University, China
Li Yanqi	University of Jinan, China
Li Yuan	Defence Innovation Institute, China
Li Zhixin	Guangxi Normal University, China
Lian Yahong	Dalian University of Technology, China
Liang Nie	Southwest University of Science and Technology, China
Liang Qi	Chinese Academy of Sciences, Beijing, China

Liang Senwei	Purdue University, USA
Liang Yuxin	Northwest University, China
Lim Nengli	Singapore University of Technology and Design, Singapore
Liu Gongshen	Shanghai Jiao Tong University, China
Liu Haolin	Chinese Academy of Sciences, China
Liu Jian-Wei	China University of Petroleum, China
Liu Juan	Wuhan University, China
Liu Junxiu	Guangxi Normal University, China
Liu Qi	Chongqing University, China
Liu Shuang	Huazhong University of Science and Technology, China
Liu Shuting	University of Shanghai for Science and Technology, China
Liu Weifeng	China University of Petroleum, China
Liu Yan	University of Shanghai for Science and Technology, China
Liu Yang	Fudan University, China
Liu Yi-Ling	Imperial College London, UK
Liu Zhu	University of Electronic Science and Technology of China, China
Long Zi	Shenzhen Technology University, China
Lopes Vasco	Universidade da Beira Interior, Portugal
Lu Siwei	Guangdong University of Technology, China
Lu Weizeng	Shenzhen University, China
Lukyanova Olga	Russian Academy of Sciences, Russia
Luo Lei	Kansas State University, USA
Luo Xiao	Peking University, China
Luo Yihao	Huazhong University of Science and Technology, China
Ma Chao	Wuhan University, China
Ma Zeyu	Harbin Institute of Technology, China
Malialis Kleanthis	University of Cyprus, Cyprus
Manoonpong Poramate	Vidyasirimedhi Institute of Science and Technology, Thailand
Martinez Rego David	Data Spartan Ltd., UK
Matsumura Tadayuki	Hitachi, Ltd., Tokyo, Japan
Mekki Asma	Université de Sfax, Tunisia
Merkel Cory	Rochester Institute of Technology, USA
Mirus Florian	Intel Labs, Germany
Mizuno Hideyuki	Suwa University of Science, Japan
Moh Teng-Sheng	San Jose State University, USA
Mohammed Elmahdi K.	Kasdi Merbah university, Algeria
Monshi Maram	University of Sydney, Australia
Moreno Felipe	Universidad Católica San Pablo, Peru
Morra Lia	Politecnico di Torino, Italy

Rusiecki Andrzej	Wroclaw University of Science and Technology, Poland
Salomon Michel	Université Bourgogne Franche-Comté, France
Sarishvili Alex	Fraunhofer ITWM, Germany
Sasi Swapna	Birla Institute of Technology and Science, India
Sataer Yikemaiti	Southeast University, China
Schaaf Nina	Fraunhofer IPA, Germany
Schak Monika	University of Applied Sciences, Fulda, Germany
Schilling Malte	Bielefeld University, Germany
Schmid Kyrill	Ludwig-Maximilians-Universität München, Germany
Schneider Johannes	University of Liechtenstein, Liechtenstein
Schwab Malgorzata	University of Colorado at Denver, USA
Sedlmeier Andreas	Ludwig-Maximilians-Universität München, Germany
Sendera Marcin	Jagiellonian University, Poland
Shahriyar Rifat	Bangladesh University of Engineering and Technology, Bangladesh
Shang Cheng	Fudan University, China
Shao Jie	University of Electronic Science and Technology of China, China
Shao Yang	Hitachi Ltd., Japan
Shehu Amarda	George Mason University, USA
Shen Linlin	Shenzhen University, China
Shenfield Alex	Sheffield Hallam University, UK
Shi Ying	Chongqing University, China
Shrestha Roman	Intelligent Voice Ltd., UK
Sifa Rafet	Fraunhofer IAIS, Germany
Sinha Aman	CNRS and University of Lorraine, France
Soltani Zarrin Pouya	Institute for High Performance Microelectronics, Germany
Song Xiaozhuang	Southern University of Science and Technology, China
Song Yuheng	Shanghai Jiao Tong University, China
Song Ziyue	Shanghai Jiao Tong University, China
Sowinski-Mydlarz Viktor	London Metropolitan University, UK
Steiner Peter	Technische Universität Dresden, Germany
Stettler Michael	University of Tübingen, Germany
Stoean Ruxandra	University of Craiova, Romania
Su Di	Beijing Institute of Technology, China
Suarez Oscar J.	Instituto Politécnico Nacional, México
Sublime Jérémie	Institut supérieur d'électronique de Paris, France
Sudharsan Bharath	National University of Ireland, Galway, Ireland
Sugawara Toshiharu	Waseda University, Japan
Sui Yongduo	University of Science and Technology of China, China
Sui Zhentao	Soochow University, China
Swiderska-Chadaj Zaneta	Warsaw University of Technology, Poland
Szandała Tomasz	Wroclaw University of Science and Technology, Poland

Šejnová Gabriela	Czech Technical University in Prague, Czech Republic
Tang Chenwei	Sichuan University, China
Tang Jialiang	Southwest University of Science and Technology, China
Taubert Nick	University Clinic Tübingen, Germany
Tek Faik Boray	Isik University, Turkey
Tessier Hugo	Stellantis, France
Tian Zhihong	Guangzhou University, China
Tianze Zhou	Beijing Institute of Technology, China
Tihon Simon	Eura Nova, Belgium
Tingwen Liu	Chinese Academy of Sciences, China
Tong Hao	Southern University of Science and Technology, China
Torres-Moreno Juan-Manuel	Université d'Avignon, France
Towobola Oluyemisi Folake	Obafemi Awolowo University, Nigeria
Trinh Anh Duong	Technological University Dublin, Ireland
Tuna Matúš	Comenius University in Bratislava, Slovakia
Uelwer Tobias	Heinrich Heine University Düsseldorf, Germany
Van Rullen Rufin	CNRS, Toulouse, France
Varlamis Iraklis	Harokopio University of Athens, Greece
Vašata Daniel	Czech Technical University in Prague, Czech Republic
Vásconez Juan	Escuela Politécnica Nacional, Ecuador
Vatai Emil	RIKEN, Japan
Viéville Thierry	Inria, Antibes, France
Wagner Stefan	Heinrich Heine University Düsseldorf, Germany
Wan Kejia	Defence Innovation Institute, China
Wang Huiling	Tampere University, Finland
Wang Jiaan	Soochow University, China
Wang Jinling	Ulster University, UK
Wang Junli	Tongji University, China
Wang Qian	Durham University, UK
Wang Xing	Ningxia University, China
Wang Yongguang	Beihang University, China
Wang Ziming	Shanghai Jiao Tong University, China
Wanigasekara Chathura	University of Auckland, New Zealand
Watson Patrick	Minerva KGI, USA
Wei Baole	Chinese Academy of Sciences, China
Wei Feng	York University, Canada
Wenninger Marc	Rosenheim Technical University of Applied Sciences, Germany
Wieczorek Tadeusz	Silesian University of Technology, Poland
Wiles Janet	University of Queensland, Australia
Windheuser Christoph	ThoughtWorks Inc., Germany
Wolter Moritz	Rheinische Friedrich-Wilhelms-Universität Bonn, Germany

Wu Ancheng	Pingan Insurance, China
Wu Dayan	Chinese Academy of Sciences, China
Wu Jingzheng	Chinese Academy of Sciences, China
Wu Nier	Inner Mongolia University, China
Wu Song	Southwest University, China
Xie Yuanlun	University of Electronic Science and Technology of China, China
Xu Dongsheng	National University of Defense Technology, China
Xu Jianhua	Nanjing Normal University, China
Xu Peng	Technical University of Munich, Germany
Yaguchi Takaharu	Kobe University, Japan
Yamamoto Hideaki	Tohoku University, Japan
Yang Gang	Renmin University of China, China
Yang Haizhao	Purdue University, USA
Yang Jing	Guangxi Normal University, China
Yang Jing	Hefei University of Technology, China
Yang Liu	Tianjin University, China
Yang Sidi	Concordia University, Canada
Yang Sun	Soochow University, China
Yang Wanli	Harbin Institute of Technology, China
Yang XiaoChen	Tianjin University of Technology, China
Yang Xuan	Shenzhen University, China
Yang Zhao	Leiden University, The Netherlands
Yang Zhengfeng	East China Normal University, China
Yang Zhiguang	Chinese Academy of Sciences, China
Yao Zhenjie	Chinese Academy of Sciences, China
Ye Kai	Wuhan University, China
Yin Bojian	Centrum Wiskunde & Informatica, The Netherlands
Yu James	Southern University of Science and Technology, China
Yu Wenxin	Southwest University of Science and Technology, China
Yu Yipeng	Tencent, China
Yu Yue	BNU-HKBU United International College, China
Yuan Limengzi	Tianjin University, China
Yuchen Ge	Hefei University of Technology, China
Yuhang Guo	Peking University, China
Yury Tsoy	Solidware, South Korea
Zeng Jia	Jilin University, China
Zeng Jiayuan	University of Shanghai for Science and Technology, China
Zhang Dongyang	University of Electronic Science and Technology of China, China
Zhang Jiacheng	Beijing University of Posts and Telecommunications, China
Zhang Jie	Nanjing University, China
Zhang Kai	Chinese Academy of Sciences, China

Zhang Kaifeng	Independent Researcher, China
Zhang Kun	Chinese Academy of Sciences, China
Zhang Luning	China University of Petroleum, China
Zhang Panpan	Chinese Academy of Sciences, China
Zhang Peng	Chinese Academy of Sciences, China
Zhang Wenbin	Carnegie Mellon University, USA
Zhang Xiang	National University of Defense Technology, China
Zhang Xuewen	Southwest University of Science and Technology, China
Zhang Yicheng	University of Lincoln, UK
Zhang Yingjie	Hunan University, China
Zhang Yunchen	University of Electronic Science and Technology of China, China
Zhang Zhiqiang	Southwest University of Science and Technology, China
Zhao Liang	University of São Paulo, Brazil
Zhao Liang	Dalian University of Technology, China
Zhao Qingchao	Harbin Engineering University, China
Zhao Ying	University of Shanghai for Science and Technology, China
Zhao Yuekai	National University of Defense Technology, China
Zheng Yuchen	Kyushu University, Japan
Zhong Junpei	Plymouth University, UK
Zhou Shiyang	Defense Innovation Institute, China
Zhou Xiaomao	Harbin Engineering University, China
Zhou Yucan	Chinese Academy of Sciences, China
Zhu Haijiang	Beijing University of Chemical Technology, China
Zhu Mengting	National University of Defense Technology, China
Zhu Shaolin	Zhengzhou University of Light Industry, China
Zhu Shuying	The University of Hong Kong, China
Zugarini Andrea	University of Florence, Italy

Contents – Part IV

Model Compression

Multi-task and Multi-label Learning

Neural Network Theory

Normalization and Regularization Methods

Person Re-identification

Recurrent Neural Networks

Model Compression

Blending Pruning Criteria for Convolutional Neural Networks

Wei He[1], Zhongzhan Huang[2], Mingfu Liang[3], Senwei Liang[4], and Haizhao Yang[4](✉)

[1] Nanyang Technological University, Singapore, Singapore
[2] Tsinghua University, Beijing, China
[3] Northwestern University, Evanston, USA
[4] Purdue University, West Lafayette, USA
yang1863@purdue.edu

Abstract. The advancement of convolutional neural networks (CNNs) on various vision applications has attracted lots of attention. Yet the majority of CNNs are unable to satisfy the strict requirement for real-world deployment. To overcome this, the recent popular network pruning is an effective method to reduce the redundancy of the models. However, the ranking of filters according to their "importance" on different pruning criteria may be inconsistent. One filter could be important according to a certain criterion, while it is unnecessary according to another one, which indicates that each criterion is only a partial view of the comprehensive "importance". From this motivation, we propose a novel framework to integrate the existing filter pruning criteria by exploring the criteria diversity. The proposed framework contains two stages: Criteria Clustering and Filters Importance Calibration. First, we condense the pruning criteria via layerwise clustering based on the rank of "importance" score. Second, within each cluster, we propose a calibration factor to adjust their significance for each selected blending candidates and search for the optimal blending criterion via Evolutionary Algorithm. Quantitative results on the CIFAR-100 and ImageNet benchmarks show that our framework outperforms the state-of-the-art baselines, regrading to the compact model performance after pruning.

Keywords: Convolutional neural networks · Network pruning

1 Introduction

Deep convolutional neural networks (CNNs) have been the prevailing methods in computer vision and brought remarkable improvement to various tasks [5, 6, 13, 14, 19, 20, 30]. However, as the CNNs are normally over-parameterized and cumbersome, it is challenging for the model deployment on devices with limited resources, and the acceleration during the inference stage becomes necessary.

W. He and Z. Huang—Equal contribution.

I. Farkaš et al. (Eds.): ICANN 2021, LNCS 12894, pp. 3–15, 2021.
https://doi.org/10.1007/978-3-030-86380-7_1

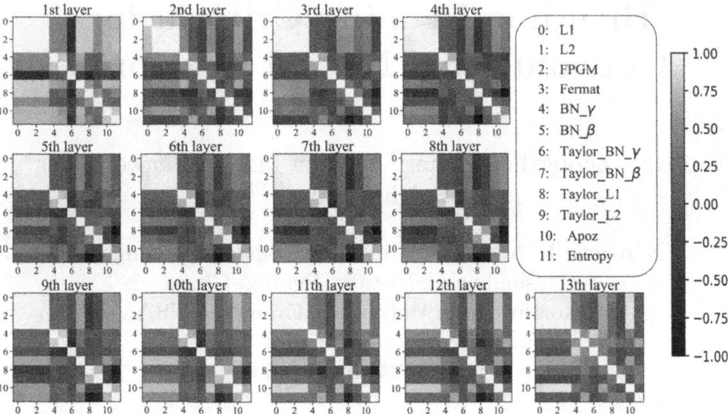

Fig. 1. The Spearman's rank correlation coefficient (Sp) of 12 pruning criteria in VGG16 [32]. The color of each pair of pruning criteria represents the value of Sp, and the lighter the color (close to 1), the stronger similarity.

Network pruning, one of the critical directions in network compression, aims at eliminating the unimportant parameters or operations without compromising the model performance. In this area, filter pruning methods [7,10,18] are more practical to deploy and easily to be implemented. Generally, the workflow of filter pruning can be divided into three steps: (1) *Normal Training*: train the original network on a specific dataset from scratch. (2) *Pruning*: prune the insignificant network components such as neurons, filters, based on a well-handcrafted criterion, where the score magnitude under the criterion reflects their "importance". (3) *Finetuning*: recover the performance loss caused by the removal of the components to a certain extent. Among all steps, an effective pruning criterion plays an essential role in one filter pruning algorithm.

Conventional pruning methods mainly concentrate on designing a better criterion to increase the viable prune ratio without harming the performance, but few of them have introspected the actual correlations among them. Recent work [15] reveals that some of the filter pruning criteria, *e.g.*, L1-Norm [18], L2-Norm [3], FPGM [9] and Fermat [15], have a substantial similarity on the "importance" index of pruned filters in most layers. That is, some pruning criteria incline to remove alike filters, though their considerations are from a different perspective. From this motivation, we further extend the comparison to more criteria. In Fig. 1, we demonstrate the filters rank similarity under assorted state-of-the-art criteria and their variants using the Spearman's correlation coefficient (Sp) [31], which is a non-parametric correlation measurement of rankings, and able to assess the relationship between two variables using a monotonic function. Specifically, for two sequences $X = \{x_1, x_2, \cdots, x_n\}$ and $Y = \{y_1, y_2, .., y_n\}$, if the rank of X and Y are $\{x_1\prime, x_2\prime, \cdots, x_n\prime\}$ and $\{y_1\prime, y_2\prime, \cdots, y_n\prime\}$ respectively, the definition of the Sp between them is

$$\rho(X,Y) = 1 - \frac{6\sum_{i=1}^{N} d_i^2}{n(n^2-1)}, \tag{1}$$

where $d_i = x_{i'} - y_{i'}$. In general, if the Sp is above 0.8, there is a strong confidence that the two sequences of variables are highly similar. Figure 1 indicates an empirical fact that although each criterion is competent for filter pruning, the Sp correlation on their measured "importance" rank has a discrepancy. For example, in the first layer, Taylor BN_γ [25] has negative Sp value with other criteria, *i.e.*, it tends to remove different filters comparing to other criteria. Additionally, in the intermediate layers, this discrepancy becomes obvious on more criteria, excluding the four criteria mentioned in [15]. These inconsistencies imply that some of the pruning criteria may prune the potentially significant filters, *e.g.*, a filter may be viewed as an important filter by one pruning criterion whereas another criterion may judge it unnecessary. Hence, each criterion may only be a partial view of the comprehensive "importance" of filters. Thus, inspired by this phenomenon, we consider a problem: can we introduce one criterion that integrates both the criteria diversity and their advantages as much as possible?

To solve this problem, we propose a novel framework to layerwise integrate the existing filter pruning criteria by examining the criteria diversity on their "importance" measurements, filters "importance" rank, and the discrepancy on their similarity. The proposed framework contains two stages: Criteria Clustering and Filters Importance Calibration. Since the searching space of the candidate combination pools will be extremely large, especially when the network is particularly deep, *e.g.*, ResNet152 has over a hundred layers, finding the solution for the blending criterion among them is non-trivial. Therefore, to ease the above problem and to ensure the variance on blending candidates, we condense the pruning criteria via layerwise clustering based on the rank of "importance" score during the first stage. Then, in each cluster, we propose a calibration factor to adjust their significance for the ensemble. In the second stage, we introduce an Evolutionary Algorithm to optimize the combination of the calibration factor and the blending candidates sampled from each cluster and ultimately generate the optimal blending criterion. Our contributions are summarized as follows:

- To the best of our knowledge, our work is the first to explore the correlation among some existing filter pruning criteria and propose a simple-yet-effective ensemble framework to integrate different pruning criteria and generate an optimal criterion.
- Compared to the conventional filter pruning methods, our method searches for the optimal pruning criteria automatically without manual interaction and empirical knowledge prior. The comprehensive experiments on benchmarks exhibit that our method can further outperform the current state-of-the-art methods. Especially, for ResNet56 pruning in CIFAR-100, our pruned model can exceed the original model performance.

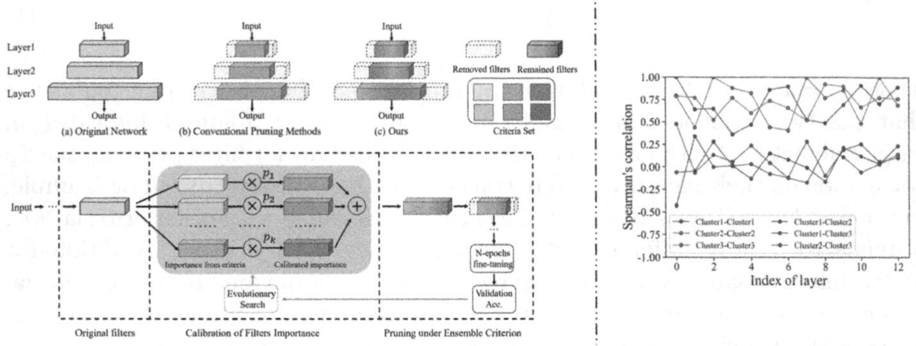

Fig. 2. Left: Overview of our framework for pruning. (a)–(c) show three layers within the original unpruned network, the pruned network under certain conventional filter pruning criterion (denoted in blue) and the pruned network under the blending criterion. The three-step blending process in one layer is illustrated in the dash-line bounding box, where the notation "⊕" denotes the element-wise addition and the notation "⊗" denotes the multiplication between each filter score and the corresponding calibration factor p. **Right**: Average Sp of the criteria score between two clusters. (Colour figure online)

2 Related Works

Filter Pruning. To perform fast inference without largely sacrificing the accuracy, filter pruning focuses on removing the insignificant filters from the original network [4,24]. Therefore, it is crucial to construct an effective criterion to evaluate the "importance" or contribution of the filters. Previously proposed criteria can be mainly categorized into four folds: (1) Filter-based criteria, which consider the property among filters as the importance indicator. The scoring metrics can be the filter's L1-Norm [18] or L2-Norm [3]. The underlying assumption of these methods is that the small norm parameters play a less informative role on the final prediction. Recent FPGM [9] and Fermat [15] advance the local filter property for the correlation of multiple filters in a layer. (2) Batch Normalization (BN) based criteria, which estimate channel importance via the value of the parameter inside each BN layer. Network Slimming [22] and SSS [12] consider taking the magnitude of the scaling factor γ to reveal the importance of their corresponding filter. (3) Feature maps activation based criteria, which take the activation value in each feature map as a proxy for its importance, for instance, the average percentage of zeros (APoZ) and the in-between entropy on the channel maps [11,23]. (4) First-order Taylor based criteria, which estimate the filter's contribution with respect to the cost function and the scoring function is designed based on the Taylor expansion [26]. One recent work is proposed to adaptively select pruning criterion for each layer to better suit the filter distribution across layers [8]. Our framework differs from [8] in two folds: (1) for each layer, we integrate different criteria based on the similarity of pruned filter selection, while [8] used only one pruning criterion for each layer; (2) according to the findings on [15] and the experiments (see Fig. 1), for L1-norm [18], L2-Norm [3] and FPGM [9] used in [8], these three criteria tend to remove the consistent set of filters in most layers. Thus, although one of them is selected, the strength of different criteria are not sufficiently utilized.

Evolutionary Algorithms. Recently, the Evolutionary Algorithms (EA) [1] and their variants are widely used in Network Compression and Neural Architecture Search (NAS) areas as the EA can flexibly solve the multi-objective optimization problem and combinatorial optimization with conflicting objectives. In Network Compression, MetaPruning [21] applied an evolutionary search to find the high accuracy pruned network under the soft or hard constraints. [16] leveraged an Evolution Strategy (ES) algorithm to find a good solution for multi-objective optimization problems. In NAS, [28] modified the EA to search for high-performance neural network architectures for large and realistic classification dataset. [27] introduced the novel aging evolution such that the tournament selection can be biased to choose the younger genotypes. In this paper, our target is totally different from all the previous work utilizing the EA. Our work leverages the EA to search for the blend of filter pruning criteria and our empirical results demonstrate the effectiveness.

3 Proposed Method

In this section, we introduce our proposed framework for filter pruning. Given a CNN, our method adaptively generates an integrated criterion to identify the model redundancy layerwise. The proposed method consists of two stages: in the first stage, we divide different pruning criteria via clustering. In the second stage, we propose the calibration factors to combine criteria sampled from each cluster. Furthermore, the heuristic Evolutionary Algorithm (EA) is applied to optimize the calibration factors and to search the optimal combination of criteria. The details of these two stages are illustrated in Algorithm 1. For notation, suppose that we are given I criteria, *e.g.*, L1-Norm, L2-Norm and FPGM, and the overall criteria set is denoted as $U_{criteria} = \{f_i\}_{i=1}^{I}$, where f_i is the mapping to filter importance score under $criterion_i$. Consider a L-layer network, the filters set in l-th convolution layer is denoted as $F^l = \{\mathbf{F}_i^l\}_{i=1}^{\lambda_l}$, where λ_l is the number of filters in layer l. The filters importance score $\mathbf{S}_i^l \in [0,1]^{\lambda_l}$ under $criterion_i$ is calculated by $f_i(\mathbf{F}_1^l, \cdots, \mathbf{F}_{\lambda_l}^l)$, where $i = 1, \cdots, I$. Each component of $\mathbf{S}_i^l$ represents the importance score of the corresponding filter given by the $criterion_i$. For each criterion, the larger the score, the more important the filter is.

3.1 Criteria Clustering

We first consider the selection complexity for blending K candidate criteria among N given criteria on a L-layer CNN. When $N = 12, K = 6$, and

Algorithm 1. Framework for Blending Pruning Criteria

Input: Unpruned model ϕ with L convolution layers; Criteria Set $U_{criteria} = \{f_i\}_{i=1}^{I}$, I is the number of included criteria; Convolution filters in layer l: $F^l = \{\mathbf{F}_i^l\}_{i=1}^{\lambda_l}, l = 1, 2, \cdots, L$; Number of clusters each layer: K;
Output: Pruned model ϕ_{blended} over the optimal integrated criterion S_{blended}.

▷ Calculation of Importance
for l from 1 to L **do**
    for i from 1 to I **do**
        $\mathbf{S}_i^l \leftarrow f_i(\mathbf{F}_1^l, \mathbf{F}_2^l, \cdots, \mathbf{F}_{\lambda_l}^l)$
    end for
    $S_{Criteria}^l \leftarrow \{\mathbf{S}_1^l, \mathbf{S}_2^l, \cdots, \mathbf{S}_I^l\}$
end for
▷ Clustering Criteria
for l from 1 to L **do**
    for i from 1 to I **do**
        ▷ Calculate the Spearman's correlation matrix
        $Sp_{ij}^l \leftarrow \rho(\mathbf{S}_i^l, \mathbf{S}_j^l), j = 1, \cdots, I$
    end for
    $(C_1^l, \cdots, C_K^l) \leftarrow \text{KM}(Sp_{1:}^l, \cdots, Sp_{I:}^l)$
end for
Obtain K-Means results: $(C_1^{:}, \cdots, C_K^{:})$
▷ Evolutionary Search
EA Hyperparameters: Population size $\mathcal{N}$, Number of iterations $\mathcal{I}$, Mutation Probability $\mathcal{M}$, Crossover Probability $\mathcal{C}$, Drop Ratio $\mathcal{D}$, Finetuned Epochs $\mathcal{E}$.
$\mathcal{G}_0 \leftarrow (\mathbf{P}_0, \mathbf{S}_0)_{\mathbf{P}_0 \sim \mathcal{U}[0,1], \mathbf{S}_0 \sim (C_1^{:}, \cdots, C_K^{:})}$
$\mathbf{P}_0, \mathbf{S}_0 \in \mathbb{R}^{\mathcal{N} \times L \times K}$
for *iter* from 1 to $\mathcal{I}$ **do**
    $\mathcal{G}_{Crossover} \leftarrow \text{Crossover}(\mathcal{G}_{iter-1}, \mathcal{C})$
    $\mathcal{G}_{Mutation} \leftarrow \text{Mutation}(\mathcal{G}_{Crossover}, \mathcal{M})$
    $\mathcal{G}_{Drop} \leftarrow \text{Drop}(\mathcal{G}_{Mutation}, \mathcal{D})$
    $\mathcal{G}_{iter} \leftarrow \mathcal{G}_{Drop}$
    $\phi_{iter} \leftarrow \text{Blending}(\mathcal{G}_{iter})$
    $\text{Acc}_{\phi_{iter}} \leftarrow \text{Finetune}(\phi_{iter}, \mathcal{E})$
end for
$\mathbf{P}_{topk}, \mathbf{S}_{topk} \leftarrow \text{TopK}(\text{Acc}_{\phi_{\mathcal{I}}})$
$\phi_{\text{blended}}, S_{\text{blended}} \leftarrow \text{Final}(\mathbf{P}_{topk}, \mathbf{S}_{topk})$
return $\phi_{\text{blended}}, S_{\text{blended}}$

$L = 13$, we have $(C_{12}^6)^{13} \approx 3^{38}$ combinations. For the commonly used model, the number of selection will be extremely large. In addition, from Fig. 1, we observe that some of the filter pruning criteria have a strong similarity on the rank of the criteria score. As a result, they tend to prune a similar set of filters in one convolution layer. Moreover, in traditional implementation of the ensemble method [2,33], its capability of achieving greater performance than an individual method comes from the diversity and effectiveness of the candidate methods that will be integrated. Given these above points, we cluster the given criteria set in each layer based on the Spearman's correlation matrix **Sp** before the blending, which is able to decrease the search space on the criteria selections efficiently. When the K candidate criteria are obtained from each cluster in one layer, using the rule of product and Arithmetic Mean-Geometric Mean Inequality, the upper bound of the search space is $\left(\frac{N}{k}\right)^k$. And $\left(\frac{N}{k}\right)^k = \prod_{j=0}^{k-1}\left(\frac{N}{k}\right) \le \prod_{j=0}^{k-1}\left(\frac{N-j}{k-j}\right) = \frac{\prod_{j=0}^{k-1}(N-j)}{k!} = C_N^k$.

When $k \in [1, N]$ is selected appropriately, we have $\left(\frac{N}{k}\right)^k \ll C_N^k$. If we sample the candidate criteria from different clusters, the Sp value between them should be relatively small (as shown in Fig. 2), *i.e.*, their filter importance rank would be dissimilar. Therefore, this clustering of criteria can not only maintain the criteria diversity but also it can reduce the search space by selecting the number of clusters. Before clustering, we assign $criterion_i$ with a correlation vector,

$$Sp^l_{i:} = (\rho(\mathbf{S}^l_i, \mathbf{S}^l_1), \rho(\mathbf{S}^l_i, \mathbf{S}^l_2), \cdots, \rho(\mathbf{S}^l_i, \mathbf{S}^l_I)), \tag{2}$$

where $i = 1, 2, \cdots, I$ and ρ is Spearman's correlation defined in Eq. 1. Subsequently, we conduct K-Means to cluster the correlation vectors of the criteria into K clusters and obtain K clustering sets $\{C^l_1, \cdots, C^l_K\}$. The two criteria in the same cluster have similar correlation vectors in the sense of Euclidean distance. We want to point out that the two criteria in the same cluster have large Sp correlation value (see Fig. 2), which indicates the rank of these two criteria is similar. Therefore, we are able to sample criteria from each cluster whose in-between Sp is relatively small and indicate the adequate diversity of basic criteria for the ensemble.

3.2 Filters Importance Calibration

After criteria clustering, we obtained K clustering sets $(C^l_1, C^l_2, \cdots, C^l_K)$ in layer l. To filter out the similar criteria, we sample the distinctive criterion score $\mathbf{S}^l_{i_k}$ from each cluster C^l_k as the candidate for ensemble, where $i_k \in \{1, 2, \cdots, I\}$, $k = 1, 2, \cdots, K$. Thus, to combine those selective criteria and integrate their importance measurements to identify the redundancy, we calibrate their filters importance with the introduced filter importance calibration factors $p^l_k \in [0, 1]$. When filters in different layer extract multi-level features, we conduct layerwise criteria blending to adaptively discover their importance $S^l_{\text{blended}} = \sum_{k=1}^{K} p^l_k \mathbf{S}^l_{i_k}$. The larger the value of p^l_k reveals that the cluster k is much significant for pruning filters in this layer. We denote $\phi(\{S^l_{\text{blended}}\}^L_{l=1}, N)$ as the network ϕ after finetuning N epochs and discarding filters according to the ensemble score. As the pruning objective is to remove redundancy without harming the model performance too much, therefore, our framework for filter pruning tends to discover the blending criterion, such that its pruned network maximizes the accuracy after N-epoch finetuning in the validation set,

$$\max_{\left\{p^l_k, \mathbf{S}^l_{i_k}; k=1,\cdots,K, l=1,\cdots,L\right\}} \text{Accuracy}\left(\phi\left(\left\{S^l_{\text{blended}}\right\}^L_{l=1}\right), N\right). \tag{3}$$

Since the objective function (3) is not differentiable, we consider using the Evolutionary Algorithm (EA) oriented by the validation accuracy to optimize it, and the superiority of EA has been mentioned in the related works section. In the evolutionary search, the optimization fitness is the model evaluation result after N-epochs finetuning over part of the training set. The validation set and train set are split from the original training set, the splitting details are discussed in the experiments section. To be specific, each evolution gene consists of the calibration combination and the pruned network in terms of the corresponding calibrated criterion. All calibration factors are initiated from the uniform distribution $\mathcal{U}[0, 1]$. Though the criteria in each cluster possess high similarity, they also have their ability to probe the network redundancy individually. To avoid

Table 1. Quantitative results on CIFAR-100 dataset

Model	Criterion	Pruned/ Finetuned Acc. (%)	Acc.↓ (%)	Model	Criterion	Pruned/ Finetuned Acc. (%)	Acc.↓ (%)
VGG16*	L1-Norm	15.76/71.29	0.93	ResNet56†	L1-Norm	52.16/69.43	0.07
	L2-Norm	16.24/71.32	0.90		L2-Norm	50.75/69.45	0.05
	Apoz	5.69/70.91	1.31		Apoz	2.03/63.68	5.82
	BN_γ	15.87/71.26	0.96		BN_γ	29.35/69.39	0.11
	BN_β	6.92/71.45	0.77		BN_β	22.44/69.32	0.18
	Entropy	11.80/71.09	1.13		Entropy	17.37/69.14	0.36
	FPGM	15.91/71.37	0.85		FPGM	51.20/69.50	0.00
	Fermat	15.39/71.39	0.83		Fermat	**51.45**/69.47	0.03
	Taylor L1-Norm	1.29/70.35	1.87		Taylor L1-Norm	15.77/69.27	0.23
	Taylor L2-Norm	16.19/71.19	1.03		Taylor L2-Norm	39.22/69.23	0.27
	Taylor_BN_γ	7.46/71.19	1.03		Taylor_BN_γ	30.41/69.34	0.16
	Taylor_BN_β	7.10/71.16	1.06		Taylor_BN_β	25.42/69.34	0.16
	Ours	**16.67/71.68**	**0.54**		**Ours**	40.38/**69.82**	**-0.32**

* VGG16 original Acc.: 72.22%

† ResNet56 original Acc.: 69.50%

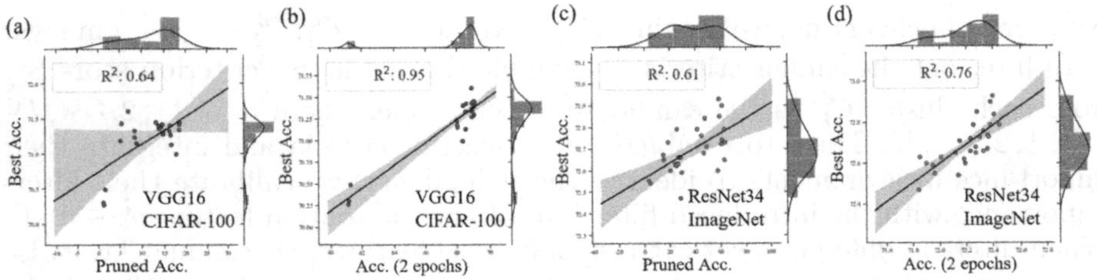

Fig. 3. The R^2 between Acc. on different finetuned epochs. (a) and (c): best finetuned Acc. vs pruned Acc.; (b) and (d): best finetuned Acc. vs Acc. after 2 epochs finetuning.

sticking to one criterion that gives high ensemble accuracy, during crossover in EA, we give other criteria in the same cluster the opportunity to be selected again via random sampling in each evolutionary process.

After iterations of crossover, mutation, and drop, the TopK genes with the highest validation accuracy are considered the potential optimal calibrated pruning criterion. Then, under these blending results, we can obtain the gene with the highest accuracy after the final one-shot pruning and finetuning, and the criterion under this gene is considered the optimal filter importance measurement to discard unimportant filters in this architecture.

4 Experiments

We evaluate the effectiveness of our proposed method over different image classification benchmarks.

Dataset. We conduct experiments on CIFAR-100 [17] and ImageNet [29] datasets. CIFAR-100 has 50k train images and 10k test images of size 32 by

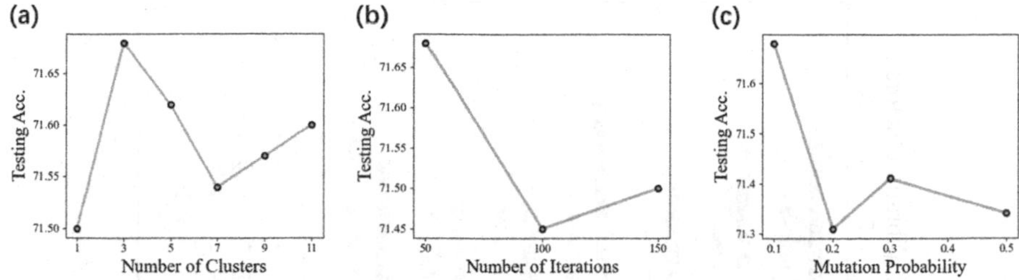

Fig. 4. The testing accuracy of VGG16 after finetuning. (a) Comparison of the performance under different number of clusters. Note that when the number of clusters equals to 1, we choose one criterion at each layer and when the number of clusters equals to number of criteria, we choose all criteria; (b) Comparison of the performance over different number of iteration in EA; (c) Comparison of the performance over mutation probability in EA.

32 from 100 classes. 10% of train images are split for validation and the remaining for training. ImageNet comprises 1.28 million train images and 50k validation images from 1000 classes. 50k out of 1.28 million train images (50 images in each class) are used for sub-validation. The cropping size 224 by 224 is used in our ImageNet experiments. Adopting the same predefined pruning configuration [18], we evaluate our method on VGG [32] and ResNet [6].

Results & Analysis. In Table 1 and Table 2, we present the quantitative comparison on CIFAR-100 and ImageNet, where the average accuracy over three repeated experiments are attached (denoted as Acc.). Comparing to the baselines, our method performs the best in the same settings.

According to Fig. 2, the optimization fitness in the evolutionary search needs N-epochs finetuning over part of the training set. Is N-epoch finetuning necessary in evolutionary search?

To illustrate, we take VGG16 on CIFAR-100 and ResNet34 on ImageNet as examples. First, we calculate the Pearson correlation coefficient (R^2) between the accuracy of the pruned model without finetuning and the best accuracy after completed finetuning. In Fig. 3 (a) and (c), the value of R^2 indicates that the accuracy between the pruned model accuracy and the best accuracy does not have a strong linear relationship. Therefore, the accuracy of the pruned model without finetuning is not suitable as a metric for our Evolutionary process in Filters Importance Calibration. However, after several epochs of finetuning (as shown in Fig. 3(b) and (d)), the R^2 improve significantly and it means that a certain amount of finetuning is necessary.

From the clustering results, pruning criteria that have strong similarity will gather in the same cluster as expected. In Fig. 5, the value of calibration factors on each cluster are illustrated. Taking the Conv7 of VGG16 on CIFAR-100 as an example, Criterion1 that consists of L1-Norm, L2-Norm, and FPGM, is calibrated with the largest factor, which indicates that the first cluster contributes more significantly in this layer.

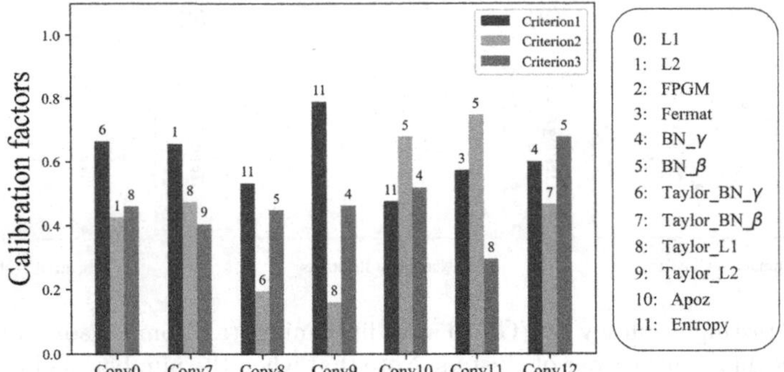

Fig. 5. The optimal value of calibration factors and the sampled criterion of each cluster at different layers of VGG16 on CIFAR-100. The annotation above each bar denotes the sampled criterion index.

Table 2. ImageNet quantitative results

Model	Criterion	Pruned/ Finetuned Acc. (%)	Acc.↓ (%)
ResNet34*	L1-Norm	59.08/72.76	1.03
	L2-Norm	61.02/72.77	1.02
	Apoz	4.70/72.19	1.60
	BN_γ	19.02/72.71	1.08
	BN_β	4.12/72.59	1.20
	Entropy	25.84/72.57	1.22
	FPGM	**62.28**/72.78	1.01
	Fermat	44.63/72.80	0.99
	Taylor L1-Norm	25.71/72.67	1.12
	Taylor L2-Norm	46.43/72.67	1.12
	Taylor BN_γ	27.47/72.65	1.14
	Taylor BN_β	18.00/72.67	1.12
	Ours	61.33/**72.85**	**0.94**

* ResNet34 original Acc.: 73.79%

Table 3. Ablation on hyperparameters

#Clusters	#Iterations	Mutation prob.	Fintuned acc.
1	50	0.10	71.50
3	50	0.10	71.68
5	50	0.10	71.62
7	50	0.10	71.54
9	50	0.10	71.57
11	50	0.10	71.60
3	100	0.10	71.45
3	150	0.10	71.50
3	50	0.20	71.31
3	50	0.30	71.41
3	50	0.50	71.34

5 Implementation Details

For the normal training and the finetuning, we use the SGD optimizer with momentum and weight decay parameter 0.9 and 0.0001 respectively. For finetuning, the learning rate is started at 0.001. On CIFAR-100, we finetune the pruned model for 40 epochs in batch size 64. On ImageNet, we finetune for 20 epochs with a mini-batch size of 256.

For the evolutionary search setting, we consider the criteria as follows: L1-Norm, L2-Norm, FPGM, Fermat, BN_γ scale, BN_β scale, Entropy, Taylor L1-Norm, Taylor L2-Norm, Taylor BN_γ, Taylor BN_β. In each evolution iteration, we set the mutation probability to 0.1, crossover constant to 0.8, and drop probability to 0.05. In CIFAR-100, the population size is 20, the number of iterations is 50 and the drop ratio is 0.08. In ImageNet, the population size is 10, the number of iterations is 30 and the drop ratio is 0.1. After pruning the network based on the weighted sum of the scores, we finetune the pruned network on the validation split for 3 epochs in CIFAR-100 experiments and 1 epoch for ImageNet. Finally, the network is pruned under the optimal blending criterion obtained by EA, where the finetuning epochs are 40 on CIFAR-100 and 20 on ImageNet over the whole training set.

6 Ablation Studies

In this section, to understand the performance of our method in different settings, we conduct the following ablation experiments on the number of clusters used in Criteria Clustering and the hyperparameters of Filters Importance Calibration. The ablation results are shown in Fig. 4. The search space of EA is related to the number of clusters. In each layer l, the larger the number of clusters K^l, the harder the optimization of the calibration factors p^l. From our experiments, the best performance appears when $K^l = 3$ for VGG16. Also, we compare the performance with different hyperparameters of EA, including the number of evolution iterations and mutation ratio. As we see in Fig. 4(b), the increment of iterations is not sufficient for the increment of performance. Therefore, we choose the relatively small number of iterations and use the top-K strategy. From Fig. 4(c), we observe that the large mutation probability may harm the search. The ablation study on the EA hyperparameters and the number of the cluster are shown in Table 3.

7 Conclusion

In this paper, we propose a novel framework for filter pruning. In the first stage, we reduce the searching space for the criteria selection and fit the requirement for the ensemble using clustering. In the second stage, the criteria blending problem is formulated as an optimization problem on filters' importance calibration. The comprehensive experiments on various benchmarks exhibit that our blended criterion is able to outperform the current state-of-the-art criteria. Besides, we explore the correlation among existing filter pruning criteria and provides a way to obtain effective criteria without manual efforts.

Acknowledgments. S. L. and H. Y. were partially supported by the NSF grant DMS-1945029 and the NVIDIA GPU grant.

References

1. Beyer, H.G., Schwefel, H.P.: Evolution strategies-a comprehensive introduction. Natural Comput. **1**(1), 3–52 (2002)

2. Dietterich, T.G.: Ensemble methods in machine learning. In: Kittler, J., Roli, F. (eds.) MCS 2000. LNCS, vol. 1857, pp. 1–15. Springer, Heidelberg (2000). https://doi.org/10.1007/3-540-45014-9_1
3. Frankle, J., Carbin, M.: The lottery ticket hypothesis: Finding sparse, trainable neural networks. In: International Conference on Learning Representations (2019)
4. Guo, J., Ouyang, W., Xu, D.: Multi-dimensional pruning: A unified framework for model compression. In: Proceedings of the IEEE/CVF Conference on Computer Vision and Pattern Recognition, pp. 1508–1517 (2020)
5. He, K., Gkioxari, G., Dollár, P., Girshick, R.: Mask R-CNN. In: Proceedings of the IEEE International Conference on Computer Vision, pp. 2961–2969 (2017)
6. He, K., Zhang, X., Ren, S., Sun, J.: Deep residual learning for image recognition. In: Proceedings of the IEEE Conference on Computer Vision and Pattern Recognition, pp. 770–778 (2016)
7. He, W., Wu, M., Liang, M., Lam, S.K.: Cap: context-aware pruning for semantic segmentation. In: Proceedings of the IEEE/CVF Winter Conference on Applications of Computer Vision (WACV), pp. 960–969, January 2021
8. He, Y., Ding, Y., Liu, P., Zhu, L., Zhang, H., Yang, Y.: Learning filter pruning criteria for deep convolutional neural networks acceleration. In: Proceedings of the IEEE Conference on Computer Vision and Pattern Recognition (CVPR) (2020)
9. He, Y., Liu, P., Wang, Z., Hu, Z., Yang, Y.: Filter pruning via geometric median for deep convolutional neural networks acceleration. In: Proceedings of the IEEE Conference on Computer Vision and Pattern Recognition, pp. 4340–4349 (2019)
10. He, Y., Zhang, X., Sun, J.: Channel pruning for accelerating very deep neural networks. In: Proceedings of the IEEE International Conference on Computer Vision, pp. 1389–1397 (2017)
11. Hu, H., Peng, R., Tai, Y.W., Tang, C.K.: Network trimming: a data-driven neuron pruning approach towards efficient deep architectures. arXiv preprint arXiv:1607.03250 (2016)
12. Huang, Z., Wang, N.: Data-driven sparse structure selection for deep neural networks. In: Proceedings of the European Conference on Computer Vision (ECCV), pp. 304–320 (2018)
13. Huang, Z., Liang, S., Liang, M., He, W., Yang, H.: Efficient attention network: Accelerate attention by searching where to plug. arXiv preprint arXiv:2011.14058 (2020)
14. Huang, Z., Liang, S., Liang, M., Yang, H.: Dianet: dense-and-implicit attention network. arXiv preprint arXiv:1905.10671 (2019)
15. Huang, Z., Wang, X., Luo, P.: Convolution-weight-distribution assumption: Rethinking the criteria of channel pruning. arXiv preprint arXiv:2004.11627 (2020)
16. Junior, F.E.F., Yen, G.G.: Pruning deep neural networks architectures with evolution strategy. arXiv preprint arXiv:1912.11527 (2019)
17. Krizhevsky, A., Hinton, G.: Learning multiple layers of features from tiny images. Technical report, Citeseer (2009)
18. Li, H., Kadav, A., Durdanovic, I., Samet, H., Graf, H.P.: Pruning filters for efficient convnets. arXiv preprint arXiv:1608.08710 (2016)
19. Liang, S., Huang, Z., Liang, M., Yang, H.: Instance enhancement batch normalization: an adaptive regulator of batch noise. In: AAAI, pp. 4819–4827 (2020)
20. Liang, S., Khoo, Y., Yang, H.: Drop-activation: implicit parameter reduction and harmonious regularization. Commun. Appl. Math. Comput. **3**(2), 293–311 (2021)
21. Liu, Z., et al.: Metapruning: meta learning for automatic neural network channel pruning. In: Proceedings of the IEEE International Conference on Computer Vision, pp. 3296–3305 (2019)

22. Liu, Z., Li, J., Shen, Z., Huang, G., Yan, S., Zhang, C.: Learning efficient convolutional networks through network slimming. In: Proceedings of the IEEE International Conference on Computer Vision, pp. 2736–2744 (2017)
23. Luo, J.H., Wu, J.: An entropy-based pruning method for cnn compression. arXiv preprint arXiv:1706.05791 (2017)
24. Luo, J.H., Wu, J., Lin, W.: Thinet: A filter level pruning method for deep neural network compression. In: Proceedings of the IEEE International Conference on Computer Vision, pp. 5058–5066 (2017)
25. Molchanov, P., Mallya, A., Tyree, S., Frosio, I., Kautz, J.: Importance estimation for neural network pruning. In: Proceedings of the IEEE Conference on Computer Vision and Pattern Recognition, pp. 11264–11272 (2019)
26. Molchanov, P., Tyree, S., Karras, T., Aila, T., Kautz, J.: Pruning convolutional neural networks for resource efficient inference. arXiv preprint arXiv:1611.06440 (2016)
27. Real, E., Aggarwal, A., Huang, Y., Le, Q.V.: Regularized evolution for image classifier architecture search. In: Proceedings of the AAAI Conference on Artificial Intelligence, vol. 33, pp. 4780–4789 (2019)
28. Real, E., Moore, S., Selle, A., Saxena, S., Suematsu, Y.L., Tan, J., Le, Q.V., Kurakin, A.: Large-scale evolution of image classifiers. In: Proceedings of the 34th International Conference on Machine Learning-Volume 70, pp. 2902–2911. JMLR. org (2017)
29. Russakovsky, O., Deng, J., Su, H., Krause, J., Satheesh, S., Ma, S., Huang, Z., Karpathy, A., Khosla, A., Bernstein, M., Berg, A.C., Fei-Fei, L.: ImageNet large scale visual recognition challenge. Int. J. Comput. Vis. **115**(3), 211–252 (2015). https://doi.org/10.1007/s11263-015-0816-y
30. C Schroff, F., Kalenichenko, D., Philbin, J.: Facenet: A unified embedding for face recognition and clustering. In: Proceedings of the IEEE Conference on Computer Vision and Pattern Recognition, pp. 815–823 (2015)
31. Sedgwick, P.: Spearman's rank correlation coefficient. Bmj **349**, g7327 (2014)
32. Simonyan, K., Zisserman, A.: Very deep convolutional networks for large-scale image recognition. arXiv preprint arXiv:1409.1556 (2014)
33. Zhou, Z.H.: Ensemble Methods: Foundations and Algorithms. CRC Press, Boca Raton (2012)

BFRIFP: Brain Functional Reorganization Inspired Filter Pruning

Shoumeng Qiu, Yuzhang Gu(✉), and Xiaolin Zhang

Bio-Vision System Laboratory, State Key Laboratory of Transducer Technology, Shanghai Institute of Microsystem and Information Technology, Chinese Academy of Sciences, Beijing, China
gyz@mail.sim.ac.cn

Abstract. Neural network pruning has attracted enormous attention since it offers a promising prospect to facilitate the deployment of deep neural networks on resource-limited devices. However, the core of most existing methods lies in the criteria of selection of filters which were pre-defined by researchers. With the advancement of network pruning research, the criteria are becoming increasingly complex. In this paper, we propose a brain-inspired filter pruning algorithm for deep neural networks, which requires no selection criteria. Inspired by the reorganization of brain function in humans when irreversible damage occurs, we treat the weight to be pruning as damaged neurons, and complete the reorganization of the network function in the novel training process proposed in this paper. After pruning, the kept parameters can take over the function of those that have been pruned. The pruning method is widely applicable to common architectures and does not require any artificially designed filter importance measurement functions. As the first attempt on weight-importance irrelevant pruning, BFRIFP provides novel insight into the network pruning problem. Experiments on CIFAR-10 and ImageNet demonstrate the effectiveness of our new perspective of network pruning compared to traditional network pruning algorithms.

Keywords: Filter pruning · Brain functional reorganization · Deep neural networks

1 Introduction

During the past years, deep neural networks (DNNs) have reached state-of-the-art performance in a variety of computer vision and natural language processing tasks. Despite their great success, they also cause the prohibitively expensive computational cost and make it more difficult to deploy the model on mobile devices. So there is a growing need for reduction of model size by parameter quantization, low-rank decomposition, and network pruning.

Among these methods, network pruning has gained tremendous attention since it can reduce the number of model parameters and operations simultaneously. The crux of filter pruning is selecting the unimportant filters to be pruned,

---

The original version of this chapter was revised: The corresponding author was corrected. The correction to this chapter is available at https://doi.org/10.1007/978-3-030-86380-7_57

I. Farkaš et al. (Eds.): ICANN 2021, LNCS 12894, pp. 16–28, 2021.
https://doi.org/10.1007/978-3-030-86380-7_2

which should yield the highest compression ratio with the lowest loss of accuracy. Many of them are based on assumption that the magnitude of weight and its importance are strongly correlated. But recent work [1] questions this assumption and observes a significant gap in the correlation between weight-based pruning decisions and empirically optimal one-step decisions. Other studies [2,3] have also shown the pruned architecture itself, rather than a set of inherited "important" weights, is more crucial to the efficiency in the final model. So filter pruning remains an open problem so far, the optimal prune rate of each layer is hard to obtain and the prune-retrain iteration is time-consuming.

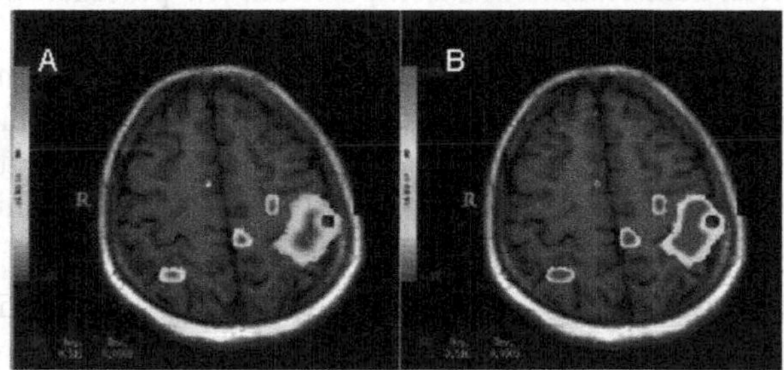

Fig. 1. The process of Brain Reorganization: Functional MRI images of brain functional activation in a stroke patient before (A) and after (B) constraint-induced movement therapy for 4 weeks. A comparison of the images in A and B indicates that the majority of areas of reduced functional activation displayed increased activation after constraint-induced movement therapy. [4].

To address the above issues, and inspired by the reorganization of brain function phenomenon when irreversible damage occurs [5], we propose a novel filter pruning approach, named Brain-inspired Filter pruning (BFRIFP). Reorganization of brain function after a disabling injury or illness has been found early [6], the process is shown in Fig. 1. Specifically, consider some regions of the brain are irreversibly injured (correspond to filters to be pruned), other regions of the brain may substitute or complement for this function (correspond to filters to be retained). More details can be referred to [7,8]. Different from the previous methods which prune filters with relatively less contribution, any filters can be considered a candidate to BFRIFP. To simplify the method, and without loss of generality, we select filters from bottom to top based on the channel index in each layer (because in general, there is no correlation between the channel index and the content in the corresponding feature map, so select filters from bottom to top equate to select filters randomly). Through theoretical analysis and experiments, we demonstrate that there is knowledge transfer from the filters to be pruned to the filters that will be retained during the pruning process.

Our contributions can be summarized as follows:

1. Inspired by the reorganization of brain function in humans when irreversible damage occurs, we propose BFRIFP (Brain Function Reorganization Inspired Filter Pruning) to effectively conduct filter pruning of deep neural networks.

2. We employ theoretical analysis and experiments to demonstrate that there is knowledge transfer from the filters to be pruned to the filters retained in the pruning process, which is not only crucial for the success of the proposed algorithm but also will deepen our understanding of the pruning process.
3. Extensive experiments demonstrate the efficiency and effectiveness of BFRIFP in both model compression and acceleration.

2 Related Works

Most previous works on accelerating neural networks can be broadly classified into four categories, namely, matrix decomposition, low-precision weights, knowledge distilling, and pruning. A comprehensive survey is provided in [9]. In this section, we mainly review the closely related work about filter pruning.

Unstructured pruning and structured pruning are two major lines of methods for Network pruning. From a broader point of view, e.g., low-precision weights and low-rank decomposition can be integrated with network pruning to achieve higher compression and speedup.

Unstructured Pruning. To compress deep neural networks, network pruning disables the weak connections in a network, which will not have substantial negative influences on model performance. [10] utilized the second-order Taylor expansion as criteria to select less important parameters for pruning. [11] introduces an iterative weight pruning algorithm by fine-tuning with a strong l2 regularization and discarding the unimportant weights with values below a predefined threshold. [12] implemented CNNs in the frequency domain and apply 2-D DCT (Discrete Cosine Transform)decomposition to sparsify the coefficients for spatial redundancy removal. Since these unstructured methods make a big network sparse rather than change the whole structure of the network, they require specialized hardware or software supports to speed up inference, due to the irregular sparsity in weight tensor.

Structured Pruning. To address the problem in Unstructured Pruning, structured pruning has no dependency on specialized hardware or software since the entire filters are removed, and thereby it has more advantages in accelerating deep neural networks. In early work on the subject, [13] proposed a group lasso to enable the structured sparsity of deep networks. [14] proposed a data-driven sparse structure selection by introducing scaling factors to scale the outputs of the pruned structure and imposed the sparsity constraint on the scaling factors. [15] proposed to minimize an objective function with l1-regularization of a soft mask via generative adversarial learning and adopted the knowledge distillation techniques for optimization.

3 The Proposed Approach

In this section, we first introduce symbols and notations. Second, we present the details of the proposed approach. Then we employ theoretical analysis and conduct experiments to evaluate the knowledge transfer from the filters to be pruned to the filters retained in the pruning process.

3.1 Notations

We formally introduce symbols and notations in this subsection, which can be summarized in Table 1 (In this paper, we are mainly interested in the CNN model, but the algorithm is adapted to other neural networks, such as the RNN model).

Table 1. Notations in this paper

n	Number of layers	c_i	Number of filters in L_i
L_i	the i-th conv layer	k_i	kernel size in L_i
$W = \{W_1, W_2, ..., W_n\}$	model parameters	b	batchsize
$W_i = w_1^i, w_2^i, .., w_{c_i}^i$	parameters in L_i	h_i	the height of feature map
$w_j^i \in \mathbb{R}^{c_{i-1} \times k_i \times k_i}$	the j-th filter in L_i	w_i	the width of feature map
$F^i \in \mathbb{R}^{b \times c_i \times h \times w}$	feature maps from L_i	K	subset to be kept
$f_c^i \in \mathbb{R}^{b \times h_i \times w_i}$	feature map generated by w_c^i	P	subset to be pruned
$G(w_j^i)$	the gradient of weight w_j^i		

3.2 BFRIFP

Conventional filter pruning methods aim to identify and remove the less important filters from W. Most prior works resort to directly designing a function on the filters to measure the importance of a filter the model. However, consider the previous studies [2,3] have shown: 1. Learned "important" weights of the large model are typically not useful for the small pruned model. 2. The pruned architecture itself, rather than a set of inherited "important" weights, is more crucial to the efficiency in the final model. We argue that function may not be necessary.

Based on the analysis above, we propose a new pruning method without filter importance measurement function. Compared with the previous methods, this greatly reduces the complexity of pruning algorithms, which also means that researchers can focus more on the design of the structure and size of the model. The whole pipeline of the algorithm is inspired by the mechanism of reorganization of brain function. The flowchart of the algorithm is shown in Fig. 2.

Given a neural network denoted as G, instead of measuring the importance of every filter to the model, we only need to determine the pruning ratio of each layer (we do not need to identify which filters should remove). Suppose the pruning ratio α_i in each layer is already known, the only thing we need to do is to transfer the knowledge from the original network to the pruned network. In the proposed algorithm, the whole transfer process is the finetune process. Specifically, during the forward propagation, we gradually decrease the value of the outputs from the candidate filters to be pruned. This can be easily accomplished by multiplying a scalar decaying with finetuning iterations. Suppose the current

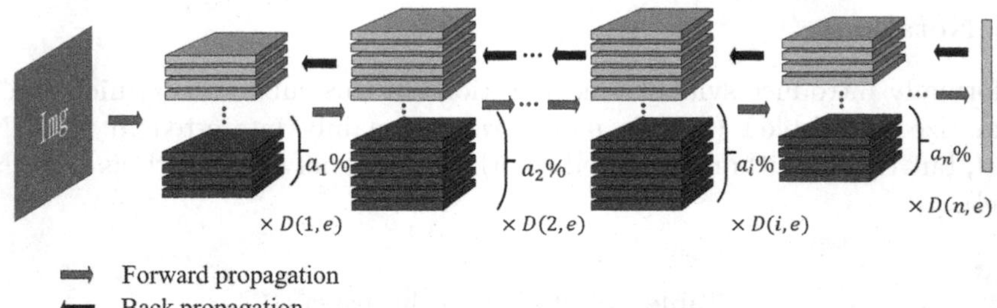

Fig. 2. An overview of the proposed filter pruning algorithm. Given a pre-trained network G, suppose the pruning ratio α_i in each layer is known. We choose the last α_i percentage of filters of each layer as candidates to be pruned. Where the orange part represents the filters to be preserved, and the green part represents filters to be pruned. In the forward propagation process, we gradually decay the output of the green part over training iterations, in the backward propagation process, the parameters that correspond to the green part are frozen. (Color figure online)

training epoch is e, and the decay parameter is obtained by $D(l, e)$, where l is the current layer, $D(.)$ is the iteration-decay function. The whole forward propagation process can be summarized in Formula (1) (here we take the convolution layer followed by the BN (Batch-Normalization) layer as an example, which is very common in convolutional networks):

$$f_j^i = \begin{cases} BN(w_j^i * F^i) & w_j^i \in K \\ BN(w_j^i * F^i) \times D(i, e) & w_j^i \in P \end{cases} \tag{1}$$

The decaying operation is put after $BN(BatchNormalize)$ because the BN layer has a scaling effect on the input. It should be noted that in other cases such as the BatchNorm layer is not present in CNN, the decay operation is applied to the input to the next convolution layer, no matter what the previous layer is. As the pruning in the bottom layer may cause the accumulation of errors in the forward propagation, so the decay function is gradually applied from top to bottom layers. In general, we consider a decay function of the form:

$$D(l, e) = exp(min(-\lambda_e \cdot e + \lambda_l(n - l)/L, 0)) \tag{2}$$

The output of the decay function is a scalar, where λ_e denotes epoch weight in decay function, λ_l denotes layer index weight in decay function, the index value keeps increasing from the bottom layers to the top layers. We choose the exponential function because it has a smooth decay process while ensuring a faster decay rate.

During the backward propagation, the gradients of filters in subset P are set to zero while keeping the gradients of filters in the subset K as the same, because the update of the filters in subset P may compensate for the decay function. This also stays consistent with the biological situation: when a neuron is damaged, it may lose the ability to learn. The whole backward propagation can be summarized as follows:

$$G(w_j^i) = \begin{cases} G(w_j^i) & w_j^i \in K \\ 0 & w_j^i \in P \end{cases} \tag{3}$$

As the decay function cannot decay to zero from 1, so the filters to be pruned may still have a certain contribution to the final result after many iterations. To solve this problem, we set the output of the filters to be pruned as random noise after a certain number of iterations (we refer it as Random Firing of Pruned Neurons, RFPN), which can force the network not to consider the output of those filters, and it can also be seen as a kind of regularization and experimental results indicated that it can further boost the performance of the proposed pruning algorithm.

The detailed algorithm is described in Algorithm 1.

Algorithm 1. Algorithm Description of BFRIFP

Require: Model M;
Pruning ratio of each layer α^i;
Decaying function $D(.)$;
Filters to be preserved in set K, filters to be pruned in set P;
Training epoch $E = 1, 2, ..., T$;
Ensure: Pruned model M^*;
for epoch e in E **do**
    if $D(l, e) > \textit{threshold}$ **then**
        Forward:
            Forward propagation with equation (1)
        Backward:
            Backward propagation with equation (2)
    end if
    if $D(l, e) < \textit{threshold}$ **then**
        if RFPN_Flag **then**
            Random firing of pruned neurons
        end if
        Finetune the subnetworks using conventional procedures
    end if
end for
Removing filters of M in subset P
$M^* = M$
Return M^*

3.3 Knowledge Transfer Theory

In this subsection, we give a theoretical analysis of the proposed method and show that there is knowledge transfer from the filters to be pruned to the filters that will be retained in the pruning process.

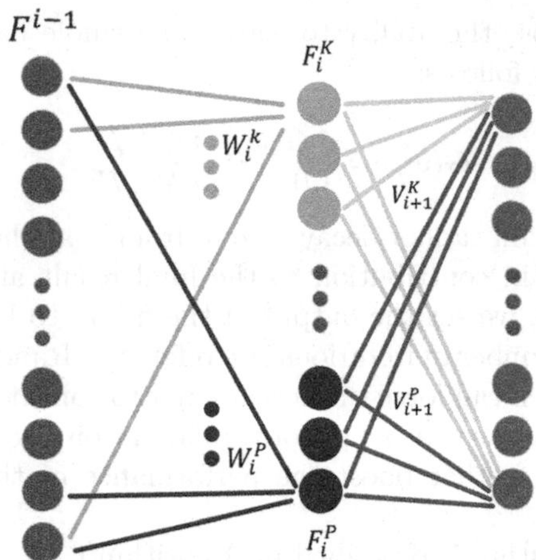

Fig. 3. Attribute-specific weights in Knowledge Transfer process.

As shown in Fig. 3, F^{i-1} represents the feature map input from the previous layer, F_i^K (orange) represents the feature map generated by filters from subset K, denoted as W_i^K, F_i^P (green)represents the feature map generated by filters from subset P, denoted as W_i^P. In the next layer, The parameters of each filter are divided into two parts, one part of the parameters correspond to the feature maps generated by filters from subset K, denoted as V_{i+1}^K, and the other part of the parameters correspond to the feature maps generated by filters from subset P, denoted as V_{i+1}^P. The differences in feature maps before and after decay operation can be easily obtained as follows:

$$\begin{aligned} \mathit{diff} &= F^{i-1} * w_i^k * v_{i+1}^k + F^{i-1} * w_i^p * v_{i+1}^p \\ &\quad - F^{i-1} * w_i^k * v_{i+1}^k - D(i,e)F^{i-1} * w_i^p * v_{i+1}^p \\ &= (1 - D(i,e))F^{i-1} * w_i^p * v_{i+1}^p \end{aligned} \tag{4}$$

Since the model has been pre-trained before pruning, we argue that minimizing the diff is consistent with minimizing the loss on the task. So that the following part should give the contribution to the gradients obtained by back-propagation.

$$grad = \frac{\partial(1 - D(i,e))F^{i-1} * w_i^p * v_{i+1}^p}{\partial w_i^k} \tag{5}$$

As seen from Eq. 5 that there does exist a knowledge transfer (the w_i^p contains in the formula) from the filters to be pruned to the filters reserved in the pruning process.

An experiment was conducted to further confirm the presence of the Knowledge Transfer phenomenon in the pruning process. We use the Wasserstein distance (EMD) for measuring the distance between the preserved and pruned filters. EMD measures the minimal effort required to reconfigure the probability mass of one distribution to recover the other distribution [16]. The p-Wasserstein distance between probability measures K and P on $\mathbb{R}^d$ is defined as:

$$W_p(K, P) = \inf_{\substack{x \sim K \\ y \sim D}} \left(\mathbb{E}\|x - y\|_p\right)^{1/p}, p \geq 1 \tag{6}$$

We considered that this can be regarded as a measurement of knowledge transfer. Specifically, with gradually decreasing distance, which means that the preserved filters are moving towards the pruned filters. From another perspective, the knowledge contained in the pruned filters is transferred to the preserved filters. We use 2-Wasserstein distance in the experiments, and x, y corresponds to filters to be preserved and pruned respectively. The ResNet56 is used in the experiment, and the 50th layer is measured, the filters to be pruned are randomly selected from the 50th layer, and the number is set to half of the total filters for measurement convenience. The experiment results are shown in Fig. 4.

Considering there might be an overlapping distribution between the weights to be pruned and preserved, the 2-Wasserstein distance dropping process is very clear and stable, which indicates that there does exist knowledge transfer in the pruning process.

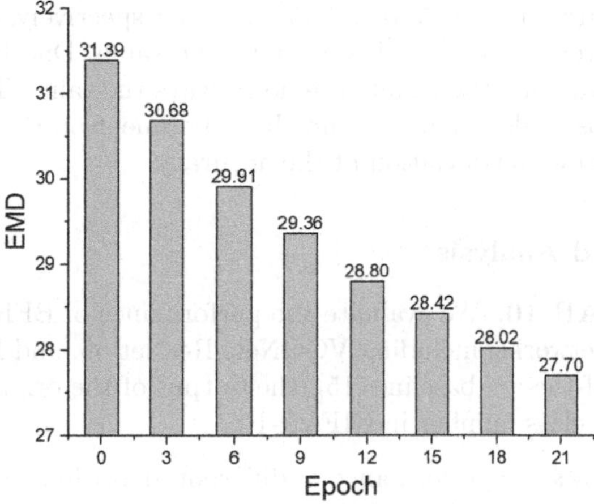

Fig. 4. The Wasserstein distance (EMD) between preserved and pruned filters in the pruning process.

4 Experiments

4.1 Experimental Settings

Datasets and Baselines: To demonstrate the algorithm's efficiency in reducing model complexity, we conduct experiments on both small and large datasets.

i.e., CIFAR-10 [17] and ImageNet [18]. Two types of popular network architectures are adopted: VGGNet [19], ResNet [20]. We report the performances on CIFAR and ImageNet datasets and compare them to the state-of-the-art. All these experiments demonstrate the effectiveness of the proposed method.

Evaluation Protocols: We adopt the widely-used protocols, i.e., number of parameters and required Float Points Operations (denoted as FLOPs), to evaluate the model size and computational requirement. For CIFAR-10, top-1 accuracy is provided. To evaluate the task-specific capabilities, for ILSVRC-2012, both top-1 and top-5 accuracies are reported.

Implementation Details: We use PyTorch to implement the proposed BFRIFP approach (+RFPN means the random firing of pruned neurons is utilized in the pruning process). We solve the optimization problem by using the Stochastic Gradient Descent algorithm (SGD) with an initial learning rate of 0.01 and divided by 10 every 30 epochs. The batchsize is set to 128, weight decay is set to 0.0005 and the momentum is set to 0.9 respectively. For the convergence rate and stability, λ_e is set to 2, and λ_l is set to 5. The *threshold* is set to 0.01, we set the distribution of random firing follows a normal distribution, multiplied by the scaling factor 0.01. We fine-tune the network for 100 epochs. All experiments are conducted on two NVIDIA GTX 1080Ti GPUs. To make the comparison fair, with the similar reductions of parameters and FLOPs, we measure the accuracy. For VGGNet, ResNet-56, ResNet-110, and ResNet-50, the pruning ratios α are set to 0.45, 0.5, 0.45 and 0.4 respectively, and the pruning ratios for each layer in the model are set to the same. Due to the stochastic nature of model training, the results are not always the same. To prove the stability of the proposed algorithm, we run the experiment on the VGGNet model three times and show the deviation of the accuracy.

4.2 Results and Analysis

Results on CIFAR-10. We evaluate the performance of BFRIFP on CIFAR-10 with popular networks, including VGGNet, ResNet-56, and ResNet-110. Following the state-of-the-art baseline [15], the output of the original networks are changed to fit the class number in CIFAR-10.

VGG: Table 2 shows the performance of different algorithms, including a property importance based method (PR denotes the percentage of FLOPs and Parameters reduction, $*$ denotes the proposed algorithm). Compared with recent state-of-the-art method HRank, BFRIFP+RFPN obtains a better accuracy (92.76 *vs.* 92.34%), while maintain the similar acceleration (66.5% *vs.* 65.3%). From the deviation of the accuracy, it can also be seen that our algorithm is very stable.

Table 2. Pruning results of VGGNet on CIFAR-10

Model	Top-1%	FLOPs (PR)	Parameter (PR)
VGGNet	93.96	313.73M(0.0%)	14.98M(0.0%)
L1 [21]	93.40	206.00M(34.3%)	5.40M(64.0%)
Zhao rt al. [22]	93.18	190.00M(39.1%)	3.92M(73.3%)
GAL-0.05 [15]	92.03	189.49M(39.6%)	3.36M(77.6%)
SSS [14]	93.02	183.13M(41.6%)	3.93M(73.8%)
GAL-0.15 [15]	90.73	171.89M(45.2%)	2.67M(82.2%)
HRank [23]	92.34	108.61M(65.3%)	2.64M(82.1%)
BFRIFP*	92.41 ± 0.015	105.68M(66.5%)	5.16M(66.4%)
BFRIFP+RFPN*	**92.78** ± 0.025	105.68M(66.5%)	5.16M(66.4%)

Resnet-56: The results for ResNet-56 are shown in Table 3. BFRIFP+RFPN yields a better compression and acceleration rate than GAL-0.8 and Random while maintaining a better accuracy (91.19% *vs.* 90.36% by GAL-0.8 and 90.55% by Random). Compared with HRank, we observe that BFRIFP+RFPN shares the same FLOPs reduction as HRank (74.7% *vs.* 74.1%), another property importance based method, but achieves a much higher reduction in parameters (74.9% *vs.* 68.1%) better accuracy (91.19% *vs.* 90.72%).

Table 3. Pruning results of Resnet-56 on CIFAR-10

Model	Top-1%	FLOPs (PR)	Parameter (PR)
ResNet	93.26	125.49M(0.0%)	0.85M(0.0%)
L1 [21]	93.40	90.90M(27.6%)	0.73M(14.1%)
NISP [24]	93.01	81.00M(35.5%)	0.49M(42.4%)
GAL-0.6 [15]	92.98	78.30M(37.6%)	0.75M(11.8%)
Random [25]	90.55	73.76M(41.5%)	0.50M(41.2%)
GAL-0.8 [15]	90.36	49.99M(60.02%)	0.29M(65.9%)
HRank [23]	90.72	32.52M(74.1%)	0.27M(68.1%)
BFRIFP*	91.11	32.02M(74.7%)	0.215M(74.9%)
BFRIFP+RFPN*	**91.19**	32.02M(74.7%)	0.215M(74.9%)

Resnet-110: Table 4 summarizes the experimental results on Resnet-110. BFRIFP+RFPN demonstrates its ability to obtain a high accuracy of 93.17%, with around 66.3% FLOPs and 66.2% parameters reduction, which is better than HRank (93.17% *vs.* 92.65%).

Table 4. Pruning results of Resnet-110 on CIFAR-10

Model	Top-1%	FLOPs (PR)	Parameter (PR)
ResNet-110	93.50	252.89M(0.0%)	1.72M(0.0%)
L1 [21]	93.30	155.00M(38.7%)	1.16M(32.6%)
GAL-0.5 [15]	92.55	130.20M(48.5%)	0.95M(44.8%)
Random [25]	89.88	92.84M(63.3%)	0.69M(59.9%)
HRank [23]	92.65	79.30M(68.6%)	0.53M(68.7%)
BFRIFP*	93.27	81.31M(66.3%)	0.55M(66.2%)
BFRIFP+RFPN*	**93.45**	81.31M(66.3%)	0.55M(66.2%)

Table 5. Pruning results of Resnet-50 on ImageNet

Model	Top-1%	Top-5%	FLOPs (PR)	Para (PR)
ResNet-50	76.15	92.87	4.09B	25.50M
GAL-0.5 [15]	71.95	90.94	2.33B	21.20M
SSS-26 [14]	71.82	90.79	2.33B	15.60M
GDP-0.6 [15]	71.19	90.71	1.88B	-
GAL-0.5-joint [15]	71.80	90.82	1.84B	19.31M
GAL-1 [15]	69.88	89.75	1.58B	14.67M
GDP-0.5 [15]	69.58	90.14	1.57B	-
HRank [23]	71.98	91.01	1.55B	13.77M
GAL-1-joint [15]	69.31	89.12	1.11B	10.21M
ThiNet-50 [26]	68.42	88.30	1.10B	8.66M
BFRIFP*	72.18	90.85	1.48B	10.40M
BFRIFP+RFPN*	**72.38**	**91.30**	1.48B	10.40M

Results on ImageNet. Experiments are also conducted on the ImageNet dataset using the ResNet50 network, and the results are shown in Table 5. Compared with HRank, which gains 71.98% top-1 accuracy and 91.01% top-5 accuracy, and 1.55 FLOPs, BFRIFP+RFPN obtain 72.38% top-1 accuracy and 91.30% top-5 accuracy, and 1.48B FLOPs.

5 Conclusions

In this paper, we propose a new approach for network pruning, which is inspired by the brain functional reorganization phenomena in people when irreversible damage of the brain occurs. instead of designing a function to measure the importance of a filter input to the CNN, our algorithm requires only a pruning rate. We employ theoretical analysis to demonstrate that there is knowledge transfer from the filters to be pruned to the filters preserved in the pruning process, so the kept parameters can take over the function of the pruned parameters after pruning. Extensive experiments have demonstrated the superiorities of BFRIFP over state-of-the-arts. As the first attempt on weight-importance irrelevant pruning, BFRIFP provides fresh insight into the network pruning problem. It should be noticed that the pruning rate for each layer is set to the same in each model, we believe that the adaptive determination of the pruning rate for each layer may yield better results. That's what we are going to do in future works.

Acknowledgments. The research presented in this paper was partially supported by the National Science and Technology Major Project from Minister of Science and Technology, China (Grant No. 2018AAA0103100), the Key Research Program of Frontier Sciences of the Chinese Academy of Sciences under Grant QYZDY-SSW-JSC034, and Shanghai Municipal Science and Technology Major Project (ZHANGJIANG LAB) under Grant 2018SHZDZX01.

References

1. Molchanov, P., Mallya, A., Tyree, S., Frosio, I., Kautz, J.: Importance estimation for neural network pruning. In: 2019 IEEE/CVF Conference on Computer Vision and Pattern Recognition (CVPR), pp. 11264–11272 (2019)
2. Frankle, J., Carbin, M.: The lottery ticket hypothesis: finding sparse, trainable neural networks. In: International Conference on Learning Representations (2018)
3. Liu, Z., Sun, M., Zhou, T., Huang, G., Darrell, T.: Rethinking the value of network pruning. arXiv preprint arXiv:1810.05270 (2018)
4. Wang, W., Wang, A., Limin, Yu., Han, X., Jiang, G., Weng, C., Zhang, H., Zhou, Z.: Constraint-induced movement therapy promotes brain functional reorganization in stroke patients with hemiplegia. Neural Regen. Res. **7**(32), 2548 (2012)
5. Leclerc, C., Saint-Amour, D., Lavoie, M.E., Lassonde, M., Lepore, F.: Brain functional reorganization in early blind humans revealed by auditory event-related potentials. NeuroReport **11**(3), 545–550 (2000)
6. Liou, S.: (2010)
7. Levin, H.S., Grafman, J.: Cerebral reorganization of function after brain damage. Oxford University Press (2000)
8. Marsh, E.B., Hillis, A.E., the role of reorganization: Recovery from aphasia following brain injury. Prog. Brain Res. **157**, 143–156 (2006)
9. Sze, V., Chen, Y.-H., Yang, T.-J., Emer, J.S.: Efficient processing of deep neural networks: a tutorial and survey. Proc. IEEE **105**(12), 2295–2329 (2017)
10. Hassibi, B., Stork, D.G.: Second order derivatives for network pruning: optimal brain surgeon. Adv. Neural. Inf. Process. Syst. **5**, 164–171 (1992)
11. Han, S., Pool, J., Tran, J., Dally, W.J.: Learning both weights and connections for efficient neural networks. In NIPS'15 Proceedings of the 28th International Conference on Neural Information Processing Systems - Volume 1, pp. 1135–1143 (2015)
12. Liu, Z., Xu, J., Peng, X., Xiong, R.: Frequency-domain dynamic pruning for convolutional neural networks. In: Advances in Neural Information Processing Systems, pp. 1043–1053 (2018)
13. Wen, W., Wu, C., Wang, Y., Chen, Y., Li, H.: Learning structured sparsity in deep neural networks. In: Proceedings of the 30th International Conference on Neural Information Processing Systems, pp. 2074–2082 (2016)

14. Huang, Z., Wang, N.: Data-driven sparse structure selection for deep neural networks. In: Proceedings of the European Conference on Computer Vision (ECCV), pp. 317–334 (2018)
15. Lin, S., et al.: Towards optimal structured CNN pruning via generative adversarial learning. In: 2019 IEEE/CVF Conference on Computer Vision and Pattern Recognition (CVPR), pp. 2790–2799 (2019)
16. Panaretos, V.M., Zemel, Y.: Statistical aspects of wasserstein distances. arXiv preprint arXiv:1806.05500, 6(1), 405–431 (2019)
17. Krizhevsky, A., Hinton, G., et al.: Learning multiple layers of features from tiny images (2009)
18. Russakovsky, O., Deng, J., Hao, S., Krause, J., Satheesh, S., Ma, S., Huang, Z., Karpathy, A., Khosla, A., Bernstein, M., et al.: Imagenet large scale visual recognition challenge. Int. J. Comput. Vision **115**(3), 211–252 (2015)
19. Simonyan, K., Zisserman, A.: Very deep convolutional networks for large-scale image recognition. arXiv preprint arXiv:1409.1556 (2014)
20. He, K., Zhang, X., Ren, S., Sun, J.: Deep residual learning for image recognition. In: Proceedings of the IEEE Conference on Computer Vision and Pattern Recognition, pp. 770–778 (2016)
21. Li, H., Kadav, A., Durdanovic, I., Samet, H., Graf, H.P.: Pruning filters for efficient convnets. arXiv preprint arXiv:1608.08710 (2016)
22. Zhao, C., Ni, B., Zhang, J., Zhao, Q., Zhang, W., Tian, Q.: Variational convolutional neural network pruning. In: Proceedings of the IEEE Conference on Computer Vision and Pattern Recognition, pp. 2780–2789 (2019)
23. Lin, M.: Hrank: filter pruning using high-rank feature map. In: 2020 IEEE/CVF Conference on Computer Vision and Pattern Recognition (CVPR), pp. 1529–1538 (2020)
24. Yu, R., et al.: Nisp: pruning networks using neuron importance score propagation. In: 2018 IEEE/CVF Conference on Computer Vision and Pattern Recognition, pp. 9194–9203 (2018)
25. Lin, M., et al.: Filter sketch for network pruning. arXiv preprint arXiv:2001.08514 (2020)
26. Luo, J.-H., Wu, J., Lin, W.: Thinet: a filter level pruning method for deep neural network compression. In: Proceedings of the IEEE International Conference on Computer Vision, pp. 5058–5066 (2017)

CupNet – Pruning a Network for Geometric Data

Raoul Heese[1,2](✉), Lukas Morand[3], Dirk Helm[3], and Michael Bortz[1,2]

[1] Fraunhofer Center for Machine Learning, 53757 Sankt Augustin, Germany
[2] Fraunhofer-Institut für Techno- und Wirtschaftsmathematik ITWM, Fraunhofer-Platz 1, 67663 Kaiserslautern, Germany
raoul.heese@itwm.fraunhofer.de
[3] Fraunhofer-Institut für Werkstoffmechanik IWM, Wöhlerstr. 11, 79108 Freiburg, Germany

Abstract. Using data from a simulated cup drawing process, we demonstrate how the inherent geometrical structure of cup meshes can be used to effectively prune an artificial neural network in a straightforward way.

Keywords: Regression · Informed learning · Pruning · Network architecture · Deep drawing

1 Introduction

The optimization of production processes can benefit from machine learning methods that incorporate domain knowledge and data from numerical simulations [1]. Typically, such methods aim to model relations between process parameters and the resulting product. In this manuscript, we consider an example from the field of deep drawing, a sheet metal forming process in which a sheet metal blank is drawn into a forming die by mechanical action.

Specifically, we study the prediction of product geometries in a cup drawing process based on data from finite element simulations [2]. For each simulation, we choose randomized process and material parameters $\mathbf{p} \in \mathbb{R}^k$ with $k \equiv 9$ and observe the resulting geometry as a set of $m \equiv 1979$ mesh coordinates $\mathbf{x} \in \mathbb{R}^d$ with $d \equiv 3m = 5937$. Thus, the machine learning task is to predict

$$\hat{\mathbf{x}}(\mathbf{p}) : \mathbb{R}^k \longmapsto \mathbb{R}^d \tag{1}$$

based on the generated data. Such a predictive regression model can be considered as a short-cut for the actual simulation. In contrast to the simulation, it is faster and always numerically stable and therefore particularly suitable to solve optimization problems. On the other hand, the model predictions are less accurate than the simulation results, which corresponds to a trade-off between calculation speed and outcome precision.

The choice of parameters affects the resulting cup quality in the sense that we can infer good, defect and cracked cups (indicated by strong deformations) from

I. Farkaš et al. (Eds.): ICANN 2021, LNCS 12894, pp. 29–33, 2021.
https://doi.org/10.1007/978-3-030-86380-7_3

the mesh geometries. In total, we ran 10000 simulations, of which two failed (for numerical reasons). Of the remaining 9998 parameter combinations, 3991 lead to good cups, 5075 lead to defect cups and 932 cause cracked cups, cf. Fig. 1.

2 Method

We propose two artificial neural networks to model Eq. (1). Our first network architecture, which we call `CupNet`, particularly takes the geometrical structure of the data into account to effectively prune the network weights. Pruning is a technique that helps in the development of smaller and more efficient networks, see, e. g., Ref. [3] and references therein. That means, instead of changing the loss function as in e. g., Ref. [4], we use expert knowledge to change the network architecture itself.

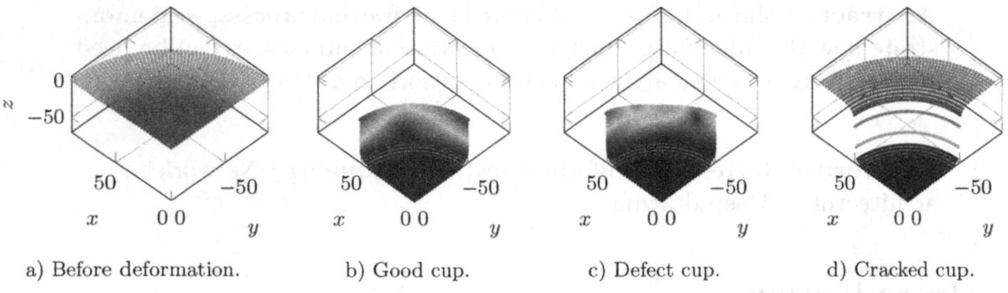

Fig. 1. Typical cup geometries, each consisting of m points. For reasons of symmetry, it is sufficient to simulate the deformation of a quarter cup segment instead of the full cup. The colors indicate the distance of each point to the reference mesh, consisting of the average coordinates of all good cups. We use a different color scale for each subfigure: 0 ▇ a) 70, b) 2, c) 6, d) 49. (Color figure online)

The proposed network consists of an input layer of size k (i. e., it contains k units), which is fully connected to an initial layer of size d, which we call *frame*. We split the frame layer into three evenly sized segments (i. e., one for each dimension denoted by x, y, and z, cf. Fig. 1), which are each connected to the following layers in a special way. Specifically, we chose the forward pass

$$\mathbf{o} \equiv A([\mathbf{C}(\alpha) \odot \mathbf{W}]^{\intercal}\mathbf{i} + \mathbf{b}). \tag{2}$$

Here $\mathbf{i} \in \mathbb{R}^{m\times 1}$ and $\mathbf{o} \in \mathbb{R}^{m\times 1}$ represent the layer inputs and outputs, whereas $\mathbf{W} \in \mathbb{R}^{m\times m}$ and $\mathbf{b} \in \mathbb{R}^{m\times 1}$ stand for the (trainable) layer weights and biases, and $A(\cdot)$ represents the activation function. The symbol $\odot$ denotes the Hadamard product (element-wise multiplication). Moreover, we have introduced the symmetric pruning matrix $\mathbf{C}(\alpha) \in \{0, 1\}^{m\times m}$ with elements

$$\mathbf{C}_{ij}(\alpha) \equiv \begin{cases} 0 & \text{if } \mathbf{D}_{ij} > \alpha \\ 1 & \text{if } \mathbf{D}_{ij} \leq \alpha \end{cases} \qquad \text{with} \qquad \mathbf{D}_{ij} \equiv ||\mathbf{x}'_\mathbf{i} - \mathbf{x}'_\mathbf{j}||_2 = \text{const.} \tag{3}$$

for $i, j = 1, \ldots, m$. It is based on the symmetric distance matrix $\mathbf{D} \in \mathbb{R}^{m \times m}_{\geq 0}$, which contains the euclidean distances $||\cdot||_2$ between different mesh points $\mathbf{x}'$ of the undeformed geometry, Fig. 1a). Thus, the pruning matrix removes the influence of all weights for which the corresponding mesh points of the undeformed geometry have a distance beyond the user-defined pruning threshold $\alpha \geq 0$.

This special layer configuration is repeated h times and concludes with a fully-connected last layer merging the three previously splitted segments into the output layer. Summarized, we use the inherent geometrical structure of the data to prune a fully connected network in such a way that correlations between spatially related mesh points are preserved. The complete architecture is sketched in Fig. 2a).

As a reference we also use a second architecture, which we call `RefNet`. It has a similar structure and complexity as the `CupNet`, but does not take advantage of the geometrical structure of the data. Specifically, it consists of an input layer of size k, $h + 1$ hidden layers of size s and an output layer of size m, all of which are fully connected. In order to obtain a comparable complexity of the two architectures we choose s in such a way that the number of trainable parameters is as close as possible. For that, we first determine the number of trainable parameters for the `CupNet` architecture

$$n_{\text{cup}}(h, \alpha) = (k \cdot d + d) + 3\,h(c(\alpha) + m) + 3(m^2 + m) \qquad \text{with} \qquad c(\alpha) \equiv \sum_{i,j=1}^{m} \mathbf{C}_{ij}(\alpha). \quad (4)$$

On the other hand, the number of trainable parameters for the `RefNet` architecture reads

$$n_{\text{ref}}(h, s) = (k \cdot s + s) + h(s^2 + s) + (s \cdot d + d) \quad (5)$$

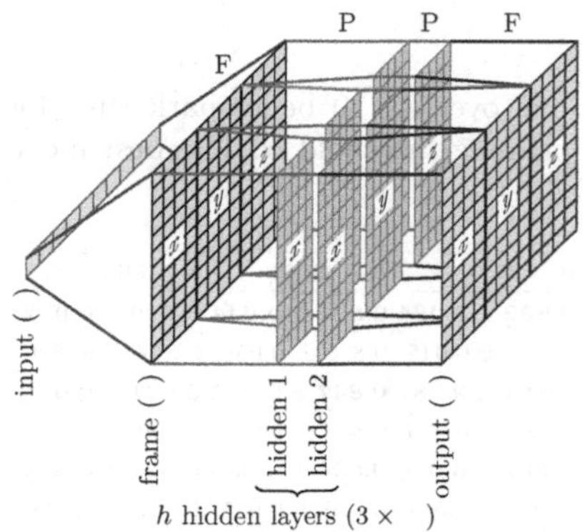

a) Our proposed `CupNet` with $n_{\text{cup}}(h, \alpha)$ trainable parameters, Eq. (4), and dimensions x, y, and z.

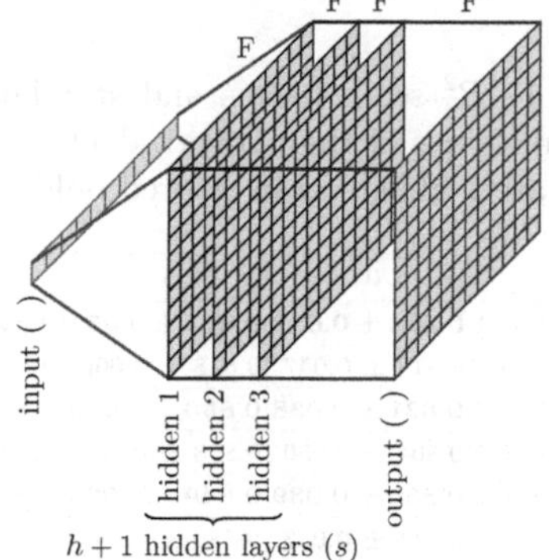

b) The reference network `RefNet` with $n_{\text{ref}}(h, s)$ trainable parameters, Eq. (5).

Fig. 2. Network architectures used to model Eq. (1). The k-dimensional simulation parameters $\mathbf{p}$ constitute the input, whereas the output corresponds to the d-dimensional mesh $\hat{\mathbf{x}}(\mathbf{p})$. Both architectures consist of a sequence of layers (number of units in brackets), which are fully connected (F) or partially connected, i. e., pruned (P). We apply a dropout after every inner layer for regularization.

so that the condition $n_{\text{ref}}(h,s) \stackrel{!}{=} n_{\text{cup}}(h,\alpha)$ leads to $s(h,\alpha) = (-u + \sqrt{u^2 - 4h(d - n_{\text{cup}}(h,\alpha))})/(2h)$, where $u \equiv k + h + d + 1$. We set the layer size s to the ceiling of this value for a given depth h and a given pruning threshold α. The complete `RefNet` architecture is sketched in Fig. 2b.

For both networks the activation function is chosen to be a ReLU for all but the output layer for which we use a linear activation. As a regularizer we apply a dropout after every inner layer, where we randomly set 20% of the units to zero.

3 Experiments

We test the performance of both network architectures, which we have implemented using Ref. [5]. For this purpose we split the standardized data into a training set with 9000 elements and a test set with 998 elements stratified according to the three cup classes of good cups, defect cups, and cracked cups. We repeat this approach for 10 benchmark runs with different data splittings and different random seeds for the network initialization. For the training we use an Adam optimizer and a mean squared error for the loss. As a result, we obtain the R^2 scores shown in Table 1.

We find that in most cases, `CupNet` is superior to `RefNet`. It performs worse only for low α and large h (i. e., strong pruning and deep nets). In these cases, the training process appears to not converge to a sufficiently good state. However, the mean scores of the two architectures are mostly within one standard deviation of each other. The best mean `CupNet` score of 0.862 is achieved for $h = 2$ and $\alpha = 5$, which corresponds to a network with $n_{\text{cup}} = 12277950$ trainable parameters. On the other hand, the best mean `RefNet` score of 0.827 is achieved for $h = 3$ and

Table 1. R^2 score means and standard deviations over all 10 benchmark runs for different values of the network depth h and the pruning threshold α. The best mean results are highlighted in colored bold.

network	$\alpha = 1.0$	$\alpha = 2.5$	$\alpha = 5.0$	$\alpha = 10.0$	$\alpha = 25.0$	$\alpha = 50.0$
`CupNet`, $h = 1$	**0.822 ± 0.042**	**0.823 ± 0.052**	**0.829 ± 0.040**	**0.832 ± 0.084**	**0.839 ± 0.044**	**0.819 ± 0.072**
`RefNet`, $h = 1$	0.818 ± 0.047	0.818 ± 0.066	0.815 ± 0.066	0.817 ± 0.045	0.818 ± 0.056	0.817 ± 0.053
`CupNet`, $h = 2$	**0.821 ± 0.038**	**0.850 ± 0.039**	**0.862 ± 0.046**	**0.851 ± 0.057**	**0.847 ± 0.047**	**0.831 ± 0.045**
`RefNet`, $h = 2$	0.804 ± 0.050	0.813 ± 0.061	0.809 ± 0.048	0.821 ± 0.036	0.803 ± 0.037	0.800 ± 0.070
`CupNet`, $h = 3$	**0.830 ± 0.039**	**0.849 ± 0.039**	**0.850 ± 0.053**	**0.861 ± 0.056**	**0.839 ± 0.053**	**0.829 ± 0.043**
`RefNet`, $h = 3$	0.811 ± 0.043	0.789 ± 0.085	0.826 ± 0.042	0.802 ± 0.064	0.810 ± 0.045	0.827 ± 0.029
`CupNet`, $h = 4$	**0.830 ± 0.040**	**0.838 ± 0.050**	**0.845 ± 0.064**	**0.849 ± 0.035**	**0.817 ± 0.114**	**0.806 ± 0.034**
`RefNet`, $h = 4$	0.797 ± 0.055	0.792 ± 0.044	0.800 ± 0.052	0.808 ± 0.041	0.779 ± 0.051	0.768 ± 0.068
`CupNet`, $h = 5$	0.478 ± 0.292	**0.835 ± 0.064**	**0.838 ± 0.048**	**0.839 ± 0.037**	**0.832 ± 0.036**	**0.805 ± 0.033**
`RefNet`, $h = 5$	**0.762 ± 0.060**	0.774 ± 0.041	0.789 ± 0.038	0.767 ± 0.050	0.778 ± 0.042	0.691 ± 0.126
`CupNet`, $h = 6$	0.052 ± 0.108	**0.832 ± 0.042**	**0.840 ± 0.046**	**0.832 ± 0.103**	**0.832 ± 0.045**	**0.787 ± 0.080**
`RefNet`, $h = 6$	**0.780 ± 0.041**	0.785 ± 0.039	0.769 ± 0.049	0.770 ± 0.045	0.765 ± 0.019	0.436 ± 0.129
`CupNet`, $h = 7$	0.053 ± 0.161	0.714 ± 0.191	**0.843 ± 0.049**	**0.857 ± 0.033**	**0.825 ± 0.051**	**0.781 ± 0.049**
`RefNet`, $h = 7$	**0.772 ± 0.034**	**0.761 ± 0.058**	0.755 ± 0.040	0.755 ± 0.031	0.592 ± 0.243	0.377 ± 0.203

$\alpha = 50$, which corresponds to a much larger network with $n_{\text{ref}} = 34898737$ trainable parameters. Thus, according to the respective optimal values for h and α, our pruning approach leads to smaller networks with a better expected score.

As an alternative approach we also test the performance of a Random Forest regressor (with 250 trees) on PCA-transformed features (with 100 components) using the implementation from Ref. [6]. This leads to a R^2 score of 0.736 ± 0.029 over 10 benchmark runs, which is worse than most results from Table 1.

4 Conclusion

Summarized, we find that our approach of pruning the network connections according to the spatial correlation of mesh points leads to a better expected performance in comparison with a reference network with similar structure and complexity. It would be an interesting point of origin for further studies to check whether this approach can also be applied to other geometrical data.

Acknowledgements. We would like to thank Alexander Butz for helpful discussions, Maria Baiker and Jan Pagenkopf for providing the simulation of the cup drawing process, and Boris Giba for data processing. This work was developed in the Fraunhofer Cluster of Excellence "Cognitive Internet Technologies" as well as the Fraunhofer lighthouse project "Machine Learning for Production".

References

1. von Rueden, L., et al.: Informed machine learning - a taxonomy and survey of integrating knowledge into learning systems. arXiv:1903.12394v2 (2020)
2. Iza-Teran, R., et al.: Learning product properties with small data sets in forming simulations. In: Submitted to: NUMISHEET 2020: 12th International Conference and Workshop on Numerical Simulation of 3D Sheet Metal Forming Processes (2020)
3. Liu, Z., et al.: Rethinking the value of network pruning (2018). arXiv: 1810.05270 (cs.LG)
4. Heese, R., Walczak, M., Morand, L., Helm, D., Bortz, M.: The good, the bad and the ugly: augmenting a black-box model with expert knowledge. In: Tetko, I.V., Kůrková, V., Karpov, P., Theis, F. (eds.) ICANN 2019. LNCS, vol. 11731, pp. 391–395. Springer, Cham (2019). https://doi.org/10.1007/978-3-030-30493-5_38
5. Abadi, M., et al.: TensorFlow: large-scale machine learning on heterogeneous systems (2015). Software available from tensorow.org. http://tensorflow.org/
6. Pedregosa, F., et al.: Scikit-learn: machine learning in Python. J. Mach. Learn. Res. **12**, 2825–2830 (2011)

Pruned-YOLO: Learning Efficient Object Detector Using Model Pruning

Jiacheng Zhang[1,2], Pingyu Wang[1,2], Zhicheng Zhao[1,2(✉)], and Fei Su[1,2]

[1] School of Artificial Intelligence, Beijing University of Posts and Telecommunications, Beijing, China
{zhangjiacheng,applewangpingyu,zhaozc,sufei}@bupt.edu.cn

[2] Beijing Key Laboratory of Network System and Network Culture, Beijing, China

Abstract. Accurate real-time object detection plays a key role in various practical scenarios such as automatic driving and UAV surveillance. The memory limitation and poor computing power of edge devices hinder the deployment of high performance Convolutional Neural Networks (CNNs). Iterative channel pruning is an effective method to obtain lightweight networks. However, the channel importance measurement and iterative pruning in the existing methods are suboptimal. In this paper, to measure the channel importance, we simultaneously consider the scale factor of batch normalization (BN) and the kernel weight of convolutional layers. Besides, sparsity training and fine tuning are combined to simplify the pruning pipeline. Notably, the cosine decay of sparsity coefficient and soft mask strategy are used to optimize our compact model, i.e., Pruned-YOLOv3/v5, which is constructed via pruning YOLOv3/v5. The experimental results on the MS-COCO and VisDrone datasets show that the proposed model achieves a satisfactory balance between computational efficiency and detection accuracy.

Keywords: Model compression · Channel pruning · Object detection · YOLO

1 Introduction

As fundamental task of computer vision, object detection is widely studied and applied. With the rapid development of deep learning, object detection models show unprecedented performance and the average precision (AP) records on large public datasets are constantly refreshed. The state-of-the-art detection models often use high complexity backbone to extract the features rich in semantic information, then the detection head is further used to locate and classify the bounding boxes. However, increasing backbone parameters will certainly limit the computational efficiency of detection models. When the model is deployed

This work is supported by Chinese National Natural Science Foundation (62076033, U1931202), and BUPT innovation and entrepreneurship support program (2021-YC-T026).

I. Farkaš et al. (Eds.): ICANN 2021, LNCS 12894, pp. 34–45, 2021.
https://doi.org/10.1007/978-3-030-86380-7_4

on mobile and edge devices, one of the biggest challenges of such networks is the high memory and computational requirements. As a representative model compression method, model pruning is often used to remove the relatively unimportant weights to lighten the model. Pruning technology can retain the model accuracy well and is complementary to other compression methods. For example, the pruned model can be further compressed by parameter quantization [16,30] or low rank factorization [17], and the accuracy can be further restored by knowledge distillation technology [5,22].

We focus on the channel pruning, which removes some relatively unimportant filters in CNNs. The key point lies in how to measure the channels' importance. The scale factor of BN layer following the convolutional layer is taken as a measure [23], and achieves satisfactory performance on the classification task. This method is extended to the object detection model YOLOv3 [36]. However, it is not enough to only use the scale factor to determine whether a channel should be reserved. Since the input feature map is processed by convolution and normalization in turn, the output feature map is weighted by convolution kernel first, and then scaled by BN layer. Therefore, the convolution kernel corresponding to the output channel of feature map should also be considered.

The popular pipeline of channel pruning is the continuous iteration of sparsity training, channel pruning and model fine-tuning. The purpose of sparsity training is to obtain channel sparsity model. According to the designed pruning strategies, some channels are removed, then fine tuning the pruned model. These three steps are iteratively applied until the compression model reaches the budget target. This process is cumbersome and time-consuming. We propose a method that combines the normal training and sparsity training. During the network training, the importance of each channel is evaluated at the same time, and the soft mask operation is adopted for the less important channels. The soft mask strategy helps the model fast sparsity. Besides, the weighting coefficient of the L1 regularization term directly affects the sparsity speed. We add cosine decay for it. The small coefficient in the later training stage is helpful to the recovery of model accuracy. The proposed method can speed up the pruning period, meanwhile improve the accuracy.

In this paper, YOLOv3/v5 [15,28] are chosen as the baseline and the proposed channel pruning method is applied to obtain compact models, namely Pruned-YOLOv3/v5. Our contributions can be summarized in three-fold. First, a channel pruning algorithm for YOLOv3/v5 is proposed. The method of measuring channel importance is optimized, and the ablation experiments demonstrate its effectiveness. Then, the combination of sparsity training and fine tuning greatly shorten the iteration period. The introduction of soft mask and sparse factor cosine decay in the training process is the key of success. Third, the experimental results on the VisDrone and MS-COCO benchmark datasets show that our method greatly reduces the model parameters, while ensuring an acceptable decline in accuracy. Our code is available at https://github.com/jiachengjiacheng/Pruned-YOLO.

2 Related Work

2.1 Series Models of YOLO

YOLO [26] regards object detection as a regression problem and uses a single neural network directly to predict the bounding box and category probability in the whole image. YOLOv2 [27] achieves better detection accuracy by the aid of a series of tricks, such as dimension clusters, multi-scale training etc. YOLO9000 [27] is a real-time framework for detection more than 9000 object categories. DC-SPP-YOLO [14] introduces dense connection and improved spatial pyramid pooling to ameliorating the detection accuracy. The powerful darknet-53 is put forward in YOLOv3 [28]. Because of its excellent speed accuracy balance, YOLOv3 becomes one of the most popular object detectors in industry. Gaussian YOLOv3 [7] models the bounding box with a Gaussian parameter and redesigning the loss function, showing a higher accuracy than previous approaches with a similar FPS. Stochastic-YOLO [1] introduces stochasticity in the form of Monte Carlo Dropout, which improves different components of uncertainty estimations. YOLOv4 [3] optimizes the model from the aspects of data processing, backbone, activation function and loss function, etc. Scaled-YOLOv4 [31] propose a network scaling approach which modifies the depth, width, resolution and architecture of the network. PP-YOLO [24] combine various existing tricks and achieve a better balance between effectiveness and efficiency than EfficientDet [29] and YOLOv4. In view of the huge application prospect, the improvement of YOLO is constantly proposed. However, the optimal combination of accuracy and speed still has large room to explore.

2.2 Model Pruning Methods

Some early approaches to pruning based on the Hessian of the loss function [12]. [11] prunes redundant connections using a three-step method and learns the important connections by an iterative process. It reduces the number of parameters of multiple large-scale networks by an order of magnitude. However, only with the help of dedicated libraries or hardware can the speedup be realized. Incremental/iterative model pruning becomes a representative procedure, and the components removed from deep models can be not only individual neural connections, but also network structures [23]. FPGM [13] chooses the filters with the most replaceable contribution through calculating the Geometric Median of the filters. Centripetal SGD [8] is a novel optimization method for seeking removed filters. MDP [10] introduces a gate for each channel to indicate its importance, which automatically learned in the searching stage. HRank [18] prunes filters with low-rank feature maps. These methods demonstrate the effectiveness on image classification datasets, but their performance in challenging object detection tasks has not been discussed. SlimYOLOv3 [36] uses the idea of network slimming [23] and applies the pruning method to the object detection model YOLOv3. It identifies automatically insignificant channels and prunes afterwards to obtain thin models. [32] further proposes an overall slimming scheme to alleviate the problem of low computation reduction rate. However, improvements in channel importance measurement and pruning pipeline are still required.

3 Methodology

An efficient deep object detector could be learned through an iterative procedure of three-step including sparsity training, channel pruning and fine tuning. Sparsity training helps to highlight the differences between channels, which is helpful to the following pruning process and model accuracy recovery. Convolution layer, BN and activation function are the smallest components of deep model. Channel-wise sparsity training is conducted by imposing weight decay on convolution kernel parameters α and L1 regularization on trainable scale factor γ of BN. Both are considered when measuring channel importance. We remove a certain proportion of the least important channels according to the ranking of the importance of them. For accuracy recover, it is crucial to keep the surviving parameters and retrain the pruned network. We propose to integrate fine tuning into sparsity training for fast iteration, which can not only shorten the pruning period, but also help to restore the model's accuracy.

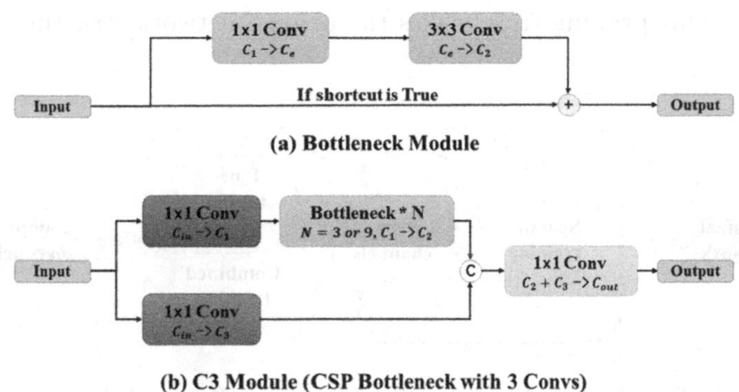

Fig. 1. The bottleneck module and C3 module in YOLOv5 [15].

3.1 Channel Importance Measurement

Assuming that C_{in} and C_{out} are the channel number of input and output feature map respectively. The convolution layer is expressed as $\{\alpha_1, \alpha_2, \ldots, \alpha_{out}\}$, where α_i is the ith filter. The ith channel response value of the output feature map is calculated by convolution of the input feature map and the ith filter. BN layer following the convolution layer normalizes convolutional features using mini-batch statistics. The channel importance is calculated by formula (1).

$$\theta_i = |\gamma_i| * \sum_{t \in \alpha_i} |t|, i \in [1, 2, ..., C_{out}], \tag{1}$$

where γ_i is the scale factor corresponding to the ith filter. The importance measurement factors of all channels in the network are sorted. It combines the pre-set pruning ratio of channels to determine the removal or retention of a channel.

Specific to YOLOv5 [15], some basic modules need customized pruning strategies. For the module called Conv, which is composed of convolution layer, BN and activation function, the channel pruning is carried out naturally according to the above method. In SPP module [6], Conv is used to reduce channel dimension before and after max-pooling, and its filters can be reduced. Upsample layer and concatenate layer are ignored during pruning process because there is no need to change their channel number. Detect layer also is discard because it outputs the final detection results and cannot be compressed. The bottleneck module and C3 module are shown in Fig. 1. If the shortcut layers do not exist in the C3 module, it degenerates into a simple cascade of multi Convs and each Conv can be pruned directly and independently. Otherwise, all the layers connected to shortcut layer are required to have a same channel number. In this case, we divide the channels needed to be removed equally among these layers. This pruning trick makes the pruned network structure relatively uniform.

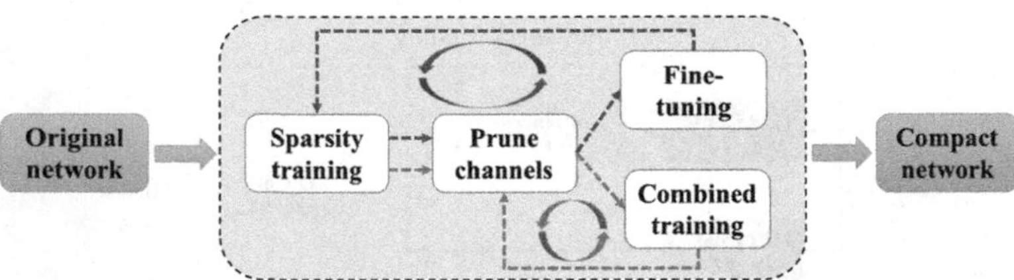

Fig. 2. The pipeline of channel pruning. The blue arrow flow and the green arrow flow indicate the classical procedure and the improved procedure respectively. (Color figure online)

3.2 Combination of Sparsity Training and Fine Tuning

When the channel pruning strategy is designed, pruning is not time-consuming in the iterative process, and almost all the time is spent on model training. In order to shorten the iteration period, we propose to combine sparsity training and fine tuning, and the pruning pipeline before and after combining the two is shown in Fig. 2. When the training epochs of the two are equal, this combined strategy reduces the time of each iteration to about half of the original.

First, the L1 regularization coefficient changes in the way of cosine decay as the training proceeds. At the early stage of training, large coefficient can help the model sparse quickly, and meanwhile the accuracy declines significantly. In the later stage of training, the small coefficient is helpful to accuracy recovery, which simulates the fine-tuning process. In addition, we add warm up strategy for it at the initial phase. Specifically, the same decay strategy as the learning rate is used directly.

Compared with the constant coefficient method, when the initial coefficient is the same, the cosine decay method leads to less sparse model at convergence. It is likely to cause precipitous accuracy reduction to prune the model with insufficient sparsity. Simply increasing the initial coefficient is not conducive to the stability of model, and increasing the training epoch goes against our purpose. We propose the soft mask strategy, which checks the sparsity in the channel level and deliberately reduces the scale factor of the nearly sparse channel during training. In our implementation, before each training epoch, we count the scale factor γ of all BN layers in the network, calculate the mean value of $\bar{\gamma}$, and set the threshold value of $\bar{\gamma}/5$. If the scale factor is less than the threshold, it is reduced to one tenth of the original. The soft mask strategy helps to speed up the sparsity process.

4 Experiments

MS-COCO 2017 [20] and VisDrone2018-Det [39] datasets are used to verify the performance of our methods on the object detection benchmark. We apply the proposed channel pruning method to compress YOLOv3/v5 [15,28]. Generous ablation studies are imported to investigate the properties of proposed method and compare it with similar state-of-the-art algorithms.

4.1 Implementation Details

Two sets of hyper-parameters are released in the implementation of YOLOv3/v5[1], one is used for training from scratch on COCO dataset, the other is used for finetuning on VOC dataset [9]. The latter is obtained by hyper-parameter evolution. When experiments are performed on the VisDrone dataset, all models are trained on training set and evaluated on validation set. We set the initial learning rate to 0.0064, the input image resolution to 640, minibatch size to 24 and others are the same as finetuning hyper-parameters. The baseline model of pruning is trained for 200 epochs. Both sparsity training and fine tuning are performed for 100 epochs. When experiments are performed on the COCO dataset, we use the default hyper-parameters directly in sparsity training. The initial learning rate is reduced to 0.0064 in fine tuning, and the others remain unchanged. We select the sparse penalty according to [34].

[1] https://github.com/ultralytics/yolov3, https://github.com/ultralytics/yolov5.

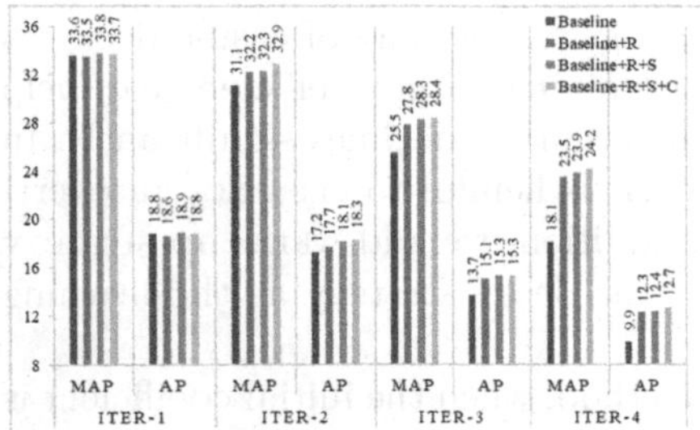

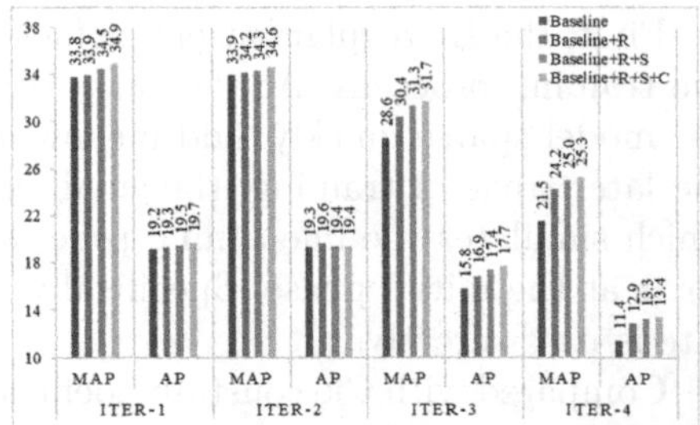

Fig. 3. The ablation results of Pruned-YOLOv3 (left) and Pruned-YOLOv5 (right) on the VisDrone dataset [39]. R, S and C represent the reweighting of channel important factors, soft mask strategy and sparsity coefficient cosine decay respectively.

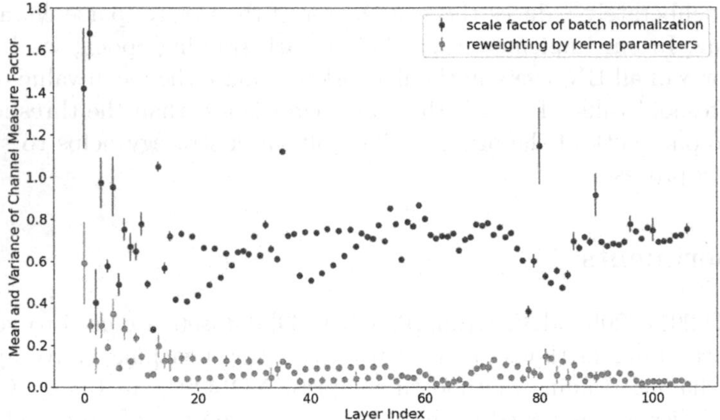

Fig. 4. The mean and variance of channel measure factors are visualized. Horizontal coordinate is the layer index. The sparse YOLOv5 model training on VisDrone dataset [39] is used.

4.2 Experimental Results on VisDrone Dataset

Ablation Studies. Firstly, we implement channel pruning algorithms for YOLO v3/v5, where the L1-norm of scale factors denote channel importance [23]. The theoretical channel pruning rate is set to 50%, and the model is pruned four times. Then, the reweighting of channel important factors by convolution kernel parameters, soft mask strategy and sparsity coefficient cosine decay are introduced in turn. Figure 3 reports the quantitative comparison. In the first iteration, the proposed method brings few accuracy improvement. When the model has a large number of parameters, some differences in the model structure are insignificant, and the small fluctuation of accuracy may be caused by the randomness in the training. With the progress of iteration, the advantage of the improved method is more and more obvious. The more iterations, the less parameters, the greater the difference of model structure after pruning, and the more important the model structure and retained weight. This proves the effectiveness of the improved method. Introducing the weight of convolution kernel into the measurement of channel importance can prune the model more reasonably.

The mean and variance of channel measure factors are visualized layer by layer in Fig. 4. It can be seen that compared with the method using only scaling factor of BN, the proposed method makes the distribution of channel measure factors more balanced. It means that channel pruning can balance the network structure, which is beneficial for the subsequent deployment. Besides, the difference between the two distribution shows that the two different measurement strategies focus on different filter sets.

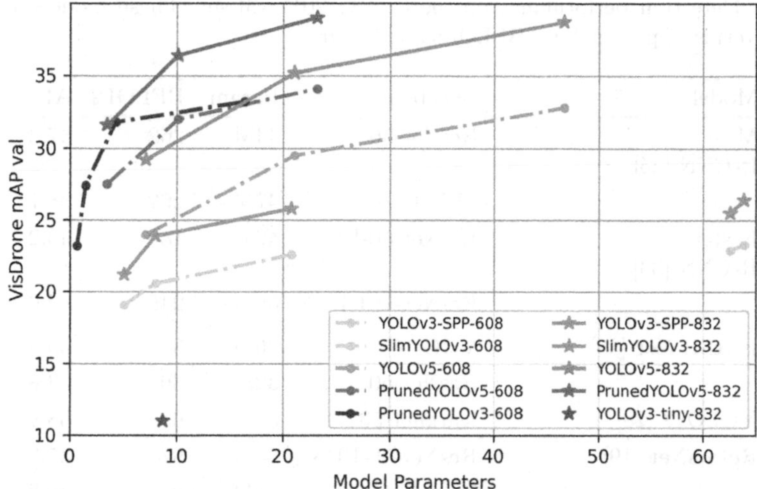

Fig. 5. Comparison of the proposed Pruned-YOLO and other state-of-the-art object detectors on the VisDrone dataset [39]. Pruned-YOLO has better parameter/accuracy trade-off than the others.

Comparison with Other Methods. The theoretical channel pruning rate is set to 25% in the iterative pruning, and the model is pruned three times. In order to make a fair comparison with SlimYOLOv3, we use the same test parameters as them [36]. Figure 5 illustrates the comparison of the proposed pruned-YOLO and other object detectors. Obviously, Pruned-YOLO has better parameter/accuracy trade-off than the other methods. Surprisingly, Pruned-YOLOv3 achieves a better performance than Pruned-YOLOv5. Pruning is a positive evolutionary process with learning new knowledge [2]. We consider that Pruned-YOLOv3 learns more effective representations than Pruned-YOLOv5 when aggressive pruning is occurring. The interpretability of evolutionary process is an open problem, which needs further study.

4.3 Experimental Results on MS-COCO Dataset

As in Sect. 4.2, we perform iterative channel pruning on the base model YOLOv5l. The comparison between it and other state-of-the-art detectors in terms of model parameters, BFLOPs and accuracy is shown in Table 1, in which the AP on the validation set is reported. Two-stage detectors have very high BFLOPs, which weakens their real-time performance. Compared with other one-stage detectors, Pruned-YOLOv5 has higher detection accuracy while BFLOPs is similar. Besides, it has obvious advantages in model volume, which reduces the overhead of model storage. In a word, Pruned-YOLOv5 achieves excellent performance in the balance of parameters, calculation and accuracy.

Table 1. Detection performance on the COCO 2017 val set. These models are compared in terms of parameters, BFLOPs and accuracy.

Model	Backbone	Param.	BFLOPs	AP
Mask R-CNN [25]	ResNet-50	44M	262	37.2
	SENet-50	47M	262	38.7
Faster R-CNN [33]	ResNet-50-FPN	42M	180	40.2
	ResNet-101-FPN	60M	246	42.0
E-RFB Net [35]	VGG-16	36M	37	30.6
	ResNet-50	32M	36	33.8
YOLOv3 [28]	Darknet-53	59M	66	38.9
RetinaNet [19]	ResNet-50-FPN	34M	97	37.8
	SpineNet-49	29M	85	40.8
DTER [4]	ResNet-50	41M	86	42.0
	ResNet-101	60M	152	43.5
Deformable DETR [40]	ResNet-50	40M	173	43.8
YOLOv5 [15]	v5l	47M	115	48.1
	v5m	21M	51	44.5
	v5s	7M	17	36.5
Pruned-YOLOv5	**v5l-I**	**17M**	**72**	**46.5**
	v5l-II	**8M**	**54**	**44.6**
	v5l-III	**3M**	**30**	**38.2**

Comparison of the results on test split with other object detectors are shown in Table 2. Almost all other state-of-the-art models use backbones with high complexity. Our Pruned-YOLOv5 has certain advantages in accuracy and complexity. If we employ multi-scale training like [3,21,24], the performance will be improved further. When running on NVIDIA GTX2080ti GPU, the end-to-end latency is about 10ms when batch size is set to 1.

Table 2. Detection performance on the COCO 2017 test-dev dataset. Size refers to the input resolution of the model.

Model	Backbone	Size	AP	AP_{50}	AP_{75}	AP_s	AP_m	AP_l
EfficientDet-D1 [29]	Efficient-B1	640	39.6	58.6	42.3	17.9	44.3	56.0
EfficientDet-D2 [29]	Efficient-B2	768	43.0	62.3	46.2	22.5	47.0	58.4
RetinaNet [19]	ResNet-101-FPN	800	39.1	59.1	42.3	21.8	42.7	50.2
FCOS [38]	ResNet-101-FPN	800	41.0	60.7	44.1	24.0	44.1	51.0
ATSS [37]	ResNet-101-FPN	800×	43.6	62.1	47.4	26.1	47.0	53.6
YOLOv3 + ASFF [21]	Darknet-53	608	42.4	63.0	47.4	25.5	45.7	52.3
		800	43.9	64.1	49.2	27.0	46.6	53.4
YOLOv4 [3]	CSPDarknet-53	512	43.0	64.9	46.5	24.3	46.1	55.2
		608	43.5	65.7	47.3	26.7	46.7	53.3
PP-YOLO [24]	ResNet50-vd-dcn	512	44.4	64.6	48.8	24.4	47.1	58.2
		608	45.2	65.2	49.9	26.3	47.8	57.2
YOLOv5 [15]	v5l	640	48.2	66.6	52.4	30.0	52.5	59.8
	v5m	640	44.4	62.9	48.3	26.4	48.6	54.8
	v5ls	640	36.6	55.3	39.8	20.3	41.1	44.5
Pruned- YOLOv5	**v5l-I**	**640**	**46.6**	**65.7**	**50.6**	**28.7**	**50.8**	**56.9**
	v5l-II	**640**	**44.9**	**63.9**	**48.9**	**27.8**	**49.3**	**53.6**
	v5l-III	**640**	**38.5**	**57.5**	**41.7**	**23.7**	**42.3**	**44.3**

5 Conclusion

We improve the representative pipeline of channel pruning. Both the kernel weight and scale factor are considered when measuring channel importance. A more comprehensive importance measure of filters can get a more reasonable structure of the pruned model. Soft mask strategy and sparse factor cosine decay play a key role in fast iteration. Generous experiments on the object detection benchmark demonstrate the effectiveness of the proposed methods.

References

1. Azevedo, T., de Jong, R., Maji, P.: Stochastic-yolo: Efficient probabilistic object detection under dataset shifts. arXiv preprint arXiv:2009.02967 (2020)
2. Blakeney, C., Yan, Y., Zong, Z.: Is pruning compression? investigating pruning via network layer similarity. In: Proceedings of the IEEE/CVF Winter Conference on Applications of Computer Vision. pp. 914–922 (2020)
3. Bochkovskiy, A., Wang, C.Y., Liao, H.Y.M.: Yolov4: optimal speed and accuracy of object detection. arXiv preprint arXiv:2004.10934 (2020)
4. Carion, N., et al.: End-to-end object detection with transformers. In: Vedaldi, A., Bischof, H., Brox, T., Frahm, J.-M. (eds.) ECCV 2020. LNCS, vol. 12346, pp. 213–229. Springer, Cham (2020). https://doi.org/10.1007/978-3-030-58452-8_13
5. Chen, G., Choi, W., Yu, X., Han, T., Chandraker, M.: Learning efficient object detection models with knowledge distillation. In: Proceedings of the 31st International Conference on Neural Information Processing Systems, pp. 742–751 (2017)

6. Chen, L.C., Papandreou, G., Schroff, F., Adam, H.: Rethinking atrous convolution for semantic image segmentation. arXiv preprint arXiv:1706.05587 (2017)
7. Choi, J., Chun, D., Kim, H., Lee, H.J.: Gaussian yolov3: An accurate and fast object detector using localization uncertainty for autonomous driving. In: Proceedings of the IEEE/CVF International Conference on Computer Vision, pp. 502–511 (2019)
8. Ding, X., Ding, G., Guo, Y., Han, J.: Centripetal sgd for pruning very deep convolutional networks with complicated structure. In: Proceedings of the IEEE/CVF Conference on Computer Vision and Pattern Recognition, pp. 4943–4953 (2019)
9. Everingham, M., Van Gool, L., Williams, C.K., Winn, J., Zisserman, A.: The pascal visual object classes (voc) challenge. Int. J. Comput. Vision **88**(2), 303–338 (2010)
10. Guo, J., Ouyang, W., Xu, D.: Multi-dimensional pruning: a unified framework for model compression. In: Proceedings of the IEEE/CVF Conference on Computer Vision and Pattern Recognition, pp. 1508–1517 (2020)
11. Han, S., Pool, J., Tran, J., Dally, W.J.: Learning both weights and connections for efficient neural networks. arXiv preprint arXiv:1506.02626 (2015)
12. Hassibi, B., Stork, D.G.: Second order derivatives for network pruning: Optimal brain surgeon. Morgan Kaufmann (1993)
13. He, Y., Liu, P., Wang, Z., Hu, Z., Yang, Y.: Filter pruning via geometric median for deep convolutional neural networks acceleration. In: Proceedings of the IEEE/CVF Conference on Computer Vision and Pattern Recognition, pp. 4340–4349 (2019)
14. Huang, Z., Wang, J., Fu, X., Yu, T., Guo, Y., Wang, R.: Dc-spp-yolo: dense connection and spatial pyramid pooling based yolo for object detection. Inf. Sci. **522**, 241–258 (2020)
15. Jocher, G.: ultralytics/yolov5. https://github.com/ultralytics/yolov5
16. Kwon, S.J., Lee, D., Kim, B., Kapoor, P., Park, B., Wei, G.Y.: Structured compression by weight encryption for unstructured pruning and quantization. In: Proceedings of the IEEE/CVF Conference on Computer Vision and Pattern Recognition, pp. 1909–1918 (2020)
17. Li, Y., Gu, S., Mayer, C., Gool, L.V., Timofte, R.: Group sparsity: the hinge between filter pruning and decomposition for network compression. In: Proceedings of the IEEE/CVF Conference on Computer Vision and Pattern Recognition, pp. 8018–8027 (2020)
18. Lin, M., et al.: Hrank: filter pruning using high-rank feature map. In: Proceedings of the IEEE/CVF Conference on Computer Vision and Pattern Recognition, pp. 1529–1538 (2020)
19. Lin, T.Y., Goyal, P., Girshick, R., He, K., Dollár, P.: Focal loss for dense object detection. In: Proceedings of the IEEE International Conference on Computer Vision, pp. 2980–2988 (2017)
20. Lin, T.-Y., Maire, M., Belongie, S., Hays, J., Perona, P., Ramanan, D., Dollár, P., Zitnick, C.L.: Microsoft COCO: common objects in context. In: Fleet, D., Pajdla, T., Schiele, B., Tuytelaars, T. (eds.) ECCV 2014. LNCS, vol. 8693, pp. 740–755. Springer, Cham (2014). https://doi.org/10.1007/978-3-319-10602-1_48
21. Liu, S., Huang, D., Wang, Y.: Learning spatial fusion for single-shot object detection. arXiv preprint arXiv:1911.09516 (2019)
22. Liu, Y., Chen, K., Liu, C., Qin, Z., Luo, Z., Wang, J.: Structured knowledge distillation for semantic segmentation. In: Proceedings of the IEEE/CVF Conference on Computer Vision and Pattern Recognition, pp. 2604–2613 (2019)
23. Liu, Z., Li, J., Shen, Z., Huang, G., Yan, S., Zhang, C.: Learning efficient convolutional networks through network slimming. In: Proceedings of the IEEE International Conference on Computer Vision, pp. 2736–2744 (2017)

24. Long, X., et al.: Pp-yolo: an effective and efficient implementation of object detector. arXiv preprint arXiv:2007.12099 (2020)
25. Qin, Z., Zhang, P., Wu, F., Li, X.: Fcanet: frequency channel attention networks. arXiv preprint arXiv:2012.11879 (2020)
26. Redmon, J., Divvala, S., Girshick, R., Farhadi, A.: You only look once: unified, real-time object detection. In: Proceedings of the IEEE Conference on Computer Vision and Pattern Recognition, pp. 779–788 (2016)
27. Redmon, J., Farhadi, A.: Yolo9000: better, faster, stronger. In: Proceedings of the IEEE Conference on Computer Vision and Pattern Recognition, pp. 7263–7271 (2017)
28. Redmon, J., Farhadi, A.: Yolov3: An incremental improvement. arXiv preprint arXiv:1804.02767 (2018)
29. Tan, M., Pang, R., Le, Q.V.: Efficientdet: Scalable and efficient object detection. In: Proceedings of the IEEE/CVF Conference on Computer Vision and Pattern Recognition, pp. 10781–10790 (2020)
30. Tung, F., Mori, G.: Clip-q: Deep network compression learning by in-parallel pruning-quantization. In: Proceedings of the IEEE Conference on Computer Vision and Pattern Recognition, pp. 7873–7882 (2018)
31. Wang, C.Y., Bochkovskiy, A., Liao, H.Y.M.: Scaled-yolov4: Scaling cross stage partial network. arXiv preprint arXiv:2011.08036 (2020)
32. Wang, Z., Zhang, J., Zhao, Z., Su, F.: Efficient yolo: A lightweight model for embedded deep learning object detection. In: 2020 IEEE International Conference on Multimedia & Expo Workshops (ICMEW). pp. 1–6. IEEE (2020)
33. Wu, Y., Kirillov, A., Massa, F., Lo, W.Y., Girshick, R.: Detectron2 (2019). https://github.com/facebookresearch/detectron2
34. Ye, J., Lu, X., Lin, Z., Wang, J.Z.: Rethinking the smaller-norm-less-informative assumption in channel pruning of convolution layers. arXiv preprint arXiv:1802.00124 (2018)
35. Zhang, J., Zhao, Z., Su, F.: Efficient-receptive field block with group spatial attention mechanism for object detection. In: 2020 25th International Conference on Pattern Recognition (ICPR), pp. 3248–3255 (2021)
36. Zhang, P., Zhong, Y., Li, X.: Slimyolov3: narrower, faster and better for real-time uav applications. In: Proceedings of the IEEE/CVF International Conference on Computer Vision Workshops, pp. 0–0 (2019)
37. Zhang, S., Chi, C., Yao, Y., Lei, Z., Li, S.Z.: Bridging the gap between anchor-based and anchor-free detection via adaptive training sample selection. In: Proceedings of the IEEE/CVF Conference on Computer Vision and Pattern Recognition, pp. 9759–9768 (2020)
38. Zhi Tian, Chunhua Shen, H.C., He, T.: FCOS: fully convolutional one-stage object detection. In: Proceedings of the IEEE International Conference on Computer Vision, pp. 9627–9636 (2019)
39. Zhu, P., Wen, L., Bian, X., Ling, H., Hu, Q.: Vision meets drones: A challenge. arXiv preprint arXiv:1804.07437 (2018)
40. Zhu, X., Su, W., Lu, L., Li, B., Wang, X., Dai, J.: Deformable detr: deformable transformers for end-to-end object detection. arXiv preprint arXiv:2010.04159 (2020)

Gator: Customizable Channel Pruning of Neural Networks with Gating

Eli Passov(✉), Eli O. David, and Nathan S. Netanyahu

Department of Computer Science, Bar-Ilan University, 5290002 Ramat-Gan, Israel
elipassov@gmail.com, mail@elidavid.com, nathan@cs.biu.ac.il

Abstract. The rise of neural network (NN) applications has prompted an increased interest in compression, with a particular focus on *channel pruning*, which does not require any additional hardware. Most pruning methods employ either single-layer operations or global schemes to determine which channels to remove followed by fine-tuning of the network. In this paper we present Gator, a channel-pruning method which temporarily adds learned gating mechanisms for pruning of individual channels, and which is trained with an additional auxiliary loss, aimed at reducing the computational cost due to memory, (theoretical) speedup (in terms of FLOPs), and practical, hardware-specific speedup. Gator introduces a new formulation of dependencies between NN layers which, in contrast to most previous methods, enables pruning of non-sequential parts, such as layers on ResNet's highway, and even removing entire ResNet blocks. Gator's pruning for ResNet-50 trained on ImageNet produces state-of-the-art (SOTA) results, such as 50% FLOPs reduction with only 0.4%-drop in top-5 accuracy. Also, Gator outperforms previous pruning models, in terms of GPU latency by running 1.4 times faster. Furthermore, Gator achieves improved top-5 accuracy results, compared to MobileNetV2 and SqueezeNet, for similar runtimes.

1 Introduction

The use of NNs, in particular, *convolutional neural networks* (CNNs), in a variety of Computer Vision applications has surged considerably in recent years. Most NNs consist of tens to hundreds of millions of weight parameters and require typically billions of *floating point operations* (FLOPs) for processing a single image. This limits their use on available hardware, especially on small devices. Consequently, many works in recent years have focused on reducing the computational cost of network architectures without severely impairing their performance, either by creating more efficient network architectures or by applying network compression. Pruning is a popular method among compression methods, where network weights and activations are removed. Pruning methods can be categorized as *unstructured*, i.e., referring to the removal of individual weights,

Nathan Netanyahu is also affliiated with the Department of Computer Science at the College of Law and Business, Ramat-Gan 5257346, Israel

I. Farkaš et al. (Eds.): ICANN 2021, LNCS 12894, pp. 46–58, 2021.
https://doi.org/10.1007/978-3-030-86380-7_5

or *structured*, i.e., referring mostly to the removal of convolutional channels. Unstructured pruning is considered much less practical, as it requires special hardware for efficient application.

More recent techniques also utilize dynamic computation in conjunction with *gating* mechanisms to control the network operations that are invoked for each input instance; thus, the computational cost is determined dynamically for each individual input. Our method utilizes dynamic gating mechanisms only during training, to learn which channels should be removed, thereby producing a pruned network without any gating mechanisms.

The effectiveness of pruning methods is usually assessed by these parameters:

- Reduction of memory required for storing weights;
- Theoretical speedup, measured by the reduction of the number of FLOPs;
- Latency/runtime on a specific hardware.

Note that latency is not commonly used as an optimization objective, and that theoretical speedup is never translated into the exact same practical speedup. For unstructured methods, this is due to the fact that most hardware does not support sparse operations, leading to no optimization in practice; for structured pruning, the sole focus on the FLOPs metric ignores hardware-specific behavior.

This paper makes the following contributions:

- Presentation of *Gator*, an innovative pruning technique that utilizes channel hard-gating to remove channels during training while also adjusting the remaining weights;
- Introduction of a novel formulation for dependencies between NN layers allowing Gator to prune non-sequential parts of NN architectures (such as ResNet's highway), which are not handled by most pruning methods;
- Presentation of a customizable cost function, which reflects various practical compression criteria, such as memory reduction, FLOPs reduction, and hardware-specific speedup;
- Obtaining new SOTA results for ResNet-50 pruning on ImageNet, in particular, 50% FLOPs reduction with 0.4% top-5 accuracy drop and runtime speedup (latency reduction) of 1.4 for the same accuracy as other methods;
- Presentation of additional results for higher pruning rates, outperforming MobileNet V2 and SqueezeNet for the same runtime.

2 Related Work

2.1 Network Compression

Most methods for NN compression can be categorized into three categories. First, tensor decomposition [15,17,20], where the convolutional operation is approximated by decomposing it to smaller operations.

Second, quantization methods [2,33,34], in particular, binary methods [3, 24], where the network weights are approximated with lower precision variables allowing for memory reduction.

And third, pruning, where parts of layer outputs or weights are removed. In early works [21] and more recent ones [8], pruning methods are characterized by weight elimination and a "fine tuning" training stage. A thorough review of pruning methods can be found in [1], which also highlights the distinction between structured and unstructured pruning. Since unstructured pruning cannot reduce computational costs on most hardware types, we will focus and compare Gator only to other structured pruning methods.

2.2 Structured Channel Pruning

Most channel pruning works differ in the criteria by which channels are pruned. In [22] the smallest sums of weights of channels from all layers are pruned, while non sequential layers are being considered. The pruning criterion in [23] is the first order Taylor expansion of the loss ($w\frac{\partial L}{\partial w}$). Weights closest to the geometric median are pruned in [9], in an iterative process for each layer. And in [32], individually trained squeeze and excitation [12] blocks are used to prune layers with the lower attention values.

Other methods, such as [11], remove the convolutional input channels with the least impact on the output. While [35] first train auxiliary classification losses on intermediate layers and define reconstruction losses on potential channels to be remove. The channels chosen to be removed are those which have the smallest impact on the sum total of all classification and reconstruction losses.

2.3 Gating

Dynamic gating modules determine, for each individual input, which parts are executed and which are skipped within a computational NN graph. In [30], squeeze and excitation blocks [12] are used with a gumbel softmax [16] gate on individual residual blocks, enabling skipping some blocks dynamically. In [4], the same gating mechanism is applied on individual channels.

Methods which do not rely on gumbel softmax, such as [7], use regression on the global pooling vector of the convolutional input to determine dynamically which channels are passed to the convolution. In [13], convolutions are divided into two parts, such that the output of the first gates the execution of the second.

A soft sigmoid gate is used in [6] to prune connections in fully-connected layers. Our method also uses a sigmoid; however, it gates entire channels, using a hard gating mechanism with a different learning process which leads to practical results on ImageNet.

2.4 Network Architecture Search

Network architecture search (NAS) first introduced in [36]. It focuses on finding an optimal network architecture within a wide search space using methods such as reinforcement learning. Many NAS works, such as [29], typically regard the number of layer channels as part of the search space while minimizing the FLOPs metric. The search space of [10] consists of layer pruning ratios minimizing either FLOPs or memory metrics for a given target accuracy. Other methods, such as [31], optimize the latency metric. Although many NAS methods also share the idea of optimizing the number FLOPs, memory footprint or latency, and even yield SOTA performance in many cases, they are extremely computationally intensive compared to pruning methods, and thus exhibit sub-optimal latency.

3 Approach

In this section we describe the components of Gator. We start with the gating mechanism in Subsect. 3.1, and then explain in Subsect. 3.2 how modeling the network architecture as a hypergraph encapsulates the channel dependency between different layers in the network architecture, thereby allowing for non-sequential pruning. Finally, in Subsect. 3.3 we present the loss function for computational cost and demonstrate how to customize it for FLOPs, memory, and latency reduction.

3.1 Channel Gating

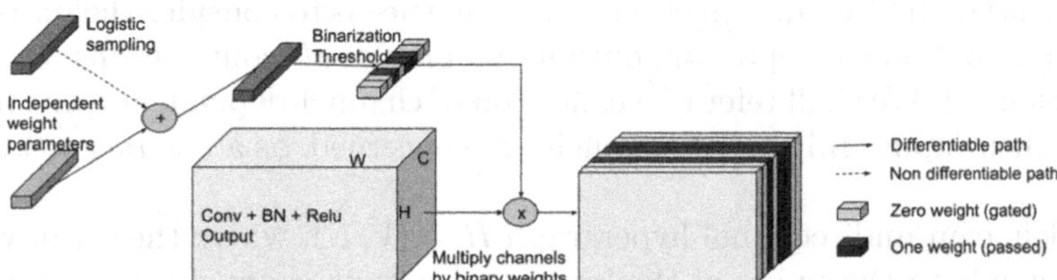

Fig. 1. Logistic sigmoid gating model for an output of a layer.

Gator utilizes a gating mechanism which determines for each individual channel whether it should be passed or gated for each individual sample within a batch. The gating mechanism (see Eq. 1) uses a binary version of the Gumbel softmax distribution (introduced in [16]), referred to as the *logistic sigmoid distribution.*

$$\begin{aligned} \sigma(\theta) &= \frac{1}{1+e^{-\frac{\theta+x}{\tau}}} \quad \text{where} \quad x \sim Logistic(0,1) \\ g(\theta) &= \begin{cases} 1 & \sigma(\frac{\theta+x}{\tau}) \geq 0.5 \\ 0 & \sigma(\frac{\theta+x}{\tau}) < 0.5 \end{cases} \simeq sign(\theta+x) \; . \end{aligned} \tag{1}$$

The gating binary value $g(\theta)$ is determined by adding the gating weight θ to a random variable x sampled from a logistic distribution. The purpose of the sigmoid function is to enable a continuous gradient while the threshold test provides a discrete output equivalent to a sign function in the forward pass. The temperature parameter τ, which controls the gradient magnitude, is set to the default value of 1 and is, henceforth, ignored. The addition of the random variable x is according to the reparameterization trick in [18], which enables a computational flow of the gradients for the gating weights as part of the backpropagation process, while providing a discrete value in the forward pass.

A gating module can be placed before or after a layer to pass or block individual channels, thereby simulating the effect of pruning input or output channels. Figure 1 illustrates gating on an output of a model.

3.2 Hypergraph of Neural Network Channels

Early pruning methods on sequential network architectures, such as VGG [27], focus naturally on individual convolutions, so they are applicable to all layers. However, most recent architectures consist of many non-sequential parts. Considering ResNet architectures, for example, note that inputs of some convolutions depend on outputs of multiple convolutions residing in different ResNet blocks, as a result of the "highway" path configuration. Thus, using a channel pruning scheme, in an attempt to remove a channel from the output of a single convolution may not remove the same channel from the input of a dependent convolution or the output of another convolution, as implied by the network's non-sequential architecture. In other words, one needs to consider the impact of a channel removal on the input and output channels of *all* convolutions dependent on that channel. We shall refer to a collection of channel-dependent convolutions, as far as their input and output channels are concerned, as a *channel dependency group*.

We define an undirectional hypergraph $H = (V, E)$, where the set of vertices V corresponds to the union of the input and output channel sets over all convolutions. Let C^{in} and C^{out} denote these input and output sets, respectively. Specifically, the vertices $c_i^{in} \in C^{in}$ and $c_i^{out} \in C^{out}$ represent the (numbers of the) input and output channels of convolution i, respectively. The set of edges E is composed of subsets of V, where an edge $e_j \in E$ corresponds to channel dependency group j. (Each edge in E is referred to as a *dependency edge*.) We represent the dependency group as $e_j = C_j^{in} \cup C_j^{out} \subseteq V$, where $C_j^{in} \subseteq C^{in}$ and $C_j^{out} \subseteq C^{out}$ denote, respectively, the input and output channel subsets associated with dependency group j. We can now define pruning as a removal of channels from each dependency edge.

For sequential networks, each dependency edge is composed of a pair of a convolutional layer's output and the following convolutional layer's input. However, we can now also map channel dependency for non-sequential networks, such as ResNet-50, as detailed in Table 1. Specifically, 53 convolutions and a fully-connected layer are mapped to 37 dependency edges, 32 of which are trivial edges representing sequential connections inside bottleneck blocks, and to 5 additional edges, which include more than two convolutions (some of which are located along the "highway" path).

Table 1. Dependency mapping for Resnet-50; Each row represent one edge composed of output and input layers (vertices); encoding used, L1B1-(example of) layer and block, C0-first convolution, C1, C2, C3-bottleneck convolutions, D-downsampling convolution, and FC-fully connected; for brevity, trivial edges inside bottlenecks are listed once

Output layers	Input layers	# Edges
c0	L1B1D, L1B1C1	1
c1	c2	16
c2	c3	16
L1B1D, L1B1C3, L1B2C3, L1B3C3	L1B2C1, L1B3C1, L2B1D, L2B1C1	1
L2B1D, L2B1C3, L2B2C3, L2B3C3, L2B4C3	L2B2C1, L2B3C1, L2B4C1, L3B1D, L3B1C1	1
L3B1D, L3B1C3, L3B2C3 L3B3C3, L3B4C3, L3B5C3, L3B6C3	L3B2C1, L3B3C1, L3B4C1, L3B5C1, L3B6C1, L4B1D, L4B1C1	1
L4B1D, L4B1C3, L4B2C3, L4B3C3	L4B2C1, L4B3C1, FC	1

3.3 Loss Function for Computational Cost

For each edge e_j we have $c_j(t)$ non-gated channels at iteration t from a total of c_j channels, computed from the binary gating values defined in Eq. (1):

$$c_j(t) = \sum_{i=1}^{c_j} g(\theta_j^i). \tag{2}$$

Let $\lambda_j(t)$ denote the per channel cost factor for iteration t. The change in cost for different iterations stems from the fact that the number of non-gated input and output channels of a convolution changes at each iteration. We now define the auxiliary computational loss as:

$$L_{computation}(t) = \sum_{j=1}^{m} c_j(t)\widehat{\lambda_j}(t) = \frac{\sum_{j=1}^{m} c_j(t)\lambda_j(t)}{\sum_{j=1}^{m} c_j\lambda_j}, \tag{3}$$

where m is the number of dependency edges, $\widehat{\lambda_j}(t)$ is the normalized, per-channel cost factor, and λ_j is the initial cost factor. The normalization sets the initial loss to $L_{computation}(0) = 1$, so that it is easier to calibrate the total loss

$$L_{total}(t) = L_{original} + \alpha L_{computation}(t), \tag{4}$$

where $L_{original}$ is the original loss and α is a global weight being calibrated.

The memory footprint cost factor is the number of weights in all layers of each individual edge, i.e.,

$$\lambda_j(t) = \sum_{q_i \in \mathbf{C_j^{in}}} k_{q_i}^w k_{q_i}^h c_{q_i}^{out}(t) + \sum_{q_i \in \mathbf{C_j^{out}}} k_{q_i}^w k_{q_i}^h c_{q_i}^{in}(t), \quad (5)$$

where $\mathbf{C_j^{out}}$ and $\mathbf{C_j^{in}}$ are the convolution sets corresponding to C_j^{out} and C_j^{in}, respectively. For each convolution q_i, $k_{q_i}^w$ and $k_{q_i}^h$ denote the kernel width and kernel height, respectively. Also, $c_{q_i}^{in}(t)$ and $c_{q_i}^{out}(t)$ denote, respectively, the number of non-gated input and output channels at iteration t.

The theoretical speed cost factor is computed for a single input pixel, by multiplying the number of weights of each layer by the downsample factor d_i, i.e., the ratio between the number of pixels in the current layer's output and the original input image. Typically $d_i = 4^{-s_i}$, where s_i is the number of stride-2 operations (e.g., convolutions, maxpooling, etc.) encountered on a computational path from the input image to the current layer i. Thus the FLOPs cost factor is given by

$$\lambda_j(t) = \sum_{q_i \in \mathbf{C_j^{in}}} d_i k_{q_i}^w k_{q_i}^h q_i^{out}(t) + \sum_{q_i \in \mathbf{C_j^{out}}} d_i k_{q_i}^w k_{q_i}^h q_i^{in}(t). \quad (6)$$

For latency, the cost factor cannot be generally defined, as it is hardware-specific. Instead, we approximate, in this case, the cost factor $\lambda_j(t)$, by measuring the latency difference between the original network and a network with 50% of the channels in e_j pruned.

4 Experiments

4.1 Methodology and Setup

The lack of a comparison standard for pruning results is discussed in [1], listing different types of pruning, different benchmark types, and a plethora of different network architectures on which various pruning methods are benchmarked. Hence, comparing between pruning methods is only relevant for compatible criteria, i.e., same pruning type (e.g., structured pruning), optimized parameter (e.g., FLOPs reduction), and architecture. (From a practical consideration, we only compared with structured channel pruning methods.) Similarly to most other works, we performed pruning on the ImageNet ILSVRC2012 [25] and CIFAR-10 [19] classification challenges. However, we believe that results for CIFAR-10 are not very indicative, due to the small dataset, the large variation in accuracy [5], and the fact that the dataset does not adequately represent "real-world" data. We chose the ResNet architecture, which enabled demonstrating Gator's pruning capability for a non-sequential architecture and comparing it to other works. Note that newer and smaller architectures would require a much greater effort in recreating proper training and pruned versions, not to mention that there are very few results to compare to.

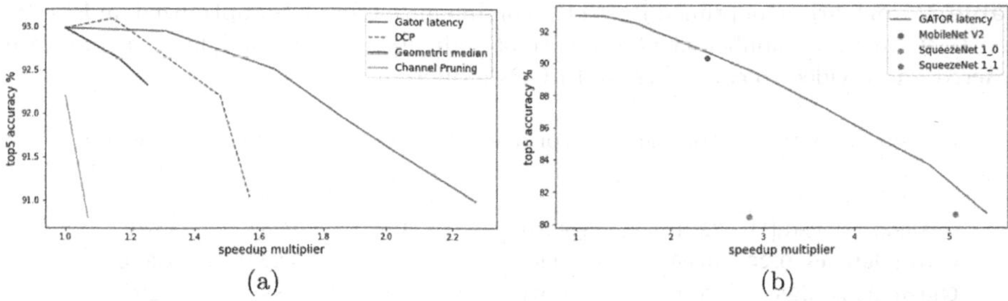

(a) (b)

Fig. 2. ImageNet (ILSVRC-12) top-5 accuracy (%) as a function of latency speedup for ResNet-50 pruning by Gator compared with (a) other pruning networks and (b) smaller networks for larger scale pruning.

In both experiments, we trained our model with the standard SGD optimizer, setting the momentum to 0.9 and the weight decay to 0.0001. We initialized the gating probability to 0.005, which was found empirically to have a low impact on the network's initial accuracy, while still enabling the pruning in a relatively low number of epochs. Note that a lower initial gating probability would have required more steps to reach the pruning threshold probability set to 0.5. Crossing the threshold probability marks a channel as permanently pruned. We performed iterative pruning with an increasing global weight α. Each pruning iteration consisted of training with gating, and of additional fine-tuning without gating. The next iteration loaded the weights produced by the gating phase.

4.2 Results for ResNet-50 on ImageNet

For pruning ResNet-50 trained on ImageNet, we used the pretrained weights. The batch size was 256, which was split between two GPUs. However, due to the lack of RAM, we used gradient accumulation and split each half batch into 4 parts, training equivalenty on 8 GPUs with sub-batches of size 32 each. (This only affects the batch normalization.) We trained with gates for 30 epochs, using learning rates of 0.01 and 0.001 for the first 20 epochs and the latter 10 epochs, respectively. Table 2 contains fine-tuning results for lower pruning rates ($\alpha \leq 2$). We trained, in this case, for 40 epochs with a learning rate step policy of 0.001, 0.0001, and 0.00001 for 20, 10, and 10 epochs, respectively. For high pruning rates, we trained for 20 epochs (given the available resources under the time constraints), with a learning rate step policy of 0.001, 0.0001, and 0.00001 for 10, 5, and 5 epochs, respectively (see Table 3). For image preprocessing, we applied mean subtraction and standard deviation normalization for each color channel. Data augmentation consisted of selecting a random 224×224 crop from the original image and applying to it a random horizontal flip. Practical speedup was measured by timing an inference run in Pytorch on GTX 1080 Ti GPU with a batch of size 32 for 224×224 images.

Table 2 contains comparative results of optimized Gator pruning on FLOPs and latency, with other methods (also illustrated in Fig. 2(a)). Note the very

Table 2. Comparison of pruned ResNet-50 on ImageNet for Gator optimized on FLOPs and GPU latency; number of Gator variant indicates pruning weight α; results are ordered and divided to categories by FLOPs reduction (%)

Pruning algorithm	Top-1 acc.%	Top-5 acc.%	FLOPs % reduction	Memory % reduction	Practical Speed-up[a]
Channel pruning [11]	72.30	90.80	24.14	15.52	1.069
Gator latency 0.25	76.00	92.94	26.75	5.22	**1.310**
Gator flops 0.25	75.89	92.93	31.48	8.88	1.200
DCP 30 [35]	**76.35**[b]	**93.09**[b]	36.04	33.45	1.145
Geometric 30% [9]	75.59	92.63	41.89	37.64	1.162
Gator latency 0.5	**75.28**	92.50	48.27	18.05	**1.647**
Gator flops 0.5	75.19	**92.61**	49.91	18.96	1.442
Geometric 40%	74.83	92.32	53.16	47.72	1.251
DCP 50	74.88	92.19	55.77	51.63	1.477
PCAS [32]	72.68	91.09	56.70	51.20	–
Gator latency 1	**74.24**	91.95	61.17	31.18	**1.857**
Gator flops 1	74.14	**91.99**	62.64	31.40	1.612
DCP 70	72.65	91.03	71.10	66.00	1.569
Gator flops 2	72.36	90.97	76.57	55.15	2.106

[a] Speedup multiplier for batch 32 on single GTX 1080 Ti GPU
[b] [2] Better accuracy then baseline ResNet-50.

Table 3. Comparison of small networks to high rate pruned ResNet-50 on ImageNet for Gator optimized on GPU latency; number of Gator variant indicates pruning weight α; results are ordered and divided to categories by speedup

Pruning algorithm	Top-1 acc.%	Top-5 acc.%	FLOPs	Speed up
Gator latency 2	**72.69**	**90.98**	973M	2.273
MobileNet V2	71.87	90.29	301M	**2.399**
squeezenet 1.0	58.10	80.42	888M	2.843
Gator latency 4	**69.48**	**89.3**	551M	**2.959**
Gator latency 16	**61.07**	**83.72**	191M	4.777
squeezenet 1.1	58.19	80.62	387M	5.070
Gator latency 20	56.89	80.67	134M	**5.404**

similar accuracy obtained by the two optimization methods and how each type is better suited for its designated reduction metric. (Although there is a single instance that outperforms Gator (optimized on FLOPs reduction) for lower pruning rates, note that the accuracy reported in this case [35] exceeds the original ResNet-50 accuracy; this could be explained by the use of auxiliary classification losses, known to enhance the performance [28]. Thus, we believe this isolated instance is not a fair comparison.)

Regarding the latency speedup, Gator outperforms all other methods, achieving a speedup of 1.4 for some pruning rates.

Table 4. Pruning results of ResNet-56 on CIFAR-10 using Gator optimization on FLOPs and memory vs. other methods; baseline network accuracy is listed for comparison as it differs across methods

Pruning algorithm	Baseline acc. %	Acc. %	FLOPs % reduction	Memory % reduction
Gator flops 1	93.63	93.58	43.39	33.50
Gator flops 2	93.63	93.14	54.62	44.39
Gator memory 0.25	93.63	93.66	33.21	42.70
Gator memory 0.5	93.63	92.59	57.98	**75.08**
DCP	93.80	93.49	49.75	49.24
DCP Adapt	93.80	**93.81**	47.09	70.33
Geometric 40	93.59	93.49	52.30	–
Channel Pruning	92.80	91.80	50.00	–
PCAS	93.04	93.58	**54.80**	53.70
Gator flops 16	93.63	91.50	**79.33**	73.40
Gator memory 2	93.63	90.99	76.05	**90.87**

Results for higher pruning rates are available in Table 3. We compared Gator's latency optimization to that of much smaller architectures, such as SqueezeNet [14] and MobileNet V2 [26], a newer architecture containing speed-efficient elements, such as inverse bottlenecks and grouped convolutions. According to Fig. 2(b), our method slightly outperforms both of these small architectures.

4.3 Results for ResNet-56 on CIFAR-10

We trained ResNet-56 on CIFAR-10 from scratch for 240 epochs with a batch size of 128. The learning rate was 0.1 for the first 120 epochs, and was changed to 0.01 and 0.001 at epochs 120 and 180, respectively. For pruning, we trained with gating for 90 epochs, starting with at a learning rate of 0.01 and decreasing it to 0.001 at epoch 60. This was followed by fine-tuning for another 30 epochs at the same learning rate. Image preprocessing consisted of mean subtraction and standard deviation division for each channel. Data augmentation consisted of random cropping and random horizontal flipping. The results are available in Table 4, where we see a significant reduction of FLOPs with little accuracy loss for Gator which also and best performance on memory reduction compared to other models. In addition Gator was able to prune entire ResNet blocks, thereby reducing the number of layers.

5 Conclusions

In this paper we presented Gator, a novel structural channel-pruning method, which utilizes dynamic channel gating during training to obtain smaller effective networks. We showed how to prune non-sequential architectures by using a hypergraph formulation to encapsulate the mapping of dependencies between input and output channels of different convolutions. We also demonstrated how Gator can accommodate a variety of auxiliary cost functions to optimize FLOPs, memory, and latency reduction due to pruning. Latency reduction, in particular, is important for allowing to produce very light networks designed for small devices. Finally, we showcased SOTA results of pruning ResNet-50, trained on ImageNet, with respect to FLOPs reduction and practical speedup on actual hardware.

References

1. Blalock, D., Ortiz, J.J.G., Frankle, J., Guttag, J.: What is the state of neural network pruning? arXiv preprint arXiv:2003.03033 (2020)
2. Chen, W., Wilson, J., Tyree, S., Weinberger, K., Chen, Y.: Compressing neural networks with the hashing trick. In: International Conference on Machine Learning, pp. 2285–2294 (2015)
3. Courbariaux, M., Hubara, I., Soudry, D., El-Yaniv, R., Bengio, Y.: Binarized neural networks: Training deep neural networks with weights and activations constrained to + 1 or -1. arXiv preprint arXiv:1602.02830 (2016)
4. Ehteshami Bejnordi, B., Blankevoort, T., Welling, M.: Batch-shaping for learning conditional channel gated networks. arXiv pp. arXiv-1907 (2019)
5. Frankle, J., Carbin, M.: The lottery ticket hypothesis: Finding sparse, trainable neural networks. arXiv preprint arXiv:1803.03635 (2018)
6. Gain, A., Kaushik, P., Siegelmann, H.: Adaptive neural connections for sparsity learning. In: The IEEE Winter Conference on Applications of Computer Vision, pp. 3188–3193 (2020)
7. Gao, X., Zhao, Y., Dudziak, Ł., Mullins, R., Xu, C.z.: Dynamic channel pruning: Feature boosting and suppression. arXiv preprint arXiv:1810.05331 (2018)
8. Han, S., Pool, J., Tran, J., Dally, W.: Learning both weights and connections for efficient neural network. Adv. Neural. Inf. Process. Syst. **28**, 1135–1143 (2015)
9. He, Y., Liu, P., Wang, Z., Hu, Z., Yang, Y.: Filter pruning via geometric median for deep convolutional neural networks acceleration. In: Proceedings of the IEEE Conference on Computer Vision and Pattern Recognition, pp. 4340–4349 (2019)
10. He, Y., Lin, J., Liu, Z., Wang, H., Li, L.J., Han, S.: Amc: automl for model compression and acceleration on mobile devices. In: Proceedings of the European Conference on Computer Vision, pp. 784–800 (2018)
11. He, Y., Zhang, X., Sun, J.: Channel pruning for accelerating very deep neural networks. In: Proceedings of the IEEE International Conference on Computer Vision, pp. 1389–1397 (2017)
12. Hu, J., Shen, L., Sun, G.: Squeeze-and-excitation networks. In: Proceedings of the IEEE Conference on Computer Vision and Pattern Recognition, pp. 7132–7141 (2018)
13. Hua, W., Zhou, Y., De Sa, C.M., Zhang, Z., Suh, G.E.: Channel gating neural networks. In: Advances in Neural Information Processing Systems, pp. 1886–1896 (2019)
14. Iandola, F.N., Han, S., Moskewicz, M.W., Ashraf, K., Dally, W.J., Keutzer, K.: Squeezenet: Alexnet-level accuracy with 50x fewer parameters and <0.5 MB model size. arXiv preprint arXiv:1602.07360 (2016)

15. Jaderberg, M., Vedaldi, A., Zisserman, A.: Speeding up convolutional neural networks with low rank expansions. arXiv preprint arXiv:1405.3866 (2014)
16. Jang, E., Gu, S., Poole, B.: Categorical reparameterization with gumbel-softmax. arXiv preprint arXiv:1611.01144 (2016)
17. Kim, Y.D., Park, E., Yoo, S., Choi, T., Yang, L., Shin, D.: Compression of deep convolutional neural networks for fast and low power mobile applications. arXiv preprint arXiv:1511.06530 (2015)
18. Kingma, D.P., Welling, M.: Auto-encoding variational bayes. arXiv preprint arXiv:1312.6114 (2013)
19. Krizhevsky, A., Hinton, G.: Learning multiple layers of features from tiny images (2009)
20. Lebedev, V., Ganin, Y., Rakhuba, M., Oseledets, I., Lempitsky, V.: Speeding-up convolutional neural networks using fine-tuned CP-decomposition. arXiv preprint arXiv:1412.6553 (2014)
21. LeCun, Y., Denker, J., Solla, S.: Optimal brain damage. Adv. Neural. Inf. Process. Syst. **2**, 598–605 (1989)
22. Li, H., Kadav, A., Durdanovic, I., Samet, H., Graf, H.P.: Pruning filters for efficient convnets. arXiv preprint arXiv:1608.08710 (2016)
23. Molchanov, P., Tyree, S., Karras, T., Aila, T., Kautz, J.: Pruning convolutional neural networks for resource efficient inference. arXiv preprint arXiv:1611.06440 (2016)
24. Rastegari, M., Ordonez, V., Redmon, J., Farhadi, A.: XNOR-Net: ImageNet classification using binary convolutional neural networks. In: Leibe, B., Matas, J., Sebe, N., Welling, M. (eds.) ECCV 2016. LNCS, vol. 9908, pp. 525–542. Springer, Cham (2016). https://doi.org/10.1007/978-3-319-46493-0_32
25. Russakovsky, O., Deng, J., Su, H., Krause, J., Satheesh, S., Ma, S., Huang, Z., Karpathy, A., Khosla, A., Bernstein, M., et al.: Imagenet large scale visual recognition challenge. Int. J. Comput. Vision **115**(3), 211–252 (2015)
26. Sandler, M., Howard, A., Zhu, M., Zhmoginov, A., Chen, L.C.: Mobilenetv 2: inverted residuals and linear bottlenecks. In: Proceedings of the IEEE Conference on Computer Vision and Pattern Recognition, pp. 4510–4520 (2018)
27. Simonyan, K., Zisserman, A.: Very deep convolutional networks for large-scale image recognition. arXiv preprint arXiv:1409.1556 (2014)
28. Szegedy, C., Vanhoucke, V., Ioffe, S., Shlens, J., Wojna, Z.: Rethinking the inception architecture for computer vision. In: Proceedings of the IEEE Conference on Computer Vision and Pattern Recognition, pp. 2818–2826 (2016)
29. Tan, M., Le, Q.V.: Efficientnet: Rethinking model scaling for convolutional neural networks. arXiv preprint arXiv:1905.11946 (2019)
30. Veit, A., Belongie, S.: Convolutional networks with adaptive inference graphs. In: Proceedings of the European Conference on Computer Vision, pp. 3–18 (2018)
31. Wu, B., et al.: Fbnet: Hardware-aware efficient convnet design via differentiable neural architecture search. In: Proceedings of the IEEE Conference on Computer Vision and Pattern Recognition, pp. 10734–10742 (2019)
32. Yamamoto, K., Maeno, K.: Pcas: pruning channels with attention statistics for deep network compression. arXiv preprint arXiv:1806.05382 (2018)
33. Zhou, A., Yao, A., Guo, Y., Xu, L., Chen, Y.: Incremental network quantization: Towards lossless cnns with low-precision weights. arXiv preprint arXiv:1702.03044 (2017)
34. Zhu, C., Han, S., Mao, H., Dally, W.J.: Trained ternary quantization. arXiv preprint arXiv:1612.01064 (2016)

35. Zhuang, Z., et al.: Discrimination-aware channel pruning for deep neural networks. In: Advances in Neural Information Processing Systems, pp. 875–886 (2018)
36. Zoph, B., Le, Q.V.: Neural architecture search with reinforcement learning. arXiv preprint arXiv:1611.01578 (2016)

Multi-task and Multi-label Learning

MMF: Multi-task Multi-structure Fusion for Hierarchical Image Classification

Xiaoni Li[1,2], Yucan Zhou[1(✉)], Yu Zhou[1], and Weiping Wang[1]

[1] Institute of Information Engineering, Chinese Academy of Sciences, Beijing, China
{lixiaoni,zhouyucan,zhouyu,wangweiping}@iie.ac.cn

[2] School of Cyber Security, University of Chinese Academy of Sciences, Beijing, China

Abstract. Hierarchical classification is significant for complex tasks by providing multi-granular predictions and encouraging better mistakes. As the label structure decides its performance, many existing approaches attempt to construct an excellent label structure for promoting the classification results. In this paper, we consider that different label structures provide a variety of prior knowledge for category recognition, thus fusing them is helpful to achieve better hierarchical classification results. Furthermore, we propose a multi-task multi-structure fusion model to integrate different label structures. It contains two kinds of branches: one is the traditional classification branch to classify the common subclasses, the other is responsible for identifying the heterogeneous superclasses defined by different label structures. Besides the effect of multiple label structures, we also explore the architecture of the deep model for better hierachical classification and adjust the hierarchical evaluation metrics for multiple label structures. Experimental results on CIFAR100 and Car196 show that our method obtains significantly better results than using a flat classifier or a hierarchical classifier with any single label structure.

Keywords: Hierarchical classification · Multi-task learning · Multiple label structures

1 Introduction

Although deep learning in text spotting [5,6,25–28], object detection [37], self-supervised learning [22,23,38–40] and image classification [10,15] has achieved dramatic performance with the increase of annotated data, the unclassifiable categories are growing and inevitable in the ear of big data. Moreover, the conventional one-hot coding in flat classifiers suggests a strict error evaluation: as

Supported by the National Natural Science Foundation of China (No. 62006221), the Open Research Project of the State Key Laboratory of Media Convergence and Communication, Communication University of China, China (No. SKLMCC2020KF004), the Beijing Municipal Science & Technology Commission (Z191100007119002), and the Key Research Program of Frontier Sciences, CAS, Grant NO ZDBS-LY-7024.

I. Farkaš et al. (Eds.): ICANN 2021, LNCS 12894, pp. 61–73, 2021.
https://doi.org/10.1007/978-3-030-86380-7_6

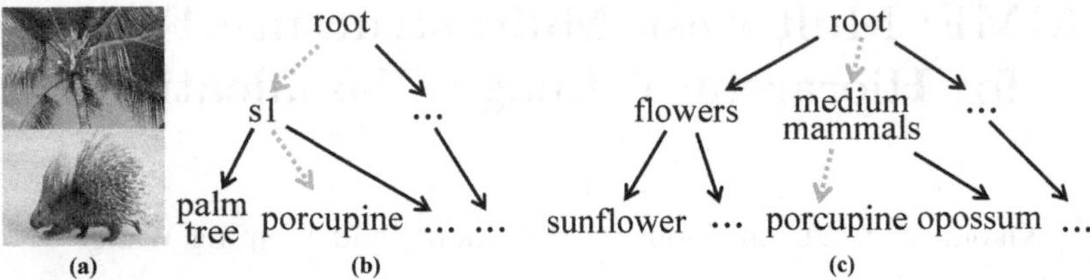

Fig. 1. The benefit of combining multiple label structures. (a) shows two samples for palm tree and porcupine, as these two categories are similar, they are easy to be misclassified. (b) and (c) are two label structures, each for the visual sturcture based on the affinity matrix and the semantic structure. The second layers in (b) and (c) are the superclasses, the third layers are the shared subclasses. The green dashed paths are the ground truth in both label structures when a "porcupine" is needed to identify. When "s1"and "medium mammals"are recognized in each label structure, "porcupine"is promoted as it belongs to both "s1"and "medium mammals". (Color figure online)

long as the predicted value is inconsistent with the real one, it will be recognized as misclassification. In fact, there are different levels of severity in mistakes [4]. As shown in Fig. 1(c), the classifier makes a less serious mistake when it classifies a "porcupine" into an "opossum" than a " sunflower" obviously, because they all belong to the superclass "medium mammals". Therefore, when misclassification is unavoidable, providing a reasonable mistake is more significant.

Recently, more and more work is devoted to using hierarchical classification methods [34,35] to make multi-granular predictions and avoid serious mistakes. In hierarchical classification, label structures play a critical role. Hence many researchers try to construct efficient label structures, which can be roughly divided into semantics-based methods and computation-based methods. The former extracts the semantic structure from WordNet [18], where categories are organized into a tree-shape structure according to their semantic relations [7,8,14,41]. However, these relations may be inconsistent with the appearances, which weakens the performance of classification tasks. Therefore, a lot of work builds visual information tree structures [3,11,13,16,19–21,29]. Some build the tree structures based on the confusion matrix [3,13,19–21], which is constructed by the results of a classifier. Others construct the label structure based on the affinity matrix [11,16,29] calculted by the similarity of any two categories.

Different label structures provide various prior knowledge for the underlying classification tasks. Hence integrating these structures can further improve the performance [33,43]. As shown in Fig. 1, in the mission of "porcupine" classification, if one has determined its superclass "s1" and "medium mammals" according to the label structure based on the affinity matrix and semantics respectively, then, "porcupine" can be easily determined by combining these two intermediate results. A straightforward strategy to fuse multiple label structures is constructing a hierarchical classifier for each structure, and the prediction is obtained by integrating the results of multiple classifiers [33]. This idea is simple and efficient, but in the deep learning scenario, it is memory-consuming and computationally redundant to design a neural network for each label structure.

In this paper, a multi-task multi-structure fusion (MMF) model is proposed to make the superclasses from different label structures instruct the subclass recognition. It achieves this by encouraging the learned feature to satisfy the multiple similarity constraints in various hierarchical label structures. Specifically, it is a deep convolutional neural network with two kinds of classification branches: the conventional classification branch (CCB) used for identifying subclasses, and the multiple superclass classification branches (MSCBs), where each branch is responsible for recognizing the superclasses defined by a specific label structure.

Our main contributions are summarized in three folds: 1) We find that integrating multiple label structures can further improve the performance of hierarchical classification, and propose a MMF model to combine different hierarchical label structures. 2) Further, various architectures of our MMF model are explored for better classification. 3) We adjust the hierarchical evaluation metrics for multiple label structures. Experimental results on CIFAR100 and Car196 are better than traditional flat classifiers and hierarchical classifiers with any single label structure.

2 Related Work

2.1 Hierarchical Classification

The traditional methods decompose the hierarchical classification task into several subtasks and train a subclass classifier for each superclass node independently [3,9,13,29]. However, this strategy is memory-consuming and computing expensive for storing and training many subclass classifiers. Therefore, these methods are not suitable for deep learning. For deep hierarchical classification, Frome *et al.* [12] constructs a deep visual-semantic model by re-training the lower layers of the pre-trained visual network to predict the vector representation of the image label text in the hierarchical label structure learned by the language model. Barz & Denzler [2] design an algorithm to map the labels into a unit hypersphere where the cosine distances between different labels are equal to the distance in the hierarchical label structure.

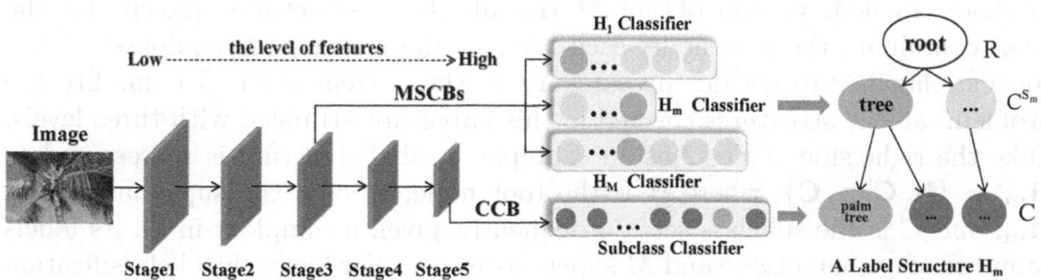

Fig. 2. The architecture of our MMF model with a five-stage CNN.

Besides the implicit label embedding, many researchers want to explicitly model the hierarchical label structure. Wu *et al.* [36] adds one fully connected softmax layer for each layer in the hierarchy to make the network recognize both the superclasses and the subclasses. But in this work, the relations between the superclasses and subclasses are underutilized. Bertinetto *et al.* [4] adds a weight matrix between the superclass classifier and the subclass classifier, thus, predictions of the superclass can be propagated to and affect the predictions of the subclass through the weight matrix. Ahmed *et al.* [1] trains a network to provide superclasses information and common knowledge through shared features to a set of expert networks, each of which devoted to recognizing the subclasses of a specific superclass. Therefore, the multi-task framework has been proved efficient for hierarchical classification.

2.2 Multiple Label Structures Fusion

As we have mentioned, different label structures provide different priori knowledge for hierarchical classification, thus, integrating these structures can further improve the performance. Wang *et al.* [33] constructs a classifier for each label structure, and the prediction of a test sample is obtained by integrating the results of multiple classifiers. This idea is simple and efficient, but in the deep learning scenario, it is memory-consuming and computationally redundant to design a neural network for each label structure. Instead of training multiple subclass classifiers, Zhao *et al.* [43] fuses multiple category similarities defined by different label structures in the kernel space, then trains one kernel SVM classifier. Inspired by this idea, we propose a multi-task multi-structure framework to make the superclasses from different label structures instruct the subclass recognition by encouraging the learned features to satisfy the multiple similarity constraints in different label structures.

3 Method

3.1 Problem Definition

Given an image dataset $\mathbf{D}$ with N classes, after M label structure construction methods applied, we can obtain M tree-like label structures. Except for the layer containing the root node, each layer in the structure is equipped with a specific classifier to decide the category in the current layer. To simplify the problem, all the structures covered in this paper are arranged with three levels. Take the right side of Fig. 2 as an example, a label structure is represented as $\mathbf{H_m} = \{\mathbf{R}, \mathbf{C^{S_m}}, \mathbf{C}\}$, where $\mathbf{R}$ is the root node, $\mathbf{C^{S_m}}$ is the superclass set in $\mathbf{H_m}$, and $\mathbf{C}$ is the subclass set. Consequently, given a sample x in $\mathbf{D}$, its labels compose of one subclass c and M superclasses c^{s_m}. For hierarchical classification with multiple label structures, all these superclasses should be predicted.

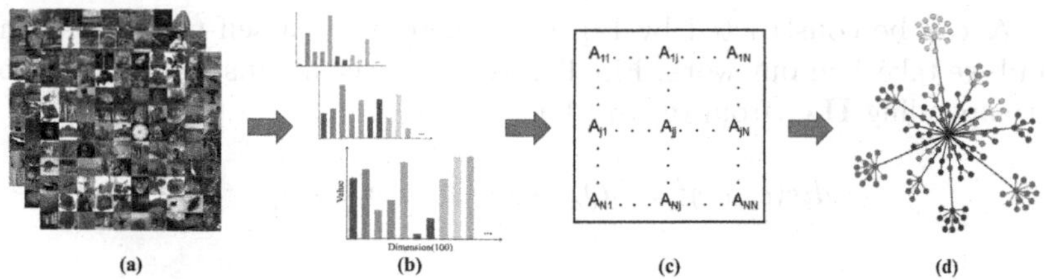

Fig. 3. The construction of $\mathbf{H_A}$ on CIFAR100. (a) Samples from CIFAR100 dataset. (b) Feature representations devided from 100 classes in images. (c) The affinity matrix obtained from the features. (d) $\mathbf{H_A}$ with 30 superclasses after spectral clustering.

3.2 Multi-task Multi-structure Fusion Framework

Assumed that multiple label structures have been obtained, the MMF model can be constructed, which includes two kinds of classification branches: CCB is a classification branch with a traditional classifier to identify the subclass, while MSCBs are several classifiers for the superclass identification. Figure 2 shows an overview of our model. All MSCBs work in parallel to encourage the features derived from the network to meet various similarity constraints in different label structures, guiding CCB to make more accurate predictions.

MSCBs The MSCBs contains multiple superclass classifiers. As shown in Fig. 2, the "$\mathbf{H_m}$ classifier" in MSCBs completes its task based on the label structure $\mathbf{H_m}$. As the superclasses are more generic than the subclasses (e.g., medium mammals and porcupine in Fig. 1(c)), and the high-level features usually contain more details to discriminate the subclasses, MSCBs should be inserted in the early stages. We will explore the influence of various network stages to attach the MSCBs in the following experiments.

3.3 Multiple Label Structures

For a dataset $\mathbf{D}$, we introduce two kinds of $\mathbf{H_m}$ to construct our MMF model: the semantic label structure $\mathbf{H_S}$ and the visual label structure $\mathbf{H_A}$ based on the affinity matrix.

$\mathbf{H_S}$ Usually, a semantic structure is adopted to organize the data. Take CIFAR100 as an example: there is a three-level semantic hierarchical label structure (one root node, 20 superclasses, and 100 subclasses) in the dataset (like $\mathbf{H_m}$ in Fig. 2). We adopt this semantic structure $\mathbf{H_S}$ inherent in the datasets in our paper.

$\mathbf{H_A}$ We construct a visual label structure based on the affinity matrix through two stages as shown in Fig. 3: feature extraction and label structure construction. For feature extraction (from (a) to (b)), we use a pre-trained VGG16 to extract features. Then, for label structure construction, we adopt sample pairwise distance to calculate the similarity between any two categories (from (b) to (c)), and simplify the calculation with [29] by Eq. (1), where c_i is the i-th class, and Q_{c_i}, σ_{c_i} are the mean and variance of features in c_i. Then the affinity matrix $\mathbf{A}$ can be constructed by Eq. (2), where δ_{ij} is a self-tuning parameter [30], and we take 1 in our work. Finally, we use spectral clustering [24] to build the corresponding $\mathbf{H_A}$ (from (c) to (d)).

$$dis(c_i, c_j)^2 = \left\|Q_{c_i} - Q_{c_j}\right\|^2 + \sigma_{c_i}^2 + \sigma_{c_j}^2. \tag{1}$$

$$A_{ij} = \exp(-\frac{dis(c_i, c_j)}{\delta_{ij}}). \tag{2}$$

3.4 Hierarchical Measures

As it is a multi-structure fusion work, we add the hierarchical information to the evaluation measures, and consider the similarity between the predicted class and the ground truth, *i.e.*, the severity of the classifier's mistakes. However, the existing evaluation measures [42] such as hierarchical F_1-measure (F_H), the tree induced loss (TIE) and the lowest common ancestor (LCA) of the prediction and the ground truth, are designed for a single label structure. Therefore, we adjust the above three measures to fit our method.

$\mathbf{F_{Ha}}$ The traditional precision P and recall R rate are extended to the hierarchical precision P_H and recall R_H rate, which can well measure the severity of mistakes, as the error in the superclasses is more serious than that in the subclasses. As our MMF deals with multiple label structures, we take the average of all P_H and R_H in each label structure. F_{Ha} is calculated from P_{Ha} and R_{Ha}:

$$P_{Ha} = \frac{1}{M}\sum_{m=1}^{M}\frac{\left|\hat{C_{aug}^m} \cap C_{aug}^m\right|}{\left|\hat{C_{aug}^m}\right|}, \; R_{Ha} = \frac{1}{M}\sum_{m=1}^{M}\frac{\left|\hat{C_{aug}^m} \cap C_{aug}^m\right|}{\left|C_{aug}^m\right|}, \tag{3}$$

$$F_{Ha} = \frac{2 \cdot P_{Ha} \cdot R_{Ha}}{P_{Ha} + R_{Ha}}, \tag{4}$$

where M is the number of the label structures, $\hat{C_{aug}^m}$ is the predicted extension set which contains the class nodes on the path from the root class to the predict subclass in $\mathbf{H_m}$, C_{aug}^m is the real extension set which contains the class nodes on the path from the root class to the real subclass in $\mathbf{H_m}$, and $|\cdot|$ is an operator to calculate the number of the elements.

$\mathbf{TIE_a}$ In the tree structure, the total number of edges from the predicted node to the real node along a specific label structure is represented as TIE distance. To deal with multiple label structures, we introduce TIE_a to average all the TIE distances in each label structure by Eq. (5), where $|Edge_m(c, \hat{c})|$ is the number of edges from the predicted node $\hat{c}$ to the real node c in $\mathbf{H_m}$. Accordingly, the smaller the TIE_a, the more similar the predicted class is to the real class.

$$TIE_a = \frac{1}{M} \sum_{m=1}^{M} |Edge_m(c, \hat{c})| \, . \tag{5}$$

$\mathbf{LCA_a}$ We modified the LCA height to the mean value of all LCA heights in each label structure to obtain LCA_a by Eq. (6), where $Height_m(c, \hat{c})$ is the lowest common ancestor height between the predicted node $\hat{c}$ and the real node c in $\mathbf{H_m}$. A smaller LCA_a means a smaller classification error.

$$LCA_a = \frac{1}{M} \sum_{m=1}^{M} Height_m(c, \hat{c}). \tag{6}$$

3.5 Traing and Inference

The multi-task loss for MMF model contains a CCB loss and several MSCBs losses denoted by Eq. (7), where $\phi(x;\theta)$ is a classification network, the parameter θ is learned by minimizing our loss function. $\hat{c}$, $c^{\hat{s}_m}$ are the predicted subclass and superclass, c, c^{s_m} are the ground truth of subclass and superclass in $\mathbf{H_m}$ respectively. λ_m is the constraint intensity of "$\mathbf{H_m}$ classifier", and $\lambda = \sum_{m=1}^{M} \lambda_m$. We use the standard cross entropy loss to compute L_{CCB} and L_{H_m}.

$$\mathcal{L}(\phi(x, \theta), c, \mathbf{C^S}) = (1 - \lambda) * L_{CCB}(\hat{c}, c) + \sum_{m=1}^{M} \lambda_m * L_{H_m}(c^{\hat{s}_m}, c^{s_m}). \tag{7}$$

When training, samples with different hierarchical label structures are input into the framework for multiple rounds of iterative training. MSCBs impose constraints on the network through the multi-task loss, affecting the prediction of subclasses. When it comes to inference, the final predicted result of subclass is decided by CCB only.

4 Experiments

4.1 Experimental Settings

Datasets. We conduct experiments on two benchmark datasets CIFAR100 and Car196. In CIFAR100, there is a total number of 100 categories belonging to 20 semantic superclasses on average. Car196 is a fine-grained dataset containing 196 subclasses from three different kinds of semantic superclasses "Make" (49 categories), "Type"(18 categories), and "Year". We choose "Make" and "Type" as the semantic label structures because "Year" is not discriminative. We also construct a three-level $\mathbf{H_A}$ for each dataset.

Backbones. The backbones of our network are VGG16 [31] and ResNet50 [32] trained from scratch. Note that there are five stages in both backbones.

Evaluation Metrics. Four evaluation metrics are considered in our work to fully analyze the classifiers' results. Besides the flat measure top-1 accuracy (Acc), we also adopt three hierarchical measures proposed before to better evaluate the performance of the classifiers.

Table 1. The subclass performance with different $\mathbf{H_A}$.

Dataset	Num_{super}	VGG16				ResNet50			
		Acc(↑)	F_{Ha}(↑)	TIE_a(↓)	LCA_a(↓)	Acc(↑)	F_{Ha}(↑)	TIE_a(↓)	LCA_a(↓)
CIFAR100	18	72.67	**84.15**	**0.9509**	**0.4754**	79.20	**88.12**	**0.7130**	**0.3565**
	20	72.51	84.07	0.9558	0.4779	79.01	88.04	0.7176	0.3588
	25	72.46	83.78	0.9733	0.4867	79.13	87.93	0.7240	0.3620
	30	**72.95**	84.04	0.9574	0.4787	**79.21**	87.91	0.7252	0.3626
Car196	15	**82.67**	**91.70**	**0.4979**	**0.2490**	**90.19**	**95.44**	**0.2738**	**0.1369**
	18	81.04	90.87	0.5478	0.2739	89.17	95.06	0.2963	0.1482
	20	82.42	91.47	0.5116	0.2558	89.69	95.22	0.2865	0.1433
	30	79.58	89.38	0.6370	0.3185	89.06	94.47	0.3321	0.1660
	40	79.09	88.66	0.6804	0.3402	89.26	94.33	0.3402	0.1701
	50	79.76	89.05	0.6569	0.3285	89.67	94.50	0.3297	0.1649

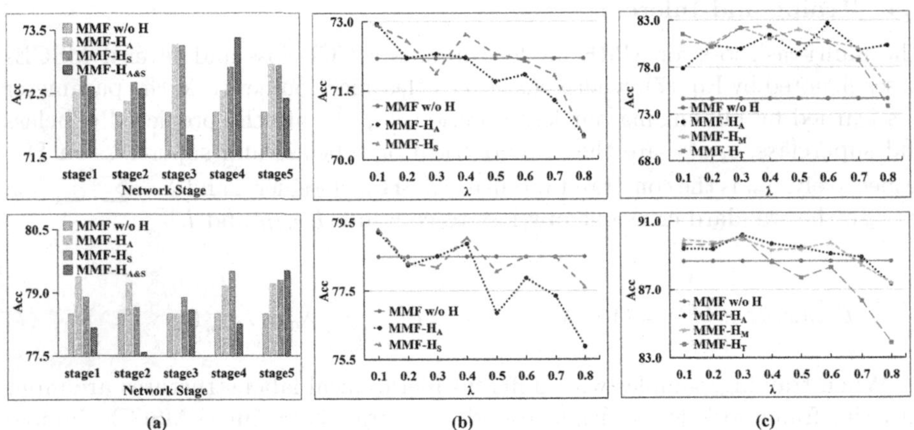

Fig. 4. (a) MSCBs attached in different stages on CIFAR100. (b) and (c) are the constraint intensities of MSCBs on CIFAR100 and Car196 respectively. Note that results in the first row are for VGG16, and the second are for ResNet50.

4.2 Ablation Study

The impact of $\mathbf{H_A}$, the network stages to attach MSCBs, and the constraint intensity λ on the model's performance is explored in the following ablation experiments. Note that all the ablation studies are adapted both VGG16 and ResNet50 backbone on CIFAR100 and Car196, in order to show the generalization of our model.

$\mathbf{H_A}$s As $\mathbf{H_A}$ is three-level, the number of superclasses decides its structure. To obtain a suitable number of superclasses, we perform a series of ablation experiments on our MMF model with a singe label structure $\mathbf{H_A}$. Referring to the number of superclasses in $\mathbf{H_S}$, We vary the number of $\mathbf{H_A}$'s superclasses in [18, 20, 25, 30] for CIFAR100 , and [15, 18, 20, 30, 40, 50] for Car196. According to the results of Table 1, we select the $\mathbf{H_A}$ with 30 superclasses for CIFAR100, and 15 for Car196.

Table 2. The subclass performance of VGG16.

Dataset	Method	Structure	Num_{class}	λ	Acc(↑)	F_{Ha}(↑)	TIE_a(↓)	LCA_a(↓)
CIFAR100	Greedy [3,17]	$\mathbf{H_S}$	100/20	–	70.09	81.98	1.0811	0.5405
	NBPath [29]	$\mathbf{H_S}$	100/20	–	70.49	82.23	1.0664	0.5332
	MMF	w/o **H**	100	–	72.20	83.35	0.9991	0.4995
		$\mathbf{H_A}$	100/30	0.1	73.27	**84.97**	**0.9015**	**0.4507**
		$\mathbf{H_S}$	100/20	0.1	73.25	84.70	0.9179	0.4590
		$\mathbf{H_{A\&S}}$	100/30/20	0.15	**73.37**	84.79	0.9127	0.4563
Car196	Greedy [3,17]	$\mathbf{H_T}$	196/18	–	51.45	73.89	1.5663	0.7832
		$\mathbf{H_M}$	196/49	–	54.05	75.40	1.4763	0.7381
	NBPath [29]	$\mathbf{H_T}$	196/18	–	52.99	74.71	1.5172	0.7586
		$\mathbf{H_M}$	196/49	–	55.30	76.05	1.4373	0.7186
	MMF	w/o **H**	196	–	74.63	87.88	0.7273	0.3637
		$\mathbf{H_A}$	196/15	0.6	82.67	91.70	0.4979	0.2490
		$\mathbf{H_T}$	196/18	0.4	82.35	91.34	0.5344	0.2672
		$\mathbf{H_M}$	196/49	0.3	82.24	91.89	0.4864	0.2432
		$\mathbf{H_{A\&T}}$	196/15/18	0.3	82.67	92.23	0.4661	0.2330
		$\mathbf{H_{A\&M}}$	196/15/49	0.3	81.62	91.77	0.4938	0.2469
		$\mathbf{H_{T\&M}}$	196/18/49	0.2	80.69	91.44	0.5134	0.2567
		$\mathbf{H_{A\&T\&M}}$	196/15/18/49	0.2	**83.67**	**92.88**	**0.4274**	**0.2137**

MSCBs. An important thing for our MMF model is where to insert the classifiers for superclasses. We explore it with $\mathbf{H_A}$, $\mathbf{H_S}$ and multiple structures $\mathbf{H_{A\&S}}$ on CIFAR100, and the results with $\lambda = 0.2$ are shown in Fig. 4(a). One interesting phenomenon can be observed in the both backbones: adding the superclass classifiers in the early stages is more effective. The reason may be that the low-level features are more generic and lose details of the high-level features for subclasses identification. So in the experiments, we insert MSCBs in the early stages to make our MMF model firstly grasp general concepts, then the CCB captures details in each concept to discriminate subclasses.
λ: We fix MSCBs on the stage where the best performance is achieved, then vary λ in [0.1, 0.8]. In Fig. 4(b) and (c), experimental results on the subclasses show that different Acc obtained by adjusting λ. With a larger λ ($\lambda \geq 0.1$), the performance on the subclasses is worse than the MMF w/o **H**. And it's not weird that results of different label structures don't coincide exactly because they have different similarity constraints, corresponding to different constraint strengths. In the following experiments with a single label structure, we set λ with the best performance. And for multiple label structures, λ_m is set to the same values for the sake of making these label structures act equally, varying within the range of the λ which achieved the best results in the single label structures.

4.3 Experimental Results and Analyses

Our deep MMF model with different single label structures and their combinations is compared with two methods based on the top-down strategy. For the top-down methods, we choose two methods which are based on the greedy selection at each hierarchy (Greedy) [3,17] and the N-Best Path (NBPath) [29]. To

Table 3. The subclass performance of ResNet50.

Dataset	Method	Structure	Num_{class}	λ	Acc(↑)	F_{Ha}(↑)	TIE_a(↓)	LCA_a(↓)
CIFAR100	Greedy [3,17]	$\mathbf{H_S}$	100/20	–	76.22	85.68	0.8594	0.4297
	NBPath [29]	$\mathbf{H_S}$	100/20	–	76.44	85.78	0.8535	0.4267
	MMF	w/o **H**	100	–	78.50	87.22	0.7668	0.3834
		$\mathbf{H_A}$	100/30	0.1	79.38	88.14	0.7114	0.3557
		$\mathbf{H_S}$	100/20	0.1	79.51	88.28	0.7034	0.3517
		$\mathbf{H_{A\&S}}$	100/30/20	0.15	**79.52**	**88.28**	**0.7029**	**0.3514**
Car196	Greedy [3,17]	$\mathbf{H_T}$	196/18	–	86.80	93.30	0.4022	0.2011
		$\mathbf{H_M}$	196/49	–	87.30	93.57	0.3855	0.1928
	NBPath [29]	$\mathbf{H_T}$	196/18	–	87.40	93.63	0.3823	0.1911
		$\mathbf{H_M}$	196/49	–	87.69	93.78	0.3732	0.1866
	MMF	w/o **H**	196	–	88.66	94.84	0.3097	0.1548
		$\mathbf{H_A}$	196/15	0.3	90.19	95.44	0.2738	0.1369
		$\mathbf{H_T}$	196/18	0.3	90.10	95.44	0.2736	0.1368
		$\mathbf{H_M}$	196/49	0.3	89.92	95.59	0.2645	0.1322
		$\mathbf{H_{A\&T}}$	196/15/18	0.1	90.20	95.72	0.2567	0.1283
		$\mathbf{H_{A\&M}}$	196/15/49	0.1	89.45	95.41	0.2756	0.1378
		$\mathbf{H_{T\&M}}$	196/18/49	0.2/0.1	**90.42**	**95.89**	**0.2468**	**0.1234**
		$\mathbf{H_{A\&T\&M}}$	196/15/18/49	0.05	90.29	95.87	0.2477	0.1239

improve the performance, we adopt features extracted from a carefully fine-tuned VGG16 or ResNet50, which is the backbone in our MMF model. Then kernel SVMs are employed as the classifiers at each hierarchy. For our MMF model, we adopt different label structures as shown in Table 2 and Tabel 3. "w/o **H**" means MMF model without any hierarchical structures, which is a traditional classification network contains a backbone and a classifier for subclass classification. "$\mathbf{H_T}$" and "$\mathbf{H_M}$" are the semantic structures based on "Type" and "Make" respectively, and "$\mathbf{H_{A\&S}}$" (i.e., $\mathbf{H_A}$ and $\mathbf{H_S}$) *etc.* are multiple label structures.

Table 2 and Table 3 show the results of VGG16 and ResNet50 on CIFAR100 and Car196, respectively. Note that in the multi-structure models, the performance of the subclass classifiers achieves the best performance when the λ_m for different structures is equal, except for $\mathbf{H_{T\&M}}$ in ResNet50. It can be concluded that: 1) For the subclass classifier performance, our MMF model with a single structure is better than the top-down methods with a considerable margin, which verifies the efficiency of the end-to-end training. 2) Besides, MMF with any single structure achieves better performance than "w/o **H**", indicating the benefit of the superclass classifiers. 3) Furthermore, MMF with multiple label structures performs better than any single one, which confirms our assumption that multiple label structures can provide richer similarity constraints to improve the performance of the subclass classifier. 4) The gain in hierarchical evaluation metrics is more obvious than the flat measure Acc, indicating that predictions in our MMF model are more closer to the ground truth (i.e., a less serious mistake).

5 Conclusion

In this paper, we have constructed a multi-task multi-structure fusion model for hierarchical classification. Various factors have been explored, such as different label structures based on the affinity matrix, the stages to attach the superclass classifiers, and theconstraint intensities. Besides, the hierarchical evaluation metrics have been adjusted to fit the classification with multiple label structures. The experimental results demonstrate that different label structures provide various prior knowledge for the subclass classifier. Meanwhile, integrating these multiple label structures can achieve better results.

In this work, relations of the subclass and its superclasses are impplicitly modeled by the weighted multi-task loss function. In the future, we will explore more direct ways to utilize multiple label structures.

References

1. Ahmed, K., Baig, M.H., Torresani, L.: Network of experts for large-scale image categorization. In: ECCV, pp. 516–532 (2016)
2. Barz, B., Denzler, J.: Hierarchy-based image embeddings for semantic image retrieval. In: WACV, pp. 638–647 (2019)
3. Bengio, S., Weston, J., Grangier, D.: Label embedding trees for large multi-class tasks. In: NIPS, pp. 163–171 (2010)
4. Bertinetto, L., Müller, R., Tertikas, K., Samangooei, S., Lord, N.A.: Making better mistakes: leveraging class hierarchies with deep networks. CoRR abs/1912.09393 (2019)
5. Chen, Y., Wang, W., Zhou, Y., Yang, F., Yang, D., Wang, W.: Self-training for domain adaptive scene text detection. In: ICPR, pp. 850–857 (2020)
6. Chen, Y., Zhou, Yu., Yang, D., Wang, W.: Constrained relation network for character detection in scene images. In: Nayak, A.C., Sharma, A. (eds.) PRICAI 2019. LNCS (LNAI), vol. 11672, pp. 137–149. Springer, Cham (2019). https://doi.org/10.1007/978-3-030-29894-4_11
7. Deng, J., Dong, W., Socher, R., Li, L., Li, K., Li, F.: ImageNet: a large-scale hierarchical image database. In: CVPR (2009)
8. Deng, J., Krause, J., Berg, A.C., Li, F.: Hedging your bets: optimizing accuracy-specificity trade-offs in large scale visual recognition. In: CVPR (2012)
9. Deng, J., Satheesh, S., Berg, A.C., Li, F.: Fast and balanced: efficient label tree learning for large scale object recognition. In: NIPS, pp. 567–575 (2011)
10. Devries, T., Taylor, G.W.: Improved regularization of convolutional neural networks with cutout. CoRR abs/1708.04552 (2017)
11. Fan, J., Zhou, N., Peng, J., Gao, L.: Hierarchical learning of tree classifiers for large-scale plant species identification. TIP **24**(11), 4172–4184 (2015)
12. Frome, A., et al.: DeViSE: a deep visual-semantic embedding model. In: NIPS, pp. 2121–2129 (2013)
13. Griffin, G., Perona, P.: Learning and using taxonomies for fast visual categorization. In: CVPR (2008)
14. Guillaumin, M., Ferrari, V.: Large-scale knowledge transfer for object localization in ImageNet. In: CVPR (2012)

15. Krause, J., Stark, M., Deng, J., Fei-Fei, L.: 3D object representations for fine-grained categorization. In: ICCV Workshops, pp. 554–561 (2013)
16. Lei, H., Mei, K., Zheng, N., Dong, P., Zhou, N., Fan, J.: Learning group-based dictionaries for discriminative image representation. Pattern Recognit. **47**(2), 899–913 (2014)
17. Li, S., Liu, Z., Chan, A.B.: Heterogeneous multi-task learning for human pose estimation with deep convolutional neural network. In: CVPR Workshops, pp. 488–495 (2014)
18. Lin, D.: WordNet: an electronic lexical database. CL **25**(2), 292–296 (1999)
19. Liu, B., Sadeghi, F., Tappen, M.F., Shamir, O., Liu, C.: Probabilistic label trees for efficient large scale image classification. In: CVPR (2013)
20. Liu, Y., Dou, Y., Jin, R., Li, R.: Visual confusion label tree for image classification. CoRR abs/1906.02012 (2019)
21. Liu, Y., Dou, Y., Jin, R., Qiao, P.: Visual tree convolutional neural network in image classification. CoRR abs/1906.01536 (2019)
22. Luo, D., Fang, B., Zhou, Y., Zhou, Y., Wu, D., Wang, W.: Exploring relations in untrimmed videos for self-supervised learning. CoRR abs/2008.02711 (2020)
23. Luo, D., et al.: Video cloze procedure for self-supervised spatio-temporal learning. In: AAAI, pp. 11701–11708 (2020)
24. Ng, A.Y., Jordan, M.I., Weiss, Y.: On spectral clustering: analysis and an algorithm. In: NIPS, pp. 849–856 (2001)
25. Qiao, Z., Qin, X., Zhou, Y., Yang, F., Wang, W.: Gaussian constrained attention network for scene text recognition. In: ICPR, pp. 3328–3335 (2020)
26. Qiao, Z., Zhou, Y., Yang, D., Zhou, Y., Wang, W.: SEED: semantics enhanced encoder-decoder framework for scene text recognition. In: CVPR, pp. 13525–13534 (2020)
27. Qin, X., Zhou, Y., Wu, D., Yue, Y., Wang, W.: FC2RN: a fully convolutional corner refinement network for accurate multi-oriented scene text detection. CoRR abs/2007.05113 (2020)
28. Qin, X., Zhou, Y., Yang, D., Wang, W.: Curved text detection in natural scene images with semi- and weakly-supervised learning. In: ICDAR, pp. 559–564 (2019)
29. Qu, Y., et al.: Joint hierarchical category structure learning and large-scale image classification. TIP **26**(9), 4331–4346 (2017)
30. Qu, Y., Wu, S., Liu, H., Xie, Y., Wang, H.: Evaluation of local features and classifiers in BOW model for image classification. Multimedia Tools Appl. **70**(2), 605–624 (2012). https://doi.org/10.1007/s11042-012-1107-z
31. Simonyan, K., Zisserman, A.: Very deep convolutional networks for large-scale image recognition. In: ICLR (2015)
32. Verma, A., Qassim, H., Feinzimer, D.: Residual squeeze CNDS deep learning CNN model for very large scale places image recognition. In: UEMCON, pp. 463–469 (2017)
33. Wang, Y., Forsyth, D.A.: Large multi-class image categorization with ensembles of label trees. In: ICME, pp. 1–6 (2013)
34. Wang, Y.: Deep fuzzy tree for large-scale hierarchical visual classification. ITFS **28**(7), 1395–1406 (2020)
35. Wang, Y., Wang, Z., Hu, Q., Zhou, Y., Su, H.: Hierarchical semantic risk minimization for large-scale classification. ITC (2021)
36. Wu, H., Merler, M., Uceda-Sosa, R., Smith, J.R.: Learning to make better mistakes: semantics-aware visual food recognition. In: ACM MM, pp. 172–176 (2016)

37. Yang, D., Zhou, Y., Wu, D., Ma, C., Yang, F., Wang, W.: Two-level residual distillation based triple network for incremental object detection. CoRR abs/2007.13428 (2020)
38. Yao, Y., Liu, C., Luo, D., Zhou, Y., Ye, Q.: Video playback rate perception for self-supervised spatio-temporal representation learning. In: CVPR, pp. 6547–6556 (2020)
39. Zhang, Y., Liu, C., Zhou, Y., Wang, W., Wang, W., Ye, Q.: Progressive cluster purification for unsupervised feature learning. In: ICPR, pp. 8476–8483 (2020)
40. Zhang, Y., Zhou, Y., Wang, W.: Exploring instance relations for unsupervised feature embedding. CoRR abs/2105.03341 (2021)
41. Zhao, B., Li, F., Xing, E.P.: Large-scale category structure aware image categorization. In: NIPS, pp. 1251–1259 (2011)
42. Zhao, H., Hu, Q., Zhu, P., Wang, Y., Wang, P.: A recursive regularization based feature selection framework for hierarchical classification. ITKDA (2020)
43. Zhao, S., Zou, Q.: Fusing multiple hierarchies for semantic hierarchical classification. IJMLC **6**(1), 47 (2016)

GLUNet: Global-Local Fusion U-Net for 2D Medical Image Segmentation

Ning Wang and Hongyan Quan(✉)

School of Computer Science and Technology, East China Normal University, Shanghai, China
51184501052@stu.ecnu.edu.cn, hyquan@cs.ecnu.edu.cn

Abstract. Medical image segmentation is a fundamental technology for computer-aided diagnosis and clinical disease monitoring. Most of existing deep learning-based methods solely focus on the region and position of objects without considering edge information which provides accurate contour of objects and is beneficial to medical image segmentation. In this paper, we propose a novel Global-Local fusion UNet model (GLUNet) to address above problem, which contains a Global Attention Module (GAM) and a Local Edge Detection Module (LEDM). In GAM, we embed residual block and convolution block attention module to capture contextual and spatial information of objects. Meanwhile, to obtain accurate edge information of objects in medical image segmentation, we devise the LEDM to integrate edge information into our model. We also propose a multi-task loss function that combines the segmentation loss and the edge loss together to train our GLUNet. Experimental results demonstrate that our proposed method outperforms the original U-Net method and other state-of-the-art methods for lung segmentation in Computed Tomography (CT) images, cell/nuclei segmentation and vessel segmentation in retinal images.

Keywords: Medical image segmentation · Neural networks · Attention mechanism · Edge detection · Multi-task learning

1 Introduction

Medical image segmentation is a vastly significant task for quantitative disease diagnosis, pathology assessment and treatment planning, which is closely related to clinical applications. Nevertheless, automatic or semi-automatic segmentation of object regions from medical images is a challenging assignment due to the high complexity of medical images, the vast difference of object regions and the lack of simple and effective linear information.

With the wide application of convolutional neural network (CNN) [8], deep learning-based methods [12,20,25] are proposed for medical image segmentation and achieve superior performance. But these methods only utilize the abstract information of the multi-scale feature maps without considering the different contributions between high-level and low-level features. Recently, massive studies

I. Farkaš et al. (Eds.): ICANN 2021, LNCS 12894, pp. 74–85, 2021.
https://doi.org/10.1007/978-3-030-86380-7_7

[5,10,13,17] have shown that attention mechanism augments the global attention capability of the model and can obtain detailed information about medical images while suppressing irrelevant information. Attention Gate (AG) for spatial attention is proposed in [10] and an image-grid based gate that makes the coefficient of attention specific to the target region is introduced. In [13], the self-supervised approach utilizes regularization constraints to generate semantically meaningful segmented maps. However, these methods solely focus on the global region and shape representation, which leads to discontinuous boundary and blurred details of segmented organs. Some methods including [16,21,24] introduce edge detection into their proposed model, which can extract the local contour feature of the object and refine the shape feature in theory.

In this paper, we combine the benefits of these models mentioned above and propose a novel method to aggregate dense pixel information and refine the global shape features. Specifically, we apply a U-like architecture as our backbone network, and augment it with attention mechanism and edge detection strategy to consider global region information and local edge information together.

The contributions of this paper are listed as follows: (1) We propose a global-local fusion U-Net to learn representation effectively. (2) To highlight the global features, we introduce the attention mechanism and residual block to make our model focus on the target region and position information. We also utilize an edge detection module to optimize the encoder of our model and assist in learning local edge features. (3) The experimental results demonstrate that our proposed GLU-Net outperforms other state-of-the-art methods on three benchmark datasets.

2 Related Work

With the emergence of the Full Convolutional Network (FCN) [14], many methods [10–13,18,24,25] have been studied for medical image segmentation. U-Net [12] is one of the encoder-decoder models based on FCN, which is composed of a contracting path and an expanding path, and the two paths are symmetric to each other. Specially, through skip connection, the different features in the contracting path and the expanding path are combined, which can help U-Net achieve high accuracy in segmentation. U-Net++ [25] propose nested dense skip connections to further narrow the semantic gap between the feature mapping of encoder and decoder.

When human vision captures an image, it obtains abundant information from the relevant areas and suppresses other irrelevant information [6]. Attention mechanism simulates human visual architecture that has been widely used in various fields, such as image processing, natural language processing or speech recognition. Attention U-Net [10] and CA-Net [5] apply attention mechanism to improve the sensitivity and accuracy of models. They suppress feature activation in irrelevant regions and realize high segmentation accuracy without additional location modules. Woo et al. [17] propose the attention mechanism of the convolution module, CBAM, where the attention maps are added to the input features for adaptive feature refinement through two independent channel and spatial dimensions. Guo et al. [19] integrate squeeze and excitation blocks into U-Net deformation network and achieve successful performance in medical image segmentation.

Edge detection methods [16,21,23,24] are gradually applied to image segmentation. Determining and extracting the image edge information is greatly important for recognizing and understanding the whole image scene. For example, Deeptour [16] proves that the features learned from CNN can improve the accuracy of edge detection. To learn more distinguishable features, Deeptour also proposes a positive-sharing loss function. To utilize the correlation between encoder and decoder, Dense R2UNet [4] introduces residual network and dense convolutional network to improve the segmentation performance. Furthermore, SUD-GAN [18] and M-GAN [11] respectively propose deep convolutional adversarial network with deep residual blocks or dense blocks to conduct accurate and precise vessel segmentation.

3 Proposed Method

Figure 1 illuminates the architecture of our proposed **G**lobal-**L**ocal fusion **U**-Net (GLUNet) which is mainly composed of two modules – a Global Attention Module (GAM) and a Local Edge Detection Module (LEDM). The overall backbone of GLUNet is similar to U-Net which is an encoder-decoder structure responsible for feature extraction and up-sampling respectively, and features are augmented by the skip connections at each resolution level. The difference between our model and U-Net is that the encoder of our GLUNet is replaced with dense blocks from DenseNet-121 [7]. Specifically, in our GLUNet, we embed the GAM in each skip connection to obtain the global region information of the object more accurately, which can extract dense pixel information and features from channel and spatial dimensions. Besides, we propose that on top of producing finer segmentation, LEDM encourages the model to learn object edge information. LEDM, explained in detail in Sect. 3.2, can supervise and optimize the encoder in the early stage, and fine-tune the image segmentation effect in the later stage.

3.1 Global Attention Module

U-Net fuses feature maps output by the encoder with the feature maps of lower decoder that capture more spatial and contextual information. Naturally, we would like to focus more on extracting image feature maps in the process of image segmentation to decrease information redundancy. Woo et al. [17] propose the convolution block attention module (CBAM), which multiplies the attention map to the input feature map for adaptive feature refinement through two independent channel and spatial dimensions, so that it can focus on the object. Inspired by them, we propose a global attention module (GAM), as shown in Fig. 2, which is comprised of two residual blocks and CBAM after the feature maps extracted by the encoder.

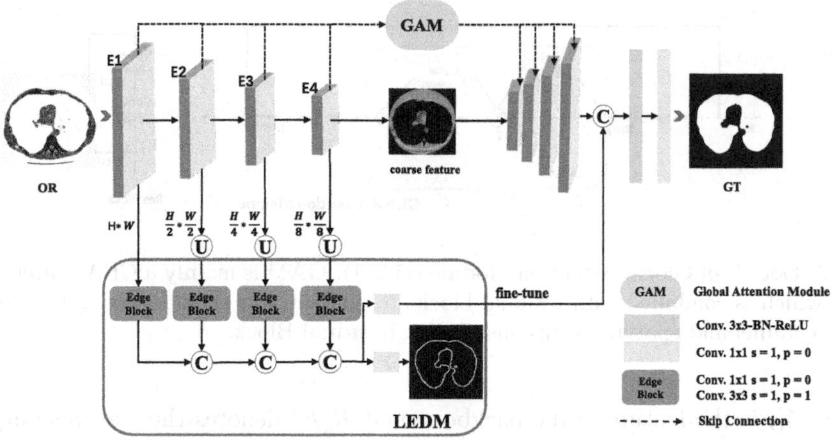

Fig. 1. Illustration of our proposed Global-Local fusion U-Net. The proposed architecture is composed of two main module - the Global Attention Module (GAM) that captures the global region information and the Local Edge Detection Module (LEDM) that learns local edge information. 'Conv.' represents the convolutional layer, while 'U' and 'C' represent the upsampling and concatenation, respectively.

CBAM is a lightweight module, including channel attention mechanism and complementary spatial attention mechanism, both of which use average-pooling and max-pooling. In the channel attention module, the feature map F performs the global average-pooling and max-pooling along the spatial dimension, generating two channel descriptors: C_a' and C_m'. Both descriptors are then input to a shared network that is composed of multi-layer perceptron with one hidden layer to produce our channel attention map M_c. In the spatial attention module, $F' = M_c \otimes F$ also performs two pooling operations along the channel dimension, generating two 2D maps: C_a'' and C_m''. Those are then concatenated and convolved by a standard convolution layer, producing 2D spatial attention map M_s. In the two attention modules, M_c and M_s multiply with the original feature to obtain the new feature after scaling. On this basis, in order to prevent the loss of information in the feature extraction process, we add residual blocks before and after the CBAM. The residual block is composed of two normalized 3×3 convolutional layers with a skip connection, which is greatly easy to learn the identity function. It not only retains the original feature information, but also learns the more abstract feature information.

Given the input feature F, GAM feeds it into residual blocks and attention mechanism to capture feature maps M_c and M_s along channel and spatial dimensions respectively. In short, our GAM is calculated as follows:

$$A_G = R(R(F) \otimes M_c \otimes M_s), \tag{1}$$

$$A_{total} = F + A_G, \tag{2}$$

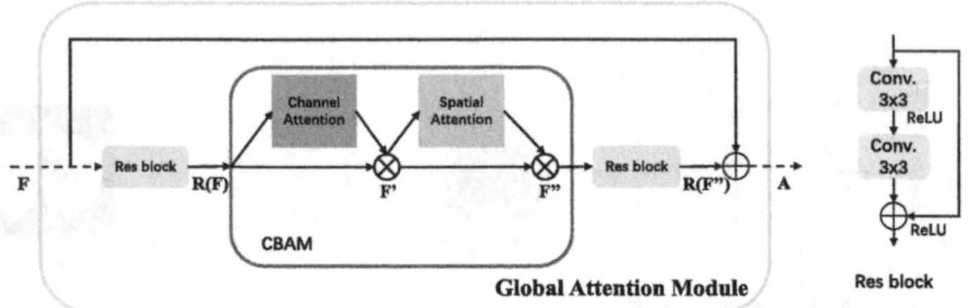

Fig. 2. Details of Glocal Attention Module (GAM). GAM is mainly a CBAM architecture, which is combined with residual blocks to extract abundant feature information along channel and spatial dimensions. Right: Residual Block.

where A_G is the feature of the backbone and $R(F)$ denotes the features output by the residual block. Operator $\otimes$ denotes element-wise multiplication.

3.2 Local Edge Detection Module

As stated in Sect. 3.1, GAM solely focuses on the object region information without considering the edge information which is beneficial to refining object edge. Hence, we devise a novel local edge detection module (LEDM) to capture local edge features. We embed the LEDM in each layer of the encoding path, as shown in Fig. 1. To our knowledge, lower-level features preserve more sufficient edge information than higher-level features. Therefore, in this module the feature weights of encoders decrease with the increase of layers, which means that the weights of earlier layers are relatively larger in the concatenation process. LEDM provides two main functions: First, it supervises and optimizes the early convolutional layers using loss functions. Furthermore, the output of LEDM refines the process of segmentation in the decoder.

As shown in Fig. 1, to ensure that the outputs of all encoder layers can be connected together, the outputs of other layers are upsampled to the same resolution as the outputs of E1 by '×2', '×4' and '×8'. After that, they are fed separately into the Edge Block which consists of $1\times1-3\times3$ convolutional layers and then concatenated together. Let $C_{1\times1}(x)$ and $C_{3\times3}(x)$ denote the normalized 1×1 and 3×3 convolution function applied on feature map x. Formally, denote the LEDM feature maps as L_k where k is the layer number in our LEDM. Then, L_k is computed as,

$$L_k = C_{3\times3}(C_{1\times1}(x)) + C_{3\times3}(C_{1\times1}(x\times2)), \tag{3}$$

where '×2' denotes that the scale factor of upsampling is 2. During concatenation, the weights of features of each edge block decrease as the number of block increases. The concatenated features flow to one of the following two branches: a 1×1 convolutional layer to predict the edge detection results for early supervision, or another 1×1 convolutional features to be conducive to the segmentation of GLUNet. In the latter branch, the output of LEDM is then concatenated with the decoder feature maps before the last normalized 3×3 convolution layer.

3.3 Multi-task Loss Function

Our proposed GLUNet adopts a multi-task learning framework with different loss functions to optimize image segmentation and edge detection. The $Lov\bar{a}sz-Softmax$ loss [3] is used in our LEDM, since it performs better than the common cross entropy loss [22] in image segmentation for the IoU index measure and class imbalanced problems. The loss can be formulated as:

$$loss(f) = \frac{1}{|C|}\sum_{c\in C}\overline{\Delta_{J_c}}(m(c)), \tag{4}$$

$$m_i(c) = \begin{cases} 1 - f_i(c) & if\ c = y_i^*, \\ f_i(c) & otherwise, \end{cases} \tag{5}$$

where C denotes the class number, i.e., 2. $f_i(c) \in [0,1]$ is the output score of class c, and $y_i^* \in \{-1,1\}$ is the ground truth label. $\overline{\Delta_{J_c}}$ is the $Lov\bar{a}sz$ extension of the Jaccard index [3].

Same as edge detection based on LEDM, our GAM also utilizes $Lov\bar{a}sz$ loss function. Thus, in GLUNet, our loss function is defined as:

$$L_{total} = \lambda L_{seg} + (1-\lambda)L_{edge}, \tag{6}$$

where L_{seg} and L_{edge} denote the loss of GAM and LEDM, respectively. λ is a hyperparameter, denoting the weight of the loss function.

4 Experiment

4.1 Datasets

To evaluate the robustness and accuracy of our model, we conduct experiments on three standard medical image datasets. Examples of these datasets are shown in Fig. 3 and the details are as follows.

Lung Segmentation in CT Images: The dataset [9] is from the Lung Nodules Analysis Competition, which contains 214 images for training and 53 images (size: 512 × 512) for testing. They are obtained by a 2D CT scan and manually labeled with a lung mask, and are used as the basis for diagnosing lung diseases.

The Nucleus Detection Challenge (DSB2018): The dataset [1] includes nuclear images under different conditions such as cell types, magnification and imaging modality, which is suitable to evaluate the performance of models. It contains 670 images (size: 256 × 256) for training and testing.

Vessel Segmentation in Retinal Images: The dataset [15] is a retinal vascular detection dataset. DRIVE [15], provides two kinds of manually annotated masks, one of which, according to our opinion, has little effect on the task of image segmentation. Therefore, we use the first mask data containing retinal blood vessels as the ground truth for performance evaluation. The dataset contains 20 images for training and 20 images (size: 565 × 584) for testing.

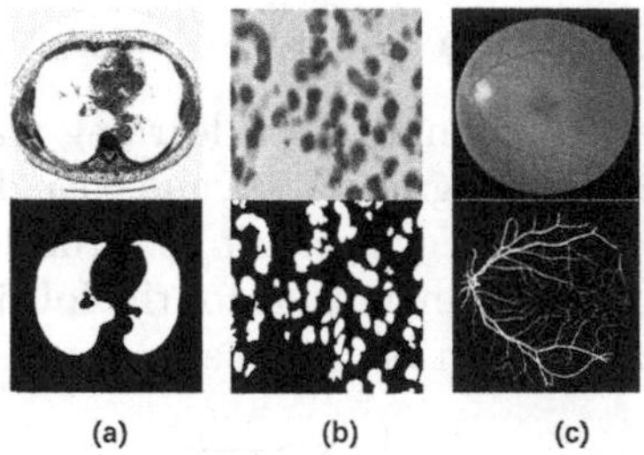

Fig. 3. Samples of three datasets. (a) Lung segmentation in CT images; (b) The Nucleus Detection Challenge; (c) Retinal Vessel Detection.

4.2 Data Processing and Implementation Details

In data processing, we resize all the input images of the three datasets to satisfy the requirements of models. In terms of data augmentation, we flip each image horizontally and vertically. Besides, we add Gaussian white noise with variances of 0.001 and 0.01 to the lung dataset and the nuclear dataset following MUNet [20]. We train our proposed GLUNet architecture from scratch on an NVIDIA GeForce GTX 1070 Ti in the experiments. The implementation is based on PyTorch (version 1.1.0), and our model is optimized with the Adam optimizer. The grid search method is adopted to select the optimal parameters of our model. According to the results, we set the learning rate as 0.0001, the batch size as 16 and the hyperparameter λ in loss function as 0.7. During training, we apply early stopping strategy. For each dataset, the network is trained for 150 epochs, after which the training loss tends to be stable. Under our experimental conditions, it takes 2.4 h to train the model once (150 epochs).

4.3 Evaluation of Our Method

Table 1. Quantitative comparison of segmentation results on Lung dataset.

Method	IoU	F1	SE	SP	ACC	AUC
U-Net	0.9352	0.9420	0.9467	0.9431	0.9663	0.9512
R2UNet	0.9421	0.9574	0.9669	0.9583	0.9740	0.9685
Attention UNet	0.9480	0.9578	0.9698	0.9610	0.9756	0.9700
EU-Net	0.9538	0.9622	0.9779	0.9610	0.9776	0.9702
SUD-GAN	0.9632	0.9656	0.9853	0.9674	0.9801	0.9725
M-GAN	0.9636	0.9653	0.9896	0.9715	0.9843	0.9765
U-Net++	0.9684	0.9723	0.9841	0.9737	0.9874	0.9809
Dense R2UNet	0.9707	0.9715	0.9920	0.9721	0.9882	0.9816
GLUNet (Ours)	**0.9745**	**0.9813**	**0.9943**	**0.9840**	**0.9906**	**0.9889**

To highlight the potential of our method, we compare our model with other state-of-the-art models on three datasets. Furthermore, to ensure the fairness of quantitative comparison, the results in the table (including Table 2 and Table 3) are trained by ourself under the environment of Sect. 4.2. We employ Intersection over union (IoU), F1-score (F1), Sensitivity (SE), Specificity (SP), Accuracy (ACC) and Area Under ROC (AUC) as measurements. It is obvious that our method outperforms most of the existing methods.

Table 2. Quantitative comparison of segmentation results on DSB2018.

Method	IoU	F1	SE	SP	ACC	AUC
U-Net	0.8731	0.8682	0.9479	0.9263	0.9314	0.9371
R2UNet	0.8772	0.8799	0.9454	0.9338	0.9367	0.9396
Attention UNet	0.8857	0.8823	0.9496	0.9313	0.9372	0.9405
EU-Net	0.8903	0.8920	0.9643	0.9625	0.9624	0.9619
Sahasrabudhe	0.8943	0.9043	0.9732	0.9765	0.9798	0.9703
U-Net++	0.8991	0.9125	0.9712	0.9769	0.9830	0.9722
Dense R2UNet	0.9024	0.9218	0.9784	0.9788	0.9821	**0.9853**
GLUNet (Ours)	**0.9175**	**0.9273**	**0.9805**	**0.9853**	**0.9842**	0.9844

Table 3. Quantitative comparison of segmentation results on DRIVE.

Method	IoU	F1	SE	SP	ACC	AUC
U-Net	0.6942	0.8174	0.7822	0.9808	0.9555	0.9752
R2UNet	0.7018	0.8149	0.7726	0.9820	0.9553	0.9779
Attention UNet	0.7132	0.8171	0.7792	0.9813	0.9556	0.9784
EU-Net	0.7184	0.8198	0.8296	0.9822	0.9560	0.9786
SUD-GAN	0.7208	0.8333	0.8340	0.9820	0.9589	0.9792
M-GAN	0.7372	0.8324	**0.8346**	0.9836	0.9706	0.9868
U-Net++	0.7518	0.8452	0.8312	0.9831	0.9772	0.9830
Dense R2UNet	0.7756	0.8618	0.8276	0.9869	0.9753	0.9878
GLUNet (Ours)	**0.8040**	**0.8686**	0.8302	**0.9930**	**0.9783**	**0.9897**

Similar to R2UNet [2] and Attention UNet [10], our model also employs the residual block and attention mechanism strategy, and applies them to skip connection. From Table 1, 2 and 3, we can see that our results are better than R2UNet and Attention UNet. Compare to them, our model can improve the performance on F1-score, SE, SP and ACC by more than 2%. Especially on the DRIVE dataset, our model increases F1-score and SE by 5.37% and 5.76% respectively.

Besides, it's obvious that EU-Net [23] and Sahasrabudhe [13] achieve competitive performance among above methods, where EU-Net adopts edge guidance strategy and Sahasrabudhe adopts self-supervised segmentation strategy. We compare our experimental results with them and all metrics are increased on the three datasets as shown in Table 1, 2 and 3.

Dense R2Unet [4], which is a synthesis of recurrent, residual and dense convolutional network, achieves high performance. Our method is a mixture of residual block, attention mechanism and edge detection, which pays attention to global and local features at the same time. On the lung dataset and DRIVE, experimental metrics are slightly improved compared to the Dense R2UNet. On the DSB2018, our method has improved on most metrics, only slightly decreased on AUC. Finally, our GLUNet is also superior to U-Net and U-Net++ in all metrics.

Table 4. Ablation study on Lung dataset and DSB2018.

Model	Dataset			
	Lung		DSB2018	
	IoU	ACC	IoU	ACC
Backbone	0.9352	0.9663	0.8731	0.9314
Backbone + LEDM	0.9479	0.9742	0.8915	0.9534
Backbone + GAM	0.9593	0.9803	0.9048	0.9736
Backbone + GAM + LEDM	0.9745	0.9906	0.9175	0.9842

4.4 Ablation Study

To verify the effectiveness of each main module in our GLUNet, we conduct ablation study on lung dataset and DSB2018 respectively, and evaluate the results with IoU and ACC metrics. Quantitative results of model with different structures are tabulated in Table 4. When the overall network only contains Backbone (U-Net), IoU and ACC are lowest. By adding GAM, the rates of IoU and ACC have improved significantly. We observe an interesting phenomenon, when we only consider LEDM, the ratio of IoU and ACC is lower than that of GAM only. As a result, we conclude that the acquisition of whole region of an object is the most important for the entire segmentation task, followed by edge information.

Furthermore, to verify strength of effect of ResBlock in GAM on our model, we carry out verification according to the following conditions, as shown in Table 5: **Single**: GAM with CBAM (without ResBlock); **Single-Res1**: GAM with CBAM and one ResBlock (Adding a ResBlock before CBAM); **Single-Res2**: Our GLUNet; (**Single-Res3**): GAM with CBAM and there ResBlocks (Adding an extra ResBlock before CBAM); **Single-Res4**: GAM with CBAM and four ResBlocks (Adding an extra ResBlock before and after CBAM).

Table 5. The IoU and ACC scores in percentage of our GAM with and without ResBlock evaluated on Lung dataset and DSB2018 validation set split.

Dataset	Metrics	Single	Single-Res1	Single-Res2	Single-Res3	Single-Res4
Lung	IoU	0.9689	0.9713	**0.9745**	0.9745	0.9751
	ACC	0.9842	0.9866	**0.9906**	0.9907	0.9910
DSB2018	IoU	0.9063	0.9104	**0.9175**	0.9182	0.9187
	ACC	0.9785	0.9821	**0.9842**	0.9849	0.9844

The quantitative experimental results are shown in Table 5. We can see that our GLUNet achieves the best results when we add two ResBlocks. It can also be seen that, in our experiment, with the continuously increasing amount of ResBlock, our time-consuming in training increases, but the results of the experiment have no improvement notably. Finally, we choose to add two ResBlocks in our model.

4.5 Visual Results

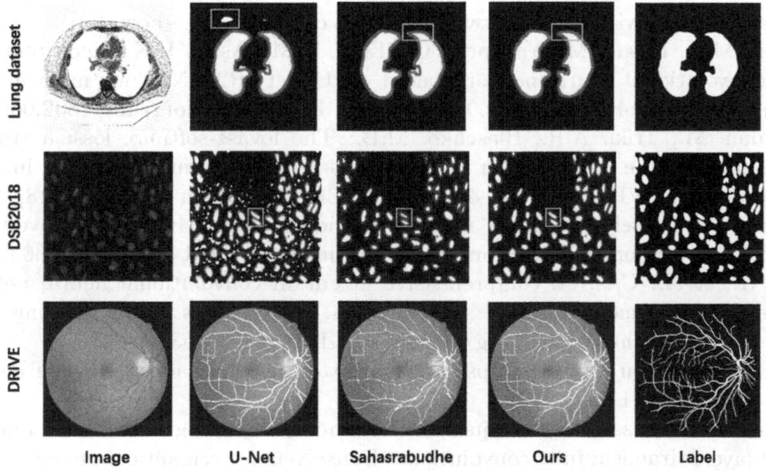

Fig. 4. Visualized results on different datasets. (The ground truth field is outlined with red, while the predicted field is filled with white. The differences in results are marked with blue blanks but are not limited to these blue blanks). (Color figure online)

In addition to the quantitative results, we also show some examples for visual comparison in Fig. 4. According to the visualization results, other state-of-the-art methods tend to focus on global segmentation, while our GLUNet is capable of focusing on both edge details and global regions. The results show that our architecture captures global region information and fuses edge information to refine our object segmentation. We mark some different areas with blue blanks in Fig. 4 to make it clear. The results also indicate that the segmentation effect of GLUNet is better than that of other state-of-the-art methods.

5 Conclusion

In this paper, we propose a Global-Local fusion U-Net (GLUNet) for medical image segmentation, the backbone of which is similar to U-Net network. In GLUNet, the backbone is used for the overall segmentation task, and the global attention module (GAM) is used to focus on the region information of the object, so that the module can extract the feature maps of the object, just like human visual attention. Meanwhile, the local edge detection module (LEDM) is used to extract the edge information mainly including the features of the shallow layers of the encoder, so as to supervise the encoder and fine-tune the region information of the whole object. Our extensive experimental results demonstrate that our method outperforms the state-of-the-art segmentation methods on various medical datasets. In future research, we will extend our approach to 3D segmentation.

References

1. Data science bowl. https://www.kaggle.com/c/data-science-bowl-2018
2. Alom, M.Z., Hasan, M., Yakopcic, C., Taha, T.M., Asari, V.K.: Recurrent residual convolutional neural network based on U-Net (R2U-Net) for medical image segmentation. CoRR abs/1802.06955 (2018). http://arxiv.org/abs/1802.06955
3. Berman, M., Triki, A.R., Blaschko, M.B.: The lovász-softmax loss: a tractable surrogate for the optimization of the intersection-over-union measure in neural networks. In: CVPR 2018, pp. 4413–4421. IEEE Computer Society (2018)
4. Dutta, K.: Densely connected recurrent residual (Dense R2UNet) convolutional neural network for segmentation of lung CT images. CoRR abs/2102.00663 (2021)
5. Gu, R., et al.: CA-Net: comprehensive attention convolutional neural networks for explainable medical image segmentation. IEEE Trans. Med. Imaging **40**(2), 699–711 (2021). https://doi.org/10.1109/TMI.2020.3035253
6. Huang, W., Zhou, F.: DA-CapsNet: dual attention mechanism capsule network. Sci. Rep. **10**(1), 1–13 (2020)
7. Jgou, S., Drozdzal, M., Vazquez, D., Romero, A., Bengio, Y.: The one hundred layers tiramisu: fully convolutional DenseNets for semantic segmentation. In: 2017 IEEE Conference on Computer Vision and Pattern Recognition Workshops (CVPRW) (2016)
8. Krizhevsky, A., Sutskever, I., Hinton, G.E.: ImageNet classification with deep convolutional neural networks. Commun. ACM **60**(6), 84–90 (2017)
9. Mader, K.S.: 2017 data science bowl. https://www.kaggle.com/kmader/finding-lungs-in-ct-data (2017)
10. Oktay, O., et al.: Attention U-Net: learning where to look for the pancreas. CoRR abs/1804.03999 (2018). http://arxiv.org/abs/1804.03999
11. Park, K., Choi, S.H., Lee, J.Y.: M-GAN: retinal blood vessel segmentation by balancing losses through stacked deep fully convolutional networks. IEEE Access **8**, 146308–146322 (2020)

12. Ronneberger, O., Fischer, P., Brox, T.: U-Net: convolutional networks for biomedical image segmentation. In: Navab, N., Hornegger, J., Wells, W.M., Frangi, A.F. (eds.) MICCAI 2015. LNCS, vol. 9351, pp. 234–241. Springer, Cham (2015). https://doi.org/10.1007/978-3-319-24574-4_28
13. Sahasrabudhe, M., Christodoulidis, S., Salgado, R., Michiels, S., Vakalopoulou, M.: Self-supervised nuclei segmentation in histopathological images using attention (2020)
14. Shelhamer, E., Long, J., Darrell, T.: Fully convolutional networks for semantic segmentation. IEEE Trans. Pattern Anal. Mach. Intell. **39**(4), 640–651 (2017). https://doi.org/10.1109/TPAMI.2016.2572683
15. Staal, J., Abràmoff, M.D., Niemeijer, M., Viergever, M.A., van Ginneken, B.: Ridge-based vessel segmentation in color images of the retina. IEEE Trans. Med. Imaging **23**(4), 501–509 (2004). https://doi.org/10.1109/TMI.2004.825627
16. Wei, S., Wang, X., Yan, W., Xiang, B., Zhang, Z.: Deepcontour: a deep convolutional feature learned by positive-sharing loss for contour detection. In: Computer Vision and Pattern Recognition (2015)
17. Woo, S., Park, J., Lee, J., Kweon, I.S.: CBAM: convolutional block attention module. In: Computer Vision - ECCV 2018–15th European Conference, 8–14 September 2018, Munich, Germany. Lecture Notes in Computer Science, vol. 11211, pp. 3–19. Springer (2018). https://doi.org/10.1007/978-3-030-01234-2_1
18. Yang, T., Wu, T., Li, L., Zhu, C.: SUD-GAN: deep convolution generative adversarial network combined with short connection and dense block for retinal vessel segmentation. J. Digit. Imaging **33**(4), 946–957 (2020)
19. Zhang, S., Yang, J., Schiele, B.: Occluded pedestrian detection through guided attention in CNNs. In: CVPR 2018, 18–22 June 2018, Salt Lake City, UT, USA, pp. 6995–7003. IEEE Computer Society (2018)
20. Zhang, W., Cheng, H., Gan, J.: MUNet: a multi-scale U-Net framework for medical image segmentation. In: 2020 International Joint Conference on Neural Networks, IJCNN 2020, 19–24 July 2020, Glasgow, United Kingdom, pp. 1–7. IEEE (2020). https://doi.org/10.1109/IJCNN48605.2020.9206703
21. Zhang, Z., Fu, H., Dai, H., Shen, J., Pang, Y., Shao, L.: ET-Net: a generic edge-attention guidance network for medical image segmentation. CoRR abs/1907.10936 (2019)
22. Zhang, Z., Sabuncu, M.R.: Generalized cross entropy loss for training deep neural networks with noisy labels. In: Advances in Neural Information Processing Systems 31: Annual Conference on Neural Information Processing Systems 2018, NeurIPS 2018, 3–8 December 2018, Montréal, Canada, pp. 8792–8802 (2018)
23. Zhao, R., Chen, W., Cao, G.: Edge-boosted u-net for 2D medical image segmentation. IEEE Access **7**, 171214–171222 (2019). https://doi.org/10.1109/ACCESS.2019.2953727
24. Zhou, Y., Onder, O.F., Dou, Q., Tsougenis, E., Chen, H., Heng, P.A.: CIA-Net: robust nuclei instance segmentation with contour-aware information aggregation. In: International Conference on Information Processing in Medical Imaging (2019)
25. Zhou, Z., Siddiquee, M.M.R., Tajbakhsh, N., Liang, J.: UNet++: Redesigning skip connections to exploit multiscale features in image segmentation. IEEE Trans. Med. Imaging **39**(6), 1856–1867 (2020)

Textbook Question Answering with Multi-type Question Learning and Contextualized Diagram Representation

Jianwei He[1,2], Xianghua Fu[1(✉)], Zi Long[1], Shuxin Wang[1], Chaojie Liang[1,2], and Hongbin Lin[1,2]

[1] Shenzhen Technology University, Shenzhen, China
fuxianghua@sztu.edu.cn, thinkjerry@icloud.com
[2] Shenzhen University, Shenzhen, China

Abstract. Textbook question answering (TQA) is a multi-modal task that requires complex parsing and reasoning over scientific diagrams and long text to answer various types of questions, including true/false questions, reading comprehension, and diagram questions, making TQA a superset of question answering (QA) and visual question answering (VQA). In this paper, we introduce a Multi-Head TQA architecture (MHTQA) for solving the TQA task. To overcome the long text issue, we apply the open-source search engine Solr to select sentences from lesson essays. In order to answer questions that have different input formats and share knowledge, we build a bottom-shared model with a transformer and three QA networks. For diagram questions, previous approaches did not incorporate the textual context to produce diagram representation, resulting in insufficient utilize of diagram semantic information. To address this issue, we learn a contextualized diagram representation through the novel Contextualized Iterative Dual Fusion network (CIDF) using the visual and semantic features of the diagram image and the lesson essays. We jointly train different types of questions in a multi-task learning manner for knowledge sharing by an efficient sampling strategy of Multi-type Question Learning (MQL). The experimental results show that our model outperforms the existing single model on all question types by a margin of 4.6%, 1.7%, 1%, 1.9% accuracy on Text T/F, Text MC, Diagram, and overall accuracy.

Keywords: Question answering · Visual question answering · Multi-task learning

1 Introduction

Question answering (QA) is a hot topic in the natural language processing (NLP) community. For many years, QA focuses on building a text processing system that can answer questions posed by humans [7]. Recently, visual question answering (VQA) has received increasing attention in the field of artificial intelligence

I. Farkaš et al. (Eds.): ICANN 2021, LNCS 12894, pp. 86–98, 2021.
https://doi.org/10.1007/978-3-030-86380-7_8

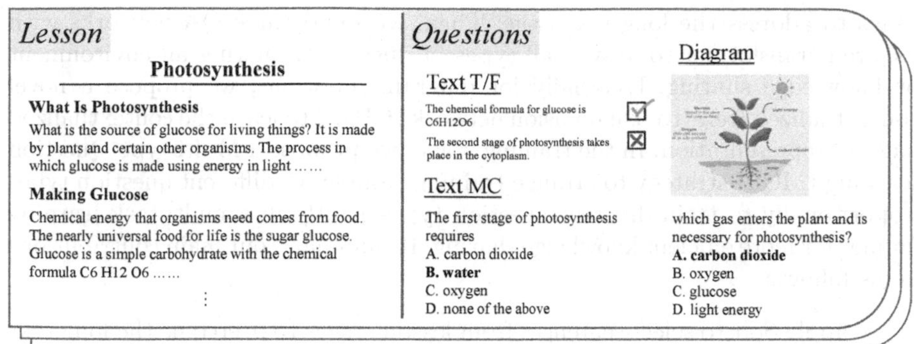

Fig. 1. Content of Photosynthesis lesson in the TQA dataset. The lesson contains abundant essays, and the following questions have three types: text T/F, Text MC, and diagram. The knowledge required for answering questions is bounded to the lesson essays.

as it is the intersection of NLP and computer vision (CV). VQA system takes a natural image and the corresponding question as input and outputs the answer in the natural language form [2]. To build a more realistic QA system, Kim et al. [10] published a new challenging dataset, the textbook question answering (TQA). The TQA dataset comprises many lessons, and each lesson contains abundant essays and three types of questions. Figure 1 shows the content of the Photosynthesis lesson in the TQA dataset, accompanying three types of questions: the true/false questions *Text T/F*, the reading comprehension questions *Text MC* and the diagram questions *Diagram*. TQA is a superset of text QA and visual QA since the text QA does not have the image, while the visual QA does not have the lesson essays.

Over 75% of TQA lessons have at least 50 sentences, making it almost impossible to load the entire lesson into memory for calculation. Previous works [11,13] use TF-IDF to select important sentences to overcome this so-called long text issue. Parsing and reasoning abilities are required to answer TQA questions, not just simple words matching. Another characteristic of the TQA that makes it rather challenging is the diagram questions. People use scientific diagrams to illustrate scientific phenomenons or processes that occur in the real world. Thus, diagrams are more abstract than natural images and hard to generalize and understand. Specifically, objects in the natural images are limited to common objects in daily life, such as persons, cars, and cats. But objects that appear in the diagram are various. For instance, we might find *microzooplankton* in a food web diagram, *mantle* in a geography diagram. We believe that the lesson essay is the key to understand what the diagram image conveys.

Although TQA has three question types, recent work [5] deal with different question types separately, ignoring the correlations between different types of questions. In this work, we introduce a Multi-Head TQA architecture (MHTQA) that can answer all categories of questions in a unified framework. First, we apply the open-source search engine Solr to select sentences from the lesson essays to address the long text issue. Then, we build three QA networks with a shared transformer to answer all types of questions, offering an environment for knowledge sharing. Especially for diagram questions, we propose a novel Contextualized Iterative Dual Fusion network (CIDF) to learn the contextualized diagram representation. In the training stage, we propose a Multi-type Question Learning (MQL) strategy to arrange training samples of different question types proportionally to train different question types jointly in a multi-task learning manner for more efficient knowledge sharing. In summary, our main contributions are as follows:

- We apply Solr to select sentences from lesson essays to overcome the long text problem in TQA. Compared to TF-IDF, Solr is more practical and accurate.
- We propose the Multi-Head TQA architecture (MHTQA) to address all types of questions and a Multi-type Question Learning strategy (MQL) to share knowledge of different question types.
- We extract the visual and semantic features of objects and texts from the diagram for better diagram representation learning.
- We propose the novel Contextualized Iterative Dual Fusion network (CIDF) to learn the contextualized diagram representation and answer diagram questions.

2 Related Work

Kembhavi et al. [10] proposed several TQA baselines based on Machine Comprehension (MC) and VQA models, such as BiDAF [20] and VQA [2]. Unsurprisingly, those famous models worked poorly on the TQA dataset, indicating that existing methods are insufficient for the TQA dataset. Kim et al. [11] use Stanford dependency parser extract context graph from lesson text and diagram image then use Graph Convolutional Networks (GCN) to extract knowledge features from context graphs. Gomez-Perez et al. [5] incorporate the RoBERTa [16] and BUTD attention with 6 models ensembled, pushes forward the research of TQA. While researchers successfully build VQA systems based on large datasets and attention mechanisms, the diagram question could not be answered properly by those approaches [10]. Therefore, Kembhavi et al. [9] proposed DsDP-net to parse the diagram image into Diagram Parsing Graph (DPG), then convert the generated DPGs to statements. However, the converted statements lose the original visual features of the diagram like shapes and colors. By contrast, Gomez-Perez et al. [5] extracts the visual features of diagram constituents and applied the Bottom-up and Top-Down (BUTD) attention [1] to answer diagram questions.

3 Method

3.1 Overview

Figure 2 shows an overview of the Multi-Head TQA architecture (MHTQA). We generate a short passage for each candidate answer by applying the open-source search engine Solr to select sentences from the lesson essays. We build a

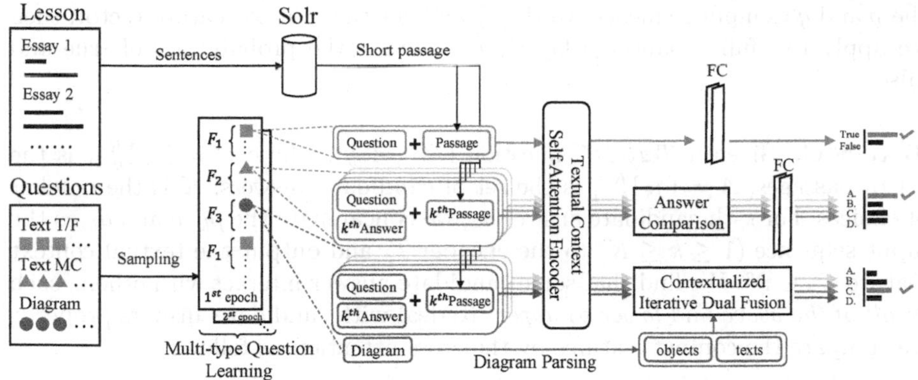

Fig. 2. An overview of the multi-head TQA architecture (MHTQA).

model with a shared transformer T_c, the textual context self-attention encoder in our architecture, and three QA networks, each QA network for answering a specific question type. For the *Text T/F* question, we use two fully connected (FC) layers to calculate the probabilities of true and false. For the *Text MC* question, we compare the candidate answers before the two FC layers. For the *Diagram* question, we learn a contextualized diagram representation of the diagram image through the novel Contextualized Iterative Dual Fusion network (CIDF). We train different types of questions jointly for knowledge sharing by arranging the training samples proportionally through the Multi-type Question Learning (MQL) strategy. Our MHTQA can be compatible with other QA and VQA models by replacing the QA network. For example, we can use BUTD to answer diagram questions instead of CIDF.

3.2 Sentences Retrieval

Most previous works use TF-IDF to select relevant sentences from the lesson essays. However, the TF-IDF is very sensitive to word morphological variations. To overcome this shortcoming, we apply the open-source search engine Solr to retrieve sentences. Given a question q and a set of candidate answers $A = \{a_k\}_{k=1}^{K}$, where K is the number of choices. For k-th candidate answer a_k, we concatenate q and a_k as a query and input it into Solr to search relevant sentences. To ensure the retrieved sentences are relevant to a_k, the retrieved sentence must have at least one overlapping and non-stop word with a_k. Finally, we concatenate the top 10 valid sentence as passage p_k and assume that p_k is the knowledge needed to answer the question.

3.3 Text Question Answering

Text T/F. Given a *Text T/F* question (p, q, y), where p is the generated passage by the sentences retrieval, q is the question and y is true or false. We concatenate the p and q as input sequences to the T_c and get the context feature vector, then we apply two fully connected layers to calculate the probabilities of true and false.

Text MC. Given a *Text MC* question (P, q, A, y), where $P = \{p_k\}_{k=1}^{K}$ is the set of passages, $A = \{a_k\}_{k=1}^{K}$ is the set of candidate answers, K is the number of choices. For k-th candidate answer a_k, we concatenate the p_k, q and a_k as the input sequence $(1 \leq k \leq K)$ to the encoder T_c and output the textual context feature $C_k \in \mathbb{R}^h$. We find that some candidate answer interact with others, such as *all of the above* and *lower* to *upper*. To deal with candidate answers properly, we compare the context features by the cross attention as follows:

$$\begin{aligned}
G &= CrossAttention(\bar{C}_1, \bar{C}_2, ..., \bar{C}_K) \\
G_{i,j} &= softmax(\frac{Q_i \bar{C}_j^T}{\sqrt{d_{\bar{C}_j}}}), i \neq j \\
\bar{C}_j &= tanh(W_c C_j) \\
Q_i &= W_{cq} \bar{C}_i \\
\hat{C}_i &= [G_{i,j} \bar{C}_i]_{j=1}^{K}, i \neq j \\
\tilde{C}_i &= ReLU(W_{cc} C_i + W_{oc} \hat{C}_i)
\end{aligned} \tag{1}$$

where W_c, W_{cq}, W_{cc}, W_{oc} are trainable weights, $G \in \mathbb{R}^{K \times K}$ is the matrix of attention scores for comparison, and $[\Delta]$ is the operation of matrix concatenation. The $\tilde{C}_i$ is the comparison features for i-th candidate answer. Then, we use two fully connected layers to select the correct answer.

3.4 Contextualized Iterative Dual Fusion Network

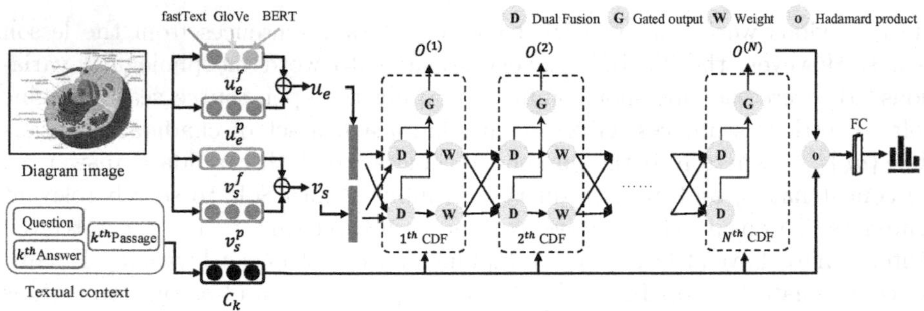

Fig. 3. An overview of the Contextualized Iterative Dual Fusion network (CIDF).

Figure 3 shows an overview of the Contextualized Iterative Dual Fusion network (CIDF). Given a *Diagram* question (P, q, I, A, y), where I is the diagram image. Firstly, similar to the *Text MC* question, for k-th candidate answer, we use T_c to encode the passage, question, and candidate answer to the textual context feature C_k. Secondly, we parse the diagram into a set of objects and texts. For objects, we apply ResNet [6] to extract visual features. For texts, previous work also uses ResNet to extract the features [5,13], resulting in insufficient utilize of text semantics in the diagram image. By contrast, we exploit several word embeddings tools to capture the semantics feature of texts. Finally, we use Contextualized Dual Fusion (CDF) layer to learn the contextualized diagram representation. After several representation learning iterations, CIDF output the final diagram representation and answers the diagram question.

Diagram Parsing. A diagram image is composed of constituents, including objects and texts. Given a diagram image I, we apply off-the-shelf object detection model Faster R-CNN [19] to extract a set of bounding boxes $\{b_s^{obj}\}_{s=1}^{N_o}$ of RoIs (Region-of-Interest) of the image, where N_o is the number of objects. Then, we recognize the words of the diagram by text detection model CRAFT [3], which is robust on character-level text detection, and text recognition model STAR-net [15]. We concatenate the word as text according to their spatial relationship and finally obtain a set of text and the bounding boxes set $\{b_e^{text}\}_{e=1}^{N_t}$, where N_t is the number of texts.

Visual and Semantic Representations. For s-th objects ($1 \leq s \leq N_o$), we exploit the ResNet to encode it to a feature vector $v_s^f \in \mathbb{R}^h$. In addition, we learn a spatial embeddings [21] v_s^p as follows:

$$v_s^p = LayerNorm(W_p b_s^{obj}) \tag{2}$$

the W_p are trainable weights, b_s^{obj} is the bounding box coordinates of s-th object. Then we take the average of vectors as the final representation $v_s = (v_s^f + v_s^p)/2$. We use three different text representations, including fastText [8], GloVe [18] and BERT [4], to extract semantic features of diagram texts. To produce a text representation $u_e^f \in \mathbb{R}^h$ for e-th ($1 \leq e \leq N_t$) text, we transform the semantic features into a same vector space:

$$u_e^f = u_e^{fasttext} W_f + u_e^{glove} W_g + u_e^{bert} W_b \tag{3}$$

where the W_f, W_g and W_b are trainable projection matrices, $u_e^{fasttext}$, u_e^{glove} are word embeddings of fastText and Glove, and u_e^{bert} is the output of the first three layers of BERT. We also learn a spatial embeddings u_e^p with b_e^{text} by Eq. 2 and output the final text representation $u_e = (u_u^f + u_e^p)/2$.

Now, We learn a contextualized diagram representation for image I by Contextualized Dual Fusion Layer (CDF). The CDF input consists of three types of features: diagram visual features, diagram semantic features, and textual context features. There are two main components in the CDF layer: the dual fusion operation and the gated output.

Dual Fusion. People learn the object by words and vise versa, suggesting this is a two-way learning procedure. To modeling this procedure, we define the Dual Fusion operation to calculate the dual representations of objects and texts. We gather the object features and text features as matrix respectively, as $V^{(0)} = [v_1; v_2; ...; v_{N_o}] \in \mathbb{R}^{N_o \times h}$ and $U^{(0)} = [u_1; u_2; ...; u_{N_t}] \in \mathbb{R}^{N_t \times h}$. For t-th CDF layer, the dual representation of object to text is calculated as follows:

$$
\begin{aligned}
a_u^{(t)} &= U^{(t)} W_u^{(t)} (V^{(t)})^T \\
\hat{a}_u^{(t)} &= softmax(\frac{a_u^{(t)}}{\sqrt{d_{U^{(t)}}}}) \\
S_u^{(t)} &= (\hat{a}_u^{(t)})^T V^{(t)} \\
Z_u^{(t)} &= ReLU(S_u^{(t)} W_{ou}^{(t)})
\end{aligned}
\tag{4}
$$

where $W_u^{(t)}, W_{ou}^{(t)}$ are trainable weights, $a_u^{(t)} \in \mathbb{R}^{N_t \times N_o}$ is bi-linear attention scores and $\hat{a}_u^{(t)}$ is its normalized version. The $Z_u^{(t)} \in \mathbb{R}^{N_t \times h}$ is the dual representation of object to text. Then, we exchange the $V^{(t)}$ and $U^{(t)}$ and calculate the dual representation $Z_v^{(t)}$ of text to object by:

$$
\begin{aligned}
a_v^{(t)} &= V^{(t)} W_v^{(t)} (U^{(t)})^T \\
\hat{a}_v^{(t)} &= softmax(\frac{a_v^{(t)}}{\sqrt{d_{V^{(t)}}}}) \\
S_v^{(t)} &= (\hat{a}_v^{(t)})^T U^{(t)} \\
Z_v^{(t)} &= ReLU(S_v^{(t)} W_{ov}^{(t)})
\end{aligned}
\tag{5}
$$

where $W_v^{(t)}, W_{ov}^{(t)}$ are trainable weights, and $a_v^{(t)}, \hat{a}_v^{(t)} \in \mathbb{R}^{N_o \times N_t}$ are attention scores. Dual representations describe the correlations between objects and texts. We need to learn a joint representation of them for diagram question answering.

Gated Output. Now we learn the joint representation $O^{(t)}$ of the two dual representations $Z_u^{(t)}$ and $Z_v^{(t)}$ under the guidance of the textual context:

$$
\begin{aligned}
\bar{Z}_u^{(t)} &= MaxPooling(Z_u^{(t)}) \\
\bar{Z}_v^{(t)} &= MaxPooling(Z_v^{(t)}) \\
g^{(t)} &= tanh(\bar{Z}_u^{(t)} W_{gu}^{(t)} + \bar{Z}_v^{(t)} W_{gv}^{(t)} + C_k W_{gc}^{(t)}) \\
O^{(t)} &= g^{(t)} * \bar{Z}_u^{(t)} + (1 - g^{(t)}) * \bar{Z}_v^{(t)}
\end{aligned}
\tag{6}
$$

where $W_{gu}^{(t)}, W_{gv}^{(t)}, W_{gc}^{(t)}$ are trainable weights. We use $MaxPooling$ to select important features and output the $\bar{Z}_u^{(t)}, \bar{Z}_v^{(t)} \in \mathbb{R}^h$. The $g^{(t)} \in \mathbb{R}^h$ controls the feature selection with the help of textual context information. For $(t+1)$-th CDF layer, we transform the dual representation $Z_v^{(t)}$ and $Z_u^{(t)}$ as the inputs by:

$$
\begin{aligned}
U^{(t+1)} &= Z_u^{(t)} W_{uu}^{(t)} \\
V^{(t+1)} &= Z_v^{(t)} W_{vv}^{(t)}
\end{aligned}
\tag{7}
$$

where $W_{uu}^{(t)}, W_{vv}^{(t)}$ are trainable weights. We compute the Hadamard product between the output of last CDF layer $O^{(N)}$ and textual context features C_k and output the answer score by two fully connected layers. We argue that after several iterations, the $O^{(N)}$ contains rich semantic information and is the high-level representation of the diagram.

3.5 Multi-type Question Learning

Traditional multi-task learning shares both input data and networks, while our MHTQA shares only networks. Therefore, we should alternatively take training samples from different tasks to optimize the MHTQA model. Previous work uses a round-robin batch-level sampling strategy (RRBS) to arrange the training samples [17]. For L tasks, and $\{b_r^{(l)}\}_{r=1}^{M_l}$ is the set of batches of the l-th task, the size of the set is M_l and $b_r^{(l)}$ is r-th batch. In an epoch of training, the RRBS strategy sample a batch from 1-th task, then a batch from 2-th task and so on, until all of the batches are visited:

$$b_1^{(1)}, b_1^{(2)}, ..., b_1^{(L)}, b_2^{(1)}, b_2^{(2)}, ..., b_2^{(L)}, ... \tag{8}$$

Obviously, the distribution of batches is unbalanced if the numbers of task batches are not equal. To address this issue, we propose the sampling strategy of Multi-type Question Learning (MQL) to distribute the batches proportionately:

$$b_1^{(1)}, ..., b_{F_1}^{(1)}, b_1^{(2)}, ..., b_{F_2}^{(2)}, ..., b_1^{(L)}, ..., b_{F_L}^{(L)}, b_{F_1+1}^{(1)}, b_{F_1+2}^{(1)}, ... \tag{9}$$

where $F_1, ..., F_N$ are task ratios. The MQL sample F_l batches from l-th task $(1 \leq l \leq L)$ until all batches are visited. The key of MQL is that we need ensure the task ratios $F_1 : ... : F_L \approx M_1 : ... : M_L$. In practical, we use the size of the minimal batch set $M_{min} = min(M_1, ..., M_L)$ as the cardinal number, and the task ratio F_i for i-th task is calculated by $F_i = floor(\frac{M_i}{M_{min}})$.

4 Experiments

4.1 Datasets

TQA. Drawn from middle school science curricula, the TQA dataset comprises 1,076 lessons distributed in Earth Science, Life Science, and Physical Science, containing 78,338 sentences and 3,455 images. The dataset is split by training, validation, and test sets, consist of 666, 200, and 210 lessons respectively, including 5,400 true/false questions, 8,293 text-related multi-choice questions, and 12,567 diagram questions.

AI2D. AI2D [9] is a diagram dataset with exhaustive annotations of constituents and relationships for over 5,000 diagrams and 15,000 multi-choice questions and answers. The diagram category is various, such as food webs, life cycles etc.

4.2 Settings

We build Solr with OpenNLP integrations[1], including tokenizer, part-of-speech filter, phrase chunking filter, and lemmatizer filter. Every sentence in Solr has tagged with lesson id, we run the query and filter the sentences with the same lesson id. In the MHTQA architecture, the T_c is RoBERTa-large [16] and we use the model weights provided by [5] for comparable results. We truncate the input sequence of T_c to 180 tokens. For object detection, we pre-training the Faster R-CNN[2] on the AI2D dataset and then apply to the TQA dataset. For word recognition, we use default settings of the CRAFT[3] and the STAR-net[4]. We set the maximum number of objects and texts to 20, 15 respectively. In MQL, the task ratio of *Text T/F*, *Text MC* and *Diagram* is 1, 6, 7, and the batch size is 8, 2, 2 respectively. We use Adam as the optimizer and the learning rate is 2×10^{-6}. We train our model for 4 epochs and take the epoch with the best validation accuracy as the final model.

4.3 Main Results

Table 1. Comparison of accuracy (%) with previous single model and ours on the TQA validation set.

Model	Text T/F	Text MC	Text all	Diagram	All
Random	50.10	22.88	33.62	24.96	29.08
MemN+VQA [10]	50.50	31.05	38.73	31.82	35.11
MemN+DPG [10]	50.50	30.98	38.69	32.83	35.62
BiDAF+DPG [10]	50.40	30.46	38.33	32.72	35.39
IGMN [14]	57.41	40.00	46.88	36.35	41.36
f-GCN1+SSOC [11]	62.73	49.54	54.75	37.61	45.77
RoBERTa+VQA [5]	76.85	62.81	68.38	41.14	54.09
ISAAQ-IR [5]	78.26	67.52	71.76	53.83	62.37
MHTQA+BUTD	80.79	67.78	72.92	53.43	62.63
MHTQA+CIDF	80.79	67.78	72.92	**54.87**	63.46
MHTQA+CIDF+MQL_{text}	**82.87**	**69.22**	**74.61**	**54.87**	**64.27**

Table 1 shows the single model performance of previous works and our work on the TQA validation set. Testing our method on the validation set is sufficient since all of the previous works do also. Note that the ISAAQ is a model ensemble approach, and the best single model in ISAAQ is ISAAQ-IR [5]. Obviously, our

[1] https://solr.apache.org/guide/7_3/language-analysis.html.
[2] https://github.com/facebookresearch/detectron2.
[3] https://github.com/clovaai/CRAFT-pytorch.
[4] https://github.com/clovaai/deep-text-recognition-benchmark.

Table 2. Comparison of different training strategies.

Training strategy	Text T/F	Text MC	Text all	Diagram	All
Independent	80.79	67.78	72.92	**54.87**	63.46
$RRBS_{all}$	80.06	67.97	72.74	53.15	62.48
MQL_{all}	81.16	68.17	73.53	53.72	63.04
$RRBS_{text}$	81.06	68.04	73.18	–	–
MQL_{text}	**82.87**	**69.22**	**74.61**	–	–
$MQL_{tf,diag}$	81.26	–	–	53.36	–
$MQL_{mc,diag}$	–	68.78	–	53.76	–

MHTQA+CIDF+MQL$_{text}$ outperforms the previous best single model by a margin of about 4.6% in true/false questions and 2% in overall accuracy. Even our base version of **MHTQA+BUTD** have about 2.5% accuracy improvement on *Text T/F* questions compare to the previous best model. We believe that our method works well on the TQA problem since our method achieves considerable margins compared to recent methods. Details of variants of our method:

- **MHTQA+BUTD**. We train different types of questions independently and use the BUTD to answer diagram questions.
- **MHTQA+CIDF**. We replace the BUTD with our CIDF.
- **MHTQA+CIDF+MQL**$_{text}$. We train *Text T/F* and *Text T/F* questions jointly with our MQL strategy. We will discuss why not train diagram questions together in Sect. 4.4.

4.4 Ablations and Analysis

Multi-type Question Learning. We first train and evaluate our model for each question type independently (see Independent in Table 2). In this setting, different question types share nothing. Next, we take all of the types of questions together to train MHTQA through our MQL strategy (see MQL_{all}). As a comparison, we also experiment with the RRBS strategy (see $RRBS_{all}$). The results show that compares to independent training, MQL_{all} slightly improves model accuracy on *Text T/F* and *Text MC* questions, but accuracy decline on *Diagram* questions.

Considering the largest proportion of diagram questions in TQA dataset, we believe that the main reason is the task correlations instead of the data scale. For diagram questions, the model needs to pay more attention to multimodal representation learning. By contrast, the model needs to focus on semantic matching and reasoning when answering text-related questions. Thus, *Text T/F* and *Text MC* questions have a strong correlation. And the correlation of diagram questions and text-related questions is weak. We can infer that it is harmful to related tasks when adding an unrelated task into multi-task learning. We make further experiments exclude a type of questions and get three

Table 3. Comparison of accuracy (%) with previous single model and ours MHTQA+CIDF in the TQA diagram questions and the AI2D dataset.

Model	AI2D	TQA	All
VQA [10]	32.90	31.82	31.10
DGGN+Dqa-Net [12]	41.55	32.83	35.10
ISAAQ-IR [5]	73.29	53.83	58.89
Our CIDF			
with $N = 0$	72.90	53.37	58.45
with $N = 2$	**74.74**	**54.87**	**60.04**
with $N = 4$	72.8	54.01	58.90

combinations: the *Text T/F* and *Text T/F* (RRBS_{text} and MQL_{text}), the *Text T/F* and *Diagram* ($\text{MQL}_{tf,diag}$), and the *Text MC* and *Diagram* ($\text{MQL}_{mc,diag}$). The results demonstrate that MQL_{text}, which excludes the diagram questions, obtain the best accuracy in text-related questions, confirming that *Text T/F* and *Text MC* have a strong correlation, and diagram questions is weakly correlate to text-related questions. We also observe that MQL_{all} and MQL_{text} outperforms RRBS_{all} and RRBS_{text}, showing that our MQL strategy is more efficient than RRBS strategy when training MHTQA (Table 3).

Number of CDF Layers. We train and evaluate our model on TQA diagram questions and the AI2D dataset separately. We experiment with multiple CDF layers ($N > 0$) and record the model accuracy relative to no CDF layers ($N = 0$). We draw Fig. 4 to observe the effects of CDF layers. When $0 \leq N \leq 2$, model accuracy increase with N on TQA dataset, and model obtained best performance on both TQA and AI2D dataset when $N = 2$. When $3 \leq N \leq 7$, for the AI2D dataset, accuracy decreases and fluctuates around $N = 0$, while for the TQA dataset, the accuracy decreased also but above $N = 0$. We believe that greater N means a higher level of diagram representation. And bigger N may harm the model as the diagram may not contain too complex relationships. The model can refine diagram representation by lesson essays of the TQA dataset. Therefore, compare to the AI2D dataset, which does not have lesson essays, the model performed more stable on the TQA dataset.

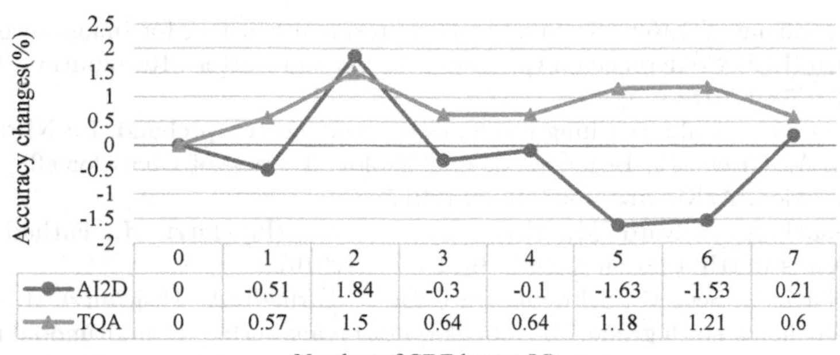

	0	1	2	3	4	5	6	7
AI2D	0	-0.51	1.84	-0.3	-0.1	-1.63	-1.53	0.21
TQA	0	0.57	1.5	0.64	0.64	1.18	1.21	0.6

Fig. 4. Accuracy changes (relative to $N = 0$) under different number of CDF layers (N).

5 Conclusion

This paper proposes a Multi-Head TQA architecture (MHTQA) integrated with Multi-type Question Learning (MQL) and Contextualized Iterative Dual Fusion Network (CIDF) to solve the TQA task. We confirmed by experiments that knowledge sharing on text-related questions is possible. The quantitative analysis clearly shows the general effectiveness of our method. The TQA remains an open research field especially the diagram questions. We believe that future works on diagram representation learning and multi-type question knowledge sharing can push forward the development of the TQA problem.

Acknowledgments. This work was supported by the Stable Support Projects for Shenzhen Higher Education Institutions (SZWD2021011) and the Scientific Research Platforms and Projects in Universities in Guangdong Province (2019KTSCX204).

References

1. Anderson, P., et al.: Bottom-up and top-down attention for image captioning and visual question answering. In: 2018 IEEE/CVF Conference on Computer Vision and Pattern Recognition, pp. 6077–6086 (2018)
2. Antol, S., et al.: VQA: visual question answering. In: 2015 IEEE International Conference on Computer Vision (ICCV), pp. 2425–2433 (2015)
3. Baek, Y., Lee, B., Han, D., Yun, S., Lee, H.: Character region awareness for text detection. In: Proceedings of the IEEE Conference on Computer Vision and Pattern Recognition, pp. 9365–9374 (2019)
4. Devlin, J., Chang, M.W., Lee, K., Toutanova, K.: BERT: pre-training of deep bidirectional transformers for language understanding. In: NAACL, pp. 4171–4186 (2019)
5. Gómez-Pérez, J.M., Ortega, R.: ISAAQ-mastering textbook questions with pre-trained transformers and bottom-up and top-down attention. In: EMNLP, pp. 5469–5479 (2020)

6. He, K., Zhang, X., Ren, S., Sun, J.: Deep residual learning for image recognition. In: 2016 IEEE Conference on Computer Vision and Pattern Recognition (CVPR), pp. 770–778 (2016)
7. Hermann, K., et al.: Teaching machines to read and comprehend. In: NIPS (2015)
8. Joulin, A., Grave, E., Bojanowski, P., Mikolov, T.: Bag of tricks for efficient text classification. ArXiv abs/1607.01759 (2017)
9. Kembhavi, A., Salvato, M., Kolve, E., Seo, M., Hajishirzi, H., Farhadi, A.: A diagram is worth a dozen images. In: ECCV (2016)
10. Kembhavi, A., Seo, M., Schwenk, D., Choi, J., Farhadi, A., Hajishirzi, H.: Are you smarter than a sixth grader? Textbook question answering for multimodal machine comprehension. In: 2017 IEEE Conference on Computer Vision and Pattern Recognition (CVPR), pp. 5376–5384 (2017)
11. Kim, D., Kim, S., Kwak, N.: Textbook question answering with multi-modal context graph understanding and self-supervised open-set comprehension. In: ACL (2019)
12. Kim, D., Yoo, Y.J., Kim, J., Lee, S., Kwak, N.: Dynamic graph generation network: generating relational knowledge from diagrams. In: 2018 IEEE/CVF Conference on Computer Vision and Pattern Recognition, pp. 4167–4175 (2018)
13. Li, J., Su, H., Zhu, J., Wang, S., Zhang, B.: Textbook question answering under instructor guidance with memory networks. In: 2018 IEEE/CVF Conference on Computer Vision and Pattern Recognition, pp. 3655–3663 (2018)
14. Li, J., Su, H., Zhu, J., Wang, S., Zhang, B.: Textbook question answering under instructor guidance with memory networks. In: 2018 IEEE/CVF Conference on Computer Vision and Pattern Recognition, pp. 3655–3663 (2018)
15. Liu, W., Chen, C., Wong, K.Y.K., Su, Z., Han, J.: STAR-Net: a spatial attention residue network for scene text recognition. In: BMVC, vol. 2, p. 7 (2016)
16. Liu, Y., et al.: RoBERTa: a robustly optimized BERT pretraining approach. ArXiv abs/1907.11692 (2019)
17. McCann, B., Keskar, N., Xiong, C., Socher, R.: The natural language decathlon: multitask learning as question answering. ArXiv abs/1806.08730 (2018)
18. Pennington, J., Socher, R., Manning, C.D.: GloVe: global vectors for word representation. In: EMNLP (2014)
19. Ren, S., He, K., Girshick, R.B., Sun, J.: Faster R-CNN: towards real-time object detection with region proposal networks. In: NIPS (2015)
20. Seo, M.J., Kembhavi, A., Farhadi, A., Hajishirzi, H.: Bidirectional attention flow for machine comprehension. In: ICLR (2017)
21. Tan, H., Bansal, M.: LXMERT: learning cross-modality encoder representations from transformers. In: EMNLP, pp. 5103–5114 (2019)

A Multi-Task MRC Framework for Chinese Emotion Cause and Experiencer Extraction

Haoda Qian[1,2(✉)], Qiudan Li[2,3], and Zaichuan Tang[1,2]

[1] The State Key Laboratory of Management and Control for Complex Systems, Institute of Automation, Chinese Academy of Sciences, Beijing 100190, China
[2] School of Artificial Intelligence, University of Chinese Academy of Sciences, Beijing 100049, China
{qianhaoda19,tangzaichuan19}@mails.ucas.ac.cn, qiudan.li@ia.ac.cn
[3] Shenzhen Artificial Intelligence and Data Science Institute (Longhua), Shenzhen, China

Abstract. Extracting emotion cause and experiencer from text can help people better understand users' behavior patterns behind expressed emotions. Machine reading comprehension framework explicitly introduces a task-oriented query to boost the extraction task. In practice, how to learn a good task-oriented representation, accurately locate the boundary, and extract multiple causes and experiencers are the key technical challenges. To solve the above problems, this paper proposes BERT-based Machine Reading Comprehension Extraction Model with Multi-Task Learning (BERT-MRC-MTL). It first introduces query as prior knowledge and obtains text representation via BERT. Then, boundary-based and tag-based strategies are designed to select characters to be extracted, so as to extract multiple causes or experiencers simultaneously. Finally, hierarchical multi-task learning structure with residual connection is adopted to combine the answer extraction strategies. We conduct experiments on two public Chinese emotion datasets, and the results demonstrate the efficacy of our proposed model.

Keywords: Emotion cause and experiencer extraction · Machine reading comprehension · Multi-task learning

1 Introduction

Extracting emotion causes and experiencers from text is a fine-grained emotion analysis task. For instance, structural emotion phrases such as "陷入回忆 (caught up in memories)" and "白金跃 (Jinyue Bai)" extracted from Fig. 1 can provide a more comprehensive description of the "激动 (excited)" emotion, which answer the questions like "What is the cause of emotion?" and "Who feels such emotion?".

I. Farkaš et al. (Eds.): ICANN 2021, LNCS 12894, pp. 99–110, 2021.
https://doi.org/10.1007/978-3-030-86380-7_9

当日，和中新网记者谈起建言献策的初衷，<情绪感受者>**白跃金**</情绪感受者><情绪原因>**陷入回忆**</情绪原因>，并略显<情绪词>**激动**</情绪词>。

On that day, when talking to a reporter from Zhongxin Net about the original intention of his advice and suggestions, <Experieincer>**Jinyue Bai**</Experiencer> was <Cause>**caught up in memories**</Cause> and slightly <Emotion keywords>**excited**</Emotion keywords>.

Fig. 1. An example of emotion cause and experiencer extraction.

The machine reading comprehension based framework provides a task-specific extraction mechanism which guides the learning of extraction by explicitly introducing target-oriented query. This framework exerts easily generated queries and does not depend on particular category features. The key issue lies in how to mine the relationship between the query and the content. Recently, pre-trained language models such as BERT [3] obtain good performance on machine reading comprehension (MRC) tasks, it contains rich linguistic knowledge [10] and can capture long-distance relations [2]. In this paper, we adopt BERT to acquire query-aware contextualized representation. In practice, there exists multiple emotion causes or experiencers for one emotion, however, traditional machine reading comprehension models can output only one answer by selecting the answer head and the answer tail with the maximum probability. We propose boundary-based and tag-based extraction strategies to extract all causes or experiencers simultaneously. Moreover, since cause phrases have complex semantic structures and are variable in length, it is hard to accurately locate their boundaries. A multi-task learning structure is designed to combine answer sequence labeling and answer boundary prediction into a unified framework, where hierarchical structure and residual connection are adopted to share the encoder parameters.

We conduct experiments on two public Chinese emotion datasets. The empirical results show that the BERT-based machine reading comprehension extraction model with multi-task learning achieves a boost over off-the-shelf sequence labeling models and named entity recognition models.

Contributions. Our contributions can be summarized as follows:

1) We propose a MRC-based framework that introduces task-oriented query to extract emotion causes and experiencers.
2) The model uses contextualized Chinese character embeddings and does not suffer from segmentation errors or out of vocabulary (OOV) problems.
3) We demonstrate the efficacy of the model on two public Chinese emotion datasets.

2 Related Work

Our work is related to structural emotion phrase extraction and machine reading comprehension framework. In this section, we review the related works.

Extracting multiple emotion related structural information such as causes, experiencers and cues can enhance the interpretability of emotion analysis [19]. [11] adopted LSTM-CRF to extract causes, experiencers, targets and cues from English fiction corpus separately. [1] proposed an English news headline emotion corpus and used BiLSTM-CRF to extract causes, experiencers, cues and targets. They formulated the extraction task as a common sequence labeling problem and did not consider the relation between emotion roles and emotion expressed in the text, which limits its performance. [20] analyzed the emotion roles by masking or preserving specific emotion roles in the text when detecting emotions.

Most of the existing works focused on extracting cause and experiencer separately from English fiction or news headline corpus. Little work has been done on extracting emotion cause and experiencer from Chinese news content in a unified framework. News headlines are usually a summary of the news content and have higher information density. In contrast, the news content provides more details of an event. Hence, extracting cause and experiencer from news content facilitates understanding of the emotion behind the event from a deeper level and enables a multi-dimensional emotion analysis.

Machine reading comprehension framework provides a mechanism to extract answer spans from the content given a query. Such formulation has two main advantages. First, since query provides important prior information, it is highly task-oriented. Second, it does not rely much on manual features, and can easily apply to many scenarios. Recently, there has been a trend of converting NLP tasks [4,13,15,16] into machine reading comprehension problem. [6] adopted memory slots to model context information in emotion cause clause identification task. Different from these works, we focus on extracting structural information related to emotion.

3 Proposed Model

3.1 Problem Definition and Formulation

Given a news fragment $C = [c_1, c_2, ..., c_n]$, where n denotes the length of the news, our purpose is to find the structural information related to emotion using task-oriented query $Q = [q_1, q_2, ..., q_m]$, where m denotes the length of the query. We assign a label $y \in Y$ to c_i , where Y is a list of predefined phrase types (e.g., cause, experiencer, etc.).

3.2 Model Architecture

The overview of the proposed model (BERT-MRC-MTL) is shown in Fig. 2. It provides a unified framework that extracts structural emotion information.

The model contains two modules: (1)A query-aware context encoder. The task-oriented query and news fragment are concatenated and put into BERT. The encoder outputs the query-fused text representation. (2)A hierarchical multi-task learning answer extraction module with two-layer BiLSTM and residual connection. The contextualized text representation is input into the lower BiLSTM to tag the answer sequence, then the representation obtained by BERT and the output sequence from the lower BiLSTM are transfered together to the higher BiLSTM to predict the answer boundary. The final extraction results are decided by the higher BiLSTM.

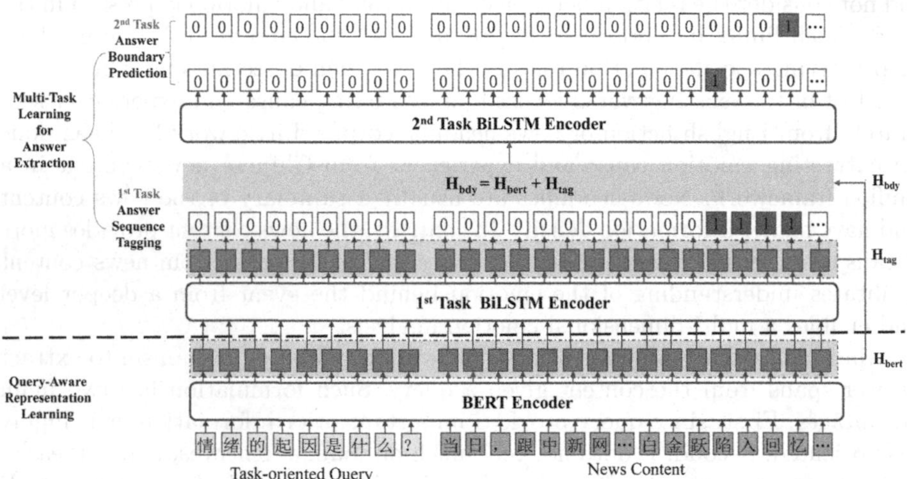

Fig. 2. The overview of the machine reading comprehension extraction framework with multi-task learning.

Query-Aware Context Encoder. Given the task-oriented query Q, we aim to extract the type y span from the news. The key issue is how to generate query related news content representation. The BERT receives the input sequence $[[\mathrm{CLS}], Q, [\mathrm{SEP}], C]$, and models the interactions between the query and the news using layer-by-layer Transformers, and outputs a context representation matrix $H_{bert} \in R^{n \times d}$, where d is the vector dimension of the last layer.

Answer Span Extraction. There may exist multiple causes or experiencers in one news fragment. Hence, two multi-span extraction strategies are adpoted to solve the problem.

Boundary-based strategy consists of two binary token classifiers. One classifier predicts the probability of each token being a start, while the other predicts the probability of each token being an end:

$$L_{start} = \mathrm{Linear}(W_{start} H) \in R^{n \times 2} \tag{1}$$

$$L_{end} = \text{Linear}(W_{end}H) \in R^{n\times 2} \tag{2}$$

Then, we apply argmax to L_{start} and L_{end} in the token level and get the starting and ending indices.

$$I_{start} = \{i \mid argmax(L^i_{start}) = 1, \quad i = 1, 2, \cdots, n\} \tag{3}$$

$$I_{end} = \{i \mid argmax(L^i_{end}) = 1, \quad i = 1, 2, \cdots, n\} \tag{4}$$

Since there is no overlap between certain category, the Nearest Match Rule is adopted to generate pairs for the starting or ending indices. The loss function for predicting the start and end indices is defined as follows:

$$\mathcal{L}_{start} = \text{BCE}(L_{start}, Y_{start}) \tag{5}$$

$$\mathcal{L}_{end} = \text{BCE}(L_{end}, Y_{end}) \tag{6}$$

$$\mathcal{L}_{bdy} = \mathcal{L}_{start} + \mathcal{L}_{end} \tag{7}$$

where BCE denotes Binary Cross Entropy, Y_{start} and Y_{end} indicate the true start and end indices.

Tag-based strategy uses a binary token classifier to predict the probability distribution of tokens belonging to the answer:

$$L_{tag} = \text{Linear}(W_{tag}H) \in R^{n\times 2} \tag{8}$$

$$I_{tag} = \{i \mid argmax(L^i_{tag}) = 1, \quad i = 1, 2, \cdots, n\} \tag{9}$$

This strategy can also extract a set of non-contiguous spans from the input text and does not need to handle the start/end matching issue. The loss function is defined as follows:

$$\mathcal{L}_{tag} = \text{BCE}(L_{tag}, Y_{tag}) \tag{10}$$

where Y_{tag} is the ground truth answer.

Multi-Task Learning Structure. Boundary-based extraction strategy predicts the start and end indice of an answer, it suffers from label imbalance problem. In contrast, tag-based extraction strategy labels the whole answer sequence, it assigns the same weight to each token in the answer and needs to put more emphasis on the boundary. Inspired by the existing multi-task learning methods in NLP tasks [5], these two extraction strategies are integrated together to enhance the performance. They share the BERT encoder, and each subtask has its corresponding classifier. Specifically, for the input in Fig. 2, to extract the cause phrase "陷入回忆 (fall into memory)", the answer tagging subtask will learn to tag the span "陷入回忆 (fall into memory)", while the answer boundary prediction subtask will learn to predict the start indice "陷 (fall)" and the end indice "忆 (memory)".

Parallel Multi-Task Learning. This multi-task learning mode puts the two subtasks in a parallel manner. Two separate BiLSTMs for each subtask share parameters of the encoding part. One BiLSTM is regarded as the answer tagger and the other is the answer boundary predictor.

$$X_{tag} = X_{bdy} = H_{bert} \tag{11}$$

$$H_{tag} = \text{BILSTM}_{tag}(X_{tag}) \tag{12}$$

$$H_{bdy} = \text{BILSTM}_{bdy}(X_{bdy}) \tag{13}$$

Here *tag* and *bdy* represent answer tagging and boundary prediction.

Heirarchical Multi-Task Learning. Hierarchial learning structure is used to make use of order information between the two subtasks. The text representation obtained by BERT is first input into the lower BiLSTM to tag answers:

$$X_{tag} = H_{bert} \tag{14}$$

$$H_{tag} = \text{BILSTM}_{tag}(X_{tag}) \tag{15}$$

Then, the output hidden states of BiLSTM_{tag} are input into the higher BiLSTM to predict the answer boundary. In addition, to share information between different layers and avoid error propagation, residual connection [8] is added between the BERT encoder and BiLSTM_{bdy}:

$$X_{bdy} = H_{bert} + H_{tag} \tag{16}$$

$$H_{bdy} = \text{BiLSTM}_{bdy}(X_{bdy}) \tag{17}$$

where BILSTM_{bdy} learns the answer boundary information. The final answer is decided by BILSTM_{bdy} using Eq.(1)(2)(3)(4).

Training Objective. The overall training objective to be minimized can be summarized as follows:

$$\mathcal{L} = \lambda \mathcal{L}_{bdy} + (1 - \lambda)\mathcal{L}_{tag} \tag{18}$$

where λ is a hyper-parameter that controls the importance of each subtask. In the experiment, we set λ to 0.5. The two losses are jointly trained in an end-to-end fashion, with parameters shared at the BERT encoder.

4 Experimental Setup

4.1 Datasets

We conduct experiments on two public Chinese emotion datasets named HLTEmotionml and CEAC. HLTEmotionml[1] is a benchmark dataset for emotion cause

[1] HLTEmotionml is available at http://119.23.18.63/?page_id=694

analysis proposed by [7]. Since there are only emotion and cause annotated on this dataset, we ask two annotators to find experiencers for HLTEmotionml. The inter-annotator agreement of the experiencer is 82%. CEAC[2] [17] labels causes, experiencers, emotion keywords and actions on news corpus. Samples that lack cause or experiencer are deleted from the two datasets. Table 1 shows the statistical information of the two datasets. During the experiment, we stochastically select 90% of the data for training and the remaining 10% for testing. The experiment is repeated 10 times and the average result is reported. Span-level micro precision, recall, and F1 score are used as evaluation measures.

Table 1. Statistical information of the two datasets.

Dataset	HLTEmotionml	CEAC
Instances	2045	2915
Instances with multiple causes	57	515
Instances with multiple experiencers	42	6
Avg. text length	64.98	88.08
Avg. cause length	9.33	10.48
Avg. experiencer length	2.19	2.79

4.2 Compared Methods

Sequence labeling models and named entity recognition models are used as baselines:

- LSTM-CRF [9]: It is a Chinese-character-based model using BiLSTM as encoder and CRF layer as decoder. Compared with word-based methods, this model does not suffer from segmentation errors.
- CAN-NER [21]: It is a convolutional attention network for Chinese named entity recognition that uses character embedding and segmentation information as features.
- BERT [3]: It uses BERT model as encoder with a token classification unit on top. This model treats extraction task as a sequence labeling problem.

We additionally propose a series of methods based on the MRC framework.

- BERT-MRC(Tag): It uses BERT to encode the query and the content, then adopts the tag-based span extraction strategy to extract the answers.
- BERT-MRC(Bdy): Similar to BERT-MRC(Tag), it adopts boundary-based answer span extraction strategy.
- BERT-MRC-MTL(Parallel): A BERT-MRC model that combines tag-based extraction strategy and boundary-based extraction strategy in a parallel way.

[2] CEAC is available at https://github.com/liupengyuan/EmotionAction_EmotionInference

- BERT-MRC-MTL(Hierarchy): A BERT-MRC model that combines tag-based extraction strategy and boundary-based extraction strategy in a hierarchical way.

4.3 Implementation Details

Under the MRC framework, the task-oriented query is instantiated as "情绪的起因是什么? (What is the cause of emotion?)" for cause extraction and "情绪的感受者是谁? (Who feels the emotion?)" for experiencer extraction. We set the max sequence length for HLTEmotionml and CEAC to 120 and 160 respectively. For non-BERT models, the Chinese character embeddings are taken from[4] [14]. The character embedding size, hidden size of CNN and BiLSTM(BiGRU) are set to 300. The window size of CNN is set to 5, which is the same as the setting in [21]. Adam [12] is used for optimization, with an initial learning rate of 0.001. For all BERT-based models, we use BEET-Base-Chinese[5] as backbone. The hidden dimension of the BiLSTM in BERT-based models is set to 768. For BERT-Tagger and BERT-MRC(Tag), we train them with a learning rate of 1e-5 for all parameters. For other models, we employ layer-wise learning rate, where BERT encoder has a learning rate of 1e-5 while the other layers have a learning rate of 1e-4. AdamW [18] is employed for optimization. Note that Pytorch 1.6.0 and Transformers 3.4.0 are used to implement the model.

5 Results and Discussions

The results are shown in Table 2. The models are categorized into non-BERT models and BERT-based models.

5.1 Model Comparison

Evaluation on HLTEmotionml. For non-BERT models, CAN-NER achieves an F1 score of 60.53 and has a relative margin of 3.21 over LSTM-CRF. BERT-based models outperform non-BERT models. BERT-MRC-MTL(Hierarchy) is the best among them with an F1 score of 74.99. BERT-MRC(Bdy) and BERT-MRC(Tag) contain target-oriented information and perform better than BERT-Tagger.

Evaluation on CEAC. CAN-NER is the best among non-BERT models and achieves an F1 score of 56.94. BERT-MRC-MTL(Hierarchy) achieves the best performance in terms of F1 score. BERT-MRC(Bdy) and BERT-MRC(Tag) perform better than BERT-Tagger.

[4] The Chinese character embedding is available at https://github.com/Embedding/Chinese-Word-Vectors

[5] BERT-Base-Chinese is available at https://huggingface.co/bert-basechinese/tree/main

Table 2. F1-score of the extraction on the two datasets.

Dataset	HLTEmotionml			CEAC		
Type	Cause	Experiencer	All	Cause	Experiencer	All
Non-BERT models						
LSTM-CRF	40.85	73.96	57.32	46.21	65.13	54.82
CAN-NER	44.75	76.1	60.53	47.61	68.29	56.94
BERT-based models						
BERT-Tagger	54.52	87.68	70.52	61.94	82.35	70.79
BERT-MRC(Tag)	53.93	88.27	70.52	62.62	84.29	72.09
BERT-MRC(Bdy)	57.93	89.87	74.22	67.06	86.61	75.83
BERT-MRC-MTL(Parallel)	59.47	90.21	74.94	69.33	**87.03**	77.32
BERT-MRC-MTL(Hierarchy)	**59.66**	**90.33**	**74.99**	**70.13**	86.95	**77.76**

It can be seen that BERT-based models perform better on CEAC than on HLTEmotionml. The reason may be that the average text length for CEAC dataset is longer and BERT can better capture long-distance dependencies.

5.2 Ablation Test

We conduct ablation tests to study the effect of different modules.

Context Encoder. In this section, different context encoders including LSTM, convolutional attention network and BERT are compared. LSTM-CRF uses BiLSTM as encoder to capture sequence-aware information. CAN-NER first combines CNNs with local attention to capture local context relations among characters, then, a GRU unit with global self-attention layer is used to capture the sentence context information. With more local and sentence context information, CAN-NER performs better than LSTM-CRF. BERT-based models outperform non-BERT models since BERT is better at capturing the long-range interactions between characters.

Answer Extraction Strategy. Compared with BERT-Tagger, BERT-MRC(Tag) achieves comparable performance on HLTEmotionml and make a slight improvement on CEAC. BERT-MRC(Bdy) outperforms BERT-Tagger on both HLTEmotionml and CEAC. The different improvement margins of the two MRC-based models imply that the chosen of span extraction strategy affects the extraction quality. The tag-based one assigns the same weight to all the answer tokens while the boundary-based one emphasizes the importance of extracting the exact spans. We select the boundary-based strategy to obtain the final answer.

Multi-Task Learning Structure. Boundary-based extraction strategy may suffer from label imbalance, while tag-based strategy can provide more category labels. To take advantage of both strategies, we co-train the two answer extraction tasks. BERT-MRC-MTL(Parallel) aims to share the parameters of the context encoder. It performs better than any single task learning model. BERT-MRC-MTL(Hierarchy) runs the two subtasks in a hierarchical order. To avoid error propagation and share the parameters of the encoder, a residual connection is added to directly link the BERT and the higher-level BiLSTM. Compared with BERT-MRC(Parallel), BERT-MRC-MTL(Hierarchy) provides a mechanism that the high-level task benefits from the low-level one.

5.3 Case Study

Table 3. A test case on HLTEmotionml.

Raw Text in Chinese and its English Translation		
S1.他愿意再去尝试。 (He is willing to try again.) S2.但是院方的建议是采用非血缘关系相匹配的骨髓或许成功率更高。 (But the hospital's advice is that using non-blood-matched marrow might have a higher success rate.) S3.如今康复出院的尹宾怡提起哥哥为了救她做5次骨髓移植的事, (When the recovered Bingyi Yin mentions the event that her brother had five hematopoietic stem cell transplantation to save her,) S4.感激的泪水就会夺眶而出。 (tears of gratitude will start from her eyes)		
Ground Truth		
Type	Cause	Experiencer
	哥哥为了救她做5次骨髓移植	尹宾怡
Prediction		
Model	Cause	Experiencer
LSTM-CRF	提起哥哥为了救她做5次骨髓移植的事(×)	尹宾怡(✓)
CAN-NER	提起哥哥为了救她做5次骨髓移植的事(×)	尹宾怡(✓)
BERT-Tagger	起(×); 哥哥为了救她做5次骨髓移植的事(×)	尹宾怡(✓)
BERT-MRC(Tag)	哥哥为了救她做5次骨髓移植的事(×)	尹宾怡(✓)
BERT-MRC(Bdy)	哥哥为了救她做5次骨髓移植的事(×)	尹宾怡(✓)
BERT-MRC-MTL(Parallel)	哥哥为了救她做5次骨髓移植(✓)	尹宾怡(✓)
BERT-MRC-MTL(Hierarchy)	哥哥为了救她做5次骨髓移植(✓)	尹宾怡(✓)

An example in Table 3 is used to illustrate the proposed model vividly. It can be seen that BERT-MRC-MTL(Parallel) and BERT-MRC-MTL(Hierarchy) extract the cause "哥哥为了救她做5次骨髓移植 (her brother had five hematopoietic stem cell transplantation to save her)" and experiencer "尹宾怡 (Bingyi Yin)" correctly, while the other models roughly locate the cause phrase and extract a longer span, such as "提起哥哥为了救她做5次骨髓移植的事 (mentions the event that her brother had five hematopoietic stem cell transplantation to save her)". The results indicate that the combination of query-related information, deep contextualized representation and multi-task learning structure can help improve the extraction performance.

6 Conclusion

We present a novel extraction framework to obtain emotion cause and experi- encer from news corpus, it generates task-oriented content representation through BERT, and adopts multi-task learning for spans extraction. Experiments on two public Chinese emotion datasets show that BERT-MRC-MTL(Hierarchy) outperforms other models. In future work, we will extract emotion cause and experiencer in more complex scenarios such as Weibo, which contains dialogue structures and rich user interactions.

Acknowledgement. This work was supported in part by the National Key Research and Development Program of China under Grant 2020AAA0103405, the National Natural Science Foundation of China under Grants 62071467,71621002 and 71902179, as well as the Strategic Priority Research Program of Chinese Academy of Sciences under Grant XDA27030100.

References

1. Bostan, L.A.M., Kim, E., Klinger, R.: GoodNewsEveryone: a corpus of news headlines annotated with emotions, semantic roles, and reader perception. In: LREC (2020)
2. Clark, K., Khandelwal, U., Levy, O., Manning, C.D.: What does bert look at? an analysis of bert's attention. In: Proceedings of the 2019 ACL Workshop BlackboxNLP (2019)
3. Devlin, J., Chang, M.W., Lee, K., Toutanova, K.: Bert: pre-training of deep bidirectional transformers for language understanding. In: NAACL-HLT (2019)
4. FitzGerald, N., Michael, J., He, L., Zettlemoyer, L.: Large-scale qa-srl parsing. ArXiv abs/1805.05377 (2018)
5. Gong, Y., et al.: Deep cascade multi-task learning for slot filling in online shopping assistant. In: AAAI (2019)
6. Gui, L., Hu, J., He, Y., Xu, R., Lu, Q., Du, J.: A question answering approach for emotion cause extraction. In: EMNLP (2017)
7. Gui, L., Wu, D., Xu, R., Lu, Q., Zhou, Y.: Event-driven emotion cause extraction with corpus construction. In: EMNLP (2016)
8. He, K., Zhang, X., Ren, S., Sun, J.: Deep residual learning for image recognition. In: 2016 IEEE Conference on Computer Vision and Pattern Recognition (CVPR), pp. 770–778 (2016)
9. Huang, Z., Xu, W., Yu, K.: Bidirectional lstm-crf models for sequence tagging. ArXiv abs/1508.01991 (2015)
10. Jawahar, G., Sagot, B., Seddah, D.: What does bert learn about the structure of language? In: ACL (2019)
11. Kim, E., Klinger, R.: Who feels what and why? annotation of a literature corpus with semantic roles of emotions. In: COLING (2018)
12. Kingma, D.P., Ba, J.: Adam: a method for stochastic optimization. In: ICLR (Poster) (2015). http://arxiv.org/abs/1412.6980
13. Levy, O., Seo, M., Choi, E., Zettlemoyer, L.: Zero-shot relation extraction via reading comprehension. In: CoNLL (2017)
14. Li, S., Zhao, Z., Hu, R., Li, W., Liu, T., Du, X.: Analogical reasoning on Chinese morphological and semantic relations. In: ACL (2018)

15. Li, X., Feng, J., Meng, Y., Han, Q., Wu, F., Li, J.: A unified mrc framework for named entity recognition. In: ACL (2020)
16. Liu, J., Chen, Y., Liu, K., Bi, W., Liu, X.: Event extraction as machine reading comprehension. In: EMNLP (2020)
17. Liu, P., Du, C., Zhao, S., Zhu, C.: Emotion action detection and emotion inference: the task and dataset. ArXiv abs/1903.06901 (2019)
18. Loshchilov, I., Hutter, F.: Decoupled weight decay regularization. In: International Conference on Learning Representations (2019). https://openreview.net/forum?id=Bkg6RiCqY7
19. Oberländer, L., Klinger, R.: Token sequence labeling vs. clause classification for english emotion stimulus detection. ArXiv abs/2010.07557 (2020)
20. Oberländer, L., Reich, K., Klinger, R.: Experiencers, stimuli, or targets: which semantic roles enable machine learning to infer the emotions? ArXiv abs/2011.01599 (2020)
21. Zhu, Y., Wang, G., Karlsson, B.F.: Can-ner: convolutional attention network for Chinese named entity recognition. In: NAACL-HLT (2019)

Fairer Machine Learning Through Multi-objective Evolutionary Learning

Qingquan Zhang[1,2], Jialin Liu[1,2], Zeqi Zhang[3], Junyi Wen[3], Bifei Mao[3], and Xin Yao[1,2(✉)]

[1] Research Institute of Trustworthy Autonomous System, Southern University of Science and Technology (SUSTech), Shenzhen, China
11930582@mail.sustech.edu.cn, {liujl,xiny}@sustech.edu.cn

[2] Guangdong Provincial Key Laboratory of Brain-inspired Intelligent Computation, Department of Computer Science and Engineering, Southern University of Science and Technology (SUSTech), Shenzhen, China

[3] Trustworthiness Theory Research Center, Huawei Technologies Co., Ltd., Shenzhen, China

Abstract. Dilemma between model accuracy and fairness in machine learning models has been shown theoretically and empirically. So far, dozens of fairness measures have been proposed, among which incompatibility and complementarity exist. However, no fairness measure has been universally accepted as the single fairest measure. No one has considered multiple fairness measures simultaneously. In this paper, we propose a multi-objective evolutionary learning framework for mitigating unfairness caused by considering a single measure only, in which a multi-objective evolutionary algorithm is used during training to balance accuracy and multiple fairness measures simultaneously. In our case study, besides the model accuracy, two fairness measures that are conflicting to each other are selected. Empirical results show that our proposed multi-objective evolutionary learning framework is able to find Pareto-front models efficiently and provide fairer machine learning models that consider multiple fairness measures.

Keywords: Fairness in machine learning · Discrimination in machine learning · AI ethics · Fairness measures · Multi-objective learning

---

This work was supported by the Research Institute of Trustworthy Autonomous Systems, the Guangdong Provincial Key Laboratory (Grant No. 2020B121201001), the Program for Guangdong Introducing Innovative and Entrepreneurial Teams (Grant No. 2017ZT07X386), the Guangdong Basic and Applied Basic Research Foundation (Grant No. 2021A1515011830), the Shenzhen Science and Technology Program (Grant No. KQTD2016112514355531), the Shenzhen Fundamental Research Program (Grant Nos. JCYJ20180504165652917, JCYJ20190809121403553) and Huawei project on "Fundamental Theory and Key Technologies of Trustworthy Systems".

I. Farkaš et al. (Eds.): ICANN 2021, LNCS 12894, pp. 111–123, 2021.
https://doi.org/10.1007/978-3-030-86380-7_10

1 Introduction

Machine learning techniques are widely applied in real life, such as image recognition [9] and job application screening [21]. However, unfairness or discrimination from training data may lead to unfair data-driven models and unfair predictions. During the last decade, there has been a significantly growing research interest in measuring and mitigating unfairness in machine learning [1,4,14,27,34].

Dozens of (un)fairness measures for determining and evaluating the fairness of machine learning models trained only for accuracy have been defined [1,4,14, 27,34] mainly based on the evaluated model's predicted outcomes, the predicted and actual outcomes, predicted probabilities and actual outcomes, similarity, and causal reasoning [27]. However, two dilemmas exist [1]: (i) the trade-off between model accuracy and its fairness has been theoretically and empirically shown [26]; (ii) some fairness measures have been shown to be conflicting with each other [3,26], such as individual fairness and group fairness [26]. To tackle the former dilemma, some approaches for mitigating unfairness take into account a single fairness measure as a regularisation term or a constraint aiming at balancing between model accuracy and fairness [1]. However, no fairness measure has been universally accepted as the single fairest measure. To our best knowledge, no one has considered multiple fairness measures simultaneously during training. Motivated by this gap, we attempt to answer the following research question in this paper: *Can we make fair machine learning fairer by considering multiple fairness measures simultaneously?* This can be divided into three questions more precisely: ($\mathcal{Q}1$) Whether multi-objective learning can simultaneously optimise the model accuracy and multiple conflicting fairness measures? ($\mathcal{Q}2$) Can multi-objective learning optimise one or several fairness measures without degenerating others? In other words, whether the obtained models will become less fair according to any of the considered measures? ($\mathcal{Q}3$) Can we obtain a group of diverse models by applying multi-objective learning so that different trade-offs can be seen clearly?

To answer those questions, in this paper, we propose a multi-objective evolutionary learning framework which trains machine learning models for accuracy and multiple fairness measures simultaneously. The main contributions of this paper are as follows. (i) We propose a multi-objective evolutionary learning framework for training fairer machine learning models. Multi-objective optimisation is applied to consider model accuracy and multiple fairness measures simultaneously during training. (ii) We have implemented our framework with a concrete instantiation which uses the model error and two conflicting but complementary unfairness measures as three objectives during model training. (iii) Empirical results on three well-known benchmark sets show that our framework is able to find Pareto-front models effectively. (iv) The obtained models can act as good candidates for human decision-makers' use with different preferences.

The remainder of this paper is organised as follows. Section 2 presents related work. Our framework is proposed in Sect. 3.1. An effective instantiation of our framework is described in Sect. 3.2. Section 4 presents and discusses empirical studies. Section 5 concludes the paper.

2 Background

Concepts of (un)fairness in machine learning have been considered in many research fields for more than half a decade [14]. Different perspectives of fairness have different preferences and there is no universal definition of fairness [1,14]. The interpretation of individual fairness and group fairness is one perspective being accepted by many studies [7,26]. Individual fairness implies that similar individuals should be treated similarly. On the contrary, group fairness considers the fairness of different groups, which often depends on sensitive (also called protected [4]) attributes. Typically, sensitive attributes are traits considered to discriminate against by law, such as gender, race, age and so on. A number of articles [4,14,27,34] have reviewed research progresses on measuring and mitigating unfairness in machine learning, in which dozens of fairness or unfairness measures have been defined.

Different (un)fairness measures have been used as a regularisation term or a constraint together with model accuracy/error during model training for balancing between model performance and fairness [1,23]. In the work of [29], the fairness-accuracy Pareto front was estimated by training models for different weighted sums of model accuracy and one single fairness measure. However, correlation and disagreement between fairness measures have been observed [3,26]. A model determined as fair under one measure could be unfair under another measure. Speicher *et al.* [26] illustrated the trade-off between model accuracy and fairness, as well as the trade-off between individual fairness and group fairness.

How to make fair machine learning fairer is a core research topic. In this paper, we intend to treat model accuracy and multiple fairness measures equally with multi-objective learning, which is significantly different from existing works.

3 Multi-objective Evolutionary Learning for Mitigating Unfairness

To make fair machine learning fairer, we propose a multi-objective evolutionary learning framework [2] to train models for accuracy and multiple fairness measures simultaneously. An instantiation of our framework is also provided.

3.1 Proposed Framework

Our general framework is presented in Algorithm 1. It takes as input a set of training data $\mathcal{D}_{train}$, a set of validation data $\mathcal{D}_{validation}$, a number of initial models $\mathcal{M}$, a multi-objective optimisation algorithm π and a set of model evaluation criteria $\mathcal{E}$, including an accuracy measure and multiple (un)fairness measures. Every time a new model is initialised or generated (line 1, 9), partial training [30,31] on $\mathcal{D}_{train}$ is always applied as a kind of local search. Each model is evaluated with criteria $\mathcal{E}$ as objectives of π. In the main loop, μ promising models are selected according to some selection strategy of π (line 6), from which λ new models $\mathcal{M}'$ are generated with the aim of inheriting information from promising

Algorithm 1. Multi-objective learning framework for fairer machine learning.

Require: Initial models $\mathcal{M}_1, \ldots, \mathcal{M}_\lambda$
Require: Set of model evaluation criteria $\mathcal{E}$
Require: Training dataset $\mathcal{D}_{train}$, validation dataset $\mathcal{D}_{validation}$
Require: Multi-objective optimiser π
1: Partially train [30, 31] $\mathcal{M}_1, \ldots, \mathcal{M}_\lambda$ over $\mathcal{D}_{train}$
2: **for** $i \in \{1, \ldots, \lambda\}$ **do**
3: $\quad \epsilon_i \leftarrow$ Evaluate $\mathcal{M}_i$ with criteria $\mathcal{E}$ on $\mathcal{D}_{validation}$
4: **end for**
5: **while** terminal conditions are not fulfilled **do**
6: $\quad \mathcal{P} \leftarrow$ Select μ promising models from $\mathcal{M}_1, \ldots, \mathcal{M}_\lambda$ with "best" $\epsilon_1, \ldots, \epsilon_\mu$ according to π
7: $\quad \mathcal{M}' \leftarrow$ Generate λ new models $\mathcal{M}'_1, \ldots, \mathcal{M}'_\lambda$ from $\mathcal{P}$ according to π
8: $\quad$ **for** $i \in \{1, \ldots, \lambda\}$ **do**
9: $\quad\quad \mathcal{M'}_i \leftarrow$ Partially train [30, 31] $\mathcal{M}'_i$ on $\mathcal{D}_{train}$
10: $\quad\quad \epsilon'_i \leftarrow$ Evaluate $\mathcal{M'}_i$ with criteria $\mathcal{E}$ on $\mathcal{D}_{validation}$
11: $\quad$ **end for**
12: $\quad < \mathcal{M}_1, \epsilon_1 >, < \mathcal{M}_2, \epsilon_1 >, \ldots, < \mathcal{M}_\lambda, \epsilon_\lambda > \leftarrow$ Select λ promising models from $\{\mathcal{M}_1, \ldots, \mathcal{M}_\lambda\} \bigcup \{\mathcal{M}'_1, \ldots, \mathcal{M}'_\lambda\}$ by π based on $\epsilon_1, \ldots, \epsilon_\lambda$ and $\epsilon'_1, \ldots, \epsilon'_\lambda$, and then update $\mathcal{M}_1, \ldots, \mathcal{M}_\lambda$ and $\epsilon_1, \ldots, \epsilon_\lambda$ accordingly
13: **end while**
14: **Return** $\mathcal{M}_1, \ldots, \mathcal{M}_\lambda$

models (line 7). After partial training and model evaluation (line 8–11), λ models are selected from $\mathcal{M} \bigcup \mathcal{M}'$ by π as new $\mathcal{M}$ (line 12). The above steps repeat until a termination criterion is reached.

The core steps of our framework are the model evaluation based on multiple criteria and the generation of new models. Multi-objective evolutionary algorithms (MOEAs) [19] are ideal for those tasks. The output models can be further selected by human decision-makers or used as an ensemble of models [2,31].

3.2 An Effective Instantiation of Our Framework

The choices of the model set, multi-objective optimisation algorithm and evaluation criteria in our proposed framework can vary according to the prediction tasks and actual preferences. We provide an instantiation of our framework and perform experimental studies with this instantiation in Sect. 4. Core ingredients of this instantiation are as follows.

Evaluation Criteria (Measuring Between- and in-group Unfairness). The mean square error (MSE), individual unfairness and group unfairness [26] are used as three evaluation criteria. In this paper, we view the conflicting but complementary in- and between- group unfairness as individual unfairness (f_I) and group unfairness (f_G), respectively, which were formulated in [26] as:

$$f_I = \sum_{g=1}^{|G|} \frac{n_g}{n} \left(\frac{\mu_g}{\mu}\right)^\alpha \epsilon^\alpha(\boldsymbol{b}^g), \tag{1}$$

$$f_G = \frac{1}{n\alpha(\alpha-1)} \sum_{g=1}^{|G|} n_g \left((\frac{\mu_g}{\mu})^\alpha - 1 \right), \tag{2}$$

where $|G|$ is the number of groups, n_g refers to the size of group g (e.g., male, female), n is the number of individuals (i.e., $n = \sum_g n_g$). The work of [26] defined the notion of *benefit vector* in group g, denoted as $\boldsymbol{b}^g$. For each individual i, its benefit is quantified as $b_i = \theta x_i - y_i + 1$ [12,26], where y_i, θ and x_i denote the true labels, parameters of models and data, respectively. The averaged benefit of a group g and the whole dataset are denoted and calculated as $\mu_g = mean(\boldsymbol{b}^g)$ and $\mu = mean(\boldsymbol{b})$ [26], respectively. α is a constant $\notin \{0, 1\}$ and set as 2 in our empirical studies as in [26]. $\epsilon^\alpha(\boldsymbol{b}^g)$ is a family of inequality indices from the perspective of economics [5], namely generalised entropy indices, which measures the degree of (un)fairness of the benefits obtained by algorithmic predictors and ground-truth, calculated as $\epsilon^\alpha(\boldsymbol{b}^g) = \epsilon^\alpha(b_1, b_2, \ldots, b_n) = \frac{1}{n\alpha(\alpha-1)} \sum_{i=1}^n \left((\frac{b_i}{\mu})^\alpha - 1 \right)$.

Model Set. Various machine learning models can be used. In this work, a set of artificial neural nets (ANNs) with an identical architecture is used.

Multi-objective Optimiser. The non-dominated sorting genetic algorithm-II (NSGA-II) [6], a well-known Pareto dominance-based MOEA, is used in our instantiation. The weights and bias of each ANN are encoded as a real-value vector. During selection and replacement, NSGA-II uses Pareto dominance mechanisms to select non-dominated solutions based on the evaluation criteria. When reproducing individuals, isotropic Gaussian perturbation $\delta \sim \mathcal{N}(0, \sigma^2)$ is added to weights and bias of each parent [11,22], where σ indicates mutation strength. During partial training [30], model parameters are updated by Adam [16].

4 Experimental Studies

To answer our research questions proposed in Sect. 1, we perform several experiments on three benchmark datasets. On each dataset, the instantiation of our framework is used to optimise simultaneously three objectives, the model error (MSE), individual and group unfairness of models (f_I and f_G, respectively). This tri-objective case is referred to as F_{EIG} in our experiments.

To our best knowledge, there is no study that directly applied individual and group unfairness [26] to mitigate model discrimination. Therefore, in order to verify the effectiveness of our framework, we perform the following three ablation studies as baselines for comparison: a bi-objective one considering MSE and f_I (referred to as F_{EI}) during model training; another bi-objective one considering MSE and f_G (F_{EG}); and a single-objective one considering MSE alone (F_E). In each case, 15 independent trials have been performed.

4.1 Experimental Setup

Datasets. Three benchmark datasets, *German* [15], *COMPAS* [18] and *Adult* [17], have been used in our experimental study. The task of *German* is predicting if a person has an acceptable credit risk. The sensitive attributes are gender and age. Both have two categories. The task of *COMPAS* (Correctional Offender Management Profiling for Alternative Sanctions) [18] is predicting whether an arrested offender will be rearrested within two years counting from taking the test. The sensitive attributes are race and gender, which have six and two categories, respectively. The task of *Adult* is predicting whether a person can get income higher than $50,000 per year or not. The sensitive attributes are race and gender, which have three and two categories, respectively. The pre-processing on each dataset is the same as in [8]. Each dataset is randomly split into 3 partitions, with a ratio of 6:2:2, as training, validation and test sets.

Parameter Setting. Our model set is composed of 50 ANN models. In our primary experiments, all models are fully connected with one hidden layer of 64, 128 and 256 nodes for *German*, *COMPAS* and *Adult*, respectively. The weights are initialised as in [10], which is commonly used. The learning rate is set as 0.001 for *German* and 0.01 for both *COMPAS* and *Adult*. The mutation strength is set as 0.01. The μ and λ of NSGA-II are 50. In the tri-objective and two bi-objective cases, the experimental setting are the same. Since F_E considers one single objective, the top λ models considering MSE only are directly selected as the new population for the next generation. The termination condition is set as a maximum number of 500 generations of NSGA-II.

Performance Measures. Three popular indicators [20], hyper volume (HV) [33], pure diversity (PD) [25] and spacing [24], are used to evaluate the solution set obtained by NSGA-II. HV is widely used as a common measure to evaluate the overall performance of a solution set in terms of convergence and diversity, while PD and spacing indicators emphasise more the diversity of solutions. In this work, due to the unknown true Pareto front, when calculating HV, all the non-dominated solutions found in all the experimental trials on the same dataset are collected as a pseudo Pareto front. Equation (7) of the work [32] is used to calculate HV, with Nadir point $\{1.1, \ldots, 1.1\}$ after normalisation. PD is calculated with Eq. (5) of [25]. Spacing is calculated with Eq. (1) on page 136 of [25].

4.2 Experimental Results and Discussions

In this section, our research questions are answered with experimental results. ($\mathcal{Q}$1) ***Whether multi-objective learning can simultaneously optimise the model accuracy and multiple conflicting fairness measures or not?***

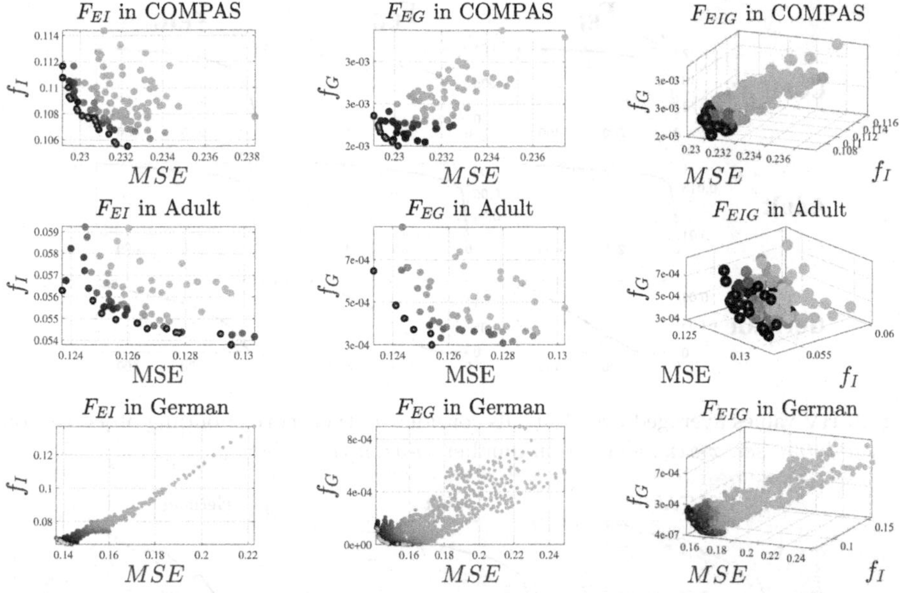

Fig. 1. Illustrative examples: evaluated values on validation set. Different colours indicate solutions at different generations. Green stars highlight the non-dominated solutions in the final generation. Left to right: F_{EI}, F_{EG} and F_{EIG}. (Color figure online)

We answer *Q*1 from two perspectives on the *validation set*: (i) visualisation of optimisation process and (ii) convergence curves of HV values.

Figure 1 illustrates the optimisation process of arbitrarily selected trials of F_{EI}, F_{EG} and F_{EIG} on the validation set, where non-dominated solutions of each generation are drawn with colour darken as the evolution progresses. It's clearly shown that, model error and one or two unfairness measures converge simultaneously towards Pareto fronts (green stars).

In addition, Fig. 2 illustrates the convergence curves of HV values obtained by F_{EI}, F_{EG} and F_{EIG} considering their corresponding objectives in calculating HV values.

In all the three studies considering two or three objectives, their HV values increase along with evolution, which implies that the model error, individual and group unfairness decrease along with evolution while the diversity significantly increases.

(*Q*2) *Can multi-objective learning optimise one or several fairness measures without degenerating others?*

*Q*2 is answered by results on the *test set*: (i) model quality measured by HV values and (ii) model unfairness (comparing the models trained for error and unfairness to the ones trained for error only).

For the first aspect, HV values of F_{EI}, F_{EG} F_{EIG}, and F_E are compared. In order to achieve fair comparison, MSE, f_I and f_G are involved as the three objectives in the calculation of HV for all the four aforementioned cases.

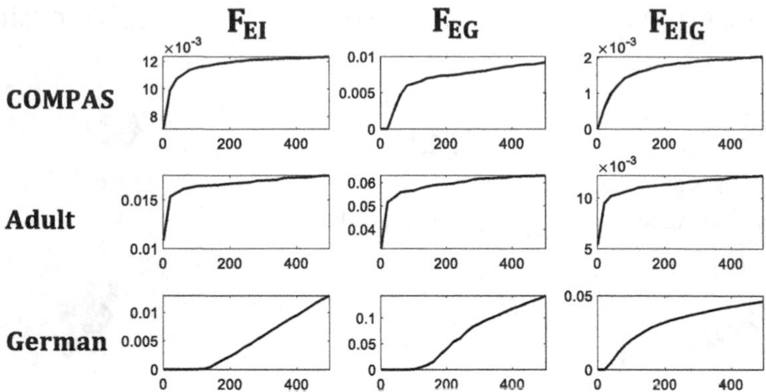

Fig. 2. HV values averaged over 15 trials considering their corresponding objectives on the *validation set*. *x-axis*: generation number; *y-axis*: HV value.

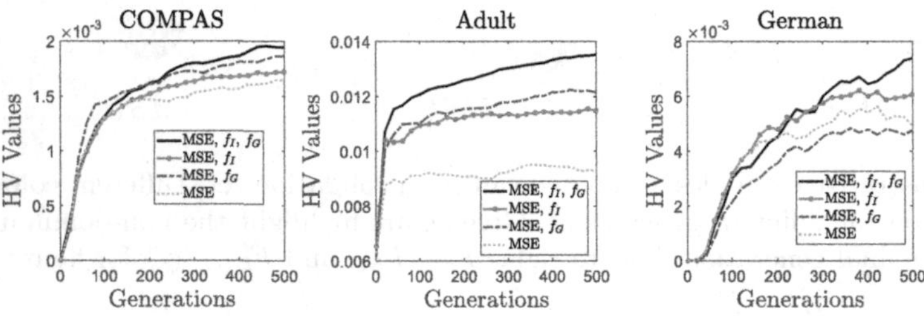

Fig. 3. HV values averaged over 15 trials considering each objective on *test* set.

Figure 3 illustrates how the average HV value changes along with evolution. In F_{EIG} (black curve), the obtained HV value is usually higher than the ones of other cases. Especially on *Adult* dataset, this tri-objective F_{EIG} significantly outperforms the bi-objective and single-objective cases. It is worth mentioning that although only MSE is optimised in F_E, the HV values of its solutions increase with the generation number. This can be easily justified. The calculations of individual and group unfairness [26] involve the true positives, true negatives, false positives and false negatives which imply the model error. According to benefit $b_i = \theta x_i - y_i + 1$, minimising MSE means making $\theta x_i - y_i$ closer to 0 and b_i closer to 1. According to Eqs. (1) and (2), f_I is minimal when $b_1 = b_2 = \dots b_n$ and f_G has the similar trend to f_I. Therefore, optimising MSE alone will decrease the individual and group unfairness but the effect is limited. This was also shown in [26]. However, on *Adult* and *German*, the contribution of solely optimising MSE to HV gradually decreases as shown in Fig. 3.

Table 1 provides the statistical analysis of HV values of the final solution sets illustrated in Fig. 3. Overall, F_{EIG}, considering simultaneously MSE, f_I and f_G, achieves statistically the best HV values in 7 out of 9 cases according to the Wilcoxon rank sum test [13] with 0.05 significance level. From the perspective of multi-objective optimisation, F_{EIG} has superior performance, in terms

Table 1. HV values of final solutions averaged over 15 trials. "+/≈/-" indicates that the average HV value of corresponding algorithm (specified by column header) is statistically better/similar/worse than the one of F_{EIG} according to Wilcoxon rank sum test with 0.05 significance level.

Dataset	F_{EI}	F_{EG}	F_E	F_{EIG}
COMPAS	0.00172–	0.00186≈	0.00165–	0.00195
Adult	0.01147–	0.01214–	0.00929–	0.01351
German	0.00606≈	0.00476–	0.00494–	0.00738

Table 2. Comparing models shown to be non-dominated on the test data and best on at least one of the metrics (MSE, f_I and f_G), in terms of the three metric values averaged over 15 runs. "NDM" stands for "non-dominated models". "+/≈/-" indicates that the average objective value (specified by row header) of corresponding algorithm (specified by column header) is statistically better/similar/worse than the one of F_{EIG} according to Wilcoxon rank sum test with 0.05 significance level.

		NDM with best MSE			NDM with best f_I			NDM with best f_G		
		Avg. MSE	Avg. f_I	Avg. f_G	Avg. MSE	Avg. f_I	Avg. f_G	Avg. MSE	Avg. f_I	Avg. f_G
COMPAS	F_{EIG}	0.22268	0.10575	0.00290	0.22585	0.10203	0.00297	0.22351	0.10371	0.00287
	F_{EI}	0.22270≈	0.10567≈	0.00297-	0.22582≈	0.10206≈	0.00299≈	0.22363≈	0.10402≈	0.00291≈
	F_{EG}	0.22246≈	0.10486+	0.00289≈	0.22296+	0.10368-	0.00285+	0.22279+	0.10446-	0.00285≈
	F_E	0.22362-	0.10610≈	0.00299-	0.22415+	0.10368-	0.00292≈	0.22333≈	0.10451-	0.00290≈
Adult	F_{EIG}	0.12565	0.05738	0.00057	0.13163	0.05396	0.00065	0.12926	0.05791	0.00027
	F_{EI}	0.12552≈	0.05810-	0.00066≈	0.13133≈	0.05411≈	0.00064≈	0.12777+	0.05540+	0.00048-
	F_{EG}	0.12546≈	0.05804-	0.00065-	0.12758+	0.05643-	0.00038+	0.12933≈	0.05807≈	0.00027≈
	F_E	0.12556≈	0.05828-	0.00066≈	0.12679+	0.05608-	0.00063≈	0.12705+	0.05709+	0.00040-
German	F_{EIG}	0.16380	0.08071	0.00115	0.16813	0.07707	0.00121	0.16449	0.08224	0.00110
	F_{EI}	0.16375≈	0.07830+	0.00125-	0.16716≈	0.07537+	0.00125≈	0.16468≈	0.07748+	0.00125-
	F_{EG}	0.16314≈	0.08302-	0.00110≈	0.16341+	0.08297-	0.00110≈	0.16476≈	0.08361≈	0.00107≈
	F_E	0.16574≈	0.08367-	0.00120≈	0.16512+	0.08172-	0.00119≈	0.16489≈	0.08294≈	0.00117≈

of convergence and diversity, in comparison with the single- and bi-objective optimisation cases.

For the second aspect, we focus on studying each unfairness measure individually for further analysis. A set of models, providing different tradeoffs among the optimised objectives, can be obtained by our proposed framework. Among the models returned at the end of each run of an F_* ("$*$" indicates the objective(s) considered during training), the models shown to be non-dominated on the test data and "best" on at least one of the metrics (MSE, f_I and f_G) are selected (in other words, extreme points are selected). The MSE, f_I and f_G values of those selected models are averaged separately over 15 runs and reported in Table 2. Statistical tests assist with the determination of dominance relation [20] when comparing to the aforementioned, selected models obtained by F_{EIG} with the ones obtained by other algorithms. Highlights are summarised as follows.

F_{EIG} **versus** F_{EI}. In only one case (German, highlighted in grey in Table 2), F_{EIG}'s "best" model has worse f_I (0.07707) than the one (0.07537) obtained by F_{EI}, while no statistically significant difference has been observed on their MSE or f_G values; in the other cases, F_{EIG}'s "best" models are not dominated by the ones of F_{EI}, and even dominate F_{EI}'s in some cases.
F_{EIG} **versus** F_{EG}. Similarly, in only one case (COMPAS, highlighted in grey in Table 2), F_{EIG}'s "best" model has worse f_I (0.10575) than the one (0.10486) of F_{EG}, while no statistically significant difference has been observed on their MSE or f_I values; in the other cases, F_{EIG}'s best models are not dominated by the ones of F_{EG}, and even dominate F_{EG}'s in some cases.
F_{EIG} **versus** F_E. "best" models of F_{EIG} are never dominated by F_E's.

To summarise, in 25 out of 27 cases, our framework is able to optimise multiple fairness measures without degenerating others.

Table 3. PD and spacing of final solutions averaged over 15 trials. "+/≈/-" indicates that the average PD or spacing value of corresponding algorithm (specified by column header) is statistically better/similar/worse than the one of F_{EIG} according to Wilcoxon rank sum test with 0.05 significance level. Larger PD values and smaller spacing values imply better performance.

		F_{EI}	F_{EG}	F_E	F_{EIG}
PD	*COMPAS*	77509–	72794–	63791–	94144
	Adult	80454–	72202–	69703–	94345
	German	76695–	51746–	68083–	97476
Spacing	*COMPAS*	0.1614≈	0.1846–	0.2599–	0.1462
	Adult	0.1518≈	0.1716–	0.2434–	0.1308
	German	0.1086–	0.1046–	0.1775–	0.0409

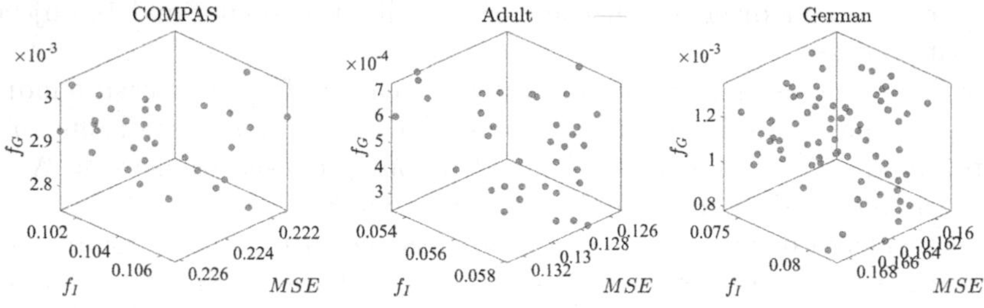

Fig. 4. Pareto fronts obtained by F_{EIG} from all the generations over 15 runs.

(*Q*3) ***Can we obtain a group of diverse models by applying multi-objective learning?***
To verify if multi-objective learning can generate a group of diverse models providing different tradeoffs among the concerned objectives, Fig. 4 illustrates the Pareto fronts generated by F_{EIG}, i.e., our algorithm considering MSE, f_I and f_G simultaneously. All the points in Fig. 4 are non-dominated solutions. Table 3 shows that tri-objective F_{EIG} obtains models with better diversity in 16 out of 18 cases than the other three algorithms according to PD [28] and spacing [24] indicators (cf. Sect. 4.1).

5 Conclusion

In this paper, we propose a novel multi-objective evolutionary learning framework for mitigating unfairness in machine learning models considering simultaneously multiple (un)fairness measures. An instantiation of the proposed framework is evaluated on three well-known benchmark datasets. Experimental results show that our framework is able to optimise one or several fairness measures without degenerating others and find Pareto-front models efficiently to provide human decision-makers with diverse candidate models for their choice.

In the future, we plan to evaluate our framework on a larger number of data sets. We will investigate (1) more appropriate multi-objective optimisation algorithm as the learning algorithm in our framework; (2) more efficient fitness evaluation methods for evaluating learning models; and (3) ensemble strategies for combining multiple models [2].

References

1. Caton, S., Haas, C.: Fairness in machine learning: a survey. arXiv preprint arXiv:2010.04053 (2020)
2. Chandra, A., Yao, X.: Ensemble learning using multi-objective evolutionary algorithms. J. Math. Model. Algor. **5**(4), 417–445 (2006)
3. Chouldechova, A.: Fair prediction with disparate impact: a study of bias in recidivism prediction instruments. Big Data **5**(2), 153–163 (2017)
4. Corbett-Davies, S., Goel, S.: The measure and mismeasure of fairness: a critical review of fair machine learning. arXiv preprint arXiv:1808.00023 (2018)
5. Cowell, F.A., Kuga, K.: Additivity and the entropy concept: an axiomatic approach to inequality measurement. J. Econ. Theory **25**(1), 131–143 (1981)
6. Deb, K., Pratap, A., Agarwal, S., Meyarivan, T.: A fast and elitist multiobjective genetic algorithm: NSGA-II. IEEE Trans. Evol. Comput. **6**(2), 182–197 (2002)
7. Dwork, C., Hardt, M., Pitassi, T., Reingold, O., Zemel, R.: Fairness through awareness. In: Proceedings of the 3rd Innovations in Theoretical Computer Science Conference, pp. 214–226 (2012)
8. Friedler, S.A., Scheidegger, C., Venkatasubramanian, S., Choudhary, S., Hamilton, E.P., Roth, D.: A comparative study of fairness-enhancing interventions in machine learning. In: Proceedings of the Conference on Fairness, Accountability, and Transparency, pp. 329–338 (2019)

9. Fujiyoshi, H., Hirakawa, T., Yamashita, T.: Deep learning-based image recognition for autonomous driving. IATSS Res. **43**(4), 244–252 (2019)
10. Glorot, X., Bengio, Y.: Understanding the difficulty of training deep feedforward neural networks. In: Proceedings of the Thirteenth International Conference on Artificial Intelligence and Statistics, pp. 249–256. JMLR Workshop and Conference Proceedings (2010)
11. Gong, Z., Chen, H., Yuan, B., Yao, X.: Multiobjective learning in the model space for time series classification. IEEE Trans. Cybern. **49**(3), 918–932 (2018)
12. Heidari, H., Ferrari, C., Gummadi, K.P., Krause, A.: Fairness behind a veil of ignorance: a welfare analysis for automated decision making. In: Proceedings of the 32nd International Conference on Neural Information Processing Systems, NIPS'18, pp. 1273–1283. Curran Associates Inc., Red Hook (2018)
13. Hollander, M., Wolfe, D.A., Chicken, E.: Nonparametric Statistical Methods, vol. 751. John Wiley & Sons, Hoboken (2013)
14. Hutchinson, B., Mitchell, M.: 50 years of test (un) fairness: lessons for machine learning. In: Proceedings of the Conference on Fairness, Accountability, and Transparency, pp. 49–58 (2019)
15. Kamiran, F., Calders, T.: Classifying without discriminating. In: 2nd International Conference on Computer, Control and Communication, pp. 1–6. IEEE (2009)
16. Kingma, D.P., Ba, J.L.: Adam: a method for stochastic gradient descent. In: ICLR: International Conference on Learning Representations, pp. 1–15 (2015)
17. Kohavi, R., Becker, B.: UCI machine learning repository: The adult income data set (1998). https://archive.ics.uci.edu/ml/datasets/adult
18. Larson, J., Mattu, S., Kirchner, L., Angwin, J.: Data and analysis for "how we analyzed the compas recidivism algorithm" (2016). https://github.com/propublica/compas-analysis
19. Li, B., Li, J., Tang, K., Yao, X.: Many-objective evolutionary algorithms: a survey. ACM Comput. Surv. **48**(1) (2015)
20. Li, M., Yao, X.: Quality evaluation of solution sets in multiobjective optimisation: a survey. ACM Comput. Surv. **52**(2) (2019)
21. Liem, C.C.S., et al.: Psychology meets machine learning: interdisciplinary perspectives on algorithmic job candidate screening. In: Escalante, H.J., Escalera, S., Guyon, I., Baró, X., Güçlütürk, Y., Güçlü, U., van Gerven, M. (eds.) Explainable and Interpretable Models in Computer Vision and Machine Learning. TSSCML, pp. 197–253. Springer, Cham (2018). https://doi.org/10.1007/978-3-319-98131-4_9
22. Minku, L.L., Yao, X.: Software effort estimation as a multiobjective learning problem. ACM Trans. Softw. Eng. Methodol. **22**(4) (2013)
23. Perrone, V., Donini, M., Zafar, M.B., Schmucker, R., Kenthapadi, K., Archambeau, C.: Fair bayesian optimization. In: Proceedings of the 2021 AAAI/ACM Conference on AI, Ethics, and Society (2021)
24. Schott, J.R.: Fault tolerant design using single and multicriteria genetic algorithm optimization. Ph.D. thesis, Massachusetts Institute of Technology (1995)
25. Solow, A., Polasky, S., Broadus, J.: On the measurement of biological diversity. J. Environ. Econ. Manag. **24**(1), 60–68 (1993)
26. Speicher, T., et al.: A unified approach to quantifying algorithmic unfairness: Measuring individual & group unfairness via inequality indices. In: Proceedings of the 24th ACM SIGKDD International Conference on Knowledge Discovery & Data Mining, pp. 2239–2248 (2018)
27. Verma, S., Rubin, J.: Fairness definitions explained. In: 2018 IEEE/ACM International Workshop on Software Fairness (FairWare), pp. 1–7. IEEE (2018)

28. Wang, H., Jin, Y., Yao, X.: Diversity assessment in many-objective optimization. IEEE Trans. Cybern. **47**(6), 1510–1522 (2017)
29. Wei, S., Niethammer, M.: The fairness-accuracy Pareto front. arXiv preprint arXiv:2008.10797 (2020)
30. Yao, X.: Evolving artificial neural networks. Proc. IEEE **87**(9), 1423–1447 (1999)
31. Yao, X., Liu, Y.: A new evolutionary system for evolving artificial neural networks. IEEE Trans. Neural Netw. **8**(3), 694–713 (1997)
32. Zhang, Q., Wu, F., Tao, Y., Pei, J., Liu, J., Yao, X.: D-MAENS2: a self-adaptive D-MAENS algorithm with better decision diversity. In: Proceedings of the 2020 IEEE Symposium Series on Computational Intelligence, pp. 2754–2761. IEEE (2020)
33. Zitzler, E., Laumanns, M., Thiele, L.: SPEA2: Improving the strength pareto evolutionary algorithm. TIK-report 103 (2001)
34. Žliobaitė, I.: Measuring discrimination in algorithmic decision making. Data Mining Knowl. Disc. **31**(4), 1060–1089 (2017). https://doi.org/10.1007/s10618-017-0506-1

Neural Network Theory

Single Neurons with Delay-Based Learning Can Generalise Between Time-Warped Patterns

Joshua Arnold[1(✉)], Peter Stratton[2], and Janet Wiles[1]

[1] The University of Queensland, Brisbane, Australia
{j.arnold4,j.wiles}@uq.edu.au
[2] University of Technology Sydney, Sydney, Australia
peter.stratton@uts.edu.au

Abstract. Spatiotemporal patterns, such as words in speech, are rarely precisely the same duration, yet a word spoken faster or slower is still easily recognisable. Neural mechanisms underlying this ability to recognise stretched or compressed versions of the same spatiotemporal pattern are not well understood. Recognition of time-varying patterns is often studied at the network level, however here we propose a single neuron using learnable spike delays for the task. We characterise the response of a single neuron to stretched and compressed versions of a learnt pattern and show that using delays leads to pattern recognition above 99% accuracy for patterns morphed by up to 50%. Additionally, we demonstrate a significantly reduced response when the pattern is reversed, a property that is often difficult to reproduce in synaptic efficacy (synaptic weight) based learning systems. With appropriate settings of the neuron membrane time constant and spike threshold, we show that a single neuron is able to generalise to time-warped patterns while discriminating temporally reversed patterns. Together, these results highlight the potential of synaptic delay-based learning rules as a robust mechanism for learning time-warped spatiotemporal patterns.

Keywords: Time-warped · Delay-based learning · Spatiotemporal pattern.

1 Introduction

Much of the information processed by brains is inherently temporal in nature. However, the temporal structure of sequences is often distorted including being temporally stretched or compressed. Neural systems are well adapted to be invariant to such temporal morphing; for example, a speech played at 1.5x the speed is still understandable.

This project was supported by a UQ scholarship to J.A. and funding from the ARC Centre of Excellence for the Dynamics of Language Project ID: CE140100041.

I. Farkaš et al. (Eds.): ICANN 2021, LNCS 12894, pp. 127–138, 2021.
https://doi.org/10.1007/978-3-030-86380-7_11

The neural mechanisms underpinning the ability to recognise patterns under temporal morphing have been studied at many levels, but are not completely understood. Spike timing-depending plasticity (STDP) has been a major focus of computational studies and has significant biological evidence (for a review see [3]). Neural learning has focused primarily on synaptic efficacy plasticity (often called weight learning). Synaptic efficacy plasticity excels at modelling spatial information in signals by reinforcing connections between correlated neurons [10]. For modelling temporal information, synaptic efficacy based rules depend on the implicit interaction of the weight efficacy with other components in the system with temporal dynamics, such as membrane dynamics or synapse transfer functions. For example, using a shorter membrane time constant can allow neurons to differentiate between a larger number of patterns [9]. However, the length of pattern that can be learnt is limited by the period over which the neuron can integrate. Using a short membrane time constant means only short sections of a pattern can be learnt if differentiating between patterns is also required [9]. Furthermore, because efficacy-based learning only requires that a set of inputs fire within a short time period, the temporal order of inputs is irrelevant, such that differentiating between temporally reversed patterns is difficult.

An alternative form of plasticity that is also based on spike-timing is conduction delay plasticity (CDP) [5]. CDP explicitly adjusts delays between neurons to cause input spikes to arrival coincidentally, evoking a larger response from the postsynaptic neuron [14]. As CDP adjusts delays for each input, it learns both the spatial (which synapses) and temporal (when they fire) information in a pattern. A dependence on both the spatial and temporal information in a pattern makes CDP a promising rule for learning spatiotemporal patterns where the temporal order matters. Conduction delays have been demonstrated as a functional learning mechanism in animals [4]. In humans, training has also been linked to increased white matter volume which is associated with axon myelination and conduction delay changes [6]. There is an increasing body of literature around computational potential of CDP rules [1,11,13,14]. In particular, the computational performance of delay learning has been studied under different amounts of time-warping using supervised learning [7] and simplified, well separated data [12]. However, the performance of unsupervised delay-learning of time-warped signals in noisy continuous spike data has not been tested.

Software simulations allow direct study of the computational advantages of using conduction delays as a learning mechanism for time-warped patterns. This work extends earlier studies using the CDP rule Synaptic Delay Variance Learning (SDVL) [2,14]. The range over which delay-based learning can generalise or discriminate between temporally morphed (stretched or compressed) versions of a learnt pattern are quantified. In particular, the aims of this work are two fold. First, to characterise the performance of a delay-based learning rule on the task of recognising stretched and compressed versions of a learnt pattern and its temporal reversal. Stretching and compression will be tested between 0.5x-2x the original learnt pattern length. Second, to demonstrate the influence of the neuron's membrane dynamics on learning by comparing the voltage responses of a neuron acting as an input spike coincidence detector or integrator.

2 Methodology

2.1 Synaptic Delay Variance Learning

The delay-based learning rule Synaptic Delay Variance Learning (SDVL) is used to train a single neuron in each experiment. Delay-based learning rules generally work by causing spikes that would arrive at a neuron asynchronously to instead arrive coincidentally by adjusting the delays (often bidirectionally). Causing multiple input spikes to arrive coincidentally evokes a large response in the neuron, even when the synaptic efficacy weights have remained the same. The performance and behaviour of SDVL has been studied in earlier works but is outlined here for completeness [14,15]. SDVL models the synaptic current transfer of a synapse using a Gaussian function. The current applied to the postsynaptic neuron, $I(t)$, from a synapse is defined as:

$$I(t) = c\exp(\frac{-(t-\mu)^2}{\sigma}), \qquad \text{for } t \geq 0 \tag{1}$$

where c is the centre (peak) of the Gaussian, with delay, μ, and variance σ. Adjusting the mean of the Gaussian function changes the delay when current is applied to the postsynaptic neuron. By adjusting the variance, SDVL can change whether the current is applied as a large short pulse (low variance) or a smaller longer term influence (high variance). SDVL changes the mean, $\Delta\mu$, and variance, $\Delta\sigma$, following the equations:

$$\Delta\mu = \begin{cases} sgn(t_0-\mu)k\eta_\mu, & if|t_0-\mu| \geq \alpha_1 \\ -k\eta_\mu, & if t_0 \geq \alpha_2 \\ 0, & otherwise \end{cases} \tag{2}$$

$$\Delta\sigma = \begin{cases} k\eta_\sigma, & if|t_0-\mu| \geq \beta_1 \\ -k\eta_\sigma, & if|t_0-\mu| < \beta_2 \\ 0, & otherwise \end{cases} \tag{3}$$

where, t_0 is the difference between the postsynaptic neuron spike time, s_n, and the presynaptic input spike time. Furthermore, sgn is the signum function, and k is a learning accelerator defined as $k(\sigma) = (\sigma + 0.9)^2$. The hyperparameters α_1, α_2, β_1, and β_2 control the regions over which SDVL changes delays and variances, while η_μ, and η_σ control the learning rate. The maximum and minimum values allowed for μ and σ are [1, 20] and [0.1, 10] respectively. As μ and σ change, the total current applied for each input spike also changes; that is, the integral of Eq. (1). To ensure each input spike delivers the same amount of current, the Gaussian peak, c, of each synapse is adjusted with μ and σ. Adjusting the peaks to give a constant integral ensures the system is performing delay learning rather than some variant of synaptic efficacy learning. As the constant integral value is used globally across all synapses, it is called the fixed global integral (FGI). Prohibiting efficacy learning in this fashion means SDVL must learn the spatial information (which synapses) as well as the temporal information (what delays) necessary for a pattern. The necessity to learn both spatial and temporal information in a signal is what makes SDVL well suited for spatiotemporal pattern learning.

A simplified version of SDVL (sSDVL) can be used by setting $\alpha_1 = \alpha_2$, $\beta_1 = \beta_2$, and $\eta_\mu = \eta_\sigma$; the value of these parameters are then referred to as α, β, and η, respectively. These simplifications are described in greater detail in [2] and allow simpler optimisation of SDVL by reducing the hyperparameter space that needs searching. This simplified rule will be used for all tasks described here with values: $\alpha = 3$; $\beta = 20$; and $\eta = 0.04$. These values were chosen through experimenter experience with SDVL following principles outlined in previous work [2].

2.2 Tasks

The experimental design consists of a single leaky-integrate and fire neuron using sSDVL to learn a repeating pattern embedded in distractor inputs (see Fig. 1. The change in membrane voltage ($v(t)$) of the neuron with membrane time constant (τ) is defined as:

$$\tau \frac{dv}{dt} = v_{rest} - v(t) + RI(t) \tag{4}$$

where $v_{rest} = 65$ mV; $R = 1\Omega$ is the resistance; and $I(t)$ is the current applied by the inputs. The current is the sum of the $N = 2000$ input afferents, of which 500 are involved in the pattern. The 500 inputs involved in the pattern are at index 1–501 sorted by ascending firing time and are called pattern inputs (see Fig. 1). Sorting pattern inputs make visualisation clearer and have no impact on the difficulty of the task from the neuron's perspective. The pattern repeats at a rate 5 Hz and consists of each pattern input firing exactly once over the pattern length, $L = 50$ ms. A spike from input i at time t is specified as s_i^t. The other 1500 distractor inputs are allowed to fire during each pattern presentation, but their firing rates are adjusted to ensure the average input to the neuron remains constant throughout the simulation. All inputs fire with a Poisson distribution 10 Hz over the length of the simulation. The neuron is allowed to train on a pattern for 300 simulated seconds and reported averages are taken over 20 s of subsequent testing.

Delay representations are studied under two conditions for the neuron: acting as an integrator or as a coincident spike detector [8]. Using a larger membrane time constant, $\tau = 20ms$, the neuron's membrane voltage is able to accumulate the influence of spikes over a longer time period and decays slowly, acting as an integrator. Neurons can also act as coincident spike detectors when using short membrane time constants, $\tau = 3ms$. Using a short time constant means the membrane voltage decays quickly, so only recent spikes can affect the voltage;

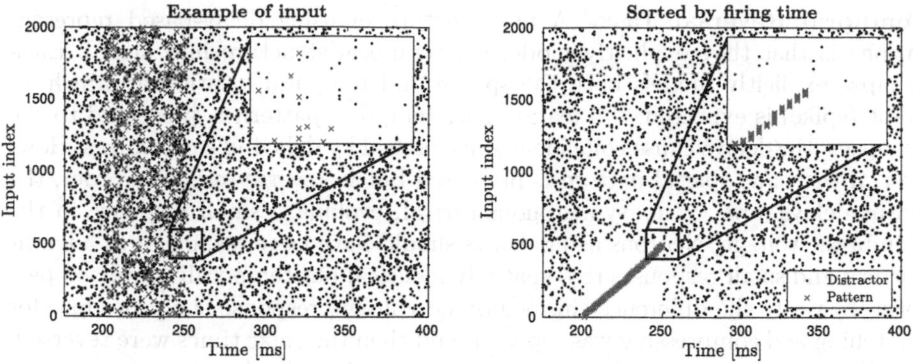

Fig. 1. Example input during training, pattern is presented between time 400–450 ms on inputs 0–500. The activity of distractor neurons firing during the pattern presentation is adjusted so the total activity remains constant. The firing rate of pattern inputs between each pattern presentation are adjusted to maintain 10 Hz firing rate.

in this case, to cause a large membrane voltage response, many spikes need to arrive within a short time period.

Testing. After the neuron has learnt a pattern, all learning is stopped and the neuron is presented with morphed instances of the pattern as described in the next sections. To observe the relative difference in response, the spike threshold is removed and the membrane voltage is measured during morphed pattern presentations. Accuracy is also used to assess performance and is defined as the product of the percentage of correctly recognised patterns and the percentage of correctly unrecognised regions between pattern presentations. That is, the percentage of patterns with at least one output spike and the percentage of between-pattern periods with no output spikes.

Stretch and Compress Task. The learnt pattern is stretched or compressed linearly such that the morphed spike time of an input m_i^t is defined as:

$$m_i^t = s_i^t * m_f \tag{5}$$

where the pattern is assumed to be starting at time 0 and m_f is the morphing factor. A morph factor of 0.5 (1.5) represents compressing (stretching) the pattern by 50% of its original length. Values for m_f were tested in the range 0.5 to 2.0 in steps of 0.5. As the pattern is stretched and compressed, the distractor inputs' firing rates are also adjusted to ensure the average input to the neuron remains constant. In the case of $m_f = 0.5$, the firing rate of the pattern inputs are high enough that no distractor inputs fire during the pattern presentation. Values of $m_f < 0.5$ would not be possible in this task without the pattern contributing a larger than average total input during the presentation and are thus excluded.

Temporal Reversal Task. A main feature of using delay-based representations is that they explicitly model the temporal structure in a signal. Each synapse explicitly models both the spatial and temporal location at which an event (spike) is expected. If a learnt spatiotemporal pattern is presented to the synapses, the delays cause coincident spike arrival by delaying early spikes. However, if the same spatial pattern is presented but in reverse temporal order, the learnt delays now cause asynchronous arrival, evoking a small response in the membrane voltage. Neurons using delays should have large responses to a learnt pattern and small responses to a spatially identical but temporally reversed pattern. To verify the differences in membrane voltage, response the procedure for stretching and compressing was repeated and then the spike times were reversed. A spike in the reversed and morphed pattern, r_i^t, is defined as:

$$r_i^t = m_f(L - s_i^t) \tag{6}$$

For simplicity, stretched and compressed patterns will be denoted as a positive m_f while temporally reversed and morphed patterns will be denoted with a negative m_f. All experiments were carried out using custom written Matlab code available with an open source licence.[1]

3 Results

3.1 Training the Neuron

A neuron was trained for 300 s as described in Sect. 2.2. Visualising the learnt delays showed a straight line with negative slope indicating the pattern had been effectively learnt, see Fig. 2A. As the pattern inputs are sorted by ascending firing time, current from spikes with smaller input indexes and larger delays arrive coincidentally with inputs which fire later but have smaller delays. A common structure learnt is a smaller set of delays just before the main feature. This smaller feature often causes an initial neuron spike before the arrival of input from the main feature, resulting in two spikes per pattern presentation (see Fig. 2C). Once the neuron has learnt the pattern it quickly stabilises its firing time and maintains it, see Fig. 2B. The final firing time of each neuron depends on random chance during learning.

3.2 Stretch and Compression Effects on Neuron Response

Presenting the learnt pattern to a trained neuron (with spiking disabled) results in a large membrane voltage response, reaching −38 mV on average, see Fig. 3A. When the neuron acts as an integrator ($\tau = 20ms$) the average response is much smaller in general, on average only achieving voltages of −52 mV on the learnt task, see Fig. 3C. When using delay-based representation there is a drop in membrane voltage just after the peak of the response. This corresponds to the pattern spikes which would have normally arrived in this period but instead have shortened delays to arrive coincidentally with the earlier input arrival times.

[1] https://github.com/jotia1/modular-spikingnets.

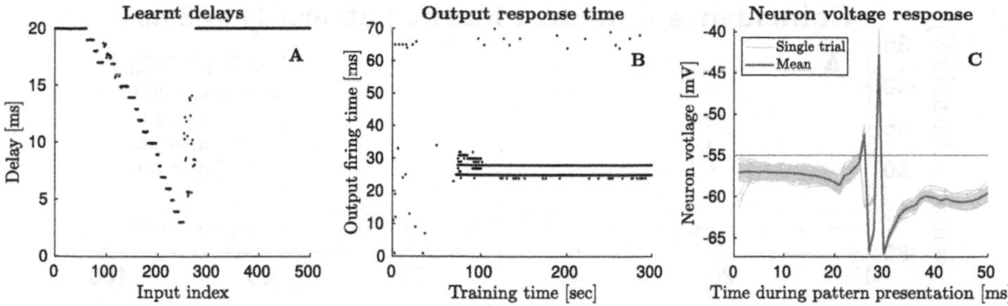

Fig. 2. The learnt delays align well with the pattern, produce consistent output firing times (26 and 28 ms), and evoke a large voltage response. (A) The final delays learnt by a neuron, early inputs fire first but have the largest delay such that all spikes arrive simultaneously. (B) Simultaneously arriving spikes cause very consistent firing times once learnt, the neuron consistently fires at 26 and 28 ms for every presentation. (C) The voltage trace of the neuron after training (averaged over 100 presentations).

Coincidence Detector. As the pattern is compressed the current from pattern spikes no longer arrive coincidentally. When the neuron is acting as a coincident detector, these asynchronous arrivals result in a diminished response, however the response still exceeds threshold allowing the neuron to generalise to these cases. An equal amount of stretching ($m_f = 1.5$) has a much smaller response (max at −52 mV) in contrast with compression ($m_f = 0.5$, max at −43 mV).

Integrator. When the neuron acts as an integrator, its response is similar to when the pattern is compressed, with a maximum of the average at −52 mV. Although the spikes are no longer arriving coincidentally the slow decay of the membrane time constant allows them to be integrated, resulting in the similar response. As the pattern is stretched ($m_f = 1.5$) the maximum of the average response drops to −54 mV. However, even when the pattern is stretched to twice its originally learnt length ($m_f = 2.0$) the maximum average response (−54.7 mV) still exceeds the voltage threshold.

3.3 Temporal Reversal Effects of Neuron Response

In both cases responses of the membrane voltage to the reversed and morphed patterns are significantly lower than to the learnt patterns, see Fig. 3B,D. The response is diminished by the morphing as well as the asynchronous spike arrival from the temporal reversal. However, while the average response to the reversed and morphed patterns is lower than the learnt case the response still exceeds threshold in some cases. These slight increases in response are due to the delay learning rule assigning a low variance to synapses with learnt delays. The current applied from each spike follows the Gaussian synapses outlined in Eq. 1, meaning a low variance results in a short but large burst of current. These short but large impulses are able to evoke a larger effect in the membrane voltage before the membrane dynamics decay it.

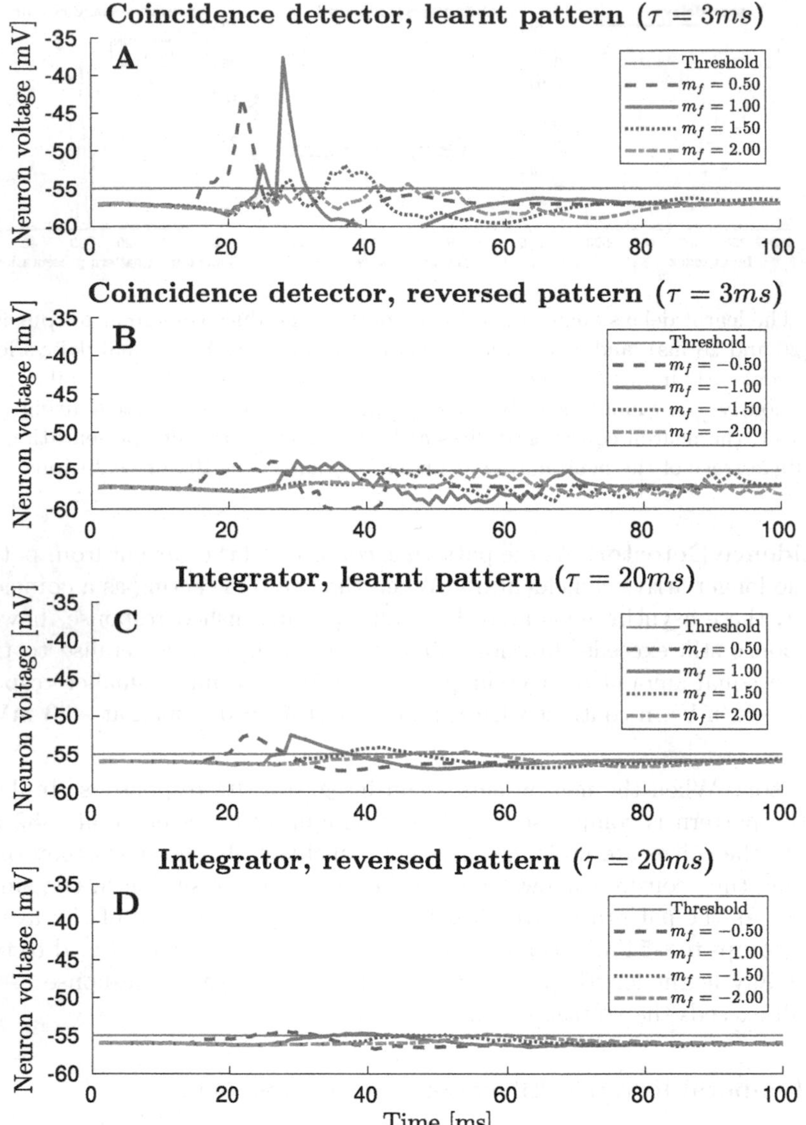

Fig. 3. Neurons acting as coincidence detectors respond more strongly then integrators when using delay-based learning and evoke larger responses to temporally morphed patterns than temporally reversed patterns. (A) The neuron's membrane voltage response to the learnt pattern is largest when the pattern is unchanged ($m_f = 1.0$), stretching or compressing the pattern diminished this response. (B) Temporally reversing the pattern severely diminished the response, however it still often exceeded threshold. (C) Using a larger membrane time constant ($\tau = 20$ ms) produced a smaller response. Compressing the pattern evokes a similar response to the learnt pattern while stretching diminished the response. (D) The average response to a temporally reversed version of a learnt pattern is smaller when using a large membrane time constant. All curves are average responses from 100 pattern presentations.

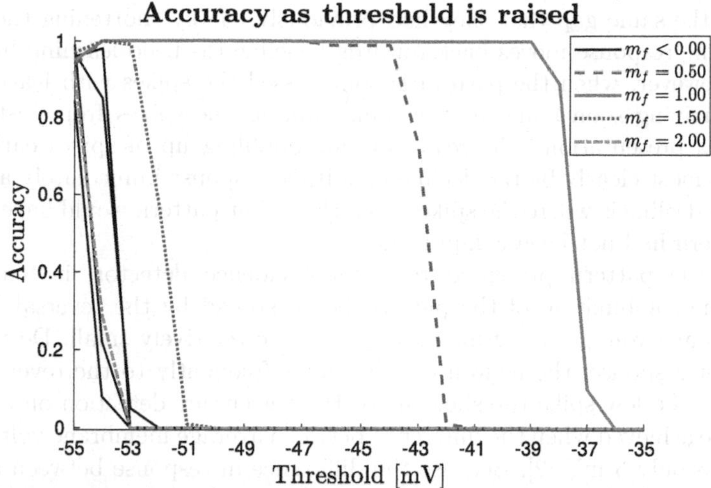

Fig. 4. Increasing the voltage threshold to −52 mV would allow near perfect generalisation to patterns stretched or compressed by up to 50% while discriminating temporally reversed patterns ($m_f < 0.00$).

4 Discussion

4.1 Learnt Features

Once trained, the neuron typically learns one large pattern that spans the delay range allowed and consisting of between 150–200 inputs. However, in some cases, smaller sub-patterns can form just before the main pattern, see Fig. 2A. These smaller features are often responsible for producing an initial spike, allowing the neuron to fire two or more times during a single pattern presentation as shown in the average response in Fig. 2C. The cause of these smaller features forming is likely linked to the parameters of sSDVL used, in particular, setting $\alpha = 3ms$. Additional details on the behaviour and parameter settings of sSDVL can be found in [2]. The reliable response of the neurons firing time (see Fig. 2B) and membrane voltage (see Fig. 2C) is an advantageous feature of this representation. In particular, it suggests that delay learning could be extended to multiple layers with early layers able to produce precise temporal structure in their outputs as inputs to deeper layers.

4.2 Coincidence Detector

Stretching and compressing the learnt pattern causes the inputs to apply current to the neuron asynchronously. When the neuron is a coincidence detector this results in a diminished response for both stretching and compression. The response to stretched patterns declines faster than the response to the same amount of compression. When the pattern is stretched, the spikes from the learnt delays fill the same gap that they had previously left by shortening the delays and thus the response moves back towards baseline (as if no learning had happened). However, when the pattern is compressed the spikes with learnt delay are now arriving sooner and at the same time as the spikes from just before the pattern presentation. The result of this doubling up of spikes earlier can be noticed most clearly by the decline in voltage response immediately after the peak. This decline is where the spikes from the learnt pattern would have arrived if the pattern had not been compressed.

When the pattern presented to the coincidence detector, it temporally reverses the combination of the pattern being spread by the reversal and the fast membrane voltage decay makes the response relatively small. Despite this much lower response, the neuron does respond frequently to the reversed pattern due to the low spike threshold used. High accuracy detection on a similar task can be achieved when the difference between average membrane voltage and threshold is only 3 mV [2]. Because the difference in response between a learnt and temporally reversed pattern is > 15 mV increasing the threshold slightly would enable whatever level of discrimination or generalisation is needed.

4.3 Integrator

When the neuron is an integrator the overall responses are much smaller. This is a consequence of there being a fixed number of pattern spikes arriving coincidentally yet the integrator still integrates all spikes (including the noise spikes) from over a longer period. Because of the accumulated noise influence, integrator neurons are not as well suited to take advantage of the simultaneous spike arrivals as coincidence detector neurons. The relative decrease in performance of integrator neurons for morphed patterns is less than in the coincidence detector case, however, it is still significantly lower in general. It is still possible for integrators to differentiate between learnt and temporally reversed patterns, however the difference is small and would have a high signal-to-noise ratio.

Membrane Time Constant Interaction. Efficacy-based systems depend on carefully setting the membrane time constant of the postsynaptic neuron to allow generalisation or discrimination between patterns [9]. Short time constants have been used in weight-based learning systems to enable them to differentiate between spatially similar but temporally different patterns [9]. However, the size of the time constant in a weight based system limits the maximum size of the pattern that can be learnt. That is, if the neuron has effectively decayed any spikes from more then 3 ms ago, then 3 ms becomes the upper limit of the length of pattern that can be learnt in a weight based system. Delay-based systems do not suffer from this same issue, even with a short membrane time constant, features up to the length of the maximum delay can be learnt by causing all of the spikes to arrive simultaneously. Using a short time constant is still advantageous in delay-based systems as this allows the effect of coincidentally arriving spikes to have a larger influence.

4.4 Discrimination Between Learnt and Reversed Patterns

While the overall response is much lower, the temporal reversal still evokes a large enough response to cause the neuron to fire regularly. This is due to the membrane voltage needing to be driven near-threshold for learning to originally occur. Once learning has occurred shifting the threshold up slightly would enable the neuron to differentiate between the learnt pattern and the temporal reversal. There are numerous methods through which the threshold could be appropriately adjusted to allow discrimination between the learnt pattern and the temporal reversal. A simple solution is to simply apply a variant of simulated annealing where the threshold (or synaptic efficacy) are adjusted slowly during learning [14]. Using an adaptive threshold or intrinsic plasticity would provide a much more robust solution but also bring added levels of complexity []. Shifting the threshold up to −52 mV from −55 mV would allow near perfect accuracy for the learnt patterns with m_f in the range [0.5, 1.5], whilst also perfectly discriminating between the temporal reversal, see Fig. 4. Methods of dynamically adjusting the threshold are left for future studies in this work. Which instead focuses on demonstrating there is a relative difference in response which could be used to differentiate between a learnt pattern and its temporal reversal.

5 Conclusion

A single neuron using delay-based learning is able generalise to patterns time-warped by up to 50% with an accuracy >99%. Further, there is a distinct difference between the response of the neuron to the learnt pattern and a spatially identical but temporally reversed pattern. The membrane time constant plays and important role in allowing the neuron to generalise to stretched and compressed patterns. Small values of the membrane time constant cause the neuron to act as a coincidence detector without hampering the neuron's ability to learn temporal structure. These results demonstrate that using delay-based representations is a promising method for allowing single neurons to generalise to time-warped versions of a pattern whilst still allowing discrimination between spatially identical but temporally distinct (reversed) patterns. Future work is needed to compare the performance of delay-based learning with network level solutions but also to study the integration of delay-based learning into network level solutions. Delay-based learning offers an explanation of how neurons can respond to spatiotemporal patterns that are temporally distorted such as words spoken faster or slower.

References

1. Afshar, S., George, L., Tapson, J., van Schaik, A., Hamilton, T.J.: Racing to learn: statistical inference and learning in a single spiking neuron with adaptive kernels. Front. Neuroscience 8 (2014). https://doi.org/10.3389/fnins.2014.00377

2. Arnold, J., Statton, P., Wiles, J.: Conduction delay plasticity can robustly learn spatiotemporal patterns embedded in noise. In: The 2021 International Joint Conference on Neural Networks (IJCNN) (in press)
3. Caporale, N., Dan, Y.: Spike timing-dependent plasticity: a Hebbian learning rule. Annu. Rev. Neurosci. **31**(1), 25–46 (2008). https://doi.org/10.1146/annurev.neuro.31.060407.125639
4. Carr, C.E., Konishi, M.: Axonal delay lines for time measurement in the owl's brainstem. Proc. Natl. Acad. Sci. **85**(21), 8311–8315 (1988). https://doi.org/10.1073/pnas.85.21.8311
5. Fields, R.D.: Myelination: an overlooked mechanism of synaptic plasticity? Neuroscientist **11**(6), 528–531 (2005). https://doi.org/10.1177/1073858405282304
6. Fields, R.D.: A new mechanism of nervous system plasticity: activity-dependent myelination. Nat. Rev. Neurosci. **16**(12), 756–767 (2015). https://doi.org/10.1038/nrn4023
7. Gütig, R., Sompolinsky, H.: The tempotron: a neuron that learns spike timing-based decisions. Nat. Neurosci. **9**(3), 420–428 (2006). https://doi.org/10.1038/nn1643
8. König, P., Engel, A.K., Singer, W.: Integrator or coincidence detector? The role of the cortical neuron revisited. Trends Neurosci. **19**(4), 130–137 (1996). https://doi.org/10.1016/S0166-2236(96)80019-1
9. Masquelier, T.: STDP allows close-to-optimal spatiotemporal spike pattern detection by single coincidence detector neurons. Neuroscience **389**, 133–140 (2018). https://doi.org/10.1016/j.neuroscience.2017.06.032
10. Masquelier, T., Thorpe, S.J.: Unsupervised learning of visual features through spike timing dependent plasticity. PLOS Comput. Biol. **3**(2), e31 (2007). https://doi.org/10.1371/journal.pcbi.0030031
11. Matsubara, T.: Conduction delay learning model for unsupervised and supervised classification of spatio-temporal spike patterns. Front. Comput. Neurosci 11 (2017). https://doi.org/10.3389/fncom.2017.00104
12. Natschläger, T., Ruf, B.: Spatial and temporal pattern analysis via spiking neurons. Netw. Comput. Neural Syst. **9**(3), 319–332 (1998). https://doi.org/10.1088/0954-898X/9/3/003
13. Tank, D.W., Hopfield, J.J.: Neural computation by concentrating information in time. Proc. Natl. Acad. Sci. U.S.A. **84**(7), 1896–1900 (1987)
14. Wright, P.W., Wiles, J.: Learning transmission delays in spiking neural networks: a novel approach to sequence learning based on spike delay variance. In: The 2012 International Joint Conference on Neural Networks (IJCNN), pp. 1–8 (2012). https://doi.org/10.1109/IJCNN.2012.6252371
15. Wright, P.: Exploring the impact of interneurons and delay learning on temporal spike computation. B.E. Thesis, The University of Queensland, Brisbane, Australia (2011)

Estimating Expected Calibration Errors

Nicolas Posocco([✉]) and Antoine Bonnefoy

EURA NOVA, Marseille, France
{nicolas.posocco,antoine.bonnefoy}@euranova.eu

Abstract. Uncertainty in probabilistic classifiers predictions is a key concern when models are used to support human decision making, in broader probabilistic pipelines or when sensitive automatic decisions have to be taken. Studies have shown that most models are not intrinsically well calibrated, meaning that their decision scores are not consistent with posterior probabilities. Hence being able to calibrate these models, or enforce calibration while learning them, has regained interest in recent literature. In this context, properly assessing calibration is paramount to quantify new contributions tackling calibration. However, there is room for improvement for commonly used metrics and evaluation of calibration could benefit from deeper analyses. Thus this paper focuses on the empirical evaluation of calibration metrics in the context of classification. More specifically it evaluates different estimators of the Expected Calibration Error (ECE), amongst which legacy estimators and some novel ones, proposed in this paper. We build an empirical procedure to quantify the quality of these ECE estimators, and use it to decide which estimator should be used in practice for different settings.

Keywords: Uncertainty · Calibration · Reliability · Classification

1 Introduction

Almost all currently used classifiers are not intrinsically well-calibrated [11], which means their output scores can't be interpreted as probabilities. This is an issue when the model is used for decision making, as a component in a more general probabilistic pipeline, or simply when one needs a quantification of the uncertainty in model's predictions, for example in high risk applications.

To overcome this calibration issue, two main tracks have been explored by either correcting the calibration of the model via some post-training procedure [7,8,11,13] or by regularizing the model to enforce calibration during training [9]. Would it be for the quantitative comparison of the performances of calibration methods or the evaluation of prediction's uncertainty, one needs to precisely quantify calibration. The recent literature trend is to use estimators of the Expected Calibration Error (ECE) [10], which we focus on in this work.

We propose a few improvements on current ECE estimators as well as a novel approach for the estimation of this metric based on kernel density estimation. We also introduce via these new estimators a continuous equivalent of

I. Farkaš et al. (Eds.): ICANN 2021, LNCS 12894, pp. 139–150, 2021.
https://doi.org/10.1007/978-3-030-86380-7_12

the reliability diagram constructed on the proposed notion of Local Calibration Error (LCE). This notion can be used in practice to evaluate the uncertainty of the predicted probabilities itself, with an optional uncertainty interval. Furthermore we designed the first experimental setup to enable the assessment of the calibration metrics, in order to identify which estimators are the most relevant.

In this paper, we first present the context of this study in Sect. 2 and set up the formal definition of calibration in Sect. 3. The theoretical calibration metric, namely the Expected Calibration Error, and its legacy and newly proposed estimators, are presented in Sect. 4, where we also introduce the concept of Local Calibration Error. We finally assess in Sect. 5 the relevance of legacy and proposed estimators empirically using a broad empirical setup.[1]

2 Context and Related Work

The oldest attempt to quantify calibration has been the reliability diagram [3,11] for binary classification. Although it has been useful for the evaluation of early calibration methods, it does not provide point estimates - a single value - required to systematically compare calibration of different models. The first point estimate proposed in [16], which exploited a decision theory framework to use a profit maximisation as a proxy for calibration quality, required a specific type of dataset to be usable in practice. Mirroring the procedure used to compute the reliability diagram, the empirical Expected Calibration Error (ECE) was designed [3], and later has been proven to be an estimator for the natural theoretical notion of calibration error [4]. Meanwhile, some works have used the negative log-likelihood (NLL) or the Brier score [16], which both are weak proxis for the calibration of classifiers [6]. Using reliability diagrams has become even more difficult in multiclass settings [17].

Recent works mostly rely on the binning based legacy estimator of the ECE to quantify calibration. Defects have been highlighted with this estimator, such as its reliance on a hyperparameter and its bias variance trade-off [12]. More recently [7] made clearer the notion of calibration for multiclass classifiers, and new estimators of the ECE with adaptive binning have been proposed in [12] along side with uncertainty aware reliability diagrams [1]. Although the notion of calibration was originally defined for classifiers, this notion is currently being generalized to regression [5,15].

In this context we aim at improving the evaluation of calibration in the setting of classification, and specifically focus on estimators of the ECE as the theoretical definition itself has been consistently adopted.

Definition 1. *Classifier*

Let us consider the random variable (X, Y), *from which are drawn i.i.d samples to build a training set, and a holdout set of size* N : $(\boldsymbol{x}, y) \in \mathcal{X} \times [1..C]$. *A classifier* $M : \mathcal{X} \rightarrow \Delta^C$ *is a function learnt from the training set which outputs*

[1] The code ensuring the reproducibility of the experiments presented in this work is available at https://github.com/euranova/estimating_eces.

scores -ideally the probabilities $\mathbb{P}(Y|X)$*- of belonging to class* c *for* $c \in [1..C]$*, where* $\Delta^C \triangleq \{\boldsymbol{s} \in [0,1]^C | \sum_{j=1}^{C} \boldsymbol{s}_j = 1\}$ *is the probability simplex that ensures the scores sum up to one. In the rest of the paper the indexed notation* $\boldsymbol{s}_c$ *represents the* c^{th} *element of any vector* $\boldsymbol{s}$ *and* $\boldsymbol{x}^i$ *denotes the* i^{th} *sample of the holdout set. For readability purpose we use the notation* $\boldsymbol{s}^i$ *for the output score* $M(\boldsymbol{x}^i)$*.*

3 Calibration

In this section we present and formalize properly the 4 different notions of calibration, and derive the corresponding Expected Calibration Errors (ECE).

Calibration characterizes how much a model is able to output scores corresponding to actual posterior probabilities. The first and simplest calibration notion [13] is focused on a specific class and extends to the simultaneous calibration of every classes considering their associated scores independent, namely the class-wise calibration [17]. This version considers a classifier is well-calibrated if all one-vs-rest submodels are calibrated. The calibration concept for binary classification is equivalent to class-specific calibration focusing on the positive class and to class-wise calibration, since the score for the negative class s_0 is determined by the score for the positive class $s_1 = 1 - s_0$. The more recently introduced *confidence calibration* [4] is only concerned about the model predicting relevant scores for the class it predicts for each sample. Throughout this paper, we only tackle the confidence and class-wise settings. Finally the most rigorous evaluation of calibration should actually take into account all classes as non-independent, the corresponding definition, the *multiclass-calibration* [13] is almost never used in practice for computability reasons. All these notions are formalized in the following definition.

Definition 2. *Different calibration notions of a probabilistic classifier. A probabilistic classifier* M*, is*

Calibrated for class c *:* $\forall s \in [0,1], \mathbb{P}(Y = c|M(X)_c = s) = s$

Class-wise calibrated: $\forall c \in [1..C], \forall s \in [0,1], \mathbb{P}(Y = c|M(X)_c = s) = s$

Confidence-calibrated: $\forall s \in [0,1], \mathbb{P}(Y = \underset{c \in [1..C]}{\operatorname{argmax}}(M(X)_c) | \max_{c \in [1..C]}(M(X)_c) = s) = s$

Multiclass-calibrated: $\forall \boldsymbol{s} \in \Delta^C, \forall c \in [1..C], \mathbb{P}(Y = c|M(X) = \boldsymbol{s}) = \boldsymbol{s}_c$

The Expected Calibration Error (ECE) of a given model M can be naturally derived from these theoretical formulations by computing the expected deviation from the perfect theoretical calibration. This concept is applied to the different calibration settings and results in the following formulations:

Definition 3. *Expected calibration error (ECE) for the different settings for a given model M on (X, Y):*

$$ECE^c(M) \triangleq \mathbb{E}_{s \sim M(X)_c}\Big[\big|\mathbb{P}(Y = c \mid M(X)_c = s) - s\big|\Big]$$

$$ECE^{cw}(M) \triangleq \frac{1}{C} \sum_{c \in [1..C]} ECE^c(M)$$

$$ECE^{conf}(M) \triangleq \mathbb{E}_{s \sim \max(M(X))}\Big[\big|\mathbb{P}(Y = \operatorname{argmax}(M(X)) \mid \max(M(X)) = s) - s\big|\Big]$$

$$ECE^{mul}(M) \triangleq \mathbb{E}_{(\mathbf{s},c) \sim (M(X),Y)}\Big[\big|\mathbb{P}(Y = c | M(X) = \mathbf{s}) - \mathbf{s}_c\big|\Big]$$

Where $ECE^c(M)$ is the class-specific ECE associated to class c, ECE^{cw} the class-wise ECE [17], $ECE^{conf}(M)$ the confidence ECE [4] and $ECE^{mul}(M)$ the multiclass ECE.

By replacing the expectation over the absolute values of the differences by a simple maximum over the absolute differences, we obtain the formulations of the Maximum Calibration Error (MCE) [10], which focus on the highest gap between posterior probabilities and the scores given by the model.

4 Estimation of Calibration Quantification

In this section we describe the challenges of calibration quantification, then present the existing tools to handle these challenges namely the reliability diagram and the legacy ECE estimator. We then introduce a new formalization of these estimators based on binning and sample mapping, which help us define new binning based estimators. Finally we present the new notion of Local Calibration Error on which we rely to build continuous estimators of the ECE based on Kernel Density Estimation. All estimators are written for the class-specific calibration setting, which can then be transposed to the other settings using Definition 3.

4.1 Challenges of Such Quantification

Quantifying calibration is challenging in practice for two main reasons: *Calibration is intrinsically a local notion.* Miscalibration is defined on the neighbourhood of a given output score. Thus any global quantification of calibration depends on an aggregation procedure of local measures. This is what differentiates the ECE, which implicitly weights all parts of the score distribution according to its local density, from the MCE, which only cares about the worst case scenario. *Since calibration depends on score distributions* , any relevant estimator relies on these scores, which means that we are limited by the amount of available validation data to perform such quantification.

A good calibration metric should *specifically quantify calibration*: contrary to the Brier score and the NLL, which values only carry a partial information on calibration, we expect a good metric to be independent of confusion factors. It should then be *theoretically well-funded* as well as *tractable in practice.* Finally, a good calibration metric should be able to *take into account cost matrices for the classification task*, when available, risk management being intrinsically linked to such cost matrices.

The ECE corresponds to the identified required properties for homogeneous cost matrices, since it directly derives from the theoretical notion of calibration and has an immediate interpretation. However, it doesn't allow heterogeneous costs matrices, and as we will see in the next sections, current estimators provide poor estimations of the true value of the ECE. For these reasons we focus on the setting of homogeneous cost classification, and try to provide better estimators for the ECE. Such estimators should *be robust to hyperparameter choice*, problem which can be solved by the use of a relevant heuristic. The estimator should be *data-efficient* too, in order to provide good estimates with a *low variance* even with few holdout labeled data points. Such estimation should provide *low-bias* estimates with a sufficient amount of available data and should finally be *consistent* and *computable in a reasonable amount of time.*

4.2 Reliability Diagram

The reliability diagram introduces the classical way of calculating the ECE. To build the reliability diagram (in the binary setting), a uniform binning scheme (the $[0,1]$ interval is split into equal bins) is used, and each holdout sample is mapped into a bin based on the score given by the model for the positive class (procedure defined below as 1-bin mapping). For each bin, the average score for the positive class and the proportion of samples belonging to the positive class are calculated. The first is then plotted against the second. If the model is well calibrated, each point should fall on the line $y = x$. The local offset of each point tells us if the model is locally over or under-confident on its scores for the positive class. Such diagram can be seen on Fig. 1 (left).

Originally designed for the binary classification case, it can be easily extended to confidence calibration in the multiclass setting. In that case, samples are sent into bins based on the score the model outputs for the class it predicts, and the ratio of correct predictions is plotted against the average over the scores given for the predicted class.

4.3 Binning Based Estimators

In order to present different binning-based estimators of the ECE, we formalize the binning and affectation mapping objects. We note s^i the score of the class of interest of the ith sample, which depends on if we consider the specific-class, class-wise (fixed class) or confidence (predicted class) calibration.

Definition 4. *Binning schemes*
The $[0,1]$ segment is split into B bins used to assign each data point to one (or more) bin. These bins are defined by their respective thresholds. Hence to

define a binning scheme one only needs to specify the increasing splitting function $t : [1..B] \rightarrow [0,1]$ *that computes the right threshold for each bin.*

Two main binning schemes have been used to compute the ECE in the literature: *Uniform binning* splits the segment into B bins of equal size : $t(i) = \frac{i}{B}$ and *Adaptive binning* splits the segment so that each split contains the same number of samples : $t(i) = \{s^{\sigma(j)} \mid \forall j \in [1..N-1], s^{\sigma(j)} \leq s^{\sigma(j+1)}\}_{\lfloor N/i \rfloor}$, σ being the permutation which sorts samples based on the score predicted for the class of interest.

Definition 5. *Affectation mapping*
Given a binning of a domain $[0,1]$, *an affectation mapping of* $\mathcal{D}$ *in these bins is a matrix* W *composed of positive weights, so that* W_{ij} *is the weight of the affectation of the sample* i *in the bin* b_j. *Rows of such matrix sum up to* 1.

Using this formalisation, we start from the *1-bin mapping* W^{1bin} for which every sample is assigned to a single bin with unit weight, to go to the new proposed *convex mapping* W^{conv} for which each sample may contribute to up to two bins for the computation of the binning based ECE estimators. This mechanism is the one referred to as *linear binning* in the kernel density estimation field. These two mappings can be respectively mathematically written, as follows, where c_j is the geometric centre of the jth bin $\frac{t_{j-1}-t_j}{2}$:

$$W_{ij}^{1bin} = \begin{cases} 1 & \text{if } s_i \in [t_{j-1}, t_j] \\ 0 & \text{otherwise} \end{cases} ; \quad W_{ij}^{conv} = \begin{cases} 1 & \text{if } s_i \in [0, c_0] \;\&\; j = 0 \\ 1 & \text{if } s_i \in [c_B, 1] \;\&\; j = B \\ \frac{s_i - c_j}{c_{j+1} - c_j} & \text{if } s_i \in [c_j, c_{j+1}] \\ 1 - \frac{s_i - c_{j-1}}{c_j - c_{j-1}} & \text{if } s_i \in [c_{j-1}, c_j] \end{cases}$$

The original estimator of the ECE is basically a weighted mean over the absolute differences calculated when the reliability diagram is computed (here expressed in the specific-class case). If W is a 1-bin mapping on a uniform binning and *1* is the indicator function, the legacy estimator is:

$$ECE_l^c = \frac{1}{N} \sum_{j=1}^{B} \left| \sum_{i=1}^{N} W_{ij} (\mathit{1}_{Y^i = c} - \mathbf{s}_c^i) \right| \tag{1}$$

Such estimator can be defined in the same way for ECE^{conf} and ECE^{cw}.

We unify binning-based estimators under Eq. (1) with different binning/mapping schemes. The ECE_a uses an adaptive binning with 1-bin mapping, while the ECE_c uses a uniform binning and a convex mapping, and finally the ECE_{ac} uses both improvements on the legacy estimator - adaptive binning and convex mapping. In the case of class-wise calibration, the ACE defined in [12] is equivalent to ECE_a, when all bins contain the same amount of samples.

4.4 Local Calibration Error

We define the notion of Local Calibration Error (LCE), and then use it to build the reliability curve, a continuous version of the reliability diagram. Let us first begin with the formal definition of the LCE:

Definition 6. *Local calibration error (LCE) for the class-specific and the confidence settings for a given model M on (X, Y)*

$$LCE_M^c(s) \triangleq \mathbb{P}(Y = c \mid M(X)_c = s) - s$$
$$LCE_M^{conf}(s) \triangleq \mathbb{P}(Y = \text{argmax}(M(X)) \mid \max(M(X)) = s) - s$$

For the class-specific case, to estimate the LCE of a model for all scores $s \in [0, 1]$, we have to estimate $\mathbb{P}(Y = c|M(X)_c = s)$. We resort to the Bayes rule to tear down this estimation to estimating the densities of $\mathbb{P}(M(X)_c = s|Y = c)$ and $\mathbb{P}(M(X)_c = s)$, and the scalar $\mathbb{P}(Y = c)$. We can then rely on kernel density estimation (KDE) to estimate the two densities. Theoretically, this approach is continuous. In our implementation however, both KDEs are evaluated numerically in Fourier space (the first one on all scores for the class c and the second one on all scores for the class c when the ground truth is the class c), which makes the computation efficient with $O(N + nlog(n))$ complexity, if n is the number of numeric subdivisions of the domain $[0, 1]$. We use steps of 0.0003 for precision, and mirrored the data around $s = 0$ and $s = 1$, which are the limits of the domain. This mirroring implies a slight bias in estimations due to a leak of density mass. Once again the LCE^{conf} can be estimated in the same way with the relevant scores and classes.

A continuous equivalent of the reliability diagram can be derived from such object. The reliability curve associated with the classifier M and the class c, for the class-specific calibration is:

$$\forall\ s_c \in [0, 1], rel_M(s_c) = LCE_M^c(s_c) + s_c \tag{2}$$

An example of such reliability curve is shown in Fig. 1 (middle).

The main benefit this proposed notion of local calibration error offers is its usability in practice to know the uncertainty of a model on a specific score, which cannot be evaluated with enough precision using previous tools (points in a reliability diagram can be used for an interpolation aiming at the same result, yet the precision of such procedure is very low, and interpolation at that scale is questionable).

We propose to compute this curve on bootstrapped versions of the holdout set, in order to quantify the uncertainty on this LCE. In this context, the median curve is considered as the reliability curve and percentiles of interest are used for uncertainty quantification. This idea, illustrated on Fig. 1 (right), allows the prediction of confidence intervals for the class probabilities instead of point estimates, by only looking at the uncertainty on the bootstrapped reliability curve at the score output by the model.

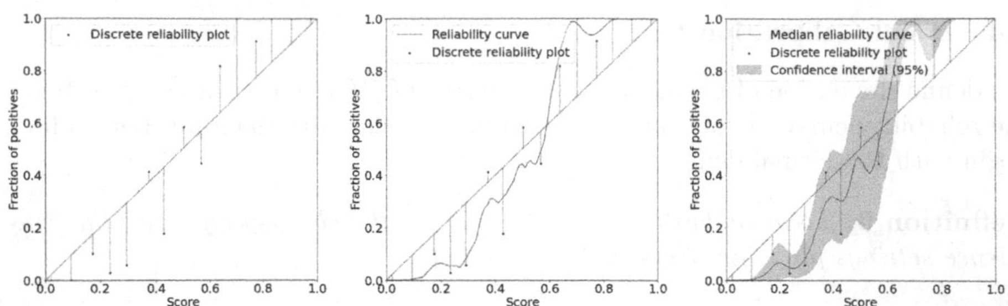

Fig. 1. Reliability diagram with 15 bins (left), reliability curve with a bandwidth of 0.03 (middle) and the bootstrapped version with the same bandwidth (right). Each plot brings one more level of insight.

4.5 Density Based Estimator: ECE_d

Based on the definition of this Local Calibration Error we can derive a new ECE estimator, which is formalized as follows:

$$ECE_d^c = \int_0^1 f_{M(X)_c}(s)\ |LCE_M(s)|\ ds,$$

where $f_{M(X)_c}$ is the probability density function of the scores given by the model for class c.

Heuristics for Hyperparameter Choices. For all binning-based estimators, we investigate the use of a simple heuristic to select the number of bins used for the estimations: the bin amount is the square root of the number of samples. For the kde-based approach, we propose to use Silverman's rule [14] to select the bandwidth (the bandwidth is estimated on $\mathbb{P}(M(X)_c = s)$, and the same bandwidth is used to estimate the density of $\mathbb{P}(M(X)_c = s|Y = c)$). Other heuristics are often used for KDE computations, yet Silverman's rule is to our knowledge the only one which provides satisfying results in small data contexts, for which legacy estimators struggle the most.

From Class-Specific to the Other Settings. To translate the class-specific estimators into the class-wise case, class-specific ECEs are estimated for all classes, and the class-wise ECE is the mean of these values. To get to the confidence case, scores for the class of interest are replaced by the score for the predicted class, and the class of interest is the ground truth label.

5 Experimental Setup

We present the assessment of a few empirical properties of the different ECE estimators. As pointed out in [12], the main difficulty with empirical evaluation of calibration methods and calibration metrics is that we don't have access to ground truths in general. This is why we worked on a setup which gives us access to arbitrarily precise estimates of the ECE considered as a the ground truth, in the class-wise and confidence settings.

5.1 Procedure

We aim at quantitatively compare the estimators in terms of approximation, data efficiency and variance. To do so we build curves which can indicate the expected performance of each estimator with its corresponding parameters, for different sizes of holdout set. In order to observe statistically robust result we introduce various degrees of variability in our experiment at distribution level, in the algorithm used to train the models, and in terms of train/holdout sets splits. The results are thus produced based on numerous realistic output score distributions.

The distribution variability is introduced by creating synthetic sample sets from Gaussian mixtures, where each class is composed of 4 modes of the mixture. For each mode we build the mean vector with elements uniformly drawn in $[0, 1]$, and the covariance matrix is built as follows: we first sample a matrix with elements uniformly drawn in $[-0.3, 0.3]$ then multiply it with its transposition to get the required positive definite matrix. This sample set generation is produced with various number of classes $(2, 5, 7)$ and dimensions of the feature space $(2, 5, 7)$ with 5 different large datasets sampled from each combination, resulting into 45 synthetic distributions.

In order to produce various relevant score distributions from these data distributions, we trained 4 different types of models (logistic regression, gaussian naïve bayes classifier, support vector classifier and random forest) on 3 train sets of size 300 sampled out from the previously generated large datasets. For each of these trained models we compute the "ground truth" ECE using the legacy estimator with high granularity (2000 bins) on the remaining holdout set (2.10^6 samples). Then, we build 200 evaluation sets which are bootstrapped versions of the holdout set of sizes taken between 30 and 500 on a logarithmic scale. The "ground truth" ECE is used as reference to compute the approximation error (the absolute value of the difference between the estimated ECE and its true value normalized by the ground truth). Among those 200 values per evaluation set size, we keep the 95th percentile of the approximation errors, below which 95% of such errors rely. For each evaluation set size and estimator, we finally plot the median over the 540 95th percentiles obtained with each score distributions. The resulting curves can be seen in Fig. 2. The number of evaluations of the learning algorithms plus the ECE estimators makes this experiment long to run, but as all the estimators have limited computation complexity the overall computation remains feasible.

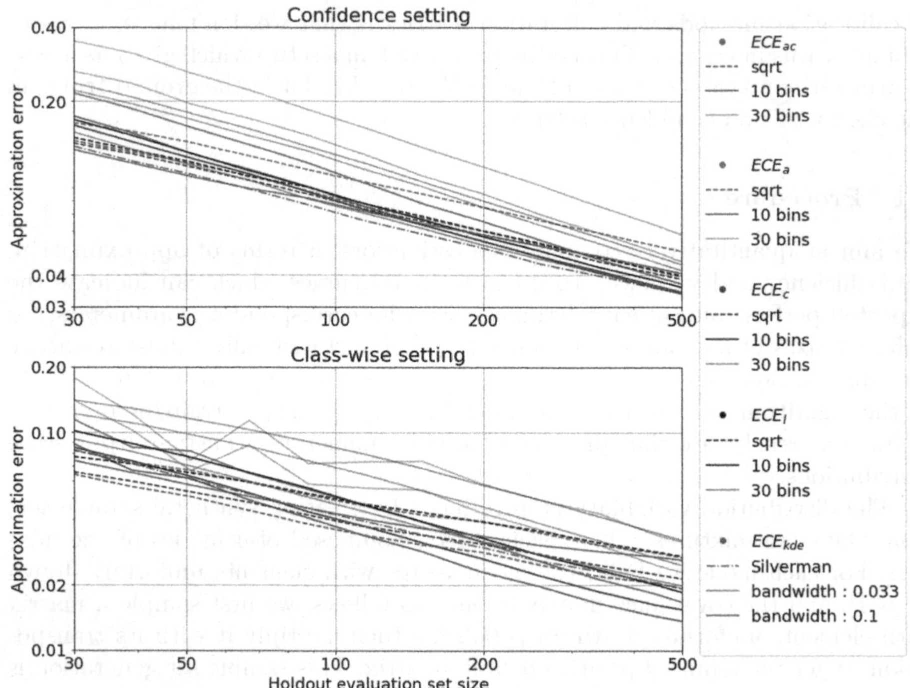

Fig. 2. Median 95th percentile of the approximation error (absolute value of the normalized relative deviation with respect to the ground truth ECE) for the different estimators of the ECE^{conf} (top) and the ECE^{cw} (bottom) (lower is better) for evaluation sets of size between 30 and 500 samples. The scale is logarithmic for both axis

5.2 Results Analysis

For All Settings, the error of all estimators is very high for small data regimes (the estimation error is around 10% of the true value), and thus one shouldn't evaluate calibration on so little data, no matter what estimator is used.

For the Confidence Setting, the best performing estimator in almost all data regimes is the ECE_d^{conf} with Silverman's rule. This is good news, since we now have a procedure to estimate the ECE which doesn't rely on a sensitive hyper-parameter choice, but instead on a simple heuristic. As far as it is concerned, the convex mapping scheme empirically improves the performance of the legacy estimator and the one using the adaptive binning, which underperforms when alone, probably because of the increased variance induced by the adaptivity. It is worth noting that above 300 samples, a lot of the estimators show similar performances. As far as the square root heuristic is concerned for the automatic choice of number of bins used, the graphs suggest that the number of bins grows slightly too fast in average with an increasing amount of samples.

For the Class-wise Setting, there is no clear outperformer in all data regimes among the tested estimators. For less than 100 samples, the ECE_{ac}^{cw} with the square root heuristic seems to be the best choice. The same estimator, this time with a fixed small number of bins, is then the most precise one. The observation made earlier about the square root heuristic still holds, and Silverman's heuristic for the bandwidth seems to be a less relevant choice in the class-wise setting than in the confidence one. We assume it is the case because of the sharpness of the score distributions for each classes in the class-wise setting (most of the density being very close to 0 and 1), which is a context in which Silverman's bandwidth is known to underperform for kernel density estimation.

6 Conclusions

We have introduced a few improvements on the legacy estimators, from the proposition of new binning schemes to the use of heuristics to automatically pick relevant values for hyperparameters of estimators of the ECE. On top of this, a novel approaches has been built to define properly the notion of local calibration error, which produces novel estimators for the ECEs. By testing all approaches on a synthetic experimental setup for which we had access to very precise estimates of the theoretical ECE, we have been able to compare all candidate estimators. This systematic evaluation, which had never been done until now, allowed us to formulate some recommendations on which estimator to use in what context.

Our proposed solutions lead to natural potential future works. First, the introduced calibration curve suggests a natural post-training calibration method, since it can be seen as a calibration map. Such method would be interesting to evaluate, yet poses the problem that the associated calibration maps are not monotonous, which is considered as a prerequisite for post-hoc calibration procedures in the literature. Then multiclass-calibration evaluation, which is still an open problem today, could potentially be evaluated in the scores space using an adapted variant of our kde approach, which we think wouldn't suffer as much as legacy estimators from the increase of dimensionality. Finally, even if this paper uses classical kernels and a mirroring approach to constrain density estimations on the domain $[0, 1]$ which allows standard and fast KDE computation, some preliminary investigations using a beta pseudo-kernel (the second one introduced in [2]) which is naturally constrained to this domain, show promising results. Because this kernel has a different shape for all support points in $[0, 1]$, it is computationally prohibitive for now, and needs further exploration.

References

1. Bröcker, J., Smith, L.A.: Increasing the reliability of reliability diagrams. Weather forecast. **22**(3), 651–661 (2007)
2. Chen, S.X.: Beta kernel estimators for density functions. Comput. Stat. Data Anal. **31**(2), 131–145 (1999)

3. DeGroot, M.H., Fienberg, S.E.: The comparison and evaluation of forecasters. J. Roy. Stat. Soc. Series D (Stat.) **32**(1–2), 12–22 (1983)
4. Guo, C., Pleiss, G., Sun, Y., Weinberger, K.Q.: On calibration of modern neural networks. In: 34th International Conference on Machine Learning, ICML 2017, vol. 3, pp. 2130–2143 (2017)
5. Keren, G., Cummins, N., Schuller, B.: Calibrated prediction intervals for neural network regressors. IEEE Access **6**, 54033–54041 (2018)
6. Kull, M., Flach, P.: Novel decompositions of proper scoring rules for classification: score adjustment as precursor to calibration. In: Joint European Conference on Machine Learning and Knowledge Discovery in Databases, vol. 9284, pp. 68–85 (2015)
7. Kull, M., Perello-Nieto, M., Kängsepp, M., Song, H., Flach, P., Others: beyond temperature scaling: obtaining well-calibrated multiclass probabilities with Dirichlet calibration. In: Advances in Neural Information Processing System, vol. 32 (2019)
8. Kull, M., Silva Filho, T., Flach, P.: Beta calibration: a well-founded and easily implemented improvement on logistic calibration for binary classifiers. In: Artificial Intelligence and Statistics, pp. 623–631. PMLR (2017)
9. Kumar, A., Sarawagi, S., Jain, U.: Trainable calibration measures for neural networks from kernel mean embeddings. In: International Conference on Machine Learning, pp. 2805–2814. PMLR (2018)
10. Naeini, M.P., Cooper, G., Hauskrecht, M.: Obtaining well calibrated probabilities using bayesian binning. In: Proceedings of the AAAI Conference on Artificial Intelligence, vol. 29 (2015)
11. Niculescu-Mizil, A., Caruana, R.: Predicting good probabilities with supervised learning. In: ICML 2005 - Proceedings of the 22nd International Conference on Machine Learning, pp. 625–632 (2005)
12. Nixon, J.V., Dusenberry, M.W., Zhang, L., Jerfel, G., Tran, D.: Measuring calibration in deep learning. In: CVPR Workshops, vol. 2 (2019)
13. Platt, J.: Others: probabilistic outputs for support vector machines and comparisons to regularized likelihood methods. Adv. Large Margin Classifiers **10**(3), 61–74 (1999)
14. Silverman, B.W.: Density Estimation for Statistics and Data Analysis, vol. 26. CRC Press, Boca Raton (1986)
15. Song, H., Diethe, T., Kull, M., Flach, P.: Distribution calibration for regression. In: Chaudhuri, K., Salakhutdinov, R. (eds.) Proceedings of the 36th International Conference on Machine Learning. Proceedings of Machine Learning Research, vol. 97, pp. 5897–5906. PMLR (2019)
16. Zadrozny, B., Elkan, C.: Obtaining calibrated probability estimates from decision trees and naive Bayesian classifiers. In: International Conference on Machine Learning (ICML), pp. 1–8 (2001)
17. Zadrozny, B., Elkan, C.: Transforming classifier scores into accurate multiclass probability estimates bianca. In: Proceedings of the ACM SIGKDD International Conference on Knowledge Discovery and Data Mining, p. 704. ACM (2002)

LipBaB: Computing Exact Lipschitz Constant of ReLU Networks

Aritra Bhowmick, Meenakshi D'Souza(✉), and G. Srinivasa Raghavan

International Institute of Information Technology Bangalore, Bangalore, India
meenakshi@iiitb.ac.in

Abstract. The Lipschitz constant of neural networks plays an important role in several contexts of deep learning ranging from robustness certification and regularization to stability analysis of systems with neural network controllers. Obtaining tight bounds of the Lipschitz constant is therefore important. We introduce LipBaB, a branch and bound framework to compute certified bounds of the local Lipschitz constant of deep neural networks with ReLU activation functions up to any desired precision. It is based on iteratively upper-bounding the norm of the Jacobians, corresponding to different activation patterns of the network caused within the input domain. Our algorithm can provide provably exact computation of the Lipschitz constant for any p-norm.

1 Introduction

The notion of Lipschitz constant for a function, in general, bounds the rate of change of outputs with respect to the inputs. For neural networks, the Lipschitz constant of the network is an useful metric to measure sensitivity, robustness and many other properties. It can be used as a regularization constraint while training or provide certified robustness bounds against adversarial perturbations. It also helps in providing guaranteed generalization bounds. Other use cases involves estimating Wasserstein distance, stabilising training of GANs, and acting as building blocks for formulating invertible neural networks and flow based generative models [4]. Hence, a provable and accurate Lipschitz constant estimation technique is important.

There have been several recent works related to the estimation of Lipschitz constants [3,6,9], etc. Sect. 2 provides a brief study on these works, including a comparison with our algorithm.

It has been shown that exactly computing the Lipschitz constant or even within any desired approximation is computationally hard [3,6]. Hence computing the exact Lipschitz constant for large networks is almost infeasible. However, any technique which provides iteratively refined bounds with convergence over time is desired. Techniques used for the verification of neural networks including

Research sponsored by DRDO Headquarters, New Delhi, India.
Extended version containing additional proofs and details [1].

I. Farkaš et al. (Eds.): ICANN 2021, LNCS 12894, pp. 151–162, 2021.
https://doi.org/10.1007/978-3-030-86380-7_13

robustness certification, output bounds estimation and calculation of the Lipschitz constant are deeply interlinked and share many similarities among them. Our work also uses some of the extensions and combinations of such related techniques like symbolic propagation, interval arithmetic and linear programming (for feasibility checking), within our proposed branch and bound framework.

Our Branch and Bound (BaB) algorithm is based on iterative space partitioning and upper bounding the local Lipschitz constant for each such partition. Each node in the BaB tree has associated with it, an input partition defined by some half-space constraints and a activation pattern of the network on which the Lipschitz upper bounds are calculated. At each iteration our algorithm provides a refined upper bound of the exact Lipschitz constant until convergence. Preliminaries and notations used are given in Sect. 3. Sections 4 and 5 provides details of our algorithm. Section 6 provides the implementation and experimental results demonstrating the performance over various parameters.

2 Related Work

We provide a brief comparison of some of the related works and the specific settings they apply to in the table below. To the best of our knowledge LipBaB is the first work which is able to calculate the **exact** local Lipschitz constant for **any** p-norm. Our algorithm can also be used to compute the **global** Lipschitz constant.

	LipBaB	**LipMIP**	**LipSDP**	**SeqLip**	**CLEVER**	**LipOpt**	**FastLip**
local/global	local,global	local	global	global	local	local	local
guarantee	exact	exact	upper	heuristic	heuristic	upper	upper
p-norms	p	1, ∞	2	p	p	p	p
activations	ReLU	ReLU	ReLU, Diff	ReLU	ReLU, Diff	Diff	ReLU

As shown in the above table, each of the approaches on estimating Lipschitz constants meet different requirements[1]. The various techniques or formulations used in these works include interval-bound propagation [9], semi-definite programming [2], extreme value theory and sampling techniques [10], combinatorial optimization [6], polynomial optimization [5] and mixed integer programming [3]. The technique LipMip [3] can be extended to work for other linear norms also.

3 Preliminaries

This section provides the preliminaries, notations and background definitions as required by the problem.

[1] We have used the names of the techniques as given in the respective papers. The column titled **LipBaB** is our algorithm.

3.1 Generalized Jacobian

The Jacobian of a function $f : \mathbb{R}^n \to \mathbb{R}^m$ at a differentiable point x is given as: $J_f(x) \in \mathbb{R}^{m \times n} : J_{f_{(ij)}} = \frac{\delta f_i}{\delta x_j}, \forall i, j$.

For functions which are not continuously differentiable, we have the notion of Clarke's generalized Jacobian. The generalized Jacobian of such a function f at a point x is defined as: $\delta_f(x) = co\{\lim_{x_i \to x} J_f(x_i) : x_i \textit{ is differentiable}\}$. In other words, $\delta_f(x)$ is the convex hull of the set of Jacobians of nearby differential points. For a differentiable point $\delta_f(x)$ is a singleton set $\{J_f(x)\}$.

3.2 Lipschitz Constant and Norms of Jacobians

For a locally Lipschitz continuous function $f : \mathbb{R}^n \to \mathbb{R}^m$ defined over an open domain $\mathcal{X} \in \mathbb{R}^n$, the local Lipschitz constant $\mathcal{L}_p(f, \mathcal{X})$ is defined as the smallest value such that $\forall x, y \in \mathcal{X} : \|f(y) - f(x)\|_p \leq \mathcal{L}_p(f, \mathcal{X}) \cdot \|y - x\|_p$. For a differentiable and locally Lipschitz continuous function, the Lipschitz constant is given as $\mathcal{L}_p(f, \mathcal{X}) = sup_{x \in \mathcal{X}} \|J_f(x)\|_p$, (Federer, 1969) [4] where $\|J_f(x)\|_p$ is the induced operator norm on the matrix $J_f(x)$.

However, in the case of ReLU-networks the function is piece-wise linear in nature and is not differentiable everywhere. For such functions, the above definition of Lipschitz constant can be extended accordingly using the notion of Clarke's generalized Jacobian [3]:

$$\mathcal{L}_p(f, \mathcal{X}) = \sup_{M \in \delta_f(x), x \in \mathcal{X}} \|M\|_p = \sup_{x_d \in \mathcal{X}} \|J_{f(x_d)}\|_p$$

where x_d is a differentiable point in $\mathcal{X}$.

It is natural that the $\sup_{M \in \delta_f(x), x \in \mathcal{X}} \|M\|_p$ is attained at a differentiable point x_d in $\mathcal{X}$. By definition, a norm $\|.\|$ is convex. Therefore, the maximal value of the norm of the elements in $\delta_f(x)$, which is itself a convex set, is attained at one of the extreme points which are the Jacobians of nearby differentiable points.

This result shows that for computing the Lipschitz constant we don't need to necessarily account for the non-differentiable points.

3.3 Upper Bounds on Jacobian Norms

Lemma 1. *If A and B are both matrices of size $m \times n$, and if for each i, j, $|A_{ij}| \leq B_{ij}$, then $\|A\|_p \leq \|B\|_p$.*

The above result can be used to upper bound the Lipschitz constant by upper bounding the absolute values of the partial derivatives [9].

Lemma 2. *Let U be a matrix of the same size as the Jacobian $J_f(x)$ of a function $f(x)$. If U is such that $sup_{x_d \in \mathcal{X}} |J_f(x_d)_{ij}| \leq U_{ij}$ for all i, j, then $\mathcal{L}_p(f, \mathcal{X}) \leq \|U\|_p$.*

3.4 Feed Forward ReLU Networks and Their Jacobians

Deep feed-forward ReLU networks (MLPs) are stacked layers of perceptrons with ReLU activation functions. They are piece-wise linear in nature.

Given an input vector x and a list of parameters $\theta \equiv \{W^{(l)}, b^{(l)}, i = 1, \ldots, n\}$ describing the network architecture, the function $f : \mathbb{R}^n \rightarrow \mathbb{R}^m$ represented by a MLP can be defined as follows:

$f(x, \theta) = W^{(L)}\phi(W^{(L-1)}(\ldots\phi(W^{(1)}x + b^{(1)})\ldots) + b^{(L-1)}) + b^{(L)}$, where ϕ denotes the ReLU activation function with $\phi(x) = max(0, x)$. To denote the input and output vectors of any layer l, we use the notations z^l and x^l respectively.

The concept of Jacobians for a network (with respect to the outputs and inputs of f) gives us an idea about how the network outputs vary with changes in inputs near a point. The Jacobian at a point x is calculated by the chain rule of derivatives and is done using back propagation. It is important to note that this Jacobian is defined only if the derivatives at every ReLU node is defined. This happens only if the input to each ReLU node is strictly positive or negative. If it is equal to zero then a sub-gradient exists which lies between $[0, 1]$. The Jacobian at a point x, if defined, can be compactly represented as

$$J_f(x) = W^{(L)}\Lambda^{(L-1)}W^{(L-1)}\ldots\Lambda^{(1)}W^{(1)}$$

where Λ^l encodes the activation pattern of a layer l caused by the input x. It is a diagonal matrix, having 1s as elements if the corresponding neuron is active and 0s for inactive neurons. The Jacobian is the same for all the points strictly inside a linear region with the same activation pattern. Since ReLU networks are piece-wise linear in nature, the Lipschitz constant is exactly equal to the p-norm of the Jacobian at one such linear region in the input domain.

4 Algorithm and Its Components

The proposed algorithm is composed of several components like initial estimation of activation pattern, calculation of Lipschitz bounds and partitioning of subproblems, which are unified within the branch and bound framework. This section describes each of these components, including the representation of the sub-problems, in relevant order. The next section combines all these components and provides the overall branch and bound framework.

4.1 Input Domain Abstraction and Interval Bound Propagation

We consider the input region $\mathcal{X}$ as a hyper-rectangle of n-dimensions. It can be represented as the Cartesian product of the following intervals, $\mathcal{X} = [\underline{x_1}, \overline{x_1}] \times [\underline{x_2}, \overline{x_2}] \times \cdots \times [\underline{x_n}, \overline{x_n}]$ where x_i denotes the ith dimension of an input x.

The aim of this section is to get an initial estimation of the activation states of neurons with respect to all the inputs in the input region. Additionally, we obtain the output bounds of the network. The activation states of the neurons can be decided by calculating the pre-activation bounds of each neuron. We mark the state of a neuron as active/inactive based on whether the pre-activation values are positive/negative respectively. If the pre-activation bounds contain both negative and positive values, it is marked as $*$ (an undecided neuron). The neurons may be active or inactive depending on the inputs.

The pre-activation bounds of each neuron can be calculated using interval bound propagation. For all $l = 1, \ldots, n$, taking $[x^{(0)}] = [z^{(0)}]$, and

$$[z^{(l)}] = W^{(l)}[x^{(l-1)}] + b^{(l)}, \ [x_i^{(l)}] = [\max(0, \underline{z_i^{(l)}}), \ \ \max(0, \overline{z_i^{(l)}})]$$

where $[z^{(0)}]$ denotes the input interval vector.

However these bounds are an over-approximation of the actual range of values and these over-approximations accumulate across the layers because of the dependency problem in interval arithmetic. The dependency problem occurs because multiple occurrences of the same variables are treated independently. This dependency problem can be reduced by using symbolic expressions. The symbolic expression makes use of the fact that the input to any neuron depends on the same set of input variables, instead of considering only the outputs from the previous layer independently as done in naive interval bound propagation. A similar approach is presented in [8], but, a crucial difference is that we maintain a single expression instead of two, per neuron. Also we create new symbols instead of concretizing the bounds completely for $*$-neurons, to reduce the dependency errors for such a neuron in deeper layers. In practice, the symbolic expressions are represented using coefficient vectors and constants.

Symbolic Propagation. We denote the symbolic counterparts of the input vector z^l and output vector x^l of the neurons in layer l, as ze^l and xe^l respectively. These expressions are symbolic linear expressions over the outputs of neurons from previous layers. To get the pre-activation bounds we calculate the lower and upper bounds of these expressions at each node. If we encounter a $*$-neuron, the linear relation breaks down and we can no longer propagate the expression from this node. Hence we introduce an independent variable for this node and hope to preserve the resultant expressions in deeper layers. $[\Lambda]^l$ is a diagonal interval matrix denoting the activation pattern of layer l, whose diagonal elements are intervals of the form $[1, 1], [0, 0]$ or $[0, 1]$ corresponding to active, inactive or $*$-neurons (undecided) respectively. All other elements of this interval matrix are $[0, 0]$. This interval matrix will be later used in calculating the Lipschitz upper bounds. Note that the number of $*$-neurons marked can only be exact or an overestimation. It is these $*$-neurons which we aim to remove successively by creating partitions.

4.2 Sub-Problem Representation

This section explains how a sub-problem, or equivalently a node in the Branch and Bound (BaB) tree, is represented. We denote a sub-problem as ρ and a

Algorithm 1. Symbolic Propagation

procedure SymProp(network N, input-domain $\mathcal{X}$)
 $//ze^l_i$ and xe^l_i are the input and output expressions respectively For ith neuron at level l
  Initialize $xe^0 = ze^0 =$ vector of input variables
  for l=1,...,L-1 **do**
    $ze^l = W^{(l)}xe^{l-1} + b^l$
    for $i = 1, ..., n_l$ **do**
      if $\underline{ze^l_i} > 0$ **then**
        $xe^l_i = ze^l_i$, $A^l_i = 1, [\Lambda]^l_{ii} = [1, 1]$ //Keep Dependency
      else if $\overline{ze^l_i} < 0$ **then**
        $xe^l_i = 0$, $A^l_i = 0, [\Lambda]^l_{ii} = [0, 0]$ //Update to 0
      else
        //Introduce new variable v^l_i
        $\overline{v^l_i} = \overline{ze^l_i}$, $\underline{v^l_i} = 0$, $xe^l_i = v^l_i$, $A^l_i = *, [\Lambda]^l_{ii} = [0, 1]$
      end if
    end for
  end for
  $ze^L = W^{(L)}xe^{L-1} + b^{(L)}$
  output-bounds=[$\underline{ze}^L \overline{ze}^L$]
end procedure

property p of that sub-problem as (p, ρ). Each sub-problem has a corresponding subset of the input space (ψ, ρ) associated with it, defined by the set of half-space constraints (H, ρ). Also, for every sub-problem there is an associated activation pattern of the network, (A, ρ), where

$$A^l_i = \begin{cases} 1 & \text{if known } z^{(l)}_i > 0 \text{ for all inputs in } \psi \\ 0 & \text{if known } z^{(l)}_i < 0 \text{ for all inputs in } \psi \\ * & \text{if known otherwise/not known} \end{cases}$$

Any sub-problem can be equivalently represented by a pair consisting of its set of half-space constraints and its activation pattern $\{H, A\}$. The half-space constraints of a sub-problem are of the form $zle^l_i < 0$ or $zle^l_i > 0$, where zle^l_i is a symbolic linear expression of only the input variables, corresponding to the ith neuron at layer l. zle^0 is the symbolic input vector.

The initial sub-problem (root node of the BaB tree) is denoted as ρ_I, whose corresponding ψ is $\mathcal{X}$ itself and activation pattern A is as determined by SymProp. The constraints corresponding to the initial hyper-rectangular input space $\mathcal{X}$ are given as $H = \bigcap\{zle^0_i < \overline{z}^{(0)}_i, i = 1, \ldots, n^{(0)}\} \cap \bigcap\{zle^0_i > \underline{z}^{(0)}_i, i = 1, \ldots, n^{(0)}\}$, which forms a bounded convex polytope. For any sub-problem, if the set of constraints H form a bounded convex polytope and a hyper plane $zle^l_i = 0$ cuts through this polytope, we get two partitions, which are also convex polytopes, given by the constraints, $\{H \cap zle^l_i < 0\}$ and $\{H \cap zle^l_i > 0\}$. It follows from induction that any feasible set of constraints generated after any number of partitioning steps as stated above, forms a bounded convex polytope.

The use of open half-spaces, or strict inequalities, makes sure that when we have a sub-problem with no $*$-neurons, any feasible point in that region is actually a differentiable point. The reason is that the strict inequalities implies that the corresponding neurons takes non-zero values as inputs for all points in the feasible region, which in turn implies that the Jacobian is well defined.

4.3 Propagating Linear Relations

In order to generate the half-space constraints corresponding to neurons at a layer l, we need to have the expressions zle^l for that layer, which is possible only if there are no $*$-neurons present in previous layers. Therefore for any sub-problem, we simply propagate the linear relations zle across the layers until we reach the last layer of the network or encounter a layer which contains a $*$-neuron (since by moving further we cannot preserve the linear relationship with the inputs anymore). xle^l_i is the output expression of a neuron corresponding to the input zle^l_i. It is computed only if there are no $*$-neurons in a layer.

$$zle^l = W^{(l)} xle^{l-1} + b^l, \; xle^l_i = \begin{cases} 0 & \text{if } A^l_i = 0 \\ zle^l_i & \text{if } A^l_i = 1 \end{cases}$$

where $xle^0 = zle^0$ is the symbolic input vector. This process, called as LinProp (as used in subsequent algorithms), is similar to SymProp except that we don't need to evaluate any bounds or introduce any new variables.

4.4 Lipschitz Bounds

In this section we describe the procedure to calculate valid upper bounds of the Lipschitz constant of a sub-problem (similar to [9]). We use interval matrix multiplication to upper bound the Lipschitz constant for a sub-problem. Similar to the Jacobian $J_f(x)$ for a single point x as described before, we can represent the notion of a Jacobian matrix for a set of points X by an interval matrix where each element is an interval which bounds the partial derivatives of all the points. We have

$$[J(X)] = W^{(L)} [\Lambda]^{(L-1)} W^{(L-1)} \ldots [\Lambda]^{(1)} W^{(1)}$$

where $[\Lambda]^l$ is an interval matrix used to denote the activation pattern for layer l, as described in SymProp. The intervals $[0, 1]$ used to represent $*$-neurons, takes into account both possible activation states to calculate the extreme cases of lower and upper bounds of the partial derivatives. Once we obtain this $[J]$ matrix, calculated using interval matrix multiplication, we construct an ordinary matrix U of the same size as that of $[J]$ where each element upper bounds the absolute values of the corresponding intervals in $[J]$. It is to be noted that the interval bounds are over-approximation of the actual values. The p-norm of the constructed U matrix gives us an upper-bound of the local Lipschitz constant for the corresponding sub-problem. In case we have no $*$-neurons (corresponds to a piece-wise linear region), we simply return the p-norm of the Jacobian at that region.

Algorithm 2. Calculating Lipschitz Bounds

procedure LIPSCHITZBOUNDS(sub-problem ρ)
  if ρ has no $*$ neurons **then**
    $//\psi$ is a linear region, hence Jacobian is defined
    return $\|J_f\|_p$
  else
    Initialize $[J]_{ij} = [W_{ij}^{(1)}, W_{ij}^{(1)}], \forall i, j$
    for $l = 2, \ldots, L$ **do**
      $[J] = W^{(l)}[\Lambda]^{(l-1)}[J]$ //interval matrix multiplication
    end for
    Define $\{U | U_{ij} = max(abs(\underline{[J]_{ij}}), abs(\overline{[J]_{ij}})), \forall i, j\}$
    return $\|U\|_p$
  end if
end procedure

4.5 Branching

The main idea behind the branching step is to create a partition in the polytope associated with the a sub-problem and compute the upper-bound of the local Lipschitz constant of each partition to get tighter estimates. The partitions are made in such a way such that inputs from one part activates a specific neuron while for the inputs from the other part, the neuron is inactive. A new set of constraints is created by adding a new constraint ($zle_i^l < 0$ in one case, $zle_i^l > 0$ in the other) corresponding to a $*$-neuron at layer l, to the existing set of half-space constraints H. A related idea of solving linear programs to get refined values after adding constraints similar to this is discussed in [7]. If the constraints set is feasible, we create a sub-problem with the new set of constraints and activation pattern (based on the new half-space constraint added). The next steps include propagating the linear expressions, zle, and also removing some of the $*$-neurons whose states can be determined to be active/inactive with respect to the new constraint set. Finally we calculate the Lipschitz bound for the newly created sub-problem and add it to the set of sub-problems. Note that the Lipschitz bounds of a branched problem can only decrease, since we reduce uncertainties.

4.6 Feasibility Filter

When a new sub-problem is created by creating a partition in a polytope, the smaller partitions may be able to decide the states (active/inactive) of more than one neuron which were marked as $*$-neurons before the partitioning. It is easy to see that identifying such a neuron early on in the BaB tree is better as it prevents repeating the process (feasbility checks) for several (in worst case, exponential) sub-problems which are generated later. We use a simple heuristic to do this. We keep on fixing the states of $*$-neurons which are decidable by the new constraints till we encounter a neuron which still maintains both active and inactive states depending on the inputs. We check the feasibility of both $(H \cap zle_i^l < 0)$ and $(H \cap zle_i^l > 0)$ for a $*$-neuron at layer l. Based on which of these two is feasible we decide the activation state of the neuron. If both of them

Algorithm 3. Branching

```
procedure BRANCH(Sub-problem ρ)
    t ← first layer with ∗-neurons
    select a ∗-neuron(ith neuron at layer t)
    H_0, H_1 ← {(H, ρ) ∩ zle_i^t < 0}, {(H, ρ) ∩ zle_i^t > 0}
    S ← S\{ρ}
    for r ∈ {0, 1} do
        if Feasible(H_r) then
            Create sub-problem ρ_r ≡ {H_r, (A, ρ)}
            (A_i^t, ρ_r) ← r, ([A]_ii^t, ρ_r) ← [r, r]
            LinProp(ρ_r)//propagating linear relations
            FFilter(ρ_r)//feasibility filter
            (L_ub, ρ_r) = LipschitzBounds(ρ_r)
            S ← S ∪ ρ_r
            if ρ_r has no ∗-neurons then
                glb ← max(glb, (L_ub, ρ_r)) //update lower bound
            end if
        end if
    end for
end procedure
```

are feasible then this is a $*$-neuron with respect to H, and we terminate this step. Later, if we need to branch on this sub-problem we shall choose to branch on the $*$-neuron which was already found to maintain both active and inactive states. This strategy will always create two feasible sub-problems. We use this process, called FFilter, in combination with LinProp (for generating half-space costraints) to reduce $*$-neurons across layers.

5 Final Algorithm

This section puts together all the individual components discussed before and provides the main branch and bound framework, as provided in Algorithm 4. Given the network parameters and the input region of interest, the first step is to run symbolic propagation to mark the state of each neurons as active, inactive or $*$. This gives us the initial activation pattern. The first sub-problem is created with this activation pattern and half-space constraints given by the bounding constraints of the input region. The corresponding Lipschitz upper bound is also calculated. The set of sub-problems is initialized with this sub-problem. We use a max heap data structure to represent the sub-problems, sorted by the Lipschitz upper-bound of the sub-problems. *glb* and *gub* are used to keep track of the lower and upper bounds of $\mathcal{L}_p(f, \mathcal{X})$ respectively. The algorithm iteratively selects a sub-problem from the set with the highest Lipschitz upper bound and branches on it. Each newly created sub-problem with its own set of half-space constraints, activation pattern and corresponding Lipschitz upper bound is pushed into the heap. Also, if a sub-problem has no $*$-neurons it is a valid lower-bound for $\mathcal{L}_p(f, \mathcal{X})$, and we use it to compare and update *glb*.

Algorithm 4. Final Algorithm

```
procedure LipBaB(network N, input domain 𝒳, approximation factor k)
    Initial constraints H ← Bounding constraints of 𝒳
    Initial activation A ← SymProp(N, 𝒳)
    Create initial sub-problem ρ_I ≡ {H, A}
    LinProp(ρ_I) //propagating linear relations
    (L_ub, ρ_I) ← LipschitzBounds(ρ_I)
    S ← S ∪ ρ_I
    gub, glb ← (L_ub, ρ_I), 0 // initialize lower and upper bounds of ℒ_p(f, 𝒳)
    if ρ_I has no ∗-neurons then
        glb ← (L_ub, ρ_I)
    end if
    while True do
        ρ' ← arg max_{ρ∈S}(L_ub, ρ)
        gub ← (L_ub, ρ')
        if gub ≤ k.glb then
            break //k=1 implies gub = glb = ℒ_p
        else
            Branch(ρ')
        end if
    end while
    return gub
end procedure
```

For an approximation factor k, we can terminate when $gub \leq k.glb$ since we know that $\mathcal{L}_p(f, \mathcal{X})$ lies between glb and gub. While calculating the exact local Lipschitz constant, the algorithm is terminated when $gub = glb$ or equivalently, the sub-problem at the top of the heap as no $*$-neurons. This means that the input region corresponding to the sub-problem is actually a piece-wise linear region and therefore the local Lipschitz upper-bound of that region is exact instead of an upper bound. Also, since this is the highest among all the other sub-problems, by definition, this is the exact local Lipschitz constant of the entire input region $\mathcal{X}$. The algorithm returns tighter estimates of the Lipschitz upper-bound iteratively until convergence. Hence terminating early because of constraints like time/memory, will always provide us with a valid upper-bound.

To compute the global Lipschitz constant we need to simply mark every neuron as $*$-neuron. This takes care of all the possible activation patterns throughout $\mathbb{R}^n$ and there is no need for any initial input constraints. The rest of the procedure is same. Note, in this case the feasible region of sub-problems are not necessarily bounded.

Note that the number of sub-problems generated in the worst case can be at most $2p - 1$, where p is the number of piece-wise linear regions in $\mathcal{X}$. This is because the BaB tree generated is a full binary tree, and there can be at most p leaf nodes (sub-problems with no $*$-neurons), representing piece-wise linear regions. In practice it is usually much less because of branch and bound.

6 Implementation and Experiments

In this section we provide experimental results to illustrate the working of our algorithm on various parameters. All the experiments were done on Google Colab notebooks. The implementation is done using Python (available in GitHub). For feasibility checking, we used the 'GLPK' Linear Programming solver with a default tolerance limit of 1e−7[2]. The MLPClassifier module from scikit-learn was used to train the networks. The local Lipschitz computation was done on the networks considering the input region $[0, 1]^4$ for the Iris data-set and $[0, 0.1]^{10}$ for the synthetic data-sets, generated using scikit-learn. Note that the choice of input region is arbitrary (Table 1).

Table 1. Lipschitz constant computation for different approximation factors.

Network	p-norm	First estimation		2-approximation		1.5-approximation		Exact	
		Time	Value	Time	Value	Time	Value	Time	Value
Iris_Network(4, 5, 5, 3)	1	0.02 s	8.776	0.06 s	6.874	0.06 s	6.874	0.11 s	5.959
	2	0.02 s	8.810	0.07 s	7.098	0.06 s	7.098	0.09 s	6.772
	inf	0.02 s	14.663	0.06 s	12.606	0.06 s	12.606	0.06 s	12.606
SD_Network1(10, 15, 10, 3)	1	0.04 s	15.105	0.17 s	12.704	0.17 s	12.704	0.25 s	10.413
	2	0.05 s	13.019	0.16 s	10.658	0.16 s	10.658	0.28 s	9.531
	inf	0.04 s	25.243	0.18 s	19.543	0.18 s	19.543	0.27 s	16.275
SD_Network2(10, 20, 15, 10, 3)	1	0.06 s	101.705	1.01 s	70.928	1.01 s	70.928	3.08 s	48.049
	2	0.07 s	101.940	1.79 s	55.969	1.79 s	55.969	3.35 s	40.057
	inf	0.06 s	182.988	2.26 s	82.938	2.26 s	82.938	2.97 s	72.286
SD_Network3(10, 30, 30, 30, 3)	1	0.20 s	131.727	9.43 s	33.890	22.24 s	25.871	56.00 s	19.370
	2	0.20 s	139.808	19.11 s	30.684	25.94 s	28.474	78.88 s	19.463
	inf	0.20 s	272.416	18.90 s	63.035	23.88 s	55.311	59.98 s	39.111

It was observed that the algorithm achieves a good approximation factor within a reasonable time, but gradually converges slowly as the number of sub-problems increases exponentially. Also, the quality of the output bounds of the networks calculated using *SymProp* in comparison to naive interval propagation was found to be much better (Fig. 1).

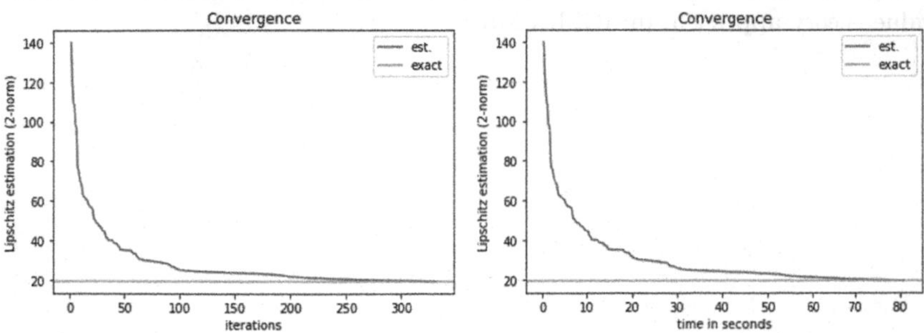

Fig. 1. Convergence of the algorithm for a network with layer sizes (10, 30, 30, 30, 3)

[2] In very rare cases where the feasibility checks demands more precision than the tolerance limit of solvers, we might get a larger value than the true exact.

7 Conclusion

We provide a technique which helps to calculate certified bounds of the Lipschitz constant of neural networks which has several important applications in deep learning. Our main contribution is that this technique can be applied for exact/approximate computation of the local/global Lipschitz constant for any p-norm. Additionally, the ideas discussed here can be applicable to other related problem areas of deep learning including verification problems like output bounds computation, robustness estimation etc., where providing formal guarantees is a requirement.

References

1. Bhowmick, A., D'Souza, M., Raghavan, G.S.: Lipbab: computing exact lipschitz constant of relu networks. arXiv preprint arXiv:2105.05495 (2021)
2. Fazlyab, M., Robey, A., Hassani, H., Morari, M., Pappas, G.J.: Efficient and accurate estimation of Lipschitz constants for deep neural networks. In: NeurIPS (2019)
3. Jordan, M., Dimakis, A.G.: Exactly computing the local lipschitz constant of relu networks. In: NeurIPS (2020)
4. Kim, H., Papamakarios, G., Mnih, A.: The lipschitz constant of self-attention. arXiv preprint arXiv:2006.04710 (2020)
5. Latorre, F., Rolland, P., Cevher, V.: Lipschitz constant estimation of neural networks via sparse polynomial optimization. In: ICLR (2020)
6. Virmaux, A., Scaman, K.: Lipschitz regularity of deep neural networks: analysis and efficient estimation. In: NeurIPS (2018)
7. Wang, S., Pei, K., Whitehouse, J., Yang, J., Jana, S.: Efficient formal safety analysis of neural networks. In: NeurIPS (2018)
8. Wang, S., Pei, K., Whitehouse, J., Yang, J., Jana, S.: Formal security analysis of neural networks using symbolic intervals. In: Proceedings of the 27th USENIX Conference on Security Symposium, pp. 1599–1614 (2018)
9. Weng, T.-W., et al.: Towards fast computation of certified robustness for ReLU networks. In: International Conference on Machine Learning (ICML) (2018)
10. Weng, T.-W., et al.: Evaluating the robustness of neural networks: an extreme value theory approach. In: ICLR (2018)

Nonlinear Lagrangean Neural Networks

Roseli S. Wedemann[1(✉)] and Angel Ricardo Plastino[2]

[1] Instituto de Matemática e Estatística, Universidade do Estado do Rio de Janeiro, Rua São Francisco Xavier 524, Rio de Janeiro, RJ 20550-900, Brazil
roseli@ime.uerj.br

[2] CeBio y Departamento de Ciencias Básicas, Universidad Nacional del Noroeste de la Provincia de Buenos Aires, UNNOBA, Conicet, Roque Saenz Peña 456, Junin, Argentina
arplastino@unnoba.edu.ar

Abstract. Recently, Fagerholm, Friston, Moran and Leech advanced a class of *linear* neural network models complying with Lagrangean dynamics. In the present effort, we explore the possibility of extending the Lagrangean approach to nonlinear models. We present a Lagrangean formalism for a family of *nonlinear* neural network models, and investigate its main mathematical features.

Keywords: Neural networks · Lagrangean and Hamiltonian dynamics · Nonlinear dynamics · Nonlinear Schrödinger equations

1 Introduction

The action variational principle, and the associated Lagrangean and Hamiltonian dynamics, are central to our present understanding of Nature [7]. At the most fundamental level, natural phenomena are described by physical theories based on the Lagrangean and Hamiltonian formalisms [10,17,19,24,27]. The fundamental description, however, is not always or necessarily the most convenient, practical or straightforward to use when studying particular problems. Scientists often use effective or phenomenological, higher level treatments formulated in terms of evolution equations that do not have a Lagrangean or a Hamiltonian form. This happens when considering systems involving drag forces or, more generally, systems that are dissipative or nonconservative. In spite of this situation, the mathematical elegance and beauty of the Lagrangean and Hamiltonian formulations, and the many conceptual and technical advantages provided by them, were strong motivations for exploring ways of recasting the higher-level, effective dynamics of non-conservative systems in a Lagrangean or Hamiltonian form. Efforts along these lines have been conducted by several researchers, and have already a long and distinguished history. We can mention a few examples of these endeavors. A Lagrangean approach to the dynamics of a dissipative oscillator was proposed by Bateman, based on the idea of introducing extra, mirror-like, dynamical variables whose evolution compensates the dissipative

I. Farkaš et al. (Eds.): ICANN 2021, LNCS 12894, pp. 163–173, 2021.
https://doi.org/10.1007/978-3-030-86380-7_14

effects associated with the oscillator's original variables [1]. A Lagrangean formulation of dissipative systems was also discussed by Lindsay and Margenau in [17]. Action-like, variational principles for the diffusion equation, based on ideas similar to those of Bateman, were studied by Morse and Feshbach in [20]. The technique of incorporating new degrees of freedom to construct action variational principles for systems whose original dynamics is not conservative has also been applied to some nonlinear wave equations [25].

Most of the fundamental models in theoretical biology exhibit a dynamics that is not conservative, and is not described by evolution equations having a Lagrangean or a Hamiltonian structure. As examples, we can mention the Lotka-Volterra models in population dynamics [18], the Hopfield and related neural network models [3,11,13], and various mathematical models for biological evolutionary dynamics [21]. There have been, however, interesting proposals for Lagrangean or Hamiltonian models in Biology, such as the Hamiltonian versions of the Lotka-Volterra dynamics investigated by Kerner [14,15], and the family of Hamiltonian neural networks proposed by De Wilde [5]. More recently, a set of Lagrangean dynamical systems, inspired in various of the basic mathematical models considered in neuroscience, have been advanced by Fagerholm, Friston, Moran and Leech (FFML) [6]. The FFML, Lagrangean, neural network systems are, however, *linear*, which constitutes a serious limitation for neural computing. The main aim of the present contribution is to advance a nonlinear extension of the FFML proposal, and explore some of its main mathematical features.

2 The Action Variational Principle and the Lagrangean and Hamiltonian Formulations of Classical Dynamics

Here, we are going to briefly review some basic aspects of the Lagrangean and Hamiltonian formalisms, as applied to classical, dynamical systems. In classical mechanics, the dynamical properties of a conservative system with N degrees of freedom are determined by its Lagrangean $\mathscr{L}(q_1,\ldots,q_n,\dot{q}_1,\ldots,\dot{q}_N)$. The Lagrangean $\mathscr{L}$ is a function of the N generalized coordinates q_i, $i=1,\ldots,N$, and the corresponding generalized velocities $\dot{q}_i = dq_i/dt$, $i=1,\ldots,N$, which are the time derivatives of the coordinates q_i. The set of generalized coordinates $\{q_1,\ldots,q_N\}$ completely describes the instantaneous configuration of the system, at a given time. For example, in a system composed of n particles in three dimensions, the total set of $N=3n$ cartesian coordinates of the particles constitutes a possible set of generalized coordinates.

The action, variational principle states that, when evolving from an initial configuration $\{q_1^{(1)},\ldots q_N^{(1)}\}$ at time $t=t_1$, to a final configuration $\{q_1^{(2)},\ldots q_N^{(2)}\}$ at time $t=t_2$, the system chooses an orbit that makes the action integral,

$$\mathcal{S} = \int_{t_1}^{t_2} \mathscr{L}\, dt \tag{1}$$

stationary. In other words, the action variational principle states that

$$\delta \mathcal{S} = \delta \int_{t_1}^{t_2} \mathscr{L}\, dt = 0. \tag{2}$$

It can be shown that a trajectory $\{q_1(t), \ldots, q_N(t)\}$ that makes the action stationary has to obey the Lagrange equations of motion,

$$\frac{d}{dt}\left(\frac{\partial \mathscr{L}}{\partial \dot{q}_i}\right) = \frac{\partial \mathscr{L}}{\partial q_i}, \quad i = 1, \ldots, N. \tag{3}$$

In classical physics, the Lagrangean of a conservative, mechanical system can be expressed as the difference between the system's kinetic and potential energies (T and V, respectively). For instance, for a system of n particles of mass m, moving in three dimensions, under the effects of interactions described by the potential function V, the Lagrangean is given by

$$\begin{aligned} \mathscr{L} &= T - V \\ &= \frac{m}{2}\left[\sum_{j=1}^{n}\left(\dot{x}_j^2 + \dot{y}_j^2 + \dot{z}_j^2\right)\right] - V(x_1, y_1, z_1, \ldots, x_n, y_n, z_n), \end{aligned} \tag{4}$$

where (x_i, y_i, z_i) are the cartesian coordinates of the ith particle.

One of the great advantages of the Lagrangean formalism is that the form (3) of the equations of motion is the same for any system of generalized coordinates $\{q_1, \ldots q_N\}$. In other words, the Lagrange equations of motion preserve their form (3) when one changes from a given system of generalized coordinates $\{q_1, \ldots q_N\}$ to a new one $\{\bar{q}_1, \ldots \bar{q}_N\}$.

Closely related to the Lagrangean formalism is the Hamiltonian one. The energy of the system can be expressed in terms of the Lagrangean as

$$E = \left(\sum_{i=1}^{N} \dot{q}_i p_i\right) - \mathscr{L}, \tag{5}$$

where the

$$p_i = \frac{\partial \mathscr{L}}{\partial \dot{q}_i}, \quad i = 1, \ldots, N, \tag{6}$$

are the generalized momenta, canonically conjugated with the generalized coordinates q_i. If the Lagragean does not depend explicitly on time (which is the case for autonomous dynamical systems), the energy is conserved: $dE/dt = 0$. If Eqs. (6) are solved for the velocities $\dot{q}_i$ (expressing them as functions of the *canonical variables* q_i's and p_i's) and the resulting expressions are used, in turn, to express E as a function of the canonical variables, one obtains the Hamiltonian function of the system $H(q_1, \ldots, q_N, p_1, \ldots, p_N)$. The system's dynamics can then be described in terms of the canonical variables and the Hamiltonian function, yielding the celebrated Hamiltonian equations of motion,

$$
\begin{aligned}
\dot{p}_i &= -\frac{\partial H}{\partial q_i}, \qquad i = 1, \ldots, N, \\
\dot{q}_i &= \frac{\partial H}{\partial p_i}, \qquad i = 1, \ldots, N.
\end{aligned} \tag{7}
$$

The abstract space whose points have as coordinates the set of $2N$ canonical variables $\{q_i, p_i\}$ is the phase space of the system. The Hamilton equations of motion (7) define a flow in phase space. One of the most important properties of a Hamiltonian, dynamical system is that the associated flow in phase space is divergenceless. This property can be interpreted as meaning that *information* is conserved under Hamiltonian evolution. The conservation of information implied by Hamiltonian dynamics is regarded, by some leading theoretical physicists, as the most fundamental law of Physics [26].

3 The FFML, Linear, Lagrangean Neural Network Models

Before we explore its nonlinear extensions, we shall briefly review the main ingredients of the original, FFML proposal for linear, Lagrangean neural network models. In a nutshell, the basic mathematical procedure behind the construction of the FFML Lagrangean networks is as follows (see [6] for details). The starting point is an appropriate (in general, nonconservative), linear, neural network, governed by the equations of motion of the form,

$$
\dot{x}_j = \sum_k \Omega_{jk} x_k + \sum_k \Gamma_{jk} V_k + W_j, \tag{8}
$$

where the variable x_j characterizes the state of neuron j, the variables V_k represent external inputs, and the quantities W_j represent noise. The symmetric matrix $\{\Omega_{jk}\}$ describes the interaction among the neurons, and the matrix $\{\Gamma_{jk}\}$ describes the effect of each input V_k on each neuron j. Equations (8) are a linear version of the widely used Dynamic Causal Modelling (DCM) equations of motion [9]. To obtain the FFML Lagrangean network, one promotes the real variables x_j to complex variables z_j. Then, one incorporates a multiplicative factor, proportional to the imaginary constant i, in front of each of the time derivatives $\dot{z}_j$ appearing in the left-hand sides of the dynamical equations of the network. At first sight, this procedure may look arbitrary. However, if properly applied, it leads to conservative neural networks complying with the structures associated with the Lagrangean and Hamiltonian formalisms which, in turn, have deep and far-reaching, conceptual implications.

4 The Lagrangean for a Nonlinear Neural Network

The DCM equations of motion, that are at the basis of the original FFML proposal, provide useful descriptions of various scenarios in neuroscience [9].

However, they are a linear approximation [6] to more general, nonlinear neuronal systems. In order to go beyond the linear approximation, we shall explore an extension of the FFML approach, leading to nonlinear, Lagrangean networks. We start by proposing an appropriate Lagrangean function, and then show how this Lagrangean leads, via the action, variational principle, to the dynamical equations governing the evolution of a nonlinear, Lagrangean network.

The neural network we are considering consists of N interacting neurons. The state of each neuron j is characterized by the complex number z_j. Alternatively, the state of this neuron can be regarded as given by two real quantities in an ordered pair (u_j, v_j), such that $z_j = u_j + iv_j$ and i is the imaginary unit. The Lagrangean of our nonlinear network is

$$\begin{aligned}\mathscr{L} = &\frac{i}{2}\sum_{j=1}^{N}(z_j^*\dot{z}_j - \dot{z}_j^* z_j) - \sum_{j,k=1}^{N} z_j^* g(|z_j|^2)\Omega_{jk} g(|z_k|^2) z_k \\ &- \sum_{j=1}^{N}\left[\left(\sum_{k=1}^{N}\Gamma_{jk}V_k\right) + W_j\right](z_j + z_j^*), \end{aligned} \tag{9}$$

where z_j^* indicates the complex conjugate of variable z_j. In the expression (9) for the Lagrangean $\mathscr{L}$, the $N \times N$ matrix Ω_{ij} is hermitian, that is,

$$\Omega_{ij}^* = \Omega_{ij}. \tag{10}$$

The function $g(x)$ characterizes the nonlinearity in the evolution equations governing the behavior of the network. The matrix $\{\Gamma_{jk}\}$ has real elements. Finally, $V_1, \dots V_N$ and $W_1, \dots W_N$ are real quantities, possibly time-dependent. Note that $\mathscr{L}$ is itself a real quantity.

The Lagrangean $\mathscr{L}$ gives rise to the action integral

$$\mathcal{S} = \int_{t_1}^{t_2} \mathscr{L} dt. \tag{11}$$

The evolution of the network can then be determined by a variational principle of stationary action [7,10,24],

$$\delta\mathcal{S} = \delta\int_{t_1}^{t_2} \mathscr{L} dt = 0. \tag{12}$$

This principle leads to the Euler-Lagrange equations of motion. We refer the reader to Chapter 19 of [7] for a descrition of the principle of least action.

To obtain the equations of motion, we can work with the real state variables (u_j, v_j). Alternatively, we can regard the complex variables z_j, and the corresponding complex conjugate quantities z_j^*, as formally independent. This last procedure is more expeditive and we thus obtain the corresponding Euler-Lagrange equations, in the form

$$\frac{d}{dt}\left(\frac{\partial \mathcal{L}}{\partial \dot{z}_j^*}\right) = \frac{\partial \mathcal{L}}{\partial z_j^*}, \qquad i = 1, \dots N,$$
$$\frac{d}{dt}\left(\frac{\partial \mathcal{L}}{\partial \dot{z}_j}\right) = \frac{\partial \mathcal{L}}{\partial z_j}, \qquad i = 1, \dots N, \tag{13}$$

yielding

$$\begin{aligned} i\dot{z}_j = {} & [g(|z_j|^2) + |z_j|^2 g'(|z_j|^2)] \sum_{k=1}^{N} \Omega_{jk} g(|z_k|^2) z_k \\ & + z_j^2 g'(|z_j|^2) \sum_{k=1}^{N} \Omega_{jk}^* g(|z_k|^2) z_k^* + \left[\left(\sum_{k=1}^{N} \Gamma_{jk} V_k\right) + W_j\right], \\ i\dot{z}_j^* = {} & [g(|z_j|^2) + |z_j|^2 g'(|z_j|^2)] \sum_{k=1}^{N} \Omega_{jk}^* g(|z_k|^2) z_k^* \\ & + z_j^{*2} g'(|z_j|^2) \sum_{k=1}^{N} \Omega_{jk} g(|z_k|^2) z_k + \left[\left(\sum_{k=1}^{N} \Gamma_{jk} V_k\right) + W_j\right]. \end{aligned} \tag{14}$$

Note that the equation of motion for z_j^* is the complex conjugate of the equation of motion for z_j. These equations of motion (14) can be formally cast under the guise

$$\begin{aligned} i\dot{z}_j = {} & a(z_j) \sum_{k=1}^{N} \Omega_{jk} b(z_k) + d(z_j) \sum_{k=1}^{N} \Omega_{jk}^* c(z_k) \\ & + \left[\left(\sum_{k=1}^{N} \Gamma_{jk} V_k\right) + W_j\right] \qquad j = 1, \dots N, \end{aligned} \tag{15}$$

and their respective complex conjugates. In (15),

$$\begin{aligned} a(z_j) &= \left[g(|z_j|^2) + |z_j|^2 g'(|z_j|^2)\right], \\ b(z_j) &= g(|z_j|^2) z_j, \\ d(z_j) &= z_j^2 g'(|z_j|^2), \quad \text{and} \\ c(z_j) &= g(|z_j|^2) z_j^*. \end{aligned} \tag{16}$$

These Eqs. (15) are clearly similar in form to the equations of motion for the continuous Hopfield model for associative memory [11,13,28].

When choosing the function g to be constant and equal to one, $g(|z|^2) = 1$, our Lagrangean network model becomes linear, and coincides with one of the models proposed by FFML [6]. It was pointed out by FFML that their Lagrangean network models have a formal structural similarity with the Schrödinger equation. This similarity has interesting consequences, because some of the techniques of quantum mechanics can then be applied to the study of the Lagrangean network. In a similar vein, the nonlinear, Lagrangean networks advanced in the present work share basic structural features with some nonlinear, Schrödinger equations that have been recently considered in the theoretical physics, research literature [16,23,29]. We have to emphasize, however, that the mathematical connection between our present network dynamics with some Schrödinger equations does not imply that our models represent quantum mechanical systems. We are not proposing these Lagrangean networks as neural networks incorporating quantum mechanical effects. The use of complex numbers to formulate our present models should be regarded only as a matter of mathematical convenience. By recourse to complex numbers, the action integral and the associated Lagrangean equations of motion can be cast in a compact way that makes their mathematical features more transparent. However, everything could be expressed using only the $2N$ real quantities (u_i, v_i), $i = 1, \ldots, N$, that constitute the state variables of a classical, dynamical system. It is worth mentioning that this de-complexification procedure can be applied to the standard, Schrödiner equation itself, which can be formally regarded as describing a classical, dynamical system [12]. The mathematical connections between the Schrödinger equation and the evolution equations describing classical systems admit diverse applications such as, for instance, to kinetic theory [8].

5 Energy Function

If the V_j and W_j are time-independent, one has the conserved quantity given by the energy

$$E = \sum_{k=1}^{N} \left(\frac{\partial \mathscr{L}}{\partial \dot{z}_k} \dot{z}_k + \frac{\partial \mathscr{L}}{\partial \dot{z}_k^*} \dot{z}_k^* \right) - \mathscr{L} \,, \tag{17}$$

which can be calculated from (9), resulting in

$$E = \sum_{j,k=1}^{N} z_j^* g(|z_j|^2) \Omega_{jk} g(|z_k|^2) z_k + \sum_{j=1}^{N} \left[\left(\sum_{k=1}^{N} \Gamma_{jk} V_k \right) + W_j \right] (z_j + z_j^*). \tag{18}$$

For autonomous neural networks (corresponding to constant V_j's and vanishing W_j's), it can be directly verified from the equations of motion (14) that the energy is conserved,

$$\frac{dE}{dt} = 0. \tag{19}$$

Otherwise, this conservation law can be derived from the celebrated Noether's theorem [24] (that relates conservation laws with symmetries), as a consequence of the invariance of the action (12), under a time shift (see, for instance, [10]).

6 Another Conservation Law

It can be verified that, under the time evolution determined by the equations of motion (14), the time derivative of the quantity

$$\mathcal{N} = \sum_{j=1}^{N} |z_j|^2 = \sum_{j=1}^{N} \left(u_j^2 + v_j^2 \right), \tag{20}$$

vanishes: $d\mathcal{N}/dt = 0$. The conservation of $\mathcal{N}$ can thus be proved directly from the equations of motion (14), or, alternatively, using Noether's theorem. The action functional (11), corresponding to the Lagrangean (9), is invariant under the transformation $z_i \rightarrow \exp(i\alpha)z_i$; $z_i^* \rightarrow \exp(-i\alpha)z_i^*$, where α is a real number and $\exp(-i\alpha)$ is a global phase. The conservation law associated, via Noether's theorem, with this invariance under a global phase change, is precisely the conservation of $\mathcal{N}$. A similar situation, of course, holds for Schrödinger's equation (see, for instance, [10]). In the case of Schrödinger equations, either linear or nonlinear, the conservation of $\mathcal{N}$ corresponds to the conservation of the normalization of the wave function, which is essential for the probabilistic interpretation of the squared modulus of the wave function (see [16] for an interesting discussion of this issue, in the context of nonlinear, Schrödinger equations). In our system, the conservation of $\mathcal{N}$ allows us to formally treat the quantities $\mathscr{P}_i = |z_i|^2/\mathcal{N}, \;\; i = 1, \ldots, N$, as constituting a normalized, probability distribution. This, in turn, permits the application of techniques based on the maximum entropy principle, to obtain approximate solutions of the equations of motion of the system. These techniques have been successfully applied in quantum mechanical scenarios (see [22] and references therein).

7 Hamiltonian Formulation

The conjugate momenta associated with z_j and z_j^* are, respectively,

$$
\begin{aligned}
\chi_j &= \frac{\partial \mathscr{L}}{\partial \dot{z}_j} = \frac{i z_j^*}{2}, \qquad i = 1, \ldots N\,, \\
\bar{\chi}_j &= \frac{\partial \mathscr{L}}{\partial \dot{z}_j^*} = -\frac{i z_j}{2}, \qquad i = 1, \ldots N\,.
\end{aligned} \tag{21}
$$

We see that the quantities z_j and $\chi_j = i z_j^*/2$ can be formaly regarded as canonically conjugate, dynamical variables. The Hamiltonian function then is given by the expression for the energy. That is,

$$
\begin{aligned}
H(z_j, \chi_j) = &\sum_{j,k=1}^{N} z_j^* g(|z_j|^2) \Omega_{jk} g(|z_k|^2) z_k \\
&+ \sum_{j=1}^{N} \left[\left(\sum_{k=1}^{N} \Gamma_{jk} V_k \right) + W_j \right] (z_j + z_j^*),
\end{aligned} \tag{22}
$$

where z_j^* is replaced by $-2i\chi_j$, and $|z_j|^2$ by $-2iz_j\chi_j$. The equations of motion then become

$$
\dot{z}_j = \frac{\partial H}{\partial \chi_j} = -2i \frac{\partial H}{\partial z_j^*}, \qquad i = 1, \ldots N\,, \tag{23}
$$

or, equivalently,

$$
\frac{i}{2} \dot{z}_j = \frac{\partial H}{\partial z_j^*}, \qquad i = 1, \ldots N\,, \tag{24}
$$

which coincides with the equations of motion (14).

As already mentioned, the equations of motion of our system can be re-expressed in terms of the real variables (u_i, v_i), adopting the form

$$\begin{aligned} \dot{u}_i &= \mathcal{U}_i(u_1, \ldots, u_N, v_1, \ldots, v_N), \\ \dot{v}_i &= \mathcal{V}_i(u_1, \ldots, u_N, v_1, \ldots, v_N), \end{aligned} \tag{25}$$

where the $\mathcal{U}_i$'s and the $\mathcal{V}_i$'s are functions of the $2N$ real quantities (u_i, v_i).

All over the biological kingdom *Animalia*, nervous systems are constituted by neurons sharing the same basic features. There are theoretical reasons to expect that this remarkable fact might hold even within astrobiological contexts [4]. In spite of this uniformity of biological neuronal systems, there are valid reasons to explore new biologically-inspired mathematical models of computation. First, it would be naive to expect that the existing mathematical models exhaust all the richness and complexity of biological computation (even if neurons are everywhere more or less alike). Second, there are theoretical reasons to explore new models of computation. We are specially interested in models that share with the fundamental laws of physics a basic information-theoretical feature. The dynamical system (25) has a divergenceless phase space flow. This divergenceless property, related to the conservation of information, is perhaps the most fundamental difference between the network models explored in this work, and those usually considered in theoretical neuroscience. In this regard, it is worth to mention a recent work by Berto, Tagliabue and Rossi (BTR) [2]. These authors investigate the deep conceptual and philosophical implications of a cellular automata admitting universal computation that, in contrast to Conway's "Game of Life", is *reversible*. We believe that Lagrangean neural networks may give rise, within the context of continuous models of computation, to similar theoretical issues, deserving further scrutiny.

8 Concluding Remarks

In a recent contribution, Fagerholm, Friston, Moran and Leech made the intriguing proposal of considering neural network models that are governed by Lagrangean equations of motion, and thus comply with the celebrated action variational principle, which is at the heart of our present understanding of fundamental physics. The Lagrangean networks studied by Fagerholm and collaborators are inspired on linear approximations to neuronal dynamics, such as the linear Dynamic Causal Modelling (DCM) equations of motion [9]. Linearity imposes a severe limitation on the computational capabilities of these Lagrangean models. The main purpose of our present work is to explore the possibility of extending the Lagrangean approach to *nonlinear* networks. We advance a Lagrangean function leading, via the action variational principle, to neural-network-like, dynamical systems governed by *nonlinear*, Lagrangean, equations of motion. These equations of motion are structurally similar to some nonlinear, Schrödinger equations that have been investigated in the recent theoretical physics literature. The analogy with Schrödinger equations makes it possible to study the Lagrangean networks taking advantage of techniques borrowed from quantum mechanics. Schrödinger-like equations admit oscillatory solutions that, as suggested in [9], may describe oscillatory phenomena in neuronal systems. Nonlinear Lagrangean models could be useful in this regard, since the oscillatory behavior in real neuronal systems is typically nonlinear. As a final remark, it is worth stressing that in spite of their formal connection with some Schrödinger equations, the neural network models considered here are dynamical systems of a strictly classical nature.

All biologically inspired models supporting universal computation are nonconservative or, in the case of discrete models, nonreversible. A paradigmatic example is Conway's celebrated "Game of Life" cellular automata. In an interesting recent work [2], Berto, Tagliabue, and Rossi explore the manyfold conceptual implications of a cellular automata admitting universal computation that, in contrast to the "Game of Life", is *reversible*. The nonlinear Lagrangean networks investigated here might play, for continuous models of computation, a role similar to the one that the reversible cellular automata of Berto and collaborators plays for discrete models. Of one thing we are certain: the Lagrangean networks and the reversible cellular automata inspire in us the same kind of intellectual curiosity. We hope that the curiosity of other researchers will be aroused as well.

References

1. Bateman, H.: On dissipative systems and related variational principles. Phys. Rev. **38**(4), 815–819 (1931). https://doi.org/10.1103/PhysRev.38.815
2. Berto, F., Tagliabue, J., Rossi, G.: There's plenty of Boole at the bottom: a reversible CA against information entropy. Mind. Mach. **26**(4), 341–357 (2016). https://doi.org/10.1007/s11023-016-9401-6
3. Cohen, M.A., Grossberg, S.: Absolute stability of global pattern formation and parallel memory storage by competitive neural networks. IEEE Trans. Syst. Man Cybern. **13**, 815–826 (1983). https://doi.org/10.1109/TSMC.1983.6313075
4. Cranford, J.L.: Astrobiological Neurosystems: Rise and Fall of Intelligent Life Forms in the Universe. Springer, Cham (2015)
5. De Wilde, P.: Class of Hamiltonian neural networks. Phys. Rev. E **47**(2), 1392–1396 (1993). https://doi.org/10.1103/PhysRevE.47.1392
6. Fagerholm, E.D., Friston, K.J., Moran, R.J., Leech, R.: The principle of stationary action in neural systems. arXiv p. 2010.02993 (2020). https://arxiv.org/abs/2010.02993
7. Feynman, R.P., Leighton, R.B., Sands, M.: The Feynman Lectures on Physics, vol. 2. Addison Wesley, Reading (2006)
8. Flego, S.P., Frieden, B.R., Plastino, A., Plastino, A.R., Soffer, B.H.: Nonequilibrium thermodynamics and Fisher information: sound wave propagation in a dilute gas. Phys. Rev. E **68**(1), 016105 (2003). https://doi.org/10.1103/PhysRevE.68.016105
9. Friston, K.J., Harrison, L., Penny, W.: Dynamic causal modelling. Neuroimage **19**(4), 1273–1302 (2003). https://doi.org/10.1016/S1053-8119(03)00202-7
10. Goldstein, H.: Classical Mechanics, 2nd edn. Addison-Wesley, New York (1980)
11. Hertz, J.A., Krogh, A., Palmer, R.G.: Introduction to the Theory of Neural Computation. Lecture Notes, vol. 1. Perseus Books, Cambridge (1991)

12. Heslot, A.: Quantum mechanics as a classical theory. Phys. Rev. D **31**(6), 1341–1348 (1985). https://doi.org/10.1103/PhysRevD.31.1341
13. Hopfield, J.J.: Neurons with graded responses have collective computational properties like those of two-state neurons. Proc. Natl. Acad. Sci. **81**, 3088–3092 (1984). https://doi.org/10.1073/pnas.81.10.3088
14. Kerner, E.H.: A statistical mechanics of interacting biological species. Bull. Math. Biophys. **19**, 121–146 (1957)
15. Kerner, E.H.: Note on Hamiltonian format of Lotka-Volterra dynamics. Phys. Lett. A **151**(8), 401–402 (1990). https://doi.org/10.1016/0375-9601(90)90911-7
16. Lenzi, E.K., de Castro, A.S.M., Mendes, R.S.: Some nonlinear extensions for the Schrödinger equation. Chin. J. Phys. **66**, 74–81 (2020). https://doi.org/10.1016/j.cjph.2020.04.019
17. Lindsay, R.B., Margenau, H.: Foundations of Physics. Dover, New York (1957)
18. Lotka, A.J.: Elements of Mathematical Biology. Dover, New York (1956)
19. Mercier, A.: Analytical and Canonical Formalism in Physics. Dover, Mineola (2004)
20. Morse, M., Feshbach, H.: Methods of Theoretical Physics. McGraw-Hill, New York (1953)
21. Nowak, M.A.: Evolutionary Dynamics. Harvard University Press, Cambridge (2006)
22. Plastino, A.R., Plastino, A.: Maximum entropy and approximate descriptions of pure states. Phys. Lett. A **181**(6), 446–449 (1993). https://doi.org/10.1016/0375-9601(93)91147-W
23. Plastino, A.R., Wedemann, R.S.: Nonlinear wave equations related to nonextensive thermostatistics. Entropy **19**(2), 60.1–13 (2017). https://doi.org/10.3390/e19020060
24. Ramond, P.: Field Theory: A Modern Primer. Taylor and Francis, New York (1997)
25. Rego-Monteiro, M.A., Nobre, F.D.: Nonlinear quantum equations: classical field theory. J. Math. Phys. **54**(10), 103302 (2013). https://doi.org/10.1063/1.4824129
26. Susskind, L., Hrabovsky, G.: The Theoretical Minimum: What You Need to Know to Start Doing Physics. Basic Books, New York (2014)
27. Wald, R.M.: General Relativity. University of Chicago Press, Chicago (1984)
28. Wedemann, R.S., Plastino, A.R.: A Nonlinear Fokker-Planck Description of Continuous Neural Network Dynamics. In: Tetko, I.V., Kůrková, V., Karpov, P., Theis, F. (eds.) ICANN 2019. LNCS, vol. 11727, pp. 43–56. Springer, Cham (2019). https://doi.org/10.1007/978-3-030-30487-4_4
29. Yamano, T.: Gaussian solitary waves for argument-Schrödinger equation. Communications in Nonlinear Science and Numerical Simulation **91**, 105449 (2020). https://doi.org/10.1016/j.cnsns.2020.105449

Normalization and Regularization Methods

Energy Conservation in Infinitely Wide Neural-Networks

Shu Eguchi(✉) and Takafumi Amaba

Fukuoka University, 8-19-1 Nanakuma, Jônan-ku, Fukuoka 814-0180, Japan
fmamaba@fukuoka-u.ac.jp

Abstract. A three-layered neural-network (NN), which consists of an input layer, a wide hidden layer and an output layer, has three types of parameters. Two of them are pre-neuronal, namely, thresholds and weights to be applied to input data. The rest is post-neuronal weights to be applied after activation. The current paper consists of the following two parts. First, we consider three types of stochastic processes. They are constructed by summing up each of parameters over all neurons at each epoch, respectively. The neuron number will be regarded as another time different to epochs. In the wide neural-network with a neural-tangent-kernel- (NTK-) parametrization, it is well known that these parameters are hardly varied from their initial values during learning. We show that, however, the stochastic process associated with the post-neuronal parameters is actually varied during the learning while the stochastic processes associated with the pre-neuronal parameters are not. By our result, we can distinguish the type of parameters by focusing on those stochastic processes. Second, we show that the variance (sort of "energy") of the parameters in the infinitely wide neural-network is conserved during the learning, and thus it gives a conserved quantity in learning.

Keywords: Wide neural-networks · Cumulative sum of parameters · Energy conservation

1 Introduction

In recent years, great developments have been made in understanding the mechanisms of training of a neural networks when the width of the network is large. The first step was given in Neal [7], where it was shown that for any NTK-parametrized NN, the output before training converges to a Gaussian process on the space of inputs as the width increases. This means that even in the case of a neural network with nonlinear transformations, Bayesian regression with this Gaussian process as its prior distribution is tractable when we take the limit of width to infinity (Williams [12] and Goldberg et al. [2]). This idea has been extended to deep neural-networks by Lee et al. [5].

The Bayesian regression and training by gradient method have been linked by Jacot et al. ([4]). They found that gradient method in a NTK-parametrized

I. Farkaš et al. (Eds.): ICANN 2021, LNCS 12894, pp. 177–189, 2021.
https://doi.org/10.1007/978-3-030-86380-7_15

NN with the large width is equivalent to kernel learning with the neural tangent kernel (NTK), and found a connection between the kernel and the maximum-a-posteriori estimator in Bayesian inference. They and Lee et al. ([6]) also showed that as the NTK-parametrized NN becomes wider, the model becomes linearized along the gradient descent or flow as the training, and the parameters become harder to be changed. This "lazy" regime appears, as shown in Chizat et al. [1], not only in over-parametrized neural-networks, but also in more abstract settings depending on the choice of scaling and initialization.

Due to the universal nature discovered in [4] and [6], we have not been able to distinguish whether they are pre- or post-neuronal if we focus on the behavior of the parameters. In this paper, we show that, during the learning, the behaviors of the cumulative sums of parameters over all neurons are different from each other according to their types of parameters. This implies that it is possible to distinguish whether the parameters are pre- or post-neuronal. When the width of the network tends to infinity, we also show that the "energy" of the cumulative sum is conserved (Theorem 2).

2 Related Works

Integral Representation of Mean-Field Parametrized NN. A mean-field parametrized NN forms like a Riemann sum, and thus has an integral representation when the width tends to infinity. In Sonoda-Murata [8] and Murata [11], the relationship between the distribution of parameters and the output is described via ridgelet transformation and their reconstruction theorem. On the other hand, in the case of our NTK-parametrized NN, the output before training is given by a *stochastic integral* when the network is infinitely wide. It would be of independent interest to investigate the reconstruction theorem in this situation.

Dynamics of Infinitely Wide Mean-Field Parametrized NN. For training of mean-field parametrized NN, another method for training is the stochastic gradient descent. It is described as a stochastic differential equation in the parameter space, in particular, it gives a gradient Langevin dynamics. When the width of the network is infinite, the parameter space is infinite-dimensional. Then the corresponding dynamics is described by an infinite-dimensional Langevin dynamics in a reproducing kernel Hilbert space, which appears as a collection of features. This infinite-dimensional model contains all models of finite width, and thus allows us to analyze them universally among all models with finite width. The convergence of this learning and the generalization error are discussed in Suzuki [9] and Suzuki-Akiyama [10].

3 Our Contribution

We consider the following NTK-parametrized NN of the width m:

$$f(x;\theta) = \frac{1}{\sqrt{m}} \sum_{j=1}^{m} b_j \sigma(a_j x + a_{0,j}).$$

Here, the input $x \in \mathbb{R}$ is one-dimensional and the activation function $\sigma : \mathbb{R} \to \mathbb{R}$ is assumed to be non-negative and Lipschitz continuous. We denote the coordinates of the parameter $\theta = (\boldsymbol{a}_0, \boldsymbol{a}, \boldsymbol{b})$ as follows.

- Pre-neuronal thresholds: $\boldsymbol{a}_0 = (a_{0,1}, a_{0,2}, \dots, a_{0,m}) \in \mathbb{R}^m$,
- Pre-neuronal weights: $\boldsymbol{a} = (a_1, a_2, \dots, a_m) \in \mathbb{R}^m$,
- Post-neuronal weights: $\boldsymbol{b} = (b_1, b_2, \dots, b_m) \in \mathbb{R}^m$.

Given a training data $\{(x_i, y_i)\}_{i=1}^n$, we put $\hat{y}_i(\theta) := f(x_i; \theta)$ and define a loss function by

$$L(\theta) := \frac{1}{n} \sum_{i=1}^{n} (\hat{y}_i(\theta) - y_i)^2.$$

The solution to the associated gradient flow equation $\frac{\mathrm{d}}{\mathrm{d}t}\theta(t) = -\frac{1}{2}(\nabla_\theta L)(\theta(t))$ is denoted by $\theta(t) = (\boldsymbol{a}_0(t), \boldsymbol{a}(t), \boldsymbol{b}(t)) = (\{a_{0,j}(t)\}_{j=1}^m, \{a_j(t)\}_{j=1}^m, \{b_j(t)\}_{j=1}^m)$, where we set its initialization by $\theta(0) = (\boldsymbol{a}_0(0), \boldsymbol{a}(0), \boldsymbol{b}(0)) \sim \mathrm{N}(\boldsymbol{0}, I_{3m})$. Here, I_{3m} is the identity matrix of order $3m$.

It is known that when the width m of the network is sufficiently large and training is performed, the optimal parameters are obtained as values close to the initial ones (Jacot et al. [4]). In this paper, we further investigate behaviors of the parameters. Specifically, we consider cumulative sums of the parameters over all neurons at each epoch, which are normalized by a scale depending on the width m. We focus on what arises when we take the normalized cumulative sums along the gradient flow, even the values of parameters are hardly varied. It is enough to consider only two cumulative sums $\sum_{j=1}^m a_j(0)$ and $\sum_{j=1}^m b_j(0)$ associated with pre- and post-neuronal weights respectively since thresholds have the same role as pre-neuronal weights by considering $\{(x_i, 1)\}_{i=1}^n$ as a two-dimensional input.

To compare their behaviors among different widths during the training, we have to consider which scale is appropriate to normalize the cumulative sums of the parameters. The initialization gives us a hint. At the initialization, variances of the cumulative sums are given by $\sum_{j=1}^m \mathrm{Var}(a_j(0)) = \sum_{j=1}^m \mathrm{Var}(b_j(0)) = m$. Thus it would be natural to normalize $\sum_{j=1}^m a_j(0)$ and $\sum_{j=1}^m b_j(0)$ by scaling of $\sqrt{m}$. Moreover, we embed them into the space of continuous functions on the interval $[0, 1]$ as follows. On the m-equidistant partition $\{s_k := \frac{k}{m}\}_{k=0}^m$ of the interval, we set $A_{s_k}^{(m)}(t) := \frac{1}{\sqrt{m}} \sum_{j=1}^k a_j(t)$ and $B_{s_k}^{(m)}(t) := \frac{1}{\sqrt{m}} \sum_{j=1}^k b_j(t)$ and then we extend them onto subintervals $[s_{k-1}, s_k]$ by linear interpolations:

$$\begin{aligned} A_s^{(m)}(t) &:= \frac{A_{s_k}^{(m)}(t) - A_{s_{k-1}}^{(m)}(t)}{s_k - s_{k-1}}(s - s_{k-1}) + A_{s_{k-1}}^{(m)}(t), \\ B_s^{(m)}(t) &:= \frac{B_{s_k}^{(m)}(t) - B_{s_{k-1}}^{(m)}(t)}{s_k - s_{k-1}}(s - s_{k-1}) + B_{s_{k-1}}^{(m)}(t) \end{aligned} \qquad \text{if } s_{k-1} \le s \le s_k.$$

For each width m and time t of the gradient flow, these embedded functions $A^{(m)}(t) = \{A_s^{(m)}(t)\}_{0 \le s \le 1}$ and $B^{(m)}(t) = \{B_s^{(m)}(t)\}_{0 \le s \le 1}$ are random continuous-functions on $[0, 1]$, namely, stochastic processes.

With this embedding, it will be necessary that they do not diverge when $m \to \infty$ in order to compare them appropriately among various widths. At the initialization, by the so-called Donsker's invariance principle, which is well known in probability theory, the stochastic processes $\{(A^{(m)}(0), B^{(m)}(0))\}_{m=1}^{\infty}$ converge to a two-dimensional Brownian motion. In general, for any time t of the gradient flow, the following is valid.

Theorem 1. *The family $\{(A^{(m)}(t), B^{(m)}(t))\}_{m=1}^{\infty}$ is tight.*

This implies that a certain subsequence $\{(A^{(m_k)}(t), B^{(m_k)}(t))\}_{k=1}^{\infty}$ converges almost surely (by replacing the probability space appropriately if necessary). In what follows, we denote the subsequence again by $\{(A^{(m)}(t), B^{(m)}(t))\}$ for simplicity of notations. The limit $(A(t), B(t))$ of this subsequence gives a dynamics on the infinite-dimensional Banach space $C([0,1] \to \mathbb{R}^2)$ and then it would be another interest to describe the dynamics. In terms of $B(t) = \{B_s(t)\}_{0 \leq s \leq 1}$, we have

$$f(x_i; \theta) = \frac{1}{\sqrt{m}} \sum_{j=1}^{m} \sigma(a_j x_i + a_{0,j}) b_j \to \int_0^1 \sigma(a_s x + a_{0,s}) \mathrm{d}B_s(0) =: \hat{y}_i^{(\infty)}$$

in probability as $m \to \infty$, and this limit is called a stochastic integral. In the above, $\{a_s\}_{0 \leq s \leq 1}$ and $\{a_{0,s}\}_{0 \leq s \leq 1}$ are mutually independent Gaussian processes on $[0,1]$ with a zero mean and the covariance function given by $\mathbf{E}[a_s a_u] = \mathbf{E}[a_{0,s} a_{0,u}] = \mathbf{1}_{\{0\}}(u - s)$. Here, $\mathbf{1}_{\{0\}}$ is the indicator function of the singleton $\{0\}$. These are also independent of $B(0)$. Although it can be smoothly expected that the dynamics of $\{(A(t), B(t))\}_{t \geq 0}$ is described by the neural tangent kernel, since $C([0,1] \to \mathbb{R}^2)$ is a non-Hilbert Banach space, it is difficult to employ the concepts of their gradient and kernel that depend on the inner product structure.

Now, among NTK-parametrized NNs of various widths, we can compare the dynamics for the cumulative sum at an "appropriate scale". Figure 1 shows outputs of neural networks widths of $m = 100, 1000, 10000$ after training. The training data are indicated by points, and we have used gradient descent. The following Figs. 2, 3, 4 and 5 show the changes of the parameters and their cumulative sums during the training. Each line in Figs. 2 and 4 represents how the corresponding parameter is varied during the training.

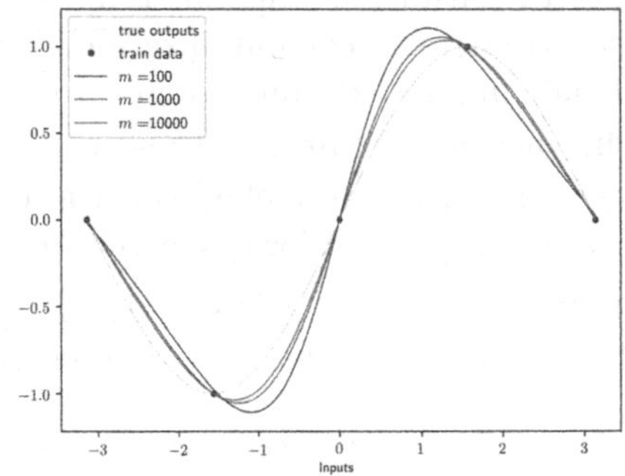

Fig. 1. Outputs after training

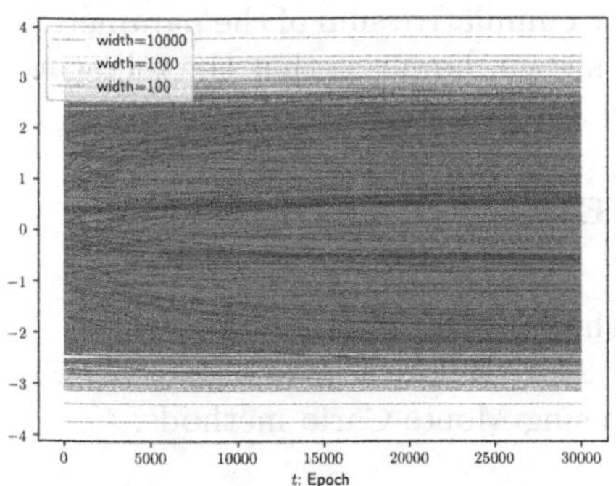

Fig. 2. Changes of parameters a_j during the training

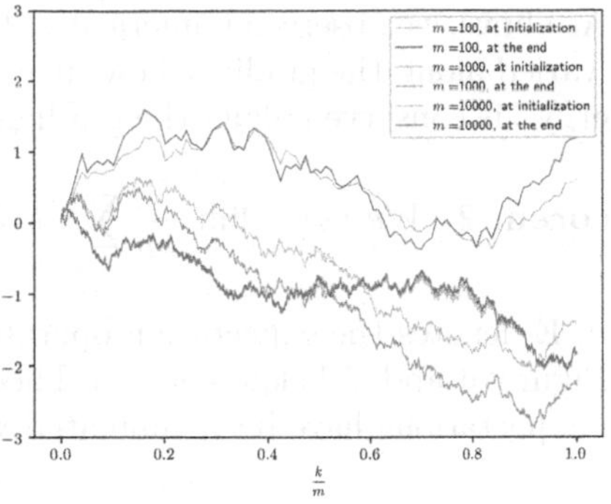

Fig. 3. Cumulative sums of parameters a_j before/after the training

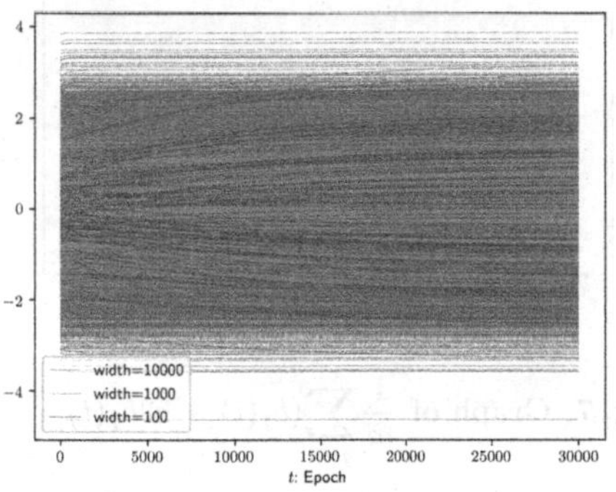

Fig. 4. Changes of parameters b_j during the training

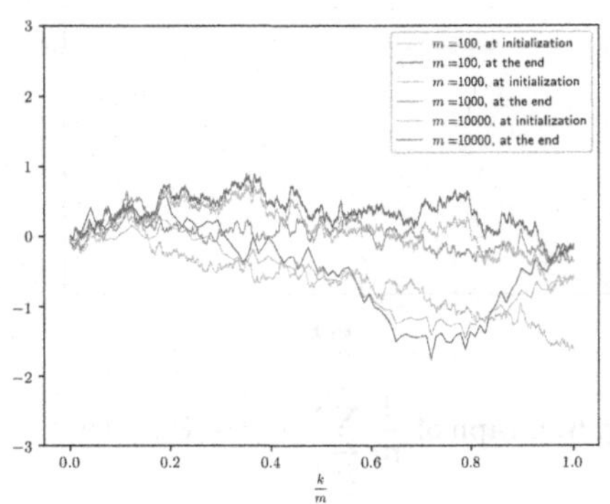

Fig. 5. Cumulative sums of parameters b_j before/after the training

From the figures, as width increases, the variation of cumulative sum becomes smaller for parameters a, while we can see it is actually varied for parameters b.

In fact, when $t = 0$ and $m \to \infty$, by the law of large numbers, we have

$$\begin{aligned}\left.\frac{\mathrm{d}}{\mathrm{d}t}\right|_{t=0} A_{s_m}^{(m)}(t) &= -\frac{1}{n}\sum_{i=1}^{n}\big(\hat{y}_i(\theta(0)) - y_i\big)\frac{1}{m}\sum_{j=1}^{m}\sigma'\big(a_j(0)x_i + a_{0,j}(0)\big)x_i b_j(0)\\ &\to -\frac{1}{n}\sum_{i=1}^{n}\big(\hat{y}_i^{(\infty)} - y_i\big)\mathbf{E}\big[\sigma'\big(a_1(0)x_i + a_{0,1}(0)\big)x_i\big]\mathbf{E}[b_1(0)] = 0.\end{aligned}$$

On the other hand, since the activation function σ is non-negative and non-zero,

$$\begin{aligned}\left.\frac{\mathrm{d}}{\mathrm{d}t}\right|_{t=0} B_{s_m}^{(m)}(t) &= -\frac{1}{n}\sum_{i=1}^{n}\big(\hat{y}_i(\theta(0)) - y_i\big)\frac{1}{m}\sum_{j=1}^{m}\sigma\big(a_j(0)x_i + a_{0,j}(0)\big)\\ &\to -\frac{1}{n}\sum_{i=1}^{n}\big(\hat{y}_i^{(\infty)} - y_i\big)\mathbf{E}\big[\sigma\big(a_1(0)x_i + a_{0,1}(0)\big)\big] \neq 0.\end{aligned}$$

As above, we observed numerically that the cumulative sum of the parameters b is varied along the gradient flow. It can be shown, however, that the following "energy" is conserved along the gradient flow.

Theorem 2. *We have* $\lim_{m\to\infty} \frac{1}{m}\sum_{j=1}^{m}\left(b_j(t) - \mathbf{E}[b_j(t)]\right)^2 = 1$ *for all* $t \geq 0$.

Here, $\mathbf{E}$ denotes the expectation operator. The same for $a_{0,j}(t)$ and $a_j(t)$.

Figures 6 and 7 below confirm Theorem 2 in the learning shown in Fig. 1. The expectations have been simulated with using Monte Carlo methods.

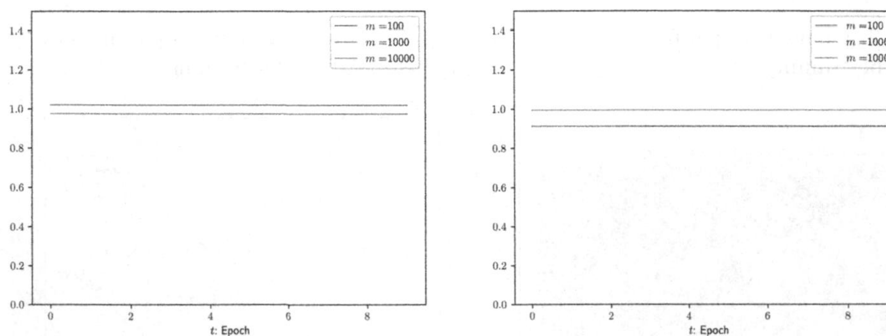

Fig. 6. Graph of $\frac{1}{m}\sum_{j=1}^{m}(a_j(t) - \mathbf{E}[a_j(t)])^2$ **Fig. 7.** Graph of $\frac{1}{m}\sum_{j=1}^{m}(b_j(t) - \mathbf{E}[b_j(t)])^2$

4 Conclusion

In this paper, we showed that in a three-layer wide neural-network, the cumulative sum of pre-neuronal parameters is hardly varied along the gradient flow, while it is varied for post-neuronal parameters. This allowed us to find a critical difference among the behaviors of the pre- and post-neuronal parameters, this is a first trial to distinguish them, which has not been so far. Furthermore, we showed that the energy is conserved along the gradient flow.

Acknowledgments. The authors would like to express their appreciation to Professor Masaru Tanaka and Professor Jun Fujiki who provided valuable comments and advices.

A Proof of Theorem 1 and Theorem 2

Recall that the activation function σ has been assumed to be non-negative and Lipschitz continuous. Then σ is differentiable almost everywhere and the Lipschitz constant can be expressed as $\|\sigma'\|_\infty := \operatorname{ess\,sup}|\sigma'|$, where σ' is the almost-everywhere-defined derivative of σ. We shall put $|\mathcal{X}| := \max_{i=1,2,\ldots,n}|x_i|$, where

$\{x_i\}_{i=1}^m$ is the input data. Note that the loss function $L(\theta) = \frac{1}{n}\sum_{i=1}^n \big(\hat{y}_i(\theta) - y_i\big)^2$ depends on the width m as does so for the outputs $\hat{y}_i(\theta) = \frac{1}{\sqrt{m}}\sum_{j=1}^m \sigma(a_j x_i + a_{0,j}) b_j$.

A.1 Equipments About Gradient Flow $\frac{\mathrm{d}}{\mathrm{d}t}\theta(t) = -\frac{1}{2}(\nabla_\theta L)(\theta(t))$

Lemma 1. *Along the gradient flow, we have $L(\theta(t)) \leq L(\theta(0))$ for $t \geq 0$.*

In the coordinate $\theta(t) = (\boldsymbol{a}_0(t), \boldsymbol{a}(t), \boldsymbol{b}(t)) = (\{a_{0,j}(t)\}_{j=1}^m, \{a_j(t)\}_{j=1}^m, \{b_j(t)\}_{j=1}^m)$, the gradient flow $\frac{\mathrm{d}}{\mathrm{d}t}\theta(t) = -\frac{1}{2}(\nabla_\theta L)(\theta(t))$ can be written as follows: for $j = 1, 2, \ldots, m$ and $t \in \mathbb{R}$,

$$\begin{aligned}
\frac{\mathrm{d}}{\mathrm{d}t} a_{0,j}(t) &= -\frac{1}{n}\sum_{i=1}^n \big(\hat{y}_i(\theta(t)) - y_i\big)\sigma'\big(a_j(t)x_i + a_{0,j}(t)\big)\frac{b_j(t)}{\sqrt{m}}, \\
\frac{\mathrm{d}}{\mathrm{d}t} a_j(t) &= -\frac{1}{n}\sum_{i=1}^n \big(\hat{y}_i(\theta(t)) - y_i\big)\sigma'\big(a_j(t)x_i + a_{0,j}(t)\big)x_i\frac{b_j(t)}{\sqrt{m}}, \\
\frac{\mathrm{d}}{\mathrm{d}t} b_j(t) &= -\frac{1}{n}\sum_{i=1}^n \big(\hat{y}_i(\theta(t)) - y_i\big)\sigma\big(a_j(t)x_i + a_{0,j}(t)\big)\frac{1}{\sqrt{m}}.
\end{aligned} \tag{1}$$

Proposition 1. *For $m = 1, 2, 3, \ldots$, $j = 1, 2, \ldots, m$ and $t \geq 0$, we have*

$$F_j(t) \leq \left(F_j(0) + \frac{\sigma(0)t}{\sqrt{m}}\sqrt{L(\theta(0))}\right)\mathrm{e}^{\frac{\|\sigma'\|_\infty(|\mathcal{X}|+1)}{\sqrt{m}}\sqrt{L(\theta(0))}\,t},$$

where $F_j(t) := |a_{0,j}(t)| + |a_j(t)| + |b_j(t)|$.

Proof. We begin with estimating $a_j(t)$. Let $\dot{a}_j(s) := \frac{\mathrm{d}}{\mathrm{d}s}a_j(s)$. By fundamental theorem of calculus, the triangle inequality and (1), we have

$$\begin{aligned}
|a_j(t)| &\leq |a_j(0)| + \int_0^t \left|\frac{1}{n}\sum_{i=1}^n \big(\hat{y}_i(\theta(s)) - y_i\big)\sigma'\big(a_j(s)x_i + a_{0,j}(s)\big)x_i\frac{b_j(s)}{\sqrt{m}}\right|\mathrm{d}s \\
&\leq |a_j(0)| + \int_0^t \frac{\|\sigma'\|_\infty|\mathcal{X}|}{\sqrt{m}}\left(\frac{1}{n}\sum_{i=1}^n |\hat{y}_i(\theta(s)) - y_i|\right)|b_j(s)|\mathrm{d}s.
\end{aligned}$$

Since it holds that

$$\frac{1}{n}\sum_{i=1}^n |\hat{y}_i(\theta(s)) - y_i| \leq \sqrt{L(\theta(s))} \leq \sqrt{L(\theta(0))} \tag{2}$$

by virtue of Jensen's inequality and Lemma 1, we obtain

$$|a_j(t)| \leq |a_j(0)| + \frac{\|\sigma'\|_\infty|\mathcal{X}|}{\sqrt{m}}\sqrt{L(\theta(0))}\int_0^t |b_j(s)|\mathrm{d}s. \tag{3}$$

Similarly, we have

$$|a_{0,j}(t)| \le |a_{0,j}(0)| + \frac{\|\sigma'\|_\infty}{\sqrt{m}}\sqrt{L(\theta(0))}\int_0^t |b_j(s)|\mathrm{d}s. \tag{4}$$

For $b_j(t)$, by estimating in a manner similar to $|a_j(t)|$, we get

$$|b_j(t)| \le |b_j(0)| + \int_0^t \frac{1}{n}\sum_{i=1}^n |\hat{y}_i(\theta(s)) - y_i| \cdot \sigma\big(a_j(s)x_i + a_{0,j}(s)\big)\frac{1}{\sqrt{m}}\mathrm{d}s.$$

By using a estimate: $\sigma\big(a_j x_i + a_{0,j}\big) \le \sigma(0) + \|\sigma'\|_\infty(|\mathcal{X}||a_j| + |a_{0,j}|)$ and (2),

$$|b_j(t)| \le |b_j(0)| + \frac{\sigma(0)t}{\sqrt{m}}\sqrt{L(\theta(0))} + \frac{\|\sigma'\|_\infty t(|\mathcal{X}|+1)}{\sqrt{m}}\sqrt{L(\theta(0))}\int_0^t (|a_j(s)| + |a_{0,j}(s)|)\mathrm{d}s. \tag{5}$$

By putting estimates (3), (4) and (5) together, we have

$$F_j(t) \le F_j(0) + \frac{\sigma(0)t}{\sqrt{m}}\sqrt{L(\theta(0))} + \frac{\|\sigma'\|_\infty(|\mathcal{X}|+1)}{\sqrt{m}}\sqrt{L(\theta(0))}\int_0^t F_j(s)\mathrm{d}s.$$

Now, by applying Grönwall's inequality, we reach the conclusion.

Proposition 2. *For every $j = 1, 2, \ldots, m$, we have*

(i) $\displaystyle\int_0^t F_j(u)\mathrm{d}u \le G_j(t)$,

(ii) $\displaystyle\int_0^t \max\{|\dot{a}_{0,j}(u)|, |\dot{a}_j(u)|, |\dot{b}_j(u)|\}\mathrm{d}u \le \sqrt{\frac{L(\theta(0))}{m}}\{\|\sigma'\|_\infty(|\mathcal{X}|+1)G_j(t) + \sigma(0)t\}$,

where $F_j(u) := |a_{0,j}(u)| + |a_j(u)| + |b_j(u)|$ and

$$G_j(t) = \left(F_j(0) + \frac{\sigma(0)}{\|\sigma'\|_\infty(|\mathcal{X}|+1)}\right)t \cdot \mathrm{e}^{\frac{2\|\sigma'\|_\infty(|\mathcal{X}|+1)}{\sqrt{m}}\sqrt{L(\theta(0))}\,t}. \tag{6}$$

Note that each $G_j(t)$ depends on the width m of the network.

Proof. (i) Put $c_1 = \frac{\|\sigma'\|_\infty(|\mathcal{X}|+1)}{\sqrt{m}}\sqrt{L(\theta(0))}$ and $c_2 = \frac{\sigma(0)}{\sqrt{m}}\sqrt{L(\theta(0))}$. Then by Proposition 1, we have

$$\int_0^t F_l(u)\mathrm{d}u \le \int_0^t (F_l(0) + c_2 u)\,\mathrm{e}^{c_1 u}\mathrm{d}u \le F_l(0)\frac{\mathrm{e}^{c_1 t} - 1}{c_1 t}t + \frac{c_2}{c_1}t \cdot \mathrm{e}^{c_1 t}.$$

Since it holds that $\frac{\mathrm{e}^x - 1}{x} \le \mathrm{e}^{2x}$ for $x > 0$, we obtain

$$\int_0^t F_l(u)\mathrm{d}u \le F_l(0)\mathrm{e}^{2c_1 t} \cdot t + \frac{c_2}{c_1}t \cdot \mathrm{e}^{c_1 t} \le \left(F_l(0) + \frac{c_2}{c_1}\right)t \cdot \mathrm{e}^{2c_1 t} = G_j(t).$$

(ii) We show only for $\int_0^t |\dot{b}_j(u)|\mathrm{d}u$. The same is for the other parameters. By (1) and (2), we get $\int_0^t |\dot{b}_j(u)|\mathrm{d}u \le \sqrt{\frac{L(\theta(0))}{m}}\int_0^t \sigma\big(a_j(u)x_i + a_{0,j}(u)\big)\mathrm{d}u$. Then by using that $\sigma\big(a_j(u)x_i + a_{0,j}(u)\big) \le \|\sigma'\|_\infty(|\mathcal{X}|+1)F_j(u) + \sigma(0)$ and by (i), we have the conclusion.

Proposition 3. *For all $p > 0$, we have the following:* $\limsup_{m\to\infty} \mathbf{E}[(\sqrt{L(\theta(0))})^p] < \infty$, $\limsup_{m\to\infty} \mathbf{E}[G_j(t)^p] < \infty$ *and* $\limsup_{m\to\infty} \mathbf{E}[(\sqrt{L(\theta(0))}\, G_j(t))^p] < \infty$.

Proof. The last estimate follows from the first two estimates and Cauchy-Schwarz' inequality. Since the first estimate is obvious, we show only the second. For this, it is sufficient to show that

$$\limsup_{m\to\infty} \mathbf{E}[\mathrm{e}^{\frac{p}{\sqrt{m}}\sqrt{L(\theta(0))}}] < \infty. \tag{7}$$

In the following, we write $a_{0,j}(0) = a_{0,j}$, $a_j(0) = a_j$ and $b_j(0) = b_j$. First, we note that $\sqrt{L(\theta(0))} \le \frac{1}{\sqrt{n}}\sum_{i=1}^n |\hat{y}_i(\theta(0)) - y_i| \le \frac{1}{\sqrt{n}}\sum_{i=1}^n |\hat{y}_i(\theta(0))| + \frac{1}{\sqrt{n}}|y_i|$. Then by using Hölder's inequality, we get

$$\mathbf{E}[\mathrm{e}^{\frac{p}{\sqrt{m}}\sqrt{L(\theta(0))}}] \le \mathrm{e}^{\frac{p}{\sqrt{nm}}\sum_{i=1}^n |y_i|}\Big(\prod_{i=1}^n \mathbf{E}\big[\mathrm{e}^{\frac{p\sqrt{n}}{\sqrt{m}}|\hat{y}_i(\theta(0))|}\big]\Big)^{1/n}$$

$$\le \mathrm{e}^{\frac{p}{\sqrt{nm}}\sum_{i=1}^n |y_i|}\max_{i=1,2,\dots,n}\mathbf{E}\big[\mathrm{e}^{\frac{p\sqrt{n}}{\sqrt{m}}|\hat{y}_i(\theta(0))|}\big] \le \mathrm{e}^{\frac{p}{\sqrt{nm}}\sum_{i=1}^n |y_i|}\sum_{i=1}^n \mathbf{E}\big[\mathrm{e}^{\frac{p\sqrt{n}}{\sqrt{m}}|\hat{y}_i(\theta(0))|}\big].$$

Since we have $(\hat{y}_i(\theta(0)) \mid \boldsymbol{a}_0, \boldsymbol{a}) \sim \mathrm{N}\big(0, \frac{1}{m}\sum_{j=1}^m \sigma(a_j x_i + a_{0,j})^2\big)$,

$$\mathbf{E}\big[\mathrm{e}^{\frac{p\sqrt{n}}{\sqrt{m}}|\hat{y}_i(\theta(0))|}\big] = \sqrt{\frac{2}{\pi}}\int_0^\infty \mathbf{E}\Big[\mathrm{e}^{\frac{p\sqrt{n}}{\sqrt{m}}\big(\frac{1}{m}\sum_{j=1}^m \sigma(a_j x_i + a_{0,j})^2\big)^{1/2} w}\Big]\mathrm{e}^{-\frac{w^2}{2}}\,\mathrm{d}w$$

$$\le \sqrt{\frac{2}{\pi}}\int_{-\infty}^\infty \mathbf{E}\Big[\mathrm{e}^{\frac{p\sqrt{n}}{\sqrt{m}}\big(\frac{1}{m}\sum_{j=1}^m \sigma(a_j x_i + a_{0,j})^2\big)^{1/2} w}\Big]\mathrm{e}^{-\frac{w^2}{2}}\,\mathrm{d}w = 2\mathbf{E}\Big[\mathrm{e}^{\frac{p^2 n}{2m}\frac{1}{m}\sum_{j=1}^m \sigma(a_j x_i + a_{0,j})^2}\Big].$$

Furthermore, by Jensen's inequality and independence,

$$\mathbf{E}\Big[\mathrm{e}^{\frac{p^2 n}{2m}\frac{1}{m}\sum_{j=1}^m \sigma(a_j x_i + a_{0,j})^2}\Big] \le \mathbf{E}\Big[\mathrm{e}^{\frac{p^2 n}{2m}\sum_{j=1}^m \sigma(a_j x_i + a_{0,j})^2}\Big]^{1/m} = \mathbf{E}\Big[\mathrm{e}^{\frac{p^2 n}{2m}\sigma(a_1 x_i + a_{0,1})^2}\Big].$$

We can show that $\sigma(a_1 x_i + a_{0,1})^2 \le 16\{\|\sigma'\|_\infty(|\mathcal{X}|+1)\}^2\{(a_{0,1})^2 + (a_1)^2\} + (\sigma(0))^2$. Hence

$$\mathbf{E}\Big[\mathrm{e}^{\frac{p^2 n}{2m}\sigma(a_1 x_i + a_{0,1})^2}\Big] \le \mathrm{e}^{\frac{p^2 n}{2m}(\sigma(0))^2}\cdot\mathbf{E}\Big[\mathrm{e}^{\frac{8p^2 n\|\sigma'\|_\infty^2(|\mathcal{X}|+1)^2}{m}((a_{0,1})^2 + (a_1)^2)}\Big].$$

The right-hand-side is finite if $\frac{8p^2 n\|\sigma'\|_\infty^2(|\mathcal{X}|+1)^2}{m} - \frac{1}{2} < 0$, that is, $m > 16p^2 n\|\sigma'\|_\infty^2(|\mathcal{X}|+1)^2$, and then it is decreasing with respect to m. By putting all together, (7) is proved.

A.2 Proof of Theorem 1

It is enough to prove that both of $\{A^{(m)}(t)\}_{m=1}^\infty$ and $\{B^{(m)}(t)\}_{m=1}^\infty$ are tight. For this, from [3, Chapter I, Section 4, Theorem 4.3], it is sufficient to show that (i) $\sup_m \mathbf{E}\big[|A_0^{(m)}(t)| + |B_0^{(m)}(t)|\big] < \infty$ and (ii) there exist $\gamma, \alpha > 0$ such that

$$\sup_m \sup_{\substack{s,u\in[0,1]:\\ s\neq u}} \left(\frac{\mathbf{E}\big[|A_s^{(m)}(t) - A_u^{(m)}(t)|^\gamma\big]}{|s-u|^{1+\alpha}} + \frac{\mathbf{E}\big[|B_s^{(m)}(t) - B_u^{(m)}(t)|^\gamma\big]}{|s-u|^{1+\alpha}}\right) < \infty.$$

(i) is clear since $A_0^{(m)}(t) = B_0^{(m)}(t) = 0$. Thus we show only (ii). We will only show the one for $A^{(m)}(t)$. Since $A^{(m)}(t)$ is a piecewise linear interpolation of values on $\{s_k = \frac{k}{m}\}_{k=0}^m$, it suffices to show that for some $\gamma, \alpha > 0$, it holds that

$$\sup_m \sup_{\substack{1 \le k,j \le m: \\ k \ne j}} \frac{\mathbf{E}\big[|A_{s_k}^{(m)}(t) - A_{s_j}^{(m)}(t)|^\gamma\big]}{|s_k - s_j|^{1+\alpha}} < \infty. \tag{8}$$

Let $k, j \in \{1, 2, \ldots, m\}$ be arbitrary. Without loss of generality, we assume that $j < k$. Then we have

$$|A_{s_k}^{(m)}(t) - A_{s_j}^{(m)}(t)| \le \frac{1}{\sqrt{m}}\Big| \sum_{l=j+1}^{k} \big(a_l(t) - \mathbf{E}[a_l(t)]\big)\Big| + \frac{1}{\sqrt{m}}\Big| \sum_{l=j+1}^{k} \mathbf{E}[a_l(t)]\Big|. \tag{9}$$

We shall make estimates for two terms on the right-hand-side.

Lemma 2. *With $G_l(t)$ defined in (6), we have*

$$\Big| \sum_{l=j+1}^{k} (a_l(t) - \mathbf{E}[a_l(t)])\Big| \le \Big| \sum_{l=j+1}^{k} a_l(0)\Big| + \frac{\|\sigma'\|_\infty |\mathcal{X}|}{\sqrt{m}} \sum_{l=j+1}^{k} \big(\sqrt{L(\theta(0))}\, G_l(t) + \mathbf{E}[\sqrt{L(\theta(0))}\, G_l(t)]\big).$$

Proof. Since $\mathbf{E}[a_l(0)] = 0$, we have $a_l(t) - \mathbf{E}[a_l(t)] = \int_0^t \dot{a}_l(u)\mathrm{d}u - \int_0^t \mathbf{E}[\dot{a}_l(u)]\mathrm{d}u + a_l(0)$. By summing up this over $l = j+1, j+2, \ldots, k$ and by using (1) and (2),

$$\begin{aligned}\Big| \sum_{l=j+1}^{k} (a_l(t) - \mathbf{E}[a_l(t)])\Big| \le \Big| \sum_{l=j+1}^{k} a_l(0)\Big| &+ \frac{\|\sigma'\|_\infty |\mathcal{X}|}{\sqrt{m}} \sqrt{L(\theta(0))} \sum_{l=j+1}^{k} \int_0^t |b_l(u)|\mathrm{d}u \\ &+ \frac{\|\sigma'\|_\infty |\mathcal{X}|}{\sqrt{m}} \mathbf{E}\big[\sqrt{L(\theta(0))} \sum_{l=j+1}^{k} \int_0^t |b_l(u)|\mathrm{d}u\big].\end{aligned}$$

Finally, by applying Proposition 2, we get the conclusion.

Lemma 3. *We have* $\Big| \sum_{l=j+1}^{k} \mathbf{E}[a_l(t)]\Big| \le \frac{\|\sigma'\|_\infty |\mathcal{X}|}{\sqrt{m}} \mathbf{E}\big[\sqrt{L(\theta(0))} \sum_{l=j+1}^{k} G_l(t)\big]$.

Proof. By (1), $\mathbf{E}[a_l(t)] = \int_0^t \mathbf{E}[-\frac{1}{n}\sum_{i=1}^n \big(\hat{y}_i(\theta(u)) - y_i\big)\sigma'\big(a_l(u)x_i + a_{0,l}(u)\big)x_i \frac{b_l(u)}{\sqrt{m}}]\mathrm{d}u$. By taking the sum over $l = j+1, j+2, \ldots, k$, we have

$$\Big| \sum_{l=j+1}^{k} \mathbf{E}[a_l(t)]\Big| \le \frac{\|\sigma'\|_\infty |\mathcal{X}|}{\sqrt{m}} \mathbf{E}\Big[\sqrt{L(\theta(0))} \sum_{l=j+1}^{k} \int_0^t |b_l(u)|\mathrm{d}u\Big].$$

Then by using Proposition 2, we reach the conclusion.

Turning back to Eq. (9), we apply Lemma 2 and Lemma 3 to get

$$|A_{s_k}^{(m)}(t) - A_{s_j}^{(m)}(t)| \le \frac{1}{\sqrt{m}}\Big| \sum_{l=j+1}^{k} a_l(0)\Big| + \frac{\|\sigma'\|_\infty |\mathcal{X}|}{m} \sum_{l=j+1}^{k} \big(2H_l(t) + \mathbf{E}[H_l(t)]\big),$$

where $H_l(t) = \sqrt{L(\theta(0))}\, G_l(t)$. By an easy estimate: $(x+y)^4 \le 2^4(x^4+y^4)$,

$$\begin{aligned}&(A^{(m)}_{s_k}(t) - A^{(m)}_{s_j}(t))^4\\ &\le \frac{2^4}{m^2}\left(\sum_{l=j+1}^{k} a_l(0)\right)^4 + 2^4\|\sigma'\|_\infty^4|\mathcal{X}|^4\left(\frac{k-j}{m}\right)^4\left(\frac{1}{k-j}\sum_{l=j+1}^{k}(2H_l(t) + \mathbf{E}[H_l(t)])\right)^4.\end{aligned}$$

Therefore $\mathbf{E}[\big(A^{(m)}_{s_k}(t) - A^{(m)}_{s_j}(t)\big)^4] = \frac{2^4}{m^2}I + 2^4\|\sigma'\|_\infty^4|\mathcal{X}|^4(s_k - s_j)^4 II$. Here,

$$I := \mathbf{E}[\Big(\sum_{l=j+1}^{k} a_l(0)\Big)^4], \quad II := \mathbf{E}[\Big(\frac{1}{k-j}\sum_{l=j+1}^{k}(2H_l(t) + \mathbf{E}[H_l(t)])\Big)^4].$$

First, we shall focus on II. By Jensen's inequality,

$$II \le \frac{1}{k-j}\sum_{l=j+1}^{k}\mathbf{E}[\big(2H_l(t) + \mathbf{E}[H_l(t)]\big)^4] = \mathbf{E}[\big(2H_1(t) + \mathbf{E}[H_1(t)]\big)^4].$$

On the other hand, for I, since $a_1(0), a_2(0), \ldots, a_m(0)$ are independent and identically distributed, and each of them is distributed in $\mathrm{N}(0,1)$, we have $I = 3(k-j)^2$. Hence

$$\begin{aligned}&\mathbf{E}[\big(A^{(m)}_{s_k}(t) - A^{(m)}_{s_j}(t)\big)^4]\\ &\le 2^4\cdot 3(s_k - s_j)^2 + 2^4\|\sigma'\|_\infty^4|\mathcal{X}|^4(s_k - s_j)^4\mathbf{E}[\big(2H_1(t) + \mathbf{E}[H_1(t)]\big)^4].\end{aligned}$$

Finally, by noting Proposition 3, we see that (8) holds for $\gamma = 4$ and $\alpha = 1$.

A.3 Proof of Theorem 2

By the law of large numbers, we see that $\frac{1}{m}\sum_{j=1}^{m}\big(b_j(0)\big)^2 \to \mathbf{E}[\big(b_j(0)\big)^2] = 1$ as $m \to \infty$. Then it suffices to show that

$$\mathbf{E}\Big[\Big|\frac{1}{m}\sum_{j=1}^{m}(b_j(t) - \mathbf{E}[b_j(t)])^2 - \frac{1}{m}\sum_{j=1}^{m}\big(b_j(0)\big)^2\Big|\Big] \to 0.$$

Since $b_j(t) - \mathbf{E}[b_j(t)] = b_j(0) + \int_0^t\big(\dot{b}_j(u) - \mathbf{E}[\dot{b}_j(u)]\big)du$, we have $(b_j(t) - \mathbf{E}[b_j(t)])^2 - (b_j(0))^2 = \big(\int_0^t\big(\dot{b}_j(u) - \mathbf{E}[\dot{b}_j(u)]\big)du\big)^2 + 2b_j(0)\int_0^t(\dot{b}_j(u) - \mathbf{E}[\dot{b}_j(u)])du$. Thus we have

$$\begin{aligned}&\Big|\frac{1}{m}\sum_{j=1}^{m}(b_j(t) - \mathbf{E}[b_j(t)])^2 - \frac{1}{m}\sum_{j=1}^{m}\big(b_j(0)\big)^2\Big|\\ &\le \frac{1}{m}\sum_{j=1}^{m}\Big|\Big(\int_0^t(\dot{b}_j(u) - \mathbf{E}[\dot{b}_j(u)])du\Big)^2 + 2b_j(0)\int_0^t(\dot{b}_j(u) - \mathbf{E}[\dot{b}_j(u)])du\Big|.\end{aligned}$$

By taking the expectation, we get

$$
\begin{aligned}
&\mathbf{E}\Big[\Big|\frac{1}{m}\sum_{j=1}^{m}\left(b_j(t)-\mathbf{E}[b_j(t)]\right)^2-\frac{1}{m}\sum_{j=1}^{m}\left(b_j(0)\right)^2\Big|\Big] \\
&\leq \frac{1}{m}\sum_{j=1}^{m}\left\{\mathbf{E}\Big[\Big(\int_0^t\left(|\dot{b}_j(u)|+\mathbf{E}\big[|\dot{b}_j(u)|\big]\right)\mathrm{d}u\Big)^2\Big]+2\mathbf{E}\Big[|b_j(0)|\int_0^t\left(|\dot{b}_j(u)|+\mathbf{E}\big[|\dot{b}_j(u)|\big]\right)\mathrm{d}u\Big]\right\}.
\end{aligned}
$$

For the term $\int_0^t |\dot{b}_j(u)|\mathrm{d}u$ appeared above, we know by Proposition 2 that

$$
\int_0^t |\dot{b}_j(u)|\mathrm{d}u \leq \sqrt{\frac{L(\theta(0))}{m}}\left\{\|\sigma'\|_\infty(|\mathcal{X}|+1)G_j(t)+\sigma(0)t\right\} =: \frac{M_j(t)}{\sqrt{m}},
$$

where note that $M_j(t)$ depends on the width m. Thus, $\int_0^t\left(|\dot{b}_j(u)|+\mathbf{E}\big[|\dot{b}_j(u)|\big]\right)\mathrm{d}u \leq \frac{M_j(t)+\mathbf{E}[M_j(t)]}{\sqrt{m}}$. By Proposition 3, we have $\limsup_{m\to\infty}\mathbf{E}\big[\left(M_1(t)+\mathbf{E}[M_1(t)]\right)^2\big] < \infty$ and $\limsup_{m\to\infty}\mathbf{E}\big[|b_1(0)|\left(M_1(t)+\mathbf{E}[M_1(t)]\right)\big] < \infty$. Hence as $m\to\infty$,

$$
\begin{aligned}
&\mathbf{E}\Big[\Big|\frac{1}{m}\sum_{j=1}^{m}\left(b_j(t)-\mathbf{E}[b_j(t)]\right)^2-\frac{1}{m}\sum_{j=1}^{m}\left(b_j(0)\right)^2\Big|\Big] \\
&\leq \frac{1}{m}\sum_{j=1}^{m}\left\{\frac{\mathbf{E}\big[\left(M_j(t)+\mathbf{E}[M_j(t)]\right)^2\big]}{m}+2\frac{\mathbf{E}\big[|b_j(0)|\left(M_j(t)+\mathbf{E}[M_j(t)]\right)\big]}{\sqrt{m}}\right\} \\
&= \frac{\mathbf{E}\big[\left(M_1(t)+\mathbf{E}[M_1(t)]\right)^2\big]}{m}+2\frac{\mathbf{E}\big[|b_1(0)|\left(M_1(t)+\mathbf{E}[M_1(t)]\right)\big]}{\sqrt{m}} \to 0.
\end{aligned}
$$

References

1. Chizat, L., Oyallon, E., Bach, F.: On lazy training in differentiable programming. In: Wallach, H., Larochelle, H., Beygelzimer, A., d'Alché-Buc, F., Fox, E., Garnett, R. (eds.) Advances in Neural Information Processing Systems, vol. 32, (NeurIPS 2019). Curran Associates, Inc (2018)
2. Goldberg, P., Williams, C., Bishop, C.: Regression with input-dependent noise: a Gaussian process treatment. In: Advances in Neural Information Processing Systems, vol. 10, NIPS 1997. MIT Press (1998)
3. Ikeda, N., Watanabe, S.: Stochastic Differential Equations and Diffusion Processes, Second edn. North-Holland Mathematical Library, 24. North-Holland Publishing Co., Amsterdam; Kodansha Ltd, Tokyo, p. xvi+555 (1989). ISBN: 0-444-87378-3
4. Jacot, A., Gabriel. F., Hongler. C.: Neural tangent kernel: convergence and generalization in neural networks. In: Bengio, S., Wallach, H., Larochelle, H., Grauman, K., Cesa-Bianchi, N., Garnett, R. (eds.) Advances in Neural Information Processing Systems, vol. 31, pp. 8571–8580. Curran Associates, Inc (2018)
5. Lee, J., Bahri, Y., Novak, R., Schoenholz, S., Pennington, J., Sohl-Dickstein, J.: Deep neural networks as Gaussian processes. In: International Conference on Learning Representations, (ICLR 2018) (2018)

6. Lee, J., et al.: Wide neural networks of any depth evolve as linear models under gradient descent. In: Wallach, H., Larochelle, H., Beygelzimer, A., d'Alché-Buc, F., Fox, E., Garnett, R. (eds.) Advances in Neural Information Processing Systems, vol. 32, (NeurIPS 2019), Curran Associates, Inc (2019)
7. Neal, R.M.: Priors for infinite networks. In: Bayesian Learning for Neural Networks, pp. 29–53. Springer, New York (1996). https://doi.org/10.1007/978-1-4612-0745-0_2
8. Sonoda, S., Murata, N.: Neural network with unbounded activation functions is universal approximator. Appl. Comput. Harmonic Anal. **43**(2), 233–268 (2017)
9. Suzuki, T.: Generalization bound of globally optimal non-convex neural network training: transportation map estimation by infinite dimensional Langevin dynamics. In: Larochelle, H., Ranzato, M., Hadsell, R., Balcan, M.F., Lin, H. (eds.), Advances in Neural Information Processing Systems, vol. 33, (NeurIPS 2020), pp. 19224–19237. Curran Associates, Inc (2020)
10. Suzuki, T., Akiyama, S.: Benefit of deep learning with non-convex noisy gradient descent: provable excess risk bound and superiority to kernel methods. To appear in International Conference on Learning Representations, 2021 (ICLR 2021) (2021)
11. Murata, N.: An integral representation of functions using three-layered networks and their approximation bounds. Neural Netw. **9**(6), 947–956 (1996)
12. Williams, C.: Computing with infinite networks. In: Mozer, M.C., Jordan, M., Petsche, T. (eds.) Advances in Neural Information Processing Systems, vol. 9, (NIPS 1996), MIT Press (1997)

Class-Similarity Based Label Smoothing for Confidence Calibration

Chihuang Liu(✉) and Joseph JaJa

University of Maryland, College Park, MD 20742, USA
chliu@umd.edu

Abstract. Generating confidence calibrated outputs is of utmost importance for the applications of deep neural networks in safety-critical decision-making systems. The output of a neural network is a probability distribution where the scores are estimated confidences of the input belonging to the corresponding classes, and hence they represent a complete estimate of the output likelihood relative to all classes. In this paper, we propose a novel form of label smoothing to improve confidence calibration. Since different classes are of different intrinsic similarities, more similar classes should result in closer probability values in the final output. This motivates the development of a new smooth label where the label values are based on similarities with the reference class. We adopt different similarity measurements, including those that capture feature-based similarities or semantic similarity. We demonstrate through extensive experiments, on various datasets and network architectures, that our approach consistently outperforms state-of-the-art calibration techniques including uniform label smoothing.

Keywords: Confidence calibration · Uncertainty estimation · Similarity measure

1 Introduction

Machine learning algorithms have progressed rapidly in recent years and are becoming the critical component in a wide variety of technologies [6]. In most of these applications, making wrong decisions could lead to very high costs, including significant business losses or even severe human injuries [2]. As a result, in real-world decision-making systems, machine learning models should not only try to be as accurate as possible, but should also indicate when they are likely to be incorrect, which allows the decision-making to be stopped or passed to human experts when the models are not sufficiently confident to produce a correct prediction. It is therefore strongly desirable that a network provides a calibrated confidence measure in addition to its prediction; that is, the probability associated with the predicted class label should reflect its ground truth likelihood of correctness [19].

However, recent works [7] have shown through extensive empirical studies that even though impressively accurate, modern deep neural networks are poorly

I. Farkaš et al. (Eds.): ICANN 2021, LNCS 12894, pp. 190–201, 2021.
https://doi.org/10.1007/978-3-030-86380-7_16

calibrated. It turns out that modern DNNs are overconfident - the prediction accuracy is likely to be lower than what is indicated by the associated confidence. Since the discovery of this challenging problem, several methods [18,25,27,31] have been explored and empirically shown to improve confidence calibration performance on the predictions, which we refer to as *prediction calibration*, for which only the model's prediction (the winning class) and its associated confidence (the maximum softmax score) are considered.

In the output of a neural network, each score represents the model's estimated probability of the current input belonging to that corresponding class. Therefore, for a well-calibrated model, each probability should be indicative of the actual likelihood of the input belonging to each class, not just the one with the maximum score [10,12]. This is significant in safety-critical applications. For example, an autonomous driving system predicts an object to be 60% a pedestrian, 30% an obstacle, and 10% a traffic sign. Clearly these probabilities should be calibrated. We refer to this as *output calibration* where the entire output probabilities are considered.

The output scores define a probability distribution over all classes, and we call the perfectly calibrated distribution as the optimal output distribution. Under the optimization scheme with cross-entropy loss that most modern DNNs adopt, a model would achieve perfect confidence calibration if directly trained using the optimal distribution as training label. Unfortunately, as one would expect, it is unclear how to directly compute the optimal distribution in general. However, under certain reasonable assumptions, we can develop good approximations. Different classes are not equally distinct, and a class can be inherently more similar to some classes than others. For example, in the CIFAR-100 dataset, we could generally agree that the class dolphin is much more similar to the class seal than to the class rose, and the probability of a seal should be higher than a rose in the output distribution of a dolphin input. Therefore, we make the following two assumptions:

1. The distribution of other (i.e. non ground-truth) classes is non-uniform in general.
2. The probability value should correlate positively with the similarity between the true class and any other class, i.e. the more similar they are the higher the value.

In this paper, we propose a novel form of the smooth labeling, called *class-similarity based label smoothing*, which uses class similarities to approximate the optimal output distribution. In the proposed smooth label of a reference class, the label for another class is based on its similarity with the reference class, and hence more similar classes result in higher values.

From the label smoothing perspective, our proposed smooth label is more intuitive than the traditional uniform smooth label. One-hot labels have all probability mass in one class, which are zero-entropy signals that admit no uncertainty about the input. When a network is trained using such labels, it inevitably becomes overconfident. With uniform smooth labels, the output of a network is trained to be a mixture of a Dirac distribution and a uniform distribution. This implies that the predicted probabilities for other classes are encouraged to be equal. As we discussed above, the label value should be based on the similarity between classes, which is not accounted for in either the one-hot or the uniform smooth labels. Relational information can be crucial and provides high-order properties that can improve performance of a model in various tasks [20].

In our proposed method, we first measure the similarity between classes which is then mixed with the one-hot labels to serve as the final smooth label. Since measuring similarity is in general an open problem [26,32], we adopt different metrics, including a new notion of semantic similarity, and evaluate their effectiveness in confidence calibration on various data benchmarks and architectures.

2 Related Work

Since the pioneering work [7], confidence calibration has raised a great interest in the machine learning community resulting in a great deal of recent work trying to address this issue. Existing calibration techniques can be broadly categorized based on whether or not they are post-hoc methods.

Post-hoc calibration methods use parametric or non-parametric models to transform the network's predictions based on a held-out validation set to improve calibration. Traditional techniques include Platt scaling [22], Isotonic Regression [30], Bayesian binning [19,30], Histogram binning [30], matrix and vector scaling [7], Beta calibration [11], and temperature scaling [7]. Among these methods, temperature scaling consistently outperforms the other methods [7]. More recent advances include Dirichlet calibration [10], ensemble temperature scaling [31], mutual information based binning [21], and spline recalibration [8]. Non-post-hoc methods are mostly based on adapting the training procedure, including modifying the training loss [17,27], label smoothing [18,24], and data augmentation [25,29].

Another line of related work is Bayesian Neural Networks [5,14,23]. Bayesian methods provide a natural probabilistic representation of uncertainty in deep learning and are well-suited for providing calibrated uncertainty estimation. However, these methods are resource-demanding and hard to scale to modern datasets and architectures [14].

3 Confidence Calibration

In this section, we formally introduce the definition of confidence calibration. We denote the input as $X \in \mathcal{X}$ and label as $Y \in \mathcal{Y} = \{1, 2, ..., K\}$. Let h be a neural network and $h(k|x)$ is the confidence estimate of the sample x belonging to class k. The prediction is the winning class $\hat{Y} = \arg\max h(Y|X)$ and its associated confidence is the maximum $\hat{P} = \max h(Y|X)$. The number of samples is n.

3.1 Prediction and Output Calibration

In prediction calibration, only the winning class and its associated confidence are considered. With perfect prediction calibration, the confidence estimate $\hat{P}$ represents a true probability that indicates the likelihood of correctness

$$\mathbb{P}(Y = \hat{Y} \mid \hat{P} = p) = p, \ \forall p \in [0, 1] \tag{1}$$

The output of a neural network $h(Y|X)$ is the confidence estimate for all classes. For a calibrated model, we would like not only the maximum but all confidences to be calibrated, which means that $h(k|X)$ represents the actual likelihood of $Y = k$ for all classes k. Perfect output calibration is defined as

$$\mathbb{P}\left(Y = k \mid h(k|X) = p\right) = p, \ \forall p \in [0, 1] \text{ and } \forall k \in \{1, 2, ..., K\} \tag{2}$$

Note that output calibration infers prediction calibration but not vice versa.

3.2 Histogram-Based ECE

Since the probabilities in (1) and (2) cannot be computed using finitely many samples, empirical approximations are developed. The most widely adopted estimator is histogram-based expected calibration error (ECE) [7,19].

The model's output probabilities $p_i^k = h(k|x_i)$ are grouped into M interval bins, where p_i^k is the model's output confidence for sample i belonging to class k. Let B_m be the set of indices of which the confidence falls into bin m, i.e. $p_i^k \in (\frac{m-1}{M}, \frac{m}{M}]$. The likelihood and confidence of B_m are defined as

$$\text{lik}(B_m) = \frac{1}{|B_m|} \sum_{(i,k) \in B_m} \mathbb{1}(y_i = k) \quad \text{and} \quad \text{conf}(B_m) = \frac{1}{|B_m|} \sum_{(i,k) \in B_m} p_i^k \tag{3}$$

where y_i is true class label for sample i. The histogram-based ECE is defined as

$$\text{Histogram ECE} = \sum_{m=1}^{M} \frac{|B_m|}{nK} |\text{lik}(B_m) - \text{conf}(B_m)| \tag{4}$$

3.3 KDE-Based ECE

While a histogram-based estimator is easy to implement, it inevitably inherits drawbacks from histograms, for example being sensitive to the binning schemes and data-inefficient [12]. KDE-based estimator is proposed in [31] by replacing histograms with density estimation using a continuous kernel.

Let $\phi : \mathbb{R} \to \mathbb{R}_{\geq 0}$ denote a kernel function and h denote the bandwidth. The density function and canonical calibration function are given by

$$f(p) = \frac{h^{-K}}{n} \sum_{i=1}^{n} \prod_{k=1}^{K} \phi\left(\frac{p - p_i^k}{h}\right) \quad \text{and} \quad c(p) = \frac{\sum_{i=1}^{n} y_i \prod_{k=1}^{K} \phi\left(\frac{p - p_i^k}{h}\right)}{\sum_{i=1}^{n} \prod_{k=1}^{K} \phi\left(\frac{p - p_i^k}{h}\right)} \tag{5}$$

and the KDE-based ECE is computed as

$$\text{KDE ECE} = \int \|p - c(p)\| f(p) dp \tag{6}$$

While KDE alleviates the dependence on histogram binning, it heavily depends on the kernel choice and may induce error from the integral approximation procedure. Therefore, we use both ECE metrics in our evaluation.

4 Learning with Different Labels

In this section, we discuss the learning objective with respect to different labels and present the intuition behind our method. The output of a neural network is a probability distribution over all classes $h(k|x) = \exp(z_k)/\sum_{i=1}^{K} \exp(z_i)$, where z_k is the activation in the last layer. Let $\pi(k|x)$ be the label corresponding to input x. The model is trained by minimizing the cross-entropy loss

$$l(x) = -\sum_{i=1}^{K} \pi(k|x) \log(h(k|x)) \tag{7}$$

With one-hot label, the cross entropy loss can be simplified to

$$l(x) = -\log(h(y|x)) \tag{8}$$

Under this loss, the model is not only trained to make a correct prediction but also with the highest confidence z_y possible to reduce the loss, which causes the model to become overconfident. Uniform smooth labels are defined by

$$\pi(k|x) = (1 - \alpha)e_y + \alpha u(k)/K \tag{9}$$

where e_y is the coordinate vector and u is a uniform distribution. The cross-entropy loss with uniform smooth label can be written as

$$l(x) = -(1 - \alpha)\log(h(y|x)) + \alpha H(u, h) \tag{10}$$

The second part of this loss encourages the model to match its output with a uniform distribution, which implies that the example is regarded to be equally probable in any other class. This is clearly not the case in general as some classes are inherently more similar than others. The intuition behind our method is that we assume there is an unknown optimal distribution for perfect calibration $q^*(k|x)$ that satisfies the two assumptions made in Sect. 1 and can be approximated by estimating the class similarities. Let $\hat{q} \approx q^*$ be the approximated optimal distribution, then our proposed smooth label is defined as

$$\pi(k|x) = (1 - \alpha)e_y + \alpha\hat{q}(k|x) \tag{11}$$

With this label, the cross entropy loss can be written as

$$l(x) = -(1 - \alpha)\log(h(y|x)) + \alpha H(\hat{q}, h) \tag{12}$$

and the model is trained to make a correct classification while matching it output with the approximated optimal probability distribution. Hence, *minimizing $H(\hat{q}, h)$ is a direct optimization for both prediction and output calibration.*

5 Approach

In this section, we describe our approach to capture class similarities in order to compute the approximation distribution $\hat{q}$ and generate our proposed smooth labels. Capturing semantic similarity has been a longstanding and still a wide-open problem [26,32]. Different metrics quantify the similarity from different perspectives, therefore we propose to use several distance metrics, including a novel one based on word2vec mapping of label words, and evaluate the performance under varying notions of the captured similarities.

5.1 Image Space

For directly computing the distance in the image space, we use L_p norms and choose $p = 1$ and $p = 2$. For two inputs x in class k and x' in class k', the pairwise distances are given by

L_p Distance

$$d(x, x') = \|x - x'\|_p \tag{13}$$

5.2 Representation Space

Studies have shown that features learned by neural networks are often surprisingly useful as a representational space for a much wider variety of tasks and match with human perception [4,32]. The latent representations of autoencoders have been shown to be useful for various downstream tasks [1]. Therefore, we also propose to use an autoencoder to map the data to the representation space and compute distances between their encodings.

Autoencoder Distance

$$d(x, x') = \|r(x) - r(x')\|_2 \tag{14}$$

where $r(x)$ is the autoencoder latent encoding of input x.

The inter-class distance between classes k and k' is determined by averaging the distances between all pairs of inputs that belong to them

$$d_k(k') = \frac{1}{|C(k)||C(k')|} \sum_{x \in C(k), x' \in C(k')} d(x, x') \tag{15}$$

where $C(k)$ is the set of data points in class k, and d_k is a vector that contains the distances between class k and all other classes.

5.3 Semantic Space

The previous distance metrics use either the original features of the objects or those generated by a neural network. In general, samples in the same class are expected to share a common semantic meaning, which may not be captured in either feature space. It was observed for example that image visual similarity is not necessarily the same as semantic similarity [3]. The problem of defining semantic similarity has been studied extensively in the NLP literature as well as in various disciplines for which knowledge can be captured through an ontology or a hierarchy of classes [13]. For most datasets, the words used to label each class capture significant semantics of the class [16]. We make use of the advances in NLP based on the labels to define the semantic similarity. Vector representation of words has been shown to successfully capture semantic similarities such that words with similar meaning are mapped to similar points in the vector space [15]. Therefore, we propose to use a word2vec model to map the label words into Euclidean space, and then compute the distances between the vectors.

Word Embedding Distance

$$d_k(k') = \|\mathcal{V}(w(k)) - \mathcal{V}(w(k'))\|_2 \tag{16}$$

where $\mathcal{V}$ is a word2vec model and $w(k)$ be the natural language word associated with class k. This notion can be generalized to the case in which each class is defined by a set of words or a sentence.

5.4 Class-Similarity Based Smooth Label

Class distances are converted into class similarities using the softmax function

$$s_k(k') = \frac{\exp(-\beta d_k(k'))}{\sum_{i=1}^{K} \exp(-\beta d_k(i))} \tag{17}$$

where $\beta \geq 0$ is a hyperparameter that controls how "uniform" the similarity distribution is. In order to ensure the consistency of β for different metrics, we normalize the distances d_k to zero mean and standard deviation of one before applying the softmax function. Note that this normalization is equivalent to scaling β and does not affect the relative relationship between classes.

Finally, the class-similarity based smooth label is defined as follows. Let e_k be the one-hot label vector, the smooth label for class k is

$$y_k = (1 - \alpha)e_k + \alpha s_k \tag{18}$$

where α is the label smoothing factor. Note that in practice we set $s_k(k) = 0$ and scale $\sum_{k' \neq k} s_k(k') = 1$ to make sure that α consistently represents the total mass in the label over the other (non ground-truth) classes. Otherwise the total mass will be different because of different values of $s_k(k)$.

6 Experiments

6.1 Setup

We compare the four variants of our proposed method with L_1 distance, L_2 distance, Autoencoder distance (AE) and Word Embedding distance (WE) to the vanilla training using one-hot labels, as well as various techniques that improve confidence calibration: temperature scaling (TS) [7], uniform label smoothing [18,24], mixup training [25], Dirichlet calibration with off-diagonal regularization (Dir-ODIR) [10], and ensemble temperature scaling (ETS) [31].

We perform experiments on CIFAR-100 and Tiny-ImageNet using DenseNet (DN), ResNet (RN), and WideResNet(WRN). For all experiments, the network architectures and all parameters are identical for all methods. For CIFAR-100, we use DenseNet-161, ResNet-18, and WRN with $\{16, 16, 32, 64\}$ filters respectively. For Tiny-ImageNet, we use DenseNet-161, ResNet-34, and WRN-50-2. The dimensionality of the latent space of the autoencoder is set to 256 for CIFAR-100 and 1024 for Tiny-ImageNet. We use a pretrained Wikipedia2Vec [28] as our word2vec model $\mathcal{V}$ with a vector of length 100. For histogram-based ECE, we set the number of interval bins $M = 15$ following [7,18]. For KDE-based ECE, we use the Triweight Kernel $K(u) = \frac{35}{32}(1 - u^2)^3$ and bandwidth $h = 1.06\sigma n^{-1/5}$ [31].

Table 1. Histogram and KDE-based ECE (%) results of prediction (P) and output (O) on CIFAR-100.

Model	ECE	One-hot	TS	Uniform	Mixup	DirODIR	ETS	L_1(Ours)	L_2(Ours)	AE(Ours)	WE(Ours)
DN	Hist P	16.40	2.08	2.41	4.58	2.10	2.04	2.39	2.65	1.96	**1.68**
DN	Hist O	35.52	3.55	8.11	8.81	3.54	3.48	4.15	4.74	3.32	**2.98**
DN	KDE P	15.28	1.90	2.68	4.52	1.95	1.88	2.61	2.72	2.08	**1.75**
DN	KDE O	28.65	7.01	15.08	13.40	7.09	**7.00**	12.85	12.92	12.44	11.32
RN	Hist P	22.96	1.98	2.35	2.70	1.85	**1.71**	2.84	2.76	2.02	1.74
RN	Hist O	50.07	3.13	3.80	5.03	2.98	2.90	5.06	5.10	3.34	**2.47**
RN	KDE P	21.13	2.16	2.60	2.83	1.84	**1.65**	2.91	2.76	2.19	1.76
RN	KDE O	39.23	9.49	15.17	12.03	10.42	9.14	11.89	11.15	10.13	**9.02**
WRN	Hist P	12.17	2.34	2.77	2.29	2.07	1.79	1.68	1.56	0.77	**0.72**
WRN	Hist O	25.71	5.11	5.41	5.02	4.54	3.91	2.91	2.60	1.64	**1.55**
WRN	KDE P	11.57	2.35	2.83	2.49	1.99	1.83	1.57	1.48	1.15	**1.11**
WRN	KDE O	21.13	9.08	9.27	9.47	6.87	6.92	7.59	7.01	4.53	**3.73**

Table 2. Histogram and KDE-based ECE (%) results of prediction (P) and output (O) on Tiny-ImageNet.

Model	ECE	One-hot	TS	Uniform	Mixup	DirODIR	ETS	L_1(Ours)	L_2(Ours)	AE(Ours)	WE(Ours)
DN	Hist P	13.98	3.45	3.77	3.70	3.23	2.16	2.93	3.07	2.54	**1.19**
DN	Hist O	29.76	11.64	13.27	12.13	10.57	8.80	9.94	10.40	7.74	**3.00**
DN	KDE P	13.38	3.46	3.72	3.76	3.21	2.21	2.95	3.13	2.60	**1.23**
DN	KDE O	27.64	18.36	21.01	19.06	17.87	17.48	17.51	18.18	17.56	**15.67**
RN	Hist P	24.95	4.83	5.24	5.87	5.15	3.12	2.95	2.86	2.49	**1.23**
RN	Hist O	58.01	9.94	10.92	11.76	10.07	6.52	5.78	5.59	5.05	**2.12**
RN	KDE P	23.55	4.93	5.21	5.80	5.17	3.01	3.02	2.82	2.57	**1.26**
RN	KDE O	46.51	22.33	27.57	24.99	23.14	13.15	27.21	28.60	29.97	**11.84**
WRN	Hist P	22.39	10.15	12.92	8.73	9.79	6.71	8.55	8.03	7.41	**4.21**
WRN	Hist O	52.14	22.19	25.10	17.00	19.17	14.36	16.87	16.59	13.82	**7.93**
WRN	KDE P	21.37	10.75	12.90	8.74	9.78	6.55	8.50	7.97	7.45	**4.13**
WRN	KDE O	43.78	28.14	37.64	26.76	27.34	19.44	25.81	24.80	24.33	**11.30**

6.2 Confidence Calibration Results

We show confidence calibration results on CIFAR-100 in Table 1 and Tiny-ImageNet in Table 2. We set $\alpha = 0.1$ and $\beta \in [0.5, 6]$. Parameter effects are discussed in detail in Sect. 6.3.

The models trained with our proposed method generally outperforms other methods. Among the four distance measures, WE performs the best in all scenarios which is expected considering that the distance in the vector space more faithfully reflects class semantic relationships than pixel-wise distances and the latent encoding distance. WE delivers better confidence calibration than all comparison methods in most cases. By comparing AE with WE, we can see the performance gap is more significant on Tiny-ImageNet than on CIFAR-100. As the complexity of a dataset and the number of classes increase, it becomes more difficult for an autoencoder to learn good representations, which leads to the performance difference. The large output ECE difference between WE and Uniform shows that the uniform distribution is not an optimal objective. We note that

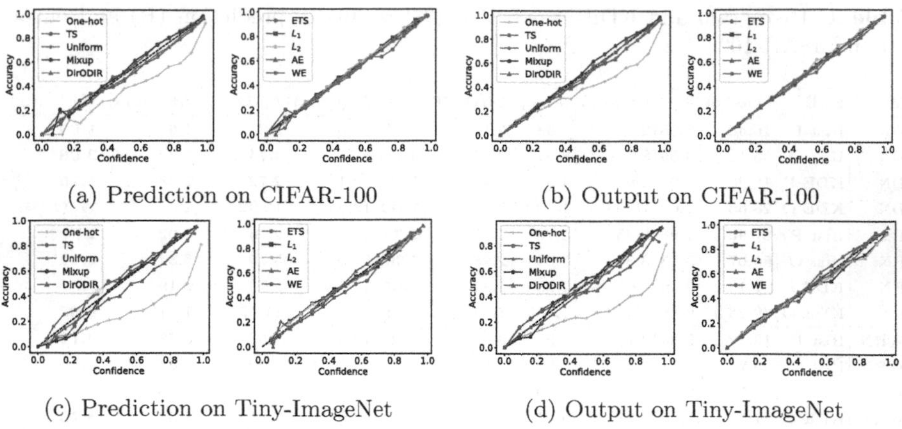

(a) Prediction on CIFAR-100 (b) Output on CIFAR-100

(c) Prediction on Tiny-ImageNet (d) Output on Tiny-ImageNet

Fig. 1. Reliability diagrams on CIFAR-100 and Tiny-ImageNet dataset.

for output ECE, the KDE estimate is significantly distinct from the histogram estimate. The output probabilities of a model contain a majority of near-zero values, thus in this case the density estimation is not very accurate.

In Fig. 1 we show the reliability diagrams for WRN on CIFAR-100 and ResNet-34 on Tiny-ImageNet. The plots confirm our findings of the ECE results. For better readability, we divide the diagrams of the ten techniques into two figures. In all the plots, the dashed black diagonal line represents perfect calibration for which the confidence matches the accuracy. The model trained using one-hot labels is clearly overconfident since the accuracy is always below the confidence. While all other methods have a better performance, diagrams from our proposed smooth labels almost identically match the diagonal line.

6.3 Effects of Parameters

In this section, we perform a series of experiments on Tiny-ImageNet to explore the effects of two important hyper-parameters α and β.

First, we test different α values that determine the strength of label smoothing. We compare WE to uniform LS and set $\beta = 2$. The results are presented in Fig. 2a and 2b. We observe that our proposed smooth label generally outperforms uniform smooth label for all α values, and the best results for both methods are achieved at $\alpha = 0.1$ which is the commonly value used in practice. When α is very small, the labels are only weakly smoothed and the model is still over-confident. When α becomes large, the labels are too noisy and the model is not well-calibrated because of the excessive smoothing.

Next, we perform experiments on different β which determines how uniform the similarity distribution is. We choose the WE model and set $\alpha = 0.1$. The results are shown in Fig. 2c. When β is too small, the similarity distribution is close to uniform and the class relation is not well represented, therefore the model is not well calibrated. As β keeps increasing when it becomes too large, the

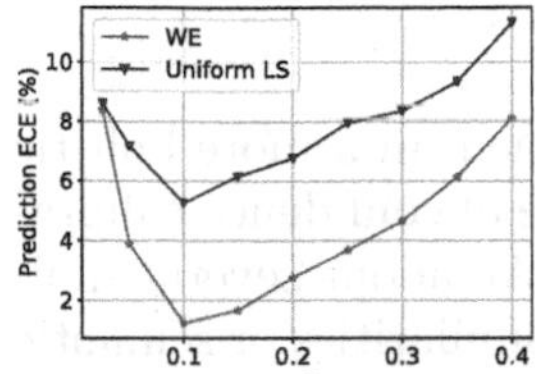

(a) Prediction ECE relative to α.

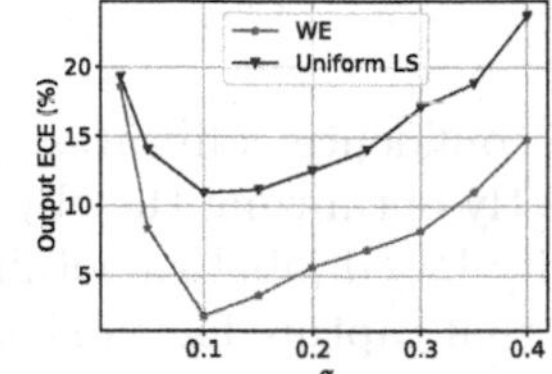

(b) Output ECE relative to α.

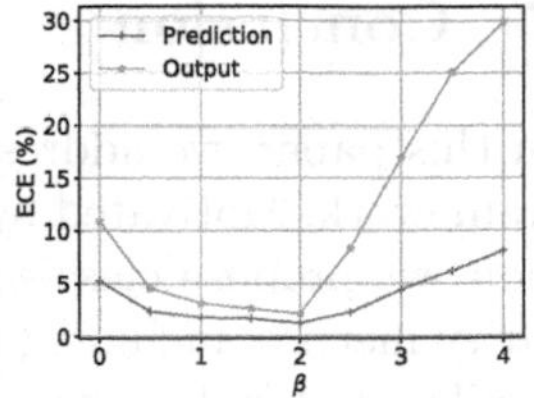

(c) Prediction and output ECE relative to β.

Fig. 2. Effects of parameters.

softmax function will produce extreme similarity values that are concentrated in only a few classes that do not represent the optimal distribution either.

6.4 Evaluation on Out-of-Distribution Data

DNNs are not only overconfident on the data they are trained on but also on unseen out-of-distribution data [9,25]. In this section, we evaluate the methods on two types of out-of-distribution data: another unseen dataset and random noise. We test the WRN models trained on CIFAR-100 in Sect. 6.2. We use the validation set of Tiny-ImageNet as the unseen dataset and generate uniformly distributed random samples as the second type of out-of-distribution data. We show the distributions of the prediction confidence values in Fig. 3.

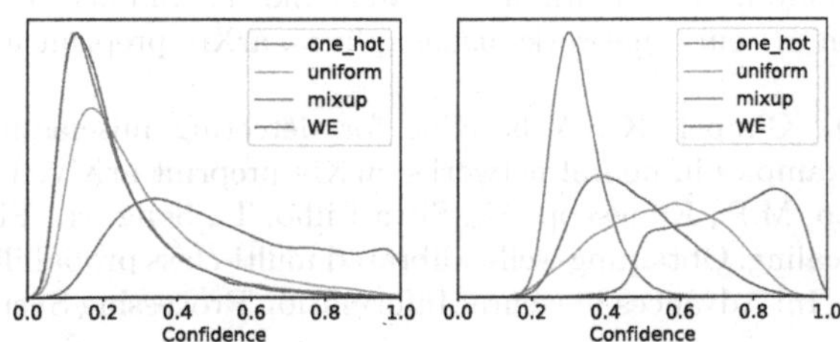

Fig. 3. Distribution of the prediction confidences on the validation set of Tiny-ImageNet (left) and uniform random noise (right).

From the left plot, we can see that our method and mixup perform the best at refraining to produce high confidence on unseen out-of-distribution data. On the random noise samples, all three methods significantly outperform the one-hot training. Note that our method is based on class similarities which is not well-suited for random noise samples where the notion of similarity does not exist. Although this application is not the main focus of our method, we note that it still significantly outperforms the uniform label smoothing in both scenarios.

7 Conclusion

In this paper, we address the confidence calibration problem in a more holistic framework. Motivated by directly optimizing the objective of confidence calibration, we propose class-similarity based label smoothing. We adopt several similarity metrics, including those that capture feature based similarities or semantic similarity. We demonstrate through extensive experiments that our method significantly outperforms state-of-the-art techniques.

References

1. Bengio, Y., Courville, A., Vincent, P.: Representation learning: a review and new perspectives. IEEE Trans. Pattern Anal. Mach. Intell. **35**(8), 1798–1828 (2013)
2. Brundage, M., et al.: The malicious use of artificial intelligence: Forecasting, prevention, and mitigation. arXiv preprint arXiv:1802.07228 (2018)
3. Deselaers, T., Ferrari, V.: Visual and semantic similarity in imagenet. In: CVPR 2011, pp. 1777–1784. IEEE (2011)
4. Dosovitskiy, A., Brox, T.: Generating images with perceptual similarity metrics based on deep networks. In: Advances in Neural Information Processing Systems, pp. 658–666 (2016)
5. Gal, Y., Ghahramani, Z.: Dropout as a bayesian approximation: representing model uncertainty in deep learning. In: International Conference on Machine Learning, pp. 1050–1059 (2016)
6. Goodfellow, I., Bengio, Y., Courville, A.: Deep learning (2016)
7. Guo, C., Pleiss, G., Sun, Y., Weinberger, K.Q.: On calibration of modern neural networks. In: Proceedings of the 34th International Conference on Machine Learning, vol. 70, pp. 1321–1330. JMLR. org (2017)
8. Gupta, K., Rahimi, A., Ajanthan, T., Mensink, T., Sminchisescu, C., Hartley, R.: Calibration of neural networks using splines. arXiv preprint arXiv:2006.12800 (2020)
9. Hendrycks, D., Gimpel, K.: A baseline for detecting misclassified and out-of-distribution examples in neural networks. arXiv preprint arXiv:1610.02136 (2016)
10. Kull, M., Nieto, M.P., Kängsepp, M., Silva Filho, T., Song, H., Flach, P.: Beyond temperature scaling: Obtaining well-calibrated multi-class probabilities with dirichlet calibration. In: Advances in Neural Information Processing Systems, pp. 12316–12326 (2019)
11. Kull, M., Silva Filho, T., Flach, P.: Beta calibration: a well-founded and easily implemented improvement on logistic calibration for binary classifiers. In: Artificial Intelligence and Statistics, pp. 623–631. PMLR (2017)
12. Kumar, A., Liang, P.S., Ma, T.: Verified uncertainty calibration. In: Advances in Neural Information Processing Systems, pp. 3792–3803 (2019)
13. Lee, W.N., Shah, N., Sundlass, K., Musen, M.: Comparison of ontology-based semantic-similarity measures. In: AMIA Annual Symposium Proceedings, vol. 2008, p. 384. American Medical Informatics Association (2008)
14. Maddox, W.J., Izmailov, P., Garipov, T., Vetrov, D.P., Wilson, A.G.: A simple baseline for bayesian uncertainty in deep learning. In: Advances in Neural Information Processing Systems, pp. 13153–13164 (2019)
15. Mikolov, T., Chen, K., Corrado, G., Dean, J.: Efficient estimation of word representations in vector space. arXiv preprint arXiv:1301.3781 (2013)

16. Miller, G.A.: Wordnet: a lexical database for English. Commun. ACM **38**(11), 39–41 (1995)
17. Mukhoti, J., Kulharia, V., Sanyal, A., Golodetz, S., Torr, P.H., Dokania, P.K.: Calibrating deep neural networks using focal loss. arXiv preprint arXiv:2002.09437 (2020)
18. Müller, R., Kornblith, S., Hinton, G.: When does label smoothing help? arXiv preprint arXiv:1906.02629 (2019)
19. Naeini, M.P., Cooper, G., Hauskrecht, M.: Obtaining well calibrated probabilities using bayesian binning. In: Proceedings of the AAAI Conference on Artificial Intelligence, vol. 29 (2015)
20. Park, W., Kim, D., Lu, Y., Cho, M.: Relational knowledge distillation. In: Proceedings of the IEEE Conference on Computer Vision and Pattern Recognition, pp. 3967–3976 (2019)
21. Patel, K., Beluch, W., Yang, B., Pfeiffer, M., Zhang, D.: Multi-class uncertainty calibration via mutual information maximization-based binning. arXiv preprint arXiv:2006.13092 (2020)
22. Platt, J., et al.: Probabilistic outputs for support vector machines and comparisons to regularized likelihood methods. Adv. Large Margin Classifiers **10**(3), 61–74 (1999)
23. Ritter, H., Botev, A., Barber, D.: A scalable laplace approximation for neural networks. In: 6th International Conference on Learning Representations, ICLR 2018-Conference Track Proceedings, vol. 6. International Conference on Representation Learning (2018)
24. Szegedy, C., Vanhoucke, V., Ioffe, S., Shlens, J., Wojna, Z.: Rethinking the inception architecture for computer vision. In: Proceedings of the IEEE Conference on Computer Vision and Pattern Recognition, pp. 2818–2826 (2016)
25. Thulasidasan, S., Chennupati, G., Bilmes, J.A., Bhattacharya, T., Michalak, S.: On mixup training: improved calibration and predictive uncertainty for deep neural networks. In: Advances in Neural Information Processing Systems, pp. 13888–13899 (2019)
26. Wang, Z., Bovik, A.C., Sheikh, H.R., Simoncelli, E.P.: Image quality assessment: from error visibility to structural similarity. IEEE Trans. Image Process. **13**(4), 600–612 (2004)
27. Xing, C., Arik, S., Zhang, Z., Pfister, T.: Distance-based learning from errors for confidence calibration. arXiv preprint arXiv:1912.01730 (2019)
28. Yamada, I., Asai, A., Shindo, H., Takeda, H., Takefuji, Y.: Wikipedia2vec: an optimized tool for learning embeddings of words and entities from wikipedia. arXiv preprint arXiv:1812.06280 (2018)
29. Yun, S., Han, D., Oh, S.J., Chun, S., Choe, J., Yoo, Y.: Cutmix: regularization strategy to train strong classifiers with localizable features. In: Proceedings of the IEEE/CVF International Conference on Computer Vision, pp. 6023–6032 (2019)
30. Zadrozny, B., Elkan, C.: Obtaining calibrated probability estimates from decision trees and naive bayesian classifiers. In: Icml, vol. 1, pp. 609–616. Citeseer (2001)
31. Zhang, J., Kailkhura, B., Han, T.: Mix-n-match: ensemble and compositional methods for uncertainty calibration in deep learning. arXiv preprint arXiv:2003.07329 (2020)
32. Zhang, R., Isola, P., Efros, A.A., Shechtman, E., Wang, O.: The unreasonable effectiveness of deep features as a perceptual metric. In: Proceedings of the IEEE Conference on Computer Vision and Pattern Recognition, pp. 586–595 (2018)

Jacobian Regularization for Mitigating Universal Adversarial Perturbations

Kenneth T. Co[1,2(✉)], David Martinez Rego[2], and Emil C. Lupu[1]

[1] Imperial College London, London SW7 2AZ, UK
{k.co,e.c.lupu}@imperial.ac.uk
[2] DataSpartan, London EC2Y 9ST, UK
david@dataspartan.com

Abstract. Universal Adversarial Perturbations (UAPs) are input perturbations that can fool a neural network on large sets of data. They are a class of attacks that represents a significant threat as they facilitate realistic, practical, and low-cost attacks on neural networks. In this work, we derive upper bounds for the effectiveness of UAPs based on norms of data-dependent Jacobians. We empirically verify that Jacobian regularization greatly increases model robustness to UAPs by up to four times whilst maintaining clean performance. Our theoretical analysis also allows us to formulate a metric for the strength of shared adversarial perturbations between pairs of inputs. We apply this metric to benchmark datasets and show that it is highly correlated with the actual observed robustness. This suggests that realistic and practical universal attacks can be reliably mitigated without sacrificing clean accuracy, which shows promise for the robustness of machine learning systems.

Keywords: Adversarial machine learning · Universal adversarial perturbations · Computer vision · Jacobian regularization

1 Introduction

Neural networks have been the algorithm of choice for many applications such as image classification [15], real-time object detection [21], and speech recognition [11]. Although they appear to be robust to noise, their accuracy can rapidly deteriorate in the face of adversarial examples – inputs that appear similar to genuine data, but have been maliciously designed to fool the model [1,25]. Thus, it is important to ensure that neural networks are robust to such attacks, especially in safety-critical applications, as this can greatly undermine the performance and trust in these models.

A concerning subset of attacks on neural networks come in the form of Universal Adversarial Perturbations (UAPs), where a single adversarial perturbation can cause a model to misclassify a large set of inputs [18]. These present a systemic risk, as many practical and physically realizable adversarial attacks are

Kenneth T. Co is supported in part by the DataSpartan research grant DSRD201801.

I. Farkaš et al. (Eds.): ICANN 2021, LNCS 12894, pp. 202–213, 2021.
https://doi.org/10.1007/978-3-030-86380-7_17

based on UAPs. These attacks can take the form of adversarial patches for image classification [2], person recognition [26], camera-based [7,8] and LiDAR-based object detection [3,9,10,28]. In the digital domain, UAPs have been shown to facilitate realistic attacks on perceptual ad-blockers for web pages [27] and machine learning-based malware detectors [16]. Furthermore, an attacker can utilize UAPs to perform query-efficient black-box attacks on neural networks [4,6].

In the literature, existing defenses to adversarial attacks focus primarily on input-specific ("per-input") attacks–where adversarial perturbations need to be crafted *for each single input*. In contrast to universal attacks, input-specific attacks fool the model on only *one input*. However, the practicality of input-specific attacks suffers in realistic settings, as the perturbations need to be constantly modified to match the current input. In contrast, defences against UAPs have not been thoroughly investigated, even if they are potentially more dangerous and should intuitively be easier to defend against because the same perturbation needs to be shared across many inputs. These are the main focus of this paper.

A number of studies have investigated the use of Jacobian regularization to improve the stability of model predictions to small changes to the input, but up to this point, studies have only considered input-specific perturbations [12, 13,20,22,24,29]. In this work, we expand the theoretical formulation of Jacobian regularization to UAPs and derive upper bounds on the effectiveness of UAPs based on the properties of Jacobian matrices for individual inputs. Our work shows that for inputs to strongly share adversarial perturbations, their Jacobians need to share singular vectors.

We empirically verify our theoretical findings by applying Jacobian regularization to neural networks trained on popular benchmark datasets: MNIST [17], Fashion-MNIST [30] and then evaluating their robustness to various UAPs. Our results show that even a small amount of Jacobian regularization drastically improves model robustness against many universal attacks with negligible downsides to clean performance. To summarize, we make the following contributions:

- We extend theoretical formulations for universal adversarial perturbations and are the first to show that the effectiveness of UAPs is bounded above by the norms of data-dependent Jacobians.
- We empirically verify our theoretical results and show that even a minimal amount of Jacobian regularization reduces effectiveness of UAPs by up to 4-times, whilst leaving clean accuracy relatively unaffected.
- We propose the use of cosine similarity for Jacobians of inputs to measure the strength of shared adversarial perturbations between distinct inputs. Our empirical evaluations on benchmark datasets demonstrate that this similarity measure is an effective proxy for measuring robustness to UAPs.

The rest of this paper is organized as follows. Section 2 introduces adversarial examples, universal adversarial perturbations, and Jacobian regularization. Section 3 formulates Jacobian regularization for UAPs and derives our key propositions. Section 4 evaluates the robustness of models trained with Jacobian regularization to various UAP attack. Finally, Sect. 5 discusses implications of our results and summarizes our findings.

2 Background

2.1 Universal Adversarial Perturbations

Let $f : \mathcal{X} \subset \mathbb{R}^n \rightarrow \mathbb{R}^d$ denote the logits of a piece-wise linear classifier which takes as input $\mathbf{x} \in \mathcal{X}$. The output label assigned by this classifier is defined by $F(\mathbf{x}) = \arg\max(f(\mathbf{x}))$. Let $\tau(\mathbf{x})$ denote the true class label of an input $\mathbf{x}$).

An *adversarial example* $\mathbf{x}'$ is an input that satisfies $F(\mathbf{x}') \neq \tau(\mathbf{x})$, despite $\mathbf{x}'$ being close to $\mathbf{x}$ according to some distance metric (implicitly, $\tau(\mathbf{x}) = \tau(\mathbf{x}')$). The difference $\delta = \mathbf{x}' - \mathbf{x}$ is referred to as an adversarial perturbation and its norm is often constrained to $\|\delta\|_p < \varepsilon$, for some ℓ_p-norm and small $\varepsilon > 0$ [25].

Universal Adversarial Perturbations (UAP) can come in targeted or untargeted forms depending on the attacker's objective. An untargeted UAP is an adversarial perturbation $\delta \in \mathbb{R}^n$ that satisfies $F(\mathbf{x} + \delta) \neq \tau(\mathbf{x})$ for sufficiently many $\mathbf{x} \in \mathcal{X}$ and with $\|\delta\|_p < \varepsilon$ [18]. Untargeted UAPs are generated by maximizing the loss $\sum_i \mathcal{L}(\mathbf{x}_i + \delta)$ with an iterative stochastic gradient descent algorithm [5,19,23,27]. Here, $\mathcal{L}$ is the model's training loss, $\{\mathbf{x}_i\}$ are batches of inputs, and δ are small perturbations that satisfy $\|\delta\|_p < \varepsilon$. Updates to δ are done in mini-batches in the direction of $-\sum_i \nabla\mathcal{L}(\mathbf{x}_i + \delta)$. Targeted UAPs for a class c are adversarial perturbations δ that satisfy $F(\mathbf{x} + \delta) = c$ for sufficiently many $\mathbf{x} \in \mathcal{X}$ and with $\|\delta\|_p < \varepsilon$. To generate this type of attack, we use the same stochastic gradient descent as in the untargeted case, but modify the loss to be minimized when all resulting inputs $\mathbf{x}_i + \delta$ are classified as c.

2.2 Jacobian Regularization

Given that $f(\mathbf{x})$ is the logit output of the classifier for input $\mathbf{x}$, we write $\mathbf{J}_f(\mathbf{x})$ to denote the input-output Jacobian of f at $\mathbf{x}$. We can linearise f within a neighbourhood around $\mathbf{x}$ as follows using the Taylor series expansion:

$$f(\mathbf{x} + \delta) = f(\mathbf{x}) + \mathbf{J}_f(\mathbf{x})\delta + O(\delta^2) \tag{1}$$

For a sufficiently small neighbourhood $\|\delta\|_p \leq \varepsilon$ with $\varepsilon > 0$, the higher order terms of δ can be neglected and the stability of the prediction is determined by the Jacobian.

$$f(\mathbf{x} + \delta) \simeq f(\mathbf{x}) + \mathbf{J}_f(\mathbf{x})\delta \tag{2}$$

and equivalently, for any q-norm, we have:

$$\|f(\mathbf{x} + \delta) - f(\mathbf{x})\|_q \approx \|\mathbf{J}_f(\mathbf{x})\delta\|_q \tag{3}$$

For a small ε, we want the δ that maximizes the right hand side of Eq. 3 in order to sufficiently change the original output and fool the model. With constraint $\|\delta\|_p \leq \varepsilon$, this is equivalent to finding the (p, q) singular vector for $\mathbf{J}_f(\mathbf{x})$ [14].

To improve the stability of model outputs to small perturbations δ, existing works have proposed regularizing the Frobenius norm [12,13,20] or the Spectral norm [22,24,29] of this data-dependent Jacobian $\mathbf{J}_f(\mathbf{x})$ for each input. Additionally, [22] show that the input-specific adversarial perturbations align with the dominant singular vectors of these Jacobian matrices.

Although [14] considered Jacobians in the context of UAPs, they only focused on the computation of δ as an attack and did not perform any theoretical or empirical analysis for mitigating the effects of UAPs. Prior studies that explore Jacobian regularization focused solely on improving robustness to single-input perturbations and did not explain nor consider the effectiveness of Jacobian regularization for UAPs. Thus, we extend these formulations [14,22] to have a more concrete theoretical understanding for how Jacobian regularization mitigates UAPs.

3 Jacobians for Universal Adversarial Perturbations

When computing a universal adversarial perturbation δ that uniformly generalizes across multiple inputs $\{\mathbf{x}_i\}_{i=1}^{N}$, one would optimize:

$$\max_{\delta:\|\delta\|_p=1} \sum_{i=1}^{N} \|\mathbf{J}_f(\mathbf{x}_i)\delta\|_q \tag{4}$$

This extends the intuition from Eq. 3 to many inputs, and due to the homogeneity of the norm, it is sufficient to solve this for $\|\delta\|_p = 1$ [14]. The solution to δ for Eq. 4 is equivalent to finding the (p, q) singular vector for the **stacked Jacobian** matrix $\overline{\mathbf{J}}_N$, the matrix formed by vertically stacking the Jacobians of the first N inputs.

$$\max_{\delta:\|\delta\|_p=1} \|\overline{\mathbf{J}}_N\delta\|_q \quad \text{where} \quad \overline{\mathbf{J}}_N = \begin{bmatrix} \mathbf{J}_f(\mathbf{x}_1) \\ \mathbf{J}_f(\mathbf{x}_2) \\ \vdots \\ \mathbf{J}_f(\mathbf{x}_N) \end{bmatrix} \tag{5}$$

3.1 Upper Bounds for the Stacked Jacobian

To obtain an upper bound for the (p, q)-operator norm shown in Eq. 5, note that it is bounded above by its Frobenius norm denoted by $\|\overline{\mathbf{J}}_N\|_F$:

$$\|\overline{\mathbf{J}}_N\delta\|_q \leq \|\overline{\mathbf{J}}_N\|_F\|\delta\| \tag{6}$$

Thus, mitigating the effectiveness of a UAP across multiple inputs can be achieved by limiting the Frobenius norm of the stacked Jacobian $\|\overline{\mathbf{J}}_N\|_F$.

Before proceeding, let us define the inner product induced by the Frobenius norm for two real matrices. Given $\mathbf{A}, \mathbf{B} \in \mathbb{R}^{m\times n}$, let the inner product in $\mathbb{R}^{m\times n}$ be defined as:

$$\langle \mathbf{A}, \mathbf{B}\rangle = \operatorname{Tr}(\mathbf{A}'\mathbf{B}) = \sum_{i=1}^{m}\sum_{j=1}^{n} a_{ij}b_{ij} \tag{7}$$

where $\mathbf{A}'$ denotes the transpose of $\mathbf{A}$, the lowercase letters a_{ij} are the entries of the matrix $\mathbf{A}$, and $\text{Tr}(\cdot)$ is the trace. This inner product is associated with the Frobenius norm $\|\cdot\|_F$. Now we introduce the following proposition.

Proposition 1. *For matrices* $\mathbf{A}, \mathbf{B} \in \mathbb{R}^{m\times n}$, *we have:*

$$\langle \mathbf{A}, \mathbf{B} \rangle \leq \|\mathbf{A}\|_F \|\mathbf{B}\|_F \tag{8}$$

with equality if and only if $\mathbf{A}$ *and* $\mathbf{B}$ *share singular directions and their singular values satisfy* $\sigma_i(\mathbf{A}) = s \cdot \sigma_i(\mathbf{B})$ *for all* i *for a constant scalar* $s > 0$, *where* $\sigma_i(\cdot)$ *is the singular value that corresponds to the i-th largest singular value.*

Proof. Consider the singular value decomposition of $\mathbf{A} = \mathbf{U}_A \mathbf{\Sigma}_A \mathbf{V}'_A$ and $\mathbf{B} = \mathbf{U}_B \mathbf{\Sigma}_B \mathbf{V}'_B$, where $\mathbf{U}_A, \mathbf{U}_B, \mathbf{V}_A, \mathbf{V}_B$ are orthogonal matrices and $\mathbf{\Sigma}_A, \mathbf{\Sigma}_B$ are diagonal matrices whose diagonal entries $\sigma_i(\mathbf{A})$ and $\sigma_i(\mathbf{B})$ are non-negative and in descending order. Let $r = \max(\text{rank}(\mathbf{A}), \text{rank}(\mathbf{B}))$.

$$\begin{aligned}
\langle \mathbf{A}, \mathbf{B} \rangle &= \text{Tr}(\mathbf{A}'\mathbf{B}) \\
&= \text{Tr}(\mathbf{V}_A \mathbf{\Sigma}'_A \mathbf{U}'_A \mathbf{U}_B \mathbf{\Sigma}_B \mathbf{V}'_B) \\
&= \text{Tr}(\mathbf{V}'_B \mathbf{V}_A \mathbf{\Sigma}'_A \mathbf{U}'_A \mathbf{U}_B \mathbf{\Sigma}_B) \qquad \text{cyclic property of trace}
\end{aligned}$$

Note that since $\mathbf{U}_A, \mathbf{U}_B, \mathbf{V}_A, \mathbf{V}_B$ are all orthogonal matrices, $\|\mathbf{U}'_A \mathbf{U}_B\|_2 \leq \|\mathbf{U}'_A\|_2 \|\mathbf{U}_B\|_2 = 1$, and in a similar way, $\|\mathbf{V}'_B \mathbf{V}_A\|_2 \leq 1$.

$$\begin{aligned}
\langle \mathbf{A}, \mathbf{B} \rangle &= \text{Tr}(\mathbf{V}'_B \mathbf{V}_A \mathbf{\Sigma}'_A \mathbf{U}'_A \mathbf{U}_B \mathbf{\Sigma}_B) \\
&= \sum_{i=1}^{r} \sum_{j=1}^{r} z_{ij} \cdot \sigma_i(\mathbf{A}) \sigma_j(\mathbf{B}) \qquad \text{where } \sum_{i=1}^{r} |z_{ij}| \leq 1, \sum_{j=1}^{r} |z_{ij}| \leq 1 \\
&\leq \sum_{i=1}^{r} \sigma_i(\mathbf{A})\, \sigma_i(\mathbf{B}) \qquad \text{equality} \iff z_{ij} \begin{cases} 1, & \text{if } i = j, \\ 0, & \text{if } i \neq j. \end{cases} \\
&\leq \left(\sum_{i=1}^{r} \sigma_i^2(\mathbf{A}) \right)^{\frac{1}{2}} \left(\sum_{i=1}^{r} \sigma_i^2(\mathbf{B}) \right)^{\frac{1}{2}} \qquad \text{Cauchy-Schwarz Inequality} \\
&= \|\mathbf{A}\|_F \|\mathbf{B}\|_F \qquad \square
\end{aligned}$$

The equality conditions for the above requires $z_{ii} = 1, \forall i$ as the σ_i are in descending order. This implies that $\mathbf{U}'_A \mathbf{U}_B$ and $\mathbf{V}'_B \mathbf{V}_A$ are identity matrices, which requires $\mathbf{U}_A = \mathbf{U}_B$ and $\mathbf{V}_A = \mathbf{V}_B$, i.e. $\mathbf{A}$ and $\mathbf{B}$ share the same singular vectors. Equality under Cauchy-Schwarz requires the singular values to be scalars of one another: $\sigma_i(\mathbf{A}) = s \cdot \sigma_i(\mathbf{B})$ for the same scalar $s > 0, \forall i$.

This proposition is significant as it gives us upper bounds for the inner product and equality conditions to achieve this upper bound. Applying this result to the stacked Jacobian matrix $\overline{\mathbf{J}}_N$ gives us the following:

$$\begin{aligned}
\|\overline{\mathbf{J}}_N\|_F^2 &= \mathrm{Tr}(\overline{\mathbf{J}}_N'\overline{\mathbf{J}}_N) \\
&= \mathrm{Tr}\left(\sum_{i=1}^{N}\sum_{j=1}^{N}\mathbf{J}_f(\mathbf{x}_i)'\mathbf{J}_f(\mathbf{x}_j)\right) \\
&= \sum_{i,j}\mathrm{Tr}(\mathbf{J}_f(\mathbf{x}_i)',\mathbf{J}_f(\mathbf{x}_j)) \\
&= \sum_{i,j}\langle\mathbf{J}_f(\mathbf{x}_i),\mathbf{J}_f(\mathbf{x}_j)\rangle && \text{Frobenius inner product} \\
&\leq \sum_{i,j}\|\mathbf{J}_f(\mathbf{x}_i)\|_F\|\mathbf{J}_f(\mathbf{x}_j)\|_F && \text{Proposition 1}
\end{aligned}$$

With equality if and only if, for all pairs of inputs $(\mathbf{x}_i, \mathbf{x}_j)$, we have $\mathbf{J}_f(\mathbf{x}_i)$ and $\mathbf{J}_f(\mathbf{x}_j)$ sharing singular vectors and their corresponding singular values are constant up to a fixed scalar $s > 0$.

Our result can be summarized with the following equation:

$$\|\overline{\mathbf{J}}_N\|_F \leq \left(\sum_{i,j}\|\mathbf{J}_f(\mathbf{x}_i)\|_F\|\mathbf{J}_f(\mathbf{x}_j)\|_F\right)^{\frac{1}{2}} \tag{9}$$

From a defense perspective, this shows that regularizing the Frobenius of the Jacobian for the $\mathbf{x}_i$ decreases the total Frobenius norm of the stacked Jacobian and hinders the overall effectiveness of a UAP. Thus, data-dependent Jacobian regularization across inputs should make it significantly more difficult to generate effective UAPs.

3.2 Measuring Alignment of Jacobians

To measure the alignment between Jacobians of two distinct inputs, we use the **cosine similarity** between their respective Jacobians under the inner product induced by the Frobenius norm:

$$\mathrm{sim}(\mathbf{x}_i, \mathbf{x}_j) = \frac{\langle\mathbf{J}_f(\mathbf{x}_i),\mathbf{J}_f(\mathbf{x}_j)\rangle}{\|\mathbf{J}_f(\mathbf{x}_i)\|_F\|\mathbf{J}_f(\mathbf{x}_j)\|_F} \leq 1 \tag{10}$$

This is precisely the formula given in Proposition 1, with the above ratio equal to one if and only if the singular vectors of their Jacobians are the same. This shows to us that alignment of Jacobians can be evaluated with this similarity measure. Also, combining this with our findings from Eq. 9, this ratio allows us to measure how strongly two inputs share adversarial perturbations.

Although the Jacobian is a first-order derivative, we show in later sections that our Jacobian similarity measure correlates with vulnerability to iterative UAP attacks. Thus, demonstrating that it is an effective measure to determine the "universality" of adversarial vulnerability even against iterative adversaries.

Having a similarity measure like this is beneficial as this allows us to easily determine if two inputs are likely to share adversarial perturbations. This is more advantageous than manually generating adversarial perturbations for each pair of inputs as one would have to consider many additional attack parameters when generating adversarial attacks, including the ε bounds, chosen ℓ_p-norm, step size, number of attack iterations, and so on.

4 Experiments

4.1 Experimental Setup

Models & Datasets. We consider the benchmark datasets MNIST [17] and Fashion-MNIST [30]. These are widely-used image classification datasets, each with 10 classes, whose images are 28 by 28 pixels, and their pixel values range from 0 to 1. For the neural network architecture, we use a modernized version of LeNet-5 [17] as detailed in [12] as it is a commonly used benchmark neural network. We refer to this model as LeNet.

Jacobian Regularization. For training with Jacobian regularization (JR), we optimize the following joint loss and use the algorithm as proposed by [12]:

$$\mathcal{L}_{\text{joint}}(\theta) = \mathcal{L}_{\text{train}}(\{\mathbf{x}_i, \mathbf{y}_i\}_i, \theta) + \frac{\lambda_{\text{JR}}}{2}\left(\frac{1}{B}\sum_i \|\mathbf{J}(\mathbf{x}_i)\|_F^2\right) \tag{11}$$

where θ represent the parameters of the model, $\mathcal{L}_{\text{train}}$ is the standard cross-entropy training loss, $\{\mathbf{x}_i, \mathbf{y}_i\}$ are input-output pairs from the mini-batch, and B is the mini-batch size. This optimization uses a regularization parameter λ_{JR}, which lets us adjust the trade-off between regularization and classification loss.

UAP Attacks. We evaluate the robustness of these models to UAPs generated via iterative stochastic gradient descent with 100 iterations and a batch size of 200. Perturbations are applied under ℓ_∞-norm constraints. The ε we consider in our attacks for this norm are from 0.1 to 0.3, this perturbation magnitude is equivalent to 10%–30% of the maximum total possible change in pixel values.

We generate untargeted and targeted attacks. For targeted UAPs, we generate one UAP for each of 10 classes of each dataset. Clean and UAP evaluations are done on the entire 10,000 sample test sets.

Robustness Metrics. The effectiveness of untargeted attacks are measured using the *Universal Evasion Rate (UER)*, defined as the proportion of inputs that are misclassified. Targeted UAPs for class c are evaluated according to their *Targeted Success Rate (TSR)*, the proportion of inputs classified as class c.

4.2 Jacobian Regularization Mitigates UAPs

Regular training without JR (i.e. $\lambda_{\text{JR}} = 0$) achieves 99.08% and 90.84% test accuracy on MNIST and Fashion-MNIST respectively. Figure 1 shows that increasing

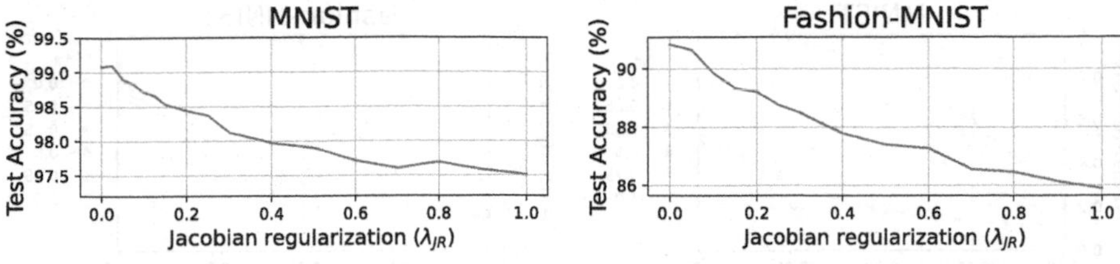

Fig. 1. Test accuracy of LeNet on MNIST (left) and Fashion-MNIST (right) for various Jacobian regularization strengths λ_{JR}.

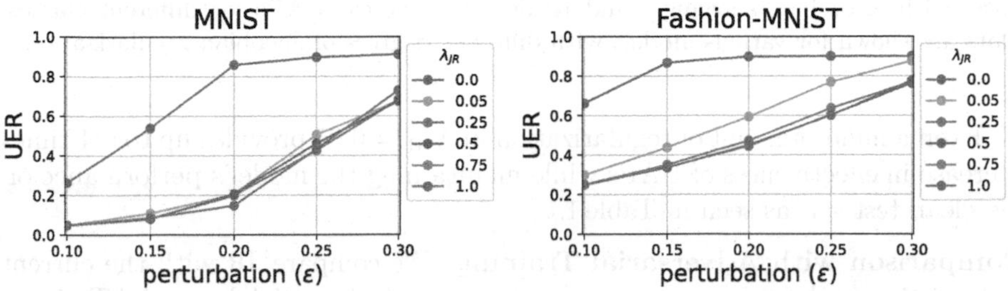

Fig. 2. Effectiveness of untargeted UAPs for various ℓ_∞-norm perturbation constraints ε. Plots are shown for various models with different degrees of Jacobian regularization.

the weight of JR decreases the resulting model's test accuracy. Note, however, that this decrease appears to be negligible for very small $\lambda_{\mathrm{JR}} \leq 0.1$.

Untargeted UAPs. Figure 2 presents the effectiveness of our untargeted UAP attacks on different LeNet with varying JR strengths. The regularly trained model is especially vulnerable to UAP attacks on both datasets, with untargeted UAPs achieving above 80% UER for $\varepsilon \geq 0.2$ on both datasets.

On MNIST, UAP attacks seem to gain reasonable success only after $\varepsilon \geq 0.25$. This is permissible as the adversary perturbs the input by 25% of its maximum possible value in this case, which entails an enormous change. What is striking is that JR has a protective effect for $\varepsilon \leq 0.2$, even for small amounts of regularization at $\lambda_{\mathrm{JR}} = 0.05$. Here, UAP effectiveness is down from 80% to 20% at $\varepsilon = 0.2$. Increasing the strength of the regularization likely has diminishing returns for robustness as stronger regularization also begins to damage clean accuracy, and thus the model's generalization. Fashion-MNIST can be seen to be less robust since it begins with a lower clean accuracy at around 91%. This means that the model is overall less robust to begin with than the model trained for MNIST, so we can expect it to be less robust to UAP attacks in general. Nonetheless, we still see a protective effect from JR for $\varepsilon \leq 0.15$ even with only a minor degree of regularization $\lambda_{\mathrm{JR}} = 0.05$.

Targeted UAPs. Figure 3 shows our results for the effectiveness of targeted UAPs. These plots follow a similar trend as with untargeted UAPs, suggesting that JR is able to improve model robustness against a diverse array of UAP attacks and not only against untargeted UAPs.

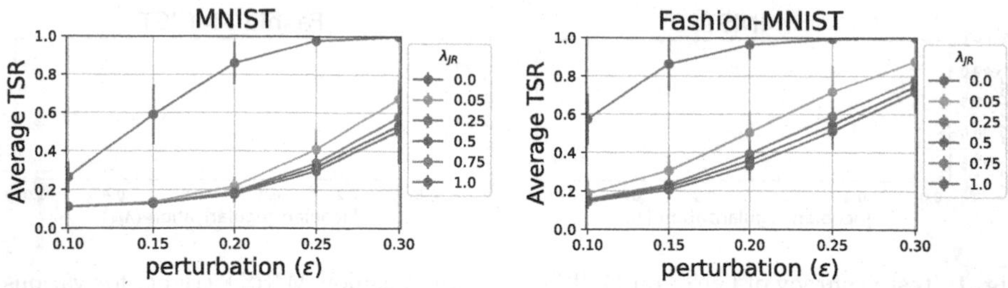

Fig. 3. Average Targeted Success Rate (TSR) of targeted UAPs generated for each class, with error bars showing standard deviation across UAPs for different classes. Plots are shown for various models with different degrees of Jacobian regularization.

Even a minor amount of regularization in $\lambda_{\text{JR}} = 0.05$ provides up to a 4-times decrease in effectiveness of UAPs while maintaining the model's performance on the clean test set, as seen in Table 1.

Comparison with Adversarial Training. We compare JR with the current state-of-the-art defense against universal attacks: Universal Adversarial Training (UAT) [23], where adversarial training is done on UAPs. UAT models in Table 1 are trained on $\varepsilon = 0.2$ and $\varepsilon = 0.15$ adversaries for MNIST and Fashion-MNIST respectively. Although UAT improves robustness to UAPs compared to standard training, it doubles the test error on both clean datasets. In contrast, JR achieves better robustness than UAT without damaging clean accuracy.

Adversarial training relies on training against specific UAP perturbations. The heuristic quality of UAT makes improving robustness against all possible perturbations computationally difficult. Our results show that regularizing a more general property of the model, in the norm of the Jacobian, leads to better robustness while maintaining accuracy.

Table 1. Performance metrics (in %) of LeNet. Jacobian regularization (JR) uses $\lambda_{\text{JR}} = 0.05$. UAP evaluations are for ℓ_∞-norm attacks at $\varepsilon = 0.2$ for MNIST and $\varepsilon = 0.15$ for Fashion-MNIST. Lowest values indicate the best robustness and are highlighted.

	MNIST			Fashion-MNIST		
	Standard	UAT [23]	JR	Standard	UAT [23]	JR
Test Error	0.92	1.81	**0.90**	9.16	16.66	**9.15**
Untargeted UER	85.88	27.49	**20.47**	86.63	34.10	**29.96**
Average TSR	85.94	24.05	**21.57**	86.33	**26.64**	30.59

4.3 Jacobian Alignment of Input Pairs

We now investigate how the cosine similarity of input Jacobians as introduced in Eq. 10 correlates with the models' robustness to UAPs. We consider LeNet with

Jacobian regularization ($\lambda_{\text{JR}} = 0.05$) and without ($\lambda_{\text{JR}} = 0.0$). The performance of the models on the test sets is the same as the ones in Table 1. For each dataset, we take a random subset of 1,000 test set images with a uniform distribution on the output classes. Thus, we measure the similarity for a million input pairs.

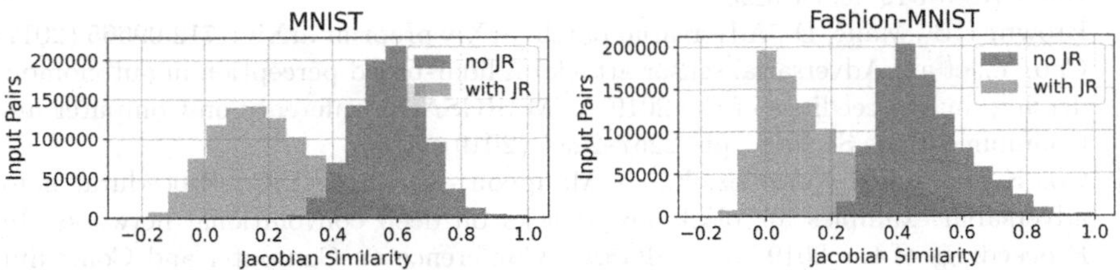

Fig. 4. Jacobian similarity for pairs of inputs on MNIST (left) and Fashion-MNIST (right) for LeNet with and without Jacobian regularization (JR). Median similarity values on MNIST are 0.18 and 0.58; and on Fashion-MNIST are 0.11 and 0.46 with and without JR respectively.

Figure 4 shows the histogram of the similarity values for the generated random pairs (cosine similarity is bounded in [−1, 1]). We observe that Jacobian regularization significantly reduces the median of the distributions by around 0.35. Although the Jacobian is only a first-order derivative, this greatly correlates with the models' robustness even for iterative stochastic gradient descent UAP attacks. This shows that observing the similarity measure we introduced can help to analyze the strength of shared adversarial perturbations, allowing defenders to better evaluate model robustness against UAPs.

5 Conclusion

In this work, we are the first to derive upper bounds on the impact of UAPs, we theoretically show and then empirically verify that data-dependent Jacobian regularization significantly reduces the effectiveness of UAPs, and finally we propose cosine similarity of Jacobians to measure the strength of shared adversarial perturbation between inputs.

In contrast to input-specific adversarial examples which have been shown to be difficult to defend against and often incur a notable decline in accuracy to achieve robustness, we show that Jacobian regularization can greatly mitigate the effectiveness of UAPs whilst maintaining clean performance through theoretical bounds and comprehensive empirical results.

These results give us confidence that applying Jacobian regularization to existing models significantly improves robustness to practical and realistic universal attacks at minimal cost to clean accuracy. Additionally, the proposed similarity metric for Jacobians can be used to further diagnose and analyze the vulnerability of models by identifying subsets of inputs with shared adversarial perturbations. Overall, these enable us to put defenses for neural networks against realistic and systemic UAP attacks on a more practical footing.

References

1. Biggio, B., et al.: Evasion attacks against machine learning at test time. In: Blockeel, H., Kersting, K., Nijssen, S., Železný, F. (eds.) ECML PKDD 2013. LNCS (LNAI), vol. 8190, pp. 387–402. Springer, Heidelberg (2013). https://doi.org/10.1007/978-3-642-40994-3_25
2. Brown, T.B., Mané, D.: Adversarial patch. arXiv preprint arXiv:1712.09665 (2017)
3. Cao, Y., et al.: Adversarial sensor attack on lidar-based perception in autonomous driving. In: Proceedings of the 2019 ACM SIGSAC Conference on Computer and Communications Security, pp. 2267–2281 (2019)
4. Co, K.T., Muñoz González, L., de Maupeou, S., Lupu, E.C.: Procedural noise adversarial examples for black-box attacks on deep convolutional networks. In: Proceedings of the 2019 ACM SIGSAC Conference on Computer and Communications Security, pp. 275–289. CCS 2019 (2019). https://doi.org/10.1145/3319535.3345660
5. Co, K.T., Muñoz-González, L., Kanthan, L., Glocker, B., Lupu, E.C.: Universal adversarial robustness of texture and shape-biased models. arXiv preprint arXiv:1911.10364 (2019)
6. Co, K.T., Muñoz-González, L., Lupu, E.C.: Sensitivity of deep convolutional networks to gabor noise. arXiv preprint arXiv:1906.03455 (2019)
7. Eykholt, K., et al.: Physical adversarial examples for object detectors. In: 12th USENIX Workshop on Offensive Technologies (*WOOT* 18) (2018)
8. Eykholt, K., et al.: Robust physical-world attacks on deep learning visual classification. In: Proceedings of the IEEE Conference on Computer Vision and Pattern Recognition (CVPR), pp. 1625–1634 (2018)
9. Hau, Z. Co, K.T., Demetriou, S., Lupu, E.C.: Object removal attacks on lidar-based 3d object detectors. arXiv preprint arXiv:2102.03722 (2021)
10. Hau, Z., Demetriou, S., Muñoz-González, L., Lupu, E.C.: Ghostbuster: Looking into shadows to detect ghost objects in autonomous vehicle 3d sensing. arXiv preprint arXiv:2008.12008 (2020)
11. Hinton, G., et al.: Deep neural networks for acoustic modeling in speech recognition: the shared views of four research groups. IEEE Signal Process. Magazine **29**(6), 82–97 (2012)
12. Hoffman, J., Roberts, D.A., Yaida, S.: Robust learning with jacobian regularization. arXiv preprint arXiv:1908.02729 (2019)
13. Jakubovitz, D., Giryes, R.: Improving DNN robustness to adversarial attacks using jacobian regularization. In: Proceedings of the European Conference on Computer Vision (ECCV), pp. 514–529 (2018)
14. Khrulkov, V., Oseledets, I.: Art of singular vectors and universal adversarial perturbations. In: Proceedings of the IEEE Conference on Computer Vision and Pattern Recognition (CVPR), pp. 8562–8570 (2018)
15. Krizhevsky, A., Sutskever, I., Hinton, G.E.: Imagenet classification with deep convolutional neural networks. In: Advances in Neural Information Processing Systems (NeurIPS), pp. 1097–1105 (2012)
16. Labaca-Castro, R., Muñoz-González, L., Pendlebury, F., Rodosek, G.D., Pierazzi, F., Cavallaro, L.: Universal adversarial perturbations for malware. arXiv preprint arXiv:2102.06747 (2021)
17. LeCun, Y., Bottou, L., Bengio, Y., Haffner, P.: Gradient-based learning applied to document recognition. Proc. IEEE **86**(11), 2278–2324 (1998)

18. Moosavi-Dezfooli, S.M., Fawzi, A., Fawzi, O., Frossard, P.: Universal adversarial perturbations. In: Proceedings of the IEEE Conference on Computer Vision and Pattern Recognition (CVPR), pp. 1765–1773 (2017)
19. Mummadi, C.K., Brox, T., Metzen, J.H.: Defending against universal perturbations with shared adversarial training. In: Proceedings of the IEEE International Conference on Computer Vision (ICCV), pp. 4928–4937 (2019)
20. Novak, R., Bahri, Y., Abolafia, D.A., Pennington, J., Sohl-Dickstein, J.: Sensitivity and generalization in neural networks: an empirical study. In: International Conference on Learning Representations (2018)
21. Redmon, J., Divvala, S., Girshick, R., Farhadi, A.: You only look once: unified, real-time object detection. In: Proceedings of the IEEE Conference on Computer Vision and Pattern Recognition (CVPR), pp. 779–788 (2016)
22. Roth, K., Kilcher, Y., Hofmann, T.: Adversarial training is a form of data-dependent operator norm regularization. In: Advances in Neural Information Processing Systems (NeurIPS) (2020)
23. Shafahi, A., Najibi, M., Xu, Z., Dickerson, J., Davis, L.S., Goldstein, T.: Universal adversarial training. arXiv preprint arXiv:1811.11304 (2018)
24. Sokolić, J., Giryes, R., Sapiro, G., Rodrigues, M.R.: Robust large margin deep neural networks. IEEE Trans. Signal Process. **65**(16), 4265–4280 (2017)
25. Szegedy, C., et al.: Intriguing properties of neural networks. In: Proceeding of the International Conference on Learning Representations (ICLR) (2014)
26. Thys, S., Van Ranst, W., Goedemé, T.: Fooling automated surveillance cameras: adversarial patches to attack person detection. In: CVPRW: Workshop on The Bright and Dark Sides of Computer Vision: Challenges and Opportunities for Privacy and Security (2019)
27. Tramèr, F., Dupré, P., Rusak, G., Pellegrino, G., Boneh, D.: Adversarial: Perceptual ad blocking meets adversarial machine learning. In: Proceedings of the 2019 ACM SIGSAC Conference on Computer and Communications Security, CCS 2019, pp. 2005–2021 (2019). https://doi.org/10.1145/3319535.3354222
28. Tu, J., et al.: Physically realizable adversarial examples for lidar object detection. arXiv preprint arXiv:2004.00543 (2020)
29. Varga, D., Csiszárik, A., Zombori, Z.: Gradient regularization improves accuracy of discriminative models. arXiv preprint arXiv:1712.09936 (2017)
30. Xiao, H., Rasul, K., Vollgraf, R.: Fashion-mnist: a novel image dataset for benchmarking machine learning algorithms. arXiv preprint arXiv:1708.07747 (2017)

Layer-Wise Activation Cluster Analysis of CNNs to Detect Out-of-Distribution Samples

Daniel Lehmann(✉) and Marc Ebner(✉)

Institut für Mathematik und Informatik, Universität Greifswald, Walther-Rathenau-Straße 47, 17489 Greifswald, Germany
{daniel.lehmann,marc.ebner}@uni-greifswald.de

Abstract. Convolutional neural network (CNN) models are widely used for image classification. However, CNN models are vulnerable to out-of-distribution (OoD) samples. This vulnerability makes it difficult to use CNN models in safety-critical applications (e.g., autonomous driving, medical diagnostics). OoD samples occur either naturally or in an adversarial setting. Detecting OoD samples is an active area of research. Papernot and McDaniel [43] have proposed a detection method based on applying a nearest neighbor (NN) search on the layer activations of the CNN. The result of the NN search is used to identify if a sample is in-distribution or OoD. However, a NN search is slow and memory-intensive at inference. We examine a more efficient alternative detection approach based on clustering. We have conducted experiments for CNN models trained on MNIST, SVHN, and CIFAR-10. In the experiments, we have tested our approach on naturally occurring OoD samples, and several kinds of adversarial examples. We have also compared different clustering strategies. Our results show that a clustering-based approach is suitable for detecting OoD samples. This approach is faster and more memory-efficient than a NN approach.

Keywords: CNN · Out-of-distribution detection · Clustering

1 Introduction

Convolutional neural network (CNN) models have increasingly been used for image classification due to their great performance [18,25]. However, a high performance is only obtained on in-distribution samples. The performance can drastically decrease in the presence of out-of-distribution (OoD) samples. In-distribution samples are samples that are drawn from the training distribution of the model. OoD samples, in contrast, are drawn from a distribution that is different from the training distribution. Distributions different from the training distribution can occur either naturally (e.g., objects presented in environments or occlusions not seen during training) [21] or in an adversarial setting (in the latter case OoD samples are usually referred to as adversarial examples) [3,16,47].

I. Farkaš et al. (Eds.): ICANN 2021, LNCS 12894, pp. 214–226, 2021.
https://doi.org/10.1007/978-3-030-86380-7_18

The vulnerability of CNN models to OoD samples makes it difficult to use CNNs in safety-critical applications (e.g., autonomous driving, medical diagnostics).

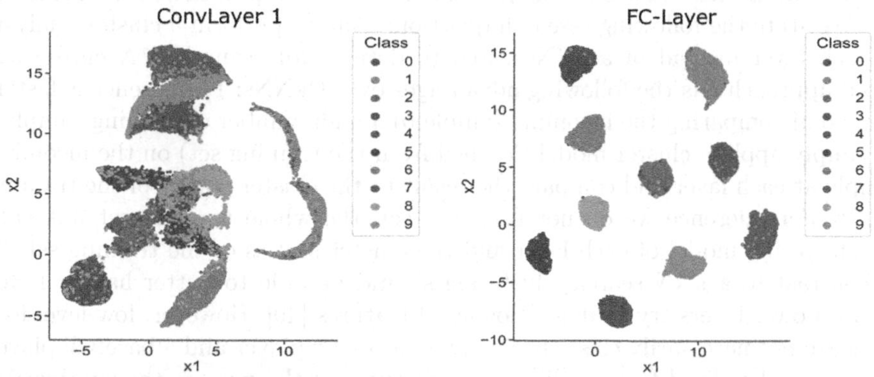

Fig. 1. 2D-Projections (created by UMAP) of the activations of the MNIST training data at the first convolutional layer (ConvLayer 1) and the output layer (FC-Layer) of the CNN (CNN setup as described in Sect. 4.1)

In safety-critical applications, the reliability of CNN models can be improved by using a confidence estimate of the predictions made by the model. This confidence estimate should be high for in-distribution samples and low for OoD samples. A naive approach to obtain such an estimate is to use the softmax scores of the network output. Unfortunately, the softmax scores do not provide a reliable confidence estimation [14,19]. To find a better confidence estimate, extensive research has been conducted. For instance, a promising approach, named Deep k-Nearest Neighbors (DkNNs), was proposed by Papernot and McDaniel [43]. Their method is based on the assumption that in-distribution samples of the same class are usually close together in feature space at each network layer. OoD samples, in contrast, can be close to in-distribution samples of a different class at each network layer. Hence, at inference, they check if an incoming sample is in-distribution or OoD (regarding a trained model) by using a k-nearest neighbor (kNN) search: When the sample is fed into the model, at each layer they identify the majority class of the kNNs of that sample among the training samples of the model (in feature space of that layer). They calculate a confidence estimate (credibility) using this majority class from each layer. If the majority class is the same among all layers, the confidence of the prediction will be high. If the majority class varies heavily between the different layers, the confidence of the prediction will be low. However, DkNNs have the following disadvantages: 1) Inference is slow because a kNN search requires comparing the incoming sample to a high number of training samples. DkNNs use an approximate kNN approach based on local-sensitive hashing [43]. An approximate approach is faster than a naive kNN search (i.e., compare with every sample), but it still requires many comparisons. Additionally, their method does not perform a kNN search only once but for each layer. This can be time-consuming for large training sets in particular. 2) To be able to perform a kNN search they need to store the whole training set for inference.

To address these issues we examine an alternative approach based on clustering. We state the following research question: Can we perform a cluster analysis at each layer instead of a kNN search to detect OoD samples? A clustering-based approach has the following advantages over DkNNs: 1) Inference is faster. Instead of comparing the incoming sample to a high number of training samples, we simply apply a cluster model (learned from the training set) on the incoming sample at each layer and compare the result to the cluster statics of the training set. 2) For inference we do not need to keep the whole training set but only the clustering model of each layer and the cluster statics of the training set. 3) In contrast to a kNN search, clustering should be able to better handle lower layers. Lower layers try to detect low-level features [49]. However, low-level features are not necessarily class-specific (e.g., a soccer player and a baseball player share some low-level features like shape features of the person, the sportswear, or the grass in the background). As a consequence, at lower layers samples of different classes are usually heavily mixed (illustrated in Fig. 1). A kNN search only tries to identify the majority class among the kNNs of a sample. At lower layers, this majority class does not need to be the same as the class of the sample (even if the sample is in-distribution). Our clustering-based approach, in contrast, tries to keep the information about all classes in the cluster by calculating a class distribution statistic of that cluster (i.e., what fraction of the samples in the cluster belongs to a certain class?). Besides these advantages, our approach keeps the following favorable properties of DkNNs: 1) OoD samples do not have to be generated for our detection approach. This would be difficult because we do not know all possible OoD samples in advance that can occur in practice. 2) The CNN model for which we want to detect OoD samples does not have to be re-trained. Our contributions are as follows: 1) We examine if a clustering-based approach is suitable to detect OoD samples for CNN models. 2) We compare different clustering strategies for the proposed approach.

2 Related Work

There have been other studies that also propose to use hidden layer activations for detecting OoD samples. Cohen et al. [9] use a kNN approach in combination with sample influence scores to detect OoD samples. Crecchi et al. [10] suggest using the hidden layer activations to learn a kernel density estimator for OoD detection. Li and Li [30] use convolutional filter statistics to learn a cascade-based OoD detector. Metzen et al. [39] propose to add a detector subnetwork at a hidden layer of the CNN. Chen et al. [6] use the hidden layer activations to train a meta-model that computes the confidence of the model prediction. Huang et al. [22] have observed that OoD samples concentrate in feature space. They propose to use a threshold on the distance to the center of the concentrated OoD samples to decide if an incoming sample is also OoD. However, in contrast to our approach, these methods are either computationally more expensive [9,43], require OoD samples to create the OoD detector [22,30,39], or are more complex [6,10]. None of these methods uses clustering to detect OoD samples. Chen et al. [5] have proposed an approach based on clustering. They try to identify if a training set was poisoned to trigger backdoor attacks on CNN models trained on this dataset. In contrast, we detect if an incoming sample, during inference, is an OoD sample for the trained CNN model. Moreover, Chen et al. apply clustering only on the last hidden layer. We apply clustering on multiple hidden layers.

A number of other approaches to detect OoD samples (especially adversarial examples) have been suggested. There are approaches that detect OoD samples based on generative models [29,38,45], using a special loss function [28,42], Baysian Neural Networks [4,15], characterizing the adversarial subspace [33], self-supervised learning [20], energy scores [32], techniques from object detection and model interpretability [7], augmenting the CNN with an additional output for the confidence estimate [12,17], or by perturbing the training images [31,48].

3 Method

A CNN model f is trained using a training dataset (X^D, Y^D) to classify samples X^I into one of C classes at inference. However, the model f can fail to predict the correct class for a sample $x^I \in X^I$, if the sample x^I is an OoD sample. To detect if x^I is OoD, we perform a layer-wise cluster analysis of the CNN model activations of x^I. Our approach is based on the work of Nguyen et al. [41]. Nguyen et al. apply clustering on the layer activations to visualize different features learned by each neuron of the model. In contrast, we use clustering to detect if a sample is OoD regarding the model f. Our approach is organized into two phases: 1) Before inference, at each layer L, we learn a clustering model g_L from the layer activations of the training data (X^D, Y^D) of f. 2) At inference, at each layer L, we apply the learned clustering model g_L on the activations of sample x^I. As a result, at each layer L, we obtain the cluster $K^L_{x^I}$ in which sample x^I falls. Finally, based on the cluster $K^L_{x^I}$ at each layer L, we determine if x^I is OoD or in-distribution. In the following, we describe both phases in detail.

Before Inference: 1) X^D has N training samples x^D. All N samples x^D are fed into model f. 2) At each (specified) layer L: (a) We fetch the activations of each sample x^D. At convolutional layers (ConvLayers), the activations of each sample x^D are in cube form. At linear layers, the activations of each sample x^D are in vector form. (b) We transform the activations of each sample x^D into vector form. However, we only need to do this for ConvLayers as the activations of linear layers are in vector form already. In either case, we obtain N vectors $A^L_{x^D}$ (one for each sample x^D) of length M_L. We concatenate all N vectors $A^L_{x^D}$ to a matrix A^L of size $N \times M_L$. (c) We need to project the activation matrix A^L from $N \times M_L$ down to $N \times 2$ using dimensionality reduction. This is a necessary preprocessing step for clustering as clustering usually does not work well in high dimensions [5]. As a result, we obtain the projected activation matrix $p_L(A^L)$ of size $N \times 2$ and the projection model p_L. (d) We try to find clusters in the projected activation matrix $p_L(A^L)$. As a result, we obtain $1, ..., k_L$ clusters and the clustering model g_L. (e) For each found cluster K_i^L ($i \in 1, ..., k_L$), we calculate a cluster statistic $S^L(K_i^L)$ expressing how much each of the C classes $c_1, ..., c_C$ is represented in cluster K_i^L at layer L in % ($cfrac^L_{K_i^L}(c_j)$).

$$\begin{aligned} S^L(K_i^L) &= \left\{ \left(c_j, cfrac^L_{K_i^L}(c_j) \right) \middle| \, c_j \in c_1, ..., c_C \right\} \\ cfrac^L_{K_i^L}(c_j) &= \frac{|(x^D, y^D_{y==c_j})|}{|(x^D, y^D)|}, \qquad \forall \, (x^D, y^D) \in K_i^L \end{aligned} \tag{1}$$

3) Finally, we store the projection model p_L, the cluster model g_L and the cluster statistic $S^L(K_i^L)$ for each found cluster K_i^L of each layer L.

At Inference: 1) The sample x^I is fed into the model f. 2) At each (specified) layer L: (a) We fetch the activations of the sample x^I. At ConvLayers, the activations of x^I are in cube form. At linear layers, the activations of x^I are in vector form. (b) We transform the activations of sample x^I to vector form. Again, we only need to do this for ConvLayers as the activations of linear layers are already in vector form. As a result, we obtain an activation vector $A^L_{x^I}$ of size $1 \times M_L$. (c) We apply the projection model p_L (that was learned from the training data (X^D, Y^D) before inference) on the activation vector $A^L_{x^I}$. As a result, we obtain a projected activation vector $p_L(A^L_{x^I})$ of size 1×2. (d) We apply the cluster model g_L (that was learned from the training data (X^D, Y^D) before inference) on the projected activation vector $p_L(A^L_{x^I})$. As a result, we determine to which cluster $K^L_{x^I}$ the sample x^I at layer L belongs (among the clusters $1, ..., k_L$ identified in the training data (X^D, Y^D) before inference). (e) We identify all classes that are in the cluster $K^L_{x^I}$ using the cluster statistic $S^L(K^L_{x^I})$ for cluster $K^L_{x^I}$. However, we only consider those classes c_j ($j \in 1, ..., c_C$) whose occurrence (in %) in the cluster is higher than a given threshold t (i.e., $cfrac$ of class c_j in cluster $K^L_{x^I}$ must be greater than t) resulting in a modified cluster statistic $S'^L(K_i^L)$. This threshold t is necessary as there are usually outliers in the training dataset (X^D, Y^D). Hence, some clusters contain only very few samples of a certain class (i.e., the occurrence of that class is low). As a result, we obtain a set of classes $cset^L(x^I)$ for the sample x^I at layer L whose occurrence in cluster $K^L_{x^I}$ is greater than a given threshold t. If x^I is an in-distribution sample, the class of x^I will probably be one of the classes in $cset^L(x^I)$.

$$\begin{aligned} cset^L(x^I) &= \left\{ c_j \middle| \, c_j \in S'^L(K^L_{x^I}) \right\} \\ S'^L(K^L_{x^I}) &= \left\{ \left(c_j, cfrac^L_{K^L_{x^I}}(c_j) \right) \middle| \, c_j \in c_1, ..., c_C \, \wedge \, cfrac^L_{K^L_{x^I}}(c_j) > t \} \right\} \end{aligned} \tag{2}$$

3) The set $cset^L(x^I)$ does most likely not contain the same classes at each layer L. The set usually contains more classes at lower layers than at higher layers.

This is caused by the type of feature each layer L tries to detect. Lower layers detect low-level features. Low-level features are typically not class-specific (e.g., a soccer player and a baseball player share some low-level features like shape features of the person, the sportswear, or the grass in the background). As a consequence, at lower layers, training samples of different classes are usually close together (illustrated in Fig. 1). Hence, the identified clusters at lower layers contain training samples of several different classes as well. Higher layers, in contrast, detect high-level features. High-level features are typically class-specific. The higher the layer, the more class-specific the features it detects. As a consequence, at higher layers, training samples of the same class are located increasingly close together, whereas training samples of different classes are located increasingly far apart (illustrated in Fig. 1). Hence, the identified clusters at higher layers only contain few classes. The clusters at the final layer ideally contain only one class [49]. This is not surprising. The goal of training a neural network-based classification model is to find a feature representation at the final layer of the network that is linearly separable (usually by softmax) regarding the different classes. As a result, the set $cset^L(x^I)$ contains more classes at lower layers than at higher layers. However, if x^I is in-distribution, all $cset^L(x^I)$ must contain at least one common class. This follows from our assumption: If a sample is in-distribution, it will usually be close to other in-distribution samples of the same class at each layer L. If a sample is OoD, it might be close to in-distribution samples of a different class at each layer L. Thus, we take the intersection of the class sets $cset^L(x^I)$ of each layer L to obtain the overall class set $cset(x^I)$ for the sample x^I.

$$cset(x^I) = \bigcap_L cset^L(x^I) \tag{3}$$

Finally, we determine if the sample x^I is OoD or in-distribution using this overall class set $cset(x^I)$ for x^I: If the class set $cset(x^I)$ is empty, it will probably be OoD. If the class set $cset(x^I)$ is not empty, it will probably be in-distribution.

$$detector(x^I) = \begin{cases} 1, & if\ cset(x^I) = \emptyset \\ 0, & otherwise \end{cases} \tag{4}$$

4 Experiments

4.1 Experimental Setup

We have conducted several experiments to find out if a clustering-based approach (as described in Sect. 3) is suitable to detect 1) natural OoD samples (Sect. 4.3), and 2) adversarial examples (Sect. 4.4). To find clusters in the activations of the training data in each layer (before inference), we need to 1) transform the activations into vector form (only ConvLayers), 2) project the activations of all samples to 2D, and 3) search for clusters in the projected activations. For each of the 3 steps, we can use several techniques. Our base configuration is based on the clustering method introduced by Nguyen et al. [41]. To transform the activations of ConvLayers into vectors, we simply flatten the activations (this approach was also used by Papernot and McDaniel [43]). Then, we concatenate the activation vectors of all samples into a matrix and normalize this matrix (subtract the mean and then divide by the standard deviation). The normalization serves as preprocessing step for projecting the activations. To project the activations, we use a combination of PCA [44] and UMAP [37]. First, we project the activations down to 50D using PCA. Then, we project the activations in 50D further down to 2D using UMAP. Theoretically, using UMAP directly should give better results because UMAP is a non-linear dimensionality reduction technique. However, the activation matrix is usually too large to apply UMAP directly. Thus, we project the matrix down to 50D using a linear method (PCA) first. A similar approach is also used by Nguyen et al. [41]. Finally, we search for clusters in the projected activations using k-Means [35]. The value for k was chosen based on the best silhouette score [46] of the identified clusters corresponding to k. The silhouette score is a metric to evaluate how well clusters are separated using the mean intra-cluster distance and the mean inter-cluster distance. We use the silhouette score to evaluate the identified clusters because, according to Chen et al. [5], it works best for evaluating clusters in CNN activations. Finally, the found clusters in each layer are used for detecting natural OoD samples and adversarial examples as described in Sect. 3. Based on our base configuration, we have also tested alternative strategies to identify clusters in layer activations (Sect. 4.2).

All experiments have been conducted using models trained on the MNIST [27] (60,000 training samples), SVHN [40] (73,257 training samples), and CIFAR-10 [24] (50,000 training samples) dataset. For MNIST and SVHN, we have used the same CNN model architecture as Papernot and McDaniel [43]: 3 consecutive ConvLayers using ReLU as activation function followed by a fully-connected output layer. The CNN model for MNIST was trained using the following training parameters: 6 epochs, learning rate (LR) of 0.001, Adam optimizer (test performance: 99.04% accuracy). The CNN model for SVHN was trained using the following training parameters: 18 epochs, base LR of 0.001, multi-step LR-schedule (gamma: 0.1, steps: (10,14,16)), Adam optimizer (test performance: 89.95% accuracy). We have used the activations from all ConvLayers (after ReLU) and the fully-connected layer for detecting OoD samples. For CIFAR-10 (not used by Papernot and McDaniel [43]), we have used a 20-layer ResNet model (using fixup initialization) introduced by Zhang et al. [50]. The ResNet model was trained using the following training parameters: data augmentation (random crop, random horizontal flip, mixup), 200 epochs, base LR of 0.1, cosine-annealing LR-schedule, SGD optimizer (test performance: 92.47% accuracy). We have used the activations from the first ConvLayer (after ReLU), the output activations of the 3 ResNet blocks, the activations from the Global-Average-Pooling layer, and the fully-connected output layer for detecting OoD samples.

4.2 Comparing Clustering Approaches

Besides our base configuration (described in Sect. 4.1), we have also examined alternative clustering strategies to find clusters in the activations of the training data at each layer. We have exchanged either the clustering algorithm, the projection technique, or the method to transform ConvLayer activations into vector form. We have tested the following approaches: 1) Clustering algorithm: DBScan [13] (we also tried OPTICS [2] and Agglomerative Clustering [1], but both did not give sufficient results). 2) Projection: (a) a combination of PCA and parametric t-SNE [34] (the original t-SNE cannot be used for our method as it does not learn a model that we can apply to incoming samples at inference), (b) only PCA. 3) Transforming ConvLayer activations: pooling the ConvLayer activations using a kernel of (2,2) followed by flattening the pooled activations (through pooling we may obtain a small translational invariance). All clustering strategies have been evaluated by the median silhouette score over all used layers. The results of our experiment are shown in Table 1.

Table 1. Silhouette scores of tested configurations (best score: 1, worst score: −1)

	DBScan	kMeans		PCA	tSNE	UMAP		Pool	Flat
MNIST	0.699	**0.733**	MNIST	0.423	0.432	**0.733**	MNIST	0.721	**0.733**
SVHN	0.535	**0.59**	SVHN	0.349	0.369	**0.59**	SVHN	0.561	**0.59**
CIFAR10	0.319	**0.677**	CIFAR10	0.378	0.382	**0.677**	CIFAR10	0.657	**0.677**

4.3 Natural OoD Sample Detection

We have conducted an experiment to find out if our clustering-based approach is suitable for detecting naturally occurring OoD samples. Before inference, we have identified the clusters in the activations of the training data for each (specified) layer of the model using our base configuration (described in Sect. 4.1). From the identified clusters we computed the cluster statistics for each (specified) layer. At inference, we have used the cluster statistics to check if samples are in-distribution or OoD. As in-distribution samples, we have used the test set of the dataset the CNN model was trained on: MNIST (10,000 test samples), SVHN (26,032 test samples), CIFAR-10 (10,000 test samples). As OoD samples we have used a test set that is different from the dataset the CNN was trained on: the KMNIST [8] test set (10,000 test samples, 7.59% test accuracy) for the MNIST model, the CIFAR-10 test set for the SVHN model (9.24% test accuracy), the SVHN test set for the CIFAR-10 model (9.35% test accuracy). We have applied our approach to each in-distribution and OoD dataset to receive the OoD detection rate for the dataset (i.e., how many samples of the dataset were recognized as OoD in %?). The threshold t was set to $t = 0.01$, $t = 0.05$ and $t = 0.1$. The results of the experiment are shown in Table 2.

4.4 Adversarial Sample Detection

Similar to our experiment in Sect. 4.3, we have also conducted an experiment to find out if our clustering-based approach is suitable for detecting adversarial examples. We have generated the adversarial examples (using the library torchattacks [23]) from the test set of the dataset the CNN model was trained on: MNIST, SVHN, CIFAR-10. The following methods to create the adversarials for MNIST have been used: FGSM [16] ($\epsilon = 0.25$, 8.05% test accuracy), BIM [26] ($\epsilon = 0.25$, $\alpha = 0.01$, $i = 100$, 0.04% test accuracy), PGD [36] ($\epsilon = 0.2$, $\alpha = 2/255$, $i = 40$, 2.46% test accuracy), PGD_{DLR} [11] ($\epsilon = 0.3$, $\alpha = 2/255$, $i = 40$, 0.85% test accuracy). The following methods to create the adversarials for SVHN have been used: FGSM ($\epsilon = 0.05$, 2.72% test accuracy), BIM ($\epsilon = 0.05$, $\alpha = 0.005$, $i = 20$, 0.79% test accuracy), PGD ($\epsilon = 0.04$, $\alpha = 2/255$, $i = 40$, 2.42% test accuracy), PGD_{DLR} ($\epsilon = 0.3$, $\alpha = 2/255$, $i = 40$, 3.48% test accuracy). The following methods to create the adversarials for CIFAR-10 have been used: FGSM ($\epsilon = 0.1$, 13.21% test accuracy), BIM ($\epsilon = 0.1$, $\alpha = 0.05$, $i = 20$, 0.84% test accuracy), PGD ($\epsilon = 0.3$, $\alpha = 2/255$, $i = 40$, 0.93% test accuracy), PGD_{DLR} ($\epsilon = 0.3$, $\alpha = 2/255$, $i = 40$, 28.0% test accuracy). We have applied our approach to each adversarial set to receive the adversarial detection rate for the dataset (i.e., how many samples of the dataset were recognized as adversarial examples in %?). The threshold t was set to $t = 0.01$, $t = 0.05$ and $t = 0.1$. The results of the experiment are shown in Table 2.

Table 2. OoD detection rates of our detection method (using the threshold t) in % for in-distribution samples (Testset), natural OoD samples (OOD) (MNIST: KMNIST, SVHN: CIFAR-10, CIFAR-10: SVHN), and several adversarial examples (FGSM, BIM, PGD, PGD_{DLR})

	MNIST			SVHN			CIFAR10		
t	0.01	0.05	0.1	0.01	0.05	0.1	0.01	0.05	0.1
Testset	3.6	5.4	5.94	1.35	19.67	42.56	4.24	19.62	63.69
OOD	81.11	86.89	86.97	12.46	70.16	81.61	22.16	42.9	83.87
FGSM	72.29	80.01	80.67	4.98	50.5	71.17	35.77	76.64	95.27
BIM	75.52	81.50	81.54	3.04	37.35	63.76	15.39	45.32	97.25
PGD	81.70	86.61	86.74	3.86	40.58	65.7	14.02	43.56	96.53
PGD_{DLR}	77.46	83.46	83.67	5.84	53.89	75.14	15.84	39.32	84.03

The best detection results, in relation to the false positive rates on in-distribution samples, have been reached using a threshold of $t = 0.05$. However, our results are not directly comparable to DkNNs as DkNNs compute a credibility score (e.g., mean scores MNIST-Test = 0.799, MNIST-FGSM = 0.136, SVHN-Test = 0.501, SVHN-FGSM = 0.237) and not a binary value. Additionally, we measured the inference times on the test sets and the FGSM adversarial examples using (a) our method (MNIST-Test: 32 s, MNIST-FGSM: 31 s, SVHN-Test: 83 s, SVHN-FGSM: 77 s, CIFAR10-Test: 145 s, CIFAR10-FGSM: 142 s), and (b) DkNNs (MNIST-Test: 296 s, MNIST-FGSM: 255 s, SVHN-Test: 1217 s, SVHN-FGSM: 1120 s, CIFAR10-Test: 783 s, CIFAR10-FGSM: 825 s). Our method was significantly faster than DkNNs.

5 Conclusion

In Sect. 1, we stated the following research question: Can we perform a cluster analysis at each layer of the CNN instead of a kNN search to detect OoD samples? Our experiments (Sect. 4) have shown that our approach is able to detect OoD samples at a higher rate than the false positive rate for in-distribution samples. As a result, an approach based on clustering is suitable to detect OoD samples. Furthermore, our experiment (Sect. 4.2) has shown that the projection technique has a crucial influence on the cluster quality. This is not surprising because without a good projection we cannot find good clusters. Best results were obtained using UMAP. This also corresponds to what we have observed visually. Using UMAP typically results in more dense clusters compared to t-SNE or PCA. However, by taking the intersection of the classes in the identified clusters of each layer, we have used a quite simple method to decide if a sample is OoD. Hence, the detection rates for SVHN and CIFAR-10 are often low. The low detection rates may be caused by noise in the data. Some form of calibration is probably needed. We have shown that clustering can be used for OoD detection. It is faster, more memory-efficient, or less complex than other state-of-the-art approaches. In future work, we plan to devise a refined clustering-based OoD detector obtaining improved detection rates. Moreover, the detector should not only give us a yes/no answer, if a sample is OoD or not. To be comparable to DkNNs, our method should compute a credibility score instead.

References

1. Ackermann, M.R., Blömer, J., Kuntze, D., Sohler, C.: Analysis of agglomerative clustering. Algorithmica **69**, 184–215 (2014)
2. Ankerst, M., Breunig, M.M., Kriegel, H.P., Sander, J.: Optics: ordering points to identify the clustering structure. In: Proceedings of SIGMOD, pp. 49–60. ACM, Philadelphia (1999)
3. Biggio, B., et al.: Evasion attacks against machine learning at test time. In: Blockeel, H., Kersting, K., Nijssen, S., Železný, F. (eds.) ECML PKDD 2013. LNCS (LNAI), vol. 8190, pp. 387–402. Springer, Heidelberg (2013). https://doi.org/10.1007/978-3-642-40994-3_25
4. Blundell, C., Cornebise, J., Kavukcuoglu, K., Wierstra, D.: Weight uncertainty in neural networks. In: Bach, F., Blei, D. (eds.) ICML, vol. 37, pp. 1613–1622. PMLR, Lille (2015)
5. Chen, B., et al.: Detecting backdoor attacks on deep neural networks by activation clustering. In: Espinoza, H., hÉigeartaigh, S.Ó., Huang, X., Hernández-Orallo, J., Castillo-Effen, M. (eds.) Workshop on SafeAI@AAAI. CEUR Workshop, vol. 2301. ceur-ws.org, Honolulu (2019)
6. Chen, T., Navratil, J., Iyengar, V., Shanmugam, K.: Confidence scoring using whitebox meta-models with linear classifier probes. In: Chaudhuri, K., Sugiyama, M. (eds.) AISTATS, vol. 89, pp. 1467–1475. PMLR, Naha (2019)
7. Chou, E., Tramer, F., Pellegrino, G.: Sentinet: detecting localized universal attacks against deep learning systems. ArXiv https://arxiv.org/abs/1812.00292 (2020)

8. Clanuwat, T., Bober-Irizar, M., Kitamoto, A., Lamb, A., Yamamoto, K., Ha, D.: Deep learning for classical Japanese literature. ArXiv https://arxiv.org/abs/1812.01718 (2018)
9. Cohen, G., Sapiro, G., Giryes, R.: Detecting adversarial samples using influence functions and nearest neighbors. In: CVPR, pp. 14441–14450. IEEE, Seattle (2020)
10. Crecchi, F., Bacciu, D., Biggio, B.: Detecting adversarial examples through non-linear dimensionality reduction. ArXiv https://arxiv.org/abs/1904.13094 (2019)
11. Croce, F., Hein, M.: Reliable evaluation of adversarial robustness with an ensemble of diverse parameter-free attacks. In: ICML, vol. 119, pp. 2206–2216. PMLR (2020)
12. DeVries, T., Taylor, G.W.: Learning confidence for out-of-distribution detection in neural networks. ArXiv https://arxiv.org/abs/1802.04865 (2018)
13. Ester, M., Kriegel, H.P., Sander, J., Xu, X.: A density-based algorithm for discovering clusters in large spatial databases with noise. In: KDD, pp. 226–231. AAAI Press, Portland(1996)
14. Gal, Y.: Uncertainty in deep learning. Ph.D. thesis, Univ of Cambridge (2016)
15. Gal, Y., Ghahramani, Z.: Dropout as a bayesian approximation: representing model uncertainty in deep learning. In: Balcan, M., Weinberger, K. (eds.) ICML, vol. 48, pp. 1050–1059. PMLR, New York (2016)
16. Goodfellow, I., Shlens, J., Szegedy, C.: Explaining and harnessing adversarial examples. In: Bengio, Y., LeCun, Y. (eds.) ICLR, San Diego, CA, USA (2015)
17. Grosse, K., Manoharan, P., Papernot, N., Backes, M., McDaniel, P.: On the (statistical) detection of adversarial examples. ArXiv https://arxiv.org/abs/1702.06280 (2017)
18. He, K., Zhang, X., Ren, S., Sun, J.: Deep residual learning for image recognition. In: CVPR, pp. 770–778. IEEE, Las Vegas (2016)
19. Hendrycks, D., Gimpel, K.: A baseline for detecting misclassified and out-of-distribution examples in neural networks. In: ICLR. Toulon, France (2017)
20. Hendrycks, D., Mazeika, M., Kadavath, S., Song, D.: Using self-supervised learning can improve model robustness and uncertainty. In: Wallach, H., Larochelle, H., Beygelzimer, A., d'Alché-Buc, F., Fox, E., Garnett, R. (eds.) NeurIPS, vol. 32, pp. 15637–15648. CAI, Vancouver(2019)
21. Hendrycks, D., Zhao, K., Basart, S., Steinhardt, J., Song, D.: Natural adversarial examples. ArXiv https://arxiv.org/abs/1907.07174 (2020)
22. Huang, H., Li, Z., Wang, L., Chen, S., Dong, B., Zhou, X.: Feature space singularity for out-of-distribution detection. ArXiv https://arxiv.org/abs/2011.14654 (2020)
23. Kim, H.: Torchattacks: A pytorch repository for adversarial attacks. ArXiv https://arxiv.org/abs/2010.01950 (2020)
24. Krizhevsky, A.: Learning multiple layers of features from tiny images. Univ of Toronto, Tech. rep. (2009)
25. Krizhevsky, A., Sutskever, I., Hinton, G.E.: Imagenet classification with deep convolutional neural networks. In: Pereira, F., Burges, C.J.C., Bottou, L., Weinberger, K.Q. (eds.) NIPS, vol. 25, pp. 1097–1105. CAI, Lake Tahoe (2012)
26. Kurakin, A., Goodfellow, I.J., Bengio, S.: Adversarial examples in the physical world. In: ICLR. Toulon, France (2017)
27. LeCun, Y., Cortes, C., Burges, C.: Mnist handwritten digit database. ATT Labs [Online]. http://yann.lecun.com/exdb/mnist 2 (2010)
28. Lee, K., Lee, H., Lee, K., Shin, J.: Training confidence-calibrated classifiers for detecting out-of-distribution samples. In: ICLR. Vancouver, CA (2018)
29. Lee, K., Lee, K., Lee, H., Shin, J.: A simple unified framework for detecting out-of-distribution samples and adversarial attacks. ArXiv https://arxiv.org/abs/1807.03888 (2018)

30. Li, X., Li, F.: Adversarial examples detection in deep networks with convolutional filter statistics. In: ICCV, pp. 5775–5783. IEEE, Venice, Italy (2017)
31. Liang, S., Li, Y., Srikant, R.: Enhancing the reliability of out-of-distribution image detection in neural networks. In: ICLR. Vancouver, CA (2018)
32. Liu, W., Wang, X., Owens, J., Li, Y.: Energy-based out-of-distribution detection. In: Larochelle, H., Ranzato, M., Hadsell, R., Balcan, M.F., Lin, H. (eds.) NeurIPS, vol. 33, pp. 21464–21475. CAI (2020)
33. Ma, X., et al.: Characterizing adversarial subspaces using local intrinsic dimensionality. In: ICLR. Vancouver, CA (2018)
34. van der Maaten, L.J.P.: Learning a parametric embedding by preserving local structure. In: van Dyk, D., Welling, M. (eds.) AISTATS, vol. 5, pp. 384–391. PMLR, Clearwater Beach (2009)
35. MacQueen, J.B.: Some methods for classification and analysis of multivariate observations. In: Cam, L.M.L., Neyman, J. (eds.) Proceedings of the Fifth Berkeley Symposium on Mathematical Statistics and Probability, vol. 1, pp. 281–297. Univ of Calif Press (1967)
36. Madry, A., Makelov, A., Schmidt, L., Tsipras, D., Vladu, A.: Towards deep learning models resistant to adversarial attacks. In: ICLR. Vancouver, CA (2018)
37. McInnes, L., Healy, J., Melville, J.: UMAP: uniform manifold approximation and projection for dimension reduction. ArXiv https://arxiv.org/abs/1802.03426 (2018)
38. Meng, D., Chen, H.: Magnet: A two-pronged defense against adversarial examples. In: SIGSAC, pp. 135–147. ACM, Dallas (2017)
39. Metzen, J.H., Genewein, T., Fischer, V., Bischoff, B.: On detecting adversarial perturbations. In: ICLR. Toulon, France (2017)
40. Netzer, Y., Wang, T., Coates, A., Bissacco, A., Wu, B., Ng, A.Y.: Reading digits in natural images with unsupervised feature learning. In: NIPS Workshop on Deep Learning and Unsupervised Feature Learning (2011)
41. Nguyen, A., Yosinski, J., Clune, J.: Multifaceted feature visualization: uncovering the different types of features learned by each neuron in deep neural networks. In: Visualization for Deep Learning workshop, International Conference in Machine Learning (2016). arXiv preprint arXiv:1602.03616
42. Pang, T., Du, C., Dong, Y., Zhu, J.: Towards robust detection of adversarial examples. In: Bengio, S., Wallach, H., Larochelle, H., Grauman, K., Cesa-Bianchi, N., Garnett, R. (eds.) NeurIPS, vol. 31, pp. 4584–4594. CAI, Montreal (2018)
43. Papernot, N., McDaniel, P.: Deep k-nearest neighbors: towards confident, interpretable and robust deep learning. ArXiv https://arxiv.org/abs/1803.04765 (2018)
44. Pearson, K.: LIII. On lines and planes of closest fit to systems of points in space. London Edinb. Dublin Philos. Mag. J. Sci. **2**(11), 559–572 (1901)
45. Qin, Y., Frosst, N., Sabour, S., Raffel, C., Cottrell, G., Hinton, G.E.: Detecting and diagnosing adversarial images with class-conditional capsule reconstructions. In: ICLR. Addis Ababa, Ethiopia (2020)
46. Rousseeuw, P.J.: Silhouettes: a graphical aid to the interpretation and validation of cluster analysis. J. Comput. Appl. Math. **20**(1), 53–65 (1987)

47. Szegedy, C., et al.: Intriguing properties of neural networks. In: Bengio, Y., LeCun, Y. (eds.) ICLR. Banff, CA (2014)
48. Xu, W., Evans, D., Qi, Y.: Feature squeezing: detecting adversarial examples in deep neural networks. ArXiv https://arxiv.org/abs/1704.01155 (2017)
49. Zeiler, M.D., Fergus, R.: Visualizing and understanding convolutional networks. In: Fleet, D., Pajdla, T., Schiele, B., Tuytelaars, T. (eds.) ECCV 2014. LNCS, vol. 8689, pp. 818–833. Springer, Cham (2014). https://doi.org/10.1007/978-3-319-10590-1_53
50. Zhang, H., Dauphin, Y.N., Ma, T.: Fixup initialization: residual learning without normalization. ArXiv https://arxiv.org/abs/1901.09321 (2019)

Weight and Gradient Centralization in Deep Neural Networks

Wolfgang Fuhl(✉) and Enkelejda Kasneci

University Tübingen, Sand 14, 72076 Tübingen, Germany
{wolfgang.fuhl,enkelejda.kasneci}@uni-tuebingen.de

Abstract. Batch normalization is currently the most widely used variant of internal normalization for deep neural networks. Additional work has shown that the normalization of weights and additional conditioning as well as the normalization of gradients further improve the generalization. In this work, we combine several of these methods and thereby increase the generalization of the networks. The advantage of the newer methods compared to the batch normalization is not only increased generalization, but also that these methods only have to be applied during training and, therefore, do not influence the running time during use. https://atreus.informatik.uni-tuebingen.de/seafile/d/8e2ab8c3fdd444e1a135/?p=%2FWeightAndGradientCentralization&mode=list.

Keywords: Neural networks · Normalization · DNN · Deep neuronal networks

1 Introduction

Deep neural networks (DNN) [21] are currently the most successful machine learning method and owe their recent progress to the steadily growing data sets [19], improvements in massively parallel architectures [17], high-speed bus systems such as PCIe, optimization methods [15,28], new training techniques [7,16], and the regularly growing fields of application. These advances in technology make it possible to train deep neural networks on huge datasets like ImageNet [19], however, further techniques had to be introduced to prevent the gradients from becoming too small [10]. The normalization of the data [13] has a huge impact on the generalization of large networks. Generalization alone is not the only quality feature of a good learning process of neural networks. Another important point is the acceleration of the learning process and the resource-saving use of the techniques. This is due to the fact that the most successful architectures already have an intrinsically high resource requirement and additional techniques to improve generalization can, therefore, only use a

Electronic supplementary material The online version of this chapter (https://doi.org/10.1007/978-3-030-86380-7_19) contains supplementary material, which is available to authorized users.

I. Farkaš et al. (Eds.): ICANN 2021, LNCS 12894, pp. 227–239, 2021.
https://doi.org/10.1007/978-3-030-86380-7_19

small number of supplementary resources. This can be seen very clearly when comparing the optimization techniques themselves. The most popular methods are Stochastic Gradient Decent (SGD) with momentum [28] and Adam [15] which introduces a second momentum. There are many other optimization algorithms [2,4,15,28], but SGD and Adam are the most popular. Both methods allow batch based learning and require only a constant multiple of the gradient (for the momentum) as additional memory. Comparing this with the Levenberg-Marquardt algorithm (LM) [22,24], which was the most popular method for training neural networks for quite some time, it is noticeable that the memory consumption in the case of LM grows quadratic to the weights. This is due to the fact that the LM algorithm calculates the exact derivatives for each weight over the whole network and not only local derivatives as is the case with back-propagation. Further procedures like the residual layers [10], weight initialization strategy [6,9], activation functions [25], gradient clipping [26,27], algorithms for adaptive learning rate optimization [15,28], and many more have been introduced and are subject to the same conditions of generalization improvement, training stabilization, and resource conservation.

In neural networks themselves, statistics are also collected and used to balance the forward and backward flow of data and errors. The best known method used directly on the activation of neurons is Batch Normalization (BN) [13]. Other procedures that work on the activation functions are instance normalization (IN) [12,34], layer normalization (LN) [1] and group normalization (GN) [35]. These procedures smooth the optimization landscape [32] and lead to an improvement of the generalization. The disadvantages of BN are that it continues to process the data in the neural network as an independent layer even after training and that it must be applied to a relatively large batch size. To avoid these disadvantages, weight normalization (WN) [11,31] and weight standardization (WS) [29] were introduced. These must only be applied during training and are independent of the batch size. WN limits the weight vectors via different standards whereas WS normalizes the weight vectors via the mean and standard deviation. A newer technique that works only on the gradient is Gradient Centralization (GC) [36], which subtracts the mean value from the gradient. All these advanced techniques smooth the error space and lead to a faster and, typically, better generalization of neural networks.

In this work, we deal with these extended techniques and seek to find a good combination of the methods. In our evaluation, it has been shown that the combination of the filter mean subtraction and the gradient mean subtraction in union is very effective for different networks. We have also tested other combinations and found that many also depend on batch normalization. Our main contributions are as follows:

1 The combination of mean gradient and mean filter subtraction
2 Publicly available CUDA implementations
3 Description of the integration into the back propagation algorithm (Supplementary material)
4 A comprehensive comparison with advanced techniques

2 Related Work

In this section, we describe the related work based on three groups. The first group is the manipulation of the data after the activation functions, which has the disadvantage that the activation functions have to be executed in the later application of the model. The second group is the manipulation of the weights during training. Here, the weights can be standardized or otherwise restricted. The last group is the manipulation of the gradients. In this instance, after each back propagation, normalizations and restrictions are applied to the gradients before they are being used to change the weights.

2.1 Manipulation of the Output of the Activations

This type of normalization is the most common use of internal manipulation in DNNs today. In batch normalization (BN) [13], the mean value and standard deviation are calculated over several batches and used for normalization. This gives the output of neurons after the activation layer a mean value of zero and uniform variance. With group normalization GN [35], groups are formed over which normalization is performed unlike BN where normalization occurs over the number of copies in a batch, this eliminates the need for large batches, which is the case with BN. Other alternatives are instance normalization IN [12,34] and layer normalization LN [1]. For IN, each specimen is used individually for the calculation of the mean and standard deviation, and for LN, the individual layers. IN and LN have been successfully used for recurrent neural networks (RNN) [33]. However, all these methods have the disadvantage that normalization has to be applied even after training.

2.2 Manipulation of the Weights of the Model

In weight normalization (WN) [11,31], the weights of the neural network are multiplied by a constant divided by the Euclidean distance of the weight vector of a neuron. This decouples the weights with respect to their length, thereby accelerating the training. An extension of this method is weight standardization (WS) [29], which does not require a constant, but calculates the mean and standard deviation thus normalizing the weights. Like the previous manipulation methods, this method smooths the error landscape, which speeds up training and levels the generalization of the final model. An advantage of these methods is that they only have to be applied during training and not in the final model. These methods, however, have a limitation and that is the fine-tuning of neural networks. If the original model was not trained with a weight normalization, these methods cannot be used for fine-tuning without creating a high initial error on the model. This is due to the fact that the restrictions and norms for the original model's weights most likely do not apply.

2.3 Manipulation of the Gradient After Back Propagation

Another very common technique is gradient manipulation over the first [28] and second moment [15]. This gradient impulse allows neural networks to be trained in a stable way without the gradients exploding, which is interpreted as a damped oscillation. The second momentum leads, in most cases, to a faster generalization, but the model's final performance is usually slightly worse when compared to training with only the first momentum. These moments are moving averages which are formed over the calculated gradients and represent a pre-determined portion of the next weight adjustment. An advanced method in this area is gradient clipping [26,27] wherein randomly selected gradients are set to zero or a small random value is added to each gradient. Another technique is to project the gradients onto subspaces [3,8,20]. Here, for example, the Riemannian approach is used to map the gradients onto a Riemannian manifold. After the mapping, the gradients are used to adjust the weights. Finally, in [36] a very simple procedure was presented which subtracts the current mean value of the gradients in addition to the moments.

3 Method

Since our approach is a combination of several previously published approaches (Weight mean subtraction and gradient centralization), we proceed as follows in this section: we formally describe the already published methods and introduce a naming convention, which we use later in the evaluation. This should make it easier for the reader to evaluate the effectiveness of different methods. In the following, we will refer to operations on the data in forward propagation as $F_{s,c,y,x}$ where s is the sample, c is the channel and y, x is the spatial position in the data. For the weights we use $W_{out,in,y,x}$. Where *out* is the output channel, *in* is the input channel and y, x is the spatial position for fully connected layers. In the case of convolution layers, y, x is the position in the two-dimensional convolution mask, which together with *in* defines the convolution tensor. To manipulate the gradient we use $\Delta W_{out,in,y,x}$ with the same indices as we used for the weights ($W_{out,in,y,x}$). Since a normalization can be applied not only to the data and the gradient, but also to the back propagated error, the error is denoted by $E_{s,c,y,x}$ where the indices are the same as the indices of the forward propagated data ($F_{s,c,y,x}$).

3.1 Weight Normalization

In this section, the equations used for weight normalization are presented. In all equations, j represents the axis to which the normalization was performed orthogonally. This means that we have calculated a separate mean value, standard deviation or Euclidean distance for each index of j.

$$W_{j,in,y,x} = W_{j,in,y,x} * \frac{k}{||W_{j,in,y,x}||} \tag{1}$$

In Eq. 1, the weight normalization [11,31] is described (WN). This normalizes each weight in a tensor with the ratio of a constant k (in our experiments 1) divided by the Euclidean distance of the tensor.

$$W_{j,in,y,x} = W_{j,in,y,x} - \overline{W}_{j,in,y,x} \tag{2}$$

Since the pure normalization over the mean value of the tensor of the weights has no separate designation, we use WC in our work. WC is defined in Eq. 2 and calculates a separate mean value for each weight tensor and subtracts it from each weight.

$$W_{j,in,y,x} = \frac{W_{j,in,y,x} - \overline{W}_{j,in,y,x}}{std(W_{j,in,y,x})} \tag{3}$$

The final normalization of the weights is the weight standardization [29] which is defined in Eq. 3. Here, as in WC, the mean value is subtracted and each weight of a tensor is also divided by the standard deviation.

3.2 Gradient Normalization

In this section, the gradient normalization is introduced. Modern optimizers already use moving averaging with momentum [15,28]. We also think that the authors exploring gradient centralization [36] already tried different approaches like the standardization. We only present the recently published approach here. Also, as in the weight normalization section, j corresponds to j against the axis along which orthogonal normalization is performed.

$$\Delta W_{j,in,y,x} = \Delta W_{j,in,y,x} - \overline{\Delta W}_{j,in,y,x} \tag{4}$$

As can be seen in Eq. 4, the mean value is subtracted from each gradient tensor. The mean value is recalculated for each output layer.

3.3 Data Normalization

In this section, we briefly describe the different data normalizations. In our analysis, we only used batch normalization [13]. In this section, j as well as j_1 and j_2 (in case of instance normalization) stand for the axis or plane to which the normalization is orthogonal. Since scal and shift is learned in data manipulation, we denote them with γ and β respectively.

$$F_{s,j,y,x} = \gamma * (\frac{F_{s,j,y,x} - \overline{F}_{s,j,y,x}}{std(F_{s,j,y,x})}) + \beta \tag{5}$$

Equation 5 describes the batch normalization[13]. As mentioned above, γ and β are the scale and shift parameters which are learned during training. Since j is on the second index, each channel has its own average and standard deviation.

$$F_{j,c,y,x} = \gamma * (\frac{F_{j,c,y,x} - \overline{F}_{j,c,y,x}}{std(F_{j,c,y,x})}) + \beta \tag{6}$$

Equation 6 is the layer normalization [1]. Compared to batch normalization [13], layer normalization is the normalization of the samples in a batch. This means that each sample has its own average and standard deviation.

$$F_{j_1,j_2,y,x} = \gamma * (\frac{F_{j_1,j_2,y,x} - \overline{F}_{j_1,j_2,y,x}}{std(F_{j_1,j_2,y,x})}) + \beta \tag{7}$$

In the case of instance normalization [12,34], each sample is normalized on its own. Equation 7 describes this procedure. It does not normalize along an axis like the other methods, but each sample and each channel separately.

The only approach still missing is group normalization [35]. Here groups are formed between the individual instances, which have their own mean values and standard deviations. Since we cannot simply describe this with our annotation, the equation for the group normalization [35] is not included in this paper.

3.4 Error Normalization

Inspired by the data normalization, we have also done some small evaluations regarding error normalization as a separate normalization approach. For this purpose, we evaluated the standardization as well as the simple mean value subtraction. The simple mean subtraction is based on the fact that, in the case of weight normalization, the simple mean has proven to be very effective. In our simple implementations we did not use the scale and shift (γ, β) parameters and applied the normalization directly.

$$E_{s,j,y,x} = \frac{E_{s,j,y,x} - \overline{E}_{s,j,y,x}}{std(E_{s,j,y,x})} \tag{8}$$

$$E_{j,c,y,x} = \frac{E_{j,c,y,x} - \overline{E}_{j,c,y,x}}{std(E_{j,c,y,x})} \tag{9}$$

The Eqs. 8 and 9 describe error normalization along the channels and samples. The procedure is the same as for batch normalization [13] and layer normalization [1]. As you can see in the equations, we have omitted the learned γ and β parameters and the remainder of the equations are the same. Thus, the standard deviation and the mean value are calculated in each iteration and normalization is performed by subtracting the mean value and dividing by the standard deviation.

$$E_{s,j,y,x} = E_{s,j,y,x} - \overline{E}_{s,j,y,x} \tag{10}$$

$$E_{j,c,y,x} = E_{j,c,y,x} - \overline{E}_{j,c,y,x} \tag{11}$$

For the two other Eqs. 10, 11, we calculated only the average value over the samples or the channels and subtracted it. This was recalculated accordingly in each iteration. An overview of the abbreviations used in the rest of the document is shown in Table 1.

Table 1. The used naming convention for our evaluation.

Name	WN	WC	WS	GC	BN	LN	IN	EBN	ELN	EB	EL
Eq.	1	2	3	4	5	6	7	8	9	10	11

4 Neural Network Models & Data Sets

Figure 1 shows the architectures used in our experimental evaluation. The first model (Fig. 1a)) is a small model with batch normalization. We used this model to show the impact of the different normalization approaches on small models with and without batch normalization. The second model (Fig. 1b)) is a ResNet-34 and a commonly used larger deep neural network. We used it with and without batch normalization during our experiments to show the impact of the normalization approaches on residual networks. The third model (Fig. 1c)) is a classical architecture for neural networks without batch normalization. This model was used to show the impact of the normalization to classical neural network architectures. The last model (Fig. 1d) is a fully convolutional neural network [23]. It uses the U-connections [30] to improve the result for semantic segmentation. We used this network, together with the VOC2012 [5] data set, in the semantic segmentation task to show the impact of the normalizations. For training and evaluation, we used the DLIB [14] library for deep neural networks. In this library we have also integrated our normalization and the state of the art approaches against which we compare our work.

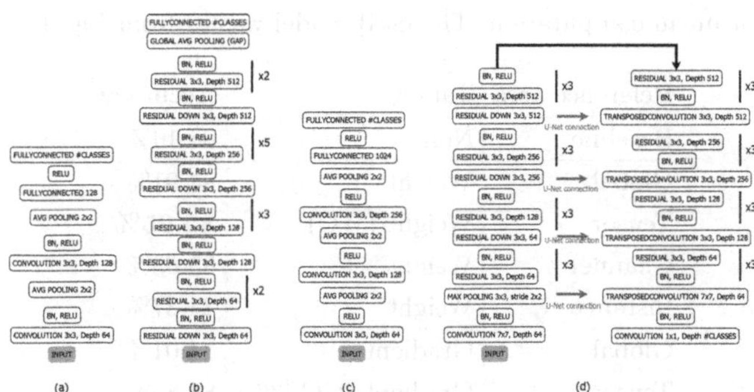

Fig. 1. All used architectures in our experimental evaluation. (a) is a small neural network model with batch normalization. (b) is a ResNet-34 architecture. (c) is a small model without batch normalization. (d) is a residual network using the interconnections from U-Net [30] for semantic image segmentation.

CIFAR10 [18] has 60,000 colour images each with a resolution of 32×32. The public data set has ten different classes. For training, 50,000 images are provided with 5,000 examples per class. The validation set consists of 10,000 images with 1,000 examples for each class.

CIFAR100 [18] is a more difficult but similar public data set like CIFAR10 and consists of color images each with a resolution of 32×32. The task here, as in CIFAR10, is to classify the given image to one of the one hundred classes provided. The training set consists of 500 examples per class and the validation set has 100 examples per class.

VOC2012 [5] is a publicly available data set which can be used for detection, classification and semantic segmentation. In our experiments we only used the semantic segmentation annotations as well as the semantic segmentation task. The training set consists of 1,464 images with 3,507 segmented objects and the validation set has 1,449 images with a total of 3,422 segmented objects on it.

ImageNet ILSVRC2015 [19] is a publicly available data set for classification with one thousand classes. The images have different resolutions and are taken everywhere on earth. The validation set consists of 50,000 images and the training set has more than a million images.

Training parameters are given in the supplementary material and under the provided link in the abstract.

5 Evaluation

In this section, we show the results on CIFAR10, CIFAR100 and VOC2012. We use the models from Fig. 1 and apply the training parameters and procedures from Sect. 4. In the first experiment, we show over which areas in the data the mean value subtraction can be used most effectively. In the following four experiments we compare the combination of GC and WC with the state of the art.

Table 2. The results for the mean subtraction normalization on CIFAR10 on different target areas for mean computation. The used model was c) from Fig. 1.

Reference area	Target	Accuracy
Baseline	Non	84.14%
Global	Weight	84.91%
Tensor	Weight (WC)	**85.95%**
Channel	Weight	85.63%
Instance	Weight	84.37%
Global	Gradient	84.01%
Tensor	Gradient (GC [36])	84.89%
Channel	Gradient	84.38%
Instance	Gradient	83.36%
Global	ERROR	79.03%
Sample	ERROR (EL)	72.15%
Channel	ERROR (EB)	75.40%
Instance	ERROR	69.73%

Table 2 shows the evaluation of mean subtraction on different areas of weights, gradients and back propagated errors. As can be seen, the mean subtraction on the error propagated back is not very effective because it significantly

Table 3. Classification accuracy on the CIFAR10 data set. The first column specifies the methods, the second column the used model from Fig. 1, and the third column is the classification accuracy. Models a) and b) where evaluated with and without batch normalization. For the models a) and c) we also used the normalization in the penultimate fully connected layer which is specified with the keyword *fully*.

Method	Model	Accuracy
Baseline	a	81.87%
WN [11,31] $k = 1$	a	71.74%
WC	a	85.01%
WS [29]	a	73.00%
GC [36]	a	81.42%
WS [29], GC [36]	a	74.51%
WC, GC [36]	a	85.75%
WC, GC [36], fully	a	**87.07%**
Baseline, BN [13]	a	84.67%
WN [11,31] $k = 1$, BN	a	82.95%
WC, BN [13]	a	85.38%
WS [29], BN [13]	a	79.65%
GC [36], BN [13]	a	84.01%
WS [29], GC [36], BN [13]	a	81.01%
WC, GC [36], BN [13]	a	85.48%
WC, GC [36], BN [13], fully	a	**85.95%**
Baseline	b	88.35%
WN [11,31] $k = 1$	b	58.77%
WC	b	80.15%
WS [29]	b	nan
GC [36]	b	69.85%
WC, GC [36]	b	**89.01%**
Baseline, BN [13]	b	91.00%
WN [11,31] $k = 1$, BN [13]	b	61.02%
WC, BN [13]	b	92.50%
WS [29], BN [13]	b	79.83%
GC [36], BN [13]	b	92.01%
WS [29], GC [36], BN [13]	b	79.71%
WC, GC [36], BN [13]	b	**92.68%**
Baseline	c	84.14%
WN [11,31] $k = 1$	c	83.73%
WC	c	85.95%
WC, fully	c	86.64%
WS [29]	c	10.05%
GC [36]	c	84.89%
GC [36], fully	c	85.37%
WS [29], GC [36]	c	10.72%
WC, GC [36]	c	87.46%
WC, GC [36], fully	c	**87.62%**

Table 4. Classification accuracy on the CIFAR100 data set. The first column specifies the methods, the second column the used model from Fig. 1 and the third column is the classification accuracy. Model a) was evaluated with and without batch normalization. For the models a) and c) we also used normalization in the penultimate fully connected layer which is specified with the keyword *fully*.

Method	Model	Accuracy
Baseline	a	46.31%
WN [11,31] $k = 1$	a	45.93%
WC	a	50.19%
WS [29]	a	41.19%
GC [36]	a	45.55%
WC, GC [36]	a	50.99%
WC, GC [36], fully	a	**52.03%**
Baseline, BN [13]	a	54.04%
WN [11,31] $k = 1$, BN	a	44.26%
WC, BN [13]	a	55.01%
WS [29], BN [13]	a	48.99%
GC [36], BN [13]	a	53.59%
WC, GC [36], BN [13]	a	56.45%
WC, GC [36], BN [13], fully	a	**56.78%**
Baseline, BN [13]	b	68.99%
WN [11,31] $k = 1$, BN [13]	b	52.97%
WC, BN [13]	b	69.89%
WS [29], BN [13]	b	63.52%
GC [36], BN [13]	b	69.34%
WC, GC [36], BN [13]	b	**70.24%**
Baseline	c	46.31%
WN [11,31] $k = 1$	c	10.31%
WC	c	52.05%
WS [29]	c	34.65%
GC [36]	c	47.95%
WC, GC [36]	c	53.16%
WC, GC [36], fully	c	**53.90%**

worsens the generalization of the deep neural network. This shows that error normalization without data normalization, as it happens in batch normalization [13], only brings disadvantages. For the weights and gradients, a convolutional tensor seems to be most effective for normalization. This means that each tensor is used for the mean calculation and this mean is subtracted only from this tensor. It is also clearly seen that weight normalization provides better results independent of gradient normalization with the exception of instance based normalization. In instance based normalization, an average value is calculated for every two dimensional mask and this average value is subtracted from the mask. Based on these results, we decided to define WC on the tensor and to discard the normalization of the back propagated error for further evaluations.

In Table 3, the results on CIFAR10 show different normalizations and the baseline, which is CNN without normalization. As you can see, the combination WC and GC can be effectively applied to all convolutions and also to the penultimate fully connected layer (indicated by the keyword *fully*). This can be seen in model a) and c) from Fig. 1. In model b), there is only one fully connected layer in which normalization is not effective because it generates the output. For model a) and b), we have also performed the evaluations with and without batch normalization. As you can see, the combination WC and GC works even better without batch normalization for model a). This is the best result for the model, especially together with normalization in the penultimate fully connected layer. In case of model b), the additional use of batch normalization is much better, because of the residual blocks. Therefore, for the additional evaluations, all residual blocks were evaluated with batch normalization only. Since model c) does not have an integrated batch normalization, we only evaluated without batch normalization.

The combination of WS and GC has not proven to be advantageous for all models, which is why we will not use it in further evaluations. In general, the best normalization across all evaluations on CIFAR10 is the combination of WC and GC. For residual blocks, batch normalization is added. Considering normalizations individually without batch normalization, WC is clearly the best, with GC a close second.

Table 4 shows the results of models a), b), and c) of Fig. 1 on the CIFAR100 data set. As you can see, again the combination WC and GC is the most effective. As with CIFAR10 (Table 3), this applies in particular to the additional use of normalization in the last fully connected layer (Indicated by the keyword *fully*). Like CIFAR10 (Table 3), the normalization WC always delivers better results in comparison to GC, if both normalizations are evaluated alone. However, there is a difference in the batch normalization for model a). The additional batch normalization is much more effective than model a) is without batch normalization. In all evaluations in Tables 3 and 4 one also sees that the normalizations WS and WN have worsened the generalization of the model. In one case, WS even led to a NaN result.

Table 5. The average pixel accuracy classification results for different normalization methods on the VOC2012 validation set using model d) from Fig. 1. We applied the normalization specified in column one to all layers except for the last convolution.

Method	Average pixel accuracy
Baseline, BN [13]	85.15%
WS [29], BN [13]	81.23%
WN [11,31] $k = 1$	75.76%
GC [36], BN [13]	85.91%
WC, BN [13]	86.92%
WC, GC [36], BN [13]	**88.98%**

Table 5 shows the evaluation of different normalization methods on the VOC2012 data set with model d) from Fig. 1. Normalization was used in all layers except the final convolution before output. As you can see, both GC and WC improve the result significantly. In combination with the batch normalization, the result is improved by more than 3%. This clearly shows that the combination of WC and GC can be used very effectively together with batch normalization for residual blocks. This can also be seen in Table 6 on the ImagNet validation set. The combination of WC and GC improves the Top-1 accuracy by 1.24% and the Top-5 accuracy by 1.46%.

Table 6. The Top-1 and Top-5 accuracy classification results for different normalization methods on the ImageNet validation set using model b) from Fig. 1.

Method	Top-1	Top-5
Baseline, BN [13]	75.37%	92.49%
GC [36], BN [13]	75.71%	92.92%
WC, BN [13]	75.89%	93.03%
WC, GC [36], BN [13]	**76.61%**	**93.95%**

6 Conclusion

In this work, we have shown that weight centralization is a very effective normalization method. Together with gradient centralization and, for residual networks, batch normalization, this combination exceeds the state of the art. We have also shown over which area mean subtraction is most effective. Our results were generated with four different nets on three public data sets and clearly show that the additional use of weight centralization is effective and improves the generalization of deep neural networks.

References

1. Ba, J.L., Kiros, J.R., Hinton, G.E.: Layer normalization. arXiv preprint arXiv:1607.06450 (2016)
2. Bottou, L.: Stochastic gradient learning in neural networks. Proc. Neuro-Nımes **91**(8), 12 (1991)
3. Cho, M., Lee, J.: Riemannian approach to batch normalization. In: Advances in Neural Information Processing Systems, pp. 5225–5235 (2017)
4. Duchi, J., Hazan, E., Singer, Y.: Adaptive subgradient methods for online learning and stochastic optimization. J. Mach. Learn. Res. **12**(7), 2121–2159 (2011)
5. Everingham, M., Van Gool, L., Williams, C.K.I., Winn, J., Zisserman, A.: The PASCAL visual object classes challenge 2012 (VOC2012) results (2012). http://www.pascal-network.org/challenges/VOC/voc2012/workshop/index.html
6. Glorot, X., Bengio, Y.: Understanding the difficulty of training deep feedforward neural networks. In: Proceedings of the Thirteenth International Conference on Artificial Intelligence and Statistics, pp. 249–256 (2010)
7. Goodfellow, I., et al.: Generative adversarial nets. In: Advances in Neural Information Processing Systems, pp. 2672–2680 (2014)
8. Gupta, H., Jin, K.H., Nguyen, H.Q., McCann, M.T., Unser, M.: CNN-based projected gradient descent for consistent CT image reconstruction. IEEE Trans. Med. Imaging **37**(6), 1440–1453 (2018)
9. He, K., Zhang, X., Ren, S., Sun, J.: Delving deep into rectifiers: surpassing human-level performance on imagenet classification. In: Proceedings of the IEEE International Conference on Computer Vision, pp. 1026–1034 (2015)
10. He, K., Zhang, X., Ren, S., Sun, J.: Deep residual learning for image recognition. In: Proceedings of the IEEE Conference on Computer Vision and Pattern Recognition (2016)
11. Huang, L., Liu, X., Liu, Y., Lang, B., Tao, D.: Centered weight normalization in accelerating training of deep neural networks. In: Proceedings of the IEEE International Conference on Computer Vision, pp. 2803–2811 (2017)
12. Huang, X., Belongie, S.: Arbitrary style transfer in real-time with adaptive instance normalization. In: Proceedings of the IEEE International Conference on Computer Vision, pp. 1501–1510 (2017)
13. Ioffe, S., Szegedy, C.: Batch normalization: accelerating deep network training by reducing internal covariate shift. arXiv preprint arXiv:1502.03167 (2015)
14. King, D.E.: Dlib-ml: a machine learning toolkit. J. Mach. Learn. Res. **10**(Jul), 1755–1758 (2009)
15. Kingma, D.P., Ba, J.: Adam: a method for stochastic optimization. arXiv preprint arXiv:1412.6980 (2014)
16. Kingma, D.P., Salimans, T., Welling, M.: Variational dropout and the local reparameterization trick. In: Advances in Neural Information Processing Systems, pp. 2575–2583 (2015)
17. Kirk, D., et al.: Nvidia CUDA software and GPU parallel computing architecture. ISMM. **7**, 103–104 (2007)
18. Krizhevsky, A., Hinton, G., et al.: Learning multiple layers of features from tiny images (2009)
19. Krizhevsky, A., Sutskever, I., Hinton, G.E.: Imagenet classification with deep convolutional neural networks. In: Advances in Neural Information Processing Systems (2012)

20. Larsson, M., Arnab, A., Kahl, F., Zheng, S., Torr, P.: A projected gradient descent method for CRF inference allowing end-to-end training of arbitrary pairwise potentials. In: Pelillo, M., Hancock, E. (eds.) EMMCVPR 2017. LNCS, vol. 10746, pp. 564–579. Springer, Cham (2018). https://doi.org/10.1007/978-3-319-78199-0_37
21. LeCun, Y., Bottou, L., Bengio, Y., Haffner, P.: Gradient-based learning applied to document recognition. Proc. IEEE **86**(11), 2278–2324 (1998)
22. Levenberg, K.: A method for the solution of certain problems in least squares Q. Appl. Math. **2**(2), 164–168 (1944)
23. Long, J., Shelhamer, E., Darrell, T.: Fully convolutional networks for semantic segmentation. In: Proceedings of the IEEE Conference on Computer Vision and Pattern Recognition, pp. 3431–3440 (2015)
24. Marquardt, D.W.: An algorithm for least-squares estimation of nonlinear parameters. J. Soc. Ind. Appl. Math. **11**(2), 431–441 (1963)
25. Nair, V., Hinton, G.E.: Rectified linear units improve restricted boltzmann machines. In: ICML (2010)
26. Pascanu, R., Mikolov, T., Bengio, Y.: Understanding the exploding gradient problem. CoRR **2**, 417 (2012). https://arxiv.org/abs/1211.5063
27. Pascanu, R., Mikolov, T., Bengio, Y.: On the difficulty of training recurrent neural networks. In: International Conference on Machine Learning, pp. 1310–1318 (2013)
28. Qian, N.: On the momentum term in gradient descent learning algorithms. Neural Netw. **12**(1), 145–151 (1999)
29. Qiao, S., Wang, H., Liu, C., Shen, W., Yuille, A.: Weight standardization. arXiv preprint arXiv:1903.10520 (2019)
30. Ronneberger, O., Fischer, P., Brox, T.: U-net: convolutional networks for biomedical image segmentation. In: Navab, N., Hornegger, J., Wells, W.M., Frangi, A.F. (eds.) MICCAI 2015. LNCS, vol. 9351, pp. 234–241. Springer, Cham (2015). https://doi.org/10.1007/978-3-319-24574-4_28
31. Salimans, T., Kingma, D.P.: Weight normalization: a simple reparameterization to accelerate training of deep neural networks. In: Advances in Neural Information Processing Systems, pp. 901–909 (2016)
32. Santurkar, S., Tsipras, D., Ilyas, A., Madry, A.: How does batch normalization help optimization? In: Advances in Neural Information Processing Systems, pp. 2483–2493 (2018)
33. Schuster, M., Paliwal, K.K.: Bidirectional recurrent neural networks. IEEE Trans. Sig. Process. **45**(11), 2673–2681 (1997)
34. Ulyanov, D., Vedaldi, A., Lempitsky, V.: Instance normalization: the missing ingredient for fast stylization. arXiv preprint arXiv:1607.08022 (2016)
35. Wu, Y., He, K.: Group normalization. In: Proceedings of the European Conference on Computer Vision (ECCV), pp. 3–19 (2018)
36. Yong, H., Huang, J., Hua, X., Zhang, L.: Gradient centralization: a new optimization technique for deep neural networks. arXiv preprint arXiv:2004.01461 (2020)

LocalNorm: Robust Image Classification Through Dynamically Regularized Normalization

Bojian Yin[1(✉)], H. Steven Scholte[2], and Sander Bohté[1,2]

[1] CWI, Machine Learning Group, Amsterdam, The Netherlands
byin@cwi.nl
[2] University of Amsterdam, Amsterdam, The Netherlands

Abstract. While modern convolutional neural networks achieve outstanding accuracy on many image classification tasks, they are, once trained, much more sensitive to image degradation compared to humans. Much of this sensitivity is caused by the resultant shift in data distribution. As we show, dynamically recalculating summary statistics for normalization over batches at test-time improves network robustness, but at the expense of accuracy. Here, we describe a variant of Batch Normalization, LocalNorm, that regularizes the normalization layer in the spirit of Dropout during training, while dynamically adapting to the local image intensity and contrast at test-time. We show that the resulting deep neural networks are much more resistant to noise-induced image degradation, while achieving the same or slightly better accuracy on non-degraded classical benchmarks and where calculating single image summary statistics at test-time suffices. In computational terms, LocalNorm adds negligible training cost and little or no cost at inference time, and can be applied to pre-trained networks in a straightforward manner.

1 Introduction

Methods that reduce internal covariate shift via learned rescaling and recentering neural activation, like Batch Normalization [8], have been an essential ingredient for successfully training deep neural networks (DNNs). In Batch Normalization, neural activation values are rescaled with trainable parameters, where summary neural activity is typically computed as mean and standard deviation over training samples. Such summary statistics however are sensitive to the input distribution, failing to generalize when novel images are outside this distribution, for example when faced with different and unseen lighting or noise conditions [5].

Where the original Batch Normalization computed statistics across the activity in a single feature map (or *channel*) [8], trainable normalizations have been proposed along a number of dimensions of deep neural network layers [2,13,18,20]. Other normalization approaches focus specifically on domain generalizability where distributions shift between source and target domains [4,12,16]. While these methods each have their merits, they do not resolve the sensitivity

I. Farkaš et al. (Eds.): ICANN 2021, LNCS 12894, pp. 240–252, 2021.
https://doi.org/10.1007/978-3-030-86380-7_20

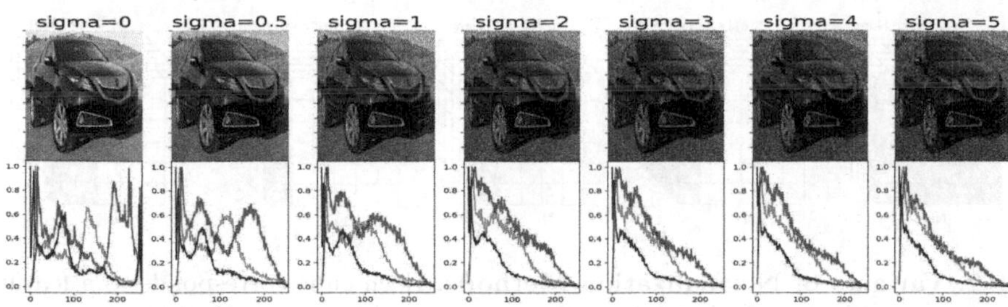

Fig. 1. RGB-histogram for increasing additive Gaussian noise (Color figure online)

of DNNs to image-degradation and the resultant distributional shifts in unseen images, which can be considered within-domain, dynamic and continuous distribution shifts.

Here, we propose a variant of Batch Normalization (BatchNorm), Local Normalization (LocalNorm): we observe that the mean and variance in channel activity changes when images are subjected to noise-related degradation. And the pixel distribution will significantly affect the network performance. Figure 1 shows an example of how the addition of Gaussian Noise flattens the color distribution for each channel in an image - other types of noise similarly affect the summary statistics. As we show, simply computing summary statistics at test-time similar to [12] – which we term *Dynamic BatchNorm* – does not resolve the problem: for large sized images, robustness increases, but accuracy decreases; for smaller sized images all accuracy is lost as the summary statistics computed from a single test-image prove too volatile.

To increase robustness of trained networks for variable summary statistics, LocalNorm regularizes the normalization parameters during training by splitting the Batch into Groups, each with their own normalization scaling parameters. At test-time, the summary statistics are then computed on the fly, either over a single image or a set (batch) of images from the test-set. For even single large images, this approach increases accuracy over and beyond both standard and dynamic Batch Normalization accuracy while retaining robustness; for single small images we demonstrate how a simple data augmentation strategy similarly fixes the accuracy while drastically increasing robustness to image degradation: the trained networks exhibit strong performance for unseen images with noise conditions that are not in the training set.

We also find that LocalNorm improves classification of distorted images in general, as measured on the CIFAR10-c and ImageNet datasets [7]. LocalNorm is straightforward to implement, also for networks already trained with standard BatchNorm - we demonstrate how a large pretrained ResNet152 network retrained further with LocalNorm significantly improves accuracy. We further show that LocalNorm achieves competitive performance on image classification benchmarks at little additional computational expense.

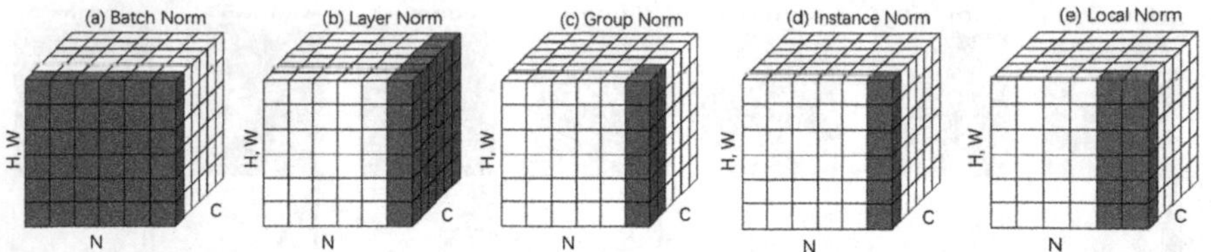

Fig. 2. Variants of Normalization Methods. Each cube corresponds to a feature map tensor, with N as the batch axis, C as the channel axis, and (H, W) as the spatial axes – height and width. The pixels in gray are normalized by the same mean and variance, computed by aggregating the values of these pixels.

2 Related Work

Lighting and noise conditions can vary wildly over images, and various preprocessing steps are typically included in an image-processing pipeline to adjust color and reduce noise. In traditional computer vision, different filters and probabilistic models for image denoising are applied [14]. More recent approaches for noise removal include deep neural networks, like Noise2Noise [11], DURR [22], and a denoising AutoEncoder [19] where the network is trained on a combination of noisy and original images to improve its performance on noisy dataset thus increasing the networks' robustness to image noise and also to train a better classifier. However, as noted in [5], training on images that include one type of noise in DNNs does not generalize to other types of noise.

Neural Normalizing Techniques. Normalization is typically used to rescale the dynamic range of input. This idea has been applied to deep learning in various guises, and notably Batch Normalization (**BatchNorm**) [8] was introduced to renormalize the mean and standard deviation of neural activations using an end-to-end trainable parametrization. **Normalization** is generally computed as

$$\hat{x}_i = \frac{x_i - \mu_i}{\sigma_i + \epsilon} * \gamma + \beta$$

where the x_i is a feature tensor of input $X = \{\cup x_i\}$ computed by the previous layer and γ and β are the (trainable) scaling parameters. For normal RGB or GBR images, $i = (i_N, i_W, i_H, i_C)$ is a 4D vector indexing the feature in $[N, W, H, C]$ order where N is the batch size(number of images per batch), H and W are the spatial height and width axes, and C is the channel axis.

The space spanned by N, H, W, C can be subdivided and subsequently normalized in multiple ways. We call the subdivision, the elements on which this normalization is performed, a group G_k: different forms of input normalization can be described as dealing with different groups. The mean μ_k and std σ_k of the certain computation group G_k are computed as:

$$\mu_k = \frac{1}{m} \sum_{x_j \in G_k} x_j; \quad \sigma_k = \sqrt{\frac{1}{m} \sum_{x_j \in G_k} (x_j - \mu_i)^2 + \epsilon}$$

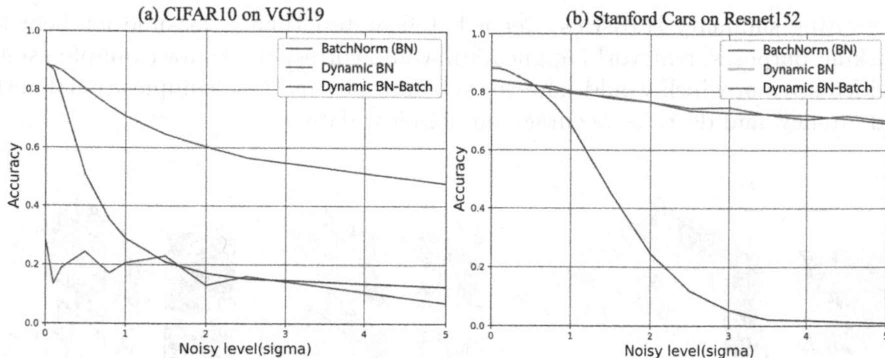

Fig. 3. Performance of VGG19 network applied to CIFAR10 (a) and a ResNet152 network to the stanford Cars dataset (b) where the test-images are subjected to increasing amounts of image degradation, here in the form of additive Gaussian noise. Blue: accuracy for standard batch normalization. Green: accuracy on dynamic batch normalization evaluated on single images. Orange: accuracy on dynamic batch normalization with summary statistics computed over a batch of test-images. (Color figure online)

where ϵ is a small constant. The computation group G_k (where $X = \{\cup G_k \mid k = 1, 2, \ldots K\}$) is a set of pixels which shares the mean μ_k and std σ_k, and m is the size of the group G_k. BatchNorm and its variants, like Layer Normalization [2], Instance Normalization [17,18] and Switchable Normalization [13], can be mapped to a computational group along various axes (Fig. 2).

Dynamic Batch Normalization. For BatchNorm, the mean μ and standard deviation (std) σ are calculated along all training samples in a channel and then fixed for evaluation on test images; as noted however, when the (test) image distribution changes, these statistical parameters will drift. As a result, DNNs with BatchNorm layers are sensitive to input that deviates from the training distribution, including noisy images. Simply computing the summary statistics on-the-fly at test-time [12], to account for potential drift, only partly solves the problem: in Fig. 3, we show what happens when the mean μ and std σ are computed as dynamical quantities also at test time for standard benchmarks CIFAR10 and Stanford Cars, using modern deep neural networks (for details, see below). For each test image (or batch of test images) we compute (μ, σ), for increasing noise (here for additive Gaussian noise).

For CIFAR10, we find that using single test images when evaluating gives poor results (Fig. 3a; Dynamic BN), as the small (32×32) images do not result in channel activity sufficient for effective summarizing statistics. However, computing these statistics over a batch shows a marked improvement (Fig. 3a; Dynamic BN-Batch): then, test accuracy exceeds standard BatchNorm for noisy images, at the expense of a slight decrease in accuracy for noiseless images. For the large images in Stanford Cars, we see that dynamically computing (μ, σ) at test time even for single images drastically improves accuracy for noise-degraded images (Fig. 3b); the classification accuracy absent noise however drops. While computing summary statistics over a batch at test-time is feasible for benchmarking purposes, real world application would correspond to for example using a video stream, which would however substantially increase computational cost and latency, and decrease accuracy on noiseless data.

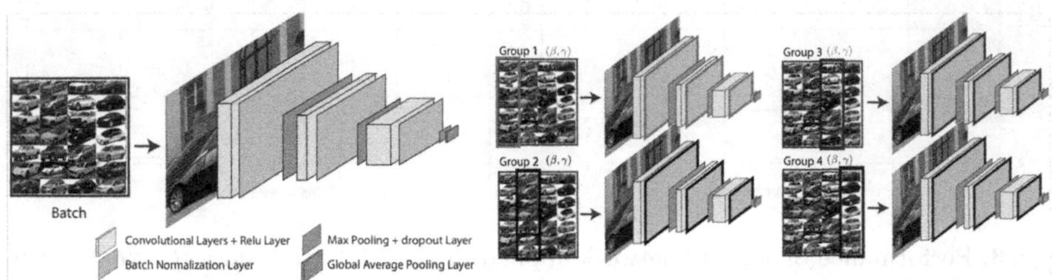

Fig. 4. LocalNet. A deep network with standard batch normalization computes single summary statistics over the entire batch. In LocalNorm, summary statistics are computed over groups, where each group k is associated with its own scaling parameters β_k, γ_k (while sharing the all other network parameters), and summary statistics (μ_k, σ_k) are dynamically computed also at test-time on the test-images.

3 Local Normalization (LocalNorm)

We develop LocalNorm, which dynamically uses the local summary statistics in a group to improve the robustness of DNNs to various noise conditions and show how resolves the loss of accuracy when computing summary statistics at test-time in Dynamic BatchNorm, while also improving the robustness to image degradation and distributional shifts at test-time.

In LocalNorm, we regularize the normalization layer for variations in μ and σ. The aim is to make the trained architecture less sensitive to changes in these statistics at test-time, such that we can dynamically recompute μ and σ on test-images. We divide the Batch into separate Groups G_k for which we each compute summarizing statistics μ_k, σ_k and associate separate scaling parameters γ_k and β_k with each Group, as illustrated in Fig. 4. For LocalNorm the computational group is defined along the $(N/K, H, W)$ axes (Fig. 2(e)):

$$G_k = \left\{ p | p_c = i_c, \lfloor \frac{p_n}{N/K} \rfloor = \lfloor \frac{i_n}{N/K} \rfloor \right\}.$$

BatchNorm computes fixed summary statistics μ, σ from the training set; for Dynamic BatchNorm and LocalNorm, we recompute these statistics at test-time.

Since LocalNorm provides both multiple independent groups and computes summary statistics at test-time, there are different variants for classifying a novel image at test-time. Given L Groups of size M each, we can evaluate an image M_i at test-time as follows: we can pass M_i through a randomly selected group L_r, use the activations of only this image M_i to compute this group's summary statistics μ_r, σ_r, and then obtain a classification c_i^r (**LN-Single**); we can pass M_i through all L groups, obtaining a set of classifications $\{c_i^l\}$ for each image, and then for each image select the class with the most votes (**LN-Single-Vote**; randomly breaking ties). We can also fill all random groups L_r with M different test-images into a batch, compute the summary statistics on the collective activations, and obtain classifications c_M^r for all M images and $M * L$ images are classified at once (**LN-Batch**), and finally we can pass the batch with M test-images through all L groups obtaining classification $\{c_M^l\}$ for each image, where voting then determines the overall classification (**LN-Voting**). For benchmark testing, **LN-Batch** is the fastest evaluation method, whereas **LN-Voting** will be most accurate; **LN-Single** will be fastest for single-image real-world application and **LN-Single-Voting** most accurate.

Implementation. LocalNorm is easily implemented in auto-different-iation frameworks like **Keras** [3] and **Tensorflow** [1] by adapting a standard batch normalization implementation[1]. For multi-GPUs, LocalNorm can map computational groups on separate GPUs which can accelerate training and allow the training of larger networks. It is moreover straightforward to adapt a model pre-trained with BatchNorm by replacing all BatchNorm layers with LocalNorm layers initialized with the BatchNorm parameters, and then continue training.

4 Image Noise

We test LocalNorm in a Noisy-object classification task where synthetic Gaussian, Poisson and Bernoulli noise is added to images, as in Noise2Noise [11]. All three kinds of independent noise ξ are added on each channel of the image x_c as follows. For **Additive Gaussian Noise (AGN)**, Gaussian noise with zero mean is added to the image on each channel, defined as $\hat{x_c} = x_c(1+\xi), \xi \sim Gaussian(0, \sigma_n)$. **Additive Poisson Noise (APN)** is one of the most dominat ing noise sources in photographs, and is easily visible in low-light images. APN is a type of zero-mean noise and is hard to remove by pre-processing because it is distributed independently at each channel. Mathematically, APN is computed as $\hat{x_c} = x_c + 255\xi$ or $\hat{x_c} = x_c(1+\xi)$ $\xi \sim Poisson(0, \sigma_n)$, where $\sigma_n \in [0, 1]$. **Multiplicative Bernoulli Noise (MBN)** removes some random pixels from the image with probability σ_n. MBN defined by $\hat{x} = x\xi, \xi \sim Bernoulli(\sigma_n)$.

5 Experimental Results

Benchmark Accuracy. We apply LocalNorm to a number of classical benchmarks: CIFAR10 [10], and Stanford Cars [9]. Where useful, we evaluate the benchmarks using all four different types of LocalNorm evaluation methods; when not explicitly mentioned otherwise, the application of LocalNorm refers

[1] Code available at https://github.com/byin-cwi/LocalNorm1.

to LN-Batch evaluation. LocalNorm has as a parameter the number of groups which, for a given batch size, determines the number of images in each group. While we did not extensively optimize for group number, we found that a smallish number of images per group, 4–8, performed best in practice for the batch sizes used in this study.

Results for all three normalization methods (BatchNorm, Dynamic BatchNorm and LocalNorm) are shown in Table 1 using otherwise identical network architectures, where we evaluate LocalNorm with LN-Single, LN-Batch and LN-Voting. We achieve high or near state-of-the-art accuracy on the original datasets, where in 3 our of 4 cases, LN-Voting and LN-Batch outperform BatchNorm and Dynamic BatchNorm. The improvement for CIFAR10 using the VGG architecture with LN-Voting in particular stands out, as accuracy improves from 88.8% to 95.3%; no such improvement is observed for the ResNet32 architecture, and only a slight improvement for the ResNet152 applied to Stanford Cars. We also observe that for the small CIFAR10 images, evaluating test-images using only a single image at a time (LN-Single) gives poor results. Comparing training time, we find that LocalNorm incurs only a small computational cost (10–20%) compared to BatchNorm.

Table 1. The accuracy on original test dataset of each network with various types of normalization on each dataset and for different LocalNorm evaluation methods.

	CIFAR10-VGG	CIFAR10-ResNet	Stanford-cars
BatchNorm	88.83%	**91.74%**	88.17%
Dyn. BatchNorm	87.64%	89.34%	85.34%
LN-Single	65.88%	32.33%	88.39%
LN-Batch	92.07%	91.15%	89.34%
LN-Voting	**95.29%**	91.65%	**89.58%**

For CIFAR10, we use two classical network architectures – VGG19 and ResNet32. The classical **VGG19** network architecture [15] is often used as a baseline to test new network architectures. **Residual Networks**, or **ResNets** [6] achieve robust and scalable accuracy on many machine learning datasets, and ResNet32 (a ResNet with 32 Layers) achieves competitive results on the CIFAR10 dataset [21]. We use a batch size of 128; for LocalNorm, we divide the batch into 8 computational groups with 16 images per group by default.

The Stanford Cars dataset contains 16,185 images of 196 classes of cars taken under various conditions, and each image is large, 224×224 pixels, allowing us to compare LocalNorm to BatchNorm and Dynamic BatchNorm when applied to large networks and large images. We use a large ResNet152For ResNet152, we use a pre-trained network[2] and continue training this network with BatchNorm, Dynamic BatchNorm or LocalNorm. For LocalNorm, 16 images are trained as a batch and divided into 4 groups.

[2] https://gist.github.com/flyyufelix/7e2eafb149f72f4d38dd661882c554a6.

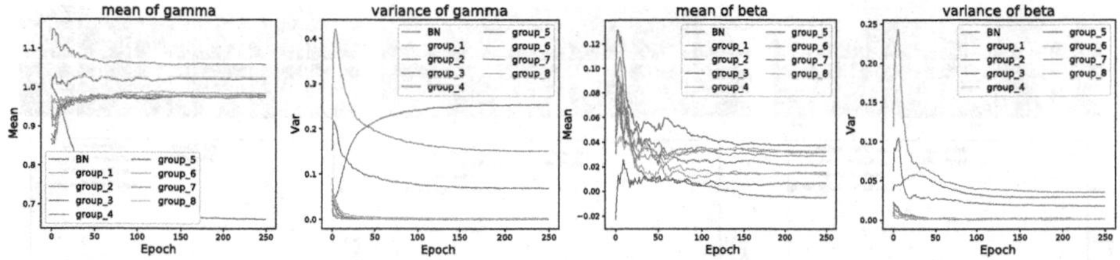

Fig. 5. Development of mean and variance of the scaling parameters γ and β for LocalNorm Groups (group_x) and BatchNorm (BN) during training on CIFAR10. The group-specific scaling parameters do not converge during training, maintaining a diverse scaling regime.

In Fig. 5 we plot the development of mean and variance of the normalization scaling parameters γ and β for LocalNorm and BatchNorm (averaged over all channels) when training VGG19 on CIFAR10 using 8 Groups for LocalNorm. We see that LocalNorm converges to a spread of γ and β values during training, maintaining a diverse normalization regime.

Noisy Image Degradation. To measure noise robustness and noise generalization, we use the networks trained with various normalization methods and the original training dataset, and test them on images degraded with different levels of noise. We evaluated the CIFAR10 and Stanford Cars dataset for all variants of LocalNorm, both where a batch of images is used at test-time (LN-Batch and LN-Voting) to obtain summary statistics, and where only a single image at a time is used at test-time to obtain summary statistics (LN-Single and LN-Single-Voting).

CIFAR10. We tested VGG19 trained on CIFAR10 with various normalization methods on noisy test images degraded with AGN. Figure 6a shows that the accuracy when using BatchNorm decreases rapidly, achieving only 29% accuracy for $\sigma_n = 1$. For the different types LocalNorm evaluation, we find that LN-Batch and LN-Voting drastically improve over BatchNorm and substantially over Dynamic Batchnorm, where for LN-Voting the network accuracy is 83% at $\sigma_n = 1$, almost three times better than the BatchNorm-based network. Evaluation using only single images, LN-Single and LN-Single-Voting, while being more robust to noise, clearly underperform for noiseless data.

Similar observations apply for the other types of noise. For APN, both BatchNorm and LocalNorm's accuracy curve dropped sharply, while LocalNorm still substantially outperforms BatchNorm and Dynamic BatchNorm in general (Fig. 6b). For MBN in Fig. 6c, BatchNorm accuracy drops exponentially and converges to random choice, while LocalNorm's performance decreases slower. Similar findings apply for a ResNet32 network (not shown).

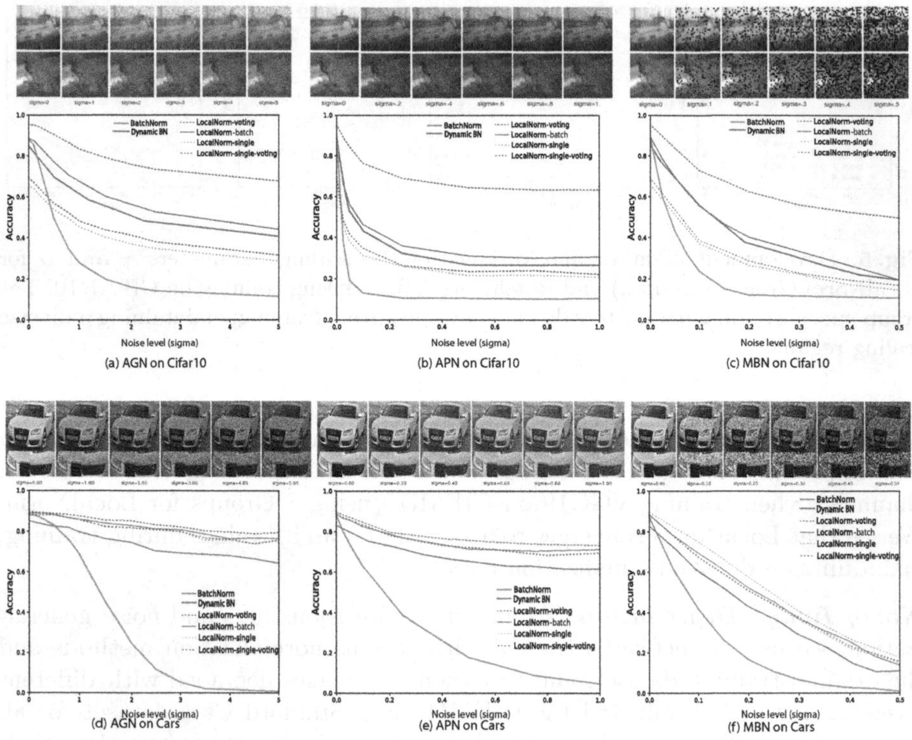

Fig. 6. Noise effect on CIFAR10 (a–c) and Stanford Cars datasets (d–f). (a–c) Top row illustrates noise-degraded CIFAR10 images for different amounts of AGN, AGN and MBN respectively. Bottom row, line graphs plot corresponding network accuracy on degraded CIFAR10 images using a VGG19 network architecture; (d–f) same noise-degradations applied to the Stanford Cars images using a ResNet152 network.

Stanford Car Dataset. For the images in the Stanford Cars dataset, we find that when testing on noisy images (Fig. 6d), all LocalNorm variants perform very similar, demonstrating that here, a single large image is sufficient to dynamically compute the summary statistics at test-time. LocalNorm maintains a test accuracy over 74% under any tested level of AGN and substantially outperforms Dynamic BatchNorm, while standard BatchNorm accuracy declines sharply to $< 20\%$ for $\sigma_n > 2.5$; similar behavior is observed for APN and BBN (Fig. 6e, f).

CIFAR10-c. The Cifar10-C dataset was published specifically to test network robustness to image corruption [7]. It contains 19 types of algorithmically generated corruptions from noise, blur, weather, and digital categories. To evaluate robustness, the networks are trained on the original CIFAR10 dataset, and evaluated on the corrupted dataset using LN-Voting. The result are shown in Fig. 7b: we find that LocalNorm outperforms both standard BatchNorm and Dynamic BatchNorm everywhere, with the largest improvements observed for those image

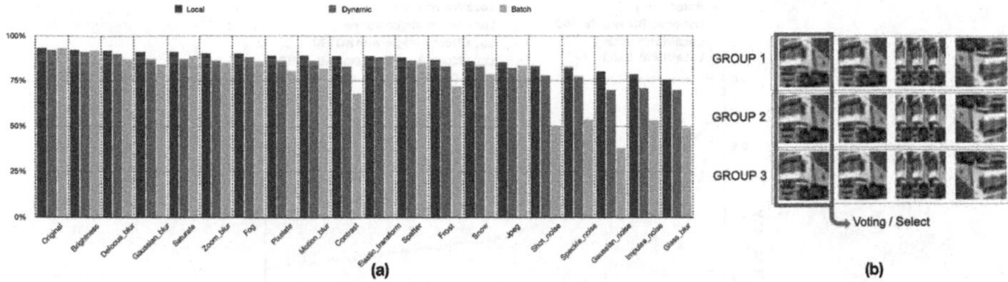

Fig. 7. (a) Comparison of LocalNorm LN-Voting to other normalization on the Cifar10-C dataset, for both Resnet32, for all the different image corruption categories. (b) Single image using data augmentation of the summary statistics through group expansion with rotated images. For a single image in each group (bracketed in green), rotated versions are created and added to the group. Summary statistics are computed for the whole group, while classification is computed for the original single image only. (Color figure online)

corruptions that incur the largest performance drop (Noise, Blur). We also see that LocalNorm improves the accuracy of the VGG-19 network much more than for the ResNet32 network, to the point that VGG becomes substantially more accurate than ResNet32.

ImageNET. We include the ImageNet dataset to test the generalization-ability improvement of VGG16 network with LocalNorm. The network was optimized based on a pre-trained network. The VGG16 with BN achieved 68% top-1 test accuracy, and LocalNorm obtained 67%. In [7], the mCE(mean of Corruption Error) was introduced to represent the generalizability of the network on various corruptions and perturbations. In [7] an mCE value of VGG16-BN of 0.8597 was reported, while the use of LocalNorm-batch improved this to 0.8036 and LocalNorm-voting achieved 0.7045.

Single Image Data Augmentation at Test-time. To improve the performance of LocalNorm-Single and LocalNorm-Single-Voting evaluation on small images, a simple suggestion is to enrich the summary statistics. Here, we propose to augment the data by adding rotated versions of the image along the width- and channel-axis (ROT90 clockwise) to the computation group to enrich the summary statistics, as shown in Fig. 7b. Adding such data will increase stability of the mean and variance derived from the computational group. During classification, the rotated images are only used to compute the summary statistics and the classification is determined for the original image only; classification can be done by either voting the prediction of each group or selecting a prediction randomly as the final result.

We find that this approach drastically improves LN-Single and LN-Single-Voting for the small images of CIFAR10. As show in Fig. 8 for AGN, thus enhancing the summary statistics for single image evaluation improves robustness and noiseless accuracy to the same level as LN-Batch - similar observations apply for

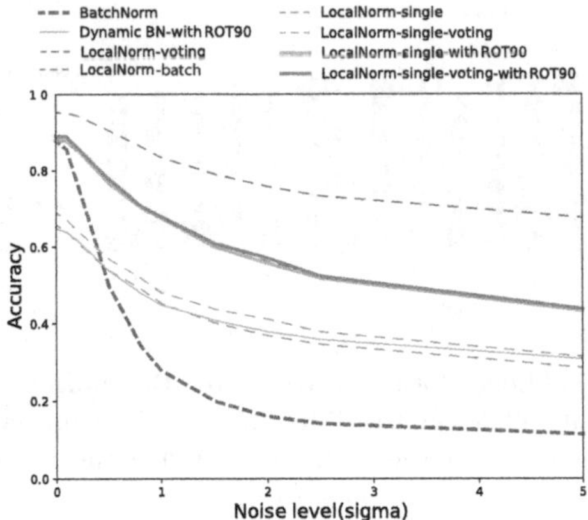

Fig. 8. Rotation-augmented summary statistics. The solid 'ROT90' lines indicate rotation data-augmented evaluation; the LN-Single-ROT90 and LN-Single-Voting-ROT90 curves now overlap with the LN-batch curve. Rotation-augmentation for Dynamic Batch Normalization on single images is insufficient (solid yellow line). (Color figure online)

APN and MBN image degradation (not shown). Applying rotation-augmentated Dynamic BatchNorm to single CIFAR10 images improves performance evaluation only modestly (DynamicBN in Fig. 8). While adding rotated images at test-time to the groups implies a substantial increase in computational cost, there is no cost to training, and evaluation on such small images tends to be very fast.

6 Conclusion

We develop an effective and robust normalization layer–LocalNorm. LocalNorm regularizes the Normaliation layer during training, and includes a dynamic computation of the Normalization layer's summary statistics during test-time. The key insight here is that out-of-sample conditions, like noise degradation, will shift the summary statistics of an image, and the LocalNorm approach makes a DNN more robust to such shifts.

We demonstrate the effectiveness of the approach on classical benchmarks, including both small and large images, and find that LocalNorm decisively outperforms classical Batch Normalization and dynamic variants like Dynamic Batch Normalization. We show that computing LocalNorm only has a limited computational cost with respect to training time, of order 10–20%. LocalNorm furthermore can be evaluated on batches of test-images, and, for large enough images, also on single images passed through only a single group, then incurring the same evaluation cost as Batch Normalization. To enable the evaluation of small images one-at-a-time at test-time, we demonstrated the addition of rotated images to the groups as a form of data augmentation to improve the summary statistics. For more general type of image distortions, we find that using LocalNorm also makes networks substantially more robust, as evidenced by the results on the CIFAR10-c dataset.

Intriguingly, the ability of regularized normalization layers to calculate sufficient summary statistics from single large-enough inputs rather than batches also suggests that correlates may be found in biological systems, where access to batch-statistics seem implausible but multiple parallel pathways may facilitate multiple independent normalizations as in LocalNorm.

Acknowledgments. BY is funded by the NWO-TTW Programme "Efficient Deep Learning" (EDL) P16-25.

References

1. Abadi, M., et al.: Tensorflow: a system for large-scale machine learning. OSDI. **16**, 265–283 (2016)
2. Ba, J.L., Kiros, J.R., Hinton, G.E.: Layer normalization. arXiv preprint arXiv:1607.06450 (2016)
3. Chollet, F., et al.: Keras. https://github.com/fchollet/keras (2015)
4. Du, Y., Zhen, X., Shao, L., Snoek, C.G.: Metanorm: learning to normalize few-shot batches across domains. In: International Conference on Learning Representations (2020)
5. Geirhos, R., Temme, C.R., Rauber, J., Schütt, H.H., Bethge, M., Wichmann, F.A.: Generalisation in humans and deep neural networks. In: NeurIPS, pp. 7549–7561 (2018)
6. He, K., Zhang, X., Ren, S., Sun, J.: Deep residual learning for image recognition. In: Proceedings of the IEEE Conference on Computer Vision and Pattern Recognition, vol. 2106, pp. 770–778 (2016)
7. Hendrycks, D., Dietterich, T.: Benchmarking neural network robustness to common corruptions and perturbations (2018)
8. Ioffe, S., Szegedy, C.: Batch normalization: accelerating deep network training by reducing internal covariate shift. arXiv preprint arXiv:1502.03167 (2015)
9. Krause, J., Stark, M., Deng, J., Fei-Fei, L.: 3D object representations for fine-grained categorization. In: 4th International IEEE Workshop on 3D Representation and Recognition (3dRR-13), Sydney, Australia (2013)
10. Krizhevsky, A., Hinton, G.: Learning multiple layers of features from tiny images. Tech. rep, Citeseer (2009)
11. Lehtinen, J., et al.: Noise2noise: learning image restoration without clean data. CoRR (2018)
12. Li, Y., Wang, N., Shi, J., Hou, X., Liu, J.: Adaptive batch normalization for practical domain adaptation. Pattern Recogn. **80**, 109–117 (2018)
13. Luo, P., Ren, J., Peng, Z.: Differentiable learning-to-normalize via switchable normalization. arXiv preprint arXiv:1806.10779 (2018)
14. Motwani, M.C., Gadiya, M.C., Motwani, R.C., Harris, F.C.: Survey of image denoising techniques. In: Proceedings of GSPX, pp. 27–30 (2004)
15. Simonyan, K., Zisserman, A.: Very deep convolutional networks for large-scale image recognition. CoRR https://arxiv.org/abs/1409.1556 (2014)
16. Summers, C., Dinneen, M.J.: Four things everyone should know to improve batch normalization. In: International Conference on Learning Representations (2019)

17. Ulyanov, D., Vedaldi, A., Lempitsky, V.S.: Improved texture networks: maximizing quality and diversity in feed-forward stylization and texture synthesis. CoRR https://arxiv.org/abs/1701.02096 (2017)
18. Ulyanov, D., Vedaldi, A., Lempitsky, V.S.: Instance normalization: the missing ingredient for fast stylization. CoRR https://arxiv.org/abs/1607.08022 (2016)
19. Vincent, P., Larochelle, H., Lajoie, I., Bengio, Y., Manzagol, P.A.: Stacked denoising autoencoders: learning useful representations in a deep network with a local denoising criterion. JMLR **11**(Dec), 3371–3408 (2010)
20. Wu, Y., He, K.: Group normalization. arXiv preprint arXiv:1803.08494 (2018)
21. Zhang, G., Wang, C., Xu, B., Grosse, R.: Three mechanisms of weight decay regularization (2018)
22. Zhang, X., Lu, Y., Liu, J., Dong, B.: Dynamically unfolding recurrent restorer: a moving endpoint control method for image restoration. CoRR https://arxiv.org/abs/1805.07709 (2018)

Channel Capacity of Neural Networks

Gen Ye[1] and Tong Lin[1,2](✉)

[1] The Key Laboratory of Machine Perception(MOE), School of EECS, Peking University, Beijing, China
{yegen,lintong}@pku.edu.cn
[2] Peng Cheng Laboratory, Shenzhen, China

Abstract. Occam's Razor principle suggests preference for simpler models and triggers an enduring question: what is the proper definition of complexity of a model? In this work, we regard neural networks as communication channels and measure the complexity of neural networks by means of their channel capacity—the maximum information reserved in the output of a neural network. Furthermore, we show a connection between the L2-norm of the weight matrix of the linear model and its channel capacity through the singular values of the weight matrix. On image classification problems, we find regularizing different neural networks by constraining their channel capacity effectively boosts the generalization performance and outperforms other information-theoretic regularization methods.

Keywords: Neural network · Channel capacity · Regularization method

1 Introduction

Inductive biases are necessary for machine learning and one of the most famous examples would be *Occam's Razor*: the simplest explanation is best. From the perspective of deep learning, a simpler model may refer to a network with fewer parameters/connections [17], a network with smaller norm [16], or a network with shorter minimal description length [12]. Following the simple intuition that the output of a simple model should contain fewer information about the input, in this work we regard neural networks or their modules/layers as communication channels and propose to view the channel capacity as a measure of model complexity.

In information theory [5], communication means messages/data/signals, denoted as a random variable W, successively get through an encoder, a communication channel, and a decoder. Analogous to this communication process,

This work was supported by NSFC Tianyuan Fund for Mathematics (No. 12026606), and National Key R&D Program of China (No. 2018AAA0100300).

I. Farkaš et al. (Eds.): ICANN 2021, LNCS 12894, pp. 253–265, 2021.
https://doi.org/10.1007/978-3-030-86380-7_21

an input to a neural network is an instantiation of a class label, and after representation learning through a neural network (corresponding to a communication channel), the recovered label is obtained by a classifier (corresponding to a decoder).

The channel capacity is defined as the maximum mutual information between channel input X and channel output Y, maximized over all possible input distributions. In this work, we define two versions of **information complexity (IC)** of neural networks. **Maximum information complexity (MIC)** of a neural network means the channel capacity of the corresponding communication channel. For boundness of this quantity, we constrain the possible distributions of the input to be those from a certain subset of absolutely continuous distributions (corresponding to a continuous random variable) and assume an extra noise added to the output. By assuming that the input distribution itself is drawn from a measure space and then changing the maximization over all distributions to expectation, we get the second version, called **expected information complexity (EIC)**, of neural networks for practical use.

It needs to be clear that analysis of **mutual information (MI)** between the input and the representation is nothing new for machine learning. **InfoMax principle** [18] argues that the goal of representation learning should be to learn a representation $Z = g(X)$ such that the MI $I(X, g(X)$ is maximized. Some recent state-of-the-art self-supervised learning methods [11,24] aim at maximizing the MI between features of different views of the input, while this objective can be treated as a lower bound of the InfoMax objective [27]. **Information bottleneck principle (IB)** [25] suggests that supervised learning should attempt to learn a representation Z being maximally expressive about the label Y while being maximally compressive about the input X, which has been recently rephrased in the context of deep learning [26]. The learning objective of IB is to minimize $L(p_\theta(z|x)) = I(Z, X) - \beta I(Z, Y)$, where model parameter θ belongs to a condition distribution and β controls the tradeoff. Following this principle, a thread of research [21,22] analyzes the training of neural networks using information planes and discusses the relationship between generalization and compression. Also IB can be directly applied to train neural networks [1,15]. Hafez-Kolahi and Kasaei [9] provides a survey about IB and its applications.

Previous works mostly draw lessons from data compression of information theory, whereas this work treats neural networks as communication channels. To verify the usefulness of this perspective, we train neural networks regularized with lower information complexity, supposing that a neural network with lower channel capacity can convey more task-relative information when it fits training data equally well as other models.

Our main contributions are as follows:

- We formally define two kinds of new complexity measures for neural networks.
- We design two regularization methods by penalizing the neural network of high channel capacity during training.

- Experiments on various settings show that our methods do improve classification performance and outperform other information-theoretic regularization methods.

2 Related Work

MacKay [19] viewed neural network learning as communication and fostered research on the capacity of a single neuron. Parameters of a neural network are treated as a message in [19] while corresponding to a communication channel in our work. Foggo and Yu [7] investigated the maximum MI $\sup_\theta I(X, Z_\theta)$, where θ is the set of parameters of a neural network, for various neural network architectures. In this work, the channel capacity of neural networks is also the maximum MI $\max_{p_X} I(X, Z)$, however, with respect to all possible input distributions.

Our work involves the calculation of MI between high dimensional random vectors, which is a notoriously hard problem. Classic techniques [8,28] proposed to estimate MI through samples are hard to scale up to dimensionality encountered in deep learning. To overcome the difficulty, recent works [1,3] develop MI estimators for DNNs with different variational bounds of MI.

In the context of supervised learning, our work is related to recently proposed information-theoretic regularization methods [1,20,23]. Szegedy et al. [23] tried to smooth the label to prevent models from assigning full probability to each training example. Similar to label smoothing, confidence penalty method of Pereyra et al. [20] proposed to regularize networks with an extra loss term, which penalizes networks for having low entropy predictive distributions. Alemi et al. [1] attempted to regularize neural networks by constraining the MI between the input and the representation.

3 Information Complexity of Neural Networks

We first introduce some concepts from information theory. We denote random vectors with capital letters such as X. All the logarithms in this paper are in base e. In this work, we use $\mathcal{AC}^n$ to denote the set of all n-dimensional continuous random vectors and $\mathcal{PD}^n$ to denote the set of all **probability density function (pdf)** of n-dimensional continuous random vectors. Beside, we use $X \sim \mathcal{N}(m, K)$ to indicate that X is a gaussian random vector with mean m and covariance matrix K. The differential entropy of the random vector X is $h(X) = -\int p(x) \log p(x) dx$, where $p(x)$ is the pdf of X. The mutual information between random vectors X and Y is $I(X, Y) = \int p(x, y) \log \frac{p(x,y)}{p(x)p(y)} dxdy$.

3.1 Information Complexity of Neural Networks

In this subsection, we give formal definitions of two version of information complexity of neural networks. In information theory, a discrete-time memoryless communication channel corresponds to a regular conditional probability mathematically, which can be used to construct a joint distribution of the input and the output. For a set $\mathcal{A}$ of all possible distributions of input, the **channel capacity** of a communication channel [5] is: $C = \max_{p_X \in \mathcal{A}} I(X, Y)$, where X is the input and Y is the output of the channel. Capacity describes the ability of the channel to transport information, which is also intuitively important to understand neural networks. Treating a neural networks as a communication channel, we need to explain how the neural network defines a regular conditional probability and what the set of possible input distributions is.

Let a n-dimensional random vector $X \in \mathcal{AC}^n$ be the input of a neural network. Let θ be the parameter of the neural network, corresponding a continuous function $f_\theta(x) : \mathbb{R}^n \to \mathbb{R}^m$. Let the m-dimensional random vector Y be the output of the neural network. In this work, we assume the output $Y(X, \theta, \varepsilon) = f_\theta(X) + \varepsilon$ is a function of the random vector X, parameter of the network θ and an extra noise ε.

Add Noises to the Output of Neural Networks. A straightforward idea making connections between a neural network and a communication channel is to define $Y = f_\theta(X)$. Because $f_\theta(x)$ is continuous, it's easy to prove that this model relates to a communication channel. In this work, we analyze neural networks with extra noise $\varepsilon \neq 0$. When the distribution of the input is absolutely continuous with respect to some convex subset of $\mathbb{R}^n$, MI between the input and the representation is infinity for some most practical deterministic neural networks and almost every choice of weight matrices [2]. To avoid the infinity of MI, we add an extra noise $\varepsilon \in \mathcal{AC}^m$ to the output of a neural network following the suggestion of [2].

Limit the Set of Possible Distributions of the Input. It's a well-known fact [5] that the channel capacity of a gaussian channel is infinite if we don't constrain the signal-to-noise rate (SNR). In this work, we follow the maximum-input-power constraint from information theory and define the allowable input pdfs as those from $\mathcal{A}_P^n = \{p(x) \mid p \in \mathcal{PD}^n, \int_{\mathbb{R}^n} x^T x p(x) dx \leq P\}$. This constraint is reasonable because the input of neural networks often takes values in intervals, e.g., $[0, 1]$.

Suppose the pdf of a fixed noise is denoted as $p_\varepsilon(\cdot)$. The joint distribution of X and Y is totally determined by the pdf of input p_X and the parameter of neural network θ, which corresponds to a conditional pdf of Y given X, $p_\theta(y|x) = p_\varepsilon(y - f_\theta(x))$. Consequently, the MI between X and Y is determined purely by p_X and θ, which can written as:

$$
\begin{aligned}
I(X, Y) &= \int_{\mathbb{R}^n \times \mathbb{R}^m} p(x, y) \log \frac{p(x, y)}{p(x)p(y)} dxdy \\
&= \int_{\mathbb{R}^n \times \mathbb{R}^m} p_\theta(y|x) p(x) \log \frac{p_\theta(y|x)}{p(y)} dxdy \\
&= \int_{\mathbb{R}^n \times \mathbb{R}^m} p_\theta(y|x) p(x) \log \frac{p_\theta(y|x)}{\int_{\mathbb{R}^n} p(x) p_\theta(y|x) dx} dxdy.
\end{aligned}
$$

Therefore we also write $MI(p_X, \theta) = I(X, Y)$ to denote MI between the input and the output. Beside a fixed noise, we restrict possible input random vectors X

to those correspond to pdfs $p_X \in \mathcal{A}_P^n$. Now we are ready to define the maximum information complexity (MIC) of neural networks.

Definition 1 (Maximum information complexity). *Given a random vector* $\varepsilon \in \mathcal{AC}^m$ *and a neural network* $f_\theta(x) : \mathbb{R}^n \to \mathbb{R}^m$*, the maximum information complexity with noise* ε *of the neural network is:*

$$MIC_\varepsilon(\theta) := \max_{p_X \in \mathcal{A}_P^n} MI(p_X, \theta).$$

Calculation of MIC requires solving an optimization problem over a function space, which makes it difficult to be used in practice. In order to overcome this difficulty, we define a similar concept called expected information complexity. Let $\mathcal{A}$ be the set of all possible pdfs of input random vectors. Assuming $\mathcal{A}$ belongs to a probability space $(\mathcal{A}, \mathcal{F}_\mathcal{A}, \mathcal{P}_\mathcal{A})$, we can define expected information complexity of neural networks in a general way:

Definition 2 (Expected information complexity). *Let a random vector* $\varepsilon \in \mathcal{AC}^m$ *and let* $(\mathcal{A}, \mathcal{F}_\mathcal{A}, \mathcal{P}_\mathcal{A})$ *be a probability space that satisfies:* (1) *the corresponding sample space* $\mathcal{A}$ *is a subset of* $\mathcal{PD}^n$ *and* (2) *the functional* $MI(\cdot, \theta) : \mathcal{A} \to [0, \infty)$ *is a random variable for all* θ. *We define the expected information complexity with noise* ε *and the probability space* $(\mathcal{A}, \mathcal{F}_\mathcal{A}, \mathcal{P}_\mathcal{A})$ *of a neural network* $f_\theta(x) : \mathbb{R}^n \to \mathbb{R}^m$ *to be:*

$$EIC_{\varepsilon, \mathcal{P}_\mathcal{A}}(\theta) := \mathbb{E}[MI(p_X, \theta)] = \int MI(p_X, \theta) d\mathcal{P}_\mathcal{A}.$$

3.2 Special Case: Single Layer Neural Networks Without Activation

In this subsection, we derive the close-form expression of MIC of a simple neural network which is just a linear function $f_\theta(x) = Wx$, where $W \in \mathbb{R}^{n \times m}$ is the weight matrix. Let X be the input whose pdf belongs to $\mathcal{A}_P^n$ and let $\varepsilon \sim \mathcal{N}(0, I_m)$ be the noise injected to the latent representation of the neural network $\hat{Y} = f_\theta(X)$. The output of the neural network is $Y = f_\theta(X) + \varepsilon$. Known as gaussian vector channel, this kind of models is well studied in the context of network information theory [6]. The next theorem gives the value of the channel capacity of a gaussian vector channel, which is also MIC of the corresponding neural network.

Theorem 1 (MIC of linear neural networks [6]**)** *Given a linear neural network* $f_\theta(x) = Wx$ *and a gaussion noise* $\varepsilon \sim \mathcal{N}(0, I_m)$. *If the rank of* W *is* d (> 0) *and the positive singular values of* W *are* $\gamma_1, \ldots, \gamma_d$ *in descenting order, the maximum information complexity is*

$$MIC_\varepsilon(W) = \frac{1}{2} \log(\lambda^k \prod_{i=1}^{k} \gamma_i^2),$$

where λ *is chosen such that* $\sum_{i=1}^d \max\{\lambda - \frac{1}{\gamma_i^2}, 0\} = P$ *(where* P *is the constant of* $\mathcal{A}_P^n$*) and* k *is the number of singular values* γ_i *that satisfies* $\lambda > \frac{1}{\gamma_i^2}$.

Proof. See the discussion in Sect. 9.1 of [6]

The MIC of linear neural networks is only related to the singular values of the weight matrix. For comparison, weight decay method [16] constrains the L2-norm of the weight matrix by introducing an extra loss $\frac{1}{2}\|W\|_F^2 = \frac{1}{2}tr(W^TW) = \frac{1}{2}\sum_{i=1}^{d}\gamma_i^2$, where $\|\cdot\|_F$ is the Frobinus norm. Yoshida and Miyato [29] proposed to constrain the spectral norm of the weight matrix by introducing an extra loss $\frac{1}{2}\|W\|_2^2 = \frac{1}{2}\gamma_1^2$, where $\|\cdot\|_2$ is the spectral norm. Note that weight decay method and spectral norm regularization show some connections to MIC of the model:

$$
\begin{aligned}
\log(\lambda^k \prod_{i=1}^{k}\gamma_i^2) &\leq \prod_{j=1}^{k}(\frac{1}{k}(P+\sum_{i=1}^{k}\frac{1}{\gamma_i^2})\gamma_j^2) - 1 \\
&\leq \prod_{j=1}^{k}(P\gamma_j^2+1) - 1 \\
&\leq (P\|W\|_F^2+1)^d - 1 \leq (Pd\|W\|_2^2+1)^d - 1.
\end{aligned}
$$

The first inequality is obtained because $\log(x) \leq x-1$ and $\lambda = \frac{1}{k}(P+\sum_{i=1}^{k}\frac{1}{\gamma_i^2})$. The second inequality holds because $\frac{1}{\gamma_i^2} - \frac{1}{\gamma_j^2} < P$ for all $1 \leq i,j \leq k$. We can see that the MIC measure is tighter than the Frobinus norm and the spectral norm of W.

3.3 Information Complexity Regularization

In this subsection, we describe how to use information complexity to regularize neural networks.

A General Learning Framework. Suppose the set of learnable parameters of a neural network is θ and the origin learning objective is to minimize a loss function $L(\theta, S)$ where S is the training dataset. Information complexity regularization methods introduce extra terms to construct a new learning objective:

$$
\min_{\theta} L(\theta, S) + \beta_e EIC_{\varepsilon,\mathcal{P}_A}(\theta) + \beta_m MIC_{\varepsilon}(\theta),
$$

where the β_e and β_m controls the strength of regularization.

A Version of EIC. At first, we show how to construct a probability space on which we can define EIC. In general, a basic idea is to parameterize the set of all possible pdfs of the input random vector and then define a prior distribution on the parameter space. We show a simple example about this strategy and use this version of EIC in our experiments. Suppose the random vector V is uniformly distributed on the n-dimensional hyperrectangle HR : $HR = \{x \in \mathbb{R}^n \mid \frac{1}{2} \leq x_i \leq 1 \text{ for all } 1 \leq i \leq n\}$. Let $G(v) = p_v : HR \to \mathcal{PD}^n$ map a vector v to the pdf of the gaussian random vector with mean 0 and covariance matrix $I_n v$. With the random vector V and the map $G(v)$, it's straightforward to construct a probability space on $\mathcal{NA} = G(HR)$, which we denote $(\mathcal{NA}, \mathcal{F}_{\mathcal{NA}}, \mathcal{P}_{\mathcal{NA}})$. In this case, the EIC of a neural network is : $EIC_{\varepsilon,\mathcal{P}_{\mathcal{NA}}}(\theta) = \mathbb{E}[MI(G(V), \theta)]$, where $G(V)$ is the pdf of the input random vector.

An Upper Bound of EIC of Neural Networks. In this work, we use a sampling method to minimize an upper bound of EIC in practice instead of minimizing the exact value of EIC. We can derive an upper bound of EIC:

$$\begin{aligned} EIC_{\varepsilon,\mathcal{P}_{\mathcal{A}}}(\theta) &= \mathbb{E}[I(X,Y)] = \mathbb{E}[h(Y) - h(Y|X)] = \mathbb{E}[h(Y)] - C \\ &\leq \mathbb{E}\left[\frac{1}{2}\log((2\pi e)^m det(K_Y))\right] - C = \mathbb{E}\left[\frac{1}{2}\log det(K_Y)\right] - C' \\ &\leq \frac{1}{2}\mathbb{E}[tr(K_Y)] - C'', \end{aligned}$$

where det means the determinant of a matrix and tr means the trace of a matrix. The first inequality holds because the maximum-entropy distribution for a given covariance is Gaussian with the same covariance [5]. The second inequality is true because $det(K_Y)$ is the product of singular values of K_Y and $tr(K_Y)$ is the sum of the singular values.

In order to minimize $\mathbb{E}[tr(K_Y)]$, we sample n pdfs $(p_X^{(1)}, \ldots, p_X^{(n)})$ of the input random vector based on $(\mathcal{A}, \mathcal{F}_{\mathcal{A}}, \mathcal{P}_{\mathcal{A}})$. Then we use each pdf $p_X^{(i)}$ to get k samples of the input $(\hat{x}_{i1}, \ldots, \hat{x}_{ik})$, which are fed into the neural network to get the samples of the output $(\hat{y}_{i1}, \ldots, \hat{y}_{ik})$. The sampled outputs are used to approximate $\mathbb{E}[tr(K_Y)]$:

$$\begin{aligned} \mathbb{E}[tr(K_Y)] &= \int \mathbb{E}_{Y\sim p_Y}\|Y - \mathbb{E}_{Y\sim p_Y}[Y]\|^2 d\mathcal{P}_{\mathcal{A}} \\ &\approx \frac{1}{kn}\sum_{i=1}^{n}\sum_{j=1}^{k}\|\hat{y}_{ij} - \frac{1}{k}\sum_{l=1}^{k}\hat{y}_{il}\|^2 \\ &\triangleq \widehat{tr}, \end{aligned}$$

where $\|\cdot\|$ means the L2-norm of a vector. It's easy to calculate the gradient of $\widehat{tr}$ with respect to model parameters.

A Surrogate of MIC of Neural Networks. We also use a sampling method to minimize a surrogate of MIC in practice. As mentioned before, the MIC of linear neural networks has an upper bound $\prod_{j=1}^{k}(\frac{1}{k}(P + \sum_{i=1}^{k}\frac{1}{\gamma_i^2})\gamma_j^2)$, which is a polynomial of singular values and the ratios between them.

Suppose the singular value decomposition of W is $U\Sigma V^T$. Let $X \sim \mathcal{N}(0, I_n)$ and let $X' = V^T X$, $X'' = \frac{X'}{\|X'\|}$. Meanwhile, we have the following equations:

$$\frac{\|Wx\|}{\|x\|} = \frac{\|U\Sigma V^T V x'\|}{\|Vx'\|} = \frac{\|U\Sigma x'\|}{\|x'\|} = \|U\Sigma x''\| = \sqrt{\sum_{i=1}^{d} \gamma_i^2 (x_i'')^2}.$$

It's straightforward to see that X'' is a random vector having uniform distribution on $\{x \in \mathbb{R}^n \mid \|x\| = 1\}$. Given $X \sim \mathcal{N}(0, I_n)$, we minimize $\mathbb{E}\left[\frac{\|Wx\|}{\|x\|}\right]$ to constrain the singular values and minimize $\mathbb{V}\left[\frac{\|Wx\|}{\|x\|}\right]$, where $\mathbb{V}[\cdot]$ means the variance, to limit the diversity of singular values.

Furthermore, we hypothesize that minimizing the surrogate of MIC of general neural networks f_θ:

$$MICS = \mathbb{E}\left[\frac{\|f_\theta(x)\|}{\|x\|}\right] + \mathbb{V}\left[\frac{\|f_\theta(x)\|}{\|x\|}\right],$$

is an effective way to constrain the MIC. The sampling method to estimate $MICS$ is straightforward and we minimize the estimator $\widehat{MICS}$ in our experiments.

Discussion. Note that we don't need to access the training data to calculate $\widehat{tr}$ and $\widehat{MICS}$. It's worth mentioning that our method is not limited to constrain the information complexity of the whole network. By viewing each block (e.g. first n layers of a neural network network) as a tiny neural network, we can impose multiple information complexity regularizer terms for more flexibility.

4 Experiments

In this section, we evaluate our methods on various image classification datasets: MNIST, Kuzushiji-MNIST, SVHN and CIFAR10[1]. All models are implemented using PyTorch and trained on a single NVIDIA GeForce RTX 2080TI GPU.

4.1 Benchmark Experiments

We first experiment our regularization methods on various image classification datasets: MNIST, Kuzushiji-MNIST, SVHN, and CIFAR-10.

[1] The code is available at https://github.com/IanyePKU/IC-Regularization-methods.

Table 1. Experimental results on benchmark datasets. The average and standard deviation of the accuracy of each method over 3 trials. We compare "baseline", "+MIC" and "+EIC" and the best one is shown in **boldface**. The best result for each dataset is shown with **underline**.

Dataset	Model & Setup	Baseline	+MIC	+EIC
MNIST	MLP	98.56%(0.03)	**98.87%(0.03)**	98.86%(0.05)
MNIST	MLP +WD	98.69%(0.02)	**98.78%(0.05)**	**98.78%(0.03)**
Kuzushiji	MLP	93.53%(0.08)	93.94%(0.13)	**94.16%(0.11)**
Kuzushiji	MLP +WD	93.40%(0.09)	93.74%(0.07)	**93.85%(0.22)**
SVHN	ResNet20	95.45%(0.12)	95.59%(0.09)	**95.60%(0.04)**
SVHN	ResNet20 +WD	95.73%(0.09)	95.89%(0.09)	**95.93%(0.05)**
CIFAR10	ResNet44	85.76%(0.23)	86.11%(0.17)	**86.56%(0.33)**
CIFAR10	ResNet44 +WD	87.91%(0.08)	87.95%(0.10)	**88.10%(0.17)**

Settings. For MNIST and Kuzushiji-MNIST, we train three-layer MLPs with fully connected layers of the form 784–1024–1024–10 and the ReLU activation function. The batchsize is set as 100. For MNIST and Kuzushiji-MNIST, all models are trained using ADAM optimizer [14] with an initial learning rate 0.001 for 200 epochs and we decay the learning rate by a factor of 0.97 every 2 epochs. We train ResNet-20 from [10] for SVHN and ResNet-44 for CIFAR10. The batchsize is set as 128. ResNets are trained using Nesterov's accelerated gradient descent [4] with momentum 0.9 for 160 epochs. For SVHN and CIFAR10, we set the initial learning rate as 0.1 and decay the learning rate by a factor of 0.1 once the half and the three quarters of the training process have passed. For all datasets, we also report results by adding weight decay (WD).

Our methods include MIC regularization method (train networks with an extra loss $\widehat{MICS}$) and EIC regularization method (train networks with an extra loss $\ddot{tr}$). We impose constraints on both the IC of whole network and the IC of each layer and assume that all noises obey the gaussian distribution. In all experiments, we perform the hyper-parameter search for β_e and β_m with candidates from $\{0.01, 0.02, 0.05, 0.1, 0.2, 0.5\}$. For EIC method, we use the probability space $(\mathcal{NA}, \mathcal{F}_{\mathcal{NA}}, \mathcal{P}_{\mathcal{NA}})$ to estimate $\widehat{tr}$, implying that we expect fewer information is preserved in the outputs of the neural network when the inputs are from a gaussian distribution.

Results. The test error rate obtained by each method is summarized in Table 1. The best result for each dataset is always achieved by the models trained with IC regularization methods. For SVHN and CIFAR10, combining our methods with weight decay has complementary effects. Introducing an extra IC regularization term always improves performance, which justify the usefulness of our methods.

As shown in Fig. 1, training curves of models trained with our methods are usually serrated, which means that our models frequently escape from the regions with low training loss. We think that this feature of our methods helps models leave local minimum and achieve better generalization performance. The phenomena is potentially related to a recent observation [13] that zero training loss is not the final goal of the training process.

4.2 Comparison Experiment with Other Regularizaion Methods

In order to verify the compatibility between our method with other regularization methods and compare our method with them, we train MLPs on MNIST using various combinations of regularizers. All settings of hyperparameters are same as the previous benchmark experiments. Other regularization methods used for comparison include:

- Weight Decay: Add an extra loss to constrain the L2-norm of parameters of the neural network. We set the regularization factor $\beta_{L2} = 10^{-4}$.

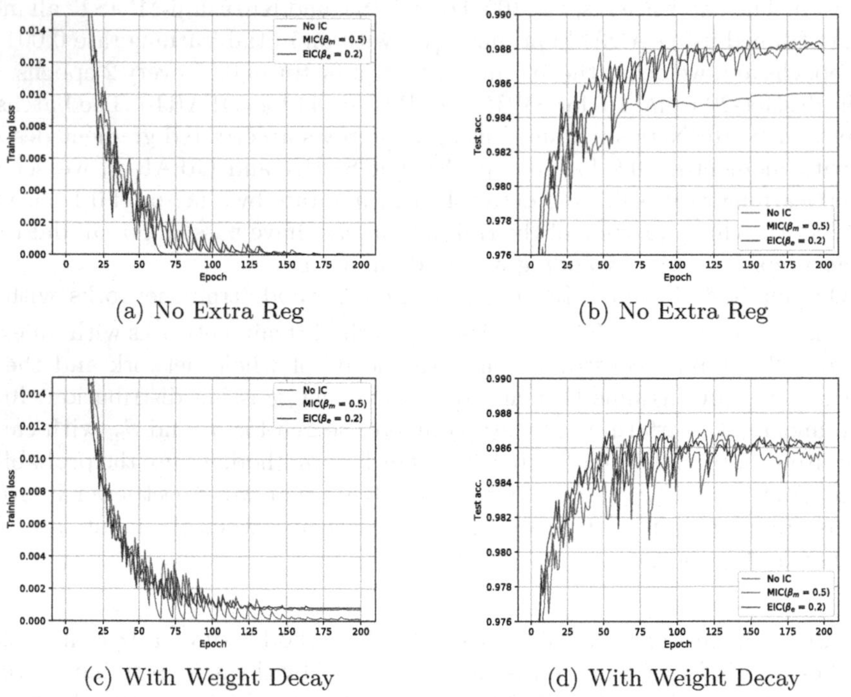

(a) No Extra Reg

(b) No Extra Reg

(c) With Weight Decay

(d) With Weight Decay

Fig. 1. Training curves of MLPs on MNIST. The top two figures show the training curves of MLPs using only our regularization terms. The bottom two figures show the training curves of MLPs using our regularization terms and weight decay.

- Confidence Penalty (CP): Penalize low entropy output distributions. We search for the best regularization factor β_{CP} from $\{0.05, 0.1, 0.2, 0.3, 0.4, 0.5\}$ as [20].
- Label Smoothing (LS): Minimize the KL divergence between uniform distribution and the network's predicted distribution.We search for the best regularization factor β_{LS} from $\{0.1, 0.3, 0.5, 1.0, 2.0, 4.0, 8.0\}$ as [20].
- Variational Information Bottleneck (VIB): Train neural networks using variational information bottleneck principle and minimize an upper bound of MI between the input of the network and the corresponding representation. We search for the best regularization factor β_{VIB} from $\{10^{-2}, 10^{-3}, 10^{-4}, 10^{-5}\}$, which is a reasonable set according to [1].

Result. The test accuracy obtained by each method is summarized in Table 2. Setup of using only MIC (average of accuracy is 98.87%, see Table 1) outperforms setups of combining other regularization terms (first two column of results from Table 2). Combining IC regularization terms further improves the performance and the model trained using CP and MIC achieves the best performance (average of accuracy is 98.97%). This experiment shows that introducing an information complexity term boosts the generalization performance of trained neural networks and is compatible with other regularization methods.

Table 2. Experimental results on MNIST. The average and standard deviation of the accuracy of each method over 3 trials. For each regularization method, we compare "No other reg", "+WD", "+MIC" and "+EIC" and the best one is shown in **boldface**.

Method	No other reg	+WD	+MIC	+EIC
CP	98.65%(0.02)	98.86%(0.03)	**98.97%(0.02)**	98.95%(0.04)
LS	98.79%(0.07)	98.85%(0.05)	**98.93%(0.05)**	**98.93%(0.01)**
VIB	98.66%(0.04)	98.80%(0.05)	**98.88%(0.01)**	98.81%(0.01)

5 Conclusion

In this paper, we have defined two kinds of new complexity measures for neural networks by linking each neural network to a communication channel. We showed a connection between the MIC of a single layer linear neural network and the L2-norm of its weight matrix. We also designed two new regularization methods using EIC and MIC. We conducted experiments on image classification datasets and showed the usefulness of our new regularization terms empirically.

References

1. Alemi, A.A., Fischer, I., Dillon, J.V., Murphy, K.: Deep variational information bottleneck. arXiv preprint arXiv:1612.00410 (2016)

2. Amjad, R.A., Geiger, B.C.: Learning representations for neural network-based classification using the information bottleneck principle. IEEE Trans. Pattern Anal. Mach. Intell. **42**(9), 2225–2239 (2019)
3. Belghazi, M.I., et al.: Mutual information neural estimation. In: International Conference on Machine Learning, pp. 531–540. PMLR (2018)
4. Bengio, Y., Boulanger-Lewandowski, N., Pascanu, R.: Advances in optimizing recurrent networks. In: 2013 IEEE International Conference on Acoustics, Speech and Signal Processing, pp. 8624–8628. IEEE (2013)
5. Cover, T.M.: Elements of Information Theory. John Wiley & Sons (1999)
6. El Gamal, A., Kim, Y.H.: Network Information Theory. Cambridge University Press (2011)
7. Foggo, B., Yu, N.: On the maximum mutual information capacity of neural architectures. arXiv preprint arXiv:2006.06037 (2020)
8. Gao, S., Ver Steeg, G., Galstyan, A.: Efficient estimation of mutual information for strongly dependent variables. In: Artificial Intelligence and Statistics, pp. 277–286. PMLR (2015)
9. Hafez-Kolahi, H., Kasaei, S.: Information bottleneck and its applications in deep learning. arXiv preprint arXiv:1904.03743 (2019)
10. He, K., Zhang, X., Ren, S., Sun, J.: Identity mappings in deep residual networks. In: Leibe, B., Matas, J., Sebe, N., Welling, M. (eds.) ECCV 2016. LNCS, vol. 9908, pp. 630–645. Springer, Cham (2016). https://doi.org/10.1007/978-3-319-46493-0_38
11. Henaff, O.: Data-efficient image recognition with contrastive predictive coding. In: International Conference on Machine Learning, pp. 4182–4192. PMLR (2020)
12. Hinton, G.E., van Camp, D.: Keeping the neural networks simple by minimizing the description length of the weights. In: Proceedings of the Sixth Annual Conference on Computational Learning Theory, pp. 5–13 (1993)
13. Ishida, T., Yamane, I., Sakai, T., Niu, G., Sugiyama, M.: Do we need zero training loss after achieving zero training error? arXiv preprint arXiv:2002.08709 (2020)
14. Kingma, D.P., Ba, J.: Adam: a method for stochastic optimization. In: International Conference on Learning Representations (2015)
15. Kolchinsky, A., Tracey, B.D., Wolpert, D.H.: Nonlinear information bottleneck. Entropy **21**(12), 1181 (2019)
16. Krogh, A., Hertz, J.A.: A simple weight decay can improve generalization. In: Advances in Neural Information Processing Systems, pp. 950–957 (1992)
17. LeCun, Y., et al.: Backpropagation applied to handwritten zip code recognition. Neural Comput. **1**(4), 541–551 (1989)
18. Linsker, R.: Self-organization in a perceptual network. Computer **21**(3), 105–117 (1988)
19. MacKay, D.J.: Information Theory, Inference and Learning Algorithms. Cambridge University Press (2003)
20. Pereyra, G., Tucker, G., Chorowski, J., Kaiser, Ł., Hinton, G.: Regularizing neural networks by penalizing confident output distributions. In: International Conference on Learning Representations Workshop (2017)
21. Saxe, A.M., et al.: On the information bottleneck theory of deep learning. J. Statist. Mech. Theor. Exp. **2019**(12), 124020 (2019)
22. Shwartz-Ziv, R., Tishby, N.: Opening the black box of deep neural networks via information. arXiv preprint arXiv:1703.00810 (2017)
23. Szegedy, C., Vanhoucke, V., Ioffe, S., Shlens, J., Wojna, Z.: Rethinking the inception architecture for computer vision. In: Proceedings of the IEEE Conference on Computer Vision and Pattern Recognition, pp. 2818–2826 (2016)

24. Tian, Y., Krishnan, D., Isola, P.: Contrastive multiview coding. arXiv preprint arXiv:1906.05849 (2019)
25. Tishby, N., Pereira, F.C., Bialek, W.: The information bottleneck method. In: Proceedings of the 37-th Annual Allerton Conference on Communication, Control and Computing, pp. 368–377 (1999)
26. Tishby, N., Zaslavsky, N.: Deep learning and the information bottleneck principle. In: 2015 IEEE Information Theory Workshop (ITW), pp. 1–5. IEEE (2015)
27. Tschannen, M., Djolonga, J., Rubenstein, P.K., Gelly, S., Lucic, M.: On mutual information maximization for representation learning. In: International Conference on Learning Representations (2020)
28. Walters-Williams, J., Li, Y.: Estimation of mutual information: a survey. In: Wen, P., Li, Y., Polkowski, L., Yao, Y., Tsumoto, S., Wang, G. (eds.) RSKT 2009. LNCS (LNAI), vol. 5589, pp. 389–396. Springer, Heidelberg (2009). https://doi.org/10.1007/978-3-642-02962-2_49
29. Yoshida, Y., Miyato, T.: Spectral norm regularization for improving the generalizability of deep learning. arXiv preprint arXiv:1705.10941 (2017)

RIAP: A Method for Effective Receptive Field Rectification

Zhenzhen Li, Kin-Wang Poon, and Xuan Yang(✉)

College of Computer Science and Software Engineering, Shenzhen University, Shenzhen, China
yangxuan@szu.edu.cn

Abstract. Receptive field (RF) plays a vital role in deep convolutional networks. Padding schemes are related to the RF closely. In this paper, we analyze the information attenuation caused by zero-padding during the convolution operations in CNNs theoretically. Moreover, the weight bias accumulated by zero-padding along the forward propagation is also analyzed. We find that in terms of each pixel's contribution to its corresponding position in output, the boundary pixels contribute less information than the pixels closer to the central area in an image. To address this issue, we propose a method for effective RF rectification (RIAP) to transmit information of the boundary pixels via augmenting path. Experimental results of glomerular microscopic image segmentation show that by using RIAP, information of all pixels can be effectively propagated forward after convolutions are performed repeatedly, and RIAP outperforms traditional padding schemes when objects locate near image boundaries.

Keywords: Convolutional neural network · Padding scheme · Segmentation

1 Introduction

In CNNs, many studies focus on various aspects of CNNs, such as optimization algorithms [12], initialization [4,7], normalization [9,18,19], shortcut connection [6,8], and receptive field [17]. The receptive field (RF) plays an essential role in network performance. Zeiler et al. [21] find that the shallower network has a smaller RF, and only local features can be learned. The network deeper, the RF larger, and the global features become easier to learn. To extract more context information, the RF is required to be enlarged successively through the convolution operations to eliminate ambiguity and improve the performance of CNNs.

Generally, there are two basic ways to enlarge the RF of CNN, i.e., increasing the filter size and increasing the depth [11]. However, filters with large sizes are not popularly used due to too many parameters. Since the RF is related to the convolution operation firmly, many approaches increase the RF by dilated

Supported by the National Natural Science Foundation of China (61871269).

I. Farkaš et al. (Eds.): ICANN 2021, LNCS 12894, pp. 266–278, 2021.
https://doi.org/10.1007/978-3-030-86380-7_22

convolution or stacking multi convolutions [20] to increase the RF. Zhou *et al.* propose multi-receptive field [23] to increase RF area by sub-networks. HAN *et al.* [5] combine a 1-D convolutional layer with dilated convolutional to enlarge the RF. Chao *et al.* [1] control the RF size with dilated temporal convolutions to align each anchor's RF with its temporal span for temporal object detection. Dadashzadeh *et al.* [2] propose the pyramid dilated convolution (PDC) to combine different scales of contextual information for semantic segmentation.

However, little attention has been paid to the analysis of the influence of padding schemes in the RF. In this paper, we find that the zero-padding results in a non-uniform RF that boundary pixels of the image contribute less information to the output feature maps than pixels located on the inner area of images. The pixels near the boundaries of the image are always involved in fewer convolution operations than those in the inner area, causing the attenuation of information. In a stack of convolutional layers, this effect is accumulated layer by layer and results in that the central pixels propagated their information through layers without attenuation, while information of the boundary pixels is weakened.

In this paper, we analyze the information attenuation caused by zero-padding and its gradual accumulation effect along with the forward propagation in theory. Next, we point out two important phenomena: 1) In terms of each pixel's contribution to corresponding positions in output, the boundary pixels contribute less than the pixels close to the central area. 2) For a convolution operation centered at a boundary pixel, the contribution center deviates to other positions instead of the position of the boundary pixel, which is not consistent with the idea of convolution. This phenomenon is called contribution deviation in this paper. Through our method, all pixels' information can be effectively propagated forward instead of contributing non-uniformly as in traditional networks. To address this issue, we propose a method to retransmit information of boundary pixels via augmenting path (RIAP). We evaluate our method on glomerular microscopic segmentation datasets with U-Net [16] and U-Net_SVC (adopting shape variant context (SVC) [3] module into U-Net). Experimental results show that the segmentation accuracy of network with RIAP is improved when objects locate near image boundaries.

Our main contributions are: 1) Analyzing the influence of the zero-padding on the RF. We find the pixel near the image boundaries contributes less information to the outputs at their corresponding positions than the pixel near the image center. It results in information attenuation and contribution deviation of the boundary pixels along with the forward propagation. 2) Proposing a method to retransmit information of boundary pixels via augmenting path (RIAP), which makes the impact of the RF uniform. Our method is conducive to extract features from the area near the image boundaries without information biases. 3) Proving the validity of RIAP in a mathematical way. We find that the derivative of each pixel in the output w.r.t. its location-corresponding pixel in the input is constant using RIAP. It implies that all pixels in RF contribute equally to output feature maps and the meanwhile, the extremum position of its output is the same as the given pixel. Hence, the central pixel contributes the most to the output, which is consistent with the idea of convolution.

2 Related Work

U-Net is a kind of fully convolution network (FCN) [14]. U-Net is composed of nine stages with different spatial resolutions: in the first/last 4 stages, the feature maps are downsampled/upsampled with stride 2 and the feature channels are doubled/halved. Each stage is composed of two 3×3 convolutions. Before each of the last four stages, there is a concatenation from the size corresponding feature maps from the first four stages.

Receptive field (RF) is first introduced by Simonyan *et al.* [17]. It is a local region on the output of the previous layer to that a neuron is connected. The theoretical size of RF can be calculated in an arithmetical way [13]. Jacobsen *et al.* [10] expressed RF in CNNs as a weighted sum over a fixed basis. However, Zhou *et al.* [22] pointed out that the actual size of the RF in a CNN is much smaller than the theoretical size, especially on high-level layers.

Effective Receptive field (ERF). Luo *et al.* [15] studied RF in CNNs, point out that not all pixels in RF contribute equally to output feature maps, and define the notation of ERF. They denote the area of the image that influences the response of a layer. However, Luo's work is based on a non-padding way. As we know, padding schemes are commonly used in CNNs that can preserve the spatial size of the image. They affect the RF significantly, especially for small images.

3 Analysis

In this section, we analyze the information attenuation and contribution deviation of boundary pixels along the forward propagation caused by the zero-padding. For simplicity, we analyze on 1-D convolution because a n-D convolution can be factorized into multiple 1-D convolutions and we remove all the non-linear functions and the bias. The initial values of all convolutions are set as one, to eliminate the influences of instability caused by random initialization.

3.1 Information Attenuation Effect

In practice, convolution operation decreases the spatial size of the feature maps. Hence, zero-padding is commonly used to make the input and output the same size. An example is demonstrated in Fig. 1. Image information is transmitted through 4 layers with a 3×3 convolution. Note that the Mixed pixel is generated by the convolution operation with Zero Pixel, which attenuates information of input image compared with Pure Pixel. Especially, it is easier to generate Mixed Pixel for the boundary pixels compared with inner pixels. That implies these boundary pixels contribute less information to the outputs at their positions, which results in information attenuation. Because of the zero-padding of each layer, boundary pixels convey more meaningless information from zero-padding pixels than the inner pixels. That means the convolution results at image boundaries lose more original image information than that at the inner image area.

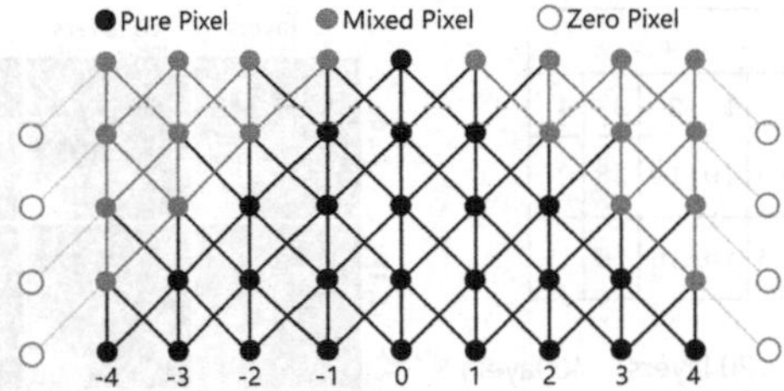

Fig. 1. Illustration of information attenuation and accumulation effect in convolution operations with zero-padding. The bottom layer denotes the input image. Points denote pixels of the image. The Pure Pixel, the Mixed Pixel, and the Zero Pixel denote the pixel not affected by zero-padding, affected by zero-padding, and zero-padding pixel, respectively.

Moreover, more mixed pixels are produced as the depth of the network increases, and more pure pixels are replaced by the mixed pixels. That is, in a stack of convolutional layers, the information attenuation effect is accumulated and gradually influences the output at the inner area of images.

Denote $x^{[l]}(r)$ as the output of the lth layer at position r. The input layer is the 0th layer, and $x^{[0]}(r)$ is the original input information of the pixel at r. $r = 0$ is the pixel located in the central area of an image. The larger r is, the far away it is from the center of an image. The partial derivative $\frac{\partial x^{[l]}(r)}{\partial x^{[0]}(r)}$ measures the contribution of $x^{[0]}(r)$ to $x^{[l]}(r)$. It is needed to emphasize that the output and the input are with the same position in above derivation. Furthermore, $\frac{\partial x^{[l]}(r)}{\partial x^{[0]}(r-1)}$ measures the contribution from the adjacent pixel $r-1$, which is close to the inner area of the image, to the output $x^{[l]}(r)$. An example of information attenuation effect in Fig. 1 is provided in Fig. 2(a), where $r = 0$ is the inner pixel and $r = 4$ is the boundary pixel. Here, $x^{[0]}(r) = 1$ for all input pixels. Figure 2(a) shows values of $\frac{\partial x^{[4]}(r)}{\partial x^{[0]}(r)}$ and $\frac{\partial x^{[4]}(r)}{\partial x^{[0]}(r-1)}$ with different position r. Noted that $\frac{\partial x^{[4]}(r)}{\partial x^{[0]}(r)}|_{r=4} < \frac{\partial x^{[4]}(r)}{\partial x^{[0]}(r)}|_{r=3} < \frac{\partial x^{[4]}(r)}{\partial x^{[0]}(r)}|_{r=2}$, which implies that the boundary pixel contributes less information to the output at its corresponding position compared with that of the inner pixel. The farther away from the central area the pixel is, the more obvious the phenomenon is. Moreover, $\frac{\partial x^{[4]}(r)}{\partial x^{[0]}(r-1)}|_{r=4} > \frac{\partial x^{[4]}(r)}{\partial x^{[0]}(r)}|_{r=4}$, that means the pixel $r-1$ contributes more information to the output at r compared with the pixel r. It demonstrates that the phenomenon of contribution deviation, that is, the central pixel in a convolution operation contributes less information than that of pixel away from the center.

Furthermore, the influence of different network depths on RF is demonstrated in Fig. 2(a). Four networks with depth 5, 10, 20, and 40 are employed. The derivation of outputs in RF for the four networks, $\frac{\partial x^{[l]}(r)}{\partial x^{[0]}(r)}$, are computed and illustrated in Fig. 2(a). The brighter the pixel is, the larger the value is. Noted the sizes of theoretical RF in the four networks are 11, 21, 41 and 81, which also

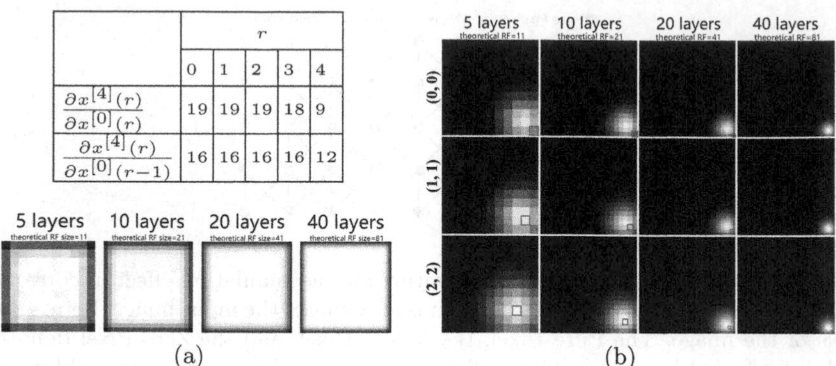

	r				
	0	1	2	3	4
$\frac{\partial x^{[4]}(r)}{\partial x^{[0]}(r)}$	19	19	19	18	9
$\frac{\partial x^{[4]}(r)}{\partial x^{[0]}(r-1)}$	16	16	16	16	12

Fig. 2. (a) Demonstration of the information attenuation effect. (b) Contributions of the given location (red rectangle) on the input to the RF on the output. Demonstration of contribution deviation for pixels located at three locations.

are the image sizes, when a 3×3 convolutional kernel is used, respectively. They are different from each other due to different network depth. It can be seen that the pixels near the boundary of the RF contribute less information to the output at their corresponding positions compared with pixels in the inner area of the RF. As the network deepens, this phenomenon is more obvious. That implies the pixels near the boundary of the RF produce an information attenuation accumulation effect. Moreover, the information attenuation accumulation effect is with a tendency to increase outward as the network deepens. However, the ratio of the influence area of the information attenuation effect to the size of the theoretical RF is getting smaller and smaller as the network deepens, which demonstrates one of the advantages of large RF.

3.2 Contribution Deviation

From Fig. 2(a), it can be seen that $\frac{\partial x^{[4]}(r)}{\partial x^{[0]}(r)}|_{r=4} < \frac{\partial x^{[4]}(r)}{\partial x^{[0]}(r-1)}|_{r=4}$. It implies the pixel at $r = 4$ contributes less information to the output $x^{[4]}(4)$ than the pixel at $r = 3$. That means, for the boundary pixel $r = 4$, the center of its contribution area deviates to the other location ($r = 3$). It is inconsistent with the idea of CNNs, where the pixel located in the center of RF should contribute the most. Similar to Fig. 2(a), we employ four networks of different depths (5, 10, 20, 40) to illustrate contribution deviation. Figure 2(b) shows the contribution from the given location (red rectangle) on the input to the output. Here, the experiment for three locations ((0,0), (1,1), (2,2)) are conducted with four networks of different depths (5, 10, 20, 40). The brightness of a pixel in Fig. 2(b) denotes its contribution (brighter is larger). It can be seen that when the network depth is given, the contribution of $(0, 0)$ is shifted farther than that of $(1, 1)$ and $(2, 2)$. Note that this shortage becomes serious when the network goes deeper, i.e., the shift of contribution being larger.

4 Method

4.1 Augmenting Path

In order to minimize information attenuation during the multi-layer convolution process, we adjust the way of padding in each layer, so that information of the boundary pixels is transmitted to the padding area of the next layer until it reaches the output layer.

The key to our method is to propagate the boundary information through an augmenting path. As shown in Fig. 3, the number of layers in a CNN is $l+1$. In $(2n+1)\times(2n+1)$ convolution, our RIAP pads zeros in the following way: $2n$ zeros marked by grey circles are padded in one side of the input layer, the 0th layer, and n augmented pixels, marked by the orange circles, are generated by convolution in the 1st layer. Next, $2n$ zeros are padded and followed the augmented pixel in the 1st layer. Corresponding, $2n$ augmented pixels are generated in the 2nd layer. Next, $2n$ zeros are padded and followed the $2n$ augmented pixels in the 2nd layer. Then, $3n$ augmented pixels are generated in the $3rd$ layer. Next, $2n$ zeros are padded and followed the $3n$ augmented pixels in the $3rd$ layer, and so on, until $\lfloor\frac{l}{2}\rfloor \times n$ augmented pixels are padded in the $\lfloor\frac{l}{2}\rfloor^{th}$ layer. Especially, when l is even, $\frac{l}{2}n$ augmented pixels are padded in the $\frac{l}{2}^{th}$ layer. When l is odd, $(\lfloor\frac{l}{2}\rfloor)n$ augmented pixels are padded in the $\lfloor\frac{l}{2}\rfloor^{th}$ layer and the $\lfloor\frac{l}{2}\rfloor+1^{th}$ layer, respectively. Since enough padding data is provided in the $\frac{l}{2}^{th}$ layer, in the following layers, traditional convolutions without padding new data are performed to produce the final output, which is same to the input in size. Noted that input boundary information is propagated along a path marked by orange, which is called an augmenting path.

Furthermore, for the pooling layers, the generated feature maps surrounded by augmented pixels provide enough supplement data, the pooling operation is performed in a usual way. Next, in the following convolutional layers, traditional convolutions are performed using padded featured maps, and a similar padding process is performed until the padding is adequate. To estimate an optimal number of padding data, a greedy algorithm is performed to supply enough padding data. For the dilated convolutions, a similar idea can be used.

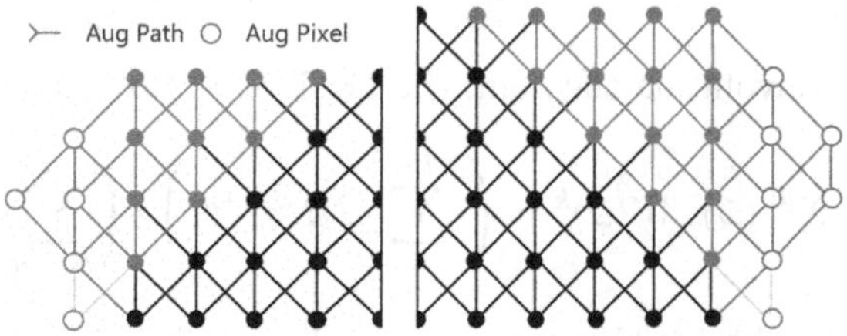

Fig. 3. Information propagation using RIAP for networks with even (left) and odd (right) layers respectively.

Note that the augmented pixel is only a padding pixel, not a neuron, and no additional neuron is needed in our approach. In fact, the augmented pixel is used to propagate the information of pixels located on boundaries to the subsequent layers, and no additional network architecture is needed.

4.2 Validity Proof

In this section, we provide the formal expression of the output for each layer in a CNN. To simplify the analysis, we focus exclusively on the 1D convolution. Here, a k layers CNN with 1-D feature map is considered, where the size of the convolution kernel in each layer is $(2n+1) \times (2n+1)$.

Define the weights of the convolution kernel is $w(t)$, then $w(t) = \begin{cases} 1, & t \in [-n,n] \\ 0, & t \notin [-n,n]. \end{cases}$ Suppose $I(r)$ is the input data, the input data in the 0th layer is,

$$x^{[0]}(r) = \begin{cases} I(r), & r \in [-kn, kn] \\ 0, & r \notin [-kn, kn]. \end{cases} \tag{1}$$

where $[-kn, kn]$ is the range of a theoretical RF in the kth layer of the CNN. The output of the lth layer is $x^{[l]} = x^{[0]} * \overbrace{w * \cdots * w}^{l}$. By introducing the augmenting path, and letting the convolution results be 0 when they are outside the region of augmented pixels, then

$$x^{[l]}(r) = \sum_{t=-(kn+l)}^{kn+l} x^{[l-1]}(r-t) \cdot w(t) = \sum_{t=-\infty}^{+\infty} x^{[l-1]}(r-t) \cdot w(t). \tag{2}$$

The discrete Fourier transform (DFT) is employed to represent $w(t)$ and $x^{[0]}(t)$ in the frequency space as,

$$\mathcal{F}(w(t)) = W(\omega) = \sum_{t=-\infty}^{+\infty} w(t) e^{-j\omega t} = \sum_{t=-n}^{n} e^{-j\omega t}. \tag{3}$$

$$\mathcal{F}(x^{[0]}(t)) = X^{[0]}(\omega) = \sum_{t=-\infty}^{+\infty} x^{[0]}(t) e^{-j\omega t} = \sum_{t=-kn}^{kn} I(t) e^{-j\omega t}. \tag{4}$$

By using the convolution theorem, the DFT of $x^{[k]}$ is

$$\mathcal{F}(x^{[k]}) = X^{[0]}(\omega) \cdot W(\omega)^k = \left(\sum_{t=-kn}^{kn} I(t) e^{-j\omega t} \right) \cdot \left(\sum_{t=-n}^{n} e^{-j\omega t} \right)^k. \tag{5}$$

Next, $x^{[k]}(r)$ can be obtained by using inverse discrete Fourier transform (IDFT),

$$x^{[k]}(r) = \frac{1}{2\pi} \int_{-\pi}^{\pi} \left(\sum_{t=-kn}^{kn} I(t) e^{-j\omega t} \right) \cdot \left(\sum_{t=-n}^{n} e^{-j\omega t} \right)^k e^{j\omega r} d\omega. \tag{6}$$

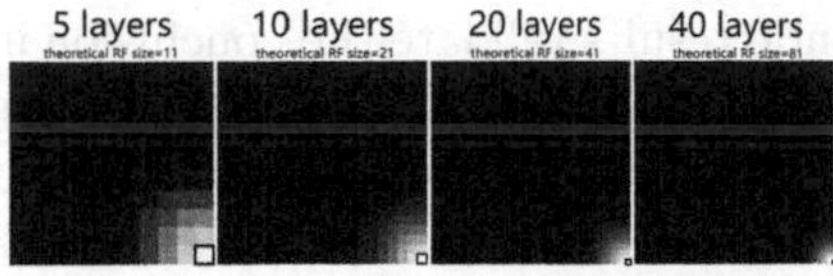

Fig. 4. Elimination of contribution deviation in the RF using RIAP.

$$\frac{\partial x^{[k]}(r)}{\partial x^{[0]}(r)} = \frac{1}{2\pi}\int_{-\pi}^{\pi} e^{-j\omega r} \cdot \left(\sum_{t=-n}^{n} e^{-j\omega t}\right)^{k} e^{j\omega r} d\omega = \frac{1}{2\pi}\int_{-\pi}^{\pi} \left(\sum_{t=-n}^{n} e^{-j\omega t}\right)^{k} d\omega. \tag{7}$$

It can be seen that $\frac{\partial x^{[k]}(r)}{\partial x^{[0]}(r)}$ is not related to r, which implies each input pixel contribute equally to the output of the kth layer in CNNs by using our RIAP.

Furthermore, for a given r_0,

$$\frac{\partial x^{[k]}(r_0)}{\partial x^{[k]}(r)} = \frac{1}{2\pi}\int_{-\pi}^{\pi} \left(\sum_{t=-kn}^{kn} e^{-j\omega t}\right)^{k} e^{j\omega(r_0 - r)} d\omega. \tag{8}$$

To estimate the extremum of $\frac{\partial x^{[k]}(r_0)}{\partial x^{[k]}(r)}$, the derivation of $\frac{\partial x^{[k]}(r_0)}{\partial x^{[k]}(r)}$ is calculated as

$$\frac{\partial \frac{\partial x^{[k]}(r_0)}{\partial x^{[k]}(r)}}{\partial r} = -\frac{1}{2\pi}\int_{-\pi}^{\pi} j\omega \left(\sum_{t=-kn}^{kn} e^{-j\omega t}\right)^{k} e^{j\omega(r_0 - r)} d\omega. \tag{9}$$

Considering the arbitrariness of k, only when the integrand is an odd function, $\frac{\partial x^{[k]}(r_0)}{\partial x^{[k]}(r)} = 0$. That is, $r = r_0$. It implies that the pixel contributing the most in the RF is itself by using our RIAP, which solves the contribution deviation issue in traditional CNNs.

5 Experiments

5.1 Eliminations of Information Attenuation and Contribution Deviation

In this experiment, four CNNs with 5, 10, 20, and 40 layers are employed. In each layer of a CNN, a single feature map is generated by using a 3×3 convolutional with weights 1. All input values are random noise with a uniform distribution in $[0, 1]$, and the size of the input is equal to that of RF $(2k+1) \times (2k+1)$ in the output layer, where k is the number of layers. Here, the pooling operation and the activate function ReLu are not used to focus on comparing the performance of RIAP in the elimination of information attenuation effect.

By using RIAP, the derivation of output w.r.t. the original input, $\frac{\partial x^{[l]}(r)}{\partial x^{[0]}(r)}$, are calculated. Values $\frac{\partial x^{[l]}(r)}{\partial x^{[0]}(r)}$ using our RIAP are same to each other by using

RIAP. These experimental results validate the conclusion in Eq. (7), that is, each pixel in the RF contributes equally to the output by using RIAP. That implies the pixels near the boundary of the RF contribute equally to the output using RIAP instead of unequally distribution using zero-padding.

Furthermore, $\frac{\partial x^{[l]}(r_0)}{\partial x^{[0]}(r)}$ is calculated for four networks respectively, which denotes the contribution of all inputs to the output at given a position r_0. Values of the derivation are illustrated in Fig. 4. It can be seen that the impact on the RF is centered at r_0 instead of being shifted to other positions as shown in Fig. 2(b).

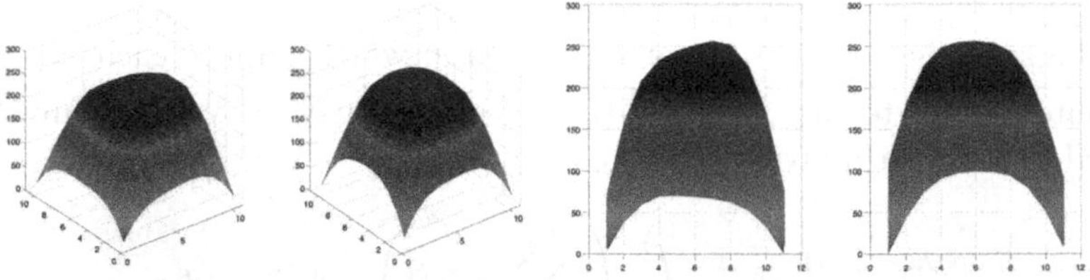

Fig. 5. Comparison of outputs of CNNs using zero-padding and using RIAP, respectively. The two sub-figures on the left show two outputs using zero-padding (left) and using RIAP (right). The two sub-figures on the right show these outputs projected onto the x-z plane.

5.2 Information Preservation

The characteristics of RIAP in preserving information of all inputs in the RF are validated in this experiment. We design a model to validate it in an unsupervised manner. We are considering a CNN with k layers all using 3×3 convolution with weights 1. Here, non-linear functions and biases are not used in the CNN. The input images are the same as the ones in Sect. 5.1. We set the ground truth as an image with all pixel intensities 0 except the central pixel intensity 1. Randomly generated images are used to train the network, and the mean square error (MSE) is used to be the loss function.

The reason why such a model is designed is explained as follows: it is supposed the mathematical operations of all convolutions on each pixel is fair; it is impossible to generate an output with significant value at the center of the output image due to the uniformly distributed noise input. For a uniformly distributed input, the network output is expected to be distributed uniformly due to the fairness of the convolution operations. This characteristic is called information preservation in this paper. Based on this assumption, the model we designed is theoretically unlearnable; that is, the loss function cannot converge. However, by using the traditional zero padding, due to the approximate Gaussian distributed EFRs, the information of boundary pixels is attenuated generally, and the network is converged and generates an output similar to a Gaussian function. Figure 5 shows outputs of networks with $k = 5$ layers using zero-padding and RIAP, respectively. It is noted that by using RIAP, the output is more similar to the input, an uniformly distributed noise image, than the one using zero-padding. Especially, the boundary parts of the output using RIAP rise more quickly than using zero-padding. That implies the input information is distorted by zero-padding, while it is preserved better by using RIAP.

5.3 Segmentation of Glomerular Microscopic Images

In this experiment, we compare the performance of CNNs using zero-padding with using RIAP for the glomerulus segmentation task. Microscopic images of the glomerulus are commonly used to diagnose kidney diseases. Histological staining is commonly used in microscopic images of the glomerulus. Due to the variations in staining methods, significant glomeruli differences exist regarding color, shape, and texture among different whole slide images, making it challenging to segment glomerulus accurately. The whole slide images of glomeruli are generally large in size. Correspondingly, these images are divided into small patches, and each patch is segmented separately. During this process, it is inevitable that a whole glomerulus is cut into fragments located on the boundaries of images. To cope with this issue, the U-Net and U-Net_SVC with RIAP are employed to be a network to segment glomeruli, especially for these objects located on the boundaries of images.

Table 1. The dice metric of segmentation results using the U-Net and the U-Net_SVC with zero-padding and with RIAP. "_Zero" and "_RIAP" represent zero-padding and RIAP, respectively, with optimal results in bold.

Test image	U-Net_Zero	U-Net_RIAP	U-Net_SVC_Zero	U-Net_SVC_RIAP
1	87.2%	**88.8%**	88.3%	**88.8%**
2	86.2%	**88.9%**	-	-
3	89.4%	**89.3%**	86.73%	**86.69%**
4	89.4%	**89.4%**	-	-
5	89.2%	**89.6%**	88.87%	**89.23%**
Average	88.28%	**89.20%**	87.97%	**88.24%**
FLOPs	63G	70G	66G	72G

We conduct the experiment on the HuBMAP kidney dataset that includes 20 samples, each of which is composed of PAS kidney images and glomeruli FTU annotation. The images are high-resolution. For example, the smallest one is 14844×31262. From the dataset, there are 15 samples shared with annotation for training, and the annotation of the other five samples is inaccessible. We randomly select 12 images from the training set to train the network, and the rest three images are used as the validation set to choose the best-trained model. Each image is evenly separated into small patches without the overlay. The resolution of each patch is 512×512. The dice is used as the measurement metric. Totally, we using five-fold cross-validation to evaluate our method on the test set. We use U-Net, U-Net_SVC and employ zero-padding, RIAP to perform glomerulus segmentation.

The CNN is evaluated using the dice metric, as listed in Table 1, which shows the advantage of RIAP in glomerular microscopic image segmentation applications. It can be seen that the performances of U-Net and U-Net_SVC with RIAP have been improved compared with these with zero-padding. The improvement indicates that more effective feature maps can be obtained by transmitting original input information, and more accurate segmentation results can be achieved in real applications. RIAP is effective because the objects on our training dataset and test dataset are possibly located on the boundary of images.

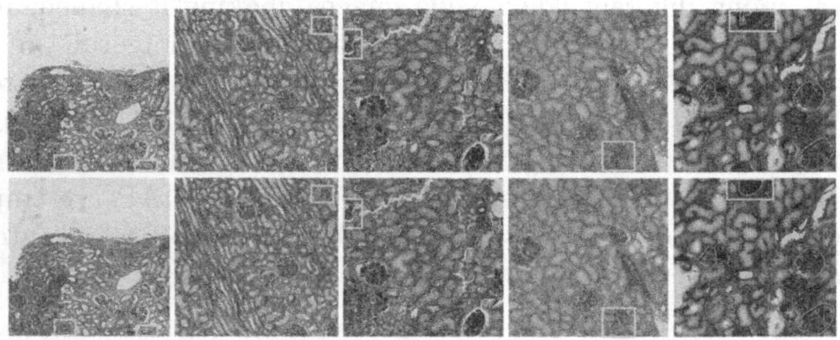

Fig. 6. Comparison of segmentation results using the U-Net with zero-padding (up) and the U-Net with RIAP (down) on the HuBMAP test set.

Segmentation examples are shown in Fig. 6. Noted the U-Net with RIAP predicts glomeruli located on the boundary of images more accurately than the U-Net with zero-padding, which illustrates advantages of RIAP in the improvement of object segmentation on the boundary of images. Moreover, we randomly select a patch from validation images and shift the selection region along the x

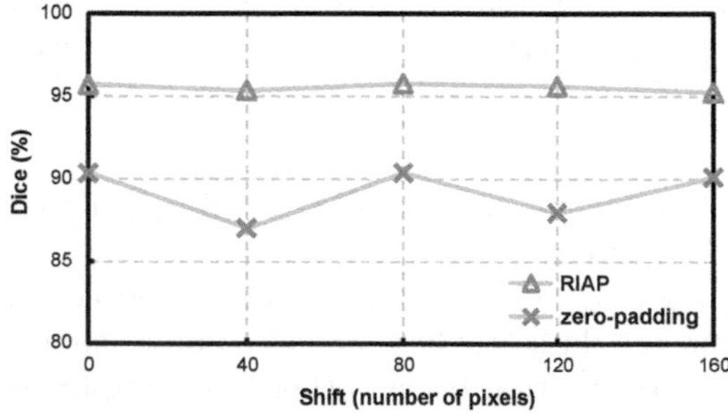

Fig. 7. The average dice of patches with different shifting offset. Note that the shift direction is horizontal.

direction to obtain patches containing glomeruli located at various positions in the image. These patches are input to the U-Net with zero-padding and the U-Net with RIAP networks to predict glomeruli. This experiment is repeated ten times to obtain the average dice of patches with the same shifting offset. Figure 7 shows the average dice of patches with different shifting offset. It can be seen that the segmentation accuracy of the U-Net with RIAP is more robust to object shifting compared with the U-Net with zero-padding.

6 Conclusion

In this paper, we propose a method, RIAP, to retransmit information of boundary pixels via augmenting path to make the impact of the RF uniform. Through our method, all pixels' information can be effectively propagated instead of being lost using zero-padding. We analyze the performance of RIAP in theory and evaluate it in the glomerular microscopic image segmentation task. Experimental results show that our RIAP achieves better performance than traditional padding schemes.

References

1. Chao, Y.W., Vijayanarasimhan, S., Seybold, B., Ross, D.A., Deng, J., Sukthankar, R.: Rethinking the faster R-CNN architecture for temporal action localization (2018)
2. Dadashzadeh, A., Targhi, A.T.: Multi-level contextual network for biomedical image segmentation (2018)
3. Ding, H., Jiang, X., Shuai, B., Liu, A.Q., Wang, G.: Semantic correlation promoted shape-variant context for segmentation. In: 2019 IEEE/CVF Conference on Computer Vision and Pattern Recognition (CVPR) (2019)
4. Glorot, X., Bengio, Y.: Understanding the difficulty of training deep feedforward neural networks. J. Mach. Learn. Res. **9**, 249–256 (2010)
5. Han, Y., Tang, B., Deng, L.: An enhanced convolutional neural network with enlarged receptive fields for fault diagnosis of planetary gearboxes. Comput. Ind. **107**, 50–58 (2019)
6. He, K., Zhang, X., Ren, S., Sun, J.: Deep residual learning for image recognition (2015)
7. He, K., Zhang, X., Ren, S., Sun, J.: Delving deep into rectifiers: surpassing human-level performance on ImageNet classification. In: Proceedings of the IEEE International Conference on Computer Vision, pp. 1026–1034 (2015)
8. Huang, G., Liu, Z., Van Der Maaten, L., Weinberger, K.Q.: Densely connected convolutional networks. In: Proceedings of the IEEE Conference on Computer Vision and Pattern Recognition, pp. 4700–4708 (2017)
9. Ioffe, S., Szegedy, C.: Batch normalization: accelerating deep network training by reducing internal covariate shift. In: International Conference on Machine Learning, pp. 448–456. PMLR (2015)
10. Jacobsen, J.H., Gemert, J.V., Lou, Z., Smeulders, A.W.M.: Structured receptive fields in CNNS (2016)

11. Kai, Z., Zuo, W., Gu, S., Lei, Z.: Learning deep CNN denoiser prior for image restoration. In: IEEE Conference on Computer Vision & Pattern Recognition (2017)
12. Kingma, D.P., Ba, J.: Adam: a method for stochastic optimization. arXiv preprint arXiv:1412.6980 (2014)
13. Le, H., Borji, A.: What are the receptive, effective receptive, and projective fields of neurons in convolutional neural networks? (2017)
14. Long, J., Shelhamer, E., Darrell, T.: Fully convolutional networks for semantic segmentation. In: Proceedings of the IEEE Conference on Computer Vision and Pattern Recognition, pp. 3431–3440 (2015)
15. Luo, W., Li, Y., Urtasun, R., Zemel, R.: Understanding the effective receptive field in deep convolutional neural networks (2017)
16. Ronneberger, O., Fischer, P., Brox, T.: U-Net: convolutional networks for biomedical image segmentation. In: Navab, N., Hornegger, J., Wells, W.M., Frangi, A.F. (eds.) MICCAI 2015. LNCS, vol. 9351, pp. 234–241. Springer, Cham (2015). https://doi.org/10.1007/978-3-319-24574-4_28
17. Simonyan, K., Zisserman, A.: Very deep convolutional networks for large-scale image recognition. Computer Science (2014)
18. Ulyanov, D., Vedaldi, A., Lempitsky, V.: Instance normalization: the missing ingredient for fast stylization. arXiv preprint arXiv:1607.08022 (2016)
19. Wu, Y., He, K.: Group normalization. In: Ferrari, V., Hebert, M., Sminchisescu, C., Weiss, Y. (eds.) ECCV 2018. LNCS, vol. 11217, pp. 3–19. Springer, Cham (2018). https://doi.org/10.1007/978-3-030-01261-8_1
20. Yu, F., Koltun, V.: Multi-scale context aggregation by dilated convolutions (2016)
21. Zeiler, M.D., Fergus, R.: Visualizing and understanding convolutional networks. In: Fleet, D., Pajdla, T., Schiele, B., Tuytelaars, T. (eds.) ECCV 2014. LNCS, vol. 8689, pp. 818–833. Springer, Cham (2014). https://doi.org/10.1007/978-3-319-10590-1_53
22. Zhou, B., Khosla, A., Lapedriza, A., Oliva, A., Torralba, A.: Object detectors emerge in deep scene CNNS. Computer Science (2014)
23. Zhou, Z., Siddiquee, M.M.R., Tajbakhsh, N., Liang, J.: Unet++: redesigning skip connections to exploit multiscale features in image segmentation. IEEE Trans. Med. Imaging **39**(6), 1856–1867 (2019)

Curriculum Learning Revisited: Incremental Batch Learning with Instance Typicality Ranking

Izabela Krysińska[1], Mikołaj Morzy[1](✉), and Tomasz Kajdanowicz[2]

[1] Poznań University of Technology, Poznań, Poland
izabela.krysinska@student.put.poznan.pl, mikolaj.morzy@put.poznan.pl
[2] Wrocław University of Science and Technology, Wrocław, Poland
tomasz.kajdanowicz@pwr.edu.pl

Abstract. The technique of *curriculum learning* mimics cognitive mechanisms observed in human learning, where simpler concepts are presented prior to gradual introduction of more difficult concepts. Until now, the major obstacle for curriculum methods was the lack of a reliable method for estimating the *difficulty* of training instances. In this paper we show that, instead of trying to assess the difficulty of learning instances, a simple graph-based method of computing the *typicality* of instances can be used in conjunction with curriculum methods. We design new batch schedulers which organize ordered instances into batches of varying size and learning difficulty. Our method does not require any changes to the architecture of trained models, we improve the training merely by manipulating the order and frequency of instance presentation to the model.

Keywords: Curriculum learning · Typicality · Batch training

1 Introduction

Although the analogy between biological neurons and their artificial counterparts is superficial, scientists still draw inspiration from human cognitive processes to introduce new mechanisms into the learning process. Imitating concepts of human cognition can be beneficial. Still, we seem to reject some of the essential approaches from psychology and cognition science when teaching models. Concepts that humans learn at particular stages of their lives are carefully arranged by experts into a *curriculum*, where the order of learned concepts is crucial for the entire process. The difficulty of tasks set for students is adapted to their maturity, and it gradually increases with their age. On the contrary, a typical assumption in machine learning is that difficulty is uniformly distributed across

M. Morzy—This work was supported by the National Science Centre, Poland, the decision no. 2016/23/B/ST6/03962.

I. Farkaš et al. (Eds.): ICANN 2021, LNCS 12894, pp. 279–291, 2021.
https://doi.org/10.1007/978-3-030-86380-7_23

all instances in the training set. Currently, the dominant approach in gradient-based optimization is *stochastic gradient descent* and *mini-batch stochastic gradient descent* [15]. As the name "stochastic" suggests, randomly chosen instances are presented to the neural network. A common practice is also to randomly shuffle instances between training epochs.

Several previous works proposed to use *curriculum learning*, i.e., to deliberately manipulate the order in which instances are presented to the neural network to improve generalization capabilities of the model [7–9]. The rationale behind this approach is to present "simpler" instances first to allow the model to gain general understanding of the relationship between input features and class labels, and then gradually progress to more "complex" instances, where this relationship might be less straightforward. More "complex" instances might represent outliers, instances close to the decision boundary, atypical examples, measurement or annotation errors, etc. The main problem of curriculum learning is the assessment of the *difficulty* of each training instance. Several proposals have been formulated in the past, including measuring prediction error rates across different classes, using errors of surrogate models, and many more. This work introduces a different approach to the curriculum learning. Rather than assessing the difficulty of an instance, we use the *typicality* of each instance as the criterion for ordering instances in the training set. A typical instance is a genuine representative of its class and has typical features and feature interactions for its class.

The original contribution of this paper is as follows:

- We introduce a simple graph-based algorithm for evaluating the typicality of each instance in the training set.
- We design three criteria which can be used to compute the typicality of each instance from the instance similarity graph.
- We develop four new scheduling strategies for curriculum learning and verify them experimentally.

2 Related Work

The first idea of learning a model with a curriculum comes from [3]. Elman proposed an approach inspired by the human cognitive process, called "starting small strategy". The motivation behind this strategy was Elman's failure with teaching neural network grammar concepts by training on a dataset consisting of compound sentences. To test his theory, Elman developed two methods of learning grammar rules: the *incremental input* method and the *incremental memory* method. The first method varied the percentage of simple and compound sentences used during training, while the second method constrained model's capacity in early phases of the training. Elman noticed that "result contrasts strikingly with the earlier failure of the network to learn when the full corpus was presented at the outset" [3].

After over 15 years, Bengio *et al.* decided to revisit Elman's approach and answer the question "when and why 'starting small' strategy can benefit machine learning algorithms" [1]. They formalized Elman's approach of starting training on easy examples first and then gradually introducing more complex examples during training, and named it *curriculum learning.* Bengio *et al.* showed the general concept of using only easy examples towards better generalization using two learners: a pair of Support Vector Machine models and a perceptron trained on increasingly noisy data. The difficulty of examples has been estimated using a Bayesian classifier.

These results have been confirmed by several followup studies [7,9,10], proposing various modifications and applications of the *curriculum learning* approach. [9] presented the *self-paced curriculum learning* (SPCL), a combination of self-paced learning (SPL) and curriculum learning (CL). The authors proved that their method outperforms self-paced learning and curriculum learning used separately, as measured by the root mean squared error (RMSE) and the mean absolute error (MAE) metrics. The conclusion is that both the prior knowledge and the learners capacity are important in the learning process, and together they give better performance than SPL and CL used separately. Various curriculum-inspired methods have been proposed for reinforcement learning [4] computer vision [6,11], or multi-task learning [14].

The main difference between previous approaches to curriculum learning and the approach advocated in this paper is the method of constructing the curriculum. Our sorting function is built on a graph-based instance weighting algorithm. Nodes in this graph represent instances while edge weights represent similarities between instances. For each node from the graph, a centrality metric is calculated and used as the sorting criterion in curriculum creation.

3 Instance Typicality

Defining the *difficulty* of a training instance is hard and it requires several additional assumptions on how to assess this measure. We propose to use instance *typicality* instead of difficulty, since it can be easily defined and does not require any hyper-parameters to be set. Intuitively, an instance is *typical* if it is similar to many instances of the same class. In other words, a typical instance is a good representative of its class. An instance is *atypical* if it is similar to many instances of other classes, so features of an atypical instance do not provide reliable information about the properties of the class. If an instance is not similar to other instances, irrespective of their class assignment, such instance is of limited importance to the training process since it does not contribute to the generalization capabilities of the learned model. We refer to such instances as *nonaligned.* Thus, our method tries to build a curriculum of training instances, starting from the most typical instances, then proceeding to nonaligned instances, to finish with atypical instances. The main idea is to focus most of the learning process on typical instances and downplay the importance of atypical instances, either by varying the number of repetitions of subsequent batches, or by manipulating the learning rate for different types of instances.

3.1 Instance Similarity Graph

Our method works provided that there is a function $sim(\mathbf{x}_i, \mathbf{x}_j)$ which computes the *similarity* between instances. The choice of a particular similarity function is irrelevant from the point of view of the procedure. Let $C = \{c_1, c_2, \ldots, c_k\}$ be the set of classes, and $\mathbf{X} = \{\mathbf{x}_1, \ldots, \mathbf{x}_n\}$ be the set of instances. Let y_i be the *label* associated with the i-th instance. Let

$$\overline{sim} = \frac{2}{n(n+1)} \sum_{i=1}^{n-1} \sum_{j=i+1}^{n} sim(\mathbf{x}_i, \mathbf{x}_j)$$

be the average instance similarity. Then the *instance similarity graph* is defined as a pair $\langle \mathbf{X}, E \rangle$, where $\mathbf{X}$ is a set of nodes (and each node represents a single training instance), and $E = \{(\mathbf{x}_i, \mathbf{x}_j) : \mathbf{x}_i, \mathbf{x}_j \in \mathbf{X} \wedge sim(\mathbf{x}_i, \mathbf{x}_j) \geq \overline{sim}\}$ is the set of edges. An edge exists if and only if the similarity between instances is greater than the average instance similarity.

3.2 Instance Typicality Measures

To measure the typicality of each instance we use the topology of the instance similarity graph. We compute three centrality indexes and treat them as proxies for instance typicality. Below we present these centrality indexes and rationale behind using them to represent instance typicality.

Degree Centrality. The *degree centrality* of an instance $\mathbf{x}_i$ is the number of instances adjacent to $\mathbf{x}_i$ in the instance similarity graph. Formally, $C_D(\mathbf{x}_i) = |\{\mathbf{x}_j : (\mathbf{x}_i, \mathbf{x}_j) \in E\}|$. Degree centrality captures the overall typicality of each instance by promoting in the curriculum instances that are similar to many other instances. Thus, training the model on these instances allows to generalize the model and cover many training instances with one selected prototype. The main drawback of degree centrality is the fact that it does not consider class assignments at all. So, ranking built on degree centrality would include an instance that is very similar to many instances belonging to other classes. We will refer to a curriculum built using this instance typicality measure as a *degree curriculum.*

Entropy Centrality. Next we introduce the *entropy centrality.* We use classical Shannon's information entropy [16] to measure the homogeneity of class assignments of a given instance nearest neighborhood. Let $N(\mathbf{x}_i) = \{\mathbf{x}_j : (\mathbf{x}_i, \mathbf{x}_j) \in E\}$ be the nearest neighborhood of $\mathbf{x}_i$. The probability of finding class c_l in $N(\mathbf{x}_i)$ is given by:

$$p(c_l, \mathbf{x}_i) = \frac{|\{\mathbf{x}_j \in N(\mathbf{x}_i) : y_j = c_l\}|}{|N(\mathbf{x}_i)|}$$

The *entropy centrality* of an instance $\mathbf{x}_i$ is simply the entropy of the distribution of classes in the nearest neighborhood of $\mathbf{x}$: $C_E(\mathbf{x}_i) =$

$-\sum_l p(c_l, \mathbf{x}_i) \ln p(c_l, \mathbf{x}_i)$. Unfortunately, this formulation of the centrality index does not safeguard against picking very atypical instances early in the curriculum, for the same reason as the degree centrality. An instance connected only to instances of the opposite class will have zero entropy, despite being a very poor representative of its class. To circumvent this problem we have to modify the entropy centrality formula. Let $c^*(\mathbf{x}_i) = \arg\max k p(c_k, \mathbf{x}_i)$ be the majority class in the nearest neighborhood of $\mathbf{x}_i$. We can define auxiliary function

$$I(\mathbf{x}_i) = \begin{cases} +1 & \textit{if } c^*(\mathbf{x}_i) = y_i \\ -1 & \textit{otherwise} \end{cases}$$

which indicates if the class of the instance $\mathbf{x}$ is the same as the majority class in its nearest neighborhood. We define the *class-adjusted entropy centrality* as follows: $C_A(\mathbf{x}_i) = \frac{I(\mathbf{x}_i)}{C_E(\mathbf{x}_i)+1}$. According to this formulation, the class-adjusted entropy of $\mathbf{x}_i$ is minimized when all instances in the nearest neighborhood of $\mathbf{x}_i$ belong to the same class as $\mathbf{x}_i$, and maximized when they belong to the opposite class. Still, this solution has a drawback: the formula does not consider the cardinality of neighborhoods of instances. We will refer to a curriculum built using this instance typicality measure as an *entropy curriculum*.

Degree-Adjusted Entropy Centrality. In order to solve the above problem we also experiment with a simple heuristic which combines both degree centrality and entropy centrality. The *degree-adjusted entropy centrality* is given by: $C_{DE}(\mathbf{x}_i) = |\{\mathbf{x}_j \in N(\mathbf{x}_i) : y_j = y_i\}| - C_A(\mathbf{x}_i)|N(\mathbf{x}_i)|$. This formula takes into account both the homogeneity of the nearest neighborhood of an instance and its size. We will refer to a curriculum built using this instance typicality measure as an *degree-adjusted entropy curriculum*.

4 Batch Schedulers

The ordering of instances does not constitute an effective learning method in itself. Learning method must define the frequency of repetitions (how often a given instance is presented to the model), the size of batches (how many instances are presented during a single iteration of the learning process), and the values of model hyperparameters used during learning. In this section we present four scheduling algorithms which vary batch sizes, and batch repetition strategies. The rationale behind all four scheduling algorithms is to consolidate the knowledge acquired by the model in early stages of learning (when the model is presented with typical instances), with the hope that it will eventually lead to better generalization of the model and faster convergence.

Ordered Gradient Descent. In traditional stochastic gradient descent the evaluation of the loss function and the updating of model parameters are performed for every single instance in the training set. Instances are randomly shuffled and read sequentially, and the true gradient of the loss function is approximated by a gradient at a single instance. The *ordered gradient descent* method

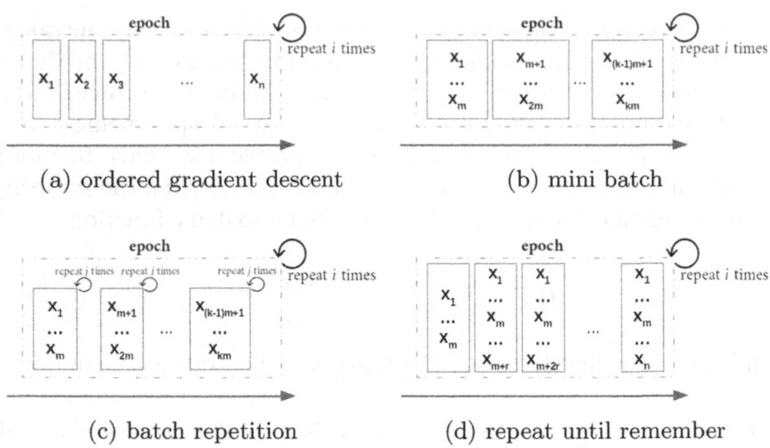

Fig. 1. Batch schedulers.

uses this mechanism, but instead of randomly shuffling the training set, it uses the curriculum of instances computed by a selected instance typicality measure (Sec. 3.2). Figure 1a depicts ordered gradient descent scheduler.

Mini-Batch. The approximation of the "true" gradient of the entire training set by a single instance is, by definition, prone to noise and outliers, but using the entire training set is usually computationally unfeasible. A reasonable compromise is to divide the training set into batches of fixed size and approximate the gradient of the loss function by the average gradient computed from the batch. This method of optimization is commonly referred to as the *mini-batch*. We slightly modify this procedure by ensuring that in each training epoch the ordering of instances in the training set is preserved and reflects the selected instance typicality measure. The size of each batch is the hyper-parameter of the method. The mini-batch scheduler is presented in Fig. 1b.

Batch Repetition. During training subsequent iterations may, to some extent, override prior knowledge encoded in parameters. Very specific, rare instances, may skew gradient approximation and adversely affect the generalization properties of the model. In order to prevent such influence, the model should master the most typical instances in the first place, and only then try to learn from more atypical and difficult instances. The *batch repetition* method tries to minimize the negative impact of atypical examples by forcing the model to the area of the parameter space defined by the most typical instances. The training set is divided into batches of a fixed size exactly as in the mini-batch method, using a selected instance typicality measure. The learning starts with repeating the first batch j times. After that, the next batch is repeated j times. The epoch ends when all batches have been processed. The ordering of instances is preserved between epochs. The method is illustrated in Fig. 1c.

Table 1. Dataset statistics.

Dataset	Instances	Attributes	Types
Audiology	200	69	Categorical
Breast cancer	569	5	Numerical
Cars	1728	21	Categorical
Credit screening	690	15	Mixed
Diagnosis	120	6	Mixed
Hepatitis	155	19	Categorical
Horse colic	300	26	Mixed
House votes	435	16	Categorical
Parkinson	195	22	Numerical

Repeat Until Remember. The fourth scheduler is inspired by the studies of Hermann Ebbinghaus, a German psychologist most famous due to his research on human memory retention over time, which resulted in the discovery of the *forgetting curve* [2] and the concept of spaced repetition. Spaced repetition is a mnemonic technique which consists in periodically refreshing newly acquired knowledge in order to retain information for a longer period of time. With each repetition the interval is extended, and, eventually, the information is permanently remembered. We incorporate the concept of spaced repetitions into the training process by introducing the *repeat until remember* (RuR) scheduler. The training set is divided into batches of gradually increasing size, each batch consists of m most typical instances (selected from the curriculum defined by the selected instance typicality measurement), and a growing number of less typical instances. Subsequent batches add r previously unseen instances from the curriculum, so that the first batch contains m instances, the second batch contains $m + r$ instances, the third batch contains $m + 2r$ instances, and so on. Final batch contains all n instances. The ordering of instances is preserved between epochs. The method is illustrated in Fig. 1d.

5 Experimental Setup

Experiments are conducted on a machine equipped with NVIDIA Tesla K80 GPU. Implementation of all learning methods is written in Python3 using `Keras` library. Experiments were carried out on 9 popular data sets from the UCI Machine Learning Repository (Table 1).

Hypotheses. Prior to conducting experiments we formulate the following research hypotheses:

- **H1**: A model trained with a curriculum performs better than a model trained without a curriculum.

- **H2**: A model trained with the *ordered gradient descent* method performs better than the *baseline* model
- **H3**: A model trained with the *batch repetition* method performs better than the *baseline* model
- **H4**: A model trained with the *repeat until remember* method performs better than the *baseline* model

These hypotheses surmise that a model trained using curriculum methods, while the architecture of a neural network remains unchanged, achieves higher accuracy than the baseline model and converges faster.

Hyper-Parameters. In order to avoid the presentation of over-optimistic results we have decided to refrain from hyper-parameter tuning for each dataset, but instead, to fix hyper-parameters for all datasets. In all experiments the Adam optimizer is applied to the same architecture of a feed-forward network. The first layer contains k inputs, where k is the number of features. The second layer is an output layer. For binary classification task the last layer contains only one node with the sigmoid activation function. For multi-label classification the final layer contains as many nodes as the number of classes and the label is determined by a softmax function. Detailed hyper-parameter values are presented in Table 2.

The baseline is a neural network model with identical architecture as the curriculum models, but trained with batches of random training instances. In addition, shuffling of instances between training epochs is applied. The batch size for the baseline method is set to 32, and training is performed for 50 epochs with Adam optimizer and learning rate set to 0.001. The same parameters are set for the curriculum methods, unless the algorithm requires parameters to be changed. The batch size for the ordered gradient descent *OGD* method is set to 1. The *mini-batch* method differs from the *baseline* method only in the order of training instances. For the *batch repetition* method each batch is repeated 4 times. The *RuR* method starts with 32-instance batch and with each iteration 4 consecutive instances are added. It is worth noticing that 32 most typical instances are examined in every iteration, while the four least typical instances are presented to the neural network only 50 times. In each run of the experiment instances are randomly split into training and validation sets to avoid bias of particularly unfavorable or favorable splits. The validation set contains 33% of all instances in the dataset.

6 Results

The key metric used in the experiments is the validation set accuracy. When validating hypotheses **H1** through **H4** we always create a similar set of groups of experimental results for the Friedman [5] and Nemenyi [13] tests: the baseline, the scheduler with degree curriculum, the scheduler with entropy curriculum, and the scheduler with degree-adjusted entropy curriculum.

Table 2. Hyper-parameters.

Method	Batch size	Epochs	Batch interval	Batch increase	Epoch increase
Baseline	32	50	1	0	1
Ordered SGD	1	50	1	0	1
Mini-batch	32	50	1	0	1
Batch rep.	32	50	4	0	1
RuR	var	50	1	4	1
LR decay	8	20	1	0	2

Table 3. Mini-batch post hoc.

	A	B	C	D
A	−1.0000	0.0010	0.0010	0.0503
B	0.0010	−1.0000	0.9000	0.1586
C	0.0010	0.9000	−1.0000	0.2980
D	0.0503	0.1586	0.2980	−1.0000

Table 4. Mini-batch ranks.

	A	B	C	D
A	−1	163	163	150
B	95	−1	130	110
C	98	130	−1	117
D	110	148	138	−1

Mini-Batch Scheduling. Our first experiment tests Hypothesis **H1**. We verify if curriculum learning alone, without dedicated batch schedulers, is able to improve the training. To answer this question we compare the baseline method to the mini-batch (MB) method, noting, that these two methods differ only in the order of training instances, with all other hyper-parameters being the same. The null hypothesis states that there is no observable difference between the groups. The significance level of the Friedman test is set to $\alpha = 0.05$, and the test yields the p-value of 3.78e−6, which allows us to reject the null hypothesis. Subsequently, we conduct the post-hoc analysis with the same significance level. Table 3 presents the results of the Nemenyi pairwise comparison: (A) baseline method (B) MB with degree curriculum (C) MB with entropy curriculum (D) MB with degree-adjusted entropy curriculum.

P-values in Table 3 indicate that there is a statistically significant difference between the baseline method and the mini-batch method with degree curriculum or entropy curriculum. The test does not detect a statistically significant difference between the baseline method and the mini-batch method with a degree-adjusted entropy curriculum. Pairwise comparisons only inform us of the difference, but not of the direction of difference, thus we follow with rank comparisons between groups. Table 4 presents the results. The baseline method is better than the mini-batch with degree curriculum in 163 comparisons (experiments), and is inferior in 95 comparisons. Since the Friedman test has shown that baseline and mini-batch with degree curriculum differ significantly, and the former outperforms the later more frequently, we can conclude that the baseline method

Table 5. Baseline vs OGD.

	A	B	C	D
A	−1	89	112	112
B	173	−1	150	143
C	146	105	−1	122
D	148	103	131	−1

Table 6. Baseline vs BR.

	A	B	C	D
A	−1	99	102	94
B	163	−1	130	113
C	161	128	−1	112
D	169	143	145	−1

Table 7. Baseline vs RuR.

	A	B	C	D
A	−1	66	86	82
B	196	−1	134	129
C	181	119	−1	126
D	179	128	133	−1

performs better than pure curriculum-based methods. Based on the results presented in Table 4 we reject Hypothesis **H1**.

Ordered Gradient Descent Scheduling. Our next experiment tries to verify if combining curriculum learning with ordered gradient descent (OGD) is beneficial for training performance. As always, the null hypothesis states that there is no statistically significant difference between the groups. The p-value yielded by the Friedman test is 1.18e−6, so we confidently reject the null hypothesis. Due to space limitations from now on we will present only the results of rank comparisons, without p-values from pairwise comparisons. Table 5 shows the performance of curriculum learning supplemented with ordered gradient descent: (A) baseline method (B) OGD with degree curriculum (C) OGD with entropy curriculum (D) OGD with degree-adjusted entropy curriculum. Every method using ordered gradient descent with curriculum learning performs better than the baseline method. Again, in each experiment the baseline method shares all hyperparameters with the OGD, with the exception of the ordering of training instances, so this ordering is the only factor influencing the performance of the model. Based on the results presented in Table 5 we accept Hypothesis **H2** that combining curriculum learning with ordered gradient descent improves the performance of the trained model.

Batch Repetition Scheduling. Hypothesis **H3** states that combining curriculum learning with batch repetition (BR) improves the performance of the model. The null hypothesis states that batch repetition does not influence the performance of the model. The Friedman test yields the p-value of 18e−6, which allows us to safely reject the null hypothesis. The Nemenyi test yield p-values below the significance level for pairwise comparison of the baseline with all batch repetition methods, and p-values above the significance level for pairwise comparisons between batch repetition methods (so there is no observable difference in performance between them). Thus, we conclude that the observed result is due to the batch repetition method rather than a particular curriculum used in the training process. Table 6 presents rank comparisons of evaluated methods: (A) baseline method (B) BR with degree curriculum (C) BR with entropy curriculum (D) BR with degree-adjusted entropy curriculum. As in the previous section, every method using the batch repetition combined with curriculum learning outperforms the baseline method. Evaluated methods share all hyper-parameters, the only difference is in the ordering of instances in the training set and the fact that subsequent batches are presented to the model multiple times. The results presented in Table 6 allow us to accept Hypothesis **H3** which states that the mini-batch method improves the performance of the model.

***Repeat Until Remember* Scheduling.** According to Hypothesis **H4**, using curriculum learning with the *repeat until remember* (RuR) scheduling improves the ability of the model to generalize. The null hypothesis states that there is no difference observable between the groups. The Friedman test yields the p-value of 1e−17, so we confidently reject the null hypothesis. The Nemenyi test yields p-values below the significance level for all pairwise comparisons of the baseline method with the *repeat until remember* (RuR) methods, and the p-values above the significance level for all pairwise comparisons between RuR methods, so, similarly to the batch repetition case, we attribute the observed differences to the RuR method rather than the particular curriculum. Table 7 presents the results of pairwise comparisons: (A) baseline method (B) RuR with degree curriculum (C) RuR with entropy curriculum (D) RuR with degree-adjusted entropy curriculum. The above results clearly show that the *repeat until remember* method outperforms the baseline method, independent of the curriculum used during training. The baseline method uses traditional mini-batches and the RuR method uses batches of increasing sizes, so the comparison of two approaches is not as straightforward as in the case of other methods. Nevertheless, based on presented evidence we accept Hypothesis **H4** that the *repeat until remember* mechanism improves the performance of the model.

7 Conclusions

This paper introduces a novel approach to curriculum learning. We advocate the use of instance typicality rather than instance difficulty when constructing the curriculum. The following observations can be made with respect to proposed curricula and cognitively-motivated training schedulers introduced in this paper:

- Changing only the order of training instances does not have a positive effect on model performance.
- The results of the *ordered gradient descent* method are better than the baseline method results. The reason for the OGD success is probably that the batch is extremely small and the backpropagation procedure is more frequent than in the *mini-batch* method.
- The *batch repetition* method outperforms the baseline method for all curricula. Confronting the results of batch repetition with the results of the *mini-batch* method we find that changing difficulty level too soon (keeping the same level of difficulty only for one iteration) can lead to worse model generalization ability, while finding a fine balance between the time that same level of difficulty is kept and introducing new instances can lead to better generalization.

- *Repeat until remember* method turns out to be the best of the examined methods. Constant repetition of the most typical instances throughout training seems to be an efficacious practice to improve model performance.

We show that the order of instances is not the only aspect that matters when constructing the curriculum. The arrangement of batches and epochs also has a significant impact on model performance. There are several avenues for future work, including introducing different centrality metrics and adopting them in the schedulers, but extending the RuR method is probably the most promising one. The *RuR* method can be extended to adapt to the learner and develop more flexible intervals between repetitions using a form of the student-teacher learning paradigm [12,17].

References

1. Bengio, Y., Louradour, J., Collobert, R., Weston, J.: Curriculum learning. In: Proceedings of the 26th ICML Conference, pp. 41–48 (2009)
2. Ebbinghaus, H.: Memory: a contribution to experimental psychology. Ann. Neurosci. **20**(4), 155 (2013)
3. Elman, J.L.: Learning and development in neural networks: the importance of starting small. Cognition **48**(1), 71–99 (1993)
4. Florensa, C., Held, D., Wulfmeier, M., Zhang, M., Abbeel, P.: Reverse curriculum generation for reinforcement learning. arXiv preprint arXiv:1707.05300 (2017)
5. Friedman, M.: The use of ranks to avoid the assumption of normality implicit in the analysis of variance. J. Am. Stat. Assoc. **32**(200), 675–701 (1937)
6. Gong, C., Tao, D., Maybank, S.J., Liu, W., Kang, G., Yang, J.: Multi-modal curriculum learning for semi-supervised image classification. IEEE Trans. Image Process. **25**(7), 3249–3260 (2016)
7. Graves, A., Bellemare, M.G., Menick, J., Munos, R., Kavukcuoglu, K.: Automated curriculum learning for neural networks. In: Proceedings of the 34th International Conference on Machine Learning, vol. 70, pp. 1311–1320. JMLR. org (2017)
8. Hacohen, G., Weinshall, D.: On the power of curriculum learning in training deep networks. In: International Conference on Machine Learning, pp. 2535–2544. PMLR (2019)
9. Jiang, L., Meng, D., Zhao, Q., Shan, S., Hauptmann, A.G.: Self-paced curriculum learning. In: Twenty-Ninth AAAI Conference on Artificial Intelligence (2015)
10. Khan, F., Mutlu, B., Zhu, J.: How do humans teach: on curriculum learning and teaching dimension. In: Advances in Neural Information Processing Systems, pp. 1449–1457 (2011)
11. Lin, L., Wang, K., Meng, D., Zuo, W., Zhang, L.: Active self-paced learning for cost-effective and progressive face identification. IEEE Trans. Pattern Anal. Mach. Intell. **40**(1), 7–19 (2017)
12. Matiisen, T., Oliver, A., Cohen, T., Schulman, J.: Teacher-student curriculum learning. IEEE Trans. Neural Netw. Learn. Syst. **31**(9), 3732–3740 (2019)
13. Nemenyi, P.: Distribution-free multiple comparisons (doctoral dissertation, Princeton University, 1963). Dissertation Abstracts International **25**(2), 1233 (1963)
14. Pentina, A., Sharmanska, V., Lampert, C.H.: Curriculum learning of multiple tasks. In: Proceedings of the IEEE Conference on Computer Vision and Pattern Recognition, pp. 5492–5500 (2015)

15. Ruder, S.: An overview of gradient descent optimization algorithms. arXiv preprint arXiv:1609.04747 (2016)
16. Shannon, C.E.: A mathematical theory of communication. Bell Syst. Tech. J. **27**(3), 379–423 (1948)
17. Wong, J.H., Gales, M.: Sequence student-teacher training of deep neural networks (2016)

Person Re-identification

Interesting Receptive Region and Feature Excitation for Partial Person Re-identification

Qiwei Meng, Te Li(✉), Shanshan Ji, Shiqiang Zhu, and Jianjun Gu

Intelligent Robotics Research Center, Zhejiang Lab, Hangzhou, Zhejiang, China
{mengqw,lite,jiss,zhusq,jgu}@zhejianglab.com

Abstract. Partial person ReID tasks have become a research focus recently for it is challenging but significant in practical applications. The major difficulty within partial person ReID is that only incomplete and even noisy person features are available for extraction and matching, which puts forward higher requirement to model robustness. To settle down this problem, our paper proposes a novel IRRFE-ReID model, which includes two major innovations, the interesting receptive region selection module and the feature excitation module. The former module can adaptively select the region of interest from original image while the latter one is applied to distinguish representative person features and weight them during matching. Proven by ablation analysis, these two modules are embeddable and considerably conducive for partial person ReID tasks. Additionally, our IRRFE-ReID model achieves the state-of-the-art performance in two mainstream partial person datasets, PartialReID and PartialiLids, with its Rank1 reaching 85.7% and 74.8% respectively.

Keywords: Partial person re-identification · Interesting receptive region · Feature excitation

1 Introduction

Person re-identification (ReID) aims to retrieve the person of interest across cameras views at different locations and times [1]. This technology has attracted increasing attention recently due to its large potential in non-cooperative video surveillance, smart city and so on [2]. According to the application scenarios of the ReID task, it can be typically classified into image based ReID and video based ReID [3]. In this paper, the image based ReID will be mainly discussed.

Since image based ReID task can hardly apply adjacent frames' information to assist person retrieval [4], it requires a more accurate and robust person feature extraction network. Recently, lots of researches have focused on this area: Cai [5] applied body part masks to guide the training of corresponding attention; Zhang [6] and Jin [7] worked on using semantic information of person to assist ReID; He [8] adopted multiple training tricks for cross-domain ReID, which improve the model robustness. Though these researches have made great progress in holistic person ReID datasets like Market1501, DukeMTMC-ReID, the research of ReID tasks in partial person datasets, like Partial-ReID and PartialiLids, is still limited [9–12]. However, for real world ReID tasks, the

I. Farkaš et al. (Eds.): ICANN 2021, LNCS 12894, pp. 295–307, 2021.
https://doi.org/10.1007/978-3-030-86380-7_24

partial or occluded persons commonly exist, and they tend to be fairly challenging to existing feature extraction and ReID algorithms [11, 13].

(a) PartialReID (b) PartialiLids

Fig. 1. Typical probe images in two partial datasets. In model test mode, we will use these partial person images to match their corresponding holistic person images in gallery.

For partial person datasets (shown in Fig. 1), the key challenge lies in only incomplete or even noisy information of target persons is available [13]. This will potentially render the matching results less satisfactory if the trained neural network is not robust enough. In order to improve this situation, researchers have tried various methods: Adam [14, 15] proposed the compositional convolutional neural networks to localize the occlusion and subsequently emphasize on the non-occluded parts for further network inference; Luo [13] designed a spatial transformer network (STN) to extract semantic features from holistic person image, and then compared them with partial images; Wang [9] proposed a skeleton based higher-order feature extraction, fusion and matching model. These methods can be typically classified into two categories: the first one is to localize the occlusions and partial parts through deep convolutional neural network (DCNN) [16] or other geometric methods [14, 15], then the ReID models can focus on the non-occluded and holistic parts for feature extraction and matching. The other category is to extract the semantic based, key-points based or skeleton based features from the partial images, and subsequently those local features are used to compare with gallery images [9, 13, 17, 18]. Instead of using global features for comparison, local features contain less occlusion noise and can improve the model performance. The abovementioned methods all can minimize the negative influences brought by occlusion and partial problems, thus considerably improving the performance in partial datasets.

However, abovementioned methods all neglect to adaptively discriminate meaningful regions and person features, resulting in their performances in partial datasets are still far from satisfactory compared with them in holistic datasets. With the SOTA ReID models can achieve 90% or higher Rank1 in mainstream holistic datasets [8, 19–22], while the SOTA partial ReID models barely get around 80% Rank1 [9, 23, 24]. This dramatically limits the wide applications of ReID in real-world scenarios.

In this paper, we innovatively propose two embeddable modules for discriminative feature extraction. The first module is interesting receptive region (IRR) selection algorithm, which would adaptively reevaluate the person images and select the region of interest (RoI) for further neural network inference. The second module is feature excitation, which can help the network attach greater importance on the discriminative local features. These two modules and their effects will be detailedly discussed in the following paper.

The main contributions of our paper are summarized as follows:

1. We propose an IRR selection algorithm, which can be applied to preprocess the person images to obtain the RoI. Using the RoI instead of the original image for person feature extraction could significantly reduce the occlusion and partial caused noise, thus improving model robustness. This module can also be embedded into other ReID models to reduce image noise.
2. We propose a feature excitation algorithm, which can be used to weight the important features during neural network inference, thus making the output person features more discriminative. Additionally, this module is also embeddable.
3. We propose an interesting receptive region and feature excitation ReID model (IRRFE-ReID). To the best of our knowledge, this model achieves the state-of-the-art performance in two partial ReID datasets, with its Rank1 reaching 85.7% in PartialReID and 74.8% in PartialiLids.

2 Related Works

2.1 Person Re-identification

Person re-identification [1, 3, 25, 26] has been studied extensively in recent years. Its main function is to find all target persons across cameras views at different locations and times [1], which would be fairly promising in non-cooperative video surveillance.

Typical person ReID can be classified into hand-crafted descriptor method [27–29] and deep learning method [13, 19]. The first method uses descriptors to interpret person images and match the same person, while the second method will mainly apply neural network and metric learning to extract person features and compare them.

Although great progress has been made in person ReID recently, it is still under development since there are lots of challenges restricting its applications in real world scenarios, like different person poses, partial and occlusion problems and so on [9].

2.2 Partial/Occluded Person Re-identification

Partial and occluded person ReID [23] is one of the major obstacles of the wide applications of person ReID in real world scenarios. It uses partial or occluded person images as probe, and finds the images of same person in gallery. Since there is noise and incomplete information within probe images, the traditional holistic ReID models achieve less satisfactory results.

Recently, researchers started to extract more discriminative features from person images to improve the robustness of ReID models under partial and occlusion scenarios. There are two typical methods to achieve this: the first method applies occlusion detection to minimize the influence of noisy areas [14–16]; and the second method extracts skeleton, key-points or semantic features of target person as local features [9, 13, 17, 18], and then matches images based on local feature alignment. Both methods could enhance the discriminability of extracted features, thereby improving the robustness and effectiveness of partial ReID models. However, the results in partial datasets are still unsatisfactory and subtler and more distinguishable features from partial persons need to be extracted.

3 Methods

In this section, we will illustrate our proposed IRRFE-ReID model. Shown in Fig. 2, our model mainly includes an interesting receptive region (IRR) selection algorithm to adaptively choose the region of interest (RoI), a feature excitation model to distinguish and weight the discriminative features, a skeleton model to extract semantic features [9, 30, 31], and a graph matching model to robustly compare person features [32–34].

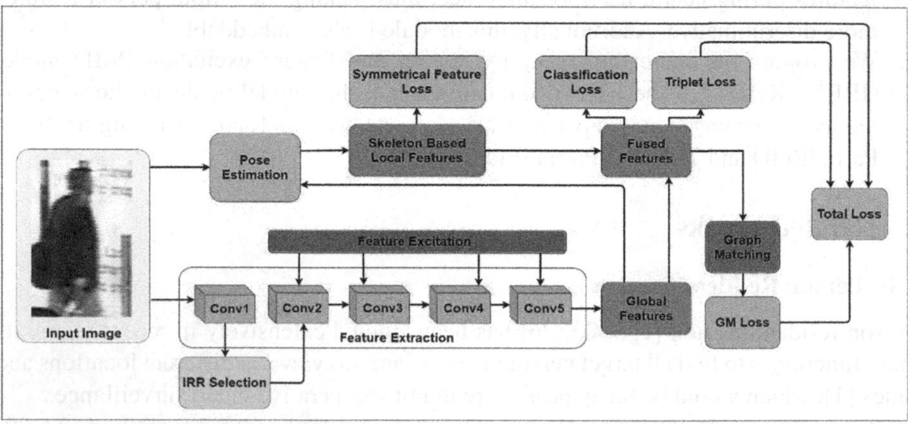

Fig. 2. The framework of IRRFE-ReID. Four major parts are included: an IRR selection algorithm; a feature excitation model; a skeleton model and a graph matching model.

3.1 Interesting Receptive Region Selection Model

The purpose of applying IRR selection before deep-network feature extraction is to aggregate meaningful information within original images. It can help deep convolutional neural network (DCNN) focus on the informative regions, so the quality and effectiveness of extracted features can be considerably improved. Besides, this module will only be applied in training mode to guide the other modules, thus not negatively influencing the speed of model inference during testing and application mode.

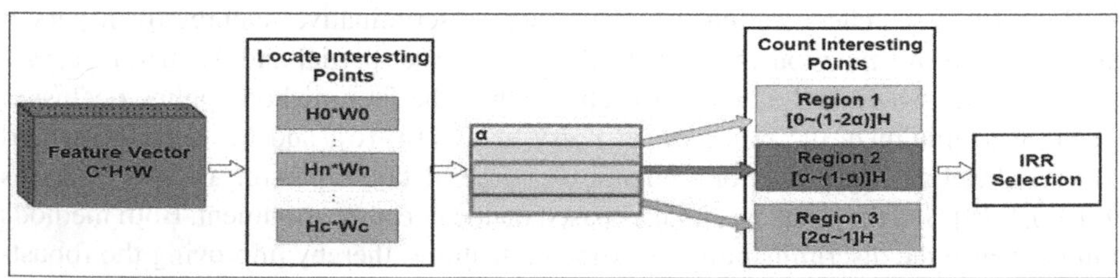

Fig. 3. The mechanism and implementation method of IRR (Color figure online).

The mechanism and implementation method of IRR is shown in Fig. 3. Firstly, given a person image, its shallow-network feature vector (C*H*W) is retrieved. Subsequently, we will find the most interesting point (point with the largest feature value) in each channel (Eq. (1)), and then obtain the point list of interesting region in all channels (Eq. (2)). For each point, it stands for a significant feature in its corresponding channel, so the point list demonstrates the informative feature distribution in the original image.

$$IRR(c_i) = (h_j, w_k) \quad \forall FeatureV(c_i, h, w) | h \neq h_j, w \neq w_k < FeatureV(c_i, h_j, w_k) \tag{1}$$

$$PointList = \{IRR(c_i)\} \;\; for\ c\ in\ C \tag{2}$$

After obtaining the point list, we then divide the original image into three horizontal regions (the purple, orange and yellow region in Fig. 3), and calculate the proportion of interesting points in each region respectively. The region with largest proportion of interesting points will be regarded as the IRR since it generally contains less noise and more discriminative body features.

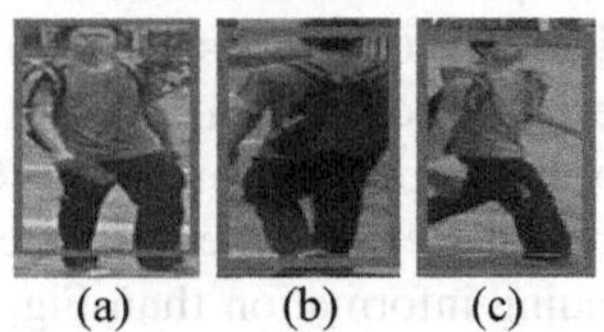

Fig. 4. Results of applying IRR. The RoI (red box) of these three images are top, middle and bottom region, respectively (Color figure online).

The results of applying IRR selection is shown in Fig. 4. It is noticeable that this algorithm could effectively remove the noise and locate the interesting and meaningful regions in original image, which means the ReID model could be better trained to extract discriminative features from images with less environmental and occlusion interference. Therefore, it is reasonable to infer that the IRR selection algorithm could improve the model performance in partial person ReID tasks.

3.2 Feature Excitation Model

The function of feature excitation module is to distinguish and weight the discriminative person features, thereby improving the quality and representability of extracted features. Note that this module will be applied in both training and testing periods.

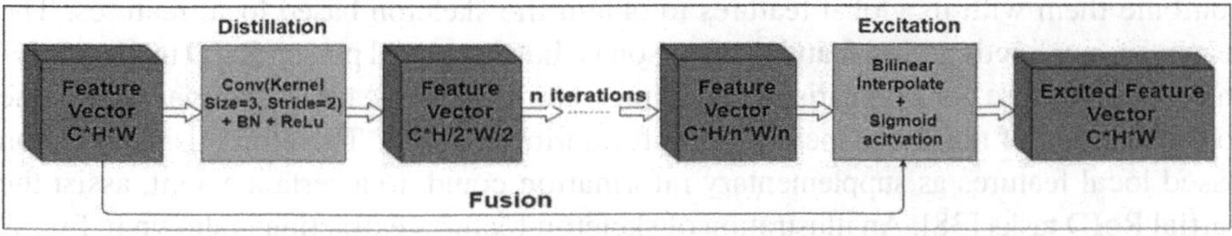

Fig. 5. The mechanism and implementation method of feature excitation.

The mechanism and implementation method of feature excitation model is shown in Fig. 5. Given an input feature vector (C*H*W), a distillation module is firstly applied, which contains n gathering modules (convolutional layers) to distill original feature vector. After that, the distilled features are interpolated and activated with the fusion of original feature vector to obtain the excited feature vector, which has the same shape like the input feature vector.

In feature excitation model, the distillation and excitation modules can be regarded as filters to wipe off the negative influences brought by environmental and occlusion noise while highlight representative features. Specifically, for the feature vector of one channel (H*W), simply apply convolutional layer or pooling layer for feature extraction tend to be terribly influenced by outliers, like noises, misleading the network to focus on the features of noise instead of the true informative features. To alleviate this problem, the distillation module applies independent convolutional layers to reduce outlier influences, and then the distilled features are excited to attach greater importance on the representative features. Therefore, the output excited feature vector is considered to contain more meaningful and discriminative person features with less environmental noises, so it is logical to infer the feature excitation module could considerably improve the model performance in partial person ReID datasets.

After applying feature excitation, the more discriminative and representative features from original image could be retrieved. Shown in Fig. 6, it is manifest that through applying feature excitation to the output of Conv2, the feature vector could become obviously smoother and more robust to environmental noise. Since the Fig. 6(c1) contains more effective and less misleading information than Fig. 6(b1), more meaningful and discriminative features from person images can be retrieved for ReID tasks.

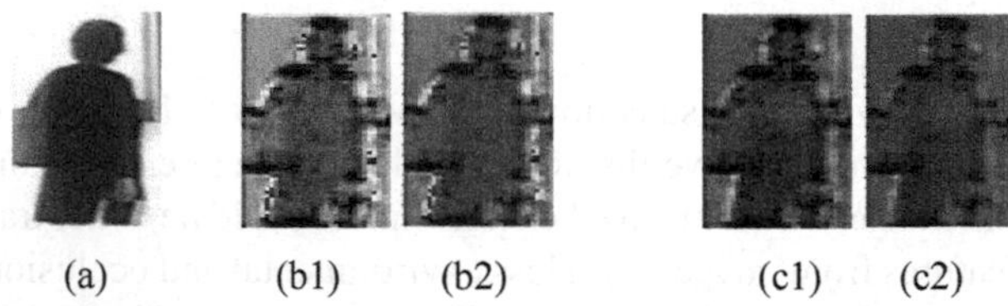

Fig. 6. The results of feature excitation. Figure 6(a) is the original image; 6(b1) and 6(b2) are the output of Resnet50 Conv2 (single channel) and its corresponding heat map; 6(c1) and 6(c2) are the output and heat map after applying feature excitation model.

3.3 Skeleton Based Local Feature Extraction Model

For skeleton model, it is used to estimate the pose and skeleton of target person, and combine them with its global features to obtain the skeleton based local features. The reasons for extracting local features of person is that for partial person ReID tasks, applying global feature for comparison sometimes could be misleading and inaccurate due to the existing of noise and incomplete information [35–37]. Therefore, using skeleton based local features as supplementary information could, to a certain extent, assist the partial ReID tasks [38]. An illustration of skeleton features extraction is shown in Fig. 7.

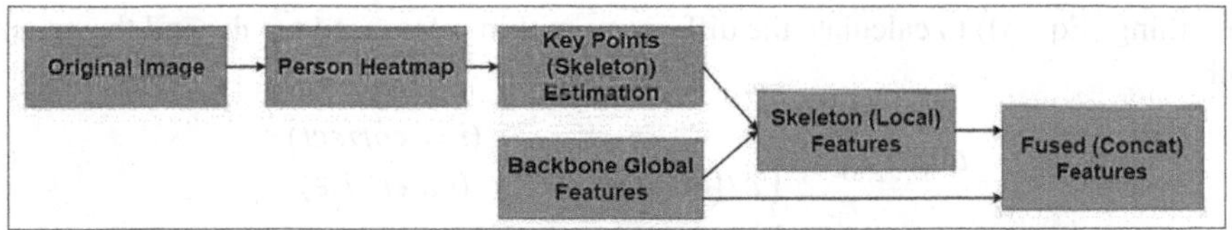

Fig. 7. The implementation method of skeleton based local features extraction.

3.4 Graph Matching Model

The graph matching model aims to match two person images using higher-order human-topology information [9] instead of simple one-to-one aligned features comparison. It is widely reported that though aligned skeleton features comparison could be straightforward and fast, it has unsatisfactory performance when noise and unsmooth information contained in target images [39–41]. Therefore, for our partial person ReID tasks, the higher-order graph matching method [32, 33] is considered to have better performance. Additionally, the graph matching model will only be applied in training period to jointly train the feature extraction and excitation models, so it will not lower the inference speed. The structure of graph matching model is shown in Fig. 8.

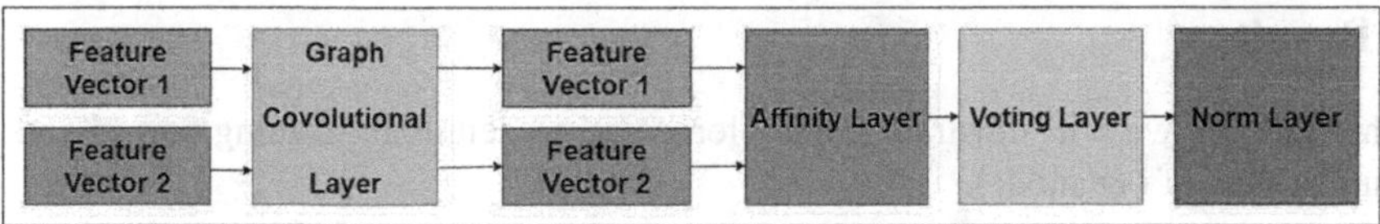

Fig. 8. The structure of graph matching model.

3.5 Loss Calculation

In this section, an illustration of loss function design is demonstrated. Shown in Fig. 2 and Eq. (3), the total loss is composed of symmetrical feature loss, classification loss, triplet loss and graph matching loss, where the α, β, γ, δ are weights of each loss.

$$Loss_{Total} = \alpha Loss_{sym} + \beta Loss_{cla} + \gamma Loss_{tri} + \delta Loss_{gm} \tag{3}$$

The symmetrical feature loss (Eq. (4)) is used to calibrate the skeleton features extraction. It evaluates the feature difference of symmetrical skeleton parts, and calculates the loss according to this difference and the confidence of skeleton segmentation.

$$Loss_{sym} = \frac{1}{num\_pairs} * \sum\nolimits_{i=0}^{num\_pairs} sum((f_{i1} - f_{i2})^2) * (1 - abs(conf_{i1} - conf_{i2}) * (conf_{i1} + conf_{i2})) \tag{4}$$

The classification loss (Eq. (6)) is used to calibrate the model parameters based on the results of person ID matching. It basically applies CrossEntropy loss with label smoothing (Eq. (5)) to calculate the difference within inferenced results and the ground truth.

$$target_{p(i)} = \begin{cases} 1 - \varepsilon & (i = correct) \\ \varepsilon / \left(num_{tagets} - 1\right) & (otherwise) \end{cases} \tag{5}$$

$$Loss_{cla} = -\frac{1}{N} \sum_{i}^{N} (LogSoftmax(i) * target\_p(i)) \tag{6}$$

The triplet loss (Eq. (7)) is used to evaluate the feature difference within positive and negative sample pairs. For a well-performed model, it is expected to have small difference within the most hard-mining positive sample pair and have big difference within the most hard-mining negative sample pair.

$$Loss_{tri} = \frac{1}{N} \sum_{i}^{N} (\max(distance(pos_i) - distance(neg_i) + margin), 0) \tag{7}$$

The graph matching loss (Eq. (8)) is used as an indicator to calibrate the similarity matrix extraction, which mainly works on the graph convolutional layer and jointly improve the quality of extracted features.

$$Loss_{gm} = -\frac{1}{N} \sum_{i}^{N} (LogSoftmax(i) * correct\_p(i)) \tag{8}$$

4 Results

In this section, we will illustrate the implementation details in training period and the testing results of our model.

4.1 Training Setting

In the best version of our model, its settings in training period are shown as follows:

For the IRR algorithm, the α value is set to be 0.02. For the feature excitation model, the excitation iterations for conv2, conv3, conv4, conv5 are 8, 4, 2, 2 respectively. For the skeleton model, local features from 13 body parts, including head, shoulders, elbows, are retrieved. For the loss calculation function, its α, β, γ, δ are 1, 1, 2, 1 respectively; the ε used in classification loss is 0.1; the margin used in triplet loss is 0.3.

Additionally, since neither PartialReID [42] nor PartialiLids [43] dataset are big enough, we train our model using Market1501 dataset and then test the model performance using these two partial person datasets.

4.2 Results in PartialReID Dataset

Applying abovementioned IRRFE-ReID model structure and training settings, to the best our knowledge, we reach the SOTA performance in PartialReID dataset. This dataset contains 600 images from 60 persons, with 5 partial images of each person as probe and the other holistic images as gallery. The PartialReID dataset is one of the most challenging and important datasets in PartialReID research, and the performance of our model is demonstrated in Table 1. It is manifest that our IRRFE-ReID model achieves the SOTA performance with improving the Rank3 and mAP by 0.4% and 1% respectively.

Table 1. Model performance in PartialReID dataset

Models	PartialReID dataset		
	Rank 1	Rank 3	mAP
CBDB-Net [44]	66.7%	78.3%	/
TSA [11]	72.7%	85.2%	/
SGAM [17]	74.3%	82.3%	/
PVPM [45]	78.3%	/	72.3%
FastReID-DSR [8]	82.7%	/	76.8%
HOReID [9]	85.3%	91.0%	/
MHSA-Net [46]	**85.7%**	91.3%	/
IRRFE-ReID (Ours)	**85.7%**	**91.7%**	**77.8%**

4.3 Results in PartialiLids Dataset

Similar to PartialReID dataset, PartialiLids is another challenging partial person dataset. In this paper, we adopt the PartialiLids dataset containing 238 images of 119 persons, and each person takes 1 image as probe and the other as gallery. Under the same training condition, its performance is shown in Table 2. From this table, we could notice that our IRRFE-ReID model reaches a better performance compared with other SOTA models, improving the Rank1, Rank3 and mAP by 1.7%, 2.7% and 2.6% respectively.

Table 2. Model performance in PartialiLids dataset

Models	PartialiLids dataset		
	Rank 1	Rank 3	mAP
STNReID [13]	54.6%	71.3%	/
SFR [47]	65.6%	81.5%	/
FPR [48]	68.1%	/	61.8%
PENet [49]	70.6%	81.3%	/
SGAM [17]	70.6%	82.4%	/
HOReID [9]	72.6%	86.4%	/
FastReID-DSR [8]	73.1%	/	79.8%
IRRFE-ReID (Ours)	**74.8%**	**89.1%**	**82.4%**

4.4 Results of Ablation Analysis

In this section, an ablation test is conducted to demonstrate the effectiveness of IRR and feature excitation modules, which are two major innovations in our paper. Results are shown in Table 3 and Table 4. It is obvious that for both PartialReID and PartialiLids datasets, applying IRR algorithm and feature excitation could effectively improve the model performance compared with the baseline (the first row in Table 3 and 4). Additionally, under the appropriate settings for IRR and feature excitation, these modules can maximize their positive effects and significantly improve the model performance in partial person ReID tasks. Therefore, the results of ablation analysis again verify the effectiveness of IRR and feature excitation, and suggest their great potential in discriminative feature extraction.

Table 3. Ablation analysis of IRRFE-ReID in PartialReID dataset

Methods					PartialReID dataset		
IRR (α value)	Feature excitation iterations				Rank 1	Rank 3	mAP
	Conv2	Conv3	Conv4	Conv5			
0	0	0	0	0	82.0%	88.0%	76.4%
0	4	4	2	2	82.7%	87.7%	75.4%
0	8	4	2	2	84.0%	87.0%	77.3%
0	8	4	4	2	83.3%	87.7%	77.5%
0	8	8	4	2	83.3%	88.0%	75.9%
0	16	8	4	2	83.0%	87.3%	76.1%
0.01	8	4	2	2	84.0%	88.0%	77.0%
0.02	8	4	2	2	**85.7%**	**91.7%**	77.8%
0.05	8	4	2	2	84.7%	89.0%	**78.0%**

Table 4. Ablation analysis of IRRFE-ReID in PartialiLids dataset

Methods					PartialiLids dataset		
IRR (α value)	Feature excitation iterations				Rank 1	Rank 3	mAP
	Conv2	Conv3	Conv4	Conv5			
0	0	0	0	0	71.4%	81.5%	78.4%
0	4	4	2	2	72.3%	79.8%	78.3%
0	8	4	2	2	73.1%	83.2%	79.0%
0	8	4	4	2	72.3%	81.5%	79.1%
0	8	8	4	2	69.7%	80.7%	77.7%
0	16	8	4	2	70.5%	82.3%	78.2%

(continued)

Table 4. (*continued*)

Methods					PartialiLids dataset		
IRR (α value)	Feature excitation iterations				Rank 1	Rank 3	mAP
	Conv2	Conv3	Conv4	Conv5			
0.01	8	4	2	2	73.1%	84.0%	79.8%
0.02	8	4	2	2	**74.8%**	**89.1%**	**82.4%**
0.05	8	4	2	2	**74.8%**	84.9%	80.6%

5 Conclusion

To summarize, our paper proposes a novel partial person re-identification model, IRRFE-ReID. This model includes two major innovations, interesting receptive region selection and feature excitation. Proven by ablation analysis, these modules can effectively weight the discriminative person features and improve the model robustness to partial and occlusion problems. Our proposed IRRFE-ReID achieves the SOTA performance in two mainstream partial person ReID datasets, PartialReID and PartialiLids, suggesting the strong potential of our work.

References

1. Gong, S., et al.: Person re-identification. Adv. Comput. Vis. Pattern Recognit. **42**(7), 301–313 (2014)
2. Leng, Q., Ye, M., Tian, Q.: A survey of open-world person re-identification. IEEE Trans. Circuits Syst. Video Technol. **30**(4), 1092–1108 (2019)
3. Zheng, L., Yang, Y., Hauptmann, A.G.: Person re-identification: past, present and future (2016)
4. Wojke, N., Bewley, A., Paulus, D.: Simple online and realtime tracking with a deep association metric. In: 2017 IEEE International Conference on Image Processing (ICIP) (2017)
5. Cai, H., Wang, Z., Cheng, J.: Multi-scale body-part mask guided attention for person re-identification. In: 2019 IEEE/CVF Conference on Computer Vision and Pattern Recognition Workshops (CVPRW) (2020)
6. Zhang, Z., et al.: Densely semantically aligned person re-identification. In: Proceedings of the IEEE/CVF Conference on Computer Vision and Pattern Recognition (2019)
7. Jin, X., et al.: Semantics-aligned representation learning for person re-identification (2020)
8. He, L., et al.: Fastreid: a pytorch toolbox for general instance re-identification. arXiv preprint arXiv:2006.02631 **6**(7), 8 (2020)
9. Wang, G.A., et al.: High-order information matters: learning relation and topology for occluded person re-identification. In: Proceedings of the IEEE/CVF Conference on Computer Vision and Pattern Recognition (2020)
10. Zhu, S., et al.: Partial person re-identification with two-stream network and reconstruction. Neurocomputing **398**, 453–459 (2020)
11. Gao, L., et al.: Texture semantically aligned with visibility-aware for partial person re-identification. In: Proceedings of the 28th ACM International Conference on Multimedia (2020)

12. Gao, Z., et al.: DCR: a unified framework for holistic/partial person ReID. IEEE Trans. Multimedia (2020)
13. Luo, H., et al.: Stnreid: deep convolutional networks with pairwise spatial transformer networks for partial person re-identification. IEEE Trans. Multimedia **22**(11), 2905–2913 (2020)
14. Kortylewski, A., et al.: Compositional convolutional neural networks: a deep architecture with innate robustness to partial occlusion. In: Proceedings of the IEEE/CVF Conference on Computer Vision and Pattern Recognition (2020)
15. Kortylewski, A., et al.: Compositional convolutional neural networks: a robust and interpretable model for object recognition under occlusion. Int. J. Comput. Vis. 1–25 (2020)
16. Jia, W., et al.: Detection and segmentation of overlapped fruits based on optimized mask R-CNN application in apple harvesting robot. Comput. Electron. Agri. **172**, 105380 (2020)
17. Yang, Q., et al.: Focus on the visible regions: semantic-guided alignment model for occluded person re-identification. Sensors **20**(16), 4431 (2020)
18. Han, C., Gao, C., Sang, N.: Keypoint-based feature matching for partial person re-identification. In: 2020 IEEE International Conference on Image Processing (ICIP). IEEE (2020)
19. Ye, M., et al.: Deep learning for person re-identification: a survey and outlook. IEEE Trans. Pattern Anal. Mach. Intell. (2021)
20. Lawen, H., et al.: Compact network training for person ReID. In: Proceedings of the 2020 International Conference on Multimedia Retrieval (2020)
21. Pathak, P.: Fine-grained re-identification. arXiv preprint arXiv:2011.13475 (2020)
22. Chen, Q., Zhang, W., Fan, J.: Cluster-level feature alignment for person re-identification. arXiv preprint arXiv:2008.06810 (2020)
23. Zhuo, J., et al.: Occluded person re-identification. In: 2018 IEEE International Conference on Multimedia and Expo (ICME). IEEE (2018)
24. Zhuo, J., Lai, J., Chen, P.: A novel teacher-student learning framework for occluded person re-identification. arXiv preprint arXiv:1907.03253 (2019)
25. Zheng, W.-S., Gong, S., Xiang, T.: Person re-identification by probabilistic relative distance comparison. In: CVPR 2011. IEEE (2011)
26. Saghafi, M.A., et al.: Review of person re-identification techniques. IET Comput. Vis. **8**(6), 455–474 (2014)
27. Liao, S., et al.: Person re-identification by local maximal occurrence representation and metric learning. In: Proceedings of the IEEE Conference on Computer Vision and Pattern Recognition (2015)
28. Ma, B., Su, Y., Jurie, F.: Covariance descriptor based on bio-inspired features for person re-identification and face verification. Image Vis. Comput. **32**(6–7), 379–390 (2014)
29. Yang, Y., Yang, J., Yan, J., Liao, S., Yi, D., Li, S.Z.: Salient color names for person re-identification. In: Fleet, D., Pajdla, T., Schiele, B., Tuytelaars, T. (eds.) ECCV 2014. LNCS, vol. 8689, pp. 536–551. Springer, Cham (2014). https://doi.org/10.1007/978-3-319-10590-1_35
30. Sun, K., et al.: Deep high-resolution representation learning for human pose estimation. In: Proceedings of the IEEE/CVF Conference on Computer Vision and Pattern Recognition (2019)
31. Cao, Z., et al.: OpenPose: realtime multi-person 2D pose estimation using part affinity fields. IEEE Trans. Pattern Anal. Mach. Intell. **43**(1), 172–186 (2019)
32. Wang, R., Yan, J., Yang, X.: Learning combinatorial embedding networks for deep graph matching. In: Proceedings of the IEEE/CVF International Conference on Computer Vision (2019)
33. Zanfir, A., Sminchisescu, C.: Deep learning of graph matching. In: Proceedings of the IEEE Conference on Computer Vision and Pattern Recognition (2018)

34. Caetano, T.S., et al.: Learning graph matching. IEEE Trans. Pattern Anal. Mach. Intell. **31**(6), 1048–1058 (2009)
35. Gao, Z., et al.: Deep spatial pyramid features collaborative reconstruction for partial person ReID. In: Proceedings of the 27th ACM International Conference on Multimedia (2019)
36. Miao, J., et al.: Pose-guided feature alignment for occluded person re-identification. In: Proceedings of the IEEE/CVF International Conference on Computer Vision (2019)
37. Sun, Y., et al.: Perceive where to focus: Learning visibility-aware part-level features for partial person re-identification. In: Proceedings of the IEEE/CVF Conference on Computer Vision and Pattern Recognition (2019)
38. Sun, Y., Zheng, L., Yang, Y., Tian, Q., Wang, S.: Beyond part models: person retrieval with refined part pooling (and a strong convolutional baseline). In: Ferrari, V., Hebert, M., Sminchisescu, C., Weiss, Y. (eds.) ECCV 2018. LNCS, vol. 11208, pp. 501–518. Springer, Cham (2018). https://doi.org/10.1007/978-3-030-01225-0_30
39. Li, J., et al.: Crowdpose: efficient crowded scenes pose estimation and a new benchmark. In: Proceedings of the IEEE/CVF Conference on Computer Vision and Pattern Recognition (2019.)
40. Zhong, Y., Wang, X., Zhang, S.: Robust partial matching for person search in the wild. In: Proceedings of the IEEE/CVF Conference on Computer Vision and Pattern Recognition (2020)
41. Fu, Y., et al.: Horizontal pyramid matching for person re-identification. In: Proceedings of the AAAI Conference on Artificial Intelligence (2019)
42. Zheng, W.-S., et al.: Partial person re-identification. In: Proceedings of the IEEE International Conference on Computer Vision (2015)
43. He, L., et al.: Deep spatial feature reconstruction for partial person re-identification: alignment-free approach. In: Proceedings of the IEEE Conference on Computer Vision and Pattern Recognition (2018)
44. Tan, H., et al.: Incomplete descriptor mining with elastic loss for person re-identification. IEEE Trans. Circuits Syst. Video Technol. (2021)
45. Gao, S., et al.: Pose-guided visible part matching for occluded person ReID. In: Proceedings of the IEEE/CVF Conference on Computer Vision and Pattern Recognition (2020)
46. Tan, H., et al.: MHSA-Net: multi-head self-attention network for occluded person re-identification. arXiv preprint arXiv:2008.04015 (2020)
47. He, L., et al.: Recognizing partial biometric patterns. arXiv preprint arXiv:1810.07399 (2018)
48. He, L., et al.: Foreground-aware pyramid reconstruction for alignment-free occluded person re-identification. In: Proceedings of the IEEE/CVF International Conference on Computer Vision (2019)
49. Miao, J., Wu, Y., Yang, Y.: Identifying visible parts via pose estimation for occluded person re-identification. IEEE Trans. Neural Netw. Learn. Syst. (2021)

Improved Occluded Person Re-Identification with Multi-feature Fusion

Jing Yang[1], Canlong Zhang[1](✉), Zhixin Li[1], and Yanping Tang[2]

[1] Guangxi Key Lab of Multi-Source Information Mining and Security, Guangxi Normal University, Guilin 541004, China
[2] School of Computer Science and Information Security, Guilin University of Electronic Technology, Guilin 541004, China

Abstract. Pedestrians are often occluded by various obstacles in public places, which is a big challenge for person re-identification. To address this issue, we propose an improved occluded person re-Identification with the feature fusion network. The new network integrates spatial attention and pose estimation (SAPE) to learn representative, robust, and discriminative features. Specifically, the spatial attention mechanism anchors the regions of interest to the unoccluded spatial semantic information. It digs out the visual knowledge that is helpful for recognition from the global structural pattern. Then, we explicitly partition the attention-aware global feature into parts and improve the recognition granularity by matching local features. On this basis, we improve a pose estimation model to extract the information of the key points and feature fusion with the attention-aware feature to eliminate the influence of occlusion on the re-identification result. We test and verify the effectiveness of the SAPE on Occluded-REID, Occluded-DukeMTMC and Partial-REID. The experiment results show that the proposed method has achieved competitive performance to the state-of-the-art.

Keywords: Attention mechanism · Pose estimation · Feature fusion · Person re-identification

1 Introduction

Person re-identification (Re-ID) [2,17] can be understood as retrieving and identifying the same pedestrian from non-overlapping cameras in different times and spaces. With the wide application of monitoring equipment, Re-ID has become an important topic in computer vision. In practical application scenarios, Re-ID can be combined with gait, face, attributes and other related technologies to carry out suspect tracking and intelligent search in police systems.

The existing methods on Re-ID [21,22] usually perform well when pedestrians are not covered. However, due to the complexity and diversity of the person's environment, many influencing factors can cause errors in the final matching

I. Farkaš et al. (Eds.): ICANN 2021, LNCS 12894, pp. 308–319, 2021.
https://doi.org/10.1007/978-3-030-86380-7_25

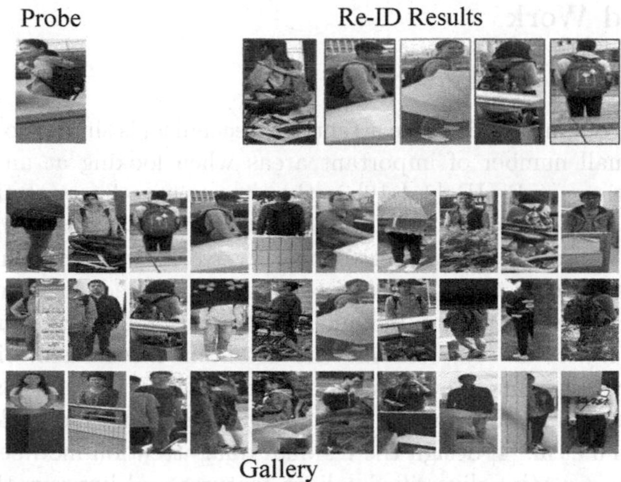

Fig. 1. The figure shows the result of incorrect re-identification by the traditional partitioning method. The red box indicates failure in identification. Under the condition that the image to be inquired is blocked by buildings, the conventional identification results are not ideal.

results. As shown in Fig. 1, the target person taken under different cameras is occluded by natural scenes. As can be seen from the Re-ID results, the existing model based on block recognition cannot effectively identify the occluded person.

A very intuitive solution is to remove the occluded parts. Some existing works [6,23] manually crop the occluded region and match the un-occluded part of the images. These methods may introduce noise. Recently, the attention mechanism has been widely used in different computer vision tasks [4,10]. By focusing on local areas, the attention mechanism can enhance the features and improve the accuracy of recognition. Besides, some methods [1,22] use pose information to accurately anchor the key points of the pedestrian's skeleton, which can avoid the alignment process of the matching process and filter the occluded regions.

Inspired by this above work, we propose a novel method that fuses the key point information feature of pose estimation with the spatial attention feature map. In summary, we make several significant contributions in this paper:

- We propose an integrated Spatial Attention and Pose Estimation (SAPE) feature fusion framework, which enriches the types of person Re-ID. It is the first time to apply spatial attention mechanism to the occluded person Re-ID.
- We improve the pose estimation model and construct a feature map with more robust recognition by combining the pose-guided attention map and spatial attention map, which guides the model to focus on the un-occluded human body area and alleviates the occlusion problem.
- We construct a multi-task network. It combines global and local features to achieve multi-granularity feature representation, thus enables the network to obtain all potential salience features.

2 Related Work

2.1 Attention-Based Person Re-ID

In the field of computer vision, the attention mechanism is similar to how humans focus on a small number of important areas when looking at an object. The main application for Re-ID [3,4,19] is that it can usually reset the weight of the convolution response map to highlight the important part of the image. Chen et al. [3] propose the attentive but diverse network, which could learn attention mask directly from data and context and redundant attention characteristics by combining attention module and diversity regularization as a mutual supplement. Tay et al. [19] combine the attention mechanism with attribute information, which unifics thc local characteristics of the image, as well as the appearance attributes of pedestrians' clothing colors, hair, and backpacks into a single frame. Fu et al. [4] design the residual dual attention module aggregation feature, which can mine diversified salient features and improve the network's capacity for salient features. These models have increased the model's attention to the human body area, but it is also prone to excessive attention to details not related to the human body. We try to transform the original image features into another space and retain the key information, which can irrelevant features can be effectively suppressed.

2.2 Pose-Drive Person Re-ID

Pose-drive person Re-ID can effectively solve the inaccurate identification caused by excessive changes in pedestrian pose [1,7,13,22]. Therefore, Liu et al. [13] propose a pose transfer framework, which uses Generative Adversarial Networks and pose skeletons for joint learning to generate new pose variants to enhance data samples. Artacho et al. [1] propose a unified pedestrian pose estimation framework based on waterfall, and single-pose estimation combines with context segmentation can effectively locate the pedestrian pose at one stage. Sarfraz et al. [16] construct the PSE model. The calculated perspective probability value would be used as the weight of the corresponding unit to get the final weighted fusion feature. However, the effect of these models is not good when they are used in an occluded scene. Our model use pose estimation to guide feature matching. The pose information of the un-occluded region guides the feature map to ignore the influence of the occluded regions.

3 The Proposed Method

Fig. 2 shows our SAPE architecture, which consists of Spatial Attention subnetwork (SAN), Horizontally Partition subnetwork (HPN) and Pose Attention subnetwork (PAN). Given an image of a person, the model firstly uses SAN to weight regions with richer semantic information, then employs PAN to predict un-occluded key points, finally fuses these features from the above two subnetworks. It is helpful to eliminate the influence of occlusion on the matching result.

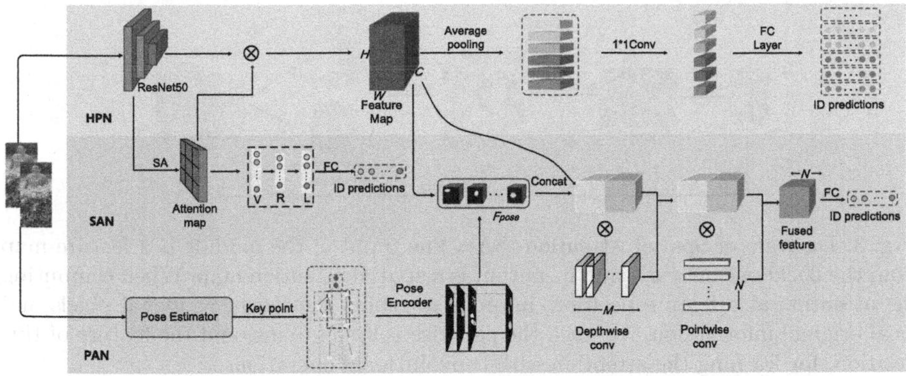

Fig. 2. A schematic overview of SAPE. It consists of Horizontally Partition subnetwork (HPN), Spatial Attention subnetwork (SAN) and Pose Attention subnetwork (PAN), where HPN is to generate features of horizontal partition, SAN is to generate spatial attention map, and PAN is to predict un-occluded key points in person pose. The outputs of three subnetworks are combined by homotopic uncertainty learning to predict the person identification.

This section elaborates on the various modules of SAPE, and finally introduces the loss function used in our work.

3.1 Spatial Attention Subnetwork

Details of spatial attention (SA) are shown in Fig. 3. The convolutional feature map extracted by the backbone network $\boldsymbol{A} \in \mathbb{R}^{C \times H \times W}$ can be used as the input of spatial attention, where C is the total number of channels and $H \times W$ is the size of the feature map. The convolutional feature map can be reshaped to a $N \times C$ 2-dim matrix $\boldsymbol{M}$, where $N = H * W$ represent the number of pixels in the convolutional feature map. Every feature vector of matrix $\boldsymbol{M}$ is expressed as $\boldsymbol{A}_i$, where $i = 1, \cdots, N$. The attention map generated by the spatial attention module as:

$$\boldsymbol{F}_s = [\mathrm{g}(\delta(\tau(\boldsymbol{W}_1\boldsymbol{A})))]©[\delta(\tau(\boldsymbol{W}_2\boldsymbol{S}_i))] \tag{1}$$

where $\boldsymbol{W}_1$ and $\boldsymbol{W}_2$ are the parameters of the spatial convolution layer. τ represents the BN layer, δ represents the ReLU activation function. $\mathrm{g}(\cdot)$ is global average pooling operation along the channel dimension. © means the connection operation. The global relationship feature $\boldsymbol{S}_i \in \mathbb{R}^{2N}$ can be expressed as:

$$\boldsymbol{S}_i = \boldsymbol{M}(i,:)©\boldsymbol{M}(:,i) \tag{2}$$

where $\boldsymbol{M}(i,:)$ is the elem at the ith row of the incidence matrix $\boldsymbol{M} \in \mathbb{R}^{N \times N}$ between pixels, and $\boldsymbol{M}(:,i)$ represent the ith column. The calculation formula of the incidence matrix S between pixels is as follows:

$$\boldsymbol{M}_{ij} = [\delta(\tau(\boldsymbol{W}_3\boldsymbol{A}_i))]^T[\delta(\tau(\boldsymbol{W}_4\boldsymbol{A}_j))] \tag{3}$$

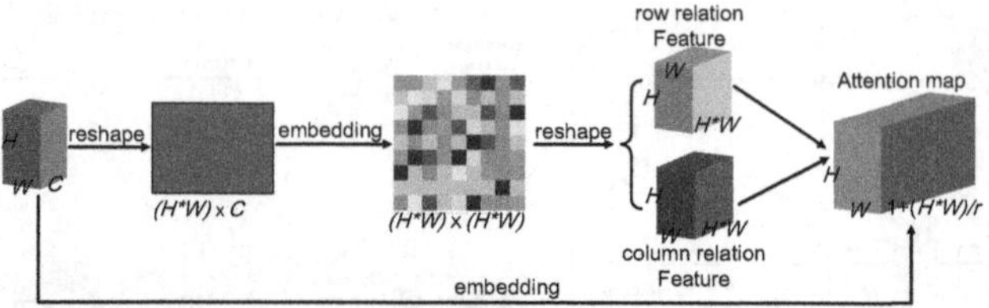

Fig. 3. Diagram of Spatial Attention (SA). The input of the module is a feature map from the backbone network, and its output is a spatial attention map. When computing the attention at a feature position, in order to fusion the relevance global pixels and local original information, we stack the pairwise relation items, and the feature of this position, for learning the attention with convolutional operations.

where $\boldsymbol{M}_{ij}$ is the ith row and j^{th} column of the incidence matrix $\boldsymbol{M}$ and indicates the effect of the ith pixel on the jth pixel, where $i, j \in [1, N]$. $\boldsymbol{W}_3$ and $\boldsymbol{W}_4$ are the parameters of the 1×1 spatial convolution layer, and the size of the convolution kernel is both $C \times (C/r) \times 1 \times 1$.

The attention map obtained through the above stages is used as the input of global average pooling. Then, a three-layer micro-network structure including convolutional layer (V), BN layer (B) and ReLU layer (R), is used to reduce the channel dimension to further increase the network depth and learn deeper semantic features.

$$\boldsymbol{F}_{out} = \delta[\tau(\boldsymbol{W}_5(g(\boldsymbol{F}_s)))] \tag{4}$$

where $\boldsymbol{W}_5$ is the parameter of the convolution layer. After getting the output of SAN, softmax is used to predict the identity of each incoming image. The training stage uses cross-entropy loss.

3.2 Horizontally Partition Subnetwork

In order to refine the network structure and further improve the characterization capability of the features, HPN is added in this paper, whose structure is shown in the upper part of Fig. 2.

In the HPN, we extract the attention-aware feature map by taking the outer product of the global feature map $\boldsymbol{A}$ output by the backbone network and the attention map $\boldsymbol{F}_s$ of the person images. Next, the attention feature map is horizontally divided into p parts, and each part is represented as $\boldsymbol{D}_p$, where $p = 1, \cdots, P$. Then global average pooling is performed for each part.

During training, the feature vectors are respectively sent to the fully connection layer for classification. After obtaining the classification result of each part, the labels that are the same as the global feature classification of person are used to calculate the cross-entropy loss. The cross-entropy loss function of multiple tasks is shown as:

$$L_h = \sum_{p=1}^{P} -\log \frac{\exp(\boldsymbol{W}_{y^p}^T \mathbf{D}_p + b_{y^p})}{\sum_{k=1}^{K} \exp(\boldsymbol{W}_k^T \mathbf{D}_p + b_k)} \tag{5}$$

where y^p represents the pedestrian identity, k is the total number of person identities in the training set, and $\{W, b\}$ denotes the weight and bias of the classification layer respectively. The total loss of a partial characteristic subnetwork with horizontal partitioning is denoted by L_h.

3.3 Pose-Guided Global Feature Subnetwork

The PAN aims to construct global features that contain pose information. The pose estimation model can extract key points and obtains confidence maps. Each key point corresponding to the visible area has a Gaussian peak, and the key points with occlusion have low confidence. We use the AlphaPose model pre-trained on the COCO [12] dataset as the pose estimator to generate key points of the human body, which predicts a total of 18 key points. In order to reduce the complexity of the pose estimation model and avoid the model paying too much attention to some details of pedestrians, we improved the model. We fuse the key points of the head area and finally obtains 14 key points, including head, neck, shoulders, elbows, wrists, hips, knees, and ankles. We set a threshold λ to filter out the key points with lower confidence.

$$LM_q = \begin{cases} (X_q, Y_q) & conf_q \geq \lambda \\ 0 & else \end{cases} \quad (q = 1, \ldots, Q) \tag{6}$$

where LM_q is the symbol of the qth key point, (X_q, Y_q) represents the corresponding coordinate, $conf_q$ is the confidence degree of the key point.

Then, we fuse the heatmaps and the spatial attention map. First, multiply heatmaps by the spatial attention map to obtain a feature map containing pose information. Then, connect the feature map containing the pose information $\boldsymbol{F}_{pose}$ with the spatial attention map $\boldsymbol{F}_s$

The convolutional neural network here uses deep convolution and point convolution, which can obtain more fine-grained fusion features, and can effectively reduce the parameters of the neural network. The fused feature map is obtained and classified after being fully connected. The whole fusion process can be expressed as:

$$\boldsymbol{F}_{fuse} = \boldsymbol{W}_7[\boldsymbol{W}_6(\boldsymbol{F}_{pose} \otimes \boldsymbol{F}_s) \copyright \boldsymbol{F}_s)] \tag{7}$$

where $\boldsymbol{W}_6$ and $\boldsymbol{W}_7$ are implemented by deep convolution and point convolution. $\otimes$ is the outer product operation. During the training of the subnetwork, same as the above network structure, softmax is used to predict the identity of each input image, and cross entropy is used as the loss function.

3.4 Loss Function

The SAPE is a multi-task network, and each subtask has different contributions to the whole model, if the weight of each subtask loss is set to the same, the final identification accuracy will be affected. Since the optimal weight of each subtask depends not only on the measurement scale, but ultimately on the size of the noise of each task. In our work, homotopic uncertainty learning [11] is used to combine the loss of multiple subtasks.

We assume that the prediction error satisfies the Gaussian distribution. The different weights of multiple tasks can be optimized by using Bayesian modeling for homotopic uncertainty. When the loss of one of the subtasks increases, the weight parameter decreases, and vice versa. This paper assumes that the prediction error satisfies the Gaussian distribution, so the minimum total task loss of this network structure is:

$$L_{total} \approx \frac{1}{\mu_1^2} L_s + \frac{1}{\mu_2^2} L_h + \frac{1}{\mu_3^2} L_p + log \mu_1 \mu_2 \mu_3 \tag{8}$$

where L_s, L_h, L_p respectively for SAN, HPN and PAN loss of three tasks. μ_1, μ_2, μ_3 are their noise factor, and they are determined by multi-task learning in training.

4 Experiments

4.1 Implementation Details

In order to verify the model in this paper is effective to occluded Re-ID, experiments are performed on the occluded datasets Occluded-DukeMTMC [14], Occluded-REID [24] and the partial dataset Partial-REID [23]. The experiment in this paper uses two evaluation indicators, the cumulative matching characteristic(CMC) and the mean average precision(mAP) to measure the performance of the model.

We use ResNet50 [8] pre-trained on the ImageNet [5] as the backbone network. In the training stage, the size of all input images is resized to 384×128, and the data is enhanced by random horizontal flipping and random erasing. The batch size is to set 32; the number of training epochs of the model is set as 120. In the SAN, the predefined positive integer r controlling the dimensionality reduction ratio is set to 8. In HPN, the feature map is horizontally divided into p parts, here p is set to 3. In the PAN, the confidence threshold λ is 0.2.

4.2 Comparison with SOTA

Comparison with attention methods [4,10,19] are illustrated in the first group of Table 1. Compared with the above attention methods, the model proposed in this paper performs well on the three datasets. The accuracy of Rank-1 is about 10% higher than the second-ranked attention method. This comparative experiment shows that the attention mechanism that lacks occlusion processing does not perform well in re-identifying occluded persons; it also shows that it is necessary to design a special occlusion processing mechanism.

The second group of Table 1 are partial methods [3,9,18]. It can be seen that compared to the existing partial-based person Re-ID methods, our model

Table 1. Compared with attention method, attitude estimation method and block method in three datasets. The 1/2 best result is red/blue.

Methods	Occluded-DukeMTMC				Occluded-REID				Partial-REID			
	Rank-1	Rank-5	Rank-10	mAP	Rank-1	Rank-5	Rank-10	mAP	Rank-1	Rank-5	Rank-10	mAP
ABD-Net [10]	44.7	60.5	67.8	34.9	54.8	60.2	73.5	50.3	60.2	78.6	87.5	55.4
AANet [19]	42.6	59.3	64.6	31.3	57.3	61.3	70.2	54.8	58.3	78.0	85.9	50.1
SCSN [4]	43.5	58.7	66.9	32.8	53.6	65.2	72.1	49.7	61.8	79.4	88.4	52.2
PCB [18]	41.8	56.9	62.5	32.8	55.8	74.4	81.2	51.3	57.5	76.9	86.8	50.7
DSR [9]	40.8	58.2	65.2	30.4	70.4	80.7	88.4	61.7	73.8	80.4	84.2	67.3
FPR [3]	–	–	–	–	75.1	79.4	87.2	60.8	79.2	82.3	89.4	70.4
PSE [15]	40.8	57.2	67.2	32.5	56.2	–	–	–	60.7	–	–	–
PGFA [14]	51.4	68.6	74.9	37.3	55.4	74.5	81.8	53.6	68.0	78.7	86.7	56.2
HOReID [20]	53.8	65.5	75.1	40.6	75.3	80.4	90.1	66.1	81.7	87.0	86.3	71.3
SAPE	55.1	70.0	74.5	42.3	76.4	82.3	89.2	68.0	82.5	89.2	90.1	72.8

shows better applicability to the occluded problem. Since the feature map of attention perception is divided into blocks in this paper, the feature map after integrating the attention mechanism enhances the attention to the unshaded area. The unshaded area can be more accurately matched after partitioning.

The third group in Table 1 shows the performance of pose estimation methods [14,15,20]. Compared with the three methods shown in the table, the model proposed in this paper achieves 55.1%, 76.4% and 82.5% of Rank-1 accuracy on the three datasets. The existing accuracy is improved. The performance improvement achieved in this paper is mainly due to partial matching is more suitable for occluded person Re-ID tasks than global feature learning.

4.3 Ablation Study

First, the effect of three subnetworks on the discernibility is verified in the Occluded-DukeMTMC dataset. The experiment results are shown in Table 2. When these related subtasks are added to the network, the network's overall recognition accuracy will increase, verifying that each subtask has a specific contribution to the model's overall performance. Besides, compared with setting the same weight for each subnetwork, the homotopic uncertainty learning we use can effectively optimize the learning objectives and effectively improve the performance.

Then, we analyze the impact of the spatial attention (SA) module at different layers of the backbone network ResNet-50. We add the proposed SA module after all residual blocks. Table 3 shows the experiment results on the Occluded-DukeMTMC and Partial-REID datasets. It can be seen from the data in the table that mAP and Rank-1 are improved after adding the SA module after different residual blocks, and the performance of the SA module after conv5_x can reach the best performance.

Figure 4 shows the effect of different of horizontal block p and threshold λ settings on the accuracy of different datasets. As shown in (a) of Fig. 4, when $p > 1$, which just proves the necessity of blocking the features extracted by

Table 2. Performance (%) comparison of different task loss combinations on Occluded-DukeMTMC dataset.

Task loss	Task loss weights			Rank-1	mAP
L_s	1	0	0	44.9	30.7
$L_s + L_h$	0.5	0.5	0	48.3	34.9
$L_s + L_h + L_p$	0.33	0.33	0.33	52.6	38.4
$L_s + L_h + L_p$	Uncertainty learning			55.1	42.3

Table 3. Experimental results (%) of placing the attention module (SA) in different positions.

Methods	Occluded-DukeMTMC		Partial-REID	
	Rank-1	mAP	Rank-1	mAP
ResNet50 (baseline)	47.5	36.8	76.3	65.6
conv2_x+SA	49.0	37.6	77.6	68.2
conv3_x+SA	53.7	40.9	80.9	70.7
conv4_x+SA	54.2	40.2	79.4	69.5
conv5_x+SA	55.1	42.3	82.5	72.8

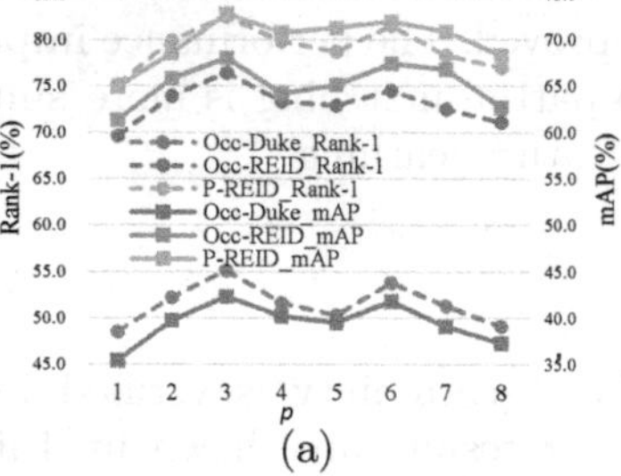

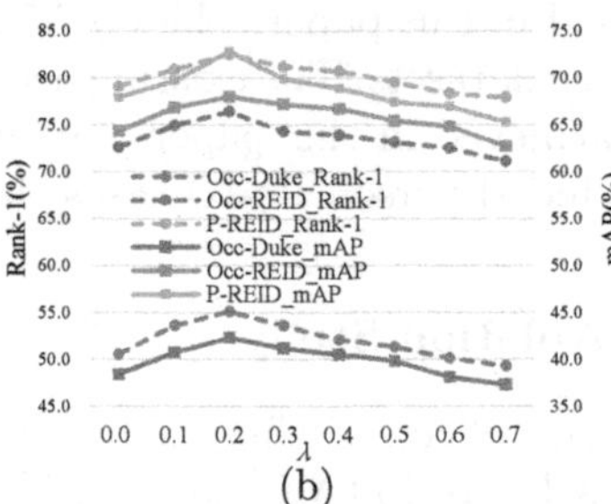

Fig. 4. The influence of setting horizontal block p and the confidence threshold λ of pose estimation on the accuracy of different datasets.

the convolutional neural network. When it is increased to 3, the performance of the model reaches the best. When it is greater than 3, the performance starts to decline slowly. Because the number of parts is too large, some un-occluded parts may not contain any key points. Otherwise, as shown in (b) of Fig. 4, when the threshold λ is too small or too large, the performance is poor. When it is too small (for example, 0), the model will select all detected markers, which will not achieve the purpose of using key points to eliminate occlusion. When the threshold is too high, many flags are discarded. It can be seen from the experimental results that when the threshold value is 0.2, the accuracy of the three data sets reaches the optimal level.

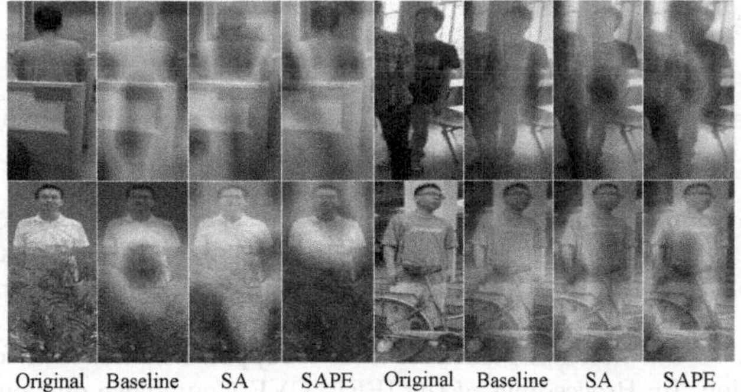

Fig. 5. The visualization results of using the attention mechanism (SA) alone and the overall model (SAPE).

4.4 Visualization

In order to feel the attention mechanism of this article more intuitively, Fig. 5 shows the visualization results of using the attention mechanism alone and the overall model using gradient response in this paper. The gradient response can identify regions that the network model considers relatively essential. In the figure, "Baseline" uses the Resnet-50 network model, and "SA" indicates that we use the spatial attention mechanism model alone. As can be seen from the Fig. 5, the model proposed in this paper can pay more attention to the un-occluded regions more accurately, showing better effects than the baseline model.

5 Conclusion

In this paper, we propose a multi-task network to solve the occluded person Re-ID. Spatial attention mechanism and pose estimation can mine recognizable fine-grained features from global features to eliminate occlusions. Moreover, local feature alignment increases the granularity of the network. Through abundant experimental analysis and verification, our model has good recognition accuracy, better robustness, and generalization ability than other advanced methods. In the following work, the occluded person Re-ID model combined with pose estimation will be further studied. The accuracy of occluded person Re-ID will be improved by suppressing background interference and using graph convolution to mine deep semantic information.

Acknowledgement. This work is supported by the National Natural Science Fo-undation of China (Nos. 61866004, 61663004, 61966004, 61962007, 61751213), the Guangxi Natural Science Foundation (Nos. 2018GXNSFDA281009, 2017GXNSFAA198365, 2019GXNSFDA245018, 2018GXNSFDA294001), Research Fund of Guangxi Key Lab of Multi-source Information Mining and Security (No. 20-A-03-01), Innovation Project of Guangxi Graduate Education JXXYYJSCXXM-2021-007 and Guangxi "Bagui Scholar" Teams for Innovation and Research Project.

References

1. Artacho, B., Savakis, A.: UniPose: unified human pose estimation in single images and videos. In: Proceedings of the IEEE/CVF Conference on Computer Vision and Pattern Recognition, pp. 7035–7044 (2020)
2. Chen, K., Chen, Y., Han, C., Sang, N., Gao, C.: Hard sample mining makes person re-identification more efficient and accurate. Neurocomputing **382**, 259–267 (2020)
3. Chen, T., et al.: ABD-Net: attentive but diverse person re-identification. In: Proceedings of the IEEE International Conference on Computer Vision, pp. 8351–8361 (2019)
4. Chen, X., et al.: Salience-guided cascaded suppression network for person re-identification. In: Proceedings of the IEEE/CVF Conference on Computer Vision and Pattern Recognition, pp. 3300–3310 (2020)
5. Deng, J., Dong, W., Socher, R., Li, L.J., Li, K., Fei-Fei, L.: ImageNet: a large-scale hierarchical image database. In: 2009 IEEE Conference on Computer Vision and Pattern Recognition, pp. 248–255. IEEE (2009)
6. Gao, Z., Gao, L., Zhang, H., Cheng, Z., Hong, R.: Deep spatial pyramid features collaborative reconstruction for partial person REID. In: MM - Proceedings ACM International Conference Multimedia, pp. 1879–1887 (2019)
7. Ge, Y., Li, Z., Zhao, H., Yin, G., Yi, S., Wang, X., et al.: FD-GAN: pose-guided feature distilling GAN for robust person re-identification. In: Advances in Neural Information Processing Systems, pp. 1222–1233 (2018)
8. He, K., Zhang, X., Ren, S., Sun, J.: Deep residual learning for image recognition. In: Proceedings of the IEEE Conference on Computer Vision and Pattern Recognition, pp. 770–778 (2016)
9. He, L., Liang, J., Li, H., Sun, Z.: Deep spatial feature reconstruction for partial person re-identification: alignment-free approach. In: Proceedings of the IEEE Conference on Computer Vision and Pattern Recognition, pp. 7073–7082 (2018)
10. Hu, J., Shen, L., Sun, G.: Squeeze-and-excitation networks. In: Proceedings of the IEEE Conference on Computer Vision and Pattern Recognition, pp. 7132–7141 (2018)
11. Kendall, A., Gal, Y., Cipolla, R.: Multi-task learning using uncertainty to weigh losses for scene geometry and semantics. In: Proceedings of the IEEE Conference on Computer Vision and Pattern Recognition, pp. 7482–7491 (2018)
12. Lin, T.-Y., et al.: Microsoft COCO: common objects in context. In: Fleet, D., Pajdla, T., Schiele, B., Tuytelaars, T. (eds.) ECCV 2014. LNCS, vol. 8693, pp. 740–755. Springer, Cham (2014). https://doi.org/10.1007/978-3-319-10602-1_48
13. Liu, J., Ni, B., Yan, Y., Zhou, P., Cheng, S., Hu, J.: Pose transferrable person re-identification. In: Proceedings of the IEEE Conference on Computer Vision and Pattern Recognition, pp. 4099–4108 (2018)
14. Miao, J., Wu, Y., Liu, P., Ding, Y., Yang, Y.: Pose-guided feature alignment for occluded person re-identification. In: Proceedings of the IEEE International Conference on Computer Vision, pp. 542–551 (2019)
15. Saquib Sarfraz, M., Schumann, A., Eberle, A., Stiefelhagen, R.: A pose-sensitive embedding for person re-identification with expanded cross neighborhood re-ranking. In: Proceedings of the IEEE Conference on Computer Vision and Pattern Recognition, pp. 420–429 (2018)
16. Sarfraz, M.S., Schumann, A., Eberle, A., Stiefelhagen, R.: A pose-sensitive embedding for person re-identification with expanded cross neighborhood re-ranking. In: Proceedings of the IEEE Conference on Computer Vision and Pattern Recognition (2018)

17. Şerbetçi, A., Akgül, Y.S.: End-to-end training of CNN ensembles for person re-identification. Pattern Recogn. **104**, 107319 (2020)
18. Sun, Y., Zheng, L., Yang, Y., Tian, Q., Wang, S.: Beyond part models: person retrieval with refined part pooling (and a strong convolutional baseline). In: Ferrari, V., Hebert, M., Sminchisescu, C., Weiss, Y. (eds.) ECCV 2018. LNCS, vol. 11208, pp. 501–518. Springer, Cham (2018). https://doi.org/10.1007/978-3-030-01225-0_30
19. Tay, C.P., Roy, S., Yap, K.H.: AANet: attribute attention network for person re-identifications. In: Proceedings of the IEEE Conference on Computer Vision and Pattern Recognition, pp. 7134–7143 (2019)
20. Wang, G., et al.: High-order information matters: learning relation and topology for occluded person re-identification. In: Proceedings of the IEEE/CVF Conference on Computer Vision and Pattern Recognition, pp. 6449–6458 (2020)
21. Zhang, Z., Lan, C., Zeng, W., Chen, Z.: Densely semantically aligned person re-identification. In: Proceedings of the IEEE Conference on Computer Vision and Pattern Recognition, pp. 667–676 (2019)
22. Zheng, F., et al.: Pyramidal person re-identification via multi-loss dynamic training. In: Proceedings of the IEEE Conference on Computer Vision and Pattern Recognition, pp. 8514–8522 (2019)
23. Zheng, W.S., Li, X., Xiang, T., Liao, S., Lai, J., Gong, S.: Partial person re-identification. In: Proceedings of the IEEE International Conference on Computer Vision, pp. 4678–4686 (2015)
24. Zhuo, J., Chen, Z., Lai, J., Wang, G.: Occluded person re-identification. In: 2018 IEEE International Conference on Multimedia and Expo (ICME), pp. 1–6. IEEE (2018)

Joint Weights-Averaged and Feature-Separated Learning for Person Re-identification

Di Su, Cheng Zhang(✉), and Shaobo Wang

Beijing Institute of Technology, Beijing 100081, China
{3220195008,zhangcheng,shao-bo.wang}@bit.edu.cn

Abstract. Although existing research has made considerable progress in person re-identification (re-id), it remains challenges due to intra-class variations across different cameras and the lack of cross-view paired training data. Recently, there are increasing studies focusing on using generative model to augment training samples. One of the main obstacles is how to use generated unlabeled samples. To address this issue, we propose a joint learning framework without label predictions, including re-id learning and data generation end-to-end. Each person encodes into a feature code and a structure code. The generative module is able to generate cross-id images by decoding structure code with switched feature code. For generated unlabeled data, we average re-id model weights instead of label predictions. Moreover, we expand the distance between inter-class feature code. Our approach improves the accuracy of the re-id model and the quality of the generated data. Experiments on several benchmark datasets shows that our method achieves competitive results with most state-of-the-art methods.

Keywords: Person re-identification · Data augmentation · Triplet loss · GAN

1 Introduction

Person re-identification (re-id) aims to retrieve images of a specified pedestrian across no-overlapping cameras, given a query person-of-interest, which is often approached as metric learning problem. It is a challenging task due to images captured by different cameras often containing significant intra-class variations in person appearance, pose, background, *etc.* Besides, pedestrian under particular view causing inapparent inter-class variations, two person may share similar looks, as shown in Fig. 1. Thus, designing powerful representations that tackle both inter-class similarity and intra-class variations has been one of the major targets in person re-id.

With the prosperity of deep convolutional network, it's discriminative representations for pedestrian images has been shown to boost the performance of person re-id into a new level. Recently, some state-of-the-art re-id methods focus

I. Farkaš et al. (Eds.): ICANN 2021, LNCS 12894, pp. 320–332, 2021.
https://doi.org/10.1007/978-3-030-86380-7_26

Fig. 1. Examples of intra-class variations and inter-class similarity on Market-1501. The two images in (a), (c) have the same identity and the two in (b), (d) have different identities.

on designing a more discriminative representations or loss functions for pedestrian feature and many other formulate re-id as metric learning. Considering inter-class similarity, [3] introduce variants of classic triplet loss and evaluate these variants.

In order to minimize the impact of intra-class variations, a number of state-of-the-art methods focus their partition strategies on part-based matching by leveraging external cues or partitioning embedding feature directly [16]. While robust metric learning strategies could alleviate the problem of insufficient data to some extent, introducing more pedestrian samples can enhance the model directly. Based on the recent development of the generative adversarial networks (GANs), generative models are widely used to introduce extra samples. Some challenging problems arises in these methods: 1) Generated samples do not contain enough discriminative information; 2) Due to the low pixel of pedestrian images and complexity of human shape, traditional strategies failed to generate identify samples with good quality.

There is a further problem with generative pipelines separating from the re-id models, bring limited improvement from the generated samples. [18] propose a joint learning framework, introducing a pretrained teacher re-id model to predict unlabeled samples generated by generative module. However, in many real-life scenarios, there is no pretrained re-id model.

To explicitly address these issues, we propose a joint weights-averaged and feature-separated learning framework which contains both discriminative and generative learning in a unified network called **WF-Net**. Our work is partly inspired by DG-Net [18], we decompose each image into a feature space and a structure space. Both encoded by generative module, feature space encodes id-related embedding and structure space encodes image structure information consisting background, pose, face, *etc.* from corresponding grayed pedestrian image. The feature encoder also act as re-id module. Generated images are taken to refine the feature encoder online. To avoid using pretrained re-id model, our strategy introduce a weights-averaged module, average model weights instead of label predictions. By switching feature codes or structure codes between two images from same/different identities, we generate intra/inter-class samples to adds sample diversity from the existing identity portfolio. Besides, we introduce a variant of the triplet loss, and it make the generated images more discriminative.

We conduct various experiments on several benchmark datasets. Analysis of the experiments showed that our framework performs very favorably and it achieves state-of-the-art results. The main contributions of this paper can be summarized as follows:

- We propose a similar semi-supervised re-id learning framework that generated unlabeled samples by itself.
- We introduce weights-averaged method to predict generated samples without additional auxiliary pretrained re-id model, and propose a variant of the triplet loss.

The rest of this paper is organized as follows: Sect. 2 briefly reviews existing related work and Sect. 3 describe the joint weights-averaged and feature-separated method. In Sect. 4, we present experimental evaluations and further analysis it. Conclusion provided in Sect. 5 lastly.

2 Related Work

Person re-identification attracts great attention due to its important application values. Most of the existing works focus on supervised learning, approach re-id as deep metric learning problems. Some exploit identification loss with classification, others introduce triplet loss with hard sample mining [3]. [14] utilize part-based matching or parsing to reduce intra-class variations and facilitate local feature learning. Similarly, [20] incorporate pose estimation into learning local features.

Generative Adversarial Networks have been widely studied after Goodfellow *et al.* first introduced the adversarial process to learn generative models. For one thing, several works explore to ameliorate model structure and optimization strategy. These lead to a more realistic samples generation. For another, many works focus on applications of GAN, [9] introduce a conditional version of GAN. Phillip Isola *et al.* focus on image style transfer. For person re-id, [19] use unconditional GAN to generate images from random vectors. Additionally, some recent methods utilize pose estimation to conduct pose-conditioned image generation.

Semi-supervised learning based on training the model predictions to be consistent to perturbation. [11] introduce DSS with a deep learning model for classification and [7] improves it through applying noise to the teacher predictions. The idea of training student by a teacher model is related to model distillation. Model distillation performed with a trained model and transfer it to a simpler model in teacher-student framework. [15] average model weights to form a target-generating teacher model.

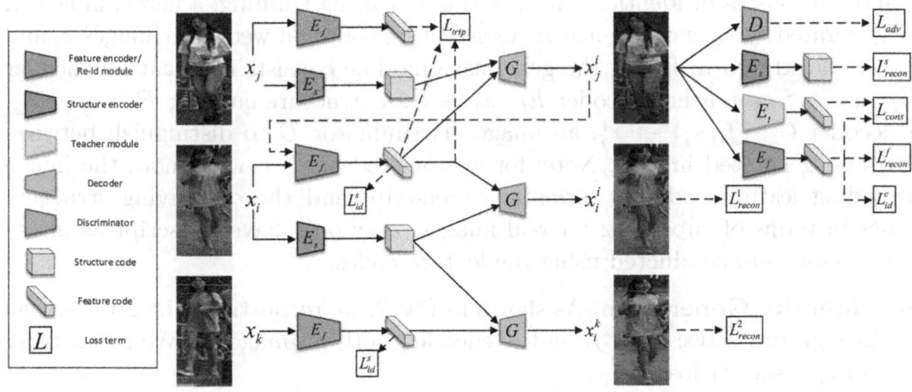

Fig. 2. The overview of WF-Net. The discriminative module share feature encoder E_f. The red line shows the generated samples are online feedback to improve E_f. The black line of dashes point to various loss terms. (Color figure online)

Our strategy differs from the above mentioned methods in following ways: 1) It does not need any pretrained re-id model to predict unlabeled samples as in [18] and does not require any pose estimation, which results in a tightly coupled relationship between feature extractors and the overall framework; 2) In contrast to [3], our approach does not require training strategies like hard mining, we process it during sample generation and feature reconstruction.

3 Method

Our proposed Joint Weights-averaged and Feature-separated Network (WF-Net) aims at learning identity-related representations through pedestrian image generation, in order to minimize the impact of intra-class variations and inter-class similarity across images in person re-id.

The overall framework of our proposed method is shown in Fig. 2, WF-Net combines the generative module and the discriminative module through feature embedding. Our generation module involves cross-identity generation and self-identity generation, synthesized samples are online fed into re-id learning. The discriminative module is co-designed with the generative module to leverage the feature embedding of generated samples directly. For the generated cross-identity samples, a weights-averaged teacher model is utilized to evaluate consistency cost, and a variant of the triplet loss is designed to guarantee its feature similarity/discrepancy with feature/structure encode source image.

3.1 Image Encoder and Image Generator

Formulation. We denote the real images and identity labels as $X = \{x_i\}_{i=1}^{N}$ and $Y = \{y_i\}_{i=1}^{N}$, where N is the number of images, $y_i \in [1, K]$ and K is the number of classes or identities in the dataset. During training, a new sample can be generated by exchanging feature or structure codes between two images x_i and x_j. As illustrated in Fig. 2, the generative module consists of a feature encoder $E_f : x_i \rightarrow f_i$, a teacher encoder $E_t : x_i \rightarrow t_i$, a structure encoder $E_s : x_j \rightarrow s_j$, a decoder $G : (f_i, s_j) \rightarrow x_j^i$, an image discriminator D to distinguish between real and generated images. Note: for synthesized images, we denote the image providing feature codes in terms of superscript and the one giving structure codes in terms of subscript; for real images, they only have subscript as image index. Our re-id conducted using the feature codes.

Self-Identity Generation. As shown in Fig. 2, we reconstruct the given image x_i through two ways: first, f_i and s_i encoded both in image x_i. We reconstruct the image using ℓ_1 loss:

$$L_{recon}^{1} = \mathbb{E}\left[\| \, x_i - G\left(f_i, s_i\right) \|_1\right]. \tag{1}$$

Second, we assume that the same person in different images possess similar feature, we utilize cross-image reconstruction between two images of the same identity. Specifically, the generator reconstruct image x_i through an image x_k with the same identity:

$$L_{recon}^{2} = \mathbb{E}\left[\| \, x_i - G\left(f_k, s_i\right) \|_1\right]. \tag{2}$$

These two ways of reconstruction acts as main regularization role to the generator, the latter promote the aggregation of feature codes of the same identity to reduce the intra-class feature variations. Besides, we introduce identification loss to force the feature codes of different images stay apart:

$$L_{id}^{s} = \mathbb{E}\left[-\log\left(p\left(y_i|x_i\right)\right)\right], \tag{3}$$

where $p\left(y_i|x_i\right)$ is consistency between the predicted probability of image x_i and the ground-truth class y_i based on its feature code.

Cross-Identity Generation. This generation task focus on image generation with different identities so that there is no constraint of ground-truth images. In this case, we utilize code reconstruction to control cross-identity generation.

Randomly choose two images x_i and x_j with different identity, the generated images $x_j^i = G(f_i, s_j)$ expected to possess similar feature/structure with image x_i/x_j. Hence, we establish code reconstruction loss by encoding the generated images x_j^i:

$$L_{recon}^{f} = \mathbb{E}\left[\| f_i - E_f\left(G\left(f_i, s_j\right)\right) \|_1\right], \tag{4}$$

$$L_{recon}^{s} = \mathbb{E}\left[\| s_j - E_s\left(G\left(f_i, s_j\right)\right) \|_1\right]. \tag{5}$$

Same as self-identity generation, we also apply identification loss to the generated image according its feature code:

$$L_{id}^{c} = \mathbb{E}\left[-\log\left(p\left(y_i|x_j^i\right)\right)\right], \tag{6}$$

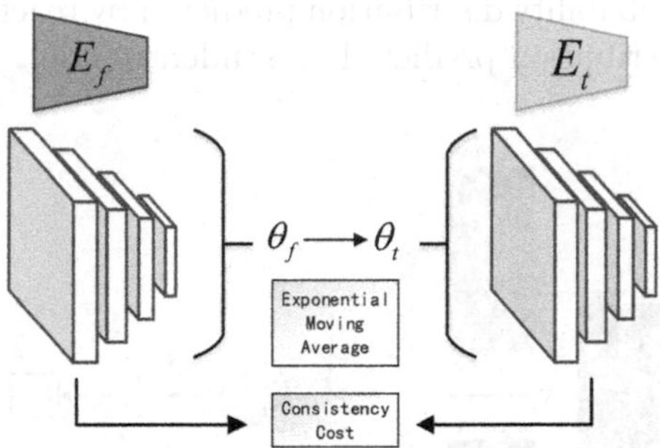

Fig. 3. The weights-averaged method. The output of encoder E_f is compared with encoder E_t using consistency cost. Both of them can be used for re-id and image generation, but the E_t performs better on image generation while the E_f performs better on re-id.

where $p\left(y_i|x_j^i\right)$ is consistency between the predicted probability of image x_j^i and the ground-truth class y_i of the one providing feature code during cross-identity image generation. Furthermore, we utilize adversarial loss to control the authenticity of the generated data:

$$L_{adv} = \mathbb{E}\left[\log D\left(x_i\right) + \log\left(1 - D\left(G\left(f_i, s_j\right)\right)\right)\right] \tag{7}$$

3.2 Weights-Averaged Teacher and Discriminative Module

Same as DG-Net, the discriminative module sharing the feature encoder as the backbone for re-id learning. Existing work show that the generated images can be used as training samples. However, we introduce weights-averaged teacher model online updating with the discriminative module instead of assigning a soft label to the generated image x_j^i, as shown in Fig. 3.

Weights-Averaged Teacher Model. Averaging model weights during training incline to train a more accurate model than using the final weights directly.

Instead of sharing weights with student model, teacher model use Exponential Moving Average to process student model. We apply weights averages to all layer output, define θ'_t at training iteration t as the processed result of θ_t:

$$\theta'_t = \alpha\theta'_{t-1} + (1-\alpha)\,\theta_t, \tag{8}$$

where α is a smoothing coefficient. Additional, the teacher model weights update with student model rather than optimize by loss functions.

Feature Learning. We assume that teacher model is more accurate than student model. Noise was apply to Increase variability in predictions. In order to make student model predictions consistent with teacher model. We define the consistency loss to value the distance between the predictions using ℓ_2 loss:

$$L_{cons} = \mathbb{E}\left[\| \, q\left(x_j^i\right) - p\left(x_j^i\right) \|_2\right], \tag{9}$$

where $q\left(x_j^i\right)$ is the probability distribution predicted by teacher model and $p\left(x_j^i\right)$ is the probability distribution predicted by student model.

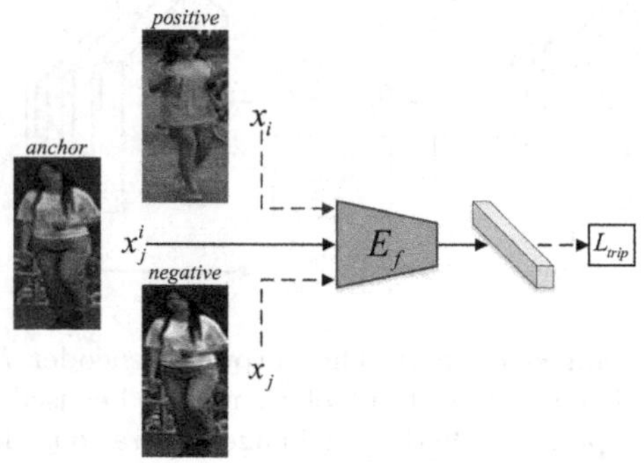

Fig. 4. The feature-separated method, depicts a variants of triplet loss.

3.3 Feature-Separated

Triplet loss is adopted extensively in retrieval tasks such as face and person re-id. This loss means that, given an anchor object x_a, the map of a positive object x_p in the same class y_a is closer to the anchor's map than a negative object x_n in another class y_n at least a margin m. Because of the generated image x_j^i is expected to maintain the information of feature code from x_i with the structure code of x_j. There is something similar to the feature code of x_j inevitably. Hence, we assume that the feature code of x_j^i, x_i and x_j as a triple, mapping is processed by the feature encoder, as illustrated in Fig. 4. The feature triplet loss is defined as follows:

$$L_{trip} = D\left(E_f\left(x_j^i\right), E_f\left(x_i\right)\right) - D\left(E_f\left(x_j^i\right), E_f\left(x_j\right)\right) + m, \tag{10}$$

where $D\left(E_f\left(x_j^i\right), E_f\left(x_i\right)\right)$ referred as the distance function between x_j^i and x_i in the feature code space.

3.4 Optimization

We jointly train the shared feature and structure encoder, decoder, as well as discriminator to optimize the total objective, which is a weighted sum of the following loss terms:

$$\begin{aligned} L_{total}\left(E_f, E_s, G, D\right) = \lambda_i L^i_{recon} + L^c_{recon} + L^s_{id} \\ + \lambda_{id} L^c_{id} + L_{adv} + \lambda_{cons} L_{cons} + L_{trip}, \end{aligned} \tag{11}$$

where $L^i_{recon} = L^1_{recon} + L^2_{recon}$ is the image reconstruction loss in self-identity generation, $L^c_{recon} = L^f_{recon} + L^s_{recon}$ is the code reconstruction loss in cross-identity generation, $\lambda_i, \lambda_{id}, \lambda_{cons}$ are the weights to control the importance of corresponding loss terms.

3.5 Comparison to DG-Net

There is an existing work, DG-Net [18] based on joint learning framework, which first propose a joint generative and discriminative learning for person re-id. It also adopts an encoder-decoder structure.

There are three key differences between the proposed WF-Net and DG-Net, which make our algorithm more general and superior. 1) We adopt a teacher student strategy and our teacher model online update by applying weights average to student model, while DG-Net use a fixed pretrained re-id model to predict label of the cross-identity generation image. 2) We utilize a variant of triplet loss to pull the feature code of image x^i_j towards x_i and push feature code of image x_j further away, while DG-Net does not have such loss term. 3) Our work devise a feasible scheme and focuses on both the problem of intra-class variability and inter-class similarity.

Fig. 5. Comparison of the generated and real images on Market-1501 across the different methods including PG^2-Net [8], DeformGAN [12], DG-Net [18], and our method. This figure is best viewed when zoom in.

4 Experiments

We evaluate the proposed framework WF-Net in PyTorch on two person Re-ID benchmark datasets, Market-1501, and DukeMTMC-reID. We report comparisons to the state-of-the-art methods and provide in-depth analysis. The qualitative results of image generation are also presented. A variety of ablation studies demonstrate the contributions of each individual component in our approach. Extensive experiments reveal that our method generate realistic images, and more importantly, is competitive with existing state-of-the-art methods over two benchmarks.

4.1 Implementation Details

E_f is modified from ResNet50 and pre-trained on ImageNet [1]. We use SGD to train E_f and Adam [6] to optimize others. Following the practice in DG-Net, we set a large weight $\lambda_i = 5$ for L^i_{recon}. At the early stage of training, the quality of cross-identity generation image is not great. Hence, we set weight $\lambda_{id} = 0.5$ for L^c_{id}. We first warm up E_f, E_t, E_s and G for 30K, then we involves the teacher consistent loss L_{cons} and the feature separated loss L_{trip}, meanwhile, we linearly increase λ_{cons} from 0 to 2 by 0.0005 per step. For feature separated learning, we set margin as 0.2 and set α as 0.999. We follow the alternative updating policy in training GANs to alternatively train E_f, E_s and G.

4.2 Qualitative Evaluations

Comparison with the State-of-the-Art. We first compare our generated result with other representative image generative approaches, including PG^2-Net [8], DeformGAN [12], DG-Net [18]. As compared in Fig. 5, PG^2-Net and DeformGAN generate image based on pose, both of them have the ability to generate images with good visual. The formal contains visible blurs and artifacts, while the latter miss body parts and in a weird pose occasionally. DG-Net can generate natural visual effect of good images, but the feature of the generated images also contains some blur.

Table 1. Comparison of FID (lower is better) and SSIM (higher is better) to evaluate fidelity and diversity of the generated and real images on Market-1501. Ours-E_f and Ours-E_t means use encoder E_f and E_t, respectively.

Method	Fidelity (FID)	Diversity (SSIM)
Real	7.22	0.350
PG^2-Net [8]	151.16	–
FD-GAN [2]	257.00	0.247
DeformGAN [12]	28.61	0.290
DG-Net [18]	18.24	0.360
Ours-E_f	18.52	0.357
Ours-E_t	**18.22**	**0.361**

4.3 Quantitative Evaluations

Generative Evaluations. Following [18], We adopt two metrics to measure fidelity and diversity of generated images: Fréchet Inception Distance (FID), Structural SIMilarity (SSIM). FID measures the distance between the distribution of generated and real images. A lower FID means that the two distributions are closer together, which means that the quality of the images produced is higher. SSIM reflect the generation diversity, we apply it to compute the intra-class similarity. As shown in Table 1, Our approach performs better in fidelity and diversity than other approach. It is worth noting that our SSIM value is higher than the real value, which means switching codes method enriches the diversity of original training set, it is also proved in DG-Net. Generated examples on Market-1501 and DukeMTMC-reID shown in the Fig. 6.

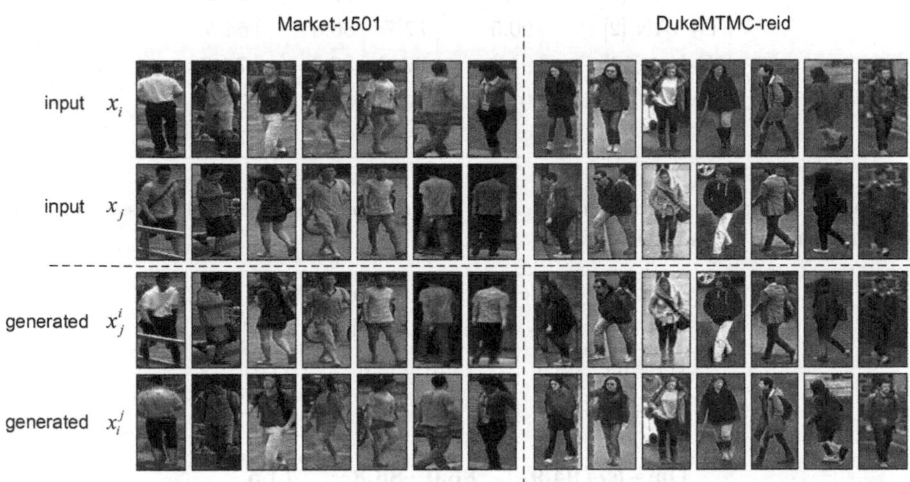

Fig. 6. Examples of the generated images on Market 1501 and DukeMTMC-reid, all input images are sampled from the test sets.

Discriminative Evaluations. We evaluate WF-Net on benchmark datasets and report it performance with other state-of-the-art results in Table 2. Our method achieved a very competitive performance on each dataset. Compare to DG-Net, similar results were obtained using a different method that does not require a pre-trained re-id model. Compare to others, our method joint image generation and re-id learning in one training phase. Meanwhile, WF-Net also achieve a better performance than other non-generative method.

4.4 Ablation Studies

Finally, we conduct some ablation studies to make certain the contributions of weights average loss and feature triplet loss. We choose ResNet50 with identification loss as our baseline. As shown in Table 3, our two loss are found to

Table 2. Comparison with the state-of-the-art methods. The top half: the methods not using generated samples. The bottom half: the methods using generated samples.

Method	Market-1501		DukeMTMC	
	Rank@1	mAP	Rank@1	mAP
GLAD [16]	89.9	73.9	–	–
Part-aligned [13]	91.7	79.6	84.4	69.3
PCB [14]	93.8	81.6	83.3	69.2
CASN+PCB [17]	94.4	82.8	87.7	73.7
IANet [4]	94.4	83.1	87.1	73.4
DeformGAN [12]	80.6	61.3	–	–
Multi-pseudo [5]	85.8	67.5	76.8	58.6
PN-GAN [10]	89.4	72.6	73.6	53.2
FD-GAN [2]	90.5	77.7	80.0	64.5
DG-Net [18]	94.8	**86.0**	86.6	**74.8**
Ours-E_f	**94.9**	**86.0**	**86.8**	74.5
Ours-E_t	94.6	85.7	86.3	73.9

Table 3. Comparison of baseline, weights average loss, feature triplet loss, and their combination on the two datasets.

Method	Market-1501		DukeMTMC	
	Rank@1	mAP	Rank@1	mAP
Baseline	89.6	74.5	82.0	65.3
L_{cons}	93.8	84.2	85.4	73.5
L_{trip}	93.1	82.5	83.9	70.8
Ours-E_f	**94.9**	**86.0**	**86.8**	**74.5**

conspicuous improve over the baseline individually. By combining these two loss, we can further improve the performance, which achieves clear gains of 5.3% for Rank@1 and 11.5% for mAP on Market-1501, 4.8% and 9.2% on DukeMTMC. This shows the merits of our method clearly.

5 Conclusion

In this paper, we have proposed an end-to-end framework that joint re-id learning and image generation without a pretrained re-id model. There exists a consistency cost between the output of the weights averaged teacher model and the feature encoder, a variant of triplet loss to separate the features from the structure. Both of them co-designed to better leverage the generated image. Experiments on two benchmarks indicate that our strategy consistently brings substantial performance gains to re-id using samples generation.

References

1. Deng, J., Dong, W., Socher, R., Li, L.J., Li, K., Fei-Fei, L.: ImageNet: a large-scale hierarchical image database. In: 2009 IEEE Conference on Computer Vision and Pattern Recognition, pp. 248–255. IEEE (2009)
2. Ge, Y., Li, Z., Zhao, H., Yin, G., Yi, S., et al.: FD-GAN: pose-guided feature distilling GAN for robust person re-identification. In: Advances in Neural Information Processing Systems, pp. 1222–1233 (2018)
3. Hermans, A., Beyer, L., Leibe, B.: In defense of the triplet loss for person re-identification. arXiv preprint arXiv:1703.07737 (2017)
4. Hou, R., Ma, B., Chang, H., Gu, X., Shan, S., Chen, X.: Interaction-and-aggregation network for person re-identification. In: Proceedings of the IEEE Conference on Computer Vision and Pattern Recognition, pp. 9317–9326 (2019)
5. Huang, Y., Xu, J., Wu, Q., Zheng, Z., et al.: Multi-pseudo regularized label for generated data in person re-identification. IEEE Trans. Image Process. **28**(3), 1391–1403 (2018)
6. Kingma, D.P., Ba, J.: Adam: a method for stochastic optimization. arXiv preprint arXiv:1412.6980 (2014)
7. Laine, S., Aila, T.: Temporal ensembling for semi-supervised learning. arXiv preprint arXiv:1610.02242 (2016)
8. Ma, L., Jia, X., Sun, Q., Schiele, B., Tuytelaars, T., Van Gool, L.: Pose guided person image generation. In: Advances in Neural Information Processing Systems, pp. 406–416 (2017)
9. Mirza, M., Osindero, S.: Conditional generative adversarial nets. arXiv preprint arXiv:1411.1784 (2014)
10. Qian, X., et al.: Pose-normalized image generation for person re-identification. In: Ferrari, V., Hebert, M., Sminchisescu, C., Weiss, Y. (eds.) ECCV 2018. LNCS, vol. 11213, pp. 661–678. Springer, Cham (2018). https://doi.org/10.1007/978-3-030-01240-3_40
11. Rasmus, A., Berglund, M., Honkala, M., Valpola, H., Raiko, T.: Semi-supervised learning with ladder networks. In: Advances in Neural Information Processing Systems, pp. 3546–3554 (2015)
12. Siarohin, A., Sangineto, E., Lathuiliere, S., Sebe, N.: Deformable GANs for pose-based human image generation. In: Proceedings of the IEEE Conference on Computer Vision and Pattern Recognition, pp. 3408–3416 (2018)
13. Suh, Y., Wang, J., Tang, S., Mei, T., Lee, K.M.: Part-aligned bilinear representations for person re-identification. In: Ferrari, V., Hebert, M., Sminchisescu, C., Weiss, Y. (eds.) Computer Vision – ECCV 2018. LNCS, vol. 11218, pp. 418–437. Springer, Cham (2018). https://doi.org/10.1007/978-3-030-01264-9_25
14. Sun, Y., Zheng, L., Yang, Y., Tian, Q., Wang, S.: Beyond part models: person retrieval with refined part pooling (and a strong convolutional baseline). In: Ferrari, V., Hebert, M., Sminchisescu, C., Weiss, Y. (eds.) ECCV 2018. LNCS, vol. 11208, pp. 501–518. Springer, Cham (2018). https://doi.org/10.1007/978-3-030-01225-0_30
15. Tarvainen, A., Valpola, H.: Mean teachers are better role models: weight-averaged consistency targets improve semi-supervised deep learning results. In: Advances in Neural Information Processing Systems (2017)
16. Wei, L., Zhang, S., Yao, H., Gao, W., Tian, Q.: GLAD: global-local-alignment descriptor for pedestrian retrieval. In: Proceedings of the 25th ACM International Conference on Multimedia (2017)

17. Zheng, M., Karanam, S., Wu, Z., Radke, R.J.: Re-identification with consistent attentive siamese networks. In: Proceedings of the IEEE Conference on Computer Vision and Pattern Recognition, pp. 5735–5744 (2019)
18. Zheng, Z., Yang, X., Yu, Z., Zheng, L., Yang, Y., Kautz, J.: Joint discriminative and generative learning for person re-identification. In: IEEE Conference on Computer Vision and Pattern Recognition (CVPR) (2019)
19. Zheng, Z., Zheng, L., Yang, Y.: Unlabeled samples generated by GAN improve the person re-identification baseline in vitro. In: Proceedings of the IEEE International Conference on Computer Vision, pp. 3754–3762 (2017)
20. Zheng, Z., Zheng, L., Yang, Y.: Pedestrian alignment network for large-scale person re-identification. IEEE Trans. Circuits Syst. Video Technol. **29**(10), 3037–3045 (2018)

Semi-Hard Margin Support Vector Machines for Personal Authentication with an Aerial Signature Motion

Takeshi Yoshida[1(✉)] and Takuya Kitamura[2]

[1] University of Tsukuba, 1-1-1 Tennodai, Tsukuba, Ibaraki, Japan
s2120791@u.tsukuba.ac.jp

[2] National Institute of Technology, Toyama College, 13 Hongo-machi, Toyama, Japan
kitamura@nc-toyama.ac.jp

Abstract. The classifiers for personal authentication needs to be robust against spoofing attacks. In this paper, we propose semi-hard margin support vector machines (SH-SVMs) for personal authentication problems with an aerial signature motion. To be robust against spoofing attacks, SH-SVMs are trained so that false acceptance rate (FAR) of training data is zero. There are three types of SH-SVMs as follows: (1) standard SHSVM based on L2-SVM, (2) semi-hard twin SVM (SH-TWSVM) based on TWSVM, (3) semi-hard support vector data description (SH-SVDD) based SVDD. In computer experiments, we compare our methods with the conventional methods, using the aerial signature dataset and show effectiveness of SH-SVMs.

Keywords: Personal authentication · Spoofing attacks · Support vector machines

1 Introduction

Lately, personal authentication is widely used such as face authentication with mobile phone [5]. Especially, biometric authentication [2] is highly safe method. However, some personal authentication systems are vulnerable to spoofing attacks [10]. Accordingly, personal authentication with an aerial signature motion [6,7,11,12] has been proposed [4,19,20]. An aerial signature is one of the behavioral features such as hand writing motion [16], keystroke [14], motion of the portable device [9], etc. Since the motion does not leave a trail, it is robust feature against spoofing attacks for personal authentication. In previous studies, the similarity measure is obtained by DP matching [8] and the threshold value is set so that false rejected rate (FRR) and false acceptance rate are low (FAR). In the results of computer experiments in [4,19,20], FAR was not enough low for personal authentication. FAR is more important than FRR to prevent spoofing attacks. To lower FAR, we try to use support vector machines (SVMs) [1] instead of DP matching. Then, FAR and FRR were lower than results of [4,19,20]. However, FAR was too high for personal authentication problem.

I. Farkaš et al. (Eds.): ICANN 2021, LNCS 12894, pp. 333–344, 2021.
https://doi.org/10.1007/978-3-030-86380-7_27

In this paper, to overcome this problem, we propose semi-hard margin support vector machines (SH-SVMs) for personal authentication. In training SH-SVMs, misclassification of training data of positive class is not allowed. Namely, in SH-SVMs, FAR of training data is zero. Then, there are three types of SH-SVMs as follows: (1) standard SH-SVM, (2) semi-hard twin SVM (SH-TWSVM), (3) semi-hard support vector data description (SH-SVDD). Standard SH-SVM is based on L2-SVM. In the optimization problem of SH-SVM, since the slack variable corresponding to only negative class data is introduced unlike the standard L2-SVM, the slack variable corresponding to positive class is zero. The data is classified into a class by using sign of decision function. SH-TWSVM is based on TWSVM [13]. SH-TWSVM calculates decision function for only negative class data unlike TWSVM. Additionally, that decision function has margin to positive class data. SH-SVDD is based on L2-soft margin two class SVDD [18]. As with SH-SVM, SH-SVDD introduces slack variable for only negative class data to calculate the hypersphere which wrap only negative class data.

We propose three types of SH-SVMs at Sect. 2, and we show result of computer experiments at Sect. 3. Section 3.1 shows the aerial signature dataset and Sect. 3.3 describe discussion of results. Finally, we conclude this paper at Sect. 4.

2 Semi-Hard Support Vector Machines

2.1 SH-SVM Based on L2 SVM

The decision function of SH-SVM is given by

$$D(\boldsymbol{x}) = \boldsymbol{w}^{\top}\boldsymbol{\phi}(\boldsymbol{x}) + b, \tag{1}$$

where $\boldsymbol{w}$, b, and $\boldsymbol{\phi}(\cdot)$ are the d-dimension weight vector, bias value, and the mapping function into the high dimension feature space whose dimension is d. Let the m-dimensional training data be $\{\boldsymbol{x}_i, y_i\}(i = 1, \ldots, M)$, where the number of the training data is M. Then, $y_i = 1$ or $y_i = -1$ if x_i belongs to negative or positive class. In SH-SVM, the optimization problem is defined as follows:

$$\min \quad Q(\boldsymbol{w}, b, \boldsymbol{\xi}) = \frac{1}{2}\boldsymbol{w}^{\top}\boldsymbol{w} + \frac{\lambda}{2}\sum_{i=1, y_i=1}^{M} \xi_i^2, \tag{2}$$

$$\text{s.t.} \quad y_i\left(\boldsymbol{w}^{\top}\boldsymbol{\phi}(\boldsymbol{x}_i) + b\right) \geq 1 - \frac{1+y_i}{2}\xi_i \quad \text{for} \quad i = 1, \ldots, M, \tag{3}$$

where $\xi_i(i = 1, \ldots, M)$ and λ are slack variable, which is a non-negative value and margin parameter. From (2) and (3), the slack variables corresponding to negative class data are not affect this problem. Moreover, for negative class data, the misclassification is not allowed by (3). Next, by introducing the Lagrange multipliers $\alpha_i (i = 1, \ldots, M)$ which is a non-negative value, we obtain the unconstrained optimization problem as follows:

$$Q(\boldsymbol{w}, b, \boldsymbol{\xi}, \boldsymbol{\alpha}) = \frac{1}{2}\boldsymbol{w}^\top \boldsymbol{w} + \frac{\lambda}{2}\sum_{i=1}^{M} \xi_i^2 - \sum_{i=1, y_i=1}^{M} \alpha_i \left(y_i \left(\boldsymbol{w}^\top \boldsymbol{\phi}(\boldsymbol{x}_i) + b \right) - 1 + \frac{1+y_i}{2}\xi_i \right). \tag{4}$$

Then, KKT conditions are given by

$$\frac{\partial Q(\boldsymbol{w}, b, \boldsymbol{\xi}, \boldsymbol{\alpha})}{\partial \boldsymbol{w}} = \boldsymbol{w} - \sum_{i=1}^{M} \alpha_i y_i \boldsymbol{\phi}(\boldsymbol{x}_i) = 0, \tag{5}$$

$$\frac{\partial Q(\boldsymbol{w}, b, \boldsymbol{\xi}, \boldsymbol{\alpha})}{\partial b} = \sum_{i=1}^{M} \alpha_i y_i = 0, \tag{6}$$

$$\frac{\partial Q(\boldsymbol{w}, b, \boldsymbol{\xi}, \boldsymbol{\alpha})}{\partial \boldsymbol{\xi}} = \lambda \xi_i - \alpha_i \frac{1+y_i}{2} = 0. \tag{7}$$

Moreover, KKT complementary conditions is defined as follows:

$$\alpha_i \left(y_i \left(\boldsymbol{w}^\top \boldsymbol{\phi}(\boldsymbol{x}_i) + b \right) - 1 + \frac{1+y_i}{2}\xi_i \right) = 0 \quad \text{for} \quad i = 1, \ldots, M, \tag{8}$$

where $\alpha_i \geq 0$ $(i = 1, \ldots, M)$. Then, $\boldsymbol{x}_i$ corresponding to $\alpha_i > 0$ is a support vector. By using the support vectors, bias value b is given by

$$b = \frac{1}{|S|}\sum_{j \in S}\left(y_j - \sum_{i \in S} \alpha_i y_i \left(K(\boldsymbol{x}_i, \boldsymbol{x}_j) + \frac{1+y_i}{2\lambda}\delta_{ij} \right) \right), \tag{9}$$

where S, $K(\cdot, \cdot)$, and δ_{ij} are index set of the support vectors, kernel function, and the Kronecker delta, defined as 0 or 1 if $i \neq j$ or $i = j$. The dual problem is defined as follows:

$$\max \quad Q(\boldsymbol{\alpha}) = \sum_{i=1}^{M} \alpha_i - \sum_{i,j=1}^{M} \alpha_i \alpha_j y_i y_j \left(K(\boldsymbol{x}_i, \boldsymbol{x}_j) + \frac{1+y_i}{2\lambda}\delta_{ij} \right) \tag{10}$$

$$\text{s.t.} \quad \alpha_i \geq 0 \quad \text{for} \quad i = 1, \ldots, M, \tag{11}$$

$$\sum_{i=1}^{M} \alpha_i y_i = 0. \tag{12}$$

With α_i and b obtained by solving above problem, the decision function is redefined as follows:

$$D(\boldsymbol{x}) = \sum_{i \in S} \alpha_i y_i K(\boldsymbol{x}_i, \boldsymbol{x}) + b. \tag{13}$$

2.2 SH-TWSVM

Unlike the standard TWSVM which determine two nonparallel hyperplanes, SH-TWSVM determine a hyperplane. Also, as with SH-SVM, misclassification of training data of positive class is not allowed. Hence, the optimization problem of SH-TWSVM can be defined as follows:

$$\min \quad Q(\boldsymbol{w}, b) = \frac{1}{2} \left\| K(A, C)\boldsymbol{w} + \boldsymbol{e}_{-} b \right\|^2, \tag{14}$$

$$\text{s.t.} \quad K(B, C)\boldsymbol{w} + \boldsymbol{e}_{+} b \leq -\boldsymbol{e}_{+}. \tag{15}$$

Here, $\boldsymbol{w}$, b, A, and B are the weight vector, the bias value, the data of negative class, the data of positive class, where the number of A and B are M and N. Additionally, C is the concatenated matrix of A and B: $C = [A, B]^{\mathsf{T}}$. $\boldsymbol{e}_{-}$ and $\boldsymbol{e}_{+}$ are the identity matrix. By introducing the Lagrange multiplier $\alpha_i (i = 1, \ldots, N)$ which is a non-negative value, we obtain the following unconstrained optimization problem:

$$Q(\boldsymbol{w}, b, \boldsymbol{\alpha}) = \frac{1}{2} \left\| K(A, C)\boldsymbol{w} + \boldsymbol{e}_{-} b \right\|^2 + \boldsymbol{\alpha} \left(K(B, C)\boldsymbol{w} + \boldsymbol{e}_{+} b + \boldsymbol{e}_{+} \right). \tag{16}$$

Then, KKT conditions are given by

$$\frac{\partial Q(\boldsymbol{w}, b, \boldsymbol{\alpha})}{\partial \boldsymbol{w}} = K(A, C) \left\| K(A, C)\boldsymbol{w} + \boldsymbol{e}_{-} b \right\| + \boldsymbol{\alpha}^{\mathsf{T}} K(B, C) = \mathbf{0}, \tag{17}$$

$$\frac{\partial Q(\boldsymbol{w}, b, \boldsymbol{\alpha})}{\partial b} = \boldsymbol{e}_{-}^{\mathsf{T}} \left\| K(A, C)\boldsymbol{w} + \boldsymbol{e}_{-} b \right\| + \boldsymbol{e}_{+}^{\mathsf{T}} \boldsymbol{\alpha} = 0. \tag{18}$$

Moreover, KKT complementary conditions is defined as follows:

$$\boldsymbol{\alpha} \left(K(B, C)\boldsymbol{w} + \boldsymbol{e}_{+} b + \boldsymbol{e}_{+} \right) = 0 \quad \text{for} \quad i = 1, \ldots, N, \tag{19}$$

where $\alpha_i \geq 0$. Matrix of the KKT conditions is given by

$$\begin{bmatrix} \frac{\partial Q(\boldsymbol{w}, b, \boldsymbol{\alpha})}{\partial \boldsymbol{w}} \\ \frac{\partial Q(\boldsymbol{w}, b, \boldsymbol{\alpha})}{\partial b} \end{bmatrix} = L^{\mathsf{T}} L \begin{bmatrix} \boldsymbol{w} \\ b \end{bmatrix} + R^{\mathsf{T}} \boldsymbol{\alpha} = \mathbf{0}, \tag{20}$$

where L is the concatenated matrix of $K(A, C)$ and $\boldsymbol{e}_{-}$: $L = [K(A, C), \boldsymbol{e}_{-}]$, and R is the concatenated matrix of $K(B, C)$ and $\boldsymbol{e}_{+}$: $R = [K(B, C), \boldsymbol{e}_{+}]$. The weight and bias are given by

$$\begin{bmatrix} \boldsymbol{w} \\ b \end{bmatrix} = -(L^{\mathsf{T}} L)^{-1} R^{\mathsf{T}} \boldsymbol{\alpha}. \tag{21}$$

The dual problem is defined as follows:

$$\max \quad Q(\boldsymbol{\alpha}) = \boldsymbol{e}_{+}^{\mathsf{T}} \boldsymbol{\alpha} - \frac{1}{2} \boldsymbol{\alpha} R (L^{\mathsf{T}} L)^{-1} R^{\mathsf{T}} \boldsymbol{\alpha} \tag{22}$$

$$\text{s.t.} \quad \alpha_i \geq 0 \quad \text{for} \quad i = 1, \ldots, N. \tag{23}$$

With $\boldsymbol{\alpha}$, b and $\boldsymbol{w}$ obtained by solving (22) and (23), the decision function is given by

$$D(\boldsymbol{x}) = K(\boldsymbol{x}, C)\boldsymbol{w} + b. \tag{24}$$

2.3 SH-SVDD

In SH-SVDD, the optimization problem is defined as follows:

$$\min \quad Q(R, \boldsymbol{a}, \boldsymbol{\xi}) = R^2 + \frac{\lambda}{2}\sum_{i=1}^{M} \xi_i^2 \tag{25}$$

$$\text{s.t.} \quad y_i \left\|\phi(\boldsymbol{x}_i) - \boldsymbol{a}\right\|^2 \leq y_i \left(R^2 - y_i + \frac{1+y_i}{2}\xi_i\right) \tag{26}$$

$$\text{for} \quad i = 1, \ldots, M.$$

Here, R^2 and $\boldsymbol{a}$ are the square of radius and the origin of the hypersphere. $\boldsymbol{\xi}(i = 1, \ldots, M)$ and λ are the slack variable and the regularization coefficient, which is a hyperparameter. By introducing the Lagrange multipliers $\boldsymbol{\alpha}_i(i = 1, \ldots, M)$ which is a non-negative value, the unconstrained optimization problem is shown as follows:

$$Q(R, \boldsymbol{a}, \boldsymbol{\xi}, \boldsymbol{\alpha}) = R^2 + \frac{\lambda}{2}\sum_{i=1}^{M} \xi_i^2 - \sum_{i=1}^{M} \alpha_i y_i \left(R^2 - y_i + \frac{1+y_i}{2}\xi_i - K(\boldsymbol{x}_i, \boldsymbol{x}_i) + 2\boldsymbol{a}^\top \boldsymbol{\phi}(\boldsymbol{x}_i) - \boldsymbol{a}^\top \boldsymbol{a}\right). \tag{27}$$

Then, KKT conditions are given by

$$\frac{\partial Q(R, \boldsymbol{a}, \boldsymbol{\xi}, \boldsymbol{\alpha})}{\partial R^2} = 1 - \sum_{i=1}^{M} \alpha_i y_i = 0, \tag{28}$$

$$\frac{\partial Q(R, \boldsymbol{a}, \boldsymbol{\xi}, \boldsymbol{\alpha})}{\partial \boldsymbol{a}} = \sum_{i=1}^{M} \alpha_i y_i \boldsymbol{\phi}(\boldsymbol{x}_i) - \boldsymbol{a} = 0, \tag{29}$$

$$\frac{\partial Q(R, \boldsymbol{a}, \boldsymbol{\xi}, \boldsymbol{\alpha})}{\partial \boldsymbol{\xi}} = \lambda\xi_i - \alpha_i y_i \frac{1+y_i}{2} = 0. \tag{30}$$

Moreover, KKT complementary conditions is defined as follows:

$$\alpha_i y_i \left(R^2 - y_i + \frac{1+y_i}{2}\xi_i - K(\boldsymbol{x}_i, \boldsymbol{x}_i) + 2\boldsymbol{a}^\top \boldsymbol{\phi}(\boldsymbol{x}_i) - \boldsymbol{a}^\top \boldsymbol{a}\right) = 0 \tag{31}$$

$$\text{for} \quad i = 1, \ldots, M,$$

where $\alpha_i \geq 0$. Then, $\boldsymbol{x}_i$ corresponding to $\alpha_i > 0$ is a support vector and also satisfy $\|\boldsymbol{\phi}(\boldsymbol{x}_i) - \boldsymbol{a}\| = R^2 - y_i$. Hence, R^2 is given by

$$R^2 = \frac{1}{\|S\|}\sum_{i \in S}\left(K(\boldsymbol{x}_i, \boldsymbol{x}_i) - 2\sum_{j \in S}\alpha_j y_j K(\boldsymbol{x}_i, \boldsymbol{x}_j) + \sum_{j,k \in S}\alpha_j \alpha_k y_j y_k K(\boldsymbol{x}_j, \boldsymbol{x}_k) - \frac{1+y_i}{2\lambda}\alpha_i y_i\right). \tag{32}$$

The dual problem is defined as follows:

$$\max \quad Q(\boldsymbol{\alpha}) = \sum_{i=1}^{M} \alpha_i y_i K(\boldsymbol{x}_i, \boldsymbol{x}_i) - \sum_{i,j=1}^{M} \alpha_i \alpha_j y_i y_j \left(K(\boldsymbol{x}_i, \boldsymbol{x}_j) + \frac{1+y_i}{4\lambda} \delta_{ij} \right) \quad (33)$$

$$\text{s.t.} \quad \alpha_i \geq 0 \quad \text{for} \quad i = 1, \dots, M, \quad (34)$$

$$\sum_{i=1}^{M} \alpha_i y_i = 1. \quad (35)$$

with $\boldsymbol{\alpha}$, R^2 and $\boldsymbol{a}$ obtained by solving above problem, the decision function is given by

$$D(\boldsymbol{x}) = R^2 - K(\boldsymbol{x}, \boldsymbol{x}) + 2 \sum_{i \in S} \alpha_i y_i K(\boldsymbol{x}, \boldsymbol{x}_i) - \sum_{i,j \in S} \alpha_i \alpha_j y_i y_j K(\boldsymbol{x}_i, \boldsymbol{x}_j). \quad (36)$$

3 Computer Experiment

In computer experiment, we confirm robustness for spoofing attack using aerial signature motion dataset. The classifier must classify the other person class which is not include training data and the person themselves class. We compare the FAR and FRR of the proposed method with those of the conventional methods. As the conventional methods, we adopted standard SVM and a classifier based on the mahalanobis distance (CM) [15]. We used the minimum value of the mahalanobis distance whose class is positive in training as the threshold of CM.

3.1 Aerial Signature Motion Dataset

Figure 1 shows the appearance of collecting the aerial signature motion data. In this study, the aerial signature trail is gotten by a Leap Motion which is hand tracking contactless device. A subject signed vertically above this while confirming to motion trail. We get the time series data which is three dimensions space coordinate values x_i, y_i, z_i $(i = 1, \dots, I)$ and velocity values $v_{x_i}, v_{y_i}, v_{z_i}$ $(i = 1, \dots, I)$ while $I/100$ seconds. Then, The signature size and position are different from signature to signature even for same persons'. Hence, at first, we normalize coordinate values range from zero to one as follows:

$$\boldsymbol{f}_i' = \frac{\boldsymbol{f}_i - \min_i \boldsymbol{f}_i}{\max_i \boldsymbol{f}_i - \min_i \boldsymbol{f}_i} \quad \text{for} \quad i = 1, \dots, I, \quad (37)$$

where $\boldsymbol{f}_i = (x_i, y_i, z_i)^\top$ $(i = 1, \dots, I)$. Next, we extract features by EfficientNet [17] pre-trained by ImageNet [3]. To input to the model, we need to convert time

Fig. 1. The appearance of collecting the aerial signature motion dataset.

series data to image. Let the all data lengths be uniform by linear interpolation as follows:

$$f'_{i'} = f_i + (f_{i+1} - f_i)\left(\frac{i'I}{I'} - i\right) \tag{38}$$

$$\text{for} \quad i < \frac{i'I}{I'} < i+1,\ i' = 1, \ldots, I',\ i = 1, \ldots, I.$$

Next, we plot the interpolated XY coordinate data to size 256 × 256 × 3. In the computer experiment, we use the eight types of datasets. Table 1 shows the image created from aerial signature motion data of time series data and used features for color and width. In Table 1, c_i is the ith value which been correspond with color by colorbar. If color of line is black, Table 1 shows c_i = BLACK. Also, w_i is the ith width.

Finally, we extract the feature by the pre-trained EfficientNet [15]. EfficientNet has eight types b0 to b7 by size of model. Each model has nine level by channel dimension. We apply an average pooling to the feature map which is gotten from each level.

The training data consists of five the person themselves data and 120 the other person data. Moreover, the test data consists of 25 the person themselves data and 150 the other person data. The other person data is written by different person in training data and test data. All aerial signature motion are same japanese characters.

3.2 Parameter Setting

We need to select the feature from Table 1, model and level of the EfficientNet. Additionally, the classifiers have some hyperparameter. Therefore, we selected each parameter by a three-fold cross validation. We selected margin parameter λ from $\{0.1, 0.5, 1, 5, 10, 50, 10^2, 5\times10^2, 10^3, 5\times10^3, 10^4, 5\times10^4, 10^5, 5\times10^5, 10^6, 5\times10^6, 10^7, 5\times10^7, 10^8, 5\times10^8, 10^9, 5\times10^9, 10^{10}\}$. Futhermore, we selected from three kernel functions: linear kernel ($K(\boldsymbol{x}, \boldsymbol{x}') = \boldsymbol{x}^\top \boldsymbol{x}'$), polynomial kernel

Table 1. The eight types of image created from aerial signature motion data and definition of color and width for each dataset.

a	b
$c_i = \text{BLACK}$ $w_i = 1$	$c_i = \sqrt{v_{x_i}^2 + v_{y_i}^2}$ $w_i = 3$
c	d
$c_i = \text{BLACK}$ $w_i = \left(v_{x_i}^2 + v_{y_i}^2\right) \times 10^{-4}$	$c_i = \sqrt{v_{x_i}^2 + v_{y_i}^2}$ $w_i = \left(v_{x_i}^2 + v_{y_i}^2\right) \times 10^{-4}$
e	f
$c_i = z_i$ $w_i = 3$	$c_i = z_i$ $w_i = \left(v_{x_i}^2 + v_{y_i}^2 + v_{z_i}^2\right) \times 10^{-4}$
g	h
$c_i = \sqrt{v_{x_i}^2 + v_{y_i}^2 + v_{z_i}^2}$ $w_i = z_i^2 \times 10$	$c_i = \text{BLACK}$ $w_i = z_i^2 \times 10$
colorbar	
$\min c_i$ $\max c_i$ for $i = 1, \ldots, I'$.	

$(K(\boldsymbol{x}, \boldsymbol{x}') = \left(\boldsymbol{x}^{\mathsf{T}}\boldsymbol{x}' + 1\right)^d)$, and radial basis function (RBF) kernel $(K(\boldsymbol{x}, \boldsymbol{x}') = \exp\left(-\gamma\|\boldsymbol{x} - \boldsymbol{x}'\|^2\right))$. where d and γ, which are the kernel parameters, is selected from $\gamma = \{10^{-10}, 5\times10^{-10}, 10^{-9}, 5\times10^{-9}, 10^{-8}, 5\times10^{-8}, 10^{-7}, 5\times10^{-7}, 10^{-6}, 5\times10^{-6}, 10^{-5}, 5\times10^{-5}, 10^{-4}, 5\times10^{-4}, 10^{-3}, 5\times10^{-3}, 10^{-2}, 5\times10^{-2}, 0.1, 0.5\}$ and $d = \{2,3,4,5,6\}$. Additionally, we use $I' = 10^4$ for data lengths in linear interpolation.

Table 2 shows the selected parameters, FAR[%], and FRR[%] in test. The feature row shows determined features: dataset-model-level.

Table 2. The determined parameters, FAR[%] and FRR[%] for personal authentication.

Class		Method				
		CM	SVM	SH-SVM	SH-TWSVM	SH-SVDD
1	Feature	g-b1-6	g-b6-5	g-b3-5	g-b3-2	g-b6-5
	kernel	–	$\gamma = 5 \times 10^{-9}$	$\gamma = 10^{-8}$	$\gamma = 5 \times 10^{-5}$	$\gamma = 5 \times 10^{-9}$
	λ	–	5×10^{6}	5×10^{6}	–	5×10^{7}
	FAR/FRR	0.67/24.00	2.67/8.00	3.33/8.00	4.67/80.00	5.33/8.00
2	Feature	d-b1-4	f-b1-5	f-b0-5	e-b0-4	f-b0-5
	kernel	–	$\gamma = 10^{-8}$	$\gamma = 5 \times 10^{-8}$	$\gamma = 10^{-10}$	$\gamma = 10^{-3}$
	λ	–	5×10^{7}	5×10^{6}	–	5×10^{6}
	FAR/FRR	0.00/96.00	2.67/40.00	1.33/60.00	0.00/100.00	1.33/56.00
3	Feature	c-b2-5	c-b5-4	c-b6-5	c-b7-3	c-b7-5
	kernel	–	$d = 3$	$\gamma = 5 \times 10^{-8}$	$\gamma = 5 \times 10^{-6}$	$\gamma = 10^{-8}$
	λ	–	5×10^{4}	10^{7}	–	5×10^{7}
	FAR/FRR	6.67/48.00	27.33/32.00	31.33/36.00	9.33/92.00	27.33/40.00
4	Feature	c-b2-4	c-b3-3	f-b1-3	f-b1-3	f-b1-3
	kernel	–	$\gamma = 5 \times 10^{-9}$	$\gamma = 10^{-4}$	$\gamma = 5 \times 10^{-6}$	$\gamma = 10^{-4}$
	λ	–	5×10^{6}	10^{4}	–	5×10^{3}
	FAR/FRR	0.00/100.00	20.00/8.00	5.33/64.00	1.33/92.00	5.33/64.00
5	Feature	f-b2-5	h-b1-2	h-b1-4	h-b2-4	h-b1-4
	kernel	–	$\gamma = 5 \times 10^{-8}$	$\gamma = 5 \times 10^{-3}$	$\gamma = 10^{-6}$	$\gamma = 5 \times 10^{-3}$
	λ	–	10^{6}	10^{6}	–	5×10^{5}
	FAR/FRR	0.00/88.00	34.00/52.00	0.00/56.00	0.67/72.00	0.00/56.00
6	Feature	c-b7-6	d-b5-5	d-b3-5	d-b2-3	d-b1-5
	kernel	–	$\gamma = 10^{-9}$	$\gamma = 10^{-8}$	$\gamma = 5 \times 10^{-6}$	$\gamma = 5 \times 10^{-8}$
	λ	–	10^{7}	5×10^{6}	–	5×10^{5}
	FAR/FRR	0.00/92.00	6.67/80.00	1.33/56.00	0.00/88.00	1.33/60.00
7	Feature	h-b7-7	a-b1-2	a-b1-6	a-b0-2	a-b1-2
	kernel	–	$\gamma = 10^{-7}$	$\gamma = 10^{-8}$	$\gamma = 10^{-4}$	$\gamma = 10^{-6}$
	λ	–	5×10^{6}	5×10^{8}	–	5×10^{6}
	FAR/FRR	4.67/64.00	7.33/20.00	2.00/32.00	1.33/60.00	6.00/20.00
8	Feature	d-b5-7	b-b5-6	b-b5-6	a-b1-2	b-b5-6
	kernel	–	$\gamma = 10^{-9}$	$d = 4$	$\gamma = 5 \times 10^{-4}$	$\gamma = 5 \times 10^{-9}$
	λ	–	10^{7}	5×10^{5}	–	5×10^{8}
	FAR/FRR	1.33/88.00	30.67/24.00	8.00/76.00	0.00/96.00	8.00/84.00
9	Feature	g-b0-6	d-b2-7	d-b2-7	b-b7-3	g-b2-7
	kernel	–	$\gamma = 10^{-10}$	$\gamma = 5 \times 10^{-9}$	$\gamma = 5 \times 10^{-6}$	$\gamma = 5 \times 10^{-4}$
	λ	–	10^{7}	10^{7}	–	5×10^{5}
	FAR/FRR	0.00/96.00	22.67/28.00	2.00/32.00	0.00/100.00	3.33/28.00
10	Feature	f-b1-6	d-b1-6	d-b7-6	d-b4-3	f-b7-6
	kernel	–	$\gamma = 10^{-9}$	$\gamma = 5 \times 10^{-9}$	$\gamma = 5 \times 10^{-4}$	$\gamma = 10^{-8}$
	λ	–	5×10^{6}	5×10^{6}	–	5×10^{7}
	FAR/FRR	0.00/76.00	2.00/80.00	0.67/92.00	10.00/96.00	4.67/48.00
Ave	FAR	1.33 ± 2.25	15.60 ± 12.00	5.53 ± 8.89	2.73 ± 3.72	6.27 ± 7.40
	FRR	77.20 ± 23.53	37.20 ± 24.85	51.20 ± 23.24	87.60 ± 12.45	46.40 ± 21.56

3.3 Discussion

In Table 2, the average FAR of CM is the lowest among that of all methods. However, in some classes, FRRs of CM and SH-TWSVM are 100%. In other words, these classifiers classified all data into positive class. In seven classes,

SH-SVM and SH-SVDD perform better than SVM from the standpoint of FAR. In particular, in class 5, FARs of SH-SVM and SH-SVDD are 0% while FRRs of them are only 4% higher than that of SVM. In this results, SH-SVM and SH-SVDD can prevent spoofing attacks than SVM only slight increase of rejection rate to the target person. In most classes, SH-SVM and SH-SVDD show about the same FARs and FRRs, to apply a RBF kernel to SH-SVM, we get same effect of SH-SVDD. In this experiment, all dataset were selected from Table 2. In other word, suitable dataset type is different for each class and classifier. The EfficientNet-b1 was most selected. Because the aerial signature image is simpler than the ImageNet which was used for pre-training of EfficientNet, small model extracts the enough feature for classification. For the same reason, the feature extracted from around level 5 was most selected.

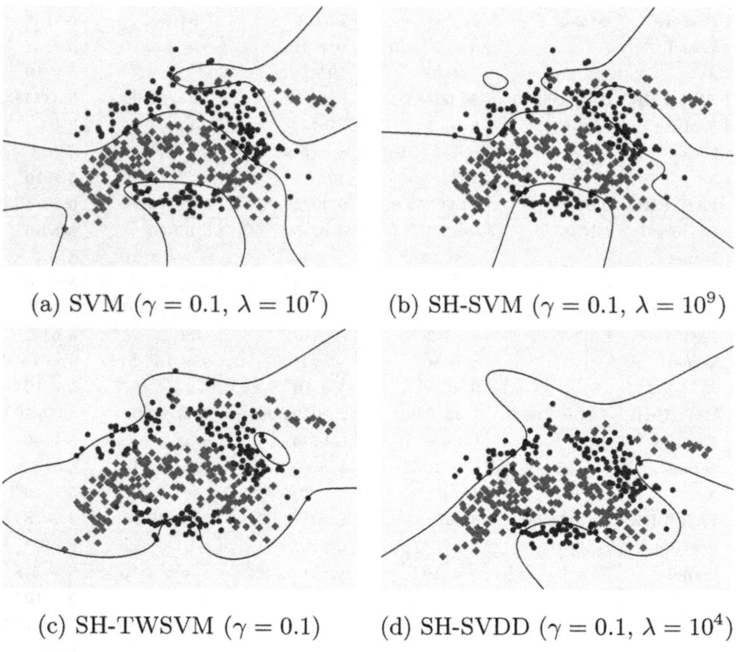

(a) SVM ($\gamma = 0.1$, $\lambda = 10^7$) (b) SH-SVM ($\gamma = 0.1$, $\lambda = 10^9$)

(c) SH-TWSVM ($\gamma = 0.1$) (d) SH-SVDD ($\gamma = 0.1$, $\lambda = 10^4$)

Fig. 2. The hyperplanes of SVM and SH-SVMs for banana dataset in training.

Figure 2 shows the hyperplanes of banana dataset, which is one of the two dimensional benchmark dataset, in training SVM and SH-SVMs. We selected hyperparameters: RBF kernel, $\gamma = 0.1$ and λ by five fold cross validation at each method. Black line in Fig. 2 shows is the hyperplane used for classification. The blue and the red correspond with negative and positive value of decision function. Futhermore, the red rhombus and blue circle are negative and positive class data. In SVM, few data of both class are misclassified. In contrast, SH-SVMs do not misclassify positive class data. All the red rhombus are on the red area. In SH-TWSVM, the red area is larger than other semi-hard margin methods. This reason is that SH-TWSVM considers only positive class data to decide margin as shown by constraint equation (15). This reason causes high FRRs of SH-TWSVM in Table 2.

4 Conclusion

In this paper, we have proposed three types of SH-SVMs to prevent proofing attack for personal authentication problems with an aerial signature motion. In SH-SVM and SH-SVDD, the slack variable of positive class is equal to zero in order to FAR $= 0$ in training.

According to the computer experiment, SH-TWSVM showed 100% FRR in a particular class same of conventional method. However, SH-SVM and SH-SVDD showed that FAR and FRR are low overall than other method. As a result of this, one can see that SH-SVM and SH-SVDD are effectiveness for classification of personal authentication with an aerial signature motion considering spoofing attack.

References

1. Cortes, C., Vapnik, V.: Support-vector networks. Mach. Learn. **20**(3), 273–297 (1995). https://doi.org/10.1007/BF00994018
2. Debnath, B., Rahul, R., Farkhod, A., Minkyu, C.: Biometric authentication: a review. Int. J. u- e- Serv. Sci. Technol. **2**(3), 13–28 (2009)
3. Deng, J., Dong, W., Socher, R., Li, L.J., Li, K., Fei-Fei, L.: Imagenet: a large-scale hierarchical image database. In: 2009 IEEE Conference on Computer Vision and Pattern Recognition, pp. 248–255 (2009)
4. Ebuchi, F., Kitamura, T.: Investigation of features for aerial signature motion personal identification systems. Institute of Electronics, Information and Communication Engineers Technical Report **116**(528), 185–189 (2017)
5. Fathy, M.E., Patel, V.M., Chellappa, R.: Face-based active authentication on mobile devices. In: 2015 IEEE International Conference on Acoustics, Speech and Signal Processing (ICASSP), pp. 1687–1691 (2015)
6. Fujii, Y., Takezawa, M., Sanada, H., Watanabe, K.: An aerial handwritten character input system. The Special Interest Group Technical Reports of Information Processing Society of Japan **50**(3), 1–4 (2009)
7. Hatanaka, I., Kahima, M., Sato, K., Watanabe, M.: Study on a individual recognition system by signature in the air using leap motion. Institute of Electronics, Information and Communication Engineers Technical Report **114**(212), 33–88 (2014)
8. Hiroaki, S., Seibi, C.: Dynamic programming algorithm optimization for spoken word recognition. IEEE Trans. Acoust. Speech Sig. Process. **26**(1), 43–49 (1978)
9. Ishihara, S., Ohta, M., Namikata, E., Mizuno, T.: Individual authentication for portable devices using motion of the devices. J. Inf. Process. (JIP) **46**(12), 2997–3007 (2005)
10. Jain, R., Kant, C.: Attacks on biometric systems: an overview. Int. J. Adv. Sci. Res. **1**(7), 283–288 (2015). https://doi.org/10.7439/ijasr.v1i7.1975

11. Katagiri, M., Sugimura, T.: Mobile personal authentication by free space signing with video capture. **25**(85), 59–64 (2001)
12. Katagiri, M., Sugimura, T.: Personal authentication by signatures in the air with a video camera. Institute of Electronics, Information and Communication Engineers Technical Report **101**(125), 9–16 (2001)
13. Khemchandani, R., Suresh, C.: Twin support vector machines for pattern classification. IEEE Trans. Pattern Anal. Mach. Intell. **29**(5), 905–910 (2007). https://doi.org/10.1109/TPAMI.2007.1068
14. Ogoshi, Y., Hinata, A., Hirose, S., Kimura, H.: Improving user authentication based on keystroke intervals by using intentional keystroke rhythm. J. Inf. Process. (JIP) **44**(2), 397–400 (2003)
15. Rippel, O., Mertens, P., Merhof, D.: Modeling the distribution of normal data in pre-trained deep features for anomaly detection. arXiv preprint arXiv:2005.14140 (2020)
16. Sugahara, S., Rokui, J.: The complex authentication system using online hand writing and password. Forum Inf. Technol. 2014: 2014 FIT **13**(4), 163–170 (2014)
17. Tan, M., Le, Q.: Efficientnet: rethinking model scaling for convolutional neural networks. In: International Conference on Machine Learning, pp. 6105–6114 (2019)
18. Tax, D.M., Duin, R.P.: Support vector data description. Mach. Learn. **54**(1), 45–66 (2004). https://doi.org/10.1023/B:MACH.0000008084.60811.49
19. Yamada, D., Kitamura, T.: Development and comparing of personal authentication systems by signature in the air. Institute of Electronics, Information and Communication Engineers Technical Report **115**(388), 105–110 (2015)
20. Yoshida, T., Kitamura, T.: Improvement of personal authentication by aerial signature. Institute of Electronics, Information and Communication Engineers Technical Report **119**(476), 45–50 (2020)

Recurrent Neural Networks

Dynamic Identification of Stop Locations from GPS Trajectories Based on Their Temporal and Spatial Characteristics

Flora Ferreira[1(✉)], Weronika Wojtak[1,2], Carlos Fernandes[2], Pedro Guimarães[1,2], Sérgio Monteiro[2], Estela Bicho[2], and Wolfram Erlhagen[1]

[1] Centre of Mathematics, University of Minho, Guimarães, Portugal
{fjferreira,wolfram.erlhagen}@math.uminho.pt

[2] Center Algoritmi, University of Minho, Guimarães, Portugal
estela.bicho@dei.uminho.pt

Abstract. The identification of stop locations in GPS trajectories is an essential preliminary step for obtaining trip information. We propose a neural network approach, based on the theoretical framework of dynamic neural fields (DNF), to identify automatically stop locations from GPS trajectories using their spatial and temporal characteristics. Experiments with real-world GPS trajectories were performed to show the feasibility of the proposed approach. The outcomes are compared with results obtained from more conventional clustering algorithms (K-means, hierarchical clustering, and HDBSCAN) which usually limit the use of the available temporal information to the definition of a threshold for the duration of stay. The experimental results show that the DNF approach not only robustly identifies places visited for a longer time but also stop locations that are visited for shorter periods but with higher frequency. Moreover, the self-stabilized activation patterns that the network dynamics develop and continuously update in response to GPS input encode simultaneously the spatial information and the time spent in each location. The impact of the obtained results on systems that automatically detect drivers' daily routines from GPS trajectories is discussed.

Keywords: Cluster · Stop location · Dynamic neural field · Trajectory data mining · Temporal and spatial properties

1 Introduction

Mobiles and GPS devices are used more and more to record people's daily trajectories. For example, a driver's daily routes can be recorded by the GPS car

The work received financial support from European Structural and Investment Funds in the FEDER component, through the Operational Competitiveness and Internationalization Programme (COMPETE 2020) and national funds, through FCT (Project **"Neurofield"**, ref POCI01-0145FEDER-031393) and ADI (Project **"Easy Ride:Experience is everything"**, ref POCI-01-0247-FEDER-039334), FCT PhD fellowship PD/BD/128183/2016, and R&D Units Project Scope: UIDB/00319/2020 and UIDB/00013/2020.

I. Farkaš et al. (Eds.): ICANN 2021, LNCS 12894, pp. 347–359, 2021.
https://doi.org/10.1007/978-3-030-86380-7_28

equipment, and useful information can be extracted from these trajectories to benefit the user's daily routine [9]. Stop locations represent the most meaningful part of the trajectories. They provide essential information for many location-based services such as destination prediction systems [12,15] and recommendation systems [3].

Many data mining methods have been used to extract these locations. Typically, clustering algorithms are adopted to the dynamic process of stop extraction from a trajectory. For example, in [28] the classical K-means clustering algorithm to identify locations of interest was used. The DBSCAN (density-based spatial clustering of applications with noise) algorithm and different derivative algorithms of the DBSCAN have been adopted in many studies in order to identify stop locations [2,12,15,20]. These density-based clustering algorithms offer some advantages over the K-means approach including the capacity of identifying clusters of varying shapes [15]. Hierarchical clustering algorithms such as agglomerative hierarchical clustering also have been used to identify different visited locations [22]. Compared to DBSCAN, hierarchical clustering methods can provide a more intuitive interpretation of clusters. More recently, a hierarchical clustering algorithm named HDBSCAN has been applied to identify regions of interest [6,9,17]. This clustering algorithm is based on DBSCAN and thus inherits the qualities of both the hierarchical clustering and DBSCAN. These methods have proven to obtain a desirable performance in many situations. However, most of them take only the spatial information about GPS points within a given distance into account, and the available temporal information is used in a very limited way. In many studies [2,11,12], a pre-defined time threshold representing the minimal amount of time spent within a region is used to select GPS points (called stop or stay points) before applying a clustering algorithm. However, by fixing a threshold value, potentially highly relevant information about stop points that a user visits for shorter periods but with higher frequency is lost.

Here, we present a recurrent neural network model [26] that supports a continuous integration of spatial and temporal information provided by raw GPS data. The model is based on the theoretical framework of Dynamic Neural Fields (DNF) which has been applied in the past to implement brain-inspired processing mechanisms supporting working memory, prediction, and decision making in cognitive systems (e.g., [7,23,24]). Recent work shows the benefits of the DNF approach for clustering analysis [18] and the encoding of temporal properties of sensory events [10,27]. A direct comparison with the more conventional clustering algorithms reveals that the identified stop points with sufficiently long stay coincide to a large extent. However, the neural integrator network is also able to automatically encode in its activation pattern the spatiotemporal properties of points of interest that have been visited more frequently for shorter periods.

The rest of the paper is organized as follows. Basic concepts concerning GPS trajectories are presented in Sect. 2. In Sect. 3, a stop point detection algorithm, three clustering algorithms used in the experiments, and the novel DNF approach are introduced. The results of the experiments with the different approaches are discussed in Sect. 4. Conclusions and future work are presented in Sect. 5.

2 Basic Concepts

Following previous work [2,11,12,20], we present some definitions and concepts which will be used throughout the paper.

Definition 1 ***GPS Trajectory:*** *A GPS Trajectory is a list of n GPS data points* (x_i, y_i, t_i) *with* $i \in \{1, \ldots, n\}$ *and* $t_i < t_i + 1$*, where* x_i*,* y_i *and* t_i *represent the longitude, latitude, and time-stamp, respectively.*

Definition 2 ***Stop Point (also known as stay point):*** *A stop point is a significant point of a trajectory where a user has spent a minimal amount of time.*

In this paper, we consider three types of stop points. Type I: the end point of each trajectory (or track) if the distance between this point and the start point of the same trajectory or of the next trajectory is less than a predefined distance. This means that the user leaves and arrives at the same place or the user arrives and leaves at the same place in two successive trajectories. Typically, a trajectory starts from a place where a user leaves and ends in a place without changing signal for a period of time. However, this might not be always true due to other factors such as signal loss or low battery. Type II: a trajectory point which is repeated for more than a predefined amount of time. Type III: The centroid of consecutive trajectory points in a region of predefined radius visited for more than a predefined amount of time.

In previous work [2,11,12], a stop location is defined as a map area that contains at least two stop points and it is obtained by a stop clustering algorithm. Here, we apply a more comprehensive stop location concept which includes the map regions with isolated stop points and the places visited repetitively but for a shorter period of time compared with the time spent in a stop point.

3 Methodology

3.1 Stop Point Detection

The algorithm proposed in [19] was used to identify the stop points. They are detected from a user's GPS trajectory based on two parameters: the distance-threshold and the time-threshold. First, the Haversine Distance (HD) formula, presented in [20], is used to calculate the distance between two sets of points in order to find those that are below the distance-threshold. Next, it is being verified whether the time the user spent in the region is longer than the time-threshold. As the last step, the algorithm calculates the stop point centroid by determining the mean of the coordinates of the set of points. In our experiments, we set the parameters distance-threshold as 200 m and the time-threshold as 20 min as suggested in [31] and used in recent work [2,12]. In other words, if a user spends over 20 min within a region of 200 m, a stop point is detected.

3.2 Clustering Algorithms

K-means clustering is a popular approach for segmenting a data set into K distinct non-overlapping clusters [16]. The objective of K-means is to minimize the within-cluster variation. In our experiments, the within-cluster variation defined by the squared Euclidean distance (also commonly known as distortion) is used to access the quality of the clustering. In K-means, the number of clusters is a parameter that must be given explicitly. It is chosen manually based on prior knowledge of the data set properties or with a cluster number determination technique (e.g., Elbow method) [13].

Agglomerative hierarchical clustering is a clustering approach in which the data points are grouped into a hierarchy, resulting in a tree-based representation called a dendrogram. The hierarchical clustering starts at the lowest level and at each subsequent level a pair of clusters is merged into a single cluster, where the pair of chosen clusters consists of the two most similar subsets [13,14]. To create the dendrogram, a measure of the distance between two clusters needs to be defined. In this work, the Ward method is applied due to its's success in a wide range of applications since its first description in 1963 [25].

HDBSCAN is a hierarchical clustering method based on the DBSCAN algorithm [4,5]. DBSCAN [8] is a classic density-based clustering method in which the density of a point is measured by the number of points within a certain distance from this point. By setting two parameters, the maximum distance between two points (*eps*) and the minimum size of points ($minPts$) that a given cluster may contain, DBSCAN is widely used for clustering and eliminating noise. A cluster is defined as the set of points with dimension higher or equal than $minPts$ and within the *eps*-neighborhood. Any point that is not part of a cluster is categorized as noise. HDBSCAN performs DBSCAN over varying *eps* values and integrates the result to find a clustering that provides the best stability over *eps*. This makes HDBSCAN identify clusters of varying densities which is the major advantage over DBSCAN. To obtain clusters of varying density, HDBSCAN builds a minimal spanning tree based on the mutual reachability distance between the points. Based on that tree, a condensed cluster hierarchy is constructed where the width of the branch represents the number of points in the cluster. HDBSCAN requires a single parameter as input: the minimum cluster size ($minPts$), which in this work is set to 2. Using this parameter, the algorithm removes connections from the tree by increasing the minimum weight of connections λ, and verifies at every juncture in the tree, whether the remaining components are larger than the $minPts$ value. If they are, they are maintained for consideration as a cluster, if they are not, they are declared noise. The parts of the tree which are the most persistent to changes of λ are considered clusters by HDBSCAN [21].

3.3 The DNF-Based Neural Integrator Model

Dynamic neural fields formalized by integro-differential equations represent a specific type of recurrent neural network in the continuum limit. The connectivity pattern is typically of lateral-inhibition type, that is, excitation dominates at shorter and inhibition at longer distances [1]. Since DNF models explain the existence of input-specific neural activation patterns that persist after the input is withdrawn, they are used as models of working memory. In applications, the fields are spanned over continuous metric dimensions such as spatial position or movement direction [7,23,24]. The evolution of a self-stabilized, bell-shaped activation pattern (or bump) in response to a transient input represents the memory of a specific parameter value. For the present study, a two-dimensional field representing the GPS coordinates latitude and longitude is used. Since we also want to support the temporal integration of inputs, we apply a novel model consisting of two coupled field equations of classical Amari-type [26,27]. It represents the accumulated input at a specific location in a continuum of bump amplitudes.

The network dynamics of the two coupled neural populations, u and v, is governed by the following equations:

$$\frac{\partial u(\mathbf{r},t)}{\partial t} = -u(\mathbf{r},t) + v(\mathbf{r},t) + I(\mathbf{r},t) + \int\int_{\Omega} w(\mathbf{r}-\mathbf{r}')f(u(\mathbf{r}',t)-\theta)d\mathbf{r}', \quad (1)$$

$$\frac{\partial v(\mathbf{r},t)}{\partial t} = -v(\mathbf{r},t) + u(\mathbf{r},t) - \int\int_{\Omega} w(\mathbf{r}-\mathbf{r}')f(u(\mathbf{r}',t)-\theta)d\mathbf{r}', \quad (2)$$

where $u(\mathbf{r},t)$ and $v(\mathbf{r},t)$ represent the activity at time t of neurons representing position $\mathbf{r} = \sqrt{x^2+y^2}$ in the spatial domain Ω, which in the present study is a subset of $\mathbb{R}^2$. The function $f(u)$ represents the firing rate function, here chosen as the Heaviside step function with threshold θ and w is the distance-dependent distribution of synaptic weights. We consider a connectivity function of "Mexican-hat" shape given by the difference of two Gaussians

$$w(\mathbf{r}) = A_{ex}e^{\left(-\mathbf{r}^2/2\sigma^2\right)} - A_{in}e^{\left(-\mathbf{r}^2/2(\gamma\sigma)^2\right)}, \quad (3)$$

where $A_{ex} > A_{in} > 0$ determine the lateral excitatory and inhibitory strength, $\sigma > 0$ determines the lateral excitatory range, and $\gamma\sigma$ with $\gamma > 1$ determines the range of lateral inhibition.
The term $I(\mathbf{r},t)$ represents a time varying external input to population u, modeled by a Gaussian function

$$I(\mathbf{r}) = A_I e^{\left(-(\mathbf{r}-\mathbf{r}_c)^2/2\sigma_I^2\right)}, \quad (4)$$

centered at position $\mathbf{r}_c$ given by the GPS coordinates, with strength A_I and standard deviation $\sigma_I > 0$.

A localized input, $I(\mathbf{r})$, with amplitude above threshold drives the evolution of a bump with a growth rate controlled by A_I. The input duration thus determines the bump height whereas the choice of the standard deviation σ_I affects the bump width. An excited region could be the result of a single input presented during a sufficiently long time interval or could be generated by different (spatially overlapping) inputs in the same region:

- a single input $I(r,t)$ for $t \in \{t_1, \ldots, t_n\}$ where $t_1, \ldots, t_n$ are successive time-stamps and the time interval $t_n - t_1$ is longer than the minimum interval necessary to reach the threshold θ for bump creation; or
- m inputs $I_i(r_i, t)$ for $t \in \{t_{i,1}, \ldots, t_{i,n}\}$ where $r_1, \ldots, r_m$ are in the same small area, $t_{i,1}, \ldots, t_{i,n}$ are successive time-stamps for all $i \in \{1, \ldots, m\}$, $t_{1,n}, \ldots, t_{m,n}$ are successive or temporally separated time-stamps and the accumulated input duration, $\sum_{i=1}^{m} (t_{i,n} - t_{i,1})$, is sufficient to reach threshold.

In the first case, the excited region corresponds to a stop location that contains a stop point of Type II. In the second case, if $t_{1,n}, \ldots, t_{m,n}$ are successive time-stamps, the excited region corresponds to a stop location that contains a stop point of Type I or Type III. If $t_{1,n}, \ldots, t_{m,n}$ represent temporally separated time-stamps, the excited region corresponds to a place visited more than once at different moments in time.

The neural integrator model is able to sustain multiple input-induced activation patterns. Their number and spatial extend depends on the kernel parameters, σ, γ, A_{ex}, and A_{in}. A larger σ induces a larger range of excitation and proximate bumps that co-exist for a smaller σ might merge in a single excited region. On the other hand, increasing the parameter γ causes a stronger lateral inhibition which may lead to a suppression below threshold of smaller bumps by larger ones.

Numerical model simulations were done in MATLAB using a forward Euler method with time step $\Delta_t = 0.1$ and spatial step $\Delta_x = 0.001$, on a finite domain $\Omega = [minLong - 0.05, maxLong + 0.05] \times [minLat - 0.05, maxLat + 0.05]$, where $minLong$, $maxLong$, $minLat$ and $maxLat$ are the minimum and maximum values of the longitude and latitude for a given set of GPS points, respectively. To compute the spatial convolution of w and f we employ a two-dimensional fast Fourier transform (FFT), using MATLAB's in-built functions `fft2` and `ifft2` to perform the Fourier transform and the inverse Fourier transform, respectively.

4 Experiments and Discussion

4.1 Dataset

Real trajectory datasets selected from GeoLife GPS Trajectory Data [29–31] were used to perform the experiments. The Geolife data contains trajectories mostly in Beijing, China, of 182 users recorded in the period from April 2007 to August 2012. A group of 73 users labeled their trajectories with transportation modes such as walk, car, taxi, bus, subway, bike and others. A GPS trajectory of this data set is represented by a sequence of time-stamped points, each of which contains the information of latitude, longitude and altitude.

4.2 Pre-processing

Since trajectories have a variety of sampling rates, first, sequences of GPS coordinates (latitude and longitude) were generated from the raw GPS trajectories with a fixed sample rate (every 30 s). The points of Type I (end trajectory points that are in the same area of the start point of the current trajectory or the next one) are repeated for a period of 20 min. Table 1 summarizes the selected trajectory datasets used in this study.

Table 1. Main characteristics of the selected trajectory datasets

User	Date	Transportation mode	Number of trajectories	Number of points	
				Raw	Sample
115	May 2007 (14 days)	Car	24	1843	3715
153	July 2008 (27 days)	Walk, Bus, Car, Taxi, Subway	60	40162	7179
128	11 February 2009	Walk, Car, Subway	5	2336	554

4.3 Stop Points

Figure 1 (a) and (d) show the scatter plot of the raw GPS points (latitude and longitude coordinates) corresponding to the trajectories recorded during a month by users 115 and 153 described in Table 1. The respective sample GPS points are presented in Fig. 1 (b) and (e). The stop points determined by the algorithm proposed in [19] and described in Sect. 3.1 are illustrated on the real map of part of Beijing city in Fig. 1 (c) and (f). The number of detected stop points was 7 and 51 for user 115 and user 153, respectively, concentrated in 3 and 7 separated regions (locations).

4.4 Stop Locations Based on Stop Points

In the following, we employ the DNF approach as well as the clustering algorithms K-means, agglomerative hierarchical, and HDBSCAN based on the stop points of user 153 found in Sect. 4.3, in order to identify the stop locations. For each stop point, inputs given by (4) with $A_I = 1$ and $\sigma_I = 0.4$, centered at the stop point coordinates, were applied sequentially to the u-field during a fixed period of time steps equal to 10. The value of θ was chosen equal to 0.5. The parameters of w given by (3) were chosen as $A_{ex} = 4$, $A_{in} = 1.5$, $\gamma = 2$ and two different σ values were considered, $\sigma = 0.5$ and $\sigma = 1$.

The DNF approach generated 7 clusters with $\sigma = 0.5$ (Fig. 2 (a)), and this number was reduced to 6 with $\sigma = 1$ (Fig. 2 (b)). Choosing the number of cluster as $k = 7$ and $k = 6$, respectively, the stop points are grouped by all three clustering algorithms (K-means, agglomerative hierarchical, and HDBSCAN) in the same 7, respectively 6, clusters obtained by the DNF model (Fig. 2 (c), (d)). For single inputs representing stop points with stay duration above threshold, the DNF approach thus produces very similar results compared with the conventional clustering algorithms.

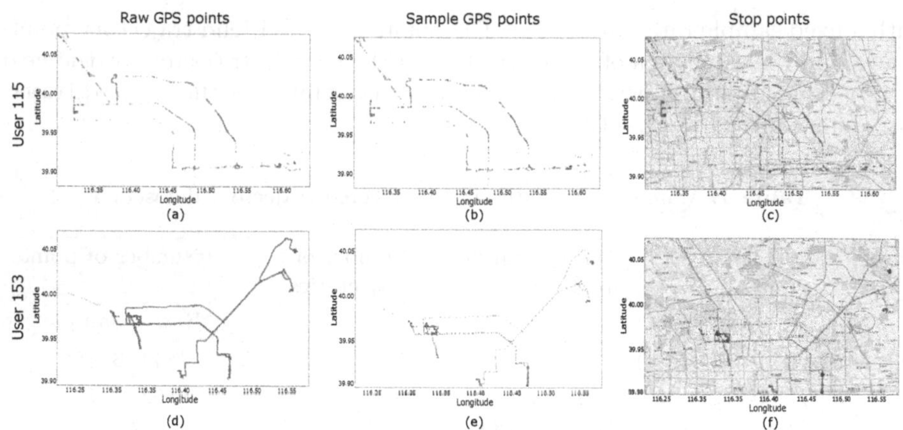

Fig. 1. Raw GPS points collected during a month by user 115 **(a)** and by user 153 **(d)** described in Table 1, the respective sample GPS points generated from the raw GPS points (**(b)** and **(e)**) and the stop points (red points) found in the subset of sample GPS points (**(c)** and **(f)**). (Color figure online)

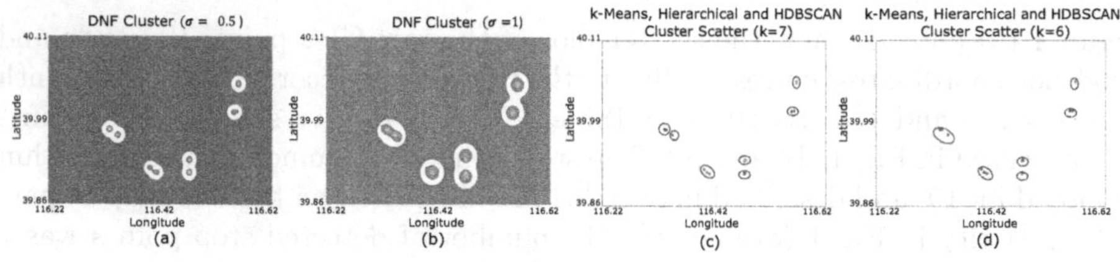

Fig. 2. Stop locations (clusters) obtained by the DNF approach with $\sigma = 0.5$ **(a)** and $\sigma = 1$ **(b)**, the K-means, agglomerative hierarchical and HDBSCAN algorithms with $k = 7$ **(c)** and $k = 6$ **(d)** based on the stop points of user 153 given in Sect. 4.3.

4.5 Stop Locations Based on GPS Trajectories

Figure 3 presents the stop locations obtained by the proposed DNF approach for two datasets: user 115 and user 153. The input is given by (4) centered at position $\mathbf{r}_c$ given by the sample GPS coordinates (3715 and 7179 points for users 115 and 153, respectively), with $A_I = 0.05$ and $\sigma_I = 0.4$ and a sample rate of 30 s (corresponding to one time step). To ensure that excitation in a region can be driven by repetitive inputs with a total duration exceeding 20 min, the activation threshold is chosen as $\theta = 0.16$. The parameters of w are the same as in Sect. 4.4. For $\sigma = 0.5$, 7 stop locations were codified for user 115 (Fig. 3 (a)) and also for user 153 (Fig. 3 (c)). Increasing the value of σ to 1, the number of stop locations decreases to six in both cases (Fig. 3 (b),(d)).

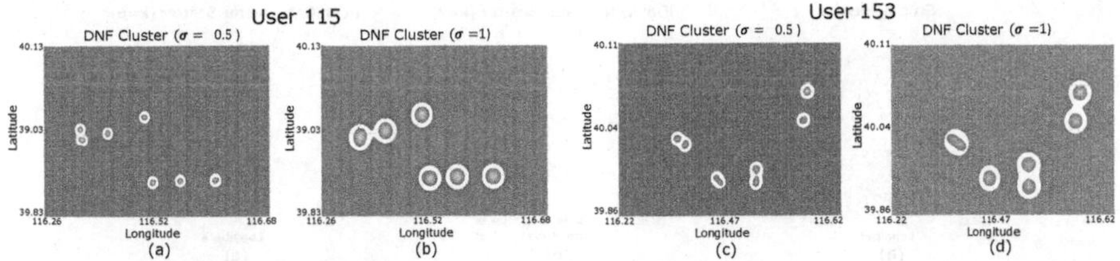

Fig. 3. Stop locations identified by the DNF approach with $\sigma = 0.5$ ((**a**) and (**c**)) and $\sigma = 1$ ((**b**) and (**d**)), for the users 115 and 153, respectively.

For user 153, all stop locations contain at least one stop point found in Sect. 4.3 (Fig. 1 (f)) and the regions are similar to the ones identified in Sect. 4.4 (Fig. 2 (a),(b)). However, for user 115 stop locations were identified in regions without stop points found in Sect. 4.3 (Fig. 1 (c)). This means that there are some places that were visited more than one time but with an accumulated stay period less than 20 min. To further analyze this situation, a new set of stop points was obtained considering now 5 min as time-threshold. By decreasing the time-threshold to 5 min, the number of stop points increases from 7 to 47 as illustrated in Fig. 4 (a). In fact, in the regions identified by the DNF approach (see Fig. 3 (a)), there exist at least 2 stop points with more than 5 min stay duration. In this case, isolated stop points can be considered as noise. Contrary to the K-means and the agglomerative hierarchical algorithms, HDBSCAN is capable of handling noise. We, therefore, run HDBSCAN on the set of stop points obtained with a 5 min time-threshold. By comparing the results of the DNF approach with $\sigma = 0.5$ (Fig. 3 (a)) and the HDBSCAN clustering result for $k = 7$ (Fig. 4 (b)), we observe that the 3 points considered as noise by HDBSCAN (gray points) do not belong to any excited region found by the DNF approach. However, some points not classified as noise by HDBSCAN due to their proximity to other points do not belong to any excited region in Fig. 3 (a). Assuming $k = 6$, the number of points classified as noise by HDBSCAN appears to be reduced to 2 (Fig. 4 (c)). In this case, if we were only interested in areas with a relatively high number of stops, HDBSCAN would give us good results for a $minPts$ value large enough to declare sparse regions as noise and dense regions as clusters. However, not all stop points in sparse environments are necessarily noise. If we were interested at the same time in areas with a higher number of stops and in areas with fewer stops or even just one stop but with a longer stay, applying HDBSCAN to a set of stop points is not sufficient. To represent the underlying data structure, the DNF approach will be more suitable.

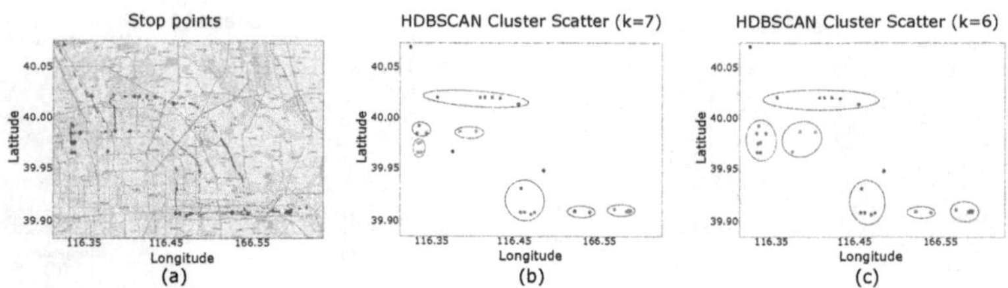

Fig. 4. **(a)** Stop points found in the subset of sample GPS points for user 115 by performing the method described in Sect. 3.1 with time-threshold of 5 min. The number of points is shown in parentheses. (b) Clustering result obtained by the HDBSCAN algorithm when choosing the number of cluster as $k = 7$ **(b)** or $k = 6$ **(c)** for the stop points in **(a)**.

4.6 Stop Locations and Time Spent in Each One

In the proposed DNF approach, the location and the time spent in each place are encoded simultaneously. As an example, consider the daily trajectories (recorded from 1:10 to 14:40 GMT) of user 128 (see Table 1). Applying the method described in Sect. 3.1, 4 stop points are found (Fig. 5 (a)). Each of the stop locations identified by the DNF approach based on the GPS trajectories contain one of these 4 stop points (Fig. 5 (b),(c)), and the time spent in each location correlates with the bump amplitude (Fig. 5 (d)).

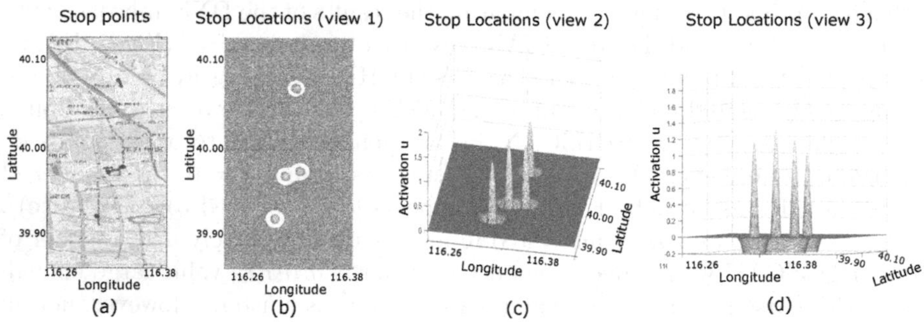

Fig. 5. **(a)** The stop points found in the subset of sample GPS points recorded during a day by user 128. **(b)**, **(c)** and **(d)** Snapshot from three different views of the stop locations identified by the DNF approach. The duration spent in each location is represented by the peak amplitude. The parameters for the nonlinearity f and the interaction kernel w are the same used in Sect. 4.5 with $\sigma = 0.5$.

The stored information could be used for instance to make predictions about the expected stay duration of a user in a specific place.

5 Conclusion and Future Work

We have presented an approach based on Dynamic Neural Fields to identify stop locations from raw GPS data. Stop location extraction occurs implicitly and it is a continuous process, taking into account not only the number of inputs (representing GPS coordinates) and the distance between them but also their temporal properties. Our approach is particularly useful when not only the duration but also the frequency of location visits have to be taken into account. If the temporal integration of GPS inputs at a specific location exceeds the threshold for bump formation, the location is memorized whereas places visited for shorter periods and with low frequency are automatically ignored. The joint representation of spatial and temporal information about stop locations offers a new perspective for driver assistant systems that are able to make predictions about the driver's daily routines. In order to further verify the feasibility of the presented DNF approach, we are currently collecting a new data set in the scope of the joint project with Bosch **"Easy Ride: Experience is everything"**, where stop locations of car trajectories are recorded. With this information, we will be able to directly compare model predictions with real driver routines.

References

1. Amari, S.: Dynamics of pattern formation in lateral-inhibition type neural fields. Biol. Cybern. **27**(2), 77–87 (1977). https://doi.org/10.1007/BF00337259
2. Andrade, T., Cancela, B., Gama, J.: Discovering common pathways across users' habits in mobility data. In: Moura Oliveira, P., Novais, P., Reis, L.P. (eds.) EPIA 2019. LNCS (LNAI), vol. 11805, pp. 410–421. Springer, Cham (2019). https://doi.org/10.1007/978-3-030-30244-3_34
3. Bao, J., Zheng, Yu., Wilkie, D., Mokbel, M.: Recommendations in location-based social networks: a survey. GeoInformatica **19**(3), 525–565 (2015). https://doi.org/10.1007/s10707-014-0220-8
4. Campello, R.J.G.B., Moulavi, D., Sander, J.: Density-based clustering based on hierarchical density estimates. In: Pei, J., Tseng, V.S., Cao, L., Motoda, H., Xu, G. (eds.) PAKDD 2013. LNCS (LNAI), vol. 7819, pp. 160–172. Springer, Heidelberg (2013). https://doi.org/10.1007/978-3-642-37456-2_14
5. Campello, R.J., Moulavi, D., Zimek, A., Sander, J.: Hierarchical density estimates for data clustering, visualization, and outlier detection. ACM Trans. Knowl. Disc. Data **10**(1), 1–51 (2015)
6. Chen, P., Shi, W., Zhou, X., Liu, Z., Fu, X.: STLP-GSM: a method to predict future locations of individuals based on geotagged social media data. Int. J. Geogr. Inf. Sci. **33**(12), 2337–2362 (2019)
7. Erlhagen, W., Bicho, E.: The dynamic neural field approach to cognitive robotics. J. Neural. Eng. **3**, 36–54 (2006)
8. Ester, M., Kriegel, H.P., Sander, J., Xu, X., et al.: A density-based algorithm for discovering clusters in large spatial databases with noise. In: KDD 1996, pp. 226–231 (1996)
9. Fernandes, C., Ferreira, F., Erlhagen, W., Monteiro, S., Bicho, E.: A deep learning approach for intelligent cockpits: learning drivers routines. In: Analide, C., Novais, P., Camacho, D., Yin, H. (eds.) IDEAL 2020. LNCS, vol. 12490, pp. 173–183. Springer, Cham (2020). https://doi.org/10.1007/978-3-030-62365-4_17

10. Ferreira, F., Wojtak, W., Sousa, E., Louro, L., Bicho, E., Erlhagen, W.: Rapid learning of complex sequences with time constraints: a dynamic neural field models. EEE Trans. Cogn. Dev. Syst. (2020). https://doi.org/10.1109/TCDS.2020.2991789
11. Fu, Z., Tian, Z., Xu, Y., Qiao, C.: A two-step clustering approach to extract locations from individual GPS trajectory data. Int. J. Geo-Inf. **5**(10), 166 (2016)
12. Hamid, R.A., Croock, M.S.: A developed GPS trajectories data management system for predicting tourists' POI. TELKOMNIKA Telecommun. Comput. Electron. Control **18**(1), 124–132 (2020)
13. Han, J., Kamber, M., Pei, J.: Data Mining - Concepts and Techniques. Elsevier, Amsterdam (2011)
14. Hastie, T., Tibshirani, R., Friedman, J.: The Elements of Statistical Learning. Data Mining, Inference, and Prediction. SSS, Springer, New York (2009). https://doi.org/10.1007/978-0-387-84858-7
15. Huang, Q.: Mining online footprints to predict user's next location. Int. J. Geog. Inf. Sci. **31**(3), 523–541 (2017)
16. James, G., Witten, D., Hastie, T., Tibshirani, R.: An Introduction to Statistical Learning. STS, vol. 103. Springer, New York (2013). https://doi.org/10.1007/978-1-4614-7138-7
17. Järv, P., Tammet, T., Tall, M.: Hierarchical regions of interest. In: 19th IEEE International Conference on Mobile Data Management (MDM), pp. 86–95. IEEE (2018)
18. Jin, D., Peng, J., Li, B.: A new clustering approach on the basis of dynamical neural field. Neural Comput. **23**(8), 2032–2057 (2011)
19. Li, Q., Zheng, Y., Xie, X., Chen, Y., Liu, W., Ma, W.Y.: Mining user similarity based on location history. In: 16th ACM SIGSPATIAL International Conference on Advances in Geographic Information Systems, pp. 1–10 (2008)
20. Luo, T., Zheng, X., Xu, G., Fu, K., Ren, W.: An improved DBSCAN algorithm to detect stops in individual trajectories. SPRS Int. J. Geo-Inf. **6**(3), 63 (2017)
21. McInnes, L., Healy, J., Astels, S.: hdbscan: hierarchical density based clustering. J. Open Source Softw. **2**(11), 205 (2017)
22. Montini, L., Rieser-Schüssler, N., Horni, A., Axhausen, K.W.: Trip purpose identification from GPS tracks. Transp. Res. Rec. J. Transp. Res. Board **2405**(1), 16–23 (2014)
23. Sandamirskaya, Y., Zibner, S.K., Schneegans, S., Schöner, G.: Using dynamic field theory to extend the embodiment stance toward higher cognition. New Ideas Psychol. **31**(3), 322–339 (2013)
24. Schöner, G.: Dynamical Systems Approaches to Cognition, pp. 101–126 (2008)
25. Ward, J.H., Jr.: Hierarchical grouping to optimize an objective function. J. Am. Stat. Assoc. **58**(301), 236–244 (1963)
26. Wojtak, W., Coombes, S., Bicho, E., Erlhagen, W.: Combining spatial and parametric working memory in a dynamic neural field model. In: Villa, A.E.P., Masulli, P., Pons Rivero, A.J. (eds.) ICANN 2016. LNCS, vol. 9886, pp. 411–418. Springer, Cham (2016). https://doi.org/10.1007/978-3-319-44778-0_48
27. Wojtak, W., Ferreira, F., Vicente, P., Louro, L., Bicho, E., Erlhagen, W.: A neural integrator model for planning and value-based decision making of a robotics assistant. Neural Comput. Appl. **33**(8), 3737–3756 (2020). https://doi.org/10.1007/s00521-020-05224-8
28. Yuan, J., Zheng, Y., Xie, X.: Discovering regions of different functions in a city using human mobility and POIs. In: 18th ACM SIGKDD International Conference on Knowledge Discovery and Data Mining, pp. 186–194 (2012)

29. Zheng, Y., Li, Q., Chen, Y., Xie, X., Ma, W.Y.: Understanding mobility based on GPS data. In: 10th International Conference on Ubiquitous Computing, pp. 312–321 (2008)
30. Zheng, Y., Xie, X., Ma, W.Y., et al.: GeoLife: a collaborative social networking service among user, location and trajectory. IEEE Data Eng. Bull. **33**(2), 32–39 (2010)
31. Zheng, Y., Zhang, L., Xie, X., Ma, W.Y.: Mining interesting locations and travel sequences from GPS trajectories. In: 18th International Conference on World wide web, pp. 791–800 (2009)

Separation of Memory and Processing in Dual Recurrent Neural Networks

Christian Oliva(✉) and Luis F. Lago-Fernández

Escuela Politécnica Superior, Universidad Autónoma de Madrid, 28049 Madrid, Spain
christian.oliva@estudiante.uam.es, luis.lago@uam.es

Abstract. We explore a neural network architecture that stacks a recurrent layer and a feedforward layer, both connected to the input. We compare it to a standard recurrent neural network. When noise is introduced into the recurrent units activation function, the two networks display binary activation patterns that can be mapped into the discrete states of a finite state machine. But, while the former is equivalent to a Moore machine, the latter can be interpreted as a Mealy machine. The additional feedforward layer reduces the computational load on the recurrent layer, which is used to model the temporal dependencies only. The resulting models are simpler and easier to interpret when the networks are trained on different sample problems, including the recognition of regular languages and the computation of additions in different bases.

Keywords: Deep learning · Recurrent neural network · Interpretability

1 Introduction

Machine learning techniques, and more specifically deep neural networks (DNNs), have become essential for a wide range of applications, such as image classification [1,17], speech recognition [11], or natural language processing [4,18,25]. Notwithstanding, these deep models are still not dominant in many applications due to the common belief that more simplistic approaches, such as linear models or decision trees, provide better interpretability. Hence techniques for interpreting DNNs are becoming popular in many fields, like image classification [19] and sequence modeling, including music composition and natural language generation [16,24]. However, the interpretation and understanding of DNNs is still an open question that deserves further research.

Recurrent Neural Networks (RNNs) are a kind of deep network aimed at sequence modeling, where the depth comes from a recurrent loop in the network architecture that forces a backpropagation through several time steps when the gradients are computed [10]. RNNs are Turing equivalent [23], and many authors have studied these networks' ability to model different kinds of formal languages [8,22,28]. The interpretability of RNNs has been often addressed by quantization

I. Farkaš et al. (Eds.): ICANN 2021, LNCS 12894, pp. 360–371, 2021.
https://doi.org/10.1007/978-3-030-86380-7_29

approaches that try to reduce the network to a set of rules (*rule extraction*) [15,22,27], usually in the form of a deterministic automaton [3,5,9].

More recently, the picture has been completed with the introduction of Memory Augmented Neural Networks (MANNs) [6], where a standard and usually recurrent neural network is enhanced with an external memory [2,12,13]. Results of these new models on complex problems seem very promising. Additionally, as much of the computational power of these networks relies on their memory, the complexity of the neural component is reduced, hence also improving the overall model interpretability. The connection with general automata seems evident, with the neural network implementing a kind of finite state neural processor and different memory schemes leading to different types of abstract models, from pushdown automata to complete Turing machines.

Following these ideas, in this article, we explore a neural network architecture that combines a feedforward processing layer with a recurrent layer that implements a sort of memory. When we train this *Dual* network to process temporal sequences, it uses its recurrent layer to keep track of only the essential information that must endure over time, without performing any additional computation. The feedforward layer combines, in turn, the input and the memory content to provide the final network's output. This separation of roles seems to be beneficial for learning since the network discharges much of the computational load from the recurrent connection and, at the same time, improves interpretability. From a more abstract point of view, we find that the network can be reduced to a Mealy machine, just as a simple recurrent network can be reduced to a stable finite automaton in the form of a Moore machine [20,21]. Mealy machines are simpler than Moore machines (lower number of states), and so the models trained using this architecture are also more understandable and interpretable. We study the network's capacity to solve several simple problems, including regular language recognition and the computation of additions in different numerical bases. We show that the Dual architecture can obtain the same prediction accuracy and at the same time generate more interpretable models.

The article is organized as follows. In Sect. 2, we introduce the network architecture. In Sect. 3, we describe the data and the experiments. Section 4 presents and analyzes the results. Finally, in Sect. 5, we present the conclusions and discuss future lines of research.

2 Networks

2.1 Elman RNN with Noisy Recurrence

The Elman RNN [7] is the simplest neural network architecture where recurrence is introduced. It adds a time dependence to the internal layer, making the activity in this layer depend on its output for the previous time step. Here we use a modified Elman RNN with a single hidden layer, where noise is introduced in the activation function of the recurrent layer units [20]. The network behavior is governed by the following equations:

$$\mathbf{h}_t = \tanh(\mathbf{W}_{xh}\mathbf{x}_t + \mathbf{W}_{hh}\mathbf{h}_{t-1} + \mathbf{X}_\nu \circ \mathbf{h}_{t-1} + \mathbf{b}_h), \tag{1}$$

$$\mathbf{y}_t = \sigma(\mathbf{W}_{hy}\mathbf{h}_t + \mathbf{b}_y), \tag{2}$$

where $\mathbf{h}_t$ and $\mathbf{y}_t$ represent the activation of the hidden and output layers, respectively, at time t, and $\mathbf{x}_t$ is the network input. The model depends on weight matrices $\mathbf{W}_{xh}$, $\mathbf{W}_{hh}$, and $\mathbf{W}_{hy}$, and also bias vectors $\mathbf{b}_h$ and $\mathbf{b}_y$. In particular, $\mathbf{W}_{hh}$ represents the weights in the recurrent connection that create an explicit dependence of $\mathbf{h}_t$ on $\mathbf{h}_{t-1}$. The recurrent connection also includes the noisy term $\mathbf{X}_\nu \circ \mathbf{h}_{t-1}$, where $\mathbf{X}_\nu$ is a random vector whose elements are drawn from a Normal distribution with mean 0 and standard deviation ν. The $\circ$ operator denotes an element-wise product. The noise effect on the overall network's behavior is to force the neurons into an almost binary regime that generates stable activation clusters [21].

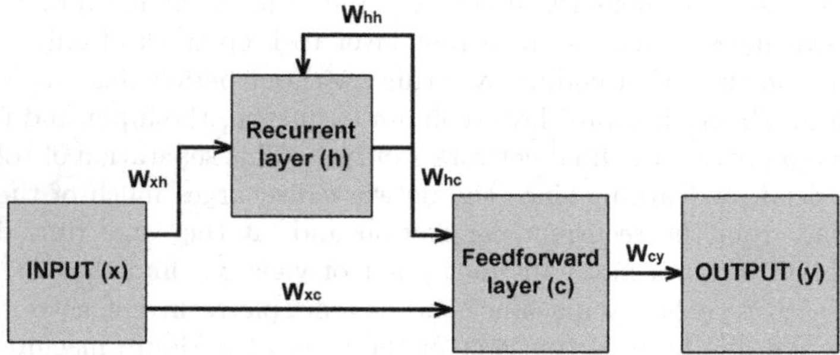

Fig. 1. Connection diagram of the Dual RNN

2.2 Dual RNN

The second network architecture that we explore combines the noisy recurrent layer described in Sect. 2.1 with a feedforward layer that receives its input from both the recurrent and the input layers. We include a final sigmoid layer on top to provide the network output (see Fig. 1). The network activity is controlled by the following set of equations:

$$\mathbf{h}_t = \tanh(\mathbf{W}_{xh}\mathbf{x}_t + \mathbf{W}_{hh}\mathbf{h}_{t-1} + \mathbf{X}_\nu \circ \mathbf{h}_{t-1} + \mathbf{b}_h), \tag{3}$$

$$\mathbf{c}_t = \tanh(\mathbf{W}_{xc}\mathbf{x}_t + \mathbf{W}_{hc}\mathbf{h}_t + \mathbf{b}_c), \tag{4}$$

$$\mathbf{y}_t = \sigma(\mathbf{W}_{cy}\mathbf{c}_t + \mathbf{b}_y), \tag{5}$$

where the symbols have the same interpretation as before. The idea behind this implementation consists of allowing the recurrent units to focus on just processing the information that must be maintained along time, while the additional feedforward layer performs all the rest of the processing. This way, we expect that the recurrent layer acts as a memory that learns to deal with time dependencies, while the feedforward layer learns to combine the input and the memory to provide an answer given the current input. We call this network a *Dual* RNN.

2.3 Network Training

We train the networks to minimize a cross-entropy loss with L1-regularization using a standard gradient descent optimizer. Regularization is applied only to the weight matrices but not to the biases. In the Dual RNN, only the weights in the recurrent layer ($\mathbf{W}_{xh}$, $\mathbf{W}_{hh}$, and $\mathbf{W}_{hc}$) are regularized.

3 Experiments and Data

We test our network on two different problems: recognition of regular grammars and addition on various numerical bases. In the following, we provide a detailed description of the data and the experiments.

3.1 Recognition of Regular Languages

The first test considers the ability of the networks to recognize the *Tomita Grammars* [26], seven Regular languages defined on the alphabet $\{a, b\}$ that are a standard in rule extraction [27]. Table 1 provides a complete description of the seven Tomita grammars. We use the experiments and results described in [20] as a reference benchmark. We generate the training and test datasets as detailed therein, including the $ symbol used as string separator. We evaluate the networks by measuring their recognition accuracy on the test set.

Table 1. Description of the 7 Tomita grammars

Name	Regular language
Tomita1	Strings with only a's
Tomita2	Strings with only sequences of ab's
Tomita3	Strings with no odd number of consecutive b's after an odd number of consecutive a's
Tomita4	Strings with fewer than 3 consecutive b's
Tomita5	Strings with even length with an even number of a's
Tomita6	Strings where the difference between the number of a's and b's is a multiple of 3
Tomita7	Strings matching the regular expression $b^*a^*b^*a^*$

3.2 Addition

The next problem consists of predicting the result of a sum of two numbers presented to the network digit by digit. We consider different numerical bases. In base B, the network inputs at a given time step are two numbers between 0 and $B-1$. The network must return a single number in the same range, which is the result (without the carry) of the two inputs addition plus the possible carry generated in the previous time step. We show one example of input and output for $B = 2$ in Table 2, where the strings must be read from left to right, contrary to the usual binary number representation. Note that we also include the separator symbol \$ in the input strings, which represents the end of a particular sum. The \$ symbol always appears in both input strings at the same position, and the expected output is the last carry.

We consider two randomly generated datasets, each consisting of two input strings of length 200000 and the corresponding output string of the same length. We set the generation probability for the \$ symbol to 0.1, and the rest of the symbols are all equally probable. We use the first dataset to train the networks, and the second one for testing. As before, we evaluate the networks by measuring their prediction accuracy on the test set.

Although the grammar associated with this problem is regular, as in the previous case, the problem complexity increases with B, and the interpretation of a standard RNN solution becomes nontrivial. As we show in the results section, this kind of problem illustrates the benefits of using a network that separates the recurrent memory from the main processing path, such as the Dual RNN. Since the only information that needs to be remembered is the carry, the discharge of computing power in the recurrent layer represents an important advantage for this problem.

Table 2. Example of input and output strings for the addition problem in base 2.

Input 1	\$0101110101011010\$01011101\$0101110101011010 11\$00111001\$
Input 2	\$11010101101010 11\$01011010\$011100111000011001\$01011010\$
Output	0101001100000110010010100010001000100111101101011011110

4 Results

4.1 Tomita Grammars

For the recognition of Tomita grammars, we compare the noisy Elman and the Dual networks. In both cases, it is not difficult to find network parameters that allow for a perfect classification with 100% accuracy in all tests. For the noisy Elman network, we use 10 units in the recurrent layer, learning rate $r = 0.01$, L1 regularization $\lambda = 0.1$, a batch size of 10, and an unfold length of 25. The Dual network uses the same parameters, with 10 additional units in the feedforward layer. We train the networks for 1000 epochs, and we use an adaptive noise level that starts at $\nu = 0.0$ and linearly increases to reach a maximum value of $\nu = 1.0$ at epoch 500. We do not use the *shocking* mechanism reported in [20].

After training, the recurrent layer is strongly regularized, with only a few neurons participating in the generation of the network's output. Additionally, the active neurons operate in a binary regime, with their activity being always very close to $+1$ or -1. We do not observe intermediate values in the activation of recurrent units (see Fig. 2). Hence the activation patterns in the recurrent layer can be interpreted as a finite set of states, and state transitions in response to input symbols define a deterministic finite automaton (DFA) that summarizes the network behavior. This observation is general for all the networks that provide satisfactory test results, independently of their architecture.

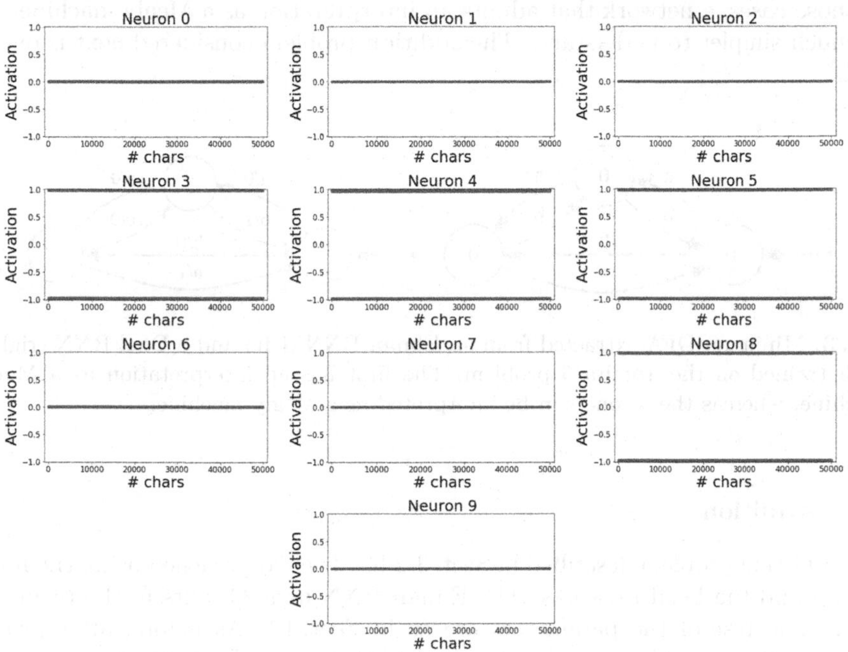

Fig. 2. Activation of the recurrent layer neurons of a Dual RNN trained on the Tomita 6 problem in response to the 50000 symbols of a test string. Only neurons 3, 4, 5 and 8 get activated, and their output is always +1 or −1.

It is, however, interesting to compare the automata obtained for the Elman and the Dual architectures. Figure 3 shows these automata for the Tomita 6 problem[1] after the application of a DFA minimization algorithm [14]. In the noisy Elman case, the network's output depends only on the recurrent layer state. This is represented by associating an output symbol to each automaton state in the figure. This way, the noisy Elman network accepts an interpretation as a Moore machine (Fig. 3, left). On the other hand, the Dual network's output depends on both the recurrent layer state and the input. We can incorporate this information into the corresponding DFA by adding the output symbol to the transition labels. In this case, the resulting automaton is a Mealy machine (Fig. 3, right).

[1] Experiments performed on the other Tomita grammars provide similar results. These can be found in our GitHub repository: https://github.com/slyder095/DualRNN_ICANN21.

Although the two automata seem, in principle, pretty similar, this observation is just valid for this particular problem. Note that, for each state, all the incoming transitions in the Mealy machine are labeled with the same output symbol. Hence the Moore and Mealy machines have the same transitions graph. This panorama changes as soon as we consider more complex problems where the separation between input and memory represents a clear benefit in terms of interpretability. In those cases, a network that admits an interpretation as a Mealy machine will be much simpler to understand. The addition problem considered next is one of such.

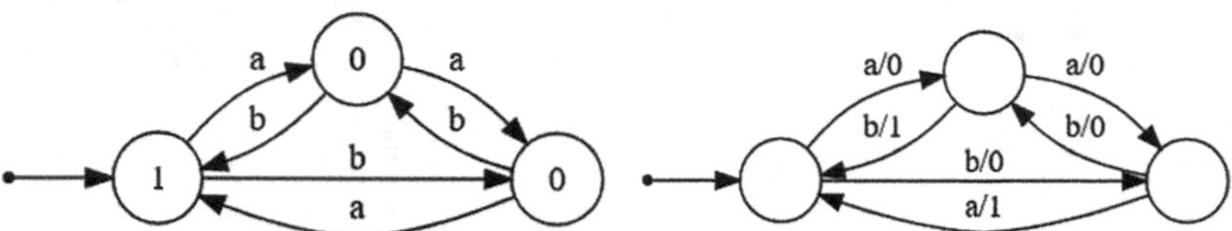

Fig. 3. Minimum DFA extracted from an Elman RNN (left) and a Dual RNN (right), both trained on the Tomita 6 problem. The first has an interpretation as a Moore machine, whereas the second can be interpreted as a Mealy machine.

4.2 Addition

The addition problem described in Sect. 3.2 has been approached using the noisy Elman and the Dual networks. The Elman RNN uses 20 units in the recurrent layer. The rest of the parameters are as in Sect. 4.1. As before, after proper training, the network can correctly predict all the samples in the test set. Regularization and binarization are also observed, with only a few recurrent units coding the solution in the form of a finite set of states. Figure 4 (left) shows the internal state space of one of these networks trained on the addition problem for $B = 2$. Only the three active units are shown (the rest are always silent). And the three of them have a clear interpretation: the first neuron (N0) is learning the carry; the second (N2) keeps track of the carry in the previous time step; and the last one (N5) is dealing with the non-linearity of the binary addition problem, behaving (in conjunction with N0) as an XOR gate. We can extract a DFA as before, and the network accepts, again, an interpretation as a Moore machine (Fig. 4, right).

From a theoretical point of view, only the state represented by the first two neurons must be kept in memory to solve the addition problem since the current input contains all the additional information needed to compute the state of N5. However, as the network has one single recurrent layer concentrating all the processing power, some recurrent units are forced to learn information that does not explicitly depend on the past. For more complex problems, this could imply an unnecessary waste of memory resources, also hindering interpretability.

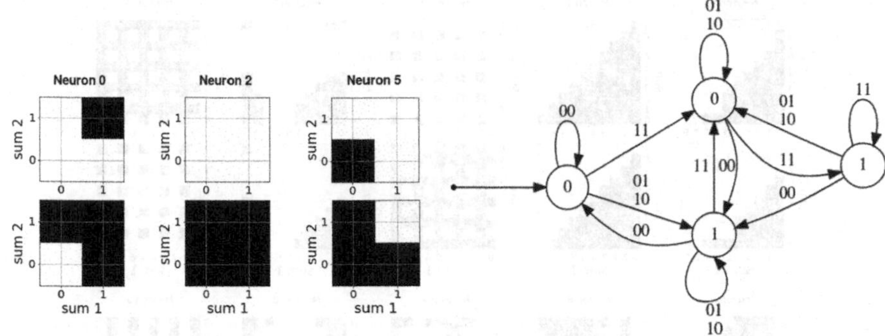

Fig. 4. Left figures represent the activation plot of the three non-regularized neurons in an Elman RNN trained on the addition problem in base 2. For each neuron, the top plot represents the activation when there is no carry, while the bottom plot represents the activation when there is a carry from the previous step. Right figure is the minimum DFA extracted from this Elman RNN.

This point is the case for the addition problem when we consider higher bases. Figure 5 shows an example for $B = 10$. The network has 20 recurrent units and we have trained it with the previous set of parameters. We observe no errors on the test dataset after training. As expected, only a few units survive the regularization, and their activation is binary. However, there is now only one neuron with a straightforward interpretation. Neuron N1 is coding the carry. The other active neurons need to be used to compute the network's output and, although their activation forms some characteristic patterns, their behavior is not meaningful at all. Note, in particular, that some neurons are not symmetric with respect to their two inputs. We do not show the extracted automaton because of its high complexity.

We have also trained a Dual network with 10 neurons in the feedforward layer, in the same conditions. After training, all the general observations extracted for the Elman case are still valid, but now only two neurons are active in the recurrent layer (Fig. 6, left). These two neurons are necessary to deal with the carry, and this is the main difference with respect to the Elman network: now, the recurrent layer only memorizes what is strictly needed to cope with time dependencies. The carry's information stored in the recurrent layer, together with the network input, is sufficient for the additional feedforward layer to compute the correct output. This observation is valid regardless of the numerical base[2].

[2] We have tested with different B values and, in all the cases, we obtain the same solution.

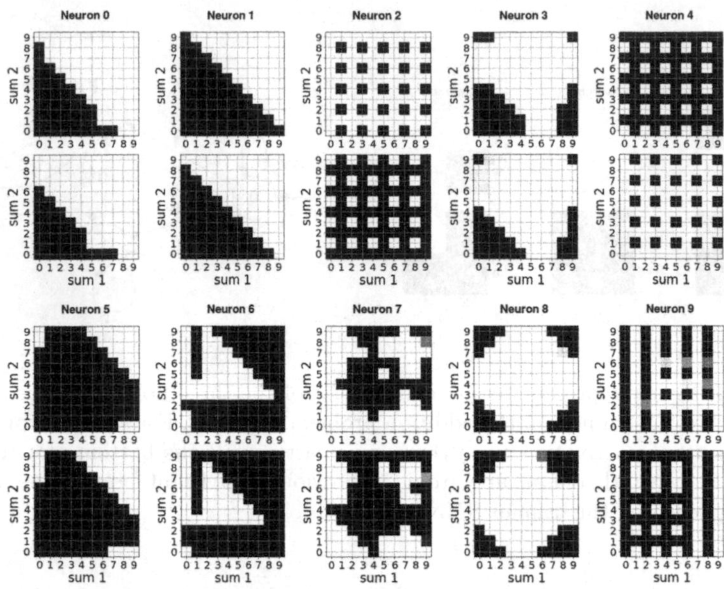

Fig. 5. Activation plot of the ten non-regularized neurons in an Elman RNN trained on the addition problem in base 10. For each neuron, the top plot represents the activation when there is no carry, while the bottom plot represents the activation when there is a carry from the previous step.

We show the corresponding automaton in Fig. 6 (right). The result for $B = 2$ is used for the sake of clarity, but networks trained with different bases provide the same transition diagram (with additional labels for different input/output pairs). The automaton extracted from the Dual network is again a Mealy machine. But the advantage over the Moore version, associated with the Elman RNN, is more evident now (compare with the DFA shown in Fig. 4). As B increases, the difference between the number of states needed by the recurrent layer in the two network architectures becomes more dramatic. While the Elman network needs more and more additional recurrent units to code the solution, the Dual RNN always uses the same memory configuration, leaving the main part of the computation to the feedforward layer. In summary, by allowing some of the processing to be carried out by the feedforward layer, the Dual RNN discharges much of the computational load from the recurrent layer, letting it concentrate on just the information that must be remembered for future time steps. This observation is a pretty exciting result that could be of general application in more complex problems.

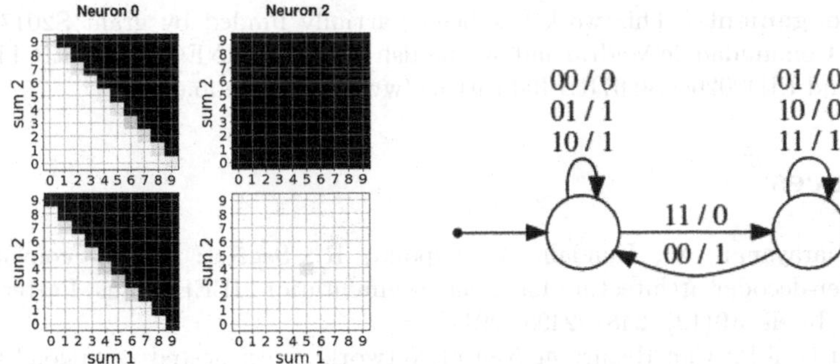

Fig. 6. Left figures represent the activation plot of the two non-regularized neurons in a Dual RNN trained on the addition problem in base 10. For each neuron, the top plot represents the activation when there is no carry, while the bottom plot represents the activation when there is a carry from the previous step. Right figure is the minimum DFA extracted from this Dual RNN.

5 Conclusions

In this article, we have explored a neural network architecture that combines a recurrent layer connected to the network input and a feedforward layer that processes both the input and the output of the recurrent layer. This way, two different processing paths may focus on distinct aspects of learning. The recurrent path concentrates its resources on remembering information that must be preserved along time, working as a kind of memory. The feedforward path can use this memory, together with the input, to provide the final network output. Networks using this architecture seem to make better use of their computational resources. The results are equivalent in accuracy to a traditional Elman RNN, but the networks are more interpretable.

The introduction of noise in the activation function of the recurrent units forces these units to behave in a binary manner, with their output being always either $+1$ or -1. Consequently, the network's time evolution can be seen as a transition through a finite set of discrete states when a given input sequence is presented. It is then possible to extract a transition map and show that the networks internally behave as deterministic finite automata. Although this observation is also valid for the Elman RNNs [21], the automata extracted from networks that use the Dual architecture are much simpler and implement a correct Mealy machine in all the problems we considered.

Despite the simplicity of the considered languages, we expect that this behavior can be extended to more complex problems, with potential applications in fields such as automatic music composition, natural language processing, or machine translation. Even if the results in these areas do not achieve state-of-the-art performance, the gain in interpretability might be worth the price.

Acknowledgements. This work has been partially funded by grant S2017/BMD-3688 from Comunidad de Madrid and by Spanish projects MINECO/FEDER TIN2017-84452-R and PID2020-114867RB-I00 (http://www.mineco.gob.es/).

References

1. Badrinarayanan, V., Kendall, A., Cipolla, R.: SegNet: a deep convolutional encoder-decoder architecture for image segmentation. IEEE Trans. Pattern Anal. Mach. Intell. **39**(12), 2481–2495 (2017)
2. Bernardy, J.P.: Can Recurrent Neural Networks learn nested recursion? In: Linguistic Issues in Language Technology, vol. 16 (2018)
3. Casey, M.: The dynamics of discrete-time computation, with application to Recurrent Neural Networks and finite state machine extraction. Neural Comput. **8**(6), 1135–1178 (1996)
4. Cho, K., et al.: Learning phrase representations using RNN encoder-decoder for statistical machine translation. In: Empirical Methods in Natural Language Processing (EMNLP), pp. 1724–1734 (2014)
5. Cohen, M., Caciularu, A., Rejwan, I., Berant, J.: Inducing regular grammars using Recurrent Neural Networks. In: International Joint Conference on Artificial Intelligence and the 23rd European Conference on Artificial Intelligence (IJCAI-ECAI-18) Workshop on Learning and Reasoning (2018)
6. Collier, M., Beel, J.: Implementing neural turing machines. In: International Conference on Artificial Neural Networks (ICANN), pp. 94–104 (2018)
7. Elman, J.L.: Finding structure in time. Cogn. Sci. **14**(2), 179–211 (1990)
8. Gers, F.A., Schmidhuber, J.: LSTM recurrent networks learn simple context-free and context-sensitive languages. IEEE Trans. Neural Netw. **12**(6), 1333–1340 (2001)
9. Giles, C.L., Miller, C.B., Chen, D., Sun, G., Chen, H., Lee, Y.: Extracting and learning an unknown grammar with Recurrent Neural Networks. In: Advances in Neural Information Processing Systems 4 (NIPS), pp. 317–324 (1991)
10. Graves, A.: Supervised Sequence Labelling with Recurrent Neural Networks. Studies in Computational Intelligence, vol. 385. Springer, Heidelberg (2012). https://doi.org/10.1007/978-3-642-24797-2
11. Graves, A., Mohamed, A., Hinton, G.: Speech recognition with deep Recurrent Neural Networks. In: IEEE International Conference on Acoustics, Speech and Signal Processing, pp. 6645–6649 (2013)
12. Graves, A., Wayne, G., Danihelka, I.: Neural turing machines. CoRR abs/1410.5401 (2014). http://arxiv.org/abs/1410.5401
13. Graves, A., et al.: Hybrid computing using a neural network with dynamic external memory. Nature **538**, 471–476 (2016)
14. Hopcroft, J.E., Motwani, R., Ullman, J.D.: Introduction to Automata Theory, Languages, and Computation, 3rd edn. Addison-Wesley Longman Publishing Co., Inc., USA (2006)
15. Jacobsson, H.: Rule extraction from Recurrent Neural Networks: a taxonomy and review. Neural Comput. **17**(6), 1223–1263 (2005)
16. Karpathy, A., Johnson, J., Fei-Fei, L.: Visualizing and understanding recurrent networks. In: International Conference on Learning Representations (ICLR) (2016)
17. Litjens, G., et al.: A survey on deep learning in medical image analysis. Med. Image Anal. **42**, 60–88 (2017)

18. Mikolov, T., Karafiát, M., Burget, L., Cernocký, J., Khudanpur, S.: Recurrent Neural Network based language model. In: International Speech Communication Association, INTERSPEECH, vol. 2, pp. 1045–1048 (2010)
19. Montavon, G., Samek, W., Müller, K.R.: Methods for interpreting and understanding deep neural networks. Digit. Sig. Process. **73**, 1–15 (2018)
20. Oliva, C., Lago-Fernández, L.F.: On the interpretation of Recurrent Neural Networks as finite state machines. In: 28th International Conference on Artificial Neural Networks (ICANN), Part I, pp. 312–323 (2019)
21. Oliva, C., Lago-Fernández, L.F.: Stability of internal states in Recurrent Neural Networks trained on regular languages. Neurocomputing **452**, 212–223 (2021)
22. Omlin, C.W., Giles, C.L.: Extraction of rules from discrete-time Recurrent Neural Networks. Neural Netw. **9**(1), 41–52 (1996)
23. Siegelmann, H.T., Sontag, E.D.: On the computational power of neural nets. J. Comput. Syst. Sci. **50**(1), 132–150 (1995)
24. Strobelt, H., Gehrmann, S., Pfister, H., Rush, A.M.: LSTMVis: a tool for visual analysis of hidden state dynamics in recurrent neural networks. IEEE Trans. Vis. Comput. Graphics **24**(1), 667–676 (2018)
25. Sutskever, I., Vinyals, O., Le, Q.V.: Sequence to sequence learning with neural networks. In: 27th International Conference on Neural Information Processing Systems, vol. 2, pp. 3104–3112 (2014)
26. Tomita, M.: Dynamic construction of finite automata from examples using hill-climbing. In: Proceedings of the 4th Annual Conference of the Cognitive Science Society, Ann Arbor, Michigan, pp. 105–108 (1982)
27. Wang, Q., Zhang, K., Ororbia, A.G., Xing, X., Liu, X., Giles, C.L.: An empirical evaluation of rule extraction from Recurrent Neural Networks. Neural Comput. **30**(9), 2568–2591 (2018)
28. Zeng, Z., Goodman, R.M., Smyth, P.: Learning finite state machines with self-clustering recurrent networks. Neural Comput. **5**(6), 976–990 (1993)

Predicting Landfall's Location and Time of a Tropical Cyclone Using Reanalysis Data

Sandeep Kumar[1,3](✉), Koushik Biswas[1], and Ashish Kumar Pandey[2]

[1] Department of Computer Science, IIIT Delhi, New Delhi, India
{sandeepk,koushikb}@iiitd.ac.in

[2] Department of Mathematics, IIIT Delhi, New Delhi, India
ashish.pandey@iiitd.ac.in

[3] Department of Mathematics, Shaheed Bhagat Singh College, Univeristy of Delhi, New Delhi, India
sandeep_kumar@sbs.du.ac.in

Abstract. Landfall of a tropical cyclone is the event when it moves over the land after crossing the coast of the ocean. It is important to know the characteristics of the landfall, well advance in time to take preventive measures timely. In this article, we develop a deep learning model based on the combination of a Convolutional Neural network and a Long Short-Term memory network to predict the landfall's location and time of a tropical cyclone in six ocean basins of the world with high accuracy. We have used high-resolution spacial reanalysis data, ERA5, maintained by European Center for Medium-Range Weather Forecasting (ECMWF). The model takes any 9 h, 15 h, or 21 h of data, during the progress of a tropical cyclone and predicts its landfall's location in terms of latitude and longitude and time in hours. For 21 h of data, we achieve mean absolute error for landfall's location prediction in the range of 66.18–158.92 km and for landfall's time prediction in the range of 4.71–8.20 h across all six ocean basins. The model can be trained in just 30 to 45 min (based on ocean basin) and can predict the landfall's location and time in a few seconds, which makes it suitable for real time prediction.

Keywords: Tropical cyclone · Landfall · Reanalysis data · LSTM · CNN

1 Introduction

Predicting natural disasters is one of the difficult prediction problems because of the complex interplay between various cause factors, which vary with space and time. One such natural disaster is a Tropical Cyclone (TC) that frequently occurs in tropical and subtropical regions of the world. TCs are also called Hurricanes or Typhoons in different parts of the world. TCs are characterized by low-pressure areas with an atmospheric circulation that brings heavy rainfall,

I. Farkaš et al. (Eds.): ICANN 2021, LNCS 12894, pp. 372–383, 2021.
https://doi.org/10.1007/978-3-030-86380-7_30

strong winds, thunderstorms, and flash floods in the coastal regions, thereby affecting human lives, property, transportation, businesses, and society. Each year TCs are responsible for the deaths of hundreds of people and billions of economic losses [15,32].

The most important event during the progress of a TC is its landfall that is when it reaches land after crossing the coast of the ocean. The economic and human losses caused by a TC are centered around few kilometers (KM) of its landfall location. Therefore, it is crucial to predict the location and time of the landfall of a TC well advance in time with high accuracy. In this study, we have used a deep learning model to predict the landfall's location and time of a TC. The model takes 9 hours (h), 15 h, or 21 h of continuous data, anytime during the course of a TC, and predicts the landfall's location and time at least 12 h before the actual landfall time. The model performance is reported for six ocean basins - North Indian (NI), South Indian (SI), West Pacific (WP), East Pacific (EP), South Pacific (SP), and North Atlantic (NA) oceans. As per our knowledge, this is the first work that directly focuses on predicting the characteristics of the landfall of a TC using reanalysis data. Predicting landfall's characteristics is a challenging problem to deal with, as discussed in [26].

There are numerous existing TC track prediction models that can be classified into numerical (or dynamical) models, statistical models, and ensemble models [29]. The numerical models rely on physical equations governing atmospheric circulations to capture the evolution of the atmospheric fields. These methods are computationally involved and need large supercomputers. The few major operational numerical models for track prediction are - European Center for Medium-Range Weather Forecasts (ECMWF), Global Forecast System (GFS), and Hurricane Weather and Research Forecasting model (HWRF). The statistical models [16] do not require high computational resources and rely on finding a relationship between historical data and cyclone specific features. The primary operational, statistical models for track prediction are - Climatology and Persistence model (CLIPER5) and Trajectory-CLIPER. The ensemble models combine numerical and statistical models for prediction. Generally, ensemble models perform better than individual models [23]. Numerical methods and statistical methods have their own limitations, and we need to make a trade-off between computational cost and capturing of the complex relationship between various cause factors. Earlier operational forecasting models for intensity prediction rely on satellite based Dvorak technique [8,9], that involves human visual inspection of temperatures infrared satellite images. This technique has inherent limitations due to human subjectivity. Recently, with the increase in the data related to tropical cyclones, various studies have appeared that have successfully applied machine learning-based models to predict various characteristics of a tropical cyclone [26,27] which we discuss in detail in the next section. The article is organized as follows: Sect. 2 describes the related work, Sect. 3 describes the data used in this study, Sect. 4 describes the proposed deep learning model, Sect. 5, describes the results and analysis of our model. Finally, in Sect. 6, we conclude and provide future directions.

2 Related Work

Initial studies regarding tropical cyclones track and intensity forecasts used Artificial Neural Networks (ANNs) [4,22]. Since the prediction problems related to atmospheric conditions involve both spatial and temporal components, deep learning models like Recurrent Neural Networks (RNNs), Long Short-Term Memory (LSTM) networks, Convolutional Neural Networks (CNNs), and combinations of these have been successfully deployed to capture the complex non-linear interplay between various atmospheric components both of spatial and temporal nature. In [27], sparse RNN with flexible topology is used for the prediction of hurricane trajectory in the Atlantic ocean. In [19], ConvLSTM is used to predict the hurricane trajectory from the past density maps of hurricane trajectories. In [1], authors have presented a fully connected RNN model to predict cyclone trajectories from historical cyclone data in the Atlantic ocean. In [11], a nowcasting model is presented based on an LSTM network to predict typhoon trajectory.

Recently, few studies have dealt with TC formation, track, and intensity prediction problems using reanalysis data [3,5,14]. In [5], reanalysis dataset has been used to forecast typhoon formation forecasting in NA, EP, and WP oceans. In [14], authors have used historical data of a TC along with reanalysis data from ERA-Interim [2] to predict the track of TC with a lead time of 24 h in six ocean basins. They propose a fusion network in which the output of CNN trained on wind fields and pressure fields from reanalysis data and output of an ANN trained on historical TC data are fed into another ANN network. Their model does not take the temporal aspect into account as they have stacked input from two-time steps t and $t - 6$ to feed into a CNN. In [3], TC intensity and track prediction task is achieved with a lead time of 24h, using reanalysis data ERA5 [10], historical TC data, and output from operational forecast models for NA and EP ocean basins. They have proposed framework Hurricast (HURR) consisting of seven different models that used different combinations of CNN, GRU, Transformers, and XGBoost models. They used data between t to $t - 21$ hours and capture the spatial and temporal aspects of data, thereby addressing the shortcoming of [14]. As there is no existing work that predicts the landfall characteristics from reanalysis data, we will try to compare our model with the models presented in [3,14].

3 Data

In this study, we have used two open-source datasets - historical cyclones data and reanalysis data. The historical track data is taken from NOAA database IBTrACS version 4 [18,21]. The dataset contains information about ocean basin, latitude, longitude, Estimated Central Pressure (ECP), Maximum Sustained surface Wind Speed(MSWS), distance to land, distance and direction of TC movement, etc. at an interval of three hours. From these features, we choose latitude, longitude, and distance to land for our study and exclude features like

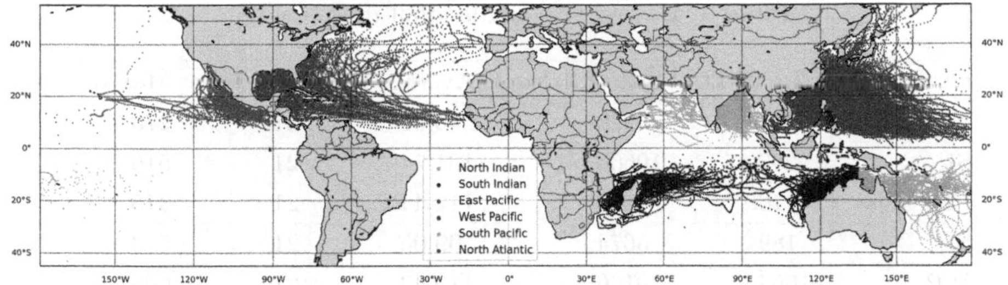

Fig. 1. Trajectory of all cyclones till landfall in six ocean basins

MSSW, ECP, distance, and direction of TC movement, which are used by two related works [3,14]. As we are predicting the landfall's location and time of a TC, our dataset consists of all those cyclones which hit the coastal region, and for all such cyclones, only data corresponding to the time points when a TC was moving over the ocean is taken into account. If a cyclone moves from ocean to land and then from land to ocean and continues like this during its course, then the data corresponding to its presence over land is not considered. Also, if a cyclone moves from ocean to land and land to ocean multiple times, then each such movement is treated as a separate cyclone while preparing the dataset. Because of this process, our dataset size is shortened. We are not using features like MSSW, ECP, distance, and direction of TC movement, which have lots of missing values to avoid further shortening of our dataset. We extracted data from 1981 to 2020 provided at an interval of three hours. The trajectory of all TCs till their landfall considered in this study are shown in Fig. 1.

The large scale atmospheric circulation of wind at different pressure levels plays a crucial role in determining the track of a TC. To capture this information, we have used ERA5 [10] reanalysis data produced by ECMWF in near to real-time. ERA5 is a fifth-generation reanalysis data covering global climate and weather since 1950. From 1979 onwards, the high-resolution data ERA5 replaces the ERA-interim. Reanalysis is a scientific way of producing globally complete and consistent data by gathering the information from various resources and validating them using the laws of physics. We extracted the u, v components of wind and z geopotential fields at three atmospheric pressure levels (225 hPa, 500 hPa, 700 hPa) for a spatial extension of $4 \times 4°$ and spatial resolution of $0.25 \times 0.25°$ (resulting in a grid of size 33×33), centered at the current TC location. The choice of these variables is inspired by [3,14] where authors have used values of these three variables at mentioned three pressure levels for a spatial extension of $25 \times 25°$ and spatial resolution of $1 \times 1°$ (resulting in a grid of size 25×25). On the world map, one degree approximately equals 110 KM. This way, we are utilizing the mentioned variables values for a spatial spread of around 440 KM (in comparison of 1320 KM by earlier two studies) with a spatial resolution of around 27.5 KM (in comparison of 110 KM by earlier two studies) around the TC center. Apart from these three variables, we extracted the sea surface temperature (SST) for the 33×33 grid centered at the TC location for each time point.

Table 1. Dataset size and landfall time (hours)

Ocean basin	No. of TCs	Size of dataset	Average time	Min time	Max time
NI	205	5920	95.61	21	270
SI	282	10600	121.74	21	516
EP	116	4000	112.44	21	315
SP	189	5674	99.06	21	513
WP	1064	39166	119.43	21	606
NA	401	11386	94.18	21	531

As we are using CNN, to feed the current location information, we have created two more 33×33 matrices lats and longs for each time point of a TC. The each row of lats is equal to vector $(\text{lat} + 0.25 * k | -16 \leq k \leq 16)$ and each column of longs is equal to vector $(\text{long} + 0.25 * k | -16 \leq k \leq 16)$ where $(\text{lat}, \text{long})$ denotes the latitude and longitude of TC's current location. Feeding this information in CNN will enable it to generate distance and direction like features between two successive time points of a TC. In Table 1, the dataset size along with average landfall time after the initiation of a TC in six ocean basins are shown for all TCs with the minimum time difference between TC formation and its landfall as 21h.

3.1 Training Dataset Preparation

Let T be the number of continuous data points (that is $3(T-1)$ hours of data) taken in the model to predict the target. For a fixed cyclone, let T_L be the number of data points between cyclone formation and its landfall. For this TC, we created $T_L - (T-1) - 3 = T_L - T - 2$ inputs, where a single input is a sequence of T vectors of the form:

$$(\text{lats}(t), \text{longs}(t), \text{u225}(t), \text{v225}(t), \text{z225}(t), \text{u500}(t)$$
$$\text{v500}(t), \text{z500}(t), \text{u700}(t), \text{v700}(t), \text{z700}(t), \text{SST}(t))$$

where $k \leq t \leq T + k - 1$ and k varies from 1 to $T_L - T - 2$. The target variables for each input are latitude and longitude at landfall or time (in hours) remaining to landfall of the cyclone from the current time t. One must note that by following the above process, we are predicting our target at least 12 h before the landfall. For example, BELNA cyclone formed at 00 h on 05 December 2019 in EP ocean, and the landfall happened at 15 h on 09 December 2019, that is $T_L = 37$. Suppose $T = 8$, then this TC will generate $37 - 8 - 2 = 27$ training data points. The collection of all such inputs across all TCs for a particular ocean basin will form the training dataset.

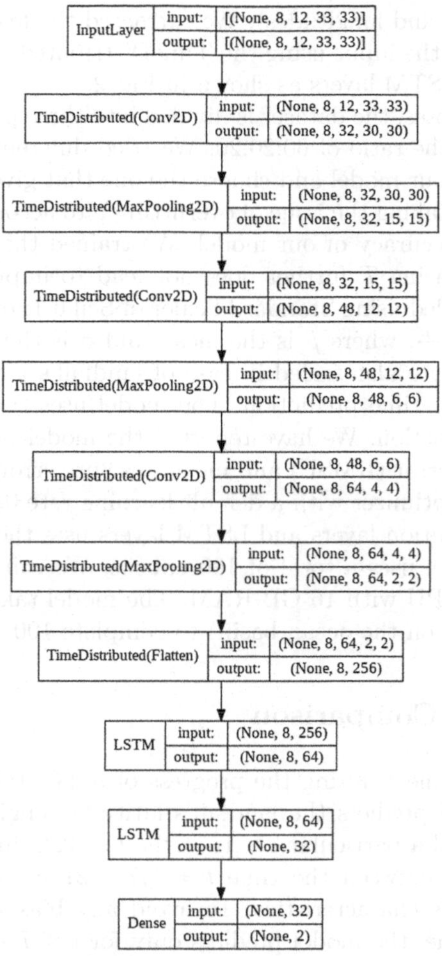

Fig. 2. Model representation for latitude/longitude prediction for $T = 8$

4 Model Implementation and Training

As we are dealing with a dataset with both spatial and temporal dimensions, we have used a combination of CNN [24,25] and LSTM [12,13,17] models to capture the spatial and temporal aspects of our prediction problem. We come up with a model that works well for each ocean basin. The structure of the model for location prediction in terms of latitude and longitude is described in the Fig. 2 for $T = 8$. The model for time prediction is the same except that the last dense layer's output size is one. The model is implemented in Keras API [6] which uses underlying low-level language TensorFlow. For $T = 8$, one training point consists of eight sequential inputs of shape $12 \times 33 \times 33$, where 12 represents the number of channels (nine channels of wind and geopotential fields, one of

SST, two of latitudes and longitudes). We extracted the features corresponding to each time point of the input using the TimeDistributed layer of Keras, which are further fed into LSTM layers as shown in Fig. 2.

For training purposes, the dataset is divided into three parts training, validation, and test set in the ratio of 60:20:20. We tried different configurations and hyperparameters for our model and choose the one that gives the best result on validation data after taking the issue of overfitting into account. Finally, we have reported the 5-fold accuracy of our model. We trained the model for T equals to 4, 6, and 8; increasing T further does not lead to improved accuracy. The input features are scaled using Standard Scaler of Scikit learn library [30], which is given by $f(x) = \frac{x-\mu}{\sigma}$, where μ is the mean and σ is the standard deviation. The target variables are also scaled in case of landfall's latitude and longitude prediction but not for time prediction. The model uses the mean square error (MSE) as the loss function. We have reported the model performance in terms of root mean square error (RMSE) and mean absolute error (MAE). The model uses the Adam [20] optimizer with a default learning rate 0.001 to minimize the loss function. Convolution layers and LSTM layers uses the activation function ReLU [28]. The model uses a total of 100 epochs. We run our experiments on Nvidia Tesla V100 GPU with 16 GB RAM. The model takes approximately 30 to 45 min (depending on the ocean basin) to complete 100 epochs.

5 Results and Comparison

Our model, at any time t during the progress of a TC, takes T number $((T-1) * 3\,\text{h})$ of data and predicts the landfall's latitude, longitude, and time. For example, if $T = 8$ and a particular TC is at the $t = 42\,\text{h}$ during its progression, then using the data between the time $t = 42 - 21 = 21$ and t. the model predicts the landfall's characteristics. To avoid any bias when time t is very close to landfall's time, the model predicts only for $t \leq L - 12$, where L is the landfall's time, which means we are remaining at least 12 h away from landfall while predicting. For each ocean basin and for different values of $T = 4, 6, 8$ (9 h, 15 h, 21 h). We have reported the size of the dataset and the 5-fold accuracy in terms of RMSE and MAE along with standard deviation in Table 2. From the predicted latitude and longitude, the distance error between actual landfall location and predicted location is also reported in Table 2.

From Table 2, we can see that we can predict the landfall's location in ocean basins NI, SI, EP, SP, WP, and NA with a distance error of 66.18 KM, 119.96 KM, 110.48 KM, 144.80 KM, 108.0 KM, and 158.92 KM respectively for $T = 8$ (21 h) with a low standard deviation (std). If we look at the landfall's time prediction results, they are quite impressive. The model predicts the landfall's time in six ocean basins NI, SI, EP, SP, WP, and NA with an MAE of 4.71 h, 6.04 h, 8.20 h, 6.74 h, 5.89 h, and 7.42 h respectively with low standard deviation.

To further demonstrate the working of our model, in Fig. 3, we have shown landfall's latitude-longitude prediction results for cyclone BUD (2018) in EP ocean basin. In Fig. 4, the landfall's time prediction results for cyclone FANI

(2019) in NI ocean basin is shown. One can note that the model start predicting at time $t = 21$ and uses data of 21 h between $t - 21$ and t to predict at time t. All these named cyclones are not part of training data.

5.1 Comparison

As per our knowledge, there does not exist any earlier work that predicts the landfall's location and time using reanalysis data. In the absence of directly related work, we will compare our results with closely related works [3,14]. In Table 3, the compassion between Fusion model [14] and our proposed model is shown. In [14] authors used TC data for 12 h at a temporal resolution of 6 h for track prediction with a lead time of 24 h. A comparison with our model with $T = 8$ is provided in Table 3. One can see that we have achieved better results for a much harder problem with arbitrary lead time depending on the time between

Table 2. 5-fold accuracy of landfall's location and time prediction for different T

Ocean basin	T (hours)	Dataset size	RMSE (std)			MAE (std)			
			Lati degree	Long degree	Time hours	Lati degree	Long degree	Time hours	Distance KM
North Indian	4 (9)	5060	0.58 (0.05)	1.03 (0.09)	10.46 (1.40)	0.38 (0.02)	0.70 (0.05)	7.33 (1.50)	93.78 (6.71)
	6 (15)	4660	0.53 (0.13)	0.90 (0.13)	8.98 (3.47)	0.36 (0.12)	0.59 (0.10)	6.05 (2.38)	81.92 (18.62)
	8 (21)	4284	0.40 (0.04)	0.76 (0.06)	6.72 (0.58)	0.26 (0.02)	0.50 (0.03)	4.71 (0.54)	66.18 (2.87)
South Indian	4 (9)	9441	0.53 (0.03)	1.78 (0.22)	13.17 (0.59)	0.36 (0.02)	1.31 (0.15)	8.32 (0.31)	150.78 (15.55)
	6 (15)	8886	0.46 (0.03)	1.44 (0.06)	11.34 (0.84)	0.30 (0.03)	1.06 (0.04)	7.24 (0.42)	123.32 (5.24)
	8 (21)	8353	0.42 (0.02)	1.42 (0.18)	9.63 (0.96)	0.27 (0.03)	1.05 (0.10)	6.04 (0.45)	119.96 (12.22)
East Pacific	4 (9)	3505	0.70 (0.23)	1.49 (0.33)	10.40 (1.03)	0.52 (0.18)	1.08 (0.24)	7.17 (0.80)	133.43 (33.42)
	6 (15)	3276	0.62 (0.04)	1.33 (0.24)	9.89 (2.17)	0.46 (0.03)	0.95 (0.10)	6.99 (1.74)	117.8 (9.76)
	8 (21)	3056	0.52 (0.03)	1.26 (0.16)	11.28 (3.69)	0.37 (0.02)	0.93 (0.03)	8.20 (2.96)	110.48 (2.86)
South Pacific	4 (9)	4885	0.89 (0.09)	2.12 (0.14)	17.44 (2.70)	0.55 (0.05)	1.50 (0.14)	11.30 (2.19)	179.03 (17.26)
	6 (15)	4520	0.89 (0.19)	2.30 (0.57)	13.24 (1.60)	0.57 (0.14)	1.57 (0.33)	7.69 (0.65)	188.81 (37.51)
	8 (21)	4182	0.72 (0.10)	1.67 (0.23)	10.07 (1.77)	0.44 (0.07)	1.23 (0.20)	6.74 (1.04)	144.80 (22.44)
West Pacific	4 (9)	34874	1.34 (0.34)	1.72 (0.37)	10.84 (0.30)	0.88 (0.24)	1.15 (0.26)	7.44 (0.41)	164.17 (40.08)
	6 (15)	32777	1.04 (0.16)	1.40 (0.22)	10.10 (2.14)	0.72 (0.13)	0.97 (0.16)	7.22 (1.62)	137.86 (24.28)
	8 (21)	30791	0.79 (0.10)	1.09 (0.10)	8.12 (0.93)	0.56 (0.08)	0.76 (0.06)	5.89 (0.72)	108.0 (11.61)
North Atlantic	4 (9)	9782	1.28 (0.12)	2.42 (0.24)	15.10 (4.20)	0.84 (0.04)	1.47 (0.11)	10.47 (3.40)	174.51 (10.68)
	6 (15)	8999	1.17 (0.15)	2.13 (0.32)	10.30 (1.26)	0.79 (0.08)	1.32 (0.14)	6.58 (0.96)	161.74 (15.36)
	8 (21)	8276	1.05 (0.04)	2.10 (0.34)	10.69 (1.14)	0.71 (0.03)	1.38 (0.13)	7.42 (0.98)	158.92 (12.62)

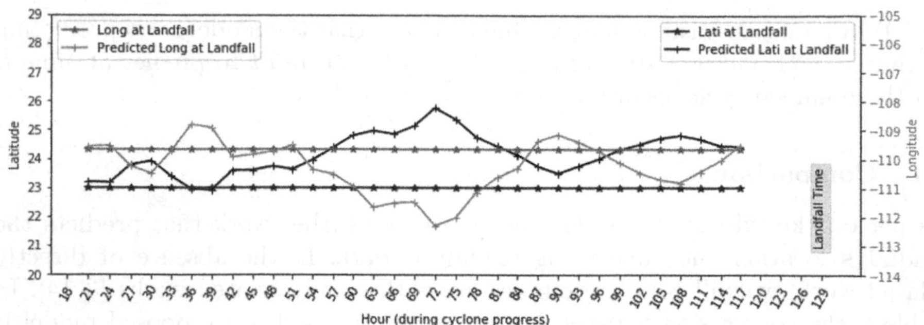

Fig. 3. Latitude and Longitude prediction for hurricane BUD (2018) in EP ocean for T = 8

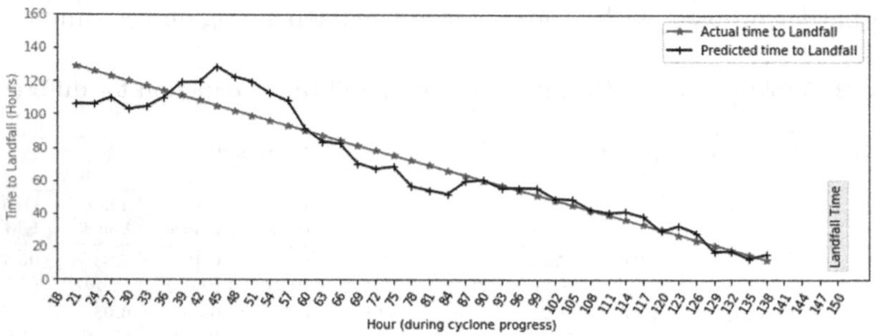

Fig. 4. Time to landfall prediction for Fani (2019) cyclone in NI ocean for T = 8

TC's initiation and its landfall. The authors of [14] have also reported the error range (std) 71 KM for a subset of cyclones in the Atlantic ocean, while our model achieves an error range (std) 2.87 KM–22.44 KM across all ocean basins. All this makes our model more robust and reliable to use for practical purposes.

In [3] authors use a combination of historical TC data, reanalysis data, and output from operational models and propose eight models for track prediction of TCs in NA and EP ocean basins for years 2017 to 2019. The model which close to our proposed model is HURR-(viz, CNN/GRU) which uses CNN-encoder and GRU-decoder [7]. The authors consider only those hurricanes in their study for which MSWS reaches 34 knots at some time t_0 and contains at least 60 h of data after t_0. Our model does not have any such restrictions. In Table 4, we have shown the results for HURR-(viz, CNN/GRU) and the operational CLIPER5 model for EP and NA ocean basin. One can see that our results are not as good as that of HURR-(viz, CNN/GRU) but quite comparable with the operational model CLIPER5. One can notice that the standard deviation of our model is quite low in comparison to these two models. Here, we would again point out that we are not making a direct comparison here as our target prediction problem is different from the above-mentioned works but, at the same time, much more challenging and important.

Table 3. Comparison in terms of distance MAE (KM)

Model/ocean basin	NI (KM)	SI (KM)	EP (KM)	SP (KM)	WP (KM)	NA (KM)	No. of parameters ($*10^6$)	Training time	Lead time
Fusion (Track) [14]	138.9	136.1	106.9	161.7	136.1	130.2	≥ 2.27	8 h	24 h
Proposed model (Landfall)	66.1	119.9	110.4	144.8	108.0	158.9	0.157	≤ 0.75 h	TC dependent ($>= 12h$)

Table 4. Track prediction MAE (std) in KM for HURR model and operational CLIPER5 model for 24 h lead time

	Model/year	2017 (10 TCs)	2018 (15 TCs)	2019 (12 TCs)
EP	HURR-(viz, cnn/gru)	74 (40)	69 (42)	73 (45)
	CLIPER5	114 (59)	109 (61)	133 (74)
NA	HURR-(viz, cnn/gru)	94 (61)	113 (77)	123 (89)
	CLIPER5	189 (135)	199 (118)	207 (171)

Table 5. 4/5 year (2015–2019) MAE reported by IMD for cyclones in NI ocean basin

Lead time (hours)	36	48	60	72
Landfall time	4.96	5.53	6.8	9.6
Landfall distance	42.84	78.08	92.6	112.5

We do not find any meteorological department across the world which reported the landfall prediction accuracy except the Indian Meteorological Department (IMD) on its website [31]. IMD has reported landfall's location error and time for a certain number of lead hours. In Table 5, we have reported the last 4/5 years (as per data availability) MAE achieved by IMD for landfall's location and time prediction. From Table 1, we can see that in the NI ocean basin, the landfall occurs on average at 95.61 h. Therefore, it is reasonable to compare our results with that of IMD for 72 lead hours. Clearly, here also, our model performs better than that of models used by IMD for both landfall's location and time. We have not included the results reported by IMD for earlier years, as errors are much higher.

6 Conclusion

We propose a model that can predict the landfall's location and time of a TC with high accuracy by observing a TC for 9 h, 15 h, or 21 h at any time of its progression in the world's six ocean basins. The model took only 30 to 45 min for training and can predict the landfall characteristics within few seconds, which makes it suitable for practical usage where the disaster managers can know the landfall location and time well in advance and can take preventive life saving and property saving measures. Our model supports the case that deep learning models like CNN and LSTM can be utilized to predict challenging and complex prediction problems like the landfall of a TC. One can further work in the direction of utilizing CNN with Attention and Transformers models for further improvement or developing Consensus models to solve the proposed prediction problem. As we are able to solve a complex landfall prediction problem using data over a small spatial extent with high resolution, it will be interesting to see to use the same kind of data for track or intensity prediction problems.

References

1. Alemany, S., Beltran, J., Perez, A., Ganzfried, S.: Predicting hurricane trajectories using a recurrent neural network. In: Proceedings of the AAAI Conference on Artificial Intelligence, vol. 33, February 2018. https://doi.org/10.1609/aaai.v33i01.3301468
2. Berrisford, P., et al.: The era-interim archive version 2.0 **1**, 23 (2011)
3. Boussioux, L., Zeng, C., Guénais, T., Bertsimas, D.: Hurricane forecasting: a novel multimodal machine learning framework (2020). https://arxiv.org/pdf/2011.06125.pdf
4. Chaudhuri, S., Basu, D., Das, D., Goswami, S., Varshney, S.: Swarm intelligence and neural nets in forecasting the maximum sustained wind speed along the track of tropical cyclones over Bay of Bengal. Nat. Hazards, p. 87, July 2017. https://doi.org/10.1007/s11069-017-2824-4
5. Chen, R., Wang, X., Zhang, W., Zhu, X., Li, A., Yang, C.: A hybrid CNN-LSTM model for typhoon formation forecasting **23**(3), 375–396 (2019). https://doi.org/10.1007/s10707-019-00355-0
6. Chollet, F.: Keras (2015). https://github.com/fchollet/keras
7. Chung, J., Gülçehre, Ç., Cho, K., Bengio, Y.: Empirical evaluation of gated recurrent neural networks on sequence modeling. CoRR abs/1412.3555 (2014). http://arxiv.org/abs/1412.3555
8. Dvorak, V.F.: Tropical cyclone intensity analysis and forecasting from satellite imagery. Mon. Weather Rev. **103**(5), 420–430 (1975)
9. Dvorak, V.F.: Tropical cyclone intensity analysis using satellite data, vol. 11. US Department of Commerce, National Oceanic and Atmospheric Administration (1984)
10. European Centre for Medium-Range Weather Forecasts: Era5 reanalysis (2017). https://doi.org/10.5065/D6X34W69
11. Gao, S., et al.: A nowcasting model for the prediction of typhoon tracks based on a long short term memory neural network. Acta Oceanologica Sinica **37**, 8–12 (2018). https://doi.org/10.1007/s13131-018-1219-z
12. Gers, F.A., Schmidhuber, J., Cummins, F.: Learning to forget: continual prediction with LSTM. In: 1999 Ninth International Conference on Artificial Neural Networks ICANN 99. Conference Publication No. 470, vol. 2, pp. 850–855 (1999)
13. Gers, F.A., Schraudolph, N.N., Schmidhuber, J.: Learning precise timing with LSTM recurrent networks. J. Mach. Learn. Res. **3**(null), 115–143 (2003). https://doi.org/10.1162/153244303768966139
14. Giffard-Roisin, S., Yang, M., Charpiat, G., Kumler Bonfanti, C., Kégl, B., Monteleoni, C.: Tropical cyclone track forecasting using fused deep learning from aligned reanalysis data. Front. Big Data **3**, 1 (2020). https://doi.org/10.3389/fdata.2020.00001

15. Grinsted, A., Ditlevsen, P., Christensen, J.H.: Normalized us hurricane damage estimates using area of total destruction, 1900–2018. Proc. Nat. Acad. Sci. **116**(48), 23942–23946 (2019). https://doi.org/10.1073/pnas.1912277116
16. Hall, T.M., Jewson, S.: Statistical modeling of North Atlantic tropical cyclone tracks. Tellus **59A**, 486–498 (2007). https://doi.org/10.1111/j.1600-0870.2007.00240.x
17. Hochreiter, S., Schmidhuber, J.: Long short-term memory. Neural Comput. **9**(8), 1735–1780 (1997). https://doi.org/10.1162/neco.1997.9.8.1735
18. IBTrACS (2020). https://www.ncdc.noaa.gov/ibtracs/index.php?name=ib-v4-access
19. Kim, S., et al.: Deep-hurricane-tracker: tracking and forecasting extreme climate events, pp. 1761–1769, January 2019. https://doi.org/10.1109/WACV.2019.00192
20. Kingma, D., Ba, J.: Adam: a method for stochastic optimization. In: International Conference on Learning Representations, December 2014
21. Knapp, K.R., Kruk, M.C., Levinson, D.H., Diamond, H.J., Neumann, C.J.: The international best track archive for climate stewardship (IBTRACS): unifying tropical cyclone data. Bull. Am. Meteorol. Soc. **91**(3), 363–376 (2010). https://doi.org/10.1175/2009BAMS2755.1
22. Kovordányi, R., Roy, C.: Cyclone track forecasting based on satellite images using artificial neural networks. ISPRS J. Photogram. Remote Sens. **64**(6), 513–521 (2009)
23. Krishnamurti, T.N., et al.: Multimodel ensemble forecasts for weather and seasonal climate. J. Climate **13**(23), 4196–4216 (2000)
24. Krizhevsky, A., Sutskever, I., Hinton, G.: ImageNet classification with deep convolutional neural networks. In: Neural Information Processing Systems, vol. 25, January 2012. https://doi.org/10.1145/3065386
25. LeCun, Y., et al.: Backpropagation applied to handwritten zip code recognition. Neural Comput. **1**(4), 541–551 (1989). https://doi.org/10.1162/neco.1989.1.4.541
26. Leroux, M.D., et al.: Recent advances in research and forecasting of tropical cyclone track, intensity, and structure at landfall. Trop. Cyclone Res. Rev. **7**(2), 85–105 (2018). https://doi.org/10.6057/2018TCRR02.02
27. Moradi Kordmahalleh, M., Gorji Sefidmazgi, M., Homaifar, A.: A sparse recurrent neural network for trajectory prediction of atlantic hurricanes. GECCO 2016, pp. 957–964. Association for Computing Machinery, New York (2016). https://doi.org/10.1145/2908812.2908834
28. Nair, V., Hinton, G.E.: Rectified linear units improve restricted boltzmann machines. In: Fürnkranz, J., Joachims, T. (eds.) Proceedings of the 27th International Conference on Machine Learning (ICML-10), 21–24 June 2010, Haifa, Israel, pp. 807–814. Omnipress (2010). https://icml.cc/Conferences/2010/papers/432.pdf
29. NOAA (2019). https://www.nhc.noaa.gov/modelsummary.shtml
30. Pedregosa, F., et al.: Scikit-learn: machine learning in Python. J. Mach. Learn. Res. **12**, 2825–2830 (2011)
31. RMSC (2020). http://www.rsmcnewdelhi.imd.gov.in/landfall-forecast.php
32. Webersik, C., Esteban, M., Shibayama, T.: The economic impact of future increase in tropical cyclones in Japan. Nat. Hazards **55**, 233–250 (2010). https://doi.org/10.1007/s11069-010-9522-9

Latent State Inference in a Spatiotemporal Generative Model

Matthias Karlbauer[1(✉)], Tobias Menge[1], Sebastian Otte[1], Hendrik P. A. Lensch[2], Thomas Scholten[3], Volker Wulfmeyer[4], and Martin V. Butz[1]

[1] University of Tübingen – Neuro-Cognitive Modeling Group, Sand 14, 72076 Tübingen, Germany
martin.butz@uni-tuebingen.de

[2] University of Tübingen – Computer Graphics, Maria-von-Linden-Straße 6, 72076 Tübingen, Germany

[3] University of Tübingen – Soil Science and Geomorphology, Rümelinstraße 19-23, 72070 Tübingen, Germany

[4] University of Hohenheim – Institute for Physics and Meteorology, Garbenstraße 30, 70599 Stuttgart, Germany

Abstract. Knowledge about the hidden factors that determine particular system dynamics is crucial for both explaining them and pursuing goal-directed interventions. Inferring these factors from time series data without supervision remains an open challenge. Here, we focus on spatiotemporal processes, including wave propagation and weather dynamics, for which we assume that universal causes (e.g. physics) apply throughout space and time. A recently introduced DIstributed SpatioTemporal graph Artificial Neural network Architecture (DISTANA) is used and enhanced to learn such processes, requiring fewer parameters and achieving significantly more accurate predictions compared to temporal convolutional neural networks and other related approaches. We show that DISTANA, when combined with a retrospective latent state inference principle called active tuning, can reliably derive location-respective hidden causal factors. In a current weather prediction benchmark, DISTANA infers our planet's land-sea mask solely by observing temperature dynamics and, meanwhile, uses the self inferred information to improve its own future temperature predictions.

Keywords: Recurrent neural networks · Graph neural networks · Latent inference · Weather prediction

Funded by the Deutsche Forschungsgemeinschaft (DFG, German Research Foundation) under Germany's Excellence Strategy - EXC number 2064/1 – Project number 390727645. Moreover, we thank the International Max Planck Research School for Intelligent Systems (IMPRS-IS) for supporting Matthias Karlbauer.

I. Farkaš et al. (Eds.): ICANN 2021, LNCS 12894, pp. 384–395, 2021.
https://doi.org/10.1007/978-3-030-86380-7_31

1 Introduction

When considering our planet's weather, centuries of past research have identified a large number of factors that affect its highly nonlinear and partially chaotic dynamics. Yet, can we ever be sure of having identified all hidden causal factors? Moreover, do we have (sufficient) data about them? These are fundamental questions in any prediction or forecasting task, including spatiotemporal processes such as soil property dynamics, traffic forecasting, energy-flow prediction (e.g. in brains or supply networks), or recommender systems. Here, we investigate how unobservable hidden factors may be inferred from spatiotemporal data streams.

When regularities in hidden causes are detectable, they may be encoded in the latent activities of recurrent neural networks [18,20], such as a long short-term memory (LSTM) [10]. The involved and conventional forward-directed inference of recurrent neural networks, however, has two main disadvantages: First, the encodings of the hidden causes form while streaming data, meaning they are not available from the beginning of a sequence. Second, learning, detecting and shaping the encodings is relatively hard, because the error signal only decreases once the unfolding data stream is suitably compressed.

To overcome these limitations, we combine and extend the recently introduced DIstributed SpatioTemporal graph Artificial Neural network Architecture (DISTANA) [13] with active tuning (AT) [7,8,17], which facilitates the determination of hidden causal states via retrospective inference over time. Projected onto stable neural states, akin to parametric bias neurons [23,24], AT searches for constant input biases, assuming that the observed dynamics are influenced by particular constant and only indirectly observable factors.

Following the idea of *relational inductive biases* [3], DISTANA is designed to model the hidden causal processes that generate spatiotemporal dynamics. Hence, DISTANA assumes that the sensed dynamics are generated by universal causal principles (e.g. physics). Moreover, we endow DISTANA with the expectation that constant, hidden factors modify the spatiotemporal processes locally. For example, weather dynamics follow the universal principles of thermodynamics from physics and are locally dependent on the topology.

The contributions we make are as follows: (A) the combination of DISTANA with active tuning (AT) to infer constant, hidden factors locally, even when these factors are never made available to the network – neither as input nor as (target) output. (B) we show that reasonable latent neural activities are inferred during training and testing via retrospective spatiotemporal analysis. (C) after having learned a distributed, generative model of the globally unfolding dynamics, we demonstrate that our planet's land-sea mask as well as other causal factors can be inferred via the retrospective analysis of unfolding weather dynamics – partially again even when the algorithm was never informed about these factors – to increase the model's prediction abilities.

We conclude that the retrospective inference of latent states via AT offers a promising method to identify hidden factors in data streams, and that graph neural networks (GNN) like DISTANA bear great potential at modeling real-world spatiotemporal processes.

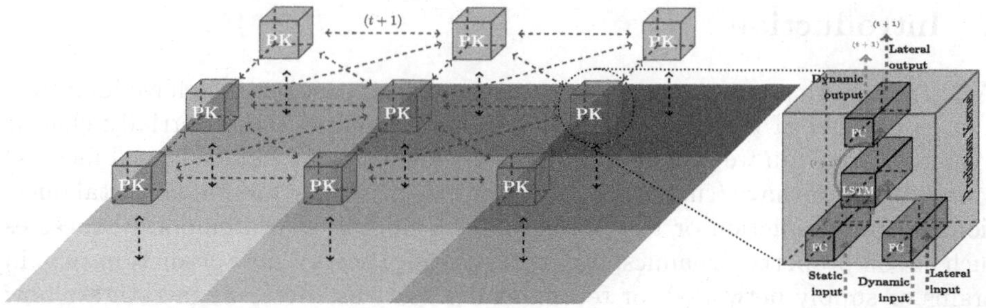

Fig. 1. 3×3 sensor mesh grid showing the connection scheme of Prediction Kernels (PKs) that model the local dynamical process while communicating laterally. Figure modified from [14].

2 DISTANA

As introduced in [13] and following the naming convention of [27], DISTANA (the DIstributed SpatioTemporal graph Artificial Neural network Architecture) can be described as a spatiotemporal graph neural network (ST-GNN). While GNNs give the designer a large amount of freedom in controlling the flow of information within the model (referred to as relational inductive biases) [3], they are reported to model physical systems with very high precision and accuracy for up to several hundreds of time steps even during closed loop prediction [2, 16,21,22,25]. Thorough surveys about GNNs and the numerous ways of creating the graph and setting up the connection schemes are written by [3,6,27].

The GNN used in this work, DISTANA, consists of prediction kernels (PKs), which are arranged in a lattice structure. PKs model local dynamics concurrently. In every time step t, each PK receives (i) local dynamic data, and (ii) lateral output activities from the neighboring PKs from $t-1$ to exchange information between PKs. Here, we extend the PKs to (iii) additionally receive location specific static inputs. The time recurrent PKs process this information, combine it with their previous latent state, and generate (i) predictions of the next local dynamic data input at $t+1$, as well as (ii) outputs to the laterally connected PKs (cf. Fig. 1). PKs are akin to a spatiotemporal convolutional kernel, since all PKs share identical weights, that is, a single set of weights is applied and optimized in every grid cell. As a result, the likelihood of overfitting local data irregularities is reduced and the emergence of a highly generalizing and universally applicable set of weights is fostered. Because of the reduction of trainable weights, less data is needed for training.

2.1 Alternative State-of-the-Art Architectures

We compared DISTANA with two well-suited deep learning approaches. First, we tested convolutional long short-term memory models (ConvLSTMs) [28] to predict circular wave dynamics (see Fig. 2). The used ConvLSTM model has

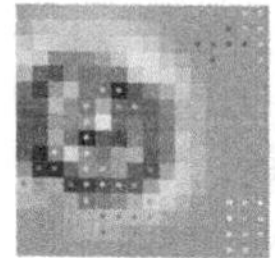

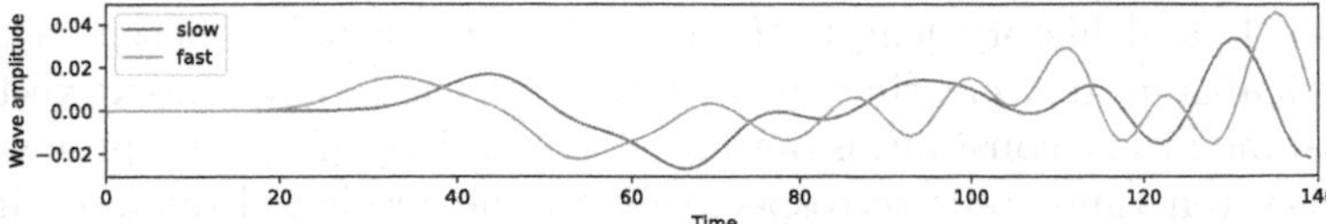

Fig. 2. Left: two-dimensional wave propagating through a 16×16 grid with obstacles. Darker dots in the grid nodes correspond to stronger blocking effect on the wave. Right: wave activity for two exemplary positions in the grid, with fast and slow propagation speeds.

2 952 free parameters to project the $16 \times 16 \times 1$ input (ignoring batch and time dimensions) via the first layer on eight feature maps (resulting in dimensionality $16 \times 16 \times 8$) and subsequently via the second layer back to one output feature map. All kernels have a filter size of $k = 3$, apply zero-padding and are implemented with a stride of one. The code was taken and adapted from[1]. Second, we tested Temporal Convolution Networks (TCN) [1,9,12]. The TCN used in this work is a three-layer network with 2 306 parameters, where the input layer projects to eight feature maps, which project their values back to one output value. A kernel filter size of $k = 3$ is used for the two spatial dimensions in combination with the standard dilation rate of $d = 1, 2, 4$ for the temporal dimension, resulting in a temporal horizon of 28 time steps, cf. [1]. Various experiments with other sizes and deeper network structures have not yielded any better performance than the one reported. Code was taken and adapted from [1].

2.2 Static Input Inference via Active Tuning

Essentially, active tuning (AT) [7,8,17] can be seen as a different paradigm for handling RNNs: instead of the usual input → compute → output scheme, a subset of the RNN's neurons is decoupled from the direct input signal. The activation of this subset of neurons is computed from the RNN's prediction-based gradients, both during training and testing. Gradient information is obtained from backpropagating the discrepancy between the RNN's predicted output $\hat{\mathbf{y}}$ and the desired output $\mathbf{y}$. Thus, the neuron dynamics of the subset is solely influenced by the target indirectly, by means of temporal gradient information induced by the prediction error.

In this work, as mentioned before, DISTANA receives dynamic and lateral input, while the static input $\mathbf{s}$ is withheld and must be inferred via AT to reasonably model the unfolding dynamics. Technically, $\mathbf{s}$ is fed to the model initially as a zero vector and optimized iteratively through the AT method. AT is applied to reduce local prediction errors, while the PK weights are updated as usual to reduce global prediction errors and model universal dynamics.

The active tuning algorithm, please refer to [17] for more information, can be applied in combination with any desired gradient optimization strategy, e.g. Adam [15]. Furthermore, an arbitrary number of optimization cycles c, here

[1] https://github.com/ndrplz/ConvLSTM_pytorch.

$c = 1$, and history length H, here $H = 10$, can be chosen, where the latter indicates up to what time in the local past the latent context vector $\mathbf{s}$, which is assumed to be constant, is optimized. The AT optimization procedure is realized every ten time steps retrospectively on the predicted dynamic input, starting from time step τ to find a converging $\mathbf{s}$.

We have modified (AT) for application on two-dimensional data in order to infer an individual, slowly changing local latent variable, denoted as $\mathbf{s}_i$, for each vertex of the two-dimensional grid. AT so far has been applied to one-dimensional time series prediction for the inference of rarely changing contextual [7,8] or dynamically changing latent states [17]. In contrast to previous applications of AT, the inferred local static input $\mathbf{s}$ is not reset between sequences during training here, assuming a constant static context.

In our initial experiments, the inferred static input frequently drifted or potentially exploded, comparable to an Intern Covariate Drift [11]. We solve this problem, similarly to [11], by normalizing the inferred latent variable (in our case the static input $\mathbf{s}$), via the mean μ_s and standard deviation σ_s with respect to all inferred static inputs $\{s_i^t\}_{i=1}^k$, where k is the number of cells or pixels in the two-dimensional field. Additionally, to remove noise from the inference process caused by inconsistent gradient signals before and after the normalization, the weights W and the bias neuron b of the static input preprocessing layer are modified such that the activation of the static input preprocessing layer remains the same before and after the normalization:

$$b \leftarrow b + W \cdot \mu_s; \qquad W \leftarrow W \cdot \sigma_s \tag{1}$$

While the activation of the network is preserved, the gradients backpropagated through the static input preprocessing layer are affected asymmetrically by the modified weights and bias. In our experiments, this has been shown to substantially improve both the inference during training and the convergence of the inference process during testing.

3 Experiments and Results

The experiments are based on two classes of spatiotemporal time series. Both are representatives of universal, but locally and temporally modifiable, spatiotemporal, causal processes that propagate dynamics over local topologies throughout a homogeneously connected graph.

3.1 2D Circular Wave

Following [13], a spatiotemporal wave propagation dataset was created to validate our approach. In comparison to [13], however, the data generation was enhanced such that the wave propagation velocity could be contextually modified locally, which intuitively resembles obstacles in the water, which affect the wave's propagation behavior (cf. Fig. 2).

This benchmark was used to (a) demonstrate and compare DISTANA's principal capability to model locally parameterized spatiotemporal dynamics and (b) determine whether DISTANA can be used in combination with AT to infer an underlying and hidden static (causal) factor, which modifies the observed dynamics locally. Adam [15] is used for training with a learning rate of 10^{-3} along with Scheduled Sampling [4] with a linear slope of 270 epochs, transitioning from a probability of $0.0 \rightarrow 0.9$ of feeding the network with its own output in the next iteration instead of the teacher signal. During each sequence, 30 teacher forcing steps are conducted to induce reasonable network activities before switching to closed loop. Network inputs $\mathbf{x}$ and the according targets $\mathbf{y}$ are exactly the same sequences shifted by one time step to train four different model types (ConvLSTM, TCN, DISTANA and DISTANA + AT) to iteratively predict the next two-dimensional dynamic wave field state (one step ahead prediction). For the static input inference, DISTANA is augmented with a parametric bias neuron, whose activity is inferred during training and testing, aiming at the identification of an unknown location-specific wave velocity-influencing factor (static context). Training was realized over 300 epochs consisting of 100 training sequences of length 120 each. The target static context vector $\mathbf{s} \in \mathbb{R}^{16\times16}$ was initialized by drawing values from $\{0.2, 0.3, 0.5, 0.6, 0.8, 0.9\}$, where small values cause the waves to propagate slower at the according pixel. An exemplary ground truth context map $\mathbf{s}_{GT}$ is visualized in Fig. 2 (left, brownish dots). Note that $\mathbf{s}_{GT}$ was used for the data generation but has never been provided to any model. The preprocessing layer size of DISTANA was set to eight neurons and the subsequent LSTM layer consisted of twelve cells, yielding 1 236 parameters. For the DISTANA + AT model, an additional static preprocessing layer with five neurons was used, resulting in 1 486 weights overall, compared to 2 952 and 2 306 weights for ConvLSTM and TCN, respectively.

To test the models' generalization capabilities, 16 new static context vectors $\mathbf{s}'$ have been generated by drawing from $\{0.2, 0.3, \ldots, 1.0\}$ (e.g. see Fig. 3, top right-most). All models were evaluated on 50 sequences – made up of 120 time steps each – per $\mathbf{s}'$. Reasonable activity was induced into the models by applying 30 steps of teacher forcing, followed by 90 steps of closed loop prediction for which an average MSE over all test examples and spatial locations was computed. For DISTANA + AT, the static context has been inferred before the testing on 50 separate sequences, using a history length of $H = 30$, one optimization cycle ($c = 1$), and an inference learning rate of $\eta = 0.1$ for the first three epochs, and $\eta = 0.01$ for the remaining seven epochs.

3.2 2D Circular Wave Results

The prediction accuracy of ConvLSTM, TCN, DISTANA and DISTANA + AT differs considerably. TCN without scheduled sampling tends to start oscillating increasingly after few steps of closed loop prediction, resulting in a mediocre MSE score of $(2.94 \pm 238) \times 10^{-2}$, while ConvLSTM $(8.69 \pm 0.87) \times 10^{-4}$ and DISTANA $(8.69 \pm 0.87) \times 10^{-4}$, both trained with scheduled sampling, tend to vanish after few steps of closed loop prediction. Solely DISTANA + AT trained

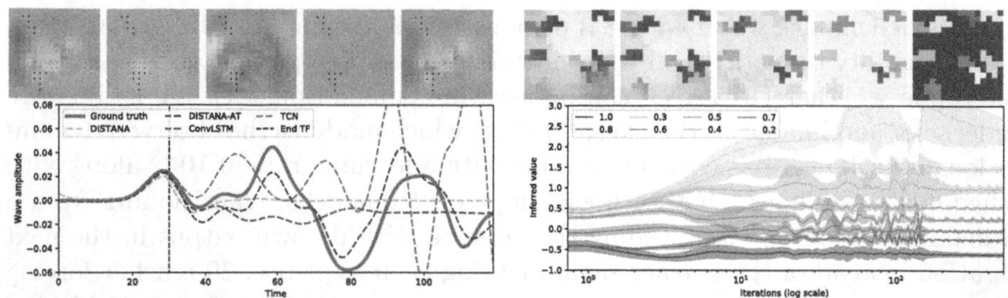

Fig. 3. Top left: ground truth and model outputs at time step 80, which is 30 time steps after the start of closed loop prediction (from left to right: ground truth, ConvLSTM, TCN, DISTANA, DISTANA + AT). Bottom left: ground truth and model outputs over time at position $x = 2$, $y = 6$ in the two-dimensional grid. Top right: inferred static context during testing with values in the range $[-0.6, 2.6]$ after 1, 2, 10, 500 iterations and ground truth with values in $[0.0, 1.0]$. For the ground truth, darker color corresponds to a stronger blocking effect on the wave, which was learned and inferred inversely by the network. Bottom right: average inferred contexts over time during testing (x-axis log scaled).

with scheduled sampling is able to preserver a stable activation pattern with an MSE of $(3.87 \pm 2.48) \times 10^{-4}$.

Furthermore, as shown in Fig. 3 (bottom right), DISTANA + AT preserves a linear ordering when inferring context values that were never encountered during training as indicated by the static context values 0.4 and 0.7, which are properly mapped to roughly -0.1 and -1.1, respectively, without violating the propagation speed order with respect to other static context values. Thus, looking at the estimated static context $\hat{\mathbf{s}}$, it turns out that the latent state inferred by AT correctly reproduced the monotonicity of the here known underlying structure. The static context map at test time, which is different to the map on which the model was trained on, is inferred correctly (see image sequence of Fig. 3, top right). When comparing the prediction accuracy of DISTANA and DISTANA + AT in Fig. 3 (top and bottom left), the self-inferred static context clearly helps DISTANA + AT to model the two-dimensional wave.

3.3 WeatherBench

Recently, [19] introduced a benchmark for comparing mid-range (that is three to five days) weather forecast qualities of data driven and physics-based approaches. While globally regularly aggregated data are provided in three spatial resolutions (5.625°, 2.8125° and 1.40525° resulting in 32×64, 64×128 and 128×256 grid points, respectively), evaluated baselines are reported for the coarsest resolution only, which in consequence we chose too for elaborating and comparing DISTANA. Baselines are generated by means of persistence (tomorrow's weather is today's weather), climatology, linear regression, and physics-based numerical weather prediction models. Moreover, convolutional neural networks (CNNs) are either applied iteratively or directly. Baselines are computed solely on three or five day predictions of the geopotential at an atmospheric pressure level of 500 hPa (roughly at 5.5 km height, called Z500) and the temperature at 850 hPa (~1.5 km height, referred to as T850). Beyond Z500 and T850, weatherBench consists of numerous additional dynamic variables (humidity, precipitation, wind direction and speed, solar radiation, etc.), partially reported on multiple vertical layers, and static variables (land-sea mask, soil type, orography, latitude and longitude).

We use weatherBench (a) to explore DISTANA's abilities to approximate real-world phenomena by comparing it to [19]'s iterative CNN approach and (b) to investigate how to apply gradient-based inference techniques in order to infer local static context (e.g. the land-sea mask) that affect Z500 and T850. The experiments we conducted on weatherBench focused on the prediction of the Z500 (geopotential) and T850 (temperature) variables. DISTANA and DISTANA + AT were trained for 2 000 epochs on weather data from 1979, using a learning rate of 10^{-4}, validated on 2016, and tested on 2017. Each year was partitioned into sequences of 96 hourly steps, yielding 91 sequences per year. Increasing the set sizes or changing the training, validation, or testing years did not seem to alter the results or model performances. DISTANA's preprocessing and LSTM layers were set to 50 neurons and cells, respectively. Furthermore, the implementation of DISTANA was enhanced to support a varying lateral communication vector size, which then was increased from one to five neurons, to enable neighboring PKs to exchange information of higher complexity, yielding ~25 000 parameters, slightly varying with the number of input variables. Moreover, the lateral connection scheme of DISTANA was specified such that information exiting the horizontal boundaries would enter at the other end of the field to match weatherBench's horizontally connected spherical data composition.

Selected static information provided by weatherBench was adapted and extended to facilitate the learning process. Changes were made to the latitude and longitude variables: latitude was transformed to be zero at the equator and non-linearly rising to one towards the poles, based on cos(lat). The longitude variable was split into its sine and cosine component, creating a circular encoding to match the spherical shape of the Earth from which the data origins. Additionally, one-dimensional north- and south-flags were provided to account for the missing neighbors in the north- and south-most rows in the grid. As has been done in [26], we also provide the top of atmosphere total incident solar radiation (tisr). All variables were normalized to the range of $[-1.0, 1.0]$. When using AT to infer a latent static context $\tilde{\mathbf{s}}$, the values were clamped to $[-1.0, 1.0]$ to prevent them from drifting or exploding. If not specified differently, we provide the models with the dynamic variable Z500 or T850 (being subject for prediction), along with nine static inputs: orography, land-sea mask (LSM), soil type, longitude (two-dimensional), latitude, tisr, and the north- and south-end flags.

3.4 WeatherBench Results

The evaluation of DISTANA being trained to predict the Z500 variable for a lead time of 72 h yielded an RSME of 816, which is better than the current best

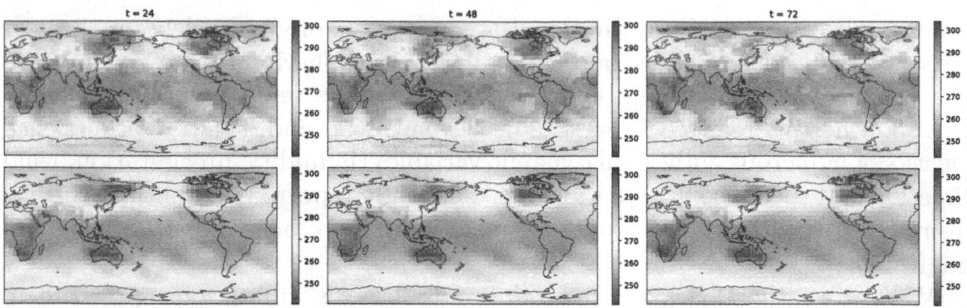

Fig. 4. Predicted temperature (T850) in degree Kelvin for 24, 48 and 72 h (corresponding to time steps) into the future (closed-loop). The first row shows the ground truth and the second row the network output.

comparable iterative approach reported on the benchmark (RMSE = 1114). However, seeing that the best numerical operational weather prediction model produces an RMSE of 154 and other machine learning approaches achieve an RMSE of 268, there is certainly room for improvement. Nonetheless, DISTANA offers the best learned generative, iterative processing model on the benchmark without applying techniques that reduce the distortion resulting from transforming the spherical Earth data to a regular two-dimensional grid.

A second experiment was conducted to (a) investigate whether DISTANA + AT is able to predict the T850 variable, see Fig. 4, and (b) simultaneously infer missing land-sea mask (LSM) values only from the observed T850 dynamics. The model thus received the same static input as in the previous experiment along with the T850 variable during training. However, only two thirds of the LSM values were provided. The other third, considered missing values, which covered America and the Atlantic ocean, were to be inferred. After training, the entire LSM vector $\hat{\mathbf{s}}_{\text{LSM}}$, initialized with zeros, was retrospectively tuned via AT such that it would best explain the observed dynamics. As visualized in Fig. 5 (top center) the missing LSM is inferred reasonably, including the American continent, which the network has never seen during training or inference. These findings suggest that the model learned a generalizable, globally applicable encoding of the LSM's influence on the T850 dynamics.

In a third experiment, we used an additional latent neuron – a parametric bias neuron – that is locally tuned during training via AT. This latent neuron is supposed to be tuned freely by the model to develop any code that helps the model to predict the observed dynamics. We were particularly interested in evaluating whether DISTANA would develop latent states $\tilde{\mathbf{s}}$ that distinctively encode prediction-relevant, hidden causal factors that correspond to observable values. For example, we wanted to see whether DISTANA would develop a latent code that resembles any land-coding quantity. Thus, in this experiment, we try to answer the question what latent states are inferred depending on the predicted variable and how the presence of land-relevant input does affect the generation of this latent code.

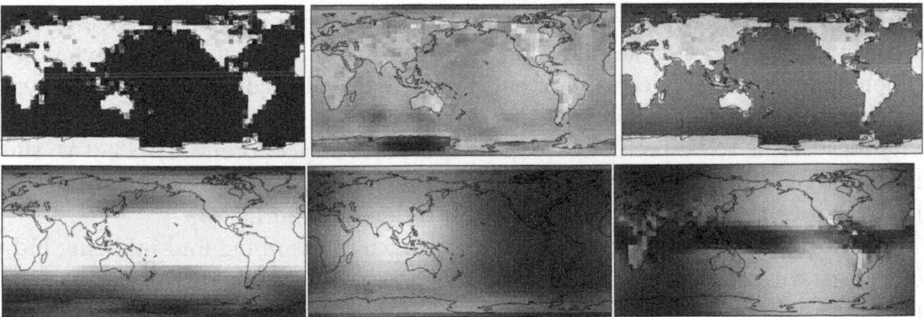

Fig. 5. Top left: original land-sea mask (LSM). Top center: global LSM inferred during testing after being trained on two thirds of the globe (the model has never seen America's LSM). Top right: a latent vector which developed during training and encodes LSM information as well as a decent latitude coding. Bottom: three latent variable codes that freely emerged during training of the Z500 (left, center) and T850 (right) variables.

Our results indicate that the nature of the developed latent states depends considerably on both the variable that is subject for prediction (Z500 or T850) and the additional static data provided. Figure 5 (top right) shows a clear tendency to encode land-sea information, augmenting it with a latitude code, when all previously mentioned static inputs (including LSM) were provided. When training a model to predict Z500, the emerging latent variables rather seem to encode latitude, albedo, monsoon [5], or humidity-distribution patterns (Fig. 5 bottom left and center). Excitingly, nuances of LSM and orography become visible when training to predict T850 without receiving any land-coding inputs (see Fig. 5 bottom right). Nevertheless, further studies are necessary to verify to which extent the inferred variables correlate with observations in detail.

4 Final Discussion

The presented results indicate that the combination of the DIstributed, SpatioTemporal graph Artificial Neural network Architecture, DISTANA, with the retrospective inference mechanism called active tuning (AT), bears large potential at predicting spatiotemporal real-world phenomena (e.g. weather). It outperforms competing deep learning algorithms by generating more accurate closed-loop predictions into the future. In addition, it can infer hidden causes by mere observation of a dynamic process. In particular, AT in DISTANA is well-suited for inferring (i) contrastive hidden causes during learning and (ii) hidden static activities while minimizing loss online. While we believe that these hidden factors tend to identify causal influences – because they form for improving the accuracy of the predicted dynamics – future research will need to investigate the robustness of this tendency.

During learning, cumulative error signals in latent parametric bias neurons at the individual prediction kernels tend to develop encodings of hidden, dynamic-influencing factors. To a certain extent, these neuronal encodings resemble physical properties, such as albedo or the land-sea mask, depending on the type of dynamics that is to be predicted (e.g. temperature or geopotential). That is, the projection of the gradient onto static neural activities identifies local parametric bias activities that best characterize local, hidden causal factors.

Overall, the results suggest that our approach of assuming and inferring hidden causes with constrained properties – such as being locally distinct, constant, but universally present – offers strong potential in fostering the development of process-explaining structures.

References

1. Bai, S., Kolter, J.Z., Koltun, V.: An empirical evaluation of generic convolutional and recurrent networks for sequence modeling. arXiv:1803.01271 (2018)
2. Battaglia, P., Pascanu, R., Lai, M., Rezende, D.J., et al.: Interaction networks for learning about objects, relations and physics. In: Advances in Neural Information Processing Systems, pp. 4502–4510 (2016)
3. Battaglia, P.W., et al.: Relational inductive biases, deep learning, and graph networks. arXiv:1806.01261 (2018)
4. Bengio, S., Vinyals, O., Jaitly, N., Shazeer, N.: Scheduled sampling for sequence prediction with recurrent neural networks. arXiv:1506.03099 (2015)
5. Boers, N., Goswami, B., Rheinwalt, A., Bookhagen, B., Hoskins, B., Kurths, J.: Complex networks reveal global pattern of extreme-rainfall teleconnections. Nature **566**(7744), 373–377 (2019)
6. Bronstein, M.M., Bruna, J., LeCun, Y., Szlam, A., Vandergheynst, P.: Geometric deep learning: going beyond Euclidean data. IEEE Signal Process. Mag. **34**(4), 18–42 (2017)
7. Butz, M.V., Bilkey, D., Humaidan, D., Knott, A., Otte, S.: Learning, planning, and control in a monolithic neural event inference architecture. Neural Netw. **117**, 135–144 (2019)
8. Butz, M.V., Menge, T., Humaidan, D., Otte, S.: Inferring event-predictive goal-directed object manipulations in REPRISE. In: Tetko, I.V., Kurková, V., Karpov, P., Theis, F. (eds.) ICANN 2019. LNCS, vol. 11727, pp. 639–653. Springer, Cham (2019). https://doi.org/10.1007/978-3-030-30487-4_49
9. Dauphin, Y.N., Fan, A., Auli, M., Grangier, D.: Language modeling with gated convolutional networks. In: Proceedings of the 34th International Conference on Machine Learning, vol. 70, pp. 933–941. JMLR. org (2017)
10. Hochreiter, S., Schmidhuber, J.: Long short-term memory. Neural Comput. **9**(8), 1735–1780 (1997)
11. Ioffe, S., Szegedy, C.: Batch normalization: accelerating deep network training by reducing internal covariate shift. In: Bach, F., Blei, D. (eds.) Proceedings of the 32nd International Conference on Machine Learning. Proceedings of Machine Learning Research, Lille, France, 07–09 July 2015, vol. 37, pp. 448–456. PMLR (2015)
12. Kalchbrenner, N., Espeholt, L., Simonyan, K., Oord, A.V.D., Graves, A., Kavukcuoglu, K.: Neural machine translation in linear time. arXiv:1610.10099 (2016)

13. Karlbauer, M., Otte, S., Lensch, H.P.A., Scholten, T., Wulfmeyer, V., Butz, M.V.: A distributed neural network architecture for robust non-linear spatio-temporal prediction. arXiv:1912.11141 (2019)
14. Karlbauer, M., Otte, S., Lensch, H.P.A., Scholten, T., Wulfmeyer, V., Butz, M.V.: Inferring, predicting, and denoising causal wave dynamics. In: Farkaš, I., Masulli, P., Wermter, S. (eds.) ICANN 2020. LNCS, vol. 12396, pp. 566–577. Springer, Cham (2020). https://doi.org/10.1007/978-3-030-61609-0_45
15. Kingma, D., Ba, J.: Adam: a method for stochastic optimization. In: International Conference on Learning Representations, December 2014
16. Kipf, T., Fetaya, E., Wang, K.C., Welling, M., Zemel, R.: Neural relational inference for interacting systems. arXiv:1802.04687 (2018)
17. Otte, S., Karlbauer, M., Butz, M.V.: Active tuning. arXiv:2010.03958 (2020)
18. Rabinowitz, N., Perbet, F., Song, F., Zhang, C., Eslami, S.M.A., Botvinick, M.: Machine theory of mind. In: Dy, J., Krause, A. (eds.) Proceedings of the 35th International Conference on Machine Learning. Proceedings of Machine Learning Research, Stockholm, Sweden, 10–15 July 2018, vol. 80, pp. 4218–4227. PMLR (2018)
19. Rasp, S., Dueben, P.D., Scher, S., Weyn, J.A., Mouatadid, S., Thuerey, N.: WeatherBench: a benchmark dataset for data-driven weather forecasting. arXiv:2002.00469 (2020)
20. Rodriguez, R.C., Alaniz, S., Akata, Z.: Modeling conceptual understanding in image reference games. In: Advances in Neural Information Processing Systems, pp. 13155–13165 (2019)
21. Sanchez-Gonzalez, A., et al.: Graph networks as learnable physics engines for inference and control. arXiv:1806.01242 (2018)
22. Santoro, A., et al.: A simple neural network module for relational reasoning. In: Advances in Neural Information Processing Systems, pp. 4967–4976 (2017)
23. Sugita, Y., Tani, J., Butz, M.V.: Simultaneously emerging Braitenberg codes and compositionality. Adapt. Behav. **19**, 295–316 (2011)
24. Tani, J., Ito, M., Sugita, Y.: Self-organization of distributedly represented multiple behavior schemata in a mirror system: reviews of robot experiments using RNNPB. Neural Netw. **17**, 1273–1289 (2004)
25. Van Steenkiste, S., Chang, M., Greff, K., Schmidhuber, J.: Relational neural expectation maximization: unsupervised discovery of objects and their interactions. arXiv:1802.10353 (2018)
26. Weyn, J.A., Durran, D.R., Caruana, R.: Improving data-driven global weather prediction using deep convolutional neural networks on a cubed sphere. arXiv:2003.11927 (2020)
27. Wu, Z., Pan, S., Chen, F., Long, G., Zhang, C., Yu, P.S.: A comprehensive survey on graph neural networks. arXiv:1901.00596 (2019)
28. Xingjian, S., Chen, Z., Wang, H., Yeung, D.Y., Wong, W.K., Woo, W.C.: Convolutional LSTM network: a machine learning approach for precipitation nowcasting. In: Advances in Neural Information Processing Systems, pp. 802–810 (2015)

Deep Learning Models and Interpretations for Multivariate Discrete-Valued Event Sequence Prediction

Gábor Kőrösi(✉) and Richárd Farkas

Institute of Informatics, University of Szeged, Szeged, Hungary
{korosig,rfarkas}@inf.u-szeged.hu

Abstract. We propose an embedding-based deep learning model architecture for raw clickstream event sequences, which has special characteristics, such as being multivariate discrete-valued. We evaluate the proposed architecture on a Stanford University MOOC dataset, which consists of clickstream-level raw log event data collected during student sessions in the MOOC. We introduce empirical results achieved by various configurations of the architecture on the student final grade regression task. Apart from the regression experiments, we also propose three visual interpretation techniques for explaining the black-box Temporal Convolutional Neural Network and Recurrent Neural Networks models. The goal is to provide easily applicable interpretations which can be used by domain experts without any Machine Learning technical expertise. Based on the visual interpretations, we were able to identify student behavior patterns from raw data, in line with educational research literature.

Keywords: Event log processing · Discrete-valued sequence prediction · TCNN · RNN · Interpretations

1 Introduction

User modelling based on users' online behavior has numerous important applications, including recommender systems and educational data mining [1, 3, 4, 12]. In this work, we analyze the online behavior of Massive Online Open Course (MOOC) students. We introduce a deep learning architecture to predict the outcome score of the students at a MOOC. We analyzed a clickstream-level raw dataset which was recorded during a Stanford University MOOC with 142,395 students. A recorded click event of the clickstream-level MOOC usage data consists of four categorical/discrete-valued attributes: action type, description of events, visited link, and the students' success on the subtask in question.

Recently, Neural Networks have been widely used as sequence predictors and time series forecasters, as they can capture complex nonlinear patterns. [9] The most commonly used model is the Recurrent Neural Network (RNN) which has outperformed statistical models, e.g., autoregressive and moving-average models. [13] Besides the dominance of RNN models, there have been Convolutional Networks (CNN) proposed for

I. Farkaš et al. (Eds.): ICANN 2021, LNCS 12894, pp. 396–406, 2021.
https://doi.org/10.1007/978-3-030-86380-7_32

time-series forecasting and sequence classification, namely Temporal CNNs (TCNN). Whereas the majority of the time series deep learning models have been applied to numerical data, event logs, such as clickstream-level MOOC data used in this instance, consists of multivariate discrete-valued sequences. Hence, time series deep learning techniques cannot be directly applied. On the other hand, most of the discrete-valued sequence prediction solutions have been published for Natural Language Processing. The raw event logs are significantly longer than natural language sentences, with their varying length, thus NLP techniques cannot be applied directly. To handle these special characteristics of the given clickstream-level MOOC dataset, we propose an embedding-based deep learning model architecture. In this study, we trained state-of-art RNN and CNN models to predict the outcome score of the students at the MOOC. We conducted experiments using various embedding layers to represent the multivariate discrete-valued data.

Recurrent and Temporal Convolutional Neural Networks provide accurate forecasts without having any access to explicit knowledge about the investigated system. Yet, deep learning methods are typically considered as 'black boxes' where it is almost impossible to fully understand what, why, and how RNN and CNN make forecasting decisions. [13] Our research aims to open the black box of RNNs and CNNs trained for time series regression. We propose three visualization techniques, which support domain-expert users in interpreting discrete-valued multivariate time series regression, neural models.

The contributions of this paper are two-fold: 1) we present experimental results on various deep learning architectures and embedding strategies, evaluated on a MOOC clickstream event, discrete-valued time-series regression task, and 2) we propose application-oriented, i.e., user-friendly visualizations for explaining the behavior of the machine-learned RNN and CNN, regression models.

2 Related Work

Analyzing student behaviour in MOOCs directly on the clickstream-level is a new field of study. Li et al. [13] and Baker et al. [3] sought to understand student behavior using log sequence from different MOOC courses. They investigated and visualized behavioral patterns of student groups by employing statistics and classic machine learning methods over hand-crafted features. To the best of our knowledge, the study by Kőrösi and Farkas [11] is the only work to date utilizing deep learning techniques to exploit raw clickstream data which have been recorded during MOOC courses. They reported that they were able to outperform hand-crafted feature-based classic machine learning approaches. In our research, we employ deep learning techniques to solve the same goal as Li et al. [13] and Baker et al. [3], i.e., to analyze student behavior. We can draw educational conclusions similar to those presented in Li et al. [13] and Baker et al. [3], but since we used raw sequences directly, our approach did not require any feature engineering of pedagogical expertise.

Recent advances in neural architectures and their application to raw time-series and sequences offer an end-to-end learning framework that is often more flexible than classic feature engineering-based approaches. [12] For example, Koehn et al. [10] showed that an RNN-based method could outperform common machine learning while using mixed continuous and discrete-valued time series to predict the order value. Guo et al. [6]

proposed the feed forward neural network and embedding layer-based DeepFM for multivariate partially raw discrete-valued clickstream data. Apart from the recurrent approaches, convolutional models capable of considering the temporal dimension have recently been proposed. Sadouk [14] proposed an exhaustive study of Convolutional Neural Networks where convolutions were applied in the sequence recognition tasks. Our work was motivated by these studies, thus we experimentally compared CNN and RNN models on discrete-valued sequences.

The embedding of discrete-valued sequences was successfully applied in user behavior analysis[10]. An et al. [2], for instance, presented their neural user embedding approach which was capable of learning informative user embeddings by using the unlabeled browsing-behavior. Cheng et al. [4] introduced the Wide and Deep feature representation method. In our work, we embed our discrete-valued attributes for enhancing the generalization capability of our neural networks.

Karpathy et al. [7] analyzed the interpretability of RNNs for language modeling, demonstrating the existence of interpretable neurons which were able to focus on specific language structures. Siddiqui et al. [15] explored the visualization techniques including input saliency by means of occlusion and derivatives, class mode visualization, and temporal outputs. In Sect. 5, we applied an approach to interpret our multivariate discrete-valued sequence forecasting model.

3 Dataset

The time-series dataset is made up of raw loglines which have been recorded during the Computer Science 101 online course at Stanford Lagunita University in the summer of 2014. It contains video lectures, optional homework assignments, discussion forums, and quizzes.

Table 1. The Stanford Lagunita's Science 101 dataset

Feature	Examples	No. unique value
Links	'courseware/z187/z172/', 'courseware/z187/z184/'	243
Events	'load_video', 'login', 'problem_check'	34
Resource	'Q1', 'Week 2 Course Survey'	35
Success	0,1,-1* (* missing value)	2

The raw data sequence includes 39.6 million loglines created by 142,395 students. Of these, only 13,574 students completed the course, so we only used the data of these students in our work. On the filtered data each logline is made up of five attributes describing a clickstream level event: event type (categorical variable), visited URL (categorical variable), resource name (categorical variable), and quiz success (binary variable). Table 1 lists some of these examples.

Table 2. Number of logged events in the different progress sections of the course

Event type/progress		20%	40%	60%	80%
Video	Load	34999	67411	97070	127552
	Play	61003	123338	182821	238408
	Seek	18862	41574	61490	80236
	Speed change	3442	5668	7600	9516
Quiz	Quiz 1	20283	42655	73102	110348
	Quiz 2	14581	33294	61091	96684
	Quiz 3	8281	21760	48636	81614
	Quiz 4	46	648	5365	9261

The aim of this research is to predict the student's final scores (from 0 to 100) achieved in the four quizzes based on the raw log sequence. The user could take the quizzes multiple times, but the final score is the sum of the first attempts. To gain a better understanding regarding the users' learning behavior and the predictive power of raw log data, we split the time series into progress sections, namely 20%, 40%, 60%, 80% of the course progress. Table 2 displays the counts of a few event types.

4 Embedding-Based Multivariate Sequence Regression

The focus of this study is on multivariate discrete-valued sequence neural regression. We propose a deep learning architecture in our MOOC scenario, which is depicted in Fig. 1, 2.

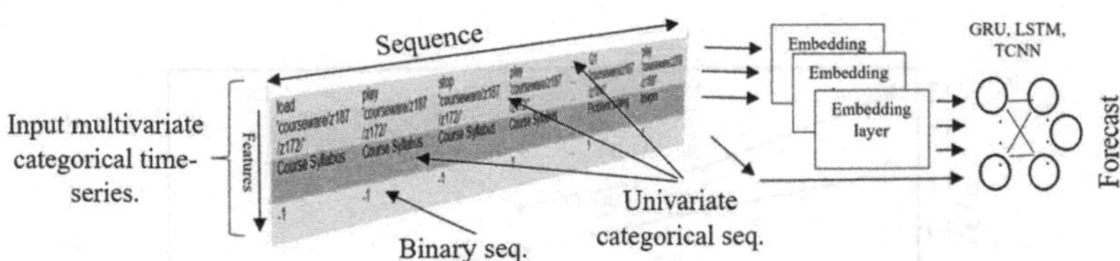

Fig. 1. A unified deep learning framework for discrete sequence forecasting. A DL architecture, where the Embedding layers are designed to encode each categorical attribute separately. Then the TCNN and RNN networks learn the hierarchical representations of the sequenced data.

Embedding layers are designed to encode each categorical attribute separately. Then the TCNN and RNN networks learn the hierarchical representations of the sequenced data. Recurrent and Temporal Convolutional Neural Networks proved their ability to discover patterns in multivariate time-series, giving forecasts without explicit knowledge of the inspected system [12].

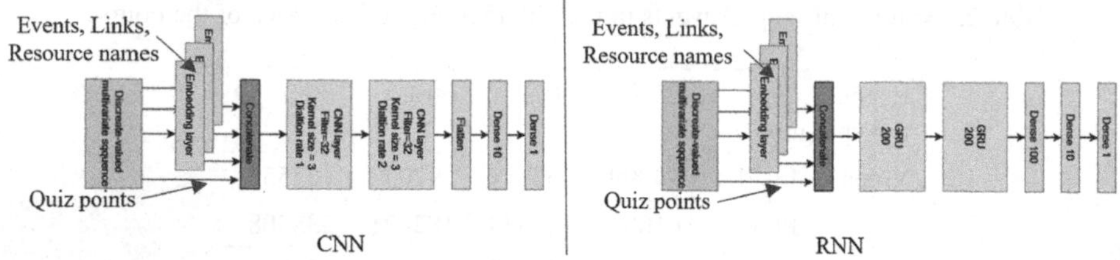

Fig. 2. Overview of the configurations for multivariate sequence prediction. TCNN architecture is seen on the left, RNN (GRU and LSTM) on the right. The numbers in boxes refers to layer sizes, i.e. number of hidden units.

Our research aims to create an accurate way to use the same methodology on discrete-valued sequences in RNN and TCNN. Our framework for discrete-valued sequence prediction is depicted in Fig. 2. We propose a representation of discrete sequence in the form of a vector embedding. Instead of any data preparations, we insert the label encoded univariate sequences themself into the embedding layer which could autonomously transform the categorical labels into a continuous space. This has the following advantages: it does not contain any artificial "human-based" parameters which could affect the behavior of the model; while the embedding layer learns without human intervention, it does not strongly depend on how many data points are available; it is suitable for the time-based discrete sequence from high-dimensional attractors.

5 Regression Results

We randomly split our student dataset into training- (9502 sequences) and evaluation (4072 sequences) datasets. The mean absolute error (MAE) of final student scores is taken as an evaluation metric.

We calibrated the size of our neural networks on a development set (random subset of the training dataset).

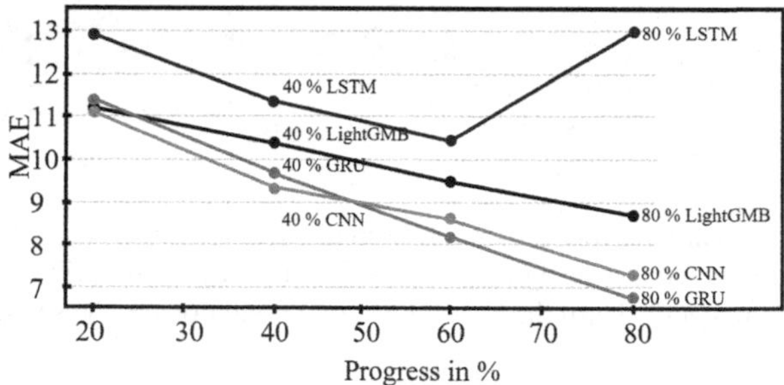

Fig. 3. Mean Absolute Errors achieved by various models at different progress state of the course

We use embedding layers of length 30 (the sizes of other layers are shown in Fig. 2). We employ tangent activation function in the GRU and LSTM experiments, while ReLU in the CNN ones. As the optimizer we used Adam with the default 0.0001 learning rate and early stopping criteria. Sequences were post padded to lengths varied in function of student progress datasets (lengths: 20%: 220, 40%: 520, 60%: 720, 80%: 920).

In our baseline model, the user's behavior in the course is encoded as a 28-dimensional feature vector. These cumulated features consist of the number of video interactions (play, stop, pause), quiz success (quiz 1, 2, 3, 4), etc. We conduct LightGMB regression [8] on the cumulated features as a baseline. Figure 3 shows that there is no significant difference among the models at 20% progress. The CNN architecture yields either the best, or the second-best performance in most of the data sets.

Table 3. Real (x axis) vs predicted (y axis) final student scores results from LightGMB, CNN, GRU, and LSTM models in different progress point of the course.

20% progress	40% progress	60% progress	80% progress
CNN - 4 features with embedding			
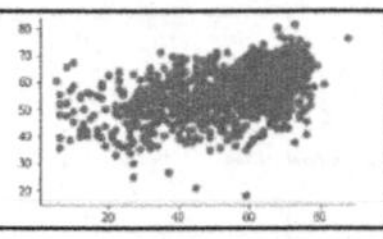	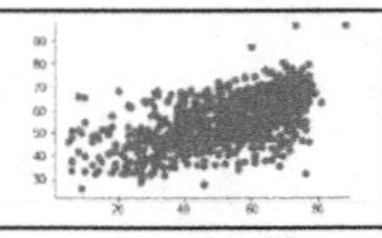	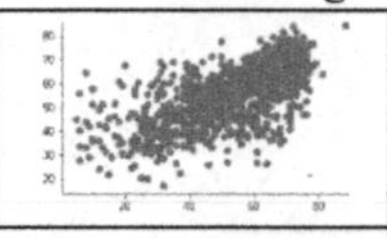	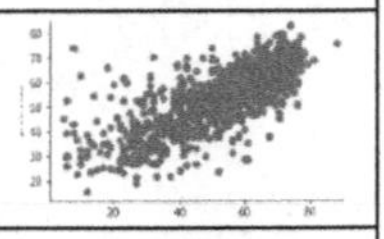
MAE 11.24	MAE 9.47	MAE 8.70	MAE 7.40
CNN - 4 features without embedding			
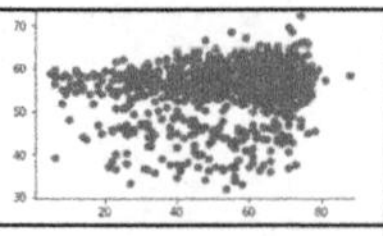	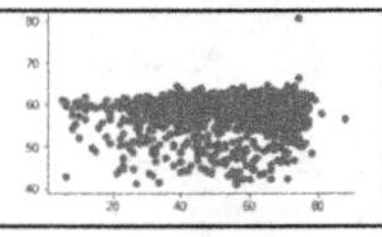	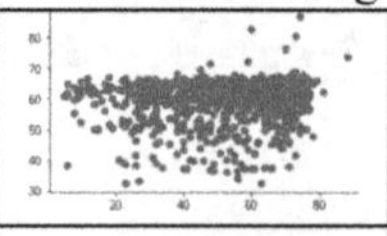	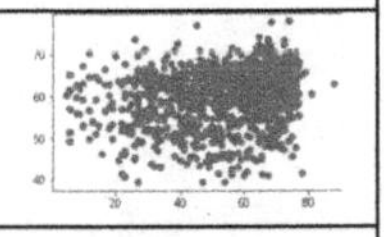
MAE 13.13	MAE 12.84	MAE 12.92	MAE 12.92
GRU - 4 features with embedding			
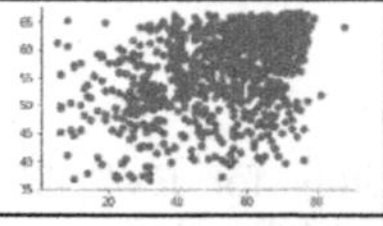	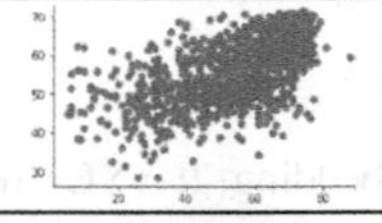	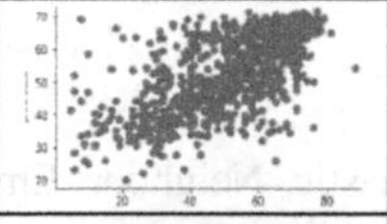	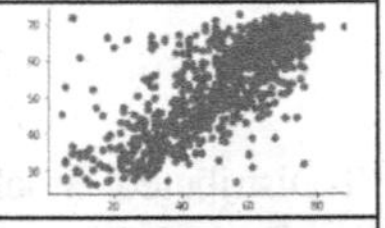
MAE 11.42	MAE 9.81	MAE 8.33	MAE 6.89
GRU – 4 features without embedding			
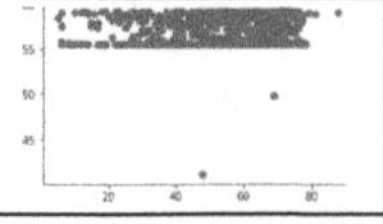	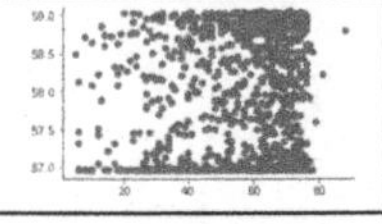	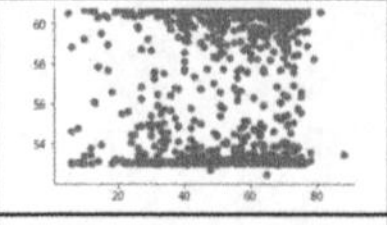	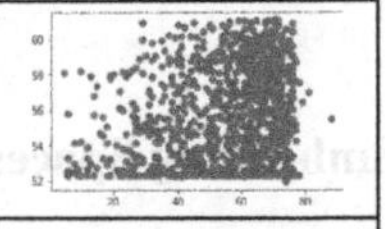
MAE 13.04	MAE 12.96	MAE 13.00	MAE 12.99
LightGMB – 27 (cumulated) feature			
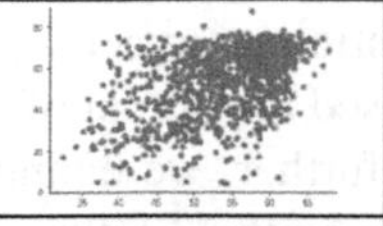	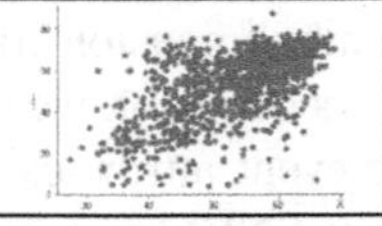	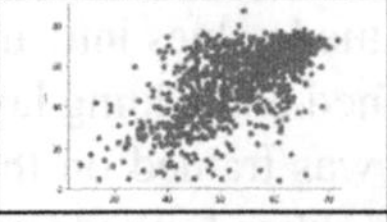	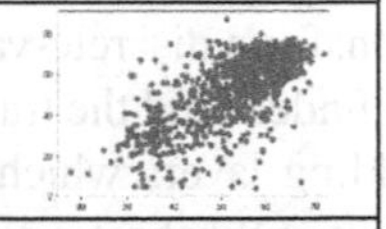
MAE 11.34	MAE 10.50	MAE 9.62	MAE 8.82

Table 3 shows that GRU and CNN with embedding has 'captured' the patterns in data better and provided a much better forecast than other implementations. We tested the

LSTM with embedding but it generated unmeasurable results. This could be explained by the amount of data because LSTM is sensitive to long sequences, and we have an average of 720 time-steps.

6 Interpretations

Recurrent and Convolutional neural network models have recently obtained state-of-the-art sequence prediction accuracy. However, for data analysis, it remains unclear what the models learned, how these approaches identify patterns and meaningful segments from time-series. This section aims to explore this black box to gain better understanding of the behavior of categorical time series prediction DNN models.

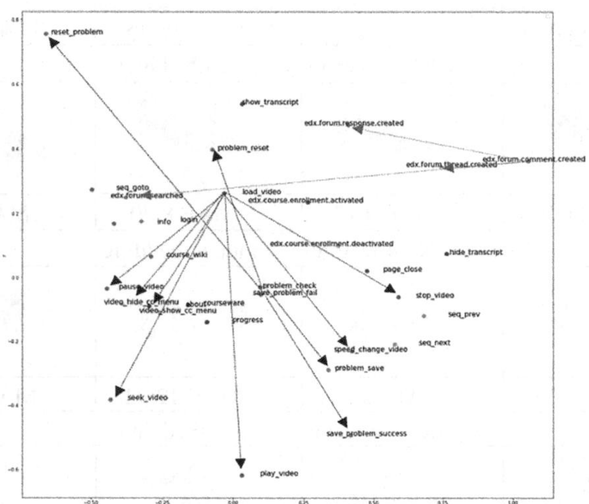

Fig. 4. T-Distributed Stochastic Neighbor Embedding (t-SNE) results for EVENT feature embedding layer. Arrows of different colors represent general groups of different event types.

6.1 Embedding Spaces

The MOOC dataset contains four attributes, including three discrete-valued variables. We transfer those three attributes to three parallel embedding layers (See Fig. 1) to learn and transform discrete-valued values into an nth dimension continuous space.

To understand the trained embedding layers behavior, we used the output of trained embedding layers which was trained on the event attributes, further, we employed t-Distributed Stochastic Neighbor Embedding (t-SNE) so as to map the 30-dimensional embedding space to 2D. Embedding with the t-SNE method is useful because embeddings are learned, thus events, links, or resources that are more similar in the context of our problem are closer to one another in the embedding. The general idea is to group each event type according to its "location" of the curriculum. For example, play, stop, pause would be in the group of video interactions, problem_check, problem_reset, save_problem_succ-es in the quiz group. However, the embedding layer processes this differently. Figure 4 highlights that both video and forum-based events are coming closer to each other, yet more peculiar is the fact that the save and play video events seem to be similar. The trained embedding layer was able to significantly improve our forecasting results (GRU-based model average increase ~8%, CNN-based model average increase ~10%), proving to be an effective aid in preprocessing discrete-sequence.

6.2 Temporal Saliency

The temporal activity of students during the MOOC is a fascinating pedagogical area to explore. The visualization below indicates how strongly the different temporal segments relate with the deep learning prediction. We also aim to detect whether students with various outcome scores display different temporal behavior.

The RNN and CNN methodology uses the output of embedding layers and one binary attribute to train the models (see Fig. 2). As a result of the training process, we use the output of CNN and RNN layers with the absolute value of the derivative of the loss function with respect to each dimension of all sequence inputs. Each row in Fig. 5 corresponds to the predicted student outcome group. Since very few users made up the first group (0–10 final student scores) and the last group (80–90 final student scores), this interpretation was omitted. The columns in the figure represent the output of CNN and GRU layers as the mean of the loss values. By visual inspection of the mean of the loss function values, we can see from the heat map (Fig. 5) that CNNs tend to focus on short contiguous subsequences ("windows/boxes") when predicting the outcomes, whereas GRU uses the whole sequence for the same task. In other words, CNN's model finds "motifs" that are important for prediction, by comparison, GRU apparently gives a different gradient for each time step. The results are almost the same as seen in Lanchantin et. Al. (2017), in their research about using CNN and RNN to understand DNA sequence. They found that the recurrent neural network tends to be spread out more across the entire sequence, indicating that they focus on all sequences together, and infer relationships among them. They also mentioned that, when using convolutional and recurrent networks for sequence forecast, those tended to have strong heat points around motifs, where one could see that there were other steps further away from the motifs that were significant for the model results. Both CNN and GRU have a considerably wide range of steps, moreover, for the low outcome final student scores (0–40) the RNN model uses the entire sequence, while for high final student scores it uses only the first part of the dataset. CNN uses windows of almost the same size as all outcome classes, and although the distribution of weights is different, it learns from the middle of sequences which is completely different from RNN.

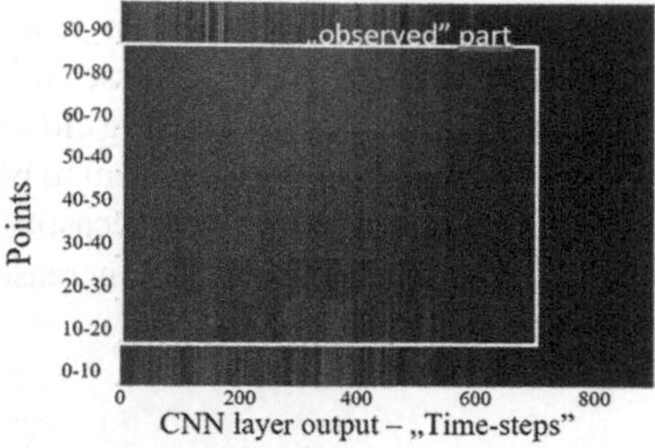

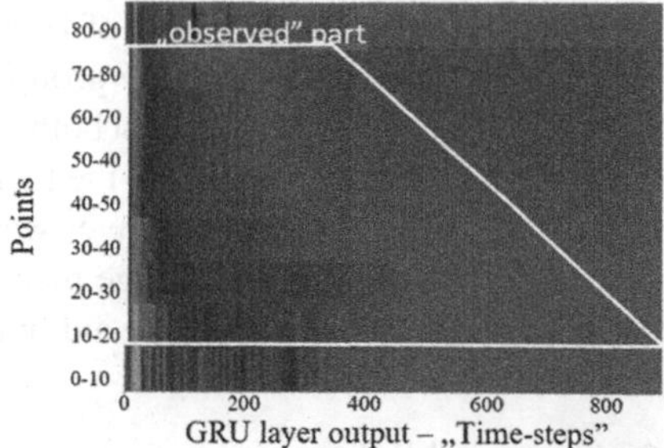

Fig. 5. Representations over time from CNNs and GRUs layers. Each row corresponds to the predicted student result group from CNN and GRU at each time-step. Each grid from the column corresponds to each dimension of the current sequence step representation. We observed only that part of the heatmap, where the data is not constant, or not too uniformly distributed. The brighter color means high activation at the output of the layer of our neural network, even the dark means weak activation.

6.3 User Behavior Clustering

In order to identify the different learning strategies and examine whether they appear in the data sequence, we conducted further studies. We investigated the best and worst 20% of student groups. We conducted a cluster analysis (Kmeans, n_clusters = 2, algorithm = Elkan), utilizing the hidden vector representation learned by our CNN and GRU models. The clustering is based on the cosine similarity of the output 50-dimensional vectors of the CNN and the GRU layers. As an interpretation of the clusters, the features introduced in Sect. 3 were accumulated from the cluster members. Figure 6 shows the boxplots of the key features by clusters. The results of the best and worst 20% clustering show that there are two different clusters among both top and worst-performing students. The first group (marked in blue) watch significantly fewer videos (rdn/Video) than the others do while achieving the same result. The feature values describing the interaction between the users and videos (numoplay_video, numostop_video, numopause_video, numoseek_vi deo) also underpin this observation. Our click-stream level raw data-driven results are in line with educational/pedagogical results. For example, Galine et al. [5] sought to understand the behavior patterns of learners in MOOC courses and they found that at the very base level, there were "All-rounders" and "Viewers", the terminology being similar to the results of our unsupervised clustering analysis: users marked blue seem to be "All-rounders".

The blue cluster members complete most assignments, watch all video lectures, and have numerous interactions with video, while "Viewers" (brown cluster) watch almost all video lectures but hardly ever make more effort than absolutely necessary to complete the course. This data-driven interpretation of MOOC log data is a promising direction for educational data mining, as we were able to show sociological-pedagogical results using only raw logline data, which has not been seen before.

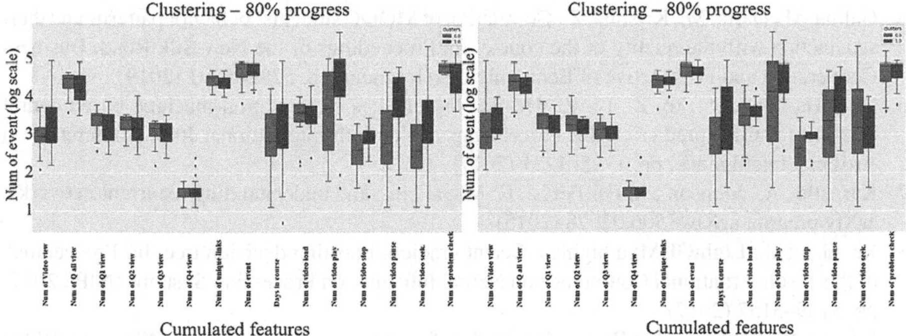

Fig. 6. Cluster analysis of the group of 20% -20% students who achieved best (left) and worst (right) final student scores during the course. The blue and orange colors are show the different clusters in the observed group. (Color figure online)

7 Conclusion

Our literature review established that the existing deep learning-based time-series prediction models could handle both continuous and discrete-valued sequences. In this work we proposed RNN and CNN based methods with embedding-based deep learning model architecture which is able to make a prediction from multivariate discrete-valued, variable-length sequences. The models were tested on a Stanford University MOOC dataset, which consisted of clickstream-level raw log event data collected during student sessions in the MOOC. Our results confirmed that RNNs and CNNs provided a better forecast than conventional methods. The interpretation section outlined that the embedding method was able to significantly improve our forecasting results and provide an effective aid in unsupervised pre-processing of discrete-valued sequence.Besides creating accurate methods, we also proposed three useful visualization of the learnt deep neural networks.

Acknowledgement. This work was supported through the Artificial Intelligence National Excellence Program (grant no.: 2018-1.2.1-NKP-2018-00008). This work was supported by the Hungarian Artificial Intelligence National Laboratory.

References

1. Aldowah, H., Al-Samarraie, H., Fauzy, W.M.: Educational data mining and learning analytics for 21st century higher education: a review and synthesis. Telematics Inform. **37**, 13–49 (2019)
2. An, M., Kim, S.: Neural user embedding from browsing events. In: Dong, Y., Mladenić, D., Saunders, C., (eds.) Machine Learning and Knowledge Discovery in Databases: Applied Data Science Track. ECML PKDD 2020 (2020)
3. Baker, R., Xu, D., Park, J., et al.: The benefits and caveats of using clickstream data to understand student self-regulatory behaviors. Int. J. Educ. Technol. High. Educ. **17**, 1–24 (2020)
4. Cheng, H., et al.: Wide & deep learning for recommender systems. In: Proceedings of the 1st Workshop on Deep Learning for Recommender Systems (2016)

5. Galina, M., Daria, M., Kristina, Z.: Correlation of MOOC students' behavior patterns and their satisfaction with the quality of the course. In: Proceedings of the New Silk Road: Business Cooperation and Prospective of Economic Development, pp. 5282–5291 (2019)
6. Guo, H., Tang, R., Ye, Z., Li, Z., He. X.: DeepFM: a factorization-machine based neural network for CTR prediction. In: Proceedings of the 26th International Joint Conference on Artificial Intelligence, pp. 1725–1731 (2017)
7. Karpathy, A., Johnson , J., Fei-Fei Li, F.: Visualizing and understanding recurrent networks. arXiv preprint arXiv:1506.02078 (2015)
8. Ke, G., et al.: LightGBM: a highly efficient gradient boosting decision tree. In: Proceedings of the 31st International Conference on Neural Information Processing Systems (NIPS 2017) pp. 3149–3157 (2017)
9. Kedem, B., Fokianos, K.: Regression models for time series analysis, vol. 488. John Wiley & Sons (2005)
10. Koehn, D., Lessmann, S., Schaal, M.: Predicting online shopping behaviour from clickstream data using deep learning. Expert Syst. Appl. **150**, 113342 (2020)
11. Kőrösi, G., Farkas R.: MOOC performance prediction by deep learning from raw clickstream data. Adv. Comput. Data Sci. 474–485 (2020)
12. Lee, J.M., Hauskrecht, M.: Recent context-aware LSTM for clinical event time-series prediction. In: Riaño, D., Wilk, S., ten Teije, A. (eds.) AIME 2019. LNCS (LNAI), vol. 11526, pp. 13–23. Springer, Cham (2019). https://doi.org/10.1007/978-3-030-21642-9_3
13. Li, Q., Baker, R., Warschauer, M.: Using clickstream data to understand, and support self-regulated learning in online courses. Internet High. Educ. (2020)
14. Sadouk, L., Gadi, T., Essoufi, E.H., Alonso-Betanzos, A.: A novel deep learning approach for recognizing stereotypical motor movements within and across subjects on the autism spectrum disorder. Intell. Neurosci. (2018)
15. Siddiqui, S., Mercier, D., Munir, M., Dengel, A., Ahmed, S.: TSViz: demystification of deep learning models for time-series analysis. IEEE Access, 1 (2019). https://doi.org/10.1109/ACCESS.2019.2912823

End-to-End On-Line Multi-object Tracking on Sparse Point Clouds Using Recurrent Convolutional Networks

Dominic Spata[1,2(✉)], Arne Grumpe[1], and Anton Kummert[2]

[1] Aptiv Services Deutschland GmbH, 42199 Wuppertal, Germany
{dominic.spata,arne.grumpe}@aptiv.com
[2] University of Wuppertal (BUW), 42199 Wuppertal, Germany
kummert@uni-wuppertal.de

Abstract. Much research has been done to leverage recent advances in deep learning for multi-object tracking, focusing mostly on data obtained from cameras and high-cost lidar sensors. Less attention has been paid to sensor types that provide low-fidelity point clouds. Such sensors provide more challenging input data, being sparser and more noisy, but may help to make the system more affordable.

In this work we present an on-line multi-object tracking system that combines and improves state-of-the-art deep learning approaches to achieve competitive performance using low-fidelity point cloud data alone. It consists of a single, end-to-end trainable recurrent convolutional neural network that simultaneously solves all tasks required to decode trajectories of bounding boxes for all cars in the scene.

Keywords: Multi-object tracking · Sparse · Point clouds · Convolutional · Recurrent

1 Introduction

Robust estimation of the trajectories of surrounding objects, including the tracking through partial or even full occlusion, is a vitally important task for driver assistance systems or autonomous driving scenarios. Deep learning techniques, especially recurrent and/or convolutional neural networks, have enabled much progress on detection and tracking problems in the domain of vision. Benchmarks like MOT16 [22] have shown the abilities of such systems for tracking pedestrians in camera images. More recent work has demonstrated similar results for the tracking of cars in bird's eye view maps generated from high-quality lidar point clouds [11,21,27].

Research has focused less on applying such deep networks on point clouds obtained from less expensive sensors. Such sensors often have lower resolution or other physical limitations, and thus the point clouds they produce are significantly sparser. They are also often prone to a lot more noise. In fact, there is usually a trade-off between sparsity and noisiness of the data. Successfully

I. Farkaš et al. (Eds.): ICANN 2021, LNCS 12894, pp. 407–419, 2021.
https://doi.org/10.1007/978-3-030-86380-7_33

detecting and tracking vehicles under such conditions is significantly more challenging, to the point where even human annotators would struggle (as can be seen from Fig. 1). Convolutional neural networks (CNNs), unquestionably the star of recent breakthroughs in machine learning, were primarily designed for camera images, which provide spatially dense features. With the right representation, CNNs can function equally well on high-quality point cloud data, though it is significantly sparser. The data we are interested in is sparser still and subject to a lot more noise than either those previous two types. It can, however, be generated by sensors that are much less expensive or have other desirable properties. Decreasing the overall cost of perception platforms is an important step in broadening the appeal of intelligent vehicles.

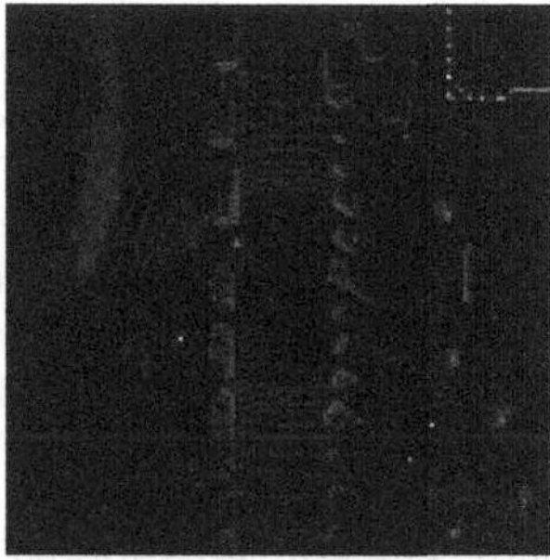

Fig. 1. Top-down view maps generated using low-fidelity point cloud data from a cheap sensor (left) and using high-fidelity point cloud data from an expensive sensor (right) for the same frame. Colour indicates point density. Even from this single high-fidelity scan, the silhouettes of cars are identifiable by eye; in the low-fidelity data substantially less so, presenting a greater challenge.

In this paper, we tackle detection and tracking based on sparse point cloud data using state-of-the-art techniques. Our proposed system is a deep learning based, end-to-end trainable on-line multi-object tracker. It operates on bird's eye view maps created from sparse and noisy point clouds and produces two-dimensional object trajectories. We demonstrate that our system can reach respectable performance in realistic driving scenarios while being fast enough to be deployed real-time.

2 Related Work

In the literature, the term "tracking" may refer inconsistently to one or a combination of either reidentification (the recognition of a previously seen target and its association with any prior information such as an active object track) or forecasting (completion of present information and prediction of future information from past information). Systems differ further in whether they consider detection as a separate, often already solved task (tracking-by-detection framework) or address tracking and detection jointly.

In the following, we will provide a brief overview over existing deep learning techniques for the various interpretations of multi-object tracking. Due to the breadth of research on this topic, that overview is superficial by necessity, and we therefore also refer the reader to [10] for a survey of deep learning multi-object tracking methods.

Reidentification: A popular technique for performing cross-frame association, especially in the vision domain, is via a learned appearance embedding or associative metric [8,13,33]. Such an embedding is usually trained using a contrastive [14], triplet [16] or quadruplet loss [30], which differ in the number of examples considered during their calculation. A related method is explored in [17], which uses a Siamese network that runs simultaneously on patches extracted for two detections and outputs a score representing the probability they show the same target. In [4], association is considered in its natural interpretation as a graph flow problem and solved by performing deep learning directly in that domain using novel Message Passing Networks. A number of systems go beyond the tracking-by-detection framework by learning the detection and appearance embedding tasks jointly within the same network [24,34,37], hoping to share computation and increase performance. MOTS [32] goes one step further still by learning detection, reidentification, and semantic segmentation in the same network.

Forecasting: An example for a forecasting system that operates on data- rather than target-level is given in the series of papers entitled *DeepTracking* [11,12,25], in which occupancy grid maps are completed and forward-predicted based on partial observations (generated from lidar scans) using stacks of convolutional gated recurrent units [9]. A similar approach is explored by the authors of [26], who perform long-term prediction of occupancy grid maps by inserting convolutional LSTM layers [36] into the lateral connections of a pyramidal architecture. Another notable example of a forecasting system is *MultiPath* [6], which predicts target-level trajectories. It captures uncertainty about its predictions by representing trajectories as a mixture of Gaussians using a Mixture Density Network [3]. *IntentNet* [5] expands upon the motion forecasting idea by also classifying driver intention, learning to output high level action labels alongside the target's future trajectory based on lidar point clouds and semantic street maps. The DESIRE system [18] combines recurrent networks with conditional variational autoencoders [29] to sample trajectories predicted into the distant future.

Full Tracking: One approach that technically falls under the tracking-by-detection umbrella but also incorporates elements of limited forecasting is a deep recurrent emulation of a Kalman filter presented in [23]. Similarly, *DeepSORT* [35] uses deep appearance embeddings to power the association step in a tracking system based on a classical Kalman filter. The system proposed in [27] extends the Complex-YOLO [28] detection pipeline using a Labelled Multi-Bernoulli Random Finite Set filter to achieve tracking in 3D lidar point clouds. The *Fast & Furious* tracker [21] performs detection and motion forecasting simultaneously and decodes object tracks based on the temporal and spatial overlap of partial trajectories. The authors of [1] extend a standard two-stage detection pipeline to perform tracking by performing the RoI pooling operation on data from the current frame using previous coordinate information.

3 Method

Our system melds recent approaches from lidar and vision into a recurrent fully-convolutional one-stage neural network that performs classification, localisation, and motion forecasting simultaneously and densely on sparse point cloud data. The main inspirations are *DeepTracking* [11], *Fast & Furious* [21], and Feature Pyramid Networks [19]. New contributions include a novel architecture that combines the strengths of and improves upon the aforementioned work, as well as adjustment of network and training details to increase performance in domains where one has to deal with sparse and noisy data. Figure 2 shows an overview diagram of the base variant of our architecture. The following sections describe the components and concepts of the system in greater detail.

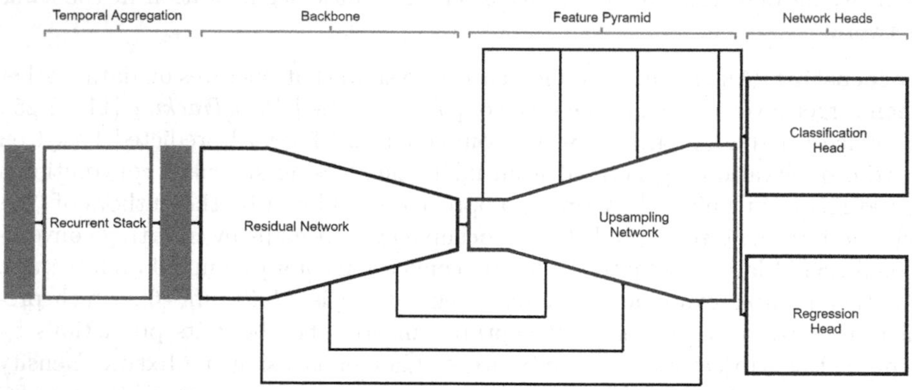

Fig. 2. A diagram overview of the basic tracker network architecture. Blue boxes denote single, regular convolutional layers and red boxes denote residual subnetworks. (Color figure online)

3.1 Temporal Aggregation

In our base architecture, the first part of the neural network consists of a stack of recurrent convolutional layers used for the temporal aggregation of information. Unlike many other recurrent systems, these layers are not used to compress a time-series of features into a single tensor (encoder architecture), but rather as a continuously updated memory. Therefore, during training useful output is expected after every update of the recurrent loop and during inference only a single frame of information is fed into the system at a time. This is a more difficult task to learn, but decreases the memory footprint and theoretically allows the network to use information from any past point in time. Reliable aggregation of temporal information is significantly more important in low-fidelity domains, as single scans often do not provide the necessary cues for the detection of vehicles, much less their tracking.

The basic setup of the recurrent layers follows that of [11]. However, dilated convolutions are foregone in favour of increasing the kernel size to achieve the same overall receptive field size, which is preferable when dealing with sparse data. Furthermore, we do not rely on the recurrence itself to produce predictions about the future as in [11]. Doing so would not easily allow for future predictions at every frame, since it corrupts the hidden states that form the network's memory of past information.

3.2 Classification and Localisation

The second part of the network is a single-shot detector that predicts object class-scores and bounding boxes for each position in the feature maps of a Feature Pyramid Network (FPN) [19]. Specifically, the bottom-up path of the network (or backbone) successively downsamples the input map using strided convolutions in a residual configuration [15]. The top-down path (or pyramid) successively upsamples the resulting map and combines it at each stage with the corresponding map from the bottom-up path via element-wise addition, forming lateral connections.

Two network heads are applied to each scale of pyramid features, providing the class-scores and bounding boxes of potential objects, respectively. Bounding boxes are predicted as offsets to a fixed set of reference bounding boxes (anchors). For training, each anchor is assigned to the ground truth object with which it has the highest intersection-over-union (IoU), provided that IoU is 0.4 or greater. Otherwise, the anchor is assigned to the background. We use anchors with a length to width ratio of 2.5 at four rotations and two scales, resulting in a total of eight anchors per position. We define bounding box regression targets as the centre position offset and relative log-size as done in [21]. However, we modify the orientation targets to include anchor rotation, giving

$$\theta_{\mathrm{T}}^{\sin} = \sin(2(\theta_{\mathrm{GT}} - \theta_{\mathrm{A}})), \tag{1}$$

$$\theta_{\mathrm{T}}^{\cos} = \cos(2(\theta_{\mathrm{GT}} - \theta_{\mathrm{A}})), \tag{2}$$

where θ_{GT} and θ_{A} are the ground truth and anchor rotation, respectively. Note that we also multiply the rotation offset by two so as to achieve 180° periodicity, which matches the rotational symmetry of rectangles. Using anchors at multiple rotations essentially amounts to performing a two-step rotation estimation consisting of a coarse initial estimate and a subsequent refinement, which we found improves stability.

3.3 Fused Architecture

Beside the basic architecture (Fig. 2), we also consider an alternative formulation in which the temporal aggregation is fused with the backbone of the feature pyramid network. Specifically, this means omitting the temporal aggregation block in front of the FPN and instead replacing the standard residual blocks in the backbone network with custom recurrent residual blocks. This allows the network to retain information at different levels of resolution and semantics.

Similar to the original ResNet [15], we propose two variants of our recurrent residual blocks with different complexities (Fig. 3). The first variant mirrors the standard two-layer residual block, simply replacing the first convolution with a convolutional recurrent layer. The second variant modifies the three-layer bottleneck design to use a convolutional recurrent layer in place of the middle 3×3 convolution. The latter design is especially attractive since the high cost of popular gated recurrent layer designs is amortised by applying them to lower-dimensional embeddings.

3.4 Motion Forecasting and Tracking

The system produces motion forecasts several time-steps into the future for each detected object in the vein of *Fast & Furious* [21]. This is done by modifying the localisation head of the single-shot detector to directly output the appropriate number of additional bounding boxes.

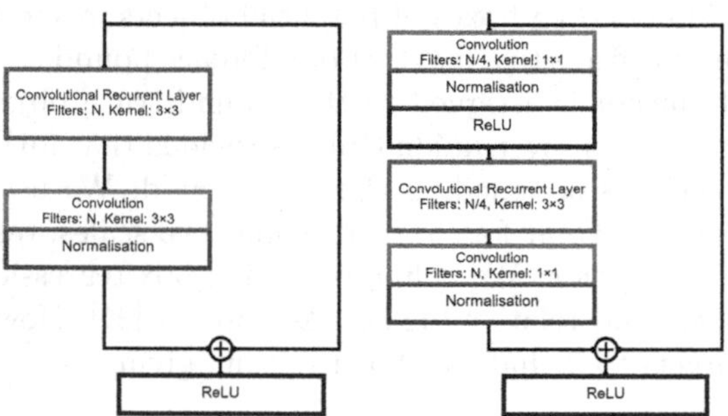

Fig. 3. A diagram showing the two variants of recurrent residual block (standard variant on the left, bottleneck variant on the right), which comprise the backbone network in the fused tracker architecture. N denotes the number of channels in the input map.

The purpose of the motion forecasting is manifold. For one, it has a regularising effect on the recurrent layers by forcing them to learn a motion model for the detected objects. It acts also as a secondary mechanism for tracking through occlusion, should the network's memory be insufficient. Lastly, it provides the necessary cues for assembling individual object detections into trajectories and allows for temporal smoothing, as each trajectory has access to multiple predicted bounding boxes per time-step.

Association of object detections across time-steps can easily be handled via the motion forecasts, since each detection already constitutes a mini-trajectory or "tracklet" (association-by-forecast as in [21]). The system therefore does not require any sophisticated recursive filtering techniques and can perform tracking instead via a greedy association pass over the temporal and spatial overlap between predictions for different time-steps. We couple this with a simple tentative track initialisation based on cumulative score: A track is considered mature when the sum of the scores accrued by all associated tracklets reaches a certain threshold.

4 Experiments

In the following, we aim to validate our tracker system on data obtained during real traffic situations. For this purpose, we have conducted recordings from a car equipped with six low-resolution short-range sensors providing point cloud data with 360° coverage. We compile these recordings into a dataset of 84 sequences containing a total of 66,245 frames recorded at 20 Hz. We use 59 sequences for training and the remaining 25 for validation.

4.1 Training

We use 128×128 bird's eye view grids with bins of size $31.25\,\text{cm} \times 31.25\,\text{cm}$. Each bin contains as features the number of points assigned to it as well as the average of any additional features the sensor provides. The network is trained using the ADAM optimiser with an initial learning rate of $3 \cdot 10^{-4}$. The learning rate remains constant for the first half of total epochs and is then linearly decayed to zero. We train for a maximum of 280,000 iterations.

Each full sequence in the dataset is divided into overlapping mini-sequences of equal length and each mini-sequence is in turn divided into batches. The order of mini-sequences within the dataset is randomised, but the order of batches within a mini-sequence is retained. During optimisation, we keep the hidden states of the recurrent layers from batch to batch and only reset them at the end of a mini-sequence. This is meant to counteract the small number of frames per batch caused by memory constraints and help the network learn dependencies between more distant points in time. We use mini-sequences with a length of 80 frames and batches with a length of 20.

The regression head is trained using a standard smooth L1 loss. The classification head is trained using a modified variant of the focal loss introduced in [20]. The original formulation normalises the loss by the total number of foreground anchors. We found this variant to grow unstable when faced with examples that contain few or no positives but many hard negatives (which is common in noisy point cloud data). We therefore normalise the loss instead using the sum of the focal weights. This has the added advantage that loss values naturally have the same scale as regular binary cross-entropy.

4.2 Metrics

The most popular choice of metric in literature is Multi-Object Tracking Accuracy (MOTA), which is part of the CLEAR MOT suite of metrics [2]. MOTA distinguishes three types of errors a tracking system can make: false positives, false negatives, and identity switches. However, in our experiments, MOTA has proven a rather unintuitive measure due to way it normalises and combines these error rates, causing its range of values to be unbounded of one side. Therefore, we will mainly employ a modified version of Multi-Camera Tracking Accuracy (MCTA) defined in [7]. We simply omit the handover term, which is not relevant to our application. MOTA will still be provided but is not used to rank the relative performance of models.

We generally follow the CLEAR MOT protocol for the calculation of the frame-wise error counts, with one notable exception. Our system predicts rotated rectangles, which naturally tend to have lower overlap, and operates on low-fidelity point cloud data, which due to its sparsity limits the localisation accuracy that reasonably can be expected. Therefore, we use a lower IoU threshold of 0.4 for ground truth to prediction matching. We report identity switches (IDSW) as a fraction of true positives. Finally, we also list displacement errors for the raw motion forecasts, which measure the mean L2 distance (in meters) between ground truth and forecasted object centres, using the average (ADE) or final (FDE) such distance.

4.3 Results

We report our results for a number of variants on our tracker architecture, including feature ablation. See Table 1 for an overview of the variants considered.

Quantitative Results: Table 2 shows a selection of performance metrics for several variants of the tracker architecture. Note that, in a bird's eye view, object bounding boxes do not pass over one another as they do in vision, and therefore identity switches are rare. Most trajectory fragmentation occurs due to false negatives, which is by far the most common type of error our tracker makes. Note here also that ground truth annotators had access to the data from auxiliary sensors for labelling, which have different mounting positions from the main sensors. Therefore, some objects included in the ground truth might not be visible in the input data, negatively affecting the reported recall values. The ablation experiments show that the method of temporal aggregation has the largest influence on the performance of the model, confirming our earlier statement on the importance of time information in low-fidelity domains. The model that runs on singe frames (model "no_temporal") performs poorly, especially in terms of recall. The model aggregating five frames via 3D convolution (model "conv3d"), which replicates the best performing fusion method from *Fast & Furious*, is a significant improvement, and yet the recurrent networks outperform it by a large margin. The feature pyramid mostly provides a boost to precision. Presumably, the addition of scene context makes distinguishing noise from signal easier, allowing the suppression of false positives. Lastly, the advanced architectures using

Table 1. Overview over variants of the tracker architecture considered during our experiments. Fames per second (FPS) are based on the execution time on an NVIDIA GeForce RTX 2080 Ti.

Model	Architecture	# Param.	FPS
Basic	Base architecture (Fig. 2)	9.0M	42
no_fpn	No feature pyramid	8.7M	43
no_temporal	No temporal aggregation	6.4M	86
conv3d	Temporal aggregation by 3D convolution ("late fusion" [21])	6.5M	54
fused_std	Fused backbone, standard recurrent residual block	9.8M	52
fused_2btln	Fused backbone, bottleneck recurrent residual block, 2 per level	6.7M	48

Table 2. Performance of the tracker models in the aspects of detection (precision (P), recall (R)), tracking (MOTA, MCTA, MOTP, IDSW, MT, ML [2,7]), and motion forecasting (ADE, FDE). Best performance for each metric in bold. "↑"/"↓" mark metrics for which larger/smaller values are better.

Model	P ↑	R ↑	MOTA ↑	MCTA ↑	MOTP ↑	IDSW ↓	MT ↑	ML ↓	ADE ↓	FDE ↓
basic	0.882	0.591	0.512	0.708	0.761	**0.00007**	0.314	0.408	0.336	0.409
no_fpn	0.793	0.602	0.445	0.684	**0.768**	**0.00007**	0.301	0.402	**0.292**	**0.322**
no_temporal	0.825	0.436	0.343	0.569	0.712	0.00226	0.189	0.513	0.403	0.493
conv3d	0.857	0.526	0.438	0.651	0.764	0.00026	0.275	0.439	0.304	0.337
fused_std	**0.886**	0.609	0.531	0.722	0.764	0.00015	0.348	**0.395**	0.306	0.349
fused_2btln	0.874	**0.623**	**0.534**	**0.728**	0.745	**0.00007**	**0.370**	0.398	0.323	0.361

recurrent residual blocks manage to increase performance by a last few percentage points, while simultaneously running faster than model "basic", which demonstrates the effectiveness of performing temporal aggregation at multiple scales.

Qualitative Results: As might be expected of this type of data, relative movement enhances the discriminative power of the system. In scenes where both the ego-car and surrounding vehicles are stopped, performance degrades substantially. Moving vehicles, on the other hand, are recognised almost unfailingly. Another scenario the tracker surprisingly seems to find difficult is turning of the ego-car, leading to a sudden increase in false positives. Figure 4 shows a few specific examples of such failure cases (as produced by the best performing model "fused_2btln"). The top-most example shows a scene in which the ego-car is currently turning, causing transient false positives and some distortion of object orientations. In the middle example, the ego-car itself and surrounding vehicles are stopped. This is a particularly hard example for the tracker, and it only manages to recognise a single object. Generally, it is difficult to distinguish stationary objects from the background given the low spatial resolution, unless the ego-car

Fig. 4. A collection of failed examples of the best performing tracker model, each example consisting of a sequence of five frames taken at five frame intervals displayed from left to right. Ground truth bounding boxes are drawn in blue. Predicted bounding boxes are drawn in red and annotated with a number indicating their identity across frames. The grayscale background visualises the point cloud. (Color figure online)

is itself moving, which can help to mitigate sparsity by providing multiple scans from different perspectives. The bottom-most example shows a scene where even the ego-car's movement was not sufficient to track the parked cars. Presumably, their close proximity to each other makes it difficult to segment instances. A set of successful examples is shown in Fig. 5. In contrast to the previous failed example with a large number of parked cars, the top-most example in Fig. 5 shows a similar scene where the tracker performs quite well, thanks to the arrangement of the cars making their shapes more recognisable. Furthermore, the orientations of the cars are estimated correctly despite the challenging situation. The middle example shows the system successfully tracking a trailer truck. Even though the tracker can only see a single side of the truck for a majority of the sequence, it is able to estimate its size and even the point of division between the two segments with surprising accuracy. Lastly, the bottom-most example shows a scene where the ego-car is driving along a multi-lane road together with other cars at similar speeds. Moving targets are recognised with high confidence and accuracy, since the feature signatures of points that belong to moving targets are easily distinguishable from the background.

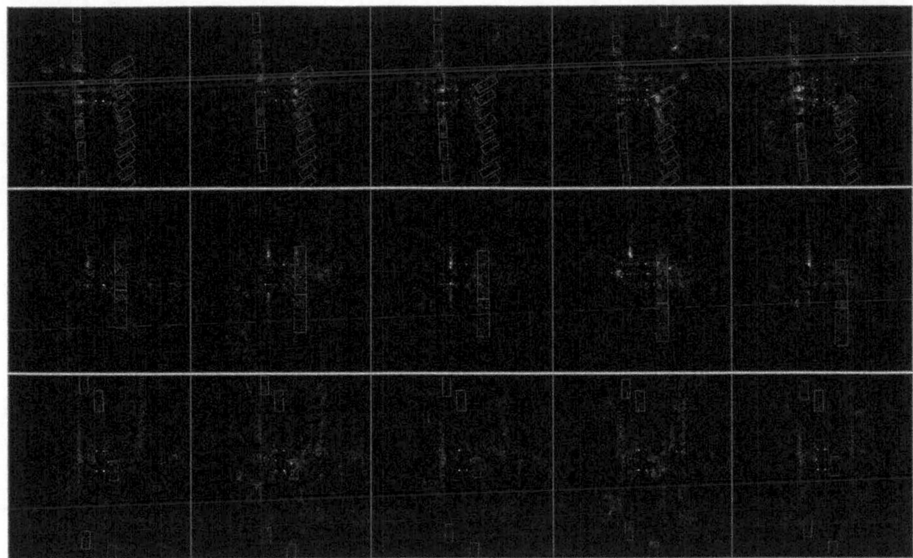

Fig. 5. A collection of successful examples from the best performing tracker model, each example consisting of a sequence of five frames taken at five frame intervals displayed from left to right. Ground truth bounding boxes are drawn in blue. Predicted bounding boxes are drawn in red and annotated with a number indicating their identity across frames. The grayscale background visualises the point cloud. (Color figure online)

5 Conclusion

In this paper, we presented a tracking system running on sparse point cloud data that consists of a single-stage neural network. It combines the strengths of convolutional recurrent layers and feature pyramid networks to perform detection and short-term motion forecasting jointly, which allows for robust estimation of two-dimensional object trajectories. We furthermore showed the effectiveness of our system in experiments on real data and demonstrated the importance of each individual component. Our final tracker variant reaches an MCTA of nearly 0.73 on sparse point cloud data alone, outperforming methods designed for other domains.

Future work might revise and extend the technique used to produce motion forecasts. The current method produces only a fixed number of future predictions and does not make the time-dependency explicit. Another avenue may be incorporating recent developments in object detection such as EfficientDet [31] and others to improve the tracker's recall. Finally, uncertainty quantisation is a promising prospect in the context of a forecasting and tracking systems.

References

1. Bergmann, P., Meinhardt, T., Leal-Taixe, L.: Tracking without bells and whistles. In: Proceedings of the IEEE International Conference on Computer Vision, pp. 941–951 (2019)

2. Bernardin, K., Stiefelhagen, R.: Evaluating multiple object tracking performance: the clear mot metrics. J. Image Video Process. **2008**, 1 (2008)
3. Bishop, C.M.: Mixture density networks (1994)
4. Brasó, G., Leal-Taixé, L.: Learning a neural solver for multiple object tracking. In: Proceedings of the IEEE/CVF Conference on Computer Vision and Pattern Recognition, pp. 6247–6257 (2020)
5. Casas, S., Luo, W., Urtasun, R.: IntentNet: learning to predict intention from raw sensor data. In: Conference on Robot Learning, pp. 947–956 (2018)
6. Chai, Y., Sapp, B., Bansal, M., Anguelov, D.: Multipath: multiple probabilistic anchor trajectory hypotheses for behavior prediction. arXiv preprint arXiv:1910.05449 (2019)
7. Chen, W., Cao, L., Chen, X., Huang, K.: An equalized global graph model-based approach for multicamera object tracking. IEEE Trans. Circuits Syst. Video Technol. **27**(11), 2367–2381 (2016)
8. Cheng, D., Gong, Y., Zhou, S., Wang, J., Zheng, N.: Person re-identification by multi-channel parts-based CNN with improved triplet loss function. In: Proceedings of the IEEE Conference on Computer Vision and Pattern Recognition, pp. 1335–1344 (2016)
9. Cho, K., et al.: Learning phrase representations using RNN encoder-decoder for statistical machine translation. arXiv preprint arXiv:1406.1078 (2014)
10. Ciaparrone, G., Sánchez, F.L., Tabik, S., Troiano, L., Tagliaferri, R., Herrera, F.: Deep learning in video multi-object tracking: a survey. Neurocomputing **381**, 61–88 (2020)
11. Dequaire, J., Ondrúška, P., Rao, D., Wang, D., Posner, I.: Deep tracking in the wild: end-to-end tracking using recurrent neural networks. Int. J. Rob. Res. **37**(4–5), 492–512 (2018)
12. Dequaire, J., Rao, D., Ondruska, P., Wang, D., Posner, I.: Deep tracking on the move: learning to track the world from a moving vehicle using recurrent neural networks. arXiv preprint arXiv:1609.09365 (2016)
13. Ding, S., Lin, L., Wang, G., Chao, H.: Deep feature learning with relative distance comparison for person re-identification. Pattern Recogn. **48**(10), 2993–3003 (2015)
14. Hadsell, R., Chopra, S., LeCun, Y.: Dimensionality reduction by learning an invariant mapping. In: 2006 IEEE Computer Society Conference on Computer Vision and Pattern Recognition (CVPR 2006), vol. 2, pp. 1735–1742. IEEE (2006)
15. He, K., Zhang, X., Ren, S., Sun, J.: Deep residual learning for image recognition. In: Proceedings of the IEEE Conference on Computer Vision and Pattern Recognition, pp. 770–778 (2016)
16. Hoffer, E., Ailon, N.: Deep metric learning using triplet network. In: Feragen, A., Pelillo, M., Loog, M. (eds.) SIMBAD 2015. LNCS, vol. 9370, pp. 84–92. Springer, Cham (2015). https://doi.org/10.1007/978-3-319-24261-3_7
17. Leal-Taixé, L., Canton-Ferrer, C., Schindler, K.: Learning by tracking: siamese CNN for robust target association. In: Proceedings of the IEEE Conference on Computer Vision and Pattern Recognition Workshops, pp. 33–40 (2016)
18. Lee, N., Choi, W., Vernaza, P., Choy, C.B., Torr, P.H., Chandraker, M.: Desire: distant future prediction in dynamic scenes with interacting agents. In: Proceedings of the IEEE Conference on Computer Vision and Pattern Recognition, pp. 336–345 (2017)
19. Lin, T.Y., Dollár, P., Girshick, R., He, K., Hariharan, B., Belongie, S.: Feature pyramid networks for object detection. In: Proceedings of the IEEE Conference on Computer Vision and Pattern Recognition, pp. 2117–2125 (2017)

20. Lin, T.Y., Goyal, P., Girshick, R., He, K., Dollár, P.: Focal loss for dense object detection. In: Proceedings of the IEEE International Conference on Computer Vision, pp. 2980–2988 (2017)
21. Luo, W., Yang, B., Urtasun, R.: Fast and furious: real time end-to-end 3D detection, tracking and motion forecasting with a single convolutional net. In: Proceedings of the IEEE Conference on Computer Vision and Pattern Recognition, pp. 3569–3577 (2018)
22. Milan, A., Leal-Taixé, L., Reid, I.D., Roth, S., Schindler, K.: MOT16: a benchmark for multi-object tracking. CoRR abs/1603.00831 (2016). http://arxiv.org/abs/1603.00831
23. Milan, A., Rezatofighi, S.H., Dick, A., Reid, I., Schindler, K.: Online multi-target tracking using recurrent neural networks. arXiv preprint arXiv:1604.03635 (2016)
24. Newell, A., Huang, Z., Deng, J.: Associative embedding: end-to-end learning for joint detection and grouping. In: Advances in Neural Information Processing Systems, pp. 2277–2287 (2017)
25. Ondruska, P., Posner, I.: Deep tracking: seeing beyond seeing using recurrent neural networks. In: Thirtieth AAAI Conference on Artificial Intelligence (2016)
26. Schreiber, M., Hoermann, S., Dietmayer, K.: Long-term occupancy grid prediction using recurrent neural networks. In: 2019 International Conference on Robotics and Automation (ICRA), pp. 9299–9305. IEEE (2019)
27. Simon, M., et al.: Complexer-YOLO: real-time 3D object detection and tracking on semantic point clouds. In: Proceedings of the IEEE Conference on Computer Vision and Pattern Recognition Workshops (2019)
28. Simon, M., Milz, S., Amende, K., Gross, H.M.: Complex-YOLO: real-time 3D object detection on point clouds. arXiv preprint arXiv:1803.06199 (2018)
29. Sohn, K., Lee, H., Yan, X.: Learning structured output representation using deep conditional generative models. In: Advances in Neural Information Processing Systems, pp. 3483–3491 (2015)
30. Son, J., Baek, M., Cho, M., Han, B.: Multi-object tracking with quadruplet convolutional neural networks. In: Proceedings of the IEEE Conference on Computer Vision and Pattern Recognition, pp. 5620–5629 (2017)
31. Tan, M., Pang, R., Le, Q.V.: EfficientDet: scalable and efficient object detection (2019)
32. Voigtlaender, P., et al.: MOTS: multi-object tracking and segmentation. In: Proceedings of the IEEE Conference on Computer Vision and Pattern Recognition, pp. 7942–7951 (2019)
33. Wang, F., Zuo, W., Lin, L., Zhang, D., Zhang, L.: Joint learning of single-image and cross-image representations for person re-identification. In: Proceedings of the IEEE Conference on Computer Vision and Pattern Recognition, pp. 1288–1296 (2016)
34. Wang, Z., Zheng, L., Liu, Y., Wang, S.: Towards real-time multi-object tracking. CoRR abs/1909.12605 (2019). http://arxiv.org/abs/1909.12605
35. Wojke, N., Bewley, A., Paulus, D.: Simple online and realtime tracking with a deep association metric. In: 2017 IEEE International Conference on Image Processing (ICIP), pp. 3645–3649. IEEE (2017)
36. Xingjian, S., Chen, Z., Wang, H., Yeung, D.Y., Wong, W.K., Woo, W.C.: Convolutional LSTM network: a machine learning approach for precipitation nowcasting. In: Advances in Neural Information Processing Systems, pp. 802–810 (2015)
37. Zhan, Y., Wang, C., Wang, X., Zeng, W., Liu, W.: A simple baseline for multi-object tracking. arXiv preprint arXiv:2004.01888 (2020)

M-ary Hopfield Neural Network Based Associative Memory Formulation: Limit-Cycle Based Sequence Storage and Retrieval

Vandana M. Ladwani[1,2] and V. Ramasubramanian[1(✉)]

[1] International Institute of Information Technology - Bangalore, Bangalore, India
{vandana.ladwani,v.ramasubramanian}@iiitb.ac.in
[2] PES University, Bangalore, India

Abstract. In this paper, we examine Hopfield network composed of multi-state neurons for storing sequence data as limit cycles of the network. Earlier, we had presented uni-modal data - particularly text, speech and audio data storage and retrieval in bipolar Hopfield based associative memory architecture. We extended this to multi-modal data and we demonstrated that Hopfield can indeed work as content addressable memory for multi-modal data. This paper is a step towards realising a more wider definition of multi-modality. We present a M-ary Hopfield associative memory model for storing limit cycle data. The proposed system uses a dual weight learning mechanism to exhibit limit cycle behavior in which sequence data can be stored and retrieved. We particularly deal with a) sequence of images and b) movie clip data as instances of limit cycle data. We also propose and use a two stage firing mechanism to retrieve the stored sequence data from the limit cycles. We present a trade-off behavior between the number of cycles and length of cycles the network can store and we demonstrate that the network capacity is still of the order of network size i.e., $O(N)$ for limit cycle data. This represents a first of its kind attempt for sequence storage and retrieval in Hopfield network as limit-cycles, particularly with image-sequence and movie-content data of real-world scales.

Keywords: Hopfield network · Limit cycle · Dual weight learning · Two stage firing · Multi-state neurons

1 Introduction

We demonstrate Hopfield based associative framework for storage and retrieval of sequence data modelled as a limit cycle. A limit cycle is a closed trajectory composed of sequence of states. Limit cycles can be used to model cyclic activities such as natural phenomenon like respiration, beating of heart, real world data like movie clips, sequence of events, audio, speech or music clips, spoken dialog etc. [1]. The original Hopfield framework was used for storing static

I. Farkaš et al. (Eds.): ICANN 2021, LNCS 12894, pp. 420–432, 2021.
https://doi.org/10.1007/978-3-030-86380-7_34

binary patterns [2]. Hopfield also extended the original model to a graded neuron model [3]. Hopfield network behaves as content addressable memory - i.e., given a corrupted partial state, the network can retrieve the complete stored pattern [4]. This important 'content addressable' property of Hopfield network has not been explored for scalable storage/retrieval of real world data. Hopfield network has been used only for storing/retrieving toy patterns and for solving optimization problems.

Our recent work focused on adapting bipolar Hopfield network for setting up content addressable retrieval system for real world uni-modal data text [5], audio [6], speech [7] and multi-modal data such as captioned images [8]. The success of the experiments on static unimodal and multimodal data unveils Hopfield network coupled with high capacity learning rules as a potential scalable associative memory architecture.

In this paper, we demonstrate M-ary Hopfield network based architecture for storage/retrieval of 'Long Sequence Data' as 'Limit Cycles' of the network under specially constructed weight learning and retrieval mechanisms. We consider two variations of such sequence data - image sequences and movie clips of long duration (e.g., 6.3 min) as limit cycle data for our experiments. Such weight-learning and retrieval mechanisms combined with large scale adoption to real world data is a first of its kind attempt. We also demonstrate the trade-off between number of limit cycles and length of limit cycle the network can support.

The general form of the proposed system is shown in Fig. 1 - given 'any' state as start state (trigger state), the system is able to retrieve the complete limit cycle (sequence). Hopfield based network consisting of multistate neurons is used to construct content addressable memory for real world sequence data. Network can be trained to store single/multiple sequences.

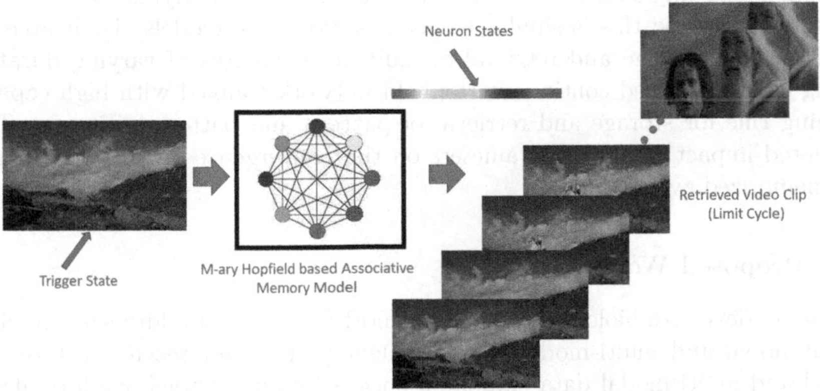

Fig. 1. M-ary Hopfield associative memory for limit cycle storage and retrieval

1.1 Associative Memory Formulation

Brain consists of massively interconnected neurons. Information is stored in brain by modifying the strength of the synaptic connections to constitute various kinds of memory mechanisms [9]. Such memory mechanisms store static information such as images, faces, scenes and pattern sequences such as movie clips, song clips, spoken sentences etc. Given a cue, e.g., a particular scene from a movie or a word from a song, the memory mechanism in the brain recalls a complete video clip or a complete song that contains the cue. This is termed as auto-association for sequence retrieval.

Auto-associative memory is a biologically plausible model for storage and content based retrieval of stored information [10]. Denizdurduran proposes attractor Neural Network Approaches in the Memory Modeling [11]. In this paper, We present Hopfield based associative memory for storing multi-valued pattern sequences.

1.2 Related Work

In this section, we focus on approaches for storage and retrieval of limit cycle based on 'Associative Memory Formulations'. Miyoshi et al. proposed Recurrent Neural Network with Delay elements for storage and retrieval of limit cycle data [12]. They demonstrated with experimental results superior performance of DRNN over RNN, bringing out the important property that delay is important for correct retrieval of limit cycle data. In another work, Miyoshi et al. proposed a DRNN based associative memory which has close resemblance to the Hopfield based model for static patterns [13]. Their proposed model uses bipolar neurons and synchronous firing (single firing rule). Maurer, Hersch and Billard presented interesting results for storage, recognition and generation of Human Gesture data [14]. They use a two layered architecture, where the first layer consists of multiple Hopfield networks each of which stores trajectory information at a particular angle and the second layer is used for classifying the gesture to a specific category; this is similar to hetero-associative models. Their architecture supports storage and retrieval of multiple sequences of varying duration. Zhang et al. proposed continuous Hopfield network coupled with high capacity learning rule for storage and retrieval of pattern and pattern sequences. They presented impact of model parameters on the convergence of retrieved orbit to the memorized cycle [15].

1.3 Proposed Work

We aim to develop a biologically plausible model for content addressable retrieval of uni-modal and multi-modal static/sequence data. Our recent work on uni-modal and multi-modal data exhibits a successful auto-associative formulation for static data storage/retrieval. In this paper, our contribution is towards developing a scalable system for sequence storage and retrieval. Given any state, i.e., a 'start state/intermediate state' as trigger state, the system retrieves the complete limit cycle. We particularly focus on

1. Modeling real world data as limit cycle
2. M-ary Hopfield network for real world data

3. Dual weight learning to store cyclic patterns in M-ary Hopfield network
4. Two stage firing procedure for sequence retrieval
5. Network size as an upper bound on length and number of cycles the network can store.

We present results of two main experiments - the first experiment deals with adapting M-ary hopfield network for storing and retrieving a long limit cycle; for this we consider a movie clip of duration (6.3 min). The second experiment deals with finding relationship between the number of limit cycles and length of limit cycles that a network of fixed size can store and retrieve with 'zero' tolerance; for this, we constructed sequences of varying lengths from 'Flickr30K' data-set images (highly uncorrelated states) [16]. We show that with high capacity learning rules, the proposed architecture supports *O(N)* number of state transitions in all for the various sequences, which is in line with the performance of Hopfield network for static patterns.

2 Basics of M-ary Hopfield Network

M-ary hopfield network is an extension of the basic bipolar Hopfield model. Bijjani and Das used it to store images as static patterns [17]. M-ary hopfield network as shown in Fig. 2 is a fully connected network in which each neuron can assume any of M values at a particular time instance as opposed to two values in case of binary or bipolar model. A state of the network at any point is represented by the vector $\xi_i = (\xi_i^1, \xi_i^2, \xi_i^3, \ldots, \xi_i^N)$, where each of ξ_i^j can take any of M values. Due to the M-ary nature of neurons, information to be stored in the network can be encoded using a large range of values which prevents loss of information that results when the data is clipped to two set of values as in case of binary neurons. This correlates well with the way human brain models information - human brain has a continuum of values while memorizing or retrieving the memorized information [18].

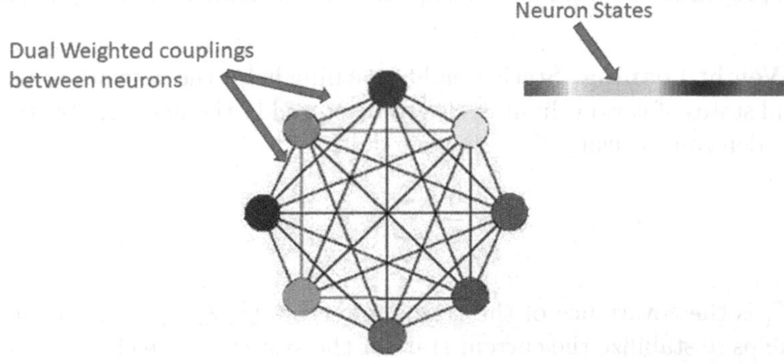

Fig. 2. Structure of M-ary hopfield neural network: network is fully connected with multi-state neurons (each can take any value from the set of permissible values) and the couplings between neurons are dual weights as they store static and transition weights

3 M-ary Hopfield Neural Network for Limit Cycle Data

Neural Network based associative memory architecture stores information by modifying the coupling strength between the neurons. The original binary Hopfield model which was used for storing static patterns uses Hebbian learning rule which is given as

$$W_{ij} = \frac{1}{N} \sum_{U} \xi_i^U \xi_j^U \tag{1}$$

where, U is the no of patterns stored in the network. Hebbian learning rule is inspired by the way human brain stores information [9]. Upper bound on the capacity, this network supports is $0.14N$ (Where N is the network size) which is achievable only when patterns are 'uncorrelated' [2]. To address this issue Personnaz et al. proposed the pseudo-inverse learning rule (high capacity learning rule) which enables network to achieve $O(N)$ capacity [19]. We could achieve the same for our experiments on static data. In the present work, we use the pseudo-inverse rule based dual weight learning which helps to store static and transition information in the network and thus can be used to store sequence data. Zhang et al. also used the pseudo-inverse learning rule [15]. In their work, they use single weight matrix to capture both static and transition information. Whereas in our work we maintain two set of weights and use them separately during the two stage retrieval procedure as opposed to the single stage retrieval presented in Zhang's work. Also, in contrast to the short synthetic constructs of data of Zhang's work, we report results of scaling our proposed model to 'very long' limit cycles which model real world data.

3.1 Dual Weight Learning

Dual weight learning helps to store 'Limit cycles' in Hopfield based associative memory network. Limit cycles can be used to model (store and retrieve) real world sequences like image sequences, movie clips, speech utterances, spoken dialogues, rhythmic signals, paired sequence data, multi-modal sequences etc.

Static Weight Leaning. Static weight Learning helps the network to memorize individual states of various limit cycles to be stored in the network. Static weight matrix is determined using the following rule.

$$S_{ij} = \frac{1}{N} \sum_{k,l} \xi_{ki} C^{-1} \xi_{lj} \tag{2}$$

Where C, is the covariance of the training vectors ξ_i^1, ξ_i^2, ξ_i^3, ... Static weight matrix helps to stabilize the current state of the system to the closest memorized state.

Transition Weight Learning. A sequence is a state of states. In order to memorize such a sequence, the system needs to capture transition information in addition to the static pattern information, e.g., the brain remembers a movie clip by memorizing individual scenes and scene to scene transitions. The transition weight matrix is determined by adapting the pseudo-inverse learning rule to capture projection of every predecessor state to its successor state in each cycle.

$$T_{ij} = \frac{1}{N} \sum_{no\ of\ cycles} \Xi_1 \Xi^+ \tag{3}$$

where, Ξ_1 is the rotated version of Ξ and Ξ^+ is the Pseudo Inverse of Ξ which represents a matrix of state vectors $\xi_i^1, \xi_i^2, \xi_i^3, \ldots, \xi_i^l$. Where l, is the length of limit cycle. The transition matrix holds information regarding the next state system should transit into. Thus T models a 'Markov process of order 1'. Using the above 'dual weight' learning, the network encodes information of cyclic sequences in the 'energy landscape'. It is this energy landscape which enables the system to behave as a content addressable memory for storage and retrieval of sequences also. Figure 3 depicts Energy landscape memorized by the system using the 'Dual Weight Learning' for two Limit Cycles.

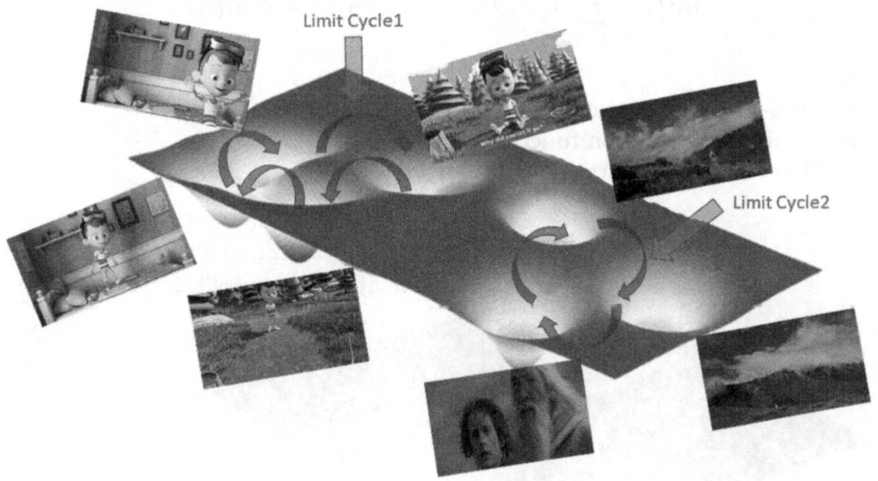

Fig. 3. Energy landscape for two limit cycles stored in M-ary hopfield network

3.2 Retrieval of Stored Limit Cycle: Two Stage Firing Procedure

Retrieval is an iterative procedure. Given a start state (also referred here as 'trigger' state) which can be the first state or any intermediate state (clean/corrupted/partial/corrupted and partial) of the stored cycle, the system switches from one state to another to retrieve the complete cycle. The network modeled for temporal processing should be capable of retaining the component of the sequence for sometime - this has a close resemblance to 'short term memory' in human brain [10]. This inspired us to come up with a two stage firing procedure. Retrieval dynamics of the proposed system is controlled by a two stage firing procedure - a) Synchronous firing which controls switching from one state to another and b) Asynchronous firing which enables system to stay in a particular state till it is stabilized. The energy landscape learnt by the system during the learning phase consists of multiple distinct regions, each corresponds to a specific limit cycle. Each region consists of multiple wells which are separated by saddle regions; each well corresponds to an attractor basin, where the bottom of the well corresponds to the attractor state of the limit cycle at a specific instance. The total energy of the region represents the energy of the stored cycle. Different cycles have different energy values associated with them. More the difference, better the retrieval.

Asynchronous Firing. Asynchronous firing uses static weight matrix to stabilize the network in the current state. As shown in Fig. 4, it is an iterative procedure which drives any state in the current basin of attraction to the minimal energy state 'within' the basin. State change during the 'asynchronous' firing is governed by the rule

$$h_i(t) = \sum_{j=1}^{N} S_{ij} x_j(t); \qquad x_i(t+1) = f(h_i(t)) \tag{4}$$

where,
$h_i(t)$ represents input potential to the ith neuron
$f()$ is a staircase activation function
$x_i(t+1)$ is the updated state of ith neuron.

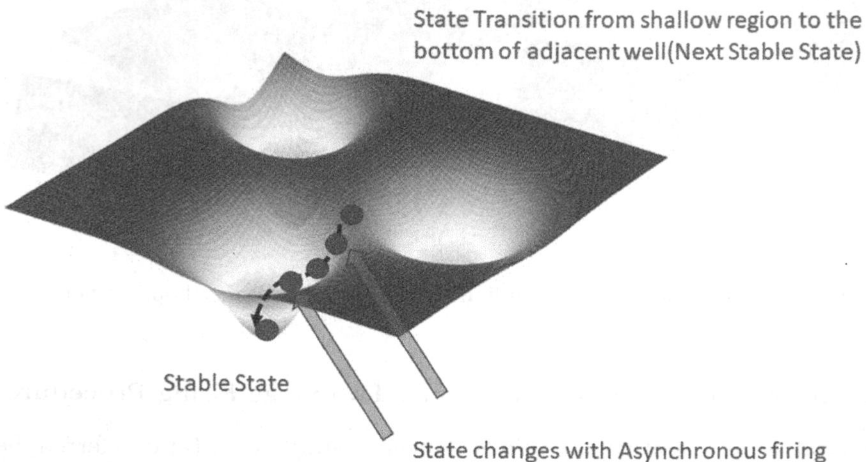

Fig. 4. Asynchronous firing: system dynamics during asynchronous firing. Circles represent state of the network at a particular instance, rolling down on the energy surface drives the system to the bottom of the basin which represents an attractor state

Synchronous Firing. Synchronous Firing helps the system to switch from one state to another state. It uses a transition weight matrix to drive the system from a valley region to the saddle region which initiates transition to the next state as demonstrated in Fig. 5. Synchronous switching is governed by the rule

$$h_i(t) = \sum_{j=1}^{N} T_{ij} x_j(t); \qquad x_i(t+1) = f(h_i(t)) \tag{5}$$

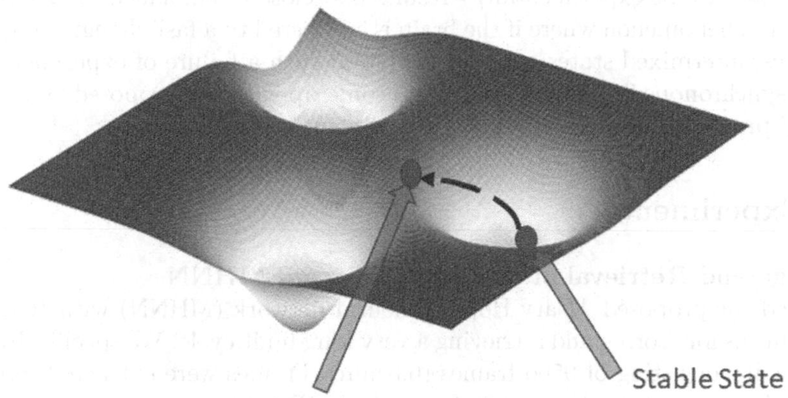

Fig. 5. Synchronous firing: movement of the circles shows transition of the current state

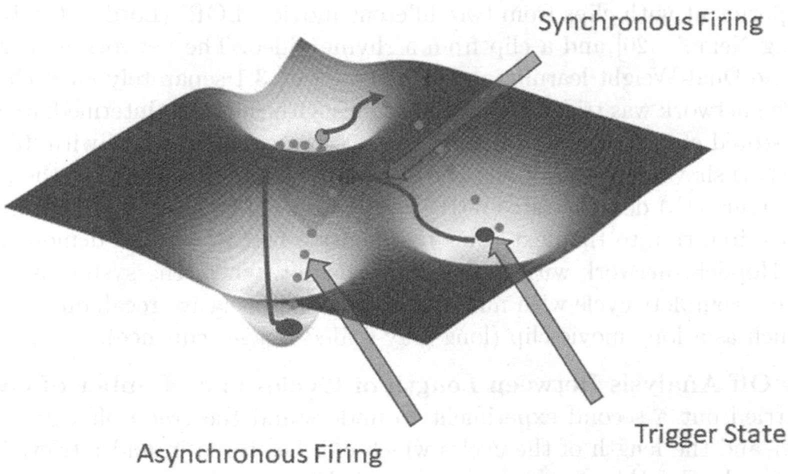

Fig. 6. System dynamics for retrieval of limit cycle of length 3, rolling of states over energy surface from one well to the another

This is again followed by asynchronous firing which rolls down the state of the system to the bottom of the adjacent well. Thus, repetition of two stage firing mechanism drives the system from one state to another and retrieves the complete cycle. Figure 6 shows rolling of states over the energy surface for retrieval of a complete limit cycle.

Advantage of Two Stage Firing Procedure. The two stage firing procedure introduces a delay in the transition from one state to another and helps network to stabilize in the current state before moving to next; this prevents mixing of states which results when we fire the network using 'only' synchronous firing. We could observe this experimentally - results had close resemblance to 'persistence of vision' phenomenon where if the brain is subjected to a fast changing sequence of states, intermixed states get perceived, and such a failure of experiment with 'only' synchronous firing motivated us to come up with the proposed 'Two Stage Firing' procedure above.

4 Experiments

Storage and Retrieval of a Movie Clip from MHNN
We used the proposed M-ary Hopfield neural network (MHNN) with 10000 M-ary neurons for storing and retrieving a very long limit cycle. We specifically used movie clip consisting of 9500 frames (6.3 min). Frames were extracted from the movie clip at a standard rate of 25 frames/s, RGB frames were converted to gray (8 bit encoding) and set to resolution 100×100 using nearest neighbor interpolation to construct a limit cycle; each rasterized frame represents a particular state in the limit cycle. We consider here Hopfield network with $M = 256$; i.e., each neuron can assume any of 256 values at a particular instance. We repeated the experiment with clips from two different movies 'LOR' (Lord of the Rings), 'Finding Nemo' [20] and a clip from a rhyme video. The network was trained using the Dual-Weight learning mentioned in Sect. 3.1 separately for each video clip. The network was triggered multiple times with the start/intermediate frame of the stored clip. The network could retrieve the complete cycle with '0' error. Figure 7(a) shows retrieval of all 9500 frames by giving first frame as the trigger state. Figure 7(b) demonstrates retrieval dynamics in terms of energy transition from one iteration to the next. This represents a first of its kind demonstration of the Hopfield network with limit-cycle behavior, where the system is able to retrieve a complete cycle with minimal cue using associative recall on real world data such as a long movie clip (long gray-scaled image sequence).

Trade Off Analysis Between Length of Cycles and Number of Cycles. We carried out a second experiment to understand the trade off between the number and the length of the cycles which can be stored in and retrieved from the network. For this experiment, we used 'Flickr 30K' data set to construct cycles of varying length starting from 100, 200 up to 2200. Limit cycles were constructed in the similar manner as in previous experiment. The network was

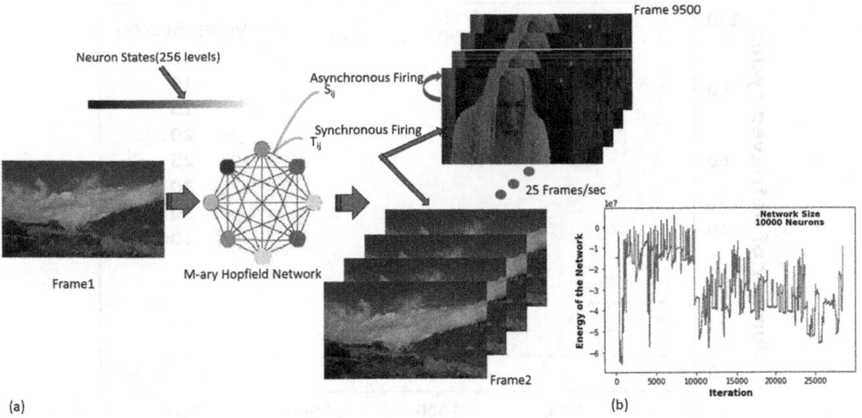

Fig. 7. Retrieval of long limit cycle (a) Limit cycle of duration 6.3 min retrieved when network is triggered with first frame (b) Energy transitions during the retrieval process

trained using the dual weight learning to store 'multiple cycles' with each cycle being of a specific length. The network was triggered with start/intermediate state from each of the cycles, and the retrieved sequence was monitored. This experiment was repeated for cycles of varying length to determine the upper bound on the number of cycles the system supports for a specific length. Figure 8 illustrates storage capacity of network for limit cycles of specific lengths. All retrievals are subjected to '0' error tolerance. For example, the 'blue' line in the figure indicates network can store 100 cycles each of length 100 in a network of 10000 neurons and retrieve all 100 cycles with '0' error. Figure 9 shows storage

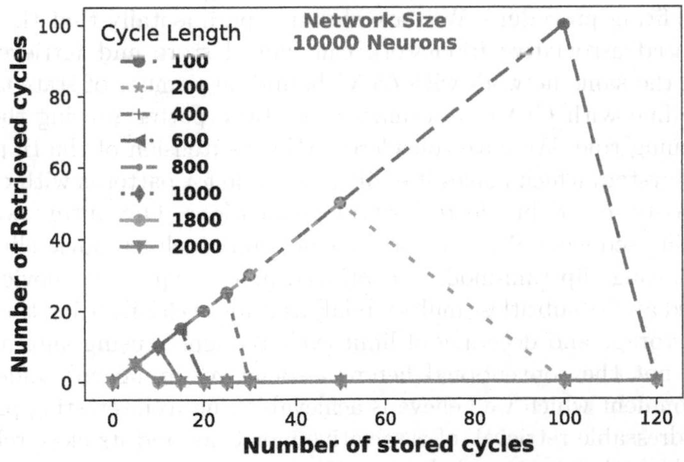

Fig. 8. Trade off between number of cycles and length of cycle supported by M-ary Hopfield associative model: storage capacity for fixed length cycles (Color figure online)

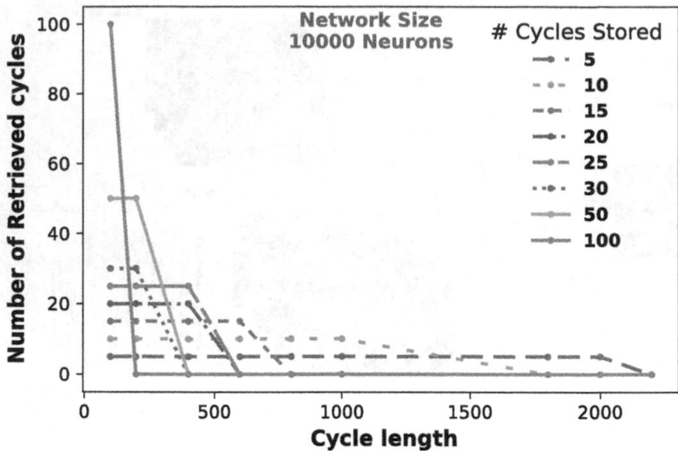

Fig. 9. Trade off between number of cycles and length of cycle supported by M-ary Hopfield associative model: storage capacity as a function of cycle length (Color figure online)

capacity of network as a function of length of the limit cycle. Example 'blue' line here shows network can store and retrieve 5 limit cycles (with 0 tolerance) for $cyclelength = 100, 200, 400, \ldots, 2000$.

5 Conclusion and Future Work

We have examined the performance of Hopfield based network to store and retrieve very long limit cycles using a novel dual weight learning mechanism and a two stage firing procedure. We have shown experimentally that the proposed Hopfield based associative framework can indeed store and retrieve multiple cycles from the same network with $O(N)$ bound on number of state transitions which is in line with $O(N)$ performance for static patterns using the pseudo-inverse learning rule. We have considered M-ary extension of the Hopfield network in our system which makes it easily adaptable for patterns with continuum of values, as observed in the real world applications. Our future works aims at i) modeling sequences in real world applications such as movie clips, spoken dialog, text, song clip (uni-modal), captioned image sequences, movie clip with synchronized audio, subtitles (multi-modal) as limit cycles ii) using the proposed system for storage and decoding of limit cycle sequences using auto-associative recall (and not the conventional hetero associative formalism) under various noisy environment which we believe is achievable due to interesting property of 'content addressable retrieval' of associative memories and its close relationship to the way biological systems behave.

References

1. Roenneberg, T., Chua, E.J., Bernardo, R., Mendoza, E.: Modelling biological rhythms. Curr. Biol. **18**(17), R826–R835 (2008)
2. Hopfield, J.J.: Neural networks and physical systems with emergent collective computational abilities. Proc. Natl. Acad. Sci. **79**(8), 2554–2558 (1982)
3. Hopfield, J.J.: Neurons with graded response have collective computational properties like those of two-state neurons. Proc. Natl. Acad. Sci. **81**(10), 3088–3092 (1984)
4. Haykin, S.: Neural Networks: A Comprehensive Foundation, 2nd edn. Prentice Hall PTR, USA (1998)
5. Ladwani, V.M., Vaishnavi, Y., Ramasubramanian, V.: Hopfield auto-associative memory network for content-based text-retrieval. In: Proceedings of 26th International Conference on Artificial Neural Networks, ICANN-2017, Alghero, Italy (September 2017)
6. Ladwani, V.M., et al.: Hopfield net framework for audio search. In: Proceedings of the 23rd National Conference on Communications (NCC), NCC-2017, pp. 1–6 (2017)
7. Vaishnavi, Y., Shreyas, R., Suhas, S., Surya, U.N., Ladwani, V.M., Ramasubramanian, V.: Associative memory framework for speech recognition: adaptation of hopfield network. In: Proceedings of the IEEE Annual India Conference, INDICON-2016, pp. 1–6 (2016)
8. Shriwas, R., Joshi, P., Ladwani, V.M., Ramasubramanian, V.: Multi-modal Associative Storage and Retrieval Using Hopfield Auto-associative Memory Network. In: Tetko, I.V., Kurková, V., Karpov, P., Theis, F. (eds.) ICANN 2019. LNCS, vol. 11727, pp. 57–75. Springer, Cham (2019). https://doi.org/10.1007/978-3-030-30487-4_5
9. Hebb, D. O. the organization of behavior: a neuropsychological theory. New York: John Wiley and Sons, Inc., 1949. 335 p. Sci. Educ. **34**(5), 336–337 (1950)
10. Wang, D.: The Handbook of Brain Theory and Neural Networks, 2nd edn. Choice Reviews Online, pp. 1163–1167 (2003)
11. Denizdurduran, B.: Attractor Neural Network Approaches in the Memory Modeling (2012)
12. Miyoshi, S., Nakayama, K.: A recurrent neural network with serial delay elements for memorizing limit cycles. In: Proceedings of the International Conference on Neural Networks, ICNN 1995. IEEE (1995)
13. Miyoshi, S., Yanai, H.-F., Okada, M.: Associative memory by recurrent neural networks with delay elements. Neural Netw. **17**(1), 55–63 (2004)
14. Maurer, A., Hersch, M., Billard, A.G.: Extended hopfield network for sequence learning: application to gesture recognition. In: Duch, W., Kacprzyk, J., Oja, E., Zadrożny, S. (eds.) ICANN 2005. LNCS, vol. 3696, pp. 493–498. Springer, Heidelberg (2005). https://doi.org/10.1007/11550822_77
15. Zhang, C., Dangelmayr, G., Oprea, I.: Storing cycles in hopfield-type networks with pseudoinverse learning rule: admissibility and network topology. Neural Netw. **46**, 283–298 (2013)
16. Plummer, B.A., Wang, L., Cervantes, C.M., Caicedo, J.C., Hockenmaier, J., Lazebnik, S.: Flickr30k entities: collecting region-to-phrase correspondences for richer image-to-sentence models. IJCV **123**(1), 74–93 (2017)
17. Bijjani, R., Das, P.: An M-ary neural network model. Neural Comput. **2**(4), 536–551 (1990)

18. Rolls, E.T., Treves, A., Foster, D., Perez-Vicente, C.: Simulation studies of the CA3 hippocampal subfield modelled as an attractor neural network. Neural Netw. **10**(9), 1559–1569 (1997)
19. Personnaz, L., Guyon, I., Dreyfus, G.: Collective computational properties of neural networks: new learning mechanisms. Phys. Rev. A **34**(5), 4217 (1986)
20. Zlatintsi, A., et al.: COGNIMUSE: a multimodal video database annotated with saliency, events, semantics and emotion with application to summarization. EURASIP J. Image Video Process. **2017**(1), 1–24 (2017). https://doi.org/10.1186/s13640-017-0194-1

Training Many-to-Many Recurrent Neural Networks with Target Propagation

Peilun Dai(✉) and Sang Chin

Department of Computer Science, Boston University, Boston, MA 02215, USA
{peilun,spchin}@bu.edu

Abstract. Deep neural networks trained with back-propagation have been the driving force for the progress in fields such as computer vision, natural language processing. However, back-propagation has often been criticized for its biological implausibility. More biologically plausible alternatives to backpropagation such as target propagation and feedback alignment have been proposed. But most of these learning algorithms are originally designed and tested for feedforward networks, and their ability for training recurrent networks and arbitrary computation graphs is not fully studied nor understood. In this paper, we propose a learning procedure based on target propagation for training multi-output recurrent networks. It opens doors to extending such biologically plausible models as general learning algorithms for arbitrary graphs.

Keywords: Artificial neural networks · Recurrent neural networks · Biologically plausible learning · Target propagation · Backpropagation

1 Introduction

Our brain has the amazing ability to use past information to set up our expectations for the future and use the actual perceived information to update synaptic weights to build a better model of the world around us. This type of sequential modelling also has been an important tasks for artificial neural networks. An important sequence model is the *Simple Recurrent Model* (SRN) proposed by [6,9] which has been the basis for many of today's successful sequence models. Usually recurrent neural network (RNN) models are trained by *backpropagation through time* (BPTT) [15,17]. However, there are two major challenges for training recurrent networks with BPTT: First, there is the well known vanishing/exploding gradient problem that the error signal received by earlier steps are either too small or to large due to the long paths of applying chain rules under certain conditions [14]. Second, it is usually considered biologically implausible [5] because it requires symmetric weights for the forward and backward passes, which has not been observed biologically. Other more biologically learning algorithms have been proposed, such as target propagation that utilizes auto-encoders for credit assignment [2,10].

I. Farkaš et al. (Eds.): ICANN 2021, LNCS 12894, pp. 433–443, 2021.
https://doi.org/10.1007/978-3-030-86380-7_35

Target propagation was originally proposed for feedforward neural networks, and there has been work to extend it to training RNNs. In [12], a step-wise inverse function is used to propagate the target activations backward in time, which is termed *Target Propagation Through Time* (TPTT). The authors have shown that target propagation is able to back propagate targets instead of error derivatives over longer ranges than backpropagation can, partially addressing the exploding/vanishing gradient problem. However, It is not straightforward to extend TPTT to RNNs with multiple outputs. For models with multiple loss terms, each loss term would have its own credit assignment path. The error back propagation in backpropagation algorithm is a linear operation, thus, we can add the error derivatives from multiple credit assignment paths and propagate the resulting accumulated derivatives only. However, due to the non-linearity in target propagation's backward pass, we cannot add up the targets from different paths directly. In this paper, we propose a method that could merge the targets from multiple loss terms, and as a result, only the merged targets need to be further propagated. This method is able to generalize target propagation to training RNNs with multiple outputs and potentially to arbitrary computation graphs with multiple credit assignment paths.

In the following section, we will give a brief introduction to backpropagation and target propagation.

2 Background

2.1 Backpropagation Through Time (BPTT)

With the help of backpropagation, recurrent neural network (RNN) models have been widely applied to solve many sequence modeling tasks in domains such as audio signal processing, natural language processing and more. The simplest recurrent network model is the Simple Recurrent Network (SRN) [6], and it is considered a precursor to many of today's state-of-the-art RNN models such as Long Short-Term Memory (LSTM) [8] and Gated Recurrent Unit (GRU) [4].

A single layer of the simple recurrent network is defined by three sets of weights $\{\mathbf{W}_{xh}\}$, $\{\mathbf{W}_h, \mathbf{b}_h\}$ and $\{\mathbf{W}_{hy}, \mathbf{b}_{hy}\}$ and an activation function for the hidden layer, such as $ReLU(\cdot)$ and $tanh(\cdot)$. Depending on the tasks, an RNN may need to produce an output at each step (many-to-many) for tasks such as language modeling and part-of-speech (POS) tagging, or may only produce one output at the last step (many-to-one) for tasks such as customer review sentiment classification. For a typical many-to-many task, the inference step is defined by a forward pass in time through the following equations for $t = 1, 2, \ldots, T$,

$$\mathbf{h}_t = \sigma_h(\mathbf{W}_h \mathbf{h}_{t-1} + \mathbf{W}_{xh} \mathbf{x}_t + \mathbf{b}_t) \tag{1}$$

$$\mathbf{y}_t = \sigma_y(\mathbf{W}_{hy} \mathbf{h}_t + \mathbf{b}_{hy}) \tag{2}$$

where $\sigma_h(\cdot)$ is the hidden activation function and σ_y is the output activation function, such as $softmax(\cdot)$ for outputting a categorical distribution for multi-class classification tasks.

When such a model is trained by backpropagation (more accurately, gradient descent, but hereafter, we will refer to the training process simply as backpropagation), it needs to be "unrolled" in time with shared weights across time steps, and then normal backpropagation can be applied to obtain the gradients of the loss with respect to all trainable weights. This way of back-propagating errors back in time is usually called *backpropagation through time* (BPTT).

BPTT works well for modeling short sequences. However, when it is applied directly to long sequences, due to the long range dependencies between inputs and outputs, it usually fails to propagate gradients across long distances due to the so-called *exploding/vanishing gradient* problem [1,14].

In order to solve this problem, more complex model architectures, such as LSTM [8] and GRU [4], and variants of BPTT, such as Truncated BPTT, gradient clipping and regularization [14] have been proposed. All these methods still use backpropagation at its core, but utilize different ad hoc tricks to make the long range credit assignment work.

Another problem with BPTT is its biological-implausibility. There is little evidence from brain research that supports backpropagation as the learning algorithm for biological learning. The main incompatibilities between backpropagation and our current understanding of biological learning include:

- Backpropagation requires precise knowledge of the non-linearity in the corresponding forward pass. But in biological learning, the feedback paths (if exist) usually consist of a different population of neurons, which makes it hard to match the feedforward counterpart.
- In the backward pass, backpropagation uses the exact symmetric weights of the forward pass (the weight transport problem [11]).
- Current mainstream neural network models use real-valued activations to convey information while most biological neurons use spikes to communicate.
- Backpropagation requires alternating between forward and backward passes.

Other more biologically plausible alternatives have been proposed mainly for feedforward networks. These models include feedback alignment (FA) and its variants [11,13], energy-based models such as equilibrium propagation [7,16] and free energy models [3]. Below, we will give a short introduction to such an algorithm, target propagation [2,10] which uses auto-encoders for credit assignment. In a later section, we will introduce our proposed method to extend target propagation to training multiple-output RNNs.

2.2 Target Propagation

Target propagation is a learning algorithm that uses learned inverse functions between layers to back-propagate activations instead of error derivatives [2,10].

For a multi-layer supervised feed-forward network being trained input $\mathbf{x}$ and label $\mathbf{t}$, we denote the hidden value at the i-th layer as $\mathbf{h}_i$, the feedforward pass sets the activations $\mathbf{h}_i$ for $i = 1, 2, \ldots, M$ where M is the depth of the network and $\mathbf{h}_M$ is the output of the network. The relationships between the activations are defined by

$$\mathbf{h}_i = f_i\left(\mathbf{h}_{i-1}\right) = s_i\left(\mathbf{W}_i\mathbf{h}_{i-1} + \mathbf{b}_i\right), \quad i = 1, \ldots, M \tag{3}$$

where s_i is a non-linear activation function such as $sigmoid(\cdot)$, $ReLU(\cdot)$, W_i and b_i are the parameters for $f_i(\cdot)$, the forward function at layer i, and $\mathbf{h}_0$ and $\mathbf{h}_M$ are the input $\mathbf{x}$ and output of the network respectively. Let's denote the parameters between the i-th layer and j-th layer $(0 \leq i < j \leq M)$ as $\theta^{i,j} = \{(\mathbf{W}_k, \mathbf{b}_k), k = i+1, \ldots, j\}$. Since $\mathbf{h}_j$ is a function of $\mathbf{h}_i$, their relationship can be written as $\mathbf{h}_j = \mathbf{h}_j(\mathbf{h}_i; \theta^{i,j})$. Then a loss function $L(\mathbf{h}_M(\mathbf{x}; \theta^{0,M}), \mathbf{t})$ is defined for the output of the network $\mathbf{h}_M$ with respect to the given label $\mathbf{t}$.

Instead of back-propagating error derivatives, if for each hidden value $\mathbf{h}_i$, we have a nearby target $\hat{\mathbf{h}}_i$ that would make the loss smaller, that is

$$L(\mathbf{h}_M(\hat{\mathbf{h}}_i; \theta^{i,M}), \mathbf{t}) < L\big(\mathbf{h}_M(\mathbf{h}_i(\mathbf{x}; \theta^{0,i}); \theta^{i,M}), \mathbf{t}\big), \tag{4}$$

then during training, we can simply update the parameters such that the hidden values get closer to the layer-wise local targets, thus decreasing the prediction loss. The local optimization problem can be set up by defining a loss function for each layer $i = 1, 2, \ldots, M$,

$$L_i(\mathbf{h}_i, \hat{\mathbf{h}}_i) = L_i(\mathbf{h}_i(\mathbf{x}; \theta^{0,i}), \hat{\mathbf{h}}_i). \tag{5}$$

We can update the weights at each layer with

$$\mathbf{W}_i \leftarrow \mathbf{W}_i - \eta_i \frac{\partial L_i(\mathbf{h}_i, \hat{\mathbf{h}}_i)}{\partial \mathbf{h}_i} \frac{\partial \mathbf{h}_i}{\mathbf{W}_i} \tag{6}$$

$$\mathbf{b}_i \leftarrow \mathbf{b}_i - \eta_i \frac{\partial L_i(\mathbf{h}_i, \hat{\mathbf{h}}_i)}{\partial \mathbf{h}_i} \frac{\partial \mathbf{h}_i}{\mathbf{b}_i} \tag{7}$$

where η_i is a layer-specific learning rate.

We then needs to define the target at the output layer.

$$\hat{\mathbf{h}}_M = \mathbf{h}_M - \hat{\eta} \frac{\partial L(\mathbf{h}_M, \mathbf{t})}{\partial \mathbf{h}_M} \tag{8}$$

where $\hat{\eta}$ is the learning rate to control how close the target is to the output. Note that although we need the derivative to define the last target, we don't need to use the chain rule as in backpropagation. To define the targets for intermediate layers, we need to use an approximate inverse functions $g_i(\cdot)$ at each layer which satisfies

$$f_i(g_i(\mathbf{h}_i)) \approx \mathbf{h}_i \quad \text{or} \tag{9}$$

$$g_i(f_i(\mathbf{h}_{i-1})) \approx \mathbf{h}_{i-1}. \tag{10}$$

These inverse functions could be obtained by training auto-encoders between adjacent layers. Once $g_i(\cdot)$ is defined for each layer, the target for earlier layers $\hat{\mathbf{h}}_i, i = M-1, M-2, \ldots, 1)$ can be obtained using

$$\hat{\mathbf{h}}_i = g_{i+1}(\hat{\mathbf{h}}_{i+1}). \tag{11}$$

or a linearly corrected version of it,

$$\hat{\mathbf{h}}_i = \mathbf{h}_i + g_{i+1}(\hat{\mathbf{h}}_{i+1}) - g_{i+1}(\mathbf{h}_{i+1}). \tag{12}$$

This linearly corrected version of target propagation is called *Difference Target Propagation* [10]. In this paper, we always use the linearly corrected version if not stated otherwise.

In the next section, we will introduce a generalization of target propagation through time for RNNs with multiple outputs and multiple credit assignment paths.

3 Generalizing Target Propagation for RNNs with Multiple Outputs

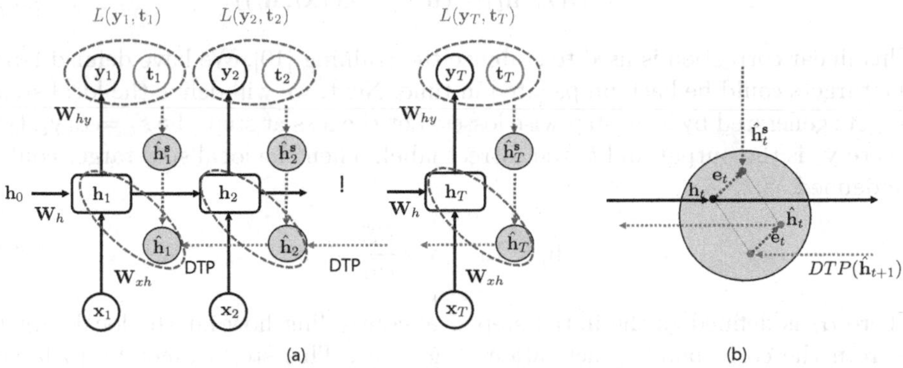

Fig. 1. (a) Propagation of merged targets back in time. For step t, $\mathbf{h}_t$ is the forward activation $\hat{\mathbf{h}}_t^s$ is the step target set with respect to the step loss $L(\mathbf{y}_t, \mathbf{t}_t)$ and $\hat{\mathbf{h}}_t$ is the updated step target used for training obtained by merging the step target and back-propagated target from future time steps. (b) Merging step target and back propagating target linearly. This merging step ensures that only one target is propagated back in time, similar to backpropagation in which the step gradients are accumulated when being back propagated.

We first need to define a simple RNN model by specifying its forward path,

$$\mathbf{h}_t = F(\mathbf{x}_t, \mathbf{h}_{t-1}) \tag{13}$$

$$= \sigma(\mathbf{W}_{xh} \cdot \mathbf{x}_t + \mathbf{W}_h \cdot \mathbf{h}_{t-1} + \mathbf{b}_h) \tag{14}$$

$$\mathbf{y}_t = \text{softmax}(\mathbf{W}_{hy} \cdot \mathbf{h}_t + \mathbf{b}_y) \tag{15}$$

where $\mathbf{W}_{xh}, \mathbf{W}_h, \mathbf{b}_h, \mathbf{W}_{hy}$ and $\mathbf{b}_y$ are the model parameters. Similar to TPTT [12], we also define a step-wise approximate inverse function,

$$\mathbf{h}_{t-1} \approx G(\mathbf{x}_t, \mathbf{h}_t) \tag{16}$$

$$= \sigma(\mathbf{V}_h \cdot \mathbf{h}_t + \mathbf{W}_{xh} \cdot \mathbf{x}_t + \mathbf{c}_h). \tag{17}$$

This approximate inverse function can be trained as the decoder of an auto-encoder, i.e. trained to reconstruct $\mathbf{h}_{t-1}$ from $\mathbf{h}_t$. In order for the proposed method to work well, and more generally for target propagation to work well, the inverse functions need to be good enough with the linear correction. It can be trained as a denoising auto-encoder [10] so that it works well in the neighborhood of the forward activations. In addition, we can also use a more complex function such as a two-layer neural network to approximate the inverse function, but in training, this requires the use of chain rule. In our derivation above, we choose the inverse function to be in the same form as the forward step function.

If the target at step t is $\hat{\mathbf{h}}_t$, then we can use difference target propagation (DTP) and the approximate inverse function $G(\cdot)$ to define the target at step $t-1$ as

$$\hat{\mathbf{h}}_{t-1} = \mathrm{DTP}(\hat{\mathbf{h}}_t) \tag{18}$$

$$= G(\mathbf{x}_t, \hat{\mathbf{h}}_t) + (\mathbf{h}_{t-1} - G(\mathbf{x}_t, \mathbf{h}_t)) \tag{19}$$

This linear correction is used to stabilize the training [10]. We have defined how the targets could be back propagated in time. Next, we will define the local step targets generated by local step-wise losses. Let the loss at step t be $\mathcal{E}_t = L(\mathbf{y}_t, \mathbf{t}_t)$ where $\mathbf{y}_t$ is the output and $\mathbf{t}_t$ the correct label. Then the local step target could be defined as

$$\hat{\mathbf{h}}_t^{\mathrm{s}} = \mathbf{h}_t - \alpha_i \cdot \frac{\partial \mathcal{E}_t}{\partial \mathbf{h}_t} \tag{20}$$

where α_i is defined as the initial step size, controlling how far the local target is from the corresponding activation (Fig. 1(a)). This step cannot be to large because the inverse functions can only work well in the neighborhood of the forward activations. Once the local step-wise targets have been defined, we then need a way to merge these local targets while the targets are being back propagated, i.e., defining the relationship between $\hat{\mathbf{h}}_t$ and $\hat{\mathbf{h}}_t^{\mathrm{s}}$.

Unlike backpropagation, in target propagation, the backward pass, like the forward pass, are non-linear, so it is hard to define a merging strategy that would make target propagation approximate backpropagation exactly. Thus, we simplify this target merging process by making it linear (Fig. 1(b)),

$$\mathbf{e}_t = \hat{\mathbf{h}}_t^{\mathrm{s}} - \mathbf{h}_t \tag{21}$$

$$\hat{h}_t = \mathrm{DTP}(\hat{h}_{t+1}) + \mathbf{e}_t \tag{22}$$

The above target merging rule has an intuitive interpretation: as the back propagating target passes through the backward path, it accumulates local errors similar to how backpropagation accumulates gradients during backward pass, but in a non-linear way. Once the merged step targets $\hat{\mathbf{h}}_t$ are defined for each step after the backward target propagation pass, we can define a local loss term (e.g., using MSE$(\cdot)$) for updating the weights $\mathbf{W}_{xh}$, $\mathbf{W}_h$ and $\mathbf{b}_h$ respectively,

$$\mathbf{W}_h \leftarrow \mathbf{W}_h - \alpha_f \sum_{t=1}^{T} \frac{\partial \operatorname{MSE}\left(F\left(\mathbf{x}_t, \mathbf{h}_{t-1}\right), \hat{\mathbf{h}}_t\right)}{\partial \mathbf{W}_{hh}} \tag{23}$$

$$\mathbf{b}_h \leftarrow \mathbf{b}_h - \alpha_f \sum_{t=1}^{T} \frac{\partial \operatorname{MSE}\left(F\left(\mathbf{x}_t, \mathbf{h}_{t-1}\right), \hat{\mathbf{h}}_t\right)}{\partial \mathbf{b}_h}. \tag{24}$$

Since the weights are shared across time steps, the updates applied to the weights are the sum of the updates cross all time steps. Note that this optimization problem is local and doesn't require chain rule as in backpropagation.

4 Experiments

4.1 Tasks

Copy Memory Task. In order to test the capability of the proposed method in training recurrent neural networks and understand its limitations, we first used the copy memory task commonly used to test the models' ability to retain information over long ranges. The first 10 elements in the input sequence are drawn uniformly randomly from k symbols, and it is then followed by $T - 1$ blank symbol. A special symbol is followed to indicate that the model should start to recall the first 10 elements in the input, which is followed by another 10 blank symbols. For the correct output, the first $(T + 10)$ elements should be blank symbols. When it receives the start recall symbol from input at the $(T + 10)$-th position, it will output the first 10 elements of the input as its last 10 elements. If, instead of 10 elements, we only consider memorizing the first 3 elements as an example, with a delay $T = 3$, the input and corresponding correct output will be $\{a, c, b, \_, \_, *, \_, \_, \_\}$ and $\{\_, \_, \_, \_, \_, \_, a, c, b\}$ where "$*$" is the start recalling signal symbol and "_" is the blank symbol. In this task, the information of the first 10 elements of the input should be kept in the model for at least T steps. Thus, as we increase the delay T, it is harder and harder for the network to recall the first 10 elements.

The model we use is a simple recurrent neural network model with 128 hidden units and $tanh(\cdot)$ activation function. We use $k = 8$ symbols for the 10 elements to be memorized and use another two special symbols as the start recalling signal symbol and blank symbol. All symbols are one-hot encoded.

In this task, a memory-less baseline method is to output blank spaces until receiving the start recalling symbol, and then output 10 random symbols. For this strategy, the expected cross-entropy loss can be calculated as $\frac{10\ln(8)}{T+20}$, which will be used as a baseline when comparing the training losses by different optimization methods. Performance at this baseline means that the recalled sequence is random and information of the first 10 elements in the input sequence has been lost.

At each delay T, we perform a hyper-parameter search to find the best learning rates for backpropagation and the proposed target propagation respectively. With a mini-batch size of 20, we generate training batches on the fly for a total of 25000 batches in total, and use the same validation set of 500 batches for validation. After training for 25000 batches in total, we report the best validation loss and accuracy.

Table 1. Results for the copy memory task using proposed target propagation method and backpropagation. The baseline is calculated using $\frac{10\ln(8)}{20+T}$. The accuracy is the percentage of correctly predicted sequences. For example, with a delay of 5 (total sequence length = 25), a baseline model that outputs random symbols in the last 10 steps and blank elsewhere will have an accuracy of $\frac{1}{8^{10}} \approx 9.31 \times 10^{-10}$ in expectation. It can be shown that our proposed target propagation managed to get a much lower loss than baseline with high recovery accuracy up to a delay of 25 steps. Backpropagation can only get loss close to the baseline, not able to propagate information for long ranges. These two methods use the same weight initialization method.

Delay (T)	Target prop		Backprop		Baseline
	Loss	Accuracy	Loss	Accuracy	Baseline loss
5	3.59×10^{-3}	100%	0.6899	0%	0.8318
10	1.30×10^{-3}	100%	0.5809	0%	0.6931
15	1.34×10^{-4}	99.99%	0.5182	0%	0.5941
20	5.70×10^{-3}	98.32%	0.5205	0%	0.5199
25	1.36×10^{-2}	92.88%	0.4625	0%	0.4621

Table 2. Results for the sequence expansion task using proposed target propagation method and backpropagation.

Sequence length (T)	Target prop		Backprop	
	Loss	Accuracy	Loss	Accuracy
10	0.0005	100.00%	0.0001	100%
20	0.0018	99.34%	0.0005	100%
30	0.3233	3.62%	0.0007	100%
40	1.0771	0%	0.0012	99.49%

The result is shown in Table 1. The accuracy is the percentage of correct sequence predictions in the validation set. As we can see, our proposed target propagation method managed to beat the baseline and achieve a high prediction accuracy until a delay of at least 25 steps. Backpropagation can only achieve a loss at a similar level as the memory-less baseline, and with an accuracy of 0%, it cannot output a single correct sequence out of the 10000 validation samples.

This results shows that target propagation is able to propagate error information over long range while backpropagation cannot. In order to see if this is due to the exploding/vanishing gradient problem, we computed the spectral radius

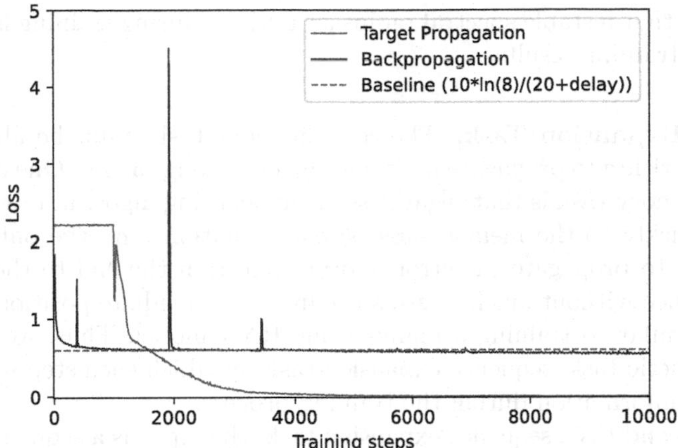

Fig. 2. The training loss of backpropagation and the proposed target propagation method for the copy memory task with a delay of 15 steps. Each step is a single weight update with a mini-batch of training examples. The baseline loss is from a memory-less strategy: outputting blanks until receiving the start-recall symbol, followed by a random sequence of 10 symbols. In target propagation, the first 1000 steps are used to train inverse function only, thus the loss doesn't change.

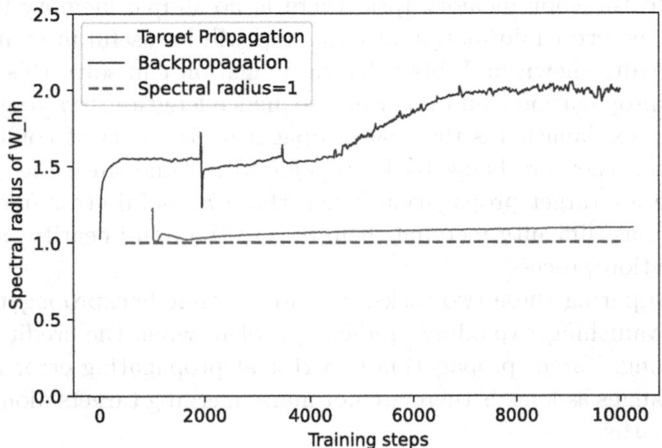

Fig. 3. The spectral radius of the transition weight matrix $\mathbf{W}_h$ during learning for proposed target propagation method and backpropagation.

of the hidden-to-hidden transition weight matrix $\mathbf{W}_h$ defined as the magnitude of the largest eigenvalue. From Fig.3, we can see that the spectral radius of the transition weight matrix $\mathbf{W}_h$ stays relatively stable around value 1.0 for target propagation. However, the spectral radius of the matrix during backpropagation is not stable and deviates significantly from 1.0. Although this figure only shows the spectral radius for one trial, this applies to other trials as well. In addition, we observed that a stable spectral radius around 1.0 during training is correlated with better training results.

Sequence Expansion Task. The copy memory task tests the ability of the learning algorithm to propagate information across long ranges. One drawback of the copy memory task is that regardless of the learning algorithm we use, it will converge quickly to the memory-less baseline solution, and the only challenge remaining is to propagate the error information from the end to the beginning of the sequence without much interference from intermediate positions along the sequence, similar to training a many-to-one RNN model. Thus, we designed a second synthetic task, sequence expansion task, in which each step will generate useful error information during the training process.

In the second task, sequence expansion task, the input is a sequence of length T. The first $T/2$ elements are drawn uniformly randomly from a set of k symbols, and the second half are all blanks represented by a special blank symbol. The task is to duplicate each element of the first half exactly once. For example, the correct output of the input sequence $\{a, c, b, *, *, *\}$ will be $\{a, a, c, c, b, b\}$. The output will have the same length as the input but without blanks. As the sequence length T increases, in order to make correct prediction, the model needs to memorize the $(T/2)$-th element in the input for at least $(T/2-1)$ steps. In contrast to the copy memory task, there is no simple memory-less baseline method and the error information at each step will be useful in training.

As the results shown in Table 2, backpropagation can solve this task easily, while target propagation could not when sequence length grows to greater than 30. The likely explanation is that backpropagation is better at combining error gradients when they are being back propagated in time since the operation is linear. While for target propagation, when there is useful error information at each step, it has difficulty merging them due to the non-linearity in the target back propagation process.

When comparing these two tasks, we can see that backpropagation usually suffers from vanishing/exploding gradient problem when the credit assignment path is too long. Target propagation is better at propagating error information across long ranges as long as there are not many merging targets along the credit assignment paths.

5 Conclusions

In this paper, we generalized target propagation to training recurrent neural networks with multiple outputs and showed that it is better at propagating long range error information compared to backpropagation, which usually suffers from the exploding/vanishing gradient problem. However, when the tasks involve many credit assignment paths that needs to be merged, such as the case in the sequence expansion task, backpropagation generally performs better. This might be due to the linear nature of backpropagation when the derivatives could be simply added along the backward pass. A potential future improvement for target propagation for RNN could be truncating the propagating targets at every a few steps, similar to truncated BPTT. The linear merging operation in the proposed method could potentially be replaced by a single many-to-one inverse function that only produce one output without the need for merging the targets explicitly. In principle, the proposed method could potentially be applied to learning in arbitrary computation graphs when there might be intersecting credit assignment paths.

References

1. Bengio, Y., Simard, P., Frasconi, P.: Learning long-term dependencies with gradient descent is difficult. IEEE Trans. Neural Netw. **5**(2), 157–166 (1994)
2. Bengio, Y.: How Auto-Encoders could provide credit assignment in deep networks via target propagation. ArXiv (July 2014)
3. Bogacz, R.: A tutorial on the free-energy framework for modelling perception and learning. J. Math. Psychol. **76**(Pt B), 198–211 (2017)
4. Chung, J., Gulcehre, C., Cho, K., Bengio, Y.: Empirical evaluation of gated recurrent neural networks on sequence modeling. ArXiv (December 2014)
5. Crick, F.: The recent excitement about neural networks. Nature **337**(6203), 129–132 (1989)
6. Elman, J.L.: Finding structure in time. Cogn. Sci. **14**(2), 179–211 (1990)
7. Ernoult, M., Grollier, J., Querlioz, D., Bengio, Y., Scellier, B.: Equilibrium propagation with continual weight updates. ArXiv (April 2020)
8. Hochreiter, S., Schmidhuber, J.: Long short-term memory. Neural Comput. **9**(8), 1735–1780 (1997)
9. Jordan, M.I.: Chapter 25 - serial order: A parallel distributed processing approach. In: Donahoe, J.W., Packard Dorsel, V. (eds.) Advances in Psychology, vol. 121, pp. 471–495. North-Holland (January 1997)
10. Lee, D.-H., Zhang, S., Fischer, A., Bengio, Y.: Difference target propagation. In: Appice, A., Rodrigues, P.P., Santos Costa, V., Soares, C., Gama, J., Jorge, A. (eds.) ECML PKDD 2015. LNCS (LNAI), vol. 9284, pp. 498–515. Springer, Cham (2015). https://doi.org/10.1007/978-3-319-23528-8_31
11. Lillicrap, T.P., Cownden, D., Tweed, D.B., Akerman, C.J.: Random feedback weights support learning in deep neural networks. ArXiv (November 2014)
12. Manchev, N., Spratling, M.W.: Target propagation in recurrent neural networks. J. Mach. Learn. Res. **21**(7), 1–33 (2020)
13. Nøkland, A.: Direct feedback alignment provides learning in deep neural networks. In: Advances in Neural Information Processing Systems, pp. 1037–1045 (2016)
14. Pascanu, R., Mikolov, T., Bengio, Y.: Understanding the exploding gradient problem. ArXiv (2012)
15. Rumelhart, D.E., McClelland, J.L.: Learning internal representations by error propagation. In: Parallel Distributed Processing: Explorations in the Microstructure of Cognition: Foundations, pp. 318–362. MIT Press (1987)
16. Scellier, B., Bengio, Y.: Equilibrium propagation: bridging the gap between energy-based models and backpropagation. Front. Comput. Neurosci. **11**, 24 (2017)
17. Werbos, P.J.: Backpropagation through time: what it does and how to do it. Proc. IEEE **78**(10), 1550–1560 (1990)

Early Recognition of Ball Catching Success in Clinical Trials with RNN-Based Predictive Classification

Jana Lang[1(✉)], Martin A. Giese[1], Matthis Synofzik[2], Winfried Ilg[1], and Sebastian Otte[3]

[1] Section for Computational Sensomotorics, Department of Cognitive Neurology, Centre for Integrative Neuroscience & Hertie Institute for Clinical Brain Research, University Clinic Tübingen, Tübingen, Germany
jana.lang@uni-tuebingen.de

[2] Department of Neurodegeneration, Hertie Institute for Clinical Brain Research & Centre for Neurology, University Clinic Tübingen, Tübingen, Germany

[3] Neuro-Cognitive Modeling Group, University of Tübingen, Tübingen, Germany

Abstract. Motor disturbances can affect the interaction with dynamic objects, such as catching a ball. A classification of clinical catching trials might give insight into the existence of pathological alterations in the relation of arm and ball movements. Accurate, but also early decisions are required to classify a catching attempt before the catcher's first ball contact. To obtain clinically valuable results, a significant decision confidence of at least 75% is required. Hence, three competing objectives have to be optimized at the same time: accuracy, earliness and decision-making confidence. Here we propose a coupled classification and prediction approach for early time series classification: a predictive, generative recurrent neural network (RNN) forecasts the next data points of ball trajectories based on already available observations; a discriminative RNN continuously generates classification guesses based on the available data points and the unrolled sequence predictions. We compare our approach, which we refer to as *predictive sequential classification* (PSC), to state-of-the-art sequence learners, including various RNN and temporal convolutional network (TCN) architectures. On this hard real-world task we can consistently demonstrate the superiority of PSC over all other models in terms of accuracy and confidence with respect to earliness of recognition. Specifically, PSC is able to confidently classify the success of catching trials as early as 123 ms before the first ball contact. We conclude that PSC is a promising approach for early time series classification, when accurate and confident decisions are required.

Keywords: Early time series classification · Recurrent neural networks (RNN) · Temporal convolutional networks (TCN) · Clinical movement control

---

W. Ilg and S. Otte—Shared authors.

I. Farkaš et al. (Eds.): ICANN 2021, LNCS 12894, pp. 444–456, 2021.
https://doi.org/10.1007/978-3-030-86380-7_36

1 Introduction

Patients suffering from neurodegenerative or neurodevelopmental disorders, including Spinocerebellar Ataxia and Autism Spectrum Disorder, are often impaired in the interaction with dynamic objects, for instance when catching a ball. Ball catching requires an intact perception-action coupling and the ability to anticipate the trajectory of an oncoming ball [16]. It is suggested that dysfunctions of predictive control which result in alterations of preparatory arm movements are the leading cause of catching impairments in these diseases [5]. In this paper, we aim to recognize changes in the relation of arm and ball movements that are predictive for the success of catching trials before the first ball contact of the catcher. To ensure clinically valuable results, we choose a confidence threshold of 75% which is commonly used for two-alternative forced choice tasks in psychophysical studies [14].

Hence, the problem at hand can be formulated as an *early time series classification* task with increased confidence requirements. Early time series classification is referred to as making classifications as early as possible, while maintaining a high classification accuracy [13]. It naturally evokes a trade-off between earliness and accuracy of classifications. Different approaches have been applied to the problem of early time series classification, including convolutional neural networks and reinforcement learning [9,15]. Surprisingly, despite the widespread application of recurrent neural network (RNN) models to sequential problems, they have rarely been used for the early classification of time series. Recent work, however, suggests that gated recurrent units can handle missing values in multivariate time series [3]. Moreover, first promising results have been achieved applying long short-term memory (LSTM) models for early classification in agricultural monitoring [12]. These approaches leave aside the confidence of decision-making, which is an important factor in various applications.

Recently, it has been shown that predictive RNNs can be employed to efficiently generate goal-directed, anticipatory behavior to support decision-making [11]. Therefore, we present a novel RNN-based approach that simultaneously optimizes accuracy, confidence and earliness in time series classification. Our approach, which we refer to as *predictive sequential classification* (PSC), incorporates two different specialized RNN models into one coupled arrangement. The first model, a predictive, generative RNN, forecasts the next data points of a time series based on already available observations. The second model, a discriminative RNN, continuously generates classification guesses based on the available data points and the unrolled sequence predictions of the first model. We compare our approach to several state-of-the-art sequence learners, including various RNN and temporal convolutional network (TCN) architectures using a motion dataset containing two-dimensional trajectories of healthy and pathological ball catching attempts. At test time, all models are confronted with incomplete catching trials of different lengths. We evaluate all architectures with regard to the accuracy of the final decision, the level of decision confidence, and the earliness of decision-making.

2 Predictive Sequential Classification

Time series classification describes the task of assigning one of two (binary classification) or one of multiple (multi-class classification) labels to a time series S, where S is defined as an ordered, uniformly spaced temporal sequence of T vectors [4]:

$$S = (\mathbf{x}^1, \mathbf{x}^2, \ldots, \mathbf{x}^T) \tag{1}$$

The here considered time series are *multivariate*, i.e. they contain more than one feature for each time step. When processing time series, two different types of processing modes can generally be distinguished. The first mode, called *many-to-one* (MTO) processing, takes an input sequence and outputs a single class label after consuming the entire input sequence. *Many-to-many* (MTM) processing, on the other hand, produces a class label for multiple steps (typically for every time step) of the input sequence, i.e. both input and output are sequences. In contrast to other types of neural networks, sequence learners, such as the recurrent neural network (RNN), expect the data to be temporally highly correlated and in sequential order [6]. By introducing circular connections (*recurrences*), RNNs allow past inputs to influence future time steps. However, in practical applications, vanilla RNNs are largely replaced by long short-term memory (LSTM) networks. This extension of RNNs overcomes the vanishing gradient problem and makes the learning of long-term dependencies possible [7].

Early time series classification is targeted at making accurate classifications based on incomplete, instead of full-length time series. To compensate for the missing time interval we propose a novel RNN-based approach to early time series classification that equips a sequence classifier with predictive power. The *predictive sequential classification* (PSC) approach entails both a predictive, generative LSTM that forecasts the next data points of a time series based on already available observations, as well as a discriminative LSTM, which continuously generates classification guesses based on the available data points and the unrolled sequence predictions. Both models are trained separately on their respective tasks. At test time the models come together to make a predictive classification guess.

With every incoming observation $\mathbf{x}^t$, the amount of available observations increases. Based on these data points, the predictor sequentially forecasts the remaining $T - t$ data points of the time series. Each predicted observation $\tilde{\mathbf{x}}^t$ is used to make a predictive classification. Finally, the classification output $\mathbf{y}_c^t$ is updated with the last predictive classification $\mathbf{y}_c^T$ (Algorithm 1). For every history size, the classifier aggregates already available observations and predicted observations to make a predictive classification guess. When all data points of the time series are available, PSC defaults to a vanilla sequence classifier (Fig. 1). In the following experiments, we show that PSC is superior to state-of-the-art sequence classifiers for the task of early and confident time series classification. In an additional study, we investigate the importance of the two-model design for PSC, revealing that directly including a predictive objective into a single model even harms the classification performance.

Algorithm 1: Predictive Sequential Classification

/* *Initialize hidden states* */
$\mathbf{h}_c^0 \leftarrow \mathbf{0}, \mathbf{h}_p^0 \leftarrow \mathbf{0}$ /* *Loop over incoming observations* */
for $t \leftarrow 1$ **to** T **do**
  /* *Update classifier and predictor with current input* */
  $\mathbf{y}_c^t, \mathbf{h}_c^t \leftarrow f_c(\mathbf{x}^t, \mathbf{h}_c^{t-1})$
  $\tilde{\mathbf{x}}^{t+1}, \mathbf{h}_p^t \leftarrow f_p(\mathbf{x}^t, \mathbf{h}_p^{t-1})$
  /* *Unroll sequence prediction and predictive classification* */
  for $t' \leftarrow t+1$ **to** T **do**
    $\mathbf{y}_c^{t'}, \mathbf{h}_c^{t'} \leftarrow f_c(\tilde{\mathbf{x}}^{t'}, \mathbf{h}_c^{t'-1})$
    $\tilde{\mathbf{x}}^{t'+1}, \mathbf{h}_p^{t'} \leftarrow f_p(\tilde{\mathbf{x}}^{t'}, \mathbf{h}_p^{t'-1})$
  end for
  /* *Use predictive classification as current classifier output* */
  $\mathbf{y}_c^t \leftarrow \mathbf{y}_c^T$
end for

Variables:

t	: current time step	$\mathbf{h}_c^t$	: the classifier's hidden state
t'	: time step within prediction loop	$\mathbf{h}_p^t$	: the predictor's hidden state
T	: sequence length	f_c	: the classifier's forward pass function
$\mathbf{x}^t$	: observation at time t	f_p	: the predictor's forward pass function
$\tilde{\mathbf{x}}^t$	: predicted observation for time t	$\mathbf{y}_c^t$	: classification output for time t

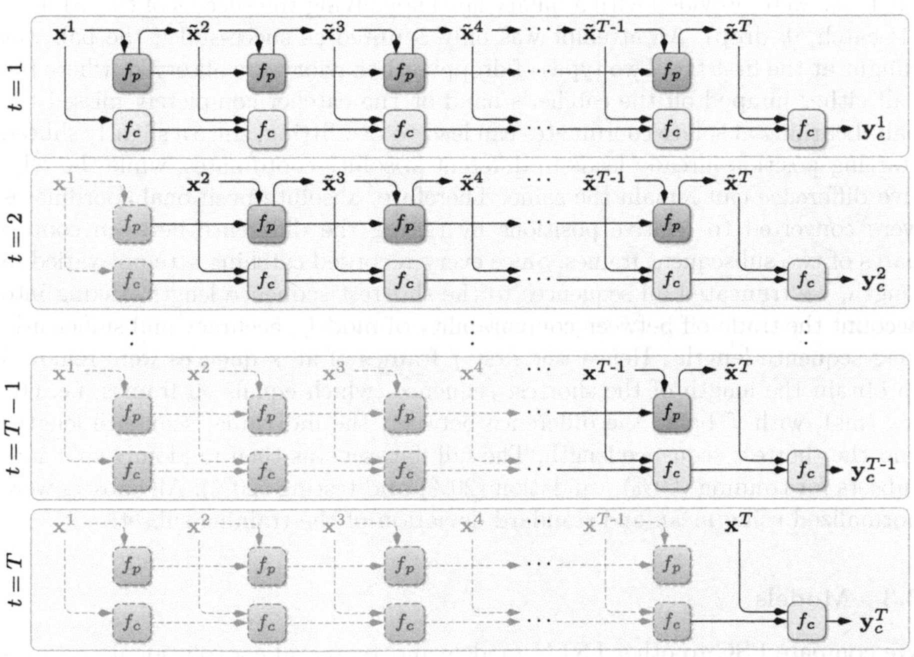

Fig. 1. Predictive sequential classification. A predictive RNN forecasts the remaining trajectories based on past observations. The classifier combines both to make informed classification guesses. Grayed out boxes indicate previously computed states.

3 Experimental Setup

3.1 Data

We recorded 63 videos of one-handed ball catching attempts by 11 healthy subjects, 13 children with Autism Spectrum Disorder and 10 patients with Spinocerebellar Ataxia at the Outpatient Clinic of Neurology and the Child and Adolescent Psychiatry in Tübingen. All experiments were admitted by the ethical committee of the University Clinic of Tübingen. Of the 1975 recorded catching trials, 1082 attempts were successful, and 893 attempts were unsuccessful. 965 trials were caught with the right hand and 1010 trials with the left hand. Videos were recorded at a frame rate of 100 frames per second. The two-dimensional position of the catcher's arm and hand joints and the trajectory of the ball were captured with two deep learning frameworks for pose estimation [2,10]. We extracted 18 hand and arm features describing the motion of the shoulder, the elbow, the wrist, the ball of the hand, each fingertip on the relevant body side, and two features specifying the ball center for each video frame.

3.2 Preprocessing

A Savitzky-Golay filter was applied to the arm and hand marker trajectories between the start and the end of each trial to smooth flickering noise. All catching trials were provided with a binary label specifying the success of the attempt (1: catch, 0: drop). An attempt was only counted as successful if the ball was caught at the first try. Two types of dropping behavior were observed, where the ball either jumped off the catcher's hand or the catcher completely missed the ball. Learning absolute coordinates can lead to overfitting, since a slightly shifted starting position already leads to different absolute coordinates, while the relative difference can remain the same. Therefore, absolute positional coordinates were converted to relative positions by taking the difference between coordinates of two subsequent frames. Since every recorded catching attempt varied in length, we truncated all sequences to the shortest sequence length, taking into account the trade-off between comparability of models, accuracy and sufficiently long sequence lengths. Hence, the first f frames of all sequences were removed to obtain the length of the shortest sequence, which equals 60 frames, i.e. 600 ms (ms), with f being the difference between the individual sequence lengths and the shortest sequence length. The full dataset was then randomly split into subsets for training (60%), validation (20%) and testing (20%). All subsets were normalized using mean and standard deviation of the training subset.

3.3 Models

We compare PSC to other LSTM models and temporal convolutional networks (TCN) [1,7]. All models are trained using the Adam optimizer with standard parameters ($\eta = 0.001$ (learning rate), $\beta_1 = 0.9$ and $\beta_2 = 0.999$, $\epsilon = 10^{-7}$) and the binary cross-entropy (BCE) loss. Dropout rates are determined heuristically, taking into account the complexity of the corresponding model architecture and the structure of the model input.

LSTM Models: All LSTM models contain two LSTM layers with 64 hidden units, one dropout layer after each LSTM layer, recurrent dropout of 20% and a fully-connected output layer with sigmoid activation. They are trained on full batches. The weights of LSTM layers are initialized according to Xavier uniform initialization. Recurrent weights are initialized in an orthogonal manner. The many-to-one model (MTO-LSTM) maps the input sequence to a single binary classification. A dropout of 50% is applied. It is trained for 250 epochs. The many-to-many model (MTM-LSTM) produces classification guesses for each time step of the input sequence. A dropout of 40% is applied. MTO-LSTM and MTM-LSTM have 54,849 trainable parameters each. The hybrid model (HYB-LSTM) extends the fully-connected layer of MTM-LSTM by an additional branch for trajectory prediction with linear activation. At each time step t, HYB-LSTM simultaneously produces a classification guess for step t and a prediction for arm, hand and ball trajectories at $t + 1$. It is trained on an equally-weighted additive loss, consisting of the BCE for classification outputs and the mean squared error for regression outputs. HYB-LSTM includes 56,149 parameters. Finally, PSC-LSTM realizes our *predictive sequential classification* approach. For classification, we use the above described MTM-LSTM model. For prediction, we train a separate LSTM on trajectory prediction which resembles the prediction branch of HYB-LSTM. MTM-LSTM, HYB-LSTM and the ancillary prediction network of PSC-LSTM are trained for 200 epochs.

TCN Models: Three TCN models are implemented, each of which covers a different receptive field size (10, 30 or 60 steps). The size of the receptive field determines the number of residual stacks, the size of the kernels and the dilation factors used (*receptive field size = number of stacks * kernel size * last dilation factor*). We examined different combinations of these factors for each receptive field size and selected the architecture that yielded the highest validation accuracy. TCN-10 is composed of one residual block, 32 filters of size 2, dilations of 1 and 5 and a dropout rate of 0.2. It is trained on batches of 32 samples and has 8,257 trainable parameters. TCN-30 holds 3 residual blocks, 20 filters of size 2, dilations of 1 and 5 and a dropout rate of 0.3 and is trained on batches of 64 samples. It contains 9,861 trainable parameters. Finally, TCN-60 contains 2 residual blocks, 20 filters of size 2, dilations of 1, 5, 10 and 15 and a dropout rate of 0.3 and is trained on batches of 64 samples. It comprises 13,141 trainable parameters. All TCN models are trained for 500 epochs and contain one final fully-connected layer with sigmoid activation to produce class probabilities for each time step. A He normal initializer is used for TCN kernels.

3.4 Evaluation Metrics

All models were tested on an unseen subset of the original data containing 395 randomly selected catching attempts. The models are rated according to the degree of correctness of a classification, as well as the earliness of decision-making.

Accuracy: We evaluate the models based on the percentage of correctly classified test trials (the percent accuracy) given different sizes of past history. We apply two different thresholds to measure the confidence of a prediction. The 50% confidence threshold rounds the final model output to 1 or 0, symbolizing a catch or a drop, respectively and compares it to the target label. When applying a 75% confidence threshold, however, trials are only considered if the final model output either exceeds 0.75 or undershoots 0.25. In the first case, the binary output is set to 1, in the latter case to 0. Trials with model outputs between 0.25 and 0.75 are disregarded. The binary output is again compared to the target label.

Ball-Hand Distance: The distance between the catcher's hand and the ball can be a first indicator to determine whether the ball will be caught or not. The metric is used to qualitatively evaluate the performance of a model by visually comparing trends in the prediction curve with the ball-hand distance over time. It is defined as the Euclidian distance between the absolute two-dimensional positions of the marker at the base of the relevant hand and at the center of the ball at a given time step t. The ball-hand distance increases when ball and hand move farther apart, while it decreases when the markers are moving closer together. However, since the ball-hand distance only considers the base of the hand, it does not necessarily give insight into the ball being grasped or not.

Mean Time to (Correct) Decision: We introduce a novel metric to quantitatively evaluate the earliness of decision-making. The time to decision (TTD_i) for a given input sequence (sample) i is defined as the time step when the model makes a final decision without switching decisions afterwards. A final decision is defined as a model prediction of larger than 0.75 or smaller than 0.25, regardless of the correctness. Values between 0.25 and 0.75 are treated as indecisive and excluded in further calculations.

$\forall \mathbf{y}_i : y_i^T \geq \theta_{hi} \vee y_i^T \leq \theta_{lo}$

$$\begin{aligned} TTD(Y) = \max\{1 \leq t \leq T \mid & \left(y^{t-1} < \theta_{hi} \wedge y^t \geq \theta_{hi}\right) \\ & \vee \left(y^{t-1} > \theta_{lo} \wedge y^t \leq \theta_{lo}\right)\} \end{aligned} \tag{2}$$

The time to correct decision ($TTcD_i$) for a given sample i equals the time to decision if the final decision is correct, i.e. if the binary model output y_{bin_i} after applying a 75% confidence threshold equals the target label z_i. Otherwise, the $TTcD_i$ is undefined:

$$TTcD(Y) = \begin{cases} TTD(Y), & y_{bin_i} = z_i \\ undefined, & y_{bin_i} \neq z_i \end{cases} \tag{3}$$

The mean time to decision ($MTTD$) and the mean time to correct decision ($MTTcD$) are defined as the arithmetic mean of all defined TTD_i and $TTcD_i$, respectively, for i in the number of data samples N. A low MTTcD indicates that a model can make the correct decision early in the time sequence, i.e. based on a small size of available past history, whereas a low MTTD only implies that a model tends to make decisions early, but not necessarily correctly.

4 Results and Discussion

All models are confronted with incomplete trajectories of catching trials. Therefore, the ready-trained models are used to make a classification based on increasing sizes of known past history. The presented results are average values based on ten repetitions with random data splits. To evaluate the correctness of the final classification, two different confidence thresholds are applied. Figure 2 depicts the percentage of correctly classified test samples for all models assuming a decision confidence threshold of 50%. This figure shows that all models start with an accuracy above chance level. MTO-LSTM is the only model that falls below chance level for history sizes between 34 and 47 time steps. However, it reaches the highest accuracy of 81.27% when the entire history is known, i.e. after 60 time steps of accumulated history. PSC-LSTM only starts to make predictions after a warm-up phase of ten time steps where history is accumulated. When the entire past history is available, it defaults to MTM-LSTM. Hence, both models reach the same final accuracy of 67.08% after 60 time steps. However, MTM-LSTM performs slightly better over time applying a 50% confidence threshold. HYB-LSTM demonstrates constant accuracies around 60% with an increase to 65.06% for the complete sequence. When applying a 50% confidence threshold, the TCN models outperform the LSTM models, especially with larger history sizes, without dropping below chance.

However, when considering a 75% confidence threshold, the picture changes significantly. Figure 3 depicts selected steps of a sample trial where the subject was able to catch the ball. In Fig. 4 the corresponding model predictions and the ball-hand distance for this trial are displayed. The latter shows a clear decrease until step 40, the point of time when the ball is first touched. Since the ball is successfully caught, the ball-hand distance stays minimal after the catcher's first ball contact. The two upper sub-figures depict the process of decision-making along the course of the trial. The point at which a model reaches the gray-shaded

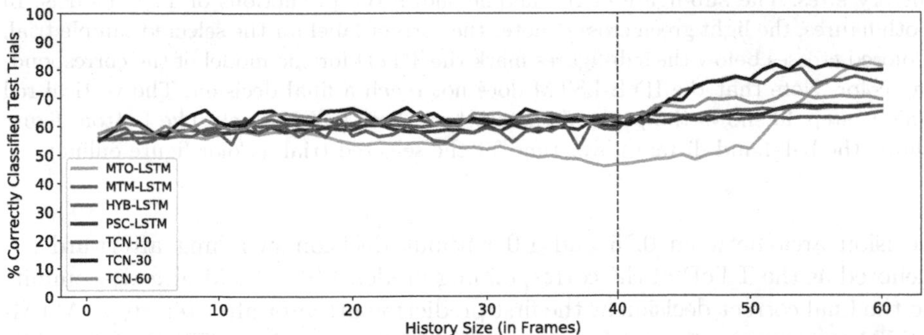

Fig. 2. Model accuracy applying a 50% decision confidence threshold. The figure illustrates the percentage of correctly classified test trials for increasing sizes of past history for all models. The vertical red line denotes the point of the catcher's first ball contact. (Color figure online)

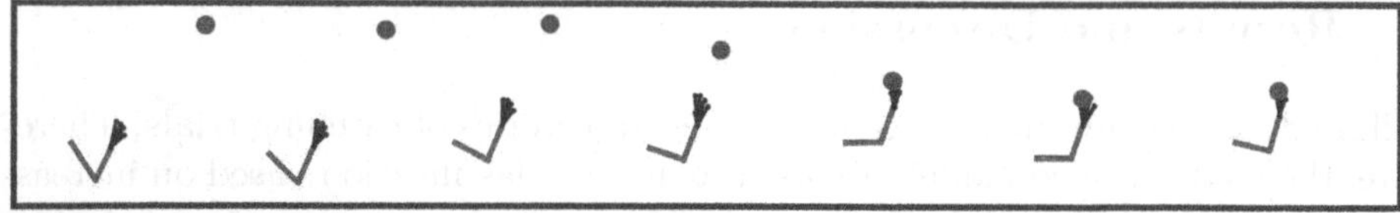

Fig. 3. Animated two-dimensional trajectories of the catcher's arm (red) and hand (blue) and the ball (green) for a successful sample trial over time. The figure illustrates the trajectories every ten time steps, starting with step 0. The fifth pose denotes the point of the catcher's first ball contact. (Color figure online)

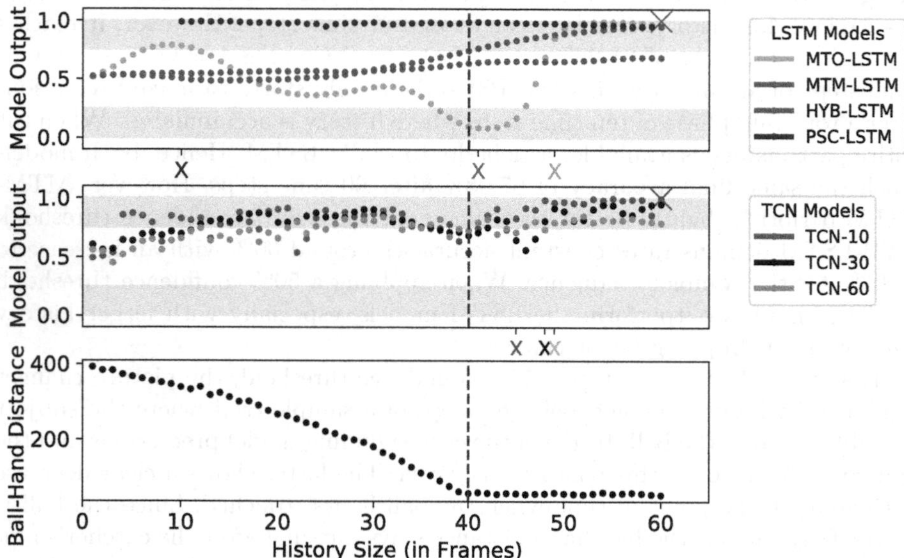

Fig. 4. Predictions of all models for a successful sample trial (cf. Fig. 3). The uppermost sub-figure illustrates the model classifications of all LSTM models for increasing history sizes. The sub-figure in the middle shows the predictions of TCN models. In both figures, the light green cross denotes the correct label for the selected sample trial. Colored crosses below the sub-figures mark the TTcD for the model of the corresponding color. Note that the HYB-LSTM does not reach a final decision. The vertical red line at step 40 shows the point of the catcher's first ball contact. The bottom figure shows the ball-hand distance over time for the selected trial. (Color figure online)

decision area between 0.75 and 1.0 without decision-switching afterwards, is denoted as the TTcD of the corresponding model. PSC-LSTM already commits to the final correct decision at the first prediction attempt after ten steps. MTM-LSTM expresses a continuously increasing confidence with a TTcD of 41, while HYB-LSTM does not reach a final confident decision and stays below 0.75. MTO-LSTM exhibits decision-switching and only comes to a final confident decision at step 49. Compared to the LSTM models, all TCN models demonstrate a more noisy prediction curve and high TTcDs (TCN-10: 45, TCN-30: 48, TCN-60: 49).

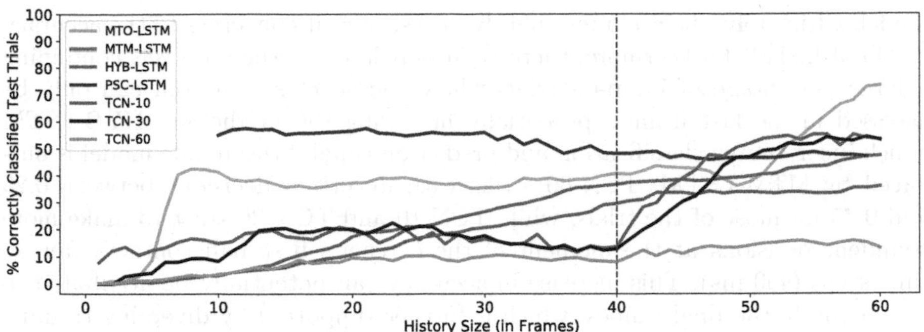

Fig. 5. Model accuracy applying a 75% decision confidence threshold. The figure illustrates the percentage of correctly classified test trials for increasing sizes of past history for all models. The vertical red line denotes the point of the catcher's first ball contact. (Color figure online)

Table 1. Comparison of the mean times to (correct) decision. Numbers in brackets denote the temporal distance to the catcher's first ball contact at frame 40 (after 400 ms). Negative distances represent classifications before the initial ball contact, and positive distances indicate classifications after the catcher's first ball contact.

Model	No. Decisions	MTTD [ms]	No. correct decisions	MTTcD [ms]
MTO-LSTM	327	475.5 (+75.5)	290	475.9 (+75.9)
MTM-LSTM	258	316.1 (–83.9)	187	313.3 (–86.7)
HYB-LSTM	191	348.4 (–51.6)	142	334.4 (–65.6)
PSC-LSTM	257	277.7 **(–122.3)**	186	276.9 **(–123.1)**
TCN-10	242	524.5 (+124.5)	211	516.2 (+116.2)
TCN-30	234	482.1 (+82.1)	210	476.0 (+76.0)
TCN-60	60	495.3 (+95.3)	52	481.3 (+81.3)

PSC-LSTM is the only model which can predict the success of the trial before the ball-hand distance reaches 0.

Figure 5 illustrates the resulting percentage of correctly classified trials across all test samples for different history sizes. First, it can be observed that PSC-LSTM is the only model which is capable of correctly classifying more than half of the test samples with history sizes smaller than 47 steps. For all other models, there is a vast discrepancy between Fig. 2 and Fig. 5 which implies that most model classifications fall between 0.25 and 0.75, especially for smaller history sizes. When comparing the LSTM models, MTO-LSTM model again performs best when the entire history is available. This indicates that MTO-LSTM does not learn to make decisions early, but rather waits for the final frames. For smaller history sizes before the first ball contact, PSC-LSTM is the dominant model. Ultimately, the accuracy slightly drops, since it converges to the accuracy of MTM-LSTM. Furthermore, there is an imbalance in the data set, containing a large percentage of jump-off trials where the success of a trial can only be assessed in the last frames, potentially hindering the prediction. HYB-LSTM which incorporates classification and prediction capabilities in one model is outpaced by MTM-LSTM. TCN-60 sticks with uncertain decisions between 0.25 and 0.75 for most of the trials, while TCN-10 and TCN-30 start to make more confident decisions at the moment of the catcher's first ball contact after 40 time steps (400 ms). This increase in accuracy can potentially be attributed to overfitting to the final frames, which is further supported by diverging training and test accuracies.

This observation is confirmed by the low percentage (15%) of confidently classified catching trials made by TCN-60 (Table 1). The highest percentage of correct decisions is made by TCN-30 and MTO-LSTM. However, both models rely on late information, while PSC-LSTM achieves the highest accuracy before the first ball contact. Considering that the first ball contact occurs at time step 40, neither the TCN models (MTTcD for TCN-10: 516.2, TCN-30: 476.0, TCN-60: 481.3), nor MTO-LSTM (MTTcD: 475.9) are capable of correctly and confidently classifying catching trials before the outcome is visually observable. The prevailing models are the recurrent networks trained on many-to-many classification. The best performance by far is achieved by PSC-LSTM which can confidently classify trials already 123 ms before the first ball contact.

HYB-LSTM performs slightly worse than MTM-LSTM, but can still make a classification 65.6 ms before the ball is first touched. In contrast to Hüsken and Stagge who argue that incorporating an additional prediction task into a classification RNN improves the learning process, we show that it does not have a positive effect on the earliness of decision-making [8]. However, the outsourced prediction approach of PSC-LSTM is superior to both the embedded prediction approach of HYB-LSTM, as well as the pure classification approach of MTM-LSTM. Hence, the inclusion of prediction capabilities into a classification model seems to harm classification performance. This finding can be a first indicator for the existence of different, possibly antagonistic internal representations and learning strategies of RNNs trained on classification versus regression tasks.

5 Conclusion

In this paper we introduced a novel RNN-based approach for early and confident time series classification: the *predictive sequential classification* (PSC). We evaluated our approach in comparison to state-of-the-art sequence learners on the early recognition of clinical ball catching trials. We consistently demonstrate the superiority of PSC over all other LSTM and TCN models in terms of the earliness and accuracy of decisions under a high confidence threshold. Specifically, PSC can on average make a final decision as early as 123 ms before the catcher's first ball contact. Hence, we show that ancillary prediction models clearly benefit classification performance. However, incorporated prediction capabilities seem to interfere with classification skills and ultimately hurt classification performance. Our findings show that PSC with its two-model design can simultaneously optimize accuracy, earliness and confidence of decision-making, thus constituting a promising approach for early and confident time series classification in manifold applications.

Acknowledgments. The authors thank Tobias Renner and Gottfried Barth (Department of Child and Adolescent Psychiatry, Psychosomatics and Psychotherapy, University Hospital of Psychiatry and Psychotherapy, Tübingen, Germany) for their support on the assessment of catching movements in children with Autism Spectrum Disorders. The authors thank the International Max Planck Research School for Intelligent Systems (IMPRS-IS) for supporting JL. Additional support was provided by BMG, project SStepKiZ, and by ERC 2019-SyG-RELEVANCE-856495 to MG.

References

1. Bai, S., Kolter, J.Z., Koltun, V.: An empirical evaluation of generic convolutional and recurrent networks for sequence modeling. arXiv:1803.01271 (2018)
2. Cao, Z., Hidalgo, G., Simon, T., Wei, S.E., Sheikh, Y.: Openpose: realtime multi-person 2d pose estimation using part affinity fields. IEEE Trans. Pattern Anal. Mach. Intell. **43**(1), 172–186 (2019)
3. Che, Z., Purushotham, S., Cho, K., Sontag, D., Liu, Y.: Recurrent neural networks for multivariate time series with missing values. Sci. Rep. **8**(1), 1–12 (2018)
4. Esling, P., Agon, C.: Time-series data mining. ACM Comput. Surv. (CSUR) **45**(1), 1–34 (2012)
5. Franklin, D.W., Wolpert, D.M.: Computational mechanisms of sensorimotor control. Neuron **72**(3), 425–442 (2011)
6. Goodfellow, I., Bengio, Y., Courville, A., Bengio, Y.: Deep Learning, vol. 1. MIT Press Cambridge (2016)
7. Hochreiter, S., Schmidhuber, J.: Long short-term memory. Neural Comput. **9**(8), 1735–1780 (1997)
8. Hüsken, M., Stagge, P.: Recurrent neural networks for time series classification. Neurocomputing **50**, 223–235 (2003)
9. Martinez, C., Perrin, G., Ramasso, E., Rombaut, M.: A deep reinforcement learning approach for early classification of time series. In: 2018 26th European Signal Processing Conference (EUSIPCO), pp. 2030–2034. IEEE (2018)
10. Mathis, A., et al.: Deeplabcut: markerless pose estimation of user-defined body parts with deep learning. Nature Neurosci. **21**(9), 1281–1289 (2018)
11. Otte, S., Schmitt, T., Friston, K., Butz, M.V.: Inferring adaptive goal-directed behavior within recurrent neural networks. In: Lintas, A., Rovetta, S., Verschure, P.F.M.J., Villa, A.E.P. (eds.) ICANN 2017. LNCS, vol. 10613, pp. 227–235. Springer, Cham (2017). https://doi.org/10.1007/978-3-319-68600-4_27
12. Rußwurm, M., Tavenard, R., Lefèvre, S., Körner, M.: Early classification for agricultural monitoring from satellite time series. arXiv:1908.10283 (2019)
13. Santos, T., Kern, R.: A literature survey of early time series classification and deep learning. In: Sami@ iknow (2016)
14. Ulrich, R., Vorberg, D.: Estimating the difference limen in 2afc tasks: Pitfalls and improved estimators. Attention Percept. Psychophysics **71**(6), 1219–1227 (2009)

15. Wang, W., Chen, C., Wang, W., Rai, P., Carin, L.: Earliness-aware deep convolutional networks for early time series classification. arXiv:1611.04578 (2016)
16. Whyatt, C.P., Craig, C.M.: Motor skills in children aged 7–10 years, diagnosed with autism spectrum disorder. J. Autism Dev. Disord. **42**(9), 1799–1809 (2012)

Precise Temporal P300 Detection in Brain Computer Interface EEG Signals Using a Long-Short Term Memory

Christian Oliva[1(✉)], Vinicio Changoluisa[1,2], Francisco B. Rodríguez[1], and Luis F. Lago-Fernández[1]

[1] Grupo de Neurocomputación Biológica, Dpto. de Ingeniería Informática. Escuela Politécnica Superior, Universidad Autónoma de Madrid, 28049 Madrid, Spain
christian.oliva@estudiante.uam.es, {f.rodriguez,luis.lago}@uam.es
[2] Universidad Politécnica Salesiana, Quito, Ecuador
fchangoluisa@ups.edu.ec

Abstract. Event-Related Potentials (ERP) detection is a latent problem in the clinical, neuroscience, and engineering fields. It is an open challenge that contributes to achieving more accurate and adaptable Brain-Computer Interfaces (BCI). The state-of-the-art typically uses simple classifiers based on Discriminant Analysis due to their little computational demand. Some more recent approaches have started using Deep Learning techniques, but these do not provide any temporal information and rarely focus on detecting the P300 at sample level in electroencephalography (EEG) signals, which would improve the Information Transfer Rate in BCIs. In other research areas, recurrent neural networks have shown high performance in those tasks that require online responses. We propose a new methodology, based on Long-Short Term Memory networks, in a sample level forecast to predict the P300 signal continuously. We get a slight improvement concerning the standard procedure, typically Bayesian Linear Discriminant Analysis, and we also show that the model predicts the occurrence of the P300 ERP at sample level in EEG signals. This brings us the possibility of evaluating the inherent variation between subjects. Our approach contributes to more agile and adaptable BCIs development, going further in the real-life usage of BCIs.

Keywords: Recurrent neural networks · Inter- and intra-subject variability · Detection of P300 at sample level · Event-related potential · P300 latency variability · Oddball paradigm · Bayesian LDA

1 Introduction

Brain-computer interface (BCI) technology allows converting the neural activity into external commands. These commands enable us to interact with the outside world, replacing the brain's normal exit pathways with this computerized interface. In recent years, this research has grown, spanning research and

I. Farkaš et al. (Eds.): ICANN 2021, LNCS 12894, pp. 457–468, 2021.
https://doi.org/10.1007/978-3-030-86380-7_37

applications from clinical to entertainment [5,28]. One of the ways to implement BCIs is through event-related potential (ERP) detection. An ERP is the stereotyped brain response, as a direct result, of a specific sensory, cognitive, or motor event. The detection of these ERPs can be carried out non-invasively in electroencephalography (EEG) signals, presenting these as characteristic positive or negative voltage deflections. These deflections appear with a certain latency after the stimulus has been presented. One of the most widely used ERPs in BCI is the P300, which stands out for its outstanding positive deflection that occurs with a latency of around 300 ms after the stimulus presentation [26]. This latency value can vary over a remarkable range and depends on several factors, as intrinsic properties of the subject (for example, age), the stimulus modality, etc. [11,22].

Its temporal-spatial structure is variable, spatial patterns appear in the posterior region of the brain, but they are also present in the central and frontal regions [4,15,18,26]. Its temporal structure changes from one trial to another, affecting its amplitude and latency [24]. This variability is recognized at the individual level (intra-subject variability), as well as between subjects (inter-subject variability) [19]. Although this variability was considered an obstacle, now it is recognized as an essential feature of brain functionality that can facilitate BCI customization. Therefore, identifying the variability can improve the precision and speed of communication of BCIs.

A common way of generating P300, in the context of BCIs, is through the well-known oddball paradigm [12,29]. In this paradigm, a set of stimuli corresponding to two categories, target and non-target, are presented to a subject. Stimuli belonging to the target category are presented with a lower frequency than stimuli from the non-target category. Hence, the subject's task is to classify each event in one of the two classes, generating a P300 signal when the least frequent category (target) is presented. Generally, the analysis of the EEG signal to locate the P300 events is carried out by trials. In a trial, all possible stimuli are presented, and only one of them is the target generating a P300 event. Thus, in the standard approach, signal analysis is carried out by trial groups and not continuously, at sample level in EEG signal, as we propose in this work. There are different techniques to detect P300s trial by trial. The most common are classifiers based on discriminant analysis (Fisher's Linear Discriminant Analysis, Bayesian Linear Discriminant Analysis, etc.), classifiers based on support vector machines, Artificial Neural Network, etc. (see [25] for a complete review of the different methods to detect visual P300-ERPs, and [20] for classification algorithms in general EEG-based BCIs).

In this work, we show how an ad-hoc design of a long short-term memory (LSTM) network manages to extract the appropriate information in a continuous mode from the input signals that contain P300-ERPs. Although there is little evidence of the use of LSTM networks in the P300-based BCI prediction [10,31] and the few works that exist on LSTM perform a combination with CNN to retrieve spatial information [1,2,17], its validity for the temporal information retrieval is already highlighted. Our results get a slight improvement concerning the standard procedures, and we also show that our new approach predicts with temporal precision (at sample level in EEG signal) when a P300 occurs. It brings us the possibility of evaluating the inherent variation between subjects.

The remaining of the article is organized as follows. First, in Sect. 2, we describe the dataset and our preprocessing to test recurrent neural networks, the machine learning approaches we use, and the experiment. In Sect. 3, we present our results, and, finally, in Sect. 4, we discuss and analyze the results and give the conclusions and further lines of research.

2 Materials and Methods

2.1 Data Description and Our Preprocessing

We base our work on a six-choice P300 paradigm dataset defined by Hoffman et al. [15]. It contains eight different users' EEG, corresponding to their answers to random image sequences with an Inter-Stimulus Interval (ISI) of 400 ms. There are only six distinct images to be shown. Each flash of an image lasted for 100 ms, and in the last 300 ms, users wait for the next one. The EEG signals were recorded at 2048 Hz sampling rate from 32 electrodes at the standard positions of the 10–20 international system. The main goal is to predict which one of these six images is the target stimulus. The state-of-the-art usually transform the P300-based BCI prediction into a trial-level prediction problem, where those images are always shown in packs of 6 (trial). However, we propose a new methodology, where Machine Learning models must solve a sample-level prediction problem. It implies the model returns its current prediction in real-time, sample by sample.

Standard Preprocessing. We filter the data with a sixth-order forward-backward Butterworth bandpass filter, and cut-off frequencies were set to 1.0 Hz and 12.0 Hz. Each run was standardized to a mean of 0 and a standard deviation of 1. Following the work in [15], we also downsample the signal from 2048 Hz to 32 Hz, and we extract single windows of duration 1000 ms, starting at stimulus onset. This extraction makes the last 600 ms of each single capture overlap with the beginning of the next one. We show in Fig. 1 an explanatory diagram of this standard preprocessing, where the overlap is manifest. In this figure, we present a single trial that begins at time 0 ms and finishes at 3000 ms. Different boxes represent the six possible image stimulation, where only one, plotted in yellow, is the target. These boxes have a duration of 1000 ms. Note that we have remarked the first 100 ms from each window, which represents the stimulus presentation.

Our Preprocessing. Our goal is to make an available methodology to train a Recurrent Neural Network, typically an LSTM network, continuously, in a sample-level way. We expect the network to return its prediction at each sample, so we directly preprocess the original continuous signal. We follow the same preprocessing as the standard (filtering, standarization and downsampling), but we do not split the signal into 1000 ms windows, avoiding the overlapping. We

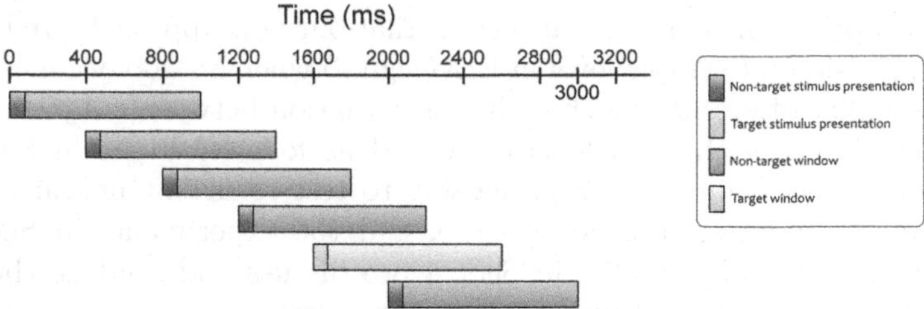

Fig. 1. Diagram of the standard preprocessing, where the overlap occurs. It represents a single trial that begins at time 0 ms and finishes at 3000 ms. Different boxes represent the six possible images, and each of them has a duration of 1000 ms. Only one window has been plotted in yellow, which means that this one is the target window. Note that we have remarked the first 100 ms from each window, which represents the stimulus presentation. (Color figure online)

show in Fig. 2-top an example to illustrate the procedure, wherein each color represents the signal since one of the six possible stimuli is presented. We represent the target stimulus in magenta (image 2). The output variable is set to *true* when the target image appears, being *false* for the rest of the images.

Once we generate the input dataset, one could ask how to well-define the final output dataset. To define the positive and negative classes (target versus non-target stimulus), we must consider that we do not know accurately where the P300 wave occurs. There is an inherent latency variation in this P300 component between the different subjects, as we have commented in the introduction. Therefore, we have defined two additional hyperparameters in the dataset generation to define a region after the target stimulus presentation: the start time of P300, measured from the image presentation (*offset*, see Fig. 2-middle), and the event duration (*window size*, see Fig. 2-bottom). We will study and adjust these hyperparameters in the learning process, where the model must learn where is the most valid information to recognize the P300 wave and then validate them in the test stage. We can not preset these two hyperparameters in the build-model phase due to the P300 latency variability.

2.2 Machine Learning Approaches

In this section, we detail the two machine learning approaches used in this work. Bayesian Linear Discriminant Analysis (BLDA) is the ML model implemented by Hoffman et al. [15] in the P300 detection problem, which makes a standard trial-level analysis, and Long-Short Term Memory (LSTM) [14] networks, which are the standard and most frequently used recurrent neural networks in the state-of-the-art. We will train these LSTM networks to make our sample-level analysis.

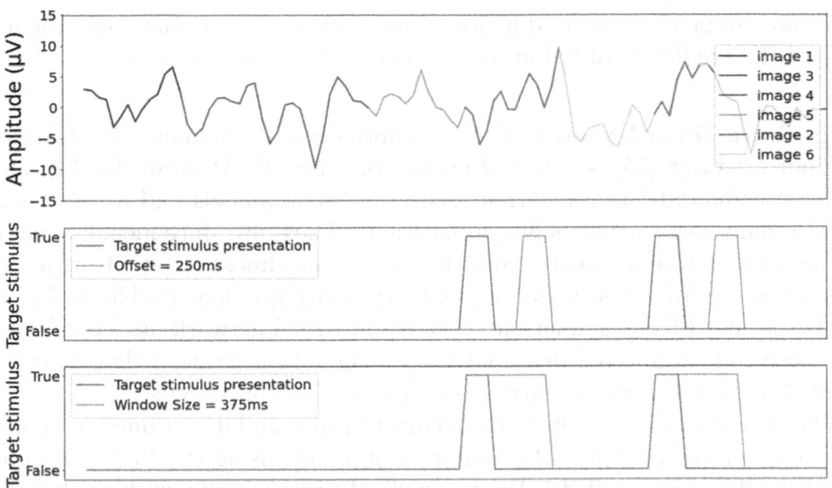

Fig. 2. Example of a continuous signal generated from the original dataset. Different colors represent different stimuli. The top signal represents the input data. The middle and bottom figures are two examples of modifying, on the one hand, the start time of the P300 wave with the *offset* hyperparameter set to 250 ms, and on the other hand, the event duration with the *window size* hyperparameter set to 375 ms. Note that the target stimulus presentation (the blue plot in middle and bottom figures) is always at the beginning of the magenta image, and it is always beginning at a multiple of 400 ms. (Color figure online)

Bayesian Linear Discriminant Analysis. As we discussed in the introduction, target signal recognition can be thought of as a binary classification problem: P300 vs non-P300 signals. Bayesian Linear Discriminant Analysis (BLDA) was proposed by Hoffman et al. [15] for such problems in P300-based BCI. BLDA is an extension of Fisher's Linear Discriminant Analysis (FLDA) [3] but runs the regression in a Bayesian framework, allowing it to automatically estimate the degree of regularization. In this way, BLDA prevents overfitting in noisy and high-dimensional datasets. BLDA considers class labels t can be expressed as a weighted sum of the features in the corresponding feature vector x, and it is assumed that this linear dependence is corrupted by a certain amount of Gaussian noise n: $t = w^T x + n$. The class probability can be obtained by calculating the probability of the target value during the training process. Class labels indicate the target (P300) and non-target (non-P300) as a number $y \in \{1, -1\}$. The EEG signal of each stimulus is a feature vector which is represented as $x \in R^D$, where D indicates the number of features. The weight vectors $w \in R^D$ are obtained by solving the parameter selection problem using maximum-likelihood estimates [15]. Once the w parameters are adjusted to different classes, this Bayesian formalism allows us to calculate the probability that a new feature vector x has class label $y = 1$ or $y = -1$. The probabilistic model used is expressed in terms of a predictive distribution, for simplicity, with a Gaussian form that can be characterized by its mean and its variance. Here only the mean value of the predictive distribution was assessed to make decisions.

Long-Short Term Memory. For our approach of continuous data EEG from Hoffman's dataset [15] (see Sect. 2.1), we consider LSTM networks [14], one of the most commonly used recurrent neural network models and a usual benchmark in many sequence modeling applications. They introduce memory cells and gate units to build an architecture that keeps an almost constant error signal along time, avoiding the vanishing and exploding gradient problems. Here we use the standard Keras implementation [8]. The final network model includes an additional fully connected dense layer with sigmoid activation that determines the final output as a probability of recognizing the P300-ERPs.

The network has 200 units in the recurrent layer, and it is trained to minimize the cross-entropy loss with a learning rate of 0.0004 using the Nadam optimizer [13] with a decay rate of 0.001. We use gradient norm clipping with a value of 1.0. We also add input and output dropout with a probability of 0.1. We train the networks with a batch size of 32, and we set the unfold length of the network to 100. Note that, because of the nature of the continuous signal, and also because we want the network to return its prediction at each sample, it has a many-to-many architecture, giving the corresponding answer for each time step. We show in Fig. 3 an example of a prediction of the network in a continuous mode for users 4 and 7. The blue plot represents the target (after applying the adequate *offset* and *window size*), the orange curve is the LSTM prediction along time, and the dotted red plot represents the target stimulus presentation. These examples have been extracted from LSTMs trained with different hyperparameters. Note the latency variability between the users: User 4 has an *offset* of 625 ms and a *window size* of 187.5 ms, and User 7 has an *offset* of 312.5 ms and a *window size* of 125 ms.

2.3 Experiments and Evaluation Criteria

Instead of calculating the accumulative accuracy as in [15], we propose to use the balanced accuracy (BA) metric: $BA = (recall + specificity)/2$. We must take into account metrics that consider unbalanced classes because the problem has intrinsic imbalance: there are five negative stimuli against only one positive stimulus. We evaluate the two models introduced in Sect. 2.2 by using the BA metric, and we compare them. We train the BLDA model with the standard preprocessing (see Sect. 2.1), and the LSTM networks with our new approach. For the BLDA model, the training phase consists of correctly classifying the P300 when the target stimulus appears (or not) in the first 100 ms of the current window of 1000 ms. For the LSTM, the training phase consists of predicting the target stimulus sample by sample in real-time. Here we perform a grid search of the best *offset* and *window size* hyperparameters for each user.

The dataset given in [15] has 8 users and four different sessions for each of them. This way, we test the models using K-Fold cross-validation (K = 4) with

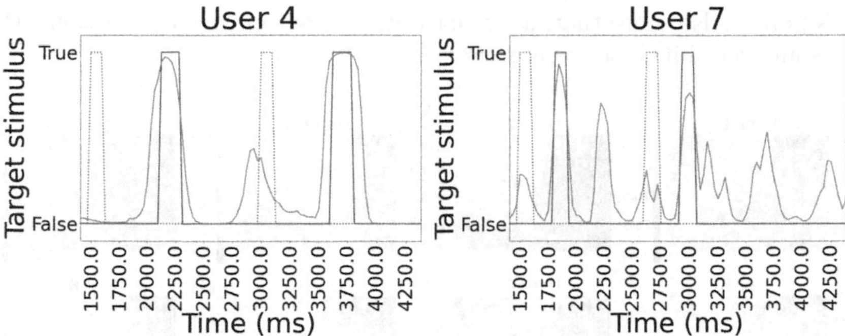

Fig. 3. LSTM output with a continuous signal along time when trained with User 4 (left figure) and with User 7 (right figure). The blue line represents the expected target, the orange one represents the LSTM output, and the dotted red curve is the target stimulus presentation. Note that, for each user, the *offset* hyperparameter is different (625 ms for User 4 and 312.5 ms for User 7). (Color figure online)

the four available sessions for each user, which means that we average the results obtained after using three of these sessions for training and the last one for the test. However, the two different training methods could make anyone argue that we can not compare the models. Despite this difference, we emphasize that the test is the same for both models. For BLDA, given a 1000 ms window, the model returns the prediction probability for being or not a P300 wave. For LSTM, the test uses the standard preprocessing, receiving as input the same 1000 ms windows. In this case, the network returns 32 predictions, corresponding to the 32 samples of the 1000 ms input signal, and we discard those which are not included in the appropriate training *offset* and *window size*. In summary, we get the maximum value in this window as the prediction probability.

We also compare the results between the usage of all the electrodes (32) against only use the eight most relevant electrodes, which is a standard selection [15,18]. We show in the next section that, for some users, the information given by the rest of the electrodes is also helpful for the LSTM to obtain better performance.

3 Results

In this section, we present the results. First, we show in Fig. 4 the grid BA matrix for each user when training the LSTM networks with the continuous mode, where we use a heat color map to identify the best configuration in the test dataset. The figures have been generated with the cross-validation balanced accuracy average of a set *offset* and *window size*. The best hyperparameter settings are usually close to the top of the figures, which indicates a *window size* always smaller than 250 ms and an *offset* greater than 300 ms. We want to highlight that a greater *offset* does not mean that the only valid information is at this point, but also the model uses all the previous signal samples to complement the final decision at this point. Also, note that, as we have mentioned in previous sections, there exists some variability between users.

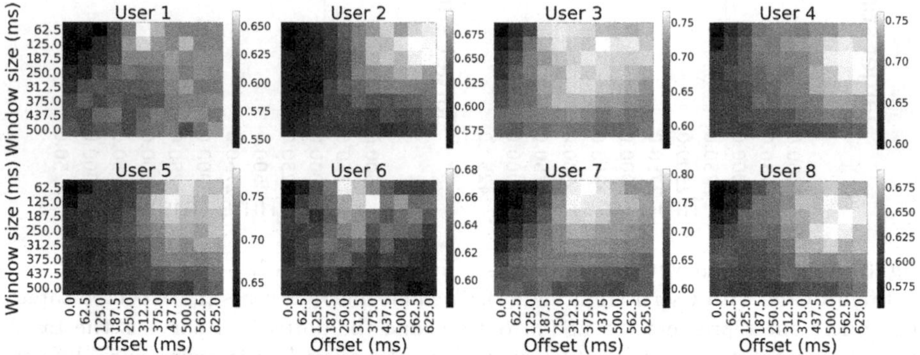

Fig. 4. Grid BA matrix for each user when training the LSTM networks with the continuous dataset. Note the different color bar scales for each figure. The figures have been generated with the cross-validation balanced accuracy average of each *offset* and *window size*. (Color figure online)

We have also observed that even with the same user, different sessions have also focus on different settings. We show an example in Fig. 5 for User 1 and the four cross-validation settings. In these figures, we can observe that test sessions 1, 2, and 4 can behave similarly, around 300 ms with some variability. However, test session 3 completely differs from the others, focusing on 600 ms and larger window size. This significant difference has led us to add the *LSTM + Best Session Settings (BSS)* model to compare with the others, choosing the proper settings for each cross-validation test. The average of the four grids in Fig. 5 results in the User 1 grid in Fig. 4. We do not plot all our results because of the paper extension limitation.

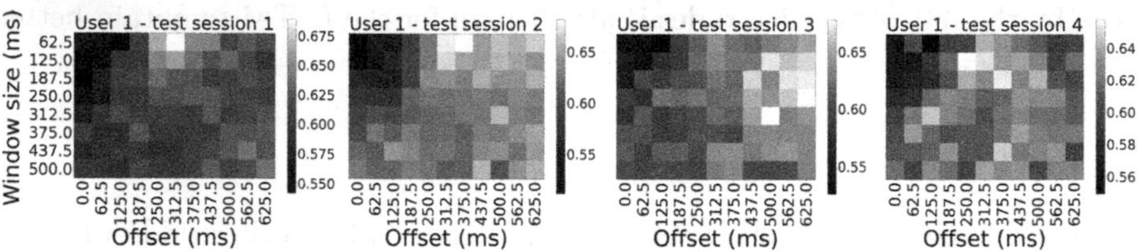

Fig. 5. Grid BA matrix for User 1 and the four cross-validation tests when training the LSTM networks with the continuous dataset. Note the difference between the white squares (Best Session Settings, BSS in Table 1). These white squares are used to define the *LSTM + BSS*.

We present in Table 1 the obtained results with the eight most relevant electrodes and all the electrodes. In both cases, we compare the balanced accuracy

(BA) computed with the models described in Sect. 3. We also add the results obtained with the *Best Session Settings* mentioned above. We include in the penultimate column the average result.

Table 1. Balanced Accuracy obtained in the cross-validation test when training with the standard 8 electrodes and all the 32 electrodes.

Model	U1	U2	U3	U4	U5	U6	U7	U8	Avg.	#Elec.
BLDA	0.628	0.703	**0.803**	0.715	0.777	**0.707**	0.772	0.625	0.716	
LSTM	0.663	0.699	0.766	0.760	0.782	0.680	0.808	0.692	0.731	8
LSTM + BSS	**0.676**	**0.711**	0.774	**0.771**	**0.789**	0.687	**0.817**	**0.703**	**0.741**	
BLDA	0.670	0.681	**0.803**	0.751	0.784	**0.733**	0.791	0.670	0.735	
LSTM	0.718	0.700	0.765	0.782	0.801	0.701	0.835	0.725	0.753	32
LSTM + BSS	**0.723**	**0.706**	0.779	**0.794**	**0.810**	0.711	**0.840**	**0.738**	**0.763**	

We observe a slight improvement in the overall result when using an LSTM network. However, the usage of all electrodes allows all the models to reach the best accuracy. LSTM, in its best configuration, gets a score of 0.763 versus the score of 0.735 obtained by BLDA. We also notice that BLDA improves the accuracy for users 3 and 6 compared to our methodology.

We have also observed a substantial difference in the first user when trained with eight or all the electrodes. It is not only about the accuracy but also the focus of the trained networks. We show in Fig. 6 the grid BA matrix for User 1 when trained on eight electrodes (left) versus User 1 when trained on all the electrodes (right). Of course, we can observe that the left figure is darker because of the accuracy. However, when we train a network with all the electrodes (right-figure), it better recognizes the signal when focusing on an offset of 550 ms and larger window size. This observation differs from the 8-electrodes situation, where the model was focusing on 300 ms.

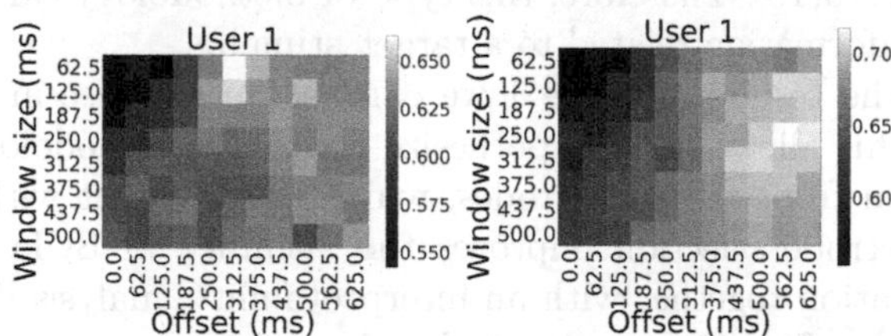

Fig. 6. Comparison between User 1 when trained on 8 electrodes (left-figure) versus User 1 when trained on 32 electrodes (right-figure). Note that the scale is not the same.

In summary, we want to highlight that, even if our results are similar to those obtained with the BLDA, our new methodology has two significant differences:

first, now the model gives a real-time evaluation sample by sample when a P300 occurs, as we show in Fig. 3. In other words, this approach provides us precise (at sample level) temporal information where the P300 event occurs. Second, our approach brings us the possibility of evaluating the well-known latency variability of P300 at the individual level (intra-subject variability), as well as between subjects (inter-subject variability) [19].

4 Conclusion and Discussion

In this work, we have presented a new methodology in P300-based BCI prediction by using Deep Learning. This method consists of making a recurrent neural network, typically a Long-short Term Memory (LSTM) network, analyze the input signal continuously, in a sample-level prediction, instead of the standard trial-level predictions. We based our work on the dataset presented by Hoffman et al. [15], with some detailed modifications and we compare our results with theirs. Besides, we show that our new methodology has a good performance in terms of accuracy, compared with the actual work for trial-level detection for this type of evoked potentials. Our results demonstrate that the LSTM network, either with 8 or 32 electrodes, extracts the appropriate information from the input signals in a continuous mode by learning the temporal dependencies to give the best prediction in real-time. We also show how the LSTM network can find, on its own, that some variability exists among different sessions in the same user and also how it preserves the previous information to give the correct prediction with a concrete offset.

This new methodology opens the way to a thorough study of the EEG signal in ERP-based BCIs that will substantially improve the information transfer rate (ITR), as has been done with other control signals in BCI [16,30].Optimizing the ITR metric is a pending challenge for BCIs [27]. Sample-level prediction methodology allows real-time monitoring of the EEG signal generation related to ERPs, which is useful since abundant scientific evidence highlights the presence of several ERPs such as N200 or P100 in P300-based BCIs that contribute to its accuracy [4,7,15,18]. Therefore, this type of methodology can help to locate that temporal information related to a target stimulus.

Comparing the results of Table 1 we can see an increase in accuracy with 32 electrodes. This allows us to hypothesize that this methodology can recover more information from other electrodes, which is consistent with the evidence that proper electrode selection improves the accuracy of BCIs [6,7,9,21]. An electrode exploration together with an interpretability analysis [23] can lead to a spatial location of the information related to the target stimulus. Consider that LSTM is currently used in combination with a CNN to retrieve spatial information to improve accuracy in P300-based BCIs. Retrieving spatial information increases the capabilities of LSTM that have been used only to retrieve temporal information in the study of the EEG signal for different purposes such as sleep study, emotion recognition, motor imagery, or mental workload [10,31].

Acknowledgement. This work has been partially funded by grant S2017/BMD-3688 from Comunidad de Madrid, by Spanish projects MINECO/FEDER TIN2017-84452-R and PID2020-114867RB-I00 (http://www.mineco.gob.es/) and by Predoctoral Research Grants 2015-AR2Q9086 of the Government of Ecuador through the Secretaría de Educación Superior, Ciencia, Tecnología e Innovación (SENESCYT).

References

1. Abibullaev, B., Zollanvari, A.: A systematic deep learning model selection for p300-based brain-computer interfaces. IEEE Trans. Syst. Man Cybern. Syst. (2021). https://doi.org/10.1109/TSMC.2021.3051136
2. Bashivan, P., Rish, I., Yeasin, M., Codella, N.: Learning representations from EEG with deep recurrent-convolutional neural networks. arXiv preprint arXiv:1511.06448 (2015)
3. Bishop, C.M.: Pattern Recognition and Machine Learning. Springer, Heidelberg (2006). ISBN 978-0-387-31073-2
4. Blankertz, B., Lemm, S., Treder, M., Haufe, S., Müller, K.R.R.: Single-trial analysis and classification of ERP components - a tutorial. Neuroimage **56**(2), 814–825 (2011)
5. Nam, C.S., Nijholt, A., Lotte, F. (eds.): Brain-Computer Interfaces Handbook_ Technological and Theoretical Advances, vol. 73. CRC Press, Boca Raton (2018)
6. Changoluisa, V., Varona, P., Rodríguez, F.B.: An electrode selection approach in p300-based BCIs to address inter-and intra-subject variability. In: 2018 6th International Conference on Brain-Computer Interface (BCI), pp. 1–4. IEEE (2018)
7. Changoluisa, V., Varona, P., Rodríguez, F.B.: A low-cost computational method for characterizing event-related potentials for BCI applications and beyond. IEEE Access **8**, 111089–111101 (2020)
8. Chollet, F., et al.: Keras. https://keras.io (2015)
9. Colwell, K., Ryan, D., Throckmorton, C., Sellers, E., Collins, L.: Channel selection methods for the p300 speller. J. Neurosci. Methods **232**, 6–15 (2014)
10. Craik, A., He, Y., Contreras-Vidal, J.L.: Deep learning for electroencephalogram (EEG) classification tasks: a review. J. Neural Eng. **16**(3), 031001 (2019)
11. van Dinteren, R., Arns, M., Jongsma, M.L., Kessels, R.P.: P300 development across the lifespan: a systematic review and meta-analysis. PloS One **9**(2), e87347 (2014)
12. Donchin, E., Coles, M.G.: Is the p300 component a manifestation of context updating. Behav. Brain Sci. **11**(3), 357–427 (1988)
13. Dozat, T.: Incorporating Nesterov momentum into Adam. In: ICLR workshop (2016)
14. Hochreiter, S., Schmidhuber, J.: Long short-term memory. Neural Comput. **9**(8), 1735–1780 (1997)
15. Hoffmann, U., Vesin, J.M., Ebrahimi, T., Diserens, K.: An efficient p300-based brain computer interface for disabled subjects. J. Neurosci. Methods **167**, 115–25 (2008)
16. Hosman, T., et al.: BCI decoder performance comparison of an LSTM recurrent neural network and a Kalman filter in retrospective simulation. In: 2019 9th International IEEE/EMBS Conference on Neural Engineering (NER), pp. 1066–1071. IEEE (2019)

17. Joshi, R., Goel, P., Sur, M., Murthy, H.A.: Single trial P300 classification using convolutional LSTM and deep learning ensembles method. In: Tiwary, U.S. (ed.) IHCI 2018. LNCS, vol. 11278, pp. 3–15. Springer, Cham (2018). https://doi.org/10.1007/978-3-030-04021-5_1
18. Krusienski, D.J., Sellers, E.W., McFarland, D.J., Vaughan, T.M., Wolpaw, J.R.: Toward enhanced p300 speller performance. J. Neurosci. Methods **167**(1), 15–21 (2008)
19. Li, F., et al.: Inter-subject P300 variability relates to the efficiency of brain networks reconfigured from resting- to task-state: evidence from a simultaneous event-related EEG-fMRI study. NeuroImage **205**, 116285 (2020)
20. Lotte, F., et al.: A review of classification algorithms for EEG-based brain-computer interfaces: a 10 year update. J. Neural Eng. **15**(3), 031005 (2018)
21. McCann, M.T., Thompson, D.E., Syed, Z.H., Huggins, J.E.: Electrode subset selection methods for an EEG-based p300 brain-computer interface. Disabil. Rehabil. Assist. Technol. **10**(3), 216–220 (2015)
22. McCarthy, G., Donchin, E.: A metric for thought: a comparison of p300 latency and reaction time. Science **211**(4477), 77–80 (1981)
23. Oliva, C., Lago-Fernández, L.F.: On the interpretation of recurrent neural networks as finite state machines. In: Tetko, I.V., Kurková, V., Karpov, P., Theis, F. (eds.) ICANN 2019. LNCS, vol. 11727, pp. 312–323. Springer, Cham (2019). https://doi.org/10.1007/978-3-030-30487-4_25
24. Ouyang, G., Hildebrandt, A., Sommer, W., Zhou, C.: Exploiting the intra-subject latency variability from single-trial event-related potentials in the P3 time range: a review and comparative evaluation of methods, April 2017
25. Philip, J.T., George, S.T.: Visual p300 mind-speller brain-computer interfaces: a walk through the recent developments with special focus on classification algorithms. Clin. EEG Neurosci. **51**(1), 19–33 (2020)
26. Polich, J.: Updating P300: an integrative theory of P3a and P3b. Clin. Neurophysiol. **118**(10), 2128–2148 (2007)
27. Ramadan, R.A., Vasilakos, A.V.: Brain computer interface: control signals review. Neurocomputing **223**, 26–44 (2017)
28. Rashid, M., et al.: Current status, challenges, and possible solutions of EEG-based brain-computer interface: a comprehensive review (2020)
29. Squires, N.K., Squires, K.C., Hillyard, S.A.: Two varieties of long-latency positive waves evoked by unpredictable auditory stimuli in man. Electroencephalogr. Clin. Neurophysiol. **38**(4), 387–401 (1975)
30. Tortora, S., Ghidoni, S., Chisari, C., Micera, S., Artoni, F.: Deep learning-based BCI for gait decoding from EEG with LSTM recurrent neural network. J. Neural Eng. **17**(4), 046011 (2020)
31. Zhang, X., Yao, L., Wang, X., Monaghan, J., McAlpine, D., Zhang, Y.: A survey on deep learning-based non-invasive brain signals: recent advances and new frontiers. J. Neural Eng. **18**(3), 031002 (2021)

Noise Quality and Super-Turing Computation in Recurrent Neural Networks

Emmett Redd(✉) and Tayo Obafemi-Ajayi

Missouri State University, Springfield, MO 65897, USA
{emmettredd,tayoobafemiajayi}@missouristate.edu

Abstract. Noise and stochasticity can be beneficial to the performance of neural networks. Recent studies show that optimized-magnitude, noise-enhanced digital recurrent neural networks are consistent with super-Turing operation. This occurred regardless of whether true random or sufficiently long pseudo-random number time series implementing the noise were used. This paper extends prior work by providing additional insight into the degrading effect of shortened and repeating pseudo-noise sequences on super-Turing operation. Shortening the repeat length in the noise resulted in fewer chaotic time series. This was measured by autocorrelation detected repetitions in the output. Similar rates of chaos inhibition by the shortening of the noise repeat lengths hint to an unknown, underlying commonality in noise-induced chaos among different maps, noise magnitudes, and pseudo-noise functions. Repeat lengths in the chaos-failed outputs were predominately integer multiples of the noise repeat lengths. Noise repeat lengths only marginally shorter than output sequences cause the noise-enhanced digital recurrent neural networks to repeat and, thereby, fail in being consistent with chaos and super-Turing computation. This implies that noise sequences used to improve neural network operation should be at least as long as any sequence it produces.

Keywords: Super-turing · Recurrent neural networks · Chaos · Pseudo-random noise

1 Introduction

It has been shown that noise injection is beneficial to the training performance of neural networks (NNs) regardless of the type of network ([3,9,12,13,20]). Varied NN applications (such as feedforward, recurrent, convolutional, etc.) have demonstrated some level of success in incorporating synthesized noise in their training model [4,5,7,9,12]. The study by Jim et al.[7] introduced and analyzed various methods of injecting synaptic noise into dynamically driven recurrent networks during training. Lim et al.[11] applied a Stochastic Differential Equation (SDE) framework to analyze recurrent NNs (RNNs) trained by injecting

I. Farkaš et al. (Eds.): ICANN 2021, LNCS 12894, pp. 469–478, 2021.
https://doi.org/10.1007/978-3-030-86380-7_38

noise into the hidden states. They focused on the impact of regularizing effects of general noise injection schemes. RNNs are important when analyzing time series data because they are designed to adaptively look backward over varying lengths of time [2]. The noise benefit experienced in NN systems could be viewed as a type of stochastic resonance (SR) effect. This is apparent, as discussed in [16,17], since in SR benefiting systems, a small amount of noise improves the performance of a nonlinear system while too much noise harms the performance [1]. The question remains, how do you determine the appropriate quality of noise beneficial for a given network?

In prior work [16], we demonstrated that optimized-magnitude, noise-enhanced digital RNNs showed consistency with super-Turing operation. This occurred regardless of whether true random or sufficiently long pseudo-random number time series were utilized to implement the noise. It showed a connection between SR and a mathematical proof of the computational complexity of an analog RNN obtained by Siegelmann [19]. Since a Turing machine (and digital computers) operate in a discrete space and their precision is too low, even pseudo-random noise will not help them access the continuous phase space of chaotic systems [19]. The simulations discussed in [16] revealed the optimum magnitude of added noise that made the varied time series consistent with chaos. (Note that noise is injected during operation of the NN model, in contrast to the noise commonly used in training.) Although both the pseudo- and true-random number noise gave chaos consistent results, the shortness of the pseudo-random sequences allowed them to pass any randomness test. Therefore, the results failed to illustrate the computational complexity limits of pseudo-noise-enhanced digital RNNs as expected. This was attributed to the pseudo-random number sequences being too short for their character to manifest itself.

This paper gives insight into the degrading effect of shortened and repeating pseudo noise on super-Turing operation and chaos consistency in noise-enhanced digital RNNs. The input data for training the NN models were generated using algebraic functions of logistic and Hénon maps. We pass the output sequences of varied time series through an autocorrelation function. Distances between peaks in its results give the lengths of repetitions in those sequences. This current work demonstrates that pseudo-noise with repeat lengths marginally shorter than a limited-precision digital RNN output sequence is detectable in that it fails to be consistent with chaos. The repeat lengths of the failed chaotic time series mainly follow the repeat lengths of the noise. When otherwise, the failing repeat lengths do not match any of the other repeat lengths involved in the simulations.

We discuss the details of SR and super-Turing complexity classes in Sect. 2. Section 3 provides an overview of the analysis framework for exploring the chaos consistency of the time series data. The results obtained as well as the related open ended problems are discussed in Sect. 4, while we conclude in Sect. 5.

2 Background

In this section, we review key concepts of stochastic resonance and super-Turing complexity classes as well as prior work on noise optimization in digital RNNs to provide a context for current work. These are all fully explored in [16].

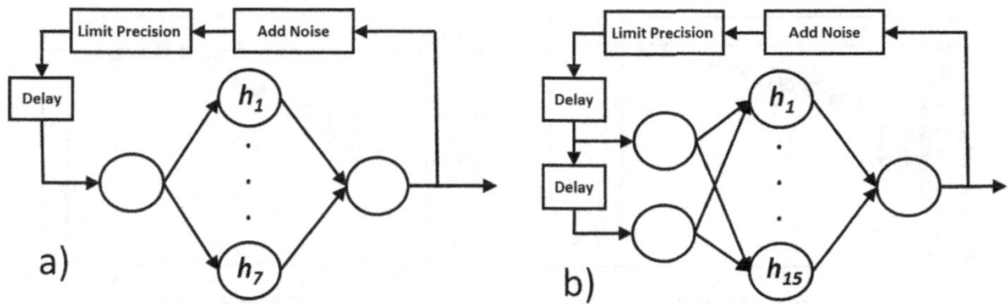

Fig. 1. The logistic (a) and Hénon (b) map RNNs used in this study. The output vector is pre-allocated to have the seed values. Other than the first one (or two) entries, the rest are overwritten as the noise-enhanced, limited-precision time series are calculated.

SR systems can be modeled using a double well potential which uses a rate equation approach to solve the temporal evolution of movement of system between two wells. A periodic forcing function and noise are required additions to the model to obtain the transitions [6,13,14]. Siegelmann [19] studied the effect of stochasticity on rational numbered RNNs. The computational complexity proof [19] models a RNN with rational neurons using the stochastic flipping of real probability unfair coins. The proof demonstrates that adding this stochasticity to these networks resulted in an improved complexity class beyond a Turing machine, the super-Turing BPP/log* class. Although Siegelmann argued against stochasticity being the same as noise, we [16] showed that noise in a SR modeled coin flip matched the stochasticity used in [19].

Given that the complexity proofs in [19] did not address whether digital RNNs could be super-Turing, we [16] proved the existence of an infinite hierarchy where these RNNs could also compute at a super-Turing level. We also demonstrated that noise-enhanced digital RNNs made calculations that were chaos-consistent, an indication of super-Turing operation. This affirmed that noise-enhanced digital RNNs exhibit some super-Turing computational power, even while not reaching the full power of the analog RNNs computing at a BPP/log* computational level.

The limited-precision digital RNNs analyzed in this paper, as shown in Fig. 1, are same as in prior work [16]. Lyapunov exponents [18] were used to quantify the consistency with chaos. Ten 10,000-long random number sequences of each noise type have magnitudes relative to the least significant bit (LSB) of each limited-precision digital RNN. They did not mimic chaos until pseudo- and true-random noise of the proper magnitude were added to their recurrent signals. As shown in Fig. 2, very small and larger magnitudes produced inconsistent and small Lyapunov exponents. Noise magnitudes of eight times LSB for the logistic map and four times LSB for the Hénon map digital RNNs best matched their accepted Lyapunov exponents. We utilized these noise magnitudes as well in this study, since they had been established as in best agreement with chaos mimicry and super-Turing consistency.

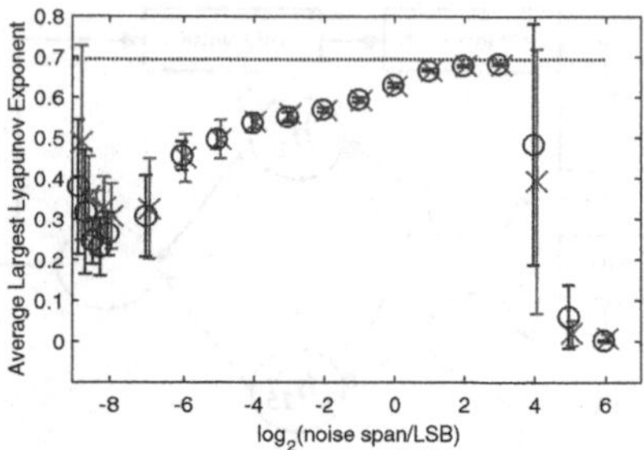

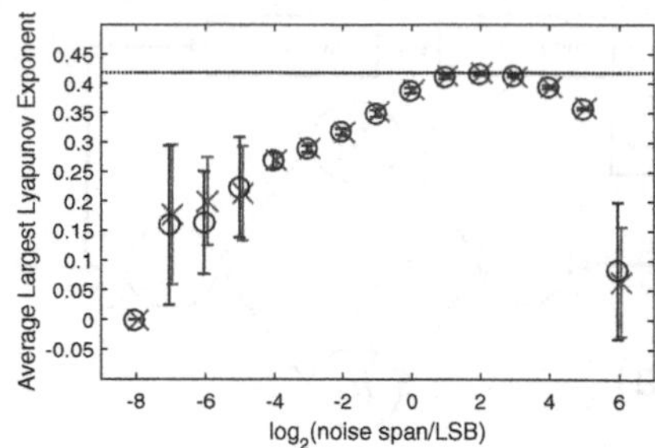

Fig. 2. Largest Lyapunov Exponent of a digital recurrent neural networks trained with a Logistic (left) and Hénon (right) map series for various noise magnitudes. The x coordinates are integers, but the plotted points and error bars are offset by ± 0.05 for the true random noise [15] (red $\times$) and for the pseudo random noise from MATLAB's `rand()` function (blue o), respectively. In both maps, the largest Lyapunov exponents are at four and eight times the least significant bits of the limited-precision digital RNNs. The dotted lines (black) represent the accepted value for the maps [18]. For more details, see Figs. 5 and 6 in [16].

3 Exploration of Repeating Noise Sequences

To investigate chaos consistency (implying super-Turing operation) of identifiable pseudo-random number time series, we utilize repeating sequences since they are readily observed to be non-random. The sequences are obtained using two pseudo-random generators: truncations of the MATLAB `rand()` sequences and an n-bit linear feedback shift register (LFSR) [10]. The LFSR sequences of comparable repeat lengths provide an alternative source of pseudo-random number sequences for a more robust comparison. We compare noise of length 10K sequences to 100K long sequences.

For the 10K experiments, different length portions of pseudo-random numbers (ranging from 64 to 8192) from the MATLAB `rand()` function are repeated to generate ten separate input sequences each of total length of 10,000. Likewise, LFSR random sequences of varying length portions (from 63 to 8191) are also generated and repeated to obtain ten different input 10K length sequences. For the 100K experiments, there are eleven sequences for each pseudo-random type. The length portions are varied from 4096 to 65536 for MATLAB generated sequences, and from 4095 to 65535 for the LFSR sequences. For both experiments, the LFSR sequences are seeded as near as possible to the initial numbers in the repeated MATLAB pseudo-number sequences. All experiments use four times and eight times noise magnitudes that have the highest Lyapunov exponent values from Fig. 2.

For each experiment, we observe the number of noise sequences which have no repeats in the digital RNNs output. This is detected by passing the output time series through the autocorrelation function which results in peaks if the sequences repeat [8] and shows a failure to mimic chaos. The distance between those peaks is the repeat length. While there can be multiple repeat lengths in

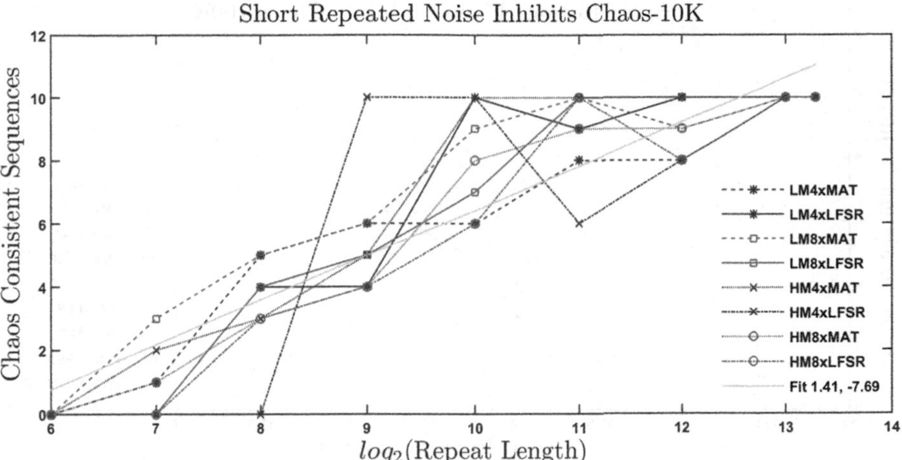

Fig. 3. Outcome of the 10K experiments. Short repeated-noise number sequences added to the recurrent digital RNN signals and, then precision limited reduces the number of output sequences which are consistent with chaos. For comparison to least square fitting parameters (green line), they are (1.39, −7.36) (1.43, −8.04) for the logistic and Hénon maps respectively.

the resulting power spectrum, the experiments only detect the shortest one in the output sequences.

Figures 3 and 4 show the number of output sequences which remain consistent with chaos (y-axis) vs. log_2 of the repeat length of the noise (x-axis) for the logistic and Hénon maps digital RNNs for both optimum and near-optimum noise magnitudes and the two noise types (MATLAB vs. LFSR). As mentioned in Sec. 2, noise magnitudes of four times LSB is regarded as optimum for the Hénon map, and eight times LSB for the logistic map. This results in eight experimental combinations of these three pairs (Figs. 3 and 4). These are coded in the legends of the figures: 'LM' denotes logistic map, 'HM': Hénon map; '4x' implies four times LSB, '8x': eight times LSB; 'MAT' denotes MATLAB generated sequences, and 'LFSR': linear feedback shift register generated sequences. Thus, the notation "LM4xMAT" implies a repeated pseudo-number sequence generated using MATLAB `rand()` function with magnitude four times relative to the least significant bit of the logistic map RNN.

For Figs. 3 and 4, all sequences converge at the right-most data point which correspond to no repeating noise sequences added to the recurrent signals. Note that all the pseudo-number experiments shown at values of log_2(noise span/LSB) = (2, 3) in Fig. 2 are contained in the converged data point in Fig. 3. We can observe that for the 10K experiment results (Fig. 3), all ten output sequences are consistent with chaos at log_2(`RepeatLength`) = `13`. But, at log_2(`RepeatLength`) = `12`, only three output sequences remain consistent. Interestingly, for the 100K experiment results (Fig. 4), at log_2(`RepeatLength`) = `16`, only two output sequences remain consistent with chaos. This seems to suggest

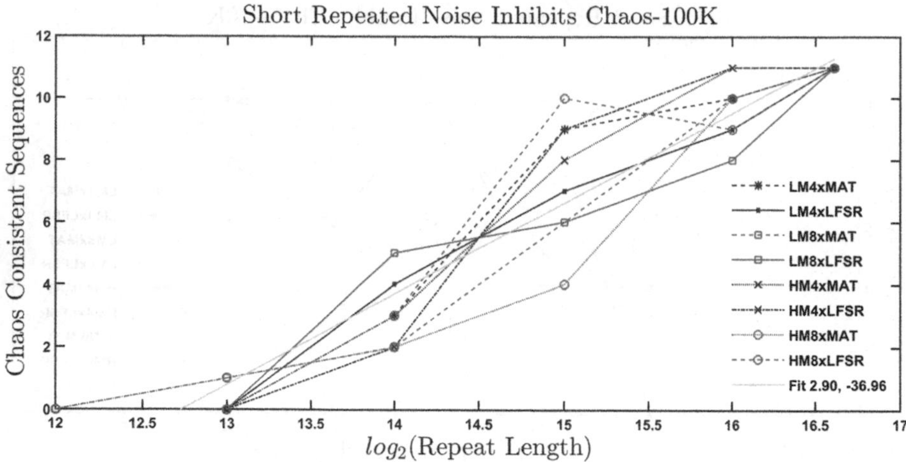

Fig. 4. Outcome of the 100K experiments. Short repeated-noise number sequences added to the recurrent digital RNN signals and, then precision limited reduces the number of output sequences which are consistent with chaos. For comparison to least square fitting parameters (green line), they are (2.80, −35.53) (3.01, −38.40) for logistic and Hénon maps respectively.

that a noise source needs to be at least as long as the digital RNN provisional chaotic sequence to maintain chaotic and super-Turing consistency.

The least square fit ($mx + b$) model for the experimental results are denoted by the green line in both figures. Combining logistic and Hénon map data in making the fit initially seemed without justification, but the separate fits for the individual maps are given in the figure captions and are very similar to the legend values. (See Figs. 3 and 4 captions.) This may suggest unknown, fundamental mechanisms underlying the relationship between noise repetition and chaos consistency.

4 Repeat Lengths and Open Questions

Tables 1 and 2 list the details of the 10K long experimental results, which were used to obtain Fig. 3. The non-zero entries indicate repeating, non-chaotic results while the number of zeroes in each column are the number of chaotic consistent sequences plotted in Fig. 3. Eighty-nine percent of the non-chaotic outputs have integer multiples of the noise repeat lengths. This indicates that lack of noise quality dominates. Seeking a contribution of the noiseless, limited-precision repeat length (83) in the non-integer multiples was unsuccessful. The 100K Tables 3 and 4 list similar data for Fig. 4. In this case, seventy-two percent of the non-chaotic sequences' repeat lengths are integer multiples of the noise repeat lengths. Similar to the 10K results, no contribution of the noiseless, limited-precision repeat length (581) could be found. The noiseless repeat lengths

Table 1. Four and eight times LSB for the logistic map RNN: ten 10K long sequences.

LM4xMAT							LM4xLFSR					LM8xMAT								LM8xLFSR			
2^7	2^8	2^9	2^{10}	2^{11}	2^{12}	2^{13}	2^8	2^9	2^{10}	2^{11}	2^{12}	2^6	2^7	2^8	2^9	2^{10}	2^{11}	2^{12}	2^{13}	2^8	2^9	2^{10}	2^{11}
30	6	4	0	0	0	0	3	0	0	0	0	4	21	6	0	0	0	0	0	19	2	0	0
36	0	0	0	1	0	0	3	0	0	0	0	27	0	0	4	0	0	0	0	18	0	0	0
0	8	0	0	2	0	0	0	6	0	0	0	6	9	0	3.53	4	0	0	0	18	0	4.78	0
14	2	0	3.77	0	0	0	0	6	0	0	0	51.27	11	14.07	9.53	0	0	0	0	14	0	0	0
22	0	0	3	0	1	0	3	1	0	1.89	0	73	34	0	0	0	0	1	0	0	0	0	0
2	0	2	2	0	0	0	0	0	0	0	0	18	28	4	0	0	0	0	0	0	2	4.78	0
14	0	0	0	0	0	0	3	9	0	0	0	30	0	0	0	0	0	0	0	19	2	0	0
32	0	5	4.77	0	0	0	3	0	0	0	0	56	0	13	1	0	0	0	0	0	2	0	0
33	4	0	0	0	0	0	3	6	0	0	0	68.27	24	0	0	0	0	0	0	0	1	1	0
1	6	6	0	0	0.44	0	0	9	0	0	0	31	38	7	0	0	0	0	0	18	0	0	0

LM4xMAT: Non-integer multiple 3.77 comes from a repeat length of 3857; 4.77 from 4881; 0.44 from 1809.
LM4xLFSR: Non-integer multiple 1.89 comes from a repeat length of 3860. Lengths beyond 2^{12} contain all zeros.
LM8xMAT: Non-integer multiple 51.27 comes from a repeat length of 3281; 68.27 from 4369; 14.066 from 3601; 3.533 from 1809; 9.533 from 4881.
LM8xLFSR: Non-integer multiple 4.78 comes from a repeat length of 4887. Lengths beyond 2^{11} contain all zeros.

Table 2. Four and eight times LSB for the Hénon map RNN: ten 10K long sequences.

HM4xMAT				HM4xLFSR					HM8xMAT							HM8xLFSR					
2^7	2^8	2^9	2^{10}	2^9	2^{10}	2^{11}	2^{12}	2^{13}	2^7	2^8	2^9	2^{10}	2^{11}	2^{12}	2^{13}	2^8	2^9	2^{10}	2^{11}	2^{12}	2^{13}
6	8	0	0	0	0	0	0	0	24	19	0	0	0	0	0	2	4	0	0	0	0
1	12	6	0	0	0	1	0	0	35.14	0	0	0	0	0	0	1	4	0	0	0	0
11	17	0	0	0	0	0	0	0	16	0	6	0	0	0	0	18	4	0	0	0	0
9	14	1	0	0	0	2	0	0	16	14	2	0	0	1	0	18	4	2	0	1	0
0	7	0	0	0	0	1	0	0	1	3	1	0	0	0	0	7	0	0	0	1	0
28	0	2	0	0	0	1	1	0	3	12	7.54	0	0	0	0	0	0	2	0	0	0
23	13	7	0	0	0	0	0	0	0	0	1	0	2	0	0	0	4	2	0	0	0
16	0	0	0	0	0	0	1	0	27	16.07	0	3	0	0	0	2	4	0	0	0	0
0	0	0	0	0	0	0	0	0	36	6	0	0	0	0	0	0	0	4.78	0	0	0
12	4	0	0	0	0	0	0	0	5	8	8.54	4	0	0	0	2	0	0	0	0	0

HM4xMAT: Lengths beyond 2^{10} contain all zeros.
HM8xMAT: Non-integer multiple 35.14 comes from a repeat length of 4498; 16.07 from 4114; 7.54 from 3858; 8.54 from 4730.
HM8xLFSR: Non-integer multiple 4.78 comes from a repeat length of 4887.

(83, 581) did not manifest themselves in these noise quality experiments, since the noise magnitude is likely too high. At zero magnitude, where noise quality is moot, they do appear [16].

To further understand the connections among the digital RNN repeat lengths that are not integer multiples of the noise repeat lengths, we summarize all instances in Table 5 . Closer analysis reveals that the Hénon noiseless repeat length is seven times that of the logistic map. However, that does not necessarily explain the three entries in Table 5 where the two maps have similar output repeat lengths since none of them share that common factor (83). All entries in Table 5 have both LSB multiplying factors. This is not surprising since the noise is optimum or near optimum in giving chaos consistency. We also observe in Fig. 2 that the Lyapunov values are nearly identical. The three entries that have

Table 3. Four and eight times LSB for the logistic map: eleven 100K long noise sequences.

LM4xMAT			LM4xLFSR			LM8xMAT				LM8xLFSR		
2^{14}	2^{15}	2^{16}	2^{14}	2^{15}	2^{16}	2^{13}	2^{14}	2^{15}	2^{16}	2^{14}	2^{15}	2^{16}
1	1.052	0	1	0	0	5	1	0	0.526	0	1.052	0
2	0	0	0	0	0	1	0	0	0	1.104	0	0.526
2	0	0	2.104	0	0	1	1.104	0	0	0	1	0
1	0	0	1	1	0	3	1	1	0	0.451	1	0
1	1.052	0	0	0	0	1	1	1.052	0	1.104	0	0.526
3	0	0	1	1	0	3	1	0	0	1.104	0	0
0	0	0	2.104	0	0.526	5	0	0	0	0	1.052	0
1	0	0	0	1	0.742	4	3	0	0	1.104	0	0
0	0	0.526	1	0	0	2	1	1	0	0	0	0
2	0	0	0	1	0	0	3	1	0	1.104	1	0.526
0	0	0	1	0	0	1	1	1	0	0	0	0

LM4xMAT: Non-integer multiples 1.052 and 0.526 come from a repeat length of 34465.
LM4xLFSR: Non-integer multiple 2.104 comes from a repeat length of 34469; 0.526 from 34466; 0.742 from 48643.
LM8xMAT: Non-integer multiple 1.104 comes from a repeat length of 18081; both 1.052 and 0.526 from 34465.
LM8xLFSR: Non-integer multiple 1.104 comes from a repeat length of 18066; 0.451 from 7391; 1.052 from 34467; 0.526 from 34466.

Table 4. Four and eight times LSB for the Hénon map: eleven 100K long noise sequences.

LM4xMAT				LM4xLFSR			LM8xMAT				LM8xLFSR		
2^{13}	2^{14}	2^{15}	2^{16}	2^{14}	2^{15}	2^{16}	2^{13}	2^{14}	2^{15}	2^{16}	2^{14}	2^{15}	2^{16}
1	1	0	0	1	0	0	3	1	0	0	2.104	1.502	0
4	1	0	0	1	0	0	1	0	0	0	2.104	0	0
5.207	1	1	0	0	1.052	0	2	1	1	0	2.104	0	0
1	1	0	0	1	0	0	1	3	1	0	3	0	0
1	3	0	0	1	0	0	1	2	1	0	2.104	0	0.526
4	2	0	0	1	0	0	3	2.104	0	0.526	2.104	0	0
3	0	1.052	0	1	1.052	0	5.207	0	1	0	3	0	0
3	0	0	0	1	0	0	0	1	0	0	0	0	0.526
1	0	0	0	1	0	0	3	1	1	0	0	0	0
3	1	0	0	0	0	0	4	1	1	0	2.104	0	0
2	1	1.052	0	1	0	0	1	1	1	0	0	0	0

HM4xMAT: Non-integer multiple 5.207 comes from a repeat length of 42658; 1.052 from 34466.
HM4xLFSR: Non-integer multiple 1.052 comes from a repeat length of 34468.
HM8xMAT: Non-integer multiple 5.207 comes from a repeat length of 42658; both 2.104 and 0.526 from 34466.
HM8xLFSR: Non-integer multiple 2.104 comes from a repeat length of 34470; 1.052 from 34468; 0.526 from 34467.

Table 5. Summary of non-integer-multiple repeat lengths.

# Of Systems	Range	Map	Times LSB	Noise source	Output length
2	1809	Logistic	Four, Eight	MAT	10K
3	3857–3860	Logistic, Hénon	Four, Eight	MAT, LFSR	10K
4	4881–4887	Logistic, Hénon	Four, Eight	MAT, LFSR	10K
11	34465–34470	Logistic, Hénon	Four, Eight	MAT, LFSR	100K
2	42658	Hénon	Four, Eight	MAT	100K

both types of noise function are reasonable since their repeat lengths result in similar quality. It is difficult to draw a conclusion about the different non-integer-multiple output lengths except the pattern that short output repeat lengths seem to occur in the short 10K experiments. Further investigation needs to be conducted to determine the underlying systematics for these non-integer-multiple results.

5 Conclusion

This work demonstrates that pseudo-noise with repeat lengths marginally shorter than a limited-precision digital RNN output sequence is detectable in that it fails to be consistent with chaos. This provides further insight beyond prior work that appeared to affirm the statement "there is no difference between pseudo- and true-random noise enhanced digital RNNs attaining consistency with chaos". It was assumed that this was probably due to pseudo-random number sequences being long enough to be indistinguishable from true-random sequences. However, as shown in this paper, repeat lengths of failed chaotic sequences mainly follow repeat lengths of the noise. When they don't, the failing repeat lengths do not seem to match the limited-precision digital RNN repeat lengths that occur without noise enhancement. The noise repeat lengths inhibiting chaos appear independent of the two chaotic functions studied (logistic and Hénon) and similar noise magnitudes. This suggests that if this independence could be extended to other chaotic-system-trained, noise-enhanced digital RNNs, a fundamental relationship between noise-enhancement and chaos mimicry could exist.

References

1. Adigun, O., Kosko, B.: Using noise to speed up video classification with recurrent backpropagation. In: 2017 International Joint Conference on Neural Networks (IJCNN), pp. 108–115. IEEE (2017)
2. Al-Jabery, K., Obafemi-Ajayi, T., Olbricht, G., Wunsch, D.: Computational Learning Approaches to Data Analytics in Biomedical Applications. Academic Press, Cambridge (2019)

3. Audhkhasi, K., Osoba, O., Kosko, B.: Noise-enhanced convolutional neural networks. Neural Netw. **78**, 15–23 (2016)
4. Chakrabarty, S., Habets, E.A.: Broadband doa estimation using convolutional neural networks trained with noise signals. In: 2017 IEEE Workshop on Applications of Signal Processing to Audio and Acoustics (WASPAA), pp. 136–140. IEEE (2017)
5. Chakrabarty, S., Habets, E.A.: Multi-speaker doa estimation using deep convolutional networks trained with noise signals. IEEE J. Sel. Topics Sign. Process. **13**(1), 8–21 (2019)
6. Harmer, G.P., Davis, B.R., Abbott, D.: A review of stochastic resonance: circuits and measurement. IEEE Trans. Instrum. Meas. **51**(2), 299–309 (2002)
7. Jim, K.C., Giles, C.L., Horne, B.G.: An analysis of noise in recurrent neural networks: convergence and generalization. IEEE Trans. Neural Networks **7**(6), 1424–1438 (1996)
8. Kaplan, D., Glass, L.: Understanding nonlinear dynamics. Springer, New York (2012)
9. Kim, J., Picek, S., Heuser, A., Bhasin, S., Hanjalic, A.: Make some noise. unleashing the power of convolutional neural networks for profiled side-channel analysis. In: IACR Transactions on Cryptographic Hardware and Embedded Systems, pp. 148–179 (2019)
10. https://en.wikipedia.org/wiki/Linear-feedback_shift_register#Some_polynomials_for_maximal_LFSRs Accessed 09 Apr 2021
11. Lim, S.H., Erichson, N.B., Hodgkinson, L., Mahoney, M.W.: Noisy recurrent neural networks. arXiv preprint arXiv:2102.04877 (2021)
12. Liu, X., Si, S., Cao, Q., Kumar, S., Hsieh, C.J.: How does noise help robustness? explanation and exploration under the neural sde framework. In: Proceedings of the IEEE/CVF Conference on Computer Vision and Pattern Recognition, pp. 282–290 (2020)
13. McDonnell, M.D., Abbott, D.: What is stochastic resonance? definitions, misconceptions, debates, and its relevance to biology. PLoS Comput. Biol. **5**(5), e1000348 (2009)
14. McNamara, B., Wiesenfeld, K.: Theory of stochastic resonance. Phys. Rev. A **39**(9), 4854 (1989)
15. https://www.random.org/ (2019)
16. Redd, E., Senger, S., Obafemi-Ajayi, T.: Noise optimizes super-turing computation in recurrent neural networks. Phys. Rev. Res. **3**(1), 013120 (2021)
17. Redd, E., Younger, A.S., Obafemi-Ajayi, T.: Stochastic resonance enables BPP/log* complexity and universal approximation in analog recurrent neural networks. In: 2019 International Joint Conference on Neural Networks. IEEE (2019)
18. Rosenstein, M.T., Collins, J.J., De Luca, C.J.: A practical method for calculating largest lyapunov exponents from small data sets. Phys. D Nonlinear Phenomena **65**(1–2), 117–134 (1993)
19. Siegelmann, H.T.: Neural Networks and Analog Computation: Beyond the Turing Limit. Birkhauser, Boston (1999)
20. Smart, A.: Is noise the key to artificial general intelligence? converging evidence indicates noise plays a fundamental role in the brain. https://www.psychologytoday.com/intl/blog/machine-psychology/201606/is-noise-the-key-artificial-general-intelligence (2016)

Reinforcement Learning I

Learning to Plan via a Multi-step Policy Regression Method

Stefan Wagner(✉), Michael Janschek(✉), Tobias Uelwer(✉), and Stefan Harmeling(✉)

Department of Computer Science, Heinrich Heine University, Düsseldorf, Germany
{stefan.wagner,michael.janschek,tobias.uelwer,stefan.harmeling}@hhu.de

Abstract. We propose a new approach to increase inference performance in environments that require a specific sequence of actions in order to be solved. This is for example the case for maze environments where ideally an optimal path is determined. Instead of learning a policy for a single step, we want to learn a policy that can predict n actions in advance. Our proposed method called policy horizon regression (PHR) uses knowledge of the environment sampled by A2C to learn an n dimensional policy vector in a policy distillation setup which yields n sequential actions per observation. We test our method on the MiniGrid and Pong environments and show drastic speedup during inference time by successfully predicting sequences of actions on a single observation.

Keywords: Deep learning · Planning · Hierarchical reinforcement learning · Policy distillation · Model inference

1 Introduction

In recent years, reinforcement learning has seen growing success due to the use of deep learning as in [12]. The reinforcement learning field has been mostly split between two major subfields: model-free and model-based reinforcement learning. In the first case we have a reactionary agent which learns directly from sampled experience, while in the latter case a model of the environment is learned from which the agent samples trajectories. Especially in model-based reinforcement learning the term of planning has come to fruition. Either prior or during agent training a model of the environment is learned. The agent then plans by simulating trajectories by using some form of tree search and thus is able to select the best actions while using fewer samples.

Recently, there have been investigations about how to plan with a model-free based approach. Guez et al. [7] trained an agent with a regular neural network with an architecture that has not been modified to enable any special planning behavior. The authors achieve state of the art performance for combinatorial problems such as Sokoban. However, after 10^9 steps the authors experiments show that a simpler CNN seems to be sufficient in order to learn several possible

I. Farkaš et al. (Eds.): ICANN 2021, LNCS 12894, pp. 481–492, 2021.
https://doi.org/10.1007/978-3-030-86380-7_39

variations of Sokoban. Another area that deals with planning in reinforcement learning is hierachical reinfocerment learning (HRL) as in [1]. The main idea of HRL is not only to predict primitive actions for every time step, but macro-actions called *options*. An option represents a policy that contains a sequence of primitive actions that are executed until a termination point. Then the agent may choose another option. HRL can be adapted to regular reinforcement learning via semi-markov decision processes (SMDPs). Policy distillation is a straightforward way of learning multiple tasks within a single policy. Policy distillation defines a *teacher policy* T and a *student policy* S where the teacher policy T is usually first trained in advance and then the student policy S is trained to match the teacher policy via supervised learning. We combine model-free reinforcement learning, HRL and policy distillation to create a new method to speed up model inference.

We take the recent advances in model-free reinforcement learning by Guez et al. [7] and take inspiration from HRL to create a method that leverages the inherent planning capability and simplicity of model-free learning, while applying the notion of options that stems from HRL to predict n actions for a single state in order to speed up model inference. That is, for a single state we want to predict the following n actions without changing the function approximator's architecture much. While the general outline in HRL is to define options over an SMDP, we learn an MDP and settle for a specific scenario, where the agent predicts a fixed number of actions for a given state. We do this by first training the environment with an extended A2C architecture that first learns a base policy via regular A2C [11] which will serve as teacher policy T. In a second training stage, in order to learn n actions for a single input, we take successful trajectories of the trained agent and regress these teacher policies on to the extended A2C architecture, so that it learns to predict n actions given a single observation. Our method can be seen as part of intra-option learning as in [17] where options are learned off-policy from experience. In this way, we can reduce the number of evaluations needed to solve the environment during inference time. We thus formulate our main contributions with this work:

Contributions

- We achieve model inference speedup in a reinforcement learning setting by leveraging the general framework of policy distillation, adding to the many use cases such as neural network compression and multi-task learning.
- We achieve a substantial inference speedup, as the prediction of the n dimensional action vector is much more efficient than evaluating the model n times.
- We show empirically that the inference speedup is due to the agent completing the environments faster than its non-PHR counterpart. Thus increasing the productivity of the agent.
- With our flexible and simple approach, we especially see a benefit in problems where the agent has limited resources during inference time or where the agents productivity should be boosted.

We propose our method as a viable option for *optimal path finding.* Popular path-finding algorithms such as A* in [8] are able to find optimal paths given a start-point and an endpoint. However it can be challenging to find a good heuristic that works for a given environment. Deep learning circumvents the need for a heuristic by learning directly from data.

We demonstrate this by training PHR on two MiniGrid environments. In the first set of experiments the agent has to find the goal in a multi room grid and a stochastic grid that changes after every episode with the only reward being the end goal. We also train PHR on the Pong-Deterministic-v4 environment, showing that reactive environments which do not follow a grid structure can be enhanced with PHR as well. Overall, we achieve twice the inference performance while learning an optimal path i.e. sequences of actions while retaining policy quality.

2 Related Work

Sequencing actions to leverage different time scales has been used in reinforcement learning to improve learning speed. Schoknecht et al. [16] improve learning speed by defining multi-step actions on different time scales. The authors argue that between important actions (decisions) there may exist more superfluous actions that have to be executed repeatedly and should therefore only be learned as a single decision. This approach has also been extended to deep learning by Lakshminarayanan et al. [9] and been formalized by Lee et al. [10]. Our approach focuses on sequencing actions as an abstraction over actions rather than for different time scales. By sequencing n actions for a single state we reduce the number of model evaluations, thus speeding up inference time.

Efroni et al. [6] look at the problem of policy improvement with multi-step actions. The algorithm h-PI tries to find the choice of actions that maximizes the joint cumulative expected reward given a sequence of actions within a defined horizon h starting from a given state. De Asis et al. [5] define a hyperparameter σ to perform policy evaluation seamlessly over multiple steps.

Panov et al. [14] used a CNN for path finding in conjunction with a custom reward function in settings that are challenging for A* with moderate results.

Contrary to the work mentioned above, our approach focuses on speeding up model inference in real word applications while maintaining policy quality. Our approach is inspired by *policy distillation* as in [15] and more generally specified in [4]. Generally, the focus in knowledge distillation is to transfer knowledge to smaller networks. We seek to achieve inference speedup in a reinforcement learning setting by leveraging the general framework of policy distillation. In this way the architecture is only affected minimally and efficiency can be improved by either accelerating workflow or reducing the power target. Policy distillation defines a *teacher policy* T and a *student policy* S where the teacher policy T is usually first trained in advance and then the student policy S is trained to match the teacher policy via supervised learning. We learn a good policy via regular policy gradient ascent which serves as the teacher policy and then map a horizon of n actions from the teacher policy to the student policy, which in this case is the function approximator which predicts n actions for a single state.

Improving inference performance for a CNN has been previously investigated by Ning et al. [13]. The authors use a collection of clustering techniques and similarity measures to compress the network and thus improve inference time. Our algorithm does not modify the network functionality, but leverages the reinforcement learning setting on an environment level.

3 Methods

In this section we describe our neural network architecture and our extension to the policy gradient called *policy horizon regression* (PHR) which allows for an n dimensional policy vector to be learned.

3.1 PHR Architecture

PHR can be understood as an extension to any function approximator that requires planning its steps ahead of time. In this particular case we use A2C as the foundation for our training algorithm which includes the baseline loss and entropy regularization. We then extend the policy gradient in order to predict n additional agent moves where $H = \{1, 2, \ldots, n\}$ is the *policy horizon.* We say our extended architecture predicts an n dimensional *policy vector.*

Policy Vector. A policy π represents a probability distribution that assigns probabilities $\pi(a|s)$ for each state $s \in \mathcal{S}$ over actions $a \in \mathcal{A}$, i.e., $\sum_a \pi(a|s) = 1$ for all $s \in \mathcal{S}$. We also write $\pi(\cdot|s)$ to denote the probability distribution over states for a fixed state $s \in \mathcal{S}$. Moreover, we denote π^θ as a policy determined by the network parameters θ. Let π_1^θ, ..., π_n^θ be a sequence of such policies, then we call the vector of these policies

$$\vec{\pi}^\theta = [\pi_1^\theta, \ldots, \pi_n^\theta]^T \tag{1}$$

a *policy vector.* Note that for a given state $s \in \mathcal{S}$ the policy vector $\vec{\pi}^\theta$ defines n probability distributions $\pi_1^\theta, \ldots, \pi_n^\theta$ over the action space that are determined by the network parameters θ.

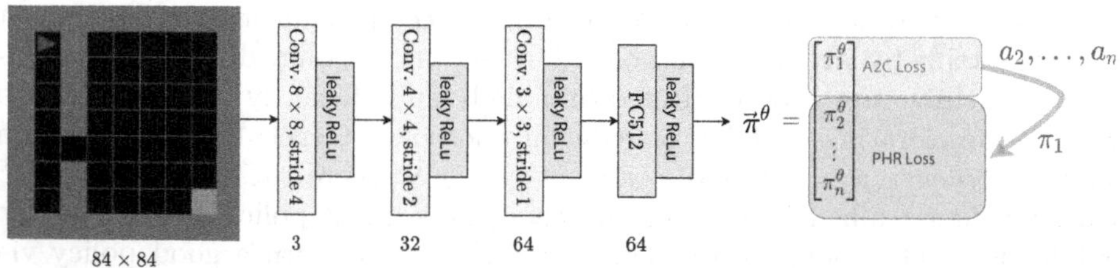

Fig. 1. Instead of predicting a single policy we predict a policy vector $\vec{\pi}^\theta$ by mapping n actions or policies from π_1^θ to the policy vector.

Figure 1 depicts the PHR architecture: for a single state $s \in S$ we seek to predict a vector of n *policies*. We use π_1^θ as the target policy to sample n actions from it, then PHR maps these n actions to the *policy vector* $\vec{\pi}^\theta$. Alternatively, the same can be done between n probability distributions of π_1^θ and of the *policy vector*. Note that the policy vector is computed only at the last layer (FC512), while the rest of the network is not any different from the usual setup to learn a single policy. Essentially, the network learns to predict the correct sequence of actions for a given input. Extension of the convolutional layers are not necessary as the learned representations are already powerful enough to learn the proposed environments with PHR successfully. Overall, extending only the last layer creates minimal overhead.

3.2 Policy Horizon Regression (PHR)

Distances Between Q-Values. Let $q^T = [q_1^T, \ldots, q_m^T]$ and $q^S = [q_1^S, \ldots, q_m^S]$ be two vectors describing the q-values corresponding to each possible action for the agent. In this case the former is the teacher policy and the latter the student policy. Then the distance between the two vectors can be measured with the squared loss d_2 or the KL-divergence d_{KL} (which is strictly speaking not a distance since not symmetric),

$$d_2(q^S, q^T) = \sum_i |q_i^S - q_i^T|^2 \qquad d_{KL}(q^S, q^T) = \sum_i \sigma(q_i^S) \log \frac{\sigma(q_i^S)}{\sigma(q_i^T)} \tag{2}$$

where σ is the softmax function. These two distance measures are considered in our experiments, however, others are possible too.

Mapping actions directly to policy vector $\vec{\pi}^\theta$. Let $a^* = \arg\max q^T$ be the index of the maximum value over the discrete values of q^T, i.e., the best action. Then the cross entropy loss between q^S and the best action a^* reads as follows,

$$L_{CE}(q^S, a^*) = \log q_{a^*}^S. \tag{3}$$

Compared to the distance measures, this approach seeks to map the teacher policy onto the student policy directly. Overall, d_2 and d_{KL} should yield a softer regression of the teachers actions, while L_{CE} is a logistic regression. We consider all three approaches as methods to map our base policy π_1^θ onto the policy vector $\vec{\pi}^\theta$. In the following, we also refer to the teacher policy as the base policy $\pi_1^\theta = q^T$ and to the student policy as the policy vector $\vec{\pi}^\theta = q^S$.

Learning Policy Vector $\vec{\pi}^\theta$ Off-Policy. We learn the policy vector off-policy in two stages as in Fig. 2: (i) First the environment is learned fully with A2C via regular policy gradient ascent defined as

$$J_{\mathrm{PG}}(\theta) = \mathbb{E}_{\pi_1}\left[\log \pi_1^\theta(s,a)\; Q^\theta(s,a)\right] \tag{4}$$

with corresponding gradient

$$\nabla_\theta J_{\mathrm{PG}}(\theta) = \mathbb{E}_{\pi_1}\left[\nabla_\theta \log \pi_1^\theta(s,a)\; Q^\theta(s,a)\right]. \tag{5}$$

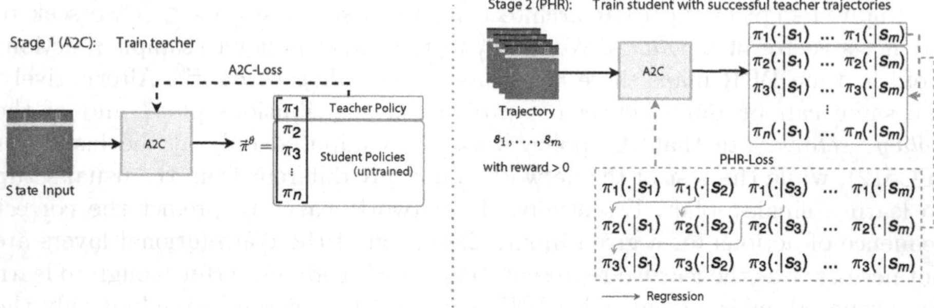

Fig. 2. Diagram depicting PHR training process. (i) First, we train the teacher policy with regular A2C. (ii) In the second stage we evaluate successful trajectories from the teacher with reward $r_{m-1} > 0$ and regress the base policy π_1^θ onto the policy vector $\vec{\pi}^\theta$.

Note that the policy vector in our extended A2C architecture predicts n policies. At this stage we have only learned the first policy π_1^θ which will serve as our *teacher policy* to learn the rest of the policy vector.

(ii) In the second stage we sample successful trajectories from our teacher policy π_1^θ (the so-called experience),

$$D = \{(s_1, \pi_1(\cdot, s_1), \ldots, s_m, \pi_1(\cdot, s_m)), \ldots\} \tag{6}$$

which will be regressed onto the policy vector, where s_m is a terminal state with reward $r_{m-1} > 0$. We then take out sub-sequences B_n of length n from D

$$B_n = \{(s_t, \pi_1(\cdot, s_t), \ldots, s_{t+n-1}, \pi_1(\cdot, s_{t+n-1})), \ldots\} \quad \text{with } 1 \leq t \leq m - n + 1. \tag{7}$$

We minimize the squared distance between the teacher policies $\pi_1^{\theta'}(\cdot|s_i)$ and the set of student policies $\pi_i^\theta(\cdot|s_t)$ of the sub-sequence

$$\sum_{i=2}^{n} \left(\pi_i^\theta(\cdot|s_t) - \pi_1^{\theta'}(\cdot|s_i)\right)^2 . \tag{8}$$

Here, we use the squared distance, but any regression function can be used. Further note that θ is the parameter of the full policy vector $\vec{\pi}^\theta$. For $\pi_1^{\theta'}$ the parameter is held fixed (denoted by θ'). So PHR implicitly defines a *semi-gradient* update method. Note, that PHR uses the rewards only to train the teacher policy π_1^θ via the A2C loss , but not for learning $\pi_2^\theta, \ldots, \pi_n^\theta$. In the second stage, the reward is only used to determine the best teacher trajectories.

Finally, we have the PHR loss which is the expectation of Eq. 8 wrt. to all sub-sequences, i.e.,

$$J_{\text{PHR}}(\theta, \theta') = \mathbb{E}_{\mathcal{D}}\left[\sum_{i=2}^{n} \left(\pi_i^\theta(\cdot|s_t) - \pi_1^{\theta'}(\cdot|s_i)\right)^2\right] \tag{9}$$

where $(s_1, \ldots, s_n)$ are the random variables that are averaged out. The gradient for the PHR loss with respect to the parameters θ is:

$$\nabla_\theta J_{\text{PHR}}(\theta, \theta') = \mathbb{E}_{\mathcal{D}} \left[\sum_{i=2}^{n} \nabla_\theta \pi_i^\theta(\cdot|s_t) \left(\pi_i^\theta(\cdot|s_t) - \pi_1^{\theta'}(\cdot|s_i) \right) \right]. \quad (10)$$

In other words, the policy vector $\vec{\pi}^\theta$ should learn to perform the same set of actions $a_2, \ldots, a_n$ just by looking at s_t as π_1^θ would choose by looking at the full state sequence. Finally, this yields the following update rule,

$$\nabla_\theta J(\theta) = \lambda \nabla_\theta J_{\text{PHR}}(\theta, \theta') \quad (11)$$

where λ is a hyperparameter that adjusts the sensitivity of PHR and must be set depending on the chosen distance measure. Overall, during the two stage process we combine the A2C gradient from Eq. 5 with the PHR gradient which yields the full gradient for the parameter θ of the policy vector $\vec{\pi}^\theta$:

$$\nabla_\theta J(\theta) = \nabla_\theta J_{\text{PG}}(\theta) + \lambda \nabla_\theta J_{\text{PHR}}(\theta, \theta') \quad (12)$$

The complete learning procedure is summarized in Algorithm 1.

Implementation Details. (i) Depending on the environment regressing every sub-sequence from Eq. 9 may lead to bad performance. Therefore, we define a hyperparameter $\alpha \in \mathbb{N}$ such that only every α-th sub-sequence is used for regression. (ii) For L_{CE} we sample the index of the best actions from the teacher policies as in Eq. 3 and calculate the cross entropy loss between these actions and the student policies, i.e., $a^* = \arg\max \pi_1(\cdot|s_t)$ and $L_{CE} = \log \pi_i(a^*|s_t)$.

4 Results

In the following experiments we investigate two contributions of PHR: (i) Is PHR able to increase inference speed in a meaningful way? (ii) Does the raw performance of the trained agent scale according to the inference speedup? For this purpose we test PHR agents with horizons $n \in \{1, 4, 8, 16\}$ on two sets of environments, gym-minigrid and Pong from the ALE emulator [2]. To test (i) we measure the wall-clock time every agent needs to complete 100,000 steps. For (ii) we measure the amount of reward the agent can collect in one second.

4.1 Experiments

The Python package gym-minigrid [3] is a collection of gridworld environments. We chose the environments depicted in Fig. 3 where the goal is to reach the green square. Only here the agent receives a reward making both environments very sparse. Changing direction and moving forward are two separate sets of actions. In addition, we chose the Pong-Deterministic-v4 environment from ALE [2]. The environment has 6 different actions to interact with the players paddle. A reward signal of 1 or -1 is given depending on which player scores a point. The episode ends when one player reaches the score of 21.

Algorithm 1: Policy Horizon Regression Algorithm

Select horizon n, hyperparameter $\alpha \in \mathbb{N}$ and randomly initialize network with π_1^θ and policy vector $\vec{\pi}^\theta = \left[\pi_1^\theta, \ldots, \pi_n^\theta\right]^T$.

Train A2C agent fully as teacher with the A2C gradient to update π_i^θ

$$\nabla_\theta J_{\mathrm{PG}}(\theta) = \nabla_\theta \log \pi_1^\theta(s_t, a_t)\; Q^\theta(s_t, a_t)$$

for *episode* $= 1, \ldots, K$ **do**

  Sample *experience* $(s_1, \pi_1(\cdot|s_1), \ldots, s_m, \pi_1(\cdot|s_m))$ from teacher policy π_1^θ where reward $r_{m-1} > 0$

  for $t = 1, \ldots, m-n+1$ **do**

    if $t \mod \alpha == 0$ **then**

      Take out sub-sequence of n states $(s_t, \ldots, s_{t+n-1})$ from *experience*

      Calculate PHR gradient to update policy vector $\vec{\pi}^\theta$

$$\nabla_\theta J_{\mathrm{PHR}}(\theta, \theta') = \sum_{i=2}^{n} \sum_{j=1}^{A} \nabla_\theta \pi_i^\theta(a_j|s_t) \left(\pi_i^\theta(a_j|s_t) - \pi_1^{\theta'}(a_j|s_{t+i-1})\right)$$

      Update model with PHR gradient

$$\nabla_\theta J(\theta) = \lambda \nabla_\theta J_{\mathrm{PHR}}(\theta, \theta')$$

    end

  end

end

MultiRoom. We adapted the MultiRoom environment to be the same as the environment in [18], also used by [16]. It is a 13 × 13 grid and has 4 crossings. This environment requires the agent to learn a long path from start to finish, thus we test how precisely PHR can map a set of actions to the policy vector.

Crossing. The SimpleCrossingS9N1 environments changes the position of the crossing after every episode with uniform probability to any position on the grid except the start and goal state. It is a 9 × 9 grid with 1 crossing. We test whether PHR is able to learn multiple paths in an environment that changes frequently.

Pong. Finally, we test PHR on a reactionary environment where the agent needs to react to an opponents actions. For this we use the Pong-Deterministic-v4 environment. We analyze whether PHR is able to learn where an agent must perform precisely timed actions and react to an opposing agents behavior.

4.2 Setup

To test PHR, we define agents that evaluate the environment every n steps. In other words, these agents perform n actions from a single state evaluation

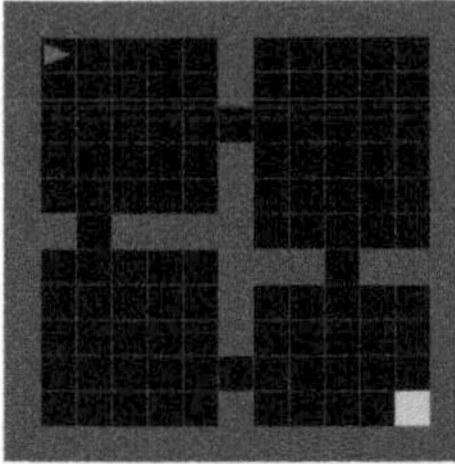
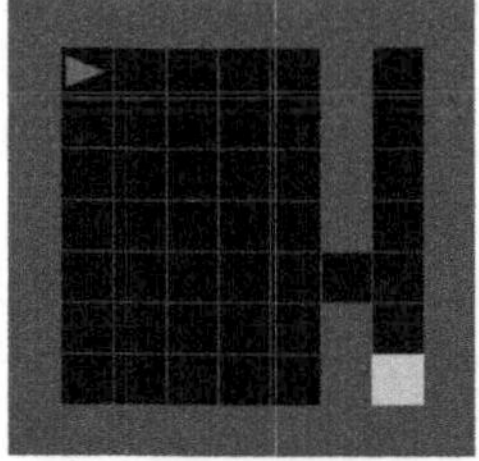
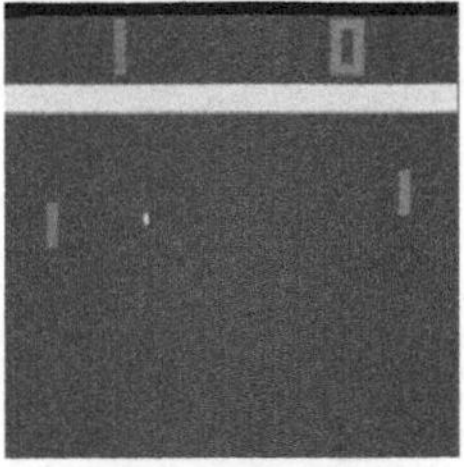

Fig. 3. Environments used in this work. First we test on a deterministic grid environment (left) MultiRoom with 4 rooms. The second environment (middle) Crossing is stochastic in the sense that the crossing changes position after every episode. Finally (right), we test on the Pong environment.

before evaluating the state again. For example: an agent that evaluates *every* state to generate a policy is denoted with $n = 1$. An agent that evaluates every *fourth* state to generate a policy is denoted with $n = 4$. Moreover, once an agent completes an episode it is allowed to evaluate the model, regardless of the current action in the policy vector. We test every environment for $n \in \{1, 4, 8, 16\}$ and perform 5 runs for every configuration. For the Crossing environment the seed for the randomization of the environment is different across all 5 runs.

Performance Metrics. We define two performance metrics for our experiments. We measure wall-clock time and score per second between different horizons n for PHR. With wall-clock time we measure the overall inference speedup provided by evaluating the policy vector instead of the complete model. The score per second measures the reward the agents can gather in one second. This allows us to measure whether the agents raw performance also scales with inference speedup. In this way we can visualize the trade-off between faster model evaluation and the agents quicker task completion due to the sequencing of actions.

Baseline. We define $n = 1$ as the baseline. This is the agent that evaluates the model at every step, i.e., regular model inference with A2C. Ideally, the PHR agents $n \in \{4, 8, 16\}$ should be more efficient to evaluate and complete the environments faster while maintaining or increasing raw performance.

4.3 Performance

Figure 4 shows the wall-clock time of the different agents and their throughput in score per second for 100k steps of inference averaged over 5 runs. We generally see that PHR is able to provide at least double the inference speedup in all 3 environments, effectively only needing at least half the time to complete 100k steps, while scaling logarithmically through the different agents (lower part of Fig. 4). Moreover, as policy quality is maintained, the agent is able to increase

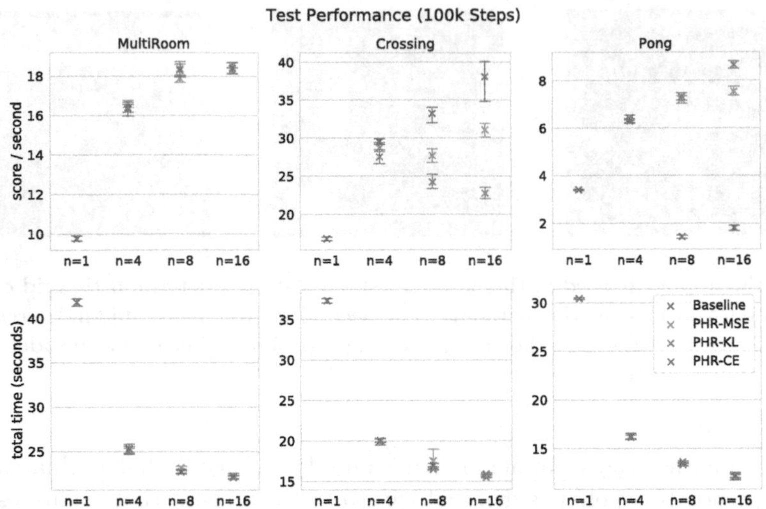

Fig. 4. Score per second and total inference time (100k steps, 5 runs) for all 3 environments. The top 3 plots show the achieved score per second (higher is better), while the lower 3 plots show the time needed to complete 100k steps (lower is better). PHR is generally able to reduce the wall-clock time at least by half, thus doubling inference speed. Moreover, PHR is able to maintain policy quality thus achieving a higher throughput.

its throughput by the same factor (upper part of Fig. 4). This means that not only is evaluating the policy vector more efficient, but predicting n actions for a single observation also effectively increases the throughput i.e. the productivity of the agent. Due to the low tolerance of error in Crossing, cross entropy leads to vastly better performance as it maps actions directly compared to the distance measures. Pong on the other hand benefits from a softer regression as this produces less jittery behavior which is counterproductive in reactive settings.

4.4 Learned Path

We analyzed the paths that are actually learned by the agent. Figure 5 shows the learned path of an agent evaluating $n = 4$, i.e., evaluating a state every 4 actions. We see that the agent is able to learn the most important decisions such as turning towards the crossing in actions 4, 8 and turning towards the goal in action 13. Moreover, these actions are determined from intermediate policies that have been learned by PHR.

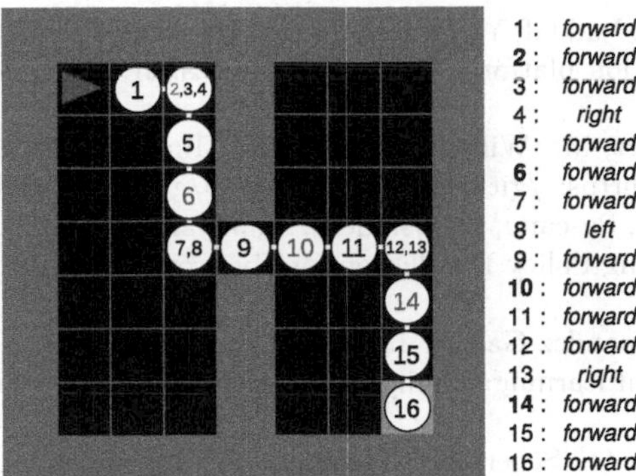

Fig. 5. Learned path for one configuration of the Crossing environment with two rooms. Crucial actions are taken at intermediate policies, thus showing that PHR has learned a path. Numbers 1 to 16 represent actions performed to land in each state. Red (**Bold**) numbers represent a state evaluation, which happens every 4 actions. (Color figure online)

5 Discussion

Limitations. A drawback to our method is that we require the tasks to be sequenceable and not highly stochastic. As the agent is committed to n steps when it evaluates the policy vector, all stochastic behavior must be observable to the agent during the first stage of training the teacher policy. However, we show with the Crossing and Pong environments that PHR is well able to handle stochasticity and reactive settings. Thus, once the teacher policy is successfully learned, learning the policy vector is straightforward and remains performant.

Conclusion. Overall, we succeeded in training an agent to predict n actions given only a single state. We showed on one hand that an optimal path can be learned with PHR in the minigrid environments. On the other hand we showed that PHR is well capable of being used in a reactive environment that is not sequenced as an optimal path in a grid, but as an optimal set of actions that have to be executed precisely. With PHR we drastically reduce the computational cost at inference time as it takes less time to evaluate the policy head with n actions than to evaluate the model n times. Furthermore, PHR sequences actions reliably such that it is able to complete the environments faster, providing an even greater inference speedup. This opens PHR up to easy implementation in real-world applications where limited computing resources are of concern.

References

1. Barto, A., Mahadevan, S.: Recent advances in hierarchical reinforcement learning. Discrete Event Dyn. Syst. Theory Appl. **13** (2002). https://doi.org/10.1023/A:1025696116075

2. Bellemare, M.G., Naddaf, Y., Veness, J., Bowling, M.: The arcade learning environment: an evaluation platform for general agents. arXiv e-prints arXiv:1207.4708, July 2012
3. Chevalier-Boisvert, M., Willems, L., Pal, S.: Minimalistic gridworld environment for openai gym. https://github.com/maximecb/gym-minigrid (2018)
4. Czarnecki, W.M., Pascanu, R., Osindero, S., Jayakumar, S.M., Swirszcz, G., Jaderberg, M.: Distilling Policy Distillation. arXiv e-prints arXiv:1902.02186, February 2019
5. De Asis, K., Hernandez-Garcia, J.F., Zacharias Holland, G., Sutton, R.S.: Multi-step reinforcement learning: a unifying algorithm. arXiv e-prints arXiv:1703.01327, March 2017
6. Efroni, Y., Dalal, G., Scherrer, B., Mannor, S.: Beyond the one step greedy approach in reinforcement learning. arXiv e-prints arXiv:1802.03654, February 2018
7. Guez, A., et al.: An investigation of model-free planning (2019)
8. Hart, P.E., Nilsson, N.J., Raphael, B.: A formal basis for the heuristic determination of minimum cost paths. IEEE Trans. Syst. Sci. Cybern. **4**(2), 100–107 (1968)
9. Lakshminarayanan, A.S., Sharma, S., Ravindran, B.: Dynamic action repetition for deep reinforcement learning. In: Proceedings of the Thirty-First AAAI Conference on Artificial Intelligence, pp. 2133–2139. AAAI 2017. AAAI Press (2017)
10. Lee, J., Lee, B.J., Kim, K.E.: Reinforcement learning for control with multiple frequencies. In: Larochelle, H., Ranzato, M., Hadsell, R., Balcan, M.F., Lin, H. (eds.) Advances in Neural Information Processing Systems, vol. 33, pp. 3254–3264. Curran Associates, Inc. (2020). https://proceedings.neurips.cc/paper/2020/file/216f44e2d28d4e175a194492bde9148f-Paper.pdf
11. Mnih, V., et al.: Asynchronous methods for deep reinforcement learning. In: International Conference on Machine Learning, pp. 1928–1937. PMLR (2016)
12. Mnih, V., et al.: Playing Atari with deep reinforcement learning. In: NIPS Deep Learning Workshop (2013)
13. Ning, L., Shen, X.: Deep reuse: streamline CNN inference on the fly via coarse-grained computation reuse. In: Proceedings of the ACM International Conference on Supercomputing, pp. 438–448 (2019)
14. Panov, A.I., Yakovlev, K.S., Suvorov, R.: Grid path planning with deep reinforcement learning: preliminary results. Procedia Comput. Sci. **123**, 347–353 (2018)
15. Rusu, A.A., et al.: Policy Distillation. arXiv e-prints arXiv:1511.06295, November 2015
16. Schoknecht, R., Riedmiller, M.: Speeding-up reinforcement learning with multi-step actions. In: Dorronsoro, J.R. (ed.) ICANN 2002. LNCS, vol. 2415, pp. 813–818. Springer, Heidelberg (2002). https://doi.org/10.1007/3-540-46084-5_132
17. Sutton, R., Precup, D., Singh, S.: Intra-option learning about temporally abstract actions, pp. 556–564 (1998)
18. Sutton, R.S., Precup, D., Singh, S.: Between MDPs and semi-MDPs: a framework for temporal abstraction in reinforcement learning. Artif. Intell. **112**(1–2), 181–211 (1999)

Behaviour-Conditioned Policies for Cooperative Reinforcement Learning Tasks

Antti Keurulainen[1,3](✉), Isak Westerlund[3], Ariel Kwiatkowski[3], Samuel Kaski[1,2], and Alexander Ilin[1]

[1] Helsinki Institute for Information Technology HIIT, Department of Computer Science, Aalto University, Espoo, Finland
antti.keurulainen@aalto.fi

[2] Department of Computer Science, University of Manchester, Manchester, UK

[3] Bitville Oy, Espoo, Finland

Abstract. The cooperation among AI systems, and between AI systems and humans is becoming increasingly important. In various real-world tasks, an agent needs to cooperate with unknown partner agent types. This requires the agent to assess the behaviour of the partner agent during a cooperative task and to adjust its own policy to support the cooperation. Deep reinforcement learning models can be trained to deliver the required functionality but are known to suffer from sample inefficiency and slow learning. However, adapting to a partner agent behaviour during the ongoing task requires ability to assess the partner agent type quickly. We suggest a method, where we synthetically produce populations of agents with different behavioural patterns together with ground truth data of their behaviour, and use this data for training a meta-learner. We additionally suggest an agent architecture, which can efficiently use the generated data and gain the meta-learning capability. When an agent is equipped with such a meta-learner, it is capable of quickly adapting to cooperation with unknown partner agent types in new situations. This method can be used to automatically form a task distribution for meta-training from emerging behaviours that arise, for example, through self-play.

Keywords: Agent behaviour · Cooperative AI · Deep reinforcement learning

1 Introduction

In many real-world applications, the ability of AI agents to cooperate with each other and humans is of crucial importance. It is especially important to have the capability to cooperate with different types of agents with different characteristics and behavioural patterns. In practice, this calls for functionalities to infer the behaviour of the partner agent and then adapting to the inferred agent type

I. Farkaš et al. (Eds.): ICANN 2021, LNCS 12894, pp. 493–504, 2021.
https://doi.org/10.1007/978-3-030-86380-7_40

for common good. Furthermore, it is useful to infer the behaviour of an unknown partner agent as fast as possible during the ongoing task. Such situations arise, for example, when self-driving cars try to adapt to the various driving styles of the surrounding (human) drivers, or when an AI teacher tries to adapt to the skill level of the human student.

Human cognition studies suggest that predictions on other peoples' behaviour are based on high-level models, such as mental states and abstractions [1,3,14]. Such high-level abstractions may be, for example, intentions, goals, desires or some other factors describing the mental state. Taking inspiration from human cognition, our goal is to enable an agent to infer the latent variable that explains the behaviour of the partner agent, and then make use of the inferred information during the ongoing task. In practice, the latent variable needs to be low-dimensional since it needs to be inferred from short-term behaviour. For example, it might be known that the behaviour of the partner agent depends heavily on the skill level of the partner agent, which may be unknown and therefore needs to be inferred.

In our method, we synthetically produce partner agent populations that are used for training a meta-learner, which can be integrated as part of the agent policy. As a result, an agent gains the capability of "learning to learn" and can quickly adapt to unknown agent types in new situations. Self-play has been shown to create an automatic curriculum for learning and to produce emerging behaviours [27,28], thus it is a good candidate to synthetically produce populations with different behavioural patterns. Since the agents are synthetically generated, the process also produces appropriate ground truth data of the partner agent behaviour that can be used for training the meta-learner.

We frame this setting as a deep meta-reinforcement learning problem [8,12,26], where the partner agent behaviour is embedded in the transition dynamics of the Markov Decision Process (MDP). During the training phase of the meta-learning process, an agent is partnered with different partner agent types in different instances of the environment. A detailed description of the meta-learning approach is described in Sect. 3.

Our method is also based on the assumption that the two tasks, of inferring the partner agent behaviour, and of conducting the actual task, have different requirements and hence need different solutions. In particular, the former requires observing the agent for some time period and hence requires memory in its policy. A common way for introducing memory in neural networks is by allowing recurrent connections, which brings challenges such as vanishing and exploding gradients and credit assignment [4]. On the other hand, many cooperative tasks can be executed without memory, once the policy network is conditioned on the partner agent behaviour. As an example, if the partner agent is closer to a specific item to be collected in a gridworld, it is useful to let the partner agent collect the item, if it is known to have the skills to do it.

In our approach, which we call the *behaviour-conditioned policy*, we suggest a separate dedicated network with memory that infers the agent behaviour quickly during the first steps of the task execution and a separate policy network without memory, which is conditioned on the inferred behaviour. As a result, the actual policy is easier to train as it can be implemented by a simpler feedforward network without recurrent connections. Both networks can be trained separately by using the synthetically produced agent populations together with the ground truth data of their behaviour. During the execution, the ground truth data is replaced by the predictions of the partner agent behaviour, resulting in a policy that is not dependent on the ground truth information that is used for training.

The contributions of this paper can be summarized as:

- A method to automatically generate a task distribution and associated ground truth data from scratch by self-play for training a meta-learner.
- An architecture and training method that can efficiently use the generated task distribution and the ground truth data.

We demonstrate the capabilities of our approach in two different types of experiments. In the first experiment, we compare the performance against the RL^2 meta-reinforcement learning architecture [8] in a simple matrix game. In the second, more complex environment, an agent solves a travelling salesman gridworld (TSG) task in cooperation with a partner agent of an unknown type, and we show higher performance when compared to an end-to-end solution with an LSTM architecture.

2 Related Work

There is a long history of research in opponent modelling [22]. For example, [25] present an idea, where one agent predicts the behaviour of the other agent by putting itself in a similar situation and [30] present a method of breaking the symmetries in the underlying task and thus improving cooperation. The former is an example where the partner agent is considered to be similar to oneself, and the latter assumes that the partner agent is optimal but might have converged to a different convention than oneself. In our case, we make weaker assumptions as the partner agent is not assumed to be optimal. In [16] and [24], methods to shape the learning of the other agent are presented. In our work, we do not try to affect the learning of the partner agent, but rather adapt to the behaviour of the agent, which is embedded in the transition dynamics.

Applying centralized training with decentralized execution (CTDE) [6,9] is an active research area and it is an open problem how to best benefit from the centralized training when private information is not available during execution. For example, MADPPG [19] uses a centralized critic with decentralized actors and [23] suggests a method based on using a centralised critic and a specific version of the baseline in an actor-critic algorithm to tackle the multi-agent credit assignment challenge. Since centralized critics appear to be beneficial, we make use of this concept in our baselines and thus reduce variance in the policy gradient estimates. Our method suggests a natural extension of CTDE to the transition dynamics of the MDP.

Self-play has been shown to be a successful method for producing an automated curriculum for learning in multi-agent reinforcement learning settings [11,27,28]. When training is conducted with a copy of itself, the cooperability with other agent types with different behaviour might be limited. One possible solution to improve generalization and robustness in self-play is to interleave old versions of the policy in the training procedure. In [11], a method to sample old opponents, which were stored during the self-play training, was used to prevent overfitting to the latest policy and for stabilizing the self-play training procedure. Also, [15] show that sampling opponents from a pool of past versions of the policy improves the performance and robustness of training agents in adversarial settings. Our method also benefits from the sampling of old opponents, but instead of adversarial training we use self-play to produce a suitable task distribution for meta-learning.

One typical way to encourage neural networks to learn more useful representations for a particular task, is to add auxiliary tasks to the learning process [2]. For example, auxiliary tasks can be used to improve representations in classification tasks [7,13], or in the context of deep reinforcement learning [10,18,29]. Our mechanism differs from the typical way of using auxiliary heads, as instead of adding an extra auxiliary head to the common representation, we train a distinct prediction network with a supervised loss, and condition the policy network with this prediction.

3 Setting

We formalize our problem as a meta-reinforcement learning setting [8,12,26]. We synthetically construct a set of MDPs by training populations of agents with self-play to obtain a distribution of agents with different behaviours. We sample MDPs from a family $\mathcal{M}$ according to a meta learning distribution $M_i \sim p(M)$. From the point of view of one agent, every MDP has a different transition dynamics dictated by the behaviour of the partnering agent. To be more specific, we define the MDP by the tuple $M = \langle \mathcal{S}, \mathcal{A}, \mathcal{P}, \mathcal{R}, \gamma, \rho_0, H \rangle$, where $\mathcal{S}$ is the state space and $\mathcal{A}$ is the action space, γ is the discount factor, $\rho_0 : \mathcal{S} \rightarrow [0, 1]$ is the initial state distribution and H is the horizon. The transition function $\mathcal{P}$ is defined as a function of the action space and the state space as $\mathcal{P} : \mathcal{S} \times \mathcal{A} \times \mathcal{S} \rightarrow [0, 1]$ and $\mathcal{R} : \mathcal{S} \times \mathcal{A} \rightarrow \mathbb{R}$ is the reward function experienced by the agent.

Under this setting, the objective is to maximize the expected sum of discounted rewards over the episodes $J(\pi_\theta) = \mathbb{E}_{\tau \sim p_\pi(\tau)}[\sum_{t=0}^{H} \gamma^t \mathcal{R}(s_t, a_t)]$, where $\tau = (s_0, a_0, ...)$ is the trajectory of states s_t and actions a_t of the agent at time step t for an episode of length H. The initial state is sampled from the distribution ρ_0 and the agent samples the action a_t from its policy function $\pi(a_t|s_t)$. The next state is sampled from the transition dynamics function $s_{t+1} \sim \mathcal{P}(s_{t+1}|s_t, a_t)$. The meta-MDP objective is to find the policy that maximizes the expected returns over the task distribution: $\arg\max_{\theta} \mathbb{E}_{p(M)}[J(\pi_\theta)]$.

4 Behaviour-Conditioned Policy

The two distinct structures of the task can be efficiently exploited by constructing separate networks for both task structures, which we name the *task prediction* and the *policy.* We synthetically produce populations of agents together with ground truth information about their behaviour. Under the meta-learning framework, each sampled MDP embeds the behaviour of the partner agent, and the task prediction refers to predicting the behaviour of the partner agent. Following the centralised training and decentralised execution (CTDE) paradigm, we use this ground truth information during training, but not during decentralised execution. The architectures for the training and execution phases are shown in Fig. 1.

The task prediction network is stateful and thus able to preserve the representation of the trajectories $\tau_i = \{s_t\}_{t=0}^{l}$, where i is the task index and l is the length of the episode. The task prediction is performed by a neural network f_ϕ as $\hat{T}_i = f_\phi(\tau_i)$, where $\hat{T}_i$ is the estimation of the task i. More specifically, the task prediction network uses a standard LSTM architecture [5]. The task prediction network is trained by minimizing the loss under the task distribution $\mathcal{L} = \mathbb{E}_{p(M)}[L_M(f_\phi)]$ by using the ground truth task labels T_i.

During the training, the policy network is a feedforward network $\pi = g_\theta(s_i, T_i)$. During the execution, the ground truth task label T_i is replaced by the prediction $\hat{T}_i$, produced by the task prediction network.

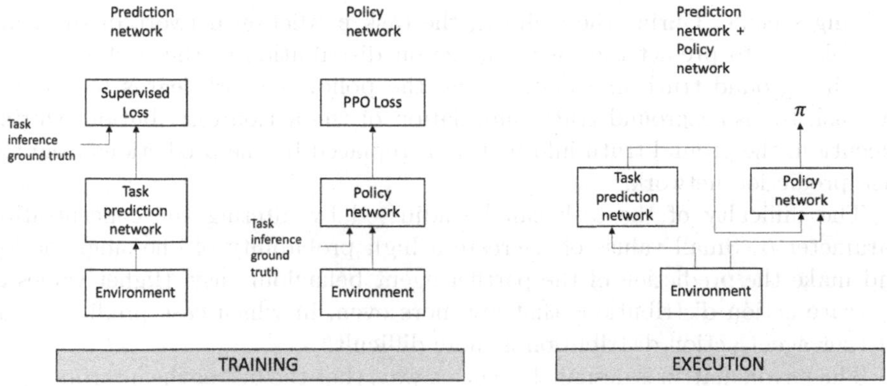

Fig. 1. Illustration of the training and execution architectures. Two separate networks are trained with ground truth data to predict the task and to run the policy. The execution is run by using the task prediction to allow decentralised execution

5 Experiments

In this section, we present the experiments and their results. In these experiments one agent (*the main agent*) is equipped with the behaviour-conditioned policy, and adapts to the behaviour of the other agent (*the partner agent*). The first experiment is a simple matrix game, where the task is to adapt to the partner policy. The purpose of this experiment is to investigate how well the suggested architecture can benefit from a synthetically generated task distribution compared to a strong meta-learning baseline. In the second experiment, we combine the behaviour conditioned policy architecture with the creation of a meta-learning task distribution with self-play. In essence, the task is a travelling salesman-type problem for which self-play produces a distribution of agents of different skill levels.

5.1 Matrix Game Experimental Setup

In this matrix game two agents perform actions sampled from their action distributions. For each time step, the shared reward of their joint action is defined by the payoff matrix, shown in Table 1.

For the partner agent, the action distributions are generated by drawing them from a symmetric Dirichlet distribution $Dir(\alpha)$ with concentration parameter α. The main agent is equipped with the behaviour-conditioned policy and it is thus able to learn during the episode the behaviour of the unknown partner agent, and adjust its own policy accordingly.

One episode is fixed to ten steps, and the partner agent uses the same sampled action distribution throughout the episode, and for each episode a new action distribution is sampled. In one training iteration, 50 partner action distributions are drawn and thus one iteration consists of 50 different tasks in the meta-training scheme. During the training, the task prediction network of the main agent learns to predict the task (the action distribution of the partner agent) by using ground truth information, and the policy network learns to conduct the task by using ground truth information of the action distribution. During execution, the ground truth information is replaced by the predictions from the task prediction network.

The difficulty of the task can be adjusted by altering the concentration parameter α. Small values of α create a high probability of one single action and make the prediction of the partner agent behaviour easy. Higher values of α create action distributions that are more even, in which case predicting the partner agent action distribution is more difficult.

The payoff matrix is designed in such a way, that the better the interpretation of the other agent behaviour, the higher the payoff. As an example, predicting the partnering agent to take an action p_0 results in high reward if predicted correctly, and a high negative reward if predicted wrongly. If the prediction of the partner agent behaviour is uncertain, the main agent is tempted to select the action m_4, a low risk but low reward option, to avoid high negative rewards.

The prediction network uses the MSE loss function $\mathcal{L} = \mathbb{E}_{p(M)}||T - \hat{T}||_2^2$ and the policy network is trained using PPO loss [21], with separate networks for policy and value predictions. In this experiment the input is augmented by the time step index, in order to allow the network to perform value prediction. More details of the network implementation is available in the appendix.

Table 1. The payoff matrix for the matrix game. The partnering agent actions represent the rows $p_0 - p_4$, and the main agent selects the columns $m_0 - m_4$.

	m_0	m_1	m_2	m_3	m_4
p_0	1.0	–0.7	–0.4	–0.1	0.0
p_1	–1.0	0.8	–0.4	–0.1	0.0
p_2	–1.0	–0.7	0.6	–0.1	0.0
p_3	–1.0	–0.7	–0.4	0.4	0.0
p_4	–1.0	–0.7	–0.4	–0.1	0.2

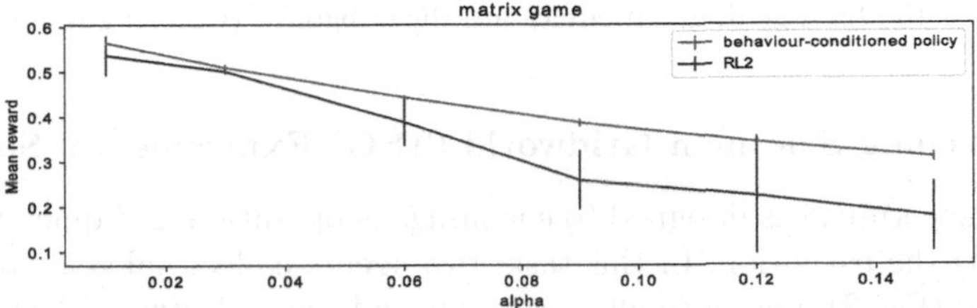

Fig. 2. Results of the matrix game experiment. The behaviour-conditioned policy is able to learn to predict the partner agent behaviour during an episode, and use that information in its policy function efficiently. The results show that the baseline RL^2 method does not reach as high mean reward, and the variance across the seeds is considerably higher. Lines are mean values over five random seeds and error bars indicate the standard deviation. The rewards are measured at the last time step of the episodes.

5.2 Matrix Game Results

We compare our algorithm against the RL^2 meta-reinforcement learning algorithm [8], which is capable of performing end-to-end training in the matrix game task. The expressive capacity of the behaviour conditioned policy was designed to be similar to the baseline RL^2 implementation, see details about the specific architectures in the appendix. Both methods receive the ground truth information of the partner agent behaviour during training by the use of a centralized critic, in order to reduce the variance of the policy gradient estimates.

In order to compare the performance for various levels of task difficulty, the experiment is run with six different values of the concentration parameter α. When $\alpha = 0.01$ or $\alpha = 0.03$, the task is easy and can be solved by both methods, but as the task is made more difficult by increasing the value of α, the behaviour-conditioned policy outperforms the end-to-end alternative (Fig. 2). The results show that if the factor that explains the behaviour is known, a separate network can infer the partner agent behaviour fast enough with sufficient accuracy during an episode, and that conditioning a simple feedforward policy with the inferred behaviour reaches higher mean reward and more stable training compared to the baseline, as is shown in Fig. 2.

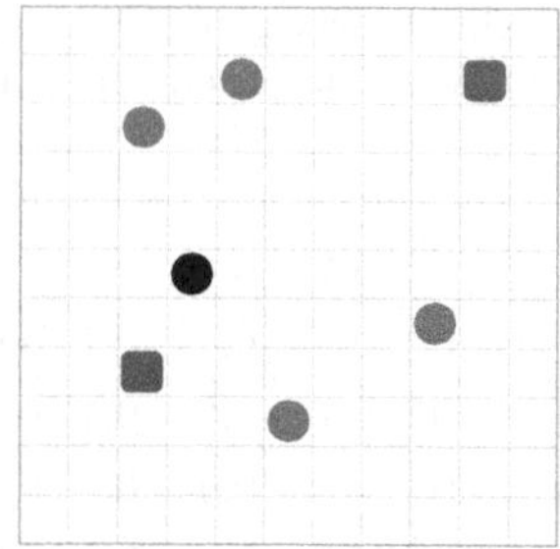

Fig. 3. Illustration of the 11×11 gridworld. Red and blue squares are the two agents, black circle is the final goal, green circles are the subgoals. (Color figure online)

5.3 Travelling Salesman Gridworld (TSG) Experimental Setup

The TSG experiment is designed to encourage cooperation and quick task inference during the execution. In this task, two agents collect subgoals together in a gridworld (Fig. 3), and once all subgoals have been collected, either one of the agents needs to collect the final goal.

Both agents have four possible actions: move up, down, left or right. The actions of both agents are fed to the environment simultaneously at each time step. Each step causes a small negative reward (–0.01), and collecting goals results in a positive reward (0.05). An episode ends when the final goal is collected or if the maximum amount of steps have been taken. As our setting is fully cooperative, both agents share the same reward.

For this task, several populations of agents with various skill levels are trained using self-play and by collecting agents from different phases of the training. Our solution tackles the non-stationarity problem [17,31] by running the training in two phases. During the first phase (*clone training*) the self-play training is conducted with the most recent versions of the policy. During the second phase, the partner is sampled from the older versions of the policy, but only the parameters of the latest version of the policy are updated. Thus, during the second phase, which we call *co-op training*, only one agent keeps on learning, thus avoiding the non-stationarity problem. We produce populations with three different skill levels: fully trained (*skilled*), untrained (*novice*) and a skill level that reaches a specified intermediate performance (*intermediate*).

The state s_t from the environment consist of the gridworld coordinates of all objects and flags indicating whether certain subgoals are already collected. We use a modified relation network [20] to produce improved representations of the states in all networks during the training and execution. In this experiment, the different tasks refer to cooperating with partner agents with various skill levels.

The skill prediction network uses a standard LSTM implementation. We minimize the negative log likelihood under the task distribution $\mathcal{L}^{XE} = \mathbb{E}_{p(M)}[-log(\hat{T}_i)]$, where $\hat{T}_i$ is the prediction of the correct task. The policy network is a feedforward network with PPO loss and with separate policy and value networks. More details of the implementation is available in the appendix.

5.4 Travelling Salesman Gridworld (TSG) Results

In the TSG experiment, we compare the behaviour-conditioned policy against a baseline LSTM policy with a similar capacity which can learn the required functionality in an end-to-end manner, see the appendix for details. As with the matrix game experiment, the baseline LSTM policy and the behaviour conditioned policy receive the ground truth information about the partner agent behaviour and use it in the form of a centralized critic. All populations that are trained with five random seeds, are partnered during evaluation with agents from an additional reference population that is not seen during the training in order to penalize overfitting to the behaviours present within the training population.

The results in Table 2 show that both the behaviour conditioned policy and baseline reach strong absolute performance with all partner types when comparing to the optimal policy. Furthermore, the performance of both methods consistently improves as the partner agent becomes more skilled. This shows that the meta-learning distribution generated through self-play not only produces strong co-operative agents, but also allows for gaining the ability to quickly adapt based on the behaviour of the partner agent in novel situations. The results also show that the behaviour conditioned policy outperforms the baseline for all partner types. This indicates that the inductive bias present for exploiting the two-fold structure of the task is useful for fast adaptation, and that the labels produced during self-play can be used as an additional training signal in parallel to their typical use for a centralized critic.

Table 2. Main results for simulations in 11×11 gridworld, two agents, four subgoals and one final goal. The results show mean values and standard deviations over five random seeds. *This is optimal when one agent collects everything. In our simulations, the other novice agent can accidentally pick up subgoals or the final goal, meaning that the simulation can exceed this value.

Method	Partner type	Mean episode length	Mean return
Behaviour-conditioned policy	Skilled	15.9 ± 0.1	0.080 ± 0.001
Behaviour-conditioned policy	Intermediate	22.9 ± 0.1	0.011 ± 0.001
Behaviour-conditioned policy	Novice	28.0 ± 0.4	-0.040 ± 0.004
LSTM policy	Skilled	17.8 ± 0.2	0.062 ± 0.002
LSTM policy	Intermediate	25.4 ± 0.8	-0.015 ± 0.009
LSTM policy	Novice	31.8 ± 0.6	-0.084 ± 0.007
Optimal	Skilled	12.9	0.121
Optimal	Novice	26.2*	−0.012*

6 Discussion

In this paper, we introduced ways to improve cooperation with an unknown partner agent type by synthetically generating population of agents and training a meta-learner by using these populations. Furthermore, we suggested an architecture that exploits efficiently the two-fold structure that is common in many real world scenarios.

The results showed that self-play can be used to construct useful task distributions for meta-learning the ability to quickly adapt to different partner types in novel cooperative situations. The results additionally indicate that utilizing data produced by self-play together with suitable inductive biases further improves the performance.

Our experiments covered cases where the latent variable that explained the behaviour of the partner agent was the skill level of the partner agent. Depending on the tasks, many other latent variables could be identified. An interesting research direction would be to explore methods for incorporating the identification of important factors as a part of the autocurriculum.

Acknowledgements. This work was supported by the Academy of Finland (Flagship programme: Finnish Center for Artificial Intelligence FCAI, grants 319264, 292334).

8 Appendix: Details of the Neural Network Implementations

8.1 Matrix Game Experiment

The baseline RL2 implementation has an LSTM layer with 32 units, followed by a MLP layer with 16 units and a linear layer with softmax. The value network does not share any weights with the policy network, and it has an LSTM layer with 16 units, followed by a MLP layer of 16 units and a linear layer.

The behaviour-conditioned policy network has two MLP layers with 6 and 16 units followed by a linear layer with softmax. The value network does not share any weights with the policy network, and it has similar structure as the policy network, except there is no softmax.

The task prediction network has an LSTM layer with 32 units, followed by one MLP layer with 16 units and a linear layer with softmax.

8.2 Travelling Salesman Gridworld Experiment

All networks use modified version of relation net [20], where the pairwise relations are processed only between the agents and other objects, instead of relations between all possible objects. The relation nets have 7 MLP layers with the hidden size of 128 before the summation operation, and 2 MLP layers of 64 hidden units after the summation. All LSTM layers have 64 hidden units.

The LSTM policy network (baseline) implementation has an LSTM layer on top of the relation net and a softmax layer to produce action distribution. The value network is a separate network with 2 MLP layers on top of the relation net. The baseline was trained 3000 iterations of clone training, and another 1000 of co-op training, with a dataset batch size of 4000 time steps.

The skill prediction network has an LSTM layer on top of the relation net and 2 MLP layers with softmax layer. It was trained with 5000 training iteration with a batch size of 4000 time steps.

The behaviour-conditioned policy network has 2 MLP layers and a softmax on top of the relation net. It was trained 3000 iterations of clone training, and another 1000 of co-op training, with a dataset batch size of 4000 time steps.

The optimizer is Adam with initial learning rate 5e–4 and scheduled learning rate decrease.

References

1. Premack, D., Woodruff, G.: Does the chimpanzee have a theory of mind? Behav. Brain Sci. **1**(4), 515–526 (1978)
2. Suddarth, S.C., Kergosien, Y.L.: Rule-injection hints as a means of improving network performance and learning time. In: Almeida, L.B., Wellekens, C.J. (eds.) EURASIP 1990. LNCS, vol. 412, pp. 120–129. Springer, Heidelberg (1990). https://doi.org/10.1007/3-540-52255-7_33
3. Gopnik, A., Wellman, H.M.: Why the child's theory of mind really is a theory. Mind & Language (1992)
4. Bengio, Y., Simard, P., Frasconi, P.: Learning long-term dependencies with gradient descent is difficult. IEEE Trans. Neural Netw. **5**(2), 157–166 (1994)
5. Hochreiter, S., Schmidhuber, J.: Long short-term memory. Neural Comput. **9**(8), 1735–1780 (1997)
6. Oliehoek, F.A.: Decentralized POMDPs. In: Wiering M., van Otterlo M. (eds) Reinforcement Learning. Adaptation, Learning, and Optimization, vol. 12. Springer, Berlin (2012). https://doi.org/10.1007/978-3-642-27645-3_15
7. Rasmus, A., Valpola, H., Honkala, M., Berglund, M., Raiko, T.: Semi-supervised learning with ladder networks. In: Advances in Neural Information Processing Systems (2015)
8. Duan, Y., Schulman, J., Chen, X., Bartlett, P.L., Sutskever, I., Abbeel, P.: RL^2: Fast reinforcement learning via slow reinforcement learning. arXiv preprint arXiv:1611.02779 (2016)
9. Kraemer, L., Banerjee, B.: Multi-agent reinforcement learning as a rehearsal for decentralized planning. Neurocomputing **190**, 82–94 (2016)
10. Mirowski, P., et al.: Learning to navigate in complex environments. arXiv preprint arXiv:1611.03673 (2016)
11. Silver, D., et al.: Mastering the game of go with deep neural networks and tree search. Nature **529**(7587), 484–489 (2016)
12. Wang, J.X., et al.: Learning to reinforcement learn. arXiv preprint arXiv:1611.05763 (2016)
13. Zhang, Y., Lee, K., Lee, H.: Augmenting supervised neural networks with unsupervised objectives for large-scale image classification. In: International conference on machine learning, ICML (2016)
14. Baker, C.L., Jara-Ettinger, J., Saxe, R., Tenenbaum, J.B.: Rational quantitative attribution of beliefs, desires and percepts in human mentalizing. Nature Hum. Behav. **1**(4), 1–10 (2017)
15. Bansal, T., Pachocki, J., Sidor, S., Sutskever, I., Mordatch, I.: Emergent complexity via multi-agent competition. arXiv preprint arXiv:1710.03748 (2017)

16. Foerster, J.N., Chen, R.Y., Al-Shedivat, M., Whiteson, S., Abbeel, P., Mordatch, I.: Learning with opponent-learning awareness. arXiv preprint arXiv:1709.04326 (2017)
17. Hernandez-Leal, P., Kaisers, M., Baarslag, T., de Cote, E.M.: A survey of learning in multiagent environments: dealing with non-stationarity. arXiv preprint arXiv:1707.09183 (2017)
18. Jaderberg, M., et al.: Reinforcement learning with unsupervised auxiliary tasks. In: 5th International Conference on Learning Representations (2017)
19. Lowe, R., Wu, Y., Tamar, A., Harb, J., Abbeel, P., Mordatch, I.: Multi-agent actor-critic for mixed cooperative-competitive environments. In: Advances in Neural Information Processing Systems (2017)
20. Santoro, A., et al.: A simple neural network module for relational reasoning. In: Advances in Neural Information Processing Systems (2017)
21. Schulman, J., Wolski, F., Dhariwal, P., Radford, A., Klimov, O.: Proximal policy optimization algorithms. arXiv preprint arXiv:1707.06347 (2017)
22. Albrecht, S.V., Stone, P.: Autonomous agents modelling other agents: a comprehensive survey and open problems. Artif. Intell. **258**, 66–95 (2018)
23. Foerster, J., Farquhar, G., Afouras, T., Nardelli, N., Whiteson, S.: Counterfactual multi-agent policy gradients. In: Proceedings of the AAAI Conference on Artificial Intelligence, vol. 32 (2018)
24. Letcher, A., Foerster, J., Balduzzi, D., Rocktäschel, T., Whiteson, S.: Stable opponent shaping in differentiable games. arXiv preprint arXiv:1811.08469 (2018)
25. Raileanu, R., Denton, E., Szlam, A., Fergus, R.: Modeling others using oneself in multi-agent reinforcement learning. In: International Conference on Machine Learning (2018)
26. Stadie, B.C., et al.: Some considerations on learning to explore via meta-reinforcement learning. In: Advances in Neural Information Processing Systems (2018)
27. Baker, B., et al.: Emergent tool use from multi-agent autocurricula. arXiv preprint arXiv:1909.07528 (2019)
28. Leibo, J.Z., Hughes, E., Lanctot, M., Graepel, T.: Autocurricula and the emergence of innovation from social interaction: a manifesto for multi-agent intelligence research. arXiv preprint arXiv:1903.00742 (2019)
29. Hu, H., Foerster, J.N.: Simplified action decoder for deep multi-agent reinforcement learning. In: ICLR (2020)
30. Hu, H., Lerer, A., Peysakhovich, A., Foerster, J.: Other-play for zero-shot coordination. In: International Conference on Machine Learning (2020)
31. Nguyen, T.T., Nguyen, N.D., Nahavandi, S.: Deep reinforcement learning for multiagent systems: a review of challenges, solutions, and applications. IEEE Trans. Cybern. **50**(9), 3826–3839 (2020)

Integrated Actor-Critic for Deep Reinforcement Learning

Jiaohao Zheng[1], Mehmet Necip Kurt[2(✉)], and Xiaodong Wang[2]

[1] Shenzhen Institute of Advanced Technology, Shenzhen, China
jh.zheng@siat.ac.cn
[2] Electrical Engineering Department, Columbia University, New York, NY, USA
m.n.kurt@columbia.edu, wangx@ee.columbia.edu

Abstract. We propose a new deep deterministic actor-critic algorithm with an integrated network architecture and an integrated objective function. We address stabilization of the learning procedure via a novel adaptive objective that roughly ensures keeping the actor unchanged while the critic makes large errors. We reduce the number of network parameters and propose an improved exploration strategy over bounded action spaces. Moreover, we incorporate some recent advances in deep learning to our algorithm. Experiments illustrate that our algorithm speeds up the learning process and reduces the sample complexity considerably over the state-of-the-art algorithms including TD3, SAC, PPO, and A2C in continuous control tasks.

Keywords: Deep reinforcement learning · Integrated actor-critic · Adaptive objective · Sample complexity

1 Introduction

Reinforcement learning (RL) is effective to learn and control over complex and uncertain environments [25]. Especially with the combination of deep learning, RL has been to shown to perform well in many fields such as robotics, games, automatic control and cybersecurity [2,3,12]. In RL, an agent interacts with an environment with the goal of learning the reward-maximizing policy. Policy-based RL directly optimizes the policy towards higher rewards. Value-based RL learns the value (i.e., expected future reward) of each environment state or state-action pair, and the optimal policy is implicitly determined as the reward-maximizing action at each state. Actor-critic RL is at the intersection of the policy-based and the value-based RL such that the policy (actor) is optimized in the direction suggested by the value function (critic).

In deep RL, actor and critic strongly interact while they are trained simultaneously towards the same objective (i.e., learning the reward-maximizing policy). We aim to use the interdependency between them more explicitly and propose an integrated actor-critic algorithm. In this framework, actor and critic share more

I. Farkaš et al. (Eds.): ICANN 2021, LNCS 12894, pp. 505–518, 2021.
https://doi.org/10.1007/978-3-030-86380-7_41

knowledge, which leads to saving lots of parameters. However, shared parameters also bring an additional challenge on stabilizing the training procedure. The integrated actor-critic can be motivated from animal brains such that although different regions in a brain are assigned to different tasks, all regions are still interconnected, and a brain can act both as actor (i.e., select an action) and critic (i.e., evaluate an action).

Deep RL algorithms suffer from slow learning and high sample complexity. We propose a new model-free off-policy deep deterministic integrated actor-critic algorithm (IAC)[1]. Our algorithm speeds up learning, and equivalently reduces sample complexity of the training procedure, compared to the state-of-the-art deep RL algorithms including the twin delayed deep deterministic policy gradient algorithm (TD3) [4], soft actor-critic algorithm (SAC) [6], proximal policy optimization algorithm (PPO) [21], and advantage actor-critic algorithm (A2C) [15] in continuous control tasks. We first design a novel integrated actor-critic network architecture. Next, we propose a novel adaptive objective function to stabilize the training procedure of the integrated network. Finally, we propose an improved exploration strategy over bounded action spaces and use a set of recent advances in deep learning to further improve the performance and stability of our algorithm.

2 Background

We consider a standard RL problem where an agent interacts with a stochastic environment in order to maximize its expected total reward. We model the problem as a Markov decision process where at each discrete time t, the environment is in a particular state $s_t \in \mathcal{S}$. Assuming a fully observable environment, the agent observes the state s_t, takes an action $a_t \in \mathcal{A}$, and receives a reward $r(s_t, a_t) \in \mathbb{R}$ in return of its action. At the same time, the environment makes a transition to the next state s_{t+1} with the probability $p(s_{t+1}|s_t, a_t)$. This process is repeated until a terminal state is reached. We assume that state and action spaces are continuous and real-valued. In addition, since the feasible action space is usually bounded, we assume $a_{t,k} \in [a_{\min}, a_{\max}]$ where $a_{t,k}$ denotes the kth element of a_t.

Return from a state is defined as the total discounted future reward, $G_t = \sum_{i=t}^{\infty} \gamma^{i-t} r(s_i, a_i)$, where $\gamma \in [0, 1]$ denotes the discount factor. In RL, the agent's goal is to learn an optimal policy $\pi : \mathcal{S} \rightarrow \mathbb{P}(\mathcal{A})$ to maximize its expected return from the start, written by $J^\pi = \mathbb{E}_{s_i \sim p^\pi, a_i \sim \pi}[G_1]$, where p^π denotes the state visitation distribution under the policy π. The agent's policy can either be stochastic or deterministic. In case the policy is stochastic, $\pi(a_t|s_t)$ denotes a probability density function over the action space given the state s_t.

The expected return from a state and action pair is called the Q value. If policy π is followed after taking action a in state s, the Q value is written by $Q^\pi(s, a) = \mathbb{E}_{s_{i>t} \sim p^\pi, a_{i>t} \sim \pi}[G_t|s_t = s, a_t = a]$. The Bellman equation provides a recursive relationship between the current and the next Q values:

$$Q^\pi(s_t, a_t) = r(s_t, a_t) + \gamma \mathbb{E}_{s_{t+1} \sim p^\pi, a_{t+1} \sim \pi}[Q^\pi(s_{t+1}, a_{t+1})].$$

[1] IAC codes are available at https://github.com/IAC-deepRL/IAC.

If the policy is deterministic, it is denoted by $\mu : \mathcal{S} \rightarrow \mathcal{A}$ and the Bellman equation is written by

$$Q^{\mu}(s_t, a_t) = r(s_t, a_t) + \gamma \, \mathbb{E}_{s_{t+1} \sim p^{\mu}}[Q^{\mu}(s_{t+1}, \mu(s_{t+1}))].$$

2.1 Deterministic Policy Gradient

Policy gradient algorithms are useful to solve the RL problems, especially over continuous action domains, in which the policy is parameterized and updated with the policy gradient. Let a deterministic policy $\mu_{\theta}(s)$ be parameterized with θ and the expected return be written by

$$J(\theta) = \mathbb{E}_{s \sim p^{\mu}}[Q^{\mu}(s, \mu_{\theta}(s))]. \tag{1}$$

In the deterministic policy gradient algorithm (DPG) [22], the parameters θ are moved towards maximizing $J(\theta)$ via the deterministic policy gradient, given by

$$\nabla_{\theta} J(\theta) = \mathbb{E}_{s \sim p^{\mu}} \left[\nabla_{\theta} \mu_{\theta}(s) \, \nabla_a Q^{\mu}(s, a)|_{a = \mu_{\theta}(s)} \right].$$

2.2 Deep Deterministic Policy Gradient

The deep deterministic policy gradient algorithm (DDPG) [13] is a model-free off-policy actor-critic algorithm that combines DPG [22] with the deep Q network algorithm (DQN) [16]. In DDPG, actor and critic are both neural networks. The critic estimates the Q values $Q_w(s, a)$ parameterized by w and the actor learns a deterministic policy $\mu_{\theta}(s)$. Moreover, separate target actor and target critic networks are kept with parameters θ' and w', respectively, that are slowly updated. These networks provide stable targets to the critic through the Bellman equation: $y_t = r(s_t, a_t) + \gamma Q_{w'}(s_{t+1}, \mu_{\theta'}(s_{t+1}))$. The critic then updates its parameters w to minimize the difference between its Q value estimates and the given targets. Let $\delta_i = y_i - Q_w(s_i, a_i)$. The critic minimizes the following loss function over a mini-batch of samples chosen uniformly from an experience replay buffer $\mathcal{D}$:

$$L(w) = \mathbb{E}_{(s_i, a_i, r(s_i, a_i), s_{i+1}) \sim \mathcal{D}} \left[\delta_i^2 \right], \tag{2}$$

where the replay buffer stores the tuples $(s_i, a_i, r(s_i, a_i), s_{i+1})$ collected during exploration. Moreover, the policy parameters are updated via the sample deterministic policy gradients, given by

$$\nabla_{\theta} J(\theta) = \mathbb{E}_{\mathcal{D}} \left[\nabla_{\theta} \mu_{\theta}(s)|_{s = s_i} \, \nabla_a Q_w(s, a)|_{s = s_i, a = \mu_{\theta}(s_i)} \right].$$

In DDPG, actor and critic network parameters, θ and w, are disjoint and updated simultaneously in turn. For exploration, actor follows a stochastic behavior policy via additive random noise $\mathcal{N}$ on the deterministic policy: $\mu'(s) = \mu_{\theta}(s) + \mathcal{N}$.

3 Integrated Actor-Critic

3.1 Network Architecture

The proposed integrated network (see Fig. 1) consists of five main building blocks: state encoder, action encoder, action decoder, Q value decoder, and an internal network connected to all encoders and decoders. The integrated network acts as actor when the green area is activated, and critic when the pink area is activated. The actor and critic share the state encoder and the internal network. The whole network is kept active during training procedure and only the green area (i.e., actor) is activated after training is done.

In the integrated network, each building block is a multilayer neural network (see Fig. 2). The encoder outputs can either be concatenated or added to obtain the internal network's input. According to our experiments, the addition operation works better to reduce the network size and speed up learning without performance loss. In this case, the encoder outputs have the same width, say m.

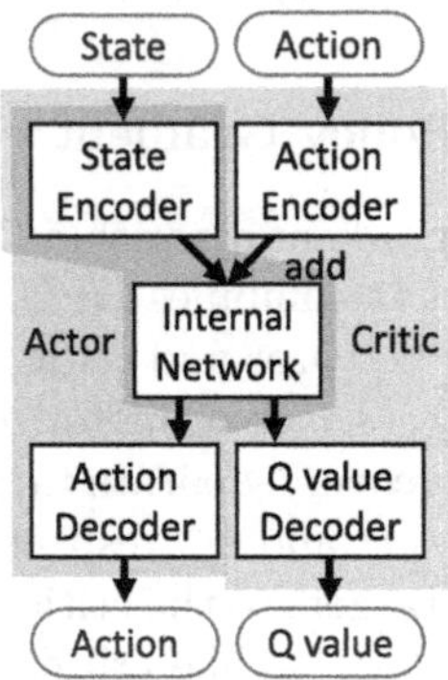

Fig. 1. Integrated actor-critic network. (Color figure online)

We design the internal network by modifying the Dense Convolutional Network (DenseNet) [9] such that all convolutional layers in the DenseNet are replaced with dense (i.e., fully connected) layers. Shortcut connections in the DenseNet architecture enable us training with fewer parameters and improve the learning performance. The internal network takes an input tensor with width m and outputs a tensor of width $4m$, which is input to both decoders.

Thanks to the shared internal network and the state encoder, the integrated network has fewer parameters compared to overall parameters of separate actor and critic networks, especially in high-dimensional tasks (e.g., when video frames form the state input). This can speed up learning. However, the shared parameters also bring an additional challenge on the training stability. The next section addresses this challenge via an adaptive objective function designed for the integrated network.

3.2 Adaptive Objective Function

Let ϕ denote parameters of the integrated network, which is the union of actor and critic parameters: $\phi = \theta \cup w$. In our algorithm, similar to DDPG, we also keep a separate target network with parameters ϕ' to provide stable targets to the critic during training. For convenience, let the policy and the value function be written in terms of ϕ by $\mu_\phi(s)$ and $Q_\phi(s, a)$, respectively. Moreover, let the expected return and the critic's loss be written by $J(\phi)$ (see Eq. (1)) and $L(\phi)$ (see Eq. (2)), respectively, additionally with the following ℓ_1 smoothing [10] on the critic's loss: $L(\phi) = E_\mathcal{D}\left[f(\delta_i)\right]$, where

$$f(x) = \begin{cases} 0.5\,x^2, & \text{if } |x| < 1, \\ |x| - 0.5, & \text{if } |x| \geq 1. \end{cases}$$

The ℓ_1 smoothing enables a more stable training, as it provides steady gradients for large δ_i and hence helps to avoid exploding gradients.

We aim to design an objective function to train the parameter-sharing integrated network in a stable manner. In the policy gradient algorithms, the policy cannot be improved if the value function estimation is wrong [4]. Hence, we introduce an adaptive variable $\lambda \in [0, 1]$ that reflects the critic's reliability level. After an initialization, we propose to update λ depending on the critic's loss (over a batch of samples) such that $\lambda \leftarrow \tau e^{-L(\phi)^2} + (1 - \tau)\lambda$, where $\tau \in (0, 1)$ is a hyperparameter. Notice that as the critic's loss $L(\phi)$ gets larger, λ gets closer to 0, and as the critic's loss gets smaller, λ gets closer to 1. A larger λ implies a more reliable critic.

Using the adaptive variable λ, we integrate $J(\phi)$ and $L(\phi)$ as well as an additional regularization term $G(\phi)$ on the policy into the following objective function:

$$Z(\phi) = L(\phi) - \lambda J(\phi) + (1 - \lambda) G(\phi), \tag{3}$$

where $G(\phi) = E_\mathcal{D}\left[f(\mu_\phi(s_i) - \mu_{\phi'}(s_i))\right]$ is a measure of how different the policy is from the target policy.

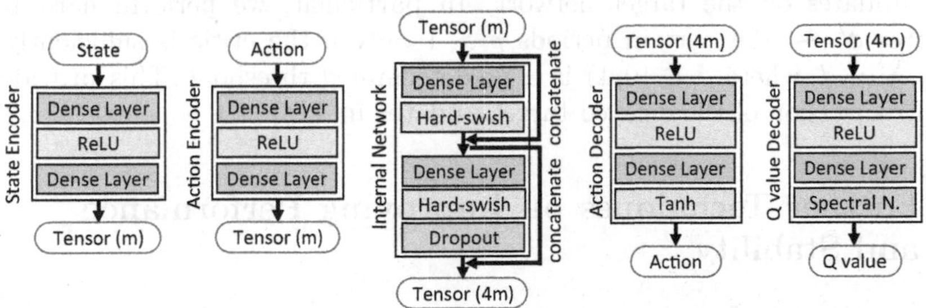

Fig. 2. Building blocks of the integrated network.

The integrated network parameters are updated towards minimizing $Z(\phi)$ via the stochastic gradient descent as follows:

$$\phi \leftarrow \phi - \alpha \nabla_\phi Z(\phi) = \phi - \frac{\alpha}{N} \sum_{i=1}^{N} \nabla_\phi Z_i(\phi),$$

where α is the learning rate, N is the batch size, and

$$Z_i(\phi) = f(y_i - Q_\phi(s_i, a_i)) - \lambda\, Q_\phi(s_i, \mu_\phi(s_i)) + (1-\lambda)\, f(\mu_\phi(s_i) - \mu_{\phi'}(s_i)).$$

We use the deterministic policy gradient theorem [22] to compute sample policy gradients as in [13].

According to the adaptive objective in Eq. (3), when the critic is less reliable (i.e., smaller λ), the actor gets a smaller learning rate. Specifically, as $\lambda \to 0$, the objective function approximates to

$$Z(\phi) \approx L(\phi) + (1-\lambda)G(\phi),$$

including only the critic's loss and the regularization term on the actor that roughly ensures keeping the policy unchanged (near the target policy) while the critic makes large errors. In this case, effectively only the critic is updated towards minimizing its loss. On the other hand, when the critic is more reliable (i.e., larger λ), actor gets a larger learning rate such that as $\lambda \to 1$, the objective function approximates to $Z(\phi) \approx L(\phi) - \lambda J(\phi)$ without including the regularization term $G(\phi)$. In this case, actor and critic are updated together.

The two-time-scale update rule (TTUR) [7,11] was shown to be useful for the convergence of the actor-critic algorithms. The TTUR suggests updating the policy with a smaller learning rate and less frequently than the value function. Notice that with the proposed objective function $Z(\phi)$, we update the policy less frequently than the value function, and moreover, we update the policy with a smaller learning rate as $\lambda \leq 1$. Hence, the proposed objective enables an adaptive version of the TTUR.

Finally, depending on the critic's reliability level, we perform adaptive periodic updates on the target network. In particular, we perform hard target updates $\phi' \leftarrow \phi$ at certain periods $p > 1$ only if the critic is sufficiently reliable: $\lambda > \beta$, where $\beta \in (0, 1)$ is a predetermined threshold. This provides an adaptive version of the delayed target updates in TD3 [4].

4 Further Techniques on Improving Performance and Stability

In this section, we first propose an improved exploration strategy and then a modified version of the target policy smoothing technique in TD3. Next, we discuss utility of a set of recent deep learning techniques that have not been commonly used in deep RL.

4.1 Exploration over Bounded Action Spaces

In deep RL, improving exploration is critical to increase data diversity, mitigate overfitting, and speed up learning. Moreover, in off-policy deterministic policy gradient algorithms, exploration can be treated independently from the learning problem [13]. Existing algorithms such as DDPG [13] use random exploration noise $\mathcal{N}_1$ such that $\mu'(s) = \mu_\theta(s) + \mathcal{N}_1$ is the behavior policy. However, since feasible actions are usually bounded to a certain interval such that $a \in [a_{\min}, a_{\max}]$, a clipping operation needs to be employed after noise addition: $\mu'(s) = \min\{\max\{a_{\min}, \mu_\theta(s) + \mathcal{N}_1\}, a_{\max}\}$. We argue that the clipping degrades the exploration efficiency since all actions exceeding the limits are set to the boundary actions, which may then be repeatedly explored by the RL agent.

We address this issue via an easy modification: whenever action exceeds the limits, choose a uniformly random action from the feasible space: $\mu'(s) = g(\mu_\phi(s) + \mathcal{N}_1)$, where

$$g(a) = a\,\mathbb{1}\{a \in [a_{\min}, a_{\max}]\} + \mathcal{U}[a_{\min}, a_{\max}]\,\mathbb{1}\{a \notin [a_{\min}, a_{\max}]\}, \tag{4}$$

$\mathbb{1}\{\cdot\}$ is an indicator function, and $\mathcal{U}[a_{\min}, a_{\max}]$ is a uniform random variable. If the action space is multidimensional, $g(\cdot)$ performs the same elementwise operation at each dimension. We choose the exploration noise $\mathcal{N}_1$ as an independent and identically distributed (iid) zero-mean Gaussian process with variance σ_1^2 at each dimension.

4.2 Target Policy Smoothing

In TD3 [4], target policy smoothing regularization forces similar actions to have similar values and for this purpose, a small random noise is clipped and added on the target policy when computing the target Q values. We find it useful to apply a modified target policy smoothing technique by computing the target y_i for $Q_\phi(s_i, a_i)$ as follows:

$$y_i = r(s_i, a_i) + \frac{\gamma}{2}\big(Q_{\phi'}(s_{i+1}, \mu_{\phi'}(s_{i+1})) + Q_{\phi'}(s_{i+1}, g(\mu_{\phi'}(s_{i+1}) + \mathcal{N}_2))\big),$$

where $g(\cdot)$ is as given in Eq. (4) and the smoothing noise $\mathcal{N}_2$ is chosen as an iid zero-mean Gaussian process with variance σ_2^2 at each action dimension.

4.3 Spectral Normalization

Since the generative adversarial networks (GANs) [5] and the actor-critic RL [11] are both bi-level optimization problems, where one model is optimized with respect to the optimum of another model, and there are many similarities in their information structures [17], techniques for improving the stability of GANs are potentially useful to stabilize the actor-critic algorithms as well. In GANs, the spectral normalization, that normalizes the spectral norm of the weight matrices of the discriminator network, is shown to improve the stability of training the discriminator [14]. Since the discriminator in GANs corresponds to the critic in actor-critic RL [17], we employ the spectral normalization on the critic network, particularly on the Q value decoder (see Fig. 2), with the goal of improving the stability of our algorithm.

4.4 Hard-Swish

In neural networks, nonlinear activation functions enable learning complex mappings from inputs to outputs, which is useful to deal with complex and high-dimensional data. Hard-swish [8] is a computationally simplified version of the swish nonlinearity [18] and it achieves a good performance especially in deep neural networks [8]. In our network design, we use the hard-swish as the activation function in the internal network and the decoders (see Fig. 2). Moreover, we use the rectified linear unit (ReLU) activation in the encoders and the hyperbolic tangent (Tanh) activation at the output layer of the action decoder.

4.5 Dropout

Dropout [24] is randomly zeroing out a certain fraction of neurons at a layer, that reduces the network capacity and forces the network to learn the most important patterns in the data. It is a widely used technique to mitigate overfitting in deep learning. We use the dropout at the last layer of the internal network (see Fig. 2) with the purpose of reducing the overfitting and improving the generalization ability of the network.

4.6 Adjusting Batch Size and Number of Iterations During Training

In [23], it is shown that increasing the batch size enables training a model with fewer parameter updates compared to reducing the learning rate in the stochastic gradient descent optimization. Based on this principle, we increase the batch size and the number of iterations during training as new samples are collected and stored in the experience replay buffer, until the buffer is full.

In our algorithm (see Algorithm 1), at each training episode, first the actor interacts with the environment, collects new samples, and saves them into the buffer. Next, the network parameters are updated via the stochastic gradient descent with a mini-batch of samples chosen uniformly from the buffer. In this process, let the parameters be updated over K iterations and the batch size be N. Moreover, let $K_0 \geq 1$ and $N_0 \geq 1$ be the initial number of iterations and the initial batch size, respectively. Furthermore, let the buffer capacity be $M \gg 1$ and the current size of the buffer be $0 \leq R \leq M$. We keep and update a parameter ρ while the buffer size gradually increases as more samples are collected: $\rho = 1 + R/M$. We then update the number of iterations and the batch size as $K = \rho K_0$ and $N = \rho N_0$, respectively.

Algorithm 1. Integrated Actor-Critic (IAC)

Initialize the integrated network with random parameters ϕ and the target network with $\phi' \leftarrow \phi$
Initialize the replay buffer $\mathcal{D}$ with size $R \leftarrow 0$ and the adaptive variable with $\lambda \leftarrow 0.5$
for episode $= 1 : E$ **do**
  I. Interact with environment
  Observe the initial state s_1
  for $t = 1 : T$ **do**
    Select action $a_t \leftarrow g(\mu_\phi(s_t) + \mathcal{N}_1)$, receive reward $r(s_t, a_t)$, and observe the next state s_{t+1}
    Save the tuple $(s_t, a_t, r(s_t, a_t), s_{t+1})$ into $\mathcal{D}$ and update the buffer size: $R \leftarrow \min\{R+1, M\}$
  II. Update network parameters
  Update the number of iterations and the batch size: $\rho \leftarrow 1 + R/M$, $K \leftarrow \rho K_0$, $N \leftarrow \rho N_0$
  Initialize the total loss of critic: $L \leftarrow 0$
  for $k = 1 : K$ **do**
    Sample uniformly a mini-batch of N tuples $(s_i, a_i, r(s_i, a_i), s_{i+1})$ from $\mathcal{D}$
    $y_i \leftarrow r(s_i, a_i) + \frac{\gamma}{2}\left(Q_{\phi'}(s_{i+1}, \mu_{\phi'}(s_{i+1})) + Q_{\phi'}(s_{i+1}, g(\mu_{\phi'}(s_{i+1}) + \mathcal{N}_2))\right)$
    Update the integrated network: $\phi \leftarrow \phi - \frac{\alpha}{N}\sum_{i=1}^{N} \nabla_\phi Z_i(\phi)$
    Update the total loss of critic: $L \leftarrow L + \sum_{i=1}^{N} f(y_i - Q_\phi(s_i, a_i))$
    if k mod p **then**
      Compute the average loss of critic: $\bar{L} \leftarrow L/pN$ and reset the total loss: $L \leftarrow 0$
      Update the adaptive variable: $\lambda \leftarrow \tau e^{-\bar{L}^2} + (1-\tau)\lambda$
      if $\lambda > \beta$ **then**
        Update the target network: $\phi' \leftarrow \phi$

5 Experiments

5.1 Comparisons with Benchmark Algorithms

We evaluate IAC (see Algorithm 1) over five continuous control tasks in the OpenAI Gym [1]. In all the tasks, feasible actions are limited to $[-1, 1]$. For comparisons, we use TD3 [4], SAC [6], A2C [15] (both with separate and shared actor-critic networks), and PPO [21] algorithms. Figure 3 illustrates the learning curves of all algorithms. We measure the sample complexity (equivalently, learning speed) of each algorithm until reaching the default target reward set at each environment. Figure 4 illustrates the average training steps until achieving the target rewards. Note that in Fig. 4, we do not present the bar charts for algorithms that could not reach the target rewards within a reasonable training period. We obtain both the learning curves and the bar charts by averaging the results over 50 random seeds. The experiments show that IAC outperforms all the benchmark algorithms in terms of learning speed.

5.2 Self-comparisons

We evaluate contributions of various IAC components on the overall algorithm performance. We specify four algorithm levels such that new components are added at each level and the level 4 corresponds to the full algorithm (see Table 1). Figure 5 illustrates the average training steps until achieving the target rewards (over 50 random seeds) for all IAC levels and TD3 as a benchmark. Figure 5 shows that the learning speed progressively improves from level 1 to level 4, which implies that all IAC components are useful. Note that in the level 1, conventional clipping operation is performed for the exploration, different from the level 2. Furthermore, the ReLU activation is used instead of hard-swish at all levels except for the level 4. Notice that the level 1 and level 2 include the novel components of IAC whereas the level 3 and level 4 incorporates some existing

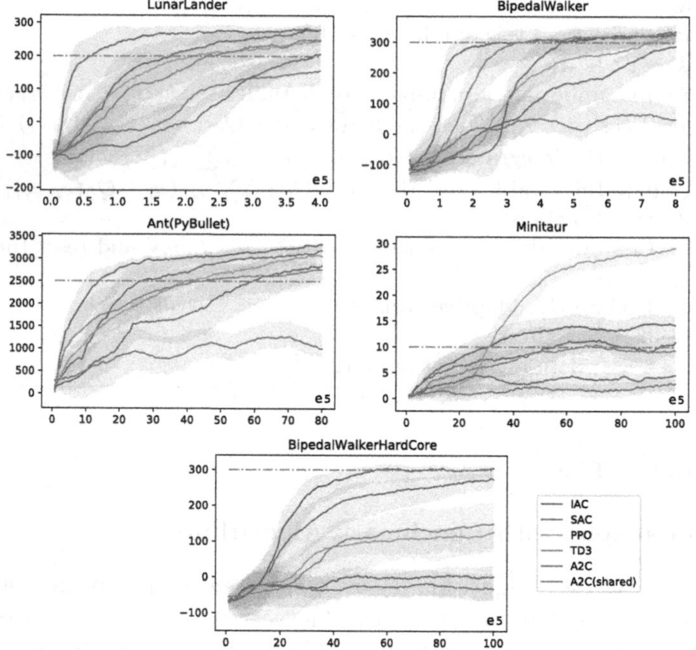

Fig. 3. Learning curves: expected return vs. number of training steps.

Table 1. Levels of IAC for self-comparisons

Level	Description
L1	Integrated network + Adaptive objective
L2	L1 + Modified exploration strategy
L3	L2 + Target policy smoothing + Spectral normalization
L4	L3 + Hard-swish + Dropout + Adjusting batch size and iteration number

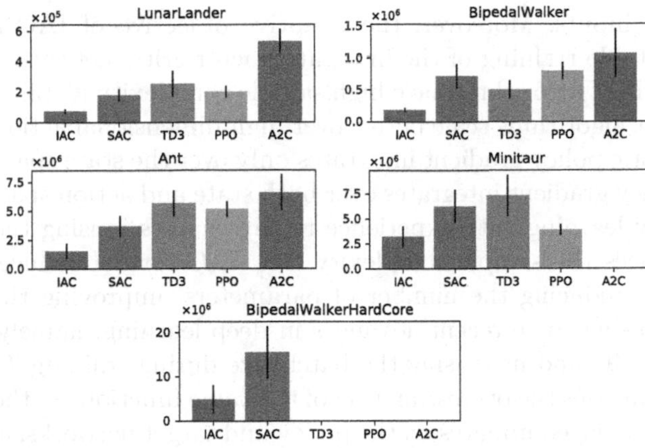

Fig. 4. Comparisons with benchmark algorithms. The bar charts illustrate the mean and standard deviation of the number of training steps until achieving the target rewards.

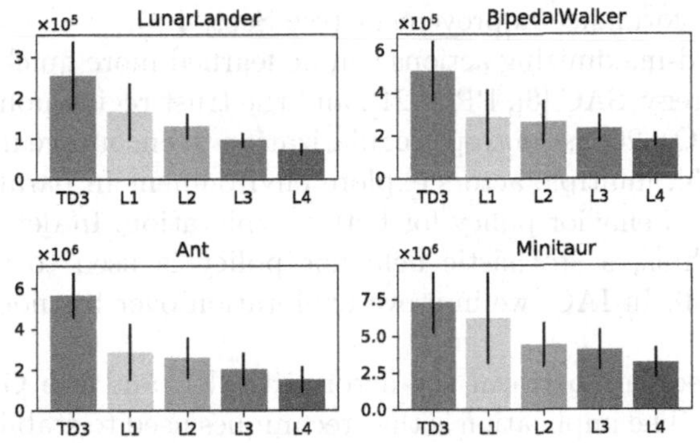

Fig. 5. Self-comparisons. The bar charts illustrate the mean and standard deviation of the number of training steps until achieving the target rewards.

deep learning techniques. Figure 5 shows that only with the novel components, IAC still significantly outperforms TD3.

6 Related Work

Parameter sharing is used for multi-task learning in neural networks [19]. In deep RL, sharing parameters between actor and critic have been discussed for A3C/A2C [15] and PPO [21] (although the PPO implementation does not share parameters) such that the network is shared except for the output layers and the objective function directly adds the actor's and critic's objectives, possibly with an additional entropy term to enable sufficient exploration. In the shared versions of both A3C/A2C and PPO, actor and critic have the same state input. In IAC, we propose a new shared network architecture where actor and critic have different inputs. Moreover, the adaptive objective of IAC is specifically designed for stable training of the integrated actor-critic network.

Policy gradient algorithms have high sample complexity [6,13]. Deterministic policy gradient algorithms scale better over high-dimensional action spaces since the deterministic policy gradient integrates only over the state space whereas the stochastic policy gradient integrates over both state and action spaces [22]. Moreover, off-policy learning with experience replay enables reusing the past experience and reduces the sample complexity [13]. IAC further reduces the sample complexity via reducing the number of parameters, improving the exploration strategy, and using some recent advances in deep learning, namely the dropout [24], DenseNet [9], and increasing the batch size during training [23].

TD3 [4] addresses the overestimation of the value function via the clipped double Q learning, delayed updates on the policy and target networks, and the target policy smoothing regularization. Our objective function enables an adaptive version of the delayed policy updates in addition to TTUR [7,11] (see Sect. 3.2). Moreover, we delay updates on the target network adaptively depending on the critic's loss (see Algorithm 1). Further, we use a modified target policy smoothing technique for performance improvement (see Sect. 4.2).

In RL, reward-maximizing actions can be learned more quickly with a better exploration strategy. SAC [6], PPO [21], and the trust region policy optimization algorithm (TRPO) [20] use entropy regularization to encourage more exploration. In A3C/A2C [15], multiple actors explore environment in parallel, each with a possibly different behavior policy for better exploration. In deterministic policy gradient algorithms, a stochastic behavior policy is used to ensure sufficient exploration [4,13]. In IAC, we improve exploration over bounded action spaces (see Sect. 4.1).

Strong connections between the actor-critic RL and the GANs have been discussed in [17]. The implication is that techniques used to stabilize and improve one of them can be useful for the other. In IAC, we use the spectral normalization that was shown to stabilize the training of GANs [14].

7 Conclusions

We have proposed an off-policy deep deterministic integrated actor-critic algorithm (IAC) based on a shared network architecture and an adaptive objective function. Sharing the network between actor and critic reduces the overall number of parameters but brings an additional challenge on the training stability. The adaptive objective enables a stable training via keeping the policy unchanged while the value estimation is wrong. We have presented an improved exploration strategy over bounded action spaces. Moreover, we have incorporated some recent advances in deep learning, namely the DenseNet, spectral normalization, target policy smoothing, dropout, hard-swish activation, and adjustment of the batch size and iteration number during training, to further improve our algorithm. The experiments have shown that IAC speeds up learning and reduces the sample complexity significantly over the state-of-the-art deep RL algorithms.

References

1. OpenAI Gym (2021). https://gym.openai.com/
2. Church, A., Lloyd, J., Hadsell, R., Lepora, N.F.: Deep reinforcement learning for tactile robotics: learning to type on a braille keyboard. IEEE Rob. Autom. Lett. **5**(4), 6145–6152 (2020)
3. François-Lavet, V., Henderson, P., Islam, R., Bellemare, M.G., Pineau, J.: An introduction to deep reinforcement learning. Found. Trends®in Mach. Learn. **11**(3–4), 219–354 (2018)
4. Fujimoto, S., van Hoof, H., Meger, D.: Addressing function approximation error in actor-critic methods. arXiv preprint arXiv:1802.09477 (2018)
5. Goodfellow, I., et al.: Generative adversarial nets. In: Advances in Neural Information Processing Systems, pp. 2672–2680 (2014)
6. Haarnoja, T., Zhou, A., Abbeel, P., Levine, S.: Soft actor-critic: off-policy maximum entropy deep reinforcement learning with a stochastic actor. arXiv preprint arXiv:1801.01290 (2018)
7. Heusel, M., Ramsauer, H., Unterthiner, T., Nessler, B., Hochreiter, S.: GANs trained by a two time-scale update rule converge to a local Nash equilibrium. In: Advances in Neural Information Processing Systems, pp. 6626–6637 (2017)
8. Howard, A., et al.: Searching for mobilenetv3. arXiv preprint arXiv:1905.02244 (2019)
9. Huang, G., Liu, Z., van der Maaten, L., Weinberger, K.Q.: Densely connected convolutional networks. In: The IEEE Conference on Computer Vision and Pattern Recognition (CVPR), July 2017
10. Huber, P.J.: Robust estimation of a location parameter. In: Breakthroughs in Statistics, pp. 492–518. Springer (1992). https://doi.org/10.1007/978-1-4612-4380-9_35
11. Konda, V.R., Tsitsiklis, J.N.: On actor-critic algorithms. SIAM J. Control. Optim. **42**(4), 1143–1166 (2003)
12. Kurt, M.N., Ogundijo, O., Li, C., Wang, X.: Online cyber-attack detection in smart grid: a reinforcement learning approach. IEEE Trans. Smart Grid **10**(5), 5174–5185 (2019)
13. Lillicrap, T.P., et al.: Continuous control with deep reinforcement learning. arXiv preprint arXiv:1509.02971 (2015)
14. Miyato, T., Kataoka, T., Koyama, M., Yoshida, Y.: Spectral normalization for generative adversarial networks. arXiv preprint arXiv:1802.05957 (2018)
15. Mnih, V., et al.: Asynchronous methods for deep reinforcement learning. In: International Conference on Machine Learning, pp. 1928–1937 (2016)
16. Mnih, V., et al.: Human-level control through deep reinforcement learning. Nature **518**(7540), 529 (2015)
17. Pfau, D., Vinyals, O.: Connecting generative adversarial networks and actor-critic methods. arXiv preprint arXiv:1610.01945 (2016)
18. Ramachandran, B.Z.P., Le, Q.V.: Searching for activation functions. arXiv preprint arXiv:1710.05941 (2017)
19. Ruder, S.: An overview of multi-task learning in deep neural networks. arXiv preprint arXiv:1706.05098 (2017)
20. Schulman, J., Levine, S., Abbeel, P., Jordan, M., Moritz, P.: Trust region policy optimization. In: International Conference on Machine Learning, pp. 1889–1897 (2015)
21. Schulman, J., Wolski, F., Dhariwal, P., Radford, A., Klimov, O.: Proximal policy optimization algorithms. arXiv preprint arXiv:1707.06347 (2017)

22. Silver, D., Lever, G., Heess, N., Degris, T., Wierstra, D., Riedmiller, M.: Deterministic policy gradient algorithms. In: Proceedings of The 31st International Conference on Machine Learning, pp. 387–395 (2014)
23. Smith, S.L., Kindermans, P.J., Le, Q.V.: Don't decay the learning rate, increase the batch size. In: International Conference on Learning Representations (2018)
24. Srivastava, N., Hinton, G., Krizhevsky, A., Sutskever, I., Salakhutdinov, R.: Dropout: a simple way to prevent neural networks from overfitting. J. Mach. Learn. Res. **15**(1), 1929–1958 (2014)
25. Sutton, R.S., Barto, A.G.: Reinforcement Learning: An Introduction. MIT Press, Cambridge (1998)

Learning to Assist Agents by Observing Them

Antti Keurulainen[1,3](✉), Isak Westerlund[3], Samuel Kaski[1,2], and Alexander Ilin[1]

[1] Helsinki Institute for Information Technology HIIT, Department of Computer Science, Aalto University, Espoo, Finland
antti.keurulainen@aalto.fi
[2] Department of Computer Science, University of Manchester, Manchester, UK
[3] Bitville Oy, Espoo, Finland

Abstract. The ability of an AI agent to assist other agents, such as humans, is an important and challenging goal, which requires the assisting agent to reason about the behavior and infer the goals of the assisted agent. Training such an ability by using reinforcement learning usually requires large amounts of online training, which is difficult and costly. On the other hand, offline data about the behavior of the assisted agent might be available, but is non-trivial to take advantage of by methods such as offline reinforcement learning. We introduce methods where the capability to create a representation of the behavior is first pre-trained with offline data, after which only a small amount of interaction data is needed to learn an assisting policy. We test the setting in a gridworld where the helper agent has the capability to manipulate the environment of the assisted artificial agents, and introduce three different scenarios where the assistance considerably improves the performance of the assisted agents.

Keywords: Deep reinforcement learning · Cooperative AI · Helper agent · Meta-learning · Modelling other agents

1 Introduction

The ability to build an AI system that can assist other AI agents and humans to reach their goals is an obviously important and ambitious goal. There are numerous possible applications that would benefit directly of such a capability. For example, helper agents could be harnessed to guide self-driving cars to allow smoother traffic flow. An example of cooperation with humans could be a helper agent, which is able to infer the goals of a human navigating a web site, and manipulate the website structure dynamically to help the human users reach their goals faster.

In this paper, we consider building such helper agents. We construct settings, where an artificial agent (*a helper agent*) observes the behavior of an

I. Farkaš et al. (Eds.): ICANN 2021, LNCS 12894, pp. 519–530, 2021.
https://doi.org/10.1007/978-3-030-86380-7_42

assisted agent (*goal-driven agent*), and learns to perform useful assisting actions by manipulating the environment dynamics.

We formulate the challenge as a meta-reinforcement learning problem. We first train a small population of goal-driven agents to reach their goals as fast as possible. The helper agent observes the goal-driven agents in many instances of the environments, and is trained by meta-reinforcement learning to perform useful assisting actions by receiving a positive reward when the goal-driven agents succeed in their tasks.

As a contribution of our work, we show that similar capabilities to inverse reinforcement learning arise spontaneously as a result of meta-learning. We demonstrate this effect and its usefulness for producing helping actions in three different scenarios:

1. By learning representations of the behavior of the goal-driven agent from the past partial trajectories in an unsupervised way.
2. By learning representations of the behavior of the goal-driven agent from the past partial trajectories in a self-supervised way, by predicting the actions of the goal-driven agent.
3. By learning representations of the behavior of the goal-driven agent from the past partial trajectories in a supervised way, by predicting the goal of the goal-driven agent.

2 Related Work

There is a rich literature on reasoning about the behavior and inferring the goals of other agents [1], which is closely related to our work. Unlike most of the work related to modelling other agents, our specific goal was to build agents which can do assisting actions, based on the inferred representations of the behavior of the other agent.

Similar settings have been studied in multi-agent scenarios. As an example, in [5] a two-agent helper-AI scenario is presented, where both agents have the same reward function, but disagree on the transition dynamics of the Markov decision process (MDP). In our setting, in contrast, the action spaces of the agents are different, and the assisted agent is unaware of the assisting agent. The authors in [8] consider learning representations of agent behaviors in multi-agent scenarios. Our approach is similar in that we also learn to represent agents' behaviors, but rather than communicating cooperatively, the helper agent attempts to change the environment in a beneficial manner.

An individual is considered to have a Theory of Mind (ToM), if they impute a mental state to themselves or others [12,19]. An inferred mental state can be used to infer goals and make predictions of behavior of other agents. Our work is inspired by Theory of Mind, as we are training behavioral embeddings of the goal-driven agents by only observing them. Examples of previous work implementing Theory of Mind in a machine learning context include [3], a Bayesian Theory of Mind model, and [20], which is based on deep learning. In our approach, a separate helper agent infers the goal-driven agent behavior and produces behavior embeddings as in [20], which are used for manipulating the environment in a beneficial way.

The problem of learning fast from limited amounts of data can be tackled with meta-learning methods, where the goal is to train a system in such a way that it is capable of performing fast adaptation to new situations [11,22]. We train the helper agent to be able to do few-shot learning of a new goal-driven agent in a new sampled environment by creating a behavior embedding of the agent based on small amounts of observations. Commonly used meta-learning methods include gradient based methods [7] and memory-based methods [6,21,24]. Our meta-learning solution resembles mostly attention-based meta-learning [14], since in our case the behavior embeddings are generated by averaging the state representations over the time steps without recurrent connections.

Our third scenario is partly inspired by the centralized training and decentralized execution (CTDE) concept [10,16], where additional information can be used during the training but not during the execution. Instead of using private information of the goal-driven agent, we use information of the goal-driven agent's goal for pre-training the helper agent policy.

Similar challenges could be solved by transfer learning or by using auxiliary tasks. In transfer learning, the goal is to transfer what has been learned in one task to some other final task, possibly by partially sharing parameters between the models [18,25]. Numerous success cases have demonstrated benefits of transfer learning in the areas of computer vision [17] and natural language processing [2,4]. Our solution is one type of transfer learning, where the goal is specifically to pre-train one specific part of the policy function to allow faster learning for producing assisting actions. When using auxiliary tasks, the common representation among the original task and auxiliary tasks can be improved by adding extra auxiliary heads to the representation [9,13,26]. In our solution, instead of adding an extra auxiliary head to the common representation, the helper agent is pre-trained on the task of making predictions of the goal-driven agents' actions in self-supervised manner or goals in a supervised manner. After completing the pre-training task, the final task training benefits from this ability.

Inverse Reinforcement Learning (IRL) [15] has similar goals, but does so by recovering the unknown reward function of the expert user or any agent it tries to model. The difference in our method is that we do not attempt to recover the reward function but rather model the agent behavior directly by observing the agent actions, and then build the helper policy, which uses the behavior embeddings. This approach is useful when moving to behavior where reward functions are complex or intractable, as often is the case when attempting to model human-like complex behavior.

3 Setting

We use a meta-reinforcement learning formulation for training both the goal-driven agents and the helper agent. The MDP is defined by a tuple $M = \langle \mathcal{S}, \mathcal{A}, \mathcal{P}, \mathcal{R}, \gamma, \rho_0, H \rangle$, where $\mathcal{S}$ is the state space and $\mathcal{A}$ is the action space, γ is the discount factor, $\rho_0 : \mathcal{S} \rightarrow [0, 1]$ is the initial state distribution,

$\mathcal{P} : \mathcal{S} \times \mathcal{A} \times \mathcal{S} \rightarrow [0, 1]$ is the transition function, $\mathcal{R} : \mathcal{S} \times \mathcal{A} \rightarrow \mathbb{R}$ is the reward function and H is the horizon.

The agents maximize the expected sum of discounted rewards over the episodes $J(\pi_\theta) = \mathbb{E}_{\tau \sim p_\pi(\tau)}[\sum_{t=0}^{H} \gamma^t \mathcal{R}(s_t, a_t)]$, where $\tau = (s_0, a_0, ...)$ is the trajectory of states s_t and actions a_t of the agent at time step t for an episode of length H. The initial state is sampled from the distribution ρ_0 and the agent j samples the action a_t from its policy function $\pi_j(a_t|s_t)$. The next state is sampled from the transition dynamics function $s_{t+1} \sim \mathcal{P}(s_{t+1}|s_t, a_t)$. The agents learn through many episodes. For each episode, a new MDP M_i is sampled from a family $\mathcal{M}$ of MDPs. The MDPs for the helper agent and the goal-driven agents share the same state space $\mathcal{S}$ but have different actions spaces and reward functions denoted as $\mathcal{A}^{helper}$ and $\mathcal{A}^{goal-driven}$, and $\mathcal{R}^{helper}$ and $\mathcal{R}_j^{goal-driven}$. From the helper agent point of view, the behavior of the goal-driven agent is embedded in the transition dynamics of the sampled MDP, and each sampled MDP refers to different task in the meta-reinforcement learning framework. The meta-learning goal is to maximize the expected returns over the task distribution.

4 Methods

4.1 The Gridworld

We test our architectures in various gridworld scenarios. Every new sampled MDP has a 7×7 gridworld environment, which includes four possible goals in random locations, an L-shaped wall in a random location and a goal-driven agent starting in a random position. Each goal-driven agent is trained to navigate to one of the goals with the shortest route. The wall has always the same basic shape, and its location is sampled but restricted so that the long edge of the wall needs to be at least two steps from the border of the gridworld. The left side of Fig. 1 illustrates a sampled gridworld environment.

The environment delivers a set of tensors as a state representation, one tensor per one time step. The state representation is a collection of $7 \times 7 \times 6$ tensors, where the different channels in one tensor represent goal-driven agent location (1 channel), wall elements (1 channel) and goals (4 channels).

The episodes are divided in two distinct stages. In the first stage, the helper agent observes several partial trajectories of the unassisted goal-driven agent navigating to its goal in different sampled environments. In the second stage, a new environment is sampled and the same goal-driven agent is set in a random location. In the beginning of the second stage, the helper agent observes the state (a single tensor) and will decide on an action based on this observation. The right side of Fig. 1 illustrates a situation where the helper agent has acted and opened a shortcut for the goal-driven agent.

4.2 The Goal-Driven Agents

The goal-driven agents, which are part of the environment of the helper agent, are trained with the Proximal Policy Optimization (PPO) algorithm [23].

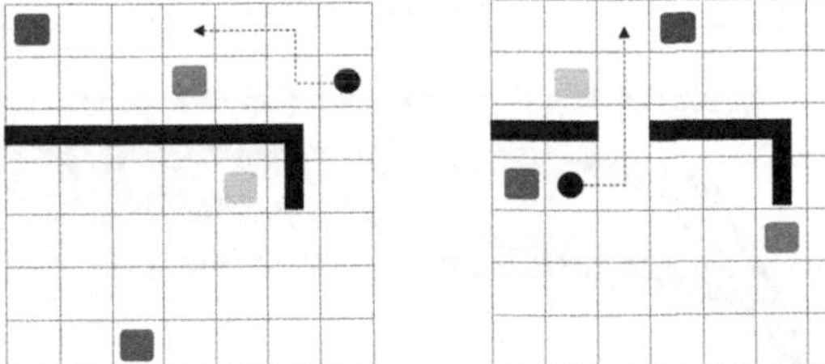

Fig. 1. Illustration of the 7 × 7 gridworld. An agent trajectory is illustrated with a dotted line, when the goal-driven agent is walking towards the red goal. Left: the helper agent has not opened a shortcut. Right: The helper agent has opened a shortcut (Color figure online)

We train four different agent types which have different target goals. The action space $\mathcal{A}^{goal-driven}$ consists of five possible actions (move up, down, left, right and stay). The episode ends with a positive reward when the agent reaches the correct goal from four possible goals. Each step has a small negative reward. During the training of the goal-driven agent, there is a shortcut in the wall with the probability 0.5.

When the goal-driven agent j follows its policy, it will produce a trajectory consisting of a list of state-action pairs

$$\tau_j = \left\{ \left(s_t, a_t \right) \right\}_{t=0}^{H}$$

where H is the length of the episode.

4.3 The Helper Agent

Once a population of goal-driven agents exists, the helper agent is trained with the PPO algorithm to infer the agent types by observing them, and to conduct an assisting action by manipulating the transition dynamics (creating a shortcut in a specified location). The action space $\mathcal{A}^{helper}$ of the helper agent consists of two actions, either to act or not to act, and the action is performed once at a specified time point depending on the scenario in question, thus the horizon H for the helper agent is a single time step. The reward function $\mathcal{R}^{helper}$, is the same as with the goal-driven agent but augmented with a negative reward for making an action to assist the goal-driven agent. In other words, the helper agent gets a reward when the goal-driven agent succeeds in its task. The helper agent has access only to the partial trajectories of τ_j of the goal-driven agents and thus not to their reward function $R_j^{goal-driven}$ or policy $\pi_j^{goal-driven}$.

5 Experiments and Results

5.1 End-to-End Training Without Agent-Specific Inference

We first evaluate the performance of the helper agent in a simplified situation where it does not have access to the past observations of unassisted behavior of

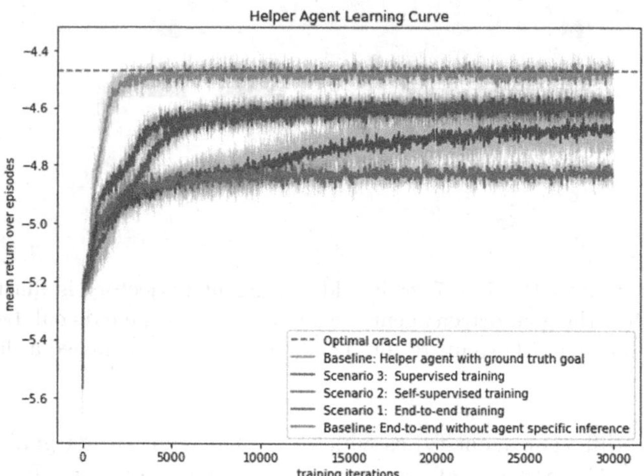

Fig. 2. The average learning curves of simulations with 8 random seeds with various helper agent architectures. The green line represents the learning curve without behavior embeddings and serves as a lower bound for the helper agent performance. The orange line shows the performance when the policy network uses ground truth information about the agent behavior, and serves as the upper bound for the helper agent performance. The blue line represents end-to-end training with embeddings (scenario 1), the purple line with action prediction pre-training (scenario 2) and the red line with goal prediction pre-training (scenario 3). The shaded region illustrates the standard deviation over 8 seeds. (Color figure online)

the goal-driven agents. The results of this experiment serve as a lower bound for the helper agent performance. The helper agent does not observe the first stage of each episode and needs to decide on its actions only based on the initial state of the second stage. Thus, in this case the helper agent does not have the capability of inferring the behavior of the goal-driven agents.

In this scenario, the helper agent is a neural network with two convolutional layers and one fully-connected layer (see Fig. 3, left). More details of the neural network implementation is available in the appendix.

The green line in Fig. 2 illustrates the training result in this setting. The helper agent learns to improve its policy slightly despite not being able to infer the agent behavior. In this case, the helper agent tries to find the optimal performance by observing the general behavior of all agent types and by finding a more general policy that does not depend on a single agent's goal. As an example, if all goals are on the other side of the wall, it would be beneficial to open the wall. Likewise, if all goals are on the same side of the wall as the goal-driven agent, it is not useful to open the wall and take the penalty. These two scenarios are illustrated in Fig. 3.

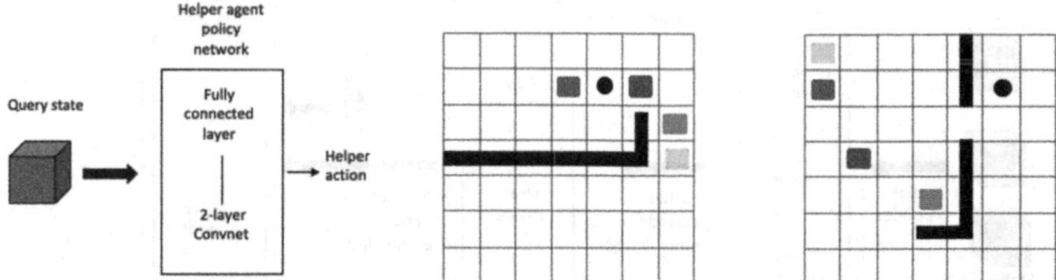

Fig. 3. Left: A simplified version of the helper agent that is not capable of inferring the goal-driven agent behavior. Middle: The helper agent has not opened the wall because all the goals are on the same side as the agent. Right: The helper has opened the wall because all the goals are on the other side. The colored squares indicate the goals, black lines represent the wall and the black circle is the location of the goal-driven agent. (Color figure online)

5.2 Scenario 1: End-to-End Training with Agent-Specific Inference

In the first scenario, the helper agent is exposed to the past observations of unassisted behavior of the goal-driven agents. In the first stage, it now observes four first steps from four different episodes of the same agent but with different sampled layout of the gridworld. By observing these partial trajectories before conducting the assisting action, the helper agent has a chance to learn about the goal-driven agents' goals based on the agents' unassisted behavior. The helper agent architecture is illustrated in Fig. 5. During the first stage, the helper agent uses the *behavior inference* part of the policy. The embeddings of partial episodes are formed by using a convolutional network, followed by mean pooling and a fully connected layer. The behavior embeddings are formed in a similar manner from the episode embeddings but without convolutional layers. During the training, the behavior inference part learns to construct 2-dimensional behavior embeddings by clustering the agents based on their goals, where each cluster contains agents with the same goal (Fig. 4).

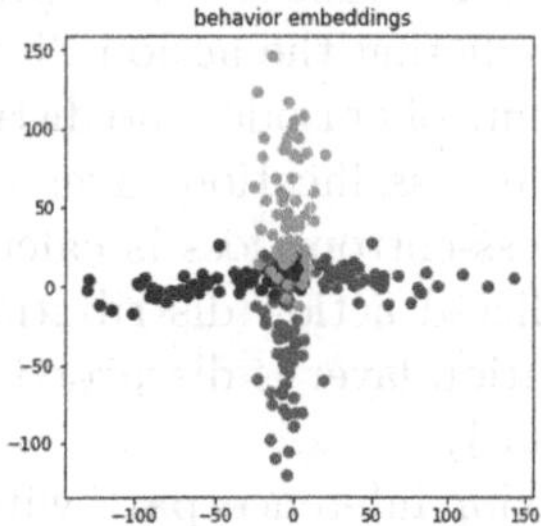

Fig. 4. Visualization of the 2-dimensional behavior embedding in scenario 1. The behavior inference part of the policy has spontaneously clustered the goal-driven agents based on their goals.

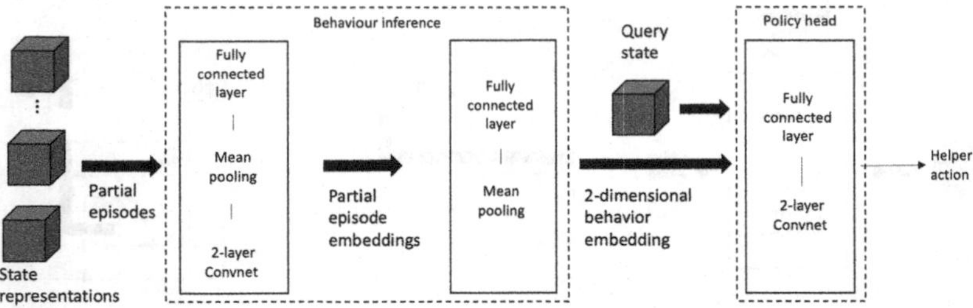

Fig. 5. Scenario 1. The helper agent architecture. The behavior inference part infers the goal driven agent behavior by observing partial unassisted behavior. The policy head produces the action distribution from a query state and the behavior embedding.

The *policy head* part of the helper agent has the same structure as the simpler case shown in the left side of Fig. 3. The task of the policy head is to produce the action distribution but now it additionally receives the behavior embedding from the behavior inference part. The training of this scenario is conducted end-to-end.

The result of this experiment is illustrated by the blue line in Fig. 2. The helper agent is capable to use the information produced by the behavior inference part and as a result the performance is improved considerably. Since there is significant variance present in simulations with different seeds, we can assume that the end-to-end training is more sensitive to the initialization than the other scenarios.

5.3 Scenario 2: Self-supervised Pre-training with Agent-Specific Inference

In this scenario the helper agent has an initial pre-training phase where it observes multiple partial episodes where the goal-driven agents behave without assistance, simulating a situation where previously collected offline data of the assisted agent behavior is available. The pre-training is conducted in a self-supervised fashion by predicting the action distributions of the goal-driven agents. After the partial rollouts of episodes the distribution over the next action is predicted by using a linear classification layer on top of the 2-dimensional behavior embedding. The cross-entropy loss is calculated between the observed one-hot action and the predicted action distribution. Once the pre-training is complete, the linear classification layer is discarded and the setting is converted to a similar one as in scenario 1.

Pre-training of the behavior inference part with action predictions clearly helps the policy function to learn assisting actions as the learning is faster and there is less variation across different seeds, as is visible by the purple line in Fig. 2.

5.4 Scenario 3: Supervised Pre-training with Agent-Specific Inference

In our final scenario the helper agent has again an initial pre-training phase where it observes multiple partial episodes where goal-driven agents behave without assistance. Inspired by the centralized training decentralized execution (CTDE) method [10,16], the helper agent is now provided with the information about the agent's goal in each episode during the pre-training phase, but not during the execution after the pre-training. The pre-training is conducted in a similar manner as in scenario 2 by using the linear classifier on top of the 2-dimensional behavior embedding, and by calculating the cross-entropy loss between the one-hot goal label and the predicted goal distribution. In this case, the pre-training has strong supervision, and the helper agent is able to cluster the goal-driven agents based on their goals already during the pre-training phase. This allows faster learning as is visible with the red line in Fig. 2.

5.5 Summary of Results

In order to evaluate the performance of the helper agent in various scenarios, we made additional measurements that are useful for gaining insight of the helper agent performance. We measured the mean return over episodes when the wall was permanently closed, when it was permanently open and the optimal policy by making rollouts from the query state. For each query state, we made a rollout both with wall open and wall closed scenarios. By selecting higher return from these rollouts, we measured the optimal policy. All key results are summarized in Table 1. The results show, that even when the helper agent does not have the possibility to observe the behavior of the goal-driven agent, the performance is improved. The performance is further increased when the helper agent can observe partial episodes of the goal driven agent (scenario 1). The self-supervised pre training (scenario 2) and supervised pre-training (scenario 3) achieve highest overall performance as they are closest to the optimal performance. Interestingly, the self-supervised scenario reach a similar performance as the supervised pre-training, which suggests that self-supervised method is a potential alternative for assessing behavior when labels are not available for the pre-training.

6 Discussion

In this paper, we introduced several scenarios, where a helper agent can assist goal-driven agents by manipulating the transition dynamics of the environment. We showed that by using meta-learning, similar capabilities to inverse reinforcement learning arise spontaneously. Our method is also an example how previously collected data can be used to enhance the performance of a helper agent when offline learning methods are not possible. This kind of situation arises if the previously collected data is from the assisted agent behavior, not from a helper agent behavior.

Table 1. Helper agents with progressively more capabilities are able to help the goal-driven agents more.

Model	Mean return
Baseline: wall always open (with penalty for opening the wall)	−5.19
Baseline: wall always closed	−5.85
Baseline: helper agent with ground truth goal	−4.48 ± 0.03
(Oracle) optimal policy	−4.47
Baseline: end-to-end without agent specific inference	−4.82 ± 0.03
Scenario 1: end-to-end with agent-specific inference	−4.66 ± 0.08
Scenario 2: self-supervised pre-training with action predictions	−4.59 ± 0.04
Scenario 3: supervised pre-training with goal predictions	−4.59 ± 0.03

The results indicated that by learning to infer the agent's behavior, the helper agent's policy can be significantly improved. Furthermore, the training can be made faster and more robust by a separate pre-training phase. The pre-training can be done either in self-supervised manner by predicting the actions of the assisted agent, or by using additional information about the agents' goals that is available during the training but not during the execution. This kind of scenario is valid when it is of interest to predict a known feature that explains the behavior, such as the goal, skill level, level of stochasticity, level of visibility, or level of memory. An interesting continuation to this work could be extending to modeling more complex human-like behaviors in scenarios that are closer to real-world human-computer interactions (for example, web-site navigation).

Acknowledgement. This work was supported by the Academy of Finland (Flagship programme: Finnish Center for Artificial Intelligence FCAI, and grants 319264, 292334).

A Neural Network details

A.1 Helper Agent

The helper agent behavior inference part has two convolutional layers, batch normalization layers, and two fully connected layers. Convolutional layers 1 and 2: 8 filters, 3 × 3 kernels, stride 1, zero padding to maintain the dimensions. Followed by ReLU activations and batch normalization. The output of the convolutional layers of each episode is averaged across the time dimension to produce the representations of the partial episodes. The representations are fed through a linear layer, averaged across the episodes of the agent and fed through another fully connected layer to produce the 2-dimensional behavior embeddings.

The policy head part of the helper agent has a shared policy and value head backbone with 2 convolutional layers with 16 filters, 3 × 3 kernels, stride 1 and zero padding. The output of the convolution is followed by a policy head with

Softmax to produce action probabilities and a separate value head to produce value estimates.

The helper agent is trained using the Adam optimizer with a learning rate of 1e–4. Reward for opening the wall: –1. Reward of every step: –1. Reward of reaching the goal +1.

Using a batch size of 256 simulations were run for 60 000 PPO training steps and pre-training was done using 10 000 classification steps. The baseline results where the wall is always closed, the wall is always open and the optimal policy were calculated as the mean return over 512 000 rollouts. The helper agent results were calculated as the mean of the last 51 200 rollouts during training.

A.2 Goal-Driven Agents

The goal-driven agent policy network has two convolutional layers and a fully connected layer.

Convolutional layer 1: 16 filters, 3×3 kernels, stride 1, ReLU activations, zero padding to maintain the dimensions. Convolutional layer 2: 32 filters, 3×3 kernels, stride 1, ReLU activations, zero padding. Fully connected layer with 32 hidden units: ReLU activation followed by a policy head with Softmax to produce action probabilities and a value head to produce value estimates.

Reward of every step: -1. Reward of reaching the goal $+1$.

References

1. Albrecht, S.V., Stone, P.: Autonomous agents modelling other agents: a comprehensive survey and open problems. Artif. Intell. **258**, 66–95 (2018)
2. Alec, R., et al.: Improving Language Understanding by Generative Pre-Training. OpenAI (2018)
3. Baker, C.L., Jara-Ettinger, J., Saxe, R., Tenenbaum, J.B.: Rational quantitative attribution of beliefs, desires and percepts in human mentalizing. Nat. Hum. Behav. **1**, 1–10 (2017)
4. Devlin, J., Chang, M.W., Lee, K., Toutanova, K.: BERT: pre-training of deep bidirectional transformers for language understanding. In: NAACL HLT 2019–2019 Conference of the North American Chapter of the Association for Computational Linguistics: Human Language Technologies - Proceedings of the Conference (2019)
5. Dimitrakakis, C., Parkes, D.C., Radanovic, G., Tylkin, P.: The helper-AI problem. In: Advances in Neural Information Processing Systems, Multi-View Decision Processes (2017)
6. Duan, Y., Schulman, J., Chen, X., Bartlett, P.L., Sutskever, I., Abbeel, P.: RL^2: fast reinforcement learning via slow reinforcement learning. arXiv preprint arXiv:1611.02779, 2016
7. Finn, C., Abbeel, P., Levine, S.: Model-agnostic meta-learning for fast adaptation of deep networks. In: 34th International Conference on Machine Learning (2017)
8. Grover, A., Ai-Shedivat, M., Gupta, J.K., Yura, B., Edwards, H.: Learning policy representations in multiagent systems. In: 35th International Conference on Machine Learning (2018)

9. Jaderberg, M., et al.: Reinforcement learning with unsupervised auxiliary tasks. In: 5th International Conference on Learning Representations (2017)
10. Kraemer, L., Banerjee, B.: Multi-agent reinforcement learning as a rehearsal for decentralized planning. Neurocomputing **190**, 82–94 (2016)
11. Lemke, C., Budka, M., Gabrys, B.: Metalearning: a survey of trends and technologies. Artif. Intell. Rev. **44**(1), 117–130 (2013). https://doi.org/10.1007/s10462-013-9406-y
12. Leslie, A.M., Friedman, O., German, T.P.: Core mechanisms in 'theory of mind'. Trends Cogn. Sci. **8**, 528–533 (2004)
13. Mirowski, P., et al. Learning to navigate in complex environments. arXiv preprint arXiv:1611.03673 (2016)
14. Mishra, N., Rohaninejad, M., Chen, X., Abbeel, P.: A simple neural attentive meta-learner. arXiv preprint arXiv:1707.03141 (2017)
15. Ng, A., Russell, S.: Algorithms for inverse reinforcement learning. In: Proceedings of the Seventeenth International Conference on Machine Learning (2000)
16. Oliehoek, F.A.: Decentralized POMDPs. Learning, and Optimization, In Adaptation (2012)
17. Oquab, M., Bottou, L., Laptev, I., Sivic, J.: Learning and transferring mid-level image representations using convolutional neural networks. In: Proceedings of the IEEE Computer Society Conference on Computer Vision and Pattern Recognition (2014)
18. Pan, S.J., Yang, Q.: A survey on transfer learning. In: IEEE Transactions on Knowledge and Data Engineering (2010)
19. Premack, D., Woodruff, G.: Does the chimpanzee have a theory of mind? Behavioral and Brain Sciences (1978)
20. Rabinowitz, N.C., Perbet, F., Song, H.F., Zhang, C., Botvinick, M.: Machine Theory of mind. In: 35th International Conference on Machine Learning (2018)
21. Santoro, A., Bartunov, S., Botvinick, M., Wierstra, D., Lillicrap, T.: Meta-learning with memory-augmented neural networks. In: 33rd International Conference on Machine Learning (2016)
22. Schmidhuber, J.: Evolutionary Principles in Self-Referential Learning. On Learning now to Learn: The Meta-Meta-Meta...-Hook. PhD thesis (1987)
23. Schulman, J., Wolski, F., Dhariwal, P., Radford, A., Klimov, O.: Proximal policy optimization algorithms. arXiv preprint arXiv:1707.06347 (2017)
24. Wang, J.X., et al.: Learning to reinforcement learn. arXiv preprint arXiv:1611.05763 (2016)
25. Yosinski, J., Clune, J., Bengio, Y., Lipson, H.: How transferable are features in deep neural networks? In: Advances in Neural Information Processing Systems (2014)
26. Zhang, Y., Lee, K., Lee, H.: Augmenting supervised neural networks with unsupervised objectives for large-scale image classification. In: International conference on machine learning, ICML (2016)

Reinforcement Syntactic Dependency Tree Reasoning for Target-Oriented Opinion Word Extraction

Yaqing Dai, Pengfei Wang(✉), and Lei Zhang

Beijing University of Posts and Telecommunications, Beijing, China
{daiyaqing97,wangpengfei,zlei}@bupt.edu.cn

Abstract. Target-oriented Opinion Word Extraction (TOWE) is a subtask of Aspect Based Sentiment Analysis (ABSA), which aims to extract fine-grained opinion terms for a given aspect term from a sentence. In TOWE task, syntactic dependency tree is useful as it provides explanation to identify opinion terms to the given aspect term. It is necessary to mine relationships between aspect and opinion terms for a better performance. Previous works introduced syntactic dependency tree into TOWE task but lacked of explicit explanation. In this paper, we propose a novel model named **MM-TOWE**, which leverages Monte-Carlo tree search to enhance **M**arkov decision process (MDP) model for **T**arget-oriented **O**pinion **W**ord **E**xtraction task. We formulate TOWE task as an MDP of reasoning over the syntactic dependency tree. By learning the dependency relationships between aspect terms and opinion terms, our model can reason a path for an explicit explanation. Extensive experimental results illustrate that our proposed model outperforms the state-of-the-art methods.

Keywords: Target-oriented opinion word extraction · Reinforcement learning · Syntactic dependency tree

1 Introduction

Target-oriented Opinion Word Extraction (TOWE) is a subtask of Aspect Based Sentiment Analysis (ABSA). The main goal of TOWE is to extract the corresponding opinion terms from a sentence for a given aspect term (also called target). For an example sentence "*The sashimi is always fresh and the rolls are innovative and delicious.*", if the given aspect term is "rolls", the goal is to extract "innovative" and "delicious". Therefore, TOWE can be used in many applications such as sentiment analysis [7] and review summarizing [4,23].

Recently, some deep learning methods [2,21] formulate TOWE task as a sequence labeling problem. Although they have good performance, they mainly learn the relationships between aspect terms and opinion terms in sequential structure. Pouran Ben Veyseh et al. [14] show that syntactic structure is useful in TOWE task, and learn the relationships implicitly. In fact, a dependency

I. Farkaš et al. (Eds.): ICANN 2021, LNCS 12894, pp. 531–543, 2021.
https://doi.org/10.1007/978-3-030-86380-7_43

path can provide an explicit explanation to identify opinion terms to the given aspect term. As shown in Fig. 1, we can find a dependency path "rolls $\xrightarrow{nusbj^{-1}}$ innovative $\xrightarrow{conj^{-1}}$ delicious" to explain the relationship between aspect term and opinion terms of the example.

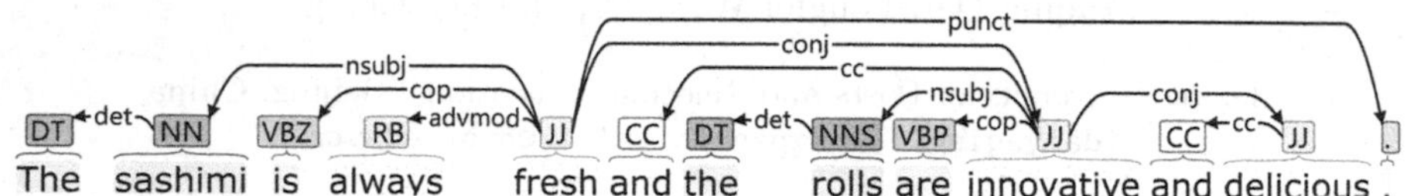

Fig. 1. The syntactic dependency tree of the example sentence - "*The sashimi is always fresh and the rolls are innovative and delicious*".

These years, reinforcement learning (RL) has been used widely in reasoning over large knowledge graph [17,22] for learning the relationships between two nodes. Therefore, RL seems to be a promising approach due to its great reasoning ability. However, many RL methods suffer from the challenges of large state space and sparse reward. AlphaGo Zero [19] uses Monte-Carlo Tree Search (MCTS) to enhance RL model for solving these two challenges during playing the game of Go. Inspired by these, we formulate TOWE task as a Markov decision process (MDP) of reasoning over the syntactic dependency tree. By learning the dependency relationships between aspect terms and opinion terms, our model can reason a path for an explicit explanation. Meanwhile, we also leverage MCTS to enhance our model.

In this paper, we propose a novel model named **MM-TOWE** to address TOWE task. We treat the syntactic dependency tree of a sentence as a graph and formulate TOWE task as an MDP. The agent starts moving from the first word of the given aspect term and reasons over this graph for opinion extraction. The reasoning path should be short and cover all opinion terms. To this end, we design a reward function to consider both of them in order to better guide the agent for reasoning path. We also leverage MCTS to enhance the model for solving the challenges of large state space and sparse reward. To evaluate the proposed model, we conduct extensive experiments on three datasets by comparing it with several competitive baselines. Experimental results show that our model can significantly outperform all the baselines in the TOWE task.

In summary, the contributions of our work are as follows:

- We formulate the TOWE task into an MDP of reasoning over syntactic dependency tree with MCTS for enhancing it.
- We design a reward function to consider both accuracy and efficiency.
- Experimental results on three real-world datasets show that our model can consistently outperform state-of-the-art baselines under different evaluation metrics and can find the dependency relationships between aspect terms and opinion terms.

2 Related Work

2.1 Target-Oriented Opinion Words Extraction

Target-oriented Opinion Words Extraction (TOWE) is a subtask of Aspect Based Sentiment Analysis (ABSA). The main goal of TOWE is to extract the opinion terms for a given aspect term from a sentence.

Early works which are related to TOWE mainly focus on doing sentiment analysis and review summarizing. There are rule-based methods which use distance rules [4] or mine high frequency rules on dependency tree [23] to extract opinion words for a given aspect word. However, these simple and effective rule-based methods can only deal with high frequency and common cases. As deep learning becomes more popular, TOWE task is formulated as a sequence labeling problem [2]. Wu et al. [21] transfer opinion knowledge from resource-rich sentiment classification task into TOWE task via an auxiliary learning signal. And Pouran Ben Veyseh et al. [14] use Graph Convolutional Networks (GCN) [6] to learn distance information from syntactic dependency tree for TOWE task.

2.2 Reinforcement Learning

Reinforcement learning (RL) is a field of machine learning and has been paid more attention by researchers. Meanwhile, reasoning over the knowledge graph with RL method also has been used widely in many areas such as recommendation [22], question and answer [1], and conversation system [9]. RL has great reasoning ability and can learn the relation rules from the start node to the target node. However, lots of works suffer from the problem of sparse reward or large state space when using RL method. Inspired by Alpha Go [18], some works [3,17] utilize Monte-Carlo Tree Search (MCTS) to enhance their models and solve these problems.

3 Methodology

In this section, we introduce our proposed MM-TOWE model. Let's denote the parameters of the model as θ.

3.1 Graph Definition

We formulate TOWE task as an MDP of walking on the syntactic dependency tree. As we show in Fig. 1, the syntactic dependency tree is a directed graph because the dependency relation edge has direction. Due to this, we add an inverse edge for each dependency relation edge, and then the agent can walk from a given word to any word in the sentence.

Specifically, for a given sentence $\mathcal{W} = \{w_1, w_2, \cdots, w_n\}$ where w_i represents the i-th word in the sentence and n is the number of words of the sentence. We use Stanza [15] to generate the syntactic dependency tree for sentence

$\mathcal{W}$ and convert the tree into a dependency tree graph $\mathcal{G}$. Let's denote graph $\mathcal{G} = \{(w_i, e_{ij}, w_j)|w_i, w_j \in \mathcal{W}, e_{ij} \in \mathcal{E}\}$, where w_i and w_j are two words in the given sentence $\mathcal{W}$ while $\mathcal{E}$ is an edge set of dependency relations. The words w_i and w_j are connected by a dependency relation edge e_{ij} according to the syntactic dependency tree of the sentence $\mathcal{W}$. Meanwhile if $(w_i, e_{ij}, w_j) \in \mathcal{G}$ and the dependency relation between word w_i and w_j is $e_{ij} = dep$, there is an inverse edge $e_{ji} = dep^{-1}$ and $(w_j, e_{ji}, w_i) \in \mathcal{G}$ (Fig. 2).

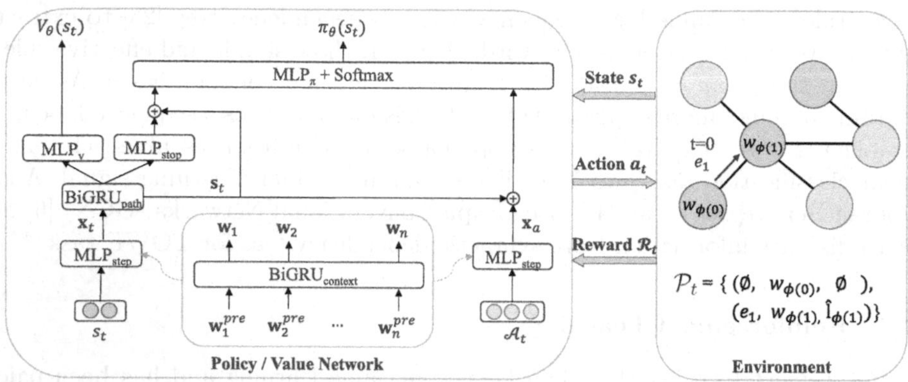

Fig. 2. The goal is to reason an explainable path from aspect term to opinion terms and predict correct label for every word to distinguish if it is an opinion word. The right part of the figure shows that the agent has chosen an action when $t = 0$ and move to word $w_{\phi(1)}$. After that, the agent will perform the next action by moving to a neighbor word through an edge and predicting the opinion label for the neighbor word.

3.2 An MDP Formulation of TOWE

We formulate the TOWE task as an MDP and let the agent reason over the dependency tree graph. The goal of TOWE task is to extract correct opinion terms from a sentence for a given aspect term. In the real cases, an aspect or opinion term may contain several words, while there may be more than one opinion term corresponding to one aspect term. Thus, the agent will learn relationships between these words on the graph, reason an explainable path to cover all opinion words and label them correctly. The model should know the position of the given aspect term in the sentence during reasoning. To this end, let's denote the information via an aspect label sequence $\mathcal{L}^a = \{l_1^a, l_2^a, \cdots, l_n^a\}$ by using BIO schema [16] ($\mathcal{L}$=$\{B$:beginning, I:inside, O:other$\}$) to label every word w_i with an aspect label l_i^a and point out the positions of the aspect words in the sentence. An opinion label sequence $\mathcal{L}^o$ which also contains opinion label l_i^o of every word is obtained in a similar way as the ground-truth.

With the information of the given sentence $\mathcal{W}$, its graph $\mathcal{G}$ and given aspect label sequence $\mathcal{L}^a$, the agent starts moving from the first word of aspect term.

For each time step, the agent chooses a neighbor word and move to it through an edge, then predicts its opinion label. When the agent chooses **STOP** action or the maximum time steps $\mathcal{T}_{max}$ has been reached, the agent stops moving over the graph and we can get the extraction result from the path with the opinion labels predicted by the agent. The states, actions, transition function, value function, and policy function of the MDP are defined as:

State $\mathcal{S}$: Let $s_t \in \mathcal{S}$ denote the state at time step t, where $\mathcal{S}$ is the state space. For each time step, the agent makes a decision based on all the information it can know, including the sentence $\mathcal{W}$, the graph $\mathcal{G}$, the given aspect label sequence $\mathcal{L}^a$ and history path $\mathcal{P}_t$. Therefore, we design the state as a tuple $s_t = (\mathcal{W}, \mathcal{G}, \mathcal{L}^a, \mathcal{P}_t)$, where $\mathcal{P}_t = \{(e_i, w_{\phi(i)}, \hat{l}^o_{\phi(i)}) | i \in [0, t]\}$ records all action information in the past (chosen edge e_i, chosen neighbor word $w_{\phi(i)}$, the predicted opinion label $\hat{l}^o_{\phi(i)}$ of $w_{\phi(i)}$) for each time step i. At time step t, the agent has reached word $w_{\phi(t)}$, where the $\phi(t)$ is the index of word $w_{\phi(t)}$ in the sentence $\mathcal{W}$. The agent starts from the first word of aspect term, thus the aspect label of $w_{\phi(0)}$ according to $\mathcal{L}^a$ must be B. And $s_0 = (\mathcal{W}, \mathcal{G}, \mathcal{L}^a, \mathcal{P}_0)$ where $\mathcal{P}_0 = \{(\varnothing, w_{\phi(0)}, \varnothing)\}$, because the agent hasn't taken any action. When the agent stops at time step $\mathcal{T}$, we get the terminal state $s_{\mathcal{T}}$ with the whole path $\mathcal{P}_{\mathcal{T}}$.

Action $\mathcal{A}$: At each time step t, $\mathcal{A}_t = \{(e, w, \hat{l}^o) | e \in \mathcal{E}, w \notin \{w_{\phi(0)}, w_{\phi(1)}, \cdots, w_{\phi(t)}\}, \hat{l}^o \in \mathcal{L}, (w_{\phi(t)}, e, w) \in \mathcal{G}\} \cup \{\textbf{STOP}\}$ is a set of possible actions according to s_t, while the whole action space is $\mathcal{A} = \cup \mathcal{A}_t$. The agent isn't allowed to go back to the word which already in the history path. If the agent performs action $a_t = (e_{t+1}, w_{\phi(t+1)}, \hat{l}^o_{\phi(t+1)}) \in \mathcal{A}_t$, it will move through an edge e_{t+1} from current word $w_{\phi(t)}$ to its neighbor word $w_{\phi(t+1)}$, and predict the opinion label $\hat{l}^o_{\phi(t+1)}$ for $w_{\phi(t+1)}$. When the agent thinks all opinion words are in the path, it will choose the **STOP** action to stop reasoning.

Reward $\mathcal{R}$: We employ the delayed reward strategy and design a reward function to consider both accuracy and efficiency to evaluate the whole path. Thus, the reward $\mathcal{R}_t$ is 0 during the reasoning process and there is a nonzero terminal reward $\mathcal{R}_{\mathcal{T}}$ to evaluate the whole path when the agent stops at time step $\mathcal{T}$. A high-quality path $\mathcal{P}_{\mathcal{T}}$ should cover all opinion words with all correct predicted labels (i.e. accuracy) based on a few actions (i.e. efficiency). To this end, we define the reward function as follows:

$$\mathcal{R}_{acc} = \frac{\hat{n}_o}{n_o} \cdot \frac{n_c}{\mathcal{T}}, \tag{1}$$

$$\mathcal{R}_{eff} = -\frac{\mathcal{T}}{\mathcal{T}_{max}}, \tag{2}$$

$$\mathcal{R}_{\mathcal{T}} = \mathcal{R}_{acc} + \mathcal{R}_{eff}, \tag{3}$$

where n_o is the number of opinion words according to the ground-truth $\mathcal{L}^o$, $\hat{n}_o$ is the number of hit opinion words in path $\mathcal{P}_{\mathcal{T}}$, n_c is the count of correct predicted labels in $\mathcal{P}_{\mathcal{T}}$. Please note that $\mathcal{T} = 0$ means the agent refuses to explore on the graph, therefore we define $\mathcal{R}_{\mathcal{T}} = -1$ for this special case.

Transition function T**:** The transition function $T : \mathcal{S} \times \mathcal{A} \rightarrow \mathcal{S}$ is defined that: $s_{t+1} = T(s_t, a_t) = (\mathcal{W}, \mathcal{G}, \mathcal{L}^a, \mathcal{P}_t \cup \{(e_{t+1}, w_{\phi(t+1)}, \hat{l}^o_{\phi(t+1)})\})$, where means state records the information of action $a_t = (e_{t+1}, w_{\phi(t+1)}, \hat{l}^o_{\phi(t+1)})$.
Value Function V_θ**:** The value function $V_\theta : \mathcal{S} \rightarrow \mathbb{R}$ is a scalar evaluation. It learns to estimate the terminal reward $\mathcal{R}_T$ for evaluating the quality of the whole path (an episode) based on the input state s_t. The same word in different sentences may represent different meanings. Thus, we input the sentence into a Bi-directional Gated Recurrent Unit (BiGRU) for encoding:

$$\mathbf{w}_i = \text{BiGRU}(\mathbf{w}_{i-1}, \mathbf{w}_i^{pre}; \theta_{context}), \tag{4}$$

where $\mathbf{w}_i^{pre}$ is the pretrained word embedding of word w_i, and $\mathbf{w}_i$ is the new word embedding of word w_i which contains the context information, $\theta_{context}$ denotes all the related parameters of the BiGRU network. We leverage a Multi-Layer Perceptrons (MLPs) to compress the information of every time step i in history path $\mathcal{P}_t = \{(e_i, w_{\phi(i)}, \hat{l}^o_{\phi(i)}) | i \in [0, t]\}$ and the aspect label $l^a_{\phi(i)}$ of word $w_{\phi(i)}$. Then, put them into a BiGRU to calculate the current state representation $\mathbf{s}_t$ and the value $V_\theta(s_t)$ is calculated by $\mathbf{s}_t$.

$$\mathbf{x}_t = \text{MLP}(\mathbf{e}_t \oplus \mathbf{w}_{\phi(t)} \oplus \mathbf{l}^o_{\phi(t)} \oplus \mathbf{l}^a_{\phi(t)}; \theta_{step}), \tag{5}$$

$$\mathbf{s}_t = \text{BiGRU}(\mathbf{s}_{t-1}, \mathbf{x}_t; \theta_{path}), \tag{6}$$

$$V_\theta(s_t) = \text{MLP}(\mathbf{s}_t; \theta_v), \tag{7}$$

where $\mathbf{e}_t$ is the embedding of edge, $\mathbf{w}_{\phi(t)}$ is the new embedding of word $w_{\phi(t)}$, $\mathbf{l}^o_{\phi(t)}$ is the embedding of predicted opinion label of $w_{\phi(t)}$, $\mathbf{l}^a_{\phi(t)}$ is the embedding of aspect label of $w_{\phi(t)}$, $\oplus$ denotes the concatenation operator, θ_{path} denotes all the related parameters of the BiGRU network, and θ_{step} and θ_v are parameters of two MLPs.

Policy π_θ**:** The policy π_θ calculates the probability distribution of all actions $a \in \mathcal{A}_t$ based on the state s_t. To this end, we calculate the representation $\mathbf{x}_a$ for every action. As we mentioned above the agent will select **STOP** action when it thinks the history path $\mathcal{P}_t$ covers all opinion words based on the state s_t. Thus, we leverage $\mathbf{s}_t$ to calculate $\mathbf{x}_a$ of the **STOP** action:

$$\mathbf{x}_a = \text{MLP}(\mathbf{s}_t; \theta_{stop}), \tag{8}$$

where θ_{stop} represents the parameters of MLP. The representation $\mathbf{x}_a$ of action $a = (e, w, \hat{l}^o)$ with the new word embedding can be written as:

$$\mathbf{x}_a = \text{MLP}(\mathbf{e} \oplus \mathbf{w} \oplus \mathbf{l}^o \oplus \mathbf{l}^a; \theta_{step}), \tag{9}$$

where $\mathbf{e}, \mathbf{w}, \mathbf{l}^o$ are the corresponding embeddings of the each element e, w, $\hat{l}^o$ of action a, $\mathbf{l}^a$ is the embedding of aspect label of word w and we also share the same parameters θ_{step} which is used in it formula (5). The probability of an action should consider both the state representation $\mathbf{s}_t$ and action representation $\mathbf{x}_a$, for any action $a \in \mathcal{A}_t$, we calculate its probability by a softmax function:

$$\pi_\theta(a|s_t) = \frac{\exp\{\mathrm{MLP}(\mathbf{s}_t \oplus \mathbf{x}_a; \theta_\pi)\}}{\sum_{a' \in \mathcal{A}_t} \exp\{\mathrm{MLP}(\mathbf{s}_t \oplus \mathbf{x}_{a'}; \theta_\pi)\}}, \tag{10}$$

where θ_π denotes as the parameters in the MLP.

3.3 Enhancing Policy by MCTS

Due to the sparse reward and large space, it is hard to sample good path at the beginning of training. Following AlpahGo Zero [19], we leverage MCTS to make a heuristic search in the whole space by using our value function V_θ and policy π_θ to get a better policy π_e. There are four steps in MCTS:

Selection: Starting from the root node s_R each time, MCTS recursively selects the child nodes by using the following function until reaches a leaf node:

$$a_t = \mathrm{argmax}_a(Q(s_t, a) + c_{puct} P(a|s_t) \frac{\sqrt{\sum_{a' \in \mathcal{A}_t} N(s_t, a')}}{1 + N(s_t, a)}), \tag{11}$$

where $Q(s_t, a)$ is an action value, c_{puct} is a hyper parameter to control the level of exploration of MCTS, $P(a|s_t)$ is a prior probability, and $N(s_t, a)$ is the visit count of the node. MCTS prefers choosing the node with small $N(s_t, a)$ at first. After simulating several times, it prefers choosing the node with higher $Q(s_t, a)$.

Evaluation: When reaching a leaf node s_t, we will estimate the value of this node. If s_t is a terminal node (i.e., the agent stops reasoning), we use the terminal reward $\mathcal{R}_T$ calculated by formula (1)-(3), else we use our value function $V_\theta(s_t)$ for estimating.

Expansion: If s_t is not a terminal leaf node, we will expand the tree by adding all child nodes (corresponding to every action $a \in \mathcal{A}_t$) for node s_t. Initializing the elements of each new child node as $P(a|s_t) = \pi_\theta(a|s_t)$, $Q(s_t, a) = 0$, $N(s_t, a) = 0$.

Backup: We recursively backup the elements $Q(s, a)$, $N(s, a)$ of all nodes from the leaf node s_t to the root node s_R according to the path $\mathcal{P}_t \in s_t$ by:

$$Q(s, a) \leftarrow \frac{V(s) + Q(s, a) \times N(s, a)}{N(s, a) + 1}, \tag{12}$$

$$N(s, a) \leftarrow N(s, a) + 1. \tag{13}$$

After reaching the maximum simulation time, we randomly choose the action according to the probabilities evaluated by searching policy π_e. A softmax function with temperature τ is used to get the probability of every action in policy π_e by using the visit count $N(s, a)$.

$$\pi_e(a_t|s_t) = \frac{\exp\{N(s_t, a_t)^{1/\tau}\}}{\sum_{a' \in \mathcal{A}_t} \exp\{N(s_t, a')^{1/\tau}\}}. \tag{14}$$

3.4 Training and Test

We use a mean square error for value function V_θ to mimic the terminal reward $\mathcal{R}_\mathcal{T}$ and a cross entropy loss for policy π_θ to mimic the searching policy π_e. The loss function $\mathcal{L}_\theta$ can be written as:

$$\mathcal{L}_\theta = (\mathcal{R}_\mathcal{T} - V_\theta(s_t))^2 - \pi_e(s_t)^\top log\pi_\theta(s_t) + \rho \|\theta\|^2, \tag{15}$$

where ρ is a parameter controlling the level of l_2 weight regularization.

After training, we also use MCTS to search a policy π by using V_θ and π_θ for testing and there are several differences. We use our value function $V_\theta(s_t)$ for estimating the value of leaf node s_t all the time because we don't know the ground-truth to calculate terminal reward $\mathcal{R}_\mathcal{T}$ during test time. And we select action $a_t = \text{argmax}_{a\in\mathcal{A}_t}\pi(a|s_t)$ for each step.

When reaching a terminal state $s_\mathcal{T}$, we generate a predicted opinion label sequence $\hat{\mathcal{L}}^o = \{\hat{l}^o_1, \hat{l}^o_2, \cdots, \hat{l}^o_n\}$ based on $\mathcal{P}_\mathcal{T} = \{(e_i, w_{\phi(i)}, \hat{l}^o_{\phi(i)}), i \in [0, T]\}$. For the words in sentence $\mathcal{W}$ which not exists in the path $\mathcal{P}_\mathcal{T}$, we assign the label O to these words. Then we use $\hat{\mathcal{L}}^o$ to extract opinion terms from sentence $\mathcal{W}$.

4 Experiment

4.1 Datasets and Metrics

We use three widely used datasets generated by Fan et al. [2] to evaluate our model. The 14lap is derived from the SemEval challenge 2014 Task4 [11], 15res is from SemEval challenge 2015 Task12 [13] and 16res is from SemEval challenge 2016 Task5 [12]. The suffixes "res" and "lap" mean that the reviews are from restaurant domain and laptop domain, respectively. We randomly sample 20% of the training data for validation.

We use the metrics precision, recall, and F1 score to measure the performance of baselines and our model. An opinion term is considered to be a correct prediction when the position (i.e., the beginning and the ending offset) of the term as well as the labels of the term are both predicted correctly.

4.2 Settings

We initialize word embedding vectors (i.e. $\mathbf{w}_i^{pre}$ in formula (4)) with 300 dimension Glove [10] vectors which are pretrained on 840 billion words and fix them during training. The dimension of edge embedding vectors is 50 and the dimension of label embedding vectors is 10. We randomly initialize the edge and label embedding vectors. The dimension of hidden states in context encoding BiGRU is set as 150 and the dimension of hidden states in BiGRU which calculates state representation is set as 50. We use Adam [5] as the optimizer and set learning rate $5e^{-4}$. The l_2 weight regularization ρ is $1e^{-5}$, hyper parameter c_{puct} in MCTS is 5.

4.3 Baselines

We compare our model with the following baselines:

Distance-rule [4]: it uses POS tags and distances by choosing the nearest adjective to the aspect term as the opinion term.

Dependency-rule [23]: it learns the dependency paths with POS tags from aspect word to opinion word, then uses the high frequency dependency templates to extract from the test data.

LSTM/BiLSTM [8]: this approach employs word embeddings to represent words, put them into a LSTM or BiLSTM, and makes a 3-class classification for every hidden state. It's a sentence-level opinion words extraction.

Pipeline [2]: it combines BiLSTM and distance rule. After getting the result of BiLSTM, choose the nearest opinion term to the aspect term as the final result.

TC-BiLSTM: this method follows the design of the work for target-oriented sentiment classification [20]. It uses the average embedding of the aspect term as the aspect vector, and concatenates it to every word embedding of the sentence. Then put them into BiLSTM to do sequence labeling.

IOG [2]: the authors use six different positional and directional LSTMs to extract opinion terms of the aspect term.

LOTN [21]: it transfers sentiment classification task into TOWE task to gather more opinion knowledge via an auxiliary learning signal.

ONG [14]: this method introduces distance information of syntactic structure into extraction. It employs BERT to get word embeddings in the paper. We reproduce the model by using Glove as word embeddings and stanza to generate syntactic dependency tree for a fair comparison.

4.4 Results

Table 1 shows the performance of our model and baselines. We can observe that our model performs best among all baselines on three datasets.

Table 1. Main experiment results(%). Best results are in bold (for P, R, and F1 score, the larger is the better).

Model	14lap			15res			16res		
	P	R	F1	P	R	F1	P	R	F1
Distance-rule	50.13	33.86	40.42	54.12	39.96	45.97	61.90	44.57	51.83
Dependency-rule	45.09	31.57	37.14	65.49	48.88	55.98	76.03	56.19	64.62
LSTM	55.71	57.53	56.52	57.27	60.69	58.93	62.46	68.72	65.33
BiLSTM	64.52	61.45	62.71	60.46	63.65	62.00	68.68	70.51	69.57
Pipeline	72.58	56.97	63.83	74.75	60.65	66.97	81.46	67.81	74.01
TC-BiLSTM	62.45	60.14	61.21	66.06	60.16	62.94	73.46	72.88	73.10
IOG	73.24	69.63	71.35	76.06	70.71	73.25	82.25	78.51	81.69
LOTN	77.08	67.62	72.02	76.61	70.29	73.29	86.57	80.89	83.62
ONG(Glove)	78.55	68.17	72.75	79.30	73.02	76.03	88.09	81.71	84.78
MM-TOWE(Our)	**81.24**	**69.49**	**74.90**	**81.00**	**75.25**	**78.02**	**89.02**	**83.43**	**86.14**

The unsupervised rule-based methods perform poorly on all datasets. Although the Dependency-rule is better than Distance-rule, it is still limited by its quality of the rules and worse than the deep-learning methods. LSTM and BiLSTM perform not well in the task because they will extract the same opinion terms for different aspect terms in the sentence. They can't extract for a special aspect term. The Pipeline combines BiLSTM and distance rule. It extracts the nearest opinion term of the aspect term and obtains a high performance as compared with LSTM/BiLSTM. TC-LSTM performs worse than Pipeline because it ignores the position of the aspect term. IOG is better than other baselines, but it suffers from the high model complexity and no supplementary information. LOTN transfers opinion knowledge from sentiment classification into TOWE and get better results, but it needs external information. ONG leverages the distance information of the dependency tree and it performs better than other baselines. However, ONG ignores the dependency relations in the syntactic structure, which results in a sub-optimal performance. Our MM-TOWE model gets great improvement and better than all baselines. The results verify the effectiveness of leveraging RL method to reason over the syntactic dependency tree and learn the dependency relationships.

4.5 Ablation Study

In order to learn the effects of different parts of our model. We compare MM-TOWE with the following variations: (i) **no context information**: we remove the BiGRU used in formula (4) from our model. We only use the pretrained word embeddings and not to aggregate the context information. (ii) **test without MCTS**: we use MCTS during training but don't use MCTS during test. We only use our policy π_θ and choose action with the maximal probability at each time when testing.

Table 2. Experiment results(%) of ablation study.

Model	14lap			15res			16res		
	P	R	F1	P	R	F1	P	R	F1
No context information	74.85	65.61	69.92	76.00	69.37	72.53	83.74	78.48	81.02
Test without MCTS	80.17	69.35	74.37	80.57	74.85	77.60	88.37	82.48	85.32
MM-TOWE(Our)	**81.24**	**69.49**	**74.90**	**81.00**	**75.25**	**78.02**	**89.02**	**83.43**	**86.14**

From Table 2, we can know that context information and testing with MCTS are all significant for opinion extraction. The performance will drop apparently when we remove any part of the model.

4.6 Case Study and Path Analysis

Table 3 shows the results of our method MM-TOWE and the best performing baseline ONG on some cases and we analyze the strengths and weaknesses of them. The first case shows that ONG only extracts the opinion word "easy" while neglect the opinion word "intuitive". However, in the second cases, ONG predicts a wrong opinion word "fast" which is not the opinion term of the aspect "graphics". In the third case, ONG extracts "not" and "enjoy" but the boundary of the opinion term is wrong. In contrast, our model correctly extracts all opinion terms for the three cases. In Table 4, we show the reasoning paths generated by our model for every sentence in Table 3.

Table 3. Cases of the extracted results of our method and the best performing baseline method (ONG). The aspect terms are red and the corresponding opinion words are blue.

SENTENCE	ONG	MM-TOWE
Everything is so easy and intuitive to setup or configure.	easy	easy, intuitive
It is super fast and has outstanding graphics.	fast & outstanding	outstanding
Did not enjoy the new Windows 8 and touchscreen functions.	not & enjoy	not enjoy

Table 4. The reasoning paths generated by our model for each sentence in Table 3. The relation types of chosen edge are shown above the arrows and the opinion labels predicted by the agent are shown in the parentheses behind the word.

configure $\xrightarrow{conj^{-1}}$ setup(O) $\xrightarrow{ccomp^{-1}}$ easy(B) $\xrightarrow{conj^{-1}}$ intuitive(B) $\longrightarrow$ **STOP**
graphics $\xrightarrow{amod}$ outstanding(B) $\longrightarrow$ **STOP**
Windows $\xrightarrow{obj^{-1}}$ enjoy(I) $\xrightarrow{advmod}$ not(B) $\longrightarrow$ **STOP**

5 Conclusion and Future Work

In this paper, we propose a novel deep reinforcement learning model for the TOWE task. To the end, we formulate the extraction task into a Markov Decision Process (MDP) of reasoning over the syntactic dependency tree. The model learns the relationships between aspect terms and opinion terms, and reasons a path to explain the result of the extraction. To better guide the reasoning process, we design a reward function to consider both accuracy and efficiency. Experimental results on three widely used datasets show that our model consistently outperforms all baselines. As transformer and BERT become more popular, future studies could fruitfully explore TOWE task further by using these structures to improve our model.

References

1. Das, R., et al.: Go for a walk and arrive at the answer: Reasoning over paths in knowledge bases using reinforcement learning. In: ICLR (2017)
2. Fan, Z., Wu, Z., Dai, X.Y., Huang, S., Chen, J.: Target-oriented opinion words extraction with target-fused neural sequence labeling. In: NAACL-HLT, pp. 2509–2518 (2019)
3. Feng, Y., Xu, J., Lan, Y., Guo, J., Zeng, W., Cheng, X.: From greedy selection to exploratory decision-making: Diverse ranking with policy-value networks. In: SIGIR, pp. 125–134 (2018)
4. Hu, M., Liu, B.: Mining and summarizing customer reviews. In: ACM SIGKDD, pp. 168–177 (2004)
5. Kingma, D., Ba, J.: Adam: A method for stochastic optimization. In: International Conference on Learning Representations (12 2014)
6. Kipf, T.N., Welling, M.: Semi-supervised classification with graph convolutional networks. In: 5th International Conference on Learning Representations, ICLR 2017, Toulon, France, April 24–26, 2017, Conference Track Proceedings (2017)
7. Liu, B.: Sentiment analysis and opinion mining. In: Synthesis Lectures on Human Language Technologies (2012)
8. Liu, P., Joty, S., Meng, H.: Fine-grained opinion mining with recurrent neural networks and word embeddings. In: EMNLP, pp. 1433–1443 (2015)
9. Moon, S., Shah, P., Kumar, A., Subba, R.: Opendialkg: Explainable conversational reasoning with attention-based walks over knowledge graphs. In: Proceedings of the 57th ACL, pp. 845–854 (2019)
10. Pennington, J., Socher, R., Manning, C.: Glove: Global vectors for word representation. In: EMNLP, pp. 1532–1543 (2014)
11. Pontiki, M., Galanis, D., Pavlopoulos, J., Papageorgiou, H., Androutsopoulos, I., Manandhar, S.: Semeval-2014 task 4: Aspect based sentiment analysis. In: SemEval, pp. 27–35 (2014)
12. Pontiki, M., et al.: Semeval-2016 task 5: Aspect based sentiment analysis. In: SemEval, pp. 19–30 (2016)
13. Pontiki, M., Galanis, D., Papageorgiou, H., Manandhar, S., Androutsopoulos, I.: SemEval-2015 task 12: aspect based sentiment analysis. In: SemEval, pp. 486–495 (2015)

14. Pouran Ben Veyseh, A., Nouri, N., Dernoncourt, F., Dou, D., Nguyen, T.H.: Introducing syntactic structures into target opinion word extraction with deep learning. In: EMNLP, pp. 8947–8956 (2020)
15. Qi, P., Zhang, Y., Zhang, Y., Bolton, J., Manning, C.D.: Stanza: a python natural language processing toolkit for many human languages. In: Proceedings of the 58th Annual Meeting of the Association for Computational Linguistics: System Demonstrations (2020). https://nlp.stanford.edu/pubs/qi2020stanza.pdf
16. Ramshaw, L., Marcus, M.: Text chunking using transformation-based learning. In: Third Workshop on Very Large Corpora (1995)
17. Shen, Y., Chen, J., Huang, P.S., Guo, Y., Gao, J.: M-walk: Learning to walk over graphs using monte carlo tree search. In: NeurIPS, pp. 6787–6798 (2018)
18. Silver, D., et al.: Mastering the game of go with deep neural networks and tree search. Nature **529**(7587), 484–489 (2016)
19. Silver, D., et al.: Mastering the game of go without human knowledge. Nature **550**(7676), 354–359 (2017)
20. Tang, D., Qin, B., Feng, X., Liu, T.: Effective LSTMs for target-dependent sentiment classification. In: COLING, pp. 3298–3307 (2016)
21. Wu, Z., Zhao, F., Dai, X.Y., Huang, S., Chen, J.: Latent opinions transfer network for target-oriented opinion words extraction. In: AAAI, pp. 9298–9305 (2020)
22. Xian, Y., Fu, Z., Muthukrishnan, S., de Melo, G., Zhang, Y.: Reinforcement knowledge graph reasoning for explainable recommendation. In: ACM SIGIR, pp. 285–294 (2019)
23. Zhuang, L., Jing, F., Zhu, X.Y.: Movie review mining and summarization. In: CIKM, pp. 43–50 (2006)

Learning Distinct Strategies for Heterogeneous Cooperative Multi-agent Reinforcement Learning

Kejia Wan[1], Xinhai Xu[2(✉)], and Yuan Li[2]

[1] Defence Innovation Insititute, Beijing, China
[2] Academy of Military Science, Beijing, China
{xuxinhai,yuan.li}@nudt.edu.cn

Abstract. Value decomposition has been a promising paradigm for cooperative multi-agent reinforcement learning. Many different approaches have been proposed, but few of them consider the heterogeneous settings. Agents with tremendously different behaviours bring great challenges for centralized training with decentralized execution. In this paper, we provide a formulation for the heterogeneous multi-agent reinforcement learning with some theoretical analysis. On top of that, we propose an efficient two-stage heterogeneous learning method. The first stage refers to a transfer technique by tuning existed homogeneous models to heterogeneous ones, which can accelerate the convergent speed. In the second stage, an iterative learning with centralized training is designed to improve the overall performance. We make experiments on heterogeneous unit micromanagement tasks in StarCraft II. The results show that our method could improve the win rate by around 20% for the most difficult scenario, compared with state-of-the-art methods, i.e., QMIX and Weighted QMIX.

Keywords: Multi-agent reinforcement learning · Heterogeneity · Transfer learning.

1 Introduction

Cooperative multi-agent reinforcement learning (MARL) has found wide applications in various areas, such as traffic light control [7], real-time strategy games [1], recommendation systems [2]. Single-agent learning methods cannot be used to train each agent independently in multi-agent settings, i.e., each agent is associated with a single-agent method. The reason is that simultaneous learning of all agents will result in a non-stationary environment from the perspective of any individual agent [6].

A natural way is to solve the multi-agent problem in a centralized manner, that is, learning an optimal joint action of agents with respect to the joint observation. However, the solution space grows exponentially with the number of agents, such that it is hard to get a good policy in a finite time [4]. To cope with this situation,

I. Farkaš et al. (Eds.): ICANN 2021, LNCS 12894, pp. 544–555, 2021.
https://doi.org/10.1007/978-3-030-86380-7_44

the paradigm of centralized training with decentralized execution [10] is proposed. The main idea is that each agent learns its policy based on its observation while a centralized mechanism is designed to guide the training of all agents. [3] proposes a multi-agent actor-critic method called counterfactual multi-agent(COMA) policy gradients, which learns a centralized critic with decentralized actor for each agent. The problem is that the global Q value is normally hard to learn for multi-agent settings with the joint state-action input. Later, value decomposition based methods (VDBMs) have gained great attention. The main idea is to decompose the global Q-value Q_{tot} to the individual Q-value for each agent. The most representative one is VDN [16], which represents Q_{tot} as a sum of individual Q-values Q_i for each agent. Each Q_i depends only on the observation of each agent, and Q_{tot} is used to compute the loss to update all neural networks. During execution, the action of each agent is selected greedily based on Q_i. VDN supposes a linear combination between Q_{tot} and Q_i, which ignores any extra state information available during the training. Then QMIX [13] is proposed by introducing a mixing neural network, which expresses Q_{tot} as a non-linear combination of Q_i. After that, many other efforts have been done to find better representations between Q_{tot} and Q_i, such as QTRAN [15], QPLEX [19], Weight Qmix [12] and so on.

The VDBMs have shown state-of-the-art performance on some challenging tasks in unit micromanagement in StarCraft II [22]. However, previous methods do not consider the heterogeneity among agents, which is in fact an important factor for MARL. In heterogeneous tasks, the strategies of heterogeneous agents vary greatly, which are hard to learn for updating simultaneously with centralized training. Moreover, parameter sharing, a technique widely used in VDBMs [20], cannot be used anymore. In parameter sharing, a neural network is shared by all agents and it is trained with experiences collected by all agents. For heterogeneous agents, it is hard to express distinct strategies with one neural network for all agents.

In this paper we firstly formulate VDBMs for multi-agent learning as an optimization problem. We classify agents to different groups based on their properties, such that each group contains only homogeneous agents. Based on the formulation, we introduce an alternating maximization technique for solving the optimization problem, and give some theoretical analysis for the properties of convergence and optimum. Then we propose a two-stage learning method for heterogeneous multi-agent reinforcement learning problems. In the first stage, we design an efficient technique to transfer existed neural networks of homogeneous agents to heterogeneous agents. We notice that existing neural networks of homogeneous agents obtained before can not be directly used for heterogeneous agents due to the change of the observation space, the action space and the environment. Although many transfer learning techniques have been studied in the area of image recognition [11], it is still a challenge for designing efficient transferring techniques for MARL. Different from previous transferring methods used in MARL, we adopt a tune method to revise existing neural networks to make them adapted to heterogeneous agents. In the second stage, we iteratively train different groups of agents until it is converged. The training process includes several iterations. In each iteration, only one group of agents is trained (named as active group) while agents in other groups (named as freezed groups) act without training. The two techniques work complementarily to improve both the convergent speed and the final performance.

We make extensive experiments in different challenging combat tasks of StarCraftII. We compare our method with popular VDBMs, i.e., Qmix and Weighted Qmix. Results show that our method significantly pushes forward state-of-the-art MARL algorithms for heterogeneous tasks. It is interesting to see that the gap between our method and traditional VDBMs increases with the increasing number of heterogeneous groups. This study reveals a new dimension, i.e., heterogeneity, for MARL, which provides a new perspective in understanding and promoting the emergence of cooperation among agents. Our main contributions are summarized as follows: (1) We provide formulations for VDBMs with heterogeneity and theoretical analyses for the solution approach; (2) We propose a novel two-stage learning method for heterogeneous multi-agent learning, including a novel transfer technique and an alternating maximization method. (3)The proposed method significantly outperforms state-of-the-art MARL method, i.e., Weighted QMIX, on hard heterogeneous tasks. (4) Our study shows that the heterogeneity is an important factor for multi-agent learning, which should be paid more attention.

2 Background

2.1 Multi-agent Markov Decision Process

In this paper we consider a cooperative multi-agent task which can be modelled by a decentralized partially observable Markov decision process(Dec-POMDP) [9].

The Dec-POMDP is characterized by the tuple $<\mathcal{N}, \mathcal{S}, \mathcal{A}, \mathcal{P}, \mathcal{O}, \mathcal{R}, \lambda>$ for N agents , where $\mathcal{N} = \{1, 2, ..., N\}$ represents a set of agents for all ally units. $\mathcal{S} = \{S^t\}_{t=0}^{T}$ is a set of game states where S^t is the state at time t. The terminal state S^T represents the final state of the task when the winning condition is satisfied or T is reached. At each time step, each agent $i \in \mathcal{N}$ chooses an action $a_i \in A_i$ and A_i represents all possible actions of agent i. It results in a joint reward $r \in \mathcal{R}$ and a state transition following the transition function $\mathcal{P}(S'|S, A)$. The joint action of all agents is denoted by $\mathcal{A} = \{A_1, A_2, ..., A_N\}$. We consider a partially observable setting, where each agent receives a partial observation $o_i \in O_i$ and $\mathcal{O} = \{O_1, O_2, ..., O_N\}$. We define $\pi_i : O_i^t \times A_i^t \to [0, 1]$ as the policy for each agent. At time step t of a game, each agent observes a partial state o_i^t and selects an action a_i^t based on its policy. To compute the optimal policy, the state value function $V^\pi(S)$ is introduced, which is calculated by cumulated rewards with the discount factor $\lambda \in [0, 1)$, see (1).

$$V^\pi(S) = \mathbb{E}\{\textstyle\sum_{t=0}^{\infty} \lambda^t r^t | S_0 = S\} \quad (1)$$

where $\mathbb{E}$ is the expectation. Based on $V^\pi(S)$, the state-action value $Q^\pi(S, A)$ is defined as (2).

$$Q^\pi(S^t, A^t) = \mathbb{E}\{r^{t+1} + \lambda V^\pi(S^{t+1})\} \quad (2)$$

2.2 Value Function Decomposition

MARL problems could be solved with VDBMs, which decompose the global state-action value Q_{tot} into the individual value Q_i for each agent. Different approaches have been proposed to study the relation between Q_{tot} and Q_i. VDN expresses Q_{tot} as a sum of Q_i, i.e., $Q_{tot} = \sum_i Q_i$ where QMIX uses a continuous monotonic function in form of a mixing network to express this relation, i.e., $Q_{tot} = f(Q_1, Q_2, ..., Q_n)$. In QMIX, each agent corresponds an independent neural network. It is used to compute Q_i based on its own local observation, which is used as the input for the mixing network. During the training, all neural networks for agents and the mixing network are trained together. The loss is computed by equation (3), where $y_k^{tot} = r + max_{a'} Q_{tot}(o, a; \theta^-)$. Here we use the mechanism of double networks which is used in DQN [8]. θ represents parameters of eval networks while θ^- represents that of target networks. b is the number of samples used to train the neural network.

$$L(\theta) = \sum_{k=1}^{b} [(y_k^{tot} - Q_{tot}(o, a; \theta))^2] \tag{3}$$

Note that for VDBMs, a general principle Individual-Global-Max (IGM) [15] should be satisfied, which is shown as equation (4). It guarantees that a global argmax performed on Q_{tot} yields the same result as a set of individual argmax operations performed on each Q_i.

$$argmax_a Q_{tot}(o, a) = \begin{pmatrix} argmax_{a_1} Q_1(o, a_1) \\ argmax_{a_2} Q_2(o, a_2) \\ \dots\dots \\ argmax_{a_N} Q_N(o, a_N) \end{pmatrix} \tag{4}$$

3 Problem Formulation

Let function f and g_i represent the mixing network and the individual network for agent i, which are parametered by $\dot{\theta}$ and $\ddot{\theta}_i$ respectively. Then we have $Q_{tot}(o, a; \dot{\theta}) = f(Q_1(o_1, a_1; \ddot{\theta}_1), ...Q_N(o_N, a_N; \ddot{\theta}_N); \dot{\theta})$ and $Q_i(o_i, a_i; \ddot{\theta}_i) = g_i(o_i, a_i; \ddot{\theta}_i)$. In the following, we use Q_{tot} and Q_i to represent $Q_{tot}(o, a; \dot{\theta})$ and $Q_i(o_i, a_i; \ddot{\theta}_i)$ respectively. The optimization problem for multi-agent learning based on VDBMs can be formulated by (5), where (o_i, a_i) belongs to the set of samples D.

Optimization Formulation for VDBM:

$$\text{maxmize } Q_{tot} = f(Q_1, Q_2, ...Q_N; \dot{\theta}) \tag{5a}$$

$$\text{subject to: } Q_i = g_i(o_i, a_i; \ddot{\theta}_i), (o_i, a_i) \in D, i \in \mathcal{N} \tag{5b}$$

$$Q_i, \dot{\theta}, \ddot{\theta}_i \in \mathbb{R}, i \in \mathcal{N} \tag{5c}$$

For heterogenous tasks, we divide $\mathcal{N}$ into different homogeneous groups $\mathcal{N}_1, \mathcal{N}_2, ..., \mathcal{N}_K$. K is the number of groups and $\mathcal{K} = \{1, 2, ..., K\}$. The number of agents in a homogeneous group is $|\mathcal{N}_k|, k = 1, 2, ..K$, and we have $|\mathcal{N}| = |\mathcal{N}_1| + |\mathcal{N}_2| + ... + |\mathcal{N}_K|$. We introduce $\delta(i) \in \mathcal{K}$ to denote the type of the ith agent, and $\epsilon(k)$ to denote the set of agents belongs to type k, i.e., if $\delta(i) = k$, then $i \in \epsilon(k)$, $i \in \mathcal{N}, k \in \mathcal{K}$. Note that agents in a homogeneous group belongs to the same type and parameter sharing could be used for homogeneous agents. The formulation of (5) could be reformulated as (6a).

Heterogenous Optimization Formulation:

$$\text{maxmize } Q_{tot} = f(Q_{\delta(1)}, Q_{\delta(2)}, ...Q_{\delta(N)}; \dot{\theta}) \tag{6a}$$

$$\text{subject to: } Q_{\delta(i)} = g_{\delta(i)}(o_i, a_i; \ddot{\theta}_i), (o_i, a_i) \in D, i \in \mathcal{N} \tag{6b}$$

$$Q_i, \dot{\theta}, \ddot{\theta}_i \in \mathbb{R}, i \in \mathcal{N} \tag{6c}$$

VDBMs solve this problem through the training with amounts of samples directly. Here we consider a non-convex optimization approach, namely the alternating maximization technique [5]. The main idea is to optimize variables for each group iteratively, which is equivalent to solve a marginal optimization problem formulated as (6a). At the beginning, $\{\dot{\theta}, \ddot{\theta}\}$ are randomly initialized. In each iteration, keeping $\{\dot{\theta}, \ddot{\theta}_l\}$ as variables while other variables $\{\ddot{\theta}_k\}$ are fixed as $\hat{\theta}_k, k \in \mathcal{K} \setminus \{l\}$. Note that Q_k can be computed by $\ddot{\theta}_k$.

Heterogenous Marginal Optimization Formulation:

$$\text{maxmize } Q_{tot} = f(\hat{Q}_{\delta(1)}, ..., Q_l, ...\hat{Q}_{\delta(N)}; \dot{\theta})$$

$$\text{subject to: } \hat{Q}_{\delta(i)} = \hat{g}_{\delta(i)}(o_i, a_i; \hat{\theta}_{\delta(i)}) \tag{7a}$$

$$Q_l = g_l(o_i, a_i; \ddot{\theta}_l), (o_i, a_i) \in D, i \in \mathcal{N} \setminus \epsilon(l) \tag{7b}$$

$$Q_l, \dot{\theta}, \ddot{\theta}_l \in \mathbb{R} \tag{7c}$$

4 Two-Stage Heterogeneous Learning

In this section we introduce a two-stage learning method for heterogeneous tasks. Firstly, to accelerate the convergent speed, we design a transfer learning technique to make homogenous models adapt to heterogeneous ones. Secondly, we adopt an alternating maximization technique to training heterogeneous groups iteratively. The framework of the proposed method is illustrated in Fig. 1.

4.1 Stage 1: Transfer Learning

In fact, we do not have to learn from the scratch for heterogenous tasks as we could reuse homogeneous models obtained before. However, it is not

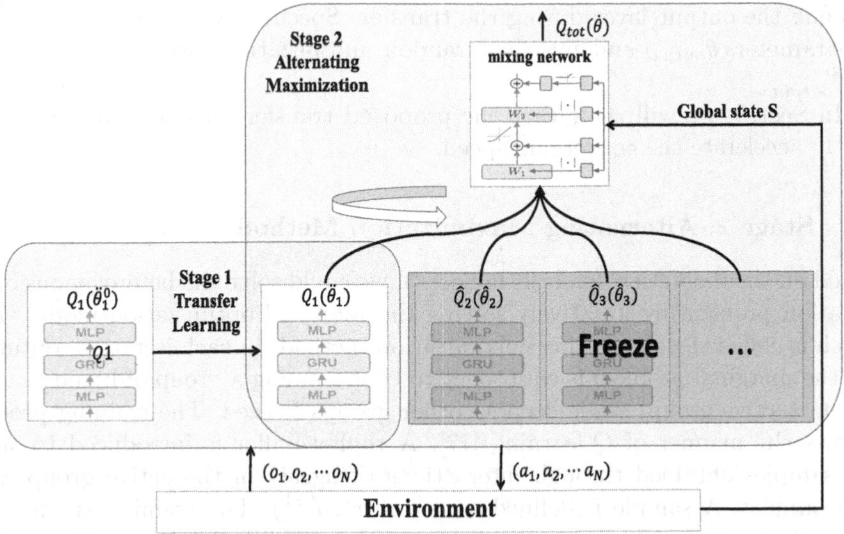

Fig. 1. The framework of the two-stage learning method. In the first stage, model parameter by $\ddot{\theta}^0$ is transferred to $\ddot{\theta}$. In the second stage, the first group is active group while others are freezed groups.

straightforward to load homogeneous models directly for heterogenous cases. The observation space and the action space are all changed when transferring existed models to heterogenous ones.

Different from previous transfer techniques used in reinforcement learning [18], we consider to refine the structure of the neural network to make them adapt to heterogeneous scenarios. This technique has been studied in the area of image recognition, which is called "finetune"[21]. The main research finding is that the first three layers of a neural network mainly include general features while the last layer mainly include features specified for certain task. Based on this intuition, we design a simple but efficient transfer method.

Suppose we have a trained model, which is a neural network consisting of an input layer, hidden layers and an output layer. The weights of the input layer is represented by $\ddot{\theta}_{input}$ while that of the output layer is $\ddot{\theta}_{output}$. To cope with the variation happened in the observation space, we consider to extend the input layer of the existed model. We use $\ddot{\theta}_{new}$ to represent the extended weights for adding new neurons in the input layer. Then the weights of the input layer for the transferred model is represented by $\ddot{\theta}'_{input} = [\ddot{\theta}_{input}, \ddot{\theta}_{new}]$. We keep the weights $\ddot{\theta}_{input}$ as it reflect general features, and then θ_{input} is initialized randomly.

When transferring a homogeneous model to the heterogeneous case, the action space may also change. Different from the way of dealing with the input layer, we tune the output layer of the exited model in another way. Since the output layer is closely related to specific task, and the homogeneous environment always differs with the heterogeneous environment greatly, we consider to redefine the output layer during the transfer. Specifically, We erase the values of parameters $\ddot{\theta}_{output}$ and give them random initializations, which is represented by $\ddot{\theta}'_{output}$.

In Sect. 5, we will show that the proposed transfer technique could significantly accelerate the converging speed.

4.2 Stage 2: Alternating Maximization Method

Based on the theoretical analysis in Sect. 3, we could solve the heterogenous optimization problem by iteratively solving the marginal optimization model (7a), which is called the alternating maximization method. In each iteration, optimizing the marginal problem is equivalent to that training a group of homogeneous agents (active group) while keeping other groups freezed. The training process follows the manner of Q-learning [17]. A replay buffer is introduced to store the samples obtained through interactions of agents in the active group with environment. A sample is defined as $(o_i^t, a_i^t, r^t, o_i^{t+1})$. The training is executed many times, and each time a batch of samples is randomly selected to update parameters of neural networks.

The two-stage heterogeneous learning is described in Algorithm 1. The input parameter θ_k^0 comes from existing models while the output is the optimized parameter. In Stage 1, $rand()$ represents randomly generating values. In Stage 2, k and l represent the iteration number and the index of active group respectively. The process of an iteration is described in Step 6–17. An episode corresponds to Step 9–15. The parameters of the neural network for the active group θ_l is updated based on VDBM every one episode.

5 Experiments

In this section we make experiments to answer the following questions: (1) Can the VDBMs perform well in heterogeneous tasks by removing the parameter sharing? (2) Can our method improve the performance of VDBMs? (3) What is the impact of transfer learning and alternating maximization on the performance of VDBMs respectively?

Our experiments are carried out on StarCraft Multi-Agent Challenge(SMAC) environment [14]. We compare our methods with two baselines: QMIX and Weighted QMIX. QMIX is a standard VDBM, which is used as the baseline for many other VDBMs. Weighted QMIX is the state-of-the-art VDBM, which has shown good performance on SMAC tasks. We use the following notations to denote different methods: (1) QMIX; (2) QMIX-THL: QMIX with two-stage heterogeneous learning; (3) QMIX-NPS: QMIX without parameter sharing; (4) OW-QMIX: Optimistically weighted QMIX, see [12]; (5) OW-QMIX-THL: Optimistically weighted QMIX with two-stage heterogeneous learning; (6) OW-QMIX-NPS: Optimistically weighted QMIX without parameter sharing.

Algorithm 1: Two-stage Heterogeneous Learning

Input: Existed parameters of models $\ddot{\theta}_i^0$ for agent $i \in \mathcal{N}$
Output: Optimized policies $g_k^*(\ddot{\theta}_k^*), k \in \mathcal{K}$
Stage 1: Set $\ddot{\theta}^* = \ddot{\theta}^0$, $\dot{\theta} = rand(), \ddot{\theta}'_{new} = rand()$
$\ddot{\theta}^*_{output} = rand()$;
$\ddot{\theta}^*_{input} = \ddot{\theta}^0_{input} \cup \ddot{\theta}'_{new}$;
Stage 2: $k = 1$
while *Non-convergent* **do**
  $l = k\%K$
  Fix the polices of groups with homogeneous agents as $\hat{g}_k(\hat{\theta}^*), k \in \mathcal{K} \setminus \{l\}$
  for $ep = 1, 2, \ldots, L$ **do**
    Initialize the task;
    for $t = 1, 2, \ldots, T$ **do**
      Obtain observations o_i^t for all agents;
      Compute individual Q values: $Q_i = \hat{g}_{\delta(i)}(o_i^t, a_i^{t-1}; \hat{\theta}_i),\ i \in \mathcal{N} \setminus \epsilon(l)$,
      $Q_l = g_l(o_j, a_j^{t-1}; \ddot{\theta}_l), j \in \epsilon(l)$;
      Compute actions following ε-greedy policy
      Get reward r^t and next observation o_i^t;
      Store samples $(o_i^t, a_i^t, r^t, o_i^{t+1}), i \in \epsilon(l)$ in the replay buffer D;
    Updating θ_l^* through VDBM
  $k = k + 1$

For all experiments, we set the discount factor $\gamma = 0.99$. The optimization is conducted using RMSprop with a learning rate of 5×10^{-4}, α of 0.99, and with no momentum or weight decay. For exploration, we use ε-greedy with ε annealed linearly from 1.0 to 0.05 over 50k time steps and kept constant for the rest of the training. Batches of 50 episodes are sampled from the replay buffer, and the whole framework is trained end-to-end on fully unrolled episodes. The percentage of these episodes in which the method defeats all enemy units within the time limit is referred to as the test win rate. All experiments use the default reward and observation settings of the SMAC benchmark.

5.1 Main Results

The comparison results of our method with two baselines, i.e., QMIX and OW-QMIX, are shown in Fig. 2. We consider three different scenarios in SMAC environments, i.e., 3s5z,1c3s5z and 1c2m3s5z, which differs in the degree of heterogeneity. c,s,z,m represent different types of units, i.e., Colossus, Stalker Zealots and Medivacs respectively. Take 1c3s5z for example, there are three different groups and nine agents in total, i.e., $K = 3$ and $|\mathcal{N}_1| = 1$, $|\mathcal{N}_2| = 3$ and $|\mathcal{N}_3| = 5$. All agents have two basic actions: move and stop. The first three types of agent have the ability of attacking. The attacking range of Colossus is the biggest while the attacking frequency of Stalker is the highest. The most different unit is Medivacs which can not attack but can heal other agents.

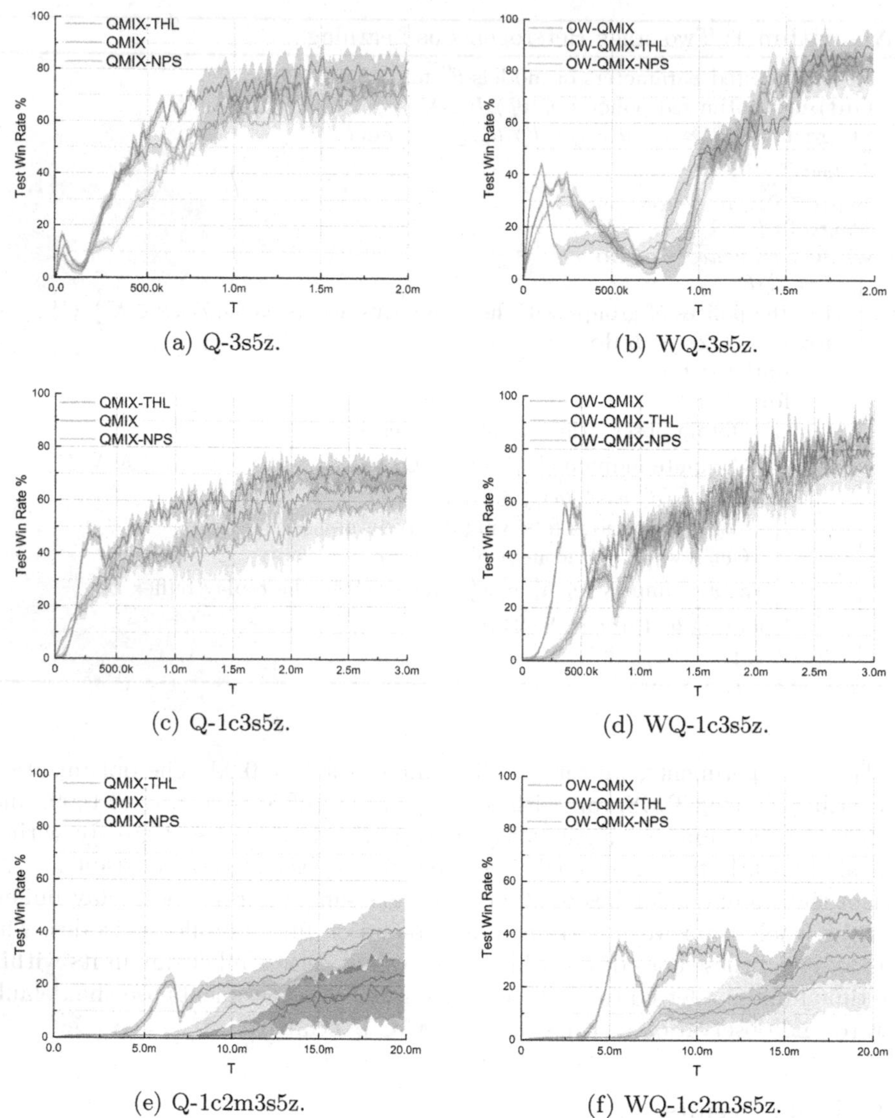

(a) Q-3s5z. (b) WQ-3s5z.

(c) Q-1c3s5z. (d) WQ-1c3s5z.

(e) Q-1c2m3s5z. (f) WQ-1c2m3s5z.

Fig. 2. Comparisons of the proposed method with QMIX and Weighted QMIX.

The first observation is that both QMIX and OW-QMIX could not get better performance by removing the parameter sharing for heterogeneous tasks. Without parameter sharing, each group of agents corresponds to a separate network, which assures that networks for heterogeneous groups update independently. However, the results show that it gets even smaller win rates than the two baselines. Secondly, THL greatly improves the performance of the two baselines. QMIX-THL increases the win rate by around 8%,10% and 20% compared to

QMIX for the three tasks while OW-QMIX-THL increases by around 5%,8% and 16% compared to OW-QMIX. Further, it is interesting to see that the increment of the win rate brought by THL becomes greater with the increase of the number of types. Especially with the emergence of Medivacs in 1c2m3s5z, the baselines are improved greatly with THL. Further, the convergent speed for VDBMs with THL is also faster that that without THL. The results show that the heterogeneity is an important factor for VDBMs.

5.2 Ablation Results

We carry out ablation studies to analyze the effectiveness of transfer learning and alternating maximization respectively. The experiments are conducted on the task 1c2m3s5z with QMIX as the baseline. The result is shown in Fig. 3. In QMIX-TL, we load a previous neural network model for each type of units and then continue training with QMIX. In QMIX-AM, we train all agents from the scratch through alternating maximization.

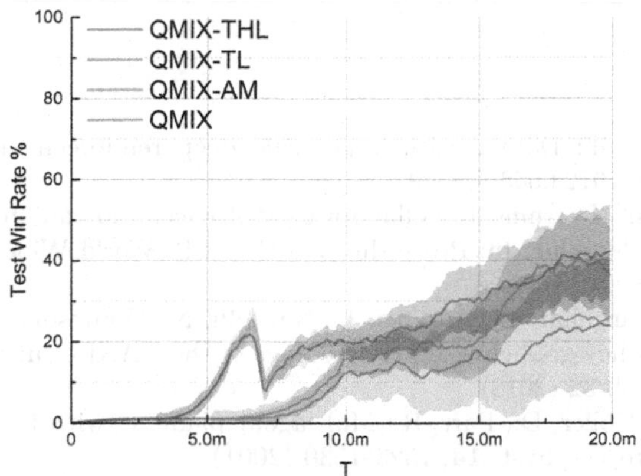

Fig. 3. Ablation Results.

As we can see, the curve for QMIX-TL and that for QMIX-THL overlap at the beginning, which are much higher than QMIX-AM and QMIX. It means that the improvements for QMIX-THL at the beginning mainly come from TL. The final win rate of QMIX-AM is similar to that of QMIX-THL, which is much bigger than that of QMIX-TL and QMIX. This shows that AM mainly contributes the final performance. Overall, the transfer learning makes contributions for accelerating the converge speed while the alternating maximization for improving the win rate. The two technologies make up the proposed effective two-stage method.

6 Conclusion

In this paper we study the heterogeneous MARL problem, for which optimization formulations are presented. Based on the formulations, we give some theoretical analysis about the convergence and the optimum of the alternating maximization technique. Then we propose an efficient two-stage heterogenous learning method, including a transferring technique based on tuning the network and an alternating maximization technique to dispose heterogeneous agents. The two techniques work complementarily, which not only accelerate the convergent speed but also improve the final performance. The experiments on heterogeneous combat tasks in StarCraft II show that our method significantly pushes forward state-of-the-art of MARL algorithms based on VDBMs. This study points that the heterogeneity is an important factor for MARL problems. It would be also interesting to investigate more heterogeneous tasks with other VDBMs in the future research.

Acknowledgement. This work was supported in part by the National Natural Science Foundation of China under Grant 61902425.

References

1. Berner, C., et al.: Dota 2 with large scale deep reinforcement learning. arXiv preprint arXiv:1912.06680 (2019)
2. Feng, J., et al.: Learning to collaborate: Multi-scenario ranking via multi-agent reinforcement learning. In: Proceedings of the 2018 World Wide Web Conference, pp. 1939–1948 (2018)
3. Foerster, J., Farquhar, G., Afouras, T., Nardelli, N., Whiteson, S.: Counterfactual multi-agent policy gradients. In: Proceedings of the AAAI Conference on Artificial Intelligence, vol. 32 (2018)
4. Guestrin, C., Koller, D., Parr, R.: Multiagent planning with factored mdps. Adv. Neural Inf. Process. Syst. **14**, 1523–1530 (2001)
5. Jain, P., Kar, P.: Non-convex optimization for machine learning. Found. Trends®Mach. Learn. **10**(3–4), 142–363 (2017). https://doi.org/10.1561/2200000058
6. Laurent, G.J., Matignon, L., Fort-Piat, L., et al.: The world of independent learners is not markovian. Int. J. Knowl. Based Intell. Eng. Syst. **15**(1), 55–64 (2011)
7. Ma, J., Wu, F.: Feudal multi-agent deep reinforcement learning for traffic signal control. In: Proceedings of the 19th International Conference on Autonomous Agents and Multiagent Systems, pp. 816–824 (2020)
8. Mnih, V., et al.: Human-level control through deep reinforcement learning. Nature **518**(7540), 529–533 (2015)
9. Nguyen, D.T., Kumar, A., Lau, H.C.: Credit assignment for collective multiagent rl with global rewards. In: Advances in Neural Information Processing Systems, pp. 8102–8113 (2018)
10. Oliehoek, F.A., Spaan, M.T., Vlassis, N.: Optimal and approximate q-value functions for decentralized pomdps. J. Artif. Intell. Res. **32**, 289–353 (2008)
11. Pan, S.J., Yang, Q.: A survey on transfer learning. IEEE Trans. Knowl. Data Eng. **22**(10), 1345–1359 (2009)

12. Rashid, T., Farquhar, G., Peng, B., Whiteson, S.: Weighted qmix: Expanding monotonic value function factorisation for deep multi-agent reinforcement learning. Adv. Neural Inf. Process. Syst. **33** (2020)
13. Rashid, T., Samvelyan, M., Schroeder, C., Farquhar, G., Foerster, J., Whiteson, S.: Qmix: monotonic value function factorisation for deep multi-agent reinforcement learning. In: International Conference on Machine Learning, pp. 4295–4304 (2018)
14. Samvelyan, M., et al.: The starcraft multi-agent challenge. In: Proceedings of the 18th International Conference on Autonomous Agents and MultiAgent Systems, pp. 2186–2188 (2019)
15. Son, K., Kim, D., Kang, W.J., Hostallero, D.E., Yi, Y.: Qtran: learning to factorize with transformation for cooperative multi-agent reinforcement learning. In: International Conference on Machine Learning, pp. 5887–5896 (2019)
16. Sunehag, P., et al.: Value-decomposition networks for cooperative multi-agent learning based on team reward. In: Proceedings of the International Conference on Autonomous Agents and Multiagent Systems, pp. 2085–2087 (2018)
17. Sutton, R., Barto, A.: Reinforcement Learning, An Introduction. 2nd edn, Bradford Books, MIT Press, Cambridge (2018)
18. Tirinzoni, A., Poiani, R., Restelli, M.: Sequential transfer in reinforcement learning with a generative model. In: International Conference on Machine Learning, pp. 9481–9492. PMLR (2020)
19. Wang, J., Ren, Z., Liu, T., Yu, Y., Zhang, C.: Qplex: Duplex dueling multi-agent q-learning (2020)
20. Wang, T., Dong, H., Lesser, V., Zhang, C.: Roma: Multi-agent reinforcement learning with emergent roles. In: Proceedings of the 37th International Conference on Machine Learning, vol. 119, pp. 9876–9886 (2020)
21. Yosinski, J., Clune, J., Bengio, Y., Lipson, H.: How transferable are features in deep neural networks? In: Advances in Neural Information Processing Systems, pp. 3320–3328 (2014)
22. Zhang, T., et al.: Multi-agent collaboration via reward attribution decomposition (2020)

MAT-DQN: Toward Interpretable Multi-agent Deep Reinforcement Learning for Coordinated Activities

Yoshinari Motokawa(✉) and Toshiharu Sugawara(✉)

Department of Computer Science and Engineering, Waseda University, Tokyo, Japan
y.motokawa@isl.cs.waseda.ac.jp, sugawara@waseda.jp

Abstract. We propose an interpretable neural network architecture for multi-agent deep reinforcement learning to understand the rationale for learned cooperative behavior of the agents. Although the deep learning technology has contributed significantly to multi-agent systems to build coordination among agents, it is still unclear what information the agents depend on to behave cooperatively. Removing this ambiguity may further improve the efficiency and productivity of multi-agent systems. The main idea of our proposal is to adopt the transformer to deep Q-network for addressing the above-mentioned issue. By extracting *multi-head attention weights* from the transformer encoder, we propose a *multi-agent transformer deep Q-network* (MAT-DQN) and show that agents using attention mechanisms possess better coordination capability with other agents despite being trained individually for a cooperative patrolling task problem; thus, they can exhibit better performance results compared with the agents with vanilla DQN (which is a baseline method). Furthermore, we indicate that it is possible to visualize heatmaps of attentions, which indicate the influential input-information in agents' decision-making process for their cooperative behaviors.

Keywords: Distributed autonomous system · Multi-agent deep reinforcement learning · Attention mechanism

1 Introduction

Recently, multi-agent systems (MASs) have gained popularity in various real-world applications. For example, thanks to the advancements made in computational technology and abundant supply of high-quality data, a swarm of drones are being increasingly used to effectively spray pesticide in agricultural fields [1,10] and sophisticated agents are being used for maintaining high levels of security in *intelligent surveillance systems* [6,12]. Furthermore, multiple robots (agents) equipped with sensors have been able to execute various complex tasks in a highly cooperative and coordinated manner [4]. In addition, MASs have benefited from the advent of deep learning; by approximating high-dimensional action-value functions with the neural networks, agents possess the capability of

I. Farkaš et al. (Eds.): ICANN 2021, LNCS 12894, pp. 556–567, 2021.
https://doi.org/10.1007/978-3-030-86380-7_45

taking appropriate actions in complicated environments and behaving cooperatively with other agents. Therefore, MASs, using deep learning methods, can be expected to further increase the productivity for real-world applications.

However, although *multi-agent deep reinforcement learning* (MADRL) has achieved the state-of-the-art performance in broad problem domains, it suffers from a crucial limitation, namely, the so-called *black box problem* [2]. The lack of transparency and algorithmic accountability is fatal, especially in critical applications, such as self-driving vehicle agents that cannot fail. Because these agents are always required to execute tasks appropriately with reasonable judgment and guarantee both robustness and safety, it is important to clarify the rationales of actions leading to such cooperation/coordination; indeed, it is almost impossible to interpret the rationales and reasons of these behaviors using the existing deep learning technology.

Thus, we introduce a novel approach to the MADRL for improving the interpretability of the multi-agent cooperation. The proposed method, the *multi-agent transformer deep Q-network* (MAT-DQN), is derived by incorporating the *transformer encoder* into the *deep Q-network* (DQN) architecture. The transformer encoder was originally proposed for natural language processing to add the *(self-)attention mechanism* [13], which can learn the relevance between tokenized vocabularies. In our approach, we extended the *multi-head attention* of vision transformer [5], which handles image classification problems in computer vision, for the MADRL in order to interpret what information is influential for the agent's decision-making process behind their coordinated behaviors. Then, the final output of the Q-values of each agent is calculated by fully connected network with the attention mechanism and the encoded environmental information.

We conducted experiments to investigate the performance and advantages of the agents using the MAT-DQN in the patrolling task, which is a coordinated object collection problem on a grid environment. To evaluate the performance, we compared these results with those of agents using vanilla DQNs as a baseline. Our experiments indicate that the MAT-DQN agents, which are the agents with their own MAT-DQNs, outperform the baseline agents. We then generated *attentional heatmaps* using the weights from the multi-head attention module in the transformer encoder, so as to understand where individual agents paid attention in their local visible areas for coordinated and cooperative behaviors with other nearby agents. The analysis shows that, for example, an agent is likely to focus on the closest object because it is easier to pick up the object, whereas if there are other agents in the local area, it actually locks on their movements and moves on to another nearby object that, although not the closest, is safer to pick, with relatively lesser chance of collision. We believe that clarifying influential features and attributes of information contribute to the interpretability as well as the efficiency of the proposed system.

2 Related Work

There are a few studies on the interpretability of the behaviors by MADRL [3,7, 8]. For example, Jiang et al. [8] proposed an *attentional communication* (ATOC) model, which comprises both attention and bidirectional long short-term memory units. After training, these agents can dynamically create a communication network with other agents to make cooperative decisions. Yet, there is still a difficulty of comprehending which information besides the information involved in communication is influential in the decision-making process of the agents. The *multi-actor-attention-critic* (MAAC) is an algorithm to train decentralized agents with their center critic network [7]. The agents selectively pay attention to relevant information from other agents after training. It also improves scalability because the decentralized critic network evaluates individual agents. Nevertheless, only the embedded information from agents is available in this approach, and thus, it is still unclear which locations/tasks are significant for decisions. Chen et al. [3] proposed the *graph attention multi-agent reinforcement learning algorithm* (GAMA) by using both a graph network and an attention mechanism to improve the scalability of the algorithm in a dynamic environment. The agents are capable of communicating with other agents selected based on the output from the attention mechanism. Although their success in the MADRL is remarkable, similar to ATOC, it is unknown what kinds of attributes of tasks are influential for the behavior decisions.

Although previous research mainly focuses on the intra-network among agents by adopting the attention mechanism, our goal in the MAT-DQN is to make the agents capable of paying attention on all agents, taking all objects into account, and executing all relevant tasks, so that we can interpret the behavior of agents based on their attentional heatmaps.

3 Background and Problem Description

3.1 Partially Observable Markov Decision Process

We introduce a discrete time step t ($\geq$0). Markov decision process (MDP) is a type of stochastic process wherein the conditional probability distribution of the next step depends on only the current state [11]. The *decentralized partially observable Markov decision process* (dec-POMDP) of n agents, $\mathcal{I} = \{1, \dots, n\}$, is stated by tuple $\langle \mathcal{I}, \mathcal{S}, \{\mathcal{A}_i\}, p_T, \{r_i\}, \{\Omega_i\}, \mathcal{O}, H \rangle$, where $\mathcal{S}$ is a finite set of available states, and $\mathcal{A}_i$ is the set of actions for agent $i \in \mathcal{I}$ with $\mathcal{A} = \mathcal{A}_1 \times \cdots \times \mathcal{A}_n$ being the set of joint actions. Function $p_T(s'|s,a)$ denotes transition probability for $a \in \mathcal{A}$ and $s, s' \in \mathcal{S}$ and $r_i(s,a)$ ($\in \mathbb{R}$) for $s \in \mathcal{S}$ and $a \in \mathcal{A}$ is the reward of i. $\Omega = \Omega_1 \times \cdots \times \Omega_n$ is the set of joint observations, where Ω_i is the set of i's observations, and $\mathcal{O}(o|s,a)$ is the observation probability $P(o|s,a)$ for $o \in \Omega$. Positive integer H is the horizon of the process and is also the maximum episode length of the patrolling task. Then, i learns the policy π_i to maximize discounted cumulative reward $R_i = \sum_{t=0}^{H} \gamma^t r_i(s,a)$ where γ is a discount factor $0 \leq \gamma < 1$.

Note that our patrolling task is the deterministic, and thus, the probabilities in this definition is 0 or 1.

In the patrolling task we use in this study, agents try to collect scattered objects in the $G_x \times G_y$ grid environment, as shown in Fig. 2. Suppose that the size of the visible area of each agent is a $R_x \times R_y$ rectangle whose center is itself. At each time step, $i \in \mathcal{I}$ observes its local area by o_i and its result is expressed by a number of (R_x, R_y) matrices, which describe the relative position of other agents, events, and other components such as walls/obstacles in the visible area. Then, in every unit time, on the basis of the local observation, i takes one of the actions $a_i \in \mathcal{A}_i = \{\text{up}, \text{down}, \text{right}, \text{left}\}$, whose elements correspond to going *upward*, *downward*, *right*, or *left*. Then, i may earn reward as follows: Once i picks up an object, meaning i is on the same coordinate as the object, it receives reward $r_e > 0$; if i collides with other agents or walls, it receives a negative reward $r_c < 0$; otherwise, no reward is given. Agents individually learn their own policies π_i to collect as many objects as possible with fewer collisions to maximize discounted cumulative reward R_i.

3.2 Self-attention

The input fed to the self-attention network can be classified into three groups of matrices describing the *query*, *key*, and *value*. Furthermore, by multiplying the query and key matrices, the network obtains the compatibility of each sequence in the query and other components in the key matrix. We then apply the softmax function to each row of the result to normalize the weights. Subsequently, the value is multiplied by the logits, which helps us to understand which information is relevant to the decision-making process of agents. The attention is calculated as

$$\text{Attention}(\mathit{Query}, \mathit{Key}, \mathit{Value}) = \text{softmax}(\frac{\mathit{Query} \cdot \mathit{Key}^T}{\sqrt{d_k}})\,\mathit{Value}, \tag{1}$$

where *Query*, *Key*, and *Value* are matrices corresponding to the query, key, and value, respectively, and d_k is the dimension of key matrix. Please see [13] for more details on this.

Furthermore, by extending the single self-attention function in parallel, the multi-head attention is derived by:

$$\begin{aligned} \text{MultiHead}(\mathit{Query}, \mathit{Key}, \mathit{Value}) &= \text{Concat}(\mathit{head}_1, \ldots, \mathit{head}_h) W^O \\ \mathit{head}_l &= \text{Attention}(\mathit{Query} \cdot W_l^Q, \mathit{Key} \cdot W_l^K, \mathit{Value} \cdot W_l^V), \end{aligned} \tag{2}$$

where W_l^Q, W_l^K, W_l^V, W_l^O are projected parameter matrices, $\mathit{head}_l (1 \leq l \leq h)$ of each attention, and h is the number of heads. Because each head encodes different information, it is expected to be able to learn the environment flexibly by increasing the number of attention heads [13].

4 Proposed Method

In our proposed method, each agent has its own transformer encoder that contains the multi-head attention network. Figure 1 depicts the structure of the MAT-DQN. The *state encoder* in each agent encodes three (R_x, R_y) matrices expressing the agents, objects and obstacles in the local area from its observation. Then, the these matrices are embedded in the C (>0) dimensional vector space and flattened by the state embedder; the query, key, and value matrices whose size is $(\frac{R_x}{P} \cdot \frac{R_y}{P} + 1, C)$ are generated where P is the patched size for the attention mechanism. Note that the dimension is extended by one in the embedder to be used as a learnable parameter called *class token* [13]. Again, by multiplying the query and key matrices, compatibility of each element in local observation, including the class token, is obtained. We then explain how the class token is associated with the decision-making process.

Then, the input to the transformer encoder is characterized L times. Finally, only the class token, which is the first row of the matrices (which is shown as the gray part of the left box Fig. 1 (b)) from the transformer encoder, is passed to a fully connected network, which is the middle block in Fig. 1 (b). Because only the class token is used as the representation of the output from the transformer encoder, analyzing its compatibility with elements in local observation by using the attention mechanism will help us to see where agents learned with the MADRL paid attention to in agents' decision-making processes.

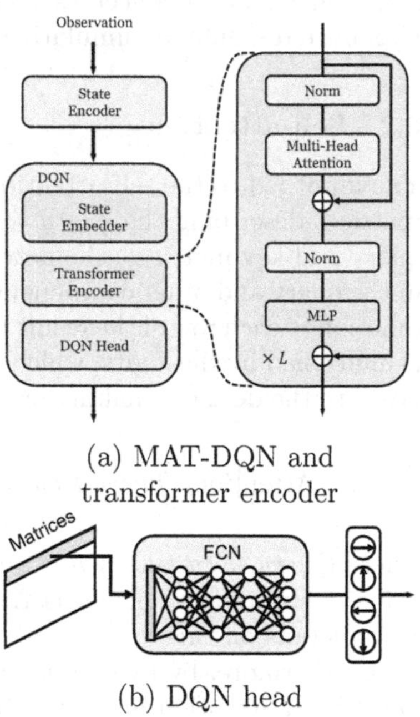

(a) MAT-DQN and transformer encoder

(b) DQN head

Fig. 1. MAT-DQN structure.

The MAT-DQN agents can benefit from the transformer encoder in two aspects. First, agents can identify which parts of information are necessary to induce better policies, including coordination. This means that agents can limit the information that should be taken into account, resulting in faster learning and efficient behaviors without collisions. Second, we can visualize such selections of information by extracting the attentional weights from the multi-head attention network. In terms of analytical studies, we can comprehend what type of information (e.g., the distance from what the agent detects in the local area, its movement direction, and its types, etc.) is influential. These extracted findings can be useful to interpret the reasons of learned behaviors and to understand the robustness and weakness of the agents to the environmental changes.

5 Experiments and Results

5.1 Experimental Setup

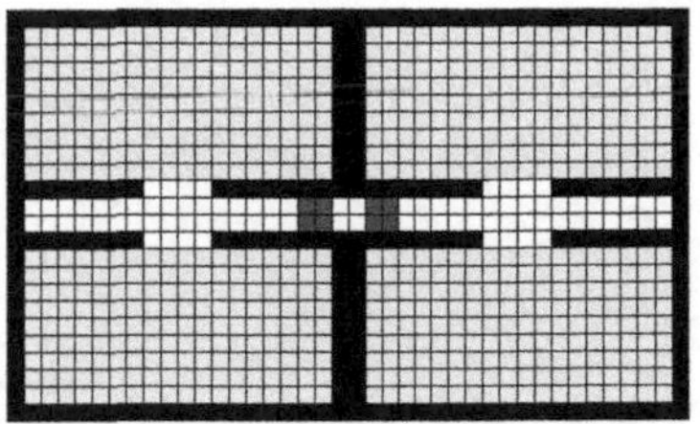

Fig. 2. Environment. (Color figure online)

We conducted experiments based on the patrolling task to investigate the performance of MAT-DQN agents and to understand what individual MAT-DQN agents focus on for their learned behaviors using the attentional mechanisms. We compared the performance results of the MAT-DQN agents with those of the vanilla DQN agents. The structure of the MAT-DQN in these experiments, as shown in Fig. 1, has four attention heads ($h = 4$). The vanilla DQN consists of two convolutional layers, two max-pooling layers, and a fully connected network. The experimental environment is a 40×24 grid (so $G_x = 40$ and $G_y = 24$) consisting of four rooms and a hallway running horizontally, as shown in Fig. 2. At the beginning of every episode, eight agents are initialized at blue cells and start exploration until the time step t reaches $H = 200$ or all objects are found. We then iterated 20,000 episodes for the training. The main purpose of agents is to collect as many objects as possible with avoiding collision with other agents and walls that are expressed by black cells. We set $r_c = -1$ and $r_e = 1$. The 40 objects are randomly scattered initially in the beige region, and when an agent collects an object, another object is placed somewhere in the same region.

We also examined how the attentions of MAT-DQN agents are affected by the input methods, using two types of observation methods: *local view* and *relative view* [9]. The local view is identical to the (R_x, R_y) matrices generated naively from the local observation, whereas the relative view is encoded into (G_x, G_y) matrices generated by embedding the observed area into the entire environment and filling the outside of the observable area with a null code; this means that agents can know their absolute position. Note that any objects behind the walls are not observable. We set the patched size to $P = 1$ for local views so that all elements in the observation are associated with the attention mechanism, and set $P = 4$ for relative views to reduce the computational complexity of attention due to the larger input. We also set the embedding dimension, which is the dimension of the class token, to $C = 64$.

5.2 Performance Comparison

Figures 3 and 4 plot the averaged values of the total number of collected objects and the earned rewards per episode by eight agents of five experimental runs when using local and relative views. Figure 3a and 4b indicate that when the input fed to the network was local views, agents with the vanilla DQNs collected 276.76 objects and earned a reward of 269.66 per episode, whereas the MAT-DQN agents could collect 310.44 events and earn 305.34 of reward per episode. Thus, the MAT-DQN agent achieved a performance improvement of approximately 12.2% in the number of collected objects and approximately 13.2% in

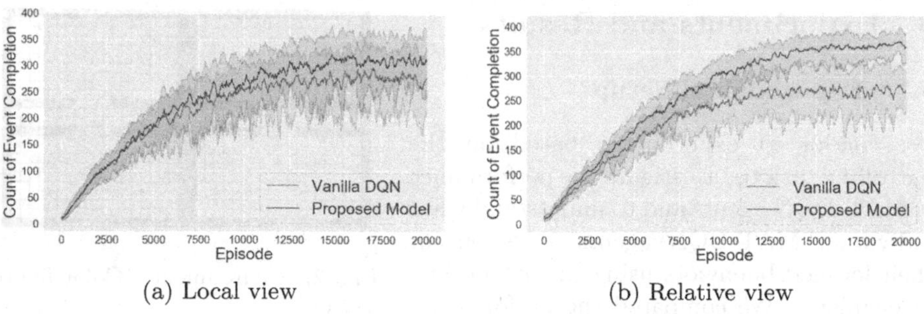

(a) Local view (b) Relative view

Fig. 3. Number of collected events per episode.

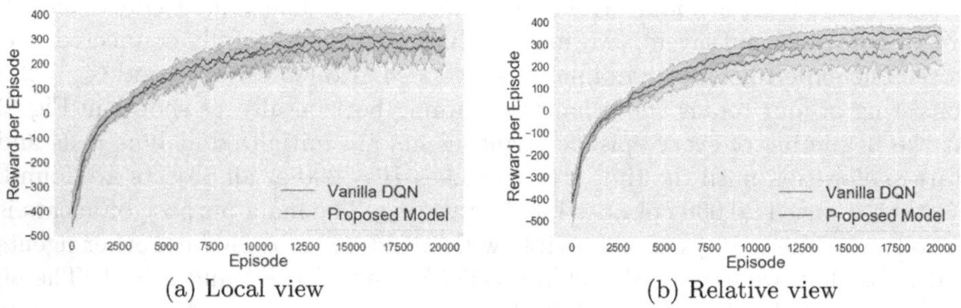

(a) Local view (b) Relative view

Fig. 4. Total reward per episode.

the reward earned, compared with the baseline method. Furthermore, by comparing the graphs in Figs. 3 and 4, we can see that the MAT-DQN agents performed approximately 15.4% better with the relative view than those of the local view, although the performance of the baseline agents with the relative view decreased approximately −2.3% . These results suggest that the MAT-DQN agents could utilize the additional information in the relative view, whereas the baseline agents could not, but rather were confused and could not learn sufficiently due to the greater amount of data in the relative view. We will discuss this in more detail in Sect. 6.

5.3 Attentional Heatmaps

We generated the heatmaps based on the output from attention heads of certain agents and analyzed which objects/cells/agents each agent focused on. Such an analysis helps us understand the agents' decision-making process after sufficient learning. We show the attentional heatmaps of agents only with the local views due to the limited number of pages, but similar patterns can be observed when they used the relative views. Figure 5a illustrates the local observation of the agent (labeled A in this figure) in a certain situation (Sit. 1) in which blue cells are agents (so the blue cell is at the center) and yellow cells are objects in the local area. Figure 5b depicts the heatmaps of the mean attention from all attentional heads indicating where the agent A paid more attention (it focuses

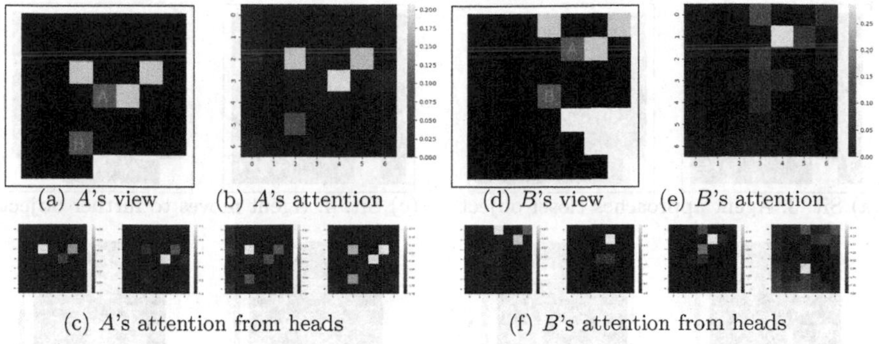

Fig. 5. Local observation and attentional heatmaps of agents A and B. (Color figure online)

on the brighter cells). Note that the attentional heatmaps from individual heads in Fig. 5c are different, which indicates that they flexibly learn actions from the observed states.

In Sit. 1, agent A pays attention to the three objects as well as agent B, as shown in Fig. 5b. In particular, the highest attention is paid to the neighboring object because A can earn reward r_e by moving to the right and there is less possibility of an immediate collision with B. Furthermore, A paid almost no attention to the walls located at the lower right, and thus, we can verify that information about walls at the further location has less significance in the decision-making process.

Figures 5 d–f, which are the maps of agent B in another situation (Sit. 2), show the different and interesting pattern of attentions of B. Figure 5d indicates that B pays more attentions to other agent A and less attentions to the nearby objects. This is because agent B's path to the close objects is affected by the movement of A, but this could not be predicted. Because if agent A pick up its local objects, B should explore other areas; this is supported by the first (leftmost) attention head in Fig. 5f. Moreover, A may move to the right to pick up the closest object; this means that A will subsequently move toward the object located at the upper right corner; thus, the first attention head in Fig. 5f focused on the object directly above B. Therefore, we can interpret that agents do not always put higher attention on objects, but selectively put attention to objects after considering other agents' locations and movements.

6 Discussion

6.1 Performance Comparison

Our experimental results clearly indicate that the MAT-DQN agents outperformed the agents with the vanilla DQN probably due to the use of the attention mechanism. During the training phase, agents successfully build tactics to identify what is the relevant information in their local areas for decision-making,

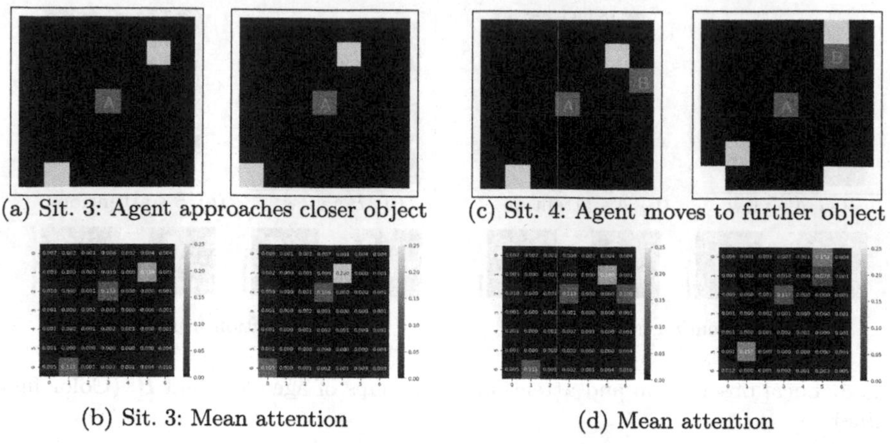

(a) Sit. 3: Agent approaches closer object (c) Sit. 4: Agent moves to further object

(b) Sit. 3: Mean attention (d) Mean attention

Fig. 6. Attentional heatmaps and cooperative behavior.

and we believe that these tactics might be provided by the attention mechanism. The experimental results when agents used the relative views also suggest another advantage of the MAT-DQN. The relative views include the map of the environment and agent's location on this map. We believe that these data are beneficial for learning. In contrast, the relative view increases the dimension of input fed to the DQNs. This is the reason for the degradation in performance of the agents that use the baseline method, and thus, the use of the relative view should be avoided.

In contrast, the MAT-DQN agents have attention mechanisms that can appropriately identify which information in their observation is necessary without getting confused because of high-dimensional data; they instead take advantage of the relative view to achieve higher efficiency compared with using the local views.

6.2 Analysis of Interpretability

We investigated how the visualized attentional heatmaps are associated with cooperative behavior. As discussed in Sect. 5.3, the heatmaps clearly indicate where agents focused. These attentions then suggested the agents' next actions. Furthermore, in Sit. 2, one of the attention heads suggested a potential action that could be triggered by the movements of another agent. We also attempt to analyze the situations where cooperative behaviors are required. The observation in the third situation (Sit. 3) and the associated heatmaps of the mean attention from the multi-heads are shown in Fig. 6a and Fig. 6b, respectively. The observations and heatmaps on the right in these figures are the state at the next time of those on the left. We also annotated the heatmap with the attentional weights. In Sit. 3, agent A saw two objects located on opposite sides; thus, it moves to the right to approach the closest object. We can recognize A's

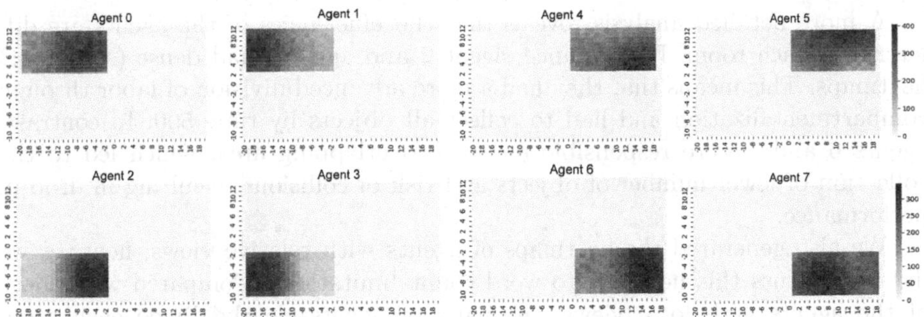

Fig. 7. Heatmaps of object collections of individual agents.

action from Fig. 6b as well; i.e., it pays attention to two objects with 0.189 (on the closest) and 0.112 (on the second closest). After moving to the right, the attentional values changed to 0.220 and 0.109, respectively.

We can observe the coordinated behavior in the fourth situation (Sit. 4), whose observations and the associated heatmaps are shown in Fig. 6c and Fig. 6d, respectively. From the left map of Fig. 6c, there were two objects located on opposite sides, as in Sit. 3, and another agent B was located near the closest object; then, A moved downward so as to approach the further object. This behavior seems rational in the sense that after leaving the collection of the closest objects for another agent, agent A headed for the object in a different direction. This action also reduced the possibility of a collision. The heatmap of the attentional weights in the left of Fig. 6d explained this situation, i.e., A put the highest attention on the closest objects, and at the same time, A focused on B. Because we can expect that the attentions on other agents work in a repulsive way, the attention mechanism directed agent A to the object below. Note that all heatmaps in Fig. 6 indicate some weak attention on the cells at the top of A. we believe that this was to avoid the collision to the wall on the lower side.

This discussion indicates that we could succeed in visualizing the sources of information in the decision-making processes of the learned agents by using the proposed MAT-DQN method.

6.3 Analysis of Coordination

Finally, we investigated the cooperative and collaborative behaviors with the learned policies from a macro perspective. For this purpose, we conducted 1,000 episodes of the same experiment after training and generated the heatmaps indicating where each agent collected objects. The result maps of eight agents are illustrated in Fig. 7. This figure shows that a pair of agents were equally distributed in each room, and the room was divided horizontally. Thus, we can say that agents individually trained without any communication and succeeded in taking charge of their respective divided region in a bottom-up manner.

A more detailed analysis reveals that the efficiencies of the agents are different for each room. For instance, agent 2 and agent 3 had dense (so darker) heatmaps. This means that they had a more advanced division of labor through compartmentalization and had to collect all objects by time 500. In contrast, agents 6 and 7 were responsible for some overlapping area, which led to the collection of fewer number of objects and risk of collisions, resulting in drop in performance.

We also generated the heatmaps of agents with relative views; however we did not discuss this here due to word count limitations. Compared with those of the agents with local views, the pairs of agents clearly divide each room horizontally to promote sharing and avoid potential conflicts. This is because they know their positions in the environment and have successfully learned the strategies to collect as many objects as possible by taking charge of only one half the sub-areas of the room with less moving load for patrolling.

These results indicate that the agents with the MAT-DQNs had the capability of selectively considering relevant information from the large input of the relative views, which leads to greater coordination efficiency; in contrast, agents with the vanilla DQN agents failed to adapt to the environment with the relative view due their larger input size.

7 Conclusion

Although deep reinforcement learning has dramatically improved the ability to learn cooperative behavior in a multi-agent system, it is still not completely clear why agents can learn policies and what parts of the input information contribute to their sophisticated decision-making.

We proposed to use the attention mechanism of the transformer architecture for MADRL, which allows us to more clearly interpret the policies and behaviors learned by the agents, as well as to identify the information that is important to them during the decision-making processes. It also enables agents to learn more efficiently and act more effectively by eliminating unnecessary information.

We experimentally substantiated the fact that MAT-DQN agents were successfully trained and adapted to the environment, resulting in better performance compared with agents with the vanilla DQN as a baseline. We also extracted the attentional weights from the transformer encoder and subsequently visualized their heatmaps. We confirmed that agents were paying attention to both objects and other agents in their local areas and selected appropriate actions depending on their situation. We found that closer objects usually had greater influences on the agents' decision-making when there were no other agents. However, when any other agents were in the visible area, agents behave differently depending on the other agents' locations and movement directions, mainly to avoid collisions or to approach an object that other agents are not likely to target.

We believe that more investigations are necessary to extend the insight drawn from this study. For instance, this research can be further extended to a more complicated and dynamic environment with a greater number of agents. In addition, we believe that incorporating our method into different types of reinforcement algorithms such as DDPG might become an important area for future work.

Acknowledgements. This work was partly supported by JSPS KAKENHI Grant Numbers 17KT0044 and 20H04245.

References

1. Amarasinghe, A., Wijesuriya, V.B., Ganepola, D., Jayaratne, L.: A swarm of crop spraying drones solution for optimising safe pesticide usage in arable lands: poster abstract. In: Proceedings of the 17th Conference on Embedded Networked Sensor Systems, SenSys 2019, pp. 410–411. ACI, USA (2019). https://doi.org/10.1145/3356250.3361948
2. Bathaee, Y.: The artificial intelligence black box and the failure of intent and causation. Harvard J. Law Technol. **31**, 889 (2018)
3. Chen, H., Liu, Y., Zhou, Z., Hu, D., Zhang, M.: GAMA: graph attention multi-agent reinforcement learning algorithm for cooperation. Appl. Intel. **50** (December 2020). https://doi.org/10.1007/s10489-020-01755-8
4. Diallo, E.A.O., Sugiyama, A., Sugawara, T.: Coordinated behavior of cooperative agents using deep reinforcement learning. Neurocomputing **396**, 230–240 (2020). https://doi.org/10.1016/j.neucom.2018.08.094
5. Dosovitskiy, A., et al.: An image is worth 16x16 words: transformers for image recognition at scale. In: International Conference on Learning Representations (2021). arXiv:2010.11929
6. Ibrahim, S.: A comprehensive review on intelligent surveillance systems. Commun. Sci. Technol. **1** (2016). https://doi.org/10.21924/cst.1.1.2016.7
7. Iqbal, S., Sha, F.: Actor-attention-critic for multi-agent reinforcement learning. In: Proceedings of the 36th International Conference on Machine Learning, 09–15 Jun 2019, vol. 97, pp. 2961–2970. PMLR (2019). http://proceedings.mlr.press/v97/iqbal19a.html
8. Jiang, J., Lu, Z.: Learning attentional communication for multi-agent cooperation. In: Proceedings of the 32nd International Conference on Neural Information Processing Systems, NIPS 2018, pp. 7265–7275. Curran Associates Inc., USA (2018)
9. Miyashita, Y., Sugawara, T.: Analysis of coordinated behavior structures with multi-agent deep reinforcement learning. Appl. Intell. **51**(2), 1069–1085 (2021). https://doi.org/10.1007/s10489-020-01832-y
10. Partel, V., Charan Kakarla, S., Ampatzidis, Y.: Development and evaluation of a low-cost and smart technology for precision weed management utilizing artificial intelligence. Comput. Electron. Agric. **157**, 339–350 (2019). https://doi.org/10.1016/j.compag.2018.12.048
11. Puterman, M.L.: Markov Decision Processes: Discrete Stochastic Dynamic Programming, 1st edn. Wiley, USA (1994)
12. Sreenu, G., Durai, M.A.: Intelligent video surveillance: a review through deep learning techniques for crowd analysis. J. Big Data **6**, 48 (2019). https://doi.org/10.1186/s40537-019-0212-5
13. Vaswani, A., et al.: Attention is all you need. In: Advances in Neural Information Processing Systems, vol. 30, pp. 5998–6008. Curran Associates, Inc. (2017)

Selection-Expansion: A Unifying Framework for Motion-Planning and Diversity Search Algorithms

Alexandre Chenu(✉), Nicolas Perrin-Gilbert, Stéphane Doncieux, and Olivier Sigaud

Sorbonne Université, CNRS, Institut des Systèmes Intelligents Et de Robotique, ISIR, 75005 Paris, France

Abstract. Reinforcement learning agents need a reward signal to learn successful policies. When this signal is sparse or the corresponding gradient is deceptive, such agents need a dedicated mechanism to efficiently explore their search space without relying on the reward. Looking for a large diversity of behaviors or using Motion Planning (MP) algorithms are two options in this context. In this paper, we build on the common roots between these two options to investigate the properties of two diversity search algorithms, the Novelty Search and the Goal Exploration Process algorithms. These algorithms look for diversity in an *outcome space* or *behavioral space* which is generally hand-designed to represent what matters for a given task. The relation to MP algorithms reveals that the smoothness, or lack of smoothness of the mapping between the policy parameter space and the outcome space plays a key role in the search efficiency. In particular, we show empirically that, if the mapping is smooth enough, i.e. if two close policies in the parameter space lead to similar outcomes, then diversity algorithms tend to inherit exploration properties of MP algorithms. By contrast, if it is not, diversity algorithms lose the properties of their MP counterparts and their performance strongly depends on heuristics like filtering mechanisms.

1 Introduction

Deep Reinforcement learning (RL) and Deep Neuro-Evolution (NE) methods have recently undergone outstanding progress, obtaining more and more impressive performance in games and robotics applications [1,16–18]. However, despite these successes, some fundamental difficulties remain in "hard exploration problems". First, when the reward signal is sparse or when the corresponding gradient is deceptive, RL agents cannot rely on the reward signal to steer their learning process, resulting in complete failure or poor performance [14]. Besides, RL agents struggle when only complex trajectories can reach the target region, as for example in a complicated maze, and when such target-reaching agents correspond to a very small domain of the policy parameter space [7,15]. In such contexts, decoupling exploration from exploitation by combining Deep RL with

I. Farkaš et al. (Eds.): ICANN 2021, LNCS 12894, pp. 568–579, 2021.
https://doi.org/10.1007/978-3-030-86380-7_46

algorithms explicitly designed to look for diversity in a relevant search space has several attractive properties. More precisely, it has been hypothesized in [6] that defining an *outcome space*[1] as the space that matters to determine whether a policy is successful and looking for diversity in that space might be the best option to tackle the sparse reward exploration problem.

We can distinguish two classes of algorithms to implement this diversity search approach and focus on exploration only: Goal Exploration Process (GEP) [8] and Novelty Search (NS) [13]. The former has been combined with RL in [3] whereas the latter is used in the same way in [2].

This paper investigates the properties of these two classes of algorithms. In a first part, based on a very general *selection-expansion* framework, we reveal a similarity between these algorithms and Motion Planning (MP) algorithms like Expansive Spaces Trees (EST) [9] and Rapidly-exploring Random Trees (RRT) [11]. In a second part, we make profit of this common framework to empirically compare both algorithms in two environments where a smoothness assumption on which MP algorithms implicitly rely either holds or not. We show that diversity algorithms are highly dependent on the design of the outcome space where the search for diversity is performed, and that the smoothness of the mapping between the policy parameter space and the outcome space plays a key role in their search dynamics. In particular, we show that if the mapping is smooth enough, GEP and NS inherit the exploration properties of RRT and EST and GEP outperforms NS. By contrast, if it is not, which is the usual case, NS and GEP perform differently depending on heuristics like filtering mechanisms that discard some of the explored policies.[2].

2 Methods

In this section we highlight that NS and GEP share properties with two well-known MP algorithms, EST and RRT. To establish the similarity between both families of algorithms, we start from a more general framework that we call *selection-expansion* algorithms which later guides our comparison of NS and GEP in Sect. 3.

2.1 Selection-Expansion Algorithms

Imagine an agent searching in some space and looking for an area it knows nothing about. What should it do? The most classical approach is to keep a memory of what has already been explored, and to progress locally, i.e. by reconsidering previous trajectories or behaviors, and by expanding or slightly modifying them to find new areas of the space to explore. This is the basis of virtually all sampling-based motion planning algorithms, and the core mechanism of Go-Explore [7]. We call this kind of algorithms selection-expansion algorithms because they share

[1] Also called *behavioral space* in the literature.

[2] Additional details are available in https://arxiv.org/pdf/2104.04768.pdf.

the common structure of maintaining an archive of previous samples and iterating over a sequence of two operators: the **selection operator** that chooses in the archive a sample from which to expand and the **expansion operator** that adds one or several new samples built from the selected sample.

Usually, selection and expansion operators are designed to efficiently expand the frontier of explored areas towards unexplored regions of the space. To do so, there are two popular selection strategies. One can either:

Strategy 1. *rank all elements in the archive in terms of distance to their neighbors, and preferentially select those far away from their neighbors, which suggests that they lie in a region with a low density of exploration; or*

Strategy 2. *randomly draw a sample anywhere in the search space and select the closest sample in the archive. This way, samples which are close to large unexplored regions have a higher chance of being selected.*

In the next section, we describe applications of the above selection-expansion algorithms in two domains, namely Motion Planning and Diversity Search algorithms. This reveals a striking similarity between both families of algorithms.

2.2 Application to Motion Planning

In Motion Planning (MP), the goal is to find a trajectory for a system navigating from a starting configuration to a goal configuration or region.

Some MP algorithms use selection-expansion algorithms to build an exploring tree eventually containing a path from the starting configuration to the goal. Nodes of the graph are configurations, and edges represent the fact that the system can navigate between two nodes. Thus, in the MP context, the need for a local expansion operator comes from the fact that the system must navigate locally from its current configuration to the next.

When the model of the system is known, finding controls to navigate between two nodes can be easy, and two successive nodes can potentially be far away from each other. We do not consider this case here. Instead, we focus on the case where the model of the system is unknown, and assume that the effects of the dynamics are not easily predictable or controllable. In that case, one must call upon random actions for a few time steps and rely on the fact that, if many random actions are tried, interesting motions may occur. Thus, the expansion operator of such "model-free" MP algorithms typically performs a random action from the selected configuration to reach a new configuration then added to the exploration tree.

For the selection operator, there exist MP algorithms corresponding to both strategies described above.

Expansive Spaces Trees. Expansive Spaces Trees (EST) corresponds to a family of algorithms where the selection operator uses Strategy 1. These algorithms select the most isolated nodes based on an estimate of the local density of nodes. Various approximations of the local density can be used. For instance, a node can be selected based on its number of neighbors within a certain range. The nodes are selected with a probability distribution such that the nodes with fewer neighbors tend to be selected with higher frequency than others. Other estimates of the local density of nodes based on nearest neighbors can also be used. In this paper, we consider the mean distance to the K-nearest nodes as an estimation of the local density. Besides, in the general case without specific knowledge on the system, a random control input is used during one or few steps to expand the selected node. If no collision occurs, the expanded node is added to the tree.

Rapidly-Exploring Random Trees. Like EST, Rapidly-exploring Random Trees (RRT) is a sampling-based path-planning algorithm. But, in contrast to EST, RRT performs selection according to Strategy 2. That is, it draws a random goal configuration s_{samp} and selects the closest node in the set of already visited nodes. Note that sampling a random configuration requires to determine the boundaries of the space where to sample from, a stronger prerequisite than in EST.

Given a set of points $\{n_i\}_{i \in \{1,\ldots,N\}}$ in a space, one can define the *Voronoi diagram* of these points as a set of *Voronoi cells* with one Voronoi cell per point, where the Voronoi cell of each point n_i is the subspace of all points that are closer to n_i than to any other point of the set. When selecting randomly, the probability for an already visited node to be selected is proportional to the volume of its Voronoi cell. After selection, without knowledge on the system, expansion is also performed by applying a random control.

Comparative Search Properties of EST and RRT. We empirically compare the exploration properties of the selection operators of EST and RRT in the “SimpleMaze” environment which is further described in Sect. 3.1.

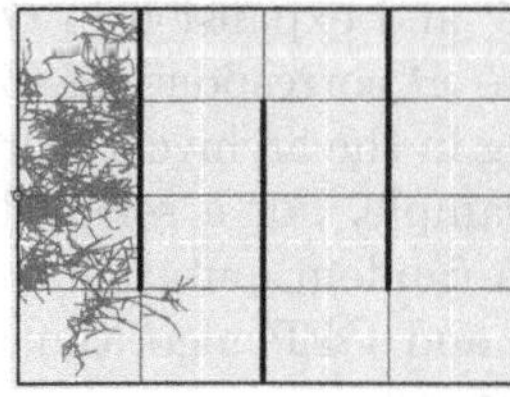

(a) EST Search tree.

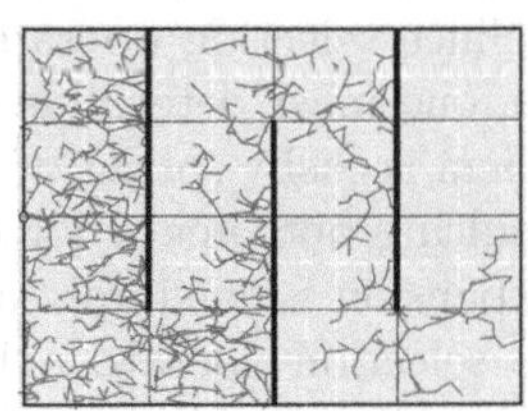

(b) RRT Search tree.

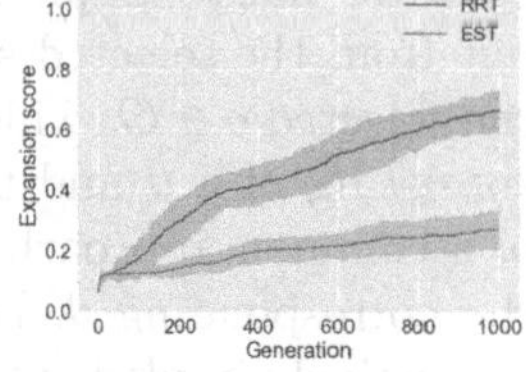

(c) Expansion score

Fig. 1. Empirical comparison of EST and RRT. The SimpleMaze environment is divided into a 4×4 grid to compute expansion scores of the MP algorithms. Search trees are shown after 1000 iterations. The means and standard deviations of the expansion scores are computed over 30 runs.

To assess expansion, we divide the maze into a 4×4 expansion grid, see Fig. 1. The expansion score corresponds to the number of zones containing at least one node over the total number of zones, i.e. 16. Both algorithms start with a single initial node in the middle of the left side (coordinates $(-1,0)$). Figures 1a and 1b display exploration trees for both EST and RRT after 1000 iterations.

The evolution of expansion presented in Fig. 1c shows that RRT explores the maze faster than EST.

2.3 Application to Diversity Search Algorithms

We now turn to the policy search context. In policy search, we consider a parametric policy π_θ where θ is a vector of parameters in a policy parameter space Θ.

Diversity algorithms, also called *divergent search* (DS) algorithms, are policy search algorithms dedicated to covering a space of solutions as widely as possible. In particular, they can be used to find a target area in the absence of a reward signal. A common feature of these algorithms is that they define an *outcome space* $\mathcal{O}$ as a generally low-dimensional space that can characterize important properties of policy runs. The target area in such policy search problems is generally defined in $\mathcal{O}$. Thus it is natural to consider that DS algorithms are performing search in that space and to define the selection operator in that space.

But a key issue in the policy search context is that one cannot directly sample in $\mathcal{O}$, as the application from outcomes to policy parameters reaching these outcomes is generally unknown. As a consequence, search in these DS algorithms considers the mapping between Θ and $\mathcal{O}$, which we call the $f : \Theta \rightarrow \mathcal{O}$ mapping hereafter.

The necessity to consider these two spaces results in key differences between MP and DS algorithms. In particular, while MP algorithms need to use a local expansion operator because they build a path to control a system from one configuration to another, DS algorithms rely on local expansions for different reasons.

Importantly, as it is not possible to sample directly in $\mathcal{O}$, the expansion operator must sample in Θ. Since selection operates in $\mathcal{O}$ and expansion in Θ but from the selected sample, one must determine the $\theta \in \Theta$ corresponding to the selected $o \in \mathcal{O}$. This problem is easily solved by storing in the archive a pair consisting of a θ and the resulting outcome o for each sample. For a selected o, a common approach for expansion is to simply apply a random mutation to the corresponding θ. For the selection operator, the NS and GEP algorithms respectively implement the two strategies described in Sect. 2.1.

Selection in NS. Novelty Search considers two sets of points in $\mathcal{O}$: the population and the archive. Only the policies contained in the population may be selected. We explain later how these sets of points are constructed. Selection in NS can be performed using various selection operators. The uniform selection operator, the score proportionate selection operator, and the tournament-based operators are the most common ones [4]. In this paper we focus on the score proportionate selection operator biased toward more novel policies.

The idea behind score proportionate selection is to construct a probability distribution according to the **novelty score** of a policy. The novelty score of a point $o \in \mathcal{O}$ is defined as the average distance to the k-nearest neighbors in the archive, k being a hyper-parameter. Given an archive containing N policies, the probability for a policy to be selected is proportional to its novelty score.

This is an instance of Strategy 1 described in Sect. 2.1 where the distance to neighbors is computed through the novelty score.

Selection in GEP. The selection operator in GEP works as follows. First, the agent draws a random target outcome o_{goal}. The agent would like to find a set of policy parameters θ_{goal} producing o_{goal}. For that, it looks in the archive for the closest outcome o_{sel} to o_{goal}, and it selects the policy parameters θ_{sel} which generated o_{sel}. This is clearly an instance of Strategy 2.

Since the GEP selection operator draws a random outcome and selects a policy corresponding to the closest outcome in the archive, the probability for a policy contained in the archive to be selected is proportional to the area of the Voronoi cell of its outcome in $\mathcal{O}$, as explained for RRT in Sect. 2.2. One can immediately see that the selection operator is exactly the same as in RRT, but acting in a different space.

Filtering in NS. In addition to their selection operators, NS also differs from GEP by using a filtering mechanism.

The notion of population differs in GEP and NS. In GEP, the population gathers all policies since the first generation. At each iteration, all expanded policies are added to the population. In NS, the population is composed of a fixed size set of policies updated at each generation. As in GEP, it is initialized with random policies. However, after expanding the policies contained in the population, only the most novel policies contained in the set { population + expanded policies } are selected to construct the new population.

Beyond the population, NS uses another set called the archive to keep track of the policies evolved in past generations. At each generation, after expanding the population, the expanded policies (or a randomly sampled subset of it) are added to the archive.

The archive in NS is only used to compute the novelty score of the policies contained in the {population + expanded policies} set. Policies from the archive are not added to the new population. If a policy contained in the set { population + expanded policies } is not selected for expansion, it is discarded and cannot be selected in future generations.

2.4 Similarities Between MP and DS Algorithms

It should now be obvious that, if we consider their most local expansion operators, NS shares similarities with EST and GEP with RRT. Indeed, the selection and expansion operators of the DS algorithms are closely related to the same operators of their MP counterparts.

Selection. From the side of NS and EST, their selection operators measure how isolated a sample is by attributing a weight to each sample proportional to the inverse of the density of the archive in its neighborhood.

The variants of EST and NS that we consider in this paper use the same weight computation based on the mean distance of outcomes/nodes to their k-nearest neighbor in the population/exploration tree. Similarly, GEP and RRT also use a similar selection operator based on the area of the Voronoi cells of the nodes/outcomes.

Expansion. In the unknown system case, a standard expansion strategy consists in applying a single random control. In order to ensure probabilistic completeness, the dynamical system is assumed to be Lipschitz-continuous [10]. This assumption means that with enough expansions from the same node, a node should finally expand in the right direction.

In DS algorithms, the standard expansion operator applies a random perturbation to the selected policy parameters, which has similarities with the use of random actions for local expansions in the MP context.

However, reasons for using a local expansion operator are different in the MP and DS contexts. In the MP context, one needs to locally control the system along a path from the current configuration to the target configuration. In GEP, a local random perturbation is applied to the selected policy hoping that, the corresponding outcome being close to the sampled goal, the perturbed policy will produce an outcome that is also close (and possibly closer) to this goal. One can see that the application of this selection-expansion strategy relies on the assumption of a smoothness property in the $f : \Theta \rightarrow \mathcal{O}$ mapping, i.e. that similar parameters yield similar outcomes. In the case of NS, the reason for using a local expansion operator relies on the assumption that, if a policy resulted in an outcome in a low density region, a perturbed version of the policy should also result in an outcome in a low density region, and thus be potentially helpful in the search of new outcomes. Again, this is equivalent to assuming a smoothness property in the f mapping.

2.5 Expansion in DS Is Often Non-local

Even though DS have good reasons to use local expansions just like MP, expansions in DS are often non-local. Indeed, there are different sources of non-locality that can be identified by dissecting the $f : \Theta \rightarrow \mathcal{O}$ mapping.

In general, the first source of non-locality originates from the use of strongly non-linear neural-network policies. Even though Multi-Layers Perceptrons (MLPs) are continuous functions, if the magnitude of the perturbation is too large, the expanded version of a policy may yield a very different policy.

The second source of non-locality lies in the nature of outcomes, which depend on policy runs, and therefore on trajectories. After selecting a pair $(\theta_{sel}, o_{sel}) \in \Theta \times O$, the expansion operator in DS perturbs the parameters of the selected policy $\pi_{\theta_{sel}}$ to obtain a new policy with parameters $\theta_{new} = \theta_{sel} + \delta\theta$

with $\delta\theta$ sampled from a spherical Gaussian distribution [17] or a more complex distributions [5]. Even if the magnitude of the mutation is kept low enough for the expanded policies to be very close to the selected one, the numerous time steps of control may result in a large deviation between the trajectories obtained by the two policies as errors accumulate over time steps. These errors may be aggravated by discontinuous dynamical systems or environments and result in a non-smooth mapping from policies to trajectories, and therefore from policies to outcomes. For instance, in maze environments, two close policies may yield very different trajectories if one trajectory gets blocked by a wall.

Preliminary Conclusion: Performance Assumptions. The similarities outlined above suggest that, if the expansion operators have similar properties, NS and GEP should share exploration abilities that are similar to those of EST and RRT respectively. However, for common $f : \Theta \rightarrow \mathcal{O}$ mappings, small perturbations in Θ may result in large changes in $\mathcal{O}$, and this lack of smoothness results in a very different situation.

If the lack of smoothness of the $f : \Theta \rightarrow \mathcal{O}$ mapping is too serious, one could hypothesize that the use of local expansions in DS should bring no advantage compared to a random sampling of policy parameters. Or, the $f : \Theta \rightarrow \mathcal{O}$ mapping could be smooth enough to let NS and GEP both outperform random sampling, but not smooth enough to inherit the search properties of EST and RRT. Below, we investigate these two possibilities experimentally.

3 Experimental Study

In this section, we experimentally study NS, GEP and a random search baseline using two environments with different locality properties to assess whether NS and GEP inherit from the properties of EST and RRT.

3.1 Experimental Setup

The experimental comparison is based on two environments: a ballistic task using a 4-DOF simulated robot arm and a maze environment called SimpleMaze, see Fig. 2. In both environments, the state space is continuous and time is discrete.

3D Ballistic Throw. The planar robot arm ballistic throw environment simulates the trajectory of a projectile thrown by a 3D 4-joint robot arm. The velocities $(\dot{\theta}_i)_{i\in[0,3]} \in [-1rad.s^{-1}, 1rad.s^{-1}]$ of the joints of the robot arm are controlled by a MLP. The throw is divided into acceleration-release phases. The acceleration phase is a single time step of control of the robot joints. After the acceleration phase, the end-effector of the robot releases the projectile which then follows a ballistic trajectory. The outcome is the (x, y) coordinates of impact. As there are no obstacles and no accumulation of differences via integration, the expansion operator of DS algorithms truly achieves local expansions in this environment: small perturbations in Θ yield small changes in $\mathcal{O}$.

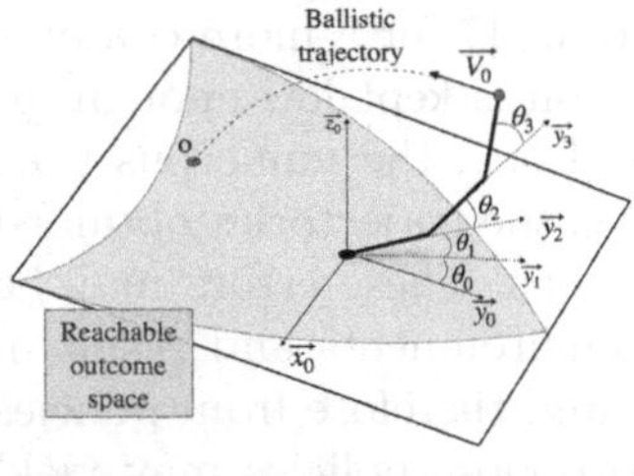

(a) 3D ballistic throw.

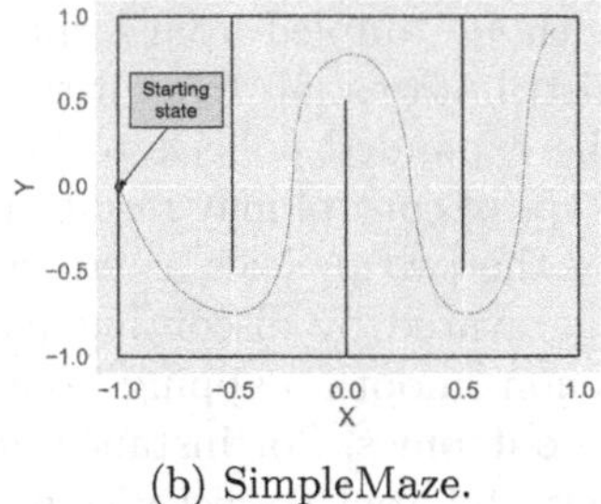

(b) SimpleMaze.

Fig. 2. Studied environments. In 3D ballistic throw, an agent controls the angular speed $(\dot{\theta}_i)_{i\in[0,3]}$ of a 4-joint 3D robot arm in order to throw a projectile. The outcome of the policy is final position of the projectile. In SimpleMaze, the agents start from a fixed position on the left and must reach the upper right corner.

SimpleMaze. We chose a Maze environment as it facilitates visualization of the exploration properties of the algorithms. A rollout lasts 50 time steps. The outcome corresponds to the final position of the agent at the end of the rollout. The agent starts from $(-1, 0)$ and receives at each time step the position of $(x, y) \in [x_{min}, x_{max}] \times [y_{min}, y_{max}]$ at the current time step as input and outputs the next displacement $(dx, dy) \in [dx_{min}, dx_{max}] \times [dy_{min}, dy_{max}]$. Let's note that the agent has no perception of the walls. The magnitude of the polynomial mutations $(\eta = 15)$, the duration of a rollout as well as the discontinuities caused by the walls result in non-local expansions, with similar policy parameters leading possibly to very different outcomes.

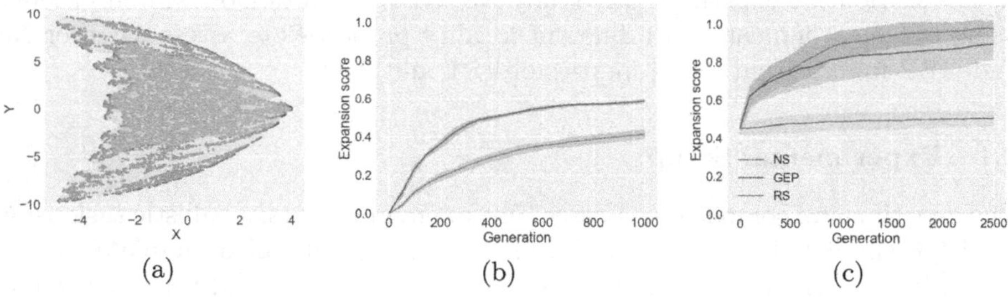

(a) (b) (c)

Fig. 3. (a) Visualisation of the concave hull of the exploration trees of NS (blue) and GEP (pink) in 3D ballistic throw. (b) Expansion scores of GEP and NS in 3D ballistic throw. As the expansion operator is local, GEP inherits exploration properties from RRT and expands faster than NS. (c) Expansion scores of GEP, NS and a random search (RS) baseline in SimpleMaze. The non-local expansions result in NS exploring slightly faster than GEP. Both NS and GEP outperform RS.

Metrics, Hyper-parameters and Technical Details. In order to assess the expansion of a DS algorithm, we use the previously defined domain expansion metric. We split $\mathcal{O}$ into a $G_{expansion} \times G_{expansion}$ expansion grid. The expansion score corresponds to the number of expansion cells filled with at least by one policy over the total number of expansion cells.

3.2 Results

Results on 3D Ballistic Throw. In this section, we evaluate NS and GEP in the robot arm ballistic throw. We previously explained why this environment conserves the locality of the expansion operators between the parameter space and $\mathcal{O}$. In this section, we verify that in this environment GEP and NS inherit the search properties of RRT and EST, and that, as expected, GEP explores $\mathcal{O}$ faster than NS.

Figure 3b presents the expansion score obtained by GEP and NS after 1000 generations. It confirms that GEP expands faster across $\mathcal{O}$ and converges quickly towards a maximum[3] that NS struggles to reach. Figure 3a presents the concave hulls obtained by the exploration trees of GEP and NS after 500 generations in one run. We observe that NS spends numerous generation paving the center of the reachable outcome space whereas GEP expands in all directions and quickly finds the limits of the reachable search space. These results are analogous to the performance of RRT and EST described above. The similarities between the selection operator of both DS algorithms and their MP counterparts enables similar exploration performance in the ballistic task, an environment that preserves the locality of expansions.

Results in SimpleMaze. We previously showed that the $\Theta \rightarrow \mathcal{O}$ mapping is non-local in SimpleMaze. In this section, we assess the consequences of non-local expansions.

Figure 3c presents the expansion and density scores obtained by NS, GEP and RS in Simple Maze. It shows that both NS and GEP outperform RS. Therefore, mapping $f : \Theta \mapsto O$ is local enough for NS and GEP to benefit from their selection operator.

However, the performances of NS and GEP in SimpleMaze differ from their performance in the ballistic throw. NS and GEP perform similarly during the first 500 generations. Then, the expansion of NS accelerates and outperforms the expansion of GEP by achieving a full exploration of the maze after about 2500 generations while GEP fails to reach the end of the maze most of the runs and only reaches an expansion score of 0.9 after the same number of generations.

The difference in expansion rates after 500 generations arises from a progressive degradation of the locality of the expansion operator. As explained in Sect. 2.5, expanding a policy which yields an outcome in the second corridor or beyond often results in a policy blocked by the first wall. Coping with this increasingly non-local expansion operator requires numerous expansions of the most advanced policies. That is exactly what NS does using its filtering mechanisms.

[3] The non-rectangular shape of $\mathcal{O}$ in the 3D ballistic throw environment makes some cells of the expansion grid unreachable, which explains why GEP eventually covers only about $\sim 60\%$ of $\mathcal{O}$.

On the contrary, GEP does not integrate any filtering mechanisms. Therefore, GEP keeps sampling policies blocked in the already well explored areas of the maze. Thus, GEP requires more generations to get past the exploration bottleneck which results in a slower increase of the expansion score.

These results show that, in an environment where the $f : \Theta \rightarrow \mathcal{O}$ mapping lacks smoothness, the properties inherited from RRT and EST are lost, which means that the selection-expansion mechanisms do not behave as originally intended. Even though both NS and GEP outperform random sampling of policies, additional heuristics such as filtering mechanisms must be exploited to overcome difficult expansions with degraded expansion operators.

4 Discussion and Conclusion

In this article, we presented a comparison between two divergent search algorithms: GEP and NS. We started by presenting a unifying framework called selection-expansion algorithms which draws a parallel between both algorithms and two Motion Planning algorithms, EST and RRT.

We made profit of this common framework to conduct an experimental study showing that in an environment like the 3D ballistic throw where the $\Theta \rightarrow \mathcal{O}$ mapping is smooth, GEP and NS inherit the exploration properties from their Motion Planning counterparts. In that case, GEP explores faster the environment than NS.

By contrast, maze results show that, even though GEP and NS share common selection-expansion properties with RRT and EST, they do not share the same exploration abilities if the expansion operator is not local. In such situations, the experimental study showed that NS outperforms GEP by using efficient filtering mechanisms.

This work opens up the question of restoring locality in complex environments where the expansion operator is non-local. Safe mutations partially restore locality [12]. However, they only tackle one source of non-localities coming from the non-linear nature of neural network policies. Discontinuities like the walls in SimpleMaze are still an important source of non-locality in the expansion operators. Based on this observation, the main research direction for future work should be to search for a generic way to restore a form of locality in environments where the expansion operator is not local.

Acknowledgements. This work was partially supported by the French National Research Agency (ANR), Project ANR-18-CE33-0005 HUSKI.

References

1. Akkaya, I., et al.: Solving rubik's cube with a robot hand. arXiv preprint arXiv:1910.07113 (2019)
2. Cideron, G., Pierrot, T., Perrin, N., Beguir, K., Sigaud, O.: Qd-rl: Efficient mixing of quality and diversity in reinforcement learning (2020)

3. Colas, C., Sigaud, O., Oudeyer, P.: GEP-PG: decoupling exploration and exploitation in deep reinforcement learning algorithms. CoRR arXiv:1802.05054 (2018)
4. Cully, A., Demiris, Y.: Quality and diversity optimization: a unifying modular framework. IEEE Trans. Evol. Comput. **22**(2), 245–259 (2018)
5. Deb, K., Deb, D.: Analysing mutation schemes for real-parameter genetic algorithms. Int. J. Artif. Intell. Soft Comput. **4**, 1–28 (2014)
6. Doncieux, S., Laflaquière, A., Coninx, A.: Novelty search: a theoretical perspective. In: Proceedings of the Genetic and Evolutionary Computation Conference, pp. 99–106. ACM, Prague Czech Republic (July 2019)
7. Ecoffet, A., Huizinga, J., Lehman, J., Stanley, K.O., Clune, J.: Go-explore: a new approach for hard-exploration problems (2019)
8. Forestier, S.: Intrinsically Motivated Goal Exploration in Child Development and Artificial Intelligence: Learning and Development of Speech and Tool Use. Ph.D. thesis, U. Bordeaux (2019)
9. Hsu, D., Latombe, J., Motwani, R.: Path planning in expansive configuration spaces. In: Proceedings ICRA, vol. 3, pp. 2719–2726 (1997)
10. Kleinbort, M., Solovey, K., Littlefield, Z., Bekris, K.E., Halperin, D.: Probabilistic completeness of RRT for geometric and kinodynamic planning with forward propagation. arXiv:1809.07051 [cs] (September 2018)
11. LaValle, S.M.: Rapidly-exploring random trees: A new tool for path planning. Technical Report, 98–11, Computer Science Department, Iowa State University (1998)
12. Lehman, J., Chen, J., Clune, J., Stanley, K.O.: Safe mutations for deep and recurrent neural networks through output gradients. arXiv:1712.06563 [cs] (May 2018)
13. Lehman, J., Stanley, K.O.: Abandoning objectives: evolution through the search for novelty alone. Evol. Comput. **19**(2), 189–223 (2011)
14. Matheron, G., Perrin, N., Sigaud, O.: The problem with DDPG: understanding failures in deterministic environments with sparse rewards. arXiv preprint arXiv:1911.11679 (2019)
15. Matheron, G., Perrin, N., Sigaud, O.: Pbcs : efficient exploration and exploitation using a synergy between reinforcement learning and motion planning (2020)
16. Silver, D.: Mastering the game of go without human knowledge. Nature **550**(7676), 354–359 (2017)
17. Such, F.P., Madhavan, V., Conti, E., Lehman, J., Stanley, K.O., Clune, J.: Deep neuroevolution: Genetic algorithms are a competitive alternative for training deep neural networks for reinforcement learning. CoRR 1712.06567, pp. 1–2 (2017)
18. Grandmaster level in starcraft ii using multi-agent reinforcement learning. Nature **575**(7782), 350–354 (2019)

A Hand Gesture Recognition System Using EMG and Reinforcement Learning: A Q-Learning Approach

Juan Pablo Vásconez, Lorena Isabel Barona López, Ángel Leonardo Valdivieso Caraguay, Patricio J. Cruz, Robin Álvarez, and Marco E. Benalcázar(✉)

Artificial Intelligence and Computer Vision Research Lab, Department of Computer Science and Informatics, Escuela Politécnica Nacional, Quito, Ecuador
{juan.vasconez,lorena.barona,angel.valdivieso,patricio.cruz, robin.alvarez,marco.benalcazar}@epn.edu.ec
https://laboratorio-ia.epn.edu.ec/en/

Abstract. Hand gesture recognition (HGR) based on electromyography (EMG) has been a research topic of great interest in recent years. Designing an HGR to be robust enough to the variation of EMGs is a challenging problem and most of the existing studies have explored supervised learning to design HGRs methods. However, reinforcement learning, which allows an agent to learn online while taking EMG samples, has barely been investigated. In this work, we propose a HGR system composed of the following stages: pre-processing, feature extraction, classification and post-processing. For the classification stage, we use Q-learning to train an agent that learns to classify and recognize EMGs from five gestures of interest. At each step of training, the agent interacts with a defined environment, obtaining thus a reward for the action taken in the current state and observing the next state. We performed experiments using a public EMGs dataset, and the results were evaluated for user-specific HGR models by using a method that is robust to the rotations of the EMG bracelet device. The results showed that the classification accuracy reach up to 90.78% and the recognition up to 87.51% for two different test-sets for 612 users in total. The results obtained in this work show that reinforcement learning methods such as Q-learning can learn a policy from online experiences to solve both the hand gesture classification and the recognition problem based on EMGs.

Keywords: Hand gesture recognition · Electromyography · EMG · Reinforcement learning · Q-learning · Experience replay

1 Introduction

Nowadays, the development of hand gesture recognition systems (HGR) that allow humans to better interact and communicate with computers and machines

Supported by Escuela Politécnica Nacional.

I. Farkaš et al. (Eds.): ICANN 2021, LNCS 12894, pp. 580–591, 2021.
https://doi.org/10.1007/978-3-030-86380-7_47

is a challenging research topic [3,7]. The use of HGR models aims to determine which hand gesture was performed, and when it was realized. Currently, the HGR systems are used for the development of intelligent prostheses, sign language recognition, rehabilitation, among others [3,7].

The EMG signals based on surface sensors can be modeled as a stochastic process that depends on two types of contractions: i) static –the muscle is contracted but there is no motion, and ii) dynamic – the muscle fibers and the joints are in motion [10,14]. However, mathematical approaches to model EMG signals are not used in HGR applications since the parameter estimation in non-stationary processes is difficult. Therefore, machine learning (ML) and deep learning (DL) techniques are typically used to classify EMG signals [4,7]. In particular, supervised methods such as support vector machine (SVM), k-nearest neighbors (K-NN), Artificial neural networks (ANN), Long short-term memory networks (LSTMs), and Convolutional neural networks (CNN) have demonstrated promising results as classifiers for HGR systems, which were able to infer hand gesture classes in real time (less than 300 ms) [6,7].

Supervised methods can achieve high classification performances for HGR applications, other methods such as reinforcement learning (RL) approaches can provide different benefits to help to improve HGR systems. In supervised learning, all the samples must be labeled in order to train a model. Meanwhile, reinforcement learning approaches find the optimal policy that allows an agent to take actions in an environment, so the cumulative reward can be maximized from online experience. Thus, this algorithm can learn from experience while using the system, which opens a wide range of new possibilities for HGR applications.

We have found in the literature a few works that have used reinforcement learning for hand gesture and arm movement recognition. Most of them use different approaches of RL for a particular experiment configuration for a hand or arm recognition application. Moreover, only a few of those approaches try to solve the HGR problem by using EMG signals. For example, in [12] the Myo armband sensor is used to obtain only raw accelerometer data from arm movement. The experiment consists of 3 arm movement, and each class has 30 samples for training and 20 for testing. The authors used Q-learning based on CNN and LSTM, and they defined the rewards of the experiments considering the human feedback. A reinforcement learning classifier for elbow, finger, and hand movement was presented in [9]. In this work, a PowerLabb 26TSystem was used to obtain EMG signals with 3 electrodes, and statistical features (variance, waveform-length, mean, and zero crossing) were extracted. Then, a Q-learning based on a neural network classifier was used to infer six elbow positions and 4 finger movement classes. For this purpose, the authors used 10 subjects, and 144 samples were taken for training and 95 for testing. Furthermore, in [13], a CNN was used to extract EMG signal features, and a dueling deep Q-learning technique was applied to learn a classification policy. Firstly, this approach was trained to learn 6 different hand gestures based on a dataset of 2700 EMG signal samples. Then, data augmentation was used to enlarge the dataset by adding Gaussian noise to the data. A gesture recognition and trajectory calculation system was developed [16]. This work proposes an interactive learning system that uses EMG and inertial information to teach a robot manipulator. The learning process is composed for a gesture recognition stage –EMG and inertial signals processed and trained off-line–; a statistical encoding stage –Gaussian mixture model–; and a reproduction and reinforcement learning stage –Gaussian Q learning model to correct the grab attitude and position of the robot–.

The current literature has some limitations and issues such us i) the small amount of data (few users and few samples per user), ii) the use of a single reward parameter to evaluate a single evaluation metric (classification accuracy), and iii) the lack of use of experience replay which can improves Q-learning performance. Considering these issues, the main contributions of this work are presented below:

- We use a public large dataset EMG-EPN-612 composed of 612 users. We used 306 users to train, validate, and test a user-specific model to find the best hyper-parameters. Then, we use them to train and test user-specific models for the other 306 users to test our model with different data and evaluate over-fitting.
- We successfully combine the EMG signals with a reinforcement learning method –Q-learning– considering two different rewards: the first reward to classify, and the second to recognize the hand gestures.
- We propose the use of experience replay that helps the Q-learning method to improve the model performance.

This work is organized as follows. In Sect. 2, the proposed architecture for an HGR system based on EMG and Q-learning is presented. Moreover, each stage of such architecture is reviewed in detail. The classification and recognition results are presented in Sect. 3. Finally, the conclusions are presented in Sect. 4.

2 Hand Gesture Recognition Architecture

In this section, we propose an architecture to solve the HGR problem based on EMG signals and Q-leaning, which is illustrated in Fig. 1. As can be observed, such architecture is conformed by a data acquisition, pre-processing, feature extraction, classification based on Q-learning, and post-processing. Following, each stage is explained in detail.

2.1 Data Acquisition

In this work, we used the public dataset EMG-EPN-612 collected by using the Myo armband device –8 channels 200 Hz– to obtain the EMG signals from 5 different gestures –wave in, wave out, fist, open, and pinch– [5]. If the gesture is not one of the above mentioned, then is considered as the no gesture (relax gesture). Such dataset is composed of 612 users, where 306 of them –training set A– are used to train, validate and test models to obtain the best possible hyper-parameter configurations, and the other 306 users –training set B– are

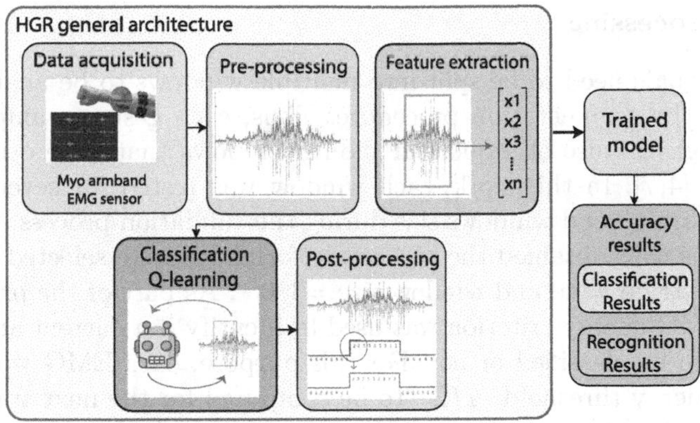

Fig. 1. Hand gesture recognition architecture based on Q-learning to learn to classify and recognize EMG signals.

used to perform an over-fitting evaluation. Each user of the training set A and B have 300 hand gesture repetitions. However, only the first 150 repetitions of training set B have the class gesture labeled and the muscular activity segmented -ground-truth-, which is key to run our tests and give rewards at each step. To access the full labeling information of the training set B it is necessary to test our model in our online web page as stated in [1]. Further details related to the dataset information, acquisition protocol, and the web page information for testing the final model can be found in [1,5]. The dataset distribution for both training set A and B that we used in this work can be observed in Table 1. It is worth mentioning that during training, samples with the no gesture (relax gesture) were not considered since most of the other signals have already several samples of such gesture. However, no gesture signal samples were considered for the final test results.

Table 1. Data set distribution to evaluate user-specific models [5].

	User-specific model (one model for each of the 306 users)			
	Number of models	Training	Validation	Test
Training set A	306 models trained (to find the best hyper-parameters)	100 samples per user	13 samples per user	12 samples per user
Training set B	306 models trained (to use the best founded hyper-parameters)	150 samples per user	–	150 samples per user

2.2 Pre-processing

The EMG signals need to be split into multiple windows to be analyzed, which is known as the segmentation procedure. Thus, each gesture sample was processed through the use of sequential sliding windows that slide over the entire EMG signal [4,7]. In this work, each window was tested for several points of separation –stride– and windows size during the validation process, but only the configurations that obtained the highest performance were selected for the testing process –stride = 40 and window size =300 –. As part of the pre-processing stage, the EMG energy criterion was used to identify if a current analyzed window is able to be classified or not. For this purpose, each EMG window has to surpass an energy threshold –17%– to be computed for the next stage, which is feature extraction. It is worth mentioning that our method is robust against the rotations of the bracelet device, as is explained in detail in [2].

2.3 Feature Extraction

Feature extraction methods are used to convert the EMG signal into a set of relevant features by extracting them in different domains, such as time, frequency, or time-frequency. In this work, five feature extraction methods in the time domain were used over every sliding window only when it surpassed the threshold of energy. The feature extraction methods that were used are: Standard deviation (SD), Absolute envelope (AE), Mean absolute value (MAV), Energy (E), and Root mean square (RMS) [2].

2.4 Classification Using Q-Learning

Q-learning is an off-policy algorithm of reinforcement learning. For any finite Markov Decision Process (MDP), Q-learning finds an optimal policy by maximizing the expected value of the total reward (i.e., return function) given both an initial state and an action [15]. For this work, we assume we have access only to observations instead of the full state of the environment. This occurs because it is not guaranteed a one-to-one mapping between the set of EMG window observations and the set of feature vectors used in this work. Therefore, it is possible a feature vector characterizes two different window observations of a EMG. Thus, this problem can be treated as a Partially Observable Markov Decision Process (POMDP), in which we apply Q-learning to the set of observations instead of the set of states. The Q-learning function is presented in the following equation:

$$Q^{(new)}\left(O_t, A_t\right) \leftarrow Q^{(old)}\left(O_t, A_t\right) + \alpha\left(R_{t+1} + \gamma \cdot \underset{a'}{max}[Q\left(O_{t+1}, a'\right)] - Q^{(old)}\left(O_t, A_t\right)\right) \quad (1)$$

where $Q^{(new)}\left(O_t, A_t\right)$ and $Q^{(old)}\left(O_t, A_t\right)$ are the updated and the old Q value, respectively, for the observation O_t and the action A_t, α is the learning rate, γ is the discount factor, $\underset{a'}{max}[Q\left(O_{t+1}, a'\right)]$ is the estimated optimal future

Q value, and R_{t+1} is the reward received when moving from the observation O_t to the observation O_{t+1} when taking the action A_t in O_t.

Q-learning can be implemented using lookup tables to store the Q values for each state and action of a given environment [15]. However, this approach is not suitable for environments with a large state-action spaces. For this case, Q-learning can be combined with function approximation to facilitate its application for large finite or infinite state-action spaces. In this work, we approximated the Q function using a feed-forward artificial neural network (ANNs) [9,15], which will be referred as QNN. To update the QNN weights, we used the following equation:

$$W \leftarrow W + \alpha\left(R_{t+1} + \gamma \cdot \max_{a'}[Q\left(O_{t+1}, a', W\right)] - Q\left(O_t, A_t, W\right)\right) \cdot \nabla Q\left(O_t, A_t, W\right) \quad (2)$$

where $\nabla Q\left(O_t, A_t, W\right)$ denotes the gradient of the outputs of the QNN with respect to W, which is a vector with the weights and biases of the QNN.

To accelerate the training of the QNN, we used experience replay [8,11]. For this purpose, we stored in a dataset $\mathcal{D} = \{E_1, E_2, \cdots, E_T\}$ the tuple $E_t = (O_t, A_t, R_t, S_{t+1})$, which contains the agent's experience at time t. During learning, we updated the parameters of the QNN using Eq. 2 computed on mini-batches of experience drawn uniformly at random from $\mathcal{D}$ [8,11].

Finally, the proposed POMDP solves the sequential decision-making problem that represents the EMG sliding window classification. The scheme of interaction between the QNN agent and the environment is shown in Fig. 2.

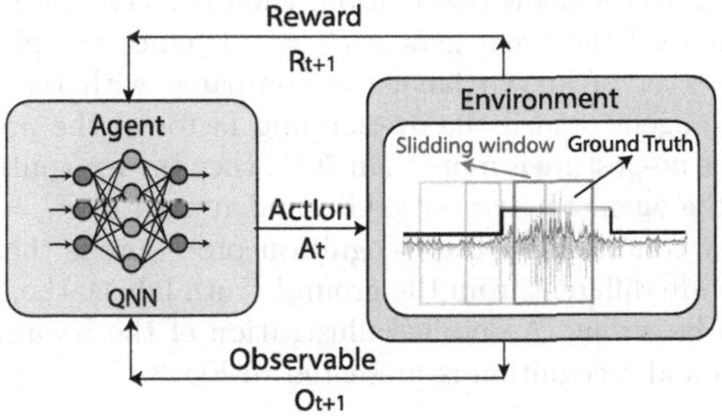

Fig. 2. Scheme of the interaction between the QNN agent and the environment. The EMG classification problem is modeled as a partially observable markov decision process (POMDP).

Below we define the elements of the proposed classification stage modeled as a Q-Learning problem:

Agent: The agent is the decision-maker entity, based on the QNN network, whose objective is to take actions, at any state of the environment, to maximize the total reward. In this work, the goal of the agent is to predict correctly as many labels as possible in the sequence of labels obtained by classifying each window observation of a given EMG. Here, the interaction between the agent and the environment is episodic.

Observable: An observable contains some information of the actual state of the environment with which the agent is interacting. In this work, we define the observable O_t for the unknown state S_t as the result of applying the feature extraction functions (SD,AE, MAV, E, and RMS) to each EMG channel observed through a window, with $t = 1, 2, \cdots, N$. In this case, N denotes the number of window observations that we can extract from an EMG using a given window length and stride. The end of an episode of interaction between the agent and the environment occurs when the last observable O_N is reached. It is worth mentioning that there is not necessarily a bijection between the set of observables and the set of states of the environment.

Action: An action is the choice or behavior A_t that the agent makes in the current observable O_t. In this work, the set of actions that the agent can take in each observable includes the classes: wave in, wave out, fist, open, pinch, and no gesture.

Environment: The environment is defined in code as the sliding window information –feature vectors and labels– extracted from each EMG signal.

Reward: The reward is the feedback information that the agent receives from its interaction with the environment. In this work, we define two rewards: one for classification and the other for recognition. If the agent predicts correctly the label for an EMG window observation, then it receives a reward $R_t = +1$; otherwise, the reward the agent gets is $R_t = -1$. Once an episode is over, the ground truth (vector of known labels) is compared with the vector of labels predicted by the agent, and if the overlapping factor of the predicted gestures different from the no-gesture is more than 70%, then the recognition is considered successful and the agent receives an additional reward of $R_t = +10$; otherwise $R_t = -10$. A key condition for the recognition procedure is that if one or more predicted labels are different from the ground truth labels, then the recognition is considered to be wrong. A detailed illustration of the reward the agent gets for classification and recognition is presented in Fig. 3.

2.5 Post-processing

To improve the accuracy of the proposed HGR system, the post-processing stage adapts the output of the classification to the final application. Most of the works found in the literature use the majority voting technique, elimination of consecutive repetitions, threshold method, the gesture mode, and velocity ramps [2, 7]. In this work, we calculate the mode on the predicted vector of classes that are different from the label no-gesture. Then, all the labels in such vectors that are different from the mode gesture are replaced with such gesture for that EMG sample.

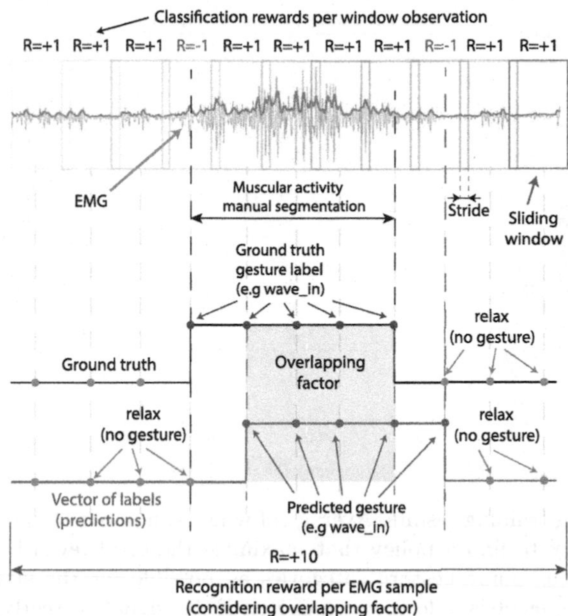

Fig. 3. Reward the agent gets for classification and recognition illustration. The classification is considered successful if each predicted window label matches the ground truth label for that point. On the other hand, each recognition reward is assigned if the recognition procedure that considers the overlapping factor between the vector of predicted labels per sample and the ground truth if higher than a threshold –70%–.

3 Results

In this section, we first present the results of training and validating the HGR user-specific proposed models on the training set A to find the best possible hyper-parameters. We illustrate in Fig. 4 a Q-learning training sample where the Average of wins vs the number of epochs can be observed. It is to be noticed that the average of wins per episode converge to their optimal value after 1000 epochs. To obtain this results, we repeat the experiences of the 100 training samples of each user 10 times through the neural network that represents the agent. The procedure of using 10 times the 100 training samples was necessary since the learning procedure is online and its performance depends on the number of experiences that the agent can use to learn.

The hyper-parameter configurations for our experiments is summarized in Table 2. It is worth mentioning that we tested 72 different hyper-parameter configurations (different number of neurons, learning rate α, momentum, and mini-batch size) to find the best fit for our models. Moreover, we tested different window sizes –150, 200, 300, and 400 points– for each of those 72 configurations during the validation process. However, only the best hyper-parameters configurations and window size are presented in Table 2.

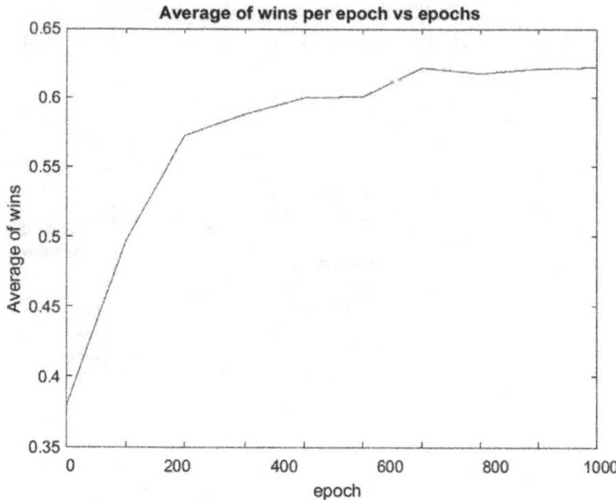

Fig. 4. Q-learning training results. Average of wins vs. number of epochs during training. The agent try to find a policy that maximize the total reward, which means to correctly predict as many gesture categories as possible for the sliding windows in the EMGs. If the agent is able to recognize an EMG signal correctly, that episode is considered as won.

In addition, by using the hyper-parameters from Table 2, we tested 160 users (since this procedure is heavily time-consuming) of the validation set from training set A. For this procedure, we changed the learning rate α as well as the window stride, and the results are presented in Fig. 5. This procedure helps us to find the best possible learning rate and stride configuration for our experiments. It can be observed that $\alpha = 0.03$ and stride $= 40$ achieve the best accuracy results with high classification and recognition as well as low variance.

Table 2. Best hyper-parameters found during tuning procedure on Training set A.

	Best hyper-parameters
Number of neurons	40, 50, 50 and 6 for the input layer, hidden layer 1, hidden layer 2, and output layer respectively
Sliding window size	300 points
Initial momentum	0.3
Mini batch size	25
ϵ-greedy value	0.2
Discount factor γ	1
Training set replay per user	10 times
Learning rate (α) decay factor	α*exp(-5*CurrentEpoch/NumEpochs)

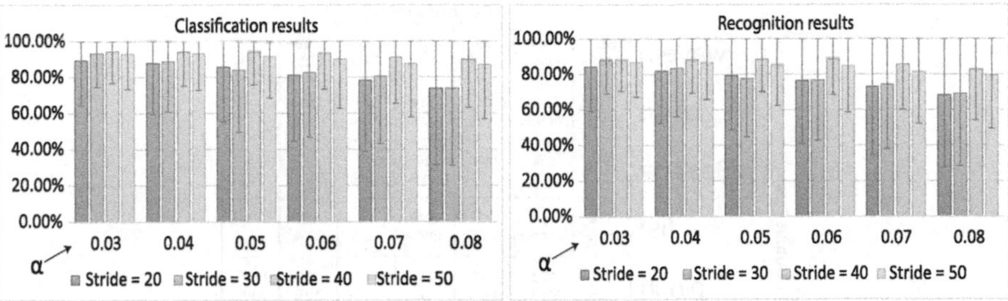

Fig. 5. User-specific HGR model classification and recognition accuracy results for 160 users for validation of training set A with different values of learning rate α and stride. It can be observed that $\alpha = 0.03$ and stride = 40 achieve the best results.

Based on the best hyper-parameters described in Table 2, and the values of $\alpha = 0.03$, and stride = 40, we used the test-set of the training set A to evaluate such models. The test accuracy results for 306 users of the training set A were 90.78% ± 20% and 84.43% ± 21% for classification and recognition respectively. Then, we use the best hyper-parameters that we found to train the 306 users of the training set B, which will help us to evaluate our models with different data and analyze over-fitting. The test results for 306 users of the training set B were 90.47% ± 20% and 87.51% ± 21% for classification and recognition respectively. We summarized the test results for 306 users for both training set A and B with the best found hyper-parameters in Table 3. Since there is barely a difference between the test results of training set A and B, we can infer that our model is robust against over-fitting. It can be seen that the standard deviation is moderate, which could be due to the variability of the data set, as the model works well for most samples and fails for a few. Finally, we also present the confusion matrix that represents the classification results on the test set of training set B in Fig. 6, which allow us to observe in detail the results for each hand gesture. It is worth mentioning that the processing time of each window observation is in average 19 ms.

Table 3. User-specific test accuracy results of the HGR best model for training set A and B (306 users for training set A and B respectively - 612 users in total).

Test results - Training set A		Test results - Training set B	
Classification	Recognition	Classification	Recognition
90.78% ± 20%	84.43% ± 21%	90.47% ± 14.24%	87.51% ± 14.1%

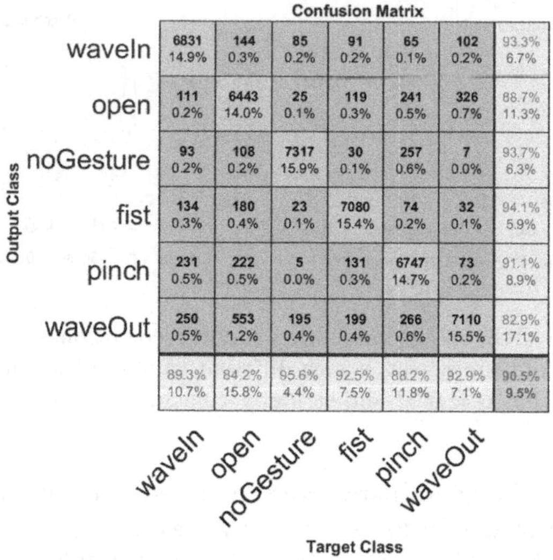

Confusion Matrix

Output Class \ Target Class	waveIn	open	noGesture	fist	pinch	waveOut	
waveIn	6831 14.9%	144 0.3%	85 0.2%	91 0.2%	65 0.1%	102 0.2%	93.3% 6.7%
open	111 0.2%	6443 14.0%	25 0.1%	119 0.3%	241 0.5%	326 0.7%	88.7% 11.3%
noGesture	93 0.2%	108 0.2%	7317 15.9%	30 0.1%	257 0.6%	7 0.0%	93.7% 6.3%
fist	134 0.3%	180 0.4%	23 0.1%	7080 15.4%	74 0.2%	32 0.1%	94.1% 5.9%
pinch	231 0.5%	222 0.5%	5 0.0%	131 0.3%	6747 14.7%	73 0.2%	91.1% 8.9%
waveOut	250 0.5%	553 1.2%	195 0.4%	199 0.4%	266 0.6%	7110 15.5%	82.9% 17.1%
	89.3% 10.7%	84.2% 15.8%	95.6% 4.4%	92.5% 7.5%	88.2% 11.8%	92.9% 7.1%	90.5% 9.5%

Fig. 6. User-specific HGR model confusion matrix for 306 users of test set B with the best hyper-parameter configuration. Each hand gesture class results can be observed in detail.

4 Conclusions

In this work, we proposed a HGR system based on Q-learning to classify and recognize five gestures using EMGs from a public dataset. The results were evaluated for user-specific HGR models. The system was tested for two different test sets for 612 users, where the classification accuracy reached up to 90.78% and the recognition accuracy reached up to 87.51%. The results obtained are encouraging, and they show that Q-learning can learn a policy from online experience to classify and recognize gestures based on EMGs. It is worth mentioning that using Q-learning for HGR allows an agent to learn from online experience. Therefore, the model can be improved at each iteration if the ground truth is defined or if we use an automatic labeling procedure. Future work includes testing other RL algorithms to create a state estimator from observations to evaluate the proposed POMDP model with belief states, as well as testing on more data-sets.

Acknowledgment. The authors gratefully acknowledge the financial support provided by the Escuela Politécnica Nacional (EPN) for the development of the research project "PIGR-19-07 Reconocimiento de gestos de la mano usando señales electromiográficas e inteligencia artificial y su aplicación para la implementación de interfaces humano—máquina y humano—humano".

References

1. EMG Gesture Recognition Evaluator. https://aplicaciones-ia.epn.edu.ec/webapps/home/session.html?app=EMGGestureRecognitionEvaluator
2. Barona López, L.I., Valdivieso Caraguay, Á.L., Vimos, V.H., Zea, J.A., Vásconez, J.P., Álvarez, M., Benalcázar, M.E.: An energy-based method for orientation correction of emg bracelet sensors in hand gesture recognition systems. Sensors **20**(21), 6327 (2020)
3. Benalcázar, M.E., Jaramillo, A.G., Zea, A., Páez, A., Andaluz, V.H., et al.: Hand gesture recognition using machine learning and the myo armband. In: 2017 25th European Signal Processing Conference (EUSIPCO), pp. 1040–1044. IEEE (2017)
4. Benalcázar, M.E., et al.: Real-time hand gesture recognition using the myo armband and muscle activity detection. In: 2017 IEEE Second Ecuador Technical Chapters Meeting (ETCM), pp. 1–6. IEEE (2017)
5. Benalcázar, M., Barona, L., Valdivieso, L., Aguas, X., Zea, J.: Emg-epn-612 dataset (2020). https://doi.org/10.5281/zenodo.4027874
6. Englehart, K., Hudgins, B.: A robust, real-time control scheme for multifunction myoelectric control. IEEE Trans. Biomed. Eng. **50**(7), 848–854 (2003)
7. Jaramillo-Yánez, A., Benalcázar, M.E., Mena-Maldonado, E.: Real-time hand gesture recognition using surface electromyography and machine learning: a systematic literature review. Sensors **20**(9), 2467 (2020)
8. Kapturowski, S., Ostrovski, G., Quan, J., Munos, R., Dabney, W.: Recurrent experience replay in distributed reinforcement learning. In: International Conference on Learning Representations (2018)
9. Kukker, A., Sharma, R.: Neural reinforcement learning classifier for elbow, finger and hand movements. J. Intell. Fuzzy Syst. **35**(5), 5111–5121 (2018)
10. McGill, K.: Surface electromyogram signal modelling. Med. Biol. Eng. Comput. **42**(4), 446–454 (2004)
11. Mnih, V., et al.: Human-level control through deep reinforcement learning. Nature **518**(7540), 529–533 (2015)
12. Seok, W., Kim, Y., Park, C.: Pattern recognition of human arm movement using deep reinforcement learning. In: 2018 International Conference on Information Networking (ICOIN), pp. 917–919. IEEE (2018)
13. Song, C., Chen, C., Li, Y., Wu, X.: Deep reinforcement learning apply in electromyography data classification. In: 2018 IEEE International Conference on Cyborg and Bionic Systems (CBS), pp. 505–510. IEEE (2018)
14. Sugiyama, M., Kawanabe, M.: Machine Learning in Non-Stationary Environments: Introduction to Covariate Shift Adaptation. MIT Press, Cambridge (2012)
15. Sutton, R.S., Barto, A.G.: Reinforcement Learning: An Introduction. MIT Press, Cambridge (2018)
16. Wang, F., et al.: Robot learning by demonstration interaction system based on multiple information. In: 2018 IEEE 8th Annual International Conference on CYBER Technology in Automation, Control, and Intelligent Systems (CYBER), pp. 138–143. IEEE (2018)

References

Reinforcement Learning II

Reinforcement Learning for the Privacy Preservation and Manipulation of Eye Tracking Data

Wolfgang Fuhl(✉), Efe Bozkir, and Enkelejda Kasneci

University Tübingen, Sand 14, 72076 Tübingen, Germany
{wolfgang.fuhl,efe.bozkir,enkelejda.kasneci}@uni-tuebingen.de

Abstract. In this paper, we present an approach based on reinforcement learning for eye tracking data manipulation. It is based on two opposing agents, where one tries to classify the data correctly and the second agent looks for patterns in the data, which get manipulated to hide specific information. We show that our approach is successfully applicable to preserve the privacy of a subject. For this purpose, we evaluate our approach iterative to showcase the behavior of the reinforcement learning based approach. In addition, we evaluate the importance of temporal, as well as spatial, information of eye tracking data for specific classification goals. In the last part of our evaluation we apply the procedure to further public data sets without re-training the autoencoder nor the data manipulator. The results show that the learned manipulation is generalized and applicable to other data too.

Keywords: Reinforcement learning · Eye tracking · Privacy · Scan path

1 Introduction

Due to the spread of the eye tracking technology over many fields and its use in everyday life, the specific information content in the eye tracking signal becomes more and more important [21]. This is mainly due to the fact that the gaze signal is very rich in information and on the other hand that it cannot be turned off or easily controlled by a human [29]. Many applications use this signal, however, still little value is placed on the anonymization of the signal. This is partly due to the fact that the topic of differential privacy has come into the focus of eye tracking research last year [18,27,28], but also to the challenge of finding specific patterns in the signal itself that make a person identifiable.

Initially in 2014 the problem of personal information in the eye tracking signal was mentioned for the first time as well as the person specific patterns contained in the signal [17]. They mentioned critical attributes that are contained in the eye tracking data like age, gender, personal preference or health [17]. This information poses a new challenge to modern eye tracking systems, which must now learn to hide this information. The basic approach of differential privacy is

I. Farkaš et al. (Eds.): ICANN 2021, LNCS 12894, pp. 595–607, 2021.
https://doi.org/10.1007/978-3-030-86380-7_48

based on adding random noise to the signal: to cover up people specific data. However, this only works in the case of prefabricated features, since modern machine learning techniques such as convolutional neuronal networks are able to adapt their feature extractors. Furthermore, it would be more interesting to find specific patterns either in the stimulus itself or, as in this paper, in the scan path, which we can remove from the signal. On the one hand, this offers an insight into important characteristics which are interesting for science. On the other hand, it can be used in many other areas such as gaze guidance [16] or expertise evaluation [15].

However, the high and unique information content in the eye tracking signal only becomes clear when biometrics applications are considered. Here, it is possible to unambiguously identify the person by means of the eye behavior. First, approaches required a moving point stimulus which was followed by the user [13] or static images [20]. Later, users were distinguished using eye movements with a task independent way [1]. In addition, model based approaches using gaze behavior with oculomotor models were proposed [14]. Furthermore, distinguishing users while performing different tasks [8] and a user authentication approach in virtual reality headsets [30] were studied using eye movements.

These works show the potential threat to a human by revealing the gaze data. It also means that raw eye tracking data should be handled carefully, especially for storage and transmission purposes. However, there are not many works focusing on privacy-preserving eye tracking. An approach for head mounted eye trackers to detect privacy sensitive situations and to disable eye tracker first person camera using a mechanical shutter was proposed in [28]. Privacy-preserving gaze estimation using a randomized encoding based framework and replacing the iris textures of the eye images using rubber sheet model were studied in [3], respectively. However, when the personal information protection is taken into account, differential privacy [7] provides privacy with theoretical guarantees by adding randomly generated noise. While differential privacy guarantees that adversaries cannot infer whether an individual participated in a database, it also decreases the data utility due to the added noise. The privacy-utility trade-off is usually tailored around a specific use case [24], which can be understood as a classification target in the eye tracking world. Recently, differential privacy was applied to static statistical eye movement features [27] and heatmaps [18] to protect privacy.

In this paper, we present an approach that is able to learn an image manipulation to hide specific information while preserving other information. Our approach uses reinforcement learning on the sparse representation learned by an autoencoder. This combination allows to manipulate general patterns in an image, since the autoencoder has to reconstruct it based on a reduced set of values. Contribution of this work:

1 An approach to remove patterns from eye tracking data.
2 No static features due to the usage of CNNs.
3 Identification of general patterns in the data instead of adding random noise as it is done in differential privacy.
4 With our method it is possible to specify the information type which has do be hidden in the data.

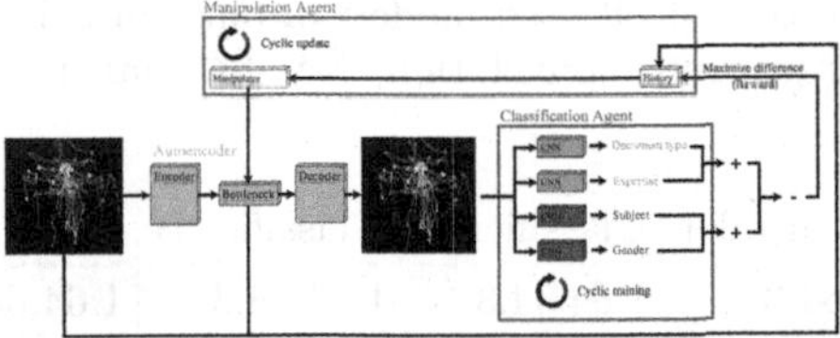

Fig. 1. The workflow used for our approach. Classification Agent holds and uses the classifiers and Manipulation Agent the manipulator. Both agents are retrained after a fixed set of steps and have a buffer to hold old and new examples. (Color figure online)

2 Method

Figure 1 shows the general workflow of our approach. The autoencoder is trained preliminary to reconstruct the image. In its central part, it holds values that correspond to general patterns for the reconstruction of the image (Bottleneck in Fig. 1). The idea behind using the autoencoder is that it reduces the input data ($64 * 64 * 3 = 12.228$ to $4 * 4 * 256 = 4096$) and thus also the possible action combinations of Manipulation Agent. Furthermore, it ensures that in the end, an image is still generated that is similar to the input image or consists of general patterns compared to a direct manipulation of the image by Manipulation Agent. Manipulation Agent is the reinforcement part of our approach. It learns a manipulation of the bottleneck from the autoencoder based on previous seen input images and the classification result from Classification Agent. This classification result is only the difference between the good (Green classifiers in Fig. 1) and bad (Red classifiers in Fig. 1) information revealed by the classifiers. This difference is used as reward in Manipulation Agent for the performed manipulation, whereas the image itself is the state. The different classification objectives (Document type, expertise, subject, gender) in Fig. 1 are intended to indicate that our approach supports any number of classifiers. Manipulation Agent tries to worsen the accuracy of the red classifiers and to keep the accuracy of the green classifiers high. In contrast to this, Classification Agent tries to adapt the classifiers to the new image manipulation by retraining them. In the following each part is described in detail.

Table 1 first row shows the architecture of the used autoencoder. Each convolution block is followed by a rectifier linear unit (ReLu) and max pooling for size reduction. For the decoder of the autoencoder, we used transposed convolutions instead of pooling. The input to the network is an image with size $64 \times 64 \times 3$. The bottleneck in the autoencoder is the block with size $4 \times 4 \times 256$. For the training, we used stochastic gradient decent with an initial learning rate of 10^{-2}, decreasing each 200 epochs by a factor of 10^{-1}. The training stops at a learning rate of 10^{-7}. Weight decay was set to $5 * 10^{-4}$ and momentum to $9 * 10^{-1}$. During training, we used a batch size of 40 and the L2 loss formulation. This autoencoder is trained only once before starting our reinforcement learning approch.

Table 1. The configuration of all used models in our work. I stands for input, C for convolution, TC for transposed convolution, MP for max pooling, and #C for the number of classes.

Autoencoder	Classifier A	Classifier B	DQL
I 64,64,3	I 64,64,3	I 64,64,3	I 64,64,3
C 7,7,32	C 7,7,32	C 7,7,32	C 7,7,32
ReLu, MP	ReLu, MP	ReLu, MP	ReLu, MP
C 7,7,64	C 7,7,64	C 7,7,64	C 7,7,64
ReLu, MP	ReLu, MP	ReLu, MP	ReLu, MP
C 5,5,128	C 5,5,128	C 5,5,128	C 5,5,128
ReLu, MP	ReLu, MP	ReLu, MP	ReLu, MP
C 5,5,256	C 5,5,256	C 5,5,256	C 5,5,256
ReLu	ReLu, MP	ReLu, MP	ReLu
TC 5,5,128	Fully 512	Fully 512	Fully 4096
ReLu	ReLu	ReLu	–
TC 5,5,64	Fully #C	Fully #C	–
ReLu	–	–	–
TC 7,7,32	–	–	–
ReLu	–	–	–
C 7,7,3	–	–	–

The classifiers used in the Classification Agent (Table 1 second and third row) use a similar structure as the autoencoder. A detailed view of the classifiers can be seen in Table 1. Each convolution block uses a ReLu together with a max pooling operation. Before the first fully connected layer, we used a dropout, which deactivates 50% randomly. A and B in Table 1 have the same structure except for the last fully connected layer, which has either eight (Subject) or four (Stimulus image) output neurons. For the training, we used stochastic gradient decent with an initial learning rate of 10^{-4} decreasing each 500 epochs by a factor of 10^{-1}. The training stops at a learning rate of 10^{-7}. Weight decay was set to $5 * 10^{-4}$ and momentum to $9 * 10^{-1}$. During training, we used a batch size of 50 and the log multi class loss with softmax.

Since these classifiers are subject to the cyclic training of Classification Agent, they are always re-trained once the reinforcement learning has stabilized. This new training is done with a random initialization. The idea behind this is that the convolutions, which learn new feature extractors, adapt to the new image manipulation and thus improve the classification result. The training itself is done using the not manipulated and all the manipulated images seen so far (only from the training set).

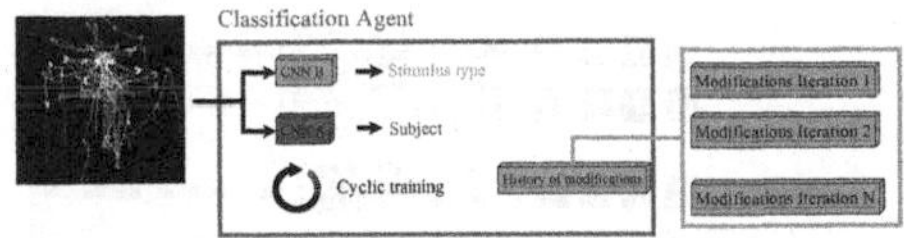

Fig. 2. Used setup of classification agent with a memory for manipulated data seen in the past.

Figure 2 shows the workflow for Classification Agent with the memory. In comparison to Fig. 1, which is a general overview, it can be seen that we now have only two classes. Those two classes are also used in our experiment for the evaluation section which is why we decided to insert them in the detailed view of the Classification Agent. In the memory (Fig. 2) are all the seen manipulated images from the training set together with their labels. Images from the validation set are discarded and therefore, not stored in the memory of Classification Agent. For the training and test set, we made a 50% to 50% split. We seperated the data to produce equal amounts of stimulus and subject classes. As can be seen in this description, Classification Agent does not use reinforcement learning. This agent can be understood as a supervised learner, which retrains its classifiers.

In contrast to the Classification Agent, the Manipulation Agent uses reinforcement learning for training. The used DQL model can be seen in Table 1 fourth row. It consists of three convolution blocks and a fully connected output layer. The input of this model is the current image, which is called the state and the output of this model (4096 fully connected neurons) are the actions. Between each convolution block, we used ReLu and max pooling as in the models before. The output of the last layer was set 1 if it was greater or equal to 0.5, otherwise it was set to 0. Meaning, our model could either deactivate a feature in the bottleneck of the autoencoder or let it unchanged. For the training we used stochastic gradient decent with a fixed learning rate of 10^{-4}. The training stops after ten epochs of training on the entire memory of Manipulation Agent. Weight decay was set to $1 * 10^{-5}$ and momentum to $9 * 10^{-1}$. During training, we used a batch size of 100 and the L2 loss formulation for reinforcement learning $(predicted - actual)^2$. The parameter *predicted* in this context means the result of DQL1 from the current input image. Since there is no ground truth in reinforcement learning, the parameter *actual* is computed based on a second network (DQL2) and the reward R. Therefore, the ground truth is formulated as $actual = R + y * DQL2$. As mentioned before, R is the reward (Result of Classification Agent), $DQL2$ is the output of a second network and y is the discount factor, which is adjusted through training so that the net explores more in the beginning. This usage of two neuronal networks is called fixed target Q-network [19]. Therefore, after ten training runs of DQL1, we set $DQL2 = DQL1$ since DQL1 has stabilized.

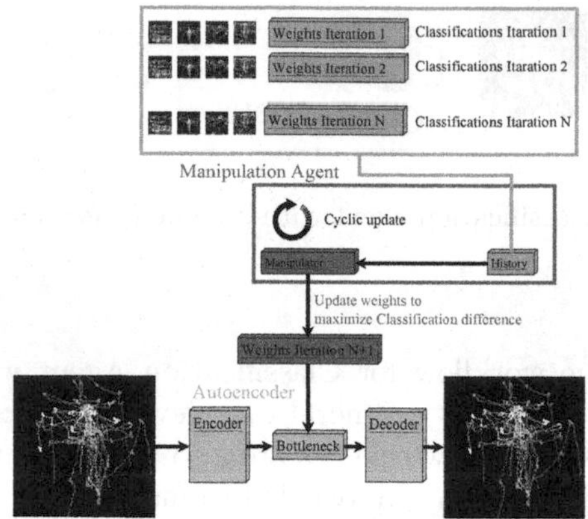

Fig. 3. Memory and setup of manipulation agent.

In addition to the fixed target network, we use the experience replay mechanism [19] as can be seen in Fig. 3. As mentioned in the related work, this concept describes the memory which holds all examples (Stimulus, actions, and classification result). In this memory, we only store examples from the training set, since we want to evaluate our approach especially for unseen data. This memory is initialized before starting the entire approach and the networks DQL1 and DQL2 are trained on it. For this initialization, we compute the change of each value in the bottleneck on the classification and store it in the memory of Manipulation Agent. In addition, we compute one hundred random changes of 2–100 values in the bottleneck. This means that for the change of two values, we compute one hundred random changes and the same for three values, four values, and so on.

For data augmentation of all models, we used random noise which was in the range of 0–20%, cropping and shifting the scanpath. Cropping in this context means that we extracted randomly 60–100% of the scanpath and draw it on the input image. With shifting, we mean a randomly selected constant shift of the entire scanpath. This shift was selected in the range of 0–30% of the stimulus size.

In order to be able to show a comparison to the state-of-the-art, we have evaluated an approach to differential privacy. Therefore, Laplacian-distributed noise based on the sensitivity (δf) of the signal is added to the raw eye tracking data (DP Raw) or to the generated image (DP Image) [5,6,26]. As sensitivity (δf) for the raw eye tracking date we used the average Manhattan distance between all gaze point recordings [25]. Since those do not have equal length we cut off the last part of the larger recording. Therefore, the scale parameter of the Laplacian-distribution is $\frac{\delta f}{\epsilon}$ [26]. For our evaluation we apllied the Laplacian Noise one hundred times to an image and computed the class using the networks. Afterwards, we selected the maximum vote as detected class. In case of the images as data we used the average maximum pixel distance (Manhatten distance between the red, green, and blue channel) between all image pairs [9]. The same formula was used to compute the scale parameter Laplacian-distribution. For a fair comparison we evaluated different values of ϵ in 0.01 steps and present the results of the best found ϵ based on the adapted classifiers. The search range of the optimal ϵ was [0.01–15.0] for the images and for the noise injection into the raw gaze data the search range was [10.00–500.0]. For the images the ϵ value has to be multiplied by the image resolution (64×64) due to the sequential composition theorem and the independecy of the image pixels [23]. Therefore, the search range for the ϵ was [40.96–61440] but the 0.01 search steps are made based on the single pixel search range ([0.01–15.0]). It also has to be mentioned that we skipped ϵ values for the raw eye tracking data if there were less than three gaze points remaining on the image. The optimal epsilon was selected based on the maximal distance between the stimulus and subject classification, where the subject classification had to be at chance level. For the DOVES [2] dataset we selected the best epsilon based on the minimal subject classification but the stimulus classification had to be over chance level. This was done for the DOVES [2] data set, because all algorithms did not work as desired for this data set.

In addition, we have also evaluated a supervised trained approach to justify the use of reinforcement learning for the manipulation. The same models as shown in Table 1 were used and trained as a Generative Adversarial Network (GAN). The autoencoder is the generator and the classifiers A and B are used as discriminators. Before we trained the GAN we initially trained the Autoencoder, Classifier A, and Classifier B for one hundred epochs with the training parameters already provided. This was done to stabilize the training of the GAN afterwards. To adapt the initial training to the training of a GAN we added the logarithmic loss from the generated image as it was done in the original GAN paper [11] with the difference, that the classifiers still had to predict the correct class.

For the generator (G) we used also the formulation of the original paper ($log(1 - D(G(I)))$) [11] but in our case the discriminator (D) consists of two networks. Therefore, Classifier A and Classifier B can only contribute 0.5 each but in inverse directions. This means if Classifier A is correct it contributes 0.5 and if Classifier B is wrong it additionally contributes 0.5 since we want the GAN to learn to perserve the information classified by Classifier A and hide the information important for Classifier B. Based on the softmax output we can simply compute the probability for the correct class for Classifier A and Classifier B and weight both with 0.5.

3 Evaluation

For the image generation out of the raw gaze data files, we used the approach from [10]. This means that the raw gaze data is in the red channel as dots, the green channel holds the time by adjusting the intensity of the dot, and the blue channel holds the relation ship of the gaze points by connecting them as lines.

ETRA [22]**:** This data is from the ETRA 2019 challenge. In this data, 8 subjects with 120 trials per subject are recorded. Therefore, it consists of 960 trials with a length of 45 s per trial. They recorded different tasks namely visual fixation, visual search, and visual exploration. Additionally, four different stimuli were presented; Which are blank, natural, where is waldo, and picture puzzle.

Gaze [4]**:** Is a huge data set with eye tracking data on dynamic scenes. The data was recorded using an SR Research EyeLink II eye tracker 250 Hz. For our experiment we only used the data provided for static images where each static image of a video was considered the same image. In addition, we had to exclude subject V01 since there was only one recording for it available. Therefore, we used the eye tracking data of 10 subjects on 9 images for our experiment with an average recording length of 2 s.

WherePeopleLook [12] **(WPL):** Is a eye tracking data set and published under the intention to integrate top down features into saliency map generation. It consists of 1003 static images with eye tracking data of 15 subjects per image with an average recording length of 3 s.

DOVES [2]**:** Contains eye tracking data of 29 subjects on 101 natural images with an average recording length of 5 s. The recordings were performed with 200 Hz high-precision dual-Purkinje eye tracker.

The first experiment shows the results of our approach for different iterations, as well as before and after the adaption of the classifiers (Classification Agent) on the ETRA data set. This experiment shows that our approach is capable of removing unwanted information in the scanpath. In this scenario, it is the information of the subject. This experiment shows the advantage of our approach to other differential privacy methods since the feature extractors (Neuronal networks in Classification Agent) adapt to the new image manipulation as well as our image manipulation technique. For all experiments, we used a 50%

Table 2. Accuracy of the classifiers after each iteration and before as well as after the adaption of the Classification Agent on the ETRA data set. RL is the proposed approach, GAN the same models trained supervised, DP Raw is the Differential Privacy applied to the raw gaze data, and DP Image is the differential Privacy applied to the image. The best results are in bold.

Iteration	No adaption		Adaption	
	Stim	Sub	Stim	Sub
RL Initial	–	–	96%	93%
RL 1	95%	13%	96%	93%
RL 2	95%	11%	95%	91%
RL 5	91%	12%	93%	52%
RL 10	88%	14%	91%	31%
RL 15	78%	12%	86%	22%
RL 20	81%	13%	**83%**	**15%**
GAN	75%	13%	81%	**15%**
DP Raw $\epsilon = 223.21$	27%	15%	30%	**15%**
DP Image $\epsilon = 10485.76$	41%	11%	59%	**15%**
Chance level	25%	12%	25%	12%

split of the data where the test and validation set contain always equal amounts of subjects and stimuli samples.

Table 2 shows the classification results per iteration. With iteration we mean that the reinforcement learning (Manipulation Agent) has stabilized, which are approximately one thousand training runs. After each iteration, Classification Agent starts to retrain the classifiers, which is indicated by the adaption rows. The first line in Table 2 shows the initial results of the pretrained classifiers. At the bottom of Table 2, the chance level is shown. As can be seen Manipulation Agent always succeeds in dropping the classification accuracy for the subject close to the chance level. Afterwards, Classification Agent adapts the classifiers, but with less success for the subject classification if the process over all iterations is considered. In the last iteration (20), the training of the subject classifier fails and is close to the chance level. This is also true for DP RAW (Differential privacy applied to the raw eye tracking data), DP Image (Differential privacy applied to the image), and the GAN (generative adversarial network) approach. When comparing the results of the different approaches, it is clear that our reinforcement learning approach is much better than differential privacy in terms of receiving the stimulus information. Compared to the GAN approach our approach gives slightly better results.

In the next experiment we will use the data manipulation (learned with reinforcement learning) and the autoencoder on other public data sets without further training to show the generalization. The classifiers, however, will be retrained on the output of the autoencoder and additionally adapted to the data manipulation in a further step.

For the classification on the data sets Gaze [4], WherePeopleLook [12], and DOVES [2] we used the same model as in Experiment 1 (Table 1). For training, we set the initial learning rate to 10^{-2} and reduced it by a factor of 10^{-1} every 100 epochs until we reached 10^{-7}. The optimizer used was stochstic gradient decent with weight decay of $5 * 10^{-4}$ and momentum of 0.9. For the data set Gaze [4] we used a batch size of twice the number of classes and made sure that there were always 2 examples of each class in a batch. For WherePeopleLook [12] we also used double the number of classes for the subject classification. For the Stimulus Classification we used only the single class number as batch size. For the last data set DOVES [2] we used twice the number of classes as batch size for both classifiers as for Gaze [4] and also made sure that there were always two examples of each class per batch.

In the first column of Table 3 the results without data manipulation on the data sets Gaze, WherePeopleLook, and DOVES can be seen. Comparing these with the results on the Challenge data set in Table 2 it can be seen that the results are significantly lower. One reason for this is that there are many more classes which increases the challenge for the classification, but the main reason is the significantly lower recording time. For the Challenge data set the average recording time is 45 s. In comparison, Gaze has an average of 2 s, WherePeopleLook an average of 3 s, and DOVES an average of 5 s. This shows that the Challenge data set provides a multiple of the information for the neural networks. This means

Table 3. Accuracy on new unseen data sets with retrained classifiers but the same data manipulation learned from experiment 1 and 2 as well as the same weights for the autoencoder. RL is the proposed approach, GAN the same models trained supervised, DP Raw is the Differential Privacy applied to the raw gaze data, and DP Image is the differential Privacy applied to the image. The best results are in bold.

Data set	Method	No manipulation		Manipulation		Adapted	
		Stim	Sub	Stim	Sub	Stim	Sub
Gaze	RL	75%	31.66%	40%	8.88%	**71.11%**	**13.33%**
	GAN	75%	31.66%	37.24%	14.32%	61.64%	19.53%
	DP Raw $\epsilon = 31.28$	75%	31.66%	15.44%	12.54%	16.25%	13.96%
	DP Image $\epsilon = 34938.88$	75%	31.66%	21.22%	11.81%	59.83%	13.61%
	Chance	11.11%	10%	11.11%	10%	11.11%	10%
WPL	RL	31.23%	30.06%	21.54%	6.39%	**30.48**	**8.28%**
	GAN	31.23%	30.06%	18.47%	14.76%	26.74%	20.37%
	DP Raw $\epsilon = 68.20$	31.23%	30.06%	0.19%	7.09%	0.4%	8.93%
	DP Image $\epsilon = 16547.84$	31.23%	30.06%	7.15%	6.72%	8.41%	8.91%
	Chance	0.099%	6.66%	0.099%	6.66%	0.099%	6.66%
DOVES	RL	10.86%	44.90%	4.3%	6.69%	**9.15%**	13.66%
	GAN	10.86%	44.90%	5.68%	6.73%	8.26%	19.55%
	DP Raw $\epsilon = 425.39$	10.86%	44.90%	1.81%	3.95%	1.42%	**12.45%**
	DP Image $\epsilon = 13762.56$	10.86%	44.90%	1.14%	5.01%	1.5%	22.11%
	Chance	0.99%	3.44%	0.99%	3.44%	0.99%	3.44%

that the data from the Challenge data set contains significantly more personal information as well as more information about the structure of the stimuli. It is also interesting how little eye tracking data is sufficient to classify a subject. If for example the data set DOVES is compared with Gaze and WherePeopleLook (Table 3 first column) it can be seen that DOVES has a higher accuracy for the subject classification although DOVES has a lower chance level but a 2–3 s longer recording time. In contrast to this the detection rate for the stimuli classification is significantly lower compared to the other data sets.

The second column in Table 3 shows the results after the data manipulation by Manipulation Agent. Manipulation Agent has not been retrained and neither has the autoencoder. As you can see, this data manipulation has a significant impact on the accuracy of the classifiers. This is true for the stimulus as well as for the subjects, although the subject classification is more influenced (except for the DOVES data set, everything is reduced below the chance level). Since this can also be purely due to data augmentation, we have also adapted the classifiers to the data manipulation via training. For this purpose, the training examples were manipulated with Manipulation Agent and both the unaltered and the manipulated data were used for the training. The results can be senn in the third column of Table 3. While the subject classification in the DOVES data set is still significantly above the chance level (13.66%), the personal information was mainly removed in the other two data sets. What can also be seen is that the

Table 4. Accuracy for the stimulus information suppression. RL is the proposed approach and GAN the same models trained supervised. DP Raw and DP Image cannot be used to suppress the stimulus information since the results would be the same as in Table 3 and Table 2. The best results are in bold.

Data set	Method	Stim	Sub
ETRA	RL	**26.55%**	**79.15%**
	GAN	26.75%	78.95%
	No manipulation	96%	93%
	Chance	25%	12%
Gaze	RL	**13.32%**	**17.76%**
	GAN	13.48%	12.25%
	No manipulation	75%	31.66%
	Chance	11.11%	10%
WPL	RL	**0.20%**	**21.98%**
	GAN	0.81%	14.49%
	No manipulation	31.23%	30.06%
	Chance	0.099%	6.66%
DOVES	RL	**1.33%**	**32.47%**
	GAN	3.33%	27.91%
	No manipulation	10.86%	44.90%
	Chance	0.99%	3.44%

Table 5. Accuracy for different and multiple information suppression targets on all data sets combined. Fields with black background represent the information to be suppressed. Fields with a white background are the information that should remain in the data. RL is the proposed approach and GAN the same models trained supervised. As in Table 4, DP Raw and DP Image can only be used for subject information suppression. The best results are in bold.

Method	Stim	Sub	Data set
RL	**2.62%**	**32.74%**	**89.05%**
GAN	2.98%	29.81%	88.07%
RL	**27.56%**	**0.11%**	**87.56%**
GAN	26.94%	0.19%	86.01%
RL	**19.82%**	**29.91%**	**26.05%**
GAN	16.79%	26.77%	27.09%
RL	**2.40%**	**0.15%**	**75.98%**
GAN	2.81%	0.21%	71.50%
RL	2.37%	**29.56%**	**26.67%**
GAN	**2.31%**	25.99%	26.91%
RL	**17.79%**	**0.19%**	**26.17%**
GAN	16.07%	0.22%	26.48%
No Manipulation	39.39%	42.73%	92.57%
Chance	1.61%	0.08%	25.0%

stimulus information was mainly retained for all data sets. This shows, at least empirically, that our approach has found generalized patterns to hide specific information.

Table 4 shows the results for the GAN and RL approach to hiding the stimulus information. As in the previous experiment, the Auroencoder and the Manipulation Agent as well as the GAN was trained only on the ETRA data to evaluate the generalization across the data set. Compared to Table 3, the reverse case also works for the DOVES data set. This is because there is generally little stimulus information in this data set. It can also be seen that the RL and GAN approaches perform equally well on the ETRA data set. However, the RL approach is significantly better when it comes to cross-data set evaluation (data sets: Gaze, WPL, DOVES in Table 4).

For the last experiment we merged the data sets ETRA, Gaze, WPL, and DOVES. This allows us to classify the stimulus, the subject, and the data set, which allows us to suppress the information from multiple classification targets. As in the previous experiments, we performed a 50% to 50% split on training and validation data. For this experiment, the GAN as well as the autoencoder and manipulation agent were trained on all training data. Table 5 shows the results for the GAN and RL approach for hiding single and multiple classification targets. The black fields in Table 5 represent the information that should be suppressed and the white fields represent the information that should remain in the data. Thus, for all black fields, a low result is better and for white fields, a higher result is better. All in all the GAN and the RL approach are similarly good, whereas the RL approach is in most cases slightly better. This is especially true when suppressing multiple classification targets in the data.

4 Conclusion

In this work, we showed the applicability of reinforcement learning for removing personal information from eye tracking data. In addition, it can be used to hide specific information and is able to adapt to an adaptive attacker (Classification Agent in Fig. 1). Our approach is theoretically also capable of removing as well as preserving the information of multiple classification targets (Table 5). In Table 3 we empirically showed that our approach has generalized and is also applicable to unseen data sets.

References

1. Bednarik, R., Kinnunen, T., Mihaila, A., Fränti, P.: Eye-movements as a biometric. In: Kalviainen, H., Parkkinen, J., Kaarna, A. (eds.) SCIA 2005. LNCS, vol. 3540, pp. 780–789. Springer, Heidelberg (2005). https://doi.org/10.1007/11499145_79
2. Bovik, A., Cormack, L., Van Der Linde, I., Rajashekar, U.: Doves: a database of visual eye movements. Spat. Vis. **22**(2), 161–177 (2009)
3. Chaudhary, A.K., Pelz, J.B.: Privacy-preserving eye videos using rubber sheet model. In: ACM Symposium on Eye Tracking Research and Applications. ETRA 2020 Short Papers, Association for Computing Machinery, New York (2020). https://doi.org/10.1145/3379156.3391375
4. Dorr, M., Martinetz, T., Gegenfurtner, K.R., Barth, E.: Variability of eye movements when viewing dynamic natural scenes. J. Vis. **10**(10), 28–28 (2010)
5. Dwork, C.: Differential privacy: a survey of results. In: Agrawal, M., Du, D., Duan, Z., Li, A. (eds.) TAMC 2008. LNCS, vol. 4978, pp. 1–19. Springer, Heidelberg (2008). https://doi.org/10.1007/978-3-540-79228-4_1
6. Dwork, C.: A firm foundation for private data analysis. Commun. ACM **54**(1), 86–95 (2011)
7. Dwork, C., McSherry, F., Nissim, K., Smith, A.: Calibrating noise to sensitivity in private data analysis. In: Halevi, S., Rabin, T. (eds.) TCC 2006. LNCS, vol. 3876, pp. 265–284. Springer, Heidelberg (2006). https://doi.org/10.1007/11681878_14
8. Eberz, S., Rasmussen, K.B., Lenders, V., Martinovic, I.: Looks like eve: Exposing insider threats using eye movement biometrics. ACM Trans. Priv. Secur. (TOPS) **19**(1), 1 (2016)
9. Fan, L.: Differential privacy for image publication (2019)
10. Fuhl, W., et al.: Encodji: encoding gaze data into emoji space for an amusing scanpath classification approach. In: Eye Tracking Research and Applications (2019)
11. Goodfellow, I., et al.: Generative adversarial nets. In: Advances in Neural Information Processing Systems, pp. 2672–2680 (2014)
12. Judd, T., Ehinger, K., Durand, F., Torralba, A.: Learning to predict where humans look. In: IEEE International Conference on Computer Vision (ICCV) (2009)

13. Kasprowski, P., Ober, J.: Enhancing eye-movement-based biometric identification method by using voting classifiers. In: Biometric Technology for Human Identification II, vol. 5779, pp. 314–323. International Society for Optics and Photonics (2005)
14. Komogortsev, O.V., Holland, C.D.: Biometric authentication via complex oculomotor behavior. In: 2013 IEEE Sixth International Conference on Biometrics: Theory, Applications and Systems (BTAS), pp. 1–8. IEEE (2013)
15. Kunze, K., Kawaichi, H., Yoshimura, K., Kise, K.: Towards inferring language expertise using eye tracking. In: CHI 2013 Extended Abstracts on Human Factors in Computing Systems, pp. 217–222. ACM (2013)
16. Latif, N., Gehmacher, A., Castelhano, M.S., Munhall, K.G.: The art of gaze guidance. J. Exp. Psychol. Hum. Percept. Perform. **40**(1), 33 (2014)
17. Liebling, D.J., Preibusch, S.: Privacy considerations for a pervasive eye tracking world. In: Proceedings of the 2014 ACM International Joint Conference on Pervasive and Ubiquitous Computing: Adjunct Publication, pp. 1169–1177. ACM (2014)
18. Liu, A., Xia, L., Duchowski, A., Bailey, R., Holmqvist, K., Jain, E.: Differential privacy for eye-tracking data. arXiv arXiv:1904.06809 (2019)
19. Luong, N.C., et al.: Applications of deep reinforcement learning in communications and networking: a survey. IEEE Commun. Surv. Tutorials **21**(4), 3133–3174 (2019)
20. Maeder, A.J., Fookes, C.B.: A visual attention approach to personal identification (2003)
21. Majaranta, P., Bulling, A.: Eye tracking and eye-based human–computer interaction. In: Fairclough, S.H., Gilleade, K. (eds.) Advances in Physiological Computing. HIS, pp. 39–65. Springer, London (2014). https://doi.org/10.1007/978-1-4471-6392-3_3
22. McCamy, M.B., Otero-Millan, J., Di Stasi, L.L., Macknik, S.L., Martinez-Conde, S.: Highly informative natural scene regions increase microsaccade production during visual scanning. J. Neurosci. **34**(8), 2956–2966 (2014)
23. McSherry, F.D.: Privacy integrated queries: an extensible platform for privacy-preserving data analysis. In: Proceedings of the 2009 ACM SIGMOD International Conference on Management of Data, pp. 19–30 (2009)
24. Pyrgelis, A., Troncoso, C., De Cristofaro, E.: Knock knock, who's there? membership inference on aggregate location data. arXiv arXiv:1708.06145 (2017)
25. Rastogi, V., Nath, S.: Differentially private aggregation of distributed time-series with transformation and encryption. In: Proceedings of the 2010 ACM SIGMOD International Conference on Management of Data, pp. 735–746 (2010)
26. Sarathy, R., Muralidhar, K.: Evaluating laplace noise addition to satisfy differential privacy for numeric data. Trans. Data Priv. **4**(1), 1–17 (2011)
27. Steil, J., Hagestedt, I., Huang, M.X., Bulling, A.: Privacy-aware eye tracking using differential privacy. In: Proceedings of the 11th ACM Symposium on Eye Tracking Research & Applications, p. 27. ACM (2019)
28. Steil, J., Koelle, M., Heuten, W., Boll, S., Bulling, A.: Privaceye: privacy-preserving head-mounted eye tracking using egocentric scene image and eye movement features. In: ACM Symposium on Eye Tracking Research & Applications, ACM (2019)
29. Stellmach, S., Dachselt, R.: Look & touch: gaze-supported target acquisition. In: Proceedings of the SIGCHI Conference on Human Factors in Computing Systems, ACM (2012)
30. Zhang, Y., Hu, W., Xu, W., Chou, C.T., Hu, J.: Continuous authentication using eye movement response of implicit visual stimuli. Proc. ACM Interact. Mobile Wearable Ubiquit. Technol. **1**(4), 177 (2018)

Reinforcement Symbolic Learning

Chloé Mercier[(✉)], Frédéric Alexandre[(✉)], and Thierry Viéville[(✉)]

Mnemosyne Team, Inria Bordeaux, LaBRI and IMN, Bordeaux, France
{chloe.mercier,frederic.alexandre,thierry.vieville}@inria.fr

Abstract. Complex problem solving involves representing structured knowledge, reasoning and learning, all at once. In this prospective study, we make explicit how a reinforcement learning paradigm can be applied to a symbolic representation of a concrete problem-solving task, modeled here by an ontology. This preliminary paper is only a set of ideas while feasibility verification is still a perspective of this work.

Keywords: Reinforcement symbolic learning · Ontology edit distances · Models for learning sciences

1 Introduction

Understanding how humans solve problems and learn is a key issue in education, and one of the transversal competencies sometimes referred to as "21st-century skills". At the cognitive level, we need to consider both exploration and exploitation strategies directed either by a stimulus-driven behavior or toward different concurrent goals in a goal-driven behavior [1]. At a computational level, the typical paradigm is reinforcement learning (RL) with a final reward (success of the task) and some intermediate rewards (discoveries of affordances, partial result regarding the goal), more precisely intrinsically motivated reinforcement learning [9]. The latter family of models is extensively used in cognitive neurosciences to model high-level executive control functions (e.g., [2,8]).

In a recent development, we have introduced the operationalization of a creative problem-solving task, via the construction of an ontology[1] [6]. The state is defined by the configuration of the objects manipulated during the task and

[1] Concretely the ontology role is to help specifying the representation of the world as conceived by the learner, i.e., what is observed and what is to be inferred during the learning activity, to solve the task. This also helps to verify the specification coherence of the model, which allows us to infer some assumptions about non observable elements of the learning process, as detailed in the supplementary material accessible here https://gitlab.inria.fr/line/aide-group/creacog

Supported by Inria, AEx AIDE https://team.inria.fr/mnemosyne/en/aide.

I. Farkaš et al. (Eds.): ICANN 2021, LNCS 12894, pp. 608–612, 2021.
https://doi.org/10.1007/978-3-030-86380-7_49

some other observables regarding the learner[2]. The key point is that, in our case, the internal state of the subject and the external state of the task material constitute a complex structure, modeled here by a set of "statements"; that is to say, in the ontological vocabulary, entities typed by classes and linked together through relationships labeled by properties. Unlike usual mechanisms based on Markov chains, the state space to consider in our RL setup is thus not reduced to an unordered finite enumeration. We would like to study here to what extent reinforcement learning could be designed on such state spaces.

In "symbolic reinforcement learning" (e.g. [3]), deep neural networks transform raw perceptual data into a symbolic representation which is then fed to a symbolic module that might perform, for instance, action selection. Other approaches such as [4] propose architectures where a numerical reinforcement algorithm communicates with a reasoner. Here we would like to explore another track and make the reinforcement algorithm work directly on the symbolic data space itself in a more integrative way, which we propose to call "reinforcement symbolic learning".

2 Symbolic State Space Specification

General Framework: An agent interacts with its environment. At a given discrete time, it perceives a part of the environment, i.e., a stimulus, including a reward. It infers elements (e.g., causes) from this input cue, including the computation of the next action. In our case, we consider a potentially hypermnesic agent for which any previous input, including rewards, might be part of the internal state. This choice is directly linked to the notion of episodic memory, an episode here being represented by an event sequence (a list of times of occurrence of atomic events). This frees us from the "Markovian" constraint taking into account not just one step in the past, at the cost of a multiplicative increase of the state space. This is going to be manageable thanks to the hierarchical structure of our state space, which encompasses a lot of information without the need for an exhaustive enumeration. Furthermore, the state space no more reduces to a flat enumeration of state values, while the number of possible ontology construction of size S on a vocabulary if size V is an order of magnitude higher (i.e. roughly in $O(V^3\, S)$).

Input Structure: The input is a hierarchical data structure time sequence, with information regarding the task and the learner. Syntactically this corresponds to tuples of named values $\{\cdots, \texttt{name} : \texttt{value}, \cdots\}$; each value has a"type" (determined by a predefined schema[3] making explicit the value set), and may be either another tuple or a literal or the meta-value `undefined` (i.e., expected by the schema, but not present in the given context). Literal values are taken among a finite enumeration of qualitative values (e.g., a color set) or quantitative values (i.e., finite precision bounded values).

[2] See here for a video illustration.
[3] In the sense of https://json-schema.org.

Comparing Two Inputs: An input s is thus a tree data structure, equipped[4] with a *a partial semi-order* compatible with an *extended semi-distance*. This means that two values may be equal, indistinguishable (i.e., too close to be ordered, thus equal or not), comparable or incomparable (i.e., too different to be compared). This mechanism not only allows to define a distance between two inputs (as the minimal cost of editing sequences transforming one input into another), but also to make explicit which node has been added, deleted, or changed. Thus, it offers a "geodesic", i.e., a path of transformation from one structure to another, allowing us to interpolate intermediate input structure between both of them.

Inferring other Elements from Input: Each data structure is translated in terms of RDF statements as follows. Each tuple is a "subject" and each named value corresponds to a relationship labeled by a "property", the value being the "object" targeted by the relationship. This transformation allows us to generate an ontology[5], offering the possibility to perform inferences, thus implementing the learner behavior at a pure symbolic level. Conversely, each RDF ontology graph may be mapped back onto the data structure, with tuples having the value `undefined` if the corresponding statement is absent from the ontology after reasoning, and defined as the property object·s otherwise—hence the need for a pre-defined schema.

3 Reinforcement Learning on Symbolic State Space

Let us consider a concrete example on the most common algorithm setup, i.e., Q-learning with ϵ-greedy exploration, namely an action-state value function $Q : S \times A \rightarrow \mathbb{R}$. At each step this function is updated, using the weighted average of the old value and the new information, while the action is chosen to either maximize the reward value, given the state, or with a small probability randomly explore new actions. This algorithm is known as "model-free", however, we are using it in a non-conventional way with inferences we generate from prior information on symbolic states, bringing it somewhat closer to model-based algorithms.

The key point is that, given the largeness of the state space, each state value is very likely different from another, so that one state value is very likely visited once, making it impossible to use the usual update rule on tabulated values $Q[s_t, a_t]$. However, given a new state value s_t and reward r_{t+1}, we can easily update all preceding Q-values in a neighborhood.

---

[4] We consider *edit operations* given an input (l+) adding, (l-) deleting or (l#) changing a value in a list, (t+) defining, (t-) undefining or (t#) changing a value in a tuple, each of these operations having a user-defined positive cost, related to the literal extended semi-distances. The key point is that we consider restricted edit distances preserving the tree filiation, computable in polynomial time [7], which would not have been the case otherwise, or if considering the tree as a general graph or ontology portion.

[5] In the sense of RDF and OWL2.

Considering an exponential weighting of radius ρ, for a learning factor α, a discount factor γ, this writes, for all Q-values:

$$Q[s, a_t] += \alpha\, e^{-d(s,s_t)/\rho}\, (r_{t+1} + \gamma\, \max_a Q(s_{t+1}, a) - Q[s, a_t])$$

where $d(s, s_t)$ stands for the predefined edit distance between both states. During an epoch of T steps, it means that we have to compute $O(T^2)$ edit distances, and Q-value updates, but this complexity depends only on the trajectory length, rather than on the state space itself.

The computation of the maximum reward prediction $\max_a Q(s_{t+1}, a)$, requires to both (i) interpolate the Q-value given available tabulated values and (ii) enumerate action candidates, including unprecedented actions. For (ii) consider a set of potential actions a_k including previous actions, predefined prototypical actions, and putative actions generated by an external process. For (i) we can use an exponential interpolation

$$Q(s, a_k) = \sum\nolimits_{s_t, a_t} e^{-(d(s,s_t)+d(a_k,a_t))/\rho}\, Q[s_t, a_t] / \sum\nolimits_{s_t, a_t} e^{-(d(s,s_t)+d(a_k+,a_t))/\rho}.$$

in coherence with the previous design choice.

4 Conclusion

We have here all ingredients to apply well-established Q-learning mechanisms not only on an enumeration of indexed states, but on a rich semantic structure, which was the goal of this preliminary work. Meanwhile, in a companion study, we explore ways to map such a semantic structure onto a neuronal vector space [5]. We are making a prospective presentation here to share the scientific idea, it goes without saying that this is only an open issue to be developed.

References

1. Alexandre, F.: A global framework for a systemic view of brain modeling. Brain Inf. **8**(1), 3 (2021)
2. Domenech, P., Koechlin, E.: Executive control and decision-making in the prefrontal cortex. Curr. Opin. Behav. Sci. **1**, 101–106 (2015)
3. Garnelo, M., Arulkumaran, K., Shanahan, M.: Towards deep symbolic reinforcement learning. arXiv:1609.05518 [cs] (Oct 2016), arXiv: 1609.05518
4. Ma, Z., et al.: Interpretable reinforcement learning with neural symbolic logic. In: ICLR 2021: 9th International Conference on Learning Representations (2020)
5. Mercier, C., Chateau-Laurent, H., Alexandre, F., Viéville, T.: Ontology as neuronal-space manifold: towards symbolic and numerical artificial embedding. In: KRHCAI 2021 Workshop @ KR 2021: 18th International Conference on Principles of Knowledge Representation and Reasoning, Hanoi, Vietnam and/or Online, submitted (2021)
6. Mercier, C., Roux, L., Romero, M., Alexandre, F., Viéville, T.: Formalizing problem-solving in computational thinking : an ontology approach. In: ICDL 2021: IEEE International Conference on Development and Learning, Beijing, China (2021)

7. Ouangraoua, A., Ferraro, P.: A constrained edit distance algorithm between semi-ordered trees. Theor. Comput. Sci. **410**(8–10), 837–846. Elsevier (2009)
8. Rmus, M., McDougle, S.D., Collins, A.G.: The role of executive function in shaping reinforcement learning. Curr. Opin. Behav. Sci. **38**, 66–73 (2021)
9. Singh, S., Lewis, R.L., Barto, A.G., Sorg, J.: Intrinsically motivated reinforcement learning: an evolutionary perspective. IEEE Trans. Auton. Mental Dev. **2**(2), 70–82 (2010)

Deep Reinforcement Learning for Job Scheduling on Cluster

Zhenjie Yao[1,2,3(✉)], Lan Chen[1,2], and He Zhang[1,2]

[1] Institute of Microelectronics, Chinese Academy of Sciences, Beijing, China
{yaozhenjie,chenlan,zhanghe}@ime.ac.cn

[2] Beijing Key Laboratory of Three-dimensional and Nanometer Integrated Circuit Design Automation Technology, Beijing, China

[3] Purple Mountain Laboratory: Networking, Communications and Security, Nanjing, China

Abstract. Job scheduling is a key function of cluster computing. Efficient job scheduling can improve hardware resource utilization and promote the execution efficiency of jobs. Conventional scheduling work is dominated by heuristic algorithms. The scheduling efficiency of the heuristic algorithm is not optimal. In this paper, we improved the deep reinforcement learning algorithm for the cluster scheduling, which named DeepCM. Test results on the simulation data shows that the DeepCM is capable of improving the performance for job scheduling on the cluster. The slowdown could be improved from 2.248 to 2.235 in a environment of 3 machines. The fusion of internal baseline and external baseline could reduce the variations of the performance on different jobsets. The experimental results demonstrate that the deep reinforcement learning get improved scheduling efficiency in cluster computing. The performance advantage is more obvious when the load gets heavier.

Keywords: Deep reinforcement learning · Schedule · Cluster · Policy gradient · Fusion baseline

1 Introduction

In computing clusters, we can access the CPU, memory, storage, software and other resources of different physical machines through the network. Computing tasks could be completed more efficiently by efficient utilization of the resources in the clusters. The establishment, lease, and even maintenance of computing clusters are expensive. Therefore, efficient utilization of computing clusters is essential. For large clusters, a small increment in utilization efficiency can save millions of investment [2].

Task scheduling is to establish the mapping relationship between tasks and computing resources. Tasks and computing resources can have a one-to-many or

Supported by National key R & D program high performance computing project (2017YFB0203501).

I. Farkaš et al. (Eds.): ICANN 2021, LNCS 12894, pp. 613–624, 2021.
https://doi.org/10.1007/978-3-030-86380-7_50

many-to-one relationship. The essence of scheduling is a combinatorial optimization problem. The mapping relationship between tasks and resources is extremely complex, and finding the optimal task scheduling strategy is complex and difficult. The existing scheduling method is dominated by heuristic algorithms. Common heuristic algorithms include Shortest Job First (SJF), fairness-based algorithms [3,5], and resource matching-based algorithms (such as Tetris [4]). Park et al. suggested to take the runtime uncertainty into consideration, and gave an end-to-end strategy for job scheduling with uncertainty [10]. Heuristic algorithms have the advantages of easy understanding, easy implementation, and strong generalization, and are widely used in various distributed systems. However, due to the lack of in-depth analysis of tasks and resources, heuristic algorithms are not optimal. In some scenarios, the scheduling efficiency is low. Task scheduling in a distributed environment still has a lot of room for improvement, especially for some specific scenarios.

Reinforcement learning has been widely used for sequential decision making in an unknown environment, where the agent learns a policy to optimize a cumulative reward by trial-and-error interactions with the environment [14]. In the last decade, the introduction of deep learning technology has promoted the rapid development of reinforcement learning, and has achieved success in games [9,13] and other scenarios. Reinforcement learning can learn the experience during the interaction with the environment and make better decisions. Task scheduling itself is also a sequential decision-making process. A natural idea is whether reinforcement learning can be used to optimize task scheduling in a distributed environment. Mao et al. implemented a task scheduling algorithm using reinforcement learning, the entire cluster was simplified into a resource pool, and tasks were allocated to the resource pool [8]. Since the whole cluster is one resource pool, the key factor is to determine the order of the tasks. In the follow-up work, Mao et al. described task dependencies through Directed Acyclic Graph (DAG), and modeled it using graph convolutional neural networks. Then reinforcement learning was adopted to schedule the tasks [7]. Compared with the heuristic scheduling algorithms, reinforcement learning algorithm has achieved significant efficiency improvements on both simulated and real data sets, which verifies the effectiveness of reinforcement learning in task scheduling. Neither of the above two algorithms restricts the task flow and they are general scheduling algorithms. Another research direction is the scheduling of dedicated task streams, such as machine learning clusters. By modeling the convergence curve of the machine learning algorithms, Peng et al. can estimate the end time of various deep learning tasks accurately. Heuristic greedy strategy is used to allocate resources, the efficiency improved more than 60% [11]. In another algorithm DL2, Peng et al. used reinforcement learning, combined with off-line initialization training and on-line learning for training, and the performance was improved by 17.5% [12]. Bao et al. tested the degree of interference between different machine learning tasks, used reinforcement learning for task scheduling, which tried to put tasks with low mutual interference in one computing unit (one or several machines). Experimental results show that compared with the traditional heuristic scheduling algorithm, the performance of this algorithm is improved by more than 25% [1]. The results showed that reinforcement learning algorithms improve the performance of machine learning clusters. Wang et al. applied a deep-Q-network model in a multi-agent reinforcement learning setting to guide the scheduling of multi-workflows over infrastructure-as-a-service clouds, which shows better performance than traditional scheduling method [16].

In Mao's works [7,8], the entire cluster is abstracted into a resource pool without considering the boundaries of physical machines. In this paper, we follow their method, the main contributions of this paper are summarized as follows:

- Applying reinforcement learning-based scheduling algorithms to more practical clusters, which taking resource boundaries of physical machines into consideration, aiming to improve resource utilization of the computing cluster.
- We propose a fusion baseline strategy, which adopt a fusion of internal baseline and external baseline as the final baseline in policy gradient algorithm, to reduce the variations of the reinforcement learning model.

The remainder of this paper is organized as follows. Section 2 presents our deep reinforcement learning model for job scheduling on cluster, Deep Cluster Management (DeepCM), in detail. Section 3 covers the experimental results on a simulation environment. Finally, Sect. 4 gives conclusions and discusses future work.

2 Deep Reinforcement Learning for Job Scheduling on Cluster

As other Reinforcement Learning (RL) system, the Deep Reinforcement Learning system for Cluster management include 3 important parts: environment(represented by state), agent and reward, which are illustrated in Fig. 1(a).

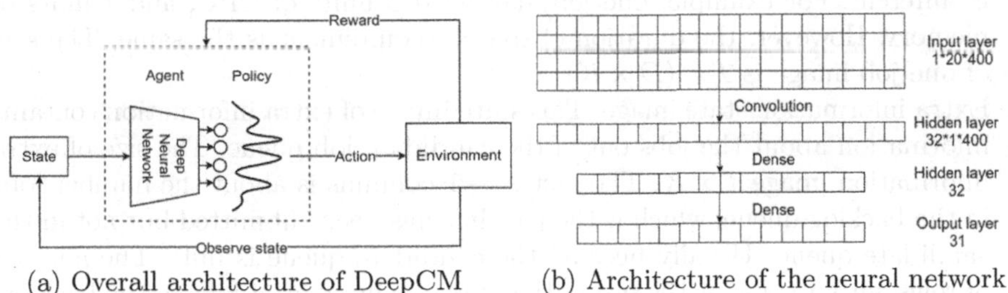

(a) Overall architecture of DeepCM (b) Architecture of the neural network

Fig. 1. System architecture of DeepCM and the architecture of the policy network.

2.1 RL Formulation for Schedule

In the application for job scheduling on cluster, the environment is the information about the jobs and the cluster. The state of the environment including the state of all the jobs that needed to schedule, and all the available resources on the nodes in the cluster. Suppose the cluster is composed of N nodes, each node contains D types of limited resources (CPU, memory, IO and disk etc.). As for the task, we suppose the resource and time requirement are known. The scheduling task is to allocate required resources of appropriate node to the jobs. **State.** The state of the system is represented by a big image composed of subimages. The subimages represent the state of candidate jobs, and nodes, and some extra information about job arriving time, and number of jobs out of the candidate queue. The image presentation of the system state is illustrated in Fig. 2. As show in the figure, the whole state image is composed by three kinds of subimages: subimage of machines, subimage of jobs and subimage of extra information. The state matrix representation is explained as follows.

1. Machine state image. Each machine image contains D images of different resources. In Fig. 2, one machine image of one resource was given for example. The size of subimage is $T \times K$, indicating the occupancy state of K units of resource in T timesteps. Each column of the image represents one unit of the resource, and each row represents a time step. The image contains the information about resource occupancy of the machine. The colored grid indicates that the resource has been occupied, which is represented by 1. The grids of the same color indicate that they are occupied by the same task. The white grids represent spare resources, represented by 0. The machine image is capable of representing the resource utilization of the machines. The size of one machine image is $T \times (D \times K)$
2. Job state image. A job stage image contains D subimages of different resources. The size of each subimage is $T \times K$, too. The colored grid indicates the resource and time the job required. For example, the job subimage in Fig. 2, the red square containing 2×2 grids, indicating executing this job require 2 units of this resource, and it will last for 2 timesteps. It should be pointed out that the amount of various resources required for the same job is different. For example, one job may need 3 units of CPU, and 1 units of memory. However, the duration of source requirement is the same. The size of one job image is $T \times (D \times K)$
3. Extra information state image. This state image of extra information contains information about the jobs out of the candidate job queue. The size of extra information image $T \times K$. The first $K - 1$ columns is about the number jobs in the backlog queue, which is the job that has been submitted but not in the candidate queue (Usually because the candidate queue is full). The number of rows with a value of 1 is proportional to the number of jobs in the backlog. The length of backlog is set to L_b, if N_b jobs in backlog, then the elements of the first $\lceil \frac{N_b}{L_b} \times T \rceil$ rows are set to 1. The blue part of the extra subimage indicates about 60% of the whole back queue are full. The last column is the number of timesteps past since last submitted job. The value of the whole column is $max(\frac{T_p}{T_w}, 1)$, where T_p is the number of timesteps past since last submitted job, T_w is a parameter.

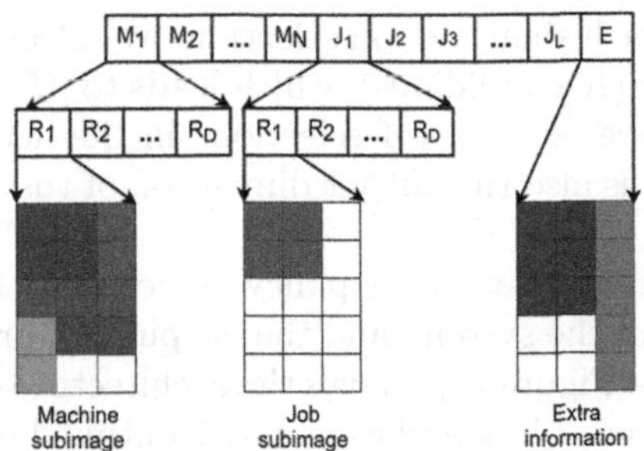

Fig. 2. Image representation of the state

Reward. Our goal is to minimize the average job slowdown. The job slowdown is defined by

$$S_j = \frac{C_j}{T_j}, \tag{1}$$

where C_j is the completion time of the job, which last from job submission to job completion, including four parts: the waiting time for entering the candidate queue, time in the candidate queue, waiting time on the scheduled machine, and time for execution. T_j is the ideal (minimum) duration of the job, including the time for execution only. It is easy to find that, $C_j > T_j$, so $S_j > 1$. The reward of each timestep is a piece of the negative slowdown, which defined as:

$$R_t = \sum_{j \in J_t} -\frac{1}{T_j}, \tag{2}$$

where J_t indicates all the jobs in the system at timestep t, including the job waiting for entering the candidate queue, the job in the candidate queue, the job scheduled on a machine (no matter it is waiting for execution or executing). The final cumulative reward is

$$R_c = \sum_{t=0}^{T_s} R_t = \sum_{t=0}^{T_s} \sum_{j \in J_t} -\frac{1}{T_j} = \sum_{j \in J} C_j \times (-\frac{1}{T_j}) = \sum_{j \in J} -\frac{C_j}{T_j}, \tag{3}$$

where R_c is the total cumulative reward of all the tasks in the T_s steps, J is the jobset of all the jobs during the T_s timesteps. The average job slowdown is defined as

$$R_a = -\frac{R_c}{|J|}, \tag{4}$$

where $|J|$ is the number of jobs in jobset J.

Agent. A reasonable schedule method should take multiple actions in one timestep. For simplicity, multiple action selection was achieved in a manner of repeat single action selections, only one action is selected at a time. Repeat the selection until a void action was selected. Suppose there are M candidate jobs and N machines. For each single action selection, we select a job (M candidates) and allocate a machine (N candidates), which leads to $M \times N$ selections and one void selection. There are $M \times N + 1$ selections in the action space for a single action selection, which is also the output dimension of the policy neural network shown in Fig. 1(a).

As shown in Fig. 1(a), the action policy is achieved by a neural network. The input is the state of the system, and the output is a probability distribution about potential actions. Figure 1(b) shows the architecture of the neural network, including the input layer, 2 hidden layers and 1 output layer.

Suppose there are 3 machines with 2 types of resources, each machine contains 10 units of either resources. At time step t, we can schedule job to $t+20$ timesteps. Under this setting, the number and size of the each layer are given in Fig. 1(b). The input layer has one input only, whose size is 20×400. The output of the convolution layer includes 32 feature maps with size of 1×400. The hidden layer as 32 neurons, with a dropout rate of 0.2. The output layer has 31 neurons with softmax activation, indicating the probability of 31 candidate actions.

2.2 Policy Gradient

We train the policy network with policy gradient descent algorithm [15]. As the name suggests, policy gradient means gradient descent of policy network. The policy neural network can be seen as a multi-class neural network. Its loss function is categorical cross-entropy. The goal of reinforcement learning is to maximize the expected cumulative reward, whose gradient is

$$\nabla E_{\pi_\theta}\left[\sum_{t=0}^{T} \gamma^t r_t\right] = E_{\pi_\theta}\left[\sum_{t=0}^{T} \nabla_\theta \log \pi_\theta(s, a) Q_\theta^\pi(s_t, a_t)\right], \tag{5}$$

where $Q_\theta^\pi(s_t, a_t)$ is the expected reward of choosing action a_t in state s_t. Its unbiased estimation obtained by Monte Carlo simulation [6] is denoted by $v_t = \widehat{Q_\theta^\pi(s_t, a_t)}$ and substitute v_t in (5), we have

$$\nabla E_{\pi_\theta}\left[\sum_{t=0}^{T} \gamma^t r_t\right] = E_{\pi_\theta}\left[\sum_{t=0}^{T} \nabla_\theta \log \pi_\theta(s_t, a_t) v_t\right], \tag{6}$$

The gradient can be decomposed into two terms, $\nabla_\theta \log \pi_\theta(s_t, a_t)$ is the gradient of conventional classification neural network, and v_t is the weight. As mention above, v_t is the expected reward of each step, we can find that the policy gradient is the conventional gradient weighted by reward. This is the key idea of policy gradient.

The policy gradient training algorithm was shown in Algorithm 1. There are J jobsets for training, each jobset run K episodes, which leads to K trajectories. Expected cumulative reward are estimated from the trajectories.

The cumulative reward has cumulative effect, which leads to heavy dependency on its time step. In order to reduce the significant difference caused by the position, a common trick of policy gradient algorithm is to adjust the rewards

Algorithm 1. Policy gradient training algorithm for cluster management

Initialize $\overrightarrow{b_e} = \overrightarrow{0.0}$
for each iteration **do**
  for each jobset $j = 1$ *to* J **do**
    for episode $k = 1$ *to* K **do**
      $\{s_1^k, a_1^k, r_1^k, s_2^k, a_2^k, r_2^k, ...s_{L_k}^k, a_{L_k}^k, r_{L_k}^k\} \sim \pi_\theta$
      Calculate returns: $v_t^k = \sum_{i=t}^{L_k} \gamma^{i-t} r_i^k$
    Calculate internal jobset baseline

$$\overrightarrow{b_a^j} = \frac{\sum_{k=1}^{K} \overrightarrow{v^j}}{K} \tag{7}$$

    Calculate jobset baseline

$$\overrightarrow{b^j} = \beta \overrightarrow{b_a^j} + (1 - \beta) \overrightarrow{b_e} \tag{8}$$

  Calculate the gradient of all the samples.

$$\triangle\theta = \nabla_\theta \log \pi_\theta(s, a)(v - b) \tag{9}$$

  Calculate **external jobset baseline**

$$\overrightarrow{b_e} = \frac{\sum_{i=1}^{J} \overrightarrow{b_a^j}}{J} \tag{10}$$

  $\theta \leftarrow \theta + \alpha \triangle \theta$

by subtracting the baseline, which is also used in [8]. The conventional baseline calculation is shown in (7), which is the average of different trajectories of the same jobset. We name it internal jobset baseline. The trajectories subtract the baseline as the reward. In the training process, we found that the differences between jobsets are also very large, and internal baseline adjustments cannot handle the difference.

We use the weighted average of the internal baselines of different jobsets as the external baseline between jobsets (10), and combine the external baseline in the last iteration and the internal baseline through linear combination (8). We use the combinational result as the final baseline for reward adjustment, expecting better learning performance. The introduction of an external baseline is a major improvement for policy gradient, and subsequent experimental results verify the effectiveness of this mechanism.

Gradients were calculate by (9), which is a cumulative gradient of all the samples in this iteration. The samples include all the trajectories of all the jobsets.

3 Experimental Results

This section contains the experimental results. First explain our test environment. Then compare the training procedure of the conventional and improved policy gradient model. Compare the schedule efficiency of our model with referenced models under different settings.

3.1 Environment Setting and Reference Models

In our setting, there are 1–3 machines in the cluster, each machine has 2 types of resources, both are divided into 10 units. Tasks are randomly generated as a batch, according to the same distribution, 20% tasks are long tasks, whose duration is uniformly from 10 to 15 timesteps. 80% of the tasks are short tasks, whose duration is from 1 to 3 timesteps. All the tasks have one dominant resource that is randomly selected. The dominant resource requirement is uniformly from 4 to 6 units of resource, and the other resource requirement is uniformly from 1 to 2 units of resource. The tasks submitted to the cluster with a probability of p_s, which is used for workload control. In the following experiments, we suppose one jobset contains 50 tasks for both training and testing.

The parameters involved in the training algorithm include: The discount parameter during cumulative reward calculation is $\gamma = 1.0$. The fusion parameter of internal baseline and external baseline β is set to 0.9. We train the network for 1000 or 1500 iterations, if the reward did not improve from the 900th to the 1000th iteration, it will stop at the 1000th iteration; Otherwise, it will stop at the 1500th iterations. Another important parameter is the learning rate, which is set to $lr = 0.003$ at the beginning, and recalculated every 30 iterations by $lr = \max(lr \times 0.8, 0.001)$.

We adopt 4 scheduling models as reference. Shortest Job First (SJF) is one of the best heuristic scheduling method. Take machines into consideration, there are two strategies for allocation: compact strategy, which allocate the job to the machine with highest resource utilization; and spread strategy, which allocate the job to the machine with lowest resource utilization. Combine SJF with compact and spread leads to SJF compact and SJF spread, together with Tetris [4] and DeepRM [8], there are the 4 reference models. Here, DeepRM was modified for cluster scheduling scenario.

Our DeepCM model has similar principle as DeepRM. However, the policy gradient algorithm is improved by a mechanism of fusion baseline, as mentioned in Algorithm 1.

3.2 Tests on Cluster with Different Number of Machines

In this part, we test the same workload on cluster with different number of machines. We set the workload control parameter $p_s = 0.8$. The number of machines is set to 1,2 and 3. Since 3 machines leads to almost no slowdown, we reduce each type of the resource on a machine from 10 units to 8 units.

The average slowdown is shown in Table 1. From the table, we can find that no matter how many machines are in the cluster, DeepCM and DeepRM achieve consistently better result than conventional heuristic methods. The performance of DeepRM is close to DeepCM. DeepCM is slightly better than DeepRM.

When there is only one machine, we have no choice, the 3 heuristic schedule models degrade to the SJF schedule. The average slowdown in the top 3 rows of the first column are the same.

Table 1. Average slowdown on cluster with different number of machines

Scheduling model	Average slowdown		
	1	2	3
SJF compact	2.833(±0.850)	1.260(±0.213)	1.147(±0.125)
SJF spread	2.833(±0.850)	1.263(±0.215)	1.149(±0.127)
Tetris	2.833(±0.850)	1.267(±0.201)	1.152(±0.130)
DeepRM	2.805(±0.846)	1.254(±0.206)	1.144(±0.128)
DeepCM	**2.773**(±0.839)	**1.245**(±0.178)	**1.143**(±0.125)

Compare the average slowdown on the same model with different number of machines, we find that the slowdown decreases as the number of machines increases. That is due to more resources are available as the number of machines increases. However, the performance improvement of DeepCM decrease as the machine number increase. When there is one machine, DeepCM outperforms the best heuristic model by 0.06, outperforms DeepRM by 0.032. When there are three machines, DeepCM outperforms the best heuristic model by 0.004, outperforms DeepRM by 0.001. We infer that as more machines get involved, resources are no longer tight, and the advantages of scheduling shrinks.

3.3 Tests Under Different Workloads

In this part, we fix the number of machines in cluster as 3, and test different workload on it. We set the workload control parameter p_s as 0.7, 0.8, 0.9 and 1.0. Each machine contains 8 units of each type of resources.

The average slowdown is shown in Table 2. From the table, we can find that no matter what value p_s is, DeepCM and DeepRM achieve consistently better result than conventional heuristic methods. The performance of DeepRM is close to DeepCM. DeepCM is slightly better than DeepRM.

Compare the average slowdown on the same model with different workload, we find that the slowdown increases as the workload increases. The performance improvement of DeepCM did increase as the workload increase. When the control parameter is 0.7, DeepCM outperforms the best heuristic model by 0.002, outperforms DeepRM by 0.001. When the control parameter is 1.0, DeepCM outperforms the best heuristic model by 0.019, outperforms DeepRM by 0.006.

Combined with the previous experimental results in Table 1, we can conclude that DeepCM can achieve better performance than conventional models, especially when the workload is heavy. Moreover, the heavier the workload, the greater performance gain can be achieved.

Table 2. Average slowdown of different workload

Scheduling model	Average slowdown			
	0.7	0.8	0.9	1.0
SJF compact	1.041(±0.042)	1.147(±0.125)	1.455(±0.265)	2.248(±0.133)
SJF spread	1.044(±0.050)	1.149(±0.127)	1.460(±0.264)	2.254(±0.139)
Tetris	1.045(±0.051)	1.152(±0.130)	1.459(±0.264)	2.254(±0.139)
DeepRM	1.040(±0.039)	1.144(±0.128)	1.450(±0.261)	2.241(±0.131)
DeepCM	**1.039**(±0.040)	**1.143**(±0.125)	**1.448**(±0.261)	**2.235**(±0.126)

Compared to scheduling on single resource pool, the scheduling on the cluster is more difficult, and we see that the improvement of DeepRM relative to the heuristic methods is small. DeepCM has further improved DeepRM. Although the numerical improvement is small, it is still important for cluster scheduling.

3.4 Benefits of the Fusion Baseline

We have seen that DeepCM has achieved better performance than conventional scheduling methods. In this section, we focus on the comparison between DeepCM and DeepRM, to demonstrate why the fusion baseline policy gradient works better than conventional policy gradient. We compared the training curve of the fusion baseline policy gradient and conventional policy gradient. Training curves of both algorithms are shown in Fig. 3. The red curve is the average slowdown of all the jobsets, the yellow region is 3σ (σ is the standard deviation) around the average curve, the blue curves are average slowdown of each jobset. The average slowdown is smoothed by moving average with 50 as the moving window width.

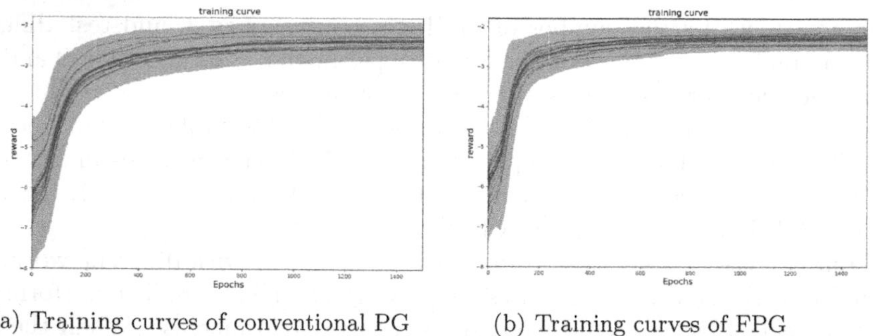

(a) Training curves of conventional PG

(b) Training curves of FPG

Fig. 3. Training curves. The red curve is the average slowdown of all the jobsets, the yellow region is 3σ (σ is the standard deviation) around the average curve, the blue curves are average slowdown of different jobset. The average slowdown is smoothed by moving average. (Color figure online)

Table 3. Statistics of the training curves

		Max	Min	Mean
PG	Mean	–2.369	–6.444	–2.812
	Std	0.692	0.157	0.218
FPG	mean	–2.300	–6.067	–2.611
	Std	0.646	0.093	0.156

Figure 3(a) is the training curves of conventional policy gradient (PG), Fig. 3(b) is the training curves of the fusion baseline policy gradient (FPG). Statistics of the training curves are listed in Table 3. By comparison, we can find that:

1. Compare the red curve in both figures. It is easy to find that the mean of rewards increase sharply at the beginning. As the training iterations increase, the growth rate decreases. Quantitatively, the average reward of PG increases from −6.444 to −2.369, while that of FPG increases from −6.067 to −2.300.
2. The curve of FPG increases more sharply than PG, PG reach −3 at 265th iteration, while FPG reach the same value at 147th iteration. Which means FPG can be trained more efficiently.
3. The standard deviation of PG is larger than that of FPG. The standard deviation of PG are reduce from 0.692 to 0.157, with mean value of 0.218. The standard deviation of FPG are reduced from 0.646 to 0.093, with mean value of 0.156.
4. By observing the blue curves, we find that the average reward on all jobsets of PG has no significant improvement after 700 iterations; while that of FPG has three significant improvements after 700 iterations, which leads to smaller deviation.

4 Conclusion and Future Works

In this paper, we improved the reinforcement learning based scheduling algorithm, and applied it for the cluster resource management, which named DeepCM. Test results on the simulation dataset shows that DeepCM is capable of improving the performance for job scheduling on the cluster, especially when the workload is heavy. Furthermore, the fusion of internal baseline and external baseline could reduce the variation of the performance on different jobsets, which makes the trained model more steady.

However, it is worth noting that, as the number of candidate jobs or the number of machines increases, both the state representation and the output dimension would increase sharply, which leads to bad scalability of the DeepCM. Poor scalability limits the application of deep reinforcement learning scheduling algorithms to large-scale clusters. In our further work, we would try to enhance the scalability of DeepCM and related algorithm.

Future work will include improving the performance of the reinforcement learning by incorporating more layers into the policy network, and considering more complex application scenarios, such as the inter dependency of the jobs, the actual resource occupation of the jobs, and the uncertainty of runtime estimation. Another possible direction is multi-objective optimization, which optimize cost, make-span and delay, etc. simultaneously.

References

1. Bao, Y., Peng, P., Wu, C.: Deep learning-based job placement in distributed machine learning clusters, pp. 505–513 (2019)
2. Barroso, L.A., Hlzle, U.: The datacenter as a computer: an introduction to the design of warehouse-scale machines. Synth. Lect. Comput. Archit. **8**(3), (2009). https://hadoop.apache.org/docs/current/hadoop-yarn/hadoop-yarn-site/FairScheduler.html
3. Ghodsi, A., et al.: Dominant resource fairness: Fair allocation of multiple resource types. In: Proceedings of the 8th USENIX Symposium on Networked Systems Design and Implementation (NSDI), vol. 11, pp. 323–336 (2011)
4. Grandl, R., Ananthanarayanan, G., Kandula, S., Rao, S., Akella, A.: Multi-resource packing for cluster schedulers. ACM SIGCOMM Comput. Commun. Rev. **44**(4), 455–466 (2014)
5. Hadoop, A.: Hadoop fair scheduler. http://hadoop.apache.org/common/docs/stable1/fair_scheduler.html (2014)
6. Hastings, W.K.: Monte carlo sampling methods using markov chains and their applications. Biometrika **57**(1), 97–109 (1970)
7. Mao, H., Schwarzkopf, M., Venkatakrishnan, S.B., Meng, Z., Alizadeh, M.: Learning scheduling algorithms for data processing clusters. In: Proceedings of the ACM Special Interest Group on Data Communication, pp. 270–288 (2019)
8. Mao, H., Alizadeh, M., Menache, I., Kandula, S.: Resource management with deep reinforcement learning. In: Proceedings of the 15th ACM Workshop on Hot Topics in Networks, pp. 50–56 (2016)
9. Mnih, V., et al.: Human-level control through deep reinforcement learning. Nature **518**(7540), 529–533 (2015)
10. Park, J.W., Tumanov, A., Jiang, A., Kozuch, M.A., Ganger, G.R.: 3sigma: distribution-based cluster scheduling for runtime uncertainty. In: Proceedings of the Thirteenth EuroSys Conference (2018)
11. Peng, Y., Bao, Y., Chen, Y., Wu, C., Guo, C.: Optimus: an efficient dynamic resource scheduler for deep learning clusters. In: Proceedings of the Thirteenth EuroSys Conference, pp. 1–14 (2018)
12. Peng, Y., et al.: Dl2: A deep learning-driven scheduler for deep learning clusters. In: arXiv preprint arXiv:1909.06040 (2019)
13. Silver, D., et al.: Mastering the game of go with deep neural networks and tree search. Nature **529**(7587), 484–489 (2016)
14. Sutton, R., Barto, A.: Reinforcement Learning: An Introduction. MIT Press, Cambridge (1998)
15. Sutton, R.S., Mcallester, D., Singh, S., Mansour, Y.: Policy gradient methods for reinforcement learning with function approximation. In: Advances in Neural Information Processing Systems, pp. 1057–1063 (1999)
16. Wang, Y., et al.: Multi-objective workflow scheduling with deep-q-network-based multi-agent reinforcement learning. IEEE Access **7**, 39974–39982 (2019)

Independent Deep Deterministic Policy Gradient Reinforcement Learning in Cooperative Multiagent Pursuit Games

Shiyang Zhou[1,2], Weiya Ren[1,2(✉)], Xiaoguang Ren[1,2], Yanzhen Wang[1,2], and Xiaodong Yi[1,2]

[1] Artificial Intelligence Research Center, Defense Innovation Institute, Beijing 100072, China
[2] Tianjin Artificial Intelligence Innovation Center, Tianjin 300457, China

Abstract. In this paper, we study a fully decentralized multi-agent pursuit problem in a non-communication environment. Fully decentralized (decentralized training and decentralized execution) has stronger robustness and scalability compared with centralized training and decentralized execution (CTDE), which is the current popular multi-agent reinforcement learning method. Both centralized training and communication mechanism require a large amount of information exchange between agents, which are strong assumptions that are difficult to meet in reality. However, traditional fully decentralized multi-agent reinforcement learning methods (e.g., IQL) are difficult to converge stably due to the dynamic changes of other agents' strategies. Therefore, we extend actor-critic to actor-critic-N framework, and propose Potential-Field-Guided Deep Deterministic Policy Gradient (PGDDPG) method on this basis. The agent uses the unified artificial potential field to guide the agent's strategy updating, which reduces the uncertainty of multi-agent's decision making in the complex and dynamic changing environment. Thus, PGDDPG which we proposed can converge fast and stably. Finally, through the pursuit experiments in MPE and CARLA, we prove that our method achieves higher success rate and more stable performance than DDPG and MADDPG.

Keywords: Reinforcement learning · Actor-critic · Potential field · Planning and learning · Predator-prey

1 Introduction

The goal of reinforcement learning (RL) is to maximize long-term returns, where a reward reflects the goal of a problem [18]. Thus, the reward is one of the core elements of RL. However, in the state-action space of many RL tasks, the reward value at any intermediate step is zero. This situation is referred to as the reward

S. Zhou and W. Ren—Contributed equally to this work.

I. Farkaš et al. (Eds.): ICANN 2021, LNCS 12894, pp. 625–637, 2021.
https://doi.org/10.1007/978-3-030-86380-7_51

sparsity problem and can cause an RL algorithm to converge slowly because an agent needs to interact with the environment many times and learn from a large number of samples to converge to the optimal solution.

Sparse rewards remain a great challenge in RL [5]. Recently, there is also substantial work in this area. Pathak, Deepak and Agrawal [12] have proposed an intrinsic curiosity mechanism to encourage agents to explore unknown states; however, the performance can be affected by randomness in the environment. In particular, there is more uncertainty caused by agents in multi-agents system. Prioritized replay buffer [15] and IGASIL [3] can replay important experiences more frequently, which enables more efficient learning. However, updating the priorities of experiences requires iterating over the buffer, which consumes considerable computing resources. In addition, this method cannot be extended to online algorithms. While the planning methods represented by artificial potential field and A* [8] only rely on environment model not the reward, which have been widely used in the traditional control field and are characterized by good stability and high sample utilization rate.

In multi-agent RL, some work make efforts to learn a communication protocol among multiple agents, such as ATOC [7], BiCNet [13]. The agents can make decisions dependent on delivering messages between each other. In reality, the problem of communication delay and bandwidth limitation hinder the application of these methods in practice. In addition, centralized training and decentralized execution is a very common paradigm, e.g., multi-agent deep deterministic policy gradient MADDPG [10]. While concentrated learning can be performed offline, the repeated process of collecting data is time consuming. Specifically, it is difficult to collect data offline, and communication is unstable and costly in practice. Therefore, these methods are more commonly used in simulators and video games [5]. Thus, a fully decentralized (decentralized training and decentralized execution) model is considered in IGASIL [3]. This approach does not require communication among the training and execution of agents, and has strong scalability and adaptability to complex environments.

Inspired by IGASIL [3], we also choose the fully distributed reinforcement learning model. At the same time, in order to solve the problem of multi-agent convergence, we combine a unified artificial potential field with deep deterministic policy gradient (DDPG) [9] through actor-critic-n framework, and propose the potential-field-guided DDPG (PGDDPG) and PGDDPG-EXP algorithm. Compared with the DDPG, MADDPG [10] and other methods in the MPE and CARLA environments, the PGDDPG performs better and is more stable. The code for this work is open source on the website (https://github.com/renweiya/PGddpg-conference).

The main contributions of this paper can be summarized as follows.

- We propose an Actor-Critic-N framework that can combine multiple critic methods and can be used in any value-based or Actor-Critic algorithm.
- We propose PGDDPG and PGDDPG-EXP algorithms guided by a unified artificial potential field, which can distribute training and distribute execution, and there is no need for communication between agents.

- Through MPE and CARLA experiments, it is proved that our method achieves better performance and more stable effect than DDPG and MADDPG.

2 Actor-Critic-N Framework

2.1 Actor-Critic-N

In order to combine the model based planning method with RL, firstly, we extend the actor-critic architecture to the **actor-critic-N** architecture, as shown in Fig. 1. We define Critic 1 based on rewards using deep function approximators. Critic 2, Critic 3, etc., can be defined using a model-based policy evaluation method. For simplicity, in this paper, we define Critic 2 based on potential fields and omit any other critics. We refer to it as actor-critic-2.

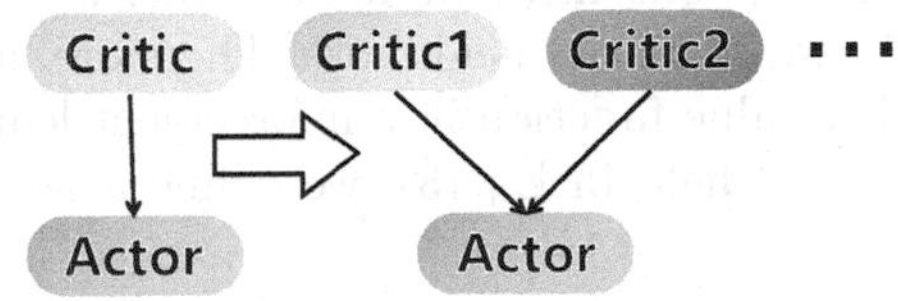

Fig. 1. Extension from the actor-critic framework to the actor-critic-N framework.

2.2 Classic Artificial Potential Field

The artificial potential field is a classical planning method, which assumes that the dynamic model of the environment is known. In this algorithm, the target and obstacle are regarded as objects with attractive force and repulsive force respectively, and the robot moves along resultant force of the attractive force and repulsive force.

In the classic artificial potential field method [14], the most commonly employed attractive potential function is

$$U_{att}(s) = \frac{1}{2}\xi d^2(s, s_{goal}) \tag{1}$$

where ξ is an attractive scaling factor and $d(s, s_{goal})$ is the distance between the point s and the goal s_{goal}.

The repulsive potential function is given by

$$U_{rep}(s) = \begin{cases} \frac{1}{2}\eta\left(\frac{1}{d(s,s_{obs})} - \frac{1}{d_0}\right)^2, & if \quad d(s, s_{obs}) \le d_0 \\ 0, & if \quad d(s, s_{obs}) > d_0 \end{cases} \tag{2}$$

where η is a repulsive scaling factor and d_0 is the maximum distance that can be affected by repulsion.

The overall potential function is given by

$$U(s) = U_{att}(s) + U_{rep}(s) \tag{3}$$

Then, the force of the artificial potential field can be calculated by $f = -\nabla U(s)$.

2.3 Potential-Field-Based Critic

The potential-field-based critic is to evaluate the current strategy of the agent from the perspective of artificial potential field. In other words, its function is to evaluate the degree of correlation between the agent's current actions (strategy) and the planned actions by the artificial potential field. In this paper, we consider that the larger the value of the artificial potential field is (the farther it is from the target or the closer it is to the obstacle), the more prior information it contains, and at this time, we should trust the planned actions of the artificial potential field more. Therefore, according to the definition of the state action value function in reinforcement learning and combined with the artificial potential field in Eq. (3), we define a *potential-field-based state-action function* as

$$q_{PF}(s,a) \triangleq -U(s)[1 - cos(\mathcal{X})]. \tag{4}$$

where $\mathcal{X}$ is the angle between the overall force $f = -\nabla U(s)$ and the actual action generated by the action policy in state s, as shown in Fig. 2.

It can be seen that as $U(s) \to +\infty$, $q_{PF}(s,a) \in [0, +\infty)$, while as $U(s) \to 0$, $q_{PF}(s,a) \to 0$.

Accordingly, $q_{PF}(s,a)$ will have a more important role when the potential value is larger, and vice versa. The overall force $f = -\nabla U(s)$ is the basis for the simplest possible single-step planning method based on the (artificial) potential field approach. More complex planning methods can be considered, but they are not the focus of this paper.

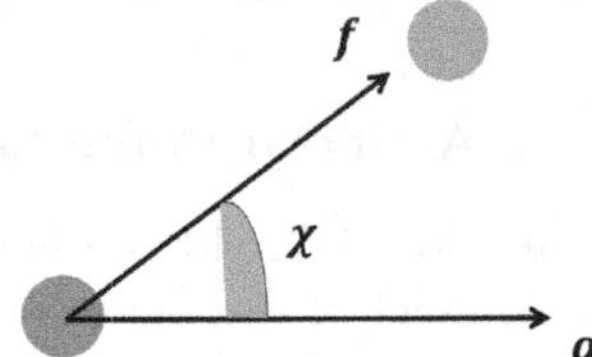

Fig. 2. A description of parameters in the potential-field-based state-action function. $\mathcal{X}$ is the angle between the overall force f and the actual action a.

Via the potential-field-based state-action function that we previously defined, we can obtain the potential-field-based critic as

$$Q^{\mu}_{PF}(s,a) \triangleq E\left[\sum_{k=1}^{\infty} \gamma_2^{k-1} q_{PF}(s_k, a_k)|s_1 = s, a_1 = a\right], \tag{5}$$

which is named **critic 2** in this paper.

Because the force calculation is the same for all agents in the artificial potential field based critic 2, we also refer to it as a **unified** artificial potential field based guidance in this paper. Each agent uses the unified artificial potential field to guide the agent's strategy update. This unified artificial potential field is known to all agents. Through the calculation of the unified artificial potential field, the agent can get the actions of other agents under the unified artificial potential field (in this paper, we call it the planned actions). That is to say, when the planned actions of agents guides its strategy update, they can also be obtained by other agents through calculation (not communication), which reduces the uncertainty of multi-agents in making decisions in the complex and dynamic changing environment and enables faster and more stable convergence of the algorithm.

3 Potential-Field-Guided Deep Deterministic PolicyGradient(PGDDPG) Approach

The actor-critic-2 framework which we designed in Sect. 2 is a combination of model-based and model-free gradients for policy improvement. A state with a large potential field often contains strong prior information, such as information pointing toward the target from a long distance or information for avoiding collision by bypassing an obstacle. In this situation, we should place more trust in the policy evaluation of the potential-field-based critic to accelerate policy improvement by guiding the action policy. For example, in practical applications, obstacle avoidance should be learned via guidance rather than by trial and error. In contrast, states with small potential fields, for example, at a local minimum point or near a moving target, often lack useful information [16]. In this case, we should place more trust in the policy evaluation of the reward-based critic to evaluate the long-term return, which will tend to encourage exploration of the action policy space. Based on these considerations, we combine the DDPG with the unified artificial potential field, which can be referred to as the PGDDPG. Then we extend it to PGDDPG-EXP(explicit).

3.1 PGDDPG

First, we consider the deterministic policy $\mu_\theta : \mathcal{S} \rightarrow \mathcal{A}$ with the parameter vector $\theta \in R^n$. The reward function is denoted by $r(s, a)$, and the density of the initial state distribution is denoted by $p_1(s)$. The density in state s' after transitioning for t time steps from state s is denoted by $p(s \rightarrow s', t, \pi)$. The (improper) discounted state distribution is denoted by

$$\rho^\mu(s', \gamma) = \int_S \sum_{t=1}^{\infty} \gamma^{t-1} p_1(s) p(s \rightarrow s', t, \pi) \mathrm{d}s, \tag{6}$$

where γ is the discount parameter.

Consider the actor-critic-2 framework and the following objective function

$$\begin{aligned} J(\mu_\theta) = \beta \int_S \rho^\mu(s, \gamma_1) r(s, \mu_\theta(s)) \mathrm{d}s \\ + (1-\beta) \int_S \rho^\mu(s, \gamma_2) q_{PF}(s, \mu_\theta(s)) \end{aligned} \tag{7}$$

where β is a parameter. When $\beta = 1$, the algorithm becomes the classic DPG [17] algorithm. The first part of the formula is the reward-based critic, and the second part of the formula is the potential-field-based critic. Note that these two critics have different discount parameters.

According to the DPG theorem and Eq. (5), we know that

$$\begin{aligned}\nabla_\theta J(\mu_\theta) = \beta E_{s\sim\rho^\mu(s,\gamma_1)}[\nabla_\theta\mu_\theta(s)\nabla_a Q_R^\mu(s,a)|_{a=\mu_\theta(s)}] \\ + (1-\beta)E_{s\sim\rho^\mu(s,\gamma_2)}[\nabla_\theta\mu_\theta(s)\nabla_a Q_{PF}^\mu(s,a)|_{a=\mu_\theta(s)}]\end{aligned} \tag{8}$$

where

$$Q_R^\mu(s,a) \triangleq E\left[\sum_{k=1}^{\infty}\gamma_1^{k-1}r(s_k,a_k)|s_1=s,a_1=a\right]. \tag{9}$$

With the introduction of the function approximator $Q^w(s,a)$, the gradient $\nabla_a Q_R^\mu(s,a)$ can be replaced by $\nabla_a Q^w(s,a)$. Note that γ_1 is usually set to a value near 1, such as $\gamma_1 = 0.99$, as the long-term reward is highly important. However, we can simply set $\gamma_2 \to 0$ as the potential field can work even without a long-term expectation. Then, $\nabla_a Q_{PF}^\mu(s,a)$ can be simply replaced by $\nabla_a q_{PF}(s,a)$ in Eq. (8).

It is important to note that even if set $\gamma_2 \to 0$, $\nabla_a q_{PF}(s,a)$ does not participate in the update of the $Q^w(s,a)$, which is substantially different from reward shaping(RS). Experiments show that our method is superior to RS. Besides $q_{PF}(s,a)$ can also be updated if we assign it a parameter. Different values of the parameter β yield different results. In this paper, we preset it to a fixed value ($\beta = 0.8$), but it can also be learned dynamically or decrease with an increasing number of training episodes.

3.2 PGDDPG-EXP (explicit)

In a non-communication environment, it is very important to simultaneously predict the actions of teammates for cooperation, as the use of such joint actions is also the main idea of Centralized Training Decentralized Execution (CTDE). Decentralized RL means that the real-time actions of other agents cannot be obtained even during the training phase.

In the PGDDPG, different agents have the same artificial potential field module, and agents calculate the potential field value in the same way, which can be regarded as a kind of internal prior knowledge that connects all agents. Based on this relationship, each agent can simultaneously calculate the planned actions of other agents. Based on the unified artificial potential field planning among agents, each agent can calculate the planned actions of other agents by its observation state. If we explicitly calculate the planned actions of teammates and add them to the agent's observation state, we can increase the amount of cooperative information and promote the cooperation among teammates. This method is referred to as PGDDPG-EXP.

Specifically, we define a extended states

$$\overline{s_t} = (s_t, a_1', \ldots, a_j', \ldots, a_n') \tag{10}$$

and replace the original s_t as the input to the neural network, extending the agent's observation. a_j' is a planned action of agent j, which can be calculated

Algorithm 1: PGDDPG-EXP algorithm

Randomly initialize policy network $\mu(s|\theta)$ and critic 1 network $Q(s,a|w)$ with weight θ and w
Initialize target network Q' and μ' with weight $w' \leftarrow w, \theta' \leftarrow \theta$
Initialize replay buffer R
for *episode = 1,M* **do**
  Initialize a random process $\mathcal{N}$ for action exploration
  Receive initial observation state s_1
  for *t=1,T* **do**
    Select action $a_t = \mu(s_t|\theta) + \mathcal{N}_t$ according to the current policy and exploration noise
    Execute action a_t and observe reward r_t and new state s_{t+1}
    Calculate $\overline{s_t}$ and $\overline{s_{t+1}}$ according to Eq. (3, 10)
    Store transition $(\overline{s_t}, a_t, r_t, \overline{s_{t+1}})$ in R
    Sample a random mini batch of N transitions $(\overline{s_i}, a_i, r_i, \overline{s_{i+1}})$ from R
    Set $y_i = r_i + \gamma Q'(\overline{s_{i+1}}, \mu'(\overline{s_{i+1}}|\theta')|w')$
    Update critic 1 by minimizing the loss: $L = \frac{1}{N}\sum_i (y_i - Q(\overline{s_i}, a_i|w))^2$
    Calculate the value of critic 2 by Eq. (4, 5)
    According to Eq. (8), update the actor policy by:

$$\nabla_\theta J(\mu_\theta) = \frac{1}{N}\sum_i \nabla_\theta \mu(\overline{s_i}|\theta)[\beta \nabla_a Q(\overline{s_i}, a_i|w) + (1-\beta)\nabla_a Q^{\mu}_{PF}(\overline{s_i}, a_i)]$$

    Update the target networks by:

$$\theta' \leftarrow \tau\theta + (1-\tau)\theta'$$
$$w' \leftarrow \tau w + (1-\tau)w'$$

  end
end

by $p(s_t)$. In this paper, the function $p()$ is based on the artificial potential field, which can be represented in Eq. (3). The value of $\overline{s_t}$ also depends on the original states s_t. However, by explicitly representing the planned actions of other agents, the artificial potential field reduces the environmental uncertainty produced by the strategies of other agents. In this way, the effect of the artificial potential field can be better mined, and the algorithm can converge more quickly and stably. The pseudo code of PGDDPG-EXP is elaborated in Algorithm 1.

4 Experimental Results

4.1 Predator-Prey Game with MPE

To evaluate the effectiveness of the proposed approach, we introduce a predator-prey game based on OpenAI's Multi-Agent Particle Environments (MPE) [10]. The goal of the predator is to catch prey **simultaneously** as quickly as possible, while the goal of the prey is to survive as long as possible. The game ends when the predator catches the prey or reaches the maximum number of steps.

A predator's maximum speed is 0.5, while the prey's maximum speed is 0.7. To highlight a larger map, the areas of the predators and prey are relatively small. The environmental rewards are sparse (a reward of +10 is earned for success) and depend only on the terminal state of each episode.

Environment and Baselines. We consider that N predators (3 predators in this paper) chase one prey in a randomly generated environment. Each predator independently learns to capture the prey, without knowing the others' policies or actions, in both training and testing. When all predators capture the prey **simultaneously**, each predator will receive a reward of +10. As long as any predator fails to catch the prey, no reward will be given to all predators. Because of the large search space and intelligence of the prey, this situation is a difficult learning problem that requires excellent tacit cooperation. Both the pure DDPG algorithm and the pure MADDPG algorithm completely fail (success rates = 0.0). In accordance with [4,11,19], by experimental comparison, we choose the best reward-shaping method, as shown in Eq. (11), which includes the change in distance and the angle between the velocity vector and the vector that points to the prey. We have also tested many other methods, including methods based on the minimum distance to the prey, in an attempt to design an effective reward-shaping function, which has been utilized in the original MPE environment. However, none can perform better than Eq. (11):

$$r_{rs} = (d_{last} - d_{now}) * \alpha * cos\theta \tag{11}$$

where r_{rs} represents the shaped reward and d_{last} and d_{now} represent the distance to the prey in the last episode and the distance to the prey in the current episode, respectively. θ is the angle between the velocity vector and the vector that points to the prey. α is a hyperparameter.

Different hyperparameter values yield different performances. Via experiments, we selected the hyperparameters with the best performance for each algorithm: $\alpha = 1$ for DDPG, $\alpha = 5$ for MADDPG and $\beta = 0.8$ for PGDDPG. Due to page limitations, analysis of the differences in performance with different hyperparameters are moved to additional material[1].

Train with Different Seeds and Preys. In this experiment, we consider ten pretrained smart prey named prey-00 to prey-09, which are pretrained models from previous battles. We consider the DDPG algorithm and MADDPG algorithm as baselines for comparison with the proposed PGDDPG algorithm. In DDPG and PGDDPG, both the predators and prey have independent observations only and do not know the actions of the other agents (except in the MADDPG algorithm, which requires observations and actions of other agents).

First, we trained DDPG (reward shaping), MADDPG (reward shaping) and PGDDPG with ten pretrained prey using the previously mentioned parameters. Each model was trained for 40,000 rounds. In Fig. 3(left), we plot the success rate

[1] https://github.com/zhoushiyang12/pgddpg.git.

(rate of successful capture based on the latest 100 episodes) for all algorithms on one graph, from which we can easily compare the convergence rate of each algorithm. (Note that to make the curves smoother, we have smoothed the values across five adjacent points; which is also valid in subsequent figures.) After training, we applied the final trained model to run 1,000 rounds of confrontation with each prey, and the average number of steps and the success rate are recorded in Table 1. From these results, we determine that only the PGDDPG achieves a success rate of 1.0 for all ten prey, and it requires the lowest average number of steps to successfully catch the prey. The PGDDPG achieves satisfactory performance for all ten prey in terms of both the convergence rate and the final performance.

Different random seeds can have different performances. Therefore, we randomly selected ten seeds from the range of 0–1,000 to re-train each algorithm (versus prey-00). Different algorithms behave differently with different seeds, but the results are relatively concentrated. The rates of successful capture are shown in Fig. 3(right). We determine that even if we train each algorithm multiple times with different seeds, the performance gaps between two algorithms are still significant.

Table 1. Average number of steps taken to successfully capture prey and the rates of successful capture for each algorithm when the final trained model runs 1,000 rounds of confrontation with each prey in the predator-prey game with MPE.

Algorithms	Metric	Prey-00	Prey-01	Prey-02	Prey-03	Prey-04	Prey-05	Prey-06	Prey-07	Prey-08	Prey-09
DDPG(RS)	Success rate	0.177	0.994	0.944	0.954	**1.000**	**1.000**	0.999	0.968	0.996	0.996
	Average step cost	182.184	75.853	101.150	84.730	81.616	65.149	72.148	84.497	62.999	74.116
MADDPG(RS)	Success rate	0.764	0.998	0.930	0.996	0.946	0.998	0.996	0.959	0.997	0.978
	Average step cost	116.627	65.304	78.630	71.281	93.840	65.224	64.648	83.250	70.005	75.282
PGDDPG	Success rate	0.996	**1.000**	**0.999**	**0.999**	**1.000**	**1.000**	**1.000**	**0.999**	**1.000**	**1.000**
	Average step cost	71.432	**56.004**	57.718	61.470	**61.531**	**53.840**	59.347	62.813	**54.002**	**53.400**
PGDDPG_EXP	Success rate	**0.999**	0.999	0.997	**0.999**	0.999	**1.000**	0.996	0.995	0.999	0.996
	Average step cost	**59.700**	57.032	**53.819**	**59.065**	62.228	54.827	**58.891**	**62.638**	55.473	55.732

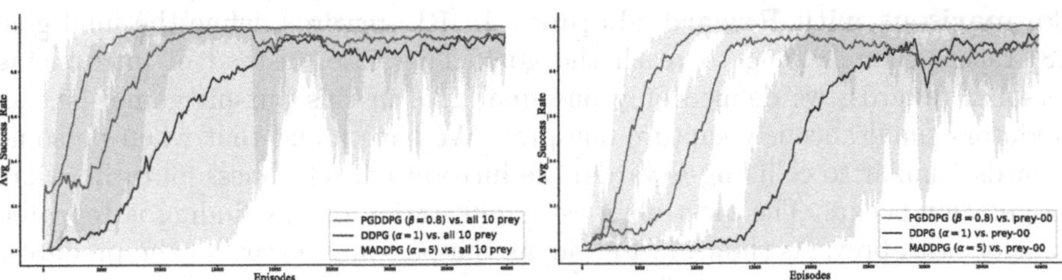

Fig. 3. left) The rates of successful capture for the PGDDPG ($\beta = 0.8$), DDPG ($\alpha = 1$), and MADDPG ($\alpha = 5$) in the predator-prey game with MPE. Each algorithm was individually trained on all ten prey. To clearly show the differences between different algorithms, we use different colours to represent different algorithms. The solid line represents the mean, while the shadow represents the variance. **right)** The rates of successful capture for each algorithm when trained with 10 different seeds in the predator-prey game with MPE. The red curves correspond to the PGDDPG ($\beta = 0.8$), the green curves correspond to MADDPG ($\alpha = 5$), and the blue curves correspond to DDPG ($\alpha = 1$). (Color figure online)

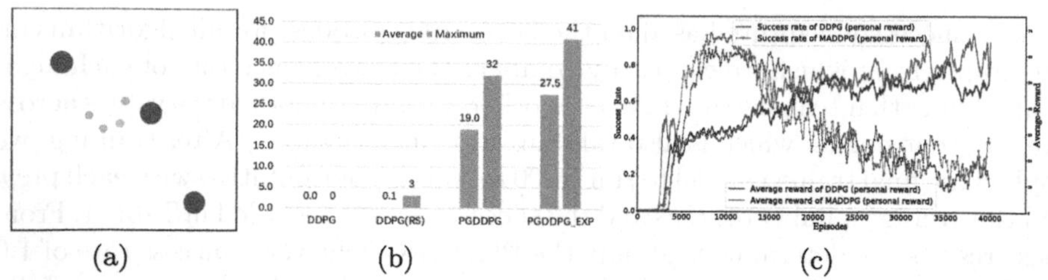

(a) (b) (c)

Fig. 4. a) The MPE environment with 3 obstacles. **b)** The number of successful capture (cooperation) for algorithms over 2,000 steps. **c)** In the predator-prey game with MPE, a personal reward of +1 is given even if only one agent catches the prey (an intermediate event before the final state). The dashed lines correspond to the average rewards for the DDPG and MADDPG with personal rewards. The solid lines correspond to the rates of successful capture for the DDPG and MADDPG with personal rewards.

Ablations. In this experiment, we randomly added 3 obstacles (size = 0.1) to increase the complexity of the environment. In order to test the contribution of reward shaping, artificial potential field guidance and explicit representation of planned actions to performance, we establish DDPG, DDPG(RS), PGDDPG and PGDDPG-EXP for comparison.

We trained 40,000 rounds of each algorithm to obtain the respective model and then utilized these models to separately hunt the prey. The prey is regenerated at a random location every time it is caught. We count the number of successful captures (cooperation) for each algorithm over 2,000 steps, as shown in Fig. 4b. With only final reward, environmental rewards are very sparse. Pure DDPG without RS completely fails. By comparing the experimental results of different algorithms, we can see that the guidance of artificial potential field plays an important role in improving the effect.

Comparisons with Reward Shaping. In RL, rewards define the final goal [18] rather than helping to reach the goal. Therefore, instead of introducing personal rewards, we defined only one final goal in this pursuit game; i.e., all predators simultaneously capture one prey. We have found that when personal rewards (similar to colliding rewards) are introduced, selfishness [6] rather than cooperation occurs. The most obvious manifestation of this finding is repeated collision with prey. As shown in Fig. 4c, as the personal reward of the predators increases, the success rate declines.

By comparing DDPG, MADDPG, DDPG (reward shaping), MADDPG (reward shaping), DDPG (personal reward), and MADDPG (personal reward), we observe that the proposed PGDDPG algorithm performs the best among all tested algorithms. That shows the beneficial effect of planning on learning.

4.2 Predator-Prey Game with CARLA

We employed the Open Urban Driving Simulator (CARLA) [2] to build a multi-car chase environment. This simulator uses the UE4 simulation engine to create a more realistic environment with more uncertainty and more complex states. First, we built an empty map with dimensions of 150 m * 150 m and placed four walls around it. Second, we set the predators (blue) and prey (red), as shown in Fig. 5a. Each car has a throttle action [0, 1], steering action [-1, 1] and braking action [0, 1] for control and four RGB cameras that point in four different directions. Similar to the reward settings in MPE, only if the three predators catch the prey **simultaneously** can they obtain a reward of +10. In these experiments, we utilized a pretrained smart prey named prey-a and trained predators with the PGDDPG, DDPG, MADDPG, and DDPG (reward shaping).

Compared to the predator-prey game with MPE, the input to the predator-prey game with CARLA is very large. Although we employed Xception [1] as a preprocessing model, 2,048 dimensions were still required for the four RGB images captured by each agent. For multiple agents, the input to MADDPG increases linearly with the number of agents. Such a large input presents an enormous challenge for the updating and training of neural networks. The MADDPG completely fails (success rate = 0.0) in this environment, and the pure DDPG algorithm with very sparse rewards also fails. The learning curves of the DDPG (reward shaping with Eq. (11)) and PGDDPG are displayed in Fig. 5b.

In this complex environment, the PGDDPG can still use the actor-critic-N framework to correctly utilize planning information and successfully accomplish tasks. This result is promising, as the real world is much more complicated than even this environment.

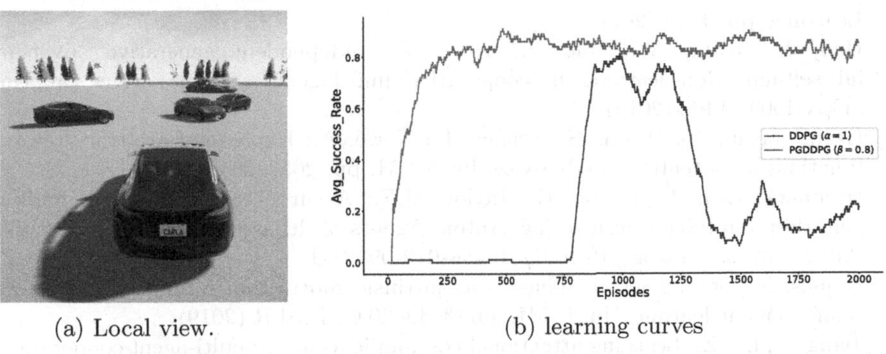

(a) Local view. (b) learning curves

Fig. 5. a) Illustrates 3-vs.-1 predator-prey game with CARLA. The blue agents are predators, and the red agent is the prey. **b)** is the rates of successful capture for PGDDPG ($\beta = 0.8$) and DDPG ($\alpha = 1$) in the predator-prey game with CARLA. PGDDPG ($\beta = 0.8$) converges faster and is more stable than DDPG ($\alpha = 1$). (Color figure online)

5 Conclusion and Future Work

In this paper, we extend the actor-critic architecture to the actor-critic-N architecture by introducing model-based policy evaluation methods. We focus on the actor-critic-2 framework and combine a reward-based critic with a potential-field-based critic for policy improvement. We place more trust in the potential-field-based critic to guide the action policy to accelerate learning when the potential field value is relatively large, whereas we place more trust in the reward-based critic to explore the action policy space and evaluate the long-term return when the potential field value is relatively small. With this approach, reward design can focus more on the final stage of the game rather than reward shaping or phased rewards. The experiments show that the PGDDPG method based on single agent RL reduces the search space with the advantages of two critics, which can not only avoid the communication problem among agents but also effectively accelerates the convergence of policy. Potential field evaluation can also compensate for a lack of communication in multiagent cooperation in both training and testing. More planning methods based on the potential field approach will also be investigated in the future. In addition, the design of the attractive and repulsive potentials is important; for example, if we have multiple goals, we might consider the minimal attractive potential generated by them.

References

1. Chollet, F.: Xception: deep learning with depthwise separable convolutions. In: CVPR (July 2017)
2. Dosovitskiy, A., Ros, G., Codevilla, F., Lopez, A., Koltun, V.: CARLA: an open urban driving simulator. In: Proceedings of the 1st Annual Conference on Robot Learning, pp. 1–16 (2017)
3. Hao, X., Wang, W., Hao, J., Yang, Y.: Independent generative adversarial self-imitation learning in cooperative multiagent systems. arXiv preprint arXiv:1909.11468 (2019)
4. Harutyunyan, A., Devlin, S., Vrancx, P., Nowé, A.: Expressing arbitrary reward functions as potential-based advice. In: AAAI, pp. 2652–2658 (2015)
5. Hernandez-Leal, P., Kartal, B., Taylor, M.E.: A survey and critique of multiagent deep reinforcement learning. Auton. Agents Multi-agent Syst. **33**(6), 750–797 (2019). https://doi.org/10.1007/s10458-019-09421-1
6. Jaques, N., et al.: Social influence as intrinsic motivation for multi-agent deep reinforcement learning. In: ICML, pp. 3040–3049. PMLR (2019)
7. Jiang, J., Lu, Z.: Learning attentional communication for multi-agent cooperation. CoRR abs/1805.07733 (2018). http://arxiv.org/abs/1805.07733
8. LaValle, S.M.: Planning Algorithms. Cambridge University Press (2006)
9. Lillicrap, T.P., et al.: Continuous control with deep reinforcement learning. arXiv preprint arXiv:1509.02971 (2015)
10. Lowe, R., Wu, Y., Tamar, A., Harb, J., Abbeel, P., Mordatch, I.: Multi-agent actor-critic for mixed cooperative-competitive environments. In: NIPS (2017)
11. Ng, A.Y., Harada, D., Russell, S.: Policy invariance under reward transformations: theory and application to reward shaping. In: ICML, vol. 99, pp. 278–287 (1999)

12. Pathak, D., Agrawal, P., Efros, A.A., Darrell, T.: Curiosity-driven exploration by self-supervised prediction. In: Proceedings of the IEEE Conference on Computer Vision and Pattern Recognition Workshops, pp. 16–17 (2017)
13. Peng, P., et al.: Multiagent bidirectionally-coordinated nets: Emergence of human-level coordination in learning to play StarCraft Combat Games. arXiv preprint arXiv:1703.10069 (2017)
14. Radmanesh, M., Kumar, M., Guentert, P.H., Sarim, M.: Overview of path-planning and obstacle avoidance algorithms for UAVs: a comparative study. Unmanned Syst. **6**(02), 95–118 (2018)
15. Schaul, T., Quan, J., Antonoglou, I., Silver, D.: Prioritized experience replay. arXiv preprint arXiv:1511.05952 (2015)
16. Siddiqui, R.: Path planning using potential field algorithm. Medium (July 2018)
17. Silver, D., Lever, G., Heess, N., Degris, T., Wierstra, D., Riedmiller, M.: Deterministic Policy Gradient Algorithms (2014)
18. Sutton, R.S., Barto, A.G.: Reinforcement Learning: An Introduction. MIT Press, Cambridge (2018)
19. Xie, L., et al.: Learning with Stochastic guidance for navigation. arXiv preprint arXiv:1811.10756 (2018)

Avoid Overfitting in Deep Reinforcement Learning: Increasing Robustness Through Decentralized Control

Malte Schilling(✉)

Machine Learning Group, Bielefeld University, 33501 Bielefeld, Germany
mschilli@techfak.uni-bielefeld.de

Abstract. Deep Reinforcement Learning is known to be brittle towards selection of appropriate hyperparameters. In particular, the selection of the structure of employed Deep Neural Networks has shown to be important and overfitting has become a common problem for DRL approaches. This study, first, analyzes how severe overfitting in DRL is in standard continuous control problems. Secondly, we argue that this might be partially due to the centralized perspective in control in which a single holistic controller is used that has to learn from all possible sensory inputs. As this is usually a high dimensional space, it appears natural that a Neural Network controller of high capacity starts to pick up non-meaningful correlations when relying on limited data during training. As a consequence, large Neural Network controller start to base their decisions on unimportant inputs. As a contrast, we offer a decentralized perspective in which control is distributed to local modules that act on local sensory inputs of much lower dimensionality. Such a prior of local inputs is biological inspired and shows, on the one hand, much faster learning, and, on the other hand, it is more robust against overfitting. Last, as decentralization impacts input (and output) dimensionality, we evaluated different common Neural Network initialization schemes and found Glorot initialization providing the most robust results.

Keywords: Deep Reinforcement Learning · Robustness · Hyperparameter selection

1 Introduction

While Deep Reinforcement Learning (DRL) has found wide application—from game playing to robot control [2]—over the last years, it still is assumed as a brittle process: adapting approaches towards new application areas requires careful and skillful tuning of hyperparameters or automated search for workable solutions [12]. Small deviations of parameters can impact results or break learning completely. This drawback—together with long computation times until possible convergence—has impacted reproducibility of DRL approaches and comparability of these approaches severely [4]. Recently, there have been multiple efforts

I. Farkaš et al. (Eds.): ICANN 2021, LNCS 12894, pp. 638–649, 2021.
https://doi.org/10.1007/978-3-030-86380-7_52

that aim for a better understanding on either small variations in implementation [10] or systematic variation of hyperparameters [1] in standard DRL algorithms. In particular, [1] showed in an extensive evaluation on Proximal Policy Optimization (PPO) which and how different hyperparameters affected learning for some typical control benchmark tasks.

These findings all point out that overfitting is a central problem for standard DRL, in particular when applied to more complex tasks. In general, overfitting is a problem observed in learning of Neural Networks (NN). NNs try to uncover possible correlations between input and output data. When the capacity of the NN models is increased, they might start to pick up specific relations in single instances without learning general structure of the underlying task. This is commonly referred to as overfitting. Overfitting is now seen as a problem in DRL control approaches [21] which negatively impacts performance, and often completely disrupts the control problem. There is still no principled approach how to deal with overfitting in DRL, instead it is required to tune a large set of hyperparameters in order to find workable solutions.

In this paper, we focus on overfitting in DRL and, accordingly, on the deep NN control models and their hyperparameters applied in DRL. While our first results will reproduce earlier results from [1], we will argue that the brittleness with respect to NN hyperparameters is partly due to the common, centralized view of current DRL approaches. In the current standard view, a single central controller is trained relying on all global available information. A consequence of this centralized approach are very high dimensional input and output spaces which makes it prone to overfitting. When the capacity of NN models increases, the models start to pick up specific relations in single instances without learning general structure of the underlying task. We will offer, as a contrast, a modularized view (Fig. 1) in which concurrent and decentralized controllers only operate on local information and only control local degrees of freedom. Such an approach is biologically inspired by the organization of animal control systems [6,16]. We will show that through this more natural scope of information learning and generalization becomes much more stable and overfitting is avoided. Last, we will discuss initialization of NNs in DRL and will show how important a suitable selection of the initialization scheme is.

2 Related Work on Robustness in DRL

Deep Reinforcement Learning (DRL) has been applied successfully in multiple areas as, for example, in locomotion control of simulated agents [9]. Still, application is often hindered by fundamental problems or a lack of principled approaches for how to apply DRL. Khadka et al. [12] summarized this as two main challenges: *"the difficulty in achieving effective exploration and brittle convergence properties that require careful tuning of the hyperparameters by a designer"*. Here, we will focus on the second challenge—selection of hyperparameters which has appeared for DRL as a difficult problem: often, already small changes of hyperparameters not only affect the results, but lead to a complete break down of learning and hinder learning any successful behavior at all.

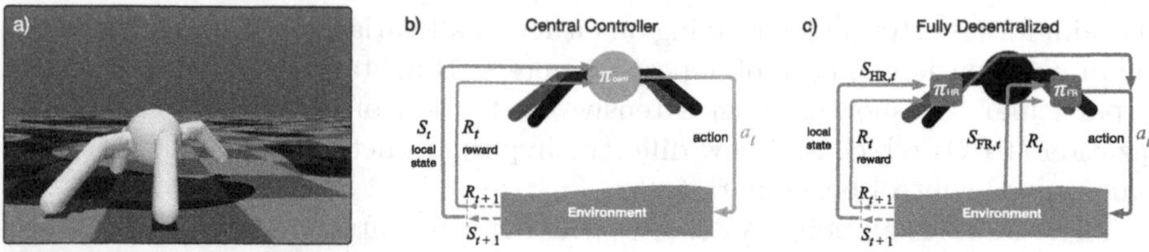

Fig. 1. a) Simulated "Ant" agent. b) Standard centralized DRL approach. c) Our decentralized approach: On the one hand, control is handled concurrently by one controller for each leg (only two are shown). This reduces the action space of each individual controller (e.g., $a_{\mathrm{HR},t}$). On the other hand, only limited local input information is used (gray arrows on the left, $S_{\mathrm{HR},t}$), stemming from that particular leg which reduces the input state space. Control policies are trained using DRL which is driven by a reward signal (R_t, as a simplification this is shown as shared between all controllers).

Therefore, there is a growing interest in more robust DRL. In continuous control tasks, there have been multiple studies on parameter selection or algorithmic variations [10] for PPO as the most prominent approach. In [1], a large set of hyperparameters were systematically tuned in multiple tasks and results were empirically evaluated through running a large number of training simulation runs. This has established some guidelines and selection of general parameters for training policy networks. Our work aims to complement this study with a—differing—focus on selection of the employed Neural Networks (NN) used for representation of the policy (and value function estimator). In particular, we analyze the selection of the size of hidden layers and how this affects learning. Our interest is understanding the fundamental problem of overfitting in the context of DRL and offering a modular perspective that helps to alleviate overfitting and, as a consequence, parameter selection. For selection of other hyperparameters (e.g. exploration rates), we stick to the recommendations in [1].

As a task, we are considering simulated locomotion (for recent overview see [11]). In this area, an earlier study [14] considered crucial design decisions for DRL applied to locomotion. They found that initialization of action distributions towards narrow and zero-centered distributions is beneficial for exploration and learning. This has been confirmed in [1] and they further considered different schemes for how to exactly initialize the NN weights [8]. Importantly, [1] did not find a difference between the different schemes. We think this is due to their specific experimental setup in which they did not focus on the employed NNs and were just able to compare these schemes for one specific network size. This makes their results misleading. Therefore, we also investigate the effect of different initialization schemes when varying NN sizes.

3 Methods

In Reinforcement Learning [19] an agent is interacting with an environment with the goal to directly learn from these interactions. When acting on the environment (selecting one out of possible actions $\mathcal{A}$), the agent is getting in response an updated state S of the environment which is used as input to the controller. Further, the agent receives a reward signal R that characterizes the task and which should guide learning of the agent. The goal is to learn—from a series of interactions—a policy $\pi(S)$ for sequential decision making that maximizes the long-term return which is understood as a Markov Decision Process.

In this article, we are considering a control problem in which the state space is given through continuous sensory inputs of the agent and in which the control policy should provide continuous control signals that actuate the joints of the agent. During learning the agent has to explore the state space with the goal of finding rewarding states and actions that lead towards these depending on its current state. As the state space is continuous and high dimensional, it can not be searched exhaustively. Therefore, in Deep Reinforcement Learning (DRL) policies (and value functions) are represented as Neural Networks (NN) that approximate and generalize over the state space. These NNs map observations to actions or action probabilities [2]. Overall, the agent has to balance exploiting already known information in order to reach known rewarding states and explore unknown parts of the state space and consequences of decision that might provide additional or higher rewards (for an introduction to DRL see [2,19]).

Simulation Environment and Control Problem Description

OpenAI is providing a set of continuous control environments which are used as benchmark for learning approaches. We chose their four legged walker environment, the 'Ant', which is simulated in Mujoco (version 1.50.1.68; simulation engine uses a step size of 10 ms, controller frequency of 20 Hz which equals a frame skip of 5) [20]. The simulated agent consists of four legs that are constituted of three segments connected by two revolute joints. As the overall control space is small with eight degrees of freedom, this is today considered an easy task that still is interesting for comparing different approaches and their learning characteristics.

A structured reward is used for this agent in which velocities (in the fixed direction of the x-axis) are rewarded linearly and keeping the simulation alive is rewarded with a constant value. Furthermore, additional costs are used that favor more efficient gaits through a control cost term and through a contact cost term. The input space (observations) is high dimensional (111 dimensions) and consists of information on body height, body orientation, and velocities of body; joint angles and velocities; external contact forces acting on the body segments (these have little impact on performance).

Control Architectures

We are comparing two different types of architectures. On the one hand, we are considering the standard paradigm as used in DRL in which one holistic controller is trained for control of an agent (**centralized approach**). In this centralized paradigm, the controller uses all available sensory information as inputs and provides control signals for all actuators as outputs which leads to high dimensional input and output spaces.

In contrast (see Table 1), we compare this to a **decentralized approach** (for details on the decentralized architecture, see [17]). A decentralized approach is biologically inspired and control is distributed into multiple local control modules [5]. This is assumed to allow for faster response times in animals [6]. For example, in insects such a decentralized control architecture has been shown crucial for adaptivity of walking behavior [3]. A decentralized control module is only responsible for controlling some of the degrees of freedom. In our approach, we are following the findings from insects [15,16] which have been applied in robotic control earlier [7]. We adapt this to the, in this case four legged, simulated agent and a DRL learning architecture: each leg is controlled by an individual controller and therefore each controller is only providing outputs for the two degrees of freedom of that particular leg. Secondly, as input local information is used for the decentralized controllers. Each control module accesses information from the controlled leg, but not from the other legs. In addition, each controller is provided some global information (current height of the body, velocity of body movement, current orientation in space as required for goal-directed behavior).

Table 1. Description of the two different control architectures: differentiation of action space, observation space, and reward function for the centralized and fully decentralized architecture.

	Centralized Controller	Decentralized Controller
Number of Controllers	1	4
Architecture	1 policy for 8 joints	4 policies, each 1 leg, 2 joints
Policy π (Action space)	$\boldsymbol{a} = \pi(obs_{\text{all}})$, 8-dim.	$\boldsymbol{a} = \text{concat}\ (\pi_{\text{FR}}(obs_{\text{FR}}), \pi_{\text{FL}}(obs_{\text{FL}}), \pi_{\text{HL}}(obs_{\text{HL}}), \pi_{\text{HR}}(obs_{\text{HR}}))$ each $\pi_x(obs_x)$, 2-dim., for one ctrl.
Observation space obs_x, dim.	global/all inf. (111)	only from controlled leg (45)
Reward fct.	$R = x_{vel} - 0.5\,\lVert\boldsymbol{a}\rVert^2 - 0.0005\,\lVert\boldsymbol{f}_{ext}\rVert^2$	$R_{\text{FL}} = 0.25x_{vel} - 0.5\,\lVert\pi_{\text{FL}}(obs_{\text{FL}})\rVert^2$ $-0.0005\,\lVert\boldsymbol{f}_{ext\_\text{FL}}\rVert^2$

DRL Approach: Training using Proximal Policy Optimization

We are using Proximal Policy Optimization (PPO) for training of all policies and architecture types [18]. In PPO, the policy is described as a function of the state (Fig. 2 a)). This is optimized using gradient ascent based on the gradient of expected return with respect to the policy parameters that has been derived from trajectory samples when using the current policy. PPO ensures—during

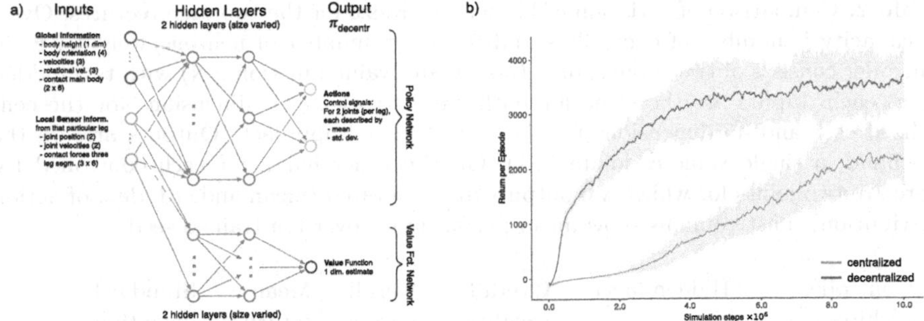

Fig. 2. a) A single leg controller in the fully decentralized approach using PPO consists of two networks: a policy network (top) and a value function network (bottom) that are both realized as NNs consisting of two hidden layers. b) Learning curves for the centralized (orange) and decentralized (blue) controller architectures over learning time (NN of two hidden layers of 64 units each). Shown is mean return per episode—calculated over 10 seeds—during learning, given in simulation steps (interactions with the environment). Standard deviation between seeds is given as shaded area. (Color figure online)

gradient steps—to change the current policy only in small and safe steps. It is implemented as an Actor-Critic method in which the policy is represented as a NN that stochastically selects actions depending on the current state, but in which another value estimate—represented as a second NN—acts as a critic in order to reduce variance of the gradients.

We used the RLlib framework [13] and Tensorflow 2 for representation and training of the NNs. RLlib offers an efficient implementation of PPO and, which is crucial for our decentralized architecture, is designed for distribution of control. As this is originally geared towards multi-agent systems, we implemented the decentralized approach as four individual agents that control one single simulated robot. RLlib handles training these agents as individual actors in a single environment efficiently. In our experiments, each control module is trained using PPO. This is straight forward for the centralized approach as a single controller is trained that has access to all information. For the decentralized case, there are four individual controllers that each are learning independently. Each of these decentralized leg controller only has access to a part of the observation space (information from the controlled leg plus some global information).

4 Results

The goal of our study is to analyze how Deep Reinforcement Learning (DRL) is affected by hyperparameter selection and, in particular, is prone to overfitting. The focus of our experiments is, therefore, on variation of the Neural Networks (NN) inside the DRL controller. We will present two experiments. First, we systematically varied the size of the NN controllers in a centralized and decentralized

Table 2. Comparison of variation of hidden layer size for the two architectures. Overall capacity is number of controllers multiplied by number of neurons/weights. Each controller consists of two subnetworks (policy and value function NN) with two hidden layers each. Inputs are the same for both subnetworks, 111 dimensions for the centralized case and 45 dimensions for the decentralized approach. Outputs are, on the one hand, a single value estimate (+1). On the other hand, for each controlled leg there are two joints for which two outputs are generated (mean and std. dev. of action distribution). Last columns show mean performance over ten trained seeds.

Controller architecture	Hidden layer size	Overall weights	Overall neurons	Mean return	Standard deviation
Centralized approach	[2, 2]	511	8	2243.5	372.6
	[4, 4]	1021	16	3040.5	592.0
	[8, 8]	2089	32	3261.9	689.0
	[16, 16]	4417	64	3986.3	591.6
	[32, 32]	9841	128	2723.8	729.1
	[64, 64]	23761	256	2168.6	484.1
	[128, 128]	63889	512	911.8	280.1
	[256, 256]	193297	1024	60.7	26.3
	[512, 512]	648721	2048	−14.7	9.2
Decentralized approach	[2, 2]	844	32	2429.3	338.7
	[4, 4]	1732	64	2909.6	376.7
	[8, 8]	3700	128	3780.8	599.2
	[16, 16]	8404	256	4386.1	342.0
	[32, 32]	20884	512	4329.4	183.9
	[64, 64]	58132	1024	3703.5	504.4
	[128, 128]	181870	2048	2932.8	406.4
	[256, 256]	625684	4096	2706.2	564.0

approach. As a consequence, we worked with NNs differing in input dimensionality, hidden layer size, and output dimensionality. Secondly, Andrychowicz et al. pointed out that DRL benefits from specific initialization schemes for the different weight matrices [1], but they did not compare how different schemes deal when changing neuron numbers in different layers. We, therefore, tested how different initialization schemes affect convergence for such variations.

4.1 Experiment 1: Variation of Hidden Layer Size

In the first experiment, we systematically varied the size of the hidden layers of the controllers. First, we are interested in how small the NN size can be in order to still deliver reasonable results. Secondly, we evaluate if larger NNs lead to worse results and exhibit overfitting. One explanation for overfitting in DRL might be the high dimensionality of input and output spaces that causes learning

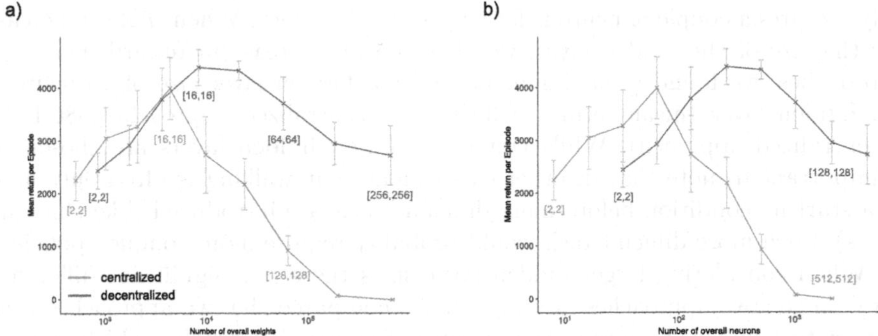

Fig. 3. Comparison of locomotion performance (after training) for different sizes of NNs when used in the centralized (orange) and decentralized (blue) architecture. Shown is mean return (y-axis) over ten seeds for different NN configurations at the end of training (after 10 million simulation steps). Horizontal axis represents size of networks: In a) given as the number of trainable weights/parameters of the NN controllers. In b) shown for the overall number of neurons of the two architectures. In the case of the decentralized architecture, it is important to note that there are always four local controllers which increased these numbers by a factor of four. (Color figure online)

of unreasonable relationships in large models. Therefore, we compare this to our decentralized DRL approach in which decentralized controllers (controlling only a limited number of actions) were trained while relying on limited information.

We chose different NN sizes around commonly applied sizes (standard approaches use two hidden layers of 64 units for action and value function network). As a smallest size, we chose two units and scaled this up to 512 units per hidden layer for the centralized approach, and 256 units for the decentralized approach. For initialization, we used Glorot initialization (see exp. 2) which we implemented for RLlib. We were considering learning to walk as fast as possible. For each condition of different hidden layer size, we trained 10 (random) seeds for each control approach for 10 million environment simulation steps.

As a first result, we replicated our findings from the hexapod walker case [17]. When considering a typical sized hidden layer (64 neurons per hidden layer as given as a default in RLlib) we found that a decentralized approach is able to learn good walking behavior (Fig. 2 b)). As one difference to our earlier results, in the decentralized approach we only relied on information of the controlled leg and were not including information from neighboring legs. Still, a decentralized controller with only limited input information and only in charge of two joints of a single leg produced stable locomotion. In particular, the decentralized approach showed much faster learning and ended up with a higher performance in the end.

Secondly, for variation of hidden layer size (see Table 2), we found that already quite small hidden layer sizes lead to walking behavior and an acceptable performance. Already with the minimal size of only two units per hidden layer, stable walking emerged for both—centralized and decentralized—approaches. This stresses that the ant environment on flat terrain is an easy DRL task that only requires a couple of neurons for acceptable behavior. When slightly increasing the size of the hidden layer, we observed an increase in reward. For both approaches, we found a maximum value for a hidden layer size of 16 neurons per hidden layer (mean return of 3986.3 for centralized approach; 4386.1 for decentralized approach). While commonly larger hidden layers are chosen, it is important to note that in other experiments flat walking is often only used as a starting condition before more difficult tasks are introduced (like climbing stairs). Such more difficult task would probably require more complex policies.

When considering larger hidden layer sizes there is a significant difference between the two approaches (see Fig. 3). We compared the two approaches with respect to number of neurons and number of connection weights which is more indicative of the learning capacity. While both approaches show a decline from an optimum value, for the centralized approach we see a very quick drop basically up to a point of zero return. This is in agreement with what is today assumed about standard DRL: it is brittle with respect to hyperparameter selection. Our results stress that a centralized approach—choosing a too large hidden layer size—might end up not gaining any positive return at all anymore and no stable behavior. Such behavior is considered as overfitting in DRL. In contrast, for the decentralized control approach, stable locomotion behavior is learned in all cases and performance staid on a reasonably high level (Fig. 3).

We already mentioned the difference in progression of learning for the two approaches for an intermediate hidden layer size (Fig. 2 b)). Figure 4 shows learning over time for different hidden layer sizes for both architectures. Again, we observe that for the decentralized approach learning progresses much faster (blue mean curves reach a high level quite early) and, overall—despite variation of the hidden layer size through a large range—for the decentralized approach the learning curves are quite close to each other.

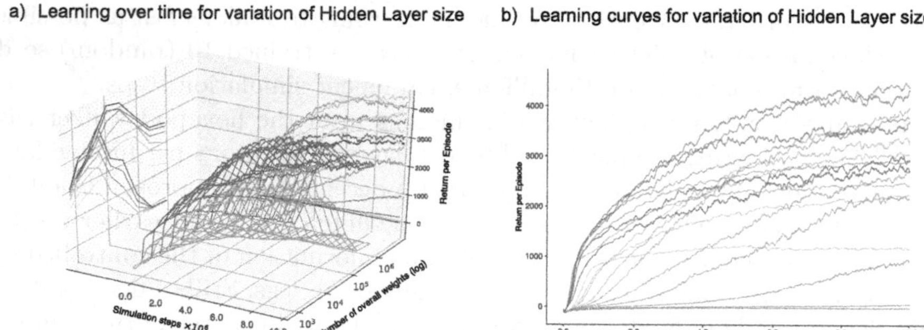

Fig. 4. Comparison of performance over the course of training for different sizes of NNs for the centralized (orange) and decentralized (blue) architecture. Shown is mean return (vertical axis) over ten seeds for different NN configurations (shown on the left as y-axis, size of NN; on the right projected onto x-z-plane) and over training time (x-axis, up to 10 million simulation steps). Size is given as the number of trainable weights/parameters of the NN controllers. (Color figure online)

4.2 Experiment 2: Impact of Initialization Schemes

Initialization of NNs has shown important for good training performance [8] in general and Andrychowicz et al. [1] analyzed the effect of initialization on DRL. Their findings are in agreement with the general notion of using small, random values for initialization and, in particular, they stressed that using very small values in the last layer for producing a zero mean action distribution is important. But, they found no difference for using different initialization schemes (Glorot/Xavier or using He initialization).

We think that their specific experiment is problematic for differentiating different initialization schemes as they were not varying the sizes of NNs. But the different initialization schemes mainly differ in how they differentially treat changes of layer sizes. While a simple (He like) normalization scheme is just scaling weights with respect to number of units in the previous layer (called fan-in), Glorot initialization is based on fan-in and fan-out (number of units in the receiving layer) for setting the mean for the random weight values. As a consequence, for typical DRL tasks—in which input spaces are high dimensional (around 100) and hidden layer sizes are as well high dimensional—these schemes should be expected to deliver quite similar initializations using small random weights. But it remains unknown how this changes when we change layer sizes. In the last experiment, we varied the dimensionality of input and hidden layer space in order to compare the effect of the initialization scheme (see results in Table 3). We are applying the Glorot and the He scheme in the same way as described in [1], i.e. weights for action outputs are further scaled down by 0.01.

First, we observed that for the decentralized case, results were only affected very little by selection of a specific initialization scheme. Secondly, for the centralized approach, we see some difference between initialization schemes when keeping high dimensional inputs and varying the hidden layer size. The difference favors Glorot initialization, but these results still are in the range reported by [1]. Last, we changed the input dimensionality to only 27 dimensions by removing

Table 3. Comparison of two common initialization schemes for deep NNs and how they affect DRL when changing hidden layer or input size.

Controller architecture	Input size	Hidden layer size	Mean return (std. dev.) Glorot init., unif. d.	Mean Return (std. dev.) He init, norm. distr.
Decentralized approach	45	16	4386.1 (342.0)	4208.2 (480.0)
		64	3703.5 (504.4)	3986.0 (268.4)
		256	2706.2 (564.0)	2480.7 (583.6)
Centralized approach	111	16	3986.3 (591.6)	3062.9 (822.6)
		64	2168.6 (484.1)	1720.1 (448.9)
		256	60.7 (26.3)	66.4 (35.3)
Centralized approach reduced obs.	27	16	4141.3 (673.5)	3554.3 (608.5)
		64	3344.0 (401.2)	2069.4 (754.1)
		256	2672.1 (462.5)	68.2 (31.0)

all contact information. These inputs have shown to only have a negligible influence on locomotion performance (as confirmed by our results). When reducing the input dimensionality, we observed a large difference between the two initialization schemes. The simple He-like normalization is very sensitive to the hidden layer size, while Glorot initialization appears more robust.

5 Discussion and Conclusion

In Deep Reinforcement Learning (DRL), selection of an appropriate size of the Neural Network (NN) is crucial. Already small variations in network size—choosing a too large network—can lead to diminished or even no returns. We assume that this overfitting is a consequence of high dimensionality input and output spaces. Larger NN models might learn non-meaningful relations in connecting input and output spaces which leads to bad results. Therefore, we analyzed this for one typical control task and found that a standard central DRL approach—in which one central control unit has access to all available information—is heavily affected by overfitting. We compared this to a decentralized approach in which—as a structural and biologically inspired prior—input spaces are restricted to local information. These smaller concurrent controllers showed more robust against overfitting and even with large network sizes provided reasonable behavior. Furthermore, the reduced input and output spaces benefitted exploration and training as decentralized controllers learned much faster.

Secondly, we found that initialization of NNs is important. As proposed by [1] using initially small weights—in particular for weights connected to the action outputs—is important. But we further analyzed robustness of initialization schemes for dimensionality changes and found that Glorot/Xavier initialization should be preferred as it takes into account all layer sizes (fan-in and fan-ought of the weight matrix) leading to more robust results.

Acknowledgements. This research was supported by the research training group "Dataninja" (Trustworthy AI for Seamless Problem Solving: Next Generation Intelligence Joins Robust Data Analysis) funded by the German federal state of North Rhine-Westphalia.

References

1. Andrychowicz, M., et al.: What Matters In On-Policy Reinforcement Learning? A Large-Scale Empirical Study. arXiv:2006.05990 [cs, stat] (2020)
2. Arulkumaran, K., Deisenroth, M.P., Brundage, M., Bharath, A.A.: A brief survey of deep reinforcement learning. IEEE Sig. Process. Mag. **34**(6), 26–38 (2017)
3. Bidaye, S.S., Bockemühl, T., Büschges, A.: Six-legged walking in insects: how CPGs, peripheral feedback, and descending signals generate coordinated and adaptive motor rhythms. J. Neurophysiol. **119**(2), 459–475 (2018)
4. Clary, K., Tosch, E., Foley, J., Jensen, D.: Let's Play Again: Variability of Deep Reinforcement Learning Agents in Atari Environments. arXiv:1904.06312 [cs, stat] (2019)

5. Clune, J., Mouret, J.B., Lipson, H.: The evolutionary origins of modularity. Proc. R. Soc. B Biol. Sci. **280**(1755), 20122863 (2013). https://doi.org/10.1098/rspb.2012.2863
6. Dickinson, M.H., Farley, C.T., Full, R.J., Koehl, M.R., Kram, R., Lehman, S.: How animals move: an integrative view. Science **288**(5463), 100–106 (2000)
7. Dürr, V., et al.: Integrative biomimetics of autonomous hexapedal locomotion. Front. Neurorobot. **13**, 88 (2019)
8. Glorot, X., Bengio, Y.: Understanding the difficulty of training deep feedforward neural networks. In: Proceedings of the 13th International Conference on Artificial Intelligence and Statistics, vol. 9, pp. 249–256 (2010)
9. Heess, N., et al.: Emergence of locomotion behaviours in rich environments. arXiv preprint arXiv:1707.02286 (2017)
10. Hsu, C.C.Y., Mendler-Dünner, C., Hardt, M.: Revisiting Design Choices in Proximal Policy Optimization. arXiv:2009.10897 [cs, stat] (2020)
11. Hwangbo, J., et al.: Learning agile and dynamic motor skills for legged robots. Sci. Robot. **4**(26), eaau5872 (2019). https://doi.org/10.1126/scirobotics.aau5872
12. Khadka, S., et al.: Collaborative Evolutionary Reinforcement Learning. arXiv:1905.00976 [cs, stat] (2019)
13. Liang, E., et al.: RLlib: Abstractions for Distributed Reinforcement Learning. arXiv:1712.09381 [cs] (2018)
14. Reda, D., Tao, T., van de Panne, M.: Learning to locomote: Understanding how environment design matters for deep reinforcement learning. In: Proceedings of the ACM SIGGRAPH Conference on Motion, Interaction and Games (2020)
15. Schilling, M., Cruse, H.: Decentralized control of insect walking: a simple neural network explains a wide range of behavioral and neurophysiological results. PLOS Comput. Biol. **16**(4), e1007804 (2020)
16. Schilling, M., Hoinville, T., Schmitz, J., Cruse, H.: Walknet, a bio-inspired controller for hexapod walking. Biol. Cybern. **107**(4), 397–419 (2013)
17. Schilling, M., Konen, K., Ohl, F.W., Korthals, T.: Decentralized deep reinforcement learning for a distributed and adaptive locomotion controller of a hexapod robot. In: IEEE/RSJ International Conference on Intelligent Robots and Systems (2020)
18. Schulman, J., Wolski, F., Dhariwal, P., Radford, A., Klimov, O.: Proximal policy optimization algorithms. arXiv preprint arXiv:1707.06347 (2017)
19. Sutton, R.S., Barto, A.G.: Reinforcement Learning: An Introduction, 2nd edn. The MIT Press (2018). http://incompleteideas.net/book/the-book-2nd.html
20. Todorov, E., Erez, T., Tassa, Y.: Mujoco: A physics engine for model-based control. In: 2012 IEEE/RSJ IROS. pp. 5026–5033 (2012)
21. Zhang, C., Vinyals, O., Munos, R., Bengio, S.: A Study on Overfitting in Deep Reinforcement Learning. arXiv:1804.06893 [cs, stat] (2018)

Advances in Adaptive Skill Acquisition

Juraj Holas(✉) and Igor Farkaš

Faculty of Mathematics, Physics and Informatics, Comenius University in Bratislava, Bratislava, Slovakia
{juraj.holas,igor.farkas}@fmph.uniba.sk

Abstract. Hierarchical Reinforcement Learning (HRL) represents a viable approach to learning complex tasks, especially those with an inner hierarchical structure. The HRL methods decompose the problem into a typically two-layered hierarchy. At the lower level, individual *skills* are created to solve specific non-trivial subtasks, such as locomotion primitives. The high-level agent can then use these skills as its actions, enabling it to tackle the overall task. The identification of an appropriate skill set, however, is a difficult problem by itself. Most current approaches solve it using a pre-training phase, in which skills are trained and fixed, before launching the training of the high-level agent. Having the skill set fixed prior to main training session can however impose flaws on the HRL system – especially if a useful skill was not successfully identified, and hence is missing from the skill set. Our *Adaptive Skill Acquisition* framework (ASA) aims specifically for these situations. It can be plugged onto existing HRL architectures and fix the defects within the pre-trained skill set. During the training of the high-level agent, ASA detects a missing skill, trains it, and integrates it into the existing system. In this paper, we present new improvements to the ASA framework, especially a new skill-training reward function, and support for skill-stopping functions enabling better integration. Furthermore, we extend our prior pilot tests into extensive experiments evaluating the functionality of ASA, in comparison to its theoretical boundaries. The source code of ASA is also available online (https://github.com/holasjuraj/asa).

Keywords: Hierarchical reinforcement learning · Skill acquisition · Adaptive model

1 Introduction

The field of Reinforcement Learning has been gaining significant attention within the past years, as being a viable pool of Machine Learning methods based on biologically motivated concepts. Thanks to its advancements, RL methods can easily surpass human-level performance in certain tasks. However, traditional ('flat') RL can still fall short if the problem at hand features several layers of abstraction.

This research was supported by KEGA grant no. 042UK-4/2019.

I. Farkaš et al. (Eds.): ICANN 2021, LNCS 12894, pp. 650–661, 2021.
https://doi.org/10.1007/978-3-030-86380-7_53

To remedy these problems, the *Hierarchical Reinforcement Learning* (HRL) was introduced [24]. HRL approaches are designed to be able to abstract a hierarchical structure of the task, and reflect it within the architecture of the model. The HRL models hence contain *skills* – actions that are temporally extended in time, which are usually specialised to perform a specific subtask. A high-level agent operates on top of them to solve the main task, using the low-level skills to abstract the peculiarities of individual subtasks. This architecture hence creates an implicit or explicit leveled hierarchy within the model.

The process of acquiring skills is typically crucial to the model, and makes a core of individual HRL algorithms. Older methods like [20,24] specify and train the skill behaviors manually, which, however, comes with high risk of engineered bias. On the other hand, all modern approaches construct the skill set in automated or semi-automated way. The most used approach is to use a pre-training phase, during which the skills are trained using a surrogate reward [6,7,10,14–16]. After the pre-training phase has finished, the skills are fixed and training of the high-level agent starts.

However, this two-phased training of a HRL architecture comes with a problems stemming from the principle of *optimality under given hierarchy* [24]. If the pre-training phase fails to produce the perfect set of skills, the high-level agent will likely fail to find an optimal overall solution, as it is bounded by the suboptimal skill set. As an example, we can imagine a locomotion robot with a task to solve a maze, which is only given skills to move forward/backward and turn left, but no skill to turn right. The high-level agent, choosing from this limited skill set, may still find a solution how to navigate through the maze, but it will clearly be suboptimal for cases it should have turned right. This principle was also experimentally proven [12].

There has been a limited amount of research focused on training the whole hierarchy jointly, with the option to adapt all skills even during the high-level training [12,13,19]. However, most of them rely on using Universal-MDP which, despite its name, is a subset of MDP class suitable mostly for spatial 'reaching' tasks.

Addressing the problem of a missing skill, we introduced our framework of *Adaptive Skill Acquisition* (ASA) [8]. Its main purpose is to identify that a skill is missing during the training of the high-level agent, formulate and train the missing skill, and integrate it to the faulty skill set. ASA is designed as a pluggable component, which can be deployed onto almost any existing HRL architecture or those yet to come. In this paper we present the improvements that have been made to the model to make it even more robust, efficient, and reusable.

Additionally, all skills generated by previous approaches can be categorized into two disjoint types. The *subgoal-based* skill identification works by selecting a state with greater importance (subgoal), and then training a skill to reach this state from its proximity [2,10,12,14,17,19]. A typical subgoal example is a doorway in a grid-world environment. On the other hand, the *behavioral* skills are crafted to execute a specific behavior which is useful in any part of state-space, not only near a subgoal – such as walking for a legged robot [6,13,15].

To the best of our knowledge, there has not been an approach which could train both *subgoal-based* and *behavioral* skills. In this work we experimentally confirm that ASA is able to train both types of skills, and it does so without the need of parameter change, or specifying which skill type it should create.

As a key contribution of this paper, we also present extended results of our method, compared to the previous pilot tests. We empirically demonstrate the successful performance of ASA on two distinctive environments, analyze the quality of the new skill, and compare our work to the HiPPO algorithm [13].

2 Preliminaries

We define a *Markov Decision Process* (MDP) as a tuple $\langle S, A, P, p_0, R, \gamma \rangle$, where $S \subseteq \mathbb{R}^{\dim(S)}$ is a set of states, A is a set of actions, $P : S \times A \times S \rightarrow [0,1]$ is a probability distribution describing the state transitions, $p_0 : S \rightarrow [0,1]$ is a probability distribution of the initial state, $R : S \times A \rightarrow \mathbb{R}$ is a (possibly non-deterministic) reward function, $\gamma \in (0,1]$ is a reward discount factor. Traditional ('flat') RL aims to find an optimal policy $\pi : S \times A \rightarrow [0,1]$ that optimizes the expected overall discounted return $G(\pi) = \mathbb{E}_\pi[\sum_{t=0}^{T} \gamma^t R(s_t, a_t)]$, where $\mathbb{E}_\pi$ denotes the expected value if an agent follows a policy π.

In Hierarchical RL, we do not optimize a single policy π, but rather a set of policies on two (or more) levels. We have a set of skills – low-level policies $\pi_1^L, \ldots, \pi_n^L$ that act using the original actions: $\pi_i^L(s_t) = a_t$. On top of them we have a manager – driven by a high-level policy π^H. Its purpose is to decide which skill will be used in a given situation, and thus its high-level actions a_t^H are in fact invocations of skill policies: $\pi^H(s_t) = a_t^H \in \{\pi_1^L, \ldots, \pi_n^L\}$. The chosen skill then selects actions until the termination criterion is met, e.g. its time limit is reached. In our paper we study variable-length sequences of skill invocations, which we denote by $\delta = [a_t^H, \ldots, a_{t+m}^H]$.

3 Related Work

The problem of automated skill discovery is the most commonly addressed issue within the field of HRL. As the cornerstone, the *Options framework* [24] laid a base for many subsequent approaches to build on. The research was originally focused mostly on approaches for discrete state-space environments [2,4,7,14, 16,20,24], as being significantly easier to tackle. Only the recent approaches, supported by the improvements in deep neural networks, were able to solve continuous domains [6,10,12,13,17,19], as we also do in our work.

The process of acquiring skills differs widely among individual works, and is often supported by a surrogate reward signal. In the simplest case, older methods [20,24] specify and train the skill behaviors manually as a series of RL agents. The frequency-based [7,14] and graph-based [16,17] approaches try to identify subgoals, and then use a simple state-based reward to train a skill for reaching them. Others employ more sophisticated rewards in order to train better specialised skills [6,13]. Analogously, we also construct a specialised reward signal for each missing skill, so that each new skill fills in the specific gap in the skill set.

The vast majority of research operates strictly on two leveled hierarchies [1,2,6,10,11,13–18,24], although there have been successful demonstrations of learning a multi-leveled hierarchy [4,12]. Our ASA framework was also designed for two levels. However, contrarily to [2,6,18], there is no fundamental constraint preventing it from being deployed on multi-level hierarchies.

In terms of a new skill-training method, our approach is similar to the *Skill-chaining* algorithm [10]. Both approaches train a skill to reach from given starting states to end states. However, their skill training is processed strictly in the pre-training phase, and produces only a linearly aligned stream of skills. Should their algorithm be deployed on a highly non-linear environment, it would most probably fail to find the suitable 'skill-chain'. On the other hand, ASA can produce versatile skills, and furthermore it can do so even after the pre-training phase is finished.

A parallel to our work can be seen in the algorithm [23], which also enables to enrich the hierarchy by new skills. However, their approach is strictly dependant on the hand-crafted curriculum of tasks supported by pre-defined stochastic grammar from which the new skills are generated, which effectively limits the capabilities of new tasks. The key advantage of ASA compared to this approach is the ability to train even behaviors that have not been considered in advance, as it is not bounded by the curriculum.

One of the latest contributions, which we consider to be the state-of-the-art for the task we are solving, is the HiPPO algorithm [13]. It also trains skills during the high-level training, as we do. It uses an approximate hierarchical policy gradient to directly train both skills *and* a high-level agent from the scratch at the same time. The only engineering choice is the latent dimension, which effectively regulates the number of skills to be trained. In their work the authors show that HiPPO consistently surpasses other similarly focused algorithms.

4 Our Approach

In this paper we present the improvements of our method *Adaptive Skill Acquisition* (ASA) [8]. The key function of ASA is to detect the inefficiencies within a current skill set, and address them by adding a new skill *in the midst* of training of the high-level agent. ASA is designed not as a closed, self-contained architecture, but rather as a component that can be plugged into almost any existing HRL architecture, or those yet to come.

As discussed in the previous section, the majority of current HRL architectures employ a pre-training phase, after which the skills are fixed – which can hurt the system if the skill set is not optimal. Some useful skills, especially in spatial tasks, can be identified only after the high-level agent explores a sufficient part of the state space, e.g. discovering a new section of a map which the original skills did not reflect upon. By generating the skills with ASA even after the pre-training phase, the system can acquire new skills according to the real current needs of the high-level agent.

The process of ASA is composed of three key conceptual steps:
1) Identification of a missing skill is performed by self-observation of the high-level agent. During the training we try to detect sequences of high-level actions which occur significantly more often than expected. Such behavior of the agent hints at a regularity in the MDP, for which no skill was trained. Hence the regularity is only modelled by reoccurring sequence of high-level actions, which can result in a highly suboptimal solution. A frequently executed sequence of skills hence serves as a candidate for a new skill.
2) Training of the new skill consists of standard RL training to solve an MDP that represents the new skill. However, this MDP has to be constructed dynamically and automatically, so that ASA can operate autonomously. The most important aspect of this step is constructing a robust reward function that will lead the new skill-agent towards the desired behavior.
3) Integration of the new skill into the overall HRL architecture will finally allow the high-level agent to use the new skill. If the agent is modelled using a neural network, this essentially means adding a new output unit to the partially trained network. Further specification of a termination criterion for the new skill will then allow it to be used more efficiently.

The described processes represent the core of Adaptive Skill Acquisition – please refer to our previous paper [8] for comprehensive description of these components. In the following sections we cover the improvements that were implemented in order to make ASA more robust, efficient, and reusable.

4.1 Normalization of Sequence Frequency

In the skill-identification phase we track the sequences of high-level actions. For each such sequence $\delta = [a_t^H, \dots, a_{t+m-1}^H]$, which is of an arbitrary length m, we gather the number of times it occurred $C(\delta)$. The most frequently used sequence, which would serve as a candidate for new skill, could be naively picked as the one with the highest $C(\delta)$.

However, the shorter sequences tend to naturally occur more often. The counts thus need to be normalized in order to account for this disproportion. We improve on our previous work by introducing a new null-count $C_H(\delta)$, which can now account for batch-training methods. We denote a batch by $\mathcal{T} = \{\tau_1, \tau_2, \dots\}$, being a set of agent's trajectories τ_j. The improved null-count for a sequence δ of length m gathered during batch $\mathcal{T}$ is computed as:

$$C_H(\delta) = \left(\sum_{\tau \in \mathcal{T}} |\tau| \; - \; (m-1)|\mathcal{T}| \right) \prod_{i=1}^{m} p(\delta_i)$$

where δ_i denotes i^{th} step of δ, and $p(\delta_i)$ is empirical probability of invoked skills.

The quantity $C_H(\delta)$ describes how many times δ is expected to occur if a random 'null' policy was used instead of real π^H. We can thus use it to normalize the count of the sequence by computing $f(\delta) = C(\delta)/C_H(\delta)$. This f-score quantity no longer favors shorter sequences, and can be used to determine the best candidate for a new skill.

4.2 Skill-Training Reward Definition

Moving on to the training of the new skill based on the selected sequence δ, we aim it to *perform the same state transition as δ did*, but to perform it more optimally. During the skill-identification step, we collect the start-states $S_{\text{start}}(\delta) = \{s_s^{(1)}, \ldots, s_s^{(C(\delta))}\}$ in which each occurrence of δ started, as well as end-states $S_{\text{end}}(\delta) = \{s_e^{(1)}, \ldots, s_e^{(C(\delta))}\}$ in which each occurrence of δ ended up. These two sets help us to specify the MDP for the new skill.

The training of the new agent is realised by spawning the agent in a randomly picked $s_s^{(i)} \in S_{\text{start}}(\delta)$, and only rewarding it upon reaching the corresponding $s_e^{(i)}$. Of course, reaching of a specific state is not achievable in continuous state-spaces, and a generalization into an *end-region* is needed. This was originally accomplished by setting a simple distance threshold, and rewarding the agent if $\|s_t - s_e^{(i)}\|_2 < \epsilon$. However, a careful tuning of ϵ had to be done for each new environment, since the relative distances of states can widely differ.

We improve on this approach by constructing a new reward function, which is agnostic to the choice of environment. First, we employ a technique of batch normalization $\phi(s)$ [9] on the state space S, typically used in deep learning. It is used to normalize each dimension of the input (i.e. state) to have zero mean and unit variance. We use it to flatten the difference between relative distances within each dimension of the state space. After the normalization, we know that the distance between any two normalized states $\phi(s_x)$ and $\phi(s_y)$ averages to ≈ 1 in each dimension.

Secondly, we define the end-region, which the agent aims to reach, as a hyper-cube centered in a normalized version of the desired end-state $\phi(s_e^{(i)})$, with a side of 2ϵ. This yields a formal definition of the reward function:

$$R(s_t, a_t) = \left[\max_{d=1..\dim(S)} \left| \phi(s_t)_d - \phi(s_e^{(i)})_d \right| < \epsilon \right]_1$$

where $\dim(S)$ is the dimensionality of state space, subscript d represents the d-th dimension of the given vector, and $[\,\cdot\,]_1$ is the indicator function. This formulation in practice means that the agent is rewarded if each dimension of the current state (after normalization) is not more than ϵ away from the desired value.

The usage of batch normalization ensures that we can set ϵ to a reasonable value, while being agnostic to the choice of the environment. E.g. setting $\epsilon = 0.1$ means that roughly 90% match between the current and the desired state in each dimension is needed for agent's success. Moreover, using this hyper-cube based reward ensures that a partial match is required in *each* dimension. This is essential if some component of a state has a greater importance, since its error cannot be ignored even if other components have a prefect match.

4.3 Skill-Stopping Criteria

Current HRL architectures usually choose to execute the skills for a fixed amount of steps [5,6,12,18,19]. Some, however, use a state-based function for skill termination [4,10,24], randomized length [13], or other criteria. In order to increase the compatibility of ASA even further and accommodate for all aforementioned methods, we introduce the concept of *skill-stopping functions* to the framework:

$$f_i^{\text{stop}}\left(s_{t-c}, a_{t-c}, \ldots, s_t, a_t\right) \in \{true, false\}$$

The skill-stopping function accepts the whole trajectory of skill since time $t-c$, at which it started, until the current time t, which can be used to implement any stopping criterion from the relevant research. Furthermore, if needed, each skill π_i^L can have separate stopping function f_i^{stop}.

The stopping-function of the new skill will directly follow what the skill was trained for – reaching the end-regions $S_{\text{end}}(\delta)$. This behavior is hence identical to terminating the episodes during the new skill's training phase, when the end of an episode was determined by the surrogate reward function $R(s_t, a_t)$. We thus alternate on R's equation to create a stopping function for the new $(n+1)$-th skill:

$$f_{n+1}^{\text{stop}}(\ldots, s_t) = \left(\exists s_e^{(i)} \in S_{\text{end}}(\delta) : \max_{d=1..\dim(S)} \left|\phi(s_t)_d - \phi(s_e^{(i)})_d\right| < \epsilon\right) \vee \left(c > t_{\max}\right)$$

We still included the condition $c > t_{\max}$ to limit the maximal execution time of the skill, in case it fails to reach the desired end-region.

5 Results

We now present new experiments and results, which significantly extended our previous pilot tests. We tested our method on two distinctive environments, and added a comparison to one of the latest HRL architectures – HiPPO [13]. Our experiments were mainly focused on two aspects:

- What is the overall ASA performance and how does it compare to HiPPO?
- What is the quality of a newly trained skill?

5.1 Environments and Training Setup

For our experiments we chose two environments which on purpose differ in numerous aspects, such as continuity, observability, skill types, etc. Our goal was to demonstrate that ASA can be used universally, not only in a single type of tasks. We thoroughly focused on sparse-reward environments.

Coin-Gatherer: The agent in Coin-gatherer environment operates in a grid-world of size 68×46 tiles depicted in Fig. 1a. There are four possible actions (N,S,W,E). Some rooms in the map contain *coins* which have to be delivered to the *drop-off area*. The agent can only carry one coin at a time, and is rewarded only upon delivering the coin. The agent knows its position and the position of all remaining coins. The HRL architecture is realised by skills trained to reach individual regions of the map, marked #1–#15 in Fig. 1a, plus four skills identical to the atomic actions. This resembles the earlier approaches [2,7,14,16,18]. Skills #14 and #15 are deliberately left out from the skill set, making a defect in the pre-trained hierarchy. Coin-gatherer environment is hence discrete, fully observable, using goal-based skills, and features a high number of 17 skills.

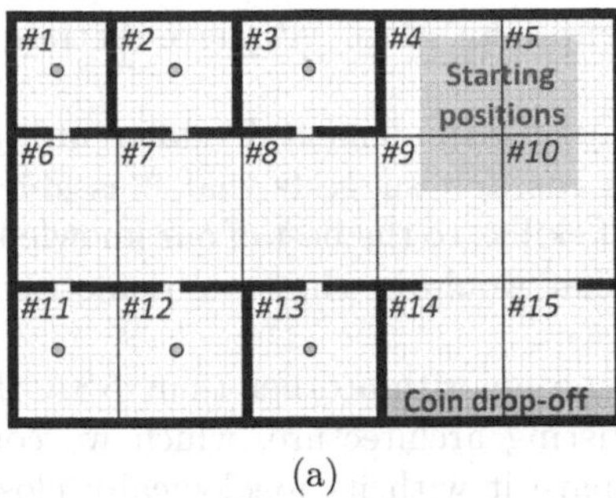

(a)

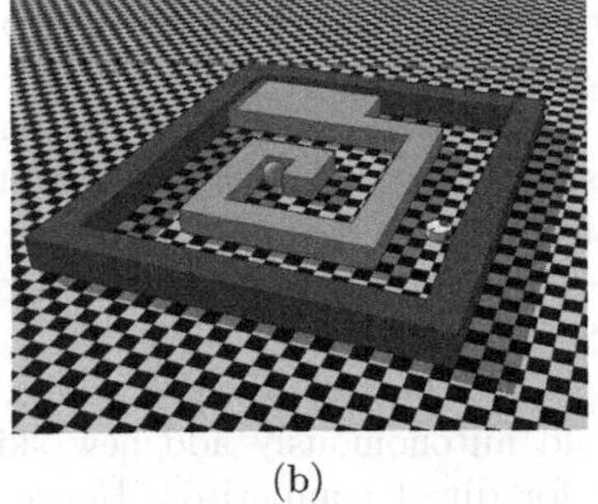

(b)

Fig. 1. Environments: (a) *Coin-gatherer* map – yellow dots are coins, numbers represent 15 ideal skill regions; (b) *Maze-bot* – one of six possible mazes, the green sphere represents the goal position. (Color figure online)

Maze-Bot: The agent represents a vacuum-cleaner-like robot in a continuous environment. Its goal is to solve a given maze, using wheel torques as atomic actions. There is a total of six different mazes (one of them shown in Fig. 1b), and a maze is chosen randomly at beginning of each episode. The agent uses only a LIDAR-like sensor to detect its surroundings, with a range roughly 6 times the robot's size. However, it does *not* have an orientation sensor (compass), or the knowledge which maze it has been placed in. A reward of 1 is given if the agent reaches the maze's goal point, and −0.05 penalty per step otherwise. The HRL architecture is realised by locomotion skills to efficiently move a larger distance forward/backward, or turn left, but not a skill to turn right. Maze-bot environment, in contrast to Coin-gatherer, is continuous, partially observable, randomized, and uses a small number of skills which are behavioral.

In both environments, all agents are trained using TRPO algorithm [22]. The policies, as well as the policy-baseline function, are modelled using neural networks with two hidden layers. They are optimised after each training iteration – batch of 5000 high-level steps ($\approx$ 50 episodes for Coin-gatherer, $\approx$ 70 episodes for Maze-bot). The metric for the evaluation of all models was the *average discounted reward*, i.e. $G(\pi) = \mathbb{E}_\pi[\sum_{t=0}^{T} \gamma^t R(s_t, a_t)]$, and the results were averaged over 8 trials with different random seeds. The implementation of ASA was made possible by the *Garage* framework [3].

5.2 Overall Performance

Since the primary goal of ASA is to *improve* an existing architecture, in Experiment 1 we focused on the overall gain of ASA to the pre-trained HRL agent ('Base run' without ASA). As seen in Fig. 2a and 3a, adding a new skill identified by ASA consistently and significantly increases the performance of the agent. In case of *Coin-gatherer*, this means an increase from 4.4 to 5.6 delivered coins, out of 6 possible. The *Maze-bot*'s increase by 0.81 translates to paths shorter by 16.2 high-level steps, on average. The shaded areas in these plots represent the 25–75 percentile for *Coin-gatherer*, and 5–95 percentile for *Maze-bot* (since its training was more stable).

As mentioned before, the two environments use fundamentally different types of skills. Since ASA was successful in both cases, it suggests that it is able to train both *goal-based* and *behavioral* types of skills. To the best of our knowledge, there has not yet been a published model that would be shown to demonstrate such behavior.

To the best of our knowledge, there is no algorithm other than ASA that would autonomously add new skills to existing architecture, which we could use for direct comparison. Hence, we compare it with its ideologically closest relative – HiPPO [13], which autonomously creates whole architecture, and is one of few models capable of skill training even *during* high-level training, as

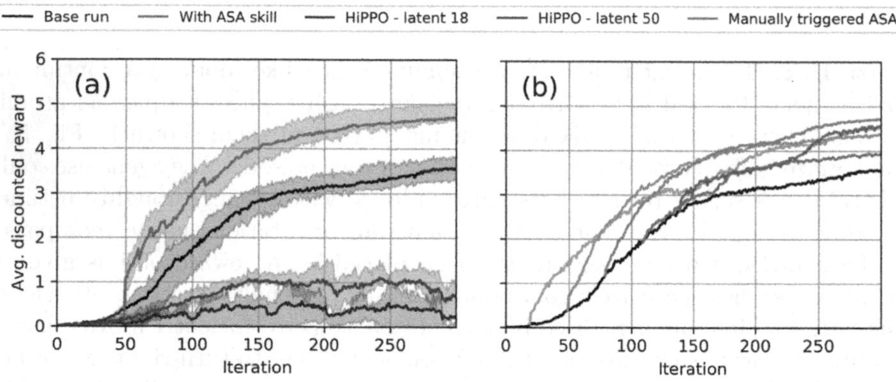

Fig. 2. *Coin-gatherer* environment – results after using ASA to add new skill. New skill was added (a) according to ASA computation, or (b) at other times overriding ASA's decision. Comparison with HiPPO for reference.

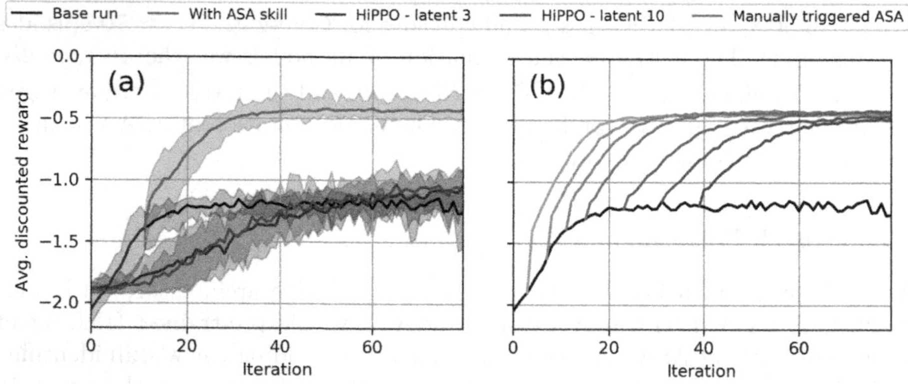

Fig. 3. *Maze-bot* environment – results after using ASA to add new skill. New skill was added (a) according to ASA computation, or (b) at other times overriding ASA's decision. Comparison with HiPPO for reference.

we do in our approach. Its slower start can be explained by initially untrained skills, compared to pre-trained (imperfect) skill set in the Base run. However, it clearly did not manage to identify all useful skills, and hence scores significantly worse compared to the ASA-powered model. We also tried to increase the latent dimension of HiPPO, which effectively controls how many skills are trained, but no further improvement was observed.

The plots in Fig. 2a and 3a show the results of a full-stack approach, i.e. all key steps (decision, training, integration) were performed by ASA. On the other hand, in Fig. 2b and 3b we depict the usage of ASA, but with deactivated component that decides *when* to add the new skill. We can see that even though ASA was triggered manually, it was still able to identify and train a reasonably useful skill.

5.3 Quality of The New Skill

Since the new skill is the key component of ASA method, in Experiment 2 we aimed to evaluate its quality. To do so, we compared it with *ideal* and *bad* skills, which serve as the upper and lower bounds for estimating the usefulness of the new skill. The *ideal* skills were manually constructed to optimally enrich the skill set: a policy for reaching regions #14 and #15 in *Coin-gatherer* environment, and a skill for turning right in *Maze-bot* environment. The *bad* skills were uniform random policies for both environments.

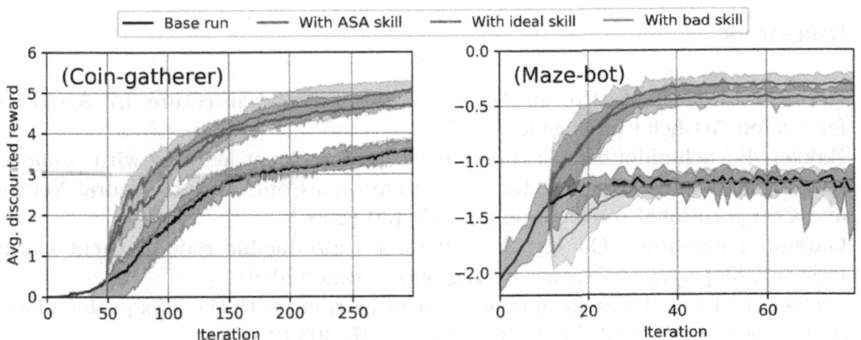

Fig. 4. Integration of ASA-trained skill, an ideal skill that optimally enriches the skill set, and an intentionally useless bad skill.

Figure 4 shows the comparison between the ideal, bad, and ASA-trained skills, from which we can draw several conclusions. First and foremost, the ASA skill identification performs very well, falling short only slightly behind the ideal skills. If we consider the ideal and bad skills as a range bounding the fitness of the skill, we can express that ASA-trained skill scored solid 73.2% of the possible performance in *Coin-gatherer*, and excellent 88.7% in *Maze-bot*. Second, the unimproved performance of a bad skill proves that adding *any* skill is not sufficient for an increased success rate, and hence the success of ASA is not only coincidental. Finally, we can see that adding a useless skill does not hurt the model performance in the long-term view. Hence, even if ASA was used on top of an optimal skill set, and would add a falsely identified missing skill, it would not decrease the overall performance.

6 Conclusion and Future Work

In this paper we presented our *Adaptive Skill Acquisition* model for adding new skills to (possibly suboptimal) HRL hierarchies, and the improvements that make it more robust, efficient, and reusable. Using two distinctive environments, both discrete and continuous, we demonstrated that the new skill trained by ASA can significantly improve the performance of a HRL agent, if it started with a suboptimal skill set. The new skills identified by ASA are only slightly inferior to the optimal ones, proving high quality of the skill-identification component. We compared our method with the state-of-the-art HiPPO algorithm [13] which trains the whole skill set, and showed that ASA skill identification outperforms the older approach by a significant margin.

As a continuation of our work, we would like to adapt the ASA framework even for UMDP-based architectures, such as [12,19]. We will also consider a pseudo-rehearsal technique [21] for the skill integration, which could help speed up the adaptation of the new skill by the high-level agent.

References

1. Bacon, P.L., Harb, J., Precup, D.: The option-critic architecture. In: AAAI Conference on Artificial Intelligence (2017)
2. Bakker, B., Schmidhuber, J.: Hierarchical reinforcement learning with subpolicies specializing for learned subgoals. In: International Conference on Neural Networks and Computational Intelligence, pp. 125–130 (2004)
3. Garage contributors: Garage: A toolkit for reproducible reinforcement learning research. https://github.com/rlworkgroup/garage (2019)
4. Dietterich, T.G.: Hierarchical reinforcement learning with the maxq value function decomposition. J. Artif. Intell. Res. **13**(1), 227–303 (2000)
5. Dillinger, V.: Abstract state space construction in hierarchical reinforcement learning. Ph.D. thesis, Comenius University in Bratislava (2019)
6. Florensa, C., Duan, Y., Abbeel, P.: Stochastic neural networks for hierarchical reinforcement learning. In: International Conference on Learning Representations (2017)
7. Goel, S., Huber, M.: Subgoal discovery for hierarchical reinforcement learning using learned policies. In: Florida AI Research Society Conference, pp. 346–350 (2003)
8. Holas, J., Farkaš, I.: Adaptive skill acquisition in hierarchical reinforcement learning. In: Farkaš, I., Masulli, P., Wermter, S. (eds.) ICANN 2020. LNCS, vol. 12397, pp. 383–394. Springer, Cham (2020). https://doi.org/10.1007/978-3-030-61616-8_31

9. Ioffe, S., Szegedy, C.: Batch normalization: Accelerating deep network training by reducing internal covariate shift. In: International Conference on Machine Learning, pp. 448–456. PMLR (2015)
10. Konidaris, G., Barto, A.G.: Skill discovery in continuous reinforcement learning domains using skill chaining. In: Advances in Neural Information Processing Systems, pp. 1015–1023 (2009)
11. Kulkarni, T.D., Narasimhan, K., Saeedi, A., Tenenbaum, J.: Hierarchical deep reinforcement learning: Integrating temporal abstraction and intrinsic motivation. In: Advances in Neural Information Processing Systems, pp. 3675–3683 (2016)
12. Levy, A., Konidaris, G., Platt, R., Saenko, K.: Learning multi-level hierarchies with hindsight. In: International Conference on Learning Representations (2018)
13. Li, A.C., Florensa, C., Clavera, I., Abbeel, P.: Sub-policy adaptation for hierarchical reinforcement learning. In: International Conference on Learning Representations (2020)
14. McGovern, A., Barto, A.G.: Automatic discovery of subgoals in reinforcement learning using diverse density. Int. Conf. Mach. Learn. **1**, 361–368 (2001)
15. McGovern, E.A., Barto, A.G.: Autonomous discovery of temporal abstractions from interaction with an environment. Ph.D. thesis, University of Massachusetts at Amherst (2002)
16. Menache, I., Mannor, S., Shimkin, N.: Q-cut—dynamic discovery of sub-goals in reinforcement learning. In: European Conference on Machine Learning, pp. 295–306 (2002)
17. Metzen, J.H., Kirchner, F.: Incremental learning of skill collections based on intrinsic motivation. Front. Neurorobotics **7**, 11 (2013)
18. Moerman, W.: Hierarchical reinforcement learning: Assignment of behaviours to subpolicies by self-organization. Ph.D. thesis, Cognitive Artificial Intelligence, Utrecht University (2009)
19. Nachum, O., Gu, S.S., Lee, H., Levine, S.: Data-efficient hierarchical reinforcement learning. In: Advances in Neural Information Processing Systems, pp. 3303–3313 (2018)
20. Parr, R., Russell, S.J.: Reinforcement learning with hierarchies of machines. In: Advances in Neural Information Processing Systems, pp. 1043–1049 (1998)
21. Robins, A.: Catastrophic forgetting, rehearsal and pseudorehearsal. Connection Sci. **7**(2), 123–146 (1995)
22. Schulman, J., Levine, S., Abbeel, P., Jordan, M., Moritz, P.: Trust region policy optimization. In: International Conference on Machine Learning, pp. 1889–1897 (2015)
23. Shu, T., Xiong, C., Socher, R.: Hierarchical and interpretable skill acquisition in multi-task reinforcement learning. In: International Conference on Learning Representations (2018)
24. Sutton, R.S., Precup, D., Singh, S.: Between MDPs and semi-MDPs: a framework for temporal abstraction in reinforcement learning. Artif. Intell. **112**, 181–211 (1999)

Aspect-Based Sentiment Classification with Reinforcement Learning and Local Understanding

Ming-Fan Li(✉), Kaijie Zhou, Hongze Wang, Long Ma, and Xuan Li

Ping An Life Insurance of China, Ltd. PAFC, No. 5033, Yitian Road, Futian District, Shenzhen, China
{limingfan409,zhoukaijie002,malong633,lixuan208}@pingan.com.cn

Abstract. Aspect-based sentiment analysis is a fine-grained classification task in natural language processing. In this paper, we propose a new framework with reinforcement learning agent to assess the importance of words in the sentence for sentiment analysis and mask out insignificant ones. Our method emphasizes on local linguistic understanding and extracts aspect-agnostic background information as well as aspect-relevant information. Experiments on three common datasets show that the proposed method is effective and achieves substantial performance improvements over comparison models.

Keywords: ABSA · Reinforcement learning · Local linguistic understanding

1 Introduction

Aspect-based sentiment analysis (ABSA, also known as aspect-level sentiment analysis) is the task of assessing the sentiment polarity of a given context sentence toward an aspect (also called target) which could be contained in the context or not. For example, "*service is slow, but the dishes are good*"; in this sentence sentiment polarities for the two aspects "*service*" and "*dishes*" are negative and positive, respectively.

Many works have done on this task and used different attention mechanisms to extract aspect-relevant information. For example, IAN [15] uses interactive attentions to generate better representation for the aspect and the sentence. TG-SAN [29] uses target-guided structured attention network to capture target-related contexts. Graph convolutional network is also utilized to find tokens that are more syntactically-proximal to the aspect, via exploiting syntactical information and word dependencies [1,27,28].

In this article, we utilize a policy network as an agent to refine the context sentence. It assesses whether tokens in the context are important or not, and masks (deletes) noisy ones. After the masking process, the context sentence is more concise and easier for sentiment analysis, and the classifier is less confused

I. Farkaš et al. (Eds.): ICANN 2021, LNCS 12894, pp. 662–674, 2021.
https://doi.org/10.1007/978-3-030-86380-7_54

by distractive narratives. Since there is no label for the task of masking, the agent cannot be trained supervisedly. We train the agent with policy gradient [20,22] in reinforcement learning. Though attention mechanism can also be used to assess importance or relevance of tokens in the sentence, it is still interesting to investigate RL for this purpose.

When doing neural language understanding, it is also important to grasp local linguistic and paralinguistic phenomena, such as idiom, negation, sarcasm, comparative, shifters, morphology and reducers, etc. [2]. For example, "*service is not exactly five star, but that's not really a big deal*"; for this instance, understanding the idioms and the negations is key to make right sentiment classification.

It can be observed that the above mentioned phenomena are mainly phrase-level, hence designing a model better poised to capture local patterns may help for sentiment analysis. So in this paper, we design a model emphasizing on local linguistic understanding. It is well known that convolutional neural network (CNN) is good at extracting local patterns [11], therefore it is promising to make use of CNN for ABSA task. Though it is interesting to use other methods to get better local linguistic understanding, we leave this kind of exploration for future work.

In another perspective toward ABSA, it can been seen that besides aspect-related snippets in the context, overall sentiment of the context is also helpful for ABSA. For example, "*it's lovely to eat here; the service is good and the food is delectable*". Two aspects can be detected in this sentence: "*service*" and "*food*". The opinion terms are "*good*" and "*delectable*" respectively. If an ABSA model only extracts aspect-relevant information, then it probably cannot make a correct classification for the sentiment toward the aspect "*food*" in case of that it cannot understand the token "*delectable*". If the opinion term is not a single token but a rare idiom, the situation is even worse.

This problem can be solved by using better token embeddings for larger vocabulary, or employing pretrained language model. Actually there have been some works adopting BERT to get better context understanding [23,26]. In this paper, we solve this problem with another approach. It can be observed that in the above example sentence, the overall sentiment is positive. This is explicitly expressed by "*lovely to eat here*". An ABSA model can make a correct classification with this fact and the conjunction "*and*" which indicates that the sentiment for the aspect "*food*" is same with the overall sentiment. In this way, information related to overall sentiment tendency of the sentence can help for aspect-based sentiment analysis. We call this kind of information as "aspect-agnostic background information (BGI)". We extract both aspect-related information and aspect-agnostic background information from the context for ABSA task.

In summary, our contributions in this paper are:

- A reinforcement learning framework is proposed to refine the context sentence. With the reinforcement learning agent, model can better catch important tokens.
- A new model is designed to understand local linguisitic phenomena, and extract both the aspect-related information and the aspect-agnostic background information.
- Experiments are conducted over 3 common datasets. The results show that the proposed method is effective and achieves substantial performance improvements.

2 Related Work

Aspect-based sentiment analysis has drawn many attentions, and many models have been proposed for this task. SVM [10] works with hand-crafted features. AOA [8] treats the aspect and the context sentence in a joint way with an attention-over-attention structure. IAN [15] generates representations for the aspect and the context with interactive attentions. TNet-LF [13] puts forward a structure calling Context-Preserving Transformation (CPT) to preserve contextual information. TG-SAN [29] captures target-related contexts for ABSA with target-guided structured attention. MCRF-SA [24] uses multiple CRFs based structured attention model to extract aspect-specific opinion spans.

ASGCN-DG [27] uses Graph Convolutional Network over directional dependency graph of the sentence to exploit syntactical information and word dependencies. ASGCN-DT [27] is same with ASGCN-DG except that undirectional dependency graph is used. ASCNN [27] is same with ASGCN-DG except that ordinary convolutional network takes the place of graph convolutional network. In [16], dependency subtree attention network (DSAN) model is proposed to extract dependency subtree and generate a more accurate aspect representation. In [19], a simple TextCNN-like model is used to approach sentence-level sentiment analysis. In [7], by using parameterized filters and parameterized gates, the authors try to incorporate aspect information into model.

Reinforcement learning deals with Markovian sequential decision process and maximizes the total reward of the whole process. Reinforcement learning has been actively explored in many NLP tasks, for example, in dependency parsing [12], seq2seq models [9], and coreference resolution [6,25]. In [30], reinforcement learning is used to learn structured representation for text classification. In [21], reinforcement learning is used to refine the context in the task of aspect sentiment classification towards question-answering.

3 Methodology

3.1 Problem and Framework

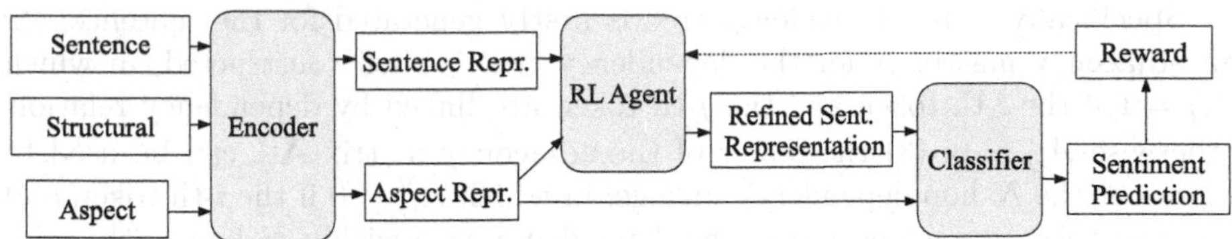

Fig. 1. Overall structure of the framework.

The problem is defined as follows: given a sentence $\mathbf{S} = \{w_1, \cdots, w_n\}$, aspect-based sentiment analysis is to predict its sentiment polarity $y \in \{positive, negative, neutral\}$ (in 3-class situation) in regard to a specified aspect term $\mathbf{A} = \{w_{a_1}, \cdots, w_{a_m}\}$. In this paper, we just consider the situation that the aspect term is contained in the sentence.

To approach this problem, we propose a framework that consists of three modules: the encoder, the classifier and the agent, as shown in Fig. 1. The encoder is used to generate representations for the sentence and the aspect; the agent aims to refine the sentence representations (to mask token representations if they are irrelated to the problem); the classifier finally predicts the sentiment polarity.

The encoder and the classifier make up the backbone model (ASBL, Aspect-based Sentiment classification with Background information and Local understanding). It can work alone for the ABSA task. In this situation, sentence representation produced by the encoder is feed directly to the classifier without refinement from the agent.

3.2 Dependency-Guided Encoder

The encoder produces an initial representation of the sentence: the sentence $\mathbf{S}$ is firstly embedded and then forwarded to a BiLSTM layer. The output of the forward and the backward LSTM layers are concatenated for the initial representation $\{\widehat{\mathbf{h}}_i\}_{i=1}^n$:

$$\begin{aligned} \{\overrightarrow{\mathbf{h}}_i\}, \{\overleftarrow{\mathbf{h}}_i\} &= \text{BiLSTM}(\text{Embed}(\{w_i\})) \\ \widehat{\mathbf{h}}_i &= [\overrightarrow{\mathbf{h}}_i; \overleftarrow{\mathbf{h}}_i] \end{aligned} \tag{1}$$

where $[\cdot\ ;\ \cdot]$ means the concatenate operation. The size of LSTM unit is d_{hidden}.

The *aspect representation* $\{\mathbf{v}_j\}_{j=1}^m$ is obtained by slicing from the sentence representation:

$$\{\mathbf{v}_j | j \in [1, m]\} = \{\widehat{\mathbf{h}}_j | j \in [a_1, a_m]\}, \tag{2}$$

where a_1 and a_m are respectively the start position and the end position of the aspect term in the context sentence.

It is intuitive that if a token is more syntactically-related to the aspect term, then it would be more informative for sentiment prediction. Hence we use multi-hop dependency linkage to adjust the initial sentence representation[1].

Specifically, (1) a dependency tree is firstly generated for the sentence; (2) an adjacency matrix $\mathbf{A}$ for the dependency tree is then constructed, in which $A_{ij} = 1$ if the i-th token and the j-th token are linked by dependency relation, otherwise $A_{ij} = 0$; (3) the power of the adjacency matrix $\mathbf{A}^N$ can be used to represent the N-hop dependency linkage, in which $A_{ij}^N \neq 0$ if the i-th token and the j-th token are connected in the dependency tree within N hops, otherwise $A_{ij}^N = 0$. (4) We believe that if a token is connected to the aspect tokens by more hops then it is less informative. Then the final *sentence representation* $\{\mathbf{h}_i\}_{i=1}^n$ can be obtained by

$$\mathbf{h}_i = \widehat{\mathbf{h}}_i \cdot \eta_i \tag{3}$$

where η_i is defined by $\eta_i = 1 - \eta_{dep}$ for $A_{ij}^N = 0, j \in [a_1, a_m]$; $\eta_i = 1$ otherwise. Here η_{dep} is an constant. A larger η_{dep} means less importance of tokens not in the N-hop neighborhood of the aspect.

3.3 Reinforcement Learning Agent

A policy network is used to work as a reinforcement learning agent. It takes the aspect representation and the initial representation of the context sentence as input and decides whether tokens in the context are important for aspect-specific sentiment analysis, and masks out noisy ones. The structure of policy network is shown in Fig. 2.

Firstly, the aspect representation $\{\mathbf{v}_j\}_{j=1}^m$ is averaged to get a vector representation: $\mathbf{v}_{aver} = (1/m)\Sigma_{j=1}^m \mathbf{v}_j$.

The vector representation is then repeated multiple times to align with the sentence representation (i.e., $\mathbf{v}_{aver}$ is repeated as $\{\overbrace{\mathbf{v}_{aver}, \cdots, \mathbf{v}_{aver}}^{n}\}$), and then it is added in the feature dimension with the sentence representation $\{\mathbf{h}_i\}_{i=1}^n$ to obtain an aspect-aware representation of the sentence: $\{\tilde{\mathbf{u}}_i\}_{i=1}^n$, with $\tilde{\mathbf{u}}_i = \mathbf{h}_i + \mathbf{v}_{aver}$.

Two self-attention layers follow:

$$\{\dot{\mathbf{u}}_i\} = \text{Attention}(\{\tilde{\mathbf{u}}_i\}, \{\tilde{\mathbf{u}}_j\}, \{\tilde{\mathbf{u}}_k\}; F_{dot}),$$
$$\{\bar{\mathbf{u}}_i\} = \text{Attention}(\{\tilde{\mathbf{u}}_i\}, \{\tilde{\mathbf{u}}_j\}, \{\tilde{\mathbf{u}}_k\}; F_{bil}).$$

Here, the attention layer is defined as a mapping from a query sequence $\{\mathbf{q}_i\}$, a key sequence $\{\mathbf{k}_j\}$ and a value sequence $\{\mathbf{v}_k\}$, to a resulting sequence $\{\mathbf{h}_i\}$, with the help of an attention score function F:

$$\{\mathbf{h}_i\} = \text{Attention}(\{\mathbf{q}_i\}, \{\mathbf{k}_j\}, \{\mathbf{v}_k\}; F). \tag{4}$$

[1] Dependency parsing tool: spaCy, https://spacy.io/.

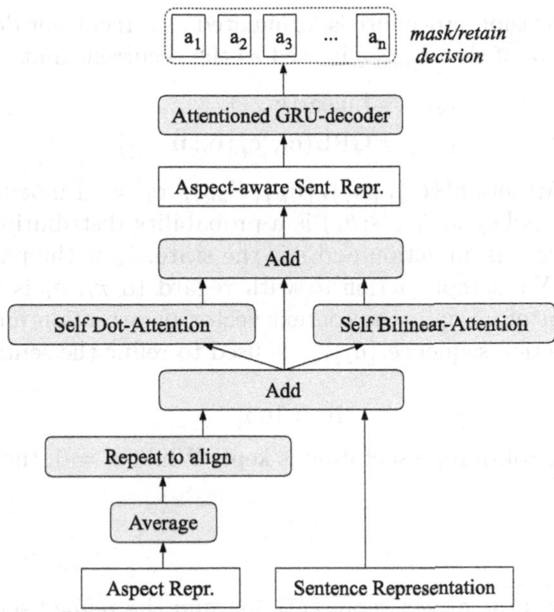

Fig. 2. Structure of the agent.

Concretely:

$$s_{ij} = F(\mathbf{q}_i, \mathbf{k}_j), \tag{5}$$

$$a_{ij} = exp(s_{ij}) / \sum_j exp(s_{ij}), \tag{6}$$

$$\mathbf{h}_i = \sum_j a_{ij} \mathbf{v}_j. \tag{7}$$

The two functions F_{dot} and F_{bil} are the dot-attention score function and the bilinear-attention score function, respectively:

$$F_{dot}(\mathbf{q}_i, \mathbf{k}_j) = \mathbf{q}_i \cdot \mathbf{k}_j, \tag{8}$$

$$F_{bil}(\mathbf{q}_i, \mathbf{k}_j) = \mathbf{q}_i^T \mathbf{W} \mathbf{k}_j, \tag{9}$$

where $\mathbf{W}$ is a trainable weight matrix.

A new representation $\{\mathbf{u}_i\}_{i=1}^n$ of the context sentence is generated by:

$$\mathbf{u}_i = \tilde{\mathbf{u}}_i + \dot{\mathbf{u}}_i + \bar{\mathbf{u}}_i. \tag{10}$$

This representation is used for following decoder to decide on tokens importance for sentiment analysis.

A sequential decision procedure is utilized to decide whether each token in the sentence is to be retained according to its importance for sentiment analysis. The action space is $\{0, 1\}$, corresponding to "mask" and "retain" respectively.

The sequential decision procedure is formulated as a recurrent decoding process, and a GRU cell [3] of size d_{hidden} is used as the recurrent unit:

$$\pi_{i+1} = \text{Linear}(\mathbf{c}_{i+1}), \tag{11}$$

$$\mathbf{c}_{i+1} = \text{GRU}(\mathbf{c}_i, [\mathbf{c}_i^x; \mathbf{e}_i; \mathbf{u}_{i+1}]), \tag{12}$$

with $\{\mathbf{c}_i^x\} = \text{Attention}(\{\mathbf{c}_i\}, \{\mathbf{u}_j\}, \{\mathbf{u}_k\}; F_{dot})$, $\mathbf{e}_i = \text{Embed}(a_i)$ and $a_i = \text{Sample}(\pi_i)$. The policy $\pi_{i+1}(a|s;\theta_\pi)$ is a probability distribution on the action space $\{0, 1\}$. Here a is an action and s is the state, θ_π is the parameters of the policy network. We sample action a_i with regard to π_i. $\mathbf{e}_i$ is the size-d_{hidden} embedding vector of a_i. $\mathbf{c}_i^x$ is the context vector by attention mechanism.

The binary action sequence $\{a_i\}_{i=1}^n$ is used to refine the sentence representation:

$$\bar{\mathbf{h}}_i = \mathbf{h}_i a_i. \tag{13}$$

When $a_i = 1$, the token representation is kept. While $a_i = 0$, the token representation is masked.

3.4 Classifier

The classifier takes the aspect representation and the refined sentence representation as input and predicts sentiment polarity. The structure is shown in Fig. 3.

The aspect representation $\{\mathbf{v}_j\}_{j=1}^m$ is averaged to $\mathbf{v}_{aver}$ and repeated to match the sentence length n. The resulting sequence is concatenated with the refined sentence representation $\{\bar{\mathbf{h}}_i\}_{i=1}^n$ in the feature dimension, to get an aspect-aware sentence representation $\{\tilde{\mathbf{h}}_i\}_{i=1}^n$, with $\tilde{\mathbf{h}}_i = [\bar{\mathbf{h}}_i; \mathbf{v}_{aver}]$.

This sentence representation $\{\tilde{\mathbf{h}}_i\}_{i=1}^n$ is then forwarded to two CNN layers. The output is a new representation $\{\mathbf{g}_i\}_{i=1}^n$ of the context sentence with local patterns emphasized. Each CNN layer uses ReLU activation.

This representation $\{\mathbf{g}_i\}_{i=1}^n$ is then aggregated via an attention-pooling layer with the aspect vector representation $\mathbf{v}_{aver}$ as the query:

$$\{\mathbf{h}_{pool}\} = \text{Attention}(\{\mathbf{v}_{aver}\}, \{\mathbf{g}_j\}, \{\mathbf{g}_k\}; F_{dot}).$$

In above, $\{\mathbf{v}_{aver}\}$ is the query sequence to the attention layer with only one element $\mathbf{v}_{aver}$. $\mathbf{h}_{pool}$ can be viewed as aspect-related information retrieved from the context.

In another branch, the refined sentence representation $\{\bar{\mathbf{h}}_i\}_{i=1}^n$ is summarized with another attention-pooling layer with a trainable vector $\mathbf{v}_{tr}$ as the query:

$$\{\mathbf{g}_{pool}\} = \text{Attention}(\{\mathbf{v}_{tr}\}, \{\bar{\mathbf{h}}_j\}, \{\bar{\mathbf{h}}_k\}; F_{dot}).$$

The resulting vector $\mathbf{g}_{pool}$ can be viewed as aspect-agnostic background information (BGI) retrieved from the context sentence.

Then $\mathbf{g}_{pool}$ and $\mathbf{h}_{pool}$ are concatenated in the feature dimension to form the final feature vector $\mathbf{r}_{all}$, which is forwarded to a feed-forward block (FFW) to get the sentiment polarity probabilities:

$$\mathbf{r}_{all} = [\mathbf{g}_{pool}; \mathbf{h}_{pool}], \tag{14}$$

$$\mathbf{p} = \text{FFW}(\mathbf{r}_{all}), \tag{15}$$

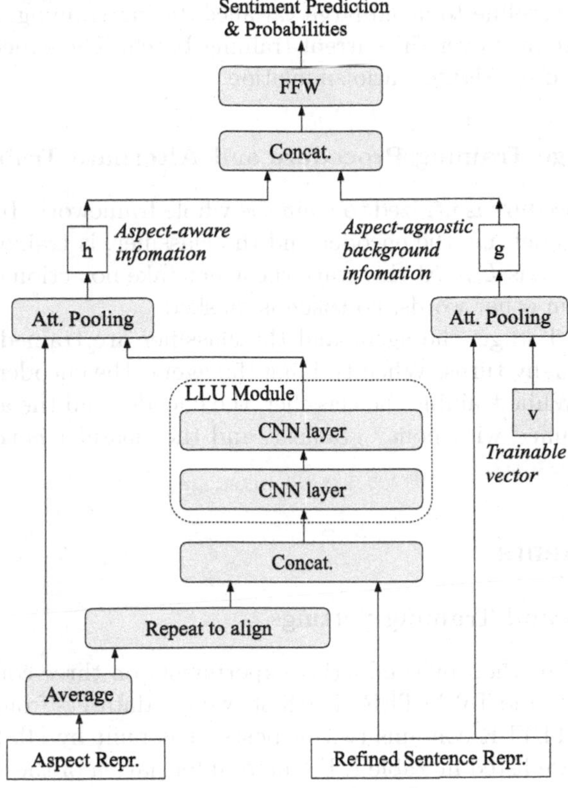

Fig. 3. Structure of the classifier.

where $\text{FFW}(\mathbf{x}) = \text{Linear}(\text{ReLU}(\text{Linear}(\mathbf{x})))$.

In the above equation, $\mathbf{p}$ is the predicted probability distribution (before normalization) over sentiment polarities. Given the ground truth $\bar{\mathbf{p}}$, the cross entropy loss used for training is calculated as:

$$L_{sa} = -\bar{\mathbf{p}} \cdot \log(\text{softmax}(\mathbf{p})). \tag{16}$$

The classification result is the polarity with highest probability. If the prediction is right, then the reward for the actions of the agent is 1. Otherwise, the reward is 0.

The policy network parameters θ_π are optimized through the policy gradient:

$$\nabla_{\theta_\pi} J = \mathsf{E}_{a\sim\pi}\{\sum_{i=1}^{n}(R-b)\nabla_{\theta_\pi}\log(\pi_i(a_i))\} \tag{17}$$

where R is the reward for the actions. There is no intermediate reward for each action in the sequential process. Only when all the actions are conducted and the sentiment polarity is predicted, then a reward is returned for all the actions.

b is the reward baseline to avoid large variance during training. It is calculated as the average reward over the current training batch. The expectation $\mathsf{E}_{a \sim \pi}$ is usually estimated by Monte Carlo simulation.

3.5 Two-Stage Training Procedure and Alternate Training

A two-stage procedure is utilized to train the whole framework. In the first stage, the backbone model, i.e. the encoder and the classifier, is trained with the loss of sentiment analysis L_{sa}. At this stage the agent take no action on the sentence representation, in other words, no token is masked.

In the second stage, the agent and the classifier are trained for one epoch alternately for many turns. When training the agent, the encoder and the classifier are frozen. While training the classifier, the encoder and the agent are frozen. The agent is trained with policy gradient, and the classifier is trained with the loss L_{sa}.

4 Experiments

4.1 Datasets and Training Settings

We evaluate our method by conducting experiments on three common datasets: LAP14, REST14, and TWITTER. The first two are datasets from SemEval 2014 task 4 [18]. TWITTER contains twitter posts, it is built by [4]. Some statistics of the datasets are listed in Table 1. For more information of the datasets, please see previous works, such as [5,13,14,27].

Table 1. Numbers of examples in the datasets.

Dataset	TWITTER		LAP14		REST14	
	Train	Test	Train	Test	Train	Test
#Positive	1561	173	994	341	2164	728
#Neutral	3127	346	464	169	637	196
#Negative	1560	173	870	128	807	196

As a common practice, accuracy and macro F1-score are used as performance metrics. 20% of the training set are randomly held out as the validation set for tuning the hyper-parameters. The word embeddings are initialized with 300-d pretrained GloVe vectors [17], and fixed during training. Xavier normal initialization is used for trainable variables initialization. d_{hidden} is set to 300. The number of output channels of the CNN layers are $d_{hidden} * 4$. The kernel sizes are 3. The padding scheme is to add "[pad]" tokens to make sequence length unchanged. The range of dependency neighborhood N_{dep} is 5. The relative neighborhood weight η_{dep} is 0.5. The optimizer used is Adam with learning rate 1e−3. The

Table 2. Model results (%). The results of TG-SAN and MCRF-SA are retrieved from the original papers. The results of other comparison models are retrieved from the work [27]. The reported results of the proposed model are averaged from those of randomly started 30 runnings with different seeds. Performance improvements of the proposed ASBL-RL model over comparison models are statistically significant with $p < 0.01$.

	Model	LAP14		REST14		TWITTER	
		Accuracy	Macro-F1	Accuracy	Macro-F1	Accuracy	Macro-F1
Comparison models	SVM [10]	70.49	–	80.16	–	63.40	63.30
	AOA [8]	72.62	67.52	79.97	70.42	72.30	70.20
	IAN [15]	72.05	67.38	79.26	70.09	72.50	70.81
	TNet-LF [13]	74.61	70.14	80.42	71.03	72.98	71.43
	ASCNN [27]	72.62	66.72	81.73	73.10	71.05	69.43
	ASGCN-DG [27]	75.55	71.05	80.77	72.02	72.15	70.40
	TG-SAN [29]	75.27	71.18	81.66	72.59	74.71	73.65
	MCRF-SA [24]	77.64	74.23	82.86	73.78	–	–
Proposed model	ASBL-RL	**78.25**	**74.37**	**83.28**	**76.14**	**75.41**	**74.03**
Ablated models	ASBL-S	77.43	73.39	82.84	75.20	74.51	73.05
	ASBL	77.41	73.35	82.84	75.16	74.51	73.03
	ASBL w/o DEP	76.52	72.53	82.68	74.70	74.37	72.93
	ASBL w/o BGI	76.32	72.00	81.83	73.78	74.31	72.76
	ASBL w/o LLU	76.03	71.80	82.23	73.98	74.15	72.48

L2-regularization coefficient is 1e−4 and the dropout probability is 0.6. Batch sizes are set to 16, 32, and 32 for datasets LAP14, REST14, and TWITTER, respectively.

4.2 Results and Ablation Study

We report our experiment results in Table 2. One can see that the proposed model ASBL-RL produces better results over all the 3 datasets than all the comparison models.

To check the effectiveness of different parts in our model, we conducted ablation study. Table 2 shows that the backbone model ASBL without reinforcement learning drops about 1.0 absolute percent in performance over all the 3 datasets. This verifies that the effectiveness of reinforcement learning for ABSA.

Experiments are also conducted when the alternate training of the agent and the classifier is changed to a single-turn one to see the impact of the training procedure. In the single-turn training, the agent is trained with policy gradient only once after the first training stage, and the resulting model is named ASBL-S. It can be observed that ASBL-S is just marginally better than ASBL. This shows that alternate training of the agent and the classifier is important for the application of RL. In the alternate training of the agent and the classifier, the agent explores to mask noisy tokens. The classifier adjusts to exploration results of the agent, and in turn, supports the agent to explore better policies. In an iterative way, the model is boosted gradually and reaches a better status.

The line "ASBL w/o DEP" lists the results of ASBL without dependency information, i.e. setting $\eta_i = 1$ for all i. There is a small drop in performance over all the 3 datasets.

The line "ASBL w/o BGI" lists the results of ASBL without aspect-agnostic background information. Without background information, accuracy and f1-score both drop about $0.4 \sim 1.0$ absolute percent over LAP14 and REST14 datasets; accuracy over TWITTER has a small drop while f1-score is nearly the same. This verifies that background information can contribute to aspect-based sentiment analysis.

The line "ASBL w/o LLU" lists the results of ASBL without local linguistic understanding. In this situation, the LLU module is replaced with a linear layer. Accuracy and f1-score both drop about $0.6 \sim 0.9$ absolute percent over LAP14 and REST14 datasets; accuracy and f1-score over TWITTER are nearly same with those of ASBL. One can see that local linguistic understanding is indeed helpful for sentiment analysis.

4.3 Case Study and Error Analysis

We also made case study to check the quality of refinement of the agent and their influence on ABSA. Some examples are listed in Table 3.

For long texts, such as the example 1, the sentence after refinement is more concise and much easier for the classifier to make prediction. In example 2, some noisy words are deleted. In example 3, narratives of another aspect with opposite sentiment polarity are deleted.

Table 3. Examples of refinement of the agent.

No.	Text refinement	Aspect	Predication	Label
1	creative dishes like ~~king crab salad with passion fruit vinaigrette and fettuccine with grilled seafood in a rosemary-orange sauce are unexpected elements on an otherwise predictable bistro menu .~~	dishes	positive ✓	positive
2	even for two ~~very hungry people there~~ is plenty of food left ~~to be taken home~~ -lrb- it reheats really well also -rrb- .	food	positive ✓	positive
3	the lack of ac and the fact that there are a million swarming bodies -lrb- although everyone is ~~polite and no one is pushing -rrb- is a slight turn off .~~	ac	negative ✓	negative
4	make more tables - ~~perhaps a rooftop bar ?~~	tables	neutral ✗	negative
5	it took 100 years for parisi to get around to making pizza -lrb- at least i do ~~n't think they ever made it before this year -rrb- ... but it was worth the wait .~~	pizza	neutral ✗	positive

There are also some badcases. In example 4, although the RL agent makes correct decisions on tokens relevance, the predicted sentiment polarity for the aspect "*tables*" is incorrect. The comment "*make more tables*" implies "*there are not enough tables*", but the model fails to catch this implicit meaning.

In example 5, the most informative part "*it was worth the wait*" is deleted and the sentiment is predicted incorrectly. To make the right prediction, coreference resolution is required: the model should understand the pronoun "*it*" is actually refering to the aspect term "*pizza*". The resolution is difficult, especially when the refering part and the antecedent are separated by a long distance.

5 Conclusion

In this article, a reinforcement learning framework is proposed for the task of aspect-level sentiment analysis. A policy network is used to refine the context representation. A novel model is designed to extract both aspect-relevant information and aspect-agnostic background information from the context sentence. It takes into account syntactic dependency information and local linguistic understanding. Experiments on three benchmark datasets demonstrate that our method is effective and achieves large improvements over comparison models.

References

1. Bai, X., Liu, P., Zhang, Y.: Investigating typed syntactic dependencies for targeted sentiment classification using graph attention neural network. In: IEEE/ACM TASLP, arXiv arXiv:2002.09685 (2020)
2. Barnes, J., Ovrelid, L., Velldal, E.: Sentiment analysis is not solved! assessing and probing sentiment classification. In: BlackBoxNLP Workshop at ACL 2019, arXiv arXiv:1906.05887 (2019)
3. Chung, J., Gulcehre, C., Cho, K.H., Bengio, Y.: Empirical evaluation of gated recurrent neural networks on sequence modeling. In: arXiv arXiv:1412.3555 (2014)
4. Dong, L., Wei, F., Tan, C., Tang, D., Zhou, M., Xu, K.: Adaptive recursive neural network for target-dependent twitter sentiment classification. ACL **2**, 49–54 (2014)
5. Fan, F., Feng, Y., Zhao, D.: Multi-grained attention network for aspect-level sentiment classification. In: EMNLP, pp. 3433–3442 (2018)
6. Fei, H., Li, X., Li, D., Li, P.: End-to-end deep reinforcement learning based coreference resolution. In: ACL, pp. 660–665 (2019)
7. Huang, B., Carley, K.: Parameterized convolutional neural networks for aspect level sentiment classification. In: EMNLP, pp. 1091–1096 (2018)
8. Huang, B., Ou, Y., Carley, K.M.: Aspect level sentiment classification with attention-over-attention neural networks. In: Thomson, R., Dancy, C., Hyder, A., Bisgin, H. (eds.) SBP-BRiMS 2018. LNCS, vol. 10899, pp. 197–206. Springer, Cham (2018). https://doi.org/10.1007/978-3-319-93372-6_22
9. Keneshloo, Y., Shi, T., Reddy, C., Ramakrishnan, N.: Deep reinforcement learning for sequence to sequence models. In: arXiv arXiv:1805.09461 (2018)
10. Kiritchenko, S., Zhu, X., Cherry, C., Mohammad, S.: Nrc-canada-2014: detecting aspects and sentiment in customer reviews. In: Proceedings of the 8th International Workshop on Semantic Evaluation (SemEval 2014), pp. 437–442 (2014)

11. Krizhevsky, A., Sutskever, I., Hinton, G.E.: Imagenet classification with deep convolutional neural networks. Commun. ACM **60**(6), 84–90 (2017)
12. Lê, M., Fokkens, A.: Tackling error propagation through reinforcement learning: a case of greedy dependency parsing. In: EACL, Long Papers, pp. 677–687 (2017)
13. Li, X., Bing, L., Lam, W., Shi, B.: Transformation networks for target-oriented sentiment classification. In: ACL, pp. 946–956 (2018)
14. Li, Z., Wei, Y., Zhang, Y., Zhang, X., Li, X., Yang, Q.: Exploiting coarse-to-fine task transfer for aspect-level sentiment classification. In: AAAI-19 (2019)
15. Ma, D., Li, S., Zhang, X., Wang, H.: Interactive attention networks for aspect-level sentiment classification. In: IJCAI, pp. 4068–4074. AAAI Press (2017)
16. Ouyang, Z., Su, J.: Dependency parsing and attention network for aspect-level sentiment classification. In: Zhang, M., Ng, V., Zhao, D., Li, S., Zan, H. (eds.) NLPCC 2018. LNCS (LNAI), vol. 11108, pp. 391–403. Springer, Cham (2018). https://doi.org/10.1007/978-3-319-99495-6_33
17. Pennington, J., Socher, R., Manning, C.: Glove: Global vectors for word representation. In: Proceedings of EMNLP, pp. 1532–1543 (2014)
18. Pontiki, M., Galanis, D., Pavlopoulos, J., Papageorgiou, H., Androutsopoulos, I., Manandhar, S.: Semeval-2014 task 4: Aspect based sentiment analysis. In: Proceedings of the 8th International Workshop on Semantic Evaluation (SemEval 2014), pp. 27–35 (2014)
19. Salinca, A.: Convolutional neural networks for sentiment classification on business reviews. In: Proceedings of IJCAI Workshop on Semantic Machine Learning (SML 2017), arXiv arXiv:1710.05978 (2017)
20. Sutton, R.S., Mcallester, D., Singh, S., Mansour, Y.: Policy gradient methods for reinforcement learning with function approximation. NIPS **1999**, 1057–1063 (1999)
21. Wang, J., et al.: Aspect sentiment classification towards question-answering with reinforced bidirectional attention network. In: ACL, pp. 3548–3557 (2019)
22. Williams, R.J.: Simple statistical gradient-following algorithms for connectionist reinforcement learning. Mach. Learn. **8**, 229–256 (1992). https://doi.org/10.1007/BF00992696
23. Xu, H., Liu, B., Shu, L., Yu, P.S.: Bert post-training for review reading comprehension and aspect-based sentiment analysis. In: NAACL-HLT (2019)
24. Xu, L., Bing, L., Lu, W., Huang, F.: Aspect sentiment classification with aspect-specific opinion spans. EMNLP 2020, arXiv arXiv:2010.02696 (2020)
25. Yin, Q., Zhang, Y., Zhang, W., Liu, T., Wang, W.: Deep reinforcement learning for chinese zero pronoun resolution. In: ACL, pp. 569–578 (2018)
26. Zeng, B., Yang, H., Xu, R., Zhou, W., Han, X.: Lcf: a local context focus mechanism for aspect-based sentiment classification. Appl. Sci. **9**(16), 3389 (2019)
27. Zhang, C., Li, Q., Song, D.: Aspect-based sentiment classification with aspect-specific graph convolutional networks. In: EMNLP-IJCNLP, pp. 4560–4570 (2019)
28. Zhang, C., Li, Q., Song, D.: Syntax-aware aspect-level sentiment classification with proximity-weighted convolution network. In: SIGIR 2019 (Short), arXiv arXiv:1909.10171 (2019)
29. Zhang, J., Chen, C., Liu, P., He, C., Leung, C.W.K.: Target-guided structured attention network for target-dependent sentiment analysis. In: TACL, 2020, vol. 8, pp. 172–182 (2020)
30. Zhang, T., Huang, M., Zhao, L.: Learning structured representation for text classification via reinforcement learning. In: AAAI (2018)

Latent Dynamics for Artefact-Free Character Animation via Data-Driven Reinforcement Learning

Vihanga Gamage(✉), Cathy Ennis, and Robert Ross

School of Computer Science, Technological University Dublin, Dublin, Ireland
vihanga.gamage@tudublin.ie

Abstract. In the field of character animation, recent work has shown that data-driven reinforcement learning (RL) methods can address issues such as the difficulty of crafting reward functions, and train agents that can portray generalisable social behaviours. However, particularly when portraying subtle movements, these agents have shown a propensity for noticeable artefacts, that may have an adverse perceptual effect. Thus, for these agents to be effectively used in applications where they would interact with humans, the likelihood of these artefacts need to be minimised. In this paper, we present a novel architecture for agents to learn latent dynamics in a more efficient manner, while maintaining modelling flexibility and performance, and reduce the occurrence of noticeable artefacts when generating animation. Furthermore, we introduce a mean-sampling technique when applying learned latent stochastic dynamics to improve the stability of trained model-based RL agents.

Keywords: Reinforcement learning · Latent dynamics · Animation

1 Introduction

An ideal data-driven virtual character animation agent would portray a reasonable variety of behaviours in a realistic manner. Work carried out examining human perception has found that realistic characters lead to more engaging and immersive virtual experiences [13,21]. However, the problem poses significant challenges when attempting to build optimal computational models for human behaviour, due to its inherent complexities and nuances [2,3].

Early work in data-driven animation involved supervised learning approaches that required a significant amount of motion capture clips as training data; however, they offer limited flexibility to generalise and capture a wider variety of behaviours [10,22]. Physics-based deep reinforcement learning approaches such as DeepMimic attempt to utilise signals from physics simulations to train animation agents [19,20]. While these agents are able to successfully learn physics-based skills, this approach cannot be applied to social behaviours, such as gestures, that do not instigate requisite feedback signals. To create neural network-based agents to portray social and interactive behaviours, motion capture clips

I. Farkaš et al. (Eds.): ICANN 2021, LNCS 12894, pp. 675–687, 2021.
https://doi.org/10.1007/978-3-030-86380-7_55

are mandatory to inform the agent being trained with what entails the ideal, realistic ways of portraying a behaviour. The results from supervised learning work carried out have demonstrated that, while supervised networks can effectively learn from motion data, applying these methods to generate more dynamic and flexible animation sequences is challenging.

A novel approach to instead use reinforcement learning to create animation agents was presented in the form of RLAnimate, which introduces data-driven RL for animation control agents, learning dynamics models for animation portraying human-like behaviour, and a compact set of motion capture clips used to inform the training algorithm [5]. RLAnimate agents learn a latent dynamics model for the behaviour portrayed that is deterministic in nature, as well as another model for character animation dynamics, universally applicable to any behaviour portrayed, which consists of deterministic and stochastic components. Agents are trained to output animation by generating a description for the next ideal pose, after which learned dynamics are applied to obtain latent representations used to calculate the rotations for the most optimal pose. The results from this intial work demonstrated that RLAnimate agents are able to generate animation portraying a variety of flexible, generalisable waving and pointing behaviours.

Trained using motion clip collection that totalled to 11482 frames (382.73 s), agents were demonstrated to be able to portray animation clips for a wide range of frame lengths, degree of exaggeration for waving, and target position and frame for pointing. However, particularly in the more subtle components of behaviours, noticeable artefacts were present. These artefacts are usually in the form of occasional twitches and tics within the animation. While these artefacts are due to the finest margins in outputs, numerically, for data-driven animation agents to be applied in applications, noticeable artefacts need to ideally be eliminated completely.

In this paper, we present work carried out to examine the learning and application of latent dynamics in model-based RL agents and introduce a novel agent architecture for RLAnimate that maintain the modelling efficiency and flexibility while eliminating artefacts. The contributions from the work presented can be summarised as follows:

- **Latent self-description** We introduce a mechanism for training model-based agents that allows for the self-description to be carried out entirely in a latent space. This leads to the agent being able to operate with a lower throughput, while enhancing the expressiveness of the latent spaces.
- **Novel agent architecture** We present a novel architecture for RLAnimate agents that learns dynamics models for a pair of parallel latent spaces, each consisting of stochastic and deterministic components.
- **Applying learnt stochastic dynamics** We examine stochastic dynamics learnt by model-based agents, and propose mean sampling for latent distributions learnt. This allows for agents to explore multiple scenarios during training to ascertain the most ideal actions, but once trained, we assumed the agents have formed a strong approximation of the dynamics involved.

The mean sampling allows for a stable application of this correct version of dynamics learnt.

2 Related Work

Early work on data-driven animation using neural networks relied heavily on the training set [11,22]. An example is the work done by Holden et al. on Phase-Functioned Neural Network, where a cyclic function was used to consider the phase of a motion [11]. While a model trained using this approach allows for efficient generation of animation portraying locomotion, adapting to different terrains, they were unable to deal with complex interactions with the environment.

Recurrent neural networks were used by Klein et al. in a methodology for data-driven gaze animation [12]. The motion clip collection of gaze behaviour, in standing, seated, and lying down actions, with a total length of 46400 frames (1546.66 s), were used, to train agents to control a subset of joints.

The authors reported that, due to only a subset of joints being controlled and the kinematic linking, artefacts were present at times, that made the behaviour portrayed appear less natural.

Supervised learning based approaches can be limited with regards to being flexible and generalisable over a wider range of behaviours. To address this, methods such as DeepMimic use reinforcement learning (RL) and physics-based simulation to portray behaviours via agents trained to learn physics-based skills [19,20]. RL was also used effectively by Liu and Hodgins to learn non-linear arm control policies that allowed the learning of robust controls for portraying behaviour involving basketball-dribbling skills [15]. However, these approaches can only be applied to tasks that feature interactions with physical surfaces and objects in the virtual environment.

Model-free RL approaches have been effective in creating agents by exploring environments effectively [7]. Learning an efficient policy is what allows these agents to function without learning a model of the environment. Thus, an ideal policy requires that the training process maximises the exploration. However, given that the goal in data-driven animation is to portray human-like behaviour and the domain provides a predictable structure, we believe model-based RL is a more suitable approach.

Recent work in model-based RL has shown that learning dynamics models for agent tasks and environments can be an effective approach [6,8,14]. Our approach to train agents to learn dynamics for animation is based on the work done by Haffner et al. [8]. To learn dynamics, the authors used a model consisting of deterministic and stochastic components. This allowed agents to make robust predictions and choose actions via online planning in a compact latent space.

3 Data-Driven RL for Virtual Character Animation

A virtual character is a three-dimensional (3D) representation, that is usually a polygon mesh with data on the material, position and textures of the points on this mesh. This mesh is attached to a skeleton, which is a hierarchically connected series of joints, through a process known as rigging, which allows for the 3D mesh to be animated through the rotation of these joints [17]. Joints may be rotated in axes heading, pitch and roll. The range of rotation available in each axes need to be constrained such that only feasible human movement is portrayed.

When creating data-driven virtual character animation control agents that can portray human-like behaviours, a recent approach has been the work done on RLAnimate to portray social behaviours [5]. Figure 1 provides an overview of RLAnimate agents and the dynamics learnt. At each timestep, the agent received an objective signal o_t from the task module in the environment. Using the portrayal model, a corresponding ideal description d_t for the next animation pose was generated. This description in conjunction with the dynamics learnt allowed an agent to obtain, from the behaviour model, latent states for task h_t and behaviour b_t. These latent states were then used to generate the animation action a_t. After applying a_t, the environment generated a real description signal d'_{t+1}, consisting of the position of all joints, and directional vectors for the finger and eye joints, which was stored in the sample buffer along with the action, objective and ideal animation per the relevant motion clip m_t.

The deterministic task state h_t was obtained via a recurrent neural network (RNN) $f(h_{t-1}, o_t)$, and the deterministic component of the behaviour state from a second RNN $f(h_t, b_{t-1}, a_{t-1})$, which was used to generate the behaviour state posterior b_t. The states h_t and b_t were computed as conditioned by d_t, and were used by the animation model to generate the next animation action a_t. RLAnimate agents thus far have been trained to portray generalisable human-like behaviours for pointing and waving with varying levels of exaggeration, target position and other parameters, with minimal noticeable artefacts in general. However, upon a closer review, a high number of artefacts occur in the more subtle waving portrayals. The most noticeable artefacts are in the form of shakiness in the neutral arm. Figure 2 demonstrates the variation in the output parameters

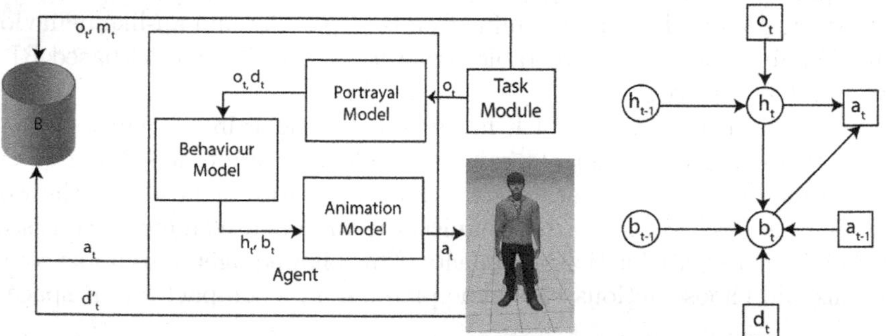

t = time step, o_t = objective signal, h_t = task state, b_t = behaviour state d_t = predicted ideal description, a_t = animation output, d'_t = real description after applying a_t, m_t = ideal animation per motion clip

Fig. 1. Overview of initial RLAnimate agent, and latent dynamics [5].

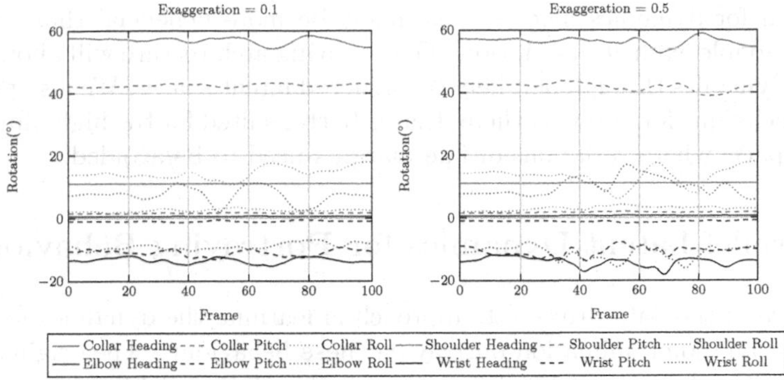

Fig. 2. Neutral arm joint rotations for waving with low and neutral exaggeration.

that lead to these, which per dimension are less than 0.05; fine margins such as these tend to be standard for RL agents, and most applications have much less dimensionality in the output/action space, as is the case in animation. For animation agents to be applied effectively in applications however, the likelihood of these artefacts need to be minimal, and preferably eliminated completely.

Figure 3 presents comparisons of the difference to the original clips across different degrees of exaggeration for neutral arm relative to the overall animation. Comparing portrayals of waving for an exaggeration factor of 0.1 compared to 0.5, throughout the episode, overall the difference per joint is higher for the 4 joints of the neutral arm compared to the average difference for the overall animation. The second plot demonstrates the difference to the original clip averaged for joint count, comparing the average difference per episode for increasing exaggeration.

We posit that while efficient latent dynamics are being constructed by the current agents, further refinements may reduce such effects by instead modelling the description in a latent space. As latent representations are a richer form of

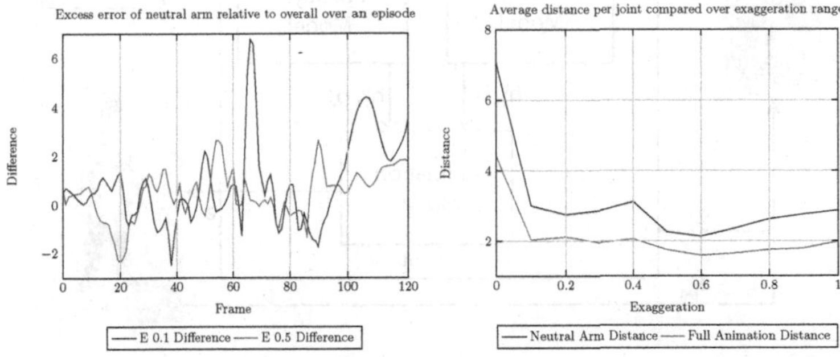

Fig. 3. Difference of Euclidean distances (averaged over number of joints), between joint positions from the motion clip and agent output, for neutral arm joints and overall animation, when waving at exaggerations 0.1 and 0.5 (left), and Euclidean distance per frame between joint positions of original clip and agent output averaged for the number of joints, compared over degrees of exaggeration (right).

expression for dynamics models, this might be more beneficial than a human-understandable explicit description. The resulting architecture will allows agents to learn dynamics through parallely constructed latent spaces. We also propose a refined technique for applying them, that is better suited for the high dimensional output space, where variations of fine margins need to be avoided.

4 Parallel Latent Dynamics for Portraying Behaviour

A key idea of the data-driven RL approach is learning the dynamics for human behaviour and joint animation portraying these behaviours. The original RLAnimate agent architecture (*A1*) relies on the behaviour model to maintain a dual latent space for dynamics, consisting of deterministic and stochastic components. The portrayal model is used to generate an estimated description for the next ideal pose, both of which are used to apply the dynamics learnt by the behaviour model and generate latent variables. The self-description process provides situational context for the present frame, for the behaviour model to apply learned dynamics. However, this might inhibit the agent overall, as an explicit medium is likely relatively less expressive. Therefore, we explore constructing this self-description entirely within a latent space.

4.1 Latent Dynamics Spaces

The novel architecture (*A2*) is depicted in Fig. 4, where the role of the portrayal model is to maintain a second latent space for portrayal dynamics. The portrayal model learns the dynamics as consisting of deterministic and stochastic components, as displayed in Eq. 1. Learning these dynamics entails the agent learning

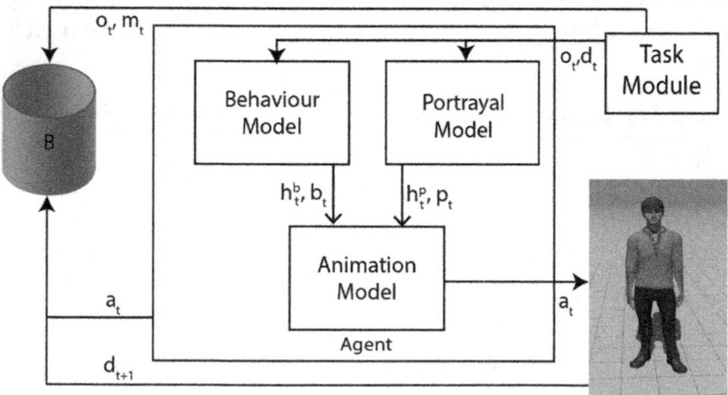

Fig. 4. Overview of novel RLAnimate agent architecture (*A2*). Upon receiving objective signal o_t and current description d_t, the agent uses the portrayal and behaviour model to generate latent portrayal states h_t^p and p_t, and behaviour states h_t^b and b_t, which are used to generate the animation a_t. The environment generates the description after a_t is applied, which is stored in the sample buffer along with the action, objective and ideal animation per the relevant motion clip.

to represent, within a latent space, dynamics for ideal behaviour. The hidden stochastic state is learned by applying the dynamics learnt for the current joint rotations a_{t-1} and objective for the next o_t.

$$\text{Deterministic Portrayal Component: } h_t^p = f(h_{t-1}^p, p_{t-1}, a_{t-1}, o_t) \quad (1)$$
$$\text{Stochastic Portrayal Component: } p_t \sim p(p_t | h_t^p)$$

The behaviour model maintains a parallel latent space for behaviour dynamics, per Eq. 2. Also made up of deterministic and stochastic components, it allows agents to gain an understanding of the dynamics concerning the animation required to actuate realistic behaviour portrayal. The behaviour model applies dynamics learnt given the animation generated in the previous step and the current description d_t.

$$\text{Deterministic Behaviour Component: } h_t^b = f(h_{t-1}^b, b_{t-1}, a_{t-1}, d_t) \quad (2)$$
$$\text{Stochastic Behaviour Component: } b_t \sim p(b_t | h_t^b)$$

4.2 Latent Self-description and Animation Generation

During training, we also train a self-description model denoted by Eq. 3. This model mandates that the agent be able to generate self-descriptions using the latent states obtained via applying the dynamics learnt by the portrayal and behaviour models.

$$f(h_{t-1}^p, p_{t-1}, h_{t-1}^b, b_{t-1}) \quad (3)$$

The animation model $p(a_t | h_t^p, p_t, h_t^b, b_t)$ is used to generate an animation action a_t, which is the agent output at each step. Animation actions, a_t, are rotations to be applied to the character skeleton. The animation model is trained to minimise a loss function that compares output animation to motion capture data. The component of the training objective relevant to the self-description model on the other hand, minimises the error relative to the description recorded by the environment.

Thus, training the self-description model results in the agent being able to imagine the result of possible animation options using the latent variables, which are then used to generate animation. And even though the self-description model is not used when generating animation, the latent dynamics are imprinted upon it to consider self-description in a latent space when operating. We use two Gated Recurrent Unit (GRU) cells for the deterministic components of the dynamics models [4]. For all other functions, we use fully connected layers with Rectified Linear Unit (ReLU) activations [16].

4.3 Applying Stochastic Dynamics

Both portrayal and behaviour models learn the stochastic components of their respective dynamics by parameterising them as normal distributions. By default,

Algorithm 1. RLAnimate

Initialise episode buffer B.
Initialise models with random parameters θ.
while not converged **do**
  if training for waving and pointing **then**
    draw at random an example $(m_t)_{t=1}^{F}$ for each from motion dataset M
  else
    draw a single example $(m_t)_{t=1}^{F}$ from motion dataset M
  end if
  for step t = 1..F **do**
    Obtain latent portrayal states h_t^p, p_t per equation 1
    Obtain latent behaviour states h_t^p, b_t per equation 2
    Generate a_t and apply to character
    Collect real description d_{t+1}
  end for
  $B \rightarrow B \cup \left\{(o_t, a_t, d_{t+1}, m_t)_{t=1}^{F}\right\}$
  for model update step s = 1..T **do**
    Draw episode chunks $\left\{(o_t, a_t, d_{t+1}, m_t)_{t=k}^{S+k}\right\}_{i=1}^{C} \sim B$ at random from data buffer
    Compute loss $L(\theta)$ per (4)
    Update model parameters $\theta \leftarrow \theta - \alpha \nabla_\theta L(\theta)$
  end for
end while

given a mean μ, and variance σ^2 over the number of samples n, the state posteriors are calculated according to Eq. 4.

$$\text{Stochastic component} \sim N\left(\mu, \frac{\sigma}{\sqrt{n}}\right) \tag{4}$$

According to the central limit theorem, as the sample size increases, the density of a random variable converges to a normal distribution. In the preliminary investigations presented in the previous section, we observed that as the agent approaches final performance, the standard deviation values are small relative to the mean, and samples drawn from the distribution approximate the mean. However, we have also established that these relatively small fluctuations can lead to significant artefacts in animation sequences.

Learning the stochastic components for dynamics models are important for the model to capture multiple options for future states. This allows an agent to explore varying animation sequences to determine which lead to the most realistic behaviours. We posit that while this is required during training, after training, we may assume that the agent has a correct understanding of which behaviours are to be used for a given objective, and which animation sequences represent the most realistic portrayals of these behaviours. Thus, when generating animation from trained agents, we use just the mean of the distribution maintained by the dynamics models.

4.4 Training Agents

Algorithm 1 describes the procedure followed when training agents: episode rollouts are generated of portrayals imitating the motion clips provided, and the models are iteratively optimised. C batches of episode chunks of size S are drawn from the sample buffer, and the training objective seeking to maximise the ideality of animation consists of components $L1$, $L2$, and $L3$ to learn latent dynamics, and $L4$ to inform agents regarding portraying human-like behaviour per the motion data provided.

$$L(\theta) = E\left[\sum_{t=0}^{n} I_t\left(a_0, ..., a_t, o_t, d_t\right)\right] = L1(\theta) + L2(\theta) + L3(\theta) + L4(\theta) \quad (5)$$

$L1$ is used to train the agent to self-describe likely next states in a latent space through the self-description model, with the loss generated as the mean squared error between the output of Eq. 6 and real description after animation is applied. $L2$ and $L3$, as denoted by Eqs. 7 and 8, are used to train the portrayal and behaviour models via Kullback-Leibler (KL) regularisation [9].

$$L1(\theta) = MSE\left[d_t, f(h_{t-1}^p, p_{t-1}, h_{t-1}^b, b_{t-1})\right] \quad (6)$$

$$L2(\theta) = E\left[q\left(p_t|o_t, a_{t-1}\right) - p\left(p_t|h_{t-1}^p, p_{t-1}, a_{t-1}\right)\right)] \quad (7)$$

$$L3(\theta) = E\left[q\left(b_t|d_t, a_{t-1}\right) - p\left(b_t|h_{t-1}^b, b_{t-1}, a_{t-1}\right)\right)] \quad (8)$$

To minimise the difference between the animation model output and the animation from the motion clip, the previous architecture used a Huber loss function. This made the training more robust, to account for the stochasticity as a result of the direct sampling of the posterior distributions and avoid artefacts. However, the use of the mean of the distribution as the latent state during operation allows for a MSE loss to be used for $L4$ as well, as denoted by Eq. 9.

$$L4(\theta) = MSE\left[M_t, p(a_t|h_t^p, p_t, h_t^b, b_t)\right] \quad (9)$$

5 Experiments

We conduct a set of experiments to evaluate the impact of the modifications we introduce to the agent architecture. The motion clips used for training and evaluation were obtained from Adobe Mixamo, consisting of 50 motion clips each for pointing and waving [1]. For all evaluations, we use a set of 5 waving and pointing clips that were withheld from the training set, that the agents recreate to establish a basis for comparison. For access to our supplementary material, that include the code and video clips demonstrating and comparing trained control agents, please visit https://virtualcharacters.github.io/links/ICANN2021.

Table 1. Performance of trained agents obtained via imitating test set motions. We compare the similarity to motion clip (S), as well as minimum, average, and maximum velocity error (V) for all control agents. The latter is not applicable for *A2_NSD* as that version fails to learn to portray behaviours adequately.

	Wave				Point				Combined			
	S	minV	avgV	maxV	S	minV	avgV	maxV	S	minV	avgV	maxV
A1	0.890	0.2	0.5	0.7	0.942	0.1	0.3	0.6	0.938	0.2	0.5	0.7
A2	0.995	0.1	0.2	0.3	0.998	0.0	0.1	0.2	0.990	0.1	0.2	0.3
A2_NSD	0.244				0.189				0.200			
A2_ESD	0.922	0.2	0.6	0.7	0.911	0.2	0.5	0.8	0.876	0.3	0.5	0.7
A1_MDY	0.900	0.2	0.4	0.5	0.955	0.0	0.2	0.4	0.941	0.2	0.4	0.5
A2_RDY	0.862	0.2	0.6	0.9	0.745	0.3	0.5	0.8	0.664	0.2	0.7	0.9

The metrics we used were similarity to motion clip and velocity error between agent output and motion clip. The similarity to motion clip acts as a measure of accuracy for the animation generated, and is based on the cosine similarity of joint positions between the agent output and motion clip. We use velocity error as an indicator of the occurrence of artefacts; velocity is calculated as the first derivative of joint positions with respect to time, and high velocity error is considered to be likely caused by twitches and similar artefacts [18]. Error values over 0.4 are indicative of noticeable artefacts. All our experiments were carried out using a workstation with an Intel Core i7-8750 H 2.2 GHz CPU and a Nvidia GeForce GTX 1070 GPU.

We evaluated control agents based on the original agent architecture (*A1*) and the novel architecture we propose in this paper (*A2*). Based on the *A1* architecture, we evaluated a control agent deployed in a mean dynamics model sampling mode (*A1_MDY*). Control agents based on the A2.0 architecture were used to examine the impact of being trained with no self-description (*A2_NSD*) and with an explicit-self description component (*A2_ESD*).

Comparison to Original Architecture: While the *A1* architecture yields animation sequences quite similar to the motion clips, there are a high degree of artefacts that appear, when particularly the neutral arm requires more subtle movement. The results show that the A2.0 agent addresses this issue, with no noticeable artefacts occurring even in the degrees of exaggeration that lead to the most subtle waving behaviours.

Latent Self-description: In Table 1, we also compare control agents to examine the role of self-description. A control based on the novel architecture (*A2_NSD*) without self-description was unable to perform as an agent cannot learn dynamics without it. The description loss is essential to inform training of what the animation generated leads to; while it is possible in theory for an agent to learn dynamics without the self-description model being trained, we observe that the latent self-description plays a key role in training efficiency. Training an agent where the portrayal model was used to generate an explicit description for the next step using the objective signal and the current animation (*A2_ESD*), lead to animation output marginally better relative to *A1*. Thus, we observe that the latent self-description helps the agent construct coherent and effective latent spaces, as dynamics can be learnt more naturally.

Sampling Latent Dynamics: We deployed the same trained control used for *A2*, but with random sampling of the dynamics models enabled when operating (*A2_RDY*). While the animations generated are overall similar, the mean being used to calculate the vectors concerning the stochastic dynamics leads to significantly smoother motions. A consistent effect is observed when an agent based on A1.0 architecture is deployed in a mean sampling mode (*A1_MDY*).

6 Conclusion

We have presented a novel agent architecture in this paper for animation generation using data-driven reinforcement learning. Relative to the former architecture, this leads to more computationally efficient agent function, as there is no extra step to generate an explicit description during operation.

We also examine the application of learned stochastic dynamics. Typically, model-based RL work involve the stochastic dynamics being modelled via a normal distribution, which is sampled randomly to generate the latent vector given the model inputs [5,6,8]. As more sample episodes are generated and training is carried out, the model is trained to maintain the distribution accurately. This leads to the values being generated by the dynamics learnt being approximately similar the mean. However, while the differences in the random sampled values and mean sampled values of the distributions are minute, we note that animation sequences carry a sensitivity to subtle twitches and other artefacts. Therefore, the stability provided by the mean sampling for the stochastic dynamics distribution is more suited to animation. During training, the agent operates using random sampling for updating model parameters and generating sample episodes. This allows for the exploration of multiple trajectories in the latent space to determine the most ideal options. We assume after training is complete, the agent has a strong understanding of the most ideal, realistic portrayal of behaviour. Mean sampling is merely a direct querying of this assumed best understanding of the dynamics. We believe that our findings on this matter can be applicable to model-based RL being used in complex domains where the state and action dimension counts are high and operation is sensitive to variations that concern similar fine margins.

The evaluation and sample output demonstrations show that the novel RLAnimate architecture can maintain modelling flexibility and performance, while eliminating the occurrence of artefacts. Previously, artefacts appeared routinely in parts of behaviour that involved subtle movement. In our future work, we plan to explore how RLAnimate agents can be trained to portray more complex behaviour such as conversational gestures, and applied to produce believable and cohesive sequences portraying composite human-like behaviour.

References

1. Adobe: Mixamo (2020). http://www.mixamo.com. Accessed 30 Jun 2021
2. Asadi-Aghbolaghi, M., et al.: Deep learning for action and gesture recognition in image sequences: a survey. In: Escalera, S., Guyon, I., Athitsos, V. (eds.) Gesture Recognition. TSSCML, pp. 539–578. Springer, Cham (2017). https://doi.org/10.1007/978-3-319-57021-1_19
3. Chakraborty, B.K., Sarma, D., Bhuyan, M.K., MacDorman, K.F.: Review of constraints on vision-based gesture recognition for human-computer interaction. IET Comput. Vis. **12**(1), 3–15 (2017)
4. Cho, K., et al.: Learning phrase representations using rnn encoder-decoder for statistical machine translation. arXiv arXiv:1406.1078 (2014)
5. Gamage, V., Ennis, C., Ross, R.: Data-driven reinforcement learning for virtual character animation control. arXiv preprint arXiv:2104.06358 (2021)
6. Ha, D., Schmidhuber, J.: World models. arXiv arXiv:1803.10122 (2018)
7. Haarnoja, T., Zhou, A., Abbeel, P., Levine, S.: Soft actor-critic: Off-policy maximum entropy deep reinforcement learning with a stochastic actor. In: International Conference on Machine Learning, pp. 1861–1870. PMLR (2018)
8. Hafner, D., et al.: Learning latent dynamics for planning from pixels. In: International Conference on Machine Learning, pp. 2555–2565. PMLR (2019)
9. Hershey, J.R., Olsen, P.A.: Approximating the kullback leibler divergence between gaussian mixture models. In: 2007 IEEE International Conference on Acoustics, Speech and Signal Processing-ICASSP 2007, vol. 4, pp. IV-317. IEEE (2007)
10. Holden, D., Komura, T., Saito, J.: Phase-functioned neural networks for character control. ACM Trans. Graph. (TOG) **36**(4), 42 (2017)
11. Holden, D., Saito, J., Komura, T.: A deep learning framework for character motion synthesis and editing. ACM Trans. Graph. (TOG) **35**(4), 1–11 (2016)
12. Klein, A., Yumak, Z., Beij, A., van der Stappen, A.F.: Data-driven gaze animation using recurrent neural networks. In: Motion, Interaction and Games, pp. 1–11 (2019)
13. Latoschik, M.E., Roth, D., Gall, D., Achenbach, J., Waltemate, T., Botsch, M.: The effect of avatar realism in immersive social virtual realities. In: Proceedings of the 23rd ACM Symposium on Virtual Reality Software and Technology, pp. 1–10 (2017)
14. Lillicrap, T.P., et al.: Continuous control with deep reinforcement learning. arXiv arXiv:1509.02971 (2015)
15. Liu, L., Hodgins, J.: Learning basketball dribbling skills using trajectory optimization and deep reinforcement learning. ACM Trans. Graph. (TOG) **37**(4), 142 (2018)
16. Nair, V., Hinton, G.E.: Rectified linear units improve restricted boltzmann machines. In: Proceedings of the 27th International Conference on International Conference on Machine Learning, pp. 807–814 (2010)
17. Parent, R.: Computer Animation: Algorithms and Techniques. Elsevier, Amsterdam (2012)
18. Pavllo, D., Feichtenhofer, C., Auli, M., Grangier, D.: Modeling human motion with quaternion-based neural networks. Int. J. Comput. Vis. 1–18 (2019)
19. Peng, X.B., Abbeel, P., Levine, S., van de Panne, M.: Deepmimic: example-guided deep reinforcement learning of physics-based character skills. ACM Trans. Graph. (TOG) **37**(4), 1–14 (2018)

20. Peng, X.B., Berseth, G., Yin, K., Van De Panne, M.: Deeploco: dynamic locomotion skills using hierarchical deep reinforcement learning. ACM Trans. Graph. (TOG) **36**(4), 1–13 (2017)
21. Wu, Y., et al.: Effects of virtual human animation on emotion contagion in simulated inter-personal experiences. IEEE Trans. Vis. Comput. Graph. **20**(4), 626–635 (2014)
22. Zhang, H., Starke, S., Komura, T., Saito, J.: Mode-adaptive neural networks for quadruped motion control. ACM Trans. Graph. (TOG) **37**(4), 1–11 (2018)

Intrinsic Motivation Model Based on Reward Gating

Matej Pecháč(✉) and Igor Farkaš

Faculty of Mathematics, Physics and Informatics, Comenius University in Bratislava, Bratislav, Slovak Republic
pechac1@uniba.sk

Abstract. Intrinsic motivation (IM) research is a promising part of reinforcement learning which can push artificial agents to completely new frontiers. Namely, from agents with a simple action repertoire, driven by the human engineered reward, to more autonomous agents with their own goals and skill development, able to act successfully in the environments which are unknown to their human designers. In this paper, we introduce an IM model, which combines via gating two different motivational signals: a prediction error estimated by the forward model and a predictive surprise estimated by the meta-critic. This approach accelerates the exploration of the environment and hence the agent is able to find sources of an external reward in a shorter time than the baseline agents, especially in case of sparse reward. We test this prediction using two environments with dense reward (HalfCheetah and Ant) and two with sparse reward (MountainCar and AerisNavigate), and show the superior performance of an agent with a gated reward in most cases as expected. The models are also compared using reliability measures related to dispersion and risk, calculated during learning. The source code is available at https://github.com/Iskandor/MotivationModels.

Keywords: Reinforcement learning · Intrinsic motivation · Prediction error · Predictive surprise · Active exploration

1 Introduction

The development of reinforcement learning (RL) methods has achieved much success over the last decade, since together with advances in computer vision [11,15], it became possible to teach agents to solve various tasks, play simple computer games [20], even surpassing human players [19]. Nevertheless, these are still concrete single tasks. A lot of computational time has to be spent, and the agents are given a lot of resources to manage to learn the aforementioned challenges in a reasonable time. However, coping with a complex (continuous) environment such as our world is still a challenge. There are several

I. Farkaš—This research was supported by KEGA grant no. 042UK-4/2019.

I. Farkaš et al. (Eds.): ICANN 2021, LNCS 12894, pp. 688–699, 2021.
https://doi.org/10.1007/978-3-030-86380-7_56

pathways offering research opportunities. One is the search for new optimization and learning methods that would shorten the learning time or reduce the amount of resources needed. Another is hardware development, which attempts to adapt to the requirements of neural networks that are currently being used in the field of reinforcement learning.

The most popular approach to make RL more efficient is based on *intrinsic motivation* (IM) [2]. IM has a strong psychological motivation [25], since children acquire skills and knowledge about the world using their own drive and experience without obvious reward from the outer environment. If we want to achieve an open-ended development with artificial agents, we have to master this first step and equip them with an ability to generate their own goals and acquire new skills. Therefore, computational approaches concerned with IMs and open-ended development are thought to have the potential to lead to the construction of more intelligent artificial systems, in particular systems that are capable of improving their own skills and knowledge autonomously and indefinitely [2].

In this paper, we introduce a new version of a IM-based agent that is shown to efficiently learn the tasks at hand. It selects between two different motivation signals generated by the forward model and the meta-critic. The selection is based on simple rule performed by the gating module and its output signal is added to external reward from the environment and serves as input for critic which in turn generates the learning signal for actor.

In particular, we provide two main contributions: First, inspired by the definition of the predictive surprise motivation [22], we propose modifications to the original formula and explored its impact on the learning process of agents. Second, we explore a *gating approach* to exploit the prediction error and predictive surprise motivation signals generated in the intrinsic module of the agent. The learning models are statistically compared using the reliability measures.

2 Related Work

The concept of intrinsic (and extrinsic) motivation was first studied in psychology [25], and later entered the RL literature where the first taxonomy of computational models appeared in [22]. Following this taxonomy, we can divide the concept of motivation into external and internal, depending on the mechanism that generates motivation for the agent. If the source of motivation comes from outside, we are talking about *external* motivation, and it is always associated with a particular goal in the environment. If the motivation is generated within the structures that make up the agent, it is an *internal* motivation.

Another dimension for the differentiation, extrinsic or intrinsic, is less obvious. *Extrinsic* motivations pertain to behaviors whenever an activity is done in order to attain some separable outcome. Some variability exists in this context, since these behaviors can vary in the extent to which they represent self-determination (see the details in [25]). On the other hand, *intrinsic* motivation is defined as doing an activity for its inherent satisfactions rather than for some separable consequence (or instrumental value). It has been operationally defined in various ways, backed up by different psychological theories, which point to some uncertainty in what IM exactly means. Nevertheless, Baldassarre [1] offers a solution of an operational definition of IMs as processes that can drive the acquisition of knowledge and skills in the absence of extrinsic motivations. Furthermore, he proposes (and explains why) a new term of *epistemic motivations* as a suitable substitution for intrinsic motivations.

According to the prevailing view, the computational approaches to IM can be divided into two main categories with adaptive motivations. *Knowledge-based* approach is focused on acquisition of knowledge of the world and draws on the theory of drives, theory of cognitive dissonance and optimal incongruity theory. *Competence-based* approach focuses on acquisition of skills by motivating the agent to achieve a higher level of performance in the environment, which means to acquire desired actions to achieve self-generated goals. Its psychological basis includes the theory of effectance and the theory of flow.

The knowledge-based category is commonly divided into *prediction-based* and *novelty-based* approaches. Prediction-based approaches often use a forward model (e.g. [3,23,28]) or a variational autoencoder [14] to compute the prediction error (for more details, see [5]). The novelty-based approaches monitor the state novelty and the intrinsic signal is based on its value. The first models were based on count-based approach [31]. This method is impractical for large or continuous state spaces and it was extended by introducing pseudo-count and neural density models [17,18,21]. A similar method to pseudo-count was used by a random network distillation model [6] with a lower complexity.

It is an empirical question what is the best IM signal for a given task [26]. The difficulty increases if an agent is supposed to learn multiple skills in the shortest time. For instance, in [26] it is shown that intrinsic reinforcements purely based on the knowledge of the system are not appropriate to guide the acquisition of multiple skills and that the stronger the link between the IM signal and the competence of the system, the better the performance. Hence, the combination of both types seems to be useful. In a recent work [24] it is shown that the combination of knowledge-based and competence-based IM signals leads to more efficient exploration and task learning.

The concept of a meta-critic (MC), or a module that learns to predict the prediction error is not new in reinforcement learning; it was introduced in early1990 s within the adaptive curiosity framework [27], and has been extended in various forms since then. Also the concept of exploration has been studied intensively, one of the first being the idea of an exploration bonus [30], later analyzed in alternative ways in [10,29]. Related work on surprise-based approaches includes Bayesian bio-inspired approach where surprise measures how data affects an observer, in terms of differences between posterior and prior beliefs about the world [12]. We use a MC module in a novel role of gating two different motivational signals, based on a prediction error and predictive surprise.

3 Preliminaries

The decision making problem in the environment using RL is formalized as a Markov decision process which consists of a state space $\mathcal{S}$, action space $\mathcal{A}$, transition function $\mathcal{T}(s,a,s') = p(s_{t+1} = s'|s_t = s, a_t = a)$, reward function $\mathcal{R}$ and a discount factor γ. The main goal of the agent is to maximize the discounted return $R_t = \sum_{k=0}^{\infty} \gamma^k r_{t+k}$ in each state. Stochastic policy is defined as a state dependent probability function $\pi : \mathcal{S} \times \mathcal{A} \rightarrow [0,1]$, such that $\pi_t(s,a) = p(a_t = a|s_t = s)$ and $\sum_{a \in \mathcal{A}} \pi(s,a) = 1$ and the deterministic policy $\pi : \mathcal{S} \rightarrow \mathcal{A}$ is defined as $\pi(s) = a$.

An agent following the optimal policy π^* maximizes the expected return R. The methods searching for the optimal policy can be divided into on-policy (family of actor–critic algorithms), and off-policy (family of Q-learning algorithms) methods. Actor–critic algorithms are based on two separate modules: an *actor* which approximates agent's policy π and generates actions and a *critic* that estimates the state value function V^π defined as:

$$V^\pi(s) = \sum_a \pi(s,a) \sum_{s'} \mathcal{T}(s,a,s') \left[\mathcal{R}(s,a,s') + \gamma V^\pi(s')\right] \tag{1}$$

or action-state value function Q^π defined as:

$$Q^\pi(s,a) = \sum_{s'} \mathcal{T}(s,a,s') \left[\mathcal{R}(s,a,s') + \gamma V^\pi(s')\right] \tag{2}$$

The actor then updates its policy to maximize return R based on critic's value function estimations.

4 Methods

In this section we describe the formal approach to the intrinsic module based on the prediction error and predictive surprise as shown in Fig. 1. The module provides for a short time a larger amount of intrinsic reward to the agent, especially in the first phases of learning. These bursts of intrinsic reward can be interpreted as predictive surprise, because there is a large difference between an estimated and the actual error of the forward model.

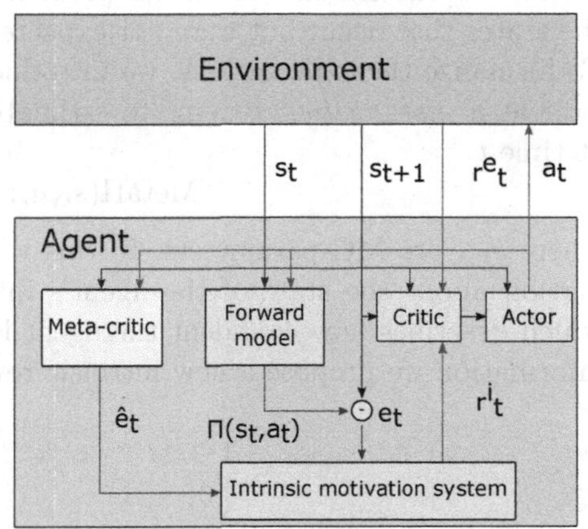

Fig. 1. Proposed intrinsic motivation model with a meta-critic module.

We propose two hypotheses: First, the gating mechanism can take the best of both reward signals and significantly improve the learning process in environments with sparse reward, so the agent should reach optimal policy in shorter time and accumulate more external reward during the training. Second, we expect that performance in environments with dense rewards will be also improved because of more rapid exploration performed mainly in the first period of learning process. Both hypotheses are tested in experiments. Now we describe its individual components.

4.1 Meta-critic

Our motivational module is based on two prediction modules. The first module is the forward model $\Pi(s_t, a_t)$ with parameters θ_{fm} which predicts the next state $\hat{s}_{t+1}$ from current state and action

$$\Pi(s_t, a_t; \theta_{\mathrm{fm}}) = \hat{s}_{t+1} \tag{3}$$

The prediction error e_t is defined as the normalized squared Euclidean distance between the predicted state $\hat{s}_{t+1}$ and the next observed state s_{t+1}

$$e_t = \frac{1}{n}\|s_{t+1} - \hat{s}_{t+1}\|_2^2 \tag{4}$$

where n is the dimensionality of the state space. The intrinsic reward based on the prediction error is defined as

$$r_t^{\mathrm{ifm}} = e_t \tag{5}$$

Such intrinsic reward decreases as the FM improves its predictions. That ideally occurs the transition from state s_t using action a_t to the next state s_{t+1} which are well-known to the agent's FM, because they were experienced several times, and hence they no longer serve as a source of intrinsic motivation.

The second module estimates predictive surprise motivation which rewards the states that occur but were not expected, or do not occur but were expected. To formalize the expectations, we introduce another predictor MetaΠ and refer to it as a *meta-critic*.[1] It aims to estimate the error e_t of the first predictor Π at time t

$$\mathrm{Meta}\Pi(s_t, a_t; \theta_{\mathrm{mc}}) = \hat{e_t} \tag{6}$$

where θ_{mc} are MC parameters. In this way, we obtain qualitatively new information about the state of the agent's internal model about the environment, which describes how confident the agent is about its predictions. Based on this information we propose a new intrinsic reward function

$$r_t^{\mathrm{imc}} = \begin{cases} e_t/\hat{e}_t + \hat{e}_t/e_t - 2, & \text{if } |e_t - \hat{e}_t| > \sigma \\ 0, & \text{otherwise} \end{cases} \tag{7}$$

If the MC correctly estimates the prediction error, the reward is close to 0 due to constant 2 which is subtracted from the term. To prevent cases where the error

[1] There is no connection to a critic estimating the value functions.

estimation and prediction error are very small, but still generate some reward, we introduced a *sensitivity* threshold σ which has to be exceeded. The reward function defined in this way can stimulate an agent if the prediction error is low and its estimate is high, or vice versa, when the prediction error is high and its estimate is low. The training of the proposed intrinsic module is straightforward and can be approached as an optimization problem, formulated as

$$\min_{\theta_{\rm fm},\theta_{\rm mc}} \left[\frac{1}{n} \|s_{t+1} - \hat{s}_{t+1}\|^2 + \|e_t - \hat{e}_t\|^2 \right] \tag{8}$$

4.2 Intrinsic Reward Gating

The proposed motivation model has two prediction modules generating two different IM signals. We decided to introduce the gating of reward signals such that in each step of an episode, only one of the two signals is passed through. This is aimed to model situations when the rarely occurring, unexpected event overrides the prediction error reward whose magnitude is much smaller. The final intrinsic reward added to an external reward is defined as

$$r_t^{\rm i} = \max(\epsilon_{\rm fm} \tanh(r_t^{\rm ifm}), \epsilon_{\rm mc} \tanh(r_t^{\rm imc})) \tag{9}$$

where the reward signals from both modules are scaled to the interval $(-1, 1)$ and then independently scaled by a respective factor ϵ. This procedure was informed by an observation that predictive surprise motivation often outperforms common prediction error motivation and leads to an effect of sudden surprise for the agent. Without surprise the agent is driven by prediction error motivation.

The final instantaneous reward r_t provided to the critic is defined as

$$r_t = r_t^{\rm e} + r_t^{\rm i} \tag{10}$$

where $r_t^{\rm e}$ is the instantaneous external reward and $r_t^{\rm i}$ was defined in Eq. 9. The above mentioned types of reward were used in four different agents listed in Table 1.

Table 1. Agents with their respective motivation signals.

Agent type	Motivation
Baseline	None
Forward model (FM)	$r^{\rm ifm}$ (Eq. 5)
Meta-critic (MC)	$r^{\rm imc}$ (Eq. 7)
Meta-critic gated (gMC)	$r^{\rm i}$ (Eq. 9)

5 Experiments

To appreciate the behavior of the proposed models, we tested them in four environments of different complexity, namely *MountainCar* available in OpenAI Gym [4], *AerisNavigate* available in gym-aeris package, then *HalfCheetah* and *Ant* from PyBullet Gym [8]. All environments have continuous state and action spaces. MountainCar present a challenge for exploration, because the agent receives a negative reward according to the magnitude of its action vector, and if it does not find a positive reward fast enough, the policy will converge into the agent's inactivity in the extreme case. AerisNavigate environment is the most difficult due to a very sparse reward obtained only at the end of an episode. The goal of MountainCar, and AerisNavigate agents is to reach a specific location in the state space: the top of the hill and the target area that changes in each episode, respectively. The next two environments (HalfCheetah, Ant) provide a dense reward signal, as a mixture of positive and negative rewards per step. Here the task of the agents is to reach the maximum distance from the starting location until the step limit is over.

We divided our experiments in two parts. The first consists of testing the agent with the MC module in described environments to compare the results with the baseline models. In the second part, we focus on a statistical analysis of all models using the specific metrics, measuring model reliability, intrinsic reward density and distribution.

5.1 Model Training Setup

All our agents are trained using DDPG algorithm [16] that has been shown to work well in many tasks. The agent's deterministic policy is approximated by an *actor* and Q-value function is approximated by a *critic*. The actor and critic are represented by three-layer neural networks and for parameter optimization of both modules we used Adam algorithm [13]. The learning rates of actor and critic in all environments were $\alpha_{\text{act}} = 0.0001$ and $\alpha_{\text{crit}} = 0.0002$, respectively. Exploration was performed by adding noise to the actor's output, generated by random variable with Gaussian distribution and monotonically decreasing standard deviation. All environments had a discount factor set to $\gamma = 0.99$ and in all our experiments, $\epsilon_{\text{fm}} = \epsilon_{\text{mc}} = 1$, except the experiments in AerisNavigate environment, where $\epsilon_{\text{fm}} = \epsilon_{\text{mc}} = 0.01$. More hyper-parameters and further details of the learning process can be found in our source codes. To model a less complex environment, with low state space dimension (MountainCar), we used three-layer neural networks (for both FM and MC) and the models were trained by Adam algorithm, in online manner adapting to actual samples experienced by the agent. We chose the learning rate values $\alpha_{\text{fm}} = 0.0001, \alpha_{\text{mc}} = 0.0002$, respectively, slightly increasing the learning speed of MC to improve the speed of estimation of FM error which represents moving target in this case. Based on preliminary tests we increased the depth of neural networks for more complex environments (HalfCheetah and Ant) to increase their capacity and we decided to use five-layer neural networks. We also employed an experience replay buffer,

Table 2. Average cumulative reward per step for all models and tasks.

Model/Env	MountainCar	AerisNavigate	HalfCheetah	Ant
Baseline	53.4 ± 58.4	0.35 ± 0.90	1021.8 ± 414.8	990.4 ± 450.8
Forward model	54.8 ± 59.3	0.44 ± 0.86	1060.1 ± 447.6	**1287.9** ± 562.0
Meta-critic	60.2 ± 52.7	0.30 ± 0.89	1010.3 ± 401.6	1178.6 ± 540.1
Meta-critic gated	**66.1** ± 55.6	**0.48** ± 0.86	**1073.7** ± 421.1	1246.6 ± 563.8

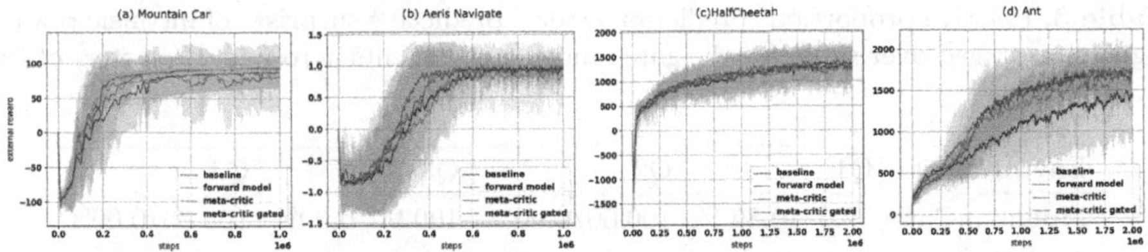

Fig. 2. Simulation results of the four agent types trained in four environments. The gMC agent was the most successful in MountainCar and AerisNavigate environments, and also reached interesting performance in Ant environment. The learned policies of IM-based agents in HalfCheetah environment do not differ much from the baseline.

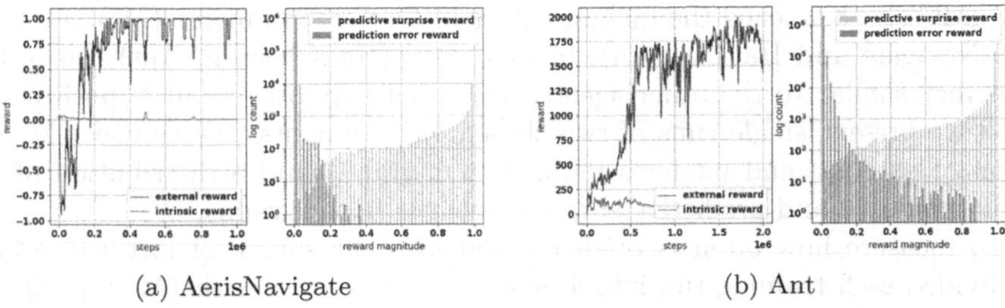

(a) AerisNavigate (b) Ant

Fig. 3. Detailed analysis of the gated meta-critic for two chosen environments showing measured quantities within a single run. The first chart of 3a shows cumulative rewards and the second chart reveals a distribution of magnitude of intrinsic reward within the entire training. The same holds for 3b. All charts are smoothed by a moving average with window size of 10,000 steps (for interpretation, see the text).

often used in off-policy learning algorithms to decorrelate the samples, e.g. [20], generating batches of size 32 used for learning of FM as well as MC (each having its own sample batch). Slightly different modules were needed for AerisNavigate environment, where the input was represented as multi-channel tensor of Lidar signals. To implement the FM we used four 1D-conv operators and then one transposed 1D-conv followed by one 1D-conv operator to create prediction about the next states. The MC module has the same structure with an additional linear layer on the top, estimating the FM error.

5.2 Model Comparison

For all the environments we performed 15 training runs of each variant: the baseline had no motivation, the FM used the prediction error motivation, MC had only predictive surprise motivation and finally the gMC combined both predictive motivations. To evaluate performance of agents we ran basic analysis in which we calculated mean and standard deviation of accumulated external reward and the results can be found in Table 2 and Fig. 2. Each curve represents an average cumulative external reward for each step smoothed by running average with window size of 10^5 steps (10 episodes). According to these met-

Table 3. Relative proportion (prediction error / predictive surprise) of intrinsic reward signals (averaged over runs) for the gated meta-critic agents across four quarters of the training.

Environment	Q1	Q2	Q3	Q4
MountainCar	99.64/0.36 %	100.00/0.00%	100.00/0.00%	100.00/0.00%
AerisNavigate	97.96/2.04%	98.71/1.29%	98.64/1.36%	98.50/1.50%
HalfCheetah	91.15/8.85%	93.73/6.27%	93.90/6.10%	94.38/5.62%
Ant	90.28/9.72%	90.78 / 9.22%	92.31/7.69%	93.03/6.97%

rics, gMC agent reached the highest values in four environments (MountainCar, AerisNavigate and HalfCheetah). In two cases (HalfCheetah, Ant) the results were very similar to the other agents, hence not supporting our hypothesis. In Fig. 3 we present single runs of two chosen environments. We can see the evolution of external and intrinsic rewards (left graph) and a distribution of the prediction error and predictive surprise rewards (right graph).

To measure how often is predictive surprise the source of intrinsic reward we divided each training run into 4 quarters (e.g. for run with 1M steps Q1: 0–0.25M, Q2: 0.25–0.5M, etc.). We evaluated average density of predictive surprise occurrence for each quarter. The results are provided in Table 3. For completeness and comparison, we also added data for prediction error based reward. In most cases, we can see a decreasing tendency of predictive surprise average density as the learning proceeds to its final phase (Q4).

5.3 Assessment of Model Reliability During Learning

To obtain a quantitative comparison of the RL models, we evaluated selected measures of reliability, following [7]. They proposed three axes of variability, of which the first two capture reliability "during training". Across Time measures the algorithm stability within each run, whereas Across Runs measures consistently reproducible performances across multiple training runs.

For both axes of variability, two kinds of measures are evaluated: dispersion and risk. Dispersion, as the width of the distribution, is taken as the Interquartile range (IQR) (i.e. the difference between the 75th and 25th percentiles), which is suitable for nonnormal distributions. Risk is defined as the heaviness and extent of the lower tail of the distribution. To measure risk, Conditional Value at Risk (CVaR) is used, measuring the expected loss in the worst-case scenarios. For motivation for these measures and more detailed explanation, the reader is referred to [7].

The RL algorithms are evaluated in Fig. 4, separately for sparse and dense rewards, in terms of dispersion and risk across runs which were found most informative. Dispersion profiles are consistent with variability of learning curves in Fig. 2 and reveal the fact the IM-based agents, and in particular gMC agent, outperform the baseline in most cases. Risk profiles provide a new information, since they focus on worst-case behaviors. Here, the evidence shows that gMC excels in two cases (MountainCar and Ant) and is never inferior to other agents.

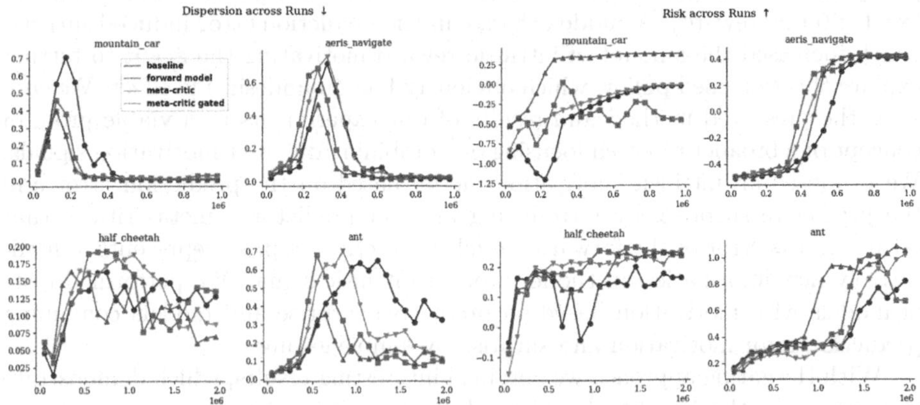

Fig. 4. Selected reliability measures (across runs) assessed for each environment and four learning agent types. Better reliability is indicated by less positive values in case of dispersion, and more positive values in case of risk.

6 Discussion

The process of learning with motivation based on gating the predictive surprise and the prediction error introduces quite complex interactions among all modules (actor, critic, forward model and meta-critic). Presented analyses suggest that it is necessary to employ a suitable FM architecture with a sufficient capacity and an appropriate training technique to take advantage of both signals. In case the FM cannot adapt quickly and hence exhibits unstable behaviour, it introduces much more noise into the model. It is also more difficult for the MC to estimate an error with higher variance, which leads to generating more surprise.

We consider the gMC agent successful in two sparse environments (MountainCar and AerisNavigate), where it outperformed the other agents. For the dense environment HalfCheetah, the external reward is sufficiently informative, and hence adding another source of reward did not induce significant improvement. A different situation occurred in Ant dense environment where the IM agents converged to more successful policies. There is also an open question of scaling the intrinsic reward. We set the scaling parameter so that the accumulated intrinsic reward had a magnitude similar to the accumulated external reward but it would be beneficial to try further experiments with different scales. One of the shortcomings of our approach is the forgetting in FM and MC despite their being trained from the replay buffer. This is noticable particularly in case of AerisNavigate (in Fig. 3). In the late phase of training, when the policy was quite stable and the agent was experiencing a smaller set of different trajectories, its actor module became overtrained and the policy collapsed for a short time. This caused large errors in FM predictions despite the fact, that this worse policy had been experienced earlier (or similar, resulting in a similar accumulated external reward). A sudden change in the prediction error induced surprise which increased the amount of intrinsic reward motivating the agent to further explore this worsened policy, which obviously had an undesirable effect. We consider the presented method and results of our experiments as a viable proof of concept of a broader research focusing on combining different motivation signals. We proposed an intrinsic motivation model based on the prediction error and the predictive surprise, by introducing another predictor – meta-critic – that estimates the error of the forward model. Predictive surprise represents a qualitatively new information in the form of an intrinsic signal. We performed tests of models with motivation based on predictive surprise and models combining prediction error motivation and surprise by simple gating.

With the gating approach we obtained interesting results, which demonstrate in three tasks the benefit of adding the IM module and also provide insight that combining two motivation signals is a viable approach with not yet fully explored potential. Further improvements of the model will be sought, based on fine-tuning its parameters and modification of its architecture.

We were able to construct intrinsic signals based on the outputs of our predictive modules which can refer to different types of behavior. We plan to identify some basic behaviours in psychology and create corresponding intrinsic signals [9]. We believe that combination of these basic rewards could lead to more complex behaviours narrowing the gap between machines and humans.

References

1. Baldassarre, G.: Intrinsic motivations and open-ended learning (2019). arXiv:1912.13263v1 [cs.AI]
2. Baldassarre, G., Stafford, T., Mirolli, M., Redgrave, P., Ryan, R.M., Barto, A.: Intrinsic motivations and open-ended development in animals, humans, and robots: an overview. Front. Psychol. (2014). https://doi.org/10.3389/fpsyg.2014.00985
3. Bellemare, M.G., Naddaf, Y., Veness, J., Bowling, M.: The arcade learning environment: an evaluation platform for general agents. J. Artif. Intell. Res. **47**, 253–279 (2013)
4. Brockman, G., et al.: OpenAI Gym (2016). arXiv:1606.01540
5. Burda, Y., Edwards, H., Pathak, D., Storkey, A., Darrell, T., Efros, A.A.: Large-scale study of curiosity-driven learning (2018). arXiv:1808.04355
6. Burda, Y., Edwards, H., Storkey, A., Klimov, O.: Exploration by random network distillation (2018). arXiv:1810.12894
7. Chan, S.C., Fishman, S., Canny, J., Korattikara, A., Guadarrama, S.: Measuring the reliability of reinforcement learning algorithms. In: International Conference on Machine Learning (2020)
8. Coumans, E., Bai, Y.: PyBullet, a Python module for physics simulation for games, robotics and machine learning. http://pybullet.org (2016–2019)

9. Csikszentmihalyi, M.: Flow: The Psychology of Optimal Experience. Harper Perennial, New York (1991)
10. Dayan, P., Sejnowski, T.: Exploration bonuses and dual control. Mach. Learn. **25**, 5–22 (1996)
11. He, K., Zhang, X., Ren, S., Sun, J.: Deep residual learning for image recognition. In: Conference on Computer Vision and Pattern Recognition (2016)
12. Itti, L., Baldi, P.: Bayesian surprise attracts human attention. Vis. Res. **49**(10), 1295–1306 (2009)
13. Kingma, D.P., Ba, J.L.: Adam: a method for stochastic optimization. In: International Conference on Learning Representations (2015)
14. Kingma, D.P., Welling, M.: Auto-encoding variational bayes (2013). arXiv:1312.6114
15. Krizhevsky, A., Sutskever, I., Hinton, G.: Imagenet classification with deep convolutional neural networks. Neural Inf. Process. Syst. **25**, 1097–1105 (2012)
16. Lillicrap, T.P., et al.: Continuous control with deep reinforcement learning (2015). arXiv:1509.02971
17. Machado, M.C., Bellemare, M.G., Bowling, M.: Count-based exploration with the successor representation (2018). arXiv:1807.11622
18. Martin, J., Sasikumar, S.N., Everitt, T., Hutter, M.: Count-based exploration in feature space for reinforcement learning (2017). arXiv:1706.08090
19. Mnih, V., et al.: Human-level control through deep reinforcement learning. Nature **518**, 529–533 (2015)
20. Mnih, V., et al.: Playing Atari with deep reinforcement learning (2013). arXiv:1312.5602
21. Ostrovski, G., Bellemare, M.G., van den Oord, A., Munos, R.: Count-based exploration with neural density models. In: International Conference on Machine Learning, pp. 2721–2730 (2017)
22. Oudeyer, P.Y., Kaplan, F.: What is intrinsic motivation? a typology of computational approaches. Front. Neurorobotics **1**, 6 (2009)
23. Pathak, D., Agrawal, P., Efros, A.A., Darrell, T.: Curiosity-driven exploration by self-supervised prediction (2017). arXiv:1705.05363
24. Rayyes, R., Donat, H., Steil, J.: Efficient online interest-driven exploration for developmental robots. IEEE Transactions on Cognitive and Developmental Systems (2020)
25. Ryan, R., Deci, E.: Intrinsic and extrinsic motivations: classic definitions and new directions. Contemp. Educ. Psychol. **25**(1), 54–67 (2000)
26. Santucci, V.G., Baldassarre, G., Mirolli, M.: Which is the best intrinsic motivation signal for learning multiple skills? Front. Neurorobotics **7**, 22 (2013)
27. Schmidhuber, J.: Curious model-building control systems. In: Proceedings of the International Joint Conference on Neural Networks, pp. 1458–1463 (1991)
28. Stadie, B.C., Levine, S., Abbeel, P.: Incentivizing exploration in reinforcement learning with deep predictive models (2015). arXiv:1507.00814
29. Stadie, B.C., Levine, S., Abbeel, P.: Incentivizing exploration in reinforcement learning with deep predictive models. In: International Conference on Learning Representations (2016)
30. Sutton, R.: Integrated architectures for learning, planning, and reacting based on approximating dynamic programming. In: Machine Learning: Proceedings of the 7th International Conference, pp. 216–224 (1990)
31. Tang, H., et al.: #Exploration: a study of count-based exploration for deep reinforcement learning. In: Advances in Neural Information Processing Systems, pp. 2753–2762 (2017)

Correction to: BFRIFP: Brain Functional Reorganization Inspired Filter Pruning

Shoumeng Qiu, Yuzhang Gu, and Xiaolin Zhang

Correction to:
Chapter "BFRIFP: Brain Functional Reorganization Inspired Filter Pruning" in: I. Farkaš et al. (Eds.): ***Artificial Neural Networks and Machine Learning – ICANN 2021*****, LNCS 12894, https://doi.org/10.1007/978-3-030-86380-7_2**

The originally published article identified the incorrect corresponding author for the paper. The correct corresponding author has been updated now.

The updated version of this chapter can be found at
https://doi.org/10.1007/978-3-030-86380-7_2

I. Farkaš et al. (Eds.): ICANN 2021, LNCS 12894, p. C1, 2022.
https://doi.org/10.1007/978-3-030-86380-7_57

Author Index